New Learning Solutions

INSTRUCTOR ANNOTATED EDITION

GLENCOE
★★★★★

CULINARY ESSENTIALS

JOHNSON & WALES
UNIVERSITY

Building Brighter Futures

New Rigor with Academic Integration

- National Academic Standards
- Academic Vocabulary
- Reading Guides
- Writing Activities
- Math, Science, and History Activities
- Certification Test Practice

Hands-On Learning

- Interpersonal and Collaborative Skills Support FCCLA and SkillsUSA
- Project-Based Learning
- Master Recipes
- Culinary Showcase
- How To Features
- Unit Culinary Projects

Technology Resources

- Lesson Planner Plus™ CD
- *ExamView® Assessment Suite* CD
- *PresentationPlus!*™ PowerPoint Presentations CD

Online Resources

- Online Learning Center
- Online Student Edition
- Graphic Organizers
- Evaluation Rubrics
- English Glossary/Spanish Glosario
- Addit_____ ources

*Esse_____ ng Center
at gle_____.com

INSTRUCTOR ANNOTATED EDITION

GLENCOE
★★★★★

CULINARY
ESSENTIALS

JOHNSON & WALES
UNIVERSITY

McGraw Hill **Glencoe**

Safety Notice

The reader is expressly advised to consider and use all safety precautions described in this textbook or that might also be indicated by undertaking the activities described herein. In addition, common sense should be exercised to help avoid all potential hazards and, in particular, to take relevant safety precautions concerning any known or likely hazards involved in food preparation, or in use of the procedures described in *Culinary Essentials*, such as the risk of knife cuts or burns.

Publisher and Authors assume no responsibility for the activities of the reader or for the subject matter experts who prepared this book. Publisher and Authors make no representation or warranties of any kind, including but not limited to, the warranties of fitness for particular purpose or merchantability, nor for any implied warranties related thereto, or otherwise. Publisher and Authors will not be liable for damages of any type, including any consequential, special or exemplary damages resulting, in whole or in part, from reader's use or reliance upon the information, instructions, warnings, or other matter contained in this textbook.

Brand Disclaimer

Publisher does not necessarily recommend or endorse any particular company or brand name product that may be discussed or pictured in this text. Brand name products are used because they are readily available, likely to be known to the reader, and their use may aid in the understanding of the text. Publisher recognizes that other brand name or generic products may be substituted and work as well or better than those featured in the text.

Printed in the United States of America.

Send all inquiries to:
Glencoe/McGraw-Hill
21600 Oxnard Street, Suite 500
Woodland Hills, California 91367

ISBN: 978-0-07-888359-0   (Student Edition)
MHID: 0-07-888359-8   (Student Edition)
ISBN: 978-0-07-888441-2   (Instructor Annotated Edition)
MHID: 0-07-888441-1   (Instructor Annotated Edition)

3 4 5 6 7 8 9   RJE/LEH   15 14 13 12 11 10

Foreword

Johnson & Wales University is known as America's Career University. The University is student centered, employment-focused, market-driven, experientially based, and globally oriented. Johnson & Wales University collaborated with Glencoe/McGraw-Hill to bring you a unique textbook filled with the essential knowledge and skills needed to become a culinary professional.

Culinary Essentials **will show you:**

- the value of quality customer service to the dining experience.
- the role of foodservice management, standards, regulations, and laws.
- why safety and sanitation must be controlled at all times.
- how to use the equipment found in the professional kitchen.
- how culinary nutrition will enable you to create successful menus.
- how to use standardized recipes to control costs.
- the cooking techniques used in quantity food preparation.

Johnson & Wales' philosophy is to learn by doing, so we hope you make good use of this learning tool and pursue a rewarding career in culinary arts. We invite you to visit **www.jwu.edu** to learn more about Johnson & Wales University and culinary arts careers.

JOHNSON & WALES
U N I V E R S I T Y

Karl Guggenmos M.B.A., GMC, AAC
WACS Global Master Chef
University Dean, Culinary Education

Paul J. McVety EdD
Dean, Culinary Academics

Johnson & Wales University Contributors

Dr. Manuel Pimentel, Jr.
Sr. Vice President Emeritus
University Relations

Bradley J. Ware Ph.D., CCE, CCC
Professor
College of Culinary Arts

Deb Bettencourt
Special Projects Coordinator
College of Culinary Arts

George O'Palenick CEC, CCE, AAC
Associate Professor
College of Culinary Arts

Marc DeMarchena M.A., WSET, FRDP, CWE
Associate Professor
College of Culinary Arts

Gary Welling A.S.
Department Chair
International Baking & Pastry
Institute
College of Culinary Arts

Suzanne Vieira M.S., RD, LDN
Department Chair
Culinary Nutrition Program
College of Culinary Arts

Mitch Stamm CEPC
Associate Instructor
International Baking & Pastry
Institute
College of Culinary Arts

Robert M. Nograd CMC
Dean Emeritus
Corporate Executive Chef

John Chiaro M.S., CEC, CCE, AAC
Associate Professor
College of Culinary Arts

Douglas Stuchel M.A.T.
Culinary Team Lead Co-op &
Employment
Career Development Office

Katrina Herold B.S., CSW
Instructor
College of Culinary Arts

Peter Vaillancourt B.S.
Instructor
College of Culinary Arts

Elaine Cwynar M.Ed.
Associate Professor
College of Culinary Arts

Rainer Heinerwadel M.A.T., GMC
WACS Global Master Chef
Department Chair
Culinary Baccalaureate Program
College of Culinary Arts

Contributors and Reviewers

Educational Reviewers

Allen B. Asch
Area Technical Trade Center
Las Vegas, Nevada

Arnell M. Currie
Welsh High School
Welsh, Louisiana

Joyce Glen
Nettleton High School
Jonesboro, Arizona

Marsha Miller
Fort Payne High School
Fort Payne, Alabama

Kimberley M. Myers M.Ed., NBPTS
Aynor High School
Aynor, South Carolina

Holly P. Nix
Blacksburg High School
Blacksburg, South Carolina

Shirley Rauh
Lutheran High School South
St. Louis, Missouri

Amanda Riggen
Walker Career Center
Indianapolis, Indiana

Denise Schaefer, CEC, CCE, AAC
Penta Career Center

Perrysburg, Ohio

Marilyn J. Schoolmeester
Edgerton High School
Edgerton, Minnesota

Wealthy Slattery
Crenshaw High School
Los Angeles, California

Kim Smith
Cary High School
Cary, North Carolina

Beverly J. Swisher
Wichita High School West
Wichita, Kansas

Susan Teelin
Camden Middle School
Camden, New York

Linda Larsen Valiga M.Ed.
Waukesha South High School
Waukesha, Wisconsin

Technical Reviewers

Stephanie Anagnoson
Mathematics Expert
Santa Clarita, California

Chef Billie DeNunzio CCE
Institute of Culinary Arts
Eastside High School
Gainesville, Florida

Emily L. Kimbrough
Lead Chef Instructor
Charleston, South Carolina

Dr. Keith Mandabach CEC, AAC
New Mexico State University
School of Hotel, Restaurant,
and Tourism Management
Las Cruces, New Mexico
Institute of Culinary Arts

Jeff Nelken M.S., RD
Food Safety/HACCP Expert
Woodland Hills, California

Chef Erik Oberholtzer
Tender Greens
Culver City, California

Sally Porter
Hinds Community College
Jackson, Mississippi

Instructor Annotated Edition
Table of Contents

Student Edition Preview

Unit Opener..TM6
Unit Culinary Project...TM7
Chapter Opener..TM8
Chapter Review TM9
Section Reading Guide...TM10
Section Review TM11
Reading Strategies and Visuals TM12
Academic Features...TM13
Other Features TM14

Instructor Annotated Edition Preview

Annotations.. TM16
Planning Guides TM17
Lesson Plans TM18
Answer Keys.. TM19

Program Resources

Lab Manual
and Instructor Annotated Edition.. TM20
Lesson Planner Plus CD TM21
ExamView® Assessment Suite CD TM22
Presentation *Plus!* PowerPoint® Presentations CD TM23
Online Learning Center.. TM24
Online Student Edition.. TM25

Classroom Solutions

Professional Development.. TM26
Academic Scope and Sequence TM28
NASAFACS Correlations TM31
Pacing Guide... TM34
Academic Rigor TM36
Relevance and Results.. TM37
Universal Access TM38
Reading Skills TM42
Academic Vocabulary TM50
Assessment.. TM52
Test-Taking Strategies... TM54
Research-Based Classroom Solutions
   Critical Thinking..TM56
   Cooperative Learning...TM57
   Technology...TM58
   Diversity..TM59
   Ethics...TM60
SkillsUSA, FCCLA TM61
Food Classroom Resources TM64
Unit/Chapter/Section Lesson Plans/Answer Keys............................ TM70

Connect Students to the Real World

Unit Opener: Create a Relevant Framework

Culinary Essentials contains 6 units that are organized into 29 chapters. Every unit begins with a list of the chapters in the unit, a description of the culinary project students will be asked to complete at the end of the unit, a journal exercise, and a photo to explore.

Cullinary Project Preview At the end of the unit, students will be assigned a culinary project based on the unit's contents. This preview allows them to think about how the information they are learning in the unit will apply to the project.

My Journal Students are asked to keep a personal journal. The suggested topics will help prepare your students for the project at the end of the unit.

UNIT 5

Culinary Applications

Chapter
15 Cooking Techniques
16 Seasonings and Flavorings
17 Breakfast Cookery
18 Garde Manger Basics
19 Sandwiches and Appetizers
20 Stocks, Sauces, and Soups
21 Fish and Shellfish
22 Poultry Cookery
23 Meat Cookery
24 Pasta and Grains
25 Fruits, Vegetables, and Legumes

EXPLORE THE PHOTO
Culinary workers must prepare a variety of foods. *What types of foods have you prepared?*

372 Unit 5 Culinary Applications

Culinary Project Preview

Local and Seasonal Foods
After completing this unit, you will know how to identify and cook a variety of foods. In your unit thematic project you will find foods from your local area. Then you will create a visual presentation on how to prepare them and prepare a dish using them.

My Journal
Write a journal entry about the different types of foods you have made.
● What ingredients have you used?
● How did you choose them?
● How did you cook them?

JOHNSON & WALES
UNIVERSITY
"Culinary school allowed me to experience a tremendous amount of new foods and spices, and even tickled taste buds I never knew I had."

Zena Harrison
Assistant Food and
Beverage Director/Catering Chef
Compass Group

Unit 5 Culinary Applications 373

Explore the Photo By examining the photo at the beginning of the unit, students will begin to think about the topics covered in the unit. It visually guides the student with an engaging question to help interpret the meaning.

of *Culinary Essentials*

Unit Culinary Project: Putting It All Together

This end-of-unit project provides an opportunity for students to apply what they learned in the unit to both academic and culinary situations. As students complete each project, they will make decisions, conduct research, connect to their communities, and develop a presentation. My Journal refers students back to their journal entries to see if their thoughts have changed.

Project Assignment This summarizes the steps students need to take to develop and complete the culinary project.

Step-by-Step Instructions There are five steps in each culinary project. Each step explains how to successfully complete a phase of the project.

Culinary Project Checklist This at-a-glance checklist allows students to effectively manage their time and resources when planning and implementing their project.

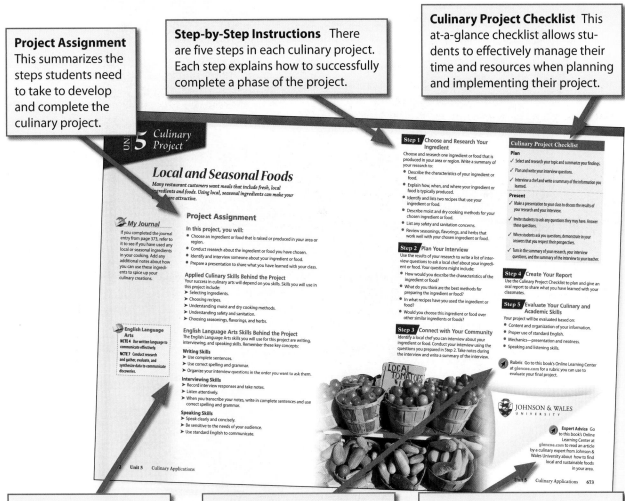

Culinary and Academic Skills These lists tell students how the information and skills they will learn in the project apply to the project.

Self Evaluation Have students go to the *Culinary Essentials* Online Learning Center at **glencoe.com** to download a rubric that they can use to create and evaluate their final projects.

Expert Advice Students can visit the *Culinary Essentials* Online Learning Center at **glencoe.com** to find articles written by Johnson & Wales University experts on topics related to each culinary project.

Chapter Opener: Promote Conceptual Understanding

Each chapter begins with a photo to explore, a preview of the main ideas in each chapter, and a writing activity that will get students thinking about what they will learn in the chapter.

Writing Activity The writing activity presents real-life writing assignments relevant to the chapter's main topics.

CHAPTER 15

Cooking Techniques

SECTIONS

15.1 How Cooking Alters Food

15.2 Dry Cooking Techniques

15.3 Moist Cooking Techniques

WRITING ACTIVITY

Cause-and-Effect Paragraph

Cause-and-effect paragraphs explain the reasons for something, or the results of something. Write a cause-and-effect paragraph about how an egg changes when it is cooked.

Writing Tips

❶ Use focusing sentences to help readers anticipate organization.

❷ Use conjunctions such as "as a result," "due to," or "because."

❸ End with a concluding sentence.

WRITING ACTIVITY ANSWER Paragraphs should follow a basic paragraph structure, with a topic sentence and supporting details.

EXPLORE THE PHOTO ANSWER Answers will vary depending on student knowledge.

374

EXPLORE THE PHOTO
Different cooking methods affect the flavor, texture, appearance, and nutritional content of food. *How many different cooking techniques can you name?*

Explore the Photo By examining the photo at the beginning of the chapter, students will begin to think about the main topics covered in the chapter.

Chapter Review: Assess Student Comprehension

The chapter closer helps your students review what they learned in the chapter and apply their learning to both their academic and real-world knowledge.

Chapter Summary Students will find the most important concepts and ideas from the chapter.

Critical Thinking If students can respond to the Critical Thinking tasks, then you will know that they understood the most important ideas in the chapter.

Academic Skills Students can use their English language arts, science, social studies, and mathematics skills to solve chapter-related problems.

Vocabulary Review Students can make sure they understand the content and academic vocabulary, and the chapter's key concepts.

Real-World Skills and Applications Help students apply what they have learned in the chapter to situations that they might encounter in a professional foodservice setting.

Certification Prep Use this section to see how students might do on standardized test questions and culinary certification tests.

Culinary Lab Students will have the opportunity to use their knowledge and skills in a culinary lab setting.

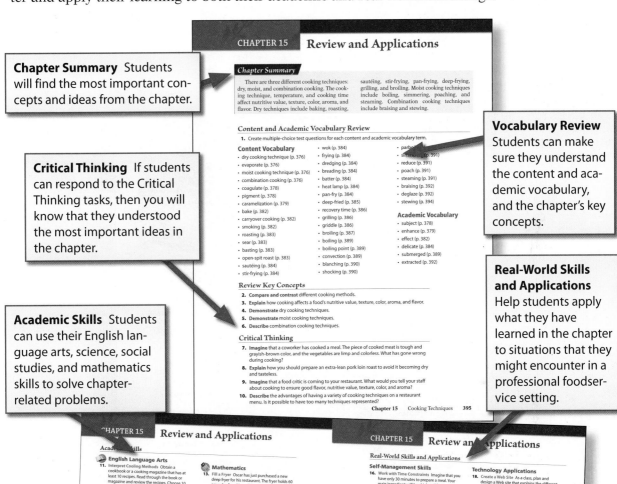

CHAPTER 15 Review and Applications

Chapter Summary

There are three different cooking techniques: dry, moist, and combination cooking. The cooking technique, temperature, and cooking time affect nutritive value, texture, color, aroma, and flavor. Dry techniques include baking, roasting, sautéing, stir-frying, pan-frying, deep-frying, grilling, and broiling. Moist cooking techniques include boiling, simmering, poaching, and steaming. Combination cooking techniques include braising and stewing.

Content and Academic Vocabulary Review

1. Create multiple-choice test questions for each content and academic vocabulary term.

Content Vocabulary
- dry cooking technique (p. 376)
- evaporate (p. 376)
- moist cooking technique (p. 376)
- combination cooking (p. 376)
- coagulate (p. 378)
- pigment (p. 378)
- caramelization (p. 379)
- bake (p. 382)
- carryover cooking (p. 382)
- smoking (p. 382)
- roasting (p. 383)
- sear (p. 383)
- basting (p. 383)
- open-spit roast (p. 383)
- sautéing (p. 384)
- stir-frying (p. 384)
- wok (p. 384)
- frying (p. 384)
- dredging (p. 384)
- breading (p. 384)
- batter (p. 384)
- heat lamp (p. 384)
- pan-fry (p. 384)
- deep-fried (p. 385)
- recovery time (p. 386)
- grilling (p. 386)
- griddle (p. 386)
- broiling (p. 387)
- boiling (p. 389)
- boiling point (p. 389)
- convection (p. 389)
- blanching (p. 390)
- shocking (p. 390)
- parboil
- simmering (p. 391)
- reduce (p. 391)
- poach (p. 391)
- steaming (p. 391)
- braising (p. 392)
- deglaze (p. 392)
- stewing (p. 394)

Academic Vocabulary
- subject (p. 378)
- enhance (p. 379)
- effect (p. 382)
- delicate (p. 384)
- submerged (p. 389)
- extracted (p. 392)

Review Key Concepts

2. **Compare and contrast** different cooking methods.
3. **Explain** how cooking affects a food's nutritive value, texture, color, aroma, and flavor.
4. **Demonstrate** dry cooking techniques.
5. **Demonstrate** moist cooking techniques.
6. **Describe** combination cooking techniques.

Critical Thinking

7. **Imagine** that a coworker has cooked a meal. The piece of cooked meat is tough and grayish-brown color, and the vegetables are limp and colorless. What has gone wrong during cooking?
8. **Explain** how you should prepare an extra-lean pork loin roast to avoid it becoming dry and tasteless.
9. **Imagine** that a food critic is coming to your restaurant. What would you tell your staff about cooking to ensure good flavor, nutritive value, texture, color, and aroma?
10. **Describe** the advantages of having a variety of cooking techniques on a restaurant menu. Is it possible to have too many techniques represented?

Chapter 15 Cooking Techniques **395**

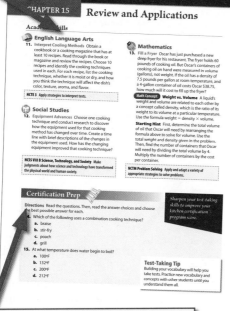

CHAPTER 15 Review and Applications

Academic Skills

English Language Arts

11. **Interpret Cooking Methods** Obtain a cookbook or a cooking magazine that has at least 10 recipes. Read through the book or magazine and review the recipes. Choose 10 recipes and identify the cooking techniques used in each. For each recipe, list the cooking technique, whether it is moist or dry, and how you think the technique will affect the dish's color, texture, aroma, and flavor.

NCTE 3 Apply strategies to interpret texts.

Social Studies

12. **Equipment Advances** Choose one cooking technique and conduct research to discover how the equipment used for that cooking method has changed over time. Create a time line with brief descriptions of the changes in the equipment used. How has the changing equipment improved that cooking technique?

NCSS VIII B Science, Technology, and Society Make judgments about how science and technology have transformed the physical world and human society.

Mathematics

13. **Fill a Fryer** Oscar has just purchased a new deep fryer for his restaurant. The fryer holds 60 pounds of cooking oil. But Oscar's containers of cooking oil on hand were measured in volume (gallons), not weight. If the oil has a density of 7.5 pounds per gallon at room temperature, and a 4-gallon container of oil costs $38.75, how much will it cost to fill up the fryer?

Math Concept **Weight vs. Volume** A liquid's weight and volume are related to each other by a concept called density, which is the ratio of its weight to its volume at a particular temperature. Use the formula weight = density × volume.

Starting Hint First, determine the total volume of oil that Oscar will need by rearranging the formula above to solve for volume. Use the total weight and density given in the problem. Then, find the number of containers that Oscar will need by dividing the total volume by 4. Multiply the number of containers by the cost per container.

NCTM Problem Solving Apply and adapt a variety of appropriate strategies to solve problems.

Certification Prep

Directions Read the questions. Then, read the answer choices and choose the best possible answer for each.

14. Which of the following uses a combination cooking technique?
   a. braise
   b. stir-fry
   c. poach
   d. grill

15. At what temperature does water begin to boil?
   a. 100°F
   b. 132°F
   c. 200°F
   d. 212°F

Sharpen your test-taking skills to improve your kitchen certification program score.

Test-Taking Tip
Building your vocabulary will help you take tests. Practice new vocabulary and concepts with other students until you understand them all.

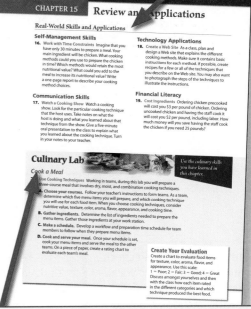

CHAPTER 15 Review and Applications

Real-World Skills and Applications

Self-Management Skills

16. **Work with Time Constraints** Imagine that you have only 30 minutes to prepare a meal. Your main ingredient will be chicken. What cooking methods could you use to prepare the chicken in time? Which methods would retain the most nutritional value? What could you add to the meal to increase its nutritional value? Write a one-page report to describe your cooking method choices.

Communication Skills

17. **Watch a Cooking Show** Watch a cooking show. Look for the particular cooking technique that the host uses. Take notes on what the host is doing and what you learned about that technique from the show. Give a five-minute oral presentation to the class to explain what you learned about the cooking technique. Turn in your notes to your teacher.

Technology Applications

18. **Create a Web Site** As a class, plan and design a Web site that explains the different cooking methods. Make sure it contains basic instructions for each method. If possible, create recipes for a few or all of the techniques that you describe on the Web site. You may also want to photograph the steps of the techniques to illustrate the instructions.

Financial Literacy

19. **Cost Ingredients** Ordering chicken precooked will cost you $3 per pound of chicken. Ordering uncooked chicken and having the staff cook it will cost you $2 per pound, including labor. How much money will you save having the staff cook the chicken if you need 25 pounds?

Culinary Lab

Cook a Meal

Use the culinary skills you have learned in this chapter.

Use Cooking Techniques Working in teams, during this lab you will prepare a three-course meal that involves dry, moist, and combination cooking techniques.

A. Choose your courses. Follow your teacher's instructions to form teams. As a team, determine which five menu items you will prepare, and which cooking technique you will use for each food item. When you choose cooking techniques, consider nutritive value, texture, color, aroma, flavor, appearance, and cooking time.

B. Gather ingredients. Determine the list of ingredients needed to prepare the menu items. Gather those ingredients at your work station.

C. Make a schedule. Develop a workflow and preparation time schedule for team members to follow when they prepare menu items.

D. Cook and serve your meal. Once your schedule is set, cook your menu items and serve the meal to the other teams. On a piece of paper, create a rating chart to evaluate each team's meal.

Create Your Evaluation
Create a chart to evaluate food items for texture, color, aroma, flavor, and appearance. Use this scale:
1 = Poor; 2 = Fair; 3 = Good; 4 = Great
Discuss amongst yourselves and then with the class how each item rated in the different categories and which technique produced the best food.

Section Reading Guide:
Enable Successful Learning

To strengthen students' reading success, each section of *Culinary Essentials* begins with a Reading Guide to preview section content.

Read to Learn By reading the Key Concepts and Main Ideas, students will know what they can expect to learn in each section.

Academic Standards Students can see which academic standards are integrated into the content of each section.

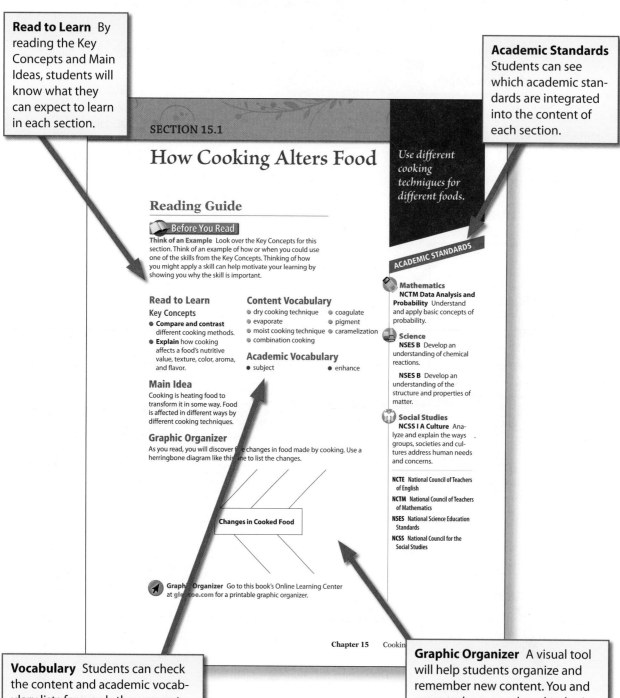

SECTION 15.1

How Cooking Alters Food

Use different cooking techniques for different foods.

Reading Guide

Before You Read

Think of an Example Look over the Key Concepts for this section. Think of an example of how or when you could use one of the skills from the Key Concepts. Thinking of how you might apply a skill can help motivate your learning by showing you why the skill is important.

Read to Learn
Key Concepts
- **Compare and contrast** different cooking methods.
- **Explain** how cooking affects a food's nutritive value, texture, color, aroma, and flavor.

Main Idea
Cooking is heating food to transform it in some way. Food is affected in different ways by different cooking techniques.

Graphic Organizer
As you read, you will discover the changes in food made by cooking. Use a herringbone diagram like this one to list the changes.

Content Vocabulary
- dry cooking technique
- evaporate
- moist cooking technique
- combination cooking
- coagulate
- pigment
- caramelization

Academic Vocabulary
- subject
- enhance

Changes in Cooked Food

Graphic Organizer Go to this book's Online Learning Center at glencoe.com for a printable graphic organizer.

ACADEMIC STANDARDS

Mathematics
NCTM Data Analysis and Probability Understand and apply basic concepts of probability.

Science
NSES B Develop an understanding of chemical reactions.

NSES B Develop an understanding of the structure and properties of matter.

Social Studies
NCSS I A Culture Analyze and explain the ways groups, societies and cultures address human needs and concerns.

NCTE National Council of Teachers of English
NCTM National Council of Teachers of Mathematics
NSES National Science Education Standards
NCSS National Council for the Social Studies

Chapter 15   Cookin

Vocabulary Students can check the content and academic vocabulary lists for words they are not familiar with, and look them up in the glossary in the back of the book before and during reading.

Graphic Organizer A visual tool will help students organize and remember new content. You and your students can download printable graphic organizers from the *Culinary Essentials* Online Learning Center at **glencoe.com**.

Section Review:
Check Comprehension

After You Read assessment at the end of each section allows you to test the students' understanding of the content before the end of the chapter. The Key Concept questions are directly related to the main topics of each section.

Review Students can organize and process their understanding of the key concepts found in each section.

Maintenance and Repairs

All equipment must be regularly and properly maintained. This will ensure that the equipment stays in top operating condition. If equipment needs to be fixed, repairs must be made promptly. This will keep the foodservice operation running smoothly. The equipment must not be used until repairs are made to maintain kitchen safety.

It is important to follow proper maintenance procedures. This is true whether you are using a deep fat fryer or a manual can opener. Managers usually create an equipment maintenance and cleaning schedule. This schedule should be followed exactly for safety.

Insurance

Owners of foodservice operations buy insurance to protect their business operations, facility, employees, and customers. There are many different types of insurance that are available. Insurance can be purchased

Small Bites

Facility Maintenance Many foodservice operations sign maintenance contracts with repair companies. Under these contracts, repair companies regularly visit the facility and perform routine maintenance.

to cover damage from fire, injury to customers, damage to equipment, employee disability, employee health, loss of life, theft, and loss of the business.

Insurance can be costly, however. Properly training employees in safety techniques and maintaining proper equipment maintenance schedules can help reduce the cost of insurance. These precautions help make the foodservice workplace a safer environment for workers and customers.

Reading Check Describe How can managers improve the safety of their facilities?

SECTION 7.2 **After You Read**

Review Key Concepts

1. **Analyze** why positive reinforcement and mentoring are good methods of employee training.
2. **Describe** the qualities of an effective work area.
3. **Explain** a manager's responsibility for equipment handling.

Practice Culinary Academics

English Language Arts

4. Read articles in trade publications about management issues such as scheduling conflicts, handling delayed orders, and equipment breakdowns. Briefly summarize each article and your thoughts in response to the article. Discuss the articles you read and your thoughts about them as a class. Attach copies of the article to your summary page and turn them in.

> **NCTE 7** Conduct research and gather, evaluate, and synthesize data to communicate discoveries.

Mathematics

5. A small deli requires four employees: two sandwich makers (who earn $10.25/hour), a cashier (who earns $9.75/hour), and a manager (who earns $850/week). If the deli is open 40 hours in a week, what are its total weekly labor costs? What is its average hourly cost?

Math Concept **Calculating Labor Costs** Calculate a company's total direct labor cost for a time period by adding all salaries and wages paid to employees over that period. Labor costs may also be averaged per hour.

Starting Hint Calculate the weekly wages paid to the three hourly employees by multiplying each pay rate ($10.25/hour, $9.75/hour) by the number of hours worked per week (40). Add these amounts to the manager's weekly salary to find the total labor costs. Divide this sum by 40 to find the average hourly cost.

> **NCTM Number and Operations** Compute fluently and make reasonable estimates.

Check your answers at this book's Online Learning Center at **glencoe.**

Practice Connect the section's content to academic skills with these English language arts, mathematics, science, and social studies activities.

Check Your Answers Students can go the *Culinary Essentials* Online Learning Center at **glencoe.com** and check their answers to ensure comprehension.

Reading Strategies and Visuals: Help Students Study Effectively

Reading strategies are offered before, during, and after each section to help enrich students' reading skills. Visuals help reinforce the concepts of each chapter.

Quick-Service Breakfasts

Breakfast foods are very popular. In the United States, many people eat breakfast foods at any meal. The standard breakfast menu includes eggs, meat, potatoes, breads, pancakes, waffles, cereals, fruit, and yogurt. Some restaurants offer customers more unusual choices, such as a special pizza or breakfast burritos. In short, anything goes!

Most restaurants that serve breakfast offer a variety of similar options and combinations. Eggs are often served either scrambled, over-easy, hard, basted, poached, or as omelets. Eggs usually come with some form of breakfast bread. This could include toast, biscuits, or an English muffin. It could also include potatoes that have been sautéed or fried. Egg dishes may also be accompanied by meat, such as bacon, ham, or sausage.

Breads such as pancakes, French toast, and waffles can be ordered in combination with eggs and a meat choice or alone. An example would be a stack of three to five pancakes with butter and syrup or fruit toppings. A small stack of two pancakes may accompany an egg dish.

Potatoes such as home fries, hash browns, and cottage fries are a common side dish for breakfast. **Home fries** are usually diced or sliced. **Hash browns** are shredded and may include onions and seasonings. For **cottage fries**, the potatoes are cut into ½-inch thick circles, and then baked or broiled.

More often than not, breakfast items may be ordered á la carte so that the customers can create their own combination of foods. This can also be profitable for the restaurant. But foodservice workers must know how to prepare a wide variety of breakfast proteins and breads. They also must learn to prepare breakfast items quickly and with skill. Most restaurant customers want their breakfast to be ready quickly.

Reading Check Determine What types of food items might be served with eggs?

Breakfast Breads and Cereals

Bread may be an even more popular breakfast item than eggs. Toast, muffins, biscuits, scones, and bagels are some of the many choices. Nearly every customer who orders an egg item will want some kind of bread with it. Many customers choose a bread item, such as pancakes, French toast, waffles, or cereal, as the mainstay, or main part, of their favorite breakfast.

Cereals appear on all breakfast menus and are served either hot or cold. Cereals are made from grains such as wheat, corn, rice, and oats, and are a good source of carbohydrates. Breakfast cereals should be stored in airtight containers to keep them from becoming stale, or being infested by pests.

Quality Breakfast Breads Cereals

Once breads are baked, they bec[...] quickly. Stale breads taste unappe[...] may become hard and dry. To avoid [...] it is necessary to consider how far in[...] you will be able to prepare and ba[...] before they are served.

Ready-Made Breads

Bread that is made in advance [...] and delivered to foodservice establis[...] called **ready-made bread**. The choic[...] ity pre-prepared breads on a breakfa[...] almost unlimited. Bagels, scones, do[...] muffins, croissants, and English mu[...] just a few examples. The only break[...] items that are routinely prepared to [...] toast, pancakes, French toast, and w[...]

Hot Cereals

Hot cereals typically fall into two c[...]
● Granular cereals, such as grits, b[...] farina.
● Whole, cracked, or flaked cereals [...] oatmeal and cracked wheat.

Chapter 17   Breakfast Cooke[...]

Hot cereals are served with milk or cream and white or brown sugar. Sometimes small ceramic bowls called ramekins filled with raisins, fresh fruit, brown sugar, or nuts are served with hot cereal. Hot cereals are a welcome menu choice for many health-conscious people.

Cold Cereals

Many cold cereals are purchased ready to eat. Some restaurants make their own special blend of granola (grə-'nō-lə). **Granola** is a blend of grains, nuts, and dried fruits. Like hot cereals, cold cereals are served with milk or cream, sugar, and sometimes fresh fruit, such as sliced strawberries or bananas. Cold cereals are a favorite breakfast choice for both children and adults. They are available in quantity portioning machines and as individual portions.

Ready-Made Breads

Breads and cereals are an essential component of breakfast menus. Rarely is an order of eggs sold without a breakfast bread. Quick

b[...]ads, such as pancakes and waffles, and [...]eakfast items like toast and French toast are [...]enerally cooked to order. Many operations [...]urchase ready-made pastries, muffins, and doughnuts. This section will introduce you to common breakfast breads and cereals.

Ready-made or convenience (kən-'vēn-yən(t)s) breads include pastries, doughnuts, and many kinds of quick breads, such as muffins. Ready-made breads can save a restaurant time during a busy breakfast rush.

Pastries

Pastries, also known as Danishes, are popular breakfast treats. They are made from yeasted, sweetened dough with butter, which gives pastries the rich flavor that makes them so appetizing. Egg is added to the dough of some kinds of pastries.

Many pastries are filled with almond paste, fruit, cream cheese, or nuts. Bear claws and strudel are two of the more well-known types of pastries. Pastries can be made from scratch, from frozen doughs, or can be purchased ready-made.

● **Breakfast Breads** Many different types of breakfast breads are available. *What kinds of specialty breakfast breads and pastries are available in your area?*

444   Unit 5   Culinary Applications

Vocabulary Students can easily identify highlighted vocabulary terms and check their definitions in the glossary.

Reading Check Students can make a quick comprehension self-check at important points in the text.

Visual Reinforcement Visuals can help reinforce the topics that your students are learning.

Features: Integrate Academics

Sections contain academic features that use students' mathematics, social studies, and science skills to connect to the chapter content.

Science à la Carte Help students connect science concepts to culinary activities they are learning. Each feature describes how science is used in everyday life.

Gourmet Math Help students connect the information in each section with mathematic concepts they are learning. Each math concept is described for them, and a starting hint is given to help them solve each problem.

Gourmet Math

Unit Prices

Unit price is the cost per unit of measure. This may be per item, per pound, per quart, or any other unit measure. When you buy food packaged in two different quantities, it is wise to know which is the better buy. To find the better buy, you need to know the unit price.
Which breadcrumbs package is the better buy: ½ pound for 75¢, or 3 pounds for $5.65? Which orange juice is the better buy: 3 quarts for $7.45, or 10 quarts for $20.25?

Math Concept **Calculating Unit Rates** A unit rate is a ratio showing how much of one quantity is needed to match 1 unit of another quantity. Unit price, a type of unit rate, is calculated by dividing the price by the quantity.
Starting Hint To find which item is the better buy, you need to calculate the unit price for each item. Do so by dividing the item's price by its quantity. The unit price of the first breadcrumbs package, for example, equals $0.75 ÷ ½, or $1.50. This means that you pay $1.50 per pound of breadcrumbs.

NCTM Number and Operations Understand numbers, ways of representing numbers, relationships among numbers, and number systems.

Academic Standards Standards are included at point of use in each of these features.

Science à la Carte

Color Fade

Do you know what gives green vegetables their color? Green vegetables, such as broccoli and spinach, contain two types of the pigment chlorophyll. One type of chlorophyll is a bright bluish-green color. The other type is a yellowish-green color. Green vegetables have about four times more of the blue-green type than the yellow-green type.
To maintain the color of a green vegetable, do not overcook it. Heat from cooking damages the vegetable's cells. This allows the acids that were in the once-living cells of the vegetable to be released. Once exposed to this acid, the chlorophyll changes to a brownish-yellow color.

Procedure

To complete the following experiment, you will need four broccoli stalks, a pot with a lid, and a second pot without a lid. Bring 3 cups of water to a boil in each uncovered pot. Separate the florets, or flowers, of the broccoli. Place half of the broccoli in one pot and cover it with the lid. Place the rest of the broccoli in the other pot without a lid. Cook both pots of broccoli for 7 minutes. After 7 minutes, drain each pot and place the broccoli into two separate bowls.

Analysis

Determine which style of cooking provided a greener vegetable. Examine each bowl. Describe the color and the texture of the broccoli in each bowl. Which dish has the greener broccoli? Explain in a short summary why you think one method of cooking had a greater impact on the color change than the other.

NSES B Develop an understanding of chemical reactions.

A Taste of History Help students learn the local, national, and international impact of history on the foodservice industry.

A TASTE OF HISTORY

2004	2007
The Spirit rover leaves Cape Canaveral, Florida, for the planet Mars	Mandatory pasteurization of all California almonds begins

Battle Against Bacteria

French scientist Louis Pasteur was a pioneer in the study of microbiology. He was the first person to understand that bacteria can cause disease, and his experiments led to a process known as pasteurization. During pasteurization, controlled heat is applied to food to kill microorganisms that could cause disease or spoilage. Pasteurization had a major impact on the food industry. Today, pasteurization is commonly used for milk and other dairy products.

History Application

Research Pasteur's discovery of how bacteria and disease are linked and how pasteurization works. Write a paragraph discussing how you believe milk and milk products have been improved because of its use.

NCSS VIII B Science, Technology, and Society Make judgments about how science and technology have transformed our understanding of human-environment interactions.

Features: The Culinary Workplace

How To Performing culinary skills in a kitchen setting is vital to a successful career in foodservice. The How To photography and step-by-step text shows students exactly how to perform culinary skills, from trussing a whole bird to making an angel food cake.

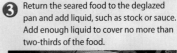

Braise
Food

1 Begin by searing the food in a frying or roasting pan. When using meats, a mixture of carrots, celery, and onions is usually added to the pan when the meat is seared.

2 Remove the food from the pan, and deglaze the pan.

3 Return the seared food to the deglazed pan and add liquid, such as stock or sauce. Add enough liquid to cover no more than two-thirds of the food.

4 Place the pan in a 350°F (177°C) oven, and cook the food slowly until it is tender when pulled apart with a fork. Turn the food every 20 to 30 minutes. Often, braised items are covered while cooking. Braising can also be done on the rangetop over low heat.

Safety Check These features offer students information on safety procedures in the professional kitchen. Each Safety Check feature is enhanced with a Critical Thinking skill question.

Sanitation Check Sanitation tips for the foodservice industry are included in this feature. Each Sanitation Check feature is enhanced with a Critical Thinking skill question.

Safety Check

✔ Egg Safety
Take the following extra precautions when you prepare eggs:

- Always store eggs and foods that contain eggs separately from raw foods. Also, store eggs away from foods that may have an undesirable odor. Eggs absorb odors easily.
- Always wash your hands before and after working with eggs and foods that contain eggs.
- Wash, rinse, and sanitize utensils, equipment, and work surfaces after you prepare eggs or products that contain eggs.
- Make sure cooked eggs do not sit out for more than a very short period of time.

CRITICAL THINKING *Why do foodservice professionals need to be extra cautious when they work with eggs?*

Sanitation Check

✔ Serve Raw Fish and Shellfish
Many restaurants offer raw fish or shellfish on the menu, such as sushi or raw oysters. Many health officials advise against serving raw fish or shellfish because of the danger of parasites and contamination from polluted water. However, if you do serve these items, follow these guidelines:

- Buy fish from reputable vendors.
- Choose only the highest quality fish because it will not be cooked.
- Handle the fish as little as possible.
- Follow state-mandated guidelines concerning the serving of raw fish and shellfish.

Critical Thinking *Why do you think you should handle the fish as little as possible?*

Features: Safety, Sanitation, and Nutrition

Master Recipes These recipes from Johnson & Wales University are made for the professional kitchen. In each recipe, students will find international alternatives, solid nutritional information, and cooking techniques.

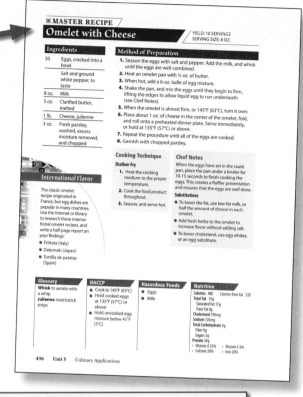

MASTER RECIPE
Omelet with Cheese

YIELD: 10 SERVINGS
SERVING SIZE: 8 OZ.

Ingredients

30	Eggs, cracked into a bowl
	Salt and ground white pepper, to taste
8 oz.	Milk
5 oz.	Clarified butter, melted
1 lb.	Cheese, julienne
3 oz.	Fresh parsley, washed, excess moisture removed, and chopped

Method of Preparation

1. Season the eggs with salt and pepper. Add the milk, and whisk until the eggs are well combined.
2. Heat an omelet pan with ½ oz. of butter.
3. When hot, add a 6-oz. ladle of egg mixture.
4. Shake the pan, and mix the eggs until they begin to firm, lifting the edges to allow liquid egg to run underneath (see Chef Notes).
5. When the omelet is almost firm, or 145°F (63°C), turn it over.
6. Place about 1 oz. of cheese in the center of the omelet, fold, and roll onto a preheated dinner plate. Serve immediately, or hold at 135°F (57°C) or above.
7. Repeat the procedure until all of the eggs are cooked.
8. Garnish with chopped parsley.

Cooking Technique

Shallow-Fry
1. Heat the cooking medium to the proper temperature.
2. Cook the food product throughout.
3. Season, and serve hot.

Chef Notes

When the eggs have set in the sauté pan, place the pan under a broiler for 10-15 seconds to finish cooking the eggs. This creates a fluffier presentation and ensures that the eggs are well done.

Substitutions
- To lower the fat, use low-fat milk, or half the amount of cheese in each omelet.
- Add fresh herbs to the omelet to increase flavor without adding salt.
- To lower cholesterol, use egg whites, or an egg substitute.

International Flavor

The classic omelet recipe originated in France, but egg dishes are popular in many countries. Use the Internet or library to research these international omelet recipes, and write a half-page report on your findings:
- Frittata (Italy)
- Datemaki (Japan)
- Tortilla de patatas (Spain)

Glossary
Whisk to aerate with a whip
Julienne matchstick strips

HACCP
- Cook to 145°F (63°C)
- Hold cooked eggs at 135°F (57°C) or above
- Hold uncooked egg mixture below 41°F (5°C)

Hazardous Foods
- Eggs
- Milk

Nutrition
Calories 480   Calories from Fat 320
Total Fat 35g
   Saturated Fat 17g
   Trans Fat 0g
Cholesterol 790mg
Sodium 720mg
Total Carbohydrate 4g
   Fiber 0g
   Sugars 3g
Protein 34g
- Vitamin A 35%   • Vitamin C 6%
- Calcium 30%   • Iron 20%

436   Unit 5   Culinary Applications

CULINARY SHOWCASE
Service Equipment

Insulated Carriers Insulated carriers are large boxes that can hold hotel pans and sheet pans filled with cooked food. Insulated carriers keep hot foods hot and cold foods cold. Some insulated carriers have wheels. If the carrier has a spigot, warm or cold beverages can be stored inside.

Chafing Dishes Chafing dishes are typically stainless steel pans used to keep food hot during service. Hotel pans of food can be inserted into the chafing dish. Chafing dishes are available in a variety of sizes.

Canned Fuel Canned fuel is used to keep food warm in chafing dishes. These small containers of solid fuel are ignited and placed beneath the chafing dish.

Coffee Systems Coffee systems can brew coffee and keep it warm during serving time. A variety of models are available. Coffee systems consist of a water tank, thermostat, warming plate, and coffee server. Systems with a hot water spigot can also be used to make hot chocolate.

Culinary Showcase Full-color photos with descriptions show students the tools, equipment, and types of ingredients that they will use in the professional foodservice industry.

Nutrition Notes Students will find tips on nutritional benefits of food and increasing nutritional value. Each Nutrition Notes feature is enhanced with a Critical Thinking skill question.

❖ Nutrition Notes ❖

Poultry Nutrition
Poultry is packed with protein. A 3½-ounce roasted chicken breast with skin has about 197 calories, 30 grams of protein, 84 milligrams of cholesterol, and 7.8 grams of fat.

CRITICAL THINKING *How does poultry fit into a well-rounded diet?*

☞ Small Bites ☜

Using Edible Flowers When you add flower petals to a salad, be sure to clean them well. Dirt and insects can hide deep down in the petals and slip unnoticed into the salad.

Small Bites These handy features offer extra information on cooking techniques, the foodservice industry, equipment and tools, and more.

Choose **Proven** **Teaching Solutions**

Annotations: Point-of-Use Answers

Point-of-use annotations within each chapter provide caption and feature answers and helpful teaching tips right as you need them.

Viruses Simple organisms that cause many food-related illnesses are called **viruses**. Viruses need a host, or another living cell, to grow. A host can be a person, animal, or plant. Once inside the host, the virus can multiply. Like bacteria, viruses can survive freezing and cooking. It is easy to **transmit**, or spread, viruses from person to person. They usually contaminate food when a foodservice worker uses poor hygiene. Poor hygiene may include sneezing on food or not washing your hands after going to the bathroom. Salads, sandwiches, milk, and other unheated foods are especially susceptible to viruses.

Parasites A **parasite** ('pàr-ə-sīt) is an organism that must live in or on a host to survive. Parasites are larger than bacteria and viruses. Parasites are often found in poultry, fish, and meats. Some common parasites found in food include protozoa, roundworms, and flatworms.

Parasites can be eliminated from food by following proper cooking methods. Freezing the food product for a number of days also can destroy parasites. Poultry, fish, and meat should be cooked until the minimum internal temperature is reached. These foods, when uncooked, should not come into contact with other foods. Carefully check the food in several different spots to be sure that the safe temperature has been reached throughout the food. If the parasites are not eliminated, they can infect anyone who eats the contaminated food.

Fungi Spore-producing organisms found in soil, plants, animals, water, and in the air are called **fungi** ('fən-gī). Fungi also are naturally present in some foods. Some fungi can be large, such as mushrooms. Some fungi can be eaten, while others cannot. Eating some fungi can cause stomach problems, or even death.

Molds A **mold** is a form of fungus. The fuzzy-looking spores produced by molds can be seen with the naked eye. Molds can grow at nearly any temperature. Even if only part of a food has mold, the whole thing should be thrown away, although some cheeses can be saved.

Yeast Another form of fungus is yeast. Yeast is most often associated with bread and the baking process. In this case, yeast is helpful. However, if yeast is present in other foods, such as sauerkraut, honey, and jelly, it can cause those foods to spoil.

Sanitation Check

Hepatitis A
Hepatitis A is a disease that causes inflammation, or swelling, of the liver. Foodservice workers with the disease can transmit the virus to food. It also can be transmitted by contact with contaminated water, or eating shellfish that has been raised in contaminated water. The symptoms of hepatitis A are similar to the flu. Hepatitis A can be prevented. You should wash your hands thoroughly after restroom use. In addition, a vaccination for hepatitis A can help protect you from infection.

CRITICAL THINKING *If you get a hepatitis A vaccination, can you forgo hand-washing procedures? Why or why not?*

Bacterial Illness Salmonella bacteria is one of the leading causes of foodborne illness. How could you help prevent the spread of salmonella in a foodservice operation?

PHOTO CAPTION ANSWER Thoroughly sanitize surfaces, keep foods at the proper temperatures, and avoid cross-contamination.

SANITATION CHECK ANSWER No. You could still spread hepatitis A to another person, or pick up other harmful microorganisms on your hands.

16 Unit 1 Culinary Safety

A TASTE OF HISTORY

1941
Breakfast cereal Cheerios is introduced as CheeriOats by General Mills

1947
First two-door refrigerator/freezer is produced

Keep Food Cool
Until the early twentieth century, people in cities who needed ice to keep their food cold purchased ice from local ice houses. The ice houses stored ice that was collected in the winter months.

The first electric refrigerators were in use by the late 1800s, but there were no mass-produced modern refrigerators until after World War II. Today, foodservice operations can choose from a large variety of refrigerators to keep food cold and fresh.

History Application
The evolution of the refrigerator/freezer had a direct connection to the frozen food industry. Create a time line about the frozen food industry that traces how the storage and shipping of frozen food has changed over time.

NCSS II B Time, Continuity, and Change Explain, analyze, and show connections among patterns of historical change and continuity.

Forms of Fungus Mold is a type of fungus. Why are some types of fungi safe to eat, but others are not?
A TASTE OF HISTORY ANSWER The time line should include early methods of freezing food by the Greeks and Romans, the days of ice cellars, and Clarence Birdseye's quick-freezing methods. Events may also include

Outbreak Response

If you have ever felt queasy several hours after eating, you may have been a victim of a foodborne illness. An outbreak of foodborne illness happens when several people become sick after eating the same food.

Any outbreak of foodborne illness must be reported to the local health department. If you think there has been an outbreak at your facility, a quick response is essential. An outbreak could cost the business thousands of dollars in legal fees, insurance costs, and loss of customers. It also could force the foodservice establishment out of business.

A laboratory analysis can tell which food made customers sick. In most areas, the public health department will investigate any outbreak of foodborne illness to protect public health. The department's job is to learn how the illness was spread and how its spread can be prevented in the future.

If you suspect a foodborne illness outbreak, take these steps:
- Tell the manager or supervisor of your suspicions immediately. It is your supervisor's responsibility to contact the appropriate authorities for an investigation.
- Avoid panic. There are many reasons why people become ill, so it is best to let the health authorities check the situation.
- Save any food you suspect may be contaminated. Wrap food in its original container or in a plastic bag. Clearly label the bag or container Do Not Use.

Reading Check Define What is the difference between direct contamination and cross-contamination?

the introduction of TV dinners and other microwavable frozen foods.
PHOTO CAPTION ANSWER Many types of fungi, such as edible mushrooms and the veins in cheeses such as Stilton or Roquefort, are safe to eat. However, some fungi are toxic to humans, and can cause serious illness or death.
READING CHECK ANSWER Direct contamination happens when food is exposed directly to harmful microorganisms. Cross-contamination means harmful microorganisms are moved from one food to another.

Chapter 1 Safety and Sanitation Principles 17

Visuals The answers to the questions for photos and figures provide you with an opportunity to discuss important topics in the chapter and reinforce content. Answers also provide additional information on real-life topics.

Feature Answers The answers to features provide you with an opportunity to discuss the chapter topics with students to help boost their reading comprehension.

Reading Check Answer Reading Checks help your students review information they have just read. Point-of-use annotation answers allow you to review these important points with them.

for **Effective** Results

Planning Guides: The Right Resources

Introduce and review each chapter in ways best suited to your students' individual needs.

Online Ancillaries Encourage your students to get more information online at this book's Online Learning Center at **glencoe.com**.

Print Ancillaries Find the additional activities, study guides, and test preparation strategies in the Lab Manual. Answers are provided in the Lab Manual Instructor Annotated Edition.

Electronic Ancillaries Have the flexibility you need to create individualized learning plans for your students with Lesson Planner Plus. Create and print tests with *ExamView® Assessment Suite*.

CHAPTER 22 Lesson Plan

Poultry Cookery

SECTION 22.1 Poultry Basics

SECTION 22.2 Cooking Poultry

Classroom Solutions

Print Resources
- Student Edition
- Instructor Annotated Edition
- Lab Manual
- Lab Manual IAE

Technology Resources

ExamView® Assessment Suite *ExamView® Assessment Suite* **CD**
Create and print unit and chapter tests.

Lesson Planner Plus **Lesson Planner Plus CD** provides access to teacher resources in one package.

Presentation Plus! provides visual teaching aids for every section.

 **Online Learning Center** includes resources and activities for students and teachers. Also includes the **Online Student Edition**.

Interactive Student Edition

SECTION 22.1 Poultry Basics

Section Overview
Students will learn about the different kinds, classes, and market forms of poultry. They will also understand USDA inspections and grading; how to purchase poultry; and how to handle, store, and prepare it for cooking.

FOCUS

Bell Ringer Activity
Poultry Pantomime Have volunteers pantomime safe poultry preparation. Have the class evaluate the accuracy of the safety procedures in the pantomimes.

D Develop Concepts
Main Idea Discuss the main idea with the students. Ask: Which kinds of poultry have the students eaten? Kinds of poultry include chicken, turkey, goose, duck, pigeon, and guinea. Have students discuss whether they liked each kind.

Professional Development MINI CLIP **Reading** Prereading Strategies

TEACH

S Skill Practice
Guided Practice
L1 List Have students make a list of qualities of Grade A poultry. Grade A poultry is plump and meaty; has clean, unblemished skin; has no broken bones; has all feathers removed.

L2 Explain Have students write a paragraph to explain why restaurants should choose Grade A poultry. Paragraphs will vary but should include quality, flavor, and appearance.

L3 Apply Have students practice cutting Grade A poultry following the examples in the book. Evaluate their technique and the result. The cut pieces should be as neat as possible, and should waste as little meat as possible.

ASSESS

Quiz
Ask students to answer the following questions:

1. How does the USDA categorize poultry? The USDA categorizes poultry by species, or kind. Each kind is then divided into classes based on age and gender.

2. What factors affect the tenderness of poultry? Maturity: older poultry is tougher. Exercise: the more exercise a bird gets, the tougher it will be.

3. How should you store fresh poultry that you will cook within a day? Place it in cold storage or pack it in ice until it is ready to use.

TM208   Chapter 22 Lesson Plan

Lesson Plans: Plan for Classroom Success

These teaching suggestions and ideas are offered to help you motivate and involve your students. They can assist you in reaching students of all levels of ability and backgrounds and make the course more rewarding for both you and your students.

Using the Six-Step Lesson Plan

Culinary Essentials makes full and effective use of a mastery approach in six steps: focus, teach, assess, reteach, assess, and close. This widely accepted instructional method provides you with a consistent framework that makes it easy for you to plan your lessons.

Reteach Different activities are provided to reinforce lesson content. Questions are designed to help your students reinforce key concepts or apply and extend what they have learned.

Close A Culminating Activity helps students make the connection between what they read and its meaning and application to the real world.

Focus A Bell Ringer Activity begins the lesson, then the pre-teaching activity, Develop Concepts, assures that all students have the same background and preparation.

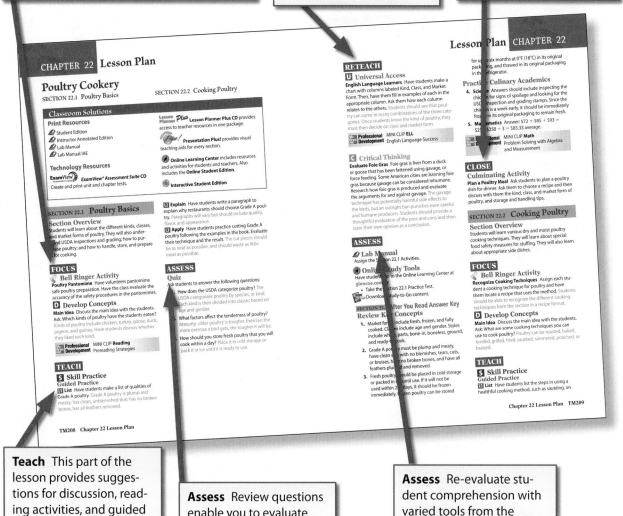

Teach This part of the lesson provides suggestions for discussion, reading activities, and guided skills practice.

Assess Review questions enable you to evaluate your students' needs.

Assess Re-evaluate student comprehension with varied tools from the *Culinary Essentials* program.

Answer Keys:
Evaluate Students' Progress

Find detailed answers to the Chapter Review and Applications questions. These answers can also help you jumpstart clasroom discussions with the students.

Key Concepts/Critical Thinking Answers Boost students' understanding of the chapter material and encourage further discussion.

Certification Prep Answers Encourage good test-taking habits in your students for success on standardized tests and culinary certification tests.

Answer Key CHAPTER 22

Grade A being the best. To be Grade A, poultry must be plump and meaty; have clean skin with no blemishes, tears, cuts or bruises; have no broken bones; and have no feathers.

4. Fresh poultry is highly perishable, and should be packed in ice or in cold storage until ready for use; if it will not be used within 2–3 days, it should be frozen immediately. Frozen poultry can be stored for up to six months at or below 0°F (18°C). Keep frozen poultry in its original packaging, and never refreeze poultry. Whole birds should be trussed to allow for even cooking, and are usually roasted.

5. Dry cooking techniques include roasting, baking, broiling, grilling, frying (pan-frying, deep-frying, and pressure-frying), and sautéing. Moist cooking techniques include simmering and poaching. Braising is a combination dry/moist cooking method.

6. Stuffing may not reach a safe temperature at the same time as the bird, creating the possibility for bacteria to grow. Poultry can become dry before the stuffing is fully cooked.

7. Answers will vary, but common poultry side dishes include stuffings, gravies, sauces, soups, salsas, vegetables, casseroles, wild rice, potatoes, and pasta.

C Critical Thinking

8. Dark meat has more muscle and connective tissue than light meat; dark meat also has more fat and generally takes a longer time to cook than light meat. Answers will vary, but can include customer preference and compatibility with the recipe chosen.

9. Answers will vary; accept any that are well thought out and supported by complete arguments.

10. Less-tender birds may be chosen because they are readily available or less expensive. They may also fit a specific recipe. Cooking methods can make this poultry tender.

Academic Skills

11. **Social Studies** Answers will vary, but students should be able to demonstrate their research skills in finding detailed recipes and knowledge of the appropriateness of spices, seasonings, and side dishes for their chosen culture.

12. **English Language Arts** The flyer should include information on when the restaurant will open, and details on specific poultry dishes.

13. **Mathematics** .30 × 500 = 150 meals should include poultry

Certification Prep

14. C. clean and sanitize the cutting board

15. A. breads

Real-World Skills and Applications

16. **Teamwork Skills** Check to see that recipes are balanced nutritionally, and that flavors, seasonings, and spreads will complement turkey. Flyers should highlight these points.

17. **Critical Thinking Skills** Answers will vary, but questions may be based on customer preferences for dishes, the general atmosphere of the event, the seasonality of available ingredients, and any specific party themes.

18. **Technology Applications** Spreadsheets should clearly display dry and moist poultry cooking methods, cooking instructions, and poultry choices appropriate to each method.

19. **Financial Literacy** Answers will depend on students' findings, but most should find that whole chicken is generally the most cost-effective option for foodservice establishments. However, labor cost, skill level of employees, and the ability to use all of the chicken parts might affect the decision.

Culinary Lab

20. **Prepare Poultry** Evaluations will vary, but dishes and evaluations should be based on knowledge of the chapter content. Students should give clear reasoning for their evaluations on appearance, flavor, and texture, and should be respectful of other teams.

Real-World Skills and Applications Answers Help students explore real-life situations using the skills they have learned from the chapter.

Evaluate Culinary Projects See how students are progressing with their culinary skills.

Chapter 22 Answer Key TM211

Utilize Time-Saving Print

Print Resources

Help Students Succeed with the Lab Manual

The *Lab Manual* includes a variety of worksheets and activities, correlated to each chapter in the text.

- Note-Taking
- Academics
- English Language Arts
- Mathematics
- Science
- Social Studies
- Study Skills
- Test-Preparation
- Test-Taking
- Content Vocabulary
- Academic Vocabulary

These worksheets and activities will help reinforce the chapter content, increasing your students' comprehension. The *Lab Manual* offers students a chance to apply what they have learned and to use their critical thinking skills.

The Instructor Annotated Edition of the *Lab Manual* includes cyan annotated answers to all of the student activities.

Lab Manual

GLENCOE
★★★★★
CULINARY ESSENTIALS
JOHNSON & WALES UNIVERSITY

and Technology Resources

Technology Solutions

Lesson Planner Plus CD

Lesson Planner Plus gives you instant access to a variety of useful program resources in one easy-to-use CD. The software provides a calendar format that allows you to plan lessons, manage daily activities, access textbook materials, and use Internet resources.

The Lesson Planner Plus program contains built-in lesson plans that can be customized to meet your individual classroom needs. It also includes links to printable program resources:

Printable Program Resources

Teacher Materials
- Lesson Plans
- Answer Keys
- Performance Rubrics
- Correlations to national standards

Student Materials
- Lesson Summaries with Key Terms and Academic Vocabulary
- Graphic Organizers
- Unit Culinary Project Self-Assessment Rubrics

Glencoe
Lesson Planner *Plus*
with **Teacher Resources**

Software Support Hotline
1-800-437-3715 or
epgtech@mcgraw-hill.com

Windows/Macintosh
Version 1.8

ISBN: 978-0-07-000000-0
MHID: 0-07-000000-0

1 2 3 4 5 6 7 8 9 10

- **Interactive Lesson Planner**
- **Student Activity Workbook IAE**
- **Lesson Plans**
- **Reproducible Tests**
- **Internet Resources**

GLENCOE
★★★★★
CULINARY
ESSENTIALS

10/08

The McGraw-Hill Companies

McGraw Hill **Glencoe**

Copyright © by The McGraw-Hill Companies, Inc. All rights reserved.

ExamView® Assessment Suite

Streamline assessment from start to finish with the *ExamView® Assessment Suite* CD. This easy-to-use software allows teachers to customize and create unique tests to conduct quizzes, chapter tests, unit tests, midterm exams, or final exams. The *ExamView® Assessment Suite* works across platforms, on the Web, and across a local area network. It offers teachers a comprehensive solution that allows them to create, administer, and score tests. The test banks, which are organized by unit and chapter, use a variety of question types to improve assessment.

Use the *ExamView® Assessment Suite* to:
- Create a paper test in fewer than five minutes.
- Print multiple versions of the same test.
- Create your own questions.
- Develop tests using state and national standards.
- Prepare online tests, study guides, and worksheets.
- Upload tests to WebCT and Blackboard.

Use the *ExamView® Test Manager* to:
- Create a class roster.
- Automatically score a paper test using a scanner.
- Administer and score an online test.
- Prepare a variety of useful class and student reports.

Presentation *Plus!* PowerPoint® Presentations

The *Culinary Essentials* Presentation *Plus!* CD provides visually motivating presentations that are helpful to both students and teachers. The presentations target key concepts by highlighting important text, providing graphic organizers, and utilizing visuals from the textbook.

How Teachers Can Use Presentation *Plus!*

The Presentation *Plus!* PowerPoint presentations are excellent teaching aids that present dynamic lessons for every section in *Culinary Essentials*. The PowerPoint presentations can be edited and customized to meet the needs of individual students. It also includes chapter assessment presentations that can be used with TurningPoint® student response systems. Teachers can use Presentation *Plus!* PowerPoint presentations in the following ways:

- To preview important concepts at the beginning of a new chapter or lesson
- To provide differentiated instruction for visual learners
- To create a customized learning experience for students

How Students Can Use Presentation *Plus!*

The Presentation *Plus!* PowerPoint presentations provide a visual overview of key concepts and vocabulary. The presentations are excellent study aids. Students can use Presentation *Plus!* PowerPoint presentations in the following ways:

- To preview important concepts, content vocabulary, and skills that are covered in a chapter before reading
- To review and reinforce difficult concepts after reading
- To prepare for quizzes and tests

Program Resources

Access the Online Learning Center

The Online Learning Center provides access to a wide variety of teacher resources. Follow these steps to access the textbook resources at the *Culinary Essentials* Online Learning Center. The Online Learning Center is password protected.

1 Go to **glencoe.com**.

2 Select **your state** from the pull-down menu.

3 Select **Teacher**

4 Select **Family & Consumer Sciences**.

5 Click **ENTER**.

6 Click *Culinary Essentials*.

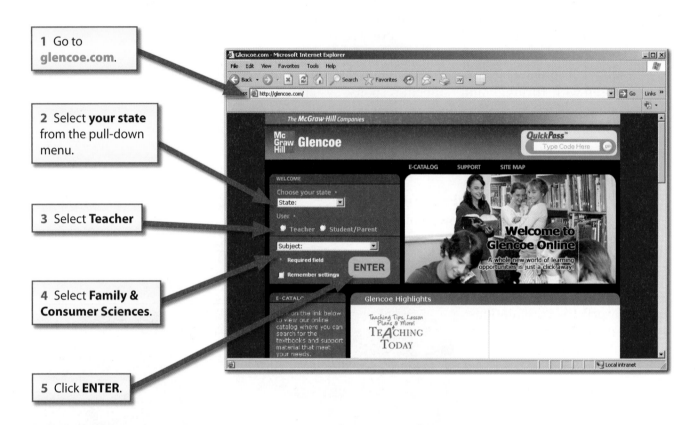

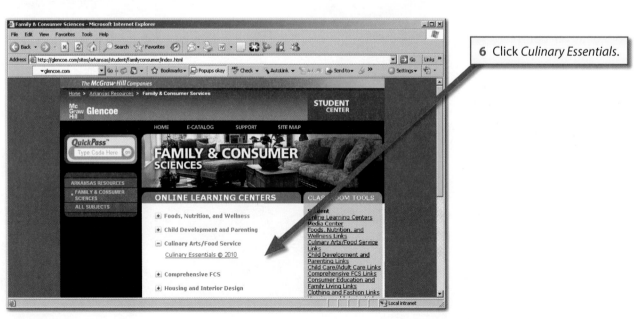

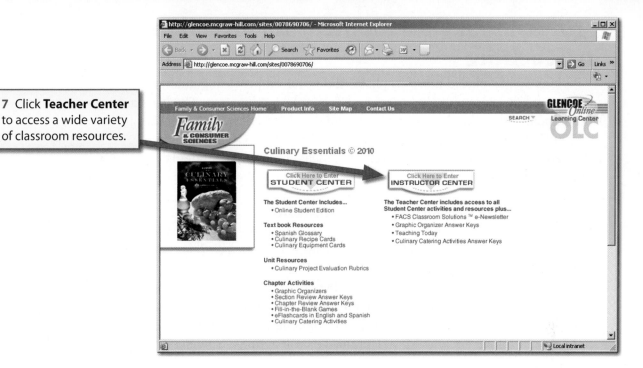

7 Click **Teacher Center** to access a wide variety of classroom resources.

Online Learning Center Web Site

The *Culinary Essentials* Online Learning Center provides resources to enrich and enhance learning. There is both a student and teacher Online Learning Center.

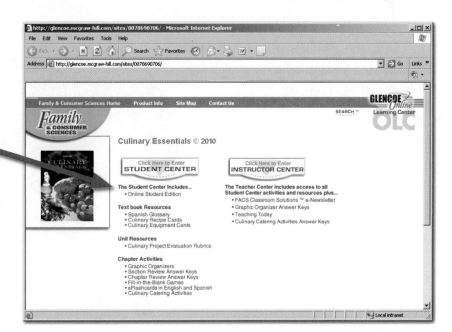

Online Student Edition

The Online Student Edition is an interactive version of the textbook that can be accessed from the Online Learning Center. This version of the textbook is as easy to read and search. It offers the same content as the printed text.

Professional Development for Excellence in Teaching

Perkins IV has placed more emphasis than ever on providing quality professional development for Career and Technology educators. The legislation mandates that the focus of professional development be the integration and reinforcement of academic competencies in order to improve student achievement. Specifically, Perkins requires measurements of students' academic success.

Glencoe and Professional Development

To support educators in their efforts to meet new professional development requirements, Glencoe now offers a new resource, *Glencoe's Online Professional Development for Integrating Academics*. This program offers a suite of online products designed to help teachers become more effective in teaching and reinforcing academic skills. The focus of this program is on instructional strategies that can help educators integrate challenging academic content seamlessly into their technical curriculum. These teaching strategies zero in on:

- Math
- Reading
- English Language Arts
- Differentiated Instruction
- English Language Learners Instruction

Glencoe's Online Professional Development for Integrating Academics

1. Professional Development Accredited Online Courses (Academic Credit available through Adams University)
2. Professional Development Web Site
3. Video Workshops
4. Mini-Clip Video Library
5. McGraw-Hill Experienced Consultants

For further pricing and ordering information, go to
mcgraw-hill-pd-online.com.

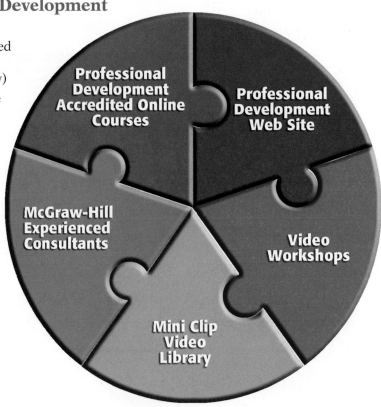

Professional Development for Academic Integration in the Glencoe 6-Step Teaching Plan

Selected online mini-clips have been integrated into this Teacher Edition's 6-step teaching plan in order to support academic instruction. These mini-clips are free and accessible online at this book's Online Learning Center at **glencoe.com**.

The Professional Development Mini Clip Video Library offers you instructional support for reading, English Language Learners, and math.

Integrate teaching strategies in your lesson plans. Mini-clip videos have been selected and matched to chapter content to help you integrate academics into your planning.

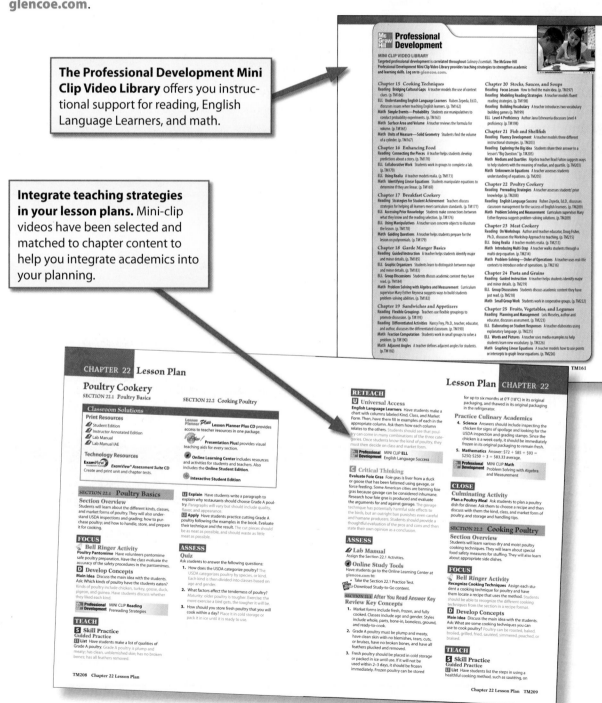

Scope and Sequence

These charts provide an overview of the academic standards covered in
Culinary Essentials.

National Council of Teachers of English Standards for English Language Arts		
NCTE 1	Students read a wide range of print and nonprint texts to build an understanding of texts, of themselves, and of the cultures of the United States and the world; to acquire new information; to respond to the needs and demands of society and the workplace; and for personal fulfillment. Among these texts are fiction and nonfiction, classic and contemporary works.	149, 194, 536, 776
NCTE 2	Students read a wide range of literature from many periods in many genres to build an understanding of the many dimensions (e.g., philosophical, ethical, aesthetic) of human experience.	515, 744
NCTE 3	Students apply a wide range of strategies to comprehend, interpret, evaluate, and appreciate texts. They draw on their prior experience, their interactions with other readers and writers, their knowledge of word meaning and of other texts, their word identification strategies, and their understanding of textual features (e.g., sound-letter correspondence, sentence structure, context, graphics).	229, 396, 428, 702
NCTE 4	Students adjust their use of spoken, written, and visual language (e.g., conventions, style, vocabulary) to communicate effectively with a variety of audiences and for different purposes.	22, 66, 110, 112, 192, 214, 319, 324, 366, 370, 426, 475, 506, 564, 610, 634, 668, 672, 700
NCTE 5	Students employ a wide range of strategies as they write and use different writing process elements appropriately to communicate with different audiences for a variety of purposes.	160, 177, 210, 223, 246, 296, 304, 326, 342, 387, 584, 686, 742, 763
NCTE 6	Students apply knowledge of language structure, language conventions (e.g., spelling and punctuation), media techniques, figurative language, and genre to create, critique, and discuss print and nonprint texts.	52, 287, 622, 666
NCTE 7	Students conduct research on issues and interests by generating ideas and questions, and by posing problems. They gather, evaluate, and synthesize data from a variety of sources (e.g., print and nonprint texts, artifacts, people) to communicate their discoveries in ways that suit their purpose and audience.	12, 52, 125, 186, 248, 370, 494, 538, 547, 672, 774
NCTE 8	Students use a variety of technological and informational resources (e.g., libraries, databases, computer networks, video) to gather and synthesize information and to create and communicate knowledge.	36, 80, 164, 414, 452, 500, 582, 658, 769, 780
NCTE 9	Students develop an understanding of and respect for diversity in language use, patterns, and dialects across cultures, ethnic groups, geographic regions, and social roles.	136, 164, 484, 726
NCTE 10	Students whose first language is not English make use of their first language to develop competency in the English language arts and to develop understanding of content across the curriculum.	All English language learner activities in IAE Lesson Plan pages.
NCTE 12	Students use spoken, written, and visual language to accomplish their own purposes (e.g., for learning, enjoyment, persuasion, and the exchange of information).	29, 48, 78, 92, 102, 138, 214, 274, 276, 302, 312, 333, 344, 364, 394, 404, 450, 461, 482, 504, 566, 593, 612, 645, 735, 753, 780

National Council of Teachers of Mathematics Standards Grades 9-12		
NCTM Number and Operations	Understand numbers, ways of representing numbers, relationships among numbers, and number systems.	20, 29, 72, 78, 80, 102, 208, 246, 304, 312, 319, 338, 355, 366, 469, 551, 593, 632
NCTM Number and Operations	Understand the meanings of operations and how they relate to one another.	74, 192, 260, 274, 428, 441, 584, 622, 761
NCTM Number and Operations	Compute fluently and make reasonable estimates.	92, 108, 112, 136, 186, 302, 323, 326, 342, 344, 351, 566, 612, 679, 686, 702, 715, 742
NCTM Algebra	Understand patterns, relations, and functions.	22, 658
NCTM Algebra	Represent and analyze mathematical situations and structures using algebraic symbols.	210, 276, 582, 726
NCTM Algebra	Use mathematical models to represent and understand quantitative relationships.	700, 711, 744
NCTM Geometry	Analyze characteristics and properties of two- and three-dimensional geometric shapes and develop mathematical arguments about geometric relationships.	154, 160, 500, 763
NCTM Geometry	Use visualization, spatial reasoning, and geometric modeling to solve problems.	48, 149, 158, 248, 253, 387, 426, 482, 506, 769, 776

NCTM Measurement	Understand measurable attributes of objects and the units, systems, and processes of measurement.	12, 36, 125, 287, 333, 494, 536, 564, 610, 724, 735
NCTM Measurement	Apply appropriate techniques, tools, and formulas to determine measurements.	220, 450, 461, 504, 525, 753
NCTM Data Analysis and Probability	Formulate questions that can be addressed with data and collect, organize, and display relevant data to answer them.	203, 774
NCTM Data Analysis and Probability	Select and use appropriate statistical methods to analyze data.	46, 240, 364, 547, 575
NCTM Data Analysis and Probability	Understand and apply basic concepts of probability.	138, 380. 419, 645, 668
NCTM Problem Solving	Build new mathematical knowledge through problem solving.	177, 223, 394, 414, 515
NCTM Problem Solving	Solve problems that arise in mathematics and in other contexts.	110, 194, 229, 404, 484, 491, 603
NCTM Problem Solving	Apply and adapt a variety of appropriate strategies to solve problems.	39, 66, 176, 296, 324, 396, 452, 475, 538, 557, 666
NCTM Reasoning and Proof	Select and use various types of reasoning and methods of proof.	634

* Standards are listed with the permission of the National Council of Teachers of Mathematics (NCTM). NCTM *does not endorse the content or validity of these alignments.*

National Council for the Social Studies Standards

I Culture

NCSS I A	Analyze and explain the ways groups, societies, and cultures address human needs and concerns.	223, 380, 414, 441, 482, 566, 584, 735, 753
NCSS I B	Predict how data and experiences may be interpreted by people from diverse cultural perspectives and frames of reference.	387, 475, 525, 593
NCSS I C	Apply an understanding of culture as an integrated whole that explains the functions and interactions of language, literature, the arts, traditions, beliefs and values, and behavior patterns.	426
NCSS I E	Demonstrate the value of cultural diversity, as well as cohesion, within and across groups.	404, 419, 474, 497, 506

II Time, Continuity, and Change

NCSS II B	Apply key concepts such as time, chronology, causality, change, conflict, and complexity to explain, analyze and show connections among patterns of historical change and continuity.	17, 254, 709, 769
NCSS II C	Identify and describe significant historical periods and patterns of change within and across cultures, such as the development of ancient cultures and civilizations, the rise of nation-states, and social, economic, and political revolutions.	63
NCSS II D	Systematically employ processes of critical historical inquiry to reconstruct and reinterpret the past, such as using a variety of sources and checking their credibility, validating and weighing evidence for claims, and searching for causality.	149, 461, 651, 693, 735, 776
NCSS II F	Apply ideas, theories, and modes of historical inquiry to analyze historical and contemporary developments, and to inform and evaluate actions concerning public policy issues.	296

III People, Places, and Environments

NCSS III H	Examine, interpret, and analyze physical and cultural patterns and their interactions, such as land use, settlement patterns, cultural transmission of customs and ideas, and ecosystem changes.	469, 765
NCSS III I	Describe and assess ways that historical events have been influenced by, and have influenced, physical and human geographic factors in local, regional, national, and global settings.	410

IV Individual Development and Identity

NCSS IV B	Identify, describe, and express appreciation for the influence of various historical and contemporary cultures on an individual's daily life.	29, 344, 515
NCSS IV E	Examine the interaction of ethnic, national, or cultural influences in specific situations or events.	142, 240, 619, 726

V Individuals, Groups, and Institutions

NCSS V A	Apply concepts such as role, status, and social class in describing the connections and interactions of individuals, groups, and institutions in society.	95, 383
NCSS V B	Analyze group and institutional influences on people, events, and elements of culture in both historical and contemporary settings.	135, 274, 309, 358, 580, 589
NCSS V C	Describe the various forms institutions take, and explain how they develop and change over time.	66, 72, 312
NCSS V F	Evaluate the role of institutions in furthering both continuity and change.	208

VI Power, Authority, and Governance

NCSS VI A	Examine persistent issues involving the rights, roles, and status of the individual in relation to the general welfare.	194
NCSS VI B	Explain the purpose of government and analyze how its powers are acquired, used, and justified.	668
NCSS VI E	Compare different political systems (their ideologies, structure, institutions, processes, and political cultures) with that of the United States, and identify representative political leaders from selected historical and contemporary settings.	102

NCSS VI H	Explain and apply ideas, theories, and modes of inquiry drawn from political science to the examination of persistent ideas and social problems.	203
NCSS VI I	Evaluate the extent to which governments achieve their stated ideals and policies at home and abroad.	182, 200
VII Production, Distribution, and Consumption		
NCSS VII A	Explain how the scarcity of productive resources (human, capital, technological, and natural) requires the development of economic systems to make decisions about how goods and services are to be produced and distributed.	666
NCSS VII B	Analyze the role that supply and demand, prices, incentives, and profits play in determining what is produced and distributed in a competitive market system.	78, 177, 324
NCSS VII F	Compare how values and beliefs influence economic decisions in different societies.	547
NCSS VII I	Distinguish between the domestic and global economic systems, and explain how the two interact.	452
VIII Science, Technology, and Society		
NCSS VIII A	Identify and describe both current and historical examples of the interaction and interdependence of science, technology, and society in a variety of cultural settings.	138, 229, 234, 333
NCSS VIII B	Make judgments about how science and technology have transformed the physical world and human society and our understanding of time, space, place, and human-environment interactions.	36, 48, 248, 294, 396, 446, 561, 564, 610, 658
NCSS VIII C	Analyze how science and technology influence the core values, beliefs, and attitudes of society, and how core values, beliefs, and attitudes of society shape scientific and technological change.	304
IX Global Connections		
NCSS IX A	Explain how language, art, music, belief systems, and other cultural elements can facilitate global understanding or cause misunderstanding.	330, 450, 774
NCSS IX C	Analyze and evaluate the effects of changing technologies on the global community.	632
X Civic Ideals and Practices		
NCSS X B	Identify, analyze, interpret, and evaluate sources and examples of citizens' rights and responsibilities.	110
NCSS X J	Participate in activities to strengthen the "common good," based upon careful evaluation of possible options for citizen action.	612

National Science Education Standards		
NSES 1	Students should develop an understanding of science unifying concepts and processes; systems, other, and organization; evidence, models, and explanation; change, constancy, and measurement; evolution and equilibrium; and form and function.	36, 80, 223, 342
NSES A	Students should develop abilities necessary to do scientific inquiry, understanding about scientific inquiry.	72, 160, 326, 404, 475, 504, 634
NSES B	Students should develop an understanding of the structure of atoms, structure and properties of matter, chemical reactions, motions and forces, conservation of energy and increase in disorder, and interactions of energy and matter.	9, 123, 203, 229, 276, 282, 287, 333, 366, 379, 380, 387, 394, 428, 437, 466, 484, 515, 518, 536, 538, 564, 607, 610, 622, 702, 711, 739, 744, 763, 774
NSES C	Students should develop understanding of the cell; molecular basis of heredity; biological evolution; interdependence of organisms; matter, energy, and organization in living systems; and behavior of organisms.	20, 210, 419, 424, 500, 645, 663
NSES E	Students should develop abilities of technological design, understandings about science and technology.	302
NSES F	Students should develop understanding of personal and community health; population growth; natural resources; environmental quality; natural and human-induced hazards; science and technology in local, national, and global challenges.	22, 46, 112, 192, 246, 260, 461, 575, 700

FACS National Standards Correlation

The following chart shows how *Culinary Essentials* meets the standards and competencies for the food and production areas of study as outlined in the Family and Consumer Sciences Education National Standards.

Food Production and Services		
Comprehensive Standard 8.0 **Integrate knowledge, skills, and practices required for careers in food production and services.**		
8.1	**Analyze career paths within the food production and food services industries.**	**Pages in Text**
8.1.1	Explain the roles, duties, and functions of individuals engaged in food production and services careers.	58–61, 84–92, 113, 116–119, 127–130, 131–134, 134–136, 456–458
8.1.2	Analyze opportunities for employment and entrepreneurial endeavors.	70–72, 74–76, 94–102, 113
8.1.3	Summarize education and training requirements and opportunities for career paths in food production and services.	63–66
8.1.4	Analyze the effects of food production and services occupations on local, state, national, and global economies.	68, 70
8.1.5	Create an employment portfolio for use with applying for internships and work-based learning opportunities.	96
8.1.6	Analyze the role of professional organizations in food production and services	90–91, 95, 274
8.2	**Demonstrate food safety and sanitation procedures.**	
8.2.1	Identify characteristics of major food borne pathogens, their role in causing illness, foods involved in outbreaks, and methods of prevention.	14–16, 143, 152, 435, 771
8.2.2	Employ food service management safety/sanitation program procedures, including CPR and first aid.	4–7, 9–12, 23
8.2.3	Use knowledge of systems for documenting, investigating, reporting, and preventing food borne illness.	14–17, 21, 23
8.2.4	Use the Hazard Analysis Critical Control Point (HACCP) and crisis management principles and procedures during food handling processes to minimize the risks of food borne illness.	31–35, 49
8.2.5	Practice good personal hygiene/health procedures, including dental health and weight management, and report symptoms of illness.	4, 26–29
8.2.6	Demonstrate proper purchasing, receiving, storage, and handling of both raw and prepared foods.	38–41, 42–44, 176–177, 359–364, 545–546, 547, 550, 551, 552, 553, 554, 555, 559, 570–575, 590–593, 599, 613, 616, 625, 638–642, 647–652, 660, 667
8.2.7	Demonstrate safe food handling and preparation techniques that prevent cross contamination from potentially hazardous foods, between raw and ready-to-eat foods, and between animal and fish sources and other food products.	42–43
8.2.8	Analyze current types of cleaning materials and sanitizers for proper uses and safety hazards.	18–19, 23
8.2.9	Use Occupational Safety and Health Administration's (OSHA) Right to Know Law and Materials Safety Data Sheets (MSDS) and explain their requirements in safe handling and storage of hazardous materials.	4, 18, 23, 201
8.2.10	Demonstrate safe and environmentally responsible waste disposal and recycling methods.	44–45, 48, 366

8.2.11	Demonstrate ability to maintain necessary records to document time and temperature control, HACCP, employee health, maintenance of equipment, and other elements of food preparation, storage, and presentation.	35–36
8.3	**Demonstrate industry standards in selecting, using, and maintaining food production and food service equipment.**	
8.3.1	Operate tools and equipment following safety procedures and OSHA requirements.	220–223, 225–229, 231–240, 242–246, 252–260, 262–274, 278–680, 681–686
8.3.2	Maintain tools and equipment following safety procedures and OSHA requirements.	185–186
8.3.3	Demonstrate procedures for cleaning and sanitizing equipment, serving dishes, glassware, and utensils to meet industry standards and OSHA requirements.	45–46, 125, 231, 234, 239–240, 274
8.3.4	Analyze equipment purchases based on long-term business needs, specific regulations, and codes related to foods.	202, 277, 686, 701
8.3.5	Demonstrate procedures for safe and secure storage of equipment and tools.	260
8.3.6	Identify a variety of types of equipment for food processing, cooking, holding, storing, and serving, including hand tools and small ware.	225–229, 231–234, 235–238, 242–246, 252–254, 262–273, 460, 633, 682–686
8.4	**Demonstrate menu planning principles and techniques based on standardized recipes to meet customer needs.**	
8.4.1	Use computer based menu systems to develop and modify menus.	327
8.4.2	Apply menu-planning principles to develop and modify menus.	305, 308–309, 314, 324, 327, 453, 507, 566, 635, 735
8.4.3	Analyze food, equipment, and supplies needed for menus.	330–331, 333, 346, 347, 458–459, 485
8.4.4	Develop a variety of menu layouts, themes, and design styles.	310–312, 317–319, 612
8.4.5	Prepare requisitions for food, equipment, and supplies to meet production requirements.	360–362, 366
8.4.6	Record performance of menu items to analyze sales and determine menu revisions.	314–317, 323
8.4.7	Apply principles of Measurement, Portion Control, Conversions, Food Cost Analysis and Control, Menu Terminology, and Menu Pricing to menu planning.	321–324, 326, 327, 335–339, 341–342, 350–351, 354–355, 356, 359–362, 505
8.5	**Demonstrate professional food preparation methods and techniques for all menu categories to produce a variety of food products that meet customer needs.**	
8.5.1	Demonstrate professional skills in safe handling of knives, tools, and equipment.	254–260, 695
8.5.2	Demonstrate professional skill for a variety of cooking methods including roasting, broiling, smoking, grilling, sautéing, pan frying, deep frying, braising, stewing, poaching, steaming, and baking using professional equipment and current technologies.	376–377, 382–387, 389–394, 397, 605–610, 619–620, 630–632, 642–645, 653, 655–657, 682–684, 721–723, 769, 777
8.5.3	Utilize weights and measurement tools to demonstrate knowledge of portion control and proper scaling and measurement techniques.	678–681, 703, 714
8.5.4	Apply the fundamentals of time, temperature, and cooking methods to cooking, cooling, reheating, and holding of variety of foods.	298–300
8.5.5	Prepare various meats, seafood, and poultry using safe handling and professional preparation techniques.	542–547, 549–557, 559–564, 567, 577–582, 585, 588–589, 595–603, 605–610, 613

8.5.6	Prepare various stocks, soups, and sauces using safe handling and professional preparation techniques.	340, 429, 510–515, 517–525, 527–536, 539
8.5.7	Prepare various fruits, vegetables, starches, legumes, dairy products, fats, and oils using safe handling and professional preparation techniques.	332, 471–475, 480, 616–622, 624–632, 635, 642–645, 652–658, 663–666, 669
8.5.8	Prepare various salads, dressings, marinades, and spices using safe handling and professional preparation techniques.	463–469
8.5.9	Prepare sandwiches, canapés and appetizers using safe handling and professional preparation techniques.	477–478, 488–494, 496–500, 502–504, 507, 585
8.5.10	Prepare breads, baked goods and desserts using safe handling and professional preparation techniques.	333, 688–700, 706–711, 713–724, 727, 730–735, 737–742, 745, 748–753, 755–763, 765–769, 771–774, 777
8.5.11	Prepare breakfast meats, eggs, cereals, and batter products using safe handling and professional preparation techniques.	432–435, 436, 437–441, 443–446, 447, 448–450, 453
8.5.12	Demonstrate professional plating, garnishing, and food presentation techniques.	421–426, 459, 461, 485, 582
8.5.13	Examine the applicability of convenience food items.	510, 571
8.5.14	Demonstrate cooking methods that increase nutritional value, lower calorie and fat content, and utilize herbs and spices to enhance flavor.	298–299, 300–302, 400–404, 406–414
8.6	**Demonstrate implementation of food service management and leadership functions.**	
8.6.1	Apply principles of purchasing, receiving, issuing, and storing in food service operations.	225–229
8.6.2	Practice inventory procedures including first in/first out concept, date marking, and specific record keeping.	229, 247, 353
8.6.3	Apply accounting procedures in planning and forecasting profit and loss.	173–175
8.6.4	Examine the areas of risk management and legal liability within the food service industry.	185
8.6.5	Apply human resource policies including rules, regulations, laws, hiring, compensation, overtime, discrimination, and harassment.	105–106, 179, 205–208
8.6.6	Apply the procedures involved in staff planning, recruiting, interviewing, selecting, scheduling, performance reviewing, and terminating of employees.	106–107, 113, 179–181, 195, 210, 222
8.6.7	Conduct staff orientation, training, consistent reinforcement of training standards, and education, and on the job training/retraining.	110, 172, 180, 185
8.6.8	Implement marketing plan for food service operations.	188–192, 195
8.6.9	Design internal/external crisis management and disaster plans and response procedures.	9–12
8.6.10	Apply principles of inventory management, labor cost and control techniques, production planning and control, and facilities management to front and back of the house operations.	175–176, 182–183, 364–366, 368, 369
8.7	**Demonstrate the concept of internal and external customer service.**	
8.7.1	Apply principles of inventory management, labor cost and control techniques, production planning and control, and facilities management to front and back of the house operations.	125, 127, 151
8.7.2	Demonstrate quality services that meet industry standards in the food service industry.	119–121, 144–149, 151–152, 157, 158, 161
8.7.3	Analyze the role of quality service as a strategic component of exceptional performance.	127, 131–134, 137, 139
8.7.4	Demonstrate quality services that meet industry standards in the food service industry.	138, 171, 177, 195
8.7.5	Analyze the relationship between employees and customer satisfaction.	303, 666, 725

90-Day Pacing Guide

18-Week Course		
	Traditional Schedule	**Block Schedule**
Week	**Student Edition**	**Student Edition**
1	Chapter 1, 2	Chapter 1
2	Unit 1 Culinary Project; Chapter 3	Chapter 2; Unit 1 Culinary Project
3	Chapter 4	Chapter 3, 4
4	Chapter 5, 6; Unit 2 Culinary Project	Chapter 5, 6
5	Chapter 7, 8; Unit 3 Culinary Project	Unit 2 Culinary Project; Chapter 7
6	Chapter 9, 10, 11	Chapter 8; Unit 3 Culinary Project
7	Chapter 12, 13, 14	Chapter 9, 10, 11
8	Unit 4 Culinary Project; Chapter 15, 16	Chapter 12, 13, 14
9	Chapter 17, 18	Unit 4 Culinary Project
10	Chapter 19, 20	Chapter 15, 16, 17
11	Chapter 21, 22	Chapter 18, 19, 20
12	Chapter 23	Chapter 21, 22
13	Chapter 24	Chapter 23, 24
14	Chapter 25	Chapter 25
15	Unit 5 Culinary Project	Unit 5 Culinary Project
16	Chapter 26	Chapter 26, 27
17	Chapter 27, 28	Chapter 28
18	Chapter 29; Unit 6 Culinary Project	Chapter 29; Unit 6 Culinary Project

Additional activities for each chapter can be found in the *Lab Manual,* Presentation *Plus!* PowerPoint® Presentation CD, *ExamView® Assessment Suite* CD and the Online Learning Center.

180-Day Pacing Guide

	Traditional Schedule	Block Schedule
	36-Week Course	
Week	**Student Edition**	**Student Edition**
1	Chapter 1, 2 (Section 2.2)	Chapter 1
2	Unit 1 Culinary Project	Chapter 2 (Section 2.2)
3	Chapter 2 (Section 2.3), 3 (Section 3.1)	Unit 1 Culinary Project
4	Chapter 3, 4(Section 4.1)	Chapter 2, 3 (Section 3.1)
5	Chapter 4	Chapter 3, 4(Section 4.1)
6	Chapter 5	Chapter 4, 5 (Section 5.1)
7	Chapter 6 (Section 6.1)	Chapter 5
8	Chapter 6	Chapter 6 (Section 6.1)
9	Unit 2 Culinary Project	Chapter 6
10	Chapter 7	Unit 2 Culinary Project
11	Chapter 8 (Section 8.1)	Chapter 7, 8 (Section 8.1)
12	Chapter 8	Chapter 8
13	Unit 3 Culinary Project	Unit 3 Culinary Project
14	Chapter 9	Chapter 9 (Section 9.1)
15	Chapter 10 (Section 10.1)	Chapter 9
16	Chapter 10	Chapter 10 (Section 10.1)
17	Chapter 11	Chapter 10, 11 (Section 11.1)
18	Chapter 12, 13 (Section 13.1)	Chapter 11, 12
19	Chapter 14	Chapter 13, 14
20	Unit 4 Culinary Project	Unit 4 Culinary Project
21	Chapter 15 (Section 15.1)	Chapter 15 (Section 15.2)
22	Chapter 15, 16	Chapter 15
23	Chapter 17 (Section 17.2)	Chapter 16, 17 (Section 17.1)
24	Chapter 17, 18 (Section 18.2)	Chapter 17, 18 (Section 18.2)
25	Chapter 19	Chapter 18, 19 (Section 19.2)
26	Chapter 20 (Section 20.2)	Chapter 19, 20 (Section 20.1)
27	Chapter 20, 21	Chapter 20, 21
28	Chapter 22	Chapter 22
29	Chapter 22 (Section 22.2)	Chapter 23
30	Chapter 23, 24 (Section 24.1)	Chapter 24, 25 (Section 25.1)
31	Chapter 25; Unit 5 Culinary Project	Chapter 25; Unit 5 Culinary Project
32	Chapter 26	Chapter 26
33	Chapter 27, 28	Chapter 27, 28
34	Chapter 29 (Section 29.2)	Chapter 29 (Section 29.2)
35	Chapter 29	Chapter 29
36	Unit 6 Culinary Project	Unit 6 Culinary Project

Raise the Bar and Help Students Clear It

Academic Integration

Academic skills are crucial for success both inside and outside the classroom. In addition to traditional academic skills, your students will need communication skills, interpersonal skills, and strong technology skills in order to succeed in the real world. Basic skills will support your students in completing the tasks that their jobs and lives will demand.

The No Child Left Behind Act

The No Child Left Behind Act of 2001 emphasizes student achievement in basic academic subjects. It introduces strict accountability measures for schools in the form of standardized testing. Traditionally, core academic subjects have been defined as language arts, science, and mathematics. No Child Left Behind names the following academic subjects:

- English
- Reading/Language Arts
- Mathematics
- Science
- World Languages
- Civics and Government
- Economics
- Art
- History
- Geography

The Importance of Integrating Academics

In a recent survey of high school graduates—many of whom had gone directly to work rather than into postsecondary education—more than half the respondents said their high schools should have placed more emphasis on basic academic skills.

Unfortunately, these students—like so many others—were not able to recognize the relevance of their course work while they were in high school. By explicitly integrating academic skills into the family and consumer sciences curriculum, you can make students aware of the connections between schoolwork and the real world.

Integrated learning offers the following additional benefits to students:

- It provides real-world learning and thus establishes patterns of lifelong learning.
- It improves the academic achievement of all students—including those who will begin their careers directly after high school, those who will go on to postsecondary education or training, and those who will obtain four-year college degrees and beyond.
- It helps students make realistic plans for their own careers and education.

Academics in the Family and Consumer Sciences Curriculum

Integrate academic skills into the classroom as a regular part of your classroom activities. For example, by having students read class assignments and texts, write letters and reports, give presentations, and perform mathematics exercises, you are helping them improve their academic skills. Make expectations clear. For example, if you ask your students to prepare a written report, explain that grammar, spelling, and presentation will be evaluated along with subject content. These are skills that students will need for success in school and at work.

To integrate academics into your course, you must incorporate principles from other subjects in a way that students can understand either on a concrete level or in metaphoric terms. This type of teaching will help those students who learn best when they are exposed to a variety of examples.

Deliver Efficient Instruction to All Students

Accountability

A consequence of the No Child Left Behind Act, and the reauthorization of the Perkins Act is that more states require testing for high school graduation. Accountability measures new to the Perkins reauthorization bill include:

- Academic proficiency as measured by the state criteria developed under NCLB;
- Graduation rates, also as defined by NCLB;
- Number of students to continue to post-secondary education;
- Number of students to complete state or industry certification or licensure; and
- Student achievement on assignments aligned with industry standards.

Connection to Relevance

With the mandatory requirements for proven test scores and graduation numbers, how can we assure that our students are learning? Most educators agree it is by connecting the relevance of education to life.

The Association for Career and Technical Education past-president Bob Scarborough says the Perkins reauthorization "ensures we are providing all students with an education that will help them succeed in the workplace and in life." William Daggett writes in *Achieving Academic Excellence through Rigor and Relevance:*

> What is important is that students enter the global economy with the ability to apply what they learned in school to a variety of ever-changing situations that they may not have been able to foresee before graduating.

The Rigor/Relevance Framework, developed at the International Center for Leadership in Education, illustrates leveled learning processes that enable students to perform high-level thinking. The learning process defines student performance in four sequential categories: acquisition, application, assimilation and adaptation.

As educators, our goal is to teach students to adapt their acquired knowledge and skills in complex ways to any situations, known and unknown. As educators, we are committed to provide the connectivity between classroom learning and real-world application.

Applications

Studies show that students understand and retain knowledge when they experience or apply it to relevant situations. The *Culinary Essentials* program is dedicated to meet the challenge. Every chapter in *Culinary Essentials* is filled with ways to engage students in experiential learning and applying their knowledge to their lives.

Features designed to help students find the relevance in content include:

- Unit Culinary Project (featuring skills self-assessment, culinary skills exploration, and connection to the community)
- How To
- Culinary Showcase
- Nutrition Notes
- Master Recipes
- Sanitation Check and Safety Check
- Science, Math, and History features
- Culinary Career Showcase
- Chapter Review and Applications, including Real-World Skills and Applications, Academic Skills, Certification Prep, and Culinary Lab

The content and teaching strategies in *Culinary Essentials* are designed to help applied learning students acclimate into the real world and to prepare them for working in the professional foodservice industry.

Designing Instruction for a Diverse Classroom

The Diverse Classroom

No two students enter a classroom with identical abilities, backgrounds, experiences, and learning preferences, yet they are all expected to master the curricular objectives. Teachers face the enormous challenge of designing instruction to better meet the diverse learning needs of students.

Universal Access and Universal Design

Universal access and universal design, as well as differentiated instruction, provide a framework for professional educators to address the challenges and opportunities of a diverse classroom.

Universal Access

Universal Access (UA) means that all people have an equal opportunity to access information, products, and services. Universal access, from an educational perspective, means that all students have an equal opportunity to education. This means access to high-quality curriculum and instruction regardless of learning diversities. UA may involve the use of specialized technology and environments.

Universal Design

Universal Design (UD) has a foundation in architecture. UD originally focused on accessibility issues for individuals with disabilities. Current UD philosophy focuses on designs that support all individuals, not just individuals with disabilities. From an educational perspective, universal design makes instructional facilities, materials, and activities available so that all learners can achieve success. The key instructional element associated with UD is variety:

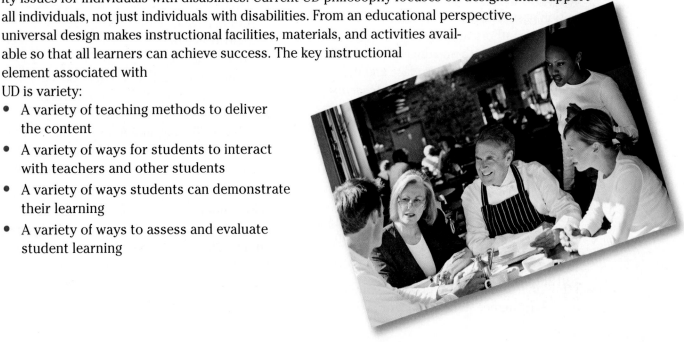

- A variety of teaching methods to deliver the content
- A variety of ways for students to interact with teachers and other students
- A variety of ways students can demonstrate their learning
- A variety of ways to assess and evaluate student learning

Differentiated Instruction

Differentiated Instruction (DI) is a planned, deliberate, sequential, and systematic instructional technique designed to maximize the learning and achievement of all students in the classroom. Because of the diversity in student learning abilities and preferences, instruction needs to be equally diverse. By recognizing and positively responding to diverse student backgrounds, languages, abilities, and learning preferences, teachers are better able to deliver instruction that creates opportunities for improved student learning, and success within the framework of universal design.

Five Key Steps for Delivering Differentiated Instruction

1. *Know your students' learning profiles.*

A student's learning profile may include information about learning disabilities, English language ability, learning preferences, customs, needs, interests, and background. To gather student learning profiles, record student inventories, take note of conversations, make observations, and connect with other education specialists. Use the Universal Access activities and suggestions found in *Culinary Essentials* to craft lessons to suit your students' needs.

2. *Use a variety of instructional methods.*

Differentiated instruction varies the way that learning expectations are delivered to the students. *Culinary Essentials* offers suggestions for modifying instructional delivery to include problem-solving activities, writing, models, demonstrations, and graphic organizers.

3. *Provide ample opportunities for student/teacher and student/student interactions.*

The varied use of small group, partner, and whole-class instruction provides a differentiated approach that can be used to support many needs, such as language skills, review, enrichment, or acceleration. Modify the independence of the activities in *Culinary Essentials* using group and partner activity suggestions throughout the book, Interpersonal and Collaborative Activities in the chapter reviews, and Guided Practice activities in the Teacher Annotated Edition Lesson Plans.

4. *Allow students to demonstrate their learning with a variety of product options.*

Students should be given the opportunity to demonstrate their learning in diverse ways. For example, some students who struggle with writing may prefer to demonstrate their learning orally (speech, skit, audio recording), visually (model, exhibit, poster, drawing), or through media applications (video, PowerPoint®, music). Use the Hands-On Labs, Technology Applications, Active Learning activities, and other creative activities throughout *Culinary Essentials* as models for alternative product options.

5. *Use varied methods to assess and evaluate student learning.*

Student assessments should be varied and frequent. They should be formal (graded, such as a test or product) and informal (non-graded, such as observations or group questioning for progress monitoring). Self-assessments allow the students to judge their own progress. Assessments should also include a range of low- to high-level thinking and responding skills in both traditional and authentic assessment formats. Use the Self-Evaluation Rubrics, quizzes, critical thinking assignments, and discussion questions in *Culinary Essentials* to assess and evaluate student learning.

Delivering Instruction to Reach All Students

Differentiated Instruction for English Language Learners

Differentiated instruction is important in virtually all classrooms. It is critical in language-diverse classrooms, where many learning activities can be and should be modified and differentiated. Before determining what level of differentiation is needed for your English language learners (ELL), ask yourself two questions:

1. Which language proficiency level best describes my English language learners?

Many schools, districts, and/or states typically place their ELL students in one of several language proficiency levels. Each level offers suggested activity verbs that support student learning. The use of verb taxonomies for differentiating both the process and product of learning can be helpful to students. Use the verbs most appropriate for the students' proficiencies, as identified below:

Language Proficiency Levels

Beginning/Early Intermediate These students typically read English at 0–2.5 grade level. They may be able to write short simple paragraphs and identify main ideas and story characters. **Activity Verbs:** tell, point, circle, underline, name, draw, change, describe, and discuss.

Intermediate These students read English at 2.6–3.5 grade level and can often write paragraphs and identify "wh" questions (who, what, when, where, and why). **Activity Verbs:** apply, show, classify, modify, explain, solve, and demonstrate.

Early Advanced These students are near proficient. They read at 3.6–5.5 grade level and may be fluent in oral English. They often need help with academic and written English. **Activity Verbs:** analyze, compare, contrast, criticize, examine, create, predict, design, manage, and prepare.

2. Is some degree of activity modification necessary to assure achievement and success?

Some activities may not need modification for ELL students, but many will. There are three common ways to modify an activity:

- **Modify the Language Rigor.**
  Change the activity verb to better align with the student's language proficiency.

- **Modify the Independence Rigor.**
  Change the students' degree of independence to align with his/her needed support. For example, an activity that directs the students to complete a task "independently" could be changed to "with a partner."

- **Provide Product Options.**
  Allow students to demonstrate their learning in multiple ways by asking them to write a report or poem; draw; orally explain; or create a game, poster, commercial, video, presentation, song, or cartoon. Students may also teach a lesson, build a model, construct a diagram, or conduct an experiment.

Prior to any activity modification, confirm that all associated vocabulary is clearly understood by all students. Whenever possible, activity modification should be supported by graphic organizers, such as T-charts, webs, sequence, hierarchical, cluster, vocabulary, and data charts.

Sample Activity Modified for ELL Students

W Writing Strategy

Make a List Ask students to create a list of questions to ask when evaluating an advertisement. Have them create a worksheet that they can fill out when looking at an advertisement that contains their questions and space to answer them.

Modified for Beginner/Early Intermediate Students
ELL Writing Strategy

As a class, ask students to think of questions to ask when evaluating an advertisement. Write each question on the board. Give the class an advertisement to evaluate. Walk students through each question as a class. Write their answers on the board.

Modified for Intermediate Students
ELL Writing Strategy

In small groups, have students list four questions to ask when evaluating an advertisement. Have students answer each question orally to their group as they evaluate an advertisement.

Modified for Early Advanced Students
ELL Writing Strategy

In pairs, have students list four questions to ask when evaluating an advertisement. Have them create a worksheet listing questions they can answer in writing when looking at an advertisement.

Empower Your Students with Reading Skills

How Can I Motivate My Students to Read?

As a teacher, your role is to help students make personal connections in order to answer the question, "Why do I need to learn this?" Emphasize that reading is not only a necessity for work and for life; it can also bring enjoyment and enlightenment.

Ask your students, "What role does reading play in your life?" You can open this discussion by modeling examples: I love historical biographies; I read menus and order meals in Spanish; I read magazines and access the Internet to stay up to date on my favorite sports teams.

Improving or Fine-Tuning Reading Skills Will Help Your Students:

- ◆ Improve grades
- ◆ Read faster and more efficiently
- ◆ Improve their study skills
- ◆ Remember more information accurately
- ◆ Improve their writing

The Reading Process

Good reading skills build on one another, overlap, and spiral in much the same way that a winding staircase goes around and around while leading readers to a higher place. The Reading Skills Handbook is designed to help your students find and use the tools to use before, during, and after reading.

Reading Strategies

- ◆ Identify, understand, and learn new words
- ◆ Understand why you read
- ◆ Take a quick look at the whole text
- ◆ Try to predict what you are about to read
- ◆ Take breaks during reading and ask questions about the text
- ◆ Take notes
- ◆ Keep thinking about what will come next
- ◆ Summarize

Vocabulary Development

Word identification and vocabulary skills are the building blocks of reading and writing. By learning to use a variety of strategies to build word skills and vocabulary, your students will become stronger readers.

Use Context to Determine Meaning

The best way for your students to expand and extend vocabulary is to read widely, listen carefully, and participate in a rich variety of discussions. When reading independently, students can often figure out the meanings of new words by looking at their context, or the other words and sentences that surround them.

They Will *Use* in the Real World

Predict a Possible Meaning

Another way to determine the meaning of a word is to take the word apart. If a reader understands the meaning of the **base, or root,** part of a word, and knows the meanings of key syllables added either to the beginning or end of the base word, it becomes easy to figure out what the word means.

Word Origins Since Latin, Greek, and Anglo-Saxon roots are the basis for much of our English vocabulary, having some background in one of these languages can be a useful vocabulary tool. For example, astronomy comes from the Greek root *astro,* which means relating to the stars. *Stellar* also has a meaning referring to stars, but its origin is Latin. Knowing root words in other languages can help readers determine meanings, derivations, and spellings in English.

Prefixes and Suffixes A prefix is a word part that can be added to the beginning of a word. For example, the prefix *semi* means half or partial, so *semicircle* means half a circle. A suffix is a word part that can be added to the end of a word. Adding a suffix often changes a word from one part of speech to another.

Using Dictionaries A dictionary provides the meaning or meanings of a word. Look at the sample dictionary entry in the student edition Reading Skills Handbook to see what other information it provides.

Thesauruses and Specialized Reference Books A thesaurus provides synonyms and often antonyms. It is a useful tool to use to expand vocabulary. Remind students to check the exact definition of the listed words in a dictionary before using a thesaurus. Specialized dictionaries such the *Barron's Dictionary of Business Terms* or *Black's Law Dictionary* list terms and expressions not commonly included in a general dictionary.

Glossaries Many textbooks and technical works contain condensed dictionaries that provide an alphabetical listing of words used throughout the text and their specific definitions.

Recognize Word Meanings Across Subjects Words often have different meanings when used for different purposes. The word *product* may mean one thing in math and another in science. For example:

Math After you multiply the two numbers, explain how you arrived at the **product.**

Science One **product** of photosynthesis is oxygen.

Economics The Gross National **Product** is the total dollar value of goods and services produced by a nation.

How Can I Help My Students Understand What They Read?

Reading comprehension means understanding—deriving meaning from—what has been read. Using a variety of strategies can help improve comprehension and make reading more interesting and more fun.

Read for a Reason

To get the greatest benefit from reading, teach students to **establish a purpose for their reading.** In school, some of the reasons for reading are to:

- learn and understand new information
- find specific information
- review before a test
- complete an assignment
- prepare (research) before you write

As reading skills improve, you will notice that your students apply different strategies to fit the different purposes for reading. For example, a person reading for entertainment may read quickly, but reading to gather information or follow directions might require reading more slowly, taking notes, constructing a graphic organizer, or rereading sections of text.

Draw on Personal Background

Drawing on personal background, or activating prior knowledge, helps students connect their culture and experiences to their reading. Before introducing a new topic, you may want to encourage students to ask:

- What have I heard or read about this topic?
- Do I have any personal experience relating to this topic?

You can also set common background knowledge with discussion before reading. For example, to prepare students to read the novel *A Farewell to Arms,* you might lead a discussion about these common background themes:

- World War I
- Italy (You might ask a student to show the location of Italy on a map)
- Other Ernest Hemingway titles
- The Nobel Prize in literature

Having this historical background will help to set the scene for students as they read.

Using a KWL Chart A KWL chart is a good device for organizing information gathered before, during, and after reading. In the first column, students list what they already know, then list what they want to know in the middle column. They use the third column to review and assess what they learned. You or your students can add more columns to record places where they found information and places where they can look for more information.

K (What I already know)	W (What I want to know)	L (What I have learned)

Adjust Your Reading Speed Reading speed is a key factor in how well students understand what they read. Reading speed can vary depending on the purpose for reading.

Scanning means running one's eyes quickly over the material to look for words or phrases. Readers scan to find a specific piece of information.

Skimming means reading a passage quickly to find its main idea or get an overview. Skim a passage as a preview to determine what the material is about.

Reading for detail involves careful reading while paying attention to text structure and monitoring understanding. Readers read for detail to learn concepts, follow complicated directions, or prepare to analyze a text.

Techniques to Help Students Understand and Remember What They Read

Preview

Previewing strategies help students begin at a visual level, then drill down to evaluate, predict, draw conclusions, and use contextual clues about what they will read.

Previewing Strategies

- ◆ Read the title, headings, and subheadings of the selection.
- ◆ Look at the illustrations and notice how the text is organized.
- ◆ Skim the selection. Take a glance at the whole thing.
- ◆ Decide what the main idea might be.
- ◆ Predict what a selection will be about.

Predict

As students read, they take educated guesses about story events and outcomes. They make predictions before and during reading. This helps them focus their attention on the text and that focus improves understanding.

Determine the Main Idea

When students look for the main idea, they are looking for the most important statement in a text. Depending on what kind of text they read, the main idea can be located at the very beginning (news stories in a newspaper or a magazine) or at the end (scientific research document).

Encourage students to ask these questions to determine the main idea:

- • What is each sentence about?
- • Is there one sentence that is more important than all the others?
- • What idea do the details support or point out?

Keep track of the text's structure (see below). Looking at headers and content structure will give students important clues about the main idea.

Taking Notes

Cornell Note-Taking System There are many methods for note taking. The **Cornell Note-Taking System** is a well-known method that can help students organize what they read. To the right is a note-taking activity based on the Cornell Note-Taking System.

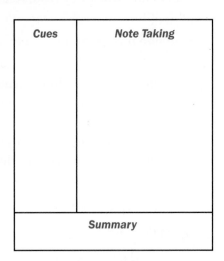

Graphic Organizers Using a graphic organizer to retell content in a visual representation will help students remember and retain content. Encourage students to make charts or diagrams to organize what they have read. Some good examples are:

Venn Diagrams A Venn diagram is a good way to organize information in a compare-and-contrast text structure. The outer portions of the circles show how two characters, ideas, or items contrast, or are different, and the overlapping part compares two things, or shows how they are similar.

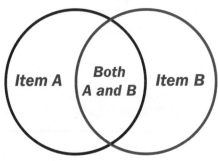

Flow Charts Students can a track sequence of events or cause and effect on a flow chart. Demonstrate how to arrange ideas or events in their logical, sequential order. Then, draw arrows between ideas to indicate how one idea or event flows into another.

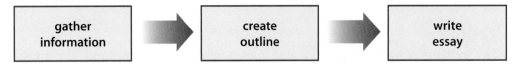

Go to **glencoe.com** for more information about note taking and additional study tools.

Visualize

Encourage students to try to form a mental picture of scenes, characters, and events as they read. This technique helps them to use the details and descriptions the author gives readers. If students can **visualize** what they read, they will become more interested and will remember the information better.

Question

Tell students to ask questions about the text while they read. Encourage them to ask about the importance of the sentences they read, how the sentences relate to one another, whether they understand what they just read, and what they think is going to come next.

Clarify

Encourage students to try these techniques when they do not understand meaning (through questioning):

What to Do When You Do Not Understand

◆ Reread confusing parts of the text.

◆ Diagram (chart) relationships between chunks of text, ideas, and sentences.

◆ Look up unfamiliar words.

◆ Talk through the text as if explaining it to someone else.

◆ Read the passage once more.

Review

Make sure students take time to stop and review what they have read. Use note-taking outlines or other graphic organizers, charts, or visual aids.

Monitor Comprehension

Teach students to continue to check their understanding using the following two strategies:

Summarize Pause and state the main ideas of the text and the key supporting details. Try to answer the following questions: Who? What? When? Where? Why? How?

Paraphrase Pause, close the book, and try to retell what they have just read using their own words. It helps students to retell, or paraphrase reading into their own words.

Understanding Text Structure

Good writers do not just put together sentences and paragraphs; they organize their writing with a specific purpose in mind. That organization is called text structure. When students understand and follow the structure of a text, it is easier to remember the information they read. There are many ways text may be structured. Each type of structure usually makes use of some specific words. Teach students to watch for these **signal words.** They will help them follow the text's organization. (Remind them to use these techniques as they write.)

Comparison and Contrast

This structure shows similarities and differences between people, things, and ideas. This is often used to demonstrate that things that seem alike are really different, or vice versa.

Signal words: similarly, more, less, on the one hand/on the other hand, in contrast, but, however

Cause and Effect

Writers use the cause-and-effect structure to explore the reasons for something happening and to examine the results or consequences of events.

Signal words: so, because, as a result, therefore, for the following reasons

Problem and Solution

When writers organize text around the question "How?", they state a problem and suggest solutions.

Signal words: how, help, problem, obstruction, overcome, difficulty, need, attempt, have to, must

Sequence

Sequencing tells readers in which order to consider thoughts or facts. Examples of sequencing are:

Chronological order refers to the order in which events take place.

Signal words: first, next, then, finally

Spatial order describes the organization of things in space (to describe the placement of objects in a room, for example).

Signal words: above, below, behind, next to

Order of importance lists things or thoughts from the most important to the least important (or the other way around).

Signal words: principal, central, main, important, fundamental

Thinking About Reading

It is important for students to think about what they are reading to get the most information from a text, to understand the consequences of what the text says, to remember the content, and to form their own opinions about what they read.

Interpret

Interpreting involves asking, "What is the writer really saying?" and then using what students already know to answer the question.

Infer

Writers do not always state exactly everything they want readers to understand. They sometimes imply certain information by providing clues and details. To infer involves using reasoning and experience to develop the idea, based on what an author implies, or suggests. What is most important when drawing inferences is to be sure that readers have accurately based their guesses on supporting details from the text. If students cannot point to a place in the selection to help back up an inference, encourage them to rethink that guess.

Draw Conclusions

A conclusion is a general statement a reader can make and explain using reasoning or supporting details from a text.

Analyze

To understand persuasive nonfiction (a text that lists facts and opinions to arrive at a conclusion), readers must analyze statements and examples to see if they support the main idea. To understand an informational text, students need to keep track of how the ideas are organized to find the main points.

Hint: Have students use graphic organizers and note-taking charts.

Distinguish Between Facts and Opinions

This is one of the most important reading skills students can learn. A fact is a statement that can be proven. An opinion is what the writer believes. A writer may support opinions with facts, but an opinion cannot be proven. For example:

Fact: California produces fruit and other agricultural products.

Opinion: California produces the best fruit and agricultural products.

Evaluate

Remind students that to rely on accurate information, they will need to consider who wrote it and why. Where did the writer get information? Is the information one-sided? Can readers verify the information?

Reading for Research

To guide students in reading actively to research a topic, encourage them to follow these directions:

- Generate an interesting, relevant, and researchable question.
- Categorize that information.
- Evaluate the information.
- Organize information in a new way for a specific audience.
- Draw conclusions about the original research question.

Link Academic Vocabulary

What Is Academic English?

by Robin Scarcella, Ph.D.

Academic English is the language commonly used in business and education. It is the language used in academics, business, and courts of law. It is the type of English used in professional books, including textbooks, and it contains specific linguistic features that are associated with all disciplines. Proficiency in reading and using academic English is strongly related to long-term success in all parts of life.

What Is Academic Vocabulary?

By the time they complete elementary school, students should acquire the knowledge they will need to understand academic vocabulary. For example, in academic texts, a full 8% of the words are academic words. A basic 2,000-word vocabulary of high-frequency words makes up 87% of the words. Three percent are technical words that vary depending on the discipline. The remaining 2% are low-frequency words.

Why Should Students Learn Academic Vocabulary?

English language learners who have mastered a basic 2,000-word vocabulary are ready to acquire the majority of general words found in their texts and on standardized tests.

Knowledge of academic words, combined with continued acquisition of general words, can significantly boost an English learner's comprehension level of academic texts. English learners who learn and practice these words before they graduate from high school are likely to master academic material with more confidence and speed. They waste less time and effort in guessing words than those students who know only the basic 2,000 words that characterize general conversation.

Academic Vocabulary and Academic English in the Family and Consumer Sciences Classroom

Teachers can provide their students with rich samples of academic vocabulary and help students understand the academic English of their text. To develop academic English, students must have already acquired a large amount of basic proficiency in the grammar of everyday English.

Academic English should be taught within contexts that make sense. Academic English arises not only from a knowledge of linguistic code and cognition but also from social practices in which academic English is used to accomplish communicative goals. The acquisition of academic vocabulary and grammar is necessary to advance the development of academic English.

Tips for Teaching Academic Vocabulary:

- **Expose Students to Academic Vocabulary**—Students learn academic vocabulary through use and in reading content. You do not need to call attention to all academic words students are learning because they will acquire them subconsciously.

- **Do Not Correct Students' Mistakes When Using Academic Vocabulary**— All vocabulary understanding and spelling errors are developmental and will disappear once the student reads more.

- **Help Students Decode the Words Themselves**—Once students learn the alphabet, they should be able to decode words. Decoding each word they do not recognize will help them more than trying to focus on sentence structure. Once they can recognize words, they can read authentic texts.

- **Do Not Ignore the English Learner in This Process**—These students can learn academic vocabulary before they are completely fluent in spoken English.

- **Helping Students Build Academic Vocabulary Leads to Broader Learning**—Students who have mastered the basic academic vocabulary are ready to continue acquiring words from the rest of the vocabulary groups. Use the Internet to find lists of appropriate vocabulary words.

Guidelines for Teaching Academic Vocabulary

There are a number of guidelines that teachers can follow when teaching academic English and vocabulary:

1. Use direct and planned instruction.
2. Employ models that have increasingly difficult language.
3. Focus attention on form by pointing out linguistic features of words.
4. Provide practice opportunities.
5. Motivate student interest and self-confidence.
6. Provide instructional feedback.
7. Use assessment tools on a regular basis.

Generate the Best Performance

Performance-Based Assessments

One good way to present a performance assessment is in the form of an open-ended question.

- **Journals**—Students write from their own perspective on topics that affect their lives.
- **Letters**—Students write a letter from themselves to friends and family, or another audience.
- **Position Paper or Editorial**—Students explain a controversial issue and present their own opinions and recommendations, supported with strong evidence and convincing reasons.
- **Newspaper**—Students write stories from the perspective of a reporter.
- **Biographies and Autobiographies**—Students write about leaders either from the third person point of view (biography) or from the first person (autobiography).
- **Creative Stories**—Students integrate family and consumer sciences topics into a piece of fiction.
- **Poems and Songs**—Students follow the conventions of a particular type of song or poem as they tell about a topic or event.
- **Research Reports**—Students synthesize information from a variety of sources into a well-developed research report.

Oral Presentations

Oral presentations allow students to demonstrate their academic and topical literacy in front of an audience. Oral presentations are often group efforts, although this need not be the case.

- **Simulations**—Students hold simulations of actual events, such as a role play in a specific scenario.
- **Debates**—Students debate two or more sides of a policy or issue.
- **Interview**—Students conduct a mock journalism interview or job interview.
- **Oral Reports**—Students present the results of research efforts in a lively oral report. This report may be accompanied by visuals.
- **Skits and Plays**—Students use specific events or topics as the basis for a play or skit.

Visual Presentations

Visual presentations allow students to demonstrate their understanding in a variety of visual formats. Visual presentations can be either group or individual projects.

- **Model**—Students make a model to demonstrate or represent a particular process.
- **Museum Exhibit**—Students create a rich display of materials around a topic. Typical displays might include models, illustrations, photographs, videos, writings, and presentation software.

from Your Students

- **Graph or Chart**—Students analyze and represent data in a line graph, bar graph, table, or other chart format.
- **Drawing**—Students represent an event or period through illustration, including cartoons.
- **Posters and Murals**—Posters and murals may include maps, time lines, diagrams, illustrations, photographs, and written explanations that reflect students' understanding of the information.
- **Videotapes**—Students film a video to show a simulation of an event.
- **Multimedia Presentation**—Students create a computer-generated presentation or slide show containing information and analysis.

How Are Performance Assessments Scored?

There are a variety of means used to evaluate performance tasks. Some or all of the following methods may be used:

- **Scoring Rubrics**—A scoring rubric is a set of guidelines for assessing the quality of a process and/or product. It sets out criteria used to distinguish acceptable responses from unacceptable ones, generally on a scale from excellent to poor. Rubrics may be used as guidelines as the students prepare their products. They are also commonly used for peer-to-peer assessment and self-assessment.
- **Models of Excellent Work**—Teacher-selected models of excellent work concretely illustrate expectations and help students set goals for their own projects.

- **Student Self-Assessment**—Common methods of self-assessment include ranking work in relation to the model, using a scoring rubric, and writing goals and then evaluating how well the goals have been met.
- **Peer or Audience Assessment**—Many of the performance tasks target an audience other than the classroom teacher. If possible, the audience of peers should give feedback. Have the class create rubrics for specific projects together.
- **Observation**—As students carry out their performance tasks, you may want to formally observe them at work. Start by developing a checklist, identifying all the specific behaviors and understandings you expect students to demonstrate. Then, observe students as they carry out performance tasks and check off behaviors as you observe them.
- **Interviews**—As a form of ongoing assessment, you may want to conduct interviews with students, asking them to analyze, explain, and assess their participation in performance tasks. When projects take place over an extended period of time, you can hold periodic interviews as well as exit interviews.

Prepare Your Students

Test-Prep Strategies

Students can follow the steps below to prepare for the standardized assessments they are required to take.

- **Read About the Test**—Students can familiarize themselves with the format, the types of questions, and the amount of time they will have to complete the test. Emphasize that it is very important for students to budget their time during test-taking.
- **Review the Content**—Consistent study will help students build knowledge and understanding. If there are specific objectives or standards that are tested on the exam, help students review facts or skills.
- **Practice**—Provide practice, ideally with real tests, to build students' familiarity with the content, format, and timing of the real exam. Students should practice all the types of questions they will encounter on the test.
- **Pace**—Students should pace themselves differently depending on how the test is administered. As students practice, they should try to increase the number of questions they can answer correctly. If students have trouble with an item, they should mark it and come back to it later.
- **Analyze Practice Results**—Help students improve test-taking performance by analyzing their test-taking strengths and weaknesses. Help students identify what kinds of questions they found most difficult. Look for patterns in errors and tailor instruction to review the appropriate test-taking skills or content.

Test-Taking Strategies

It's not enough for students to learn facts and concepts. They must be able to show what they know in a variety of test-taking situations.

Objective Tests

Apply the following strategies to help students do their best on objective tests.

Multiple-Choice Questions

- Students should read the directions carefully to learn what answer the test requires—the best answer or the right answer. This is especially important when answer choices include "all of the above" or "none of the above."

- Students should watch for negative words, such as not, except, and unless.
- Students should try to mentally answer the question before answering.
- Students should eliminate answer choices that are obviously wrong.

True/False Questions
- It is important that students read the entire question before answering. For an answer to be true, the entire statement must be true. If one part of a statement is false, the answer should be marked false.
- Remind students to watch for words such as all, never, every, and always. Statements containing these words are often false.

Matching Questions
- Students should read through both lists before they mark any answers.
- Unless an answer can be used more than once, students should cross out each choice as they use it.
- Students can use grammar to find the right answer. When matching word/definition, the definition is often the same part of speech (noun, verb, adjective, or adverb) as the word.

Essay Tests

Essay tests require students to provide thorough and well-organized written responses, in addition to telling what they know. Help students use these strategies on essay tests.

Read the Question

The key to writing successful essay responses lies in reading and interpreting questions correctly. Teach students to identify and underline key words to guide them in understanding what the question asks.

Plan and Write the Essay

Students should follow the writing process to develop their answer. Encourage students to follow these steps to plan and write their essays.

1. Map out an answer. Make lists, webs, or an outline to plan the response.
2. Decide on an order in which to present the main points.
3. Write an opening statement that directly responds to the essay question.
4. Write the essay. Expand on the opening statement. Support key points with specific facts, details, and reasons.
5. Write a closing statement that brings the main points together.
6. Proofread to check spelling, grammar, and punctuation.

Base Your Teaching on Best Practices

Critical Thinking

One of the factors that determines students' success is a their ability to deal with the varied demands of day-to-day life. This requires insightful decision making, creative problem solving, and interactions with diverse groups. Thus, teaching critical thinking equips your students with the skills necessary to achieve success.

Cognitive Development

All learning requires thinking. Benjamin Bloom's Taxonomy of the Cognitive Domain is probably the most widely recognized schema of levels of thinking. Each of Bloom's six cognitive categories lists various thinking skills and indicates the types of behavior students are expected to perform to fulfill specific learning goals. See the chart below.

The Value of Critical Thinking

Critical thinking is the process of reasonably or logically deciding what to do or believe. It involves the ability to:

- Compare and contrast
- Solve problems
- Make decisions
- Analyze and evaluate
- Synthesize and transfer knowledge
- Engage in metacognition

CATEGORY	GOAL	EXPECTED STUDENT RESPONSE	APPROPRIATE QUESTIONS/PROMPTS
Knowledge	Identify and recall information	Define, recognize, recall, identify, label, show, collect, understand, examine	Who…? What…? When…? Where…? How…? Describe….
Comprehension	Organize and select facts and ideas	Translate, interpret, explain, describe, summarize, extrapolate	Retell in your own words…. What is the main idea of…?
Application	Use facts, rules, and principles	Apply, solve, show, experiment, predict	How is…an example of…? How is…related to…?
Analysis	Separate a whole into component parts	Connect, relate, differentiate, classify, arrange, check, group, distinguish, organize, categorize, detect, compare, infer	Classify…according to…. How does… compare/contrast with…?
Synthesis	Combine ideas to form a new whole	Produce, propose, design, construct, combine, formulate, compose, plan, hypothesize	What would you predict/infer from…? What might happen if you combined…with…?
Evaluation	Develop opinions, judgments, or decisions	Appraise, judge, criticize, decide	What do you think about…? Prioritize….

Your and Students Will Benefit

Critical thinking skills are important for these reasons:

- They help students investigate their own problem-solving mechanisms.
- They help students find creative resolutions.
- They lead students to compare and contrast what they know with unknowns.
- They allow students to make decisions about their own learning while making them aware of their learning processes.

Cooperative Learning

Studies show that students learn faster and retain more information when they are actively involved in the learning process. Cooperative learning is one method that gets students actively involved in learning and at the same time allows for peer teaching.

Using Cooperative Learning

Your family and consumer sciences course provides many opportunities for students to learn and apply the skills necessary for positive interpersonal relationships. Through the use of cooperative learning, you can offer a structured method of teaching team-building, collaborative social skills, and team decision making while teaching basic concepts—essential skills for making nutrition and wellness choices.

Cooperative Learning in This Text

In *Culinary Essentials,* students and teachers have a variety of materials to assist with cooperative learning activities. Many of the features and section and chapter assessment activities can be completed in a cooperative learning environment.

The Benefits of Cooperative Learning

- Cooperative learning emphasizes working toward group goals rather than the traditional emphasis on individual competition and achievement.
- Students discover that not only must they learn the material themselves, but they are also responsible for helping everyone in the group learn the material.
- Cooperative learning increases academic achievement and develops essential social skills.
- Students learn valuable problem-solving, team-building, and creativity skills that transfer to real-world environments and situations.
- People who help each other and work together toward a common goal generally begin to feel more positive about themselves and each other.
- Students have the opportunity to perceive other students as colleagues rather than competitors. As a result, they recognize the value of helping others rather than working competitively.

Technology

Technology affects how all people work, interact, and live. Technology will affect your students in the real world. For example, they may keep records using a computer or apply for a job over the Internet. It will also affect your students as consumers. An increasing number of people market, buy, and sell products on the Web. It is critical that your students become familiar and comfortable with technology now in order to prepare for success in life.

Activities

Culinary Essentials helps you integrate technology into your teaching with technology-based activities:

- Features and assessments provide a link to the *Culinary Essentials* Online Learning Center (OLC) at **glencoe.com** to assist students in finding answers and to further research the topic or find a project.

- The section-opening **Reading Guide** provides a link to the OLC for students to download the printable graphic organizer.
- The **Unit Culinary Project** sends students to the OLC for extra information on each project topic.
- Each **Real-World Skills and Applications** section in the Chapter Review and Applications assessment contains at least one Technology Application. Extra activities are also available on the OLC.
- Students can use assessment rubrics on the OLC to self-evaluate their Unit Culinary Projects.

Using the Internet Effectively

Give these tips to your students to help them use the Internet effectively in the classroom:

- Look for sites that are created by the government or universities (their URLs typically end in .gov or .edu). These are reliable sites with factual integrity and stability.
- Find out who created the site. If the purpose and creator of the Web site are unclear, its content may be unreliable.
- Use multiple search engines when looking for information on a topic. This will call up as many of the pertinent sites as possible.
- Combine Internet research with traditional research methods. Have students ask librarians and experts for information and sources. Use books and magazines.

Diversity

Culinary Essentials is designed to help students recognize and discuss issues of cultural diversity. During class activities, you may also find it appropriate to integrate questions related to cultural diversity. For example, you might expand a class discussion by asking:

- Would your response change if a classmate did not speak the same native language as you speak? If so, how?
- Would you speak to your classmate differently if his or her ethnic background were different from yours?
- Would your decision change if your classmate were a male or female? From your own ethnic background? From a different background? Why?

Integrating Cultural Diversity

Your students will be faced with a diverse world, meeting people of many different cultures. Cultural knowledge may be the difference between success and failure in our global economy. For students to become productive and responsible citizens, they must be open to cultural differences.

As students learn about skills needed to be successful, they should keep in mind the wide diversity of the people they are likely to encounter in every aspect of their working and personal lives. In the classroom and in one-on-one conferences, you can help your students consider the diversity of the U.S. population, not only in terms of ethnicity, but also in terms of customs, attitudes, religious beliefs, language backgrounds, and physical capabilities. High school students need to understand that ability and success are not related to skin color or gender.

Multicultural Education

Multicultural education incorporates the idea that all students—regardless of their gender and social class, and their ethnic, racial, or cultural characteristics—should have an equal opportunity to learn in school. Learning about other cultures concurrently with their own culture helps students recognize similarities and appreciate differences, without perceiving inferiority or superiority of one or the other. To foster cultural awareness:

- Recognize that all students are unique, having special talents and abilities.
- Promote uniqueness and diversity as positive traits.
- Know, appreciate, and respect the cultural backgrounds of your students.
- Use authentic situations to provide cultural learning and understanding.
- Make sure people of all cultures are represented fairly and accurately.
- Make sure that historical information is accurate and nondiscriminatory.
- Make sure that materials do not include stereotypical roles.
- Make sure there is gender equity.
- Welcome family and community involvement.
- Use current news stories, advertisements, or other forms of media to call students' attention to cultural differences that influence businesses, communities, and families.

Ethics

Helping students learn about ethical behavior and how to consider the effects of a decision before it is made are important life skills for your students preparing for the real world.

The Benefits of Integrating Ethics

The goal of teaching ethical decision-making skills is not to teach values. It is to help students clarify their ethical beliefs and learn how to evaluate ethical situations. Make your classroom a risk-free environment in which students can discuss issues and make ethical decisions. Students need to learn how to evaluate their actions and to ask questions such as, "Will I be proud of myself if I take this action?" and "Would I want others to know about my actions?"

The Ethical Decision Model

Your students will learn to analyze ethical situations better if they have a model to use in deliberating the issues that helps them to understand how a decision can affect others. Several decision models exist, but the basic steps for an ethical decision model are as follows:

1. Determine the ethical issue.
2. Identify the actions for handling the situation.
3. Identify the people affected by the situation.
4. Analyze how the situation affects the people involved.
5. Decide which of the actions to take.

Classroom Strategies

Culinary Essentials provides real-world situations that sometimes pose ethical conundrums. These can be catalysts for lively classroom discussion. In addition, you might lead discussion about topical ethics issues or have students bring in newspaper or magazine articles that suggest ethical dilemmas. Have students analyze the situations in class and, perhaps, write short reports on their analyses and conclusions. Some formats, such as learning groups, role plays, and debates, are particularly well suited to teaching students about ethics.

Cooperative Learning Groups

Small groups of students are especially well suited to discuss cases and share their ideas about ethical issues. Divide students into groups of four or five. Observe groups and encourage all students to participate. Allow each group to reach its own conclusions, and then ask a member of each group to share the group's ideas with the class.

Role Plays and Debates

Have your students role play ethical situations, using their own ideas about how to respond to a given situation. Discuss class responses to the role play, guiding students in using the ethical decision model. Set up debate teams to present different sides of an ethical issue.

Preparing for Culinary Competitions

Participation in culinary competitions is a great way for students to move forward in their culinary career. Working with students as they prepare for various culinary competitions can be a rewarding process. Throughout the year you will see your students increase their culinary skills while developing their leadership and teamwork skills, while preparing for the world of work.

Preparing Yourself

After committing the time to prepare students for competitions you will need to prepare yourself:

- Attend advisor workshops or meetings about local competitions.
- Talk with other teachers who have attended competitions.
- Obtain copies of competition requirements from organizations such as Johnson & Wales University, SkillsUSA, and FCCLA.
- Attend a competition to see what skills students need to master.
- Talk to administrators, parents, and students about upcoming events.
- Locate resources in your community to help raise money for the event.

Your preparations will also include assisting at the competitions. For competitions to be successful, all advisors need to help at these events. You may be asked to help set up rooms, escort judges, and tally score sheets.

Preparing Your Students

Talk with your students about the goals of the competition and how they can benefit from competing. Explain the commitment involved in preparing for competition.

Help determine their strengths and select competitions which they will enjoy and benefit from. In, addition, review the competition requirements and evaluation processes for each event.

Practicing for the Competitions

To help your students practice, demonstrate an event or show a video of students competing. Discuss the steps students go through at competitions, the equipment they will use, and procedures they must follow. After they are comfortable with their events, have them perform for their classmates.

Going to Competitions

As a final step, proofread all paperwork for proper spelling and grammar. Have students prepare a checklist of items they will need to take to the competition. On the day of the competition, you will need to help students register for their events and help them find their assigned locations.

SkillsUSA

SkillsUSA is a national organization that prepares students interested in technical, skilled, and service occupations. One of the most visible programs of SkillsUSA is the annual SkillsUSA Championships. Thousands of students compete in more than 70 occupational and leadership skill areas. Competing against the clock and each other, participants display their expertise in food service-related skills. Students benefit from this competition no matter how they place in the finals.

Culinary Arts

During the six-hour competition, Culinary Arts contestants are judged on both hot and cold food preparation and their presentation skills. The contestants are rated in technical skills, sanitation and food safety techniques, and the quality of the prepared item.

Food and Beverage Service

In the Food and Beverage Service competition, contestants demonstrate their skills in front of the house service. The skills contestants must demonstrate include table set-up, greeting guests, reservation procedures, menu presentations, descriptions of food, drinks, soups, and daily specials, taking orders, serving each course, clearing the table, and the preparation and presentation of the check. The contestants are also judged on their personal appearance, table-side manner, professionalism, ease with customers, courtesy, and verbal skills.

Commercial Baking

Contestants in Commercial Baking are judged on a variety of production techniques as well as their knowledge of the modern baking industry. The contestants are required to take a written test that covers basic baking science. Then, during the performance test, contestants must prepare and present their final products for judging. The competition includes presenting baked goods in yeast breads and rolls, quick breads, sweet dough products, cookies, and basic icing and cake decoration.

FCCLA

Family, Career and Community Leaders of America is a nonprofit national career and technical student organization for young men and women in Family and Consumer Sciences education in public and private schools through grade 12. Everyone is part of a family, and FCCLA is the only national

Career and Technical Student Organization with the family as its central focus. Since 1945, FCCLA members have been making a difference in their families, careers, and communities by addressing important personal, work, and societal issues through Family and Consumer Sciences education.

STAR Events

STAR Events are competitive events in which members are recognized for proficiency and achievement in chapter and individual projects, leadership skills, and career preparation. National STAR Event participants are selected by each state

before moving on to the national event. Culinary students participate in a team event that will judge their ability to work to produce a quality meal.

Leaders at Work

Leaders at Work is a national program that recognizes FCCLA student members who create projects that strengthen their leadership roles on the job. The program is open to any FCCLA member who has a paid or ongoing volunteer job related to one of the FCCLA career areas.

Career Connections

Through individual and group events, members discover and target their career goals. FCCLA offers recognition to chapters that complete a Career Connection project. Special recognition for the best project is given at the National Leadership Conference.

FCCLA Supervisor

Any teacher who wishes to be a supervisor must be a current member of FCCLA and possess a credential in a Family and Consumer science subject. Benefits include networking with other teachers, ongoing professional development, and maximizing leadership skills.

MyPyramid Information

Introduced in 2005, MyPyramid is part of an overall food guidance system that emphasizes the need for a more individualized approach to improving diet and lifestyle. MyPyramid incorporates recommendations from the 2005 Dietary Guidelines for Americans. Use this information to reinforce the concept of balanced, individualized nutrition and activity with your students.

Moderation The wider base of each food group band stands for foods with little or no solid fats or added sugars. The narrower top stands for foods containing more added fats and sugars.

Proportionality The different widths of each food group band show proportionally how much of their food from that group a person should choose.

Activity The person climbing the steps is a reminder to add daily physical activity.

Variety The six color bands represent the Grains, Vegetables, Fruits, Milk, and Meat and Beans Food Groups, as well as the Oils category. They illustrate that foods from all groups are needed daily for good nutrition.

Personalization MyPyramid encourages students to take owner-ship of the program.

Gradual Improvement "Steps to a healthier you" suggests that students can take small steps to improve their diet and lifestyle every day.

MyPyramid.gov
STEPS TO A HEALTHIER YOU

MyPyramid Resources

The U.S. Department of Agriculture's MyPyramid program, designed for the general public ages 2 and up, offers several interactive tools on its Web site (**mypyramid.gov**) to help you and your students plan and assess food choices.

MyPyramid Menu Planner

Menus can be added to this interactive tool to show whether a student's food choices are balanced for the day, or on average over a week.

- Helps students plan upcoming meals to meet MyPyramid goals.
- Provides suggestions for ways to improve food choices.

MyPyramid Plan

This tool provides a quick estimate of what and how much food should be eaten from the different food groups.

- Students can enter age, gender, and activity level information to receive a customized food guide.

MyPyramid Tracker

The tracker provides detailed information by comparing a day's worth of foods eaten with current nutrition guidance.

- Provides information on diet quality, physical activity status, related nutrition messages, and links to nutrient and physical activity information.
- Automatically calculates students' energy balance by subtracting the energy you expend from physical activity from your food calories/energy intake.

Food Safety Rules

Food safety is everyone's responsibility. Share these general food safety rules with your students. They can learn to keep food fresh and safe and to keep everyone healthy.

Wash Hands Properly Wet hands and forearms with hot water. Apply soap, and rub hands and arms for at least 15 seconds. Rinse under hot water. Dry hands and arms, and use the paper towel to turn off the faucet.

Avoid Spreading Bacteria Do not handle other people's food if you are sick. Cover an open cut or sore on your hands with a clean waterproof bandage. Cover your nose and mouth with clean tissue when you sneeze or cough. Handle food with clean utensils. Tie back any long hair before preparing food. Wear clean clothes and roll up the sleeves. Wear a clean apron. Use a clean spoon for each tasting. Do not taste foods containing raw or partly cooked meat, poultry, fish, or eggs.

Keep the Kitchen Clean Use a disinfectant, a mixture of chlorine bleach and water, or hot, soapy water to clean kitchen surfaces. Wipe up spills right away. Sweep the floor whenever needed. Keep dirty dishes, pots, and pans away from food preparation areas. Wash dirty dishes immediately in hot soapy water and rinse in hot water. Clean the can opener after each use. Use different towels for drying dishes and your hands. Keep kitchen garbage in a tightly covered can.

Avoid Cross-Contamination Keep raw meat, poultry, fish, and their juices away from ready-to-eat foods. Use color-coded cutting boards just for raw meat, poultry, and fish. Wash everything that touches raw food before reusing it. Use paper towels to wipe up food scraps, spills, or meat juices. Then, wash the counter and your hands right away.

Thaw and Cook Food Properly Never thaw food at room temperature. Cook food fully. Check internal temperature with a clean thermometer. Avoid raw or partly cooked eggs. Keep foods out of the temperature danger zone (41°F to 135°F; 5°C to 57°C)

Safety in the Kitchen

Accidents in the kitchen can happen—but they are easily prevented. The main cause of kitchen accidents is carelessness. Teach students the following rules to help prevent accidents:

Basic Kitchen Safety Rules

For General Safety Pay attention to the task. Use the right tool for the job. Do not let hair, jewelry, or clothing dangle. They could catch fire or get tangled in equipment.

To Prevent Cuts Store knives in a container or block designed for them. Do not soak any sharp utensils in a sink where you may not see them. Always use a cutting board. Clean up broken glass carefully using a broom and dustpan for big pieces, and a wet paper towel for glass dust.

To Prevent Falls and Other Injuries Keep drawers and doors closed. Wipe up spills, splatters, and peelings on the floor immediately. Use a sturdy stool to reach higher shelves. Store heavy items within easy reach.

To Prevent Electrical Shock Keep small electrical appliances away from water. Keep cords away from heat sources. Unplug small appliances before cleaning them and do not immerse them in water. Do not plug too many appliances into one outlet. Keep utensils such as forks out of toasters and other electrical appliances.

To Prevent Burns Keep potholders within easy reach and use them to handle hot items. Turn the handles of pots and pans toward the inside of the range to prevent accidental spills. Carefully lift the cover of a hot pan to prevent steam from burning you. Wait until a spill cools before wiping it up.

To Prevent Fires Keep flammable items away from the range. Watch foods as they cook on the range. Store aerosol cans away from heat. Keep a fire extinguisher at hand and know how to use it.

To Prevent Accidental Poisoning Store all household chemicals away from food and out of children's reach. Keep chemicals in a locked cabinet if possible and clearly labeled. Follow label directions when you use household chemicals.

Minor Wounds

A wound is any break in the skin. Wounds are caused by forceful contact with just about anything, such as a knife, a tool, glass or the ground. Even with a minor wound there will be bleeding. Some examples of minor wounds are:

- A puncture wound from stepping on a nail

- An abrasion from scraping a knee on concrete

- An incision from a sharp object such as broken glass or a knife

Rinse the wound with clean water, and apply a bandage or clean cloth. Apply mild pressure to control bleeding. If blood soaks through, apply another bandage over the one already on the wound. Elevating the wounded body part to the level of the heart may reduce bleeding. Keep the wound clean, dry and protected. Many minor wounds will heal completely with first aid only. However, contact a doctor if the wound:

- is on the lip and/or face

- bleeds even after applying pressure for a while

- is from a bite (animal or human)

- does not heal and becomes infected

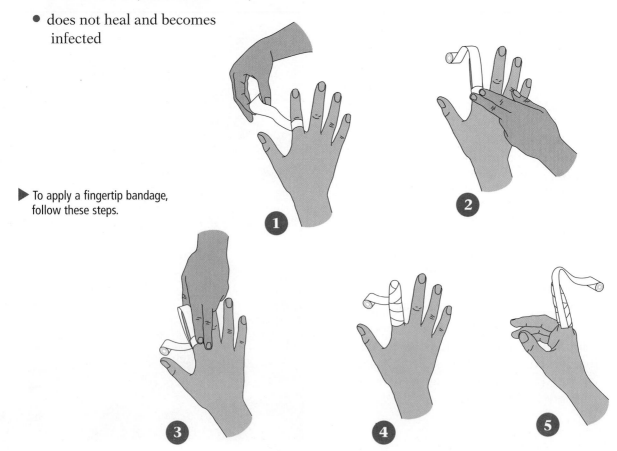

▶ To apply a fingertip bandage, follow these steps.

Glencoe FACS Classroom Solutions™ e-Newsletter

Subscribe to Glencoe's free e-newsletter and receive the latest information about strategies, trends, and technology in family and consumer sciences. Special features include insightful interviews with FACS educators, valuable information to help you meet Perkins IV mandates and obtain funding, professional development tools, technology solutions to FACS-specific challenges, plus news, event updates and more! Subscribe at **GlencoeFACSNews.com**.

Unit Overview

Introduce the Unit This unit focuses on safety in the kitchen and around food. Students will learn how to avoid personal injury, contamination, and foodborne illness in the kitchen. They will also learn about fire safety, emergency procedures, first aid, personal hygiene, and protective clothing. Finally, they will learn what the HACCP system is, about the flow of food, and how to receive, handle, and store food safely.

Chapter

1 Safety and Sanitation Principles

2 HACCP Applications

Unit Culinary Career Spotlight Answer Key (found on page 51)

Get Certified Sandwich recipes should contain a variety and balance of ingredients including grains, vegetables, fruits, milk, meats, and/or beans. The spread should be nutritious and used in proportion to the sandwich. The sandwich should be appealing and flavorful.

Competition Practice Students should be given a one-hour time limit to complete their sandwiches. Students will rate their own efforts, based on their timing, the sandwich flavor, and the presentation of the finished sandwich on the plate, including any garnishes.

SkillsUSA competitions provide important ways for your students to hone their technical skills. In the Culinary Arts competition, students are rated on sanitation and food safety techniques.

Explore Sanitation Before beginning this unit, discuss with students what appearance guidelines a person might need to meet to work in a professional kitchen to prepare food. Keep a list of ideas for clothing, hair, protective clothing, jewelry, and personal hygiene. Once you have finished this unit, have students revisit the list and add any additional changes and correct any misinformation. Answers will vary, but some adjustments might include cleaning and trimming fingernails, washing hands thoroughly, removing nail polish, changing into a uniform, changing into more comfortable or close-toed shoes, putting on gloves and/or an apron, removing jewelry, tying back hair or wearing a hairnet, and reporting any injuries or illnesses.

As part of its mission, FCCLA emphasizes cooperation learned through individuals working together as a team to accomplish specific goals.

Teamwork Form students into small groups. Tell each group that they are receiving a shipment of fresh meat in a restaurant. Groups must inspect the meat to ensure that they can serve it to their customers. As a team, students must identify the factors that would make the meat shipment acceptable or unacceptable. They should work together to make a list of what they would do during receiving. Students should work as a team to identify that they must inspect the meat's temperature, color, odor, texture, and packaging. They should communicate that beef and lamb should be fresh in appearance. The meat should have no offensive or sour odor, and it should not feel slimy or sticky. Finally, packaging should not be broken, soiled, or leaking.

McGraw Hill
Professional Development

MINI CLIP VIDEO LIBRARY
Targeted professional development is correlated throughout *Culinary Essentials*. The McGraw-Hill
Professional Development Mini Clip Video Library provides teaching strategies to strengthen academic
and learning skills. Log on to **glencoe.com**.

Chapter 1 Safety and Sanitation Principles

Reading Strategic Readers Author Scott Paris discusses the characteristics of strategic readers. (p. TM72)

Reading Building Vocabulary A teacher introduces and plays two vocabulary building games with her students. (p. TM74)

ELL Collaborative Work Students work in groups to complete a lab. (p. TM73)

Math Understanding Fractions Algebra teacher Brad Fulton discusses the importance of fraction concepts in algebra instruction. (p. TM75)

Math The Meaning of Variable Students and teacher discuss the meaning of variable. (p. TM76)

Chapter 2 HACCP Applications

Reading English Language Success Ruben Zepeda, Ed.D., discusses the role of classroom management in the success of English learners. (p. TM78)

Reading During and After Reading A teacher models for students what a good reader "thinks about." (p. TM79)

Reading Planning and Classroom Management Nancy Frey, Ph.D., teacher, educator, and author, discusses instructional strategies that support a differentiated classroom. (p. TM79)

Reading Another Point of View Lois Moseley, author and educator, discusses the benefits of teacher collaboration. (p. TM80)

Reading Assessment Planning and Management Lois Moseley, author and educator, discusses planning for, and evaluation of, an assessment. (p. TM81)

ELL Words in Action Students act out or mime the words they are trying to learn. (p. TM78)

Math Fraction Computation Students work in small groups to solve and share soultions for a fraction problem. (p. TM78)

Math Multiple Approaches to Problem Solving A teacher and students discuss various options for problem solving. (p. TM80)

Math Solving Equations Students use manipulatives and symbols to solve simple equations. (p. TM81)

Safety and Sanitation Principles

SECTION 1.1 Safety Basics   **SECTION 1.2 Sanitation Challenges**

Classroom Solutions

Print Resources

- Student Edition
- Instructor Annotated Edition
- Lab Manual
- Lab Manual IAE

Technology Resources

ExamView® Assessment Suite CD
Create and print unit and chapter tests.

Lesson Planner Plus Lesson Planner Plus CD provides access to teacher resources in one package.

Presentation Plus! provides visual teaching aids for every section.

Online Learning Center includes resources and activities for students and teachers. Also includes the **Online Student Edition**.

Interactive Student Edition

SECTION 1.1 Safety Basics

Section Overview

In this section, students will learn to identify potential sources of injury or fire. They will also learn about the proper equipment and emergency procedures to deal with fires and first aid measures for burns, wounds, and choking.

FOCUS

Bell Ringer Activity

Protective Clothing Bring in examples of protective clothing that might be worn in a kitchen, such as aprons, gloves, hats, or hair restraints. Ask volunteers to demonstrate how to wear the protective clothing, and discuss the function of each piece with the class.

D Develop Concepts

Main Idea Discuss the main idea with the students. Ask: How can procedures for dealing with fires and injuries prevent and minimize damage? Proper procedures can prevent injuries by warning of potential hazards, minimizing the risk of accident, and enabling employees to be able to react quickly to an emergency.

 **Professional Development** MINI CLIP **Reading** Strategic Readers

---

TEACH

S Skill Practice
Guided Practice

L1 List Ask students to list the four types of open wounds, or cuts, and give examples of each. The four types of wounds are abrasions, or scrapes, such as rug burns; lacerations, such as knife wounds; avulsions, such as a severed finger; and puncture wounds, such as damage from a pointed object.

L2 Explain Have students explain how to help someone who has a minor wound. Wear disposable gloves; clean the wound with soap and running water; place a bandage or sterile gauze on the cut; apply direct pressure to stop bleeding; and raise the limb above the heart to slow blood flow.

L3 Apply Have students design a procedure for minor and major wound emergencies for your classroom lab. Students should design a step-by-step procedure on how to treat major and minor wounds, how to know when to call for help, and what to do while help is on the way.

ASSESS

Quiz

Ask students to answer the following questions:

1. What is one of the most common workplace injuries? Back injuries from improper lifting and bending are some of the most common workplace injuries.

---

2. What is the first step in fire prevention? The first step in fire prevention is to keep the workplace clean, focusing especially on built-up grease.

3. Where can you learn hands-on information about first aid in the workplace? The American Red Cross offers courses that teach hands-on practical information about first aid in the workplace.

RETEACH

 Universal Access

Students with Hearing Impairments Place foods in receiving containers on the floor. Have students review the proper lifting procedures given in the text, and practice using those procedures to lift the containers. Students should demonstrate the ability to remember and follow the directions given in the text. Practicing the procedures they have read should help kinesthetic learners understand and remember the procedures.

 **Professional Development** | MINI CLIP **ELL** Collaborative Work

 Critical Thinking

Identify Potential Hazards Have students examine the classroom foods lab and identify potentially hazardous areas. Have them write an assessment of the potential hazards and the procedures needed to avoid emergencies in those areas. Students should apply what they have learned in the chapter to an actual kitchen setting to identify potential sources of fire or injury. They should then use their analytic and problem-solving skills to create workable procedures to prevent fire and injury in the space.

ASSESS

 Lab Manual

Assign the Section 1.1 Activities.

Online Study Tools

Have students go to the Online Learning Center at **glencoe.com** to:

- Take the Section 1.1 Practice Test.
- **STUDY TO GO** Download Study-to-Go content.

SECTION 1.1 After You Read Answer Key
Review Key Concepts

1. The four types of personal injuries that foodservice workers have a responsibility to help prevent in the kitchen are slips and falls; cuts; burns and scalds; and back injuries and strains.

2. Hold the extinguisher upright and remove the safety pin. Direct the nozzle at the bottom of the fire, and push down the handle. This will release the contents that can extinguish the fire.

3. First-degree burns are the least severe of all burns. The skin becomes red, sensitive, and sometimes swollen. Second-degree burns cause deeper, more painful damage, and blisters form on the skin. Third-degree burns are the most serious type of burn. These burns may be white and soft or black, charred, and leathery. The burned area may have no feeling because of damage to nerves. Third-degree burns must be treated at a hospital.

Practice Culinary Academics

4. **English Language Arts** Students may find accounts of kitchen injuries on the OSHA website (**www.osha.gov**), from news sources, or by speaking to people who have worked in the foodservice industry. Their reports should describe the injury, its cause, and any consequences the employer faced as a result of the injury. Using the information in the section, students should come to a conclusion as to how the injury might have been prevented.

5. **Mathematics** $150°F = 65.55556°C$, which may be rounded up to $66°C$. Following the conversion formula, $150 − 32 = 118$. Then, $118 × 5 = 590$. $590 ÷ 9 = 66°C$. As an alternative, students may convert $\frac{5}{9}$ to a decimal (0.555556) and multiply that decimal by 118 to get the final result.

CLOSE
Culminating Activity

Learn CPR Locate resources in your community that offer CPR certification courses at little to no cost. Create a handout with a list of resources. Explain the classes offered and the cost, if any, of the various resources to the students, and encourage students to become certified in CPR.

SECTION 1.2 | **Sanitation Challenges**

Section Overview

In this section, students will learn how to keep food safe to eat. They will learn the difference between direct contamination and cross-contamination. They will also learn to identify the biological, chemical, and physical sources of food contamination. Finally, they will learn how to respond to a foodborne illness.

FOCUS

Bell Ringer Activity

Identify Chemical Hazards Make photocopies of warning labels from various cleaning products, and hand them out to students. Discuss what might happen if these products got into food. Reading these warnings should help students understand the danger posed by chemical contamination.

 **Professional Development** MINI CLIP **Reading** Building Vocabulary

D Develop Concepts

Main Idea Discuss the main idea with the students. Ask: How can insects and rodents contaminate food? Insects and rodents can be carriers of bacteria. They can get into ingredients or food that is being prepared. Their feces can also spread bacteria.

TEACH

S Skill Practice

Guided Practice

L1 List Have students list the six different types of biological hazards. The six types are bacteria, viruses, parasites, fungi, molds, and yeast.

L2 Explain Ask students to explain how to safely store cleaning products. Cleaning products should be stored away from food, clearly labeled, and kept in their original containers. Storage areas should be neat and well organized.

L3 Apply Have students design a system to document, investigate, and report incidents of a foodborne illness. Students should create a form for documentation, a checklist for investigation, a designated employee, and reporting contact information.

ASSESS

Quiz

Ask students to answer the following questions:

1. Who is the most at risk for foodborne illness? Those most at risk for foodborne illnesses are children, the elderly, pregnant women, and those with compromised immune systems.

2. How should you properly dispose of cleaning supplies? Cleaning supplies must be disposed of according to local regulations. Local health departments can give disposal advice.

3. Where should you store pesticides? Pesticides should be stored away from food in a secure, locked area.

RETEACH

R Reading Strategy

Plan a Storage Area Have students review the information on the potential dangers of cleaning supplies and the advice about storing them. Have them create a floor plan for a cleaning equipment storage area. Plans should take the section's advice and implement it into a plan for a storage area that minimizes risk. The storage area should be arranged to avoid spills, be away from food, and provide for easy identification of and access to cleaning supplies.

U Universal Access

Gifted Students There is disagreement about whether organically grown foods are safer than conventionally grown foods. Have students research this issue and write an opinion piece with the results of their research and their opinion supported by their reasoning. Students may agree with either side. Their sources should be reliable and their reasoning sound. People who believe organic farming is safer are concerned about pesticides and the dangers of large operations. On the other hand, food contamination can also come from natural sources, such as manure and contaminated water, which can affect organic farms.

ASSESS

 ExamView® Assessment Suite *ExamView® Assessment Suite* Create a test for this chapter.

Lab Manual

Assign the Section 1.2 Activities.

Online Study Tools

Have students go to the Online Learning Center at **glencoe.com** to:

- Take the Section 1.2 Practice Test.
-  Download Study-to-Go content.

SECTION 1.2 After You Read Answer Key

Review Key Concepts

1. Biological sources of food contamination include bacteria (tiny-celled microorganisms that can make people ill), viruses (microorganisms that grow in other living cells and cause food-related illness), parasites (larger organisms that live off a host), fungi (parasitic plants that grow in food), mold (a form of fungus that often grows on spoiled food), and yeast (another form of fungus that causes food to spoil).

2. Common cleaning products include detergents, hygiene detergents, degreasers, abrasive cleaners, and acid cleaners.

3. If you suspect the workplace has become infested with pests, you should report the situation to a supervisor so he or she can call a professional exterminator. Follow procedures to make areas less attractive to pests by keeping storage areas clean, sanitary, and dry; disposing of garbage quickly; keeping food stored at least 6 in. (15 cm) off the floor and away from walls; removing items from cardboard boxes before storing; and maintaining appropriate temperatures in storage areas.

Practice Culinary Academics

4. **Science** Students should observe that molds grow best in conditions that are moist, dark, and warm. They should conclude that bread is best stored someplace cool, dry, and light. In a professional kitchen, the refrigerator is probably the best place to store bread to avoid mold growth. However, storing bread in a refrigerator can affect the quality of the bread.

5. **Mathematics** To find the ratio, create a fraction using the bleach as the numerator (½ oz.) and the water as the denominator (512 oz.). To convert the bleach fraction to a whole number, multiply both the numerator and denominator by 2:

$$\frac{\frac{1}{2} \times 2}{512 \times 2} = \frac{1}{1,024}$$

One oz. of bleach to 1,024 oz. of water is the correct ratio, with the fraction in its lowest terms.

 **Professional Development** MINI CLIP **Math** Understanding Fractions

CLOSE

Culminating Activity

Review Current Events Find a recent news article about foodborne illness that discuses how to prevent them or describes a particular outbreak. Discuss the students' reactions to the articles based on what they have learned in this section.

Chapter Review and Applications

Vocabulary Review

1. Students should write complete sentences using each term correctly.

Review Key Concepts

2. Avoid food contamination; avoid falls, cuts, burns, and back injuries; clean kitchen equipment safely.

3. Fire extinguishers are canisters containing chemicals to fight fires. A properly ventilated hood system removes excess heat, smoke, and vapors. A sprinkler system douses the room with water. Fire emergency procedures include clearly marked exits, a place for employees to meet outside for a head count, and a plan to direct customers out of the building.

4. Burns: remove heat source, cool burned area, bandage, monitor victim's temperature, and wait for medical professionals to arrive. Wounds: put on disposable gloves, clean wound, bandage, apply pressure to stop bleeding, and elevate. Choking: use the Heimlich maneuver if the victim is conscious, but do not use on unconscious or pregnant victims. If necessary, perform CPR.

5. Biological hazards, such as bacteria, viruses, parasites, fungi, mold, and yeast; chemical hazards, such as cleaning supplies, pesticides, food additives, and toxic metals; and physical hazards, such as glass chips, metal shavings, hair, and bits of wood.

6. Cleaning products, such as detergents, degreasers, abrasive cleaners, and acid cleaners; and pesticides.

7. Keep the kitchen clean and sanitary. Make sure garbage is disposed of quickly and in the appropriate containers. Report signs of insects or rodents.

C Critical Thinking

8. The right shoes can help prevent slips and protect your feet from injury. Wearing inappropriate footwear can make you more likely to slip or be injured from hot ingredients or dropped equipment.

9. A restaurant has the potential to spread a foodborne illness to many people. A quick response can stop the foodborne illness from passing to more than a few customers. Contaminated food should be removed as quickly as possible. The local health department can inform consumers and trace the source of contaminated food.

10. Students should accurately describe the cause of the outbreak and suggest appropriate methods for food handling, cleaning, storage, or cooking techniques that may have prevented the outbreak.

Academic Skills

11. **English Language Arts** Presentations should be creative and informative, perhaps incorporating checklists, illustrations, or pantomiming. The information should be presented in a style appropriate for someone with no prior knowledge of the subject.

12. **Science** Students should find that it takes longer to remove paint using just water. Students should create a hand-washing procedure that uses soap and provides an appropriate length of time based on their experience. They may include special instructions, such as cleaning under fingernails. Have them keep their results to compare to those in the next chapter.

13. **Mathematics** 7.5 tablespoons of vinegar are needed. The ratio of vinegar to water for the original quantities is 3/1 (3 Tbsp. vinegar to 1 gallon water), so the ratio of vinegar to water (x/2.5) in the larger batch must equal 3/1. This results in the equation $3/1 = x/2.5$. To solve for x, you can re-write the equation using cross products. This results in the new equation (1) $\times$ (x) = (3) $\times$ (2.5). $x = 7.5$.

McGraw Hill | **Professional Development** | MINI CLIP **Math**
The Meaning of Variable

Certification Prep

14. c. hepatitis A

15. b. call your boss and tell him that you are sick.

Real-World Skills and Applications

16. **Management Skills** Student plans should include a way to discover foodborne illnesses, such as providing a number for patrons to call if they get ill. Methods to document and investigate might include a checklist of questions to ask customers who get ill. All plans should include a procedure to isolate possible sources of foodborne illness and to report it.

17. **Critical Thinking Skills** Students should discover that the detergent is less effective to remove grease when it has been diluted with water.

18. **Financial Literacy** 25% = .25. $500 $125. $500 − $125 = $375. You may spend up to $125 on a extinguisher, and $375 on other supplies.

19. **Technology Applications** Posters should be clear, easy to read, and organized. They should specify tasks for each type of employee (for example, servers might be in charge of moving customers out of the building in a fire). They should also contain step-by-step procedures and specify locations for emergency procedures.

Culinary Lab

20. **Develop a Safety Manual** Manuals should contain the information listed in the instructions, and be organized in a logical manner. Contributions from members should be revised into a consistent style, and the manual should look neat and attractive. The information should reflect the advice in the chapter and should be presented in a simple, clear manner.

mala video

HACCP Applications

SECTION 2.1 The Safe Foodhandler
SECTION 2.2 The HACCP System
SECTION 2.3 The Flow of Food

Classroom Solutions

📖 Student Edition
📖 Instructor Annotated Edition
📖 Lab Manual
📖 Lab Manual IAE

Technology Resources

ExamView Assessment Suite
ExamView® Assessment Suite CD
Create and print unit and chapter tests.

Lesson Planner Plus **Lesson Planner Plus CD** provides access to teacher resources in one package.

Presentation Plus! provides visual teaching aids for every section.

Online Learning Center includes resources and activities for students and teachers. Also includes the **Online Student Edition**.

Interactive Student Edition

SECTION 2.1 The Safe Foodhandler

Section Overview

In this section, students will learn appropriate grooming practices for the workplace. They will also learn about protective clothing. In particular, they will learn when and why gloves are used in the workplace. Finally, they will learn about the importance of hand washing and proper hand-washing procedures.

FOCUS

🔔 Bell Ringer Activity

Proper Hand Washing Demonstrate proper hand-washing techniques to the class. Explain what you are doing as you complete each step. Have the class count with you as you rub your hands and arms for 15 seconds so that they can get a sense of how long that is.

D Develop Concepts

Main Idea Discuss the main idea with the students. Ask: How can good grooming habits prevent food-borne illnesses? Practicing good grooming habits can prevent you from bringing bacteria you have picked up outside into the kitchen and then spreading it to the food.

TEACH

S Skill Practice

Guided Practice

L1 List Have students list times when people should wash hands when in a kitchen. After coughing, using the restroom, or taking out garbage.

L2 Explain Ask students to explain what can happen if they do not properly wash hands before handling food. Harmful bacteria can be spread.

L3 Apply Tell students to practice washing their hands. They should follow proper hand-washing steps, including rubbing for at least 15 seconds.

ASSESS

Quiz

Ask students to answer the following questions:

1. How often should you change gloves during continual use? You need to change gloves approximately every four hours during continual use.

2. What is the most important thing you can do to prevent the transfer of foodborne bacteria? Hand washing is the most important thing you can do to prevent the transfer of foodborne bacteria.

3. What should you do if you start to feel ill at work? If you feel ill while at work, you must immediately tell your supervisor.

RETEACH

Universal Access

English Language Learners Ask students to imagine they are the manager of a restaurant. One of their employees has a cut on his or her hand and must be assigned to a station where he or she will not touch food. Ask them to think about different jobs in the kitchen and figure out which jobs their employee can still do. Students should come up with non-food-handling tasks such as cleaning, trash duty, washing dishes, expediting/announcing, foodrunner, or cook-stations such as grilling, where food can be handled with tongs.

Professional Development MINI CLIP **English** English Language Success

Critical Thinking

Understand Hand-Washing Rules The section states that one should never use a hand sanitizer in place of hand washing on the job. Ask students to guess why this is a rule, then conduct research to find the answer. Not all commercial hand sanitizers contain a high enough concentration of alcohol to kill bacteria. In addition, hand sanitizers do not work well when hands are dirty, or have bodily fluids on them. Hands must be washed first to remove dirt and grime before hand sanitizers can be most effective.

ASSESS

 Lab Manual

Assign the Section 2.1 Activities.

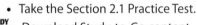 Online Study Tools

Have students go to the Online Learning Center at **glencoe.com** to:

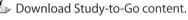

- Take the Section 2.1 Practice Test.
- Download Study-to-Go content.

SECTION 2.1 After You Read Answer Key

Review Key Concepts

1. Always wear clean gloves to perform a task. Never wear torn gloves. Change gloves after each separate operation. Change gloves every four hours during continual use. Also, change gloves immediately after handling raw food.

2. If you have a wound, wash your hands and the wound thoroughly. Keep cuts completely covered. Keep the bandage clean and dry. If you have a wound on your hand, tell your supervisor so you can be reassigned if necessary.

Practice Culinary Academics

3. **Social Studies** Early versions of the toque-blanche date back to the 13th century. It was popularized in the 1800s by French chef Marie-Antoine Carême. He believed chefs should wear white hats to demonstrate cleanliness. He also believed that chefs' hats should be different heights to show different ranks: the taller the hat, the higher the rank. The number of pleats is also a status symbol. Many toques have exactly 100 pleats, which supposedly represents the number of ways a chef can prepare an egg.

4. **English Language Arts** Students should pay close attention to what their partner says and check the book to determine whether any steps were missing, as well as time to make sure he or she was scrubbing long enough. Students should communicate clearly and courteously with their partner during evaluations.

5. **Mathematics** $1 \div 16 = 0.0625$. $0.11 - 0.0625 = 0.0475$ inch should be trimmed.

Professional Development MINI CLIP **Math** Fraction Computation

CLOSE

Culminating Activity

Share Ideas Have students stand up, one at a time, and share one thing they learned about safe food handling from this section. If their idea has already been mentioned, ask them how they will remind themselves to practice what they learned.

Professional Development MINI CLIP **ELL** Words in Action

SECTION 2.2 The HACCP System

Section Overview

In this section, students will learn what the HACCP system is. They will also learn about different hazards in the workplace and how to find the critical control points in the flow of food. Finally, they will learn about the processes of monitoring, corrective action, record keeping, and verification.

FOCUS

Bell Ringer Activity

Why Systems are Useful Discuss with students why having a system can be useful. Ask them to think about systems in their own life, such as emergency drills at school, or assignment of chores at home. What are the benefits of having a system in place?

 Develop Concepts

Main Idea Discuss the main idea with the students. Ask: How can a system help prevent hazards in a professional kitchen? Having a system makes sure that every worker is following the same steps, and also provides a means for monitoring what is happening in the kitchen and reviewing records to determine corrective action if something goes wrong later.

Professional Development	MINI CLIP **Reading** During and After Reading

TEACH

S Skill Practice
Guided Practice

L1 List Ask students to list the most frequent foodborne hazards in a kitchen. Poor personal hygiene, contaminated raw foods, cross-contamination, improper cooking, improper holding, improper cooling, improper reheating, and improper cleaning.

L2 Explain Have students explain how to take corrective action in response to a foodborne hazard. To take corrective action, you must recognize the source of a potential hazard and eliminate it.

L3 Apply Have students practice using different thermometers to check for minimal internal temperature. Students should be provided with thermometers and should become comfortable with taking the temperature of different foods.

ASSESS
Quiz

Ask students to answer the following questions:

1. What does HACCP stand for? Hazard Analysis Critical Control Point.

2. What is the safe internal cooking temperature for poultry? The safe internal cooking temperature for poultry is 165°F (74°C).

3. What types of record-keeping systems are used in HACCP? Flow charts, policy and procedure manuals, written logs, and spot-check temperature readings.

RETEACH
U Universal Access

Students with Hearing Impairments To better understand the concept of a critical control point, have students write down the definition of each word. Critical means essential, and can also mean dangerous. Control means to exercise influence over

or direct. Point means a specific moment. Analyzing the meaning of each of these words can help students better understand the meaning of the phrase as a moment in time during the flow of food that is essential or potentially dangerous over which they can exercise influence to reduce the danger.

C Critical Thinking

Find Critical Control Points Have students select a recipe and add critical control points to the appropriate places. Students should mark or add temperatures for storage, cooking, holding, transporting, cooking, and reheating. They should also consider inspection of ingredients, hygiene and sanitation, and other safety considerations.

Professional Development	MINI CLIP **Reading** Planning and Classroom Management

ASSESS

Lab Manual

Assign the Section 2.2 Activities.

Online Study Tools

Have students go to the Online Learning Center at **glencoe.com** to:

- Take the Section 2.2 Practice Test.
- Download Study-to-Go content.

SECTION 2.2 After You Read Answer Key

Review Key Concepts

1. HACCP shows how to properly handle food, monitor food safety, and keep accurate records.

2. At the end of each shift, the chef or manager should trace foods through the operation. Then, he or she should examine record-keeping logs of temperature and time, note any errors and the corrective action taken.

Practice Culinary Academics

3. **Science** Students should first identify the potential hazards associated with the control point. Then they should brainstorm corrective actions to avoid those hazards. Finally, using the corrective actions, they should create a step-by-step procedure that could be used in a professional kitchen to avoid those hazards. The procedure should be thorough and take into account all aspects of the HACCP system, including monitoring.

4. **English Language Arts** Students should find three different examples of bimetallic and digital thermometers. The thermometers should be able to be calibrated. When listing the pros and cons, students should think about the special needs of a restaurant kitchen. A good thermometer will be portable, easy to read quickly, guarantee a high degree of accuracy, and not be easily damaged. Students should take into account price when making their decision as to the best option.

5. **Mathematics** $17.5 \times \frac{9}{5} = 31.5$. $31.5 + 32 = 63.5°F$. This is in the danger zone ($41°F$ to $135°F$), so 15 minutes should be deducted from the 4 hours of total danger zone time. $4 \times 60 = 240$ minutes; $240 - 15 = 225$ minutes; $225 \div 60 = 3.75$. There are 3 hours and 45 minutes of danger zone time remaining.

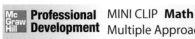 **Professional Development** MINI CLIP **Math** Multiple Approaches to Problem Solving

CLOSE

Culminating Activity

Evaluate Each Other Students should mark or add temperatures for storage, cooking, holding, transporting, and reheating. They should also consider inspection of ingredients, hygiene and sanitation, and other safety considerations that apply to the recipe they have chosen.

Section 2.3 The Flow of Food

Section Overview

In this section, students will learn why it is important to inspect all food products for damage and spoilage when they are received. They will also learn about the safety measures to take when preparing, holding, and serving food. Finally, they will learn the steps involved in cleaning and sanitizing.

FOCUS

Bell Ringer Activity

What Is the Flow of Food? Ask students to think about all of the steps that food must go through from receiving to service and have volunteers name the different steps they can think of in chronological order. See how many steps they can come up with on their own and which they miss.

D Develop Concepts

Main Idea Discuss the main idea with the students. Ask: What food safety issues should you think about when serving food? When serving food, you must make sure the food has been maintained at the correct temperature, that the plate is clean, and that no physical hazards come in contact with the food on the way to the table.

TEACH

S Skill Practice
Guided Practice

L1 List Have students list potential problems when receiving food. Thawed and refrozen foods, insect infestation, damaged food or containers, repacked or mishandled items, foods handled at incorrect temperatures.

L2 Explain Ask students to explain how to properly handle eggs. Egg cartons or cases must have USDA inspection stamp and eggs must be clean, dry, and uncracked. Store eggs immediately in a refrigerated storage area.

L3 Apply Students should imagine they work at a restaurant and receive a shipment of meat. What should they look for to ensure that the meat is okay? Students should check for temperature, color, odor, texture, and packaging.

 **Professional Development** MINI CLIP **Reading** Another Point of View

ASSESS

Quiz

Ask students to answer the following questions:

1. What are the signs that food has been thawed and refrozen? Food may be discolored or dry, it may have liquid at the bottom of the container, or ice crystals inside the carton.

2. How can you be sure meat, poultry and eggs are from a government-approved supplier? Look for the USDA inspection stamp.

3. How can you avoid contamination during food handling? Use recommended utensils rather than your hands. Always make sure equipment, utensils, cutting boards, and other surfaces are clean and sanitary. Keep foods covered when possible.

RETEACH

 Reading Strategy

Sink Diagrams Ask students to draw a three-compartment sink, with a scrape/rinse area, drain boards, and drying racks; label the tasks performed at each section; and identify chemicals and temperatures. Each diagram should contain a compartment for washing, rinsing, and sanitizing and should be labeled with appropriate tasks, temperatures, and chemicals. The wash area requires 110°F (43°C) water and detergent. The rinse area requires 110°F (43°C) water. The sanitize area needs 171°F–180°F (77°C–82°C) or cooler water with sanitizing chemicals.

Professional Development MINI CLIP **Reading** Assessment Planning and Management

Universal Access

Students with Visual Impairments Ask students to discuss why you should never mix a fresh batch of food with food that has been in holding. Because you could no longer control how long food is held. For example, if food has been holding for two hours, and you mix in fresh food, after another two hours, you will not know which food needs to be discarded and which can remain holding.

ASSESS

 *ExamView Assessment Suite*
Create a test for this chapter.

Lab Manual

Assign the Section 2.3 Activities.

Online Study Tools

Have students go to the Online Learning Center at **glencoe.com** to:

- Take the Section 2.3 Practice Test.
- Download Study-to-Go content.

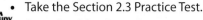

SECTION 2.3 After You Read Answer Key

Review Key Concepts

1. Inspect all of the packages for damage. Keep the goods in tightly sealed containers. Keep the food dry. Watch for signs of insects and rodents in packaging and the storage space. Check the food regularly for signs of spoilage. Check canned goods for bulges, leaks, rust, and dents.

2. Food must be reheated to a minimum internal temperature of 165°F (74°C) for 15 seconds within two hours of being removed from the refrigerator. If adding previously cooked food, the mixture must be reheated to 165°F (74°C).

3. Before loading dishes into a dishwasher, the following steps must be taken: scrape and rinse soiled dishes and pre-soak flatware; pre-rinse dishes to remove visible food and soil; rack dishes and flatware so that water will spray all surfaces.

Practice Culinary Academics

4. **Science** The properly stored dish should be appealing in texture and smell, and look ready to serve with reheating. The improperly stored dish may have a bad texture and smell or it may not. Students should learn that improper storage is dangerous, even if it is sometimes not obvious.

5. **Mathematics** The highest is 143.2°F, while the lowest is 136.1°F. 143.2°F − 136.1°F = 7.1°F.

Professional Development MINI CLIP **Math** Solving Equations

CLOSE

Culminating Activity

Monitor the Flow of Food Have students prepare a simple meal, such as pasta or soup, while thinking about the steps in the flow of food, from inspection of ingredients to serving. Remind them to be aware of each step as it occurs and practice the food safety advice they learned in the section.

Chapter Review and Applications

Vocabulary Review

1. Have students use the glossary at the back of this book to assist in creating their fill-in-the-blank sentences.

Review Key Concepts

2. Appropriate grooming habits include bathing daily, wearing deodorant, and trimming fingernails.

3. Following proper hand-washing techniques; wearing gloves when necessary and changing them often; and coming to work in good physical health.

4. HACCP was originally designed by NASA to ensure food safety for astronauts. It is now used in the foodservice industry as a self-inspection system.

5. Foodservices workers must monitor to ensure that proper procedures are followed and to spot potential problems. Corrective action is action taken when a problem occurs. Record keeping means keeping accounts in the form of flow charts, policy and procedure manuals, and written logs. Verification is when the flow of food is traced and records are examined to verify that the system is working.

6. All foods must be inspected for signs of damage, leaks, insect infestation, repackaging, and mishandling and stored quickly in dry storage, the refrigerator, or the freezer. Perishable food must be kept below 41°F (5°C).

7. Held food must be kept warm. Keep food covered, monitor temperature, and do not mix fresh and non-fresh food. Hold foods for no more than 4 hours. Do not touch the food or tableware, do not let plates overlap, and use cleaning cloths only for cleaning. Food must be reheated to 165°F (74°C) for 15 seconds within 2 hours. If adding a precooked food to fresh, the mixture must be heated to 165°F (74°C).

8. Remove leftover food and rinse dishes. Follow proper procedures for the equipment. Air dry dishes. Do not touch dish surfaces that will touch food. Wash hands, and then store items in a clean, dry area.

C Critical Thinking

9. Human hair can be a contaminant. It is a physical hazard. It can also carry bacteria, which also makes it a biological hazard. Correct the situation immediately by throwing away the sauce. Investigate where the hair came from.

10. Records ensure that there is a way to check the system. If a problem is discovered, records can help determine how to solve the problem.

Academic Skills

11. English Language Arts Procedures should be thorough and minimize hazards at the disposal and cleaning points. An employee with no previous knowledge of the HACCP system should be able to follow the procedure.

12. Social Studies The information in the report will depend on the chosen topic. Reports should be well researched and cite information sources. Students should describe the hazard that their topic addresses, the discovery and development of the solution to the hazard, and how the solution has improved human health as a result of widespread implementation.

13. Mathematics Three containers are needed. Each 12 in. by 10 in. by 2 in. container can hold 240 cu. in. of soup. Because 693 cu. in. of soup must be stored, a total of 693 ÷ 240 = 2.8875 containers are needed. Students should round up to the next whole number.

Certification Prep

14. a. 41°F to 135°F (5°C to 57°C).

15. a. receiving.

Real-World Skills and Applications

16. Time Management Skills The schedule should take into account all steps necessary, including grooming, dressing, and putting on protective clothing. Students should allot a reasonable amount of time for each task, working backwards from the time they need to arrive at work for their shift.

17. Civic Responsibility To preserve the business of a regular customer, students might assure him or her that there are systems to minimize the risk of foodborne illness. Students might describe the precautions taken in receiving, storing, and handling food.

18. Technology Applications Student spreadsheets should list the control points: menu items and recipes, receiving, storing, food preparation, cooking, food holding and serving, cooling, and reheating, and appropriate tasks under each control point. For example, under receiving, tasks might be checking fish for firm texture and springy flesh.

19. Financial Literacy You pay one employee dishwasher $58/day ($7.25 × 8). You pay 3 employee dishwashers $174/day ($58 × 3). Each day, you save $116 using only one employee dishwasher ($174 − $58). The commercial dishwasher will become cost-effective once you have saved $4,000; it will take 35 days to save $4,000 ($4,000 ÷ $116 = 34.48).

Culinary Lab

20. Your HACCP System Evaluations should provide a compare-and-contrast section, as well as an evaluation of the effectiveness. Students should answer the two questions, providing an explanation of changes they might make to their own system.

Culinary Project Lesson Plan

FOCUS

Introduce the Project

In this project, students will research restaurant safety and sanitation inspection sheets to learn what to look for during a safety and sanitation inspection. Students will also learn how to create a restaurant inspection sheet that they can use to identify anything that may violate the health and safety of restaurant staff and patrons. Have them brainstorm possible safety and sanitation violations that they may find in a restaurant.

Build Background

Inspection Research Ask students to discuss what they know about safety and sanitation in a restaurant. What are some common concerns in the kitchen and in the dining room? Write them on the board. Then, ask the students to brainstorm ways to counteract these issues. Write these solutions on the board. Ask the students to think about these issues as they begin their project.

TEACH

S Skill Practice
Guided Practice

L1 Identify Ask students to identify safety and sanitation concerns in the kitchen or the dining room. The list should include whether the issue is a safety or sanitation concern. It should also include details about how each concern can be addressed.

L2 Construct Have students construct a detailed checklist of safety and sanitation issues that may present themselves in a restaurant. Checklists will vary, but may include improper receiving and storage of food, dirty conditions in a restaurant, unsafe conditions such as wet floors, and improper waste disposal.

L3 Describe Have students choose one inspection issue, and describe potential problems about that issue in detail. Then, have them suggest solutions for that issue. Answers will vary based on the issue chosen, but an example might be: Unsafe working conditions in a kitchen, such as keeping knives loose in a drawer or on a countertop. A solution would be to purchase a storage system, such as a knife block or knife kit, that will contain knives.

C Critical Thinking

Evaluate Safety and Sanitation Concerns Hold a discussion about safety and sanitation in a restaurant. Why do these concerns matter, and how can they be prevented to maintain a restaurant experience that is enjoyable and safe for the staff and patrons? Have students explain their answers. Safety and sanitation concerns matter because of the importance of the health and safety of the employees and customers. An unsafe restaurant will soon be out of business. Concerns can be prevented by proper maintenance, cleaning, and the implementation of an HACCP system.

ASSESS

Quiz

Ask students to answer the following questions:

1. What are the advantages of understanding an inspection sheet when working in a restaurant? When employers and employees understand the inspection sheets, they will better understand the sanitation and safety standards that they are required to maintain. This, in turn, can help them work proactively toward a safe work environment.

2. What is the goal of the HACCP system? The goal of the HACCP system is to ensure that biological, chemical, and physical hazards associated with food production and practices are identified, assessed, and contained according to risk and severity.

3. Why are safety measures in a restaurant kitchen and dining room important? Safety measures are important because they ensure that the food that is produced, and the employees who serve it, are protected from direct contamination, cross-contamination, and other hazards while preparing, storing, and serving food.

CLOSE

Culminating Activity

Practical Knowledge Divide students into groups and have them choose a safety or sanitation issue. Then, have them demonstrate to the class how to avoid injury and illness from this issue. Student presentations should focus on the correct way to complete a process, rather than the wrong way. Student presentations may also include tips to other students that will help them remember the safe way to complete a task.

Unit Overview

Introduce the Unit In this unit, students will learn about various job opportunities in the foodservice industry, including those in service, management, and entrepreneurship. Students will also learn how to identify foodservice trends and what skills are important to get a foodservice job. Additionally, they will learn how to search for and apply for a foodservice job and about the importance of customer service. Finally, students will learn about the different types of dining establishments and meal services and how to properly maintain a restaurant dining room.

Chapter

3 Foodservice Career Options

4 Becoming a Culinary Professional

5 Customer Service

6 The Dining Experience

Unit Culinary Career Spotlight Answer Key (found on page 163)

Get Certified Dish descriptions should include crucial information about the dish and make the dish should tempting and appetizing. Students should be able to describe the dish, ensuring that all the information is accurate, while also enticing the reader of the advertisement.

Competition Practice Students should create a salable dish that can be pleasingly photographed and would be appropriate to place in an advertisement. Students will rate their own efforts based on the attractiveness of the finished dish, how the finished food tastes, and whether or not the finished dish was photogenic from all angles.

SkillsUSA competitions provide important ways for your students to hone their technical skills. In the Food and Beverage Service competition, students are rated on their knowledge of how to set up a table.

Table Setup Before beginning this unit, have students create a diagram of how they would set up a table to prepare for a customer. They should consider where to place tableware, glassware, and flatware to ensure customer comfort, cleanliness, and consistency. Diagrams should be neat and detailed, with each item clearly labeled. Once you have finished this unit, have students revisit their diagrams and make any necessary adjustments or corrections. Answers will vary depending on the menu and the type of dining environment, but in general, students should follow these guidelines: place a chair in front of each place setting; set forks on the left side and knives and spoons on the right side of each setting; place knives with the cutting edge toward the center of the setting; ensure that flatware does not hang over the edge of the place mat or table; place the bread plate on the left, above the fork(s); and place the water glass above the tip of the dinner knife.

FCCLA

As part of its mission, FCCLA tries to help students discover their strengths, target career goals, and initiate a plan for achieving the lifestyle they desire.

Career Connection Tell students to imagine they are looking for a job in the foodservice industry. First, have them identify sources that might contain foodservice industry jobs. Then, have students use each source to look for a foodservice industry job. Have them find a job from each and write up a summary of what the source was, how they accessed it, what the experience of using that source was like, and what job they found through that source. The job can be any job related to the foodservice industry. Students should summarize the qualifications necessary for each job they find and any other pertinent information. Students should identify that foodservice industry jobs can be found through networking, professional organizations, trade publications, employment agencies, the Internet, and telephone leads. Answers will vary depending on students' experiences, but students should access each of these sources to find a foodservice industry job. They should summarize their experience with each source, what jobs they found, the necessary qualifications for each job, and any other additional information about each job.

McGraw Hill Professional Development

MINI CLIP VIDEO LIBRARY

Targeted professional development is correlated throughout *Culinary Essentials*. The McGraw-Hill Professional Development Mini Clip Video Library provides teaching strategies to strengthen academic and learning skills. Log on to **glencoe.com**.

Chapter 3 Foodservice Career Options

Reading **Flexible Groupings** Teachers use strategies of flexible groupings and partner sharing to encourage student discussions. (p. TM87)

Reading **Exploring the Big Idea** Students share, in the format of their choice, their answer to a lesson's "Big Question." (p. TM88)

Reading **Connecting the Pieces** A teacher helps students develop predictions and inferences about characters in a story. (p. TM88)

Reading **Comprehension of English Learners** Author Josefina Tinajero discusses comprehension strategies that are appropriate for English learners. (p. TM89)

ELL **Academic Language** Authors Jana Echevarria and Josefina Tinajero discuss the importance of addressing academic language when teaching English language learners. (p. TM86)

ELL **Group Discussions** Students discuss academic content they have just read. (p. TM88)

ELL **Language Practice** Students of varying language proficiencies work together to review the content they have just read. (p. TM89)

Math **Introducing Multi-Step Equations** A teacher walks students through the process of solving multi-step equations. (p. TM87)

Math **Sampling** Algebra teacher Brad Fulton explains the need for random sampling. (p. TM89)

Chapter 4 Becoming a Culinary Professional

Reading **Obstacles to Achievement** Teachers work together to determine why their students are struggling with a particular standard. (p. TM92)

Reading **Planning and Classroom Management** Nancy Frey, Ph.D., teacher, educator, and author, discusses the instructional strategies that support a differentiated classroom. (p. TM94)

Reading **Options for Learning** Two teachers explain to their students multiple ways to read and respond to the assigned text. (p. TM94)

ELL **Level 1 Proficiency** Jana Echevarria discusses the characteristics of Level 1 proficiency English learners. (p. TM92)

Math **Multiple Representations in Mathematics** Dr. Gilbert Cuevas explains the three steps of introducing mathematical concepts. (p. TM95)

Chapter 5 Customer Service

Reading **Differentiated Activities** A teacher models for students how to create vocabulary cards that will support the students' many different learning styles. (p. TM98)

Reading **Strategies for Student Achievement** Teachers meet to discuss strategies for helping all learners meet curriculum standards. (p. TM99)

ELL **Strategies for English Learners** Author Jana Echevarria discusses strategies for teaching English learners. (p. TM98)

ELL **Words in Action** Students act out or mime the words they are trying to learn. (p. TM100)

Math **Cooperative Groups in Mathematics** Bea Moore-Harris discusses the use of cooperative groups in the mathematics classroom. (p. TM100)

Chapter 6 The Dining Experience

Reading **Prereading Strategies** A teacher assesses students' prior knowledge about a text selection they are about to read. (p. TM105)

Reading **Modeling Reading Strategies** A teacher uses a "read-aloud" to model fluent reading strategies. (p. TM105)

ELL **Scaffolding Questions** A teacher uses a series of questions to lead a student to an appropriate verbal response. (p. TM103)

ELL **Using Realia** A teacher uses realia to make lesson concepts more real to students. (p. TM106)

Math **Solving Equations** Students use manipulatives and symbols to solve simple equations. (p. TM104)

Math **Problem Solving with Algebra and Measurement** Curriculum supervisor Mary Esther Reynosa suggests various ways to build students' problem-solving abilities. (p. TM107)

Foodservice Career Options

SECTION 3.1 Careers in Foodservice
SECTION 3.2 Foodservice Trends
SECTION 3.3 Entrepreneurship Opportunities

Classroom Solutions

Print Resources

- Student Edition
- Instructor Annotated Edition
- Lab Manual
- Lab Manual IAE

Technology Resources

ExamView® Assessment Suite **ExamView® Assessment Suite CD**
Create and print unit and chapter tests.

Lesson Planner Plus **Lesson Planner Plus CD** provides access to teacher resources in one package.

Presentation Plus! provides visual teaching aids for every section.

Online Learning Center includes resources and activities for students and teachers. Also includes the **Online Student Edition**.

Interactive Student Edition

SECTION 3.1 Careers in Foodservice

Section Overview

In this section, students will learn about food production and service opportunities. They will also learn about career opportunities related to food production and service, such as management, sales, and purchasing. Finally, they will learn about the education and training available to prepare for a career in the foodservice industry.

FOCUS

Bell Ringer Activity

Jobs We Know Ask students to name jobs they know of in the food industry. Write the jobs on the board. Are most of the jobs they name food production jobs? Or are they foodservice jobs? Ask them to notice the wide variety of jobs available in the foodservice industry as they read the section.

D Develop Concepts

Main Idea Discuss the main idea with the students. Ask: Are there careers for people who are interested in both science and food? Yes there are. Someone who is interested in science and food could become a research chef, a culinary scientist, or food scientist. A research chef cooks as well as uses scientific skills, and a food scientist uses scientific methods to try to improve food products.

TEACH

S Skill Practice
Guided Practice

L1 List Have students list the different management opportunities in the foodservice industry. Management opportunities include: executive chef, research chef, culinary scientist, foodservice director, catering director, kitchen manager, dining room supervisor, and restaurant manager.

L2 Explain Ask students to explain how an apprenticeship works. An apprentice works under the guidance of an experienced chef to learn the trade.

L3 Apply Have students work together to set up a kitchen brigade and prepare a meal. Students should get an idea of what it is like to work in a kitchen by preparing a meal together.

Quiz

Ask students to answer the following questions:

1. What does a prep cook do? A prep cook prepares ingredients to be used on the food line.

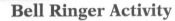 **Professional Development** MINI CLIP **ELL** Academic Language

2. What does a purchaser do? A purchaser buys goods according to his or her clients' current needs.

3. What should you consider when choosing a certificate program? When enrolling in a certificate program, you should consider the reputation of the school and the available job opportunities as well as your career goals.

RETEACH

R Reading Strategy

Real-World Connections Ask students to conduct an interview with someone who works in the food-service industry. They should find out their job duties and the rewards and demands of the position. They should transcribe or write a summary of the interview. Students should connect the real-world experience of the interviewee with what they have learned from the section to gain a deeper understanding of the experience of working in the foodservice industry and the rewards and demands.

U Universal Access

Students with Learning Disabilities Have students choose one job in the production or service category and one job in the management category. Ask them to compare and contrast the two jobs and write a summary of the similarities and differences between them. They should consider factors such as salary, experience and training needed, job location, job duties, and responsibility. Answers will vary depending on which jobs are chosen, but in general, students should have an accurate idea of what the job duties are for each job, where the job takes place, who they are working for, the education and experience needed, and the relative pay and responsibility.

 **Professional Development** MINI CLIP **Reading** Flexible Groupings

ASSESS

✎ Lab Manual

Assign the Section 3.1 Activities.

⊕ Online Study Tools

Have students go to the Online Learning Center at **glencoe.com** to:

- Take the Section 3.1 Practice Test.
- **STUDY TO GO** Download Study-to-Go content.

SECTION 3.1 After You Read Answer Key

Review Key Concepts

1. The traditional kitchen brigade includes: sous chef; chefs de partie/line chefs; saucier/sauce cooks; poissonier/fish cooks; grillardin/grill cooks; friturier/fry cooks; rotisseur/roast cook; entremetier/vegetable cook; potager/soup cook; tournant/swing cook; garde manger/pantry chef; patissier/pastry chef; and boucher/butcher.

2. You can prepare for a career in the foodservice industry through high school culinary arts classes, certification programs, associate's degree programs, bachelor's degree programs, entry-level jobs, apprenticeships, corporate training programs, military training programs, and on-the-job training programs.

Practice Culinary Academics

3. **English Language Arts** Student ads should display an understanding of which interpersonal and technical skills are required to do the jobs described in the section, as well as the education level that might be required for each job. Ads should fit the style of a recruiter looking to hire employees.

4. **Social Studies** Students should be able to discover some general information about historical and modern kitchen brigades through research. Escoffier was in the French army before working as a chef at the Savoy Hotel, where he developed the brigade system. He based his system on his experiences in the military for maximum efficiency. Over time, the kitchen brigade has been simplified in many restaurants, with fewer hierarchies of chefs who are trained to do many different tasks.

5. **Mathematics** No. The required number of hours/year is $240 \times 8 = 1{,}920$ hours. However, you will work only $120 \times 12 = 1{,}440$ hours so will fall 480 hours short ($1{,}920 - 1{,}440 = 480$).

 **Professional Development** MINI CLIP **Math** Introducing Multi-Step Equations

CLOSE

Culminating Activity

What Job Do You Want? Discuss the different career opportunities from the section with the students. After reading about the different opportunities, what career paths are they now interested in? Have they discovered career ideas they had not thought of before? What attracts them to the careers they are interested in?

SECTION 3.2 Foodservice Trends

Section Overview
In this section, students will learn how foodservice trends affect foodservice and food production operations. They will also learn about available job opportunities in various commercial and noncommercial foodservice operations.

FOCUS

🔔 Bell Ringer Activity
Identify Trends Explain to students what a trend is and ask if they can name any recent trends, such as trends in fashion, music, or language. Once they identify several trends, explain that there are trends in all businesses, including the food industry. A successful business owner must keep track of trends.

D Develop Concepts
Main Idea Discuss the main idea with the students. Ask: What might be some cultural trends that affect the food industry? Examples of cultural trends include avoidance of carbohydrates, a desire for foods that appear healthful, ready-to-eat foods or ready-to-make foods, exotic foods, or trends in desired portion sizes.

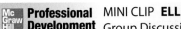 **Professional Development** MINI CLIP **ELL** Group Discussions

TEACH

S Skill Practice
Guided Practice

L1 List Ask students to list the job opportunities available in a quick-service restaurant. Quick-service restaurants hire managers, assistant managers, cashiers, prep cooks, and line cooks.

L2 Explain Have students explain how work trends affect the foodservice industry. When people work more, they have less time. They are more likely to purchase take-out, delivery, or ready-to-eat meals.

L3 Apply Tell students to find foodservice industries in their community other than restaurants and make a list. Students should locate foodservice opportunities outside of the restaurant setting, such as hotels or bakeries.

Professional Development MINI CLIP **Reading** Exploring the Big Idea

ASSESS

Quiz
Ask students to answer the following questions:

1. How did the hospitality industry begin? As traders traveled through different regions, people began offering food and shelter to them on their journey.

2. Why do industry experts analyze societal, cultural, demographic and economic trends? They analyze these trends to better understand how their operation can meet customers' needs.

3. What are the requirements for working in a fine-dining establishment? Staff members in fine-dining must be exceptionally skilled and must have prior work experience and training.

RETEACH

W Writing Support
Menu Trends Have students review the information about trends, and then collect menus from restaurants in the community. Have them examine the menus and list at least three trends found in the menu offerings. Trends that students find in the restaurant menus might include ethnic foods, low-fat or low-carb dishes, locally sourced products, or take-out offerings, among other things. Students should list at least three.

U Universal Access
Gifted Students Have students read an issue of a current foodservice magazine and look for trends. Have them identify trends indicated in the articles and formulate ideas for using these trends in the foodservice industry. Students should be able to find trends mentioned either explicitly or implicitly in the magazine. They should also be able to translate the trends they find into practical ideas for implementing in a foodservice operation. For example, if it is indicated that customers prefer several small dishes instead of one main course, students might suggest that a restaurant add a Small Plates section to its menu.

Professional Development MINI CLIP **Reading** Connecting the Pieces

ASSESS

📖 Lab Manual
Assign the Section 3.2 Activities.

🧭 Online Study Tools
Have students go to the Online Learning Center at **glencoe.com** to:

- Take the Section 3.2 Practice Test.
- Download Study-to-Go content.

SECTION 3.2 **After You Read Answer Key**

Review Key Concepts

1. As the number of single and single-parent households increase, parents will increasingly look to outside sources for help with meals. In addition, children are spending more money outside the home on food, which creates trends focused on children's preferences.

2. Hotels and resorts offer traditional foodservice positions such as chefs, servers, caterers, and management, and can also offer special opportunities such as dietitians.

Practice Culinary Academics

3. **Social Studies** Presentations should show important events in restaurant development, starting with its invention. Photos should show examples of the chosen restaurant type.

4. **Science** Students should create survey questions that will draw out information about how teenagers eat and where they would like to eat. Their sample size should be large enough to give meaningful information. From the answers they get, they should design a plan for a restaurant to be opened near the school.

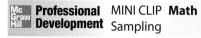 **Professional Development** MINI CLIP **Math** Sampling

5. **Mathematics** $1,750 - $1,000 = $750. $750 ÷ $1,000 = 0.75. 0.75 × 100 = 75\%$.

CLOSE

Culminating Activity

Work in the Foodservice Industry After learning about the different foodservice opportunities, ask students if any of them learned of any new types of foodservice jobs that they might be interested in, for example, working at hotels or in catering.

SECTION 3.3 **Entrepreneurship Opportunities**

Section Overview

In this section, students will learn about the different small-business opportunities available in the foodservice industry. They will also learn about the governmental requirements for starting and running a foodservice business. Finally, they will learn what a business plan is and what the basic components of a business plan are.

 **Bell Ringer Activity**

Become an Entrepreneur Ask the class to discuss what type of business they would start if they could start their own business in the foodservice industry. Encourage them to be creative and give details about the product, the location, the decor, and any other aspects of the business that would make it unique.

Professional Development MINI CLIP **Reading** Comprehension of English Learners

D **Develop Concepts**

Main Idea Discuss the main idea with the students. Ask: What are some reasons someone would become an entrepreneur? People might become entrepreneurs because they have ideas they think could be successful, they want to be their own boss and control the direction of their business, or they want to keep all of their profits.

TEACH

S **Skill Practice**

Guided Practice

L1 **List** Ask students to list types of businesses one can own. Business types include sole proprietorship, partnership, or corporation.

L2 **Explain** Have students explain what should go in the executive summary section of a business plan. The executive summary is a brief recounting of all of the points in a business plan.

L3 **Apply** Have students speak to local city officials or conduct research on the Internet to determine some requirements for starting their own businesses. Students should learn how to seek and find information from government sources and how to discover legal requirements for businesses.

 **Professional Development** MINI CLIP **ELL** Language Practice

ASSESS

Quiz

Ask students to answer the following questions:

1. How many employees does a small business have? A small business has fewer than 100 employees.

2. What are the advantages of a corporation? A corporation is easier to finance than other businesses, and the financial liability of the shareholders is limited.

3. Who updates and maintains records in a business? Records are updated or maintained by the business owner or an accountant.

RETEACH
Writing Support

Conduct Research Have students research food service or restaurant products that began as the result of entrepreneurship. Have them write descriptions of their own products that might compete with their research items in the marketplace. Almost every business began with entrepreneurship, but recent businesses that have not grown into large corporations or chains will be easier to compete with. Students should learn something about the origin of the business and from there, come up with ideas that add something to the concept and are able to compete.

U Universal Access

Students with Physical Challenges Locate or create a sample business plan and provide students with a copy. Ask them to review the business plan and critique the business idea. What are the strengths and weaknesses of this idea? Do they think this idea is likely to succeed? Why or why not? Answers will depend on the content of the business plan and students' opinions about what makes a successful business. Students should use their analytical skills to identify strengths and weaknesses in a business idea and business plan and predict the likelihood of success.

ASSESS

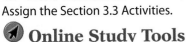 ***ExamView® Assessment Suite***
Create a test for this chapter.

✐ Lab Manual
Assign the Section 3.3 Activities.

◉ Online Study Tools
Have students go to the Online Learning Center at **glencoe.com** to:
- Take the Section 3.3 Practice Test.
- Download Study-to-Go content.

SECTION 3.3   After You Read Answer Key
Review Key Concepts

1. Entrepreneurs who want to work in foodservice management can become chef-consultants and advise corporations in opening or marketing their restaurants, or become an employee recruiter to staff restaurants.

2. The components of a business plan include an executive summary, a management team plan, a company description, a product and service plan, vision and mission statements, industry overview, a market analysis, a competitive analysis, a marketing analysis, an operational plan, a financial plan, a growth plan, a contingency plan, and a cover page, title page, table of contents, and supporting documents.

Practice Culinary Academics

3. **Social Studies** Answers should note that the demand for a particular type of foodservice business will determine that business's success. A new business may be able to supply the demand. If demand is strong enough, there may be room for more than one business.

4. **English Language Arts** Student business plans should contain basic elements of a business plan. They should be written in a style that is appropriate to present to potential lenders and investors, and should contain correct grammar, spelling, and punctuation. It should be apparent in the content that thought and consideration were put into the plan as if it were to represent a real business.

5. **Mathematics** $5 - $4 = $1 profit per cupcake. $1 \div $5 = 0.2. 0.2 \times 100 = 20\%$ profit margin.

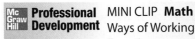 **Professional Development**   MINI CLIP **Math** Ways of Working—Solving Equations

CLOSE
Culminating Activity

Entrepreneurship Appeal Now that students have completed the chapter, ask them to discuss how they feel about the idea of entrepreneurship. Which students would like to open their own businesses someday? Which ones would prefer to work for someone else? What are the reasons for their decisions?

Chapter Review and Applications

Vocabulary Review

1. Once students have completed their crossword puzzles, have them trade and solve each other's puzzles.

Review Key Concepts

2. Foodservice jobs involve working directly with the public and include host, cashier, and server. Food production jobs require cooking or baking skills and include line cook, sous chef, and pastry chef.

3. Educational opportunities include certification programs, degree programs, entry-level work, apprenticeships, and training programs.

4. Foodservice trends reflect the desires of the consumers. Managers study trends so they can adjust their business practices to attract and keep customers.

5. Noncommercial operations work to pay for daily expenses, such as wages and food costs. Commercial operations earn more than enough for daily expenses, creating a profit.

6. Ownership, sales of food you produce to retailers, and management consulting.

7. Gives information about the future of a business and helps business owners estimate their financial, equipment, and staffing needs.

C Critical Thinking

8. You can hold the debate in a team format or as a discussion with students contributing as individuals. Management jobs are more demanding because managers also have to think about customer service, finances, hiring, regulatory compliance, and more.

9. Students should explain their predictions. For example, a restaurant that has televisions at the table or ways that technology, such as the Internet or cell phones, will change restaurant service.

10. Zoning laws help keep business and residential homes separate. This helps keep residential neighborhoods quiet, and helps ensure that businesses have enough room to grow.

Academic Skills

11. **English Language Arts** Each presentation should contain a description of the jobs along with a statement of why the student chose the jobs. The information presented should be accurate and presented in a manner that is understandable to the audience.

12. **Science** After completing the meals, students should compare the ease and efficiency of preparing the meal when everyone has an assigned task and when there are no assigned tasks. Students may notice that less time is wasted, and that steps are not skipped when everyone is assigned a task.

13. **Mathematics** Bakeries: $270 - 240 = 30$ more locations; $30 \div 240 = 0.125$; $0.125 \times 100 = 12.5\%$ increase. Fast-food: $5,125 - 5,000 = 125$ more locations; $125 \div 5,000 = 0.025$; $0.025 \times 100 = 2.5\%$ increase. Frozen yogurt: $48 - 32 = 16$; $16 \div 32 = 0.5$; $0.5 \times 100 = 50\%$ increase. Fast-food had highest total increase (125); frozen yogurt was fastest growing (with a 50% increase).

Certification Prep

14. c. restaurant manager.

15. b. independent restaurant

Real-World Skills and Applications

16. **Information Literacy** Students should discover factors in the different categories and explain how they might affect the food industry. For example, they may discover that concerns about health and the environment affect how people eat.

17. **Research Skills** Students should be able to locate at least one training program in each category and the contact information and basic requirements for attendance.

18. **Technology Applications** E-mails should be written in a tone that is appropriate to a business communication and should politely request an interview and contain a brief explanation of the applicant's skills and training.

19. **Financial Literacy** $\$10,000 \times 0.3 = \$3,000$ for food and supplies; $\$10,000 \times 0.5 = \$5,000$ for wages; $\$10,000 \times 0.15 = \$1,500$ for overhead costs; $\$10,000 \times 0.05 = \$500$ for insurance.

Culinary Lab

20. **Foodservice Careers** Student evaluations should show that they paid attention to each report. Evaluations should be fair, contain both positive comments and constructive criticism, and have notes about the presentation subjects, such as questions they still have and impressions of the job itself.

Becoming a Culinary Professional

SECTION 4.1 Employability Skills

SECTION 4.2 Seeking Employment

SECTION 4.3 On the Job

Classroom Solutions

- Student Edition
- Instructor Annotated Edition
- Lab Manual
- Lab Manual IAE

Technology Resources

 ExamView® Assessment Suite CD
Create and print unit and chapter tests.

Lesson Planner Plus Lesson Planner Plus CD provides access to teacher resources in one package.

Presentation Plus! provides visual teaching aids for every section.

Online Learning Center includes resources and activities for students and teachers. Also includes the **Online Student Edition**.

Interactive Student Edition

SECTION 4.1 Employability Skills

Section Overview

In this section, students will learn the basic skills necessary for employment in the foodservice industry. They will also learn what work ethic is and how to demonstrate a positive work ethic. Finally, they will learn how to develop leadership skills to advance in the foodservice industry.

FOCUS

Bell Ringer Activity

Job Skills Ask students to name the traits that define a good student. Why do those particular traits lead to success in school? Explain that many of those same traits define a good worker. Have the students discuss how those same traits might lead to success in the workplace.

Professional Development MINI CLIP **ELL** Level 1 Proficiency

D Develop Concepts

Main Idea Discuss the main idea with the students. Ask: What skills are helpful in finding a job? Finding a job requires good interpersonal and communication skills as well as good writing skills. Technological skills will help in the job search, and critical thinking skills will help in an interview.

TEACH

S Skill Practice
Guided Practice

L1 List Ask students to list basic reading skills you will use on the job. Basic reading skills include previewing, skimming, focusing, visualizing, and checking.

L2 Explain Have students explain why honesty is part of good work ethic. Honesty is part of a good work ethic because it helps solve problems quickly and keeps the workplace more efficient.

L3 Apply Have students role-play situations in which leadership skills are necessary, such as accidents or customer complaints. Students should demonstrate good leadership and problem-solving skills when addressing the situations presented during the role-play.

Professional Development MINI CLIP **Reading** Obstacles to Achievement

ASSESS

Quiz

Ask students to answer the following questions:

1. What kind of basic skills are helpful in any job? Basic job skills include math, listening, speaking, writing, reading, and thinking.

2. What qualities make up a strong work ethic? A strong work ethic is characterized by responsibility, flexibility, honesty, reliability, teamwork, and commitment.

3. What type of resources must leaders use effectively on the job? Leaders must effectively

use their time, energy, money, equipment, and employees.

RETEACH

R Reading Strategy

Model Skills Have students choose one of the basic job skills at the beginning of the section and demonstrate that skill. They may use a partner, if necessary. For example, a partner might be necessary to demonstrate a listening skill. Students might demonstrate how to calculate percentages, how to be an active listener, how to speak clearly, how to write a particular business communication, or how to solve a problem. Student demonstrations should display an understanding of the material presented in the section. Students may choose a skill that is a strong skill for them, or they may choose one they are trying to improve. Demonstrations should reflect the advice given in the book and should model effective use of the skills demonstrated.

U Universal Access

Students with Behavioral Challenges Ask students to think about the information in the section as it relates to themselves. Explain that before they seek a job, they must know their strengths and skills and what they can best contribute the job. Have students list and discuss their own strengths and skills and then decide what jobs are available to and best suited for a person with this skill set. Students should be able to understand and apply the information in the section to their own skills and abilities to assess their own strengths and weaknesses and determine what jobs they are and are not qualified for at the present time.

ASSESS

 Lab Manual

Assign the Section 4.1 Activities.

Online Study Tools

Have students go to the Online Learning Center at **glencoe.com** to:

- Take the Section 4.1 Practice Test.
- Download Study-to-Go content.

SECTION 4.1 After You Read Answer Key

Review Key Concepts

1. To work in the foodservice industry, one must know how to calculate percentages, make change, and work with weights and measures.

2. A reliable employee is punctual, works his or her full shift, works well without supervision or promoting, takes on extra work when necessary, gets enough rest to work effectively, and maintains good physical and mental health.

3. A leader must use the following resources effectively to be successful: time, energy, money, things, and people.

Practice Culinary Academics

4. **English Language Arts** The flyer should be eye-catching and to the point. It should clearly express the different team jobs available and the skills associated with each job. The skills chosen should match the job description and should be important skills for success in that particular job. Traits may include good attendance, reliability, honesty, and a positive attitude.

5. **Mathematics** $0.0825 \times \$86.25 = \$7.115625$. The sales tax due is $7.12.

CLOSE

Culminating Activity

Re-Evaluate Goals Now that students have learned more about the skills required for working in the foodservice industry, have them revisit their prior employment goals. Have their goals changed at all based on what they have learned about skills and their own self-assessment of their skills? How have they changed?

SECTION 4.2 Seeking Employment

Section Overview

In this section, students will learn how to look for employment in the food production, management, and service industry. They will learn practical job-search skills and how to use them. They will also learn how to prepare a résumé and how to complete a job application.

FOCUS

Bell Ringer Activity

Get a Job Ask students if any of them have a job or have had a job. Ask any students that have had a job to describe how they got their job. Discuss with the class the ways these students got their jobs and how these methods of job-seeking might be applied to the food industry.

D Develop Concepts

Main Idea Discuss the main idea with the students. Ask: What is the first step in seeking a job? The first step is to find job opportunities to apply for by looking in classifieds, online, checking with professional organizations, reading industry trade magazines, or networking.

TEACH

S Skill Practice
Guided Practice

L1 List Ask students to list five sources for job leads. Five sources for job leads are networking, professional organizations, trade publications, agencies, and the Internet.

L2 Explain Have students explain why the employment outlook for the foodservice industry is so positive. The outlook for the foodservice industry is positive because the foodservice industry employs more people than any other segment of the service and sales world, and it continues to grow.

L3 Apply Obtain sample job applications and have students practice completing them. This practice should prepare students to apply for jobs, and they should become comfortable with completing such documents.

 **Professional Development** MINI CLIP **Reading** Planning and Classroom Management

ASSESS

Quiz

Ask students to answer the following questions:

1. What are two services offered by professional organizations? Services offered by professional organizations are employment listings, job placement services, scholarships, and networking opportunities.

2. What are three tips to remember when completing a job application? Tips to keep in mind when completing an application: print neatly; read instructions carefully; carry important information with you; do not leave anything blank; always tell the truth; and be specific.

3. How may interviewers signal the end of the interview? Interviewers will signal the end of the interview in one of the following ways: they may tell you they will contact you later; they may ask you to contact them later; they may offer you the job; or they may not offer you the job.

RETEACH

U Universal Access

Students with Hearing Impairments Have students review the section on networking and ask them to apply what they have learned. First, they should look at the list of networking sources and determine which people in their life would be good networking sources. Encourage them to start talking to those people about their future plans and goals. Students should read the subsection on networking and determine how it applies to their own life and relationships. Then, they should put the advice into practice and start to build relationships with the people they choose, even if they are not currently looking for a job.

C Critical Thinking

Evaluate Job Offers Remind students that once you are offered a job, you must then decide whether to accept the offer, ask for time to consider, or turn down the job offer. Ask them to formulate a plan for evaluating job offers that they receive. What factors would they consider when making the decision of whether to accept the offer, and how would they rank those factors? Students should carefully assess what is most important to them when choosing among job offers. It could be salary, job duties, hours, opportunities for advancement, or something else. Their evaluations should contain a description of the factors that will be important to them and why, as well as a ranking of those factors and reasons for the ranking.

 Professional Development MINI CLIP **Reading** Options for Learning

ASSESS

Lab Manual

Assign the Section 4.2 Activities.

Online Study Tools

Have students go to the Online Learning Center at **glencoe.com** to:

• Take the Section 4.2 Practice Test.

• Download Study-to-Go content.

SECTION 4.2 **After You Read Answer Key**

Review Key Concepts

1. Networking sources include family members and relatives, friends and classmates, teachers and mentors, employers and coworkers, and organizations.

2. Print neatly, and use blue or black ink. Read instructions before responding, and try not to make errors. Have important information available. Fill out the application completely. Be truthful.

Practice Culinary Academics

3. English Language Arts Answers will vary, but students' presentations should include politeness, confidence, and completeness of information given as important behaviors during a job interview. Students might also list good grooming and a good attitude as important.

4. Social Studies While apprenticeships are no longer common in most industries, apprenticeships are still a part of the foodservice industry. In particular, apprenticeship programs can help low-income young people who may not be able to afford educational training to gain on-the-job training combined with education without having to enroll in a college or certificate program.

5. Mathematics $12.50/hour × 160 hours = $2,000 for the month. $2,000 × ¹⁄₁₀ = $2,000⁄10 = $200 is the total fee.

CLOSE
Culminating Activity

Find Job Opportunities Have students use the resources listed in the section to look for job opportunities in the foodservice industry. Have them find three job listings for jobs that appeal to them, and have them share the listings and a description of how they found the listings with the class.

SECTION 4.3 On the Job
Section Overview

In this section, students will learn the rights and responsibilities of employees and employers. They will also learn how to perform calculations related to wages and benefits. They will learn proper workplace etiquette. Finally, they will learn to identify opportunities for advancement in foodservice and the qualifications needed for advancement.

FOCUS
Bell Ringer Activity

On the Job Ask students who have or have had a job how they behave when on the job. What types of behavior or decision making have earned them praise? Which have they regretted? Explain that in this

section, they will learn about good work etiquette. If they follow this advice, they could be promoted.

D Develop Concepts

Main Idea Discuss the main idea with the students. Ask: What are some responsibilities an employee has? Employees are responsible for showing up on time, working when they are supposed to, and working responsibly. Students might think of other responsibilities.

TEACH
S Skill Practice
Guided Practice

L1 List Ask students to list three benefits an employer might offer. Any three of health and accident insurance; paid vacation; discounts; life insurance; disability insurance; tuition reimbursement; and savings and investment plans.

L2 Explain Have students explain the difference between a salary and an hourly wage. An hourly wage is a set amount per hour worked; a salary is a set amount regardless of hours worked.

L3 Apply Reward students who behave courteously with tokens that represent benefits such as free time, extra credit, or free homework. Explain that professional behavior is rewarded on the job as well, with bonuses, tips, raises, and promotions.

 **Professional Development** MINI CLIP **Math** Multiple Representations in Mathematics

ASSESS
Quiz

Ask students to answer the following questions:

1. What are the main responsibilities of an employee and an employer? Employees should do the best job possible by using time responsibly, respecting the rules, working safely, and earning their pay. Employers should provide adequate compensation, employee support, safe working conditions, fair employment practices, and performance evaluations.

2. What does it mean to show initiative at work? Volunteer to take on new tasks and responsibilities.

3. How much notice should be given prior to terminating employment? Always give at least two weeks' notice prior to leaving a job.

RETEACH

Universal Access

Students with Physical Challenges Have students write an employee evaluation for an entry-level food-service job by using sample evaluations gathered from local operations. Discuss the skills needed to be successful in these entry-level positions. Students should connect the skills discussed in the section to real-life working situations. They should also learn the types of skills that are important for entry-level foodservice workers by noticing the skills being evaluated in this exercise.

C Critical Thinking

Employee Ethics Ask students to think of some situations where they might have to make an ethical choice while working. Ask them to describe the situation, the possible choices, and then go through the questions listed in the section and explain the choice they would make. There are many possible situations in which ethics may come up at work. These are generally situations in which another employee asks you to do something, a mistake has been made, or even possibly when an employer asks you to do something. Students should use their decision-making and critical thinking skills to examine ethical choices.

ASSESS

 ExamView® Assessment Suite
Create a test for this chapter.

Lab Manual

Assign the Section 4.3 Activities.

Online Study Tools

Have students go to the Online Learning Center at **glencoe.com** to:

- Take the Section 4.3 Practice Test.
- Download Study-to-Go content.

SECTION 3.3 After You Read Answer Key

Review Key Concepts

1. Workers' compensation requires an employer to provide financial help to cover medical expenses and lost wages when an employee is injured on the job and cannot work.

2. Among the benefits an employer may offer are health and accident insurance, paid vacation, meal discounts, life insurance, disability insurance, tuition reimbursement, and retirement benefits.

Practice Culinary Academics

3. **English Language Arts** Students should draw on the information from the section to act as responsible employers and employees. Students should do their best to communicate in a manner that is appropriate to their respective roles.

4. **Social Studies** Students should use print and Internet resources to research the history and development of one aspect of fair labor practices. They should write a short report that describes the development of their chosen subject clearly and concisely. They should cite their sources of information.

5. **Mathematics** Base wages for the week: 38 × $8.75 = $332.50. Total for the week: $332.50 + $326.86 = $659.36. Hourly rate: $659.36 ÷ 38 = $17.35158, rounded to $17.35 per hour.

CLOSE

Culminating Activity

Plan for the Future Have students think of jobs that interest them in the food industry and then research what other jobs come either below or above that job in the foodservice hierarchy. This might help them plan where to start out and make goals for where they would like to end up.

Chapter Review and Applications

Vocabulary Review

1. Check students' vocabulary to ensure that each has been labeled with the correct part of speech.

Review Key Concepts

2. Math, listening, speaking, writing, reading, and thinking skills. Students should describe and demonstrate how these skills are used.

3. Flexibility, honesty, reliability, teamwork, and commitment. Students should describe and assess of each of these characteristics.

4. Effective use of resources, information, and technology. Students should identify and describe these skills.

5. Networking, professional organizations, trade publications, employment agencies, and the Internet.

6. The ability to fill out an application, respond by telephone and in writing, and prepare a résumé and cover letter.

7. The responsibilities of an employee include using time responsibly, respecting the rules, working safely, and earning your pay. The responsibilities of employers include employee support, safe working conditions, workers' compensation, fair labor practices, and performance evaluations.

8. Tips are bonuses given to an employee by a customer for good service. Deductions are money withheld from pay for taxes, insurance, and other fees. Benefits are services and bonuses that an employer provides to an employee besides wages.

C Critical Thinking

9. You should call the restaurant to tell your supervisor that you are running late and ask if someone can fill in until you arrive. If the restaurant is shorthanded, customer service will not be as good and work will be more difficult for your coworkers.

10. Students should tell Carla that her friendliness is a good trait to highlight, as she will have to interact with customers. However, her tendency to be late may hurt her. Responses to Carla should be tactful.

Academic Skills

11. English Language Arts Role-plays should demonstrate professional speaking, listening, and customer service skills. Students portraying the employee should be courteous and listen to the customer. Students should speak clearly.

12. Science Analyses should contain a list of areas in the foods lab that require safety checks, such as around stoves, near sinks, chemical storage areas, and emergency exits. The summary should include ideas for making the foods lab safer for workers.

13. Mathematics Customer A's tip percentage: $\$35/\$245 = p/100$, or $3{,}500 = 245p$; $p = 3{,}500/245$; $p = 14.28571\%$. Customer B's tip percentage: $\$17.50/\$112.50 = p/100$, or $1{,}750 = 112.5p$; $p = 1{,}750/112.5$; $p = 15.55556\%$. Customer C's tip percentage: $\$40/\$260 = p/10$, or $4{,}000 = 260p$; $p = 4{,}000/260$; $p = 15.38462\%$. Customer B left the highest percentage tip.

Certification Prep

14. b. server

15. d. to make change

Real-World Skills and Applications

16. Communication Skills Students should communicate with the employee well enough to gain valuable information, and in turn should communicate that information to the class. Encourage students to keep in touch with the person they interviewed as a potential networking contact.

17. Interpersonal and Collaborative Skills Students should come up with realistic situations and use the applicable skills described in the book to come up with a reasonable solution to each situation.

18. Technology Applications Students should use their technology skills to figure out how to navigate the resource and determine how to locate foodservice job opportunities. They should be able to use the summary in the future to start their job hunt.

19. Financial Literacy $\$7.25 \times (40 \times 2) = \$580$ gross pay per paycheck. $\$580 \times 0.15 = \$87$ to be deducted from each paycheck. Each month they will earn $(\$580 \times 2) - (\$87 \times 2) = \$986$.

Culinary Lab

20. Interview Practice Evaluations should be fair and should include assessments of both strengths and weaknesses. Students' self-assessments should show that they paid attention not only to their own evaluation but also to the comments of others and that they have given careful consideration to how they may improve upon their weaknesses.

Customer Service

SECTION 5.1 Service Basics   **SECTION 5.2** Serving Customers

Classroom Solutions

Print Resources

- Student Edition
- Instructor Annotated Edition
- Lab Manual
- Lab Manual IAE

Technology Resources

ExamView
Assessment Suite
ExamView® Assessment Suite CD
Create and print unit and chapter tests.

Lesson Planner *Plus* **Lesson Planner Plus CD** provides access to teacher resources in one package.

Presentation *Plus!* **Presentation Plus!** provides visual teaching aids for every section.

Online Learning Center includes resources and activities for students and teachers. Also includes the **Online Student Edition**.

Interactive Student Edition

SECTION 5.1   Service Basics

Section Overview

In this section, students will learn the role and duties of each member of a service staff. They will also learn to demonstrate customer service skills that provide exceptional customer service. In addition, they will learn how to operate and maintain hot and cold beverage equipment and how to prepare beverages.

FOCUS

Bell Ringer Activity

Restaurant Critiques Have students anonymously write summaries of their full-service restaurant dining experiences on index cards and place cards in a bowl. Randomly draw, read them orally, and discuss the importance of quality customer service.

D Develop Concepts

Main Idea Discuss the main idea with the students. Ask: Why does quality customer service draw repeat business from customers? When people go out to eat, they want good food but also want to have a good time and feel special. Customers will return to a place where they feel comfortable, happy, and valued.

Professional Development MINI CLIP **Reading** Differentiated Activities

TEACH

S Skill Practice

Guided Practice

L1 List Have students list six qualities that all foodservice employees must possess. Foodservice employees should have a positive attitude, a neat appearance, communication and teamwork skills, job knowledge, the ability to manage time, and the ability to resolve customer complaints.

L2 Explain Ask students to explain how to effectively use verbal communication as a service staff member. A service staff member must speak clearly, loudly, and not too fast. He or she should use a professional, pleasant, and friendly tone.

L3 Apply Divide students into groups and have them practice serving, looking for ways to be efficient. Have them time each other. Students should come up with ways to use less time, energy, and motion. Then, they should time each other to see if their ideas are working or not.

Professional Development MINI CLIP **ELL** Strategies for English Learners

ASSESS

Quiz

Ask students to answer the following questions:

1. How do servers function as the sales staff? Servers are the sales staff of an operation because they help set the tone of the dining experience. They also help customers make

beverage and food decisions by recommending menu items.

2. Give one example of how an employee could use time or motion effectively. Students may come up with several answers, including avoiding making empty-handed trips to and from the kitchen, refilling water at all tables at the same time, and checking on all tables at the same time.

3. What steps should you take to clean an espresso machine? To clean an espresso machine, use an approved cleaner. Dispense the recommended amount of cleaner into a filter with a blind screen. Once the blind filter has been inserted into the machine's group or housing, turn on the brewing cycle up to eight times. Leave the cleaner in the system for 15 minutes or according to the manufacturer's instructions. Remove the blind filter. Flush out by running two or more brewing cycles.

RETEACH

U Universal Access

Students with Physical Challenges Have students make a ranked list of ways in which they could exceed their customers' expectations for their beverage service. Students should think of ideas that would make beverage service better for the customer, such as serving cold or hot drinks immediately so they are at optimum temperature, getting the best hot beverage equipment, hiring specialized servers, or getting a variety of ingredients to add to hot drinks.

C Critical Thinking

Compare and Contrast Have students observe a service staff and keep track of the service from greeting to payment. What are the reasons for any differences from the book's advice? A server at a typical restaurant will follow many of the guidelines given in the book but probably not all. Students should identify where the server's behavior matches the guidelines in the book, and where it does not. They should also come with possible reasons, such as: certain behaviors may not be necessary in certain restaurants or the server may not be a good server.

 **Professional Development** MINI CLIP **Reading** Strategies for Student Achievement

ASSESS

✍ Lab Manual
Assign the Section 5.1 Activities.

◉ Online Study Tools
Have students go to the Online Learning Center at **glencoe.com** to:

- Take the Section 5.1 Practice Test.
- **STUDY TO GO** Download Study-to-Go content.

SECTION 5.1 After You Read Answer Key

Review Key Concepts

1. The busser helps maintain an inviting table and keeps the service station stocked with supplies. As customers finish eating, the busser clears the table. The busser also cleans and resets the table prior to seating the next customer and keeps the dining room tidy.

2. Be sure your uniform fits properly and is clean and pressed; keep work shoes clean and polished; remove nail polish; and keep jewelry to a minimum.

3. Clean nozzle and rubber holster daily. Place nozzle in warm water with a sanitizer for 15 minutes and allow to air dry. Soda lines are maintained by the supplier, according to state sanitation laws.

Practice Culinary Academics

4. **English Language Arts** Students should read several articles pertaining to customer service in trade magazines and summarize the points and ideas contained within them. They should also form their own opinions based on what they have read. Then, as a class, they should communicate what they have learned and their own opinions.

5. **Mathematics** 0.5 gal. $\times$ 128 oz./gal. = 64 oz. of coffee. 64 oz. $\div$ 32 oz./carafe = 2 carafes are needed.

CLOSE

Culminating Activity

Personal Hygiene Fill a bag with the following items: nail polish, belt, fake nails, perfume, tie, soap, baseball hat, hair accessories, razor, jewelry, and other similar items. Remind the students that appearance is a part of service. Have them discuss the pros and cons of each item as related to foodservice.

SECTION 5.2 Serving Customers

Section Overview

In this section, students will learn more details about the role and duties of the server. They will learn how to use selling techniques to increase sales and how to serve food and beverages properly. Finally, they will learn how to calculate customer checks.

FOCUS

 **Bell Ringer Activity**

Make Connections Ask students to think of real life experiences in restaurants and times when they had good service and bad service. What made the good service stand out? What made the bad service seem so bad? How did the service make them feel about the restaurant?

D **Develop Concepts**

Main Idea Discuss the main idea with the students. Ask: Why do servers have a key role in how a customer rates dining experiences? Servers are often the only people customers talk to during the meal. Even if the food is good, if the customer feels ignored by the server, they will not have a good dining experience.

TEACH

S **Skill Practice**

Guided Practice

L1 **List** Tell students to list three ways a server may place an order. 1) Write out a customer check; 2) recite the order from memory; or 3) use a computerized point-of-sale system.

L2 **Explain** Ask students to explain how a good server should present the check to leave a good impression. Make sure the check is accurate and legible, and place it in the center of the table. Check back frequently.

L3 **Apply** Using a customer check notebook, have students practice taking orders and transmitting those to a third student who is the kitchen. Students should practice taking and transmitting orders so that they can experience any problems that might arise.

| **Professional Development** | MINI CLIP **Math** Cooperative Groups in Mathematics |

ASSESS

Quiz

Ask students to answer the following questions:

1. What is a technique servers can use to enhance sales? Students may answer with any of the following: highlighting, open-ended questions, or upselling.

2. What are the guidelines you should follow when using service trays or tray stands? Carry the tray on your fingertips or palm, depending on the weight; use your shoulder to help balance the tray; carry the folded tray stand while walking in the dining room.

3. In what ways can a point-of-sale system be a benefit? Through fewer errors, increased efficiency, better marketing, and theft reduction.

RETEACH

U **Universal Access**

English Language Learners Have students review the information on setting and clearing tables and then model the process. When setting the table, students should first make sure the table is clean and then cover it with a tablecloth. After that, they should set the table by putting each dish, glass, and piece of flatware in its correct place. They should then clear the table, following the instructions in the section.

| **Professional Development** | MINI CLIP **ELL** Words in Action |

C **Critical Thinking**

Computer vs. Written Many restaurants are moving toward a computerized point-of-sale system, rather than a written system. Analyze the pros and cons of each. A computer system is less likely to make an error than a human, and information is less likely to get lost if it is computerized. Also, computer systems allow the entire business to be run more efficiently by simplifying record keeping. On the other hand, computers can crash or lose data, so it is important to have employees who can operate without them and to keep paper backup records.

ASSESS

 **ExamView® Assessment Suite**
Create a test for this chapter.

 Lab Manual
Assign the Section 5.2 Activities.

 **Online Study Tools**
Have students go to the Online Learning Center at glencoe.com to:

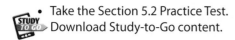

- Take the Section 5.2 Practice Test. Download Study-to-Go content.

SECTION 5.2 After You Read Answer Key

Review Key Concepts

1. There are three ways to place an order in the kitchen: writing out the check, reciting the order, or using a computerized system. When using a computer, you key in each item, press the appropriate button, and the order is sent to the kitchen. Handwritten orders are usually only a backup to the computer system. When writing, write clearly and list courses in the appropriate order.

2. Preset butter or olive oil. Place bread in the center of the table. Do not touch the bread with your hands. Serve enough for each customer to have 1½ servings.

3. Check the card for the customer's signature. Check the expiration date. Make sure the customer signs the credit slip. Compare the signatures to see that they match. Return the credit card to the correct customer. Never leave credit cards lying around.

Practice Culinary Academics

4. **English Language Arts** Encourage students to look on travel sites or in travel books, as they will often have information about local tipping customs. Students should discuss what they have learned of the culture and how that might influence tipping practices.

5. **Mathematics** $13.57 is due: 2 pennies, 1 nickel, 2 quarters, 3 dollar bills, and 1 10-dollar bill. Students should count out change to get from $86.43 to $100, beginning with pennies (2 needed to get to $86.45), then nickels (1 needed to get to $86.50), then quarters (2 needed to get to $87.00), then dollar bills (3 needed to get to $90.00), and finally, 10-dollar bills (1 needed to get to $100.00).

CLOSE

Culminating Activity

Role-Play Create a list of duties included in the order of service. Cut the list into separate duties, and place them into a hat. Have the students draw a technique out of the hat and role-play the correct procedure for the class.

Chapter Review and Applications

Vocabulary Review

1. Students should have logical reasons to explain their chosen vocabulary groupings.

Review Key Concepts

2. The host greets customers, keeps track of reservations, and tracks tables. The server represents the business, sells the menu, serves menu items, and receives payment. The busser maintains the table, keeps the service stations stocked, serves water and bread, and clears and resets the table. The cashier processes payment and makes change.

3. Servers must have a positive attitude, a neat and clean appearance, good communication, teamwork skills, thorough job knowledge, and the ability to use time wisely and resolve customer complaints.

4. When serving cold beverages, use a beverage napkin and keep the beverage to be served first near the rim of the tray. Keep the tallest, heaviest glasses near the center. Carry trays at waist level with your left hand, using your right hand to serve. Serve from the right side. Keep your fingers away from the rims. When serving water, place the glass above the entrée knife and in line with its tip. Do not allow the serving pitcher to touch the rim of the glass. Warm the mug before serving hot beverages.

5. First, give the customer a moment to settle in; then approach the table, smiling and maintaining eye contact. If there is a special event, determine who the guest of honor is. Use a pleasant tone of voice. Listen carefully. Confirm the order before moving on to the next customer. Take the menu from each customer after you have taken the order.

6. Bread, appetizers, soup, salad, entrées, and dessert.

7. Hand totaling: Do it away from the table and use a calculator; list all charges and double-check; add prices; add sales tax to get grand total. Computer: The computer automatically totals for you. Payment can be cash or credit. Cash: Take directly to the cash register; be sure the change is correct; place the money to the left of the person who paid the bill. Credit card: Double-check the information; swipe the card; enter amount; return card to customer with the receipt for signature.

C Critical Thinking

8. Students should obtain information from personal experience, looking at company Web sites, or speaking to company representatives. They should determine which aspects of the practices they learn about would help improve customer service.

9. The host makes sure the customer is seated and comfortable; the server and busser make sure the customer receives his or her meal quickly and efficiently; the cashier makes sure the payment is processed quickly and correctly. All this ensures that the customer remains content throughout the meal.

10. Good communication skills, friendly personality, and some knowledge of the food industry so that they are able to make the customers feel at ease, promote the menu, and respond to customer questions.

Academic Skills

11. English Language Arts Good service might include an apology, staying calm, and offering compensation, such as a free drink or dessert. Poor service might include ignoring the customer, getting angry, or refusing to seat the customer.

12. Social Studies Reports should be thorough, clearly written, well organized, have an introduction, body, and a conclusion, and site sources.

13. Mathematics There is a 4/7 probability of selecting sourdough, since 4 of the 7 are sourdough.

Certification Prep

14. b. metal or plastic scoop

15. c. about 1 inch

Real-World Skills and Applications

16. Communication Skills Students should learn the menu, address the customer courteously, answer all questions, and make suggestions. If they do not know an answer, they should come up with a polite response that indicates they will get the information.

17. Critical Thinking Skills Customer satisfaction depends not only on food, but also on the customer's interaction with the staff. This makes customer service extremely important.

18. Technology Applications Student charts should be designed to convey information clearly and in an organized fashion. They should contain information from the chapter and should be useful to someone wanting to be reminded of customer service skills.

19. Financial Literacy $100 - $39.77 = $60.23; $50 - $42.50 = $7.50; $20 - $11.23 = $8.77

Culinary Lab

20. Practice Table Service Student evaluations should show that they were attentive to what the servers were doing and that they learned enough from the chapter to observe the components of good service in action. The evaluations should answer each question posed for each server and then determine which areas were problem areas.

The Dining Experience

SECTION 6.1 Dining Today

SECTION 6.2 The Dining Room Environment

Classroom Solutions

Print Resources

- Student Edition
- Instructor Annotated Edition
- Lab Manual
- Lab Manual IAE

Technology Resources

ExamView *ExamView® Assessment Suite* **CD**
Create and print unit and chapter tests.

Lesson Planner *Plus* **Lesson Planner Plus CD** provides access to teacher resources in one package.

PRESENTATION *Plus!* **Presentation Plus!** provides visual teaching aids for every section.

Online Learning Center includes resources and activities for students and teachers. Also includes the **Online Student Edition**.

Interactive Student Edition

SECTION 6.1 Dining Today

Section Overview

In this section, students will learn about the main types of dining establishments. They will also learn about the different types of meal service.

FOCUS

Bell Ringer Activity

Favorite Restaurant Types Ask students to describe their favorite restaurants. Have them look over the different restaurant types and discuss which types are their favorites. Then, have them discuss why they like a certain restaurant type. Do they think this will always be their favorite restaurant type, or do they think their tastes will change?

Professional Development MINI CLIP **ELL** Scaffolding Questions

D Develop Concepts

Main Idea Discuss the main idea with the students. Ask: Why do we need different types of dining establishments? Different types of dining establishments serve different needs. Sometimes people need to eat quickly; sometimes people want a special experience; other times people want a casual, social atmosphere.

TEACH

S Skill Practice
Guided Practice

L1 List Ask students to list the service staff members in a classical French service team. The team members in a typical service team in the classical French style are the captain, front waiter, back waiter or runner, and busser.

L2 Explain Have students explain the difference between a family-style restaurant and a neighborhood establishment. A family-style restaurant serves a limited menu that often caters to children. A neighborhood establishment serves simple, inexpensive food usually in large portions.

L3 Apply Move a table next to a wall and have students practice serving from a focal point as required by booth service. Students should serve the customers in the back of the booth first; keep hands as close to table level as possible; avoid handing items to customers; instead, place the item on the table.

ASSESS

Quiz

Ask students to answer the following questions:

1. What is the captain responsible for in a typical French brigade? The captain is responsible for supervising and organizing all aspects of classical French service in his or her station.

2. How is the food served in Russian service? In Russian service, the server plates the food for customers from a large platter.

3. Who serves the customer in butler service?
In butler service, the food is brought to the customers, and then they serve themselves.

RETEACH

R Reading Strategy

Recognize Restaurant Types Have students look through local restaurant listings and categorize them as one of the restaurant types described in the section. If they are not sure, they should guess and explain the reason for their guess. Use Yellow Pages ads or Internet restaurant listings that give enough detail about the restaurants for students to determine the type of restaurant. Students may determine the type of restaurant based on clues in the ad or restaurant description.

U Universal Access

Gifted Students For each restaurant type listed in the section, write a description of the type of neighborhood that a new restaurant owner would want for that type of restaurant. Describe the types of people who would live in the neighborhood and why they would be desirable neighbors for a restaurant owner. Students should analyze the restaurant types and determine the types of people that would likely be customers. For example, a family restaurant might want to open in a neighborhood where many young families live. A coffee house might want to be in a college area that has young residents.

ASSESS

Lab Manual

Assign the Section 6.1 Activities.

Online Study Tools

Have students go to the Online Learning Center at **glencoe.com** to:

- Take the Section 6.1 Practice Test.
- Download Study-to-Go content.

SECTION 6.1 After You Read Answer Key

Review Key Concepts

1. Casual-dining establishments: family-style restaurants, limited menu with traditional, child-friendly favorites; neighborhood establishments, lunch counter or coffee shop with simple, inexpensive, and generously-portioned food; grills and buffets, self-service meals at budget prices, often all-you-can-eat; vending machines, low-cost food and beverages 24 hours a day.

2. Both classical French service and Russian service are elaborate and elegant styles of service. In classical French service, some foods are prepared tableside, while in Russian/English service, each course is prepared in the kitchen and served on large platters. Two different servers perform Russian/English service, while French service has a four-member team. Both types of service require highly skilled servers.

Practice Culinary Academics

3. **Social Studies** Students should use at least two sources to come up with information about a historical restaurant. They might use personal anecdotes of family or community owners who ate there, experiences of employees or owners of the restaurant, news items about the restaurant, or historical information found in local records or museums.

4. **English Language Arts** Students should analyze the information provided on the menu about food preparation, ingredients, price, and the design and presentation of the menu to assign a demographic to each menu using the information about types of dining establishments from the section.

| McGraw Hill **Professional Development** | MINI CLIP **Math** Solving Equations |

5. **Mathematics** The perimeter of 1 table = $(2 \times 42$ in.$) + (2 \times 30$ in.$) = 84$ in. $+ 60$ in. $= 144$ in. Two tables pushed together is still 30 in. wide, but is now 84 in. long. The perimeter of this combined table = $(2 \times 84$ in.$) + (2 \times 30$ in.$) = 168$ in. $+ 60$ in. $= 228$ in.

CLOSE

Culminating Activity

Demonstrate Service As a final activity, divide students into groups, and have them demonstrate one of the styles of service that they learned in the chapter.

SECTION 6.2 | The Dining Room Environment

Section Overview

In this section, students will learn about the side work that must be done before a service. They will also learn about the different types of glassware, dishware, and flatware. They will learn how to set a table for different situations and, finally, will learn about the different centerpieces.

FOCUS

Bell Ringer Activity

Table Settings Have students think about how a typical restaurant table looks and the things that are on it. Have they ever thought about the effort that goes into setting up and keeping the dining environment maintained? Why is this task so important? Discuss how a restaurant might change if the dining environment is not well maintained.

D Develop Concepts

Main Idea Discuss the main idea with the students. Ask: Why is keeping stations stocked important? Keeping stations stocked makes the server's job more efficient. If the stations remain stocked, then a server will not have to interrupt serving a customer to restock them.

| Professional Development | MINI CLIP **Reading** Prereading Strategies |

TEACH

S Skill Practice

Guided Practice

L1 List Have students list the common pieces of tableware you might find on a restaurant table. Common tableware includes a charger, dinner plate, salad plate, bread and butter plate, soup cup, soup bowl, cup, and saucer.

L2 Explain Ask students to explain how to fold napkins for service. Place the linen on a clean surface; make sure your hands are clean before handling the linen; and handle the customers' napkins as little as possible.

L3 Apply Practice changing table linens as described in the subsection on table preparation. The instructions in the book can seem confusing, but as the students practice, the process should begin to make sense.

ASSESS

Quiz

Ask students to answer the following questions:

1. Why is it important to ensure that salt and pepper shakers are completely dry before filling them? If the tops of the shakers are not dry, the salt and pepper will not flow properly and may clump.

2. How should you hold glassware? Always hold glassware by the base or the stem.

3. What are the three most important factors for setting tables? The three most important factors for setting tables are customer comfort, cleanliness, and uniformity.

RETEACH

U Universal Access

Students with Learning Disabilities Have students review the information on side work and create a list of side duties for a dining room staff as if they were creating it for actual restaurant employees. Lists should include the basic side work activities: cleaning and refilling salt shakers, cleaning and refilling sugar containers, and cleaning and refilling glass and metal containers used to hold condiments.

| Professional Development | MINI CLIP **Reading** Modeling Reading Strategies |

C Critical Thinking

Understand Place Settings Ask students: Why are there standard place settings? Why do different situations call for different place settings? Why not just put the tableware anywhere on the table? A standard place setting is not simply decorative. The tableware flatware and glasses are arranged for ease of use of the diner. They are arranged so that the first utensils used are closer at hand and in a way that helps prevent accidents by keeping items out of each other's way.

ASSESS

ExamView® Assessment Suite Create a test for this chapter.

Lab Manual

Assign the Section 6.2 Activities.

Online Study Tools

Have students go to the Online Learning Center at **glencoe.com** to:

- Take the Section 6.2 Practice Test.
- Download Study-to-Go content.

SECTION 6.2 After You Read Answer Key

Review Key Concepts

1. To refill salt and pepper shakers, collect the shakers on a tray, and then empty them in the kitchen. Wash the shakers using a bottlebrush, and wash the shaker tops, unplugging the holes. Let tops and shakers dry completely. Fill the shakers, using the right grain size. Tap shakers to clear out air pockets. Then, return them to tables.

2. Lead crystal glassware is hard, clear, and bright. It is expensive and easily chipped, and therefore is usually used only in fine-dining establishments. Heat-treated glassware is strong and resists breaking and chipping.

This type of glassware is used by most foodservice operations.

3. To change a table linen, start with a tabletop covered only by the soiled cloth. Fold back the soiled cloth by ¼ of its length. Place the clean cloth over the folded portion, so that it is opened one fold and hangs over the edge. Hold the corners of both cloths and pull them toward the other end of the table. Let go when you reach the end. Bring the hanging corners of the soiled cloth to the other corners of the folded cloth. Hold all corners and drop the top edge of the new cloth over the table. Fold the soiled cloth, and place it on a tray. Empty the crumbs in a trash can, and then place the soiled linen in a linen bag.

4. An edible centerpiece is made from items that can be eaten, such as fruit or carved vegetables. These centerpieces can also be sugar-based creations, which showcase the artistic skills of the chef.

Practice Culinary Academics

5. **Mathematics** The area of the place mat: 20 in. × 14 in. = 280 square in.

CLOSE

Culminating Activity

Demonstrate Knowledge As a final activity, have students demonstrate one of the new things they learned from this chapter. For example, the activity could be napkin folding, place setting, changing linens, or stocking items.

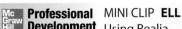 **Professional Development** MINI CLIP **ELL** Using Realia

Chapter Review and Applications

Vocabulary Review

1. After students have created their multiple-choice questions, have them trade papers and answer another student's questions.

Review Key Concepts

2. Dining environments: fine dining, theme restaurant, casual dining, quick service, and catering.

3. Styles of meal service: In modern American plated service, food is prepared, plated and garnished in the kitchen. Servers take food from the kitchen and place it in front of diners.

In booth service, servers serve from a single focal point. Banquette service is like booth service, but with two focal points. Classical French service is an elaborate service style accomplished by a four-person brigade, with several dishes partially prepared and served tableside. In Russian/English service, food is prepared in the kitchen and served from platters by two-person teams. In butler service, food is carried on a tray to customers. In buffet service, food is served from a table to diners, who carry it to their own table.

4. Service members must clean and refill salt and pepper shakers, sugar containers, and condiment containers; stock bus stations with all materials needed for service; clean the menus, seats, table, table base, and floor; fold napkins; and set the table.

5. Glassware: Used for serving beverages; divided into lead crystal and heat-treated glassware. Tableware: Plates, bowls, cups, and saucers; made of china, porcelain, or ceramic. Flatware: Dining utensils, such as spoons, forks, and knives; can be made of different grades of stainless steel or of silver.

6. Napkin goes to the left side, 1 inch from place mat or table, except for a formal dinner, when it is placed on the dinner plate. The appropriate forks go on the left side of the place setting, knives and spoons on right. The bread plate goes on the left, above the forks, with the butter knife placed on top with the cutting edge facing down. The dinner plates go in the center. Glasses and stemware go above the tip of the dinner knife. Coffee cups go to the right of the knives and spoons, with handles at the 4 o'clock position.

7. Types of centerpieces: Lighting gives off illumination; floral, made from fresh, dried, or artificial flowers, leaves and branches; edible, made from items that can be eaten; sculpted, made from ice, butter, chocolate, or beeswax formed into a shape.

C Critical Thinking

8. Tableware, glassware, and flatware in fine-dining restaurants are high-quality. These restaurant customers expect the best. In quick-service restaurants, they are chosen for durability and price.

9. Side work ensures that equipment is in its proper place, everything customers need is available, and the dining area is clean. It makes

service more efficient, as the server will not have to interrupt service.

10. A centerpiece provides something beautiful and interesting for the diners to look at and can serve as a conversation piece. A pleasing atmosphere provides a more pleasant experience for diners.

Academic Skills

11. English Language Arts The guide should be clear and lead a person who is not familiar with the process through the steps of setting a table with language appropriate to the audience (supervisor to employee).

12. Science Students should notice several problems that arise. This exercise should emphasize the importance of testing and developing procedures to eliminate potential problems.

13. Mathematics Since $c^2 = a^2 + b^2$, $c = \sqrt{a^2 + b^2}$. Plugging in 20 in. for a and for b, we get $\sqrt{20^2 + 20^2}$, or $\sqrt{400 + 400}$, or $\sqrt{800}$, or $c =$ 28.28427 inches. The triangle perimeter is 20 in. + 20 in. + 28.28427 in. = 68.28427 in.

 **Professional Development** MINI CLIP **Math Problem Solving with Algebra and Measurement**

Certification Prep

14. b. guéridon

15. a. daily

Real-World Skills and Applications

16. Interpersonal and Collaborative Skills By working together, students should see how service works in a simulated situation and learn the value of working with a team. After a few times of working with the same people, students should find it becomes easier to work together.

17. Time-Management Skills Students should practice folding napkins until they can do it quickly while retaining the proper shape and neatness.

18. Technology Applications The checklist should state the style of restaurant and service type and be neat and easy to follow. The procedure should be appropriate to the restaurant and service type.

19. Financial Literacy 100 lead crystal glasses cost $1,050. 100 heat-treated glasses cost $315. $1,050 − $315 = $735 total savings.

Culinary Lab

20. Plan a New Restaurant Evaluations should provide clear explanations of why students preferred the restaurants they did. Reasons can be personal preference or based on the marketing in the presentation. Discuss which aspects of the restaurants were successful or popular and which were not.

UNIT 2 — The Foodservice Industry

Culinary Project Lesson Plan

FOCUS

Introduce the Project

In this project, students will explore career options in the foodservice industry, and will act out a scene from a restaurant. Ask students to think about foodservice jobs that sound interesting to them. Make a list of these jobs on the board. What academic and culinary skills do students think they will need for those jobs? Have students discuss the pros and cons of each job type.

Build Background

Learn from Observing Have students search employment ads for the particular foodservice job type that interests them. Ask them to compile a list of skill and experience requirements that are listed in the employment ads. Have students revisit their lists after they have completed their observation for the unit culinary project to see if the skills they observed are on the list.

TEACH

S Skill Practice

Guided Practice

L1 List Ask students to list front of the house and back of the house job opportunities. Front of the house opportunities include server, host, busser, cashier, and manager. Back of the house opportunities might include kitchen assistant, line cook, sous chef, garde manger chef, executive chef, pastry chef, and more.

L2 Explain Have students explain the differences between employee and management jobs. Generally, management jobs require a higher skill level and have greater responsibilities than employee jobs. Management jobs also usually pay more than employee jobs, and may have more benefits. Students may list specific management duties, such as balancing receipts, training workers, marketing the business, and scheduling workers.

L3 Apply Ask students to demonstrate their knowledge of different job requirements. Have students write a letter of introduction for one of the job listings they found. Students should include a list of skills that are important for that job within the letter. Letters should be written in a business format, and should contain information about skills needed to hold that job. Although students may not have all the requirements for the chosen job listing, they may pretend that they do for the purposes of the exercise.

C Critical Thinking

Determining Job Levels Listing job skills on a résumé is important. Hold a discussion in which students must decide how skills should be discussed, and whether emphasizing skills on a résumé is acceptable. Students will have different opinions, but should note that while emphasizing appropriate skills for a particular job is an acceptable technique, adding skills that an applicant does not have is unacceptable, and illegal.

ASSESS

Quiz

Ask students to answer the following questions:

1. How will choices you make for your job affect your personal life? Answers will vary, but may include the amount of money a student will make, the amount of time away from the job a student will have, and how well the job will work with other responsibilities a student might have.

2. What are some of the demands that a foodservice career might make on your life? Foodservice businesses are often open for long hours and on holidays. Foodservice jobs also require training.

3. How would you learn new skills while on the job? Many foodservice workplaces offer training to employees. Students may be able to find a mentor, or may be able to work in an apprenticeship or work program to gain new skills.

CLOSE

Culminating Activity

Analyze Career Choices Lead students in a discussion on whether their scene and the information they learned has changed their opinion of their job choice. Have they found that different skills are needed than they originally thought? Are there aspects of the job for which they were unprepared? Students should be able to give specific examples of why their opinions have changed, or why they have remained the same. You may wish to ask other students if they learned more about or were interested by jobs that they did not originally choose.

3 Quality Foodservice Practices

Planning Guide

Unit Overview

Introduce the Unit This unit focuses on management, marketing, and employment laws in the foodservice industry. Students will learn about effective managing, cost control, and marketing strategies. They will also learn about standards, government laws, and regulations as they apply to food safety and the foodservice industry. Finally, they will learn about workers' rights, workers' safety, and laws that protect workers against discrimination.

Chapter

7 Foodservice Management

8 Standards, Regulations, and Laws

Unit Culinary Career Spotlight

Answer Key (found on page 213)

Get Certified Job descriptions should include appropriate education, experience, training, and personality requirements that are necessary to be a successful dining room manager. They should be written in a format and tone appropriate for a job listing.

Competition Practice Students should successfully role-play a situation in which they are a dining room manager who must deal with a customer who has a complaint. Students should rate their own efforts, based on their communication skills, word choice, professional demeanor, and the solution they came up with to offer to the customer.

SkillsUSA competitions provide important ways for your students to hone their technical skills. In the Food and Beverage Service competition, students are rated on their communication abilities in relation to guest service and guest relations.

Guest Relations Tips Before beginning this unit, have students imagine they are training workers in the foodservice industry on how to communicate with customers and manage customer complaints. Have students create a poster with tips and guidelines on how to handle customer complaints that would be appropriate to use when training foodservice workers. Once you have completed the unit, have students add to or adjust the content of their posters to integrate what they learned in the unit. Poster content will vary, but generally, the posters should include tips such as: listen attentively to the customer's concerns; demonstrate an understanding of the customer's frustration; address the concern quickly; offer compensation if necessary; offer reassurance that the problem will not happen again; and find and fix the cause of the problem to prevent it from happening again. The posters should be engaging and easy to read.

As part of its mission, FCCLA encourages its student members to develop and strengthen leadership skills on the job to prepare for career success.

Leaders at Work Have students name the two types of leadership styles mentioned in the text and define them. Then, have them think about the pros and cons of each. Finally, students should come up with two different scenarios that could occur in the foodservice industry, one that the students think would lend itself to one of the leadership styles and one that they think would be better handled by the other. The two leadership styles are autocratic and democratic. Autocratic leadership involves one person having all the power and not including others in the decision-making process. Although a democratic leader will make the final decision, he or she invites other members of the team to contribute to the decision-making process. Situations will vary, but examples should indicate an understanding of the pros and cons of each leadership style and when each might be useful.

McGraw Hill Professional Development

MINI CLIP VIDEO LIBRARY
Targeted professional development is correlated throughout *Culinary Essentials*. **The McGraw-Hill Professional Development Mini Clip Video Library provides teaching strategies to strengthen academic and learning skills. Log on to glencoe.com.**

Chapter 7 Foodservice Management

Reading Strategic Readers Author Scott Paris discusses the characteristics of strategic readers. (p. TM111)

Reading Vocabulary Author Josefina Tinajero describes the importance of academic language. (p. TM113)

Reading Guided Instruction A teacher helps students identify major and minor details from a selection she has read to them. (p. TM113)

Reading Connecting the Pieces A teacher helps students develop predictions and inferences about characters in a story. (p. TM114)

ELL Level 2 Proficiency Author Jana Echevarria discusses the characteristics of Level 2 proficiency English learners. (p. TM112)

Math Small Group Work Students work in cooperative groups to graph an equation. (p. TM112)

Math Independent and Dependent Events Algebra teacher Brad Fulton gives clear explanations of independent and dependent events. (p. TM115)

Chapter 8 Standards, Regulations, and Laws

Reading Attentive Reading A teacher uses read aloud and direct questioning to help her students identify elements of an essay. (p. TM117)

Reading Interacting with Text Students work in small groups to make connections and ask higher order questions. (p. TM118)

Reading Bridging Cultural Gaps A teacher models the use of context clues to determine the meaning of an unknown word. (p. TM119)

ELL Accessing Prior Knowledge A teacher helps students make connections between what they already know and the topic of the reading selection. (p. TM119)

ELL Scaffolding Questions A teacher leads a student to an appropriate verbal response. (p. TM119)

ELL Words and Pictures A teacher uses words and media examples to help students learn new vocabulary. (p. TM120)

Math Solving Equations Students use manipulatives and symbols to solve simple equations. (p. TM121)

Foodservice Management

SECTION 7.1 Management Basics
SECTION 7.2 Managing People and
             Facilities
SECTION 7.3 Foodservice Marketing

Classroom Solutions

Print Resources

- Student Edition
- Instructor Annotated Edition
- Lab Manual
- Lab Manual IAE

Technology Resources

ExamView *Assessment Suite* **ExamView® Assessment Suite CD**
Create and print unit and chapter tests.

Lesson Planner Plus Lesson Planner Plus CD provides access to teacher resources in one package.

Presentation Plus! provides visual teaching aids for every section.

Online Learning Center includes resources and activities for students and teachers. Also includes the **Online Student Edition**.

Interactive Student Edition

SECTION 7.1 Management Basics

Section Overview

In this section, students will learn the qualities necessary to be an effective manager. They will also learn how to manage time and human resources within a foodservice operation. They will learn how management is structured, and they will also learn the manager's role in implementing cost control techniques.

FOCUS

Bell Ringer Activity

A Good Manager Ask the students to imagine they are hiring a life manager who would make sure that their lives run smoothly. What kind of person would they look for? Would those same qualities transfer to managing a foodservice operation?

D Develop Concepts

Main Idea Discuss the main idea with the students. Ask: Why is cost control part of a manager's job? Cost control is part of a manager's job because the manager has the most control over the daily operations of a foodservice establishment and is in the best position to oversee overall costs.

TEACH

S Skill Practice

Guided Practice

L1 List Have students list the qualities of an effective manager. Good communication, time management, and resource management skills.

L2 Explain Ask students to explain the duties of a first-line manager. To be directly responsible for the day-to-day supervision of the employees.

L3 Apply Tell students to imagine they are the manager of a restaurant that is going to start hosting children's birthday events. Have them forecast the cost and what they must charge to make a profit. Students should find out the cost of supplies and entertainment, and determine the extra charge needed to make a profit.

 Professional Development MINI CLIP **Reading** Strategic Readers

ASSESS

Quiz

Ask students to answer the following questions:

1. What is involved in managing human resources? A manager must know the strengths and weaknesses of each employee.

2. What are the responsibilities of middle managers? To direct the activities of first-line managers; coordinate activities; and facilitate communication between first- and top-line managers.

3. What does it mean for a manager to forecast?
Forecasting means anticipating what things will costs, money needed, staffing needs, and profits.

RETEACH

U Universal Access

Students with Physical Challenges Have students review effective management and come up with personality traits of a good manager. Since an effective manager must have good communication, time management, and resource management skills, he or she would likely need to be friendly, a good listener, efficient, responsible, fair, and hard-working.

C Critical Thinking

Problem-Solving Role-Play Pair students and have one student play a complaining customer and the other play a manager who must resolve the customer's problem. Ask the student playing the customer to imagine a problem and present it so that the student playing the manager does not know what it will be. Then, have them switch places. Students playing the manager should be fair and diplomatic. They should try to come up with a solution that will satisfy the customer, such as an apology, an offer of a free dessert, or a discount on their bill.

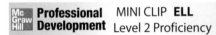 **Professional Development** MINI CLIP **ELL** Level 2 Proficiency

ASSESS

✍ Lab Manual

Assign the Section 7.1 Activities.

Online Study Tools

Have students go to the Online Learning Center at **glencoe.com** to:

- Take the Section 7.1 Practice Test.
- Download Study-to-Go content.

SECTION 7.1 After You Read Answer Key

Review Key Concepts

1. Changes that can make a business more profitable include: changes in the way a task is done, reorganizing storage space, changing staff or schedules, or adding employee training.

2. Food must be inspected to ensure that quality is as described, that you received the correct product in the correct amount and unit size, that the prices on the invoice and purchase order match, that the product is not damaged, and that it was shipped properly.

Practice Culinary Academics

3. Social Studies Students should either already know, or should learn, that supply is the amount of a product available, and demand is the amount of product people want. The relationship between the two is an important figure in determining how to price an item. A manager needs to consider supply and demand when making purchasing decisions and determining pricing.

4. English Language Arts The language used in the letter should be responsive to the customer's specific complaint, respectful and polite, and use correct spelling and grammar.

5. Mathematics Purchases for the month: $10,000 per day $\times$ 30 days = $300,000. Cost of sales = $25,000 + $300,000 − $20,000 = $305,000.

 **Professional Development** MINI CLIP **Math** Small Group Work

CLOSE

Culminating Activity

Do You Have What it Takes? Discuss the material in this section with the students. Now that they have learned the qualities and duties of a manager, are they interested in perhaps becoming a manager someday? What do they have to do to reach that goal?

SECTION 7.2 Managing People and Facilities

Section Overview

In this section, students will learn about managing both employees and facilities. They will learn decision-making and problem-solving skills for management. They will learn how to select, train, evaluate, and supervise employees. They will also learn about facility design and loss prevention.

FOCUS

Bell Ringer Activity

Develop a Management Strategy Ask students to imagine they are managers of foodservice operations. Have them brainstorm and list strategies they would use to manage effectively. List the ideas that students come up with on the board.

D Develop Concepts

Main Idea Discuss the main idea with the students. Ask: Why is a manager responsible for loss prevention? A manager is responsible for loss prevention because employee training and supervision are major factors in loss prevention, and these things are a manager's responsibility.

 Professional Development MINI CLIP **Reading** Vocabulary

TEACH

S Skill Practice
Guided Practice

L1 List Have students list factors to be considered when designing a foodservice operation. Factors to consider when designing a foodservice operation include balance, menu, traffic paths, bypassing, and production space.

L2 Explain Ask students to explain how to analyze their customer base. To analyze customer base, one must examine the type of people one wants to attract as customers.

L3 Apply Have students pair up and practice training techniques by teaching their partners how to do something they know well. Students may teach a food-related task or something else. They should use positive reinforcement and be very clear in their training instructions.

ASSESS

Quiz
Ask students to answer the following questions:

1. What is the first step a manager takes to review job applications? The first thing the manager does is make sure the job applications are neatly, completely, and correctly filled out.

2. Who are mentors and what do they do? Mentors are employees who have a solid understanding of their job and can help train new employees.

3. What are the responsibilities of a risk management coordinator? A risk management coordinator implements and oversees safety procedures.

RETEACH

R Reading Strategy
Give Examples Have students review the section on loss prevention, give examples of what could go wrong within each sector, and come up with ways to avoid those problems. Answers will vary, but should present a realistic problem that might occur in the areas of safety, sanitation, food handling, equipment

handling, maintenance and repairs, or insurance. They should also come up with a solution to help prevent that problem, such as proper training, supervision, or other measures.

 Professional Development MINI CLIP **Reading** Guided Instruction

U Universal Access
Students with Visual Impairments Have students imagine that a large piece of equipment has broken down during the dinner shift. Have a class discussion and ask the students to explain how a manager could keep the business running smoothly while the equipment is being repaired. Ways to handle this situation might include determining which tasks that the equipment usually performs can be handled manually and which cannot. The manager would also want to figure out which menu selections will not be available due to the equipment failure, and make sure servers inform customers of unavailable dishes and potential time delays in available dishes.

ASSESS

Lab Manual
Assign the Section 7.2 Activities.

Online Study Tools
Have students go to the Online Learning Center at **glencoe.com** to:
- Take the Section 7.2 Practice Test.
- Download Study-to-Go content.

 **SECTION 7.2 After You Read Answer Key**

Review Key Concepts

1. Positive reinforcement helps build employee confidence. It makes employees feel appreciated and rewarded, so they will learn better and work hard to earn recognition. Mentoring helps employees learn faster by giving them one-on-one attention from someone who already knows the job well.

2. An effective work area will allow for easy maintenance and inventory access. It will also provide a safe and productive environment for employees. It will allow work to be flexible, and it will protect equipment from damage.

3. Managers are responsible for training employees in the correct use of equipment. Managers must make sure employees are

properly trained to operate each piece of equipment they will use on the job.

Practice Culinary Academics

4. **English Language Arts** Student article summaries should demonstrate an understanding of what they read. Their responses should be both critical and analytical, not just a restatement of the articles. Student discussion should focus on the most effective ways to handle common management problems based on what they learned and their own opinions.

5. **Mathematics** The total weekly labor cost is $2,060, which averages $51.50/hour. Each of the two sandwich makers makes $10.25 × 40 = $410 in a week. The cashier makes $9.75 × 40 = $390 in a week. The manager makes $850 in a week. Therefore, the total weekly labor cost is $410 + $410 + $390 + $850 = $2,060. The average hourly cost equals $2,060 per week ÷ 40 hours per week = $51.50/hour.

CLOSE

Culminating Activity

Safety Slogans Have students write motivational safety slogans that could be used in a restaurant kitchen to remind employees of safety procedures. If you wish, you may turn it into a contest with a prize for the most clever and most effective slogan.

 **Professional Development** MINI CLIP **Reading** Connecting the Pieces

---

SECTION 7.3 | **Foodservice Marketing**

Section Overview

In this section, students will learn about marketing and why it is done. They will learn how to analyze location, customer base, competition, and trends to develop a marketing strategy. They will also learn how positioning, atmosphere, and customer needs influence marketing. Finally, they will learn about public relations.

FOCUS

Bell Ringer Activity

Marketing Plan Ask students to write the title Marketing Plan and three columns labeled Location, Customer, and Product on a sheet of paper. They should imagine a foodservice business they might want to start and fill each column with their business's characteristics.

D Develop Concepts

Main Idea Discuss the main idea with the students. Ask: Why is analyzing a location an important part of developing a marketing strategy? Analyzing a location is an important part of developing a marketing strategy because the location will determine how many people have easy access to your establishment. The type of people in the location will also be the first potential customers toward whom you will want to direct your marketing and promotional efforts.

TEACH

S Skill Practice
Guided Practice

L1 List Have students list factors to be analyzed when creating a marketing strategy. Factors to be analyzed when creating a marketing strategy include location, customer base, competition, and trends.

L2 Explain Have students explain how to analyze the competition. Business owners must determine which businesses are their competition, where their competition is located, and how they will be different and more attractive than these establishments.

L3 Apply Hold a class bake sale at the school and have students decide how best to promote it. Students should come up with creative ways to promote the sale, such as posters, announcements, live advertising, and other methods.

ASSESS

Quiz

Ask students to answer the following questions:

1. What are two marketing strategies that provide information to give an operation the best possible start? Possible marketing strategies include analyzing the location, customer base, competition, and trends.

2. Why is strong and accurate positioning important? Strong and accurate positioning attracts new customers and keeps existing customers coming back.

3. What is one advantage and one disadvantage of direct marketing? An advantage is that it allows the message to reach its desired audience. A disadvantage is that it is expensive, and people often do not read every piece of mail they receive.

 **Professional Development** MINI CLIP **Math** Independent and Dependent Events

RETEACH

U Universal Access

Students with Hearing Impairments Have students review the section on marketing strategies and write a short report on the benefits and limitations of doing market research. Doing market research prior to opening a business allows you to predict what business will be like and prepare for the type of customers you will be serving. However, you cannot predict everything, and sometimes unexpected situations will change these factors dramatically.

C Critical Thinking

Analyze a Restaurant As part of a class discussion, have students analyze the location, customer base, competition, and trends affecting a restaurant in your area. Also discuss whether the students think this restaurant will or will not continue to be successful. Answers will vary depending on the restaurant, but should be thoughtful analyses of the characteristics that might affect the restaurant's business and whether the restaurant will be successful in the location and with the customers and local trends. In addition, students should recognize that customers might not respond as predicted.

ASSESS

 ExamView® Assessment Suite
Create a test for this chapter.

Lab Manual
Assign the Section 7.3 Activities.

Online Study Tools
Have students go to the Online Learning Center at **glencoe.com** to:
- Take the Section 7.3 Practice Test.
 Download Study-to-Go content.

SECTION 7.3 After You Read Answer Key

Review Key Concepts

1. When analyzing a location, you should consider traffic patterns, as well as how accessible the location is to the general public. Prospective business owners should also think about whether the location is affordable, whether a new structure will have to be built, if an existing structure can be renovated, and why the last owner vacated the premises.

2. Direct marketing is a form of marketing in which materials, such as letters and advertisements, are mailed directly to potential customers.

Practice Culinary Academics

3. **English Language Arts** Students should be creative with their promotional plans. The plan should consider the type of restaurant chosen and the needs and desires of the people in the neighborhood. The promotion should focus on making neighborhood residents aware of how the restaurant can meet their needs. For example, a good promotional plan might be a 2-for-1 deal to appeal to low-income residents or families.

4. **Science** Students should use the strategies they learned in the section about analyzing the marketplace and apply them to determine what they believe the marketplace will look like in their community in the near future. For example, if people of a higher economic class are moving to the community, there may soon be a demand for more fine-dining restaurants.

5. **Mathematics** Pretend the office location has 1,000 customers who each spend $2, for a total of $1,000 \times \$2 = \$2,000$. To determine the residential location revenue, increase customers by 30% to 1,300 ($1,000 \times 0.30 = 300$; $1,000 + 300 = 1,300$), and decrease spending by 20% to $1.60 ($\$2 \times 0.8 = \$1.60$). The revenue for the residential location is $1,300 \times \$1.60 = \$2,080$, which is greater than the revenue for the office location.

CLOSE

Culminating Activity

Marketing Discussion Discuss with students what they have learned in this section. What do they know about marketing that they did not know before? Also, explain that creative marketing often works better than standard advertising. As a class, brainstorm creative marketing ideas for a restaurant.

Chapter Review and Applications

Vocabulary Review

1. Memos should have at least 12 vocabulary terms and be written in a business-like style.

CHAPTER 7 Answer Key

Review Key Concepts

2. An effective manager is a good communicator and leader. He or she must manage both time and resources.

3. The foodservice manager must establish an effective record-keeping system; keep food, beverage, and labor costs low; maintain profit and loss statements; make wise purchasing decisions; inspect food upon receipt; and follow standard inventory procedures.

4. The manager creates job descriptions, reviews applications, interviews prospective candidates, and hires. When training, the manager must use positive reinforcement and assign mentors. When supervising, the manager must create and enforce standards of conduct, keep customers satisfied, enforce policies regarding drug and alcohol use, and create work schedules.

5. Space is divided to meet customer, staff, and menu needs; maintain a desired turnover rate; ease movement; minimize bypass; and provide adequate production space.

6. Properly train employees in safety and sanitation procedures and the correct use of equipment; implement risk management procedures; make sure food-handling regulations are followed; establish equipment maintenance and cleaning schedules; and get necessary insurance.

7. Analyze the location, customer base and diversity, competition, and trends.

8. Promotional and public relations techniques include advertising (a paid form that persuades and informs the public about the facility) and direct marketing (materials, such as letters, are mailed directly to customers).

C Critical Thinking

9. Students should consider the type of restaurant and employees. A quick-service restaurant means employees need to perform duties efficiently. There will probably be a high turnover rate, so the manager should develop a training procedure using positive reinforcement.

10. Factors may include family needs, school/homework schedule, financial need, extracurricular activities, and sleep.

Academic Skills

11. **English Language Arts** Summaries should point to information in the advertising that targets a particular market segment and lists the advantages of using the business's services.

12. **Social Studies** Students should locate state guidelines through research and use them to create a well-organized checklist. Discuss the role of management in correcting safety violations. How would the students handle safety violations? Explain the importance of inspections in protecting customers.

13. **Mathematics** Assets: 10,000 + $20,000 + $150,000 = $180,000. Liabilities: $30,000 + $70,000 = $100,000. $180,000 − $100,000 = $80,000 in owner's equity.

Certification Prep

14. d. Foodservice Management Professional

15. b. federal, state, and local governments

Real-World Skills and Applications

16. **Communication Skills** Students may choose two positive ways of dealing with the customer or one positive and one negative way. They should predict possible outcomes and identify pros and cons of each solution.

17. **Management Skills** Students should create 5–10 questions, appropriate to the chosen position. Questions about customer service and prior experience are appropriate to all positions. A cashier may be asked about math skills.

18. **Financial Literacy** Beverage cost: $15,000 + $13,500 + $14,000 + $15,000 + $13,700 + 14,500 = $85,700. Income: $50,000 + $45,000 + $47,000 + $52,000 + $49,000 + $50,000 = $293,000. Divide beverage cost by beverage sales: $85,700 ÷ $293,000 = 0.29, or 29% beverage cost ($0.29 for every dollar received in sales.)

19. **Technology Applications** Flyers should be creative. Students may include information on pricing, special deals, and sample menu items.

Culinary Lab

20. **Market a Foodservice Operation** Each mini-review should assess the advertisements; give positives and negatives; give information not included; and be constructive.

Standards, Regulations, and Laws

SECTION 8.1 Foodservice Standards and Regulations
SECTION 8.2 Employment Laws

Classroom Solutions

Print Resources
- Student Edition
- Instructor Annotated Edition
- Lab Manual
- Lab Manual IAE

Technology Resources
ExamView® Assessment Suite CD
Create and print unit and chapter tests.

Lesson Planner Plus **Lesson Planner Plus CD** provides access to teacher resources in one package.

Presentation Plus! provides visual teaching aids for every section.

Online Learning Center includes resources and activities for students and teachers. Also includes the **Online Student Edition**.

Interactive Student Edition

SECTION 8.1 Foodservice Standards and Regulations

Section Overview
In this section, students will learn the standards of quality used to evaluate food. They will also learn the role of various government agencies in the foodservice industry. They will learn what food grading and food inspections are. Finally, they will learn about standards and regulations for facilities maintenance.

FOCUS
Bell Ringer Activity
Purpose of Regulation Ask students to give examples of some rules they have to follow at school. Discuss with them the purpose of these rules. Explain that foodservice employees and managers also have to follow rules at work. These rules ensure the safety of themselves and their customers.

D Develop Concepts
Main Idea Discuss the main idea with the students. Ask: How might government laws and regulations increase the safety level of food products? Government laws and regulations are based on research about the safest way to handle food. These laws ensure that food is handled at a certain safety level and allows corrective action to be taken when food is not handled safely.

Professional Development MINI CLIP **Reading** Attentive Reading

TEACH
S Skill Practice
Guided Practice
L1 List Have students list the government agencies that are involved in standards and regulations for the foodservice industry. The government agencies involved include the FDA, the USDA, OSHA, and the FSIS.
L2 Explain Ask students to explain how food is graded. A product receives a grade based on its quality when packaged. The package is then stamped with the grading seal.
L3 Apply Have students imagine they are safety inspectors. Have them inspect the foods lab and write an evaluation. Inspections should point out any areas they believe are unsafe or unsanitary. Evaluations should be specific and reflect what students have learned in this section.

ASSESS

Quiz

Ask students to answer the following questions:

1. **What does USDA stand for?** USDA stands for the United States Department of Agriculture.

2. **What is one function of the USDA?** Students may list any one of the following: grade and inspect poultry, eggs, egg products, meats, and meat products; supervise food grading; process plant inspections; or supervise use of pesticides, preservatives, and food additives.

3. **What are the main responsibilities of the Occupational Safety and Health Administration (OSHA)?** The main responsibilities of OSHA are to set standards and to inspect workplaces to ensure that employers provide a safe and healthful environment.

RETEACH

R Reading Strategy

Conduct Research Review the section on environmental regulations, and have students locate information on an environmental regulation that affects the foodservice industry. Students should summarize the regulation and explain how it affects the foodservice industry. Student answers will vary depending on the regulation chosen. Regulations chosen might include waste disposal, certain cleaning products, or additives used in food.

U Universal Access

Students with Visual Impairments In teams, students should research food irradiation. Remind them to evaluate their sources for potential bias. Have each team give an oral report, taking either a pro or con stand, and share their findings with the class. Food irradiation is regulated by the FDA to ensure that it is safe, and independent scientific reviews have concluded that the process is safe. Nonetheless, some groups feel that food irradiation is potentially dangerous because of concerns about the safety of radiation and concerns that radiation may be used to cover up poor food quality. Students should persuasively describe the reasoning and factual data supporting their chosen point of view.

 Professional Development MINI CLIP **Reading** Interacting with Text

ASSESS

Lab Manual

Assign the Section 8.1 Activities.

Online Study Tools

Have students go to the Online Learning Center at **glencoe.com** to:

STUDY TO GO Take the Section 8.1 Practice Test. Download Study-to-Go content.

SECTION 8.1 After You Read Answer Key

Review Key Concepts

1. Standards of quality have been developed so that managers and food safety professionals can judge the performance of a foodservice operation.

2. The FDA requires nutrition labels to be placed on food packaging. The label must show the percent of the daily dietary value in the food based on a 2,000- or 2,500-calorie intake. The label must also show the number of calories per serving, total calories, and the amount of certain nutrients in the food.

3. The three main areas that must meet industry standards of facilities maintenance are: floors, walls, and ceilings; equipment; and facility design.

Practice Culinary Academics

4. **Social Studies** Answers will vary depending on the subject chosen, but students should discuss whether they researched a standard, law, or regulation, and which government agency enforces that standard, law, or regulation. They should accurately summarize the standard, law, or regulation and demonstrate an understanding of its purpose. They might also want to discuss differences at the local, state, and federal levels.

5. **Mathematics** The horizontal scale (x-axis) should list the names of the months, from January through June. The vertical scale (y-axis) should list the number of injuries, from 0 to 6. Students should draw a bar above each month that indicates the number of injuries that occurred in that month.

CLOSE

Culminating Activity

Follow Regulations Have students locate information on local regulations or standards that affect foodservice operations and make a list of ten rules to follow in their foods lab that will ensure the foods lab operates on a level that would be required of a local foodservice operation. Post the rules in the foods lab.

SECTION 8.2 Employment Laws

Section Overview

In this section, students will learn about laws that ensure equal opportunity for employment for everyone. They will also learn about laws that are related to protecting workers' rights and worker safety. Finally, they will learn about ergonomics and the responsibilities of employees and employers in the workplace.

FOCUS

🔔 Bell Ringer Activity

How Laws Protect Us Ask students to describe laws that protect people. For example, traffic laws protect people from dangerous drivers, and criminal laws attempt to protect citizens by deterring criminal acts. Explain that the government also makes employment laws to protect workers while they are on the job.

 Professional Development MINI CLIP **Reading** Bridging Cultural Gaps

D Develop Concepts

Main Idea Discuss the main idea with students. Ask: Why do we have laws that protect people from discrimination? Laws that protect people from discrimination exist because historically, certain groups of people have had a harder time finding employment because of racial stereotypes, prejudice, or a perception of weakness due to physical disability. These laws seek to correct those injustices.

TEACH

S Skill Practice

Guided Practice

L1 List Ask students to list laws that govern equal employment opportunities. The Civil Rights Act, Equal Employment Opportunities Act, Age Discrimination in Employment Act, and Americans with Disabilities Act.

L2 Explain Ask students to explain the concept of affirmative action. Affirmative action programs are designed to locate, hire, train, and promote women and minorities to help prevent discrimination.

L3 Apply Tell students to look at each of the types of laws that affect the workplace and come up with a

real life situation that law would govern. Answers will vary. One example could be that workers' compensation laws would help a construction worker if he or she were injured on the job, ensuring that he or she has income while recovering and not being able to work.

ASSESS

Quiz

Ask students to answer the following questions:

1. What role does OSHA play in changing the workplace? OSHA monitors and investigates workplace accidents and injuries.

2. What law governs the hiring of older people? The Age Discrimination in Employment Act makes it illegal to discriminate against older employees.

3. Name three laws all foodservice workers should be aware of and the rights each law protects. Answers can vary and may include affirmative action, sexual harassment, disabilities act, wage and labor laws, and workers' compensation.

 Professional Development MINI CLIP **ELL** Accessing Prior Knowledge

RETEACH

U Universal Access

Students with Learning Disabilities Have students work in teams to create a standard operating manual for their school restaurant or foods lab. It should include policies for handling work absences, wage and salary review, resolving grievances, safety rules, sick leave, and disability. The policies that students come up with should be fair and reasonable and should also comply with the information given about existing laws in the section.

C Critical Thinking

Position Statement Have students write an essay explaining their position regarding minimum wage laws, discussing whether the government should continue to raise the minimum wage and whether changes in this law would have positive or negative impacts on the foodservice industry. Students should answer this question thoughtfully, using logical reasoning for their position. Since this is an opinion question, there is no right or wrong answer, but the reasons given must support the conclusion reached.

 **Professional Development** MINI CLIP **ELL** Scaffolding Questions

ASSESS

 ExamView® Assessment Suite
Create a test for this chapter.

Lab Manual
Assign the Section 8.2 Activities.

Online Study Tools
Have students go to the Online Learning Center at **glencoe.com** to:

- Take the Section 8.2 Practice Test.
- Download Study-to-Go content.

SECTION 8.2 After You Read Answer Key
Review Key Concepts

1. The Equal Employment Opportunities Act requires businesses to have affirmative action programs. It applies to restaurants with at least 15 employees who work at least 20 weeks per year.

2. The IRCA states that only U.S. citizens and people who are authorized to work in the United States may be legally hired. The INA states that employers must fill out an I-9 form for each employee.

3. Employee responsibilities include being aware of their rights under the law, following the laws, and providing correct information about themselves and their jobs to their employers and the government.

Professional Development MINI CLIP **ELL** Words and Pictures

Practice Culinary Academics

4. **Social Studies** Students should choose a law and think about how the law has affected businesses in their area. They may want to search news archives from the time the law was passed or interview local business owners. The changes should be a related effect of the passage of the law, not just a coincidental occurrence after the law was passed.

5. **Mathematics** Subtract the current depth from the required depth. Since the lowest common denominator is 6, the problem can be rewritten as $4\frac{4}{6} - 4\frac{3}{6}$. This yields the answer $\frac{1}{6}$ foot (or 2 inches).

CLOSE

Culminating Activity
Real-World Connections If you can, have someone from the foodservice industry come in and talk to the class about how he or she applies the law in his or her own workplace. If this is not possible, encourage students to talk to someone in the foodservice industry about laws that affect that person's workplace.

Chapter Review and Applications
Vocabulary Review

1. Before discussing vocabulary, ask students if they can define any of the words based on their own real-world experience.

Review Key Concepts

2. Safety, nutritional value, appearance, consistency, flavor, texture, convenience, ease of handling, packaging, and storage.

3. Government agencies enforce minimum standards of quality through inspection and grading of food products and supervising processing plant inspections, pesticides, preservatives, and additives.

4. By making sure that floors, walls, and ceilings are well constructed, light-colored, and in good condition, that equipment meets sanitation standards, and that facility design encourages effective workflow, minimizes risk of contamination, and allows easy access to equipment.

5. The Civil Rights Act, the Equal Employment Opportunities Act, the Age Discrimination in Employment Act, and the Americans with Disabilities Act.

6. Wage and labor laws, which determine a minimum wage employers must pay to employees; immigration laws, which govern who is authorized to legally work in the United States; workers' compensation laws, which provide benefits for those injured on the job.

7. Employees must be aware of their rights under the law, follow laws, and provide correct information about themselves and their jobs. Managers must post the required notices, keep accurate records, know and enforce the law, and train employees to follow it.

C Critical Thinking

8. Genetically engineered foods are still a fairly new technology, and while they may be a solution to food supply problems, there are also issues with patenting and how they will affect ecosystems. Irradiation is less controversial now, but is still debated. Students should come up with reasonable points to support their side and should debate in a respectful manner.

9. Food kept outside of a safe temperature can spoil or harmful bacteria can grow. This results in food being thrown out, which wastes money, or spreading foodborne illnesses to customers.

10. No. You should still inspect food products received, as they are graded at packaging so they may have lost quality or been contaminated since then.

Academic Skills

11. **English Language Arts** Memos should be in the proper format with a formal tone. Students should summarize employment equality laws covered in this section, and may also summarize immigration laws, since those would affect hiring decisions as well.

12. **Science** Students should explore the development and use of one genetically engineered product, explaining its purpose and how it is used in agriculture. Any related controversies, such as being able to patent a genetically modified food or certain countries not trusting the safety of the foods, should be described. Students should cite sources.

13. **Mathematics** Students should write $x - y = 30$, where x represents the total weight and y represents the container weight. The net weight, 30 oz, is known. If the total weight, or x, is 31.5 ounces, then the container weight can be determined by making $x = 31.5$ and solving for y. So, $y = x - 30$. Substituting 31.5 for x, $y = 31.5 - 30$, or $y = 1.5$ ounces.

Mc Graw Hill **Professional Development** MINI CLIP **Math** Solving Equations

Certification Prep

14. c. federal employees

15. d. the Food Safety and Inspection Service

Real-World Skills and Applications

16. **Civic Responsibility** Regulations chosen should be ones students understand and that are observable to a restaurant customer. Interviews should have information on how restaurants can comply with local or state standards.

17. **Critical Thinking Skills** Some items on a restaurant inspection checklist can be applied to a home kitchen, while some cannot. For example, items related to waste disposal, cleanliness, and safe food handling can generally be transferred to a home kitchen, while items regarding special equipment, such as fryers or drink dispensers, generally cannot.

18. **Technology Applications** Students should work with slide show software to make a simple presentation about their chosen topic. They should use text and graphics. The text should simply outline the topic, not attempt to display an entire report.

19. **Financial Literacy** 10% of $5.85 is 58.5 cents. $5.85 + $0.585 = $6.435. Round up to $6.44.

Culinary Lab

20. **Know the Law** Evaluations should determine how well each poster conveys information. If a poster is colorful or humorous, but does not provide enough information that a foodservice employee who has no knowledge of the law could follow, it is not useful.

Culinary Project Lesson Plan

FOCUS

Introduce the Project

In this project, students will research the job responsibilities of a foodservice manager. They will then interview a person who is a foodservice manager, and create a visual presentation to show skills a manager would need. As a class, ask students to list job responsibilities of a foodservice manager. Ask them what skills they think they might need to meet those responsibilities.

Build Background

Role Reversal Break students into teams, and have them role-play a situation between a manager and an employee. Have them imagine that the employee was late to work and the manager must make sure the employee is not late again. Then, have students switch roles. Afterward, ask students as a class how easy or difficult it was to play the part of the manager.

TEACH

S Skill Practice

Guided Practice

L1 List Ask students to list the three levels of management in most foodservice organizations. Levels of management include first-line managers, or supervisors; middle managers; and top managers, or administrators.

L2 Explain Have students explain the differences between the three levels of management. First-line managers are directly responsible for managing kitchen and service employees. They may have charge over a particular part of an operation. Middle managers usually manage the first-line managers, and help them communicate with top managers. Top managers control the business, create policies and procedures, and make financial decisions.

L3 Apply Ask students to redo their role-plays, but this time between a first-line manager and a middle manager. The middle manager should communicate a new overtime policy to the first-line manager, whose employees may not like the new policy. Was there any difference in how they felt in the role of the manager? Student answers will vary. Some students may feel less comfortable discussing policies and directing others, while some may feel no difference at all.

C Critical Thinking

Determining Job Levels Hold a discussion in which students must decide what qualities are essential in a good manager. Ask them if any qualities are different for good managers and for good employees. Many qualities, such as honesty, work ethic, and responsibility, may be the same. Students may note some differences, however, such as enhanced communication and financial skills for managers.

ASSESS

Quiz

Ask students to answer the following questions:

1. How important is time management control for a manager? Time management is very important, as an efficient business tends to be a successful one.

2. How might a manager successfully train an employee? Managers might hold on-the-job training sessions for the new employee, assign a mentor, or send the employee for further education outside the business.

3. How might a manager maintain the profitability of a foodservice business? Answers may include keeping costs under control, marketing the business to the right customers, managing resources effectively, planning new promotions to increase business, and not overstaffing the business.

CLOSE

Culminating Activity

Analyze Management Skills Lead students in a discussion on whether their ideas of the skills needed to be a successful foodservice manager have changed since the completion of their projects. Were there skills that were not part of the original list made by the class? Students should be able to give specific examples of why their opinions have changed, or why they have remained the same. You may wish to ask other students if they learned more about the qualities of a successful manager.

Introduce the Unit In this unit, students will learn about the necessary preparation that takes place before cooking. They will learn about commercial kitchen work stations and work flow. They will also be introduced to the different types of receiving, storage, preparation, cooking, holding, and service equipment, along with knives and smallwares. Additionally, they will learn about the basics of nutrition and how to incorporate government guidelines, dietary recommendations, and different lifestyles into meal planning. Finally, students will learn how to plan, design, and price menus and how to use standardized recipes.

Chapter

9 Equipment and Technology
10 Knives and Smallwares
11 Culinary Nutrition
12 Creating Menus
13 Using Standardized Recipes
14 Cost Control Techniques

Unit Culinary Career Spotlight Answer Key (found on page 369)

Get Certified Students should successfully develop an idea for a main dish that would be appropriate for a 100-guest wedding and is balanced and healthful. It should be appealing and appropriate to the festive atmosphere of a wedding.

Competition Practice Students should develop and design a three-course menu for a wedding that will have 100 guests. They should incorporate ideas on menu items, decorations, table set-up, and design. Students will evaluate their work based on their menu's design and overall appearance, the items on the menu, and the appropriateness of the menu for the occasion.

SkillsUSA competitions provide important ways for your students to hone their technical skills. In the Culinary Arts competition, one category students are rated on is their knowledge and ability in food safety techniques.

Knife Safety Before beginning this unit, have students write down all the rules and tips they can think of for handling knives safely in the kitchen. Once you have completed this unit, pair up students, and have them exchange their lists. Students should then review each other's lists, making any necessary changes or additions to incorporate what they learned in the unit. Once you are sure the lists are accurate, have students demonstrate safe knife skills and techniques, using the rules and tips from their lists. The lists may vary slightly, but in general, safety guidelines for knife use include: using the correct knife for the task; being sure the knife is sharp; cutting with the blade facing away from you; using a cutting board; never trying to catch a falling knife; never using knives for tasks other than the ones for which they are designed; never leaving a knife in a full sink; and always washing and sanitizing knives before putting them away.

As part of its mission, FCCLA encourages its student members to develop, plan, and carry out projects that improve the quality of life in their communities.

Community Connection Split your students into groups, and have each group come up with a creative way to teach elementary students about carbohydrates, fiber, proteins, fats, cholesterol, vitamins, minerals, and water. The presentations should be engaging, appropriate, and interesting to the age group, but they must also provide accurate information about the various aspects of nutrition. Then, arrange for your students to visit an elementary school class to teach students about the basics of nutrition. Presentations will vary, but students may choose to do a play, musical, dialogue, role-play, contest, game, or any other creative idea that will engage the children while teaching them about nutrition. Each student in the group should participate, and the presentations should contain accurate information from the text about the various nutritional elements discussed.

Professional Development

MINI CLIP VIDEO LIBRARY
Targeted professional development is correlated throughout *Culinary Essentials*. **The McGraw-Hill Professional Development Mini Clip Video Library provides teaching strategies to strengthen academic and learning skills. Log on to glencoe.com.**

Chapter 9 Equipment and Technology

Reading Planning for the Future Teachers collaborate to develop new instructional strategies. (p. TM127)

Reading Flexible Groupings Teachers use flexible groupings and partner sharing to promote student discussion. (p. TM129)

Reading Differentiated Instruction Nancy Frey, Ph.D., teacher, educator, and author, discusses elements of a differentiated classroom. (p. TM129)

Reading Differentiated Activities A teacher models vocabulary cards to support different learning styles. (p. TM130)

ELL Comprehension and English Learners Author Josefina Tinajero discusses comprehension strategies for English learners. (p. TM125)

ELL Direct Vocabulary Instruction A teacher has students create vocabulary cards to build a personal dictionary. (p. TM126)

ELL Collaborative Work Students work in groups to complete a lab. (p. TM127)

ELL Using Manipulatives A teacher uses concrete objects to illustrate lesson concepts. (p. TM127)

ELL Using Realia A teacher uses realia to make lesson concepts more real to students. (p. TM128)

Math Medians and Quartiles Algebra teacher Brad Fulton helps students understand the meaning of median, and quartile. (p. TM129)

Math Real-Life Ratios A teacher discusses real-life applications of ratios. (p. TM131)

Chapter 10 Knives and Smallwares

Reading Flexible Groupings Teachers use flexible groupings and partner sharing to promote student discussions. (p. TM133)

ELL Level 3 Proficiency Author Jana Echevarria discusses the characteristics of Level 3 proficiency. (p. TM134)

Math Understanding Fractions Algebra teacher Brad Fulton discusses the importance of fractions. (p. TM134)

Math Communication in Mathematics Bea Moore-Harris explains the importance of communication in the classroom. (p. TM136)

Math Solving Equations Students use manipulatives to solve equations. (p. TM136)

Chapter 11 Culinary Nutrition

Reading Another Point of View Emily M. Schell, Ed.D., educator and author, discusses standards-based instruction. (p. TM138)

ELL Language Practice Students work together to review content they have read. (p. TM138)

ELL Group Discussions Students work together to decide where to place illustrations on a chart. (p. TM139)

Math Sampling Algebra teacher Brad Fulton explains the need for random sampling. (p. TM141)

Math Exponent Rules Algebra teacher Brad Fulton suggests ways to illustrate exponent rules. (p. TM142)

Chapter 12 Creating Menus

Reading Prereading Strategies A teacher assesses students prior knowledge about a selected reading. (p. TM145)

ELL Elaborating on Student Responses A teacher elaborates using explanatory language. (p. TM143)

ELL Using Manipulatives A teacher uses concrete objects to illustrate lesson concepts. (p. TM145)

Math Fraction Computation Students work in small groups to solve a fraction problem. (p. TM144)

Chapter 13 Using Standardized Recipes

Reading Guided Instruction A teacher helps students identify details from a selected reading. (p. TM150)

ELL Level 4 Proficiency Author Jana Echevarria discusses the characteristics of Level 4 proficiency. (p. TM149)

Math Real-World Ratios A teacher has students create and compare ratios. (p. TM150)

Math Small Group Work Students work in cooperative groups to graph an equation. (p. TM151)

Chapter 14 Cost Control Techniques

Reading Another Point of View Lois Moseley, author and educator, discusses the benefits of teacher collaboration. (p. TM155)

ELL Scaffolding Questions A teacher uses a series of questions to direct students to a response. (p. TM154)

ELL Providing Clear Directions A teacher provides clear written and oral directions for an assignment. (p. TM156)

Math Ways of Working—Solving Equations A teacher uses partner and whole group instruction. (p. TM155)

Equipment and Technology

SECTION 9.1 The Commercial Kitchen

SECTION 9.2 Receiving and Storage Equipment

SECTION 9.3 Preparation and Cooking Equipment

SECTION 9.4 Holding and Service Equipment

Classroom Solutions

Print Resources

- Student Edition
- Instructor Annotated Edition
- Lab Manual
- Lab Manual IAE

Technology Resources

ExamView® Assessment Suite CD
Create and print unit and chapter tests.

Lesson Planner Plus CD provides access to teacher resources in one package.

Presentation Plus! provides visual teaching aids for every section.

Online Learning Center includes resources and activities for students and teachers. Also includes the **Online Student Edition.**

Interactive Student Edition

SECTION 9.1 The Commercial Kitchen

Section Overview

In this section, students learn what the different work sections and work stations in a professional kitchen are. They will also learn about the different types of cooking lines that may be used in a professional kitchen and the importance of efficiency.

FOCUS

Bell Ringer Activity

The Commercial Kitchen Ask students which of them have seen a professional kitchen. For those who have, ask them to describe what the kitchen or kitchens they have seen looked like. What do they remember about the equipment and the way it was arranged? Have they seen different kitchens that are arranged differently?

D Develop Concepts

Main Idea Discuss the main idea with the students. Ask: Why is the type of cooking line set-up important? The cooking line set up will determine how workers move through the kitchen. A good set-up will create efficient and safe workflow. A bad set-up will be inefficient and could be dangerous as well.

TEACH

S Skill Practice
Guided Practice

L1 List Ask students to list the different cooking line set-ups. Single, straight line; L-shaped; U-shaped; Parallel, back-to-back; and Parallel, face-to-face.

L2 Explain Have students explain the difference between a work section and a work station. A work station is a work area that is set up to prepare a certain type of food. A work section is a larger group of several work stations.

L3 Apply Have students imagine that they are preparing a Caesar salad at the salad station. Have them demonstrate how they would perform mise en place prior to making the salad. If possible, students should demonstrate in the foods lab. Otherwise, they may simply describe how they would arrange the ingredients, equipment, tools, and serving pieces to prepare the salad.

 **Professional Development** MINI CLIP **ELL** Comprehension and English Learners

ASSESS

Quiz

Ask students to answer the following questions:

1. **What is the most common cooking line arrangement?** The most common cooking line arrangement is a single, straight line.

2. **Why is mise en place important?** Mise en place is important in a kitchen because it improves workflow, efficiency, and time management.

3. **How does a kitchen design affect time management?** Kitchen design can improve workflow and create more efficient time management.

RETEACH

 Writing Support

Mise en Place Have students create a general list of mise en place steps for each section of the foods lab. Working in teams, students should select a recipe from their team's assigned station. The teams should carefully study their recipes. Then, they should write the mise en place that needs to be done for the recipe before preparation. The general list of mise en place should be a list that prepares the station for work before any recipes are ordered or prepared. The mise en place for the recipe selected will expand on the general mise en place, containing steps that apply to the particular ingredients, equipment, and dishes needed to prepare the recipe.

> **Mc Graw Hill Professional Development** MINI CLIP **ELL** Direct Vocabulary Intruction

U Universal Access

Gifted Students Kitchen technology is constantly changing, with new equipment being developed all the time. How can the development of new technology affect efficiency and kitchen design? New technology can make work more efficient by eliminating or speeding up tasks. New technology also affects kitchen design because new types of equipment may mean that a different design is needed to keep the kitchen working at its most efficient.

ASSESS

🖎 Lab Manual

Assign the Section 9.1 Activities.

✈ Online Study Tools

Have students go to the Online Learning Center at **glencoe.com** to:

- Take the Section 9.1 Practice Test.
-  Download Study-to-Go content.

Review Key Concepts

1. Range of motion means using the fewest body movements possible while avoiding unnecessary stress or strain. When your equipment, tools, and ingredients are easily accessible, you eliminate unnecessary stops and starts, which saves time. An efficient range of motion also eliminates wasted time and energy.

Practice Culinary Academics

2. **Science** Students should observe each movement as well as where each piece of equipment is. Using these observations, they should come up with ideas for eliminating unnecessary movements or moving equipment so that it takes less time and effort to use it.

3. **Social Studies** Biographies should be clear, concise, and accurate, and should deepen the class's understanding of how the person's contributions to work flow can improve a business.

4. **English Language Arts** The report should be written in a professional tone that is appropriate for a business communication. It should clearly delineate between the analysis and the recommendations. Students should use the information about different cooking line arrangements from the section to evaluate which they think would work best in the foods lab, and explain why.

5. **Mathematics** Dessert should be served at 7:04 (6:15 + 49). Since it takes 37 (10 + 25 + 2) minutes of total preparation time for the soufflé, preparation should begin at 6:27 (7:04 − 37).

CLOSE

Culminating Activity

Field Trip If possible, arrange for students to tour local foodservice kitchens. Ask them to observe how the equipment is arranged in each kitchen. Ask them to look at menus for each establishment to see if those with similar menus have similar arrangements. Discuss student observations on return to the class.

SECTION 9.2   Receiving and Storage Equipment

Section Overview

In this section, students will learn about equipment used in the process of receiving and inspecting food products. They will also learn what the first in, first out (FIFO) procedure is and how to implement it. Finally, they will learn about the different equipment used in a professional kitchen to store food.

Mc Graw Hill Professional Development   MINI CLIP **Reading** Planning for the Future

FOCUS

🔔 Bell Ringer Activity

Equipment at Home and Work Ask students to think of the equipment they have in their home kitchen for storing fresh, frozen, and dry foods. What types of storage equipment do they have? Would this equipment be good to use in a restaurant kitchen? Why or why not?

D Develop Concepts

Main Idea Discuss the main idea with the students. Ask: Why is the type of storage equipment chosen for a professional kitchen important? It is very important for a professional kitchen to have the appropriate storage equipment to fit the space and store all necessary ingredients in a safe manner. The menu will be limited by storage availability.

TEACH

S Skill Practice

Guided Practice

L1 List Have students list the types of equipment used in receiving. The types of equipment used in receiving include scales, thermometers, and dollies.

L2 Explain Ask students to explain how the FIFO process works. Receivers should mark each item with the delivery date. Older items should be moved to the front, and newer items should be moved to the back.

L3 Apply Give examples of food products, and have students match them with the proper storage equipment for that product. Choose items for each type of storage unit, and have students correctly determine where each item should be stored.

Mc Graw Hill Professional Development   MINI CLIP **ELL** Collaborative Work

ASSESS

Quiz

Ask students to answer the following questions:

1. **What is a purchase order?** A purchase order is a document asking a supplier to ship food or supplies at a predetermined price.

2. **What is the proper storage temperature for frozen goods?** The proper temperature for frozen goods is 0°F (−18°C).

3. **What is freezer burn?** Freezer burn is surface drying on frozen food.

RETEACH

W Writing Support

Create a List Ask students to imagine that a shipment of fresh, frozen, and dry food products has been delivered to the restaurant where they work. Ask them to create a list of ten different food products that were delivered. Then, they should determine where each product should be stored. Students may choose whatever they like for the food products, as long as there is a mixture of fresh, frozen, and dry food. They should then use what they read in the chapter to determine where each product should be stored, with fresh foods being refrigerated, frozen stored in the freezer, and dry foods on shelving units.

U Universal Access

English Language Learners Have the class break into groups and discuss the types of storage equipment a restaurant might need, based on information from the chapter. Students may list refrigerators, freezers, shelving units, and storage containers. They may decide on several types, or they may limit their answers due to budgetary concerns.

Mc Graw Hill Professional Development   MINI CLIP **ELL** Using Manipulatives

ASSESS

📖 Lab Manual

Assign the Section 9.2 Activities.

🧭 Online Study Tools

Have students go to the Online Learning Center at **glencoe.com** to:

- Take the Section 9.2 Practice Test.
- Download Study-to-Go content.

Review Key Concepts

1. The different types of refrigerators and freezers are a walk-in refrigerator (a refrigerated room); a reach-in refrigerator (one, two- or three-door unit with sliding shelves); a roll-in refrigerator (has a rack of sheet pans that can be rolled up a ramp into the unit); a lowboy refrigerator (a half-size refrigerator); and a freezer (a unit that can store foods for longer periods of time and at lower temperatures than a refrigerator).

Practice Culinary Academics

2. **Science** The tomatoes cooked in aluminum will have a faded color and a metallic odor. The aluminum pot may become pitted and discolored from the acid in the tomatoes. Students may taste a slight metallic taste in the tomato sauce from the aluminum pot.

3. **English Language Arts** Students should identify common invoice terms and abbreviations, such as PO number, Qty, and unit price. Use class discussion to ensure everyone understands how to read invoices.

4. **Social Studies** The term FIFO (first in, first out) was developed in the computer science industry as a way of describing computer processing algorithms. FIFO is also used in accounting as a method of evaluating the inventory of a business. It is also used in the military. Businesses often take aspects of other industries and adopt them when they can see a way that it could be useful in their own businesses.

5. **Mathematics** Annual depreciation amount: $6,300 \div 7 = $900. First-year depreciation: $6,300 - $900 = $5,400. Second-year depreciation: $5,400 - $900 = $4,500.

CLOSE

Culminating Activity

Practice Receiving Have students work in teams to check in a food order. Bring in some items to serve as their shipment. Then, have them check for quality, insects, damaged goods, and correct temperatures. Have students label and date all items to ensure FIFO.

SECTION 9.3
Preparation and Cooking Equipment

Section Overview

In this section, students will learn about the different types of food preparation, cooking, and clean-up equipment. They will also learn about the different heat sources used in cooking. Finally, they will learn how to clean and maintain the equipment to keep it in safe, working condition.

FOCUS

Bell Ringer Activity

Equipment at Home and Work Have students recall the previous discussion about storage equipment at home and in a professional kitchen. Now, have them compare and contrast the preparation, cooking, and cleaning equipment they have at home and similar cleaning equipment found in a professional kitchen. What are the similarities and differences?

D Develop Concepts

Main Idea Discuss the main idea with the students. Ask: Why is clean-up equipment included in a section about preparation? Clean-up equipment is included in a section about preparation because cleaning dishes is the last step in the process of preparing food. Cleaning dishes also serves as a preparation step for the next time you will use those dishes.

TEACH

S Skill Practice

Guided Practice

L1 List Ask students to list the different heating sources used in cooking equipment. The different heating sources used in cooking are gas, electricity, radiation, microwave, and light.

L2 Explain Have students explain how to clean a griddle. To clean a griddle, first polish the top with a griddle cloth or stone, going with the metal's grain. Then, wash the remaining area with warm soapy water, rinse, dry, and recondition the cooking surface.

L3 Apply Have students practice using a piece of food preparation equipment that is available in the foods lab. Students should practice using whatever is available to prepare ingredients for cooking.

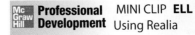 **Professional Development** MINI CLIP **ELL** Using Realia

ASSESS

Quiz

Ask students to answer the following questions:

1. **What is the first step in cleaning preparation equipment?** The first step in cleaning preparation equipment is to make sure the equipment is unplugged.

2. **How does radiation cook food in a microwave?** Invisible waves of energy cause water molecules to rub against each other.

3. **How does a convection oven cook more efficiently?** A convection oven cooks more efficiently because a fan circulates the heated air, causing all portions of the food to be heated evenly.

RETEACH

Universal Access

Students with Hearing Impairments Divide students into teams to clean and polish a large piece of equipment, following safety and sanitation guidelines. Supervise students carefully to see that they are following the instructions provided by the text for cleaning equipment. Be sure to provide both positive and negative feedback.

 **Professional Development** MINI CLIP **Reading** Flexible Groupings

C Critical Thinking

Analyze Recipes Have students choose five recipes and analyze each one to determine which types of preparation and cooking equipment will be needed to prepare each recipe. Have them list the equipment needed for each recipe. Answers will depend on which recipes are chosen, but students should examine each step carefully for clues as to which equipment will be needed. Review the recipe to make sure the student did not miss anything.

ASSESS

 Lab Manual

Assign the Section 9.3 Activities.

Online Study Tools

Have students go to the Online Learning Center at **glencoe.com** to:

- Take the Section 9.3 Practice Test.
- Download Study-to-Go content.

Review Key Concepts

1. To clean a mixer or food processor, you must first ensure that the equipment has been turned off and unplugged. Next, remove the attachment and bowl and wash them in hot, soapy water. Then, rinse and sanitize each piece. Finally, dry all of the pieces thoroughly.

2. Radiation transfers energy from the equipment to the food. The waves change to heat when they contact the food. Infrared and microwaves are two types of radiation used to cook food.

3. Commercial sinks are used to manually rinse, wash, and sanitize dishes. Commercial dishwashers automate the process of rinsing, washing, and sanitizing dishes.

Practice Culinary Academics

4. **Social Studies** Students can choose a piece of cooking equipment from any region of the world. Ideas might be tandoor ovens, earth ovens or cooking pits, hibachi grills, hayboxes, samovars, shichirins, or many others. The report should include a description of how the equipment works, how it is used, as well as the typical dishes cooked with this equipment. Students should connect knowledge about the culture to the equipment to explain how it may have developed as a commonly used piece of cooking equipment.

5. **Mathematics** The median is 14 minutes, since 14 is the middle number in the list of 7, 14, and 20.

 **Professional Development** MINI CLIP **Math** Medians and Quartiles

CLOSE

Culminating Activity

Equipment Scavenger Hunt Number the preparation, cooking, and clean-up equipment in your foods lab, and have the students identify each piece of equipment on a sheet of paper. You may wish to turn this exercise into a contest, in which the first student to turn in a completed sheet with correct answers wins a prize.

 **Professional Development** MINI CLIP **Reading** Differentiated Instruction

SECTION 9.4 Holding and Service Equipment

SECTION 9.4 Holding and Service Equipment

Section Overview

In this section, students will learn about the different types of hot food holding equipment and their uses. They will also learn about the different types of service equipment and their proper use.

FOCUS

 ### Bell Ringer Activity

Hold Food Explain to the class that even in foodservice operations, food is not always served immediately as it is prepared. Ask students to think of examples of foodservice situations in which food would need to be held. Can they think of examples they have seen of food being held?

D Develop Concepts

Main Idea Discuss the main idea with the students. Ask: Why does the temperature of hot foods need to be maintained? The temperature needs to be maintained to preserve the flavor and texture of the food. It also prevents bacteria from growing and keeps food safe.

TEACH

S Skill Practice

Guided Practice

L1 List Ask students to list the different types of holding equipment. The different types of holding equipment are steam tables, bain maries, overhead warmers, and proofing/holding cabinets.

L2 Explain Have students explain how canned fuel is used. Canned fuel is used to keep food warm in chafing dishes.

L3 Apply Have students work in teams to practice using pieces of holding and service equipment. Students should work together to become proficient in the use of the pieces of equipment. Observe and provide feedback.

Mc Graw Hill Professional Development	MINI CLIP **Reading** Differentiated Activities

ASSESS

Quiz

Ask students to answer the following questions:

1. At what minimum temperature should hot food remain during holding? Hot food should be held at a minimum temperature of 135°F (57°C).

2. What does the number on a scoop represent? The number on a scoop represents the number of scoops that will fill a quart.

3. What can happen if plated food sits under an overhead warmer for an extended period of time? If plated food sits under an overhead warmer for an extended period of time, the food will dry out and the plate will get hot.

RETEACH

R Reading Strategy

Demonstrate Measurements To demonstrate how many scoops are in a quart, place a bowl of water, empty quart measure, and scoop in the demonstration area. Have the students count the scoops of water it takes to fill the quart measure. How well does it correspond to the number on the scoop? The amount of scoops to fill the quart measure should match the number on the scoop. The class should understand that a scoop will give them an exact measurement of how much they are serving.

U Universal Access

Students with Visual Impairments Have students imagine that they are catering an off-site event. They will need to provide an entrée, a starch, a vegetable, and a hot dessert. Have them choose recipes for each of these items and then analyze their chosen menu to determine what types of holding and serving equipment they need to bring with them. Answers will vary depending on the recipes chosen, but students should consider how each dish will need to be held and also how they will be serving each dish. Their equipment list should contain all necessary equipment and should show that they considered the food and did not just list all of the equipment.

ASSESS

  **ExamView® Assessment Suite**
Create a test for this chapter.

Lab Manual

Assign the Section 9.4 Activities.

Online Study Tools

Have students go to the Online Learning Center at **glencoe.com** to:

- Take the Section 9.4 Practice Test.
- Download Study-to-Go content.

SECTION 9.4 After You Read Answer Key

Review Key Concepts

1. A proofing/holding cabinet keeps sheet pans of food warm by holding them in an enclosed, airtight metal container, controlling temperature and humidity levels. It is generally used for yeast dough products or to keep food at 135ºF (57°C).

2. Scoop the amount of food you want and then use the lever to mechanically release the food. Look at the number on the scoop to determine the appropriate size to use.

Practice Culinary Academics

3. **Science** Students should note a steady decline in temperature as the soup sits. Summaries should conclude that proper holding is important to keep food at a safe temperature.

4. **English Language Arts** Student guides should describe each piece of holding equipment and its appropriate use. Language should be appropriate for new employees in a foodservice establishment. Students may use illustrations to help explain.

5. **Mathematics** The ratios are not equal. For the 4 in.-deep pan, the ratio of capacity to depth is $\frac{13}{4}$. For the 6 in.-deep pan, it is $\frac{20}{6}$. Cross-multiplying yields $13 \times 6 = 78$, and $20 \times 4 = 80$. Since the two products are not equal, the ratios are not equal.

 **Professional Development**   MINI CLIP **Math** Real Life Ratios

CLOSE

Culminating Activity

Class Pot Luck Hold a class potluck. Have volunteers prepare dishes to bring to class or prepare dishes in class. Any food that drops below 135˚F (57˚C) in transit must be reheated to 165˚F (74˚C) before being placed in holding equipment. Then, have the class put the food in the proper holding equipment and take turns serving to their classmates. Remind them to watch the temperature of the food as they serve it. Remember the temperature danger zone (41˚F to 135˚F, 5˚C to 57˚C). Keep hot food hot and cold food cold. Reheat all foods meant to be served hot to 165˚F (74˚C) for at least 15 seconds.

Chapter Review and Applications

Vocabulary Review

1. Write the vocabulary terms on the board and encourage students to use descriptive language in their sentences.

Review Key Concepts

2. Work stations organize a kitchen so that staff does not have to leave a station to perform a task. They have all of the necessary tools, equipment, work space, and power sources to operate efficiently.

3. Receiving equipment includes scales, thermometers, and dollies. Storage equipment includes refrigerators and freezers, shelving units, storage bins, and storage containers.

4. Follow safety precautions. Turn off and unplug first. Refer to instruction manual before cleaning.

5. Gas, a natural heat, cooks evenly. Electricity also cooks with intense heat, but not as evenly. Radiation transfers energy, which changes to heat. Microwaves use radiation to make water molecules rub against each other and produce heat. Light emits energy that generates heat and is used to keep food warm. Induction uses electricity to heat cookware by magnetic energy.

6. Commercial sinks rinse, wash, and sanitize dishes. Garbage disposals eliminate scraps of food leftover from preparation. Multi-tank dishwashers pre-wash, wash, rinse, sanitize, and dry dishes. Single-tank dishwashers wash small loads of dishes.

7. Steam tables keep foods warm in serving lines. Bain maries keep foods, such as soup, warm. Overhead warmers keep foods hot until the server picks them up. Holding cabinets proof yeast dough products and keep food at 135ºF (57°C) or above during service.

8. Insulated carriers keep hot foods hot and cold foods cold. Chafing dishes keep food hot during service. Canned fuel keeps food warm in chafing dishes. Coffee systems brew coffee and keep it warm. Scoops measure amounts. Airpot brewing systems make hot beverages and keep them hot. Utility carts display food, bus tables, or move heavy items.

C Critical Thinking

9. A well-designed kitchen facilitates work flow. Serving time in a well-designed kitchen is faster, making customers happier. A poorly designed kitchen can create poor work flow and impede service.

10. First in, first out helps to ensure the safety of the food you serve. It reduces wasted product that must be discarded due to spoilage because it was not used in time. The size of the business does not affect the rate of food spoilage, so FIFO should still be followed.

Academic Skills

11. **English Language Arts** Students should examine factors such as price, durability, size, features, and warranties. Their choice should be appropriate to a commercial kitchen and be supported by reasoning that explains why this is the best choice.

12. **Social Studies** Answers will vary depending on the technology chosen. For example, new refrigerators have several different temperature zones in which the temperature can be set to exactly what you wish. This might help work flow by allowing for more precise storage of different foods, and eliminating the need for different refrigerators.

13. **Mathematics** Reach-in width: $25 - 2.5 - 2.5 = 20$ in.; depth: $25 - 2.5 - 2.5 = 20$ in.; height: $68 - 5.5 - 2.5 = 60$ in. Reach-in capacity: 20 in. $\times$ 20 in. $\times$ 60 in. = 24,000 cubic in. Lowboy width: $55 - 2.5 - 2.5 = 50$ in.; depth: $25 - 2.5 - 2.5 = 20$ in.; height: $44 - 5.5 - 2.5 = 36$ in. Lowboy capacity: 50 in. $\times$ 20 in. $\times$ 36 in. = 36,000 cubic in. Ratio of capacity of lowboy to capacity of reach-in: $^{36,000}/_{24,000}$, or $\frac{3}{2}$.

Certification Prep

14. a. thermometers

15. b. mixer and food processor

Real-World Skills and Applications

16. **Interpersonal and Collaborative Skills** Students should work together to plan how each workstation will coordinate to accomplish their task and put out a final product. Students should work together as a group while accomplishing individual tasks.

17. **Critical Thinking Skills** Lists should include things like adequate walking and storage space, equipment arrangement appropriate to tasks performed, easy interaction between staff. Students should identify benefits that derive from each feature. For example, adequate walking space can prevent accidents.

18. **Technology Applications** Students should figure out how to use the program to create a legible facsimile of a cooking line floor plan. The plan should be arranged logically and contain cooking equipment found in a commercial kitchen.

19. **Financial Literacy** $\$5,000 \div 7 = \$714.29$. The stove will lose $714.29 of value each year.

Culinary Lab

20. **Design a Kitchen** Students should use their knowledge of the menu and their own designs to answer questions, not just with a yes or no, but with reasoning for the response. For example, if they answer no to the first question, they should explain which equipment was extraneous or missing.

Knives and Smallwares

SECTION 10.1 Knives   **SECTION 10.2** Smallwares

Classroom Solutions

Print Resources

- Student Edition
- Instructor Annotated Edition
- Lab Manual
- Lab Manual IAE

Technology Resources

ExamView® **ExamView® Assessment Suite CD**
Create and print unit and chapter tests.

Lesson Planner Plus **Lesson Planner Plus CD** provides access to teacher resources in one package.

Presentation Plus! provides visual teaching aids for every section.

Online Learning Center includes resources and activities for students and teachers. Also includes the **Online Student Edition**.

Interactive Student Edition

SECTION 10.1 Knives

Section Overview

In this section, students will learn the different parts of a knife, how to select appropriate knives for specific tasks, and how to perform basic cutting techniques. They will also learn knife safety, sanitation, and storage guidelines.

FOCUS

Bell Ringer Activity

Use Knives Discuss with students the kind of knives they have used before in cooking. What kind of knives do they have at home? How do they care for the knives they have at home?

D Develop Concepts

Main Idea Discuss the main idea with the students. Ask: Why is it important to know the different parts of a knife? It will help you evaluate knives for quality and understand how to use them better.

TEACH

S Skill Practice

Guided Practice

L1 List Have the students list the different types of knife cuts. The different types of knife cuts are slicing (including chiffonade, rondelle, and diagonal cuts), mincing, dicing, julienne, batonnet, and brunoise.

L2 Explain Ask students to explain how to sanitize a knife. To sanitize a knife, wipe down the blade and clean with sanitizing solution.

L3 Apply Have students practice sharpening and trueing knives under your supervision. Students should practice sharpening and trueing until they become confident in the action.

ASSESS

Quiz

Ask students to answer the following questions:

1. What are the two most common metals used for knives? Stainless steel and high-carbon stainless steel.

2. Why should knives have a full tang? A full tang gives more strength and power to knives.

3. Why are uniform shapes important in a commercial kitchen? Uniform shapes help guarantee even cooking and improve the appearance of a dish.

RETEACH

R Reading Strategy

Create a List Without looking back at the chapter, have students create a list of the types of knives they can remember and what they are used for. Then, have them compare their list to the information in the book. Lists will vary but will provide a tool for the students to evaluate their knowledge retention so they know which information they still need to study.

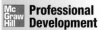 **Professional Development** MINI CLIP **Reading** Flexible Groupings

Universal Access

Students with Hearing Impairments Have students examine the knife-use guidelines and predict the possible consequences if each guideline is not followed. There will be several possible consequences for each guideline if it is not followed. In general, not following the guidelines can lead to injuries, food contamination, or poor-quality food.

ASSESS

Lab Manual

Assign the Section 10.1 Activities.

Online Study Tools

Have students go to the Online Learning Center at **glencoe.com** to:

- Take the Section 10.1 Practice Test.
- Download Study-to-Go content.

SECTION 10.1 After You Read Answer Key

Review Key Concepts

1. A boning knife is used to remove bones from meat, fish, and poultry, and to trim fat from meat.

2. Dice, julienne, batonnet, and brunoise. To dice, a chef's knife is used to cut food into ⅛ – ⅝ inch cubes. Julienne cuts are ⅛-inch thick matchstick-shaped cuts. Batonnet cuts are ¼-inch matchstick-shaped cuts. Batonnet and julienne cuts are done prior to dicing. Brunoise cuts are ⅛-inch thick cubes.

 **Professional Development** MINI CLIP **Math** Understanding Fractions

3. To safely store knives, the storage medium must hold knives in place and keep blades protected. Three common types of knife storage are slotted knife holders, knife kits, and custom drawers. Slotted knife holders should be hung on a wall.

Practice Culinary Academics

4. **Science** The cinnamon coating should transfer to the knife and then to the clean piece of cheese. This is a visual representation of cross-contamination. This activity should reinforce the importance of keeping knives sanitary.

5. **Mathematics** The stack is 2 ¼ inches tall. A medium dice will create a cube that is ⅜ inches on each side. Therefore, a stack of six of these cubes will equal $\frac{6}{1} \times \frac{3}{8} = \frac{18}{8} = \frac{9}{4} = 2\frac{1}{4}$ inches.

CLOSE

Culminating Activity

Practice Your Cuts Have students practice the different knife cuts they learned in this section on fruits or vegetables. Review the guidelines for using knives and the instructions on appropriate techniques for achieving the correct size and shape. With practice, they should be able to cut uniform pieces.

SECTION 10.2 Smallwares

Section Overview

In this section, students will learn what NSF certification standards are and how they relate to smallwares. They will learn how to select smallwares and cookware. They will also learn the proper cleaning and sanitizing of smallwares.

FOCUS

Bell Ringer Activity

What Are Smallwares? Ask students if they have heard the term smallwares before. If any of them have, ask them to explain it as they understand it. Then, define smallwares and ask students to think of examples.

D Develop Concepts

Main Idea Discuss the main idea with the students. Ask: Why must a chef know about the proper care for smallwares? The chef should be able to tell whether the smallwares are maintained properly, because poorly maintained smallwares will affect the quality of the food. Also, replacing damaged or lost smallwares can be expensive. The chef is responsible for the financial management of the kitchen.

TEACH

S Skill Practice
Guided Practice

L1 List Ask students to list the different types of measuring equipment. Portion scales, electronic scales, balance scales, volume measures, liquid measures, measuring spoons, and ladles.

L2 Explain Have students explain what NSF International is. NSF International is an organization that certifies that tools and equipment meet certain standards for construction, comfort, and safety.

L3 Apply Have students practice cleaning and sanitizing smallwares. Supervise students as they clean and sanitize smallwares until they are proficient.

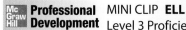 **Professional Development** MINI CLIP **ELL** Level 3 Proficiency

ASSESS

Quiz

Ask students to answer the following questions:

1. **What does an NSF seal certify?** The NSF seal certifies that equipment is designed, constructed, and installed to safety standards.

2. **Why would a kitchen have both a balloon and a rigid whisk?** A balloon whisk is used for lighter work such as whipping cream or egg whites; a rigid whisk is used for sauces and thicker batters. A restaurant that makes all of these items would need both types.

3. **How does heat transfer affect the purchase of pots and pans?** Copper is a good conductor of heat but is expensive to purchase and maintain. Aluminum is also a good conductor and is inexpensive, but cannot be used for all applications. Stainless steel is durable and safe for all uses but does not conduct heat.

RETEACH

U Universal Access

English Language Learners Place a selection of hand tools on a table. Have students identify the tools and explain their uses. See how many tools students can identify by sight and how many they can remember from their reading. Students should be able to identify the equipment discussed in the chapter and recall something about their uses. Have them check the chapter to see how well they answered.

C Critical Thinking

Analyze a Recipe Ask students to choose a dessert recipe that is appealing to them. Then, have them analyze the recipe to determine all of the smallwares needed to prepare their recipe. Have students write down each piece of equipment and how it will be used. Students should study the recipe carefully. They should infer the smallwares they will need from the directions given.

ASSESS

 ExamView® Assessment Suite
Create a test for this chapter.

Lab Manual

Assign the Section 10.2 Activities.

Online Study Tools

Have students go to the Online Learning Center at **glencoe.com** to:

- Take the Section 10.2 Practice Test.
- Download Study-to-Go content.

Review Key Concepts

1. Kitchen tools for a professional kitchen must be well constructed, comfortable to hold, and safe. Ideally, the tools will be certified by NSF International.

2. Aluminum cookware is lightweight, inexpensive, and rust-free. Aluminum is fairly heat efficient. Stainless steel is also virtually rust-free, but is a poor and uneven heat conductor.

Practice Culinary Academics

3. **English Language Arts** First, demonstrate the use of the tools for the students. Then, allow them to choose foods available in the food labs for demonstration. Demonstrations should be clear and easy to follow for the audience. They should accurately show and describe the use of the object as well as present any important cleaning, storage, and safety tips for the items they use.

4. **Social Studies** Reports should explain the chosen program and connect it to the foodservice industry. For example, NSF International offers safety audits to produce vendors.

5. **Mathematics** $6/1 \div 3/16$, which is $6/1 \times 16/3 = 96/3$, which reduces to 32. You will get 32 slices.

CLOSE

Culminating Activity

Practice Measuring Have students practice using different types of measuring equipment. In particular, have them become familiar with tools they may not have used before, such as the different types of scales.

Chapter Review and Applications

Vocabulary Review

1. Students should write complete definitions, using each term correctly.

Review Key Concepts

2. Chef's knife: all-purpose knife; used for variety of tasks. Slicer: cuts large foods like meat and poultry. Serrated slicer: cuts coarse food without tearing. Boning knife: removes bones from meat. Paring knife: pares or peels produce. Tournée knife: trims vegetables into a football shape. Fillet knife: fillets fish. Butcher knife: cuts meat, poultry, fish.

3. Knife should be gripped firmly. Index finger should not be placed on top of blade. Grip by placing four fingers on bottom of handle and thumb against back of blade, or with thumb against side of blade, or by placing three fingers on bottom of handle, index finger flat against blade on one side, and thumb on other. To control, guide knife with one hand while holding food with the other. Use smooth strokes, and never force blade through food.

4. Sharpen knives with a whetstone; true blade by using a steel to keep the blade straight and smooth. After each task, wash knives in hot, soapy water. Rinse and sanitize them, and air dry. Store knives in a slotted knife holder, knife kit, or custom-built drawer.

5. Tools must be specially selected for heavy use. Selected tools must be well-constructed, comfortable to hold, and safe. Ideally, they will be certified by NSF International. Some states require this.

6. Scrape and pre-rinse if necessary. Wash and rinse to remove detergent. Submerge in sanitizing solution at the proper temperature and concentration recommended by the manufacturer for at least 30 seconds. Air dry.

C Critical Thinking

7. A chef's knife or a utility knife, and a vegetable peeler. These are the right shape and size for vegetables.

8. Each ingredient, one after another, can be added to a portion scale. This allows you to create a more precise mixture of ingredients.

9. An 8-inch chef's knife is the most likely answer because it can be used for almost all chopping/slicing/cutting needs. A paring knife might be the second choice because it may be used for detail work that a chef's knife cannot handle.

10. The stainless steel pot. The aluminum pot may chemically react with the milk, which is slightly acidic. The stainless steel pot will not react.

Academic Skills

11. **English Language Arts** Scripts should be fun, but students should remember the main task is to make the product sound attractive to chefs and emphasize its useful qualities.

12. **Science** Results will depend on the different cooking materials used. Students should pay careful attention to the temperature of the food heated and note which food heats the fastest, and the most evenly if possible. From the data they record, they should conclude which materials conduct heat faster.

13. **Mathematics** A block weighs 6 lbs. The equation should be: $x = (\frac{2}{3})(x) + 2$, where x equals the weight of a block of cheese. (Note that each side of the equation represents each side of the balance scale.) Combine like terms by subtracting $(\frac{2}{3})(x)$ from each side, yielding $(\frac{1}{3})(x) = 2$, or $x = 6$.

McGraw Hill Professional Development MINI CLIP **Math** Communication in Mathematics

Certification Prep

14. a. 20 degrees

15. b. tongs

Real-World Skills and Applications

16. **Self-Management Skills** Answers for salad may include: chef's knife, paring knife, vegetable peeler, tomato corer, cutting board, tongs, and vegetable brush; for stew: chef's knife, slicer, cutting board, and meat tenderizer; and for shortcake: paring knife, chef's knife, and pastry tools.

17. **Interpersonal and Collaborative Skills** Students should decide what factors they will consider and which will be most important, expressing reasons for their choices. Factors may include cost, durability, or brand reputation.

18. **Technology Applications** Students should use software to create a chart that contains both illustrations and descriptions of the items and their uses.

19. **Financial Literacy** The knife-sharpening kit is more cost-effective once the service costs more than $50. Students should determine that 15×4 weeks $= \$60$ so the kit is then more cost-effective.

McGraw Hill Professional Development MINI CLIP **Math** Solving Equations

Culinary Lab

20. **Choose Knives and Smallwares** Evaluations should show that students were listening and participating in the discussion. They should note any revisions they would make to their list along with an explanation of why they chose to revise. They should also explain any changes they did not make and why they did not change positions.

Culinary Nutrition

SECTION 11.1 Nutrition Basics

SECTION 11.2 Meal Planning Guidelines

SECTION 11.3 Keep Food Nutritious

Classroom Solutions

Print Resources

- Student Edition
- Instructor Annotated Edition
- Lab Manual
- Lab Manual IAE

Technology Resources

ExamView® **ExamView® Assessment Suite** CD
Create and print unit and chapter tests.

Lesson Planner *Plus* **Lesson Planner Plus CD** provides access to teacher resources in one package.

 Presentation Plus! provides visual teaching aids for every section.

Online Learning Center includes resources and activities for students and teachers. Also includes the **Online Student Edition**.

Interactive Student Edition

SECTION 11.1 Nutrition Basics

Section Overview

In this section, students will learn what the six categories of nutrients are and how and why they are essential to the body. They will also learn about ways that foodservice operations can serve more healthful meals. Finally, they will learn about common additives used in food service.

FOCUS

Bell Ringer Activity

Describe a Healthy Meal Ask for volunteers to describe a healthy meal. What types of foods do they think of as healthy? What makes the meals they describe healthy? Tell students that in this section, they will learn the basics of nutrition and how this information will help them create more healthful meals.

D Develop Concepts

Main Idea Discuss the main idea with the students. Ask: Why would foodservice employees need to know how to give healthful meal suggestions? If foodservice employees know how to give healthful meal suggestions, they will be able to better serve customers who are concerned about eating healthfully. They will also be better able to serve customers who have special dietary needs because of health conditions.

TEACH

S Skill Practice

Guided Practice

L1 List Have students list examples of foods high in protein. Lists will vary, but may include meats, eggs, beans, nuts and seeds, peanut butter, and cheese.

L2 Explain Ask students to explain why a skinless chicken breast sautéed in olive oil is more healthful than a breaded, deep-fried chicken breast. Removing the skin reduces fat, and olive oil is lower in saturated fat and cholesterol than frying oils. Additionally, cooking without the breading means there will be fewer calories and carbohydrates.

L3 Apply Create a meal that contains all of the six nutrient types. Meals will vary, but the food combinations should contain all of the six nutrient types: carbohydrates, protein, fat and cholesterol in a small amount, vitamins, minerals, and water.

ASSESS

Quiz

Ask students to answer the following questions:

1. What is cholesterol? Cholesterol is a fatlike substance that is present in all body cells and animal foods.

2. What types of foods are high in fats? Answers will vary, but examples of foods that are high in fats include butter, salad dressing, fried foods, and some meats.

3. Which is more healthful: Whole-grain bread or white bread made of refined flour? Whole-grain bread is more healthful than white bread made with refined flour.

RETEACH

 **Reading Strategy**

Special Food Needs After reading the section on basic nutrition, have students work in teams to plan either a low-fat menu or a menu appropriate to some other health concern of the team's choice. Students should use the information in the section on basic nutrition to plan a menu that addresses the health concern they choose. If they choose to create a low-fat menu, students may choose to start, for example, with a garden salad with a low-fat dressing. Students' menus should reflect an understanding of the information on basic nutrition included in the book.

 **Professional Development** MINI CLIP **ELL** Language Practice

U Universal Access

Gifted Students Suggest a more healthful alternative for each of these foods: fried chicken, French fries, a cheeseburger, white rice, coconut oil, whole milk, and scrambled eggs. Explain how each change would improve the food's nutritional value. Answers will vary, but may include substituting baked or boiled chicken with the skin removed for the fried chicken; substituting fruit juice or milk for the soda; substituting baked potato wedges for the French fries; altering the cheeseburger by eliminating the cheese, including lower fat ingredients, or adding vegetables; substituting skim or low-fat milk for the whole milk; or altering the scrambled eggs by using egg whites or adding vegetables.

ASSESS

 **Lab Manual**

Assign the Section 11.1 Activities.

Online Study Tools

Have students go to the Online Learning Center at **glencoe.com** to:

- Take the Section 11.1 Practice Test.
- Download Study-to-Go content.

SECTION 11.1 After You Read Answer Key

Review Key Concepts

1. Water-soluble vitamins dissolve in water, so the body loses them each day, and they must be replaced daily. Fat-soluble vitamins are stored in the liver. For this reason, you do not have to consume fat-soluble vitamins every day.

2. Coloring agents may be found in cheese, soft drinks, baked items, cereals, and candy.

Practice Culinary Academics

3. Science Foods containing starch, such as potatoes, should turn a dark blue-black in reaction to the iodine. Explain to students that this is a chemical reaction. Food scientists often use chemistry to determine the nutrients that are in various food items.

4. English Language Arts Posters should be creative, but should also contain substantial information about the nutrients and the sources of the nutrients. The information should be presented in a manner appropriate to a poster for a classroom or work space to teach students or employees about nutrients.

5. Mathematics 41 grams/can × 9 cans = 369 grams of sugar/week. 369 grams ÷ 454 = 0.812775 pounds, so 0.81 pounds of sugar coming from the soda/week.

 Professional Development MINI CLIP **Reading** Another Point of View

CLOSE

Culminating Activity

Guest Speaker If possible, invite a nutritionist to your class to discuss the role of nutrients in healthful eating. Ask the nutritionist to discuss how restaurant menus can help people meet healthful eating guidelines. Encourage the class to discuss their own career and health goals with the nutritionist and get his or her advice.

SECTION 11.2 Meal Planning Guidelines

Section Overview

In this section, students will learn about tools that help consumers make healthful, informed choices about what they eat. They will also learn how age, activity level, lifestyle, and health influence a person's dietary needs. Finally, they will learn how to accommodate different dietary needs in a foodservice operation.

FOCUS

Bell Ringer Activity

Plan a Meal Ask students to describe how they decide what to eat when they must plan a meal for themselves. What are the factors they consider when deciding what to eat? How does health play into their decision-making process? Explain that in this section, they will discover tools to help them plan healthful, balanced meals.

D Develop Concepts

Main Idea Discuss the main idea with the students. Ask: How might a chef use government guidelines to plan a healthful menu? A chef could use the government recommendations to create a menu for a restaurant that would allow people to meet all of their recommended dietary needs by dining there for a day. He or she could also use the recommendations to determine serving sizes.

TEACH

S Skill Practice
Guided Practice

L1 **List** Ask students to list the types of vegetarians and what they eat. Lacto-vegetarians eat dairy products but no eggs or meat; ovo-vegetarians eat eggs but no meat or dairy products; lacto-ovo-vegetarians eat dairy products and eggs but no meat; and vegans eat food only from plant sources (no eggs, dairy products, or meat).

L2 **Explain** Have students explain how a healthful eating plan can help prevent and treat health conditions. Following a healthful eating plan can provide the necessary beneficial nutrients and moderate food items that can contribute to future health problems.

L3 **Apply** Have students use the Dietary Guidelines and MyPyramid to create a vegetarian menu. Menus will vary, but should be designed for one or more specific vegetarian diets. Meal plans should follow MyPyramid recommendations.

 Professional Development MINI CLIP **ELL** Group Discussion

ASSESS
Quiz

Ask students to answer the following questions:

1. How can a nutrition label help you to eat healthfully? A nutrition label tells you the amount of total fat and saturated fat and nutrients in prepared food. It also tells the calories per serving and serving size.

2. What are the effects of a high activity level on dietary needs? High-level activity requires more energy, so an active person needs to eat more complex carbohydrates. Activity also dehydrates you, so an active person must be sure to drink a lot of water before, during, and after exercise.

3. What are the dietary needs of an infant? Infants need a plentiful supply of nutrients, including breast milk or formula, for the first 4–6 months. They will eventually eat cut-up table foods.

RETEACH

R Reading Strategy

Practice Quizzes Divide students into small groups. Have them create five-question quizzes based on the section, and then have them take one another's quizzes. Creating the quizzes should help solidify the section information, and taking each other's quizzes can help them evaluate their knowledge of the section content.

U Universal Access

Students with Physical Challenges Obtain a copy of today's school lunch menu. How does it address MyPyramid and the Dietary Guidelines? What suggestions would you make to complete your food intake for a day? Student answers will vary and will depend on the school lunch menu, but in general, students should be able to compare the food on the menu to the recommendations of MyPyramid and the Dietary Guidelines. They should then note what nutrient and dietary needs still need to be fulfilled, if any, and create appropriate meals or snacks to fulfill those needs.

ASSESS

 Lab Manual

Assign the Section 11.2 Activities.

Online Study Tools

Have students go to the Online Learning Center at **glencoe.com** to:

- Take the Section 11.2 Practice Test.
-  Download Study-to-Go content.

SECTION 11.2 **After You Read Answer Key**

Review Key Concepts

1. Nutrition labels provide information on serving size, calories, and nutrients. Nutrients are

measured both in grams and the percentage of daily values the product contains.

2. Lacto-vegetarians eat or drink some dairy products, such as cheese and milk, but do not eat eggs. Ovo-vegetarians eat eggs in addition to foods from plant sources. Lacto-ovo-vegetarians include dairy and eggs in their diet. Vegans do not eat any meat or animal products.

Practice Culinary Academics

3. **Social Studies** The Food Guide Pyramid was developed in 1992 to show basic food groups and their relationships to each other. MyPyramid was introduced in 2005 to update the information in the Food Guide Pyramid and illustrate the Dietary Guidelines for Americans.

4. **English Language Arts** Critiques should be done in the format and tone of a newspaper column. They should explain how the menu meets the government recommendations and point out any areas where it fails to meet the recommendations. They should also provide some suggestions to the restaurant owner for improvement.

5. **Mathematics** Wesley should not exceed 93.3 grams of fat per day. $2,800 \times 0.3 = 840$ fat calories. $840 \div 9 =$ approximately 93.3 grams.

CLOSE
Culminating Activity

Student Panel Discussion Have students discuss how to make healthful selections from restaurant menus. Have students collaborate on how restaurant operators can better meet the needs of people with different dietary needs. Provide some sample menus and have the students explain which items they would choose and why.

SECTION 11.3	**Keep Food Nutritious**

Section Overview

In this section, students will learn how foods are prepared, cooked, and stored to preserve nutritional content. They will also learn how time and water can cause foods to lose nutrients. Finally, they will learn that reducing the amount of fat and cholesterol in recipes improves nutritional value.

FOCUS
Bell Ringer Activity

Healthy Cooking Ask students for their opinions on which ways to cook food are the healthiest and which are the unhealthiest. Ask students to explain their opinions. Why did they choose some methods as healthy and others as not healthy? Tell students that in this section, they will learn about healthy cooking methods.

D Develop Concepts

Main Idea Discuss the main idea with the students. Ask: Why is it important to know the effects of storage, preparation, and cooking on the nutritional value of a food? Chefs must know how these things affect nutritional value, so that they can make sure their meals remain healthful after preparation.

TEACH
S Skill Practice
Guided Practice

L1 List Have students list procedures chefs can use to reduce fat in dishes on their menu. Use reduced fat versions, offer more plant foods, use low-fat cooking techniques, reduce portion size, and use purées and seasonings for flavor instead of fat.

L2 Explain Ask students to choose one procedure to reduce fat and explain how it works. Answers will vary, but explanations should discuss how fat can be lowered.

L3 Apply Prepare a vegetable dish in a way that preserves nutrients and is low in fat, cholesterol, and sodium. Preparations will vary, but might include steamed or grilled vegetables with seasonings instead of added fat.

ASSESS
Quiz

Ask students to answer the following questions:

1. How does storage time affect nutrient loss? Foods lose nutrients with age. This means the longer foods are stored, the more nutrients they will lose.

2. How can substituting equipment improve nutritional content? Coated pans, cast iron skillets, or woks allow food to be cooked with less fat.

3. What is the smoking point of most vegetable oils? The smoking point of most vegetable oils is 400°F (204°C).

RETEACH

R Reading Strategy

Business Applications Have students think about what they learned about preparing healthful meals in this section. Then have them discuss current health trends. Collect menus from area restaurants, and evaluate them as a class in light of current health trends. Try to determine how restaurants have responded to current health trends by looking at the menus. Students should identify trends such as low-fat diets, low-carb diets, vegetarian and vegan diets, or organic foods and look for indicators of these things on menus, such as hamburgers in a lettuce wrapper instead of a bun, scrambled tofu or egg whites instead of whole egg dishes, special vegetarian menus, or menus specifying organic foods.

 **Professional Development** MINI CLIP **Math** Sampling

U Universal Access

Students with Behavioral Challenges Ask students to imagine that they want to retain the maximum amount of nutrients in sautéed spinach and mushrooms. Have them describe how they would prepare and store vegetables to keep the harmful effects of time and water to a minimum. Student answers will vary, but good suggestions include: purchase the vegetables fresh and use them within 3 to 4 days; store them covered in a refrigerator until ready for use; quickly clean them in water; and prepare the dish close to cooking time by using batch cooking.

ASSESS

 ExamView® Assessment Suite Create a test for this chapter.

Lab Manual

Assign the Section 11.3 Activities.

Online Study Tools

Have students go to the Online Learning Center at **glencoe.com** to:

- Take the Section 11.3 Practice Test.
- Download Study-to-Go content.

SECTION 11.3 After You Read Answer Key

Review Key Concepts

1. Healthful cooking techniques include steaming, grilling, poaching, stir-frying, and microwaving.

2. Replace fat in a dish by replacing part or all of whole eggs with egg whites or egg substitutes, using high-quality reduced-fat products, or using puréed fruits.

Practice Culinary Academics

3. **Science** Student reports will vary based on the product they choose, but in general, reports should provide useful information about what the product is, how it was created or developed, how it addresses a particular health need, and any controversies, benefits, and drawbacks of the product.

4. **English Language Arts** Demonstrations should accurately incorporate information from the section into a presentation that is clear, educational, and appropriate in tone to an audience of working chefs.

5. **Mathematics** Oat cereal has more fat. One cup of the oat cereal has 3.5 grams ÷ 0.75 = approximately 4.67 grams. One cup of the puffed cereal has 5 grams ÷ 1.25 = 4 grams.

CLOSE

Culminating Activity

Healthful Baking Contest Have students select a favorite cookie formula. Have them reduce or substitute at least two ingredients to make the product more healthful. The substitutions should reduce fat, salt, and sugar, and increase fiber. Have students invite another class or other guests to the lab to judge the flavor of the products.

Chapter Review and Applications

Vocabulary Review

1. Student brochures will vary but should include at least ten vocabulary terms. Terms should be used correctly and the brochure should demonstrate an understanding of personal nutrition.

Review Key Concepts

2. Carbohydrates (body's main source of energy); Proteins (build, maintain, and repair body tissues); Fats and Cholesterol (help keep body healthy); Vitamins (regulate body functions, assist other nutrients in their jobs); Minerals (essential parts of bones and teeth; regulate body processes); Water (essential for sustaining life).

3. Thickeners and stabilizers (fillings, puddings, sauces); gelling agents (desserts, fillings, sherbets, jellies, glazes); nutrients (enriched foods, cereals, flours, juices); coloring agents (cheese, soft drinks, cereals, candy); flavoring agents (baked items, candy, Asian foods, soups); fat substitutes (snacks, frozen desserts, sour cream, margarine, salad dressings); sugar substitutes (tabletop sweeteners, gelatin, sweets, beverages, jams, jellies).

4. Dietary Guidelines offer recommendations on healthful daily food choices from the MyPyramid food groups. Nutrition labels provide information on serving size, calories, and nutrients.

5. Age influences the amount of food and the balance of nutrients needed. Activity level influences the amount of energy needed and therefore the amount of nutrient-dense foods and carbohydrates needed. Lifestyle influences the types of foods people are willing to eat. Health influences the nutrients needed.

6. Steaming prevents nutrients from leaching into cooking water. Grilling and poaching require no fat to be added. Stir-frying uses only a little oil and cooking is quick so nutrient loss is minimized. Microwaving eliminates the need to keep food hot for a long period of time, and no added fat is needed.

7. Replace fat with lower-fat options, offer plant-based foods instead of animal-based, change cooking techniques, use seasonings and flavorings instead of adding salt, use special equipment, and reduce portion size.

C Critical Thinking

8. A restaurant will benefit from serving as many customers as possible. More people will be able to eat there, and you may gain customers from competitors who do not cater to these needs.

9. Consumers can be more informed about the ingredients and nutrient content of their food. They can plan food purchases to meet nutritional needs.

10. Questions are likely to be about the nutrient or fat content of food, cooking techniques used, number of calories, or suggestions for healthy ordering. Servers should learn basic nutritional facts about the menu and cooking techniques used, and be able to make suggestions for people with different dietary needs.

Academic Skills

11. **English Language Arts** Student life plans should be well-organized and easy to understand for someone who does not know much about nutrition, with a business-like tone. Life plans should contain information on generally healthful eating and also about eating with less fat to avoid heart disease.

12. **Social Studies** Students should locate technology that helps with nutritional information. Summaries should describe these technologies and explain how they help people lead healthier lives. For example, there are Web sites that allow you to record your daily food and nutrient intake.

13. **Mathematics** 5.8×10^5. Students may check their answer by multiplying 5.8×10^5 ($5.8 \times 100,000$), which restores the original number, 580,000.

 Professional Development MINI CLIP **Math** Exponent Rules

Certification Prep

14. c. Recommended Dietary Allowances

15. d. MyPyramid

Real-World Skills and Applications

16. **Research Skills** More people are becoming concerned with farming practices that produce their food so a foodservice professional should understand and evaluate the farm-to-table process. Posters should be accurate, appealing, and easy-to-understand.

17. **Critical Thinking Skills** Substituting a liquid oil for a solid fat would lower saturated fats in the pie crust, but it would also make it denser and less appealing.

18. **Technology Applications** Students should list ingredients and cooking steps in the spreadsheet, side by side with suggestions for lowering fat and sodium.

19. **Financial Literacy** $\$3.50 \div \$6.75 = 0.518518$, rounds to 0.52, and converts to 52%.

Culinary Lab

20. **Plan Nutritious Meals** Evaluations should reflect an understanding of MyPyramid and what constitutes variety in a meal. Students should use the knowledge they gained from this chapter to make recommendations for substitutions.

Creating Menus

SECTION 12.1 The Menu

SECTION 12.2 Menu Planning and Design

SECTION 12.3 Pricing Menu Items

Classroom Solutions

Print Resources

- Student Edition
- Instructor Annotated Edition
- Lab Manual
- Lab Manual IAE

Technology Resources

ExamView *ExamView® Assessment Suite CD* Create and print unit and chapter tests.

Lesson Planner Plus **Lesson Planner Plus CD** provides access to teacher resources in one package.

Presentation Plus! provides visual teaching aids for every section.

Online Learning Center includes resources and activities for students and teachers. Also includes the **Online Student Edition**.

Interactive Student Edition

SECTION 12.1 The Menu

Section Overview

In this section, students will learn the role of a menu. They will also learn how different factors influence a menu. Finally, they will learn about each type of menu used by foodservice establishments and when it is appropriate to use each type of menu.

FOCUS

Bell Ringer Activity

Review Menus Bring in several different menus from local foodservice establishments. Have the students look at each menu and then discuss what they like and what they do not like about each menu. Discuss the format, the design, the food items, and the pricing, and get the students' opinion on each.

D Develop Concepts

Main Idea Discuss the main idea with the students. Ask: Why is a foodservice establishment's chosen menu type important? The type of menu is important because the correct menu type will help service run smoothly. An inappropriate menu type may be too difficult to implement and cause customer dissatisfaction if the kitchen has difficulty creating dishes on the menu.

TEACH

S Skill Practice

Guided Practice

L1 List Have students list things a menu can determine for a restaurant. A menu can determine the type of customers attracted, the layout and equipment needed in the restaurant, the types of workers needed and their level of skill, and what supplies are necessary.

L2 Explain Ask students to explain how kitchen equipment can influence a menu. Kitchen equipment can influence a menu because a restaurant cannot have items on its menu if it does not have the equipment necessary to prepare those items.

L3 Apply Have students imagine that they are opening an ethnic restaurant. Have them determine the ethnicity and decide the type of menu they would use and why. Ethnicity and menu type will vary, but in many ethnic restaurants that serve traditional dishes, a fixed menu is used. Students should think about the layout and design of the menu as well.

 Professional Development MINI CLIP **ELL** Elaborating on Student Responses

CHAPTER 12 Lesson Plan

ASSESS

Quiz

Ask students to answer the following questions:

1. **How do à la carte and semi-à la carte menus differ?** Semi-à la carte includes an entrée, salad or soup, starch, and vegetable for one price. On an à la carte menu, everything is priced separately.

2. **In what type of establishment would you find a fixed menu?** Hotels, ethnic restaurants, and fast-food operations.

3. **What is a table d'hôte menu?** A menu that offers a complete meal for a set price.

RETEACH

U Universal Access

Students with Behavioral Challenges Have students collect menus from various sources. Then, have them work in pairs to evaluate the types of customers that would likely eat at the location, the employee skill level needed, and the equipment and layout needed. Which menu is their favorite? Why? Students should use the information they learned in the section. For example, a hospital menu would serve employees, patients, and visitors and would need many employees but not require a high skill level. It most likely would require equipment capable of preparing large quantities and plenty of food storage space.

C Critical Thinking

Evaluate a Menu Have students evaluate a local restaurant menu while thinking of the factors that influence menu planning. Ask them to determine how each factor might have influenced this menu. Ask them to explain their responses. Students should be able to apply what they have learned about the factors to an actual menu and detect possible influences. For example, if there are only a few items available, they may say that the restaurant is in a small space with few employees and limited equipment.

ASSESS

Lab Manual

Assign the Section 12.1 Activities.

Online Study Tools

Have students go to the Online Learning Center at **glencoe.com** to:

- Take the Section 12.1 Practice Test.
- Download Study-to-Go content.

Review Key Concepts

1. The location of a restaurant can impact the types of ingredients available. In addition, the culture of the area and ethnicity can affect the types of foods that are popular in the area.

2. A cycle menu is used for a set period of time. At the end of the period, the menu repeats daily dishes in the same order. Cycle menus are often found in institutions that serve the same people day after day.

Practice Culinary Academics

3. **Social Studies** Students may find that certain areas have similar types of businesses that indicate a certain ethnicity or type of person is heavily located in that area. Speaking to older residents may allow students to guess at how the culture has changed. Perhaps businesses catering to a certain population have been replaced by businesses for new populations. This exercise should show students how the local businesses can give them information about the culture of an area or neighborhood.

4. **English Language Arts** Plans should be formatted in a manner appropriate to a business communication. They should contain a brief evaluation of each of the seven factors listed in the section that influence menus. The evaluations should reflect the advice in the book and should be consistent with their imagined restaurant and the characteristics of the area.

5. **Mathematics** The ratio of prix fixe to à la carte is $^{500}/_{3,500}$, which can be reduced to $\frac{1}{7}$. There was a total of $500 + 3,500 = 4,000$ dinners, so the fraction of prix fixe customers is $^{500}/_{4,000}$, which can be reduced to $\frac{1}{8}$.

 Professional Development MINI CLIP **Math** Fraction Computation

CLOSE

Culminating Activity

Choose a Menu Type As a class, imagine that you are going to open a restaurant on the school campus. Discuss the influences that would be most important to consider when planning your menu. Then, choose a menu type as a group, making sure to discuss why you might choose a certain type of menu.

SECTION 12.2 Menu Planning and Design

Section Overview

In this section, students will learn basic menu planning principles. They will learn how to plan interesting menus that offer good nutrition and variety. They will also learn the elements that influence menu style and design. Finally, they will learn the basic menu formats and the basic menu categories.

FOCUS

Bell Ringer Activity

Plan a Meal Ask students to describe a meal that is aesthetically pleasing and that is appropriate to be served by the school cafeteria. Have them describe the food items, the preparation, and the presentation. Could they also serve this meal in a nursing home or hospital? Why or why not?

D Develop Concepts

Main Idea Discuss the main idea with the students. Ask: How can good menu organization help the customer? A menu that is well organized will help the customer make decisions. If the menu is disorganized, then the customer has to figure out the menu before he can decide on his meal. This wastes time and can lead to customer dissatisfaction.

Mc Graw Hill Professional Development MINI CLIP **ELL** Using Manipulatives

TEACH

S Skill Practice

Guided Practice

L1 List Have students list menu planning principles. Principles include variety, balance, truthfulness, nutrition, and flexibility.

L2 Explain Ask students to choose one menu planning principle and explain how to use it in a successful menu. Answers will vary according to principle chosen, but a sample may be having a variety of food types, cooking techniques, and garnishes.

L3 Apply Select a meal from a menu, or create a meal, and describe how each menu planning principle is demonstrated. Students should be able to point to specific examples of principles from a menu.

Mc Graw Hill Professional Development MINI CLIP **Reading** Prereading Strategies

ASSESS

Quiz

Ask students to answer the following questions:

1. How do truth-in-menu guidelines impact menu planning? Truth-in-menu guidelines mean that menus must be accurate, and nutritional claims must be legitimate.

2. How does the concept of visual appeal affect plate presentation? When putting a plate together, one should think of color, shapes, and sizes. Visual appeal will get customers excited about eating the dish before tasting it.

3. How do customer food allergies impact employee training? Servers should be made aware of ingredients with high allergy potential and proper procedures if customers ask about ingredients or tell the server that they have specific allergies.

RETEACH

R Reading Strategy

Conduct Research Have students use Internet or print resources to investigate a list of common food allergies and their symptoms. Discuss how to handle potential food allergies when planning a menu. What precautions need to be taken by the kitchen workers and the server? Some allergies will be easy to locate, such as allergies to nuts or shellfish. Students should find resources that list those as well as other common allergies. Since the effects of allergies are potentially severe, a restaurant owner will want to take precautions to avoid the most common allergens, and may even instruct servers to ask about food allergies. There must also be care and planning in the kitchen to prevent potential allergens from contaminating other foods.

U Universal Access

Students with Visual Impairments Tell students to imagine that they have just discovered that a support group for people with heart disease will be eating at your diner tonight. Today's special was supposed to be fried chicken, French fries, and sweet peas. Use the same ingredients to create a low-fat alternative. Answers will vary, but students should suggest more healthful cooking methods such as grilling or baking the chicken, making a baked or roasted potato, and steaming the peas. Another idea is a stir-fry that combines all of the ingredients in a healthful way.

ASSESS

Lab Manual

Assign the Section 12.2 Activities.

Online Study Tools

Have students go to the Online Learning Center at
glencoe.com to:

- Take the Section 12.2 Practice Test.
- **STUDY TO GO** Download Study-to-Go content.

SECTION 12.2 After You Read Answer Key

Review Key Concepts

1. When planning which foods make a good combination on the plate, think about the following: 1) Placement: Visualize how each element will appear on the plate and how it will be presented to the customer; 2) Serving size: Do the portions appear too small or too large on the plate? 3) Proportion: Is the ratio of one food to another and to the plate pleasing to the eye? 4) Number of foods on a plate: Odd numbers of items are more appealing than even numbers.

2. In the spoken menu format, after a customer is seated, a server states what foods are available and the prices of each. In some restaurants that have a printed menu, daily specials are presented as a spoken menu.

3. Hot entrées are main dishes that usually include meat, poultry, fish, or seafood. They also can include casseroles and other extenders or hot vegetarian dishes.

Practice Culinary Academics

4. **English Language Arts** Students should be descriptive, using detail to help the reader picture the restaurant, its atmosphere, its style, and the food it would serve. The menu items should match the restaurant's theme.

5. **Mathematics** For entrées, $^{40}/_{100} = {}^4/_{10} = {}^2/_5$ are vegetarian. For appetizers, 62.5 should first be converted into the improper fraction $^{125}/_2$. Multiplying $^{125}/_2$ by $^1/_{100}$ yields $^{125}/_{200}$, which can be reduced to $^5/_8$.

CLOSE

Culminating Activity

Menu Comparison Locate restaurant menus from as long ago as possible. Have students contrast today's menus with the older menus. What types of changes are there? What might be the reasons for these changes?

SECTION 12.3 Pricing Menu Items

Section Overview

In this section, students will learn how to identify the influences that impact menu prices. They will also learn to use different pricing methods to determine the selling price of food items, including the factor method, markup-on-cost method, contribution margin method, average check method, competitors' pricing method, and psychological method.

FOCUS

Bell Ringer Activity

Set Prices Ask students to imagine that they are going to hold a bake sale. Discuss with them how they would determine the price for each item. What factors would they consider? How would they come up with a fair price? Explain that in this chapter, they will learn how foodservice establishments determine their pricing.

D Develop Concepts

Main Idea Discuss the main idea with the students. Ask: How can choosing prices that are too low or too high affect a foodservice establishment? If prices are too low, the establishment will not be profitable. If prices are too high, people may choose not to eat there, especially if there are competitors that are offering lower prices for similar items.

TEACH

S Skill Practice

Guided Practice

L1 List Ask students to list five factors that influence menu pricing. Five factors that influence menu pricing include labor, competition, customers, atmosphere, and location.

L2 Explain Have students explain how competition affects menu pricing. You cannot set menu prices much higher or lower than competitors with similar operations.

L3 Apply Find a recipe for cookies. Determine the item cost to make them, and use the markup-on-cost pricing method to determine the selling price. Item costs will vary depending on the recipe, and therefore selling prices will vary. Students should correctly use the markup-on-cost pricing method to determine the cost of their cookies.

ASSESS

Quiz

Ask students to answer the following questions:

1. If sales are $32,658 and food cost is $10,600, what is your food cost percentage?
   $^{$10,600}/_{$32,658} = 32.46\%$

2. How does atmosphere affect menu pricing? With a nice or elegant atmosphere, customer expectations rise, and they may be willing to pay more money for the enjoyment of the atmosphere.

3. What other factors should you consider besides cost of food when calculating a menu price? When calculating a menu price, you should consider labor cost, overhead cost, and profit in addition to cost of food.

RETEACH

U Universal Access

Gifted Students Have students research food product information and prices from the vendor who supplies food for your school restaurant or school cafeteria. Have students price a menu item from each menu category served at the restaurant or cafeteria. Have them use one or more of the pricing methods described in the text. Once the students have all of the information they need (item costs, sales, information about similar items on other menus), they should be able to follow the instructions in the text to use any of the pricing methods described in the section. If it is difficult to obtain the information needed, you may wish to provide a set of fictional information for students.

C Critical Thinking

Customer Response Why should customer response be considered when pricing menu items? Customer response is one of the most important things to consider when pricing menu items because if your customers cannot afford the price, or do not feel the meal is worth the cost, they will not visit your establishment.

ASSESS

 ExamView® Assessment Suite
Create a test for this chapter.

📖 Lab Manual

Assign the Section 12.3 Activities.

🧭 Online Study Tools

Have students go to the Online Learning Center at **glencoe.com** to:

- Take the Section 12.3 Practice Test.
- Download Study-to-Go content.

Review Key Concepts

1. The cost of living is higher in some locations than others. In locations where people have more disposable income, restaurants can usually have higher menu prices.

2. To find the selling price using the markup-on-cost method, take the food cost of the item and divide it by the desired food cost percent.

Practice Culinary Academics

3. **English Language Arts** The business reports should be professional in tone, and care should be taken with spelling, grammar, and punctuation. The format should be appropriate to a business communication. Students should accurately assess the character of the surrounding community and logically relate it to pricing based on the type of customers and amount of money they might reasonably be able to spend.

4. **Social Studies** Students should locate articles about how the price of different food items is being affected either by weather events, political events, or other factors that might increase or decrease the cost. In general, they should understand that the cost of an ingredient will affect the price of the dish. Foodservice establishment operators may choose not to include items that use ingredients whose price has increased or they may need to increase the price of those dishes.

5. **Mathematics** The price should be $5.97. Using the markup-on-cost method yields $2.09 ÷ 0.35 = $5.971429, which is rounded to $5.97.

CLOSE

Culminating Activity

Guest Speaker If possible, invite a food and beverage director from a large hotel chain or local business to come and speak to the class about their business plans and menu prices. Ask students to compare this process to how a smaller business might plan and price a menu and discuss why the processes differ.

Chapter Review and Applications

Vocabulary Review

1. Students should offer logical explanations for why terms were grouped as related terms.

Review Key Concepts

2. Needs and lifestyles of an establishment's target customers; appropriate price range; type of food

served; equipment available; staff's skill level; location of operation; and current eating trends.

3. Fixed: same dishes every day for long period. Cycle: used for a set period, then repeat. À la carte: each item priced separately. Semi-à la carte: appetizers and desserts priced separately from entrées. Table d'hôte: complete meal for set price. Prix fixe: complete meal for set price, customers choose selections. Du jour: change daily.

4. Variety in meals offered and preparation types; balance of foods from food groups; truthfulness about the food; healthful choices; ability to change.

5. Restaurants can use printed menus with clip-ons or table tents to advertise specials; a menu board that lists items and can be easily changed; or a spoken menu. Designs should reflect the atmosphere of the restaurant.

6. Appetizers, soups, salads, cold entrées, hot entrées, sandwiches, accompaniments, desserts, cheeses and fruits, and beverages. Categories are typically listed in the order that they would be eaten.

7. Labor costs, competitors' prices, type of customer who eats at the establishment, style of the food-service operation, cost of living in the location.

8. Factor: Food cost percentage divided into 100% multiplied by cost of menu item = selling price. Markup-on-cost: Divide food cost by desired food cost percentage. Contribution margin: Add average contribution margin per guest to item's standard cost. Average check: Price items near average check you want each customer to spend. Competitors' pricing: Charge what competition charges. Psychological pricing: Based on how customers react to prices.

C Critical Thinking

9. Students' reasons should reflect type of restaurant and customers expected. For example, a good reason for choosing a fixed menu might be that it is more economical for a large dining room.

10 When you plan for food allergies, you must consider not just what is in the meals, but if the allergens will contact other dishes. A person who is allergic may not be able to eat in an establishment at all if the menu is not planned taking this into account.

Academic Skills

11. English Language Arts Modifications made to menus should be appropriate to the dietary need chosen and should be easily implemented without overhauling the menu. For example, for vegans, students might modify one dish in each course.

12. Science Students should create three different menus and note which aspects make certain dishes attractive. They should note the common reasons for choosing a certain dish and decide which could be applied to menu design to improve it in the future.

13. Mathematics Salmon has the highest revenue ($20,400); steak has the most profit ($7,500); pasta has the highest profit margin (40%). Steak: revenue = $26.00 × 750 = $19,500; costs = $16.00 × 750 = $12,000; profit = $19,500 − $12,000 = $7,500; profit margin = $7,500 ÷ $19,500 = 0.384615 ≈ 38.5%. Salmon: revenue = $34.00 × 600 = $20,400; costs = $22.00 × 600 = $13,200; profit = $20,400 − $13,200 = $7,200; profit margin = $7,200 ÷ $20,400 = 0.352941 ≈ 35.3%. Pasta: revenue = $22.50 × 400 = $9,000; cost = $13.50 × 400 = $5,400; profit = $9,000 − $5,400 = $3,600; profit margin = $3,600 ÷ $9,000 = 0.4 = 40%.

Certification Prep

14. c. cafeteria

15. d. dessert

Real-World Skills and Applications

16. Interpersonal and Collaborative Skills Students should work together to create menu format and content and follow truth-in-menu guidelines. It should be possible for a foodservice establishment to use and should be appealing to customers.

17. Communication Skills Students should turn their conversations and evaluations of the menu into constructive criticism for the cafeteria manager. The letter should be polite, clear, and business-like.

18. Technology Applications Menu should be appropriate to a small cafe. Menu size should be limited and focus on inexpensive dishes that can be prepared with limited equipment and a small staff.

19. Financial Literacy The total cost is $3.50. If the food cost percentage is 50%, then the factor is 2 ($^{1.00}/_{.50}$). The item cost times the factor is $6 ($3 × 2) for the pizza, and $1 (.50 × 2) for the iced tea.

Culinary Lab

20. Create a Menu Evaluations should provide both praise and constructive criticism that are useful and applicable to the menus they are evaluating.

Using Standardized Recipes

SECTION 13.1 Standardized Recipe Basics

SECTION 13.2 Recipe Measurement and Conversion

Classroom Solutions

Print Resources

- Student Edition
- Instructor Annotated Edition
- Lab Manual
- Lab Manual IAE

Technology Resources

ExamView Assessment Suite **ExamView® Assessment Suite CD**
Create and print unit and chapter tests.

Lesson Planner Plus **Lesson Planner Plus CD** provides access to teacher resources in one package.

Presentation Plus! provides visual teaching aids for every section.

Online Learning Center includes resources and activities for students and teachers. Also includes the **Online Student Edition**.

Interactive Student Edition

SECTION 13.1 Standardized Recipe Basics

Section Overview

In this section, students will learn what a standardized recipe is and the role of standardized recipes in maintaining product consistency. They will also learn the different parts of a standardized recipe. Finally, they will learn the difference between a recipe and a formula used in baking.

FOCUS

Bell Ringer Activity

Use a Recipe Ask students if they have ever prepared something from a recipe, followed the instructions correctly, and still had the product turn out poorly. Why do they think this happens? Explain that in the foodservice industry, standardized recipes are used to attempt to avoid this outcome.

D Develop Concepts

Main Idea Discuss the main idea with the students. Ask: What is the advantage of using a recipe when cooking? Recipes have generally been tested, so if you follow the instructions, you have a better chance of successfully making a dish the first time you try than if you try to figure it out on your own.

TEACH

S Skill Practice

Guided Practice

L1 List Ask students to list three ways that a formula differs from a recipe. 1) Ingredients are listed by decreasing weight; 2) Precise weight measurements are used; and 3) Formulas may not include instructions.

L2 Explain Have students explain how a standardized recipe maintains product consistency. A standardized recipe contains precise instructions and is tested to ensure that the result is the same when prepared by different people.

L3 Apply Break the class into groups and have each prepare the same standardized recipe. Taste test the results. If the directions are followed correctly, the dishes should be very similar.

Mc Graw Hill Professional Development MINI CLIP **ELL** Level 4 Proficiency

ASSESS

Quiz

Ask students to answer the following questions:

1. How does consistent quality and quantity help ensure return business and customer satisfaction? If quantity and quality are consistent, customer expectations will be met, and they will come back for their favorite dishes.

2. How does a standardized recipe affect cost control positively? A standardized recipe allows a foodservice professional to gauge how much food to purchase and reduces waste.

3. Why are both product yield and portion size important in a standardized recipe? Portion size is important because cooking the right portion size ensures that customers do not get too much and waste food, or get too little and leave hungry. Yield is important because creating the right yield ensures that you have enough food to serve everyone, and also that you do not have too much food that goes to waste.

 **Professional Development** MINI CLIP **Math** Real World Ratios

RETEACH
R Reading Strategy

Recipe Comparison Have students compare a standardized recipe with one from a cookbook that could be used at home. Ask them to examine the differences between the recipes. Will all products made from each recipe be consistent? Why or why not? While a home recipe provides a general guide for preparing a dish, a standardized recipe is more specific and has precise measurements. A standardized recipe is more likely to yield consistent results than a home recipe.

U Universal Access

Gifted Students Discuss with students whether, when preparing a standardized recipe, the chef needs to use any judgment. Will the recipe be perfect for all cooks? Why or why not? What are the limitations of a standardized recipe? When preparing a standardized recipe, the chef will still need to use judgment, as food products are not uniform, kitchens do not always have the same equipment, and not all instructions may be exact.

ASSESS
Lab Manual

Assign the Section 13.1 Activities.

Online Study Tools

Have students go to the Online Learning Center at **glencoe.com** to:

- Take the Section 13.1 Practice Test.

 Download Study-to-Go content.

SECTION 13.1 After You Read Answer Key
Review Key Concepts

1. Each standardized recipe must go through quality control. This process ensures that everything in the recipe meets the establishment's standards. To do this, recipes are repeatedly tested for consistency before they are used. They are tested for directions that are clear and easy to follow and an accurate listing of ingredients.

Practice Culinary Academics

2. **Science** Products baked with a different type of flour than specified may turn out denser than a product baked with the specified flour. The reason for this is that the gluten level in flour affects the density of baked goods.

3. **English Language Arts** All recipes should match the format given in the section for organizing a recipe and should contain each element. The recipes should be clear and easy to follow, and any alterations made should not alter the outcome of the recipe.

4. **Social Studies** Students may locate examples of technology such as equipment that helps standardize cooking, such as ovens that have more consistent cooking temperatures. They may also find software that can aid in standardizing recipes by helping to determine purchasing decisions, costs, and yield.

5. **Mathematics** Total yield: 20×4 oz. $= 80$ oz. Total pounds: 80 oz. $\div$ 16 oz./lb. $= 5$ lbs.

CLOSE
Culminating Activity

Prepare a Recipe Select a standardized recipe and label the different parts. Break into teams, and have each team prepare the recipe, following the instructions as closely as possible. Compare the results. How consistent are they? If the results are not consistent, what might be the reason for that?

 **Professional Development** MINI CLIP **Reading** Guided Instruction

SECTION 13.2 Recipe Measurement and Conversion

Section Overview

In this section, students learn the standard recipe measurements and when each one is used. They will also learn how to convert standard recipes to increase or decrease portion size or yield. Finally, they will learn about factors that can affect recipe conversion.

FOCUS

Bell Ringer Activity

Convert a Recipe Ask students if they have ever wanted to prepare a recipe, but found that the yield was too much for their needs. What did they do? Did they try to alter the recipe to get the correct yield? How did they alter the recipe? What was the result?

| McGraw Hill **Professional Development** | MINI CLIP **Math** Small Group Work |

D Develop Concepts

Main Idea Discuss the main idea with the students. Ask: Why might foodservice professionals need to adjust a recipe? Foodservice operations have different needs. The yield of a recipe may be too much or too little. In addition, they may choose to serve smaller or larger portion sizes, depending on the type of restaurant.

TEACH

S Skill Practice

Guided Practice

L1 List Have students list the equipment to measure weight. Pieces of equipment used to measure weight include a balance scale, a portion scale, and a electronic scale.

L2 Explain Ask students to explain how to measure liquids. Put a volume measure on a flat surface, and then fill with liquid to the specified line.

L3 Apply Have students practice using weight and volume measure equipment to measure different ingredient types. Students should practice with the weight and volume measure equipment in the foods lab until they are proficient.

ASSESS

Quiz

Ask students to answer the following questions:

1. How do equipment changes affect cooking times? The conductivity of the equipment will shorten or lengthen cooking times.

2. When should you use a balance scale, and when should you use a portion scale? A balance scale is for measuring ingredients for baking, and a portion scale is for measuring sliced meats in a deli.

3. Why would you change the portion size and not the total yield quantity in a recipe? Portion size may be too large or too small for the customers, or portion size might need to be changed to maximize profits.

RETEACH

U Universal Access

Students with Physical Challenges Using the recipe provided in the section, increase the yield to 50 servings and then increase portion size to 10 oz. To increase the yield to 50 servings from 10 servings, divide the desired yield (50 servings) by the existing yield (10 servings) to get the conversion factor (5). Then, multiply the existing quantity of each ingredient by the conversion factor to obtain the new quantity. To increase the portion size, multiply the existing portions (10) by the existing portion size (8 oz.) to get total yield (80 oz.). Then, multiply desired portions (10) by desired portion size (10 oz.) to determine the new yield (100 oz.) Divide the new yield (100 oz.) by the existing yield (80 oz.) to get the conversion factor (1.25). Multiply each ingredient by the conversion factor to obtain the new quantity.

C Critical Thinking

Evaluate Recipes Choose three recipes from food magazines or cookbooks and evaluate them for their ability to be converted for use in a foodservice establishment. If you were a professional chef, would you attempt to convert and standardize these recipes? Why or why not? Magazine and cookbook recipes are created for use in a home kitchen. Some might lend themselves to use in a professional kitchen. Factors to look for might include whether the yield could be increased easily without prohibitive cost, the preparation time involved, the equipment needed, and the ability to prepare in a busy kitchen under pressure.

ASSESS

 ExamView® Assessment Suite
Create a test for this chapter.

Lab Manual
Assign the Section 13.2 Activities.

Online Study Tools
Have students go to the Online Learning Center at
glencoe.com to:

• Take the Section 13.2 Practice Test.
• Download Study-to-Go content.

SECTION 13.2 After You Read Answer Key

Review Key Concepts

1. A balance scale is a scale with two platforms, one for the item being weighed, and the other for weights. The weights are added and removed until the platforms are balanced. These are used when precise measurement is important. A portion scale is similar to a bathroom scale. It measures how much the spring is depressed when an item is placed on it, and then a needle indicates the weight. An electronic scale also has a spring, but the weight is displayed by digital numbers. The readout is more accurate.

2. Shrinkage is the percentage of food lost during storage and preparation. The amount of shrinkage affects both cost and portion size. Knowing how much shrinkage will occur allows a foodservice professional to purchase the correct amount.

Practice Culinary Academics

3. **English Language Arts** Student guides should explain clearly and correctly how to adjust a recipe to change portion size or total yield of the recipe. It should be written in a style and format that could be easily comprehended by a beginning cook. It should also be organized in a way that is easy to follow.

4. **Science** Students should determine the volume of various objects using the water displacement method. This should give them a better understanding of volume as the amount of space a substance or object occupies.

5. **Mathematics** Conversion factor: $18 \div 4 = 4.5$. Potatoes: $6 \times 4.5 = 27$. Bacon: $5 \times 4.5 = 22.5$ strips (round to 23). Cheddar cheese: $4 \times 4.5 = 18$ ounces.

CLOSE

Culminating Activity

Standardized Recipes Choose a standardized recipe and as a class. First, convert the recipe to get a yield that is appropriate to feeding the class size. Adjust for portion size as well, if desired. Then, working as a class, prepare the recipe, following the instructions carefully.

Chapter Review and Applications

Vocabulary Review

1. Have students test each other using the index cards they have created.

Review Key Concepts

2. Standardized recipes are tested before they are used to ensure consistency each time. Portion size and cost are controlled. The preparation process is clear and efficient, and errors are less likely. There is less waste because food is not overproduced, and customers' expectations are more likely to be met.

3. Standard measurements are weight, volume, and count. Weight measures heaviness and is the most accurate way of measuring foods. Volume refers to the amount of space a substance occupies and is used most often with liquids. Count is the number of items and is used for foods that come in standard sizes.

4. If a recipe is altered, equipment may be the wrong size for the new recipe. A decreased formula could be affected by over-mixing, and an increased formula could be affected by under-mixing. Cooking temperatures can be affected. Shrinkage can affect cost and portion sizes. Minor recipe errors can become major.

Critical Thinking

5. Retesting means trying a recipe again for consistency. Retesting might be required if an ingredient required a substitution, if the recipe was being converted, or if there was new kitchen equipment.

6. A recipe might need to be converted to increase or decrease yield or portion size. For example, for a special event, yield may need to be increased.

7. A simple doubling of ingredient amounts may work in some situations, but as the recipe yield becomes larger, the proportion of ingredients might not be correct, and the final product may turn out poorly.

8. Some possibilities are that you can raise prices, notifying customers that it is necessary to support local farmers; look for produce from other sources; or change your menu so there is less produce in the dishes.

9. You should retest your standardized recipes with the new oven, even though it is the same type. The new oven may not have the same consistency of temperature, which could affect cooking time.

10. Weight is more accurate and consistent. Even though ingredients may be similar in size, they may have different weights, meaning different amounts of ingredient can be used, even if the same number of the item is used. Measuring by weight ensures that you use the same amount of the ingredient each time.

Academic Skills

11. **English Language Arts** Plans should be in chronological order and clear enough that a catering team could follow them and successfully prepare and deliver a dish to an event.

12. **Social Studies** Many people contributed to the development of the modern recipe. Students can find ideas in the 1800s in America, when domestic science was on the rise and women like Fannie Farmer and Isabella Beeton began writing cookbooks for use in the home.

13. **Mathematics** Total yield, old recipe: 8 × 20 oz. = 160 oz. Total yield, new recipe: 20 × 11.5 oz. = 230 oz. Conversion factor: 230 ÷ 160 = 1.4375. New quantities: asparagus—4 lbs. × 1.4375 = 5.75 lbs ≈ 6 lbs.; chicken broth—12 cups × 1.4375 = 17.25 cups ≈ 17 cups; onions—2 × 1.4375 = 2.875 ≈ 3; cream—1 cup × 1.4375 = 1.4375 cups ≈ 1.5 cups; lemon juice—¾ tsp. × 1.4375 = 1.078 tsp. ≈ 1 tsp.

Certification Prep

14. a. volume measurement

15. b. 38.4

Real-World Skills and Applications

16. **Critical Thinking Skills** Students should locate differences between the regular recipe and what is appropriate for a standardized recipe and alter the recipe to standardize ingredient measurements, refine instructions, and clarify any vague areas.

17. **Self-Management Skills** Students should use the yield of the recipes to determine how much of each ingredient they will need to prepare 100 breakfasts.

18. **Technology Applications** Students should create a blank template that has space for each section of a recipe and can be used to handwrite recipes or fill them in using a computer.

19. **Financial Literacy** To find item cost per sandwich, add ingredient costs to get total cost; then divide it by the yield. 2.25 + 5 + 7 + 3 + 3 = $20.25. $20.25 ÷ 12 sandwiches = $1.69 per sandwich.

Culinary Lab

20. **Weigh Dry Ingredients** The existing portion size is 5.99 ≈ 6 oz. Conversion factor is 13 ÷ 25 = .52. New ingredient amounts should be: bread flour—28 oz. × .52 = 14.56 oz.; pastry flour—12 × .52 = 6.24 oz.; baking powder—2.75 × .52 = 5.29 oz.; salt—1 × .52 = .52 oz.; dry milk solids—6 × .52 = 3.12 oz.; cornmeal—16 × .52 = 8.32 oz.; granulated sugar—26 × .52 = 13.52 oz.; water—30 × .52 − 15.6 oz.; eggs—16 × .52 = 8.32 oz.; vegetable oil—12 × .52 = 6.24 oz. If students measure correctly, corn bread should have good flavor, texture and color.

Cost Control Factors

SECTION 14.1 Calculate Food Costs

SECTION 14.2 Manage Food Cost Factors

Classroom Solutions

Print Resources

- Student Edition
- Instructor Annotated Edition
- Lab Manual
- Lab Manual IAE

Technology Resources

ExamView *ExamView® Assessment Suite* **CD**
Create and print unit and chapter tests.

Lesson Planner *Plus* Lesson Planner Plus CD provides access to teacher resources in one package.

Presentation Plus! provides visual teaching aids for every section.

Online Learning Center includes resources and activities for students and teachers. Also includes the **Online Student Edition**.

Interactive Student Edition

SECTION 14.1 Calculate Food Costs

Section Overview

In this section, students will learn about the different methods of portion control used by foodservice operations and why portion control is important. They will also learn how to calculate unit cost, yield percentage, percent of shrinkage, and cost per portion. Finally, they will learn how to complete and use a recipe costing form.

FOCUS

Bell Ringer Activity

Calculate Food Cost at Home Discuss with students how the food budget is handled in their homes. If they are unsure, ask them to discuss it with the adults at home. How does their family maintain a food budget and control the cost of the food they purchase? Explain that this section will focus on controlling food cost in foodservice operations.

D Develop Concepts

Main Idea Discuss the main idea with the students. Ask: What factors might influence the cost of menu items? *The cost of menu items could be influenced by food costs, equipment needed, staff needed, storage space needed, and ingredient availability.*

TEACH

S Skill Practice
Guided Practice

L1 List Ask students to list the guidelines for controlling portions. *Purchase items according to standard specifications; follow standardized recipes; and use standardized portioning tools and equipment.*

L2 Explain Have students explain why portion control is important. *Portion control helps control costs, keep customers satisfied, control number of employees needed, and manage food use.*

L3 Apply Have students find simple recipes and calculate the unit cost of each ingredient based on local supermarket prices or online prices. *Students should choose recipes with few ingredients, locate prices for those ingredients, and use the formula in the book to calculate the unit cost of each ingredient.*

 **Professional Development** MINI CLIP **ELL** Scaffolding Questions

ASSESS

Quiz

Ask students to answer the following questions:

1. What are the advantages of following standardized recipes? *Following standardized recipes helps ensure a consistent product, helps control costs, and keeps customers satisfied.*

2. How does portion control affect customers? Customers expect to each get the same size and quality of portion in return for the cost of the meal.

3. What are two examples of foods purchased in bulk? Any food that can be purchased in a large quantity at once can be a bulk food. Examples might include canned foods, dry goods, and frozen foods.

RETEACH

U Universal Access

Students with Hearing Impairments Demonstrate to students how to figure yield percentage. Purchase several types of vegetables and fruits. Weigh the AP produce. Then, peel, trim, and core them as needed for recipe production. Weigh the trim loss. Subtract the trim loss from the AP weight to determine the yield weight. Divide the yield weight by the AP weight to determine the yield percentage. Ask: How does accurately determining the yield percentage affect the bottom line in a foodservice operation? The demonstration should show students how yield percentage is determined. The discussion should focus on how accurately determining yield percentage will help prevent waste.

Mc Graw Hill **Professional Development**	MINI CLIP **Reading** Another Point of View

C Critical Thinking

Decision Making Ask the class to imagine that they are restaurant managers and they need to standardize portion control in their foodservice operation. What information, utensils, and tools would they use to aid in the process? What type of staff training is needed? Answers will vary, but may include: speaking to other managers of similar businesses; purchasing standardized measuring and serving tools, such as scoops; and developing portion sizes with the cooks. Then, staff will need to be trained on how to apportion ingredients to the agreed-upon size using the equipment. Demonstration is probably the best way to train for this.

ASSESS

✏ Lab Manual
Assign the Section 14.1 Activities.

✈ Online Study Tools
Have students go to the Online Learning Center at **glencoe.com** to:

• Take the Section 14.1 Practice Test.

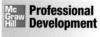 • Download Study-to-Go content.

SECTION 14.1 After You Read Answer Key
Review Key Concepts

1. Following standardized recipes allows you to determine portion size before you begin preparing the food items. The exact nature of the directions enables you to predict portion sizes if the instructions are followed correctly.

2. Product yield is the amount of the food product left after preparation. Foods can lose volume or weight as they are prepared, which means you will need to purchase a larger amount of food than the size of the portion you want to serve.

3. The cooking loss test determines how cooking affects yield percentage. First, identify the net cost and net weight of the raw food product. Next, note how many portions are produced after cooking the product. Finally, multiply the number of portions by the portion weight when served. This gives the total weight as served.

4. To find the cost-per-portion of a recipe, divide the recipe cost by the number of portions or servings.

Practice Culinary Academics

5. Mathematics The decrease in weight is $12 - 4.5 = 7.5$ oz. The percent decrease (shrinkage percentage) is $7.5 \div 12 = 0.625 = 62.5\%$. The decrease in cost is $\$3.95 - \$3.50 = \$0.45$ so the percent decrease in price is $\$0.45 \div \$3.95 = 0.113924 = 11.4\%$.

Mc Graw Hill **Professional Development**	MINI CLIP **Math** Ways of Working—Solving Equations

CLOSE

Culminating Activity

Costing Recipes Create blank recipe costing forms. Choose several simple recipes, and working together as class, fill out a recipe costing form for each. Complete each portion of the form to come up with the ingredient cost total, the Q factor, the total recipe cost, and the portion cost.

SECTION 14.2 Manage Food Cost Factors

Section Overview

In this section, students will learn the steps, methods, and types of products involved in purchasing. They will learn about the tools and equipment to use and procedures to follow when receiving goods. They will learn techniques for storing and issuing goods. Finally, they will learn how kitchen waste and customer service affect cost control.

FOCUS

Bell Ringer Activity

Complete Forms Obtain blank copies of some of the forms discussed in this section, such as food purchasing specification orders and inventory forms, and go over the different parts of each one and how to fill them out. Then, have the students practice filling out each form. Explain that forms like these are useful tools for managing food cost factors.

D Develop Concepts

Main Idea Discuss the main idea with the students. Ask: Why are management and control of food cost factors essential to running a foodservice operation? These factors are essential because if they are not managed and controlled, food will go to waste or be stolen, and the foodservice operation will lose money.

TEACH

S Skill Practice
Guided Practice

L1 List Have students list the five items needed for effective receiving. The five items needed for effective receiving are heavy-duty gloves, scales, a calculator, a cutting device, and a thermometer.

L2 Explain Ask students to explain why a yield test is important in purchasing. Doing a yield test ensures that the proper amount of food will be ordered.

L3 Apply In pairs, have students practice taking inventory in the foods lab, with one person counting and the other recording. Compare totals. Pair totals for the same ingredients should match. If not, come up with ways to be more accurate in the future.

ASSESS

Quiz

Ask students to answer the following questions:

1. What would you look for in a physical inspection of frozen items? You need to look for whether the item has thawed and been refrozen and whether the item has been tampered with.

2. What information would be included on the spec for a nonperishable good? The information that should be included includes the name of the supplier; the package size, quantity, or item count to be purchased; the form of the item to be purchased; and costs and quality limitations.

3. What is a perpetual inventory? A perpetual inventory is a continuously updated record of what is on hand for each item in an inventory.

RETEACH

R Reading Strategy

Product Types Have students identify the following as perishable, semiperishable, nonperishable, or nonedible: canned green beans, salami, paper napkins, and fresh strawberries. Explain how to inspect each item for quality and safety. Which items should be stored first? Canned green beans: nonperishable; paper napkins: nonedible; fresh strawberries: perishable; salami: semiperishable. When inspecting, check for mishandling, improper storage, and pest infestations; weigh the packages; check that packaging is clean and intact; check for cross-contamination. Store strawberries and salami first.

 Professional Development MINI CLIP **ELL** Providing Clear Directions

U Universal Access

Students with Visual Impairments Ask the class to discuss what might happen to a foodservice operation if it does not enforce issuing controls. Things that could happen include that the operation would be unable to track what products the kitchen is using and what needs to be ordered or re-ordered. In addition, there is a risk of employee theft. If the restaurant runs out of certain foods, it will also negatively affect customer service.

ASSESS

 ExamView Assessment Suite
Create a test for this chapter.

 Lab Manual
Assign the Section 14.2 Activities.

🖈 Online Study Tools
Have students go to the Online Learning Center at
glencoe.com to:

- Take the Section 14.2 Practice Test.
- Download Study-to-Go content.

SECTION 14.2 After You Read Answer Key

Review Key Concepts

1. Open market or competitive buying is where the operation gets price quotes from several vendors and chooses from among them. Single-source buying is where an operation purchases most of its products from a single vendor.

2. The proper tools and equipment include: heavy-duty gloves with non-slip fingertips, scales, a calculator, cutting devices, and a thermometer.

3. Limiting storage access helps prevent theft, which is a problem for many foodservice operations and results in loss to the business.

Practice Culinary Academics

4. **English Language Arts** Students should use the information given in the section to create food specification sheets that resemble the example in Figure 14.3. They should inspect the menu for the school restaurant or cafeteria, determine three ingredients that are used, and create specification sheets for each ingredient that contain all of the necessary information. They may need to do some research to complete the information.

5. **Mathematics** Average price is $40.50. Calculate average (mean) by adding the prices and dividing by 4. $35 + $42 + $46 + $39 = $162. $162 ÷ 4 = $40.50.

CLOSE

Culminating Activity

Receive and Store Obtain several types of products that might be purchased by a foodservice operation. Have students take turns demonstrating how to inspect and store the products. Have them explain what they are doing as they inspect each product and why they chose to store the product in a certain way.

Chapter Review and Applications

Vocabulary Review

1. Make sure that students have labeled each vocabulary word with the proper part of speech.

Review Key Concepts

2. Purchase items according to standard specifications, follow standardized recipes, and use standardized portioning tools and equipment.

3. Figure out the unit of measure used and determine how many of those units are in the item purchased. Then, divide the bulk, or as-purchased (AP), price of the item by the number of units.

4. Factors include leftover parts and by-products from food items, cooking loss, and shrinkage.

5. Fill out recipe costing form with portion size, yield, ingredients, edible portion, as-purchased amount, unit purchase price, cost per unit, ingredient cost, and Q factor. Add ingredient costs to get ingredient cost total. Add ingredient cost total to Q factor to get total recipe cost. Divide total recipe cost by number of portions to get portion cost.

6. Buyers consider the type of product the operation needs, specifications requested, desired yield, available storage space, and perishability.

7. Check the purchase order and invoice to ensure that correct items have been received. Inspect goods for quality, freshness, and signs of damage, and make sure the weights match the order.

8. To control inventory, keep physical inventory and perpetual inventory records, use computerized point-of-sale systems, and use storeroom controls like FIFO, and issuing controls like requisitions and limited access to storage. To minimize waste, use leftovers and track product history as used.

C Critical Thinking

9. Ignoring portion guidelines may result in loss of profit, upset customers due to inconsistent portions, and running out of food.

10. A good vendor provides high-quality products consistently; meets customer specifications; and makes deliveries on time.

Academic Skills

11. English Language Arts Students should create an effective system for inventory control with procedures for taking inventory and keeping records. It may include sample forms, like inventory cards.

12. Science Adding rice can help cut costs by increasing the yield of the more expensive meat, but may sacrifice flavor or texture.

13. Mathematics The weight per portion before cooking is 9 oz. ÷ (1 − 0.25) = 9 oz. ÷ 0.75 = 12 oz. The weight per portion as purchased is 12 oz. ÷ (1 − 0.10) = 12 oz. ÷ 0.90 = 13.33 oz. You need 27 × 13.33 oz. = 360 oz., or 360 oz. ÷ 16 oz./lb. = 22.5 pounds per night. At $4.50/pound, it costs $101.25 a day. The total monthly cost is $101.25 × 24 = $2,430.

Certification Prep

14. b. edible portion

15. c. parstock

Real-World Skills and Applications

16. Interpersonal and Collaborative Skills Students should refer to the chapter for information about processes and discuss how best to translate the information to a restaurant setting. Their checklists should reflect the decisions they reached as a group.

17. Communication Skills Role-plays should be potential business partners having a discussion. The vendor should sell his or her business by listing benefits of their products and services without exaggerating. Purchasers should be polite and communicate the needs of their operation.

18. Technology Applications This exercise familiarizes students with the possibility of using this type of software if employed in the foodservice industry.

19. Financial Literacy 1): 30 × 12 = 360 eggs; $25.50/360 = $0.07 (unit cost); 2): $4.67 (total recipe cost)/8 (servings) = $0.58 (cost per portion).

Culinary Lab

20. Conduct a Yield Test Results will vary because the food items will not be of uniform size, the unusable parts will be more substantial on some items, and amount trimmed will vary.

FOCUS

Introduce the Project

In this project, students will research standardized recipes, and will interview a chef or cook on the subject. They will learn the difference between a formula and a recipe, and begin to understand the important role of the standardized recipe in maintaining consistency in cooking results. They will learn the different parts of a standardized recipe, and how to develop their own standardized recipe.

Build Background

Establish Consistency Ask students to share an experience they had with following a recipe and getting disappointing results. Use this discussion to introduce the idea of a standardized recipe that can be followed repeatedly with successful results. Distribute a copy of a standardized recipe for students to review. Have them observe what is different about its contents and format from a cookbook recipe.

TEACH

S Skill Practice

Guided Practice

L1 Identify Ask students to list the parts of a cookbook recipe in one column and the parts of a standardized recipe in another column. Answers for a cookbook recipe should generally include ingredients, cooking instructions, and a serving size. Parts of a standardized recipe include product name, yield, portion size, ingredient quantity, preparation procedures, cooking time, and temperature.

L2 Contrast Have students compare a cookbook bread recipe to a similar formula in standardized form. Ask them to explain how the standardized formula helps to guarantee results. Students should notice that the formula may not have a defined procedure, but will include baker's percentages of all ingredients. The measurements for the formula will be more exact, and so the formula should work as predicted each time.

L3 Hypothesize Have students create a hypothesis of a method for creating a standardized recipe. What logistical factors would have to be considered? What academic skills might be required? Hypotheses should be complete and well thought out. Logistical factors that might be considered would include specifying a yield and serving size, ensuring that all parts of the recipe are present, that ingredients are listed in the proper order, and more.

Academic skills required include English language arts and mathematics. Science may be required for baking skills.

C Critical Thinking

Constructive Critique Have students read each other's newly created standardized recipes, and offer constructive feedback as to what they think will work and what may not, and why. They should consider chosen ingredients, ingredient proportions, methods, equipment, temperatures, and timing. Have them write their constructive critiques on a separate piece of paper. Students' comments should specify challenges in recipes. The tone of student critiques should be respectful.

ASSESS

Quiz

Ask students to answer the following questions:

1. Why does every standardized recipe contain the same elements in the same format? A standardized recipe must be similar to a universal language. It must look familiar to any chef who needs to follow it. Otherwise, creating the dishes would be more difficult, time-consuming, and potentially unsuccessful.

2. In what settings and circumstances are standardized recipes most essential? Standardized recipes are most essential in professional foodservice settings, where portion size and yield of the recipe are vital for business.

3. How do standardized recipes cut down on costs? Knowing the exact quantity that will be needed prevents under- or over-purchasing, often enabling you to buy bulk ingredients, which are less expensive.

CLOSE

Culminating Activity

Apply New Knowledge Divide students into groups and have each group follow the same standardized recipe. Have students compare their results. Are all of the finished products identical? Why or why not? If students have followed the standardized recipe, all results should be the same. If there are differences, it may be because directions were not followed exactly, or ingredient measurements were not exact.

Unit Overview

Introduce the Unit This unit introduces students to cooking methods, and the basics of cooking various types of ingredients, including meats, poultry, fish, vegetables, fruits, and grains. They will also learn to prepare basic foods, including sandwiches, stocks, sauces, soups, and some quick breads.

Chapter

15 Cooking Techniques

16 Seasonings and Flavorings

17 Breakfast Cookery

18 Garde Manger Basics

19 Sandwiches and Appetizers

20 Stocks, Sauces, and Soups

21 Fish and Shellfish

22 Poultry Cookery

23 Meat Cookery

24 Pasta and Grains

25 Fruits, Vegetables, and Legumes

Unit Culinary Career Spotlight Answer Key (found on page 671)

Get Certified Students should come up with their own pasta recipes, which are both healthful and imaginative. The recipes should incorporate a variety of ingredients. The finished pasta dishes should be flavorful and visually appealing.

Competition Practice Students should be given a two-hour time limit to complete their pasta dishes. Students will rate their own efforts, based on their timing, the flavor of their pasta dish, the variety of the ingredients they included, and the visual appeal of their finished pasta dish.

SkillsUSA competitions provide important ways for your students to hone their technical skills. In the Culinary Arts competition, students are rated on sanitation and food safety techniques as well as technical culinary skills, food quality, and presentation.

Develop Skills Before beginning this unit, bring a recipe to class. Ask students to keep a list of the sanitation and food safety concerns they must consider before and during preparation of this recipe. Once you have finished the unit, have students study the recipe again, and add cooking skill techniques needed for the recipe to their lists. Sanitation and food safety concerns might include keeping raw meats, poultry, and fish separate from other foods, keeping foods at the correct temperature, and sanitizing all dishes and utensils. Cooking skill techniques might include various dry and moist cooking methods, knife skills, and presentation techniques.

As part of its mission, FCCLA encourages its student members to make decisions and assume different responsibilities.

Take Responsibility Form students into small groups. Tell students that they own a restaurant together. Ask them to decide who will take responsibility for the different areas of the business: management, service, kitchen, and marketing. Ask students to describe to you how they decided on their individual responsibilities, and what skills they think they will need for those responsibilities. Students may express their individual preferences or specialized skills for certain types of work as the basis for their choices. Skills might include organization, leadership, customer service, writing skills, math skills, and culinary skills.

McGraw Hill **Professional Development**

MINI CLIP VIDEO LIBRARY

Targeted professional development is correlated throughout *Culinary Essentials*. The McGraw-Hill Professional Development Mini Clip Video Library provides teaching strategies to strengthen academic and learning skills. Log on to **glencoe.com**.

Chapter 15 Cooking Techniques

Reading Bridging Cultural Gaps A teacher models the use of context clues. (p. TM166)

ELL Understanding English Language Learners Ruben Zepeda, Ed.D., discusses issues when teaching English learners. (p. TM162)

Math Simple Events—Probability Students use manipulatives to conduct probability experiments. (p. TM163)

Math Surface Area and Volume A teacher reviews the formula for volume. (p. TM165)

Math Units of Measure—Solid Geometry Students find the volume of a cylinder. (p. TM167)

Chapter 16 Seasonings and Flavorings

Reading Connecting the Pieces A teacher helps students develop predictions about a story. (p. TM170)

ELL Collaborative Work Students work in groups to complete a lab. (p. TM170)

ELL Using Realia A teacher models realia. (p. TM173)

Math Identifying Linear Equations Students manipulate equations to determine if they are linear. (p. TM169)

Chapter 17 Breakfast Cookery

Reading Strategies for Student Achievement Teachers discuss strategies for helping all learners meet curriculum standards. (p. TM177)

ELL Accessing Prior Knowledge Students make connections between what they know and the reading selection. (p. TM176)

ELL Using Manipulatives A teacher uses concrete objects to illustrate the lesson. (p. TM178)

Math Guiding Questions A teacher helps students prepare for the lesson on polynomials. (p. TM179)

Chapter 18 Garde Manger Basics

Reading Guided Instruction A teacher helps students identify major and minor details. (p. TM185)

ELL Graphic Organizers Students learn to distinguish between major and minor details. (p. TM183)

ELL Group Discussions Students discuss academic content they have read. (p. TM184)

Math Problem Solving with Algebra and Measurement Curriculum supervisor Mary Esther Reynosa suggests ways to build students' problem-solving abilities. (p. TM182)

Chapter 19 Sandwiches and Appetizers

Reading Differentiated Activities Nancy Frey, Ph.D., teacher, educator, and author, discusses the differentiated classroom. (p. TM190)

Reading Flexible Groupings Teachers use flexible groupings to promote discussion. (p. TM193)

Math Fraction Computation Students work in small groups to solve a problem. (p. TM190)

Math Adjacent Angles A teacher defines adjacent angles for students. (p. TM192)

Chapter 20 Stocks, Sauces, and Soups

Reading Focus Lesson How to find the main idea. (p. TM197)

Reading Modeling Reading Strategies A teacher models fluent reading strategies. (p. TM198)

ELL Building Vocabulary A teacher introduces two vocabulary building games (p. TM199)

ELL Level 4 Proficiency Author Jana Echevarria discusses Level 4 proficiency. (p. TM198)

Chapter 21 Fish and Shellfish

Reading Fluency Development A teacher models three different instructional strategies. (p. TM203)

ELL Exploring the Big Idea Students share their answer to a lesson's "Big Question." (p. TM205)

Math Medians and Quartiles Algebra teacher Brad Fulton suggests ways to help students with the meaning of median, and quartile. (p. TM203)

Math Unknowns in Equations A teacher assesses students' understanding of equations. (p. TM205)

Chapter 22 Poultry Cookery

Reading Prereading Strategies A teacher assesses students' prior knowledge. (p. TM208)

Reading English Language Success Ruben Zepeda, Ed.D., discusses classroom management for the success of English learners. (p. TM209)

Math Problem Solving and Measurement Curriculum supervisor Mary Esther Reynosa suggests problem-solving solutions. (p. TM209)

Chapter 23 Meat Cookery

Reading On Workshops Author and teacher educator, Doug Fisher, Ph.D., discusses the Workshop Approach to teaching. (p. TM215)

ELL Using Realia A teacher models realia. (p. TM213)

Math Introducing Multi-Step Equations A teacher walks students through a multi-step equation. (p. TM214)

Math Problem Solving—Order of Operations A teacher uses real-life contexts to introduce order of operations. (p. TM216)

Chapter 24 Pasta and Grains

Reading Guided Instruction A teacher helps students identify major and minor details. (p. TM219)

ELL Group Discussions Students discuss academic content they have just read. (p. TM218)

Math Small Group Work Students work in cooperative groups. (p. TM222)

Chapter 25 Fruits, Vegetables, and Legumes

Reading Planning and Management Lois Moseley, author and educator, discusses assessment. (p. TM223)

ELL Elaborating on Student Responses A teacher elaborates using explanatory language. (p. TM225)

ELL Words and Pictures A teacher uses media examples to help students learn new vocabulary. (p. TM226)

Math Graphing Linear Equations A teacher models how to use points or intercepts to graph linear equations. (p. TM226)

Cooking Techniques

SECTION 15.1 How Cooking
Alters Food

SECTION 15.2 Dry Cooking Techniques
SECTION 15.3 Moist Cooking Techniques

Classroom Solutions

Print Resources

- Student Edition
- Instructor Annotated Edition
- Lab Manual
- Lab Manual IAE

Technology Resources

ExamView *ExamView® Assessment Suite* **CD**
Create and print unit and chapter tests.

Lesson Planner *Plus* **Lesson Planner Plus CD** provides access to teacher resources in one package.

Presentation Plus! provides visual teaching aids for every section.

Online Learning Center includes resources and activities for students and teachers. Also includes the **Online Student Edition**.

Interactive Student Edition

SECTION 15.1 How Cooking Alters Food

Section Overview

In this section, students will learn what dry, moist, and combination cooking techniques are. Students will also learn how cooking affects a food's nutritive value, texture, color, aroma, and flavor, as well as how to prepare foods to make these qualities more appealing.

FOCUS

Bell Ringer Activity

Make Choices Ask students to imagine that they have a chicken breast and a head of fresh broccoli to use in preparation for dinner. How many different ways can they think of to prepare each item and the combination of those items? How would each preparation affect the taste and texture of the different possible dishes?

D Develop Concepts

Main Idea Discuss the main idea with the students. Ask: What types of food qualities might people want to change by cooking it? We cook food to improve texture, flavor, and aroma and in some cases, cooking food makes it safe to eat.

TEACH

S Skill Practice
Guided Practice

L1 List Have students list qualities of food that are affected by cooking. The qualities of food affected by cooking are nutritive value, texture, color, aroma, and flavor.

L2 Explain Have students explain how coagulation affects the texture of meat. Coagulation makes proteins more solid, and as a result, food containing proteins becomes firmer or tougher.

L3 Apply Choose a vegetable and cook it for different lengths of time. Note any effects on color and texture of the vegetable. Answers will vary depending on students' experiences, but in general, the longer the vegetable is cooked, the more unappealing the texture and color should become.

 **Professional Development** MINI CLIP **ELL** Understanding English Language Learners

ASSESS

Quiz

Ask students to answer the following questions:

1. How do flavors change when cooking with moist heat? Cooking with moist heat brings out the natural flavors in food.

2. What is the objective of combination cooking?
The objective of combination cooking is to build upon the food's flavors by subjecting it to different cooking methods.

3. What is color fade, and how can you prevent it?
Color fade is heat damage to the chlorophyll in green vegetables. You can prevent color fade by being sure to not overcook vegetables. .

RETEACH

R Reading Strategy

Identify Cooking Methods Provide students with several menus from different restaurants. As a class, identify the cooking methods used on the menu. Does the restaurant use one basic cooking method or are there several methods on the menu? Discuss the advantages and disadvantages of each approach. The students should be able to identify the dry, moist, and combination cooking methods on the menu. A restaurant that focuses on one cooking method might be able to save money by requiring less equipment and perhaps less staff, but it would also have less variety on its menu, which may result in fewer customers.

U Universal Access

Students with Physical Challenges How might the size of the pan used affect the food being cooked? Predict the effects of using a pan that is too small or too large to cook food items. Using a pan that is too large can affect the cooking time. Food might cook more slowly or more quickly if it is spread out. Using a pan that is too small crowds the food together, leading to uneven cooking.

ASSESS

✍ Lab Manual

Assign the Section 15.1 Activities.

🧭 Online Study Tools

Have students go to the Online Learning Center at **glencoe.com** to:

• Take the Section 15.1 Practice Test.

 Download Study-to-Go content.

SECTION 15.1 After You Read Answer Key

Review Key Concepts

1. A dry cooking technique uses oil, fat, the radiation of hot air, or metal to transfer heat. No moisture is used. Any moisture that comes from the food evaporates.

2. During cooking, moisture is lost, the food tissue breaks down, and proteins coagulate. The longer proteins are subjected to heat, the firmer and more solid they become.

Practice Culinary Academics

3. **Science** Generally, moist and combination (steam, sear/braise) techniques produce a tender texture and keep original color due to the retention of moisture. Dry techniques create a firm texture, and brown the carrots, creating a strong aroma and flavor due to caramelization.

4. **Social Studies** Answers will vary depending on the country chosen, but students should describe one or more cooking techniques and identify what type of cooking technique it is. They should use the information in the book to predict how these techniques will affect food. Discuss with the class the similarities and differences between the techniques from different regions of the world.

5. **Mathematics** First egg: 12 hard-cooked, 24 overall; probability is $^{12}/_{24}$, or $\frac{1}{2}$. Second egg: if the first was hard-cooked, there will be 11 hard-cooked eggs, and 23 overall; the probability of selecting a hard-cooked egg is $^{11}/_{23}$. To find the probability of both events, multiply $\frac{1}{2} \times {}^{11}/_{23} = {}^{11}/_{46}$.

 Professional Development MINI CLIP **Math** Simple Events—Probability

CLOSE

Culminating Activity

Food Research Make up cards with different items on them, one for each student. Have each student draw a card and research the food listed on the card to learn about suggested cooking techniques for that food. Students should then locate one or more recipes using the suggested cooking techniques for their item.

SECTION 15.2 Dry Cooking Techniques

Section Overview

In this section, students will learn the various dry cooking techniques, including baking, roasting, sautéing, frying, grilling, and broiling. They will also learn about the ways to fry foods using different methods, including stir-frying, pan-frying, and deep-frying.

FOCUS

Bell Ringer Activity

Dry Cooking Now that the class has learned the basic definition of the dry cooking methods, have them name types of dry cooking techniques and how each technique might be used. Explain that they will learn more about all of the dry cooking techniques and how to use them in this section.

D Develop Concepts

Main Idea Discuss the main idea with the students. Ask: Can you describe evaporation? Evaporation is what happens when water is converted from liquid to a vapor by heat. When you see steam coming off of a hot liquid, such as tea or coffee, evaporation is occurring.

TEACH

S Skill Practice

Guided Practice

L1 List Have students list different ways to prepare food for frying. Food can be prepared for frying by dredging the food in flour or bread crumbs, breading the food with eggs and crumbs, or battering the food.

L2 Explain Ask students to explain how to broil a piece of meat. To broil a piece of meat, place the meat directly under the heat source. Thicker pieces should be placed farther away from the heat source.

L3 Apply Stir-fry some chicken and then pan-fry some chicken. What are the differences between the resulting dishes? Stir-fried chicken will be lighter in color. The pan-fried chicken will have a richer flavor due to the fat.

ASSESS

Quiz

Ask students to answer the following questions:

1. How does carryover cooking affect the cooking process? Carryover cooking is a process during which food continues to cook at a temperature of 5°F to 15°F (−15°C to −9°C) after the food is removed from the heat. This must be taken into account when planning cooking time.

2. What positive effects does searing meat have on the final product? Searing browns the outside of the meat, adding color and flavor to the surface.

3. Why should meat not be salted prior to broiling or grilling? Salting meat prior to broiling or grilling is not a good idea because it will draw moisture from the center of the meat, making it browner on the outside, but less juicy in the center.

RETEACH

U Universal Access

English Language Learners After reading the information about dry cooking techniques, divide the class into teams to prepare a meal that includes three foods prepared with different moist cooking techniques. Explain to the class how each item was prepared, and then have them taste and evaluate the meals. Students should use the advice and information from the section to prepare their meal using the different cooking techniques. Once they are prepared, they should determine what worked and what needs to be improved.

C Critical Thinking

Carryover Cooking Ask students how they can account for carryover cooking when preparing a meat dish. Students could try to calculate the potential carryover cooking time based on the thickness and density of the meat. Once they have calculated the time, take the meat out of the oven and let it rest for the appropriate amount of time. This should help prevent the meat from being overcooked due to the carryover.

ASSESS

Lab Manual

Assign the Section 15.2 Activities.

Online Study Tools

Have students go to the Online Learning Center at **glencoe.com** to:

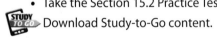

- Take the Section 15.2 Practice Test.
- Download Study-to-Go content.

SECTION 15.2 After You Read Answer Key

Review Key Concepts

1. A griddle is a solid, flat piece of metal with a gas or electric heat source. Griddles are commonly used to make sandwiches, such as grilled cheese and breakfast items, such as pancakes and eggs. Heat the griddle to 350°F (177°C), add fat if necessary, and then place the item or items on the griddle. Turn the food to cook all parts of the food.

Practice Culinary Academics

2. **English Language Arts** The advice column should offer practical advice for everyday cooks about using dry cooking techniques, such as what carryover cooking is, how to stir-fry, or tips to follow after frying.

3. **Science** The larger and denser the object, the greater the carryover cooking. Larger objects retain heat because they have a lower surface area to volume ratio. Denser objects retain moisture. Water has a higher heat capacity inside the food. The potato, being denser, will take longer to cool.

4. **Social Studies** Many cooking techniques go as far back as the ancient Egyptians. Changes in the technique occur as equipment is invented or improved that allows more control over the process. Some techniques are used all over the world now, while some places have unique versions of techniques, such as yakitori, or Japanese grilling, that are distinctive.

5. **Mathematics** The diameter of the pan is 10 inches, so the radius is 5 inches. Total volume of oil is (3.14)(5 in.)(5 in.)(0.5 in.) = 39.25 cu. in. Converted to fluid ounces, the volume is 39.25 × 0.554 = 21.7445, or about 22 fl. oz.

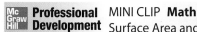

McGraw Hill **Professional Development** MINI CLIP **Math** Surface Area and Volume

CLOSE
Culminating Activity

Sauté Practice Have students take turns flipping slices of bread in a cold sauté pan to learn about holding and moving a sauté pan. Then have them practice sautéing onions. Have them carefully observe the changes in appearance and aroma of the onions so that they can determine how to recognize a properly sautéed onion.

SECTION 15.3 Moist Cooking Techniques

Section Overview
In this section, students will learn the various moist cooking techniques, including boiling, blanching, parboiling, simmering, poaching, and steaming. They will also learn about combination cooking methods, such as braising and stewing. Finally, they will learn what each of the methods is and how to perform each method.

FOCUS
Bell Ringer Activity

Moist Cooking Now that the class has learned the basic definition of moist cooking methods, have them name types of moist cooking techniques and how each technique might be used. Explain that they will learn more about all of the moist cooking techniques and how to use them in this section.

D Develop Concepts

Main Idea Discuss the main idea with the students. Ask: Why might you want to use a dry technique in combination with a moist technique? A combination dry and moist cooking technique may be the best way to improve both the flavor and texture of certain food items.

TEACH
S Skill Practice
Guided Practice

L1 List Ask students to list ways that blanching is used. Blanching is used to pre-cook foods, soften herbs, lock in color, preserve nutrients, remove salt, remove blood, and remove strong flavors.

L2 Explain Have students explain the advantages of simmering a food. Some of the advantages of simmering include less shrinkage, less evaporation and more control over evaporation, and less breakup.

L3 Apply Try using a combination cooking method on a tough piece of meat. How does the method improve the meat? The browning adds flavor, and the long, slow cooking process tenderizes the meat.

ASSESS
Quiz
Ask students to answer the following questions:

1. Why should you shock foods after blanching them? You would shock foods after blanching them because shocking foods completely stops the cooking process and prevents overcooking.

2. How does pressure affect the steaming process? Pressure will raise the temperature above the steam temperature of over 212°F (100°C).

3. What effect does braising have on the flavor of a meat? Braising concentrates the flavors by pulling the juices from the meat and mixing them with the cooking liquid.

RETEACH
R Reading Strategy

Prepare a Meal After reading the information about moist cooking techniques, divide the class into teams to prepare a meal that includes three foods prepared with different moist cooking techniques. Explain to the class how each item was prepared, and then have them taste and evaluate the meals. Students should use the advice and information from the section to prepare their meal using the different cooking techniques. Once they are prepared, they should determine what worked and what needs to be improved.

 Professional MINI CLIP **Reading**
Development Bridging Cultural Gaps

Universal Access

Students with Physical Challenges Before serving a braised food, why do you think you would strain, thicken, and add salt, pepper, and other spices to the liquid before serving? Putting the cooking liquid through this process transforms it into a flavorful sauce, which, when added to the dish, makes the dish more appealing.

ASSESS

 ExamView® Assessment Suite
Create a test for this chapter.

Lab Manual

Assign the Section 15.3 Activities.

Online Study Tools

Have students go to the Online Learning Center at **glencoe.com** to:

- Take the Section 15.3 Practice Test.
- Download Study-to-Go content.

SECTION 15.3 **After You Read Answer Key**

Review Key Concepts

1. To blanch a food, completely submerge it in a boiling liquid and briefly cook it, and then remove it. Plunge it immediately into ice water to stop the cooking.

2. Braising is a process of cooking a food item slowly for a long time in a liquid, after first searing it. It is used to make tough cuts tender. To braise, first sear the food. Then, remove it, and deglaze the pan. Then, return the food to the pan and add liquid. Finally, place the pan in the oven, and cook until tender.

Practice Culinary Academics

3. **Science** The Maillard reactions occur when the protein and the sugars on the surface of the meat combine due to the high heat. It causes the meat to brown and the flavor to become stronger. Meat is browned before stewing or braising to make it more flavorful.

4. **English Language Arts** Posters should describe braising using the steps given in this section and should illustrate each step with a drawing, picture, or illustration. Students may want to use the How To feature on braising for ideas on how to format their posters.

5. **Mathematics** 20 minutes ÷ 3.5 = 5.714286 minutes. 0.714286 is converted into seconds by multiplying 0.714286 × 60 = 42.85714 ≈ 43 seconds. The rice will cook in 5 minutes and 43 seconds.

CLOSE

Preparation Charts Working together as a class or in groups, have students prepare reference charts with instructions and tips for poaching, simmering, boiling, and steaming. Include correct temperatures and uses. Complete one set of reference charts for the class, and then put the posters up in the foods lab for reference.

Chapter Review and Applications

Vocabulary Review

1. Students should create multiple-choice questions with possible answers for each term.

Review Key Concepts

2. A dry cooking technique uses oil, fat, or the radiation of hot air or metal to transfer heat. No moisture is used, and moisture in the food evaporates. Moist cooking uses liquid to create heat. Combination techniques use both moist and dry cooking techniques.

3. The length of time cooked and the cooking technique used determine how much nutritive value is retained, how firm or soft a food is, and how tough or tender a meat is. They can change or maintain the color of food and enhance the flavor of foods. Fats and sugars can be cooked to create a pleasing aroma.

4. Dry cooking techniques are baking, smoking, roasting, sautéing, stir-frying, frying, pan-frying, deep-frying, and grilling. Baking, smoking, and roasting are cooking in an enclosed space. Sautéing, stir-frying, frying, pan-frying, and deep-frying are cooking in oil. Broiling is cooking by direct radiant heat from above. Grilling is cooking on radiant heat from below on a grill surface.

5. Moist cooking techniques are boiling, blanching, parboiling, simmering, poaching, and steaming. Boiling, blanching, and parboiling are cooking in boiling liquid. Simmering and poaching are cooking in liquid at gentler heat than boiling. Steaming is cooking in steam in an enclosed environment.

6. Braising is browning food and cooking it slowly for a long time partially covered in a liquid. Stewing is browning food and cooking it for a shorter amount of time completely covered in liquid.

C Critical Thinking

7. The food was overcooked. The meat became tough as the proteins coagulated and became discolored. The vegetables grew limp and colorless as their tissues broke down too much and they lost pigment.

8. Sear the pork before cooking it. The browning creates more flavor on the surface. Do not overcook the meat. You could also baste it with a fat while cooking.

9. The staff should be given instructions in properly storing, cooking, and holding the food, particularly on proper cooking times and temperatures so that food is not overcooked or undercooked.

10. Having many cooking techniques ensures no staff member or piece of equipment is overburdened and allows for a variety of flavors and textures. Opinions may differ about having too many techniques.

Academic Skills

11. **English Language Arts** Answers should demonstrate the ability to identify moist, dry, and combination cooking techniques and also demonstrate an understanding of how different cooking techniques affect different foods.

12. **Social Studies** Answers should explain the development (for example, how a roasting spit developed into the modern grill) and demonstrate the ability to determine how changes in equipment have improved cooking techniques (for example, increased control over temperature and cooking time).

13. **Mathematics** It will cost $77.50. Plugging weight and density into $W = (d)(V)$ yields 60 lbs. = (7.5 lbs./gal.)(V), or V = 60 ÷ 7.5 = 8 gallons. Oscar will need 8 ÷ 4 = 2 containers of oil, at a total cost of 2 × $38.75 = $77.50.

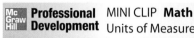 **Professional Development** MINI CLIP **Math** Units of Measure—Solid Geometry

Certification Prep

14. a. braise

15. d. 212ºF (100ºC)

Real-World Skills and Applications

16. **Self-Management Skills** Broiling, pan-frying, deep-frying, sautéing, or stir-frying will ensure that the chicken is cooked in time. Stir-frying or broiling will retain the most nutrition. Add vegetables to the stir-fry to increase nutritional value of the meal. Or use a vegetable side dish with other cooking methods.

17. **Communication Skills** Students should be able to identify the cooking technique used. Their notes should describe the technique and any tips they learned. They should then pass on what they learned in a manner that is clear and easy to understand.

18. **Technology Applications** The class should create a Web site that focuses on teaching different methods of cooking. It should clearly and accurately show how to perform different cooking techniques.

19. **Financial Literacy** $3 × 25 lbs. = $75. $2 × 25 lbs. = $50. You save $25 by having the staff cook it.

Culinary Lab

20. **Cook a Meal** Students should fill out each rating chart completely. In discussion, the groups should give reasons for why they gave the ratings they did and which techniques gave the best results. For foods that rated poorly, discuss with the group how the food could have been improved.

Seasonings and Flavorings

SECTION 16.1 Enhancing Food

SECTION 16.2 Herbs and Spices

SECTION 16.3 Condiments, Nuts, and Seeds

SECTION 16.4 Sensory Perception

Classroom Solutions

Print Resources

📖 Student Edition

📖 Instructor Annotated Edition

📖 Lab Manual

📖 Lab Manual IAE

Technology Resources

ExamView **ExamView® Assessment Suite CD**
Create and print unit and chapter tests.

Lesson Planner *Plus* **Lesson Planner Plus CD** provides access to teacher resources in one package.

Presentation Plus! provides visual teaching aids for every section.

🧭 **Online Learning Center** includes resources and activities for students and teachers. Also includes the **Online Student Edition**.

💿 **Interactive Student Edition**

SECTION 16.1 Enhancing Food

Section Overview

In this section, students will learn the difference between seasonings and flavorings. They will also learn to identify the common ingredients used to enhance flavor. Finally, they will learn when it is appropriate to add seasonings and flavorings to food.

FOCUS

🔔 Bell Ringer Activity

Experience Flavor Enhancers Have students taste small amounts of salt, pepper, onion, and lemon. Have them describe the flavor of each and predict how each might be used to enhance the flavor of a dish. Have them think of dishes in which they might use each item to enhance flavor.

D Develop Concepts

Main Idea Discuss the main idea with the students. Ask: Why is learning which seasonings and flavorings work well with certain food items an important cooking skill? It is an important skill because chefs and cooks may need to improve a bland dish by adding seasonings and flavorings. Knowing which are likely to work will save time, materials, and effort.

TEACH

S Skill Practice

Guided Practice

L1 **List** Ask students to list common seasonings and flavorings. Seasonings and flavorings include salt, pepper, onion, lemon, and monosodium glutamate.

L2 **Explain** Have students explain how flavor enhancers work. Flavor enhancers increase the way you perceive the food's flavor without changing the actual flavor or adding flavor.

L3 **Apply** Working as a class, gather several different flavorings and seasonings and make a broth or soup. Have students add the seasonings or flavorings one at a time, recording the name and amount added, until you like the soup's flavor. Through this exercise, students should learn about experimenting with seasonings and flavorings and how they affect the flavor of food.

ASSESS

Quiz

Ask students to answer the following questions:

1. Why should you wear gloves when working with hot peppers? The juices from the peppers can burn your hands and your eyes if you touch them.

2. Why might you need to adjust an amount of fresh onion substituted for dried onion in terms of flavor? Fresh onion is stronger in flavor than dried onion.

3. When using lemon zest, why should you make sure not to get any pith in it? The pith is very bitter and could ruin the flavor of food.

RETEACH

R Reading Strategy

When to Season After reading the subsection on when to season, have students prepare a dish. Ask them to choose a seasoning that is not in the recipe to add to the dish. They should consider flavor when choosing their seasoning. Then, they should prepare the dish, adding the seasoning at the proper time. Students should choose an appropriate seasoning that does not clash with the existing flavors. Most seasonings should be added during the cooking process, except for salt, which is added at the end. Dried seasonings should be added earlier than fresh.

U Universal Access

Gifted Students Have students imagine they are working on a recipe that calls for a seasoning, but their kitchen has run out. They have other seasonings, however. What adjustments do they need to make? Answers will vary, but students should determine new seasonings based on their knowledge of flavors. Suggestions should reflect knowledge from the section.

ASSESS

Lab Manual

Assign the Section 16.1 Activities.

Online Study Tools

Have students go to the Online Learning Center at **glencoe.com** to:

- Take the Section 16.1 Practice Test.
-  Download Study-to-Go content.

SECTION 16.1 After You Read Answer Key

Review Key Concepts

1. Table salt is a fine-grain salt most commonly used in food preparation and to season food at the table. Rock salt is large pieces of salt used as a bed during baking for foods such as clams, oysters, and potatoes. Sea salt has a strong distinctive flavor. Kosher salt is a coarser salt that is free of iodine and preferred by many chefs to season food during preparation.

Practice Culinary Academics

2. **Science** Adding salt to the water does not have a noticeable effect on how fast pasta cooks. Salt is added to the pasta water so that the pasta can absorb the flavor. Pasta cooked with salt will be more flavorful than pasta cooked without it. It does not matter when the salt is added as long as the pasta cooks in it for some period of time.

3. **English Language Arts** As time goes by and cultures become more integrated, more and more seasonings become commonplace in kitchens. A recipe written 40 or 50 years ago may be improved by spices that were not commonly used in American kitchens then, but are now. Encourage students to be creative in adding new seasonings and flavorings to old recipes.

4. **Social Studies** The recipe may contain seasonings or flavorings that are unfamiliar to the student. For example, many Thai recipes contain galangal, which is similar to ginger, but recipes all around the world use salt and different types of pepper. Discuss why some cultures may use seasonings and flavorings that others do not.

5. **Mathematics** The shaker weighs 80 grams. Half of the salt must equal $152\,g - 116\,g = 36\,g$. Since half of the salt plus the shaker equals 116 g, the shaker must equal $116\,g - 36\,g = 80$ g. Algebraically: If x is the weight of the salt, and y is the weight of the shaker, $x + y = 152$, and $(\frac{1}{2})x + y = 116$. Rewrite to solve for x: $x = 152 - y$ and $x = 232 - 2y$. Thus, $152 - y = 232 - 2y$. Rewrite to solve for y: $y = 232 - 152 = 80$.

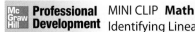

Professional Development	MINI CLIP **Math** Identifying Linear Equations

CLOSE

Culminating Activity

Make a Dish Have the class choose a recipe that has seasonings and flavorings, and make it as a group. Then, have them evaluate the overall flavor. Did the seasonings and flavorings do a good job of enhancing the flavor? Are there any changes they would make for next time to improve the flavor?

SECTION 16.2 Herbs and Spices

Section Overview

In this section, students will learn how to identify different herbs and spices. They will be given descriptions of the various forms of herbs and spices, and they will also learn how herbs and spices are used. Finally, they will learn how to store herbs and spices.

CHAPTER 16 Lesson Plan

FOCUS

 Bell Ringer Activity

Use Your Senses Bring in examples of different herbs and spices, both fresh and dried. Have the students look at, touch, smell, and taste them to become familiar with the herbs and spices. Discuss their impressions of them. Have them compare and contrast any instance when both the dried and fresh forms are available.

> **Mc Graw Hill** | **Professional Development** MINI CLIP **Reading** Connecting the Pieces

D Develop Concepts

Main Idea Discuss the main idea with the students. Ask: How could herbs and spices ruin a dish if incorrectly used? If incorrectly used, herbs and spices could drastically change the flavor of a dish in an unappealing way.

TEACH

S Skill Practice
Guided Practice

L1 List Ask students to list 10 different herbs. Answers will vary, but some examples of herbs are anise, basil, bay leaf, chervil, chives, cilantro, dill, garlic chives, lemongrass, marjoram, mint, oregano, parsley, rosemary, sage, savory, tarragon, and thyme.

L2 Explain Have students explain how to use a bouquet garni. A bouquet garni is dropped into a stockpot with liquid ingredients and allowed to simmer and infuse the dish with flavor of the herbs. It is removed before serving.

L3 Apply Have students come up with their own herb and spice blend and explain how they would use it. Blends will vary based on students' tastes. They should have an idea of what foods their blend could be used with and why their combination would go well with their chosen dish or dishes.

ASSESS
Quiz

Ask students to answer the following questions:

1. **How do you make and use a sachet?** To make a sachet, put herbs and spices in cheesecloth and tie it closed with twine. Tie the other end of the twine to a pot handle and allow the sachet to mix with the ingredients in the pot. Remove at the end of cooking.

2. **When should you add fresh herbs to uncooked dishes?** You should add fresh herbs to uncooked dishes a few hours before service.

3. **When should whole spices be added to cooked foods?** You should add whole spices to cooked foods very early in the cooking process.

RETEACH

U Universal Access

English Language Learners After reading about sachets and bouquets garni, demonstrate how to make one of each. Then, have students practice making them on their own. Supervise their attempts, and correct any mistakes. Using the information in the section and your demonstration, students should be able to learn how to make a sachet and a bouquet garni.

> **Mc Graw Hill** | **Professional Development** MINI CLIP **ELL** Collaborative Work

C Critical Thinking

Avoiding Waste Tell students to imagine that they have several bunches of fresh basil that are beginning to wilt. Ask them to come up with things they can do with the basil to avoid having to throw it out. Answers will vary, but may include making basil oil or vinegar, freezing the basil, drying the basil, making pesto or another sauce, or creating a nightly special that uses basil.

ASSESS

Lab Manual

Assign the Section 16.2 Activities.

Online Study Tools

Have students go to the Online Learning Center at **glencoe.com** to:

• Take the Section 16.2 Practice Test.

 Download Study-to-Go content.

SECTION 16.2 After You Read Answer Key
Review Key Concepts

1. Fresh herbs should be wrapped loosely and refrigerated. Store at temperatures between 34°F (1°C) and 40°F (4°C). Dried herbs should be kept in opaque, airtight containers. Store dried herbs in a cool, dry place at temperatures between 50°F (10°C) and 70°F (21°C). Do not expose stored herbs to heat, light, or excess moisture.

2. Spices should be stored in airtight containers and kept away from direct sunlight. Light can rob spices of their flavor. Spices are best kept in a cool, dry place at temperatures of 50°F to 70°F (10°C to 21°C). Check spices periodically to ensure that they are still fresh.

Practice Culinary Academics

3. **Social Studies** There are several examples of spice blends that characterize a region. For example, Cajun spices come from the American South, harissa comes from North Africa, curry comes from India, and the five spice powder comes from China. Students should explain what is in the blend, what it tastes like, and how it is used.

4. **English Language Arts** Presentations should include information on the herb that is relevant to the herb's use in cooking. Information should be clearly presented and well organized.

5. **Mathematics** The plant grew 1 foot and 6 inches. The difference in feet is $4 - 2 = 2$. The difference in inches is $1 - 7 = -6$. Subtract one from the feet and add 12 to the inches to get 1 foot, 6 inches.

CLOSE

Culminating Activity

Cooking Show Locate an episode of a cooking show that features at least one herb or spice. Have students watch the show, specifically watching for how the herbs and spices are used during the food preparation process. As a class, discuss what the students observed about the use and treatment of the herbs or spices.

SECTION 16.3 Condiments, Nuts, and Seeds

Section Overview

In this section, students will learn about the various types of condiments and the foods they accompany. They will also learn how to properly store condiments. Finally, they will learn how to identify a variety of nuts and seeds and learn how to use nuts and seeds in cooking.

FOCUS

Bell Ringer Activity

Use Your Senses Bring in examples of different condiments, nuts, and seeds. Have the students look at, touch, smell, and taste them so that they become familiar with the various condiments, nuts, and seeds. As a class, discuss the students' impressions of them. What type of foods might they pair the different condiments with?

D Develop Concepts

Main Idea Discuss the main idea with the students. Ask: How do nuts enhance flavor? Nuts not only contribute their nutty flavor, but can also add texture to a dish.

TEACH

S Skill Practice
Guided Practice

L1 List Have students list five varieties of condiments. Answers may vary, but possible answers include salsa, ketchup, steak sauce, prepared mustards, pickles, relishes, vinegars, and flavored oils.

L2 Explain Ask students to explain how flavored oils are created. They are made by extracting oils of certain ingredients and pouring them into olive or canola oil.

L3 Apply Have students choose a recipe for a baked good and add nuts to the recipe. How does this affect the final product? Students should observe the effects of adding nuts to a recipe. Often, adding nuts to a recipe will improve the flavor and texture, but it will not always be successful.

ASSESS

Quiz

Ask students to answer the following questions:

1. What are relishes? Relishes are coarsely chopped or ground pickled items.

2. If condiments come in cans, what must you do after opening them? Canned condiments should be removed from the can and stored in the refrigerator in airtight plastic containers. You should never store them in their original cans.

3. What are the standard ingredients for salsa? The standard ingredients for salsa are chilies, tomatoes, onions, and cilantro.

RETEACH

U Universal Access

Students with Hearing Impairments Have students read about the varieties of condiments and choose a condiment from the list in the section. Then, have them locate a recipe for that condiment and prepare it. Have students identify the dominant flavors and which foods they would pair their condiment with and why. Students should compare the condiments they make with the description in the book. They should be able to identify the dominant flavor and think of suitable food pairings for the condiment. How do their choices compare with the information in the section?

C Critical Thinking

Making Choices Ask students to imagine that they are the garde manger chef of a restaurant. The executive chef has asked them to choose some garnish ideas for the house salad. Have the students come up with five ideas from the ingredients they learned about in this section for salad garnishes. Answers may vary, but in general, any of the nuts and seeds discussed in the chapter might make good garnishes.

ASSESS

 Lab Manual

Assign the Section 16.3 Activities.

 Online Study Tools

Have students go to the Online Learning Center at glencoe.com to:

- Take the Section 16.3 Practice Test.
- Download Study-to-Go content.

SECTION 16.3 After You Read Answer Key

Review Key Concepts

1. Pickles are made from vegetables that are fermented in brines or vinegars flavored and seasoned with dill, garlic, sugar, peppers, or salt. Cucumbers, tomatoes, and peppers are the most common pickled vegetables.

2. In addition to adding flavor, color, and texture, nuts and seeds are also healthful because they are good sources of B vitamins, vitamin E, protein, and omega-3 fatty acids.

Practice Culinary Academics

3. **Mathematics** Probability: 1 in 6; odds: 5:1. There are 20 + 14 + 8 + 6 = 48 total nuts in the bag; 8 of them Brazil, 40 of them something else. The probability of selecting a Brazil nut is $^8/_{48} = ^1/_6$. The odds of selecting a Brazil nut are 40:8, which simplifies to 5:1.

4. **Science** The fruit punch will absorb into the pickle, turning it a bright red color. Osmosis happens because substances tend to move through a membrane from an area of high concentration to an area of low concentration. The brine creates an area of higher concentration outside the pickle, causing the water to flow out. Replacing the brine with fruit punch changes the concentration again, causing the fruit punch to absorb into the pickle.

5. **Social Studies** Salsas, pickles, mustards, and vinegars are examples of condiments that take different forms in different cultures. Yet, usually, the basic forms remain similar. Students should note the similarities and differences among condiments in different cultures and discuss possible reasons for these similarities and differences (such as different ingredients being available).

CLOSE

Culminating Activity

Experiment with Nuts Break students into groups, and have them select three nuts or seeds and then experiment with different ways of preparing them, such as blanching, roasting, or sugaring. As a class, discuss the results of their preparations. Were they successful? If not, why do they think they were unsuccessful?

SECTION 16.4 Sensory Perception

Section Overview

In this section, students will learn the sensory properties of food. They will also learn how the sensory property of flavor is actually a combination of three different sensory experiences. They will learn how to perform a sensory evaluation. Finally, they will learn to identify the factors that affect sensory evaluation.

FOCUS

Bell Ringer Activity

Sensory Perception Ask students to describe how they use their senses when eating food. Which senses are affected and how? Try to elicit answers about all five of the senses. Explain that in this chapter, they will learn about the sensory properties of food and how they can use them to improve their cooking skills.

D Develop Concepts

Main Idea Discuss the main idea with the students. Ask: How can understanding sensory perception improve your ability to taste and to create enjoyable dishes? Understanding sensory perception can help you predict what will work in a dish and what will not. This will save you time and effort in creating or altering recipes.

TEACH

S Skill Practice

Guided Practice

L1 List Have students list the sensory properties of food. The sensory properties of food are color and appearance, flavor, and texture.

L2 Explain Ask students to explain the process of sensory evaluation. Sensory evaluation is the systematic tasting of food by consumers and foodservice professionals to determine what customers like and dislike.

L3 Apply Bring in several brands of a food item, such as ketchup. Have the class perform a blind sensory evaluation of the different brands, noting what they like and dislike about each brand. By doing a mock evaluation, students should understand more about how the process helps foodservice professionals improve their products.

 **Professional Development** MINI CLIP **ELL** Using Realia

ASSESS

Quiz

Ask students to answer the following questions:

1. How does the type of lighting affect visual appeal? Different types of light will affect the perception of color of foods and can make them look more or less appealing.

2. How does the shape of foods play an important role in plate composition? Food items should not be similar in shape. Variety in products creates visual appeal.

3. Why should hot food be served on hot plates and cold food be served on cold plates? Different temperature foods should be served on plates of similar temperatures because this helps keep the food at the appropriate temperatures.

RETEACH
U Universal Access

Gifted Students Have students search through food magazines and select pictures of dishes that have appealing plate presentation. Discuss the pictures and what appeals to them about the presentation. Discuss how plate presentation impacts sensory evaluation and plate composition. Have students suggest alternate ways to present the food. Food presentation may appeal to people for many different reasons. It may be unique or eye-catching, or it may be traditional and rustic. Either of those can make a dish appealing. Unique presentation may make the customer curious about what the dish will be like, while traditional presentation may evoke good memories or romantic ideas about food.

C Critical Thinking

Blind Taste Test Ask students to imagine that they are doing a blind taste test of different tomato sauces made with similar ingredients. What are some reasons they might have different flavors? Answers will vary, but might include: they are different temperatures, they are different consistencies, they have some different types of the ingredients, factors are present that suppress the ability to perceive flavor, flavor enhancers may be used, or the amount of oil and water may vary.

ASSESS

 ExamView® Assessment Suite Create a test for this chapter.

Lab Manual
Assign the Section 16.4 Activities.

Online Study Tools
Have students go to the Online Learning Center at **glencoe.com** to:

- Take the Section 16.4 Practice Test.
- Download Study-to-Go content.

SECTION 16.4 After You Read Answer Key
Review Key Concepts

1. Different types of lighting affect the perception of the food's color. If lighting distorts the perceived color of a food, it may appear less appetizing to a customer.

2. Products that are served warm typically have a stronger flavor and aroma than those that are served chilled.

Practice Culinary Academics

3. **English Language Arts** Descriptions should provide details about all of the sensory perceptions the students experienced. In describing texture, students should answer the questions provided by the section.

4. **Social Studies** Students should learn about aspects of Japanese food presentation and considerations of food's sensory properties in Japanese culture, and then determine how they might be applied to improve their own food preparation skills.

5. **Mathematics** The radius of the dinner plate is ½ of its 11-inch diameter, or 5.5 inches. The area of the dinner plate is 3.14×5.5 in. + 5.5 in. = 94.985 sq. in. The area of the potatoes should be $0.5 \times 94.985 = 47.4925$ sq. in. Substituting that

into the area formula yields 47.4925 = 3.14r², or r² = 15.125. Take the square root of both sides to get r ≈ 3.889. The diameter of the potatoes = 2r, or 2 × 3.889 ≈ 7.8 inches.

CLOSE
Culminating Activity

Identify Seasonings Have students practice identifying seasonings by aroma. First, have them smell the seasonings and view the labels. Then, have them identify the seasonings by aroma only. Next, have them taste the seasonings. Finally, have them identify the seasonings by taste only. How many can they identify by aroma or taste? You might want to turn this into a contest to see who can best identify the seasonings.

Chapter Review and Applications

Vocabulary Review

1. Groupings will vary but students should offer logical reasons for how the terms are related.

Review Key Concepts

2. Seasonings enhance the natural flavor of food without changing it and include salt and pepper. Flavorings change the natural flavors of a food and include onion and lemon, as well as extracts such as almond or vanilla. MSG is an example of a flavor enhancer.

3. Fresh herbs should be minced or crushed close to cooking or serving time. They can be added to liquid foods in a sachet or bouquet garni. They should be loosely wrapped and refrigerated at 34–40ºF (1–4ºC). Dried herbs should be added at the beginning of cooking. They should be kept in airtight containers in a cool, dry place at 50–70ºF (10–21ºC).

4. Spices can be used whole, ground, sliced, or in chunks. The form depends on the cooking time. Spices should be added to cold food hours before serving. Add ground spices to cooked foods near the end. Measure accurately. Store in an airtight container in a cool, dry place at 50–70ºF (10–21ºC).

5. Common condiments are sauces; prepared mustards; pickled condiments; vinegars; and flavored oils. Sauces go with meats, vegetables, and salads. Mustards go with meats, vegetables, and sandwiches. Cucumbers, tomatoes, and peppers are the most commonly pickled vegetables. Vinegars can be used for salad dressings, marinades, and sauces. Flavored oils can be used as dressings or added before serving.

6. Nuts are hard-shelled dry fruits or seeds and include almonds, cashews, chestnuts, hazelnuts, peanuts, pecans, pine nuts, pistachios, and walnuts. A seed is a plant grain and includes poppy seeds, pumpkin seeds, sesame seeds, and sunflower seeds.

7. The three sensory properties of food are color and appearance, flavor, and texture. Color and appearance indicate the possible flavor and texture of the food before you eat it. Flavor is a combination of tastes, aromas, and feeling. Texture is the feel in the mouth.

8. Sensory factors can enhance different characteristics of food items, changing the customer's perception of its flavor, texture, and appearance. These small changes can make a food more enjoyable or less enjoyable to the customer.

C Critical Thinking

9. Common answers may include salt, pepper, rosemary, mint, and chives, which are often used to complement lamb. Students may choose other seasonings, if they can justify their choice.

10. Fresh herbs are not always available. Also, it takes more of a fresh herb to equal the potency of dried, so fresh herbs are usually more expensive to use. Finally, dried herbs are easier to store.

Academic Skills

11. **English Language Arts** Students should answer each question for each article. Answers will vary. Articles may range from a general article about the food item to a narrow focus about a particular use or health benefit. Writing styles may be more informational or more literary.

12. **Science** This experiment demonstrates the importance of aroma to the flavor of food. When the smell is muted, it becomes more difficult to distinguish foods of similar texture. When you smell an onion, then eat an apple, the apple may taste like an onion, because the aroma contributes to the perception of flavor.

13. **Mathematics** $4\frac{5}{12}$ ounces of salt were placed in the shaker. The expression showing the total amount of salt placed in the shaker is $2 + (\frac{1}{4} \times 2) + (\frac{1}{8} \times 2) + (\frac{1}{3} \times 2) + (\frac{1}{2} \times 2)$, which simplifies to $2 + \frac{1}{2} + \frac{1}{4} + \frac{2}{3} + 1$. Changing the fractions into the lowest common denominator (twelfths) results in $2 + \frac{6}{12} + \frac{3}{12} + \frac{8}{12} + 1 = 3 + \frac{17}{12} = 4\frac{5}{12}$.

Certification Prep

14. c. 3 months

15. a. appearance

Real-World Skills and Applications

16. Critical Thinking Skills Salt is added to many foods. Some possible substitutions are adding barbecue sauce or steak sauce to meat; adding garlic, ketchup, or chili powder to French fries; or adding salsa to tortilla chips.

17. Interpersonal and Collaborative Skills Students should work together to gather recipes and determine into which category they best fit. They should also agree on the form and creation of the classroom recipe file.

18. Technology Applications Students should successfully use spreadsheet software to create an organized, easy-to-read chart listing the herbs, spices, condiments, nuts, and seeds and uses for those items.

19. Financial Literacy The total amount of the separate ingredients is $24. By purchasing the blend, you will save $4 for each 20 oz. purchased.

Culinary Lab

20. Herbs and Spices in Action Student ratings should be fair and supported by their explanations. Different ratings should give students an idea of where their sauces do and do not work. Encourage students to revise their recipe based on the evaluations.

Breakfast Cookery

SECTION 17.1 **Meat and Egg Preparation**

SECTION 17.2 **Breakfast Breads and Cereals**

Classroom Solutions

Print Resources

📖 Student Edition
📖 Instructor Annotated Edition
📖 Lab Manual
📖 Lab Manual IAE

Technology Resources

ExamView® *Assessment Suite* CD
Create and print unit and chapter tests.

Lesson Planner *Plus* **Lesson Planner Plus CD** provides access to teacher resources in one package.

Presentation Plus! provides visual teaching aids for every section.

🧭 **Online Learning Center** includes resources and activities for students and teachers. Also includes the **Online Student Edition**.

💿 **Interactive Student Edition**

SECTION 17.1 **Meat and Egg Preparation**

Section Overview

In this section, students will learn about common breakfast protein foods. They will also learn how to prepare the most common breakfast meats. Finally, they will become familiar with several different ways to prepare eggs.

FOCUS

🔔 Bell Ringer Activity

Egg Basics Demonstration In front of the class, demonstrate how to crack eggs while explaining egg quality and the different parts of the egg. Show the students basic egg cooking techniques, and allow students to practice them. As you demonstrate, go over basic safety precautions for preparing egg dishes.

D Develop Concepts

Main Idea Discuss the main idea with the students. Ask: Why do you think people have started to eat breakfast foods at other meals? Foods that are traditionally breakfast foods can make a hearty or nutritious meal at any time of the day. They can also be healthful, depending on the foods.

TEACH

S Skill Practice
Guided Practice

L1 List Ask the students to list the different types of fried eggs. The different types of fried eggs are sunny-side up, basted, over-easy, over-medium, and over-hard.

L2 Explain Have students explain how to make a frittata. To make a frittata, a filling is mixed in with the egg, and then everything is cooked over low heat without stirring.

L3 Apply Ask the students to practice simmering eggs in the shell to different levels of doneness. Students should practice until they are familiar with the technique and are capable of achieving different levels of doneness.

Professional Development MINI CLIP **ELL** Accessing Prior Knowledge

ASSESS

Quiz

Ask students to answer the following questions:

1. How is bacon cooked in a commercial kitchen? In a commercial kitchen, bacon is arranged in single strips on a parchment-lined sheet pan. It is then cooked at 300°F – 350°F (149°C – 177°C) until almost done. Next, it is removed from the oven (with care not to spill hot grease).

Finally, it is cooked on a griddle. It is blotted to remove excess grease and serve.

2. What steps can you take to ensure scrambled eggs do not turn green? To ensure scrambled eggs do not turn green, use stainless steel pans and low heat, cook in small batches, and serve as soon as possible after cooking.

3. What is the difference between French and American omelets? For French omelets, you stir the egg mixture and shake the pan. For American omelets, you add the eggs to the pan and lift the edges to allow the uncooked portion to run underneath.

RETEACH

U Universal Access

Students with Hearing Impairments Have students review the materials available from the American Egg Board Web site (www.aeb.org) regarding eggs and the foodservice industry. Have students research egg safety and preparation. Students should successfully navigate the Web site, gather information, and understand the information presented on the Web site.

C Critical Thinking

Prioritize Tasks Imagine that you are a short-order cook in a diner. All of the following are outstanding orders. List the order in which you prepare these dishes: quiche, eggs to order, sausage and bacon, garnish, pancakes, waffles, oatmeal, toast, biscuits with sausage gravy, and hash browns. List them from first to last. Answers from first to last: biscuits with sausage gravy, quiche, sausage and bacon, hash browns, oatmeal, waffles, pancakes, garnish, eggs to order, and toast.

 Professional Development MINI CLIP **Reading** Strategies for Student Achievement

ASSESS

Lab Manual

Assign the Section 17.1 Activities.

Online Study Tools

Have students go to the Online Learning Center at glencoe.com to:

- Take the Section 17.1 Practice Test.
- Download Study-to-Go content.

SECTION 17.1 After You Read Answer Key

Review Key Concepts

1. An egg has three main parts: shell, yolk, and white. The shell is a hardened layer that protects the contents. The yolk is the yellow center part, which contains fat, proteins, iron, and vitamins. The white surrounds the yolk and contains most of the protein in the egg.

2. As a breakfast meat, ham is usually pre-cooked. If it is pre-cooked, it needs only to be warmed and browned slightly under the broiler or on the griddle before it is served.

3. Break the egg into a bowl, add milk if desired, and whisk until well blended. Heat butter on the cooking surface, and when it is hot, add the egg mixture. Cook over low to medium heat, stirring slowly and allowing uncooked egg to run under the cooked portion. When the egg mixture is set, but not yet hard, it is done. Remove from the heat immediately.

Practice Culinary Academics

4. Social Studies Answers will probably vary, but students may choose to report on dishes such as egg drop soup (Chinese), pad thai (Thai), crêpes (French), huevos rancheros (Mexican-American), huevos reales (Spanish), quiche (French), or flan (Spanish).

5. Mathematics Neal will get 64 slices from the 1-foot slab of applewood-smoked bacon. One foot is equivalent to 12 inches, and 12 inches divided by $\frac{3}{16}$ inches equals $\frac{12}{1} \times \frac{16}{3} = \frac{192}{3} = 64$.

CLOSE

Culminating Activity

Prepare an Egg Dish Working in teams, have the students prepare and plate one of the following egg dishes: fried eggs, scrambled eggs, shirred eggs, an omelet, and soft-, medium-, and hard-cooked eggs. Students should share what they learned about cooking eggs through this experience. Discuss as a class how easy or difficult each dish was to prepare.

SECTION 17.2 Breakfast Breads and Cereals

Section Overview

In this section, students will learn about the different items commonly served at breakfasts. They will also learn about the different types of quick breads and cereals. Finally, they will learn about ready-made breads, pancakes, waffles, French toast, and hot and cold cereals.

FOCUS

🔔 Bell Ringer Activity

Brainstorm Have students brainstorm a list of ready-made breads they often see on breakfast menus. List them on the board, and come up with reasons why they may be popular in the quick-service food industry. Discuss factors such as convenience, no labor cost, consistency, variety, preparation, and popularity.

D Develop Concepts

Main Idea Discuss the main idea with the students. Ask: Why would a restaurant purchase pastries ready-made? Restaurants may purchase ready-made pastries because they may not have a chef trained in making pastries or because it will save time.

TEACH

S Skill Practice

Guided Practice

L1 List Have students list three kinds of quick breads served for breakfast. Answers may include any of the following quick breads: muffins, scones, loaf-style quick breads, doughnuts, biscuits, pancakes, and waffles.

L2 Explain Ask students to explain how to plate French toast. To plate French toast, it is usually cut in half diagonally. Then, it may be topped with something and/or served with eggs or meat sides.

L3 Apply Have students practice preparing hot cereal according to the instructions in the section. Students should follow instructions to prepare hot cereal, including those for preventing lumps, until they can prepare it successfully.

ASSESS

Quiz

Ask students to answer the following questions:

1. What are quick breads? Quick breads are breads made from quick-acting leavening agents.

2. When making pancakes, what is the visual sign that it is time to turn them? When bubbles appear on the top surface of the pancakes, it is a visual sign that you should turn them.

3. How can you make French toast crunchy? To make French toast crunchy, dip the bread into crushed cereal after dipping it into the batter.

RETEACH

R Reading Strategy

Prepare a Breakfast Bread or Cereal In teams, read the instructions for preparing pancakes, waffles, French toast, and hot cereal. Choose one of these items, and prepare it. Serve your item to your classmates and evaluate the results. Ask your classmates for feedback. How well did the instructions in the section help you? Students should put the advice from the section into practice by preparing the item of their choice. If the item does not turn out well, they should evaluate the steps they took to figure out what went wrong.

U Universal Access

Students with Physical Challenges Ask students to imagine that they are in charge of making pancakes for the morning buffet line, and the pancakes are turning out very hard. Have them list possible mistakes they might have made. The pancakes may have been flipped more than once, the batter may have been overmixed, or the pancakes might have been held too long.

 **Professional Development** MINI CLIP **ELL** Using Manipulatives

ASSESS

 ExamView Assessment Suite Create a test for this chapter.

📖 Lab Manual

Assign the Section 17.2 Activities.

✈ Online Study Tools

Have students go to the Online Learning Center at **glencoe.com** to:

- Take the Section 17.2 Practice Test.
- Download Study-to-Go content.

After You Read Answer Key

Review Key Concepts

1. Quick bread choices include muffins, biscuits, sweet loaf breads, and scones. Pancakes and waffles are also considered quick breads.

2. Breakfast cereals include both hot and cold cereals. Hot cereals are made from whole, cracked, or flaked grains cooked and served hot. Oatmeal is a common hot cereal choice. Cold cereals require no preparation and are served cold with milk and other accompaniments. Granola is a common cold cereal choice.

Practice Culinary Academics

3. **English Language Arts** The essays should describe the basic procedure for making a quick bread. They may include a recipe as well. The body of the essay should describe the procedure in chronological order and give examples of tips and tricks. Students should turn in their outlines and rough drafts.

4. **Social Studies** Many cultures have fried bread products that would be appropriate for breakfast, such as beignets, churros, malasadas, or funnel cakes. Fried bread items that may not be appropriate as a breakfast item include poppadums, curry bread, and hush puppies.

5. **Mathematics** The areas are 50 square inches and 5 square inches. The area of the larger pancake = (3.14)(4 in.)(4 in.) = 50.24 sq. in. ≈ 50 sq. in. The area of the smaller pancake ≈ (3.14)(1.25 in.)(1.25 in.) = 4.90625 = 5 sq. in.

 **Professional Development** MINI CLIP **Math** Guiding Questions

CLOSE

Culminating Activity

Create Breakfast Menus Divide students into teams, and have each team create three different breakfast menus. Have them include eggs, meat, potatoes, and breads as menu selections. Then, have the teams switch and regroup the menus into a fourth menu option. Discuss the choices each team made as a class.

Chapter Review and Applications

Vocabulary Review

1. Review the definition for each vocabulary word to help students build their puzzles.

Review Key Concepts

2. Ham is generally pre-cooked. Bacon may be served thin- or thick-sliced. Canadian bacon comes from boneless pork loin that is smoked and brined with a thin layer of fat on its surface. Sausage is ground meat that has been seasoned and stuffed in casings. It is served in links or formed into patties. Eggs can be prepared in a variety of ways.

3. Ham typically needs only to be warmed and browned slightly before serving. Bacon is cooked at a low temperature in the oven and finished on the griddle. Sausage is cooked the same way as bacon. It must be cooked until well done, but not dry and hard.

4. Ways to cook fried eggs include cooked in a fat in a pan; poached, cooked in simmering water with an acid; scrambled, cooked in a pan until set; omelets, whipped and cooked at high heat until set then filling is added; shirred, baked in a ramekin with other ingredients and covered with cream or milk and bread crumbs; simmered in the shell, simmered in water to the desired level of doneness.

5. A quick-service breakfast often includes eggs, a breakfast meat, a bread item, and potatoes or fruit.

6. Breakfast quick breads include ready-made bread products such as doughnuts, muffins, and scones, as well as easy-to-prepare items such as pancakes and waffles.

C Critical Thinking

7. Answers might include substituting low-fat spreads for butter; using turkey bacon, lean turkey sausage, or tofu for protein; serving oatmeal, granola, or low-fat bran muffins, substituting egg whites for eggs.

8. Adding milk or cream can make the scrambled eggs smoother and creamier.

9. Eggs are considered a potentially hazardous food and should be discarded.

10. Purchasing a pre-cooked ham saves time as it needs only to be warmed briefly before serving.

Academic Skills

11. **English Language Arts** Students should look at MyPyramid and choose balanced meals. For example, a healthful breakfast might include two slices of whole-wheat toast, a two-egg omelet with vegetables, a small fruit salad, and a glass of milk.

12. **Social Studies** Students should list a few examples of foods that may come from other countries. Reasons might include: the food is out of season here, but in season elsewhere; the food may be a specialty of a certain region; the food or ingredient may only be available elsewhere; and the item may be less expensive to produce in another country.

13. **Mathematics** Each slice should be ⅛ inches (or 0.125 inches) thick. With a $40 total cost and a 50% profit margin, the total selling price must be $40 ÷ (1 − 0.5) = $80. If Leilani is to make $80, she needs to sell a total of $80 ÷ $5 = 16 orders of bacon. At four slices per order: 4 × 16 = 64 slices of bacon needed. Each slice must be ⁸⁄₆₄ inches, or ⅛ inches thick.

Certification Prep

14. c. white

15. a. grade AA

Real-World Skills and Applications

16. **Self-Management Skills** Possible trade-offs include purchasing some convenience foods to save labor costs or making some items from scratch to lower food costs; controlling overproduction to minimize waste; using less-expensive garnishes; and shopping for less-expensive side breads or meats without reducing quality.

17. **Collaborative and Interpersonal Skills** Students should agree upon a menu, plan for the ingredients and amounts they need to get, and plan for the work flow on the day of preparation. They should also work with their guests of honor to plan a suitable place and time for the breakfast.

18. **Technology Applications** Students should research ingredients costs and determine the menu cost and item cost. The coffee house menu might consist of quick breads, pastries, and maybe cereals. The diner meal might consist of quick breakfast combinations. The upscale menu might include more complex egg dishes, quick breads, and meats.

19. **Financial Literacy** Breakfast at school costs $2 × 5 = $10/week. Breakfast at home costs $1.10 × 5 = $5.50/week. By making your own breakfast, you would save $10 − $5.50 = $4.50/week.

Culinary Lab

20. **Prepare an Omelet** Students should answer each question honestly, giving concrete reasons for their decisions. The evaluations of each student in the group should be somewhat similar in their answers.

Garde Manger Basics

SECTION 18.1 What Is Garde Manger?

SECTION 18.2 Salads and Salad Dressings

SECTION 18.3 Cheese

SECTION 18.4 Cold Platters

Classroom Solutions

Print Resources

- Student Edition
- Instructor Annotated Edition
- Lab Manual
- Lab Manual IAE

Technology Resources

ExamView® *ExamView® Assessment Suite* CD
Create and print unit and chapter tests.

Lesson Planner Plus **Lesson Planner Plus CD** provides access to teacher resources in one package.

Presentation Plus! provides visual teaching aids for every section.

Online Learning Center includes resources and activities for students and teachers. Also includes the **Online Student Edition**.

Interactive Student Edition

SECTION 18.1 What is Garde Manger?

Section Overview

In this section, students will learn which items a garde manger chef needs to consider in preparing food. They will also learn to identify and use the tools and techniques of a garde manger. Finally, they will learn the different types of garnishes and how to prepare them.

FOCUS

Bell Ringer Activity

Plate and Tray Presentation Discuss with students what they think makes an attractive plate or tray presentation. What types of colors, shapes, and items can make the difference between a dull, unappealing presentation and an interesting, appealing one? How does the tableware affect the presentation? Explain that in this section, students will learn more about presenting cold items and hors d'oeuvres.

D Develop Concepts

Main Idea Discuss the main idea with the students. Ask: In what settings would you eat foods prepared by a garde manger chef? In a restaurant, foods you might eat prepared by a garde manger chef include salads, sandwiches, and other cold foods. Additionally, you might eat foods prepared by a garde manger chef at a buffet or at a special event.

TEACH

S Skill Practice

Guided Practice

L1 List Have students list four guidelines a garde manger chef uses when menu planning. The four guidelines a garde manger chef uses when menu planning are economics, ingredient variety, color and texture, and practical aspects of customers and staff.

L2 Explain Ask students to explain how a garnish is used. A garnish is used to decorate a serving or plate of food. It should complement food and add nutritional value.

L3 Apply Have students design a plate that is garnished attractively and explain what the garnishes are made of, how they look, and the tools used to make them. Students should describe their plate thoroughly, as well as describe the garnishes and how they are made.

ASSESS

Quiz

Ask students to answer the following questions:

1. What is the garde manger chef's responsibility? The garde manger chef's responsibility is the planning, preparation, and artistic presentation of cold foods.

2. What is a brigade? A brigade is a team of kitchen workers with each member having a different job and expertise.

3. What is a quenelle? A quenelle is a purée of chopped food formed into a shape.

RETEACH

R Reading Strategy

Demonstration Have each student choose a tool and an appropriate ingredient. Have them read about their tool in the book and, if they like, in outside sources as well. Then, students should demonstrate for the class how to use their selected tool to make a garnish. Students should be able to successfully determine how to use the various garnishing tools based on their reading and research. They should then be able to incorporate and pass on their knowledge through demonstration.

U Universal Access

Students with Learning Disabilities Ask students to imagine that they are preparing a potato salad for a banquet. Ask for volunteers to describe how they would garnish the potato salad. Answers will vary, but common garnishes for potato salad include tomato slices, egg slices, parsley, paprika, scallions, or lemon.

ASSESS

 Lab Manual

Assign the Section 18.1 Activities.

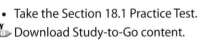 Online Study Tools

Have students go to the Online Learning Center at **glencoe.com** to:

- Take the Section 18.1 Practice Test.
- Download Study-to-Go content.

SECTION 18.1 After You Read Answer Key
Review Key Concepts

1. The garde manger chef considers the cost of ingredients and time required to prepare specific dishes, the use of different food items to keep the menu interesting, the use of different colors and textures to increase variety, the appeal of the food, and the ability of the brigade to prepare the dishes in a timely manner.

Practice Culinary Academics

2. **Science** Explain to the students that freeze-dried foods are preserved by removing the food's moisture. Once the food's moisture is removed, bacteria cannot survive or grow.

Freeze-dried fruits and vegetables can make a unique garnish, or they can be reconstituted with water for use in salads or other dishes.

3. **English Language Arts** Charts should provide accurate pictures and descriptions for each of the garnishes. Hang the charts on the classroom wall for students to use as a guide when they prepare garnishes.

4. **Social Studies** Garde manger means keeping to eat in French. This was the name that was given to cold rooms and cellars in French castles where preserved foods were stored. A trusted member of the household managed this room and issued food items from the room. The modern role of garde manger chef evolved from this position.

5. **Mathematics** A ¾-inch melon baller produces spheres with a diameter of ¾ inch, or a radius of ½ × ¾ = ⅜ inches (or 0.375 inches). The volume of one sphere, in cubic inches, is (4 × 3.14 × 0.375 × 0.375 × 0.375) ÷ 3 = 0.220781 cubic inches. The volume of four spheres 4 × 0.220781 = 0.883125 cubic inches. Multiply by 1.1 to convert to tablespoons: 1.1 × 0.883125 = 0.971438 ≈ 1. Each table should receive about 1 tablespoon of butter.

 **Professional Development** MINI CLIP **Math** Problem Solving with Algebra and Measurement

CLOSE

Culminating Activity

Prepare Garnishes Prepare garnishes using the following foods: butter, radishes, carrots, oranges, and melons. Be sure to follow safe knife handling and garnishing tool techniques. Display the garnishes on plates so that students can see everyone's work. Have students discuss their favorite garnishes with one another.

SECTION 18.2 Salads and Salad Dressings

Section Overview

In this section, students will learn how to prepare salads made from a variety of greens. They will learn about each of the main types of salad served during a meal. They will also learn how to build a salad. Finally, they will learn how to prepare salad dressings.

Lesson Plan CHAPTER 18

FOCUS

Bell Ringer Activity

Choose Greens Bring in examples of different types of greens. Speak with the class about the various types of greens, and give tips and advice about how to select quality greens. Explain what to look for, and have the class sample the different greens so they begin to understand the different flavors and textures.

D Develop Concepts

Main Idea Discuss the main idea with the students. Ask: What kinds of salads can you think of besides mixed green salads? Answers will vary, but students might describe various pasta salads, potato salads, whole-grain salads, bean salads, fruit salads, or vegetable salads.

TEACH

S Skill Practice

Guided Practice

L1 List Have students list the three guidelines for planning a salad. The three guidelines for planning a salad are combine colors, textures, and flavors that look and taste good together; do not repeat ingredients from other courses; and match the dressing to the ingredients.

L2 Explain Ask students to explain the function of a salad dressing. The function of salad dressing is to add flavor to a salad and to hold the parts of the salad together.

L3 Apply Have students practice washing and preparing greens for a salad. Students should practice adequately washing, drying, and preparing greens to be assembled into a salad.

 **Professional Development** MINI CLIP **ELL** Graphic Organizers

ASSESS

Quiz

Ask students to answer the following questions:

1. How can you refresh slightly wilted greens? You can refresh slightly wilted greens by submerging them in ice water for 30 to 60 minutes.

2. What is an emulsion? An emulsion is a mixture of two liquids that do not typically blend.

3. Why is drying the greens an important step in salad preparation? Drying the greens is important because it ensures that the dressing will stick to the greens and that your salad does not turn out too watery.

RETEACH

U Universal Access

Students with Hearing Impairments Divide students into teams, and have them evaluate the different types of salads. Then, have them locate a recipe for each type of salad. Out of the recipes they have located, have them choose one and prepare five servings of their chosen salad. Have the teams explain their choices. Finally, have students taste and evaluate one another's salads. Students should use the information in the section to help them choose the type of salad they wish to prepare and then to aid them in preparing the recipe.

C Critical Thinking

Improve a Salad Ask students to imagine that their employer has asked them to improve their restaurant's standard house salad to make a more upscale salad for a catered function. Ask students to describe methods and suggestions to make a standard house salad more flavorful, attractive, and appealing. Student answers will vary, but suggestions may include adding flavorful greens like arugula or watercress; adding herbs or specialty items such as fennel or endive; garnishing the salad with colorful items such as edible flower petals; or creating a more flavorful salad dressing.

ASSESS

Lab Manual

Assign the Section 18.2 Activities.

Online Study Tools

Have students go to the Online Learning Center at glencoe.com to:

- Take the Section 18.2 Practice Test.
- Download Study-to-Go content.

SECTION 18.2 **After You Read Answer Key**

Review Key Concepts

1. Salad arrangements consist of a foundation, a body, a garnish, and a salad dressing that are arranged attractively on a plate.

2. It is best to use up salad greens every day. However, if you need to store greens, keep them in their original packaging, and store them at three to four degrees above freezing, away from ripening fruits.

Chapter 18 Lesson Plan   TM183

3. Fruit dressings come in different flavors including sweet, tart, and spicy. They may be made with puréed fruit or fruit juice.

Practice Culinary Academics

4. Social Studies Rice vinegars are usually found in Asian recipes but can be found in many other recipes as well. Discuss with the class how ingredients and recipes move from place to place as people of different cultures settle around the world and how increased globalization has resulted in different types of foods spreading across the world.

5. Mathematics Originally, $0.4 \times 50 = 20$ customers ordered bleu cheese dressing, while $0.3 \times 50 = 15$ ordered vinaigrette dressing and Thousand Island dressing. The new total for vinaigrette dressing becomes $15 + 10 = 25$, while the total number of customers becomes $50 + 10 = 60$. So $25 \div 60 = 0.4167 \approx 42\%$ ordered vinaigrette dressing, $20 \div 60 = 0.3333 \approx 33\%$ ordered bleu cheese dressing, and $15 \div 60 = 0.25 = 25\%$ ordered Thousand Island dressing.

CLOSE

Culminating Activity

Prepare a Dressing In teams, have students prepare one of the following dressings: vinaigrette dressing, fatty dressing, cooked dressing, or fruit dressing. Then, have the students evaluate the dressing and make any necessary adjustments. Next, have them serve the dressing on mixed salad greens to another team in the class. Finally, have the teams evaluate one another's dressing.

SECTION 18.3 Cheese

Section Overview

In this section, students will learn how to identify the different types of cheeses and how they are produced. They will also learn how each type of cheese is best used. Finally, they will learn how to store cheese so it is sanitary and well-preserved.

FOCUS

🔔 Bell Ringer Activity

Cheese Tasting Have students taste a variety of cheeses that are often used in foodservice. While students are tasting the cheeses, identify the different types (including hard, firm, semisoft, soft, fresh soft, ripened soft, and specialty) so they become familiar with them. Discuss the various ways cheeses are used in food production and in garde manger.

D Develop Concepts

Main Idea Discuss the main idea with the students. Ask: How would you describe the flavor of the cheese you like? Answers will vary depending on students' preferences, but students may come up with several adjectives to describe their favorite cheese, such as salty, pungent, nutty, buttery, stinky, or rich, among others.

 **Professional Development**   MINI CLIP **ELL** Group Discusions

TEACH

S Skill Practice
Guided Practice

L1 List Have students list the different types of cheese. The different types of cheeses are hard, firm, semisoft, soft, fresh soft, ripened soft, and specialty.

L2 Explain Ask students to explain how to bring out the full flavor of ripened cheese. To bring out the full flavor of ripened cheese, take it out of the refrigerator 30 to 60 minutes before serving.

L3 Apply In teams, have students prepare a cheese-based food product that could be served as part of a cold buffet. Students should be able to successfully prepare the item, and the item prepared must be able to be served cold.

ASSESS

Quiz

Ask students to answer the following questions:

1. What happens during the ripening process of cheese? During the ripening process, healthful bacteria and mold change the cheese's texture and flavor. Ripening can occur from the surface of the cheese to the inside or from the inside of the cheese outward.

2. Why is an emulsifier used in processed cheese? An emulsifier is added so that the different cheese products combine uniformly.

3. What is the cheddaring process? During the cheddaring process, slabs of cheese are stacked and turned to squeeze out the whey.

RETEACH

R Reading Strategy

Conduct Research Have students research the history of cheesemaking. Then, have students work in teams to research the various categories of cheese. Next, teams should locate foodservice hors d'oeuvre recipes for the cheeses in their category. Finally, they should share what they discovered with the rest of the class.

Students should work together to discover more about both the history of cheesemaking and about the types of cheese. They should choose a cheese that they think they will like and that they can work with. As they share recipes, the students should also share what they learned from their research about cheesemaking.

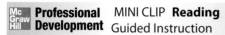
Professional Development MINI CLIP **Reading** Guided Instruction

U Universal Access

Students with Physical Challenges Ask students to imagine that they are planning a cheese tray for a reception. What factors would they consider as they plan their tray? Answers will vary, but factors that the students may want to consider could include selecting cheeses for shape and color, ease of cutting, type of utensils needed, and what accompaniments would go well with the chosen cheeses.

ASSESS

Lab Manual

Assign the Section 18.3 Activities.

Online Study Tools

Have students go to the Online Learning Center at **glencoe.com** to:

- Take the Section 18.3 Practice Test.
- Download Study-to-Go content.

SECTION 18.3 After You Read Answer Key

Review Key Concepts

1. Soft cheeses have a thin skin and a creamy center. Farmer's cheese has a slightly tangy flavor and is milky white in color. Some soft cheeses are ripened, while others are not.

Practice Culinary Academics

2. **Science** Generally, cheeses that contain more moisture will begin to mold first. The types of cheese that grow mold more quickly might be best purchased in small quantities and used right away.

3. **English Language Arts** Scripts should contain accurate advice about cheese. The dialogue should be written to sound natural, performances should be clear and well spoken, and the scripts should be appropriate for the media of radio.

4. **Social Studies** Students' presentations should show cheesemaking processes from different

areas of the United States or from other parts of the world. The presentations should include information and images of the process as well as information and images of the different dairy sources (cow, sheep, goat, and others).

5. **Mathematics** For the Cheddar: $\$7.50 \div 16 = \$0.46875$/ounce, or $\$0.46875 \times 4 = \$1.88$ for 4 ounces. For the Stilton: $\$8.99 \div 16 = \$0.561875$/ounce, or $\$0.561875 \times 3 = \$1.69$ for 3 ounces. For the brie: $\$13.99 \div 16 = \$0.874375$/ounce, or $\$0.874375 \times 2 = \$1.75$ for 2 ounces. $\$1.88 + \$1.69 + \$1.75 = \$5.32$ total cost.

CLOSE

Culminating Activity

Cheese Tasting Obtain several different types of cheese. Try to get at least one of each of the types of cheese described in the section. Have students taste and identify the different types of cheese. Have them share what they have learned about cheese and cheesemaking as compared to what they knew at the beginning of the section.

SECTION 18.4 Cold Platters

Section Overview

In this section, students will learn what hors d'oeuvres are and when they are served. They will learn the main types of hors d'oeuvres. They will also learn how to prepare fancy sandwiches, fruit and cheese trays, and cold hors d'oeuvre platters. Finally, they will learn what a relish tray is and what kind of dips accompany a relish tray.

FOCUS

Bell Ringer Activity

How Easy Is It? Ask students if any of them have prepared a cold platter before. For those students who have not, ask them how difficult they think it would be to prepare one. For those students who have, ask them to talk about how easy or difficult it was to prepare. Tell students that in this section, they will learn that while cold platters may seem simple, a lot of planning and preparation goes into a good cold platter.

D Develop Concepts

Main Idea Discuss the main idea with the students. Ask: In what types of settings may a cold platter be a desirable option? Cold platters are good options for parties and events where there are many guests and food will be served continuously over a long period of time.

TEACH

S Skill Practice

Guided Practice

L1 List Have students list the two optional parts of a canapé. *The two optional parts of a canapé are a liner and a garnish.*

L2 Explain Ask students to explain what aspic is. *Aspic is a savory jelly made from meat or vegetable stock and gelatin.*

L3 Apply Have students plan a simple antipasto platter. Have them draw a picture of their platter and label all of the components. *Students' drawings of their platters should contain common ingredients found on an antipasto platter and demonstrate that they thought their platter through based on what they learned in the book.*

ASSESS

Quiz

Ask students to answer the following questions:

1. **What are the parts of a canapé?** *The parts of a canapé are the base, the topping, and the spread.*

2. **What are the main elements of a cold platter?** *The main elements of a cold platter are the centerpiece, the serving portions, and the garnish.*

3. **Why are fruit and cheese often paired on platters?** *Fruit and cheese are often paired on platters because their flavors complement each other. Additionally, pairing fruits and cheeses on a platter enhances eye appeal.*

RETEACH

U Universal Access

Students with Physical Challenges Have students investigate fancy sandwich, hors d'oeuvre, and dip recipes. Then, have them pool their recipes and work together to plan a cold food buffet for a class party. *Students should use what they learned in the section to locate appropriate recipes. Then, they should work together to plan a buffet that they could prepare for a class party. If you want, plan this party and let the class prepare the cold food buffet.*

C Critical Thinking

Plan a Buffet Ask students to imagine that they are teaching a class on preparing a a cold platter buffet, including preparing the food and plating the trays. What factors would they consider when planning

the buffet? *Answers will vary, but examples might include the ease of picking up and eating the food with your hands; how to arrange platters attractively; how to season each hors d'oeuvre; what shapes, sizes, and number of items to have on each tray; and the appropriate sauces and utensils.*

ASSESS

 ExamView® Assessment Suite
Create a test for this chapter.

Lab Manual

Assign the Section 18.4 Activities.

Online Study Tools

Have students go to the Online Learning Center at **glencoe.com** to:

- Take the Section 18.4 Practice Test.
- Download Study-to-Go content.

SECTION 18.4 After You Read Answer Key

Review Key Concepts

1. First, cut several day-old loaves of bread into slices lengthwise with a slicing machine. Next, cut the crust from the slices using a serrated knife. Then, roll each piece flat with a rolling pin to less than $\frac{1}{8}$-inch thick.

2. A typical antipasto tray includes cold meats, assorted cheeses, olives, and marinated vegetables. It may also include fruits.

Practice Culinary Academics

3. **English Language Arts** Proposals should be written in an appropriate tone for a business communication. They should provide details on what types of foods will be on the platter, as well as their preparation and presentation. The diagram should clearly indicate where each food item will rest on the platter.

4. **Social Studies** Vietnamese summer rolls, carpaccio, baba ghanoush, hummus, and tzatziki are all items that could be served as hors d'oeuvres or dips on a cold platter. Students may find other items that could be adapted to make a fancy sandwich or other hors d'oeuvre.

5. **Mathematics** The area of each triangle is $3\frac{1}{8}$ square inches (3.125 square inches). The base and height of each triangle will be the same length as the sides of the square, or $2\frac{1}{2}$ inches ($\frac{5}{2}$ in.). The area of each triangle is $(\frac{1}{2})(\frac{5}{2})(\frac{5}{2}) = \frac{25}{8} = 3\frac{1}{8}$ square inches.

CLOSE

Culminating Activity

Create a Platter Divide students into teams. Have each team create a cold platter that would be appropriate for a graduation party. As a team, they should plan the items for the platter, preparation, and presentation. Then, they should prepare the platter and present it for evaluation. Teams should be able to explain why their platter is appropriate. At the end, have teams sample one another's platters.

Chapter Review and Applications

Vocabulary Review

1. Read the definitions of the vocabulary aloud. As you read each definition, ask students to write their sentences.

Review Key Concepts

2. The garde manger chef and brigade prepare cold foods, including hors d'oeuvres, salads, canapés, fancy sandwiches, and cold platters. They must plan, prepare, and plate these dishes.

3. The main types of salads are appetizer, accompaniment, main-course, separate-course, and dessert salads.

4. To prepare a salad, choose quality greens, clean them and tear into bite-size pieces, and build from the base up.

5. The different types of salad dressings include vinaigrette (vinegar and oil), fatty dressings (including mayonnaise or dairy products), cooked dressings (with a cooked ingredient and thickening agent), and fruit dressings (with puréed fruit or fruit juice).

6. Five main cheese categories are: hard (dense and dry), firm (not brittle, hard, or soft, may be flaky or dense), semisoft (smooth, easy to slice, may be buttery or softer, veined, and pungent), soft (thick skin, creamy center), and specialty (processed or cold-packed). Cheeses are well wrapped and stored in a refrigerator. Soft cheeses are loosely wrapped in greaseproof or waxed paper.

7. Canapés: Cut bread into a basic shape; toast; cover bread with spread and/or liner; add toppings and garnish. Rolled fancy sandwich: Use a slicer to cut lengthwise slices of day-old bread; cut off crust; roll bread flat; cover bread with spread; place interior items at one end of bread and roll tightly; wrap in plastic and refrigerate for several hours; once cold, unwrap and cut into $\frac{1}{2}$-inch slices.

8. Season items carefully. Seasoning should complement, not overpower, the flavor. Slice, shape, and portion items. Consider the overall color, shape, and look of the platter. Include sauces and utensils.

C Critical Thinking

9. Factors may include ingredient cost and preparation time. You may want to choose ingredients that complement the main course. You might consider the color and texture of foods in both courses and the customers' preferences.

10. You might choose a heavier salad, since fish is a light dish. A pasta or bean salad, or a green salad with added cheese or nuts might be appropriate choices.

Academic Skills

11. **English Language Arts** In addition to words found in this chapter, such as crudités, tournée, or quenelle, a garde manger chef might use the words pâté, charcuterie, terrine, chaud-froid, and others. Have students explain what the words they find mean in English.

12. **Science** Melting point is the point at which a substance changes from solid to liquid. The more fat a cheese has, the lower its melting point. Low-fat cheeses take longer to melt, or may not melt at all. Some cheeses, like halloumi, are heated and partially cooked in their production, so they will not melt.

13. **Mathematics** It will take them about 8.57 minutes to finish cutting the four blocks of cheese. Working together, Robyn and Antonio can cut $\frac{1}{15} + \frac{1}{20} = \frac{4}{60} + \frac{3}{60} = \frac{7}{60}$ of the block in 1 minute. If $\frac{7}{60} = 1/x$, then $x = \frac{60}{7}$ minutes $\approx$ 8.57 minutes.

Certification Prep

14. c. main-course salad
15. a. hard cheese

Real-World Skills and Applications

16. Self-Management Skills Factors to consider include how the salad would work as part of a meal, whether it could be a meal on its own, how the salad would be served and presented, and the cost. Students should describe the salad, explain its nutritional value, and describe potential buyers of the salad.

17. Interpersonal and Collaborative Skills Encourage teams to create ads that are catchy, informative, and appealing. Students should work together to come up with the characteristics of their cheese and decide how to present it to appeal to consumers. Ads should contain accurate, truthful information.

18. Technology Applications Students should use their online research skills to locate a variety of salad recipes. To make a more attractive recipe book, students may want to type the recipes.

19. Financial Literacy The first purchase was less expensive, but $1.25 was wasted (.25 × $4.99). The second choice was more cost-effective because although the Cheddar cost $1.00 more, none was wasted. The extra $1.00 is less than the $1.25 wasted.

Culinary Lab

20. Create Garnishes Students should recognize what did and did not work when creating their garnishes. They should understand whether the tool chosen was appropriate for the garnish ingredient. They should also suggest ways to improve the garnishes.

Sandwiches and Appetizers

SECTION 19.1 Sandwich-Making Basics   SECTION 19.3 Hot Appetizers

SECTION 19.2 Sandwiches

Classroom Solutions

Print Resources

- Student Edition
- Instructor Annotated Edition
- Lab Manual
- Lab Manual IAE

Technology Resources

ExamView *ExamView® Assessment Suite* **CD**
Create and print unit and chapter tests.

Lesson Planner Plus **Lesson Planner Plus CD** provides access to teacher resources in one package.

Presentation Plus! provides visual teaching aids for every section.

Online Learning Center includes resources and activities for students and teachers. Also includes the **Online Student Edition**.

Interactive Student Edition

SECTION 19.1 Sandwich-Making Basics

Section Overview

In this section, students will learn about the different types of sandwiches. They will also learn about the different types of breads and spreads used in sandwiches. Finally, they will learn about the different sandwich fillings, including meats, poultry, seafood, and cheese.

FOCUS

🔔 Bell Ringer Activity

Preparation Demonstration Ask the cafeteria if your students can come and observe the staff as they prepare lunch one day. Have the students observe the process of preparing food items in quantity. Explain to them that in this section, they will learn how to prepare sandwiches in quantity.

D Develop Concepts

Main Idea Discuss the main idea with the students. Ask: What types of skills might be needed to make sandwiches? Answers will vary, but skills needed to make sandwiches might include organization skills so one can work quickly; attention to detail to make sure ingredients are uniform; and cooking skills for hot sandwiches.

TEACH

S Skill Practice

Guided Practice

L1 List Have students list the three main types of sandwich spreads. The three main types of sandwich spreads are butter, mayonnaise, and vegetable purées.

L2 Explain Ask students to explain how sandwiches should be cut for presentation. For presentation, sandwiches should be cut into shapes as close to the serving time as possible. Be sure not to push down on the sandwich when cutting, as this will leave an imprint and compress the sandwich.

L3 Apply Have students make a simple sandwich, such as a peanut butter and jelly sandwich, and then practice cutting the sandwich following the guidelines. Students should practice cutting sandwiches neatly to preserve the presentation until they feel comfortable with this skill.

ASSESS

Quiz

Ask students to answer the following questions:

1. What guidelines should be followed when choosing bread for sandwiches? Bread for sandwiches should not be too hard or crusty, should not overpower the filling, and should be thick enough to hold the filling without tearing.

2. What is pita? Pita is a round-shaped flatbread cut open to form a pocket.

3. What guidelines should you follow when handling cheese? When handling cheese, you should wash your hands well, keep the workspace and equipment clean and sanitized, and keep the cheese tightly wrapped in plastic wrap in the refrigerator.

 **Professional Development** MINI CLIP **Reading** Differentiated Activities

RETEACH

R Reading Strategy

Demonstrate Spreads Have students review the types of spreads used on sandwiches. Then, have them choose one spread and demonstrate for the class how to prepare that spread. They may either demonstrate by preparing it themselves or by describing how to prepare it. After reading the section and some recipes, students should understand how to prepare a simple spread. They should then be able to demonstrate the process to their classmates.

U Universal Access

Gifted Students Ask students to imagine that they are working at a sandwich station. They have been assigned to the lunch rush for the first time. Have them explain how they would set up their work station to prepare for the busy shift. Answers will vary, but possible answers might include: organize the work station so that all necessary utensils and ingredients are close at hand and within your range of motion; include utensils such as chef's and bread knives, serving spoons and scoops, spatulas for spreading fillings and spreads, as well as a toaster, tongs, and cutting board.

ASSESS

Lab Manual

Assign the Section 19.1 Activities.

 Online Study Tools

Have students go to the Online Learning Center at **glencoe.com** to:

- Take the Section 19.1 Practice Test.
- Download Study-to-Go content.

SECTION 19.1 After You Read Answer Key

Review Key Concepts

1. Open-face sandwiches have one or two slices of bread placed side by side, with the spread and fillings on top of each. Closed sandwiches have the bread slices stacked on top of each other, with the filling and spread in between the slices of bread.

2. When choosing breads, select breads that are not too hard or crusty and that do not overpower the fillings. Also, be sure to choose breads that are thick enough to hold the sandwich filling without tearing or breaking apart.

3. Appropriate sandwich accompaniments include chips, French fries, vegetables, greens, pickles, olives, or fruit.

Practice Culinary Academics

4. English Language Arts The first sandwich is attributed to a Jewish rabbi, who put food items between pieces of matzoh at Passover. During the Middle Ages, thick pieces of bread were used as dishes. The sandwich grew popular in the United States as bread became a staple in the American diet. Students should compare American sandwiches with typical sandwiches of other countries, such as the Italian panini or the Vietnamese bahn mi.

5. Mathematics Each slice of bread should be $2\frac{5}{8}$ inches wide. Students should convert the 7-foot length into inches by multiplying $7 \times 12 = 84$ inches. Dividing 84 inches by 32 yields the per-slice measurement: $84 \div 32 = 2\frac{20}{32}$, which can be reduced to $2\frac{5}{8}$ inches.

 **Professional Development** MINI CLIP **Math** Fraction Computation

CLOSE

Culminating Activity

Quantity Preparation Practice Group students into teams, and have them prepare 15 sandwiches per team. Have them choose from the following sandwich types: a) one meat and one cheese; b) tuna, chicken, or ham salad; c) more than one meat. Ask them to use a variety of breads and spreads. Provide feedback.

SECTION 19.2 Sandwiches

Section Overview

In this section, students will learn the basics of preparing both hot sandwiches and cold sandwiches. They will learn about the different types of hot sandwiches, how to prepare them, and how to plate them. They will also learn about the different types of cold sandwiches and how to prepare, plate, and garnish them.

FOCUS

🔔 Bell Ringer Activity

What Is Your Favorite? Ask students to discuss their favorite sandwiches. Is their favorite sandwich hot or cold? Do they know how to prepare their favorite sandwich? Have students describe their favorite sandwich and how to make it. What are the similarities and differences between the types of sandwiches they like?

D Develop Concepts

Main Idea Discuss the main idea with the students. Ask: What kind of ingredients might be used in both hot and cold sandwiches? Answers will vary, but may include cheeses, meats, onions, tomatoes, lettuce, various other vegetables, mustard, mayonnaise, and various other spreads.

TEACH

S Skill Practice

Guided Practice

L1 List Have students list the different types of hot sandwiches. The different types of hot sandwiches are basic sandwiches, grilled sandwiches, and fried sandwiches.

L2 Explain Ask students to explain why you should not prepare salad sandwiches in advance. You should not prepare salad sandwiches in advance because the moisture from the salad will soak into the bread, and the sandwich bread will become soggy.

L3 Apply Have students find five sandwich recipes and then list a garnish and one accompaniment that they would serve with each sandwich. Answers will vary, but garnishes should have a shape, texture, or color that adds interest, and accompaniments should complement the sandwich ingredients.

ASSESS

Quiz

Ask students to answer the following questions:

1. When making grilled sandwiches, why do you need to make sure the fillings are cooked? Since the fillings will only be heated, and not completely cooked at the time the sandwich is grilled, they must be cooked beforehand.

2. What is jus? Jus is the natural juices derived from roasting that can later be used as a sauce or dip.

3. How does a club sandwich differ from a closed sandwich? Club sandwiches use three slices of bread and are cut into four triangles. Closed sandwiches use only two slices of bread and are usually only cut in half.

RETEACH

U Universal Access

Students with Hearing Impairments After reading the section on preparing hot and cold sandwiches, have students create an original sandwich. Then, have them write out the recipe for their sandwich and encourage them to prepare and test their sandwich. If possible, they should have friends, family, or fellow students try their sandwich and provide feedback. Students should use the advice in the section, combined with their own creativity, to come up with an original sandwich creation. They should then translate their creation into a recipe format. If possible, they should make their original sandwich and have others try it. Find out what responses students received.

C Critical Thinking

Plating Puzzle Ask students to imagine that they are working the sandwich station and an order comes in for a hot, open-faced sandwich. Ask students to discuss what they would keep in mind as they plate the sandwich. Answers will vary, but some things to keep in mind when plating a hot, open-face sandwich include not letting the sauce run onto any of the cold items on the plate; being sure not to over-sauce items; making sure the sauce is not too thick or too thin; and putting garnishes on the side instead of directly on the sandwich.

ASSESS

 ExamView Assessment Suite CD
Create a test for this chapter.

Lab Manual
Assign the Section 19.2 Activities.

Online Study Tools
Have students go to the Online Learning Center at **glencoe.com** to:

- Take the Section 19.2 Practice Test.
- Download Study-to-Go content.

SECTION 19.2 After You Read Answer Key

Review Key Concepts

1. Hot sandwiches may be served either open-face or closed. Hot turkey or crab sandwiches are usually served open-face with gravy or sauce spooned over the top. Hot sandwiches are often served with a side salad, soup, or French fries.

2. Choose items whose shape, color, and texture add interest to the dish. Some popular garnishes include fruit, radishes, and parsley.

Practice Culinary Academics

3. **English Language Arts** Answers will vary, but some additional examples of eponyms include: Alzheimer's disease, boycott, diesel, Honda, Jacuzzi, leotard, Mattel, mausoleum, the Morse code, and shrapnel.

4. **Science** Sprouts can be grown in about two weeks, no matter what the season is. Students' evaluations should be descriptive about how they thought the sprouts affected the taste and texture of the sandwich.

5. **Mathematics** The angle of each slice on the first pizza is $360° \div 10 = 36°$. For the second pizza, since each angle is $45°$, there must be $360° \div 45° = 8$ slices of pizza.

Professional Development MINI CLIP **Math** Adjacent Angles

CLOSE

Culminating Activity

Prepare a Hot Sandwich Have students prepare a hot sandwich with the ingredients and equipment on hand in your foods lab. Have students present their sandwiches and describe possible garnishes and accompaniments for their sandwiches. Then, have students sample one another's hot creations and provide feedback.

SECTION 19.3 Hot Appetizers

Section Overview

In this section, students will learn how to make hot appetizers, such as brochettes, filled pastry shells, meatballs, rumaki, stuffed potato skins, and chicken wings. They will also learn how to plate and serve hot appetizers, including table service, buffet service, and butler service.

FOCUS

Bell Ringer Activity

Guest Speaker If possible, have a restaurant manager come in to speak to the class about how appetizers fit into their menu and business. Ask them to talk about the percent of sales from appetizers and how it affects their overhead. Also, ask them to discuss the benefit to the restaurant when customers order appetizers.

D Develop Concepts

Main Idea Discuss the main idea with the students. Ask: Why would someone want to have an appetizer? Customers order appetizers for various reasons, including because appetizers stimulate the appetite, because it allows customers to sample various dishes in addition to their entrée, and because appetizers provide something to eat while waiting for the main course.

TEACH

S Skill Practice
Guided Practice

L1 List Have students list the main foods that are served on brochettes. The main foods that are served on brochettes are meat, poultry, fish, and vegetables.

L2 Explain Ask students to explain how to make brochettes from scratch. Before assembling, soak the bamboo skewers in water to help keep them from burning. Put a combination of meat, poultry, fish, and vegetables on a skewer, marinate them, and cook them.

L3 Apply Split students into groups of two, and have each group practice making brochettes from scratch. Be sure to look at the finished result and give feedback. Students should become comfortable making brochettes from scratch. They should follow the steps listed in the text including cutting all items into consistent shapes and sizes and soaking the bamboo skewers in water to prevent burning. Be sure to provide feedback.

ASSESS

Quiz

Ask students to answer the following questions:

1. **What is the difference between an appetizer and an hors d'oeuvre?** Appetizers are served as the first course of a meal, while hors d'oeuvres are small bites of food served before the meal or at a separate reception.

2. **Why are many appetizers prepared just before service?** Many appetizers are prepared just before service because this practice keeps them fresh in appearance and results in their being moist but not soggy.

3. **Why is presentation important when serving appetizers?** Presentation is very important when serving appetizers because appetizers need to be visually stimulating, with contrasts in color and texture.

RETEACH

R Reading Strategy

Appetizer Buffet After reading this section, have students plan and prepare a small appetizer buffet featuring the appetizer types they learned about in this section. Have them choose a style and serve the appetizers in that style to a group of teachers or another class. Students should use the advice in the chapter to create a delicious and attractive appetizer buffet. They can either serve it as a buffet or choose to serve through butler style or through table service. Have the group that they serve their appetizers to provide feedback on both taste and presentation.

 **Professional Development** MINI CLIP **Reading** Flexible Groupings

U Universal Access

Students with Learning Disabilities Break students into groups, and have them discuss the most appropriate styles of service for the following appetizers: meatballs, filled pastry shells, rumaki, stuffed potato skins, and shrimp brochettes. Answers will vary, but appropriate service styles include buffet service for meatballs; table service for filled pastry shells; butler service for rumaki; table service for stuffed potato skins; and buffet service for shrimp brochettes.

ASSESS

 ExamView Assessment Suite
Create a test for this chapter.

Lab Manual

Assign the Section 19.3 Activities.

Online Study Tools

Have students go to the Online Learning Center at **glencoe.com** to:

- Take the Section 19.3 Practice Test.
- Download Study-to-Go content.

SECTION 19.3 After You Read Answer Key

Review Key Concepts

1. A meatball is a ball of ground beef, poultry, veal, pork, or a combination. Meatballs are usually served with a sauce.

2. In table service, hot appetizers are served to each individual at the table. In contrast, in butler service, appetizers are carried on a tray and served to standing guests.

Practice Culinary Academics

3. **English Language Arts** The public service announcement should clearly, creatively, and accurately reflect a persuasive pitch for serving more healthful appetizers along with multiple examples of healthful appetizers.

4. **Science** Answers should focus on the ways in which the appetizer stimulates the senses and the appetite. One important factor will be portion size, since an appetizer should be large enough to provide a teaser, but not so large that it lessens the appetite and takes away from the enjoyment of the entrée.

5. **Mathematics** Carlo needs approximately 7 cups of the meatball mixture. The radius of each meatball is half of its diameter, or 0.5 inches. The volume of one meatball = $(\frac{1}{3})(3.14)(0.5)(0.5)(0.5) \approx 0.523$ cubic inches. The volume of all 200 meatballs is $200 \times 0.523 = 104.6$ cubic inches. Converting to cups results in $104.6 \div 14.4 = 7.26 \approx 7$ cups.

CLOSE

Culminating Activity

Plan a Display Ask students to imagine that a large corporation is looking for a caterer to provide appetizers for 100 people at an event. Divide students into teams, and have them prepare a presentation for the corporation that describes a display of hot appetizers they would prepare for the event. They should imagine that they are competing with the other teams for the job. You may want to turn this into a contest and choose a winner.

Chapter Review and Applications

Vocabulary Review

1. Students should write complete sentences using each term correctly.

Review Key Concepts

2. The different types are closed, open-face, triple-decker, finger sandwiches, and wraps.

3. Sandwich breads include sliced loaves (white, rye, and wheat); rolls (hot dog, hamburger, and Kaiser); flatbreads (pita and focaccia); or specialty breads (tortilla, bagels, croissants, chapatti, phyllo, and crêpes). Spreads include butter, mayonnaise, and vegetable purées.

4. Fillings include meat, poultry, fish, cheese, or vegetables and should be prepared, cooked, and sliced carefully. Grilled and marinated vegetables make nutritious fillings. Cream cheese and chopped vegetables make a good filling for finger sandwiches.

5. First, cook hot meat fillings. Then, assemble the sandwich. Make sure the cold fillings are crisp and cold, or set to the side. Do not overload hot wraps. Place a grilled sandwich on a warm plate. It can be served either open-face or closed. Some sandwiches might have gravy or sauce on top. They might be served with a side salad, cup of soup, or potatoes.

6. Cold sandwiches consist of bread, spread, and fillings. Use the freshest bread possible. Mayonnaise or butter will keep moisture from wetting the bread. Other spreads, such as mustard, can add flavor. Do not prepare salad sandwiches in advance.

7. Hot appetizers include brochettes, filled pastry shells, meatballs, rumaki, and stuffed potato skins.

8. Methods of serving hot appetizers include table service, buffet service, and butler service.

C Critical Thinking

9. Possible answers include using leftovers in sandwiches or using equipment that guarantees consistent portion sizes.

10. Answers will vary. Students do not have to use all of the ingredients in a dish. They should develop appetizers that use one or more of the items.

Academic Skills

11. **English Language Arts** Students should effectively communicate verbally and by demonstrating how to create the chosen sandwich.

12. **Social Studies** There are many possible answers to this question. Appetizers should be small enough to be appropriate as an appetizer. Examples might be bruschetta, chicken wings, egg rolls, and pakora.

13. **Mathematics** The hamburger patties must be at least 5 inches in diameter. If the four corners of a rectangle intercept the outer edge of a circle, then a diagonal line running through two opposing corners will also represent the diameter of the circle. The diagonal line will also divide the rectangle into two right triangles, with the diagonal line acting as the hypotenuse of each. Since students know that one side of the rectangle is 3 inches and another is 4 inches, they can use those as a and b in the Pythagorean Theorem, and solve for c, which represents the hypotenuse and the diameter of the circle. Since $c^2 = a^2 + b^2$, we get $c^2 = 3^2 + 4^2$, or $c^2 = 9 + 16$, or $c^2 = 25$. Taking the square root of each side of the equation, $c = 5$.

Certification Prep

14. b. open-face sandwich

15. a. blanched bacon

Real-World Skills and Applications

16. **Management Skills** Examples of sandwiches that provide these groups: cheeseburger with lettuce and tomato; chicken wrap with mango and red peppers; grilled cheese sandwich with tomato; peanut butter and banana sandwich; or taco or burrito with lettuce, tomato, and cheese.

17. **Interpersonal and Collaborative Skills** Vegetarian appetizer examples include: brochette with mushroom, basil, mozzarella and bell pepper; whole-wheat spanakopita with spinach and cheese; eggplant/mushroom "meatballs;" vegetarian rumaki with mushrooms, water chestnuts and soy bacon; potato skins with broccoli, red pepper, and cheese; and tofu chicken wings with buffalo sauce.

18. **Technology Applications** The nutrition database should be created in a spreadsheet or database program and show calories and nutrient amounts for each sandwich included, based on the nutrition information students located for each ingredient.

19. **Financial Literacy** Divide $5.00 and $2.00 by 2 to get the cost for 4 oz. ($2.50 and $2.00). Divide $4.50 by 18 to get the cost per slice of bread. Multiply by 2 to get the cost for 2 slices ($0.50). Add those together to get the cost for each sandwich. $2.50 + $2.00 + $0.50 = $4.50. Each sandwich will cost $4.50 to make.

Culinary Lab

20. **Quantity Sandwich Production** Students should evaluate each plan for its pros and cons and locate potential problems within the plans before they are implemented. As a group, they should agree on the plan that is likely to be most successful. In the second discussion, they should recognize what went well and what did not and draw conclusions about planning and preparing sandwiches in quantity.

Stocks, Sauces, and Soups

SECTION 20.1 Stocks

SECTION 20.2 Sauces

SECTION 20.3 Soups

Classroom Solutions

Print Resources

- Student Edition
- Instructor Annotated Edition
- Lab Manual
- Lab Manual IAE

Technology Resources

ExamView® Assessment Suite CD
Create and print unit and chapter tests.

Lesson Planner Plus **Lesson Planner Plus CD** provides access to teacher resources in one package.

Presentation Plus! provides visual teaching aids for every section.

Online Learning Center includes resources and activities for students and teachers. Also includes the **Online Student Edition**.

Interactive Student Edition

SECTION 20.1 Stocks

Section Overview

In this section, students will learn about the four basic types of stocks: white stock, brown stock, fish stock, and vegetable stock. They will also learn the basic method for preparing stock, which is to simmer the ingredients in water for a set amount of time while skimming off the impurities, and then straining the stock.

FOCUS

Bell Ringer Activity

Introduction to Stock Ask students if they know the base ingredient of every soup. The answer is stock. Briefly explain what stock is and what the different types of stock are to the students. Then, see if students can figure out what type of stocks are the base of their favorite soups.

D Develop Concepts

Main Idea Discuss the main idea with the students. Ask: How might a good stock make a soup or sauce more flavorful? A well-made stock will have a rich flavor that will deepen the flavor of a soup or sauce it is used in.

TEACH

S Skill Practice

Guided Practice

L1 List Have students list the types of stock. The types of stock are white stock, brown stock, fish stock, and vegetable stock.

L2 Explain Ask students to explain how to cool stock. To cool stock, use a Rapid Kool container; pour the stock into a shallow container and place it in refrigerator; or vent the pot over a sink of cold water.

L3 Apply Have students prepare glazes out of stocks and then taste each one. Discuss as a class how each glaze might be used. Students should successfully create a glaze and understand how it could be used.

ASSESS

Quiz

Ask students to answer the following questions:

1. Why should the liquid be cold before starting a stock? The liquid should be cold before starting a stock to prevent cloudiness.

2. Why might you blanch bones before making a stock? You might blanch bones before making a stock to remove impurities from the bones so the stock will be clearer.

3. Why do you roast bones for a brown stock? You roast bones for a brown stock to brown

the bones, which will add color and flavor to the stock.

 **Professional Development** MINI CLIP **Reading** Focus Lesson

RETEACH

W Writing Support

Demonstrate Techniques Divide the students into three teams, and have each team demonstrate one of the following techniques: mirepoix, bouquet garni, and browning bones. Discuss the demonstrations as a class. Students should be able to take the techniques they learned in the section and put them into practice in a demonstration. The discussion should focus on how well the demonstrations conveyed how to perform the technique and any suggestions for improvement.

U Universal Access

Students with Visual Impairments Tell students to imagine that they have made a brown stock, but the flavor is very weak. How could they have produced a heartier stock? Answers will vary, but might include browning the bones more, cutting the bones into smaller pieces, cooking the stock longer, adding more mirepoix, adding a bouquet garni, or using less water.

ASSESS

Lab Manual

Assign the Section 20.1 Activities.

 Online Study Tools

Have students go to the Online Learning Center at **glencoe.com** to:

- Take the Section 20.1 Practice Test.
- Download Study-to-Go content.

SECTION 20.1 After You Read Answer Key

Review Key Concepts

1. Items that may be nourishing elements include any one or a combination of the following: fresh bones, meat trimmings, fish trimmings, or vegetables.

2. Fish stock is made by slowly cooking the bones of lean fish or shellfish in the same way as a white stock, but for a shorter length of time. One can sometimes add lemon juice or other acids to liquid and reduce it further to make a fish stock called a fumet.

Practice Culinary Academics

3. **English Language Arts** The stone soup is closest to a vegetable stock. Versions of the fable may differ, but some versions may not contain elements such as a complete mirepoix or a bouquet garni. The stone soup described in the fable may not be as flavorful as a stock prepared as described in the section.

4. **Science** When stock is started in cold water, the proteins in the ingredients escape as solids and coagulate slowly, and then rise to the top in large clumps. When stock is started in boiling water, protein particles remain separate. Because they are so small, they also remain suspended in the water rather than rise. These particles are then churned with fat droplets by the boiling and form an emulsion, which makes the stock cloudy.

5. **Mathematics** The pot contained 326.82 cubic inches of fish parts. The volume of the combined water and fish parts equals (3.14)(6 inches)(6 inches)(8 inches) = 904.32 cubic inches. The volume of the fish parts equals the volume of the mixture minus the volume of the water, or 904.32 cubic inches − 577.5 cubic inches = 326.82 cubic inches.

CLOSE

Culminating Activity

Comparing Stocks Divide students into four teams, and have each team make one of the following stocks: white stock, brown stock, fish stock, and vegetable stock. Then, have them heat up a commercial base and compare the fresh stock with the commercial stock. Ask students to describe the differences in color, flavor, texture, and nutritional value.

SECTION 20.2 Sauces

Section Overview

In this section, students will learn that there are five basic sauces, called mother sauces. They will also learn about other sauces, such as compound sauces, independent sauces, and sauces made from purées, meat juice, or butter. Finally, students will learn how to thicken and flavor sauces.

FOCUS

Bell Ringer Activity

Name That Sauce Ask for volunteers to name dishes they know that have a sauce. Have them discuss the type of sauce that goes with that dish. Explain that in this section, they will learn about the basic types of sauces and how to make them.

D Develop Concepts

Main Idea Discuss the main idea with the students. Ask: How can sauces liven up a bland dish? Sauces can liven up a bland dish by adding flavor, moisture, and texture.

TEACH

S Skill Practice

Guided Practice

L1 List Have students list the types of sauces. The different types of sauces include mother sauces, compound sauces, salsa, relish, gravy, compound butters, and independent sauces.

L2 Explain Ask students to explain how to thicken a sauce by reduction. To thicken a sauce by reduction, simmer it down to between one-half and one-fourth of its original amount.

L3 Apply Have students prepare a compound sauce out of their choice of mother sauces. Students should successfully prepare a compound sauce using their choice of mother sauce. This exercise should make them feel comfortable and confident preparing a compound sauce.

 **Professional Development** MINI CLIP **ELL** Level 4 Proficiency

ASSESS

Quiz

Ask students to answer the following questions:

1. What qualities should you look for in a sauce thickened through gelatinization? A sauce thickened through gelatinization should be smooth with no lumps, have no floury flavor, adhere to the spoon, and not break.

2. Why should you use a clarified butter when making a roux? A clarified butter should be used when making a roux because a non-clarified butter will not create the correct consistency.

3. How does reduction improve a sauce? Reduction improves a sauce because it thickens the sauce and concentrates the sauce's flavor.

RETEACH

U Universal Access

Students with Physical Challenges After having the students read the section and discussing the many types of thickening agents, demonstrate to the class how to make a roux. Include a white and brown roux in

the presentation, and explain when you would use each. Have students ask questions during the demonstration, and then at the end, have a class discussion about what they learned. This demonstration should supplement the reading so that students who are visual learners can gain a better understanding of the process. Through the discussion, elicit what students learned to assess their understanding.

C Critical Thinking

Creative Solutions Have students imagine that they are creating a chicken dish that is low-fat. What can they do while creating the sauce to make sure that the dish is healthful and low in fat? Answers will vary, but some things that students can do to ensure that the chicken dish is healthful and low in fat include thickening the sauce with a non-starch vegetable purée, thickening the sauce by reduction, using a higher flour content in the roux, or using cornstarch/arrowroot, or salsa.

 Professional Development MINI CLIP **Reading** Modeling Reading Strategies

ASSESS

Lab Manual

Assign the Section 20.2 Activities.

Online Study Tools

Have students go to the Online Learning Center at **glencoe.com** to:

- Take the Section 20.2 Practice Test.
- Download Study-to-Go content.

SECTION 20.2 After You Read Answer Key

Review Key Concepts

1. The ingredients that can be used as thickening agents include flour, cornstarch, arrowroot, instant starches, bread crumbs, and vegetable purées.

2. Sauce espagnole is made from thickened brown stock and a tomato product with few added seasonings.

3. When preparing a roux, it is important to always remember not to use aluminum cookware, not to use very high or very low temperatures, and not to overthicken liquids with the roux.

Practice Culinary Academics

4. **Social Studies** Students should choose a country and then describe at least two sauces that are traditional to that country. They should note similarities and differences in liquid ingredients, thickening agents and seasonings

and flavorings, and between the international sauces and the mother sauces.

5. **Mathematics** Each cone can hold about 4 fluid ounces of sauce. Since the cone's diameter is 3 inches, its radius is 1.5 inches, and so the volume of one cone equals $(\frac{1}{3})(3.14)(1.5$ inches$)(1.5$ inches$)(3$ inches$) = 7.065$ cubic inches, or $7.065 \div 1.8 = 3.925$ fluid ounces $\approx$ 4 fluid ounces.

CLOSE
Culminating Activity
Make Sauces Divide students into five teams, and have each team make one mother sauce. Then, have students prepare a compound sauce using the mother sauce. Finally, have them compare results by tasting each team's sauce, both by itself and on a dish. Discuss the results as a class.

SECTION 20.3 Soups
Section Overview
In this section, students will learn about the different types of soups, including clear soup, thick soup, and specialty soups. They will also learn how to present and garnish soup, including how to add toppings and accompaniments. Finally, they will learn how to properly store and reheat soups.

FOCUS
Bell Ringer Activity
Favorite Soups Have the class discuss together their favorite soups. Ask volunteers to name and describe their favorite soup. As a class, try to match students' various favorite soup to the categories of soup in the section. How many soups can students describe and identify?

D Develop Concepts
Main Idea Discuss the main idea with the students. Ask: What are the nutritional benefits of soups? Soups can be very hearty and contain foods from several food groups in one dish. Depending on how they are made, they can be low-fat, low in calories, and/or high in nutritional value.

TEACH
S Skill Practice
Guided Practice
L1 List Have students list the types of soups. The types of soups are clear soups, thick soups, specialty soups, and international soups.

L2 Explain Ask students to explain how to clarify a consommé. To clarify a consommé, skim the particles from the surface as they float to the top.

L3 Apply As a class, have students prepare the beef consommé recipe as described in this section. Students should work together as a class to successfully prepare the recipe. This exercise should make them feel comfortable in preparing consommés. Be sure to provide feedback.

ASSESS
Quiz
Ask students to answer the following questions:

1. What are the two categories of thick soups? The two categories of thick soups are purée soups and cream soups.

2. What is the difference between bisque and chowder? A bisque is made with shellfish (like lobster, crab, shrimp, or crayfish), and cream, while a chowder is a hearty soup that is made with fish, seafood, or vegetables.

3. Why do you sweat vegetables when making soup? You sweat vegetables when making soup because sweating vegetables releases the moisture and flavor from them.

RETEACH
U Universal Access
Students with Hearing Impairments Prepare two sets of cards: one with the names of the categories of soups, and one with the descriptions of the categories of soups. Have students try to match the category cards to their correct descriptions by playing the memory game. Students should use their memory of the section information to successfully match the soup categories to their descriptions. You might want to turn this activity into a contest.

 **Professional Development** MINI CLIP **Reading** Building Vocabulary

C Critical Thinking
Problem Solving Have students imagine that they want to make a thick soup but have realized that they have about $\frac{1}{3}$ of the cream needed. How would they thicken the soup? What are other ways to thicken soups besides adding cream? Answers will vary, but might include making the soup a purée that uses little cream, puréeing the main ingredients of the soup itself, or adding some béchamel sauce in addition to the cream to thicken the soup.

ASSESS

 ExamView® Assessment Suite
Create a test for this chapter.

 Lab Manual

Assign the Section 20.3 Activities.

Online Study Tools

Have students go to the Online Learning Center at **glencoe.com** to:

- Take the Section 20.3 Practice Test.
- Download Study-to-Go content.

SECTION 20.3 After You Read Answer Key

Review Key Concepts

1. Some examples of specialty soups include bisques, chowders, cold soups, and international soups.

2. A soup garnish should be attractively arranged. Each garnish should be cut to the same size and shape, and the flavor and texture should complement the soup. Cook vegetables and starches separately, and do not overcook them.

Practice Culinary Academics

3. **English Language Arts** Reading an article about a particular soup may give students additional information about that type of soup, and they may also learn new tips or instructions to augment their knowledge of how to prepare the soup.

4. **Science** The process of puréeing releases the starch and fibers in the vegetables, which thicken the soup. Students should notice and come to understand this process by comparing two soups of the same ingredients and the variance in thickness between the two soups.

5. **Mathematics** The restaurant will need a minimum of 7 quarts of soup per night. On a typical night, the restaurant serves 20 × 6 fluid ounces = 120 fluid ounces in cup-size portions, and 9 × 11 fluid ounces = 99 fluid ounces in bowl-size portions, for a total of 120 + 99 = 219 fluid ounces. There are 32 ounces in one quart, so a minimum of 219 ÷ 32 = 6.84375 ≈ 7 quarts of soup are needed.

CLOSE

Culminating Activity

Practice Making Soup Divide the students into three teams. Assign each team to make either a clear soup, a specialty soup, or a thick soup. Remind them to taste the soups as they are making them to assess the flavor and seasonings. Once the soups are complete, taste each soup and evaluate them. Have the teams taste the other teams' soups and provide feedback.

Chapter Review and Applications

Vocabulary Review

1. Ensure that memos use vocabulary terms correctly.

Review Key Concepts

2. The nourishing element, such as bones, meat, fish trimmings, or vegetables; mirepoix, a mix of chopped vegetables; bouquet garni, a combination of fresh herbs and vegetables; and a liquid, such as water.

3. White stock is made by simmering bones with mirepoix and bouquet garni and straining. Brown stock is made the same way, except the bones and mirepoix are first browned. Fish stock is made the same way as white stock except the cooking time is shorter, and sometimes an acid is added. Vegetable stock is made by simmering vegetables with herbs, spices, and water for 30 to 45 minutes.

4. The main ingredients are the liquid ingredients, thickening agents, and seasonings and flavorings.

5. The five mother sauces are: sauce espagnole, made from thickened brown sauce and tomato products; tomato sauce, made by simmering a tomato product with flavorings, seasonings, and a liquid; béchamel, made by thickening milk with a white roux, seasonings, and flavorings; velouté, made by thickening a light-colored stock with a light-colored roux; hollandaise sauce, made from emulsified egg yolks, clarified butter, seasonings, and lemon juice.

6. The steps in making roux are: 1) Heat fat in a heavy saucepan; 2) Make a paste by adding flour and stirring; 3) Cook the paste on medium heat until it is the consistency of wet sand and the correct color; 4) Stir roux to keep from burning, until stiff.

7. Clear soups: vegetable and consommé; thick soups: purée and cream soups; specialty soups: bisques, chowders, international, and cold soups.

8. Serve in the proper bowl. The bowl should be heated for hot soups and chilled for cold. Cold soup should be served at 41°F (5°C) or below; serve hot soups at 165°F (74°C) or above. To

store, cool and refrigerate thick soups before adding milk or cream. Heat only small batches while holding the rest in a steam table. Stir and taste often.

C Critical Thinking

9. The long cooking time allows ingredients to fully release their flavors. Cutting the cooking time will result in a poor or weak flavor.

10. Though both soups may be good nutritional sources, a gazpacho will likely have more nutritional value because more nutrients are retained in vegetables that are cooked less. Gazpacho is made primarily of vegetables. There are few, if any, nutrients in stock.

Academic Skills

11. **English Language Arts** Answers will vary. Essays should be written in proper format, with an introduction, body, and conclusion. Sources should be cited. The essay should contain all of the information requested in the activity description.

12. **Science** Using fresher vegetables will add more flavor because the pectin becomes more soluble. Explain that soluble means a substance can dissolve in liquids. Since the pectins in fresher vegetables are more soluble, they will release their flavors into the stock more easily.

13. **Mathematics** The concentrate is cheaper. If x represents the cost of producing 60 gallons of stock, then, for the concentrate, $x/60$ gal. = $11.25/5 gal. Solving for x results in $x = (\$11.25 \times 60)/5 = \$135$. For the powder, each $14.50 four-pack produces (4 containers) $\times$ (22 servings/container) $\times$ (8 oz./serving) = 704 fl. oz. of stock, or 704 ÷ 128 = 5.5 gal. Thus, $x/60$ gal. = $14.50/5.5 gal., or $x = (\$14.50 \times 60)/5.5 = \$158.18$. The concentrate is about $23 per month cheaper.

Certification Prep

14. c. a mix of coarsely chopped vegetables and herbs.

15 d. equal parts of fat and flour by weight.

Real-World Skills and Applications

16. **Self-Management Skills** Answers might include: minestrone, gazpacho, vegetable gumbo, or chicken noodle soup.

17. **Collaborative Interpersonal Skills** Students should add new flavorings and ingredients to these classic soups that will complement the existing ingredients. They might add spices, vegetables, or meats that will change the flavor, or croutons, bacon bits, or other elements that can change the texture.

18. **Technology Applications** The menu should be either one or two pages and be organized. Each soup should be described so that you can recognize the type of soup and major ingredients. Each main dish should include a description of the type of sauce.

19. **Financial Literacy** Canned tomato: $0.08 \times 80 = \$6.40$. Homemade tomato: $0.11 \times 80 = \$8.80$.

Culinary Lab

20. **Make a Béchamel Sauce** Each card should contain an evaluation of the taste, texture, and appearance of each sauce, as well as suggestions for improvements. The discussion should focus on both the positive and negative qualities of the sauces.

Fish and Shellfish

SECTION 22.1 **Fish Basics**   SECTION 22.3 **Cooking Fish and Shelfish**
SECTION 22.2 **Shellfish Basics**

Classroom Solutions

Print Resources

- Student Edition
- Instructor Annotated Edition
- Lab Manual
- Lab Manual IAE

Technology Resources

ExamView® Assessment Suite CD
Create and print unit and chapter tests.

Lesson Planner Plus **Lesson Planner Plus CD** provides access to teacher resources in one package.

Presentation Plus! provides visual teaching aids for every section.

Online Learning Center includes resources and activities for students and teachers. Also includes the **Online Student Edition**.

Interactive Student Edition

SECTION 21.1 Fish Basics

Section Overview

In this section, students learn the structure and market forms of fish. They will also learn that fish is made up of protein, fats, and water, and has very little connective tissue. Finally, they will learn that fish is available fresh, frozen, or canned, and may come whole or in the various forms in which it will be cooked.

FOCUS

Bell Ringer Activity

Demonstration Discuss fat fish and lean fish, and flat fish and round fish with students. Demonstrate how to fillet flat fish and round fish. If time allows, follow up with student practice on filleting fish. Allow them to practice with one flat and one round fish and then give them feedback and suggestions for improvement.

D Develop Concepts

Main Idea Discuss the main idea with the students. Ask: Why do you think fish is becoming more and more popular with diners? Answers will vary, but in general, fish is becoming more popular with diners as people become more health conscious. Also, fish's popularity is increasing because of recent information about the benefits to your heart from eating fish.

TEACH

S Skill Practice
Guided Practice

L1 List Have students list the quality checks for frozen fish. Quality checks for frozen fish are to make sure there is no freezer burn, make sure there is no fishy smell, and make sure fish is coated with a thin layer of ice.

L2 Explain Ask students to explain how to butterfly a fish. To butterfly a fish, dress the fish, and then cut the fish so the two sides lie open, yet are still attached by skin.

L3 Apply Bring in fresh fish and frozen fish, and have students practice performing quality checks and then butterflying. Students should practice the quality checks listed in the book appropriate for both fresh fish and frozen fish, and then butterfly them.

ASSESS

Quiz

Ask students to answer the following questions:

1. What are the three categories of fish based on skeleton type? The three categories of fish based on skeleton type are flat fish, round fish, and boneless fish.

2. Why is fish often cooked by moist heat techniques? Fish is often cooked by moist heat techniques to help retain the natural moisture in the fish.

3. Why are fish rarely bought whole? Fish are rarely bought whole because the shelf life of a whole fish is shorter, so they must be used more quickly. Additionally, some fish are very large and difficult to use quickly.

RETEACH

 Writing Support

Find a Recipe Have students choose three of the types of fish from the list in this section. They may look in magazines, the food section of newspapers, or on the Internet to find out how that type of fish is commonly cooked and also to obtain a recipe for preparing each type of fish. Have them share their recipes with the class. Answers will vary depending on the fish chosen. For example, if the student chose catfish, he or she might discuss how it is often breaded with cornmeal and fried, and provide a recipe for such a dish.

McGraw Hill **Professional Development**	MINI CLIP **Reading** Fluency Development

U Universal Access

Students with Physical Challenges Ask the students to imagine that they have been put in charge of purchasing fish for their foodservice establishment. What qualities would they look for when choosing a vendor? Answers will vary, but might include looking for a vendor with a good reputation, a vendor with the freshest fish, and a vendor who can demonstrate knowledge about the product.

ASSESS

Lab Manual

Assign the Section 21.1 Activities.

Online Study Tools

Have students go to the Online Learning Center at **glencoe.com** to:

- Take the Section 21.1 Practice Test.
- Download Study-to-Go content.

SECTION 21.1 **After You Read Answer Key**
Review Key Concepts

1. Flat fish have a backbone that runs horizontally through the center of the fish. They have both eyes on the top of their head. Flat fish have dark skin on their upper side to hide from predators.

2. Fillets are the sides of a fish. Round fish produce one fillet from each side, while flat fish produce two fillets from the top and two from the bottom. Steaks are cross-section cuts of dressed fish.

Practice Culinary Academics

3. **English Language Arts** Fish is high in omega-3 fatty acids, which are good for the health of your heart. However, fish also absorb things from the water around them, and some fish have been shown to contain heavy metals and pollutants. Brochures should be clear and understandable and include both positive and negative aspects about including fish in one's diet.

4. **Social Studies** Students' research should address the endangerment of fish species and the impact on ocean ecology caused by commercial fishing, as well as the controversies surrounding fish farming, such as the fish feed used, potential parasites, and environmental impact.

5. **Mathematics** The median is 6 ounces, while the mode is 6 ounces. Arranged in order, the lengths are 4, 4, 5, 5, 5, 6, 6, 6, 6, 6, 7, 7, 7, 8, and 8. The middle number (the mode) in this series is 6. Six also appears the most times (5) out of all the numbers, which makes it the median.

McGraw Hill **Professional Development**	MINI CLIP **Math** Medians and Quartiles

CLOSE
Culminating Activity

Go Fish Create a set of playing cards using the definitions, composition and structure, species, market forms, and purchasing of fish. Write one of each on each card and make four versions of each card. Have students play the game Go Fish as a review of the information in this section. You may want to turn this into a contest.

SECTION 21.2 **Shellfish Basics**
Section Overview

In this section, students will learn about the structure of shellfish. They will also learn about the inspection and grading process for shellfish. Finally, they will learn about the different types of mollusks and crustaceans and their market forms, as well as how to handle and store them.

FOCUS

🔔 Bell Ringer Activity

Types of Shellfish Ask students to list the types of shellfish they are aware of. List the types on the board as they think of them. After the list is complete, verify that each one is actually a shellfish. Then, compare the list to the list in the book to see if there are any they missed.

D Develop Concepts

Main Idea Discuss the main idea with the students. Ask: Why do you think shellfish are expensive compared to fish meat? Shellfish are expensive compared to fish meat because shellfish are smaller in size, so a larger quantity must be purchased to make a portion.

TEACH

S Skill Practice
Guided Practice

L1 List Ask students to list the steps for peeling and deveining shrimp. To devein shrimp: 1) Use your forefinger to remove the legs; 2) Peel and remove the shell; 3) Leave the tail on if the shrimp will be broiled or deep-fried (remove the tail for most other preparations); 4) Cut down the back of the shrimp with a paring knife and remove the vein just below the surface; and 5) Make the cut deeper to butterfly the shrimp.

L2 Explain Ask students to explain the difference between a Type 2 and Type 3 inspection of fish and shellfish. Type 2 inspections cover labeling, weight, and packaging. Type 3 inspections cover sanitary conditions only.

L3 Apply Have students choose one type of shellfish and prepare it using a simple preparation. Students should choose a minimal preparation style. This exercise is to practice handling and preparing shellfish. Provide feedback after observing the students.

ASSESS
Quiz

Ask students to answer the following questions:

1. What is a Type 1 inspection of fish and shellfish? A Type 1 inspection of fish and shellfish covers processing methods and the processing plant.

2. What are the criteria for fish grading? The criteria for grading fish are as follows: Grade A is of the highest quality, with no physical defects and good odor and flavor. Grade B is good quality. Grade C is fairly good quality.

3. How do you determine if bivalves are alive? Bivalves are alive if the shells are closed. If the shells are open, they should close quickly when tapped. If the shell remains open when tapped, the bivalve is not alive and should not be used.

RETEACH

U Universal Access

English Language Learners Purchase several types of mollusks and crustaceans, such as shrimp, oysters, clams, or lobsters. Demonstrate how to prepare them for cooking. Then, allow students to practice different preparation techniques themselves. Students can practice peeling and deveining shrimp, shucking oysters, opening clams, and cleaning and preparing lobster tails and crab legs. Be sure to monitor closely for safety and provide feedback to the students while observing them. Students with shellfish allergies should sit out this exercise.

C Critical Thinking

Decision Making Ask students to imagine that they are the manager of a hotel food operation. It is their decision to order either fresh fish or frozen fish to be served fried. Ask them to explain which they will choose and why. Answers will vary, and either can be correct as long as the answer is supported logically. Some students may choose to buy the fish frozen because of the longer shelf life, easier handling, and ready-to-use portions that can be fried without thawing. Some students may choose to buy the fish fresh so they can market fresh fish to customers.

ASSESS

Lab Manual

Assign the Section 21.2 Activities.

Online Study Tools

Have students go to the Online Learning Center at **glencoe.com** to:

- Take the Section 21.2 Practice Test.
- Download Study-to-Go content.

SECTION 21.2 After You Read Answer Key
Review Key Concepts

1. Grade A is shellfish of the highest quality with no physical defects and a good odor and flavor. Grade B is shellfish of a good quality, but not the highest. Grade C is shellfish of fairly good quality.

2. Univalves have a single shell. Bivalves have two shells that are hinged together. Cephalopods have a thin internal shell.

3. Crustaceans have a hard outer shell and jointed skeletons.

4. Methods of cooking squid include simmering the squid in a seasoned sauce or liquid or quickly frying the squid.

Practice Culinary Academics

5. Mathematics The fifth crab should weigh 15 ½ pounds. If *x* represents the weight of the fifth crab, then $(12 + 14 + 16.5 + 17 + x) \div 5 = 15$, or $59.5 + x = 15 \times 5$. This equation further reduces to $59.5 + x = 75$, or $x = 15.5$.

 **Professional Development** MINI CLIP **Math** Unknowns in Equations

CLOSE

Culminating Activity

Work in Teams Divide the students into groups, and have them prepare different forms of shellfish for cooking. For example, one team might peel, devein, and cook shrimp. Another team might prepare oysters or clams. Remind them to follow safety and sanitation guidelines. Students with shellfish allergies should sit out this exercise.

SECTION 21.3 Cooking Fish and Shellfish

Section Overview

In this section, students learn how to cook fish and shellfish while still retaining moisture and tenderness. They will also learn a variety of options for cooking fish and shellfish, including baking, broiling, sautéing, deep frying, and pan frying. Finally, they will learn how to garnish fish and shellfish with sauces, citrus wedges, or seasoned butter.

FOCUS

Bell Ringer Activity

Many Ways to Prepare Ask students to list the ways they know that fish and shellfish can be prepared. Ask them to think of as many dishes as they can, in as many menu categories as they can. Write the students' ideas on the board. Discuss the variety of fish and shellfish dishes and why this variety makes fish and shellfish popular with foodservice operations.

Professional Development MINI CLIP **ELL** Exploring the Big Idea

D Develop Concepts

Main Idea Discuss the main idea with the students. Ask: What is your favorite cooking method for fish, and why? Answers will vary depending on personal taste. Some students might prefer the crunchy crust of a fried fish, while others might prefer the flavor of a grilled fish.

TEACH

S Skill Practice
Guided Practice

L1 List Ask students to list the guidelines for determining if fish is thoroughly cooked. To determine if a fish is thoroughly cooked, check that the fish flakes, that the flesh pulls away easily from bones and shells, that the flesh springs back when pressed, and that and flesh is opaque.

L2 Explain Ask students to write a paragraph explaining the en papillote method of cooking. To cook using the en papillote method, seal the fish in parchment paper along with vegetables, herbs, sauces, and butters. Then, steam the fish and other ingredients in the paper.

L3 Apply Have students practice cooking fish for doneness by cooking one fish correctly, undercooking one, and overcooking another. The students should compare the appearance and texture of the correctly cooked fish to the overdone and underdone fish. This exercise should give students a sense of how to cook fish for the correct amount of time and how to identify the levels of doneness of fish.

ASSESS

Quiz

Ask students to answer the following questions:

1. Why is a fatty fish better to broil than a lean fish? Fatty fish is better to broil than lean fish because lean fish can dry out very quickly with direct heat cooking methods.

2. Why is fish commonly floured or breaded prior to sautéing and pan-frying? Fish is commonly floured or breaded prior to sautéing and pan-frying to keep the fish from sticking to the cooking surface and to form a crust.

3. What happens to shellfish when it is overcooked? When shellfish is overcooked, the shellfish will become tough and unappetizing.

RETEACH

U Universal Access

Students with Behavioral Challenges Demonstrate for the class how to cook lobster. Explain the parts of the lobster and their various uses during cooking. As you go through each step, explain what you are doing, and allow the opportunity for questions. When you have finished, let the students taste the lobster. As you demonstrate how to cook lobster, have students follow along with the material about lobster in the book to connect what they read to the visual demonstration.

C Critical Thinking

Getting Prepared Imagine that you are in charge of catering at a hotel. A group of clients has asked to have a sushi station at their banquet. What preparations and precautions would you take before providing a sushi station? Answers will vary, but might include purchasing the freshest, best quality fish from reputable vendors; hiring skilled sushi chefs; and making sure food safety procedures and guidelines are followed at all times.

ASSESS

 ExamView® Assessment Suite Create a test for this chapter.

Lab Manual

Assign the Section 21.3 Activities.

Online Study Tools

Have students go to the Online Learning Center at **glencoe.com** to:

- Take the Section 21.3 Practice Test.
- Download Study-to-Go content.

SECTION 21.3 After You Read Answer Key

Review Key Concepts

1. For sautéing, use just enough fat to cover the bottom of the pan. Pan-frying requires more fat. Use flour or breading to form a crust to prevent sticking. Brown the presentation side first, turn once, and then cook quickly over high heat until done.

Practice Culinary Academics

2. **Science** Students may observe that the shrimp marinated for a short time is more tender than the other groups of shrimp. An acid marinade tenderizes the shrimp by denaturing the proteins in it. It is actually a very mild form of cooking. However, marinating too much can overcook the shrimp and it can become tough again. It is important to find a balance.

3. **English Language Arts** Groups should choose one method of cooking fish or shellfish and take the guidelines given in this section and transfer them to a poster in a manner that is easily readable and visually appealing.

4. **Social Studies** Commercial fishermen today usually use surrounding nets, seine nets, trawls, dredges, hooks and lines, lift nets, gillnets, entangling nets and traps. They also often process the fish and shellfish right on the boat. Students may talk about any of these pieces of equipment and how they compare to traditional fishing gear.

5. **Mathematics** The restaurant can get 60 sheets of parchment paper from the roll. 40 yards is the equivalent of $40 \times 3 = 120$ feet, and $120 \times 12 = 1{,}440$ inches. $1{,}440$ inches $\div 24$ inches $= 60$.

CLOSE

Culminating Activity

Work in Teams Divide students into teams, and have them prepare a garnished fish or seafood dish from a simple recipe. Then, have them exchange dishes with each other and evaluate the quality of each other's dishes. Discuss the results of the evaluation as a class, giving both positive feedback and suggestions for improvement.

Chapter Review and Applications

Vocabulary Review

1. Students should explain their vocabulary word groupings in a logical manner.

Review Key Concepts

2. Fish have backbones, an internal skeleton of cartilage and bones, gills for breathing, and fins for swimming. Fish are divided into three categories: flat, round, and boneless. Fish also have very little connective tissue.

3. Whole fish refers to the entire fish as it comes out of the water. Fish that have had their gills and entrails removed are called drawn fish. Drawn fish that have had their fins, scales, and sometimes their head removed are called dressed fish. The sides of fish are the fillets. A butterflied fish is dressed, then cut so the two sides lay open, but attached. Cross-section cuts of dressed fish are

called steaks. Leftover pieces from large fish are called cubes. Small, leftover pieces of fish that are pressed together form sticks.

4. Shellfish have no bones. They have hard shells covering their bodies. Most shellfish are lean and composed primarily of water, vitamins, minerals, protein, and fats. The USDA inspects fish and shellfish in three ways. Fish are graded based on standards for flavor and appearance. Grading is optional, but inspection is mandatory.

5. Univalves have a single shell. Bivalves have two shells that are hinged together. Instead of an outer shell, cephalopods have a thin internal shell. Cephalopods have tentacles, or false legs, attached to the head near the mouth.

6. Lobsters have two large claws, four pairs of legs, and a large, flexible tail. Shrimp are smaller than lobster and may be purchased raw in the shell, fresh or frozen. Crab may be shipped canned, fresh, or frozen. Crayfish are freshwater crustaceans that look like miniature lobsters from 3½ to 7 inches in length.

7. Other types of seafood include squid, frog legs, escargot, surimi, and eel.

8. Baking: Cooking with dry heat. Moist baking: Cooking with dry heat and moisture. Broiling or grilling: Cooking over or under direct heat, or on a grill rack. Pan-frying: Frying in a pan or skillet with a small amount of fat. Deep-frying: Breading and submerging in hot fat.

C Critical Thinking

9. Fish and shellfish are naturally low in fat. Avoiding methods that introduce fat, such as pan-frying and deep-frying, will be more healthful.

10. A restaurant that is not serving the highest-quality fish as sushi may run the risk of foodborne illness, as the fish will not be cooked. Students may wish to warn the restaurant, or impose a fine if careless food handling is found.

Academic Skills

11. **English Language Arts** Menus should contain items in all five categories. The menu descriptions should be clearly and creatively written, but truthful. The menu should mention the type of fish or shellfish used for each item, as well as the cooking method.

12. **Social Studies** Student responses can feature any recipe with fish or shellfish that is rarely served in the United States. Students should locate a recipe for the dish and provide a thorough description of the location it comes from, how the dish is made, what is in it, and how it is served and eaten.

13. **Mathematics** The market handles about 4,409,000 pounds of fish per day. 2,000 metric tons $= 2,000 \times 1,000$ kg $= 2,000,000$ kg. Two million kilograms divided by .4536 kg/lb. yields 4,409,171.08. The 9 is in the thousands place, since it is the fourth digit to the left of the decimal point. Since the digit to the right of the 9 is less than 5, rounding to the nearest thousand results in 4,409,000.

Certification Prep

14. a. fillets

15. b. bivalve

Real-World Skills and Applications

16. **Self-Management Skills** Broiling and pan-frying are both fast cooking methods. Broiling can be more healthful. To add nutritional value, the fish could be served with a side of vegetables and/or a whole grain. Also, make sure not to overcook the fish.

17. **Interpersonal and Collaborative Skills** The shows should be rehearsed and scripted prior to performing, and students should know the recipe by the time they perform.

18. **Technology Applications** The Web site should be eye-catching but easy to read. It should be organized and easy to navigate. The information should be accurate, as presented in the chapter.

19. **Financial Literacy** Yield from a whole salmon: $5 \times .50 = 2.5$ pounds. 10 pounds $\div 2.5 = 4$. You will need to purchase 4 whole salmon.

Culinary Lab

20. **Prepare Fish Dishes** Students should answer each question thoroughly and fairly. Discuss the evaluations with the class, making sure each team receives positive feedback and constructive criticism.

Poultry Cookery

SECTION 22.1 **Poultry Basics**   SECTION 22.2 **Cooking Poultry**

Classroom Solutions

Print Resources

📖 Student Edition
📖 Instructor Annotated Edition
📖 Lab Manual
📖 Lab Manual IAE

Technology Resources

ExamView **ExamView® Assessment Suite CD**
Assessment Suite
Create and print unit and chapter tests.

Lesson Planner *Plus* **Lesson Planner Plus CD** provides access to teacher resources in one package.

Presentation *Plus!* **Presentation Plus!** provides visual teaching aids for every section.

🔆 **Online Learning Center** includes resources and activities for students and teachers. Also includes the **Online Student Edition**.

💿 **Interactive Student Edition**

SECTION 22.1 **Poultry Basics**

Section Overview

Students will learn about the different kinds, classes, and market forms of poultry. They will also understand USDA inspections and grading; how to purchase poultry; and how to handle, store, and prepare it for cooking.

FOCUS

🔔 Bell Ringer Activity

Poultry Pantomime Have volunteers pantomime safe poultry preparation. Have the class evaluate the accuracy of the safety procedures in the pantomimes.

D Develop Concepts

Main Idea Discuss the main idea with the students. Ask: Which kinds of poultry have the students eaten? Kinds of poultry include chicken, turkey, goose, duck, pigeon, and guinea. Have students discuss whether they liked each kind.

McGraw Hill Professional Development MINI CLIP **Reading** Prereading Strategies

TEACH

S Skill Practice
Guided Practice

L1 List Have students make a list of qualities of Grade A poultry. Grade A poultry is plump and meaty; has clean, unblemished skin; has no broken bones; has all feathers removed.

L2 Explain Have students write a paragraph to explain why restaurants should choose Grade A poultry. Paragraphs will vary but should include quality, flavor, and appearance.

L3 Apply Have students practice cutting Grade A poultry following the examples in the book. Evaluate their technique and the result. The cut pieces should be as neat as possible, and should waste as little meat as possible.

ASSESS

Quiz

Ask students to answer the following questions:

1. How does the USDA categorize poultry? The USDA categorizes poultry by species, or kind. Each kind is then divided into classes based on age and gender.

2. What factors affect the tenderness of poultry? Maturity: older poultry is tougher. Exercise: the more exercise a bird gets, the tougher it will be.

3. How should you store fresh poultry that you will cook within a day? Place it in cold storage or pack it in ice until it is ready to use.

RETEACH

 Universal Access

English Language Learners Have students make a chart with columns labeled Kind, Class, and Market Form. Then, have them fill in examples of each in the appropriate column. Ask them how each column relates to the others. Students should see that poultry can come in many combinations of the three categories. Once students know the kind of poultry, they must then decide on class and market form.

| McGraw Hill **Professional Development** | MINI CLIP **ELL** English Language Success |

C Critical Thinking

Evaluate Foie Gras Foie gras is liver from a duck or goose that has been fattened using gavage, or force feeding. Some American cities are banning foie gras because gavage can be considered inhumane. Research how foie gras is produced and evaluate the arguments for and against gavage. The gavage technique has potentially harmful side effects to the birds, but an outright ban punishes even careful and humane producers. Students should provide a thoughtful evaluation of the pros and cons and then state their own opinion as a conclusion.

ASSESS

Lab Manual

Assign the Section 22.1 Activities.

Online Study Tools

Have students go to the Online Learning Center at **glencoe.com** to:
- Take the Section 22.1 Practice Test.
- Download Study-to-Go content.

SECTION 22.1 After You Read Answer Key
Review Key Concepts

1. Market forms include fresh, frozen, and fully cooked. Classes include age and gender. Styles include whole, parts, bone-in, boneless, ground, and ready-to-cook.

2. Grade A poultry must be plump and meaty, have clean skin with no blemishes, tears, cuts, or bruises, have no broken bones, and have all feathers plucked and removed.

3. Fresh poultry should be placed in cold storage or packed in ice until use. If it will not be used within 2–3 days, it should be frozen immediately. Frozen poultry can be stored for up to six months at 0°F (−18°C) in its original packaging, and thawed in its original packaging in the refrigerator.

Practice Culinary Academics

4. **Science** Answers should include inspecting the chicken for signs of spoilage and looking for the USDA inspection and grading stamps. Since the chicken is a week early, it should be immediately frozen in its original packaging.

5. **Mathematics** Answer: $72 + $85 + $93 = $250; $250 ÷ 3 = $83.33 average.

| McGraw Hill **Professional Development** | MINI CLIP **Math** Problem Solving and Measurement |

CLOSE
Culminating Activity

Plan a Poultry Meal Ask students to plan a poultry dish for dinner. Ask them to choose a recipe and then discuss with them the kind, class, and market form of poultry, and storage and handling tips.

SECTION 22.2 Cooking Poultry

Section Overview

Students will learn various dry and moist poultry cooking techniques. They will learn about special food safety measures for stuffing. They will also learn about appropriate side dishes.

FOCUS
Bell Ringer Activity

Recognize Cooking Techniques Assign each student a cooking technique for poultry and have them locate a recipe that uses the method. Students should be able to recognize the different cooking techniques from the section in a recipe format.

D Develop Concepts

Main Idea Discuss the main idea with the students. Ask: What are some cooking techniques you can use to cook poultry? Poultry can be roasted, baked, broiled, grilled, fried, sautéed, simmered, poached, or braised.

TEACH
S Skill Practice
Guided Practice

L1 List Have students list the steps in using a healthful cooking method, such as sautéing, on poultry. Students should select a method and list the steps as described in the section.

L2 Explain Have students write a paragraph explaining the health risks of stuffing poultry. The stuffing may not reach a safe temperature to kill bacteria. This could cause a foodborne illness.

L3 Apply Have students create a complete and balanced poultry meal that includes ingredients from all food groups. Students may choose any side dishes, so long as the combination of side dishes and poultry contains something from each food group.

ASSESS
Quiz
Ask students to answer the following questions:

1. How do bones affect poultry during cooking? Bones affect flavor and they also help the bird retain some of its moisture.

2. How should you store stuffing? Keep it refrigerated in a shallow baking pan. Never store stuffing in the same container as poultry.

3. Identify the types of poultry best suited to poaching and simmering. Poaching is usually used to cook whole, young, tender birds. Simmering is used for older, tougher birds that are cut into pieces.

RETEACH
R Reading Strategy
Apply Cooking Methods Have students review the different cooking methods and create a menu, including side dishes, for each cooking method. Students should provide examples of complete meals using each cooking type. For example, sautéed chicken strips chopped into a Greek salad with a piece of crusty bread and fruit is a complete meal.

U Universal Access
Students with Learning Disabilities In the section, students learn that poultry must be well done to be safe. As a class, discuss the dangers of poultry that is not cooked well enough. Poultry must be cooked to 165°F (74°C) eliminate pathogens and viruses that can cause illness.

ASSESS
 ExamView Assessment Suite Create a test for this chapter.

Lab Manual
Assign the Section 22.2 Activities.

Online Study Tools
Have students go to the Online Learning Center at **glencoe.com** to:
- Take the Section 22.2 Practice Test.
- Download Study-to-Go content.

SECTION 22.2 After You Read Answer Key
Review Key Concepts

1. Poultry can be roasted, baked, broiled, grilled, pan-fried, deep-fried, pressure-fried, sautéed, simmered, poached, or braised.

2. Use a dry cooking method for younger, tender poultry. Use a moist cooking method for older, tougher poultry to maintain moisture.

3. A stuffing is a seasoned food mixture often made with bread, and used as an accompaniment with poultry.

Practice Culinary Academics

4. **English Language Arts** Answers will vary, but accept paragraphs that discuss various fruits, grains, legumes, vegetables, stuffings, and breads.

5. **Mathematics** 8 × 0.30 = 2.40; 2.40 × 245 = $588 total food cost.

CLOSE
Culminating Activity
Menu Creation Ask students to imagine they are a sous chef. The executive chef wants to expand beyond standard chicken dishes. Have the class brainstorm ideas for dishes made with other kinds of birds.

Chapter Review and Applications
Vocabulary Review

1. Students should write complete sentences using each term correctly.

Review Key Concepts

2. Kinds: chicken, turkey, goose, duck, guinea, and pigeon. Classes: age and gender. Market forms: fresh, frozen, and fully cooked.

3. Poultry must be federally inspected by the USDA to see that it is processed in sanitary conditions and is safe to eat. Poultry should be free of visible signs of disease. Poultry that passes inspection earns the USDA Inspection Stamp of Approval. USDA grading is optional, and uses letters to show quality level, with

Grade A being the best. To be Grade A, poultry must be plump and meaty; have clean skin with no blemishes, tears, cuts or bruises; have no broken bones; and have no feathers.

4. Fresh poultry is highly perishable, and should be packed in ice or in cold storage until ready for use; if it will not be used within 2–3 days, it should be frozen immediately. Frozen poultry can be stored for up to six months at or below 0°F (18°C). Keep frozen poultry in its original packaging, and never refreeze poultry. Whole birds should be trussed to allow for even cooking, and are usually roasted.

5. Dry cooking techniques include roasting, baking, broiling, grilling, frying (pan-frying, deep-frying, and pressure-frying), and sautéing. Moist cooking techniques include simmering and poaching. Braising is a combination dry/ moist cooking method.

6. Stuffing may not reach a safe temperature at the same time as the bird, creating the possibility for bacteria to grow. Poultry can become dry before the stuffing is fully cooked.

7. Answers will vary, but common poultry side dishes include stuffings, gravies, sauces, soups, salsas, vegetables, casseroles, wild rice, potatoes, and pasta.

C Critical Thinking

8. Dark meat has more muscle and connective tissue than light meat; dark meat also has more fat and generally takes a longer time to cook than light meat. Answers will vary, but can include customer preference and compatibility with the recipe chosen.

9. Answers will vary; accept any that are well thought out and supported by complete arguments.

10. Less-tender birds may be chosen because they are readily available or less expensive. They may also fit a specific recipe. Cooking methods can make this poultry tender.

Academic Skills

11. **Social Studies** Answers will vary, but students should be able to demonstrate their research skills in finding detailed recipes and knowledge of the appropriateness of spices, seasonings, and side dishes for their chosen culture.

12. **English Language Arts** The flyer should include information on when the restaurant will open, and details on specific poultry dishes.

13. **Mathematics** .30 × 500 = 150 meals should include poultry.

Certification Prep

14. c. clean and sanitize the cutting board

15. a. breads

Real-World Skills and Applications

16. **Teamwork Skills** Check to see that recipes are balanced nutritionally, and that flavors, seasonings, and spreads will complement turkey. Flyers should highlight these points.

17. **Critical Thinking** Answers will vary, but questions may be based on customer preferences for dishes, the general atmosphere of the event, the seasonality of available ingredients, and any specific party themes.

18. **Technology Applications** Spreadsheets should clearly display dry and moist poultry cooking methods, cooking instructions, and poultry choices appropriate to each method.

19. **Financial Literacy** Answers will depend on students' findings, but most should find that whole chicken is generally the most cost-effective option for foodservice establishments. However, labor cost, skill level of employees, and the ability to use all of the chicken parts might affect the decision.

Culinary Lab

20. **Prepare Poultry** Evaluations will vary, but dishes and evaluations should be based on knowledge of the chapter content. Students should give clear reasoning for their evaluations on appearance, flavor, and texture, and should be respectful of other teams.

Meat Cookery

SECTION 23.1 Meat Basics

SECTION 23.2 Meat Cuts

SECTION 23.3 Principles of Cooking Meat

Classroom Solutions

Print Resources

- Student Edition
- Instructor Annotated Edition
- Lab Manual
- Lab Manual IAE

Technology Resources

ExamView *ExamView® Assessment Suite* **CD**
Create and print unit and chapter tests.

Lesson Planner *Plus* **Lesson Planner Plus CD** provides access to teacher resources in one package.

 Presentation Plus! provides visual teaching aids for every section.

Online Learning Center includes resources and activities for students and teachers. Also includes the **Online Student Edition**.

Interactive Student Edition

SECTION 23.1 Meat Basics

Section Overview

In this section, students will learn about the structure of meat. They will also learn how to identify the different cuts of meat. Finally, they will learn how meat is inspected and graded and how to properly and safely handle and store meat to avoid foodborne illness and spoilage.

FOCUS

Bell Ringer Activity

Favorite Dishes Have students describe their favorite meat dish. Ask them what type of meat it uses, if they know the cut of meat, and what cooking method is used. Write a list of dishes on the board and compare the different tastes of the class. Is one type of meat or preparation more common than others? Explain that in this section, they will learn more about the different cuts of meat.

D Develop Concepts

Main Idea Discuss the main idea with the students. Ask: Why do you think meat is so popular as a food item? Answers will vary, but in general, meat is tasty, a good source of protein, and can be very healthful. There are also many forms of meat available at a variety of prices. Additionally, restaurants often use difficult preparations that are sometimes too complex or time consuming to cook at home, so people enjoy ordering these when out to eat.

TEACH

S Skill Practice

Guided Practice

L1 List Ask students to list the two types of meat cuts. The two types of meat cuts are primal cuts and fabricated cuts.

L2 Explain Have students write a paragraph explaining how carcasses are cut. Beef carcasses are split into the forequarter and the hindquarter, while veal and lamb are divided into foresaddle and hindsaddle.

L3 Apply Ask the students to imagine they are purchasing meat, and ask them to explain what they will look for when purchasing. Answers will vary but might include the meat's cut, the tenderness, the marbling, the color, and the type of meat.

ASSESS

Quiz

Ask students to answer the following questions:

1. Why would you leave the fat cap on during cooking? You would leave the fat cap on to keep the meat moist and juicy and to keep the flavor contained.

2. How does marbling affect the quality of meat? The more marbling in the meat, the more tender and flavorful it will be.

3. How does yield grade affect purchasing? The yield grade tells you the percentage of usable

meat, which is important during purchasing to predict how much you will need to buy.

RETEACH

R Reading Strategy

Model Meat Storage Safety Discuss with students how to properly store raw roasts, ground meat, and ready-to-eat meats in the refrigerator following procedures approved by your local health department. Then have students demonstrate proper procedures for one another. After the discussion, students should be able to re-create what they learned in a demonstration. During the demonstrations, make sure to correct any incorrect behaviors and praise correct ones. The other students should provide feedback as well.

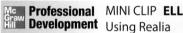 **Professional Development** MINI CLIP **ELL** Using Realia

U Universal Access

Gifted Students Ask students to imagine that they are putting together the meat order for their foodservice operation. One of the things they must decide is which market forms of the meat to purchase. What information would they use to choose the correct products? Answers will vary, but may include things like including a variety of dishes on the menu; the cooking method for each dish; the meat prices; and how the meat will be used.

ASSESS

Lab Manual

Assign the Section 23.1 Activities.

Online Study Tools

Have students go to the Online Learning Center at **glencoe.com** to:

• Take the Section 23.1 Practice Test.

STUDY TO GO Download Study-to-Go content.

SECTION 23.1 After You Read Answer Key
Review Key Concepts

1. Barding is wrapping lean meat with fat. It provides an alternate layer of fat to keep the meat moist, tender, juicy, and flavorful. Larding is inserting long, thin strips of fat or vegetables into the center of lean meat. This adds moisture, flavor, and visual appeal to the meat.

2. When purchasing meat, things to consider include: the menu, the cooking methods to be used, the price, and the quality and value.

Practice Culinary Academics

3. **English Language Arts** Student guides should be thorough, using all information from the chapter to create a well-organized and informative guide that would be helpful to a new employee who needs to purchase meats.

4. **Social Studies** There are many examples of dishes made from offal or the tougher cuts of meat that are not purchased often in our society, such as hearts, brains, and bone marrow. Students should research one such dish and create a visual presentation to show the recipe and the meat cut it uses.

5. **Mathematics** The pounded cutlets are $\frac{3}{16}$, or 18.75%, of the original thickness. The new thickness of the veal cutlets is ($\frac{1}{8}$ inches)/($\frac{2}{3}$ inches) of the original thickness. This expression is the same as dividing $\frac{1}{8}$ by $\frac{2}{3}$, which can be done by multiplying $\frac{1}{8}$ by the reciprocal of $\frac{2}{3}$, or $\frac{3}{2}$. Thus, $\frac{1}{8} \times \frac{2}{3} = \frac{3}{16}$. Convert $\frac{3}{16}$ into a percentage by dividing: $3 \div 16 = 0.1875 = 18.75\%$.

CLOSE
Culminating Activity

Tenderize Meat Divide students into teams, and have them use one of the five tenderizing methods in the section to tenderize pork, lamb, veal, or beef. Then, have them cook the meat and evaluate each other's products. Which tenderizing method worked best for each meat?

SECTION 23.2 Meat Cuts
Section Overview

In this section, students will learn the quality characteristics and cuts for pork, lamb, veal, and beef. They will also learn about processing methods such as curing, aging, and irradiation. Finally, they will learn about safe handling and storage for each of these types of meat.

FOCUS
Bell Ringer Activity

Field Trip or Presentation If possible, tour a butcher shop or processing plant to allow students to see first-hand how meats are inspected, cut, processed, and distributed to commercial operations. If this is not possible, invite a local butcher or meat processor to come to the class to speak in detail about his or her work.

D Develop Concepts

Main Idea Discuss the main idea with the students. Ask: Why is meat divided into fabricated cuts before being prepared? Meat is divided into fabricated cuts before being prepared because the primal cuts are too large to be prepared for a single serving.

TEACH

S Skill Practice

Guided Practice

L1 List Ask students to list the techniques used to process meat. The techniques used to process meat are curing, smoking, irradiating, or aging the meat.

L2 Explain Have students write a paragraph explaining the quality characteristics of veal. Veal should have a firm texture, a light pink color, and just a little bit of fat.

L3 Apply Ask students to demonstrate appropriate storage procedures for lamb. Lamb is to be stored in the refrigerator or freezer, for no more than 2–5 days in the refrigerator and no more than 6–9 months in the freezer. You might want to discuss what happens if these procedures are not followed correctly.

ASSESS

Quiz

Ask students to answer the following questions:

1. What does processing mean? Processing is changing or altering meat by artificial means.

2. What is the difference between smoking and curing meat? Smoking meat involves exposing the meat to the smoke of fragrant hardwood, while curing involves preserving the meat with salt, sugar, spices, flavoring, and nitrites.

3. Where does veal come from? Veal comes from calves that are fewer than nine months old.

RETEACH

U Universal Access

Students with Hearing Impairments After reviewing the different bones, commercial cuts, and visual differences in the kinds of meat, lay out a variety of meat cuts for students to identify. Evaluate each student's response, and check for understanding. Students should be able to successfully identify the meat cuts and have knowledge about the bones and visual differences between meats based on their reading.

C Critical Thinking

Choose a Cut Ask students which cut of meat they would choose for each of the following dishes: beef stew, roasted lamb, broiled veal, beef steak, and barbequed pork. Ask them to explain their decisions. Answers will vary, but might include: cuts from the chuck or round for the beef stew; loin or leg for the roasted lamb; rack or loin for the broiled veal; rib or loin for the beef steak; and loin, shoulder, or butt for the barbequed pork.

ASSESS

Lab Manual

Assign the Section 23.2 Activities.

Online Study Tools

Have students go to the Online Learning Center at **glencoe.com** to:

- Take the Section 23.2 Practice Test.
- Download Study-to-Go content.

SECTION 23.2 After You Read Answer Key

Review Key Concepts

1. Pork can be cured, aged, and smoked. Curing the pork is preserving the pork with salt, sugar, spices, flavoring, and nitrites. Smoking the pork is exposing the pork to the smoke of a fragrant hardwood after aging and curing.

2. The primal cuts of lamb are the shoulder, the shank/breast, the rack, the loin, and the leg.

3. The primal cuts of veal are the shoulder, the shank/breast, the rack, the loin, and the leg.

4. The chuck is a cut of beef that comes from the shoulder. It contains part of the backbone, rib bones, blade bones, and arm bones.

Practice Culinary Academics

5. **Mathematics** There are 8 ounces of steak uneaten. In the first 2 hours, customers fail to eat $1 - \frac{1}{2} = \frac{1}{2}$ of the steak. In the next 2 hours, they fail to eat $1 - \frac{2}{3} = \frac{1}{3}$ of the remaining meat. In the final 2 hours, they fail to eat $1 - \frac{1}{3} = \frac{2}{3}$ of the remaining steak. Overall, they leave $\frac{1}{2} \times \frac{1}{3} \times \frac{2}{3} = \frac{2}{18} = \frac{1}{9}$ of the steak uneaten. This equates to $\frac{1}{9} \times 72$ ounces $= \frac{72}{9} = 8$ ounces of the steak remaining.

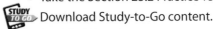

Professional Development MINI CLIP **Math** Introducing Multi-Step Equations

CLOSE

Culminating Activity

Meat Processing Safety Ask the students to research the pros and cons of irradiated or genetically engineered meat. Then, have them prepare a report about the advantages and disadvantages of each process. Have a class discussion and debate about this issue with students using information from their report to support their positions.

SECTION 23.3 Principles of Cooking Meat

Section Overview

In this section, students will learn how to cook for optimal tenderness using high- and low-heat cooking methods. They will also learn how to determine the doneness of meat by checking the meat's internal temperature and the color of the meat. Finally, they will learn how to properly plate a meat dish.

FOCUS

🔔 Bell Ringer Activity

Combination Cooking Have students find recipes for meat that use a combination cooking method. Discuss the recipes as a class. In what situations might one prepare these recipes? What would you need to think about beforehand? Discuss with students when combination cooking is desirable and when it is not.

D Develop Concepts

Main Idea Discuss the main idea with the students. Ask: Why do you think meat is a relatively expensive ingredient? Meat is a relatively expensive ingredient because the quantity of quality meat is limited, especially the prime cuts of meat.

TEACH

S Skill Practice

Guided Practice

L1 List Ask students to list the factors that determine meat's doneness. The factors include the cooking method, heat, type of meat, internal temperature, color, size, and cooking time.

L2 Explain Have students write a paragraph explaining how cooking impacts meat. Cooking impacts the tenderness of meat. Dry cooking firms proteins without breaking down connective tissue. Moist cooking tenderizes the meat.

L3 Apply Divide the class into groups, and ask them to demonstrate one cooking method for meat. Students should work together to prepare a piece of meat using one of the methods in the section. They should then observe the effects of this method and be able to decide if their chosen cooking method was successful.

 Professional Development MINI CLIP **Reading** On Workshops

ASSESS

Quiz

Ask students to answer the following questions:

1. When should you use low-heat cooking methods? Low-heat cooking methods are best used with large cuts of meat.

2. Why should you carve roasted meat against the grain? Carving roasted meat against the grain keeps the meat from being tough and stringy.

3. Why should you set up a grill with different temperatures? Setting up the grill with different temperatures will help you control cooking by moving meat to different areas of the grill.

RETEACH

R Reading Strategy

Grilled Meat Demonstration Demonstrate to the students how to charbroil steaks. Be sure to demonstrate how to create crosshatch grill marks, or grill lines, and how to cook to different levels of doneness. Also, demonstrate how to check the internal temperature with a meat thermometer. Use the demonstration to supplement the reading. Encourage students to ask questions as you demonstrate, and be sure to explain what you are doing as you do it.

U Universal Access

Students with Physical Challenges Ask students to imagine that they are roasting a prime rib for tonight's dinner menu. Ask them how they would season the meat and what their procedure for seasoning would be. Ask them to explain their decisions. Answers will vary, but may include seasonings such as salt, garlic, pepper, herbs, citrus zest, or spice blends. Students should add the seasonings to the meat surface after trimming the fat or insert seasonings, such as garlic or pepper, into the meat. This should be done several hours prior to roasting. The meat should be seasoned again after cooking.

ASSESS

 ExamView® Assessment Suite
Create a test for this chapter.

Lab Manual
Assign the Section 23.3 Activities.

 Online Study Tools
Have students go to the Online Learning Center at
glencoe.com to:

- Take the Section 23.3 Practice Test.
- Download Study-to-Go content.

SECTION 23.3 After You Read Answer Key
Review Key Concepts

1. Doneness is determined by internal temperature and color. Pork should be cooked to an internal temperature of 145°F (63°C) for 15 seconds. Steaks/chops should be cooked to an internal temperature of 145°F (63°C) for 15 seconds. Ground beef should be cooked to an internal temperature of 155°F (68°C) and held at that temperature for 15 seconds.

Practice Culinary Academics

2. **English Language Arts** The cooking guides should be creative, well organized, and visually appealing. They should reflect the information from the lesson about cooking meat. Additionally, they should combine written instructions with illustrations.

3. **Social Studies** Sous vide was originally developed for cooking on trains and airplanes, but many professional chefs have picked it up because of the way it preserves the quality of the meat. Bacteria that produce botulism can grow in the absence of oxygen, so food safety is very important with this method. Special equipment has been developed to cook this way safely. Some health departments require a special variance or permit to use sous vide cooking.

4. **Science** What students are witnessing is the Maillard reactions. The amino acids react with the sugar in the corn syrup and the flavor, smell, and color change.

5. **Mathematics** Marco should cook the pork to 62.8°C. 70°C (158°F) is enough for the hamburger, which must be cooked to 155°F. For the pork, using the F to C formula results in C = (145° − 32) × 5/9, or C = 113 × 5/9, or C = 565/9 ≈ 62.8. For the hamburger, using the C to F formula results in F = (9/5 × 70°) + 32, or F = (630/5) + 32, or F = 126 + 32 = 158.

 **Professional Development** MINI CLIP **Math**
Problem Solving—Order of Operations

CLOSE
Culminating Activity

Prepare a Pork Loin Divide the students into teams, and have the teams roast, broil, grill, sauté, pan-fry, or braise a pork loin. Set a goal for doneness, and have them try to reach that goal. Evaluate each team's product. Compare the results of the different team efforts.

Chapter Review and Applications
Vocabulary Review

1. Definitions for multiple-choice questions should be contained in one of the answers per question.

Review Key Concepts

2. The three components of meat are muscle fibers, connective tissue, and bones. Cuts include primal, large pieces of meat separated from the animal, and fabricated, smaller portions taken from primal cuts.

3. Meat that crosses state lines must be inspected, and it must have the USDA stamp to be fit for human consumption. Inspection does not indicate quality. Meat must be graded to indicate quality. Yield grades measure the amount of usable meat. Fresh meat should be stored in the refrigerator at 41°F (5°C) or below. Place meat on trays to catch juice. Store raw meats on the lowest shelf. Place fresh meat in a freezer at 0°F (−18°C) or below. Wrap in airtight, moisture-proof packaging to prevent freezer burn.

4. The cuts of pork include loin, picnic shoulder, shoulder or Boston butt, spareribs/belly, and ham. Pork can be nearly as lean as skinless chicken. Hogs are butchered young and are more tender than older animals.

5. Lamb should be pinkish to deep red, firm, finely textured, and have marbling. Fresh lamb spoils quickly and should be kept no more than 2–5 days in the refrigerator at 41°F (5°C) or below or 6 to 9 months in the freezer at 0°F (−18°C) or below.

6. Veal should have a firm texture, little fat and be light pink.

7. The best quality beef will be bright red. Fat marbling ranges from slight to moderately abundant.

8. When roasting, meat is seasoned and placed in a hot oven. Broiling is cooking directly under a high heat, while grilling is cooking on a rack with heat from below. Sautéing is frying in a small amount of fat in a shallow, open pan, while pan-frying uses more fat. Braising involves searing meats and then partially covering them with liquid and cooking them until they become tender. Stewing is similar to braising, but the meat is usually cut into smaller pieces and totally covered with liquid.

C Critical Thinking

9. The meat might not be at the correct temperature or might not have been covered properly.

10 It was probably cooked using a dry heat method, as indicated by the weight loss, due to moisture loss.

Academic Skills

11. English Language Arts Menus should use a creative design, and convey information clearly. Menu items should use the cooking techniques described in the book and describe meat cuts.

12. Social Studies Students should research humane farming and how to locate farms that treat livestock well. If they are interested in the issue, encourage them to volunteer.

13. Mathematics The ground beef is cheapest. The per-hamburger cost of the pre-formed patties is $44.99 ÷ 50 ≈ $0.90. For ground beef, if x represents the beef cost of 1 quarter-pound patty, $32.99/10 = x/.25$, or $x = ($32.99 \times 0.25) ÷ 10 = $0.82. The ground beef must be formed into patties. If the employee can form 200 patties/hour, it costs $12 to form 200 patties, or $12 ÷ 200 = $0.06 to form 1 patty. So total per-hamburger cost for the ground beef is $0.82 +

$0.06 = $0.88. For beef chuck, if x represents the beef cost of 1 quarter-pound patty, then $8.99/3 = x/0.25$, or $x = ($8.99 \times 0.25) ÷ 3 = $0.75. The chuck must be ground and formed into patties. It costs $12 to grind 120 pounds, or $12 ÷ 120 = $0.10 to grind 1 patty. So the total per-hamburger cost for the beef chuck is $0.75 + $0.10 + $0.06 = $0.91.

Certification Prep

14. b. choice

15. d. loin

Real-World Skills and Applications

16. Critical Thinking Skills Students could choose to either make the regular entrée until the meat runs out and then take it off the menu for the night, or they could choose to offer an alternate dish that uses less meat.

17. Interpersonal and Collaborative Skills Students should look for a bright red color, the grade, the proper fat content, and proper inspection stickers. They may choose to purchase irradiated beef. They should store the beef in the refrigerator at 41°F (5°C) or below, wrapped airtight on a tray on the lowest shelf. The ground beef must be cooked to 155°F (68°C) before layering into the lasagna. The lasagna must be cooked to an internal temperature of 165°F (74°C) and held at 135°F (57°C) or above during service.

18. Technology Applications Students should show how to use a thermometer to check the temperatures. They should also explain color and appearance.

19. Financial Literacy Purchasing another 10 lbs. of pork loin costs $79.90 ($7.99 \times 10). Adding extra rice and vegetables to the dish costs $120 ($1.50 \times 80). You may wish to discuss nutritional implications of both choices with your students.

Culinary Lab

20. Prepare Quality Meats Students should give comments that explain their number rating. Discuss with the class how the cut of meat chosen impacted the flavor and texture of the final dish.

Pasta and Grains

SECTION 24.1 Pasta

SECTION 24.2 Rice and Other Grains

Classroom Solutions

Print Resources

- Student Edition
- Instructor Annotated Edition
- Lab Manual
- Lab Manual IAE

Technology Resources

ExamView **ExamView® Assessment Suite CD**
Create and print unit and chapter tests.

Lesson Planner Plus **Lesson Planner Plus CD** provides access to teacher resources in one package.

Presentation Plus! provides visual teaching aids for every section.

Online Learning Center includes resources and activities for students and teachers. Also includes the **Online Student Edition**.

Interactive Student Edition

SECTION 24.1 Pasta

Section Overview
In this section, students will learn about the different types of pasta and how to cook and serve pasta. They will also learn the quality characteristics of pasta and how to purchase and store both dried and fresh pasta. Finally, they will learn how to determine the doneness of pasta and also how to make stuffed pasta.

FOCUS

Bell Ringer Activity
Potluck Pasta Ask the students to imagine they are making a pasta dish. What is one ingredient they would add to the dish? Have the students reveal their ingredients and list each ingredient on the board. Then, have students come up with pasta dishes using different combinations of the ingredients listed on the board.

D Develop Concepts
Main Idea Discuss the main idea with the students. Ask: Why do you think pasta is a staple in commercial kitchens? Pasta is a staple in commercial kitchens because it is easy to store, has a long shelf life, and is not easily contaminated or spoiled.

TEACH

S Skill Practice
Guided Practice
L1 List Ask students to list five types of pasta. Students may list any five of the following: elbow macaroni, spaghetti, egg noodles, lasagna, capellini, linguine, farfalle, fettucine, orzo, fusilli, manicotti, soba, penne, or conchiglie.
L2 Explain Ask students to write a paragraph explaining how to store fresh and dried pasta. Dried pasta should be stored in a cool, dry place. Fresh pasta should be tightly wrapped and kept refrigerated.
L3 Apply Have students demonstrate how to boil pasta. Students should practice boiling pasta and testing for doneness. They should do this activity until they are comfortable with the task. Observe the students, and provide feedback.

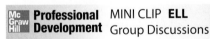

Professional Development MINI CLIP **ELL** Group Discussions

ASSESS

Quiz
Ask students to answer the following questions:
1. What type of flour is preferred in pasta? Semolina flour is the preferred type of flour for pasta.

2. Why should pasta be cooked al dente? When pasta is al dente, it is neither overcooked nor undercooked and will be more pleasant to eat.

3. How do you keep pasta from sticking as it cooks? To keep pasta from sticking as it cooks, use a combination of rapid convection movement, a large amount of water, and stirring.

RETEACH

U Universal Access

Students with Learning Disabilities Bring in a variety of fresh, dried, and frozen pasta. Have students prepare the different varieties of pasta using the same recipe. Have them compare the texture and flavor differences. Then, have them compare the cost per portion for each type of pasta. Students should experience the difference between the different forms of pasta, which will help them make decisions when preparing pasta recipes in the future. Discovering the cost per portion will help them make purchasing decisions.

C Critical Thinking

Problem Solving Ask students to imagine that they are working for a cafeteria. After the lunch period, they have a large amount of pre-cooked pasta left over. Have students brainstorm ways they can use the leftover pasta, assuming pasta is not on the dinner menu. Answers will vary, but might include things like planning a special for dinner using the pasta, adding the pasta to a soup or salad, or creating an employee meal with the pasta.

 Professional Development MINI CLIP **Reading** Guided Instruction

ASSESS

Lab Manual

Assign the Section 24.1 Activities.

Online Study Tools

Have students go to the Online Learning Center at **glencoe.com** to:

- Take the Section 24.1 Practice Test.
- Download Study-to-Go content.

After You Read Answer Key

Review Key Concepts

1. Pasta can be purchased either in dried or fresh form.

2. Determine the type of pasta to be used and prepare it. In the meantime, make the filling and then chill the filling in the refrigerator. Drain and shock the pasta when it is done. Use a pastry bag to fill the pasta.

3. Pasta must be served immediately, so the sauce and other ingredients must be ready to add, and any side vegetables and garnishes must be ready to be plated.

Practice Culinary Academics

4. English Language Arts The ads may use any form of media. Students should choose an advertising media, and make an ad appropriate to that type. They should showcase a new type of pasta created by the student after research on the qualities of good pasta. The ads should be targeted to a certain audience and use language that is clear, accurate, and convincing.

5. Mathematics You can make 22 full servings from a 5-pound bag. Since there are 16 ounces in 1 pound, the 5-pound bag of dry pasta is equivalent to $5 \times 16 = 80$ ounces. If x represents the number of cups of cooked pasta that can be made from 80 ounces of dry pasta, then 2 cups/4 ounces = x cups/80 ounces. Multiplying both sides by 80 results in $\frac{160}{4} = x$, or $x = 40$ cups. Forty cups of pasta is the same as $40 \div 1\frac{3}{4} = 40 \div \frac{7}{4} = 40 \times \frac{4}{7} = 22.86$ servings.

CLOSE

Culminating Activity

Practice Techniques Divide students into teams, and have them practice cooking cannelloni, manicotti, or conchiglie pasta until the pasta is al dente. Then, have them practice stuffing the pasta and baking it. Have the teams serve their finished products to the class, and have the class provide feedback on the results.

SECTION 24.2 **Rice and Other Grains**

Section Overview

In this section, students will learn about the different types of rice and other grains and how to cook them. They will also learn how rice is processed and how to properly handle and store rice and grains. Finally, they will learn about the appropriate cooking methods, including the risotto method, and how to serve rice and grains.

FOCUS

📣 Bell Ringer Activity

What Are These Foods? Present the following grain foods to students, and ask for volunteers to describe what they are: bulgur, muesli, couscous, pitas, basmati, and farfalle. If there are no volunteers, explain what the different types are. Explain that these foods can make good additions to a menu and can often add an exotic touch to more ordinary dishes.

D Develop Concepts

Main Idea Discuss the main idea with the students. Ask: Can you name some of the nutrients found in grains? Grains are rich in dietary fiber, B vitamins, and minerals.

TEACH

S Skill Practice
Guided Practice

L1 List Ask students to list the different varieties of rice. The different varieties of rice are brown rice, white rice, converted rice, and specialty rice.

L2 Explain Ask students to write a paragraph explaining how rice is processed. Processing rice is a procedure during which the hull is removed and the grain is polished.

L3 Apply Divide students into groups and ask them to demonstrate one cooking method for rice. Students should work together to prepare rice using one of the methods listed in the section. Observe the students, and provide feedback.

ASSESS
Quiz

Ask students to answer the following questions:

1. How does cooking brown rice differ from cooking white rice? Cooking brown rice differs from cooking white rice because cooking brown rice takes longer and requires more water.

2. What is the advantage of using enriched rice in a recipe for white rice? Using enriched rice in a recipe for white rice can be advantageous because the nutrients that were removed during processing have been replaced, so the dish will be more nutritious and balanced.

3. What is the first step in the pilaf method of making rice? The first step in making pilaf is to sauté the grains in fat.

RETEACH

W Writing Support

Rice Comparison Have students cook several different types of rice. Hold the types of rice on the steam table at a certain temperature for the same amount of time. Write a paragraph about which rice holds up the best and which qualities appear to make it the most successful for holding. Students should observe how well the different rice types stand up to holding and make conclusions about which types would be appropriate for serving at a banquet-style meal and which types would not.

U Universal Access

Gifted Students Give students a list of the following grains: cracked wheat, semolina, couscous, kasha, quinoa, triticale, kamut, spelt, and amaranth. Ask them to come up with a creative dish for each grain. Discuss the dishes they created and why they chose as they did. Answers will vary, but students should use the descriptions of these grains in the book to come up with creative dishes that are appropriate to the type of grain. Have students share their ideas with the rest of the class.

ASSESS

ExamView Assessment Suite Create a test for this chapter.

📓 Lab Manual

Assign the Section 24.2 Activities.

🧭 Online Study Tools

Have students go to the Online Learning Center at **glencoe.com** to:

- Take the Section 24.2 Practice Test.
- Download Study-to-Go content.

Review Key Concepts

1. Uncooked rice should be stored in airtight containers at room temperature in a room that is both dry and dark.

2. Hominy can be made into grits and masa harina. Grits are made from cracked hominy and are served as a side dish or as a breakfast cereal. Masa harina is a finely ground hominy used for making tortillas and breads.

3. All grains should be served as soon as possible after being cooked so that they do not lose their texture. Any grains not used immediately after being cooked should be cooled properly, labeled, dated and refrigerated in an air-tight container.

Practice Culinary Academics

4. **Social Studies** Rice has been genetically modified to add nutrients. For example, a type known as golden rice adds vitamin A. Grains can also be modified to be more resistant to pests or pesticides. While these modified grains have the potential to help some poorer populations, there is also uncertainty about unintended effects of genetic modification and the ability of corporations to exploit the technology. For these reasons, the issue is controversial.

5. **Mathematics** The 20-pound bag is the best buy because it has the lowest price per pound. The 20-pound bag sells for $19.59 \div 20 = \$0.9795 \approx \$0.98$ per pound. The 12-pound bag sells for $12.99 \div 12 = \$1.0825 \approx \$1.08$ per pound. The 5-pound bag sells for $7.75 \div 5 = \$1.55$ per pound.

CLOSE

Culminating Activity

Prepare Grains Divide students into teams and have them boil, steam, or braise a grain. Each team should prepare a different dish. They may add whatever other ingredients they like. Then, have them serve their finished products to the class. Have the other students provide feedback on the finished product.

Chapter Review and Applications

Vocabulary Review

1. Have students quiz each other using their index cards.

Review Key Concepts

2. Types of pasta include elbow macaroni, spaghetti, egg noodles, lasagna, capellini, linguine, farfalle, fettucine, orzo, fusilli, manicotti, soba, penne, and conchiglie. The quality characteristics include: 1) flour: dry pasta should be made with 100% semolina flour; 2) freshness: pasta should be hard and brittle and snap cleanly instead of bending easily. Dried pasta can be stored in a cool, dry place for several months. The storage area should be between 50-70°F (10-21°C). Fresh pasta must be tightly wrapped and kept refrigerated or frozen.

3. The best ways to cook pasta are boiling and baking. To boil, bring water to a boil with salt added. Then, add the pasta, and stir as it cooks until al dente. Cooked pasta can be baked in a casserole form or stuffed and covered with sauce and then baked in the oven.

4. Pasta must be plated and served immediately. All accompaniments must be ready to go when the pasta is finished. Add sauce and ingredients, sides and vegetables, and then serve immediately. It can be served on a plate, in soup plates, or as a side dish.

5. Brown rice has had the hull removed and has a tan color, chewy texture, and slightly nutty taste. White rice has had the outer layers of the grain removed and has a lighter texture, but is also lower in vitamins and minerals. Converted rice is rice that has been partially cooked with steam and then dried. Specialty rice offers many different textures and flavors.

6. Common grains include barley, oats, wheat products, corn products, polenta, and hominy.

7. Cooking methods used for rice and other grains include boiling, steaming, braising, and risotto.

C Critical Thinking

8. When partially cooking the pasta before stuffing, the noodles may have been overcooked and become soft and mushy while baking.

9. Answers will vary depending on the products analyzed, but students should evaluate each product based on price, available features, durability, and other relevant considerations.

10. Answers will vary, but equipment might include a saucepan or hotel pan and/or a bain marie. Rice can be kept hot in the bain marie.

Academic Skills

11. **English Language Arts** Charts should be well organized and easy to read. They should contain information that is accurate and useful. Illustrations should accurately convey the correct grain type.

12. **Science** Student lab reports should contain their hypothesis, procedure, methods, materials used, results, analysis, interpretation of their results, and their conclusions. In general, their experiment will probably involve researching the possible effects of cooking the starches in rice and cooking different types of rice and observing what happens to them over time to determine the starch content.

13. **Mathematics** Both original statements are true. The converse of statement (a) is "If a customer was charged $12, he ordered spaghetti." This is false, since he could have ordered any one of the 15 pastas for $12; he did not necessarily order spaghetti. The converse of statement (b) is "If a customer ordered a fish special, then she paid $18 for food." This is true, since both fish specials cost $18.

| Mc Graw Hill **Professional Development** | MINI CLIP **Math** Small Group Work |

Certification Prep

14. c. 1 gallon

15. a. arborio

Real-World Skills and Applications

16. **Interpersonal and Collaborative Skills** Students should work together to agree on suggestions that use grains that are healthful, and are appropriate for a school cafeteria. Their report should be professional in format and tone.

17. **Critical Thinking Skills** The substitutions students make should not only provide variety, but also be healthful. For example, it would be better to substitute whole-grain bread for white bread.

18. **Technology Applications** The report should summarize, in the student's own words, what the student learned. The information should be synthesized, organized, and explained logically.

19. **Financial Literacy** $5.00 \div 11$ oz. $= 0.45$ per oz.; $9.00 \div 24$ oz. $= 0.38$ per oz.; $2.00 \div 8$ oz. $= 0.25$ per oz.

Culinary Lab

20. **Prepare Polenta** Students should answer each question thoroughly, providing logical reasoning for their choices. Encourage them to discuss their cooking experiences with each other to gain more information to make their decisions.

Fruits, Vegetables, and Legumes

SECTION 25.1 Fruits

SECTION 25.2 Vegetables

SECTION 25.3 Legumes

Classroom Solutions

Print Resources

- Student Edition
- Instructor Annotated Edition
- Lab Manual
- Lab Manual IAE

Technology Resources

ExamView *ExamView® Assessment Suite* CD
Create and print unit and chapter tests.

Lesson Planner *Plus* Lesson Planner Plus CD provides access to teacher resources in one package.

Presentation Plus! provides visual teaching aids for every section.

Online Learning Center includes resources and activities for students and teachers. Also includes the **Online Student Edition**.

Interactive Student Edition

SECTION 25.1 Fruits

Section Overview

In this section, students will learn about the types of fruit and how to cook fruit. They will also learn about the grading, purchase, and storage of frozen, fresh, canned, and dried fruits. Finally, they will learn how to use dry and moist cooking methods with fruit and how to garnish and plate fruit dishes.

FOCUS

Bell Ringer Activity

Fruit Snacks Imagine that you have a business idea for a convenience store that will offer healthful snacks as an alternative to junk food. Ask students to brainstorm and come up with ideas for healthful snacks that use fruit as an ingredient and that you could sell in the store. Have the students share their ideas with one another.

D Develop Concepts

Main Idea Discuss the main idea with the students. Ask: What nutrients can be found in fruit? Fruits are important sources of many nutrients, including potassium, dietary fiber, vitamin C, and folate (folic acid).

TEACH

S Skill Practice

Guided Practice

L1 List Ask students to list the types of fruit. The types of fruit include citrus, melons, berries, drupes, pomes, grapes, tropical fruits, and exotic fruits.

L2 Explain Have the students explain how to store canned fruit. Store canned fruit on shelves in a cool, dry area. After opening the canned fruit, transfer any leftover fruit to a container, label, date, and refrigerate. Never leave the leftover fruit in its original can.

L3 Apply Divide students into groups and ask them to demonstrate one method of cooking fruit. Students should work together to prepare fruit using the cooking methods described in the section. After, have students share what they learned through this experience.

McGraw Hill Professional Development MINI CLIP **Reading** Planning and Management

ASSESS

Quiz

Ask students to answer the following questions:

1. What criteria are used to grade fresh fruit? The criteria used to grade fresh fruit include the fruit's shape, size, texture, color, and defects.

2. How can you prevent fruit from ripening after purchase? To prevent fruit from ripening after purchase, keep the fruit chilled and isolated from other fruits.

3. Which fruits produce the most ethylene gas? The fruits that produce the most ethylene gas are apples, melons, and bananas.

RETEACH

U Universal Access

Students with Physical Challenges Bring in a variety of fruits from the different fruit categories. Have the students identify the fruits and name three facts about each type. As a class, discuss appropriate ideas for how to serve each fruit. Students should be able to identify each fruit and remember information from the section when looking at the fruit. They should also come up with appropriate ways to prepare each fruit.

C Critical Thinking

Dealing with Setbacks Ask students to imagine that they are planning to prepare a poached pear dessert that will be served as part of a special event menu in four days. When they retrieve the pears from storage, they realize that they are not fully ripe. What would they do? To hasten the ripening of the pears, students should put them in a sealed container with fruits high in ethylene gas, such as bananas, melons, or apples, and store them in a warm area.

ASSESS

Lab Manual
Assign the Section 25.1 Activities.

Online Study Tools
Have students go to the Online Learning Center at **glencoe.com** to:

- Take the Section 25.1 Practice Test.
- Download Study-to-Go content.

SECTION 25.1 After You Read Answer Key

Review Key Concepts

1. Dried fruits can be added to baked goods or used in compotes or chutneys.

2. To prepare fruit for cooking, first wash the fruit in cold water and drain well. Then, remove any stems and peel or pull the skin. Next, cut the fruit into appropriately sized pieces. Finally, remove any seeds, pits, or cores. If fruit will brown, dip it in lemon juice to prevent this.

Practice Culinary Academics

3. **English Language Arts** Letters should be written in a business letter format. They should clearly describe the three fruit dishes and their cooking methods. Letters should be persuasive as to why the three suggested dishes would make good choices.

4. **Science** Fruit changes texture when heated because the heat kills the living cells in the fruit, which breaks down the cell membranes and causes moisture to flow out. The pectin that supported the cells dissolves, which causes the cells to loosen. This process makes the fruit softer and makes it lose shape.

5. **Mathematics** There are 720 ways that Alex can arrange the names of the sorbet flavors. Since there are 6 items, the number of arrangements is $6! = 6 \times 5 \times 4 \times 3 \times 2 \times 1 = 720$.

CLOSE

Culminating Activity

Fruit Preparation and Service Divide students into teams and have them choose a fruit to cook. Ask them to complete the necessary mise en place. Then, students should prepare their dishes. Have the teams serve their finished products to the class. Have the students evaluate each other's fruit dishes, providing positive and negative feedback.

SECTION 25.2 Vegetables

Section Overview

In this section, students will learn the basics about vegetables and cooking vegetables. They will also learn how vegetables are classified and how to purchase and store fresh vegetables, preserved vegetables, and potatoes. Finally, they will learn how to prepare vegetables for cooking, how to determine doneness, and how to plate and garnish vegetable dishes.

FOCUS

Bell Ringer Activity

Eat Your Vegetables Young children often do not like to eat vegetables. Have students imagine that their foodservice operation wants to add vegetable dishes to the children's menu that will be appealing to young children. Ask the class to brainstorm and come up with ideas for vegetable dishes that children might be interested in eating. Write the students' ideas on the board.

 **Professional Development** MINI CLIP **ELL** Elaborating on Student Responses

D Develop Concepts

Main Idea Discuss the main idea with the students. Ask: How can vegetables add variety to a main course? Answers will vary, but in general, vegetables come in different colors, flavors, and textures, and using different vegetables can change those aspects of a main course. Vegetables are also very versatile and can be cooked in many ways.

TEACH

S Skill Practice

Guided Practice

L1 List Ask students to list the classifications of vegetables. The classifications of vegetables include squash; roots and tubers; seeds and pods; cabbage; stems, stalks, and shoots; onion family; fruit-vegetables; and leafy greens.

L2 Explain Have students write a paragraph explaining how to store frozen vegetables. Frozen vegetables should be stored in the freezer. Once the vegetables have thawed and heated, they should be stored in the refrigerator.

L3 Apply Divide students into groups, and ask them to demonstrate one cooking method for vegetables. Students should work together to prepare vegetables using the cooking methods described in the section. Be sure to observe the students and provide feedback.

ASSESS

Quiz

Ask students to answer the following questions:

1. What is a tuber? A tuber is the short, fleshy, underground stem of a plant.

2. On what criteria are vegetable grades based? The criteria that vegetable grades are based on include the appearance, quality, and condition of the vegetables when they arrive on the market.

3. What is drained weight in reference to canned vegetables? In reference to canned vegetables, drained weight refers to the actual weight of the vegetable product without the packing medium.

RETEACH

R Reading Strategy

Vegetable Prep Lab Have students wash, peel, and trim assorted vegetables. Weigh all of the peels and trimmings for each vegetable. Calculate the edible portions, and determine the amounts needed for each recipe. This exercise will help students practice the preparation techniques they learned from the text, and it will also give them experience with calculating edible portions and amounts needed, which will help them with purchasing decisions.

U Universal Access

Students with Behavioral Challenges Ask students to imagine that they have checked their storeroom and noticed that some of the sweet potatoes are getting soft at the ends. How can they prepare them to avoid having to discard all their sweet potatoes? Answers will vary, but students should come up with creative solutions, such as making the sweet potatoes into sweet potato chips, a sweet potato pie, candied sweet potatoes, sweet potato casserole, sweet potato fries, or a puréed sweet potato soup.

ASSESS

Lab Manual

Assign the Section 25.2 Activities.

Online Study Tools

Have students go to the Online Learning Center at **glencoe.com** to:

- Take the Section 25.2 Practice Test.
- Download Study-to-Go content.

 **SECTION 25.2 After You Read Answer Key**

Review Key Concepts

1. Potatoes can be purchased fresh, canned, frozen, or dehydrated.

2. For the pre-preparation process for vegetables, the vegetables should be washed first in the manner appropriate to their type. Then, they should be peeled, if necessary, and then cut or shaped into the form appropriate to the cooking method that is being used.

Practice Culinary Academics

3. **English Language Arts** Students should provide all of the information requested by the activity description in their report (nutritional value, when it is in season, how to prepare and

store it, the flavor, and the texture). They should create an original dish, although they may look at existing recipes for inspiration. They should also provide a drawing or photograph that they have created to illustrate their report.

4. **Social Studies** Students should speak with a farmer or produce manager to learn how they raise and store their vegetables, and what technology is used to help the vegetables grow more easily. Then, students should accurately convey the information they learned to their classmates.

5. **Mathematics** The total order cost will equal the number of pounds multiplied by $2, plus a $5 delivery charge. If y is the total cost, and x is the number of pounds, the equation representing this relationship is $y = 2x + 5$. Students should draw a graph of this equation, which will look like a diagonal line sloping upward from left to right. The line will cross the y-axis at $y = 5$.

 **Professional Development** MINI CLIP **Math** Graphing Linear Equations

CLOSE
Culminating Activity
Create Vegetarian Dishes Ask students to create vegetarian dishes that could be added to a café lunch menu. The menu items should include an appetizer, a soup, and two entrées. Ask the students to describe how they would select, prepare, cook, and store the vegetables for each of these new menu items. They should also be able to explain why they chose the items they did.

SECTION 25.3 Legumes

Section Overview
In this section, students will learn about the types of legumes and how to cook them. They will also learn about the quality characteristics of legumes and how to purchase and store them. Finally, they will learn how to prepare legumes for cooking by soaking and simmering them.

FOCUS
🔔 Bell Ringer Activity
Assess What You Know Put a large piece of butcher paper or poster board on the wall or a table. Have students write all that they know about legumes on the butcher paper. When each student has completed his or her information, display the butcher

paper and discuss the information already known by the class. Tell students that in this section, they will be learning much more about legumes.

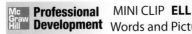 **Professional Development** MINI CLIP **ELL** Words and Pictures

D Develop Concepts
Main Idea Discuss the main idea with the students. Ask: Why do legumes have a long shelf life? Legumes have a long shelf life because they can be dried and then rehydrated for preparation. Once they are dried, they can be kept for a long time without going bad.

TEACH
S Skill Practice
Guided Practice

L1 List Ask students to list various types of legumes. Some types of legumes include lima beans, black-eyed peas, cannelini, fava, garbanzo, lentils, peanuts, split peas, and soy beans.

L2 Explain Have students explain how to store legumes. Legumes should be stored in a cool, dark, dry place with good ventilation.

L3 Apply Divide students into groups, and ask them to prepare one type of legume. Students should work together to practice preparing the legume of their choice. Observe students, and provide feedback. You may want to have students taste one another's dishes.

ASSESS
Quiz
Ask students to answer the following questions:

1. What is a legume? Legumes are a group of plants that have double-seamed pods containing a single row of seeds.

2. What is a pulse? A pulse is a dried legume.

3. Why must legumes be cooked? Legumes must be cooked to make them digestible and to make nutrients more accessible to the body. Cooking can also destroy some toxins in uncooked legumes.

RETEACH
U Universal Access
Students with Hearing Impairments Legumes are often a major part of a vegetarian menu. Have students research the use of legumes in vegetarian cooking and create a vegetarian menu that features dishes that have legumes as ingredients. Answers will vary, but students might include dishes such as hummus,

split pea soup, tofu stir-fry, black bean sauce, lentil salad, tabbouleh, and peanut butter balls for dessert.

C Critical Thinking

How to Prepare Legumes Ask students to imagine that their restaurant manager wants to promote legumes to the customers and wants them to come up with ideas for dishes that include legumes and that will appeal to the customers. Ask students to choose five different legumes and come up with a preparation for each legume that is unique and delicious. Answers will vary, but the dishes should be interesting and flavorful, as well as appealing to both timid and adventurous eaters. Students should be able to support their choices with explanations.

ASSESS

 ExamView® Assessment Suite
Create a test for this chapter.

Lab Manual

Assign the Section 25.3 Activities.

Online Study Tools

Have students go to the Online Learning Center at **glencoe.com** to:

- Take the Section 25.3 Practice Test.
- Download Study-to-Go content.

SECTION 25.3 After You Read Answer Key

Review Key Concepts

1. Some types of legumes include baby lima beans, black-eyed peas, cannellini beans, fava beans, garbanzo beans, Great Northern beans, green and brown lentils, navy beans, peanuts, pinto beans, black beans, red kidney beans, soybeans, and yellow and green split peas.

2. To prepare and cook legumes, legumes must first be rehydrated through soaking and simmering. First, sort through the legumes and remove the shriveled or discolored ones or any foreign objects. Next, rinse the legumes repeatedly until the water runs clear. Soak the legumes as desired and remove any that float. Finally, simmer the legumes until tender, but not too soft.

Practice Culinary Academics

3. **English Language Arts** Student ads should be accurate and persuasive, and contain information about the health benefits of legumes and the advantages of eating legumes instead

of meat. Ads should promote legumes and make people want to try them.

4. **Social Studies** Nitrogen used to fertilize fields has increased in price about 150% in the last decade. Legumes could provide a far cheaper method of fertilizing fields. Additionally, legumes complement the growth of grasses and extend the growth period to provide forage for livestock for a longer time. Students should be able to represent their research visually/pictorially.

5. **Mathematics** Russell can get 20 servings from a 5-pound package of dry beans. If there are 2 cups of volume for every pound, then 5 pounds is $2 \times 5 = 10$ cups of dry beans. If dry beans triple in volume when cooked, then 10 cups of dry beans results in $10 \times 3 = 30$ cups of cooked beans. The 30 cups of cooked beans can be used to make $30 \div 1.5 = 20$ servings of salad.

CLOSE

Culminating Activity

Prepare Legumes Divide students into teams and have them prepare and cook legumes. Have each team share their finished product with the other teams. Discuss the results with the class, and have students provide feedback. In particular, discuss the preparation process and how it contributed to the final product. Ask students what other dishes might use these legumes.

Chapter Review and Applications

Vocabulary Review

1. Check to see that students have correctly labeled each vocabulary word by part of speech.

Review Key Concepts

2. Fruits are available fresh, canned, frozen, or dried, and can be canned in heavy syrup, water, fruit juice, or in solid pack cans that contain little or no water. Frozen fruits are available sliced; packed in sugar syrup; whole; pitted; peeled; and sliced. Dried fruits are vacuum packed for purchasing and shipping.

3. Dry methods include broiling and grilling; baking; sautéing; and deep-frying. Moist methods include poaching and simmering.

4. Pay attention to grading for fresh vegetables, and choose ripeness based on the type of vegetable and storage. Canned vegetables will be softer, and the color may be duller. Look

for the USDA grade to denote quality. Get rid of any cans that are swollen or dented. Frozen vegetables can retain their color and texture. They use the same grading system and come in a variety of package sizes. Keep them in a freezer at a steady temperature of 0°F (−18°C) or below.

5. Dry cooking methods: broiling and grilling (cooked quickly over high heat); baking (cooked at a low temperature for a long period of time); sautéing (cooked in a little butter or oil in a hot pan); deep-frying (coated in batter and submerged in hot oil). Moist cooking methods: blanching (plunged in boiling water and then in cold water); parboiling (partially cooked); steaming (placed above boiling water in a perforated container); and poaching and braising (cooked in simmering liquid).

6. Types of legumes include lima beans, black-eyed peas, cannelini, fava, garbanzo, lentils, peanuts, split peas, and soy beans. Quality characteristics are that they should be brightly colored, uniformly sized, and not be marked, shriveled, damaged, or broken.

7. First, rinse the legumes and soak until they are three times their volume or quick soak for one hour. Then, put them in cooking liquid and bring to a simmer. When tender but not too soft, they are ready to be used for food preparation.

C Critical Thinking

8. First, consider the menu and know which fruit is in season. These are more likely to be of high quality. Then, make a visual inspection to look for the quality characteristics. Ask about grades, if any, to help you determine quality.

9. Transfer the mashed potatoes into bain marie inserts until the main entrée is done.

10. Store leafy greens and oranges in the cooler. Store tomatoes at room temperature. Store frozen corn in the freezer. Store potatoes, bananas, and dried split peas in the storeroom.

Academic Skills

11. **English Language Arts** Memorandums should provide information about fruit to support students' positions as well as healthful dessert ideas, such as fruit fondue. Writing should be persuasive and appropriate for a communication to an employer.

12. **Social Studies** Students should look into how the program works and how it was begun by the 2002 farm bill. They might also look into how schools are chosen and where the program is available to determine whether your school is eligible.

13. **Mathematics** There are 504 ways to line up three fruits. Since 3 items are being selected out of 9, the permutation formula results in $9!/[(9 − 3)!]$, or $9!/6!$. This expression is the equivalent of $(9 \times 8 \times 7 \times 6 \times 5 \times 4 \times 3 \times 2 \times 1)/(6 \times 5 \times 4 \times 3 \times 2 \times 1)$. You can cancel out the common factors from the numerator and denominator, resulting in $9 \times 8 \times 7 = 504$.

Certification Prep

14. a. U.S. Fancy

15. a. russet

Real-World Skills and Applications

16. **Interpersonal and Collaborative Skills** Dishes should be well researched, and students should know the cultural background, ingredients, and preparation.

17. **Self-Management Skills** To feed 25 customers, you will need 150 ounces of orange juice (6×25). Each orange will give you 3 ounces of juice, so you will need two oranges per glass. You will need at least 50 oranges (2×25 or $^{150}/_3$).

18. **Technology Applications** Answers should include five facts from reputable sources about legumes. Students should present at least one of their facts to the class, along with the source.

19. **Financial Literacy** The 8-ounce package is around 0.19/ounce ($1.50/8). The 12-ounce container is about 0.15/ounce ($1.75/12), and the 16-ounce package is about 0.13/ounce ($2.00/16). The 16-ounce package is the best bargain.

Culinary Lab

20. **Cook Fruits and Vegetables** Students' answers to the questions will vary depending on their preferences and the fruit or vegetable they chose. In general, the longer the fruit or vegetable is cooked, the less it will retain its texture, shape, and color.

Culinary Project Lesson Plan

FOCUS

Introduce the Project

In this project, students will learn how to choose a local and/or regional, seasonal ingredient or food, and how to incorporate that ingredient or food into a recipe. Ask students to name places where they typically purchase ingredients and food. Students may describe grocery stores, farmers' markets, or specialty food stores. Have them brainstorm which food sources they think provide the best selection of local and/or regional ingredients.

Build Background

Recipe Research Bring in a simple recipe. List the ingredients in the recipe on the board. Ask students what ingredients or foods they might add to or take away from the recipe to make it different. As students suggest ingredients and foods, write them on the board. You may discover trends of the types of ingredients and foods that students suggest, such as fruits and vegetables, meats and poultry, or cheeses. Ask students which season they think each of these ingredients becomes available, and which ones they think are available fresh locally.

TEACH

S Skill Practice

Guided Practice

L1 List Ask students to list ingredients and foods that can be found in their area/region. The list should include details on where to find these ingredients and foods.

L2 Explain Have students write two or more paragraphs about their favorite recipe, and how they might choose to use local/regional ingredients and foods in that recipe. Suggestions should be based on local/regional food availability, and should enhance the chosen recipe.

L3 Apply Have students think of three local/regional ingredients or foods that are available during the year, and what types of dishes they might complement. Sample answer: Locally grown corn might be useful in stews, as a side dish with other meats and vegetables, or in a corn chowder.

C Critical Thinking

Evaluate Cooking Methods Hold a discussion about different types of cooking methods that can be used with the local/regional ingredients and foods students have described. Are some methods better than others for specific ingredients or foods? Have students explain their answers. Answers may include moist methods to help soften tough foods, sautéing or stir-frying for more healthful cooking, or frying for a crispy texture.

ASSESS

Quiz

Ask students to answer the following questions:

1. What are the advantages of using local/regional and seasonal ingredients and foods in cooking? They can support local industry add variety and freshness to dishes, and appeal to local restaurant customers.

2. What are the factors you need to consider when you add a local/regional ingredient to a recipe? You must consider cooking time and method, seasonal availability of the ingredient, and what seasonings, flavorings, and herbs work well with your chosen ingredient or food.

3. What safety and sanitation rules do you need to follow when working with local/regional ingredients? Store and cook food at the proper temperature, avoid allowing uncooked meats and poultry to mingle with ready-to-eat foods, and thoroughly sanitize cooking surfaces and utensils.

CLOSE

Culminating Activity

Local Flavor Divide students into groups and have them decide which local/regional ingredients and foods are the most popular and easy to use in a variety of recipes. Have them decide which ingredients and foods they would use on a regular basis in a restaurant. Students may realize that local/regional ingredients and foods that are readily available will be easiest to use.

Unit Overview

Introduce the Unit In this unit, students are introduced to baking techniques and the special equipment and basic ingredients involved in quality baking. Students will also learn the proper mixing techniques and careful preparation involved in making yeast dough and bread. Additionally, students will be introduced to quick breads, focusing on biscuits and muffins. Finally, students will learn how to make cookies, cakes, pies, and specialty desserts.

Chapter

26   Baking Techniques

27   Yeast Breads and Rolls

28   Quick Breads

29   Desserts

SkillsUSA competitions provide important ways for your students to hone their technical skills. In the Commercial Baking competition, students are rated on their ability to scale, mix, prepare, and bake various baked goods.

Baked Good Choices Before beginning this unit, have students think of their favorite baked good (for example, a type of bread, cookie, pie, or cakes). Then, have them try to recreate the baking formula as best they can, including what basic ingredients they think are included and what special baking equipment they think would be necessary to make this baked good. Once you have completed this unit, have students return to the rough draft of their baking formula and adjust and correct it as much as they can. Remind students that their formula will probably not be exact, but that after reading the unit, they should be able to make it more precise. Answers will vary depending on the students' chosen baked good, but students should be able to identify most of the basic ingredients their baked good's formula would include (for example, flour, liquid, fat, sugar, eggs, leavening agent, salt, flavorings, and/or cocoa). Students should also be able to identify which special types of baking equipment their baked good might require. For example, cookies will require a sheet pan and an oven; a cake might require a mixer, an oven, and a pastry bag for frosting.

Unit Culinary Career Spotlight Answer Key (found on page 779)

Get Certified Students should successfully develop a new or modified recipe for any type of pie of their choice, deciding on the filling and types of dough and crust. Their idea should be creative, and students should have an idea of what they want their finished pie to look like.

Competition Practice Students should be given two and a half hours to complete their pies. Students should rate their own efforts based on whether they finished the pie on time, the pie's flavor, and the visual presentation of the finished pie.

As part of its mission, FCCLA encourages its student members to develop individual, teamwork, communication, and leadership skills through competitive activities.

Baking Contest Have a baking contest in class. Split students into groups. Each group should pick a baked good it wants to make. They can choose whatever they want, as long as the baked good can be made in class. Remind students that they will be judged on taste and completion, as well as creativity and presentation, so picking a more complicated dish is not necessarily better than making a simpler one well. Perhaps you can invite guest judges to the class (for example, other teachers, other students, or parents). You may want to give prizes to the winning team. The teams will be judged their ability to work as a team, the level of individual contribution, technical skill demonstrated, creativity, and the finished baked good's taste and appearance.

McGraw Hill Professional Development

MINI CLIP VIDEO LIBRARY

Targeted professional development is correlated throughout *Culinary Essentials*. The McGraw-Hill Professional Development Mini Clip Video Library provides teaching strategies to strengthen academic and learning skills. Log on to **glencoe.com**.

Chapter 26 Baking Techniques

Reading Strategies for Student Achievement Teachers discuss strategies to help all learners meet standards. (p. TM234)

ELL Understanding Proficiency Author Jana Echevarria discusses English proficiency. (p. TM233)

Math The Meaning of Variable Students and teacher discuss the meaning of variable. (p. TM235)

Chapter 27 Yeast Breads and Rolls

Reading Differentiated Activities A teacher models vocabulary cards that will support different learning styles. (p. TM240)

ELL Understanding Proficiency Author Jana Echevarria discusses the meaning of proficiency. (p. TM237)

ELL Using Manipulatives A teacher uses concrete objects to illustrate lesson concepts. (p. TM239)

Math The Meaning of Equality Curriculum supervisor Mary Esther Reynosa suggests how students can master this concept. (p. TM238)

Chapter 28 Quick Breads

Reading Strategic Readers Author Scott Paris discusses the characteristics of strategic readers. (p. TM242)

Reading Guided Instruction A teacher helps students identify major and minor details. (p. TM243)

Math Communication in Mathematics Bea Moore-Harris explains the importance of communication. (p. TM244)

Math Classroom and Instructional Management Dr. Gilbert Cuevas discusses issues that teachers face in the classroom. (p. TM245)

Chapter 29 Desserts

Reading Interacting with Text Students work in small groups to discuss higher order questions. (p. TM248)

Reading Vocabulary Author Josefina Tinajero describes the importance of academic language. (p. TM250)

ELL Building the Context A teacher models an activity that helps students understand a selected reading. (p. TM249)

Math Problem Solving—Order of Operations A teacher uses real-life examples to introduce order of operations. (p. TM250)

Baking Techniques

SECTION 26.1 Bakeshop Formulas and Equipment

SECTION 26.2 Bakeshop Ingredients

Classroom Solutions

Print Resources

- Student Edition
- Instructor Annotated Edition
- Lab Manual
- Lab Manual IAE

Technology Resources

ExamView® Assessment Suite CD
Create and print unit and chapter tests.

Lesson Planner Plus **Lesson Planner Plus CD** provides access to teacher resources in one package.

Presentation Plus! provides visual teaching aids for every section.

Online Learning Center includes resources and activities for students and teachers. Also includes the **Online Student Edition**.

Interactive Student Edition

SECTION 26.1 Bakeshop Formulas and Equipment

Section Overview

In this section, students will learn what baking formulas are and why they are used. They will also learn about volume and weight measurements and how to use a baker's scale. Finally, they will learn how to convert a baking formula to a new yield and the function of various bakeshop equipment and tools.

FOCUS

Bell Ringer Activity

Making Baked Goods Ask students to write down five of their favorite baked goods. Then, have them list what ingredients might go into each product and what equipment would be needed to make each product. Discuss the answers as a class, and determine which of the products could be made at home and which ones would require a commercial kitchen.

D Develop Concepts

Main Idea Discuss the main idea with the students. Ask: Why do you think baking requires precise measurement and accuracy? Baking requires precise measurement and accuracy because even the slightest inaccuracy can change the flavor or texture of the baked item.

TEACH

S Skill Practice
Guided Practice

L1 List Have students list three pieces of large bakeshop equipment, three pieces of bakeshop smallwares, and three baking tools. Large bakeshop equipment includes mixers, sheeters, proofing cabinets, and bakery ovens. Bakeshop smallwares include pans, molds, and rings. Baking tools include pastry bags, pastry brushes, pastry pattern cutters, bench scrapers, and rolling pins.

L2 Explain Ask students to explain the two ways that bakeshops measure ingredients. Bakeshop ingredients are measured either by weight or by volume. Volume is the space an ingredient occupies. Weight measures the mass or heaviness of something.

L3 Apply Have students practice using a baker's scale to measure various ingredients. Students should practice following the procedure in the text until they are comfortable measuring various ingredients using the scale.

ASSESS

Quiz

Ask students to answer the following questions:

1. What are two pieces of equipment found in a commercial bakeshop that you might not see in a regular commercial kitchen? Two pieces of equipment found in commercial bakeshops that are normally not found in commercial kitchens are a sheeter and a bread molder.

2. What are the basic attachments of a bench mixer? The basic attachments of a bench mixer are a spiral dough hook, a flat beater or paddle, and a whip.

3. What is a springform pan, and for what is it commonly used? A springform pan is a pan with a clamp that is used to release the pan's bottom from its circular wall. It is commonly used when making cheesecakes.

RETEACH

Universal Access

English Language Learners Divide students into teams, and have them gather all of the equipment and tools necessary to prepare a formula that you assign them. Have them share their equipment selections with the class. Did they gather all of the necessary equipment? Discuss the use of each piece of equipment in the formula. Students should select all of the necessary equipment and not leave anything out. They should also be able to explain how the equipment will be used.

Professional Development MINI CLIP **ELL** Understanding Proficiency

C Critical Thinking

Choose Your Equipment Have the students assume that they are opening a bakeshop that will specialize in cinnamon rolls. Ask them to choose the ten most important pieces of equipment and hand tools they will need to run their shop successfully. Have them explain why they made their choices. Students might choose any combination of: balance or digital scale, bench mixer, proofing cabinet, deck oven, reel oven, pastry cutters, pastry brushes, bench scraper, baking pans, molds and rings, and rolling pins. They should be able to explain why they made their specific choices.

ASSESS

Lab Manual

Assign the Section 26.1 Activities.

Online Study Tools

Have students go to the Online Learning Center at **glencoe.com** to:

- Take the Section 26.1 Practice Test.
- **STUDY TO GO** Download Study-to-Go content.

SECTION 26.1 After You Read Answer Key
Review Key Concepts

1. To use a balance scale, you must first place the scale scoop on the left side of the scale. Compensate for the weight of the scoop by balancing the right side with weights. Then, add weights to the right side of the scale to equal the desired weight of ingredients. Finally, add the ingredient to the scoop on the left side of the scale until the scale is balanced.

2. A proofing cabinet can be used to keep baked products warm or to proof yeast dough. It allows dough to rise slowly in a humidity-controlled, low-heat environment before baking.

3. Pans used in a bakeshop include cake pans, springform pans, tart pans, and sheet pans.

Practice Culinary Academics

4. **English Language Arts** The letter should provide specific information about the equipment needed and why it is necessary for making commercial cupcakes. Students should use proper grammar and spelling, and the letter should be written in a business letter format and tone.

5. **Mathematics** The baker's percentages are as follows: Bread flour = 3 kg ÷ 4 kg = 0.75 = 75%. Rye flour = 1 kg ÷ 4 kg = 0.25 = 25%. Water = 2.8 kg ÷ 4 kg = 0.7 = 70%. Yeast = 0.08 kg ÷ 4 kg = 0.02 = 2%. Salt = 0.12 kg ÷ 4 kg = 0.03 = 3%. Total = 7 kg ÷ 4 kg = 1.75 = 175%.

CLOSE

Culminating Activity

Use a Formula Divide students into groups, and have them use a formula to bake something. Encourage them to follow the measurements as accurately as possible. Once they have baked their item, have them compare the results with one another and evaluate the final products. How accurate were they with their measurements? How did their baked goods turn out?

CHAPTER 26 Lesson Plan

SECTION 26.2 Bakeshop Ingredients

Section Overview

In this section, students will learn the importance of using exact ingredients. They will also learn about the different categories of ingredients and their roles in the baking process. Finally they will learn about the techniques used to mix batters and doughs.

FOCUS

🔔 Bell Ringer Activity

Illustrate Ingredients Have students choose one ingredient type and make a poster of a creative visual representation of the various kinds of that ingredient. They can choose to draw pictures and label them with the names or they might choose to provide additional information along with the illustration.

D Develop Concepts

Main Idea Discuss the main idea with the students. Ask: How can ingredients determine the visual appeal of a baked good? Ingredients can determine the visual appeal of a baked good by adding color and determining how smooth the texture is.

TEACH

S Skill Practice
Guided Practice

L1 List Ask students to list the different types of chocolates and cocoas. The different types of chocolates and cocoas are unsweetened chocolate, semisweet chocolate, white chocolate, cocoa powder, and Dutch-process cocoa powder.

L2 Explain Have students explain what white chocolate is. White chocolate contains cocoa butter, sugar, vanilla, lecithin, and dried or condensed milk. There is no chocolate liquor in white chocolate.

L3 Apply Bring in examples of different chocolates and cocoas and have students compare the flavor, appearance, and texture. Discuss with students their impressions of the differences between the various types of chocolates and cocoas and how their use might affect baked goods.

ASSESS

Quiz
Ask students to answer the following questions:

1. What is the difference between vegetable shortenings and emulsified shortenings? Vegetable shortenings are oils that have been hydrogenated to make them solid. Emulsified shortenings have emulsifiers added and look like creamy oils.

2. What is the role of yeast during the fermentation process? During the fermentation process, yeast breaks down sugars into carbon dioxide gas and alcohol, which are necessary for the rising process in bread.

3. How do fats tenderize baked goods? During baking, fats surround the flour particles and prevent long strands of gluten from forming.

RETEACH

U Universal Access

Students with Hearing Impairments Show students how to measure various bakeshop ingredients using a balance scale and volume measures. After the demonstration, have the students practice these techniques for themselves. Students should become proficient in handling and measuring various types of ingredients.

 **Professional Development** MINI CLIP **Reading** Strategies for Student Achievement

C Critical Thinking

Account for Carryover Baking The text warns that carryover baking can lead to overbaked products. How can students prevent this from happening? To prevent overbaking, take the carryover time into account when thinking of the cooking time. In addition, cool the product in a well-ventilated area on a rack that allows air to circulate all around the dish.

ASSESS

 ExamView® Assessment Suite Create a test for this chapter.

✍ Lab Manual
Assign the Section 26.2 Activities.

🧭 Online Study Tools
Have students go to the Online Learning Center at **glencoe.com** to:

- Take the Section 26.2 Practice Test.

 Download Study-to-Go content.

SECTION 26.2 After You Read Answer Key
Review Key Concepts

1. The most common types of fat used in a bakeshop are vegetable shortening, emulsified shortening, oil, butter, and margarine.

2. Folding is gently adding light ingredients into heavier ingredients with a smooth circular movement, while kneading is working dough by hand or in a bench mixer with a dough hook to develop gluten and evenly distribute the ingredients.

Practice Culinary Academics

3. **English Language Arts** The dialogue should use language appropriate to a teacher and student and should provide accurate information from the chapter about one type of common bakeshop ingredient. It should be written in a dialogue form, with the name of the speaker, followed by what they say.

4. **Science** Answers may vary, but according to nutritiondata.com: 1 cup of unsweetened chocolate has around 660 calories, 69 g of fat, and 1 g sugar; 1 cup of semisweet chocolate has around 800 calories, 50 g of fat, and 92 g sugars; 1 cup of white chocolate has around 916 calories, 55 g fat, and 100 g sugars; 1 cup cocoa powder has around 197 calories, 12 g fat, and 2 g sugars; and in 1 cup of Dutch-process cocoa powder is around 240 calories, 8 g fat, and 0 g sugar.

5. **Mathematics** Erica needs 16 cups of 1% milk and 8 cups of 4% milk. If $x =$ cups of 1% milk and $y =$ cups of 4% milk, then $x + y = 24$ cups, or $x = 24 - y$. We also know that $0.01x + 0.04y = (0.02)(24) = 0.48$, or, multiplying both sides by 100 to remove the decimals, $1x + 4y = 48$. Substituting $(24 - y)$ for x in the second formula gives $24 - y + 4y = 48$, or $3y = 48 - 24$, or $3y = 24$, or $y = 8$. Since $x = 24 - y$, then $x = 24 - 8 = 16$.

 Professional Development MINI CLIP **Math** The Meaning of Variable

CLOSE

Culminating Activity

Research an Ingredient Have students choose a bakeshop ingredient to research. Then, have them use and print Internet resources to create a poster that explains where the ingredient comes from and how it is used to create baked products. Have the students discuss their findings as a class.

Chapter Review and Applications
Vocabulary Review

1. Have students test each other using the index cards they made.

Review Key Concepts

2. Baking formulas are recipes that include precise amounts of ingredient, often listed as percentages.

3. Mixers mix, knead, or whip batters and dough. Sheeters roll out dough to a desired thickness. Proofing cabinets keep baked products warm or proof yeast dough. Bakery ovens cook baked goods. Pans are containers to cook baked goods in. Molds and rings help form a product to a certain shape.

4. Bakeshop tools include pastry bags, pastry brushes, pastry pattern cutters, bench scrapers, and rolling pins.

5. Wheat flour gives baked goods their structure. Liquids affect texture. Fats tenderize the baked good. Sugars and sweeteners add flavor. Eggs add richness and tenderness. Leavening agents cause baked goods to rise. Flavorings enhance the flavor. Chocolate and cocoa add body, bulk, and a unique color and flavor. Additives color, thicken, provide texture, and replace fat. Nuts provide color, flavor, and texture.

6. Beating is agitating ingredients vigorously. Blending is mixing or folding ingredients together until evenly combined. Creaming is vigorously combining softened fat and sugar to add air. To cut in, mix solid fat with dry ingredients until lumps of the desired size remain. Folding is gently adding light, airy ingredients, such as eggs, to heavier ingredients by using smooth circular movements. Kneading is working dough by hand or in a bench mixer with a dough hook to develop gluten and evenly distribute ingredients. Sifting is passing dry ingredients through a wire mesh. Stirring is gently blending ingredients until they are combined. Whipping is beating ingredients to add air.

C Critical Thinking

7. Measuring dry ingredients in measuring cups instead of weighing them on a scale could lead to poor results because weight and volume produce different results in baking.

8. Answers will vary, but may include price, available features, the type of product being produced, and available space.

9. The higher the protein in a flour, the more potential the flour has to form gluten, which will alter the structure of the baked good.

10. Although you followed the correct temperature guidelines in the formula, the pies may have overbaked because the oven was too hot. Also, the formula may not be correct. Check the oven and recalibrate if necessary. Evaluate the formula to alter it.

Academic Skills

11. **English Language Arts** Baking formulas do not look like regular recipes. By looking at formulas and reading about baking formulas, students should be able to decipher how to use a formula.

12. **Science** The more gluten, the chewier the product will be. The less gluten, the softer it will be.

13. **Mathematics** Danielle will need: 54 lbs., 1 oz. of bread flour, 35 lbs., 2 oz. of water, 1 lb., 1 oz. of salt, 1 lb., 1 oz. of yeast, 2 lbs., 11 oz. of shortening, 2, lbs. 3 oz. of sugar, and 3 lbs., 13 oz. of dry milk solids. The weight of the flour equals 100 lbs. ÷ 185% = 100 ÷ 1.85 = 54.05405 lbs. Multiply this weight by each ingredient's baker's percentage to find the weights of the individual ingredients: For example, water = $0.65 \times 54.05405 = 35.13514$ lbs. Each decimal weight should be converted to pounds and ounces. For example, to find the ounce portion of the flour weight, multiply .05405 × 16 = 0.8648, which rounds up to 1. Thus, 54 lbs. 1 oz. of flour is needed.

Certification Prep

14. b. ramekin

15. b. hydrogenation

Real-World Skills and Applications

16 **Interpersonal and Collaborative Skills** Students should work together to provide five ideas with creative marketing names and nutrition information.

17. **Information Literacy** Students should be able to determine the gluten content of the different flours and read the ingredients list for additives. Self-rising flours will have additives to help the dough rise. Flours will generally have a small amount of fat and a larger amount of carbohydrates, while flours with additives will have other nutrients as well.

18. **Technology Applications** The information from the text about different baking equipment should be adapted into a PowerPoint format. It may include a title page and pages with information about the equipment, organized to make it easy to follow.

19. **Financial Literacy** There are 30 shell eggs per flat. $7.50/30 = 0.25 per egg. There are 16 eggs per 32 oz. container (½ × 32 = 16). $6.00/16 = 0.38 per egg. The shell eggs have the best price.

Culinary Lab

20. **Measure Ingredient Yields** Student's evaluations of the ingredients should include an assessment of the relative difficulty of measuring for each and reasons for the assessment.

Yeast Breads and Rolls

SECTION 27.1 Yeast Dough Basics   SECTION 27.2 Yeast Dough Production

Classroom Solutions

Print Resources

- Student Edition
- Instructor Annotated Edition
- Lab Manual
- Lab Manual IAE

Technology Resources

ExamView Assessment Suite
ExamView® Assessment Suite CD
Create and print unit and chapter tests.

Lesson Planner Plus **Lesson Planner Plus CD** provides access to teacher resources in one package.

Presentation Plus! **Presentation Plus!** provides visual teaching aids for every section.

Online Learning Center includes resources and activities for students and teachers. Also includes the **Online Student Edition**.

Interactive Student Edition

SECTION 27.1 Yeast Dough Basics

Section Overview

In this section, students will learn about the characteristics of quality yeast dough products. They will also learn about the different types of yeast and the various types of yeast dough. Finally, they will learn the difference between products made from regular yeast dough and products made from rolled-in fat yeast doughs.

FOCUS

Bell Ringer Activity

Identify Ingredients Set out small containers of the common ingredients of a yeast dough. See how many of the students can identify the ingredients by sight. Go through each ingredient, and allow students to smell, examine, and feel them. Then, have them guess which ingredient it is. You may wish to offer rewards to the first student to guess each ingredient correctly.

D Develop Concepts

Main Idea Discuss the main idea with the students. Ask: What are some examples of how bread might appear on a menu? Bread can be served as an appetizer to the table or it can appear as part of a sandwich, in a salad as croutons, as a side with soup, or as part of a dessert, among other ideas.

TEACH

S Skill Practice

Guided Practice

L1 List Have students list the functions of the ingredients in yeast dough. The functions of the various ingredients include: binding ingredients; absorbing liquids; adding to shelf life, structure, and/or nutritional value; and affecting eating quality, flavor, gluten, shape, and/or tenderness.

L2 Explain Ask students to explain how much dry yeast they would substitute if a bakery formula called for 2 ounces of compressed yeast and why. You would substitute 1 ounce of active dry yeast, because it is twice as strong as compressed yeast.

L3 Apply Have students sample breads made from each different type of dough and discuss the differences between them. Students should notice the differences in texture, appearance, and flavor caused by the use of different dough types.

 **Professional Development** MINI CLIP **ELL** Understanding Proficiency

ASSESS

Quiz

Ask students to answer the following questions:

1. What are the three most commonly used baking yeasts? The three most commonly used baking yeasts are compressed yeast, active dry yeast, and quick rise yeast.

2. What are the basic ingredients in a starter? The basic ingredients in a starter are flour, yeast, and a warm liquid.

3. How do you soften compressed yeast? To soften compressed yeast, mix it with a liquid that is about 85°F (29°C).

RETEACH
 Writing Support

Field Trip After reading the section, have students write down the questions they would ask a professional baker about careers, hours, equipment, baking formulas, ingredients, use of convenience products, and display techniques. If possible, tour a local bakeshop, and have students ask their questions during the tour. Students should start with what they have learned so far and use that to think of questions about information they would like to learn next to deepen their understanding of the subject.

U Universal Access

Students with Visual Impairments Obtain samples of different types of bread. Have students perform a taste test to compare the breads. Ask students to express their impressions of the appearance, flavor, and texture of the bread. Have them determine how they would use each of the breads. Students should report their assessments of the different breads for each category. They should then determine which uses are appropriate based on the characteristics of each bread type.

ASSESS
Lab Manual

Assign the Section 27.1 Activities.

Online Study Tools

Have students go to the Online Learning Center at **glencoe.com** to:

* Take the Section 27.1 Practice Test.
* Download Study-to-Go content.

SECTION 27.1 After You Read Answer Key
Review Key Concepts

1. A starter is a mixture of flour, yeast, and a warm liquid. It begins the leavening action.

2. Pullman bread and dinner rolls, such as cloverleaf and Parker House rolls, can be made from soft medium dough.

3. A freshly baked croissant should be light golden brown. It should have a flaky, layered texture and an open grain or crumb.

Practice Culinary Academics

4. **Science** Students should observe that the balloon expands as the carbon dioxide is released by the yeast and fills the balloon. Students should record these observations in their log and support their conclusion.

5. **Mathematics** Christine must sell at least 39 croissants during the day to cover her product cost. Christine's expenses will equal $80 \times \$0.60 = \$48$ regardless of how many croissants are sold (since all 80 croissants will have already been baked). If x represents the number of croissants sold, then Christine will break even at $\$1.25(x) = \$48$, or $x = \$48 \div \$1.25 = 38.4$ croissants sold. Thus, if she sells 39 croissants, she will cover her ingredient cost.

 Professional Development MINI CLIP **Math** The Meaning of Equality

CLOSE
Culminating Activity

Review Ask students to explain information they learned in the section that they did not know before. Have each student name at least one piece of information they learned from this section, and write each piece of information on the board so that the class can review as you discuss.

SECTION 27.2 Yeast Dough Production
Section Overview

In this section, students will learn about the proper methods for preparing yeast bread and rolls. They will learn how the process of fermentation works in yeast doughs. They will also learn the common causes of failure in yeast bread production. Finally, they will learn the steps involved in preparing quality yeast breads.

FOCUS
Bell Ringer Activity

Guest Speaker If possible, invite a local bread maker to speak to the class. Ask him or her to demonstrate the many techniques used to create yeast products. Have students practice the techniques with the guest speaker observing. Encourage students to ask questions of the guest speaker about anything they do not understand or anything they would like to know more about.

D Develop Concepts

Main Idea Discuss the main idea with the students. Ask: What do you think might be common causes of failure when making a yeast bread product? Answers will vary, but might include predictions such as using the wrong amount of ingredients, overcooking, not letting the dough rise for a long enough length of time, or skipping a step.

TEACH

S Skill Practice
Guided Practice

L1 List Ask students to list the basic steps in the sponge method. The steps of the sponge method are as follows: 1) Combine 50% water with 50% flour. 2) Add the yeast. Sugar or malt may also be added to this mixture to promote faster yeast growth. 3) Cover the sponge. Let it rise in a warm place for two to three hours or until it doubles in bulk. 4) Combine the sponge with the remaining ingredients either by hand or in a mixer.

L2 Explain Have students explain the benefits of the sponge method and when you might want to use it. The sponge method allows the yeast to develop separately before it is mixed with the other ingredients, which results in a more intense flavor and a lighter, airy texture. You might want to use it when making crusty hearth breads or sweeter doughs.

L3 Apply Ask students to practice the sponge method of mixing. Students should practice the sponge method of mixing as described in the book so that they understand how it is done and become comfortable with the process.

 **Professional Development** MINI CLIP **ELL** Using Manipulatives

ASSESS
Quiz

Ask students to answer the following questions:

1. What are two benefits of punching dough? Any two of: maintaining even temperature, releasing carbon dioxide, introducing oxygen, and developing gluten.

2. What are two principles to follow in shaping yeast dough? Any two of: work quickly, shape pieces in order, use very little flour, and place any seams at the bottom.

3. What are two ways to prevent staling? Any two of: add special ingredients or chemicals, proof adequately, and avoid refrigeration.

RETEACH

U Universal Access

English Language Learners Demonstrate quantity formulas of hard and soft roll doughs. Discuss basic principles while the dough is fermenting. Give each student a portion of the dough to work with and shape following demonstrated procedures. The visual demonstration and hands-on practice should enhance the information in the text for different types of learners.

C Critical Thinking

Troubleshoot Ask students to imagine that they are starting a loaf of yeast bread and the dough will not rise. What are some possible causes for this? Which things would they check to try to determine the cause? Answers will vary, but possible causes are that the yeast may have expired, they may have used the wrong temperature water to dissolve the yeast, they may have used the wrong type of flour, they may not have waited long enough for the dough to rise, they may not have kneaded enough, or they may have left out an ingredient.

ASSESS

 ExamView® Assessment Suite Create a test for this chapter.

Lab Manual
Assign the Section 27.2 Activities.

Online Study Tools

Have students go to the Online Learning Center at **glencoe.com** to:

- Take the Section 27.2 Practice Test.
- Download Study-to-Go content.

SECTION 27.2 After You Read Answer Key
Review Key Concepts

1. The straight-dough method calls for mixing all ingredients together in a single step either by hand or with a bench mixer.

2. The stages in mixing and kneading are: pickup (ingredients are added to the mixer); cleanup (ingredients come together in a ball); development (oxygen is incorporated and gluten is developed); and final clear (verify gluten formation and remove dough from mixer).

3. The factors that determine oven temperature and baking time are dough type, dough richness, portion size, desired color, and weather/altitude.

4. Let the bread cool before wrapping. Then, wrap tightly in a moisture-proof wrapping and store in the freezer to prevent staling.

Practice Culinary Academics

5. Mathematics The first baguette is $55 \times 10 = 550$ mm, while the second is $61 \times 10 = 610$ mm. The first baguette is $55 \div 100 = 0.55$ m, while the second is $61 \div 100 = 0.61$ m. The first baguette is $0.55 \div 1,000 = 0.00055$ km, while the second is $0.61 \div 1,000 = 0.00061$ km.

CLOSE

Culminating Activity

Prepare a Yeast Dough Working as a team, have students prepare a yeast dough and then bake it into a bread or rolls. Have them work together to plan the type of product they will make, find a baking formula, and then prepare the item. Enjoy the finished product together and evaluate the result.

 **Professional Development** MINI CLIP **Reading** Differentiated Activities

Chapter Review and Applications

Vocabulary Review

1. Write terms on separate sheets of paper; hand each to a student. Have them write what they think the definition is and pass to the next student, who should add to the definition, correct it, or confirm it. Do this at least three times; then have the last person use the textbook's glossary to write the correct definition.

Review Key Concepts

2. Yeast dough ingredients are: flour, salt, sugar, fat, milk solids, water and yeast. Yeast causes the dough to rise. The functions of the various ingredients include: binds ingredients; absorbs liquids; adds to shelf life, structure, or nutritional value; and affects eating quality, flavor, gluten, shape, or tenderness.

3. Hard lean doughs have 0-1% fat and sugar. They are often made solely from flour, water, salt, and yeast. Soft medium doughs produce items with a soft crumb and crust. The percentage of fat and sugar is 6-9%. Sweet rich doughs

incorporate up to 25% of fat and sugar. Their structure is soft and heavy.

4. Rolled-in fat yeast doughs yield a rich, flaky product. Two popular uses of this kind of dough are croissants and Danish pastries.

5. The straight-dough method calls for mixing ingredients together in a single step by hand or with a bench mixer. The modified straight-dough method breaks the straight-dough method into steps. The sponge method allows the yeast to develop separately before it is mixed with the other ingredients.

6. The stages in preparing yeast doughs are scaling, mixing, kneading, fermentation, punching, dividing, rounding, bench rest, shaping, panning, final proofing, washing, slashing, and docking.

7. Baking takes place in four stages: 1) oven spring, in which the dough rises and expands, 2) structure begins to develop, 3) crust forms, and 4) the product is finished.

8. To cool yeast breads, remove them from the pan immediately and place them on cooling racks at room temperature. You can leave rolls on the sheets to cool. Cool completely, glaze, take staling prevention measures, then if keeping them longer than a day, wrap tightly and store in the freezer.

C Critical Thinking

9. Italian bread would fit the best into a low-fat diet because it is a hard lean dough with 0-1% fat content.

10. Answers will vary, but might include adding nuts, herbs, or fruits, or a glaze or wash to the bread.

Academic Skills

11. English Language Arts Students should find different types of yeast breads from other countries, such as baguette, country bread, ciabatta, brioche, fougasse, challah, pumpernickel, babka, and panettone. They should also research the names to see if they have particular meaning.

12. Social Studies Students should find examples of how culture contributes to local bread products. For example, the Spanish brought their bread, or pan, to the places they colonized, where it survives as pan dulce, a sweet bread eaten at breakfast in Mexico; pandesal, a salt bread, in the Philippines, also eaten at breakfast; and pan de agua in the Dominican Republic.

13. **Mathematics** Bob sold 55 discounted donuts. The starting equation $(\$0.95)(265 - d) + (\$0.70)(d) = \$238$ can be rewritten as $(0.95 \times 265) - (0.95 \times d) + 0.70d = 238$, which reduces to $251.75 - 0.95d + 0.70d = 238$, or $13.75 = 0.25d$, or $d = 13.75 \div 0.25 = 55$.

Certification Prep

14. a. 78–82°F (26–28°C)

15. c. bagel

Real-World Skills and Applications

16. **Interpersonal and Collaborative Skills** Encourage teams to create ads that are catchy and informative. Remind students that their ads should be visually appealing as well. Students should use information from the text to create their ads.

17. **Self-Management Skills** Suggestions for substitutions may include eating whole wheat toast instead of croissants or Danishes at breakfast; or using rolls or sandwich breads made from hard lean dough rather than medium soft dough. Ingredients that may boost fat intake include butter, shortening, and add-ins such as nuts.

18. **Technology Applications** Students should identify the ingredients, preparation, texture, appearance, and flavor of one type of yeast bread product using the Internet.

19. **Financial Literacy** Samara spent $3 and used 6 ounces of yeast. Her cost was $0.50 per ounce. Anita used 8 ounces of yeast and spent $5 for a total of $0.63 per ounce. Despite the fact that Samara wasted some yeast, she still made the more cost-effective choice.

Culinary Lab

20. **Bake Soft Rolls** Students should be able to provide logical reasoning and criticism to support their scores.

Quick Breads

SECTION 28.1 Making Biscuits   SECTION 28.2 Making Muffins

Classroom Solutions

Print Resources

- Student Edition
- Instructor Annotated Edition
- Lab Manual
- Lab Manual IAE

Technology Resources

ExamView® **ExamView® Assessment Suite CD**
Assessment Suite
Create and print unit and chapter tests.

 Lesson Planner Plus **Lesson Planner Plus CD** provides access to teacher resources in one convenient package.

Presentation Plus! provides visual teaching aids for every section.

Online Learning Center includes resources and activities for students and teachers. Also includes the **Online Student Editions**.

Interactive Student Edition

SECTION 28.1 Making Biscuits

Section Overview

In this section, students will learn the characteristics and functions of quick breads. They will also learn about the biscuit method of mixing. Finally, they will learn the quality characteristics of biscuits and how to prepare quality biscuits.

FOCUS

🔔 Bell Ringer Activity

Quick Breads Throughout the Day Ask the class for examples of quick breads that could be served at each meal throughout the day. Try to collect as many examples as you can for each of the three meals. Make columns on the board for each meal, and list the quick bread examples under the appropriate column heading. Can any of them fit in more than one column?

D Develop Concepts

Main Idea Discuss the main idea with the students. Ask: How would you describe a cake-like texture? A cake-like texture is soft, moist, and sometimes crumbly.

TEACH

S Skill Practice
Guided Practice

L1 List Ask students to list the quality standards you should aim to meet when baking biscuits. The quality standards to meet when making biscuits are appearance, color, texture, separation, and flavor.

L2 Explain Ask students to explain the role of eggs in the biscuit-making process. In the biscuit-making process, eggs help improve the quality and flavor of biscuits. They also build the structure and increase the volume of the biscuits.

L3 Apply Have students practice the biscuit method of mixing, taking care with every step. Students should practice following the instructions carefully to learn what the dough should look like at each step. Once finished, have students share their finished biscuits with one another and provide feedback.

 **Professional Development** MINI CLIP **Reading** Strategic Readers

ASSESS

Quiz

Ask students to answer the following questions:

1. **What are typical ingredients in quick breads?** Typical ingredients include flour, eggs, fat, sugar, salt, a chemical leavening agent, and a liquid.

2. **What can cause biscuit dough to deflate?** Overkneading of dough or twisting of the hand cutters are both things that can cause biscuit dough to deflate.

3. **What color should biscuits be when they are done baking?** When done, biscuits should be a light, golden-brown color.

RETEACH

R Reading Strategy

Scone Variations Lab In teams, have students prepare a variety of scone formulas, adding different flavors of ingredients. Have students make the scones, and once they are completed, have students taste and evaluate all of the scones. Students should successfully improvise on a scone formula and evaluate their results based on what they know about quality from the text.

U Universal Access

Gifted Students Imagine that you run a small coffee shop where you serve homemade quick breads at breakfast time. Your shop is near a gym, and many of your customers are health conscious. What types of items might you offer that would appeal to these types of customers? Answers will vary, but students might choose bran or flax muffins, breads with nuts and fruits added, whole-wheat scones, low-carb products, or any other healthful ideas.

 Professional Development MINI CLIP **Reading** Guided Instruction

ASSESS

 Lab Manual

Assign the Section 28.1 Activities.

Online Study Tools

Have students go to the Online Learning Center at **glencoe.com** to:

- Take the Section 28.1 Practice Test.
- Download Study-to-Go content.

Review Key Concepts

1. The biscuit method of mixing requires cutting or rubbing fat into the dry ingredients. This is done until the fat and dry ingredients resemble cornmeal. Then, the liquid ingredients are added.

2. Quality standards to aim for when making biscuits include that the biscuits should all be the same size and have flat tops and straight sides. They should have a golden brown crust and be creamy or flaky. They should be light and tender. Flaky biscuits should easily separate into multiple layers when broken apart.

Practice Culinary Academics

3. **English Language Arts** Students should locate recipes for several types of quick breads. Their menu descriptions should be clearly and creatively written and the description should match the recipe.

4. **Social Studies** Student responses should feature quick breads from countries other than the United States. They should name and describe the quick bread product and what significance it has, if any, in the culture of origin. Students should create a chart to show the characteristics of the quick breads they researched.

5. **Mathematics** The finished biscuits will be $2 \times \frac{5}{8} = \frac{10}{8} = \frac{5}{4} = 1.25$ inches in height. Converting to centimeters yields $1.25 \times 2.54 = 3.175$ centimeters.

CLOSE

Culminating Activity

Prepare a Biscuit Dough Divide the students into teams, and have them prepare a biscuit dough. Have them practice rolling and cutting the biscuit dough. Then, have students bake the dough and serve the biscuits to the class. Have other teams evaluate each team's product for tenderness, flakiness, and flavor of their biscuits.

SECTION 28.2 Making Muffins

Section Overview

In this section, students will learn about the blending method of mixing and the creaming method of mixing. They will also learn how to successfully prepare quick bread loaves. Finally, they will learn the steps involved in preparing quality muffins and how to cool and serve them.

FOCUS

 Bell Ringer Activity

Favorite Muffins Ask each student to think of one kind of muffin that is his or her favorite. Ask for volunteers to name their favorite muffin and explain why they like that specific muffin so much. Write each muffin type on the board, and tally the amount of times each muffin is chosen to see which is the class's favorite.

D **Develop Concepts**

Main Idea Discuss the main idea with the students. Ask: What types of jobs could you get if you know how to make quality muffins? If you know how to make quality muffins, you might be able to find work in a restaurant that specializes in breakfast, a bakeshop, or a coffee shop that makes homemade baked goods, among other places.

TEACH

S **Skill Practice**

Guided Practice

L1 **List** Ask students to list the basic ingredients in muffins. The basic ingredients in muffins are flour, oil, eggs, sugar, salt, a leavening agent, and a liquid.

L2 **Explain** Ask students to explain how to cool muffins after they are done. The muffins should be cooled in the pan until they are warm. The muffins should be placed on top of wire racks to allow air to circulate all the way around.

L3 **Apply** Have students form teams, choose a type of muffin, and practice making that type of muffin. Each team should select a type of muffin, and then they should practice making that type of muffin. You might want to turn this into a contest with the class voting on which team's muffins turned out the best.

ASSESS

Quiz

Ask students to answer the following questions:

1. What quick bread products use the blending method? The quick bread products that use the blending method are muffins, loaf breads, pancakes, and waffles.

2. What is a sign of overmixing in baked muffins? If your muffins have tunnels and/or a dry or brittle texture, these are signs of overmixing.

3. How do you test muffins for doneness? To test a muffin for doneness, press the top of the muffin. If it springs back, that muffin is done.

RETEACH

U **Universal Access**

Students with Physical Challenges Using their knowledge of formulas and percentages, have students write an original muffin formula. Then, have students bake and serve muffins following their original formulas and share them as a class. Students should come up with their formulas very carefully. Encourage them to look at other muffin formulas or recipes to determine the correct percentages to use. Then, students should make muffins following their formulas and evaluate the results.

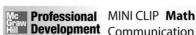 **Professional Development** MINI CLIP **Math** Communication in Mathematics

C **Critical Thinking**

Healthful Muffins Locate three different recipes for healthful muffins. Evaluate the ingredients and determine the nutrition information. Which recipe is the most healthful? How healthy are the other recipes by comparison? Students should be able to determine an estimate of the nutrition information based on the ingredients and amounts of ingredients. It is also possible that the recipe might have some nutrition information.

ASSESS

 ExamView® Assessment Suite Create a test for this chapter.

 Lab Manual

Assign the Section 28.2 Activities.

Online Study Tools

Have students go to the Online Learning Center at **glencoe.com** to:

• Take the Section 28.2 Practice Test.

 Download Study-to-Go content.

SECTION 28.2 **After You Read Answer Key**
Review Key Concepts

1. Use a portion scoop or drop the batter into the pan by hand. When filling the pans, fill them only ½ to ¾ full.

2. To check loaf breads for doneness, touch the loaf. If the loaf is firm to the touch and springs back, it is done.

3. Cool muffins in the pan until warm. Remove the muffins from the pan and let them continue to cool on a wire rack. Serve them warm or cool.

Practice Culinary Academics

4. **English Language Arts** Posters should be mostly visual and should keep textual information brief and easy to read. They should contain enough information about the muffin or loaf quick bread product to make customers interested and curious, but not so much that they do not want to take the time to read it.

5. **Mathematics** The food cost per slice is $0.50. Divide 13 ¾ by 1 ¼ by multiplying $\frac{55}{4} \times \frac{4}{5} = 11$. Thus, there are 11 slices in one loaf. Dividing $5.50 by 11 results in $0.50.

CLOSE

Culminating Activity

Make Muffins Divide students into teams, and have the teams make a variety of muffins. Evaluate the quality characteristics of each team's finished product. Then, have the students compare their results with each other. Encourage students to keep practicing by making muffins for their families for breakfast.

> **Mc Graw Hill Professional Development** MINI CLIP **Math** Classroom and Instructional Management

Chapter Review and Applications

Vocabulary Review

1. Have students check the glossary to check their sentences.

Review Key Concepts

2. Biscuit method: Cut or rub fat into dry ingredients until the ingredients resemble corn meal. Then, add liquid ingredients. Blending method: Combine liquid, sugar, liquid fat, and eggs at the same time. Then, add dry ingredients. Creaming method: Use solid shortening instead of liquid fat. Cream sugar and pre-softened shortening together with a mixer on low speed until light and fluffy. Then, add eggs one by one. Then, add dry and liquid ingredients alternately.

3. Gather and assemble ingredients and equipment. Prepare the sheet pan. Scale or measure ingredients. Sift dry ingredients. Cut or rub shortening into dry ingredients. Whisk eggs and milk into a separate stainless steel bowl. Add liquid ingredients to the flour mixture. Take the dough to a floured bench. Knead it lightly, then rotate and repeat. Allow the dough to rest before rolling. Then, roll and cut the dough, place the biscuits on a sheet pan, brush the tops with egg wash and then bake.

4. Blending method: Sift dry ingredients in mixing bowl. Combine and blend liquid ingredients with sugar until smooth. Then, add dry ingredients to liquid. Mix until just moistened. Creaming method: Gather ingredients and equipment. Scale ingredients. Sift dry ingredients. Combine solid fat and sugar until fluffy and creamy. Add eggs one by one. Add flour and liquid ingredients alternately in approximately three parts. Continue to mix until smooth.

5. Gather ingredients and equipment. Grease bottom of the deep pans. Prepare the loaf bread batter using creaming or blending method. Heat a conventional oven to 400°F (204°C). Scale the appropriate amount of batter into the greased pans. Allow the batter to rest. Place loaf pans in oven. Put a shallow trough of oil down the center of the top. Bake for specified time. Check for doneness. Remove loaves from oven.

6. Mix, divide and garnish batter, place pans in the oven, and bake for indicated time. Test for doneness. Remove pans from oven and let cool slightly on wire racks. Turn muffins out of pan onto cooling rack.

C Critical Thinking

7. You will have to dispose of the batter and start over, because the yeast will ruin the batch.

8. Improvise and locate a similar smallwares to use, such as a large spoon.

9. Do research to find similar formulas or consult with an experienced chef to decipher the formula.

10. The grandmother is probably an experienced baker who has learned from years of baking how to estimate the proper measurements. A beginning baker should always measure all ingredients carefully.

Academic Skills

11. **English Language Arts** Students should locate and read a text that deals with quick breads, which they should briefly and accurately summarize.

12. **Science** Batches with less baking powder will be too dense, while those with more will have too many bubbles.

13. **Mathematics** She can fit 24 biscuits. If x = the number of biscuits that will fit across the length of the baking sheet, then $(x + 1)$ = the number of gaps between biscuits. Thus, the biscuits will occupy (2 in.)(x) total space on the sheet, and the gaps will account for (2 in.)$(x + 1)$ total space. Since the sheet is 26 inches in length, the equation is (2 in.)(x) + (2 in.)$(x + 1)$ = 26 in. Using the distributive property of multiplication, rewrite the equation as $2x + 2x + 2 = 26$, reducing to $4x = 24$, and $x = 6$. Similarly, for the width of the baking sheet (2 in.)(x) + (2 in.)$(x + 1)$ = 18 in., or $2x + 2x + 2 = 18$, or $4x = 16$, or $x = 4$. If 6 biscuits fit the long way, and 4 fit the short way, then a total of $6 \times 4 = 24$ biscuits will fit on the full sheet.

Certification Prep

14. c. 15 minutes
15. c. 385°F–400°F (196°C–204°C)

Real-World Skills and Applications

16. **Critical Thinking Skills** Use a smaller muffin pan, and make two batches of smaller muffins.

17. **Interpersonal and Collaborative Skills** Students should identify food safety issues including washing hands; keeping hair tied back; and making sure dough is mixed properly, not left out too long, and cooked at the right temperature to doneness.

18. **Technology Applications** Students should speak clearly, model in a way that viewers can see what they are doing, and model each test correctly.

19. **Financial Literacy** Quick bread loaf: first, convert pounds to ounces: $2.5 \times 16 = 40$ oz.; $40 \div 3.5 = 11.43 \approx 11$ full servings; $3.20 \div 11 = \$0.29$ per serving. Muffins: $3.60 \div 24$ full servings = $0.15 per serving. Making the muffins would be more cost-effective and would provide you with more servings. The muffins would also provide customers with a larger serving size.

Culinary Lab

20. **Make Banana Nut Bread** Students should observe each version and account for the differences in flavor, texture, and preparation time by figuring out how each variation affected those items.

Desserts

SECTION 29.1 Cookies

SECTION 29.2 Cakes

SECTION 29.3 Pies

SECTION 29.4 Speciality Desserts

Classroom Solutions

Print Resources

- Student Edition
- Instructor Annotated Edition
- Lab Manual
- Lab Manual IAE

Technology Resources

ExamView *ExamView® Assessment Suite* CD
Create and print unit and chapter tests.

Lesson Planner Plus **Lesson Planner Plus CD** provides access to teacher resources in one package.

Presentation Plus! provides visual teaching aids for every section.

Online Learning Center includes resources and activities for students and teachers. Also includes the **Online Student Edition**.

Interactive Student Edition

SECTION 29.1 Cookies

Section Overview

In this section, students will learn about the different characteristics and types of cookies. They will also learn how to mix, pan, and bake cookies. Finally, they will learn how to cool, serve, and store cookies properly.

FOCUS

Bell Ringer Activity

Moderate Sugar Intake Cookies and other desserts are often quite high in sugar. Ask students if they can think of ways to moderate sugar content in cookie recipes or, alternatively, find cookie recipes that are low in sugar. Discuss ideas and/or low-sugar recipes with the class.

D Develop Concepts

Main Idea Discuss the main idea with the students. Ask: What are some occasions where cookies would make a good dessert? Answers will vary, but might include outdoor events like picnics and sporting events, children's parties, as a snack, or casual celebrations.

TEACH

S Skill Practice

Guided Practice

L1 List Ask students to list the types of cookies. The types of cookies are drop cookies, rolled cookies, icebox cookies, molded cookies, and bar cookies.

L2 Explain Have students explain how to store cookies. Cookies should be stored in an airtight container, or they may be stored in the freezer for up to three months.

L3 Apply Ask students to practice making one of the specific types of cookies. Students should select one of the types of cookies and practice making that type of cookie. Observe the students as they bake, and provide feedback.

ASSESS

Quiz

Ask students to answer the following questions:

1. What are the characteristics of bar cookies? Bar cookies are made from dough shaped into long bars, baked, then cut.

2. How should cookies look when they are done baking? You can tell that a cookie is done baking when the bottoms and edges become golden brown, but not too dark.

3. What is the easiest way to classify cookies? It is easiest to classify cookies by type rather than by mixing method.

RETEACH

U Universal Access

Students with Behavioral Challenges Prepare a basic sugar cookie dough, and demonstrate to students how to properly roll and cut cookies. Have them follow along in the text. Then, have them practice rolling and cutting the dough on their own. Demonstrating the technique will supplement what students learned in the text. After reading the appropriate section and watching the demonstration, students should be able to practice on their own. Provide feedback as the students practice on their own.

C Critical Thinking

Problem Solving Tell students to imagine that they are baking cookies to serve at lunch in the school restaurant. However, the cookies are spreading too thin and burning on the bottom. What factors may be contributing to the failed cookies? How would the students solve the problem? Answers will vary, but possible contributing factors include the type of flour used, the type of sugar used, the amount of sugar used, the amount of baking soda used, the type of fat used, or the oven temperature. The problem could be solved by adjusting the temperature and/or by using the double pan method. Students would need to make sure the formula is followed, or retest the formula to see if it is correct.

 Professional Development MINI CLIP **Reading** Interacting with Text

ASSESS

Lab Manual

Assign the Section 29.1 Activities.

Online Study Tools

Have students go to the Online Learning Center at **glencoe.com** to:

- Take the Section 29.1 Practice Test.

 Download Study-to-Go content.

SECTION 29.1 After You Read Answer Key

Review Key Concepts

1. The gluten in the flour used develops during the mixing stage. Gluten provides both stretch and flexibility, which gives the cookie its chewy characteristic.

2. Do not remove cookies from baking sheets until they are sfirm enough to handle.

Practice Culinary Academics

3. English Language Arts Display cards should be brief but informative and persuasive. They should describe the cookie in an appealing manner and give information about type and ingredients. For example: "Snickerdoodle: This snickerdoodle is a soft sugar cookie rolled in cinnamon sugar. The distinctive flavor is provided by the balance of cinnamon and cream of tartar, which give the cookie its sweet and savory flavor."

4. Social Studies Students can research a cookie from any part of the world and should find both a country of origin and the story of creation. For example, the fortune cookie, despite its inclusion with Chinese food, seems to have originated in Kyoto, Japan. There are competing origin stories for the first American fortune cookie, and there is also a Chinese folklore legend about the fortune cookie's origin.

5. Mathematics The circumference of a raw cookie is $(3.14)(2.5 \text{ inches}) = 7.85$ inches. The circumference of a baked cookie is $(3.14)(3 \text{ inches}) = 9.42$ inches. Using these numbers, each cookie's circumference increased by $9.42 - 7.85 = 1.57$ inches during baking.

CLOSE

Culminating Activity

Make Cookies Divide the students into teams, and have them produce a batch of one of the types of cookies introduced in this section. Sample each team's cookies. Evaluate each team's cookies for spread, consistency, and texture. Have the teams sample each other's cookies and discuss and evaluate them as a class.

SECTION 29.2 Cakes

Section Overview

In this section, students will learn about the five types of cakes and the different methods used to mix each type. They will also learn how to scale and pan cakes. Finally, they will learn how to bake, cool, and serve cakes.

FOCUS

🔔 Bell Ringer Activity

Cakes for Different Occasions Ask students what type of cake they would make on the following occasions: a birthday party, a picnic luncheon, and a wedding anniversary. Students' answers will vary, but they might choose high-ratio layer cakes for the birthday party, a pound cake for the picnic luncheon, and an angel food cake for the wedding anniversary.

Professional Development MINI CLIP **ELL** Building the Context

D Develop Concepts

Main Idea Discuss the main idea with the students. Ask: Why do you think panning the cake is so important? Panning the cake is a very important process because the way the cake is panned will determine whether or not it is of a uniform shape and size.

TEACH

S Skill Practice

Guided Practice

L1 List Ask students to list the different types of cakes. The five types of cakes are pound cakes, sponge or foam cakes, angel food cakes, chiffon cakes, and high-ratio layer cakes.

L2 Explain Ask students to explain how to use the creaming method of mixing for cakes. To use the creaming method of mixing for a cake, cream the fat, salt, and sugar together. Next, add eggs and liquids gradually, beating on low. Finally, add sifted dry ingredients, and mix on low.

L3 Apply Have students practice icing and decorating a cake. Students should follow the text directions on how to ice a cake, but they should also figure out how to insert their own creativity. You might want to turn this into a contest, having the class vote on which decorated cake is best.

ASSESS

Quiz

Ask students to answer the following questions:

1. How does starch function in cake production? Starch helps stabilize the cake by absorbing liquid when it is mixed. Liquids, such as milk or water, help form gluten when they combine with flour. When mixed, gluten gives structural support to cake.

2. How long should cakes cool before being removed from the pan? After baking, cakes should be cooled for at least 15 minutes before being removed from the pan.

3. What is the best temperature for creaming? The best temperature for creaming is when the fat or shortening is at 70°F (21°C). If the shortening is too cold, it will not bind and hold the air cells. If the shortening is too warm, it will be too soft to hold enough air or give volume.

RETEACH

U Universal Access

English Language Learners Have students divide into groups, and have each of the groups demonstrate one of the following: different types of icings, how to ice a cake, and how to decorate a cake using pastry bag techniques. Have the teams taste and evaluate each other's products. Students should practice together in the group to create a demonstration that is clear, well spoken, and accurately demonstrates the appropriate skill. Other students should be able to learn by watching the demonstrations.

C Critical Thinking

Make Substitutions Have students imagine that they are making a cake recipe and suddenly realize they have no milk. What can they substitute for milk, and how would they determine the correct amount to use? Answers may vary, but students may say they can substitute soy milk, rice milk, water or juice, dry milk powder added to water, or evaporated milk plus water. The substitutions can all be added in the same amount as the milk. For the evaporated milk, add ⅔ the original amount of milk added to water, equaling ⅓ the original amount of milk.

ASSESS

📖 Lab Manual

Assign the Section 29.2 Activities.

🧭 Online Study Tools

Have students go to the Online Learning Center at **glencoe.com** to:

- Take the Section 29.2 Practice Test.

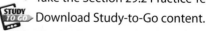 Download Study-to-Go content.

SECTION 29.2 After You Read Answer Key
Review Key Concepts

1. A pound cake contains a pound each of butter, flour, sugar, and eggs. Sponge cakes are airier and lighter because they have air whipped into the eggs. The base of the cake is whole, whipped eggs, rather than fat.

2. The pan should be prepared before the batter is mixed. It should be filled as soon as possible after mixing. Most pans are either buttered or sprayed with oil and dusted with flour. Extra flour should be tapped out. Some baked items can be placed on pans lined with parchment paper.

Practice Culinary Academics

3. **English Language Arts** Students should research different cake options for those with special diets, such as low-sugar/sugar-free cake, eggless cake, gluten-free cake, vegan cake, or any other special diet. They should present the cake and the recipe. They should give information about the special diet and how the cake fits into the diet while still retaining a pleasant texture and flavor.

4. **Science** Students should discover that the heat of the oven reacts with each ingredient, causing several reactions. The heat helps the baking powder produce gas bubbles, which make the cake light and fluffy. The heat solidifies the proteins in the egg to make the cake firm. The oil keeps the heat from drying out the cake.

5. **Mathematics** No. The perimeter of the square cake is ⅔ the perimeter of the original cake. The perimeter of the rectangular cake is (2 × 18 in.) + (2 × 9 in.) = 36 + 18 = 54 in. The perimeter of the square equals 4 × 9 in. = 36 in. $^{36}/_{54}$ = ⅔ = ⅔, not ½.

 Professional Development MINI CLIP **Math** Problem Solving—Order of Operations

CLOSE

Culminating Activity

Make A Cake Divide students into teams, and have them produce a cake. Remind them to add an icing or topping. Evaluate each team's cake on appearance, texture, and flavor. Have the students sample each of the cakes, discuss the different cakes, and evaluate them as a class.

SECTION 29.3 **Pies**

Section Overview

In this section, students will learn how to prepare both mealy pie dough and flaky pie dough. They will also learn about the different types of pie fillings and how to prepare pie fillings and crusts. Finally, they will learn how to store pies properly.

FOCUS

🔔 Bell Ringer Activity

American as Apple Pie There is a saying that goes, "As American as apple pie." As a class, investigate the history of apple pie to find out how American it really is. Students may discover that recipes for apple pie appear as early as 1381 in England. The Dutch have also been known for apple pie since the 17th century.

 **Professional Development** MINI CLIP **Reading** Vocabulary

D Develop Concepts

Main Idea Discuss the main idea with the students. Ask: What different types of pie fillings can you think of? Students should list examples of various fruit fillings, cream fillings, custard fillings, soft fillings, and chiffon fillings.

TEACH

S Skill Practice

Guided Practice

L1 **List** Ask students to list the ingredients of pie dough. Pie dough is made from pastry flour, vegetable shortening, water, and salt.

L2 **Explain** Ask students to explain how to bake a pie. Pies are baked in an oven until the crust is golden brown and the filling is cooked. Some fruit pies are baked at a consistent temperature of 400°F (204°C) while many soft or custard pies are baked at 400°F to 425°F (204°C to 218°C) for 10 minutes, and then the oven is reduced to 325°F to 350°F (163°C to 177°C) to finish baking.

L3 **Apply** Have students practice making one or both types of pie dough. Students should practice making the dough according to the instructions in the text. Have students observe each other and provide feedback.

ASSESS

Quiz

Ask students to answer the following questions:

1. What is fluting? Fluting is a manner of decorating the pie crust by making uniform folds around the edge of the pie.

2. What is the role of salt in pie dough? Salt is used in pie dough because it tenderizes the gluten and enhances the flavor.

3. What are the steps involved in shaping pie dough? To shape pie dough, scale the dough, dust the bench and rolling pin with flour, roll out the pie dough, pan the dough, and either flute or seal and flute.

RETEACH

R Reading Strategy

Demonstration Demonstrate how to prepare a pie crust, how to roll dough, and how to make decorative pie crusts. Encourage students to ask questions as you go along and to follow along in their texts. After the demonstration, have the students try these tasks on their own. Demonstrating the technique will supplement what students learned in the text. After reading the appropriate section and watching the demonstration, they should be able to practice on their own.

U Universal Access

Students with Visual Impairments Have the students imagine that they are baking custard pies for a special bakeshop order. How would they set the oven temperature to achieve a nicely browned crust without overbaking the custard filling? Students might begin the baking process in a hot oven, 400°F–425°F (204°C–218° C), for the first 10 minutes to set the crust. Then, they should bake the filling slowly by reducing the oven temperature to between 325°F–350°F (163°C–177°C).

ASSESS

Lab Manual

Assign the Section 29.3 Activities.

Online Study Tools

Have students go to the Online Learning Center at **glencoe.com** to:

- Take the Section 29.3 Practice Test.
- Download Study-to-Go content.

SECTION 29.3 After You Read Answer Key
Review Key Concepts

1. The basic ingredients of pie dough are pastry flour, vegetable shortening, water, and salt.

2. To determine the doneness of a pie, gently shake a custard or soft pie. If no liquid shakes, it is done. Another way to determine the doneness is to stick a knife in the pie's center. If it comes out clean, the pie is done. The best way to judge if a fruit pie is done is to follow the guidelines in the formula. The crust should be golden brown.

Practice Culinary Academics

3. **English Language Arts** Students should at the very least describe the pie and its ingredients.

They might also include more detailed preparation information, and history, as well as any interesting cultural information, or variants.

4. **Social Studies** There are several sources that reveal historical information about pie, as well as several significant dates that could be added to a time line. For example, in the 14th century, the Duke of Burgundy's chef made a giant pie that contained musicians and a woman who came out during the meal as entertainment.

5. **Mathematics** Approximately 13.23 inches. Each straight side of the slice is equal to the radius of the circle, or ½ the diameter of 9.5 in. = 4.75 inches. The third, curved, side is equal to ⅛ of the circumference of the circle. The circle's circumference is (3.14)(9.5 inches) = 29.83 inches, and 29.83 ÷ 8 ≈ 3.73 inches. Thus, the perimeter of the slice = 4.75 inches + 4.75 inches + 3.73 inches = 13.23 inches.

CLOSE

Culminating Activity

Make Pie Divide students into teams, and have them work together to make pies. Ask them to choose the best type of pie dough to accompany their choice of fruit pie, cream pie, or custard pie. Have the teams share their finished pies with the class. Evaluate each team's pie dough and filling.

SECTION 29.4 Specialty Desserts

Section Overview

In this section, students will learn about the different types of frozen desserts and how they compare. They will also learn how to make custards and puddings. Finally, they will learn how to store and serve these specialty desserts properly.

FOCUS

Bell Ringer Activity

Think of Examples The desserts in the previous sections have all been baked goods. Ask students if they can list any dessert items that are not baked goods. List the examples they come up with on the board as they name them. Explain that in this section, they will learn more about some of these specialty desserts.

D Develop Concepts

Main Idea Discuss the main idea with the students. Ask: What are the ideal textures for a frozen dessert, a custard, and a pudding? Frozen desserts should be firm, but creamy or smooth, not hard and icy.

Custards should be smooth and rich, and puddings should also be soft and smooth and thick, but not too runny.

TEACH

S Skill Practice
Guided Practice

L1 List Ask students to list specialty desserts. Specialty desserts include dessert crêpes and soufflés, ice cream, gelato, frozen yogurt, sherbet, sorbet, ices, stirred custards, baked custards, smooth custards, puddings, Bavarians, chiffons, and mousses.

L2 Explain Ask students to explain how to make a Bavarian. To make a Bavarian, the gelatin must be softened and then dissolved in hot custard and cooled. Then, whipped cream is folded in. Finally, this mixture is put in a mold to set.

L3 Apply Have students practice making a basic ice cream. Locate a simple ice cream recipe, and have students practice preparing it. Observe the students as they work, providing both positive feedback and any necessary suggestions.

ASSESS

Quiz
Ask students to answer the following questions:

1. What is the difference between sherbet and sorbet? Sherbet contains fruit juices, sugar, water, and a small amount of cream or milk. Sorbet contains no cream or milk.

2. Why is accurate gelatin measurement crucial in making a good Bavarian cream? Accurate gelatin measurement is crucial because too much gelatin will make a Bavarian cream rubbery and overfirm, while too little gelatin will make a Bavarian too soft to hold shape.

3. Which two ingredients often serve as a base for mousse? Fresh fruit or melted chocolate often serve as bases for mousse.

RETEACH

U Universal Access

Students with Learning Disabilities If possible, invite a local pastry chef to demonstrate several specialty desserts for students. Have the students work with the chef to plate the desserts to serve to other students. Demonstrating the technique will supplement what students learned in the text. Encourage

students to ask questions of their guest to learn more about these specialty desserts and cement what they learned in this section.

C Critical Thinking

Evaluate Circumstances Tell students to imagine that their foodservice operation has decided to serve a frozen dessert at a summer reception that will be held in a nearby park. What dessert would they recommend, and how will they store it until they are ready to serve it? Answers will vary, but may include storing the dessert in ice or on dry ice or leaving the dessert at the foodservice operation's kitchens and transporting at the last minute. Students should try to pick sturdier frozen desserts that require little assembly.

ASSESS

 ExamView® Assessment Suite Create a test for this chapter.

✍ Lab Manual
Assign the Section 29.4 Activities.

Online Study Tools
Have students go to the Online Learning Center at **glencoe.com** to:

- Take the Section 29.4 Practice Test.
-  Download Study-to-Go content.

SECTION 29.4 After You Read Answer Key
Review Key Concepts

1. A Bavarian cream is made of whipped cream, gelatin, and a flavored custard sauce. The gelatin is softened, dissolved in the custard sauce, and cooled. Then, the whipped cream is folded into the mixture, and the dessert is set in a mold. Chiffons are similar to Bavarians, but use meringue instead of whipped cream. Mousse is made with both meringue and whipped cream.

Practice Culinary Academics

2. **Science** Students should observe that the gelatin will not set when it is made with the raw pineapple. Pineapple contains the enzyme bromelain, which will digest the proteins in the gelatin, preventing it from setting.

3. **English Language Arts** A pastry chef specializes in making dessert items. Gourmet restaurants and other upscale foodservice establishments often have a separate pastry

kitchen with its own hierarchy, just as in the main kitchen. Pastry chef jobs usually require early morning hours, strict attention to detail, and creativity.

4. **Social Studies** Answers will vary, but students should discover three desserts that are not baked goods from other countries. For example, in China, they eat ginger milk curd, which is a hot, solidified milk dessert with ginger and sugar. This dessert originated in southern China. It is made by squeezing juice from a piece of ginger and filtering the juice into a bowl. Then, dissolve sugar in milk, heat, stir, and pour the mixture quickly into the bowl of ginger juice. Next, wait for two to three minutes. The milk will then solidify and may then be eaten with a spoon.

5. **Mathematics** Students should draw and label a pie chart with five sections, one for each flavor of ice cream sold. Mr. Kim sold a total of 180 scoops of ice cream. Chocolate accounted for $90 \div 180 \times 100\% = 50\%$ of the scoops, so the chocolate section of the graph should have an angle of $50\% \times 360° = 180°$. The percentages and degrees for the other sections are vanilla: 25% and 90°; pistachio: 15% and 54°; peach and blackberry: each 5% and 18°.

CLOSE

Culminating Activity

Make a Dessert Divide students into teams, and have each team prepare a dessert to present to the class as a plated dish. Evaluate each team's dessert. Then, have the students compare and evaluate each other's desserts. Finally, have students discuss what they learned from this experience and what did and did not work.

Chapter Review and Applications

Vocabulary Review

1. Letters should be in a business format, and contain at least 12 vocabulary terms.

Review Key Concepts

2. Crisp cookies have little moisture in the batter and a high ratio of sugar. Soft cookies have low amounts of fat and sugar in the batter and a high proportion of liquid. Chewy cookies have a high ratio of eggs, sugar, and liquid, but a low amount of fat.

3. Types of cookies: drop, rolled, icebox, molded, and bar cookies. Mixing methods: one-stage and creaming methods. To bake cookies, line baking pan with parchment paper. Underbake, or double pan, cookies to prevent overcooking due to carryover cooking. They are done when the bottoms and edges turn golden brown.

4. Pound cakes contain a pound each of butter, flour, sugar, and eggs. Sponge cakes have large amounts of air whipped into a base of whole eggs. Angel food cakes are made with egg whites instead of whole eggs and contain no fat. Chiffon cakes use egg yolks, sugar, flour, and egg whites whipped in for extra lightness. High-ratio layer cakes contain a high ratio of liquids and sugar and use emulsified shortening.

5. The mixing methods are creaming, blending, sponge or foam, angel food, and chiffon methods. After mixing, prepare the pan and scale the batter. Then, bake the cake until it tests successfully for doneness, and let it cool. Finally, ice the cake uniformly, starting in the center and moving outward.

6. Pie dough ingredients are pastry flour, vegetable shortening, water, and salt. Types of pie dough are mealy pie dough and flaky pie dough.

7. Mix the pie dough; shape the pie dough; bake the pie shells; make the pie filling; bake the pie, and finally store and/or serve the pie.

8. Make frozen desserts by mixing ingredients and freezing them. They may be served in a dish or cone and may have toppings. Sorbet is sometimes served between courses. Custards are baked or cooked in a double boiler and served alone or as the base for other desserts. Make puddings by mixing ingredients and cooling them as they thicken. Bavarians, chiffons, and mousses are whipped desserts and are often served molded or in special containers.

C Critical Thinking

9. Possibilities are water, fruit juice, or soy milk.

10. Because of the emulsifying agents, which cause the shortening to absorb more sugar and water.

CHAPTER 29 Answer Key

Academic Skills

11. **English Language Arts** Students should read and summarize a text that instructs on how to make a dessert. They should deepen their knowledge of that dessert with this new information.

12. **Social Studies** Students should research the history of their dessert and create a presentation that is clear and conveys the information they learned. Students should cite sources. If there are not enough desserts for each student, have them work in groups.

13. **Mathematics** 282.6 sq. in. will be covered. The radius of the cake is ½ of its diameter, or ½ × 8 in. = 4 in. Each of the three layers has a top surface area of (3.14)(4 in.)(4 in.) = 50.24 sq. in. The total height of the cake equals the height of each of the three cake layers plus the height of each of the three frosting layers, or 1.5 in. + 0.25 in. + 1.5 in. + 0.25 in. + 1.5 in. + 0.25 in. = 5.25 in. The circumference equals (3.14)(8 in.) = 25.12 in., so the surface area of the side of the cake equals (25.12 in.)(5.25 in.) = 131.88 sq. in. Thus, the total surface area to be covered with frosting equals 50.24 + 50.24 + 50.24 + 131.88 = 282.6 sq. in.

Certification Prep

14. a. high-fat cakes
15. a. sorbet

Real-World Skills and Applications

16. **Interpersonal and Collaborative Skills** Students should work together to create and accurately answer five multiple-choice and five true-false questions based on material in the chapter.

17. **Decision Making Skills** Cakes with the least fat and sugar will be at the higher end of the chart, while those with more fat, sugar, and other rich ingredients, such as egg yolks, will be at the lower end.

18. **Technology Applications** Students should create a blog entry about the dessert they choose, geared toward a casual audience with correct spelling and grammar.

19. **Financial Literacy** The apple pie à la mode costs $10 + ($0.84 × 50) + ($0.75 x 50) = $89.50. The chocolate mousse costs ($1.39 × 50) + ($0.43 × 50) = $91. The apple pie à la mode is less expensive to produce.

Culinary Lab

20. **Make Cream Puffs** Students should explain why they choose the topping and filling combination and what makes it appealing, such as texture, flavor combinations, or appearance. They should also give their cream puff a rating and explain.

Culinary Project Lesson Plan

FOCUS

Introduce the Project

In this project, students will learn how to research frozen desserts and how to find a chef whom they can observe in action creating a frozen dessert. Students will take notes as they observe. Propose that students think of ideas for their own frozen dessert that will be especially eye-catching. Have them share experiences with frozen desserts they have seen or eaten.

Build Background

Learn from Observing Discuss with students techniques used in the preparation of frozen desserts. Write these techniques as action words on the board. Have students rate these techniques by degree of difficulty, with 1 as the easiest and 5 as the most challenging. Revisit these ratings after students have completed their observations, to see if they still agree with their ratings.

TEACH

S Skill Practice
Guided Practice

L1 List Ask students to list the ingredients and tools that are used in the preparation of frozen desserts. Answers will vary, but ingredients generally will include milk, sugar, flavorings and extracts such as vanilla or almond, fruit, cream, eggs, and yogurt. Tools might include saucepans, ice cream makers, molds, spatulas, and more.

L2 Explain Have students explain their thought processes in choosing their particular frozen dessert. Students should be able to articulate the reasons for choosing a particular dessert, such as its flavor, the ability to plate it in a creative way, and the ease of making it.

L3 Apply Ask students to demonstrate their newly gained knowledge of frozen desserts to evaluate other frozen desserts. Arrange to bring in several different types of frozen desserts, and ask students to evaluate each for flavor, texture, and consistency. Generally, student evaluations should note differences between different frozen desserts. Students may wish to describe the experience of eating these desserts, such as a dessert rolling off one's tongue, or leaving a pleasant coating behind.

C Critical Thinking

Judge Suitability Hold a discussion in which students must discriminate between settings where a frozen dessert would work well, and settings where it would not. Talking points should include the demographic of the customers, the time of year, how long guests must wait before eating, and the availability of proper storage equipment.

ASSESS

Quiz

Ask students to answer the following questions:

1. What are some of the skills that might prove useful in preparing a professional quality frozen dessert? Skills include following a recipe, mixing, blending, whipping, folding, and garnishing.

2. What are some of the advantages of serving a frozen dessert rather than a cooked or baked dessert? Frozen desserts are often easy to assemble, and they work well in an environment where baking equipment is limited. Many frozen desserts require fewer preparation steps and ingredients. Also, frozen desserts have a wide appeal.

3. What ingredients and preparation factors can affect safety when working with frozen desserts? The dairy products that are often central to frozen desserts must be kept at appropriate temperatures to avoid foodborne illness. Many ice creams use eggs that must be cooked to an appropriate temperature.

CLOSE

Culminating Activity

Understand Appeal Ask students what is so appealing about frozen desserts. Divide students into groups of three or four and have each group give a presentation about why they think frozen desserts are so popular. Encourage students to use photos, dialogue, or even role-plays in their presentations. Presentations should outline specific reasons for frozen desserts' popularity. Encourage students to give specific examples of certain frozen desserts and their special appeal, such as unique toppings, coldness, creaminess, or attractiveness.

GLENCOE
★★★★★
CULINARY ESSENTIALS

JOHNSON & WALES
UNIVERSITY

Mc Graw Hill **Glencoe**

Safety Notice

The reader is expressly advised to consider and use all safety precautions described in this textbook or that might also be indicated by undertaking the activities described herein. In addition, common sense should be exercised to help avoid all potential hazards and, in particular, to take relevant safety precautions concerning any known or likely hazards involved in food preparation, or in use of the procedures described in *Culinary Essentials*, such as the risk of knife cuts or burns.

Publisher and Authors assume no responsibility for the activities of the reader or for the subject matter experts who prepared this book. Publisher and Authors make no representation or warranties of any kind, including, but not limited to, the warranties of fitness for particular purpose or merchantability, nor for any implied warranties related thereto, or otherwise. Publisher and Authors will not be liable for damages of any type, including any consequential, special or exemplary damages resulting, in whole or in part, from reader's use or reliance upon the information, instructions, warnings, or other matter contained in this textbook.

Brand Disclaimer

Publisher does not necessarily recommend or endorse any particular company or brand name product that may be discussed or pictured in this text. Brand name products are used because they are readily available, likely to be known to the reader, and their use may aid in the understanding of the text. Publisher recognizes that other brand name or generic products may be substituted and work as well or better than those featured in the text.

The McGraw·Hill Companies

Copyright © 2010 The McGraw-Hill Companies, Inc. All rights reserved. No part of this publication may be reproduced or distributed in any form or by any means, or stored in a database or retrieval system, without the prior written consent of The McGraw-Hill Companies, Inc., including, but not limited to, network storage or transmission, or broadcast for distance learning.

Printed in the United States of America.

Send all inquiries to:
Glencoe/McGraw-Hill
21600 Oxnard Street, Suite 500
Woodland Hills, California 91367

ISBN: 978-0-07-888359-0   (Student Edition)
MHID: 0-07-888359-8   (Student Edition)
ISBN: 978-0-07-888441-2   (Instructor Annotated Edition)
MHID: 0-07-888441-1   (Instructor Annotated Edition)

3 4 5 6 7 8 9   RJE/LEH   15 14 13 12 11 10

Foreword

Johnson & Wales University is known as America's Career University. The University is student centered, employment-focused, market-driven, experientially based, and globally oriented. Johnson & Wales University collaborated with Glencoe/McGraw-Hill to bring you a unique textbook filled with the essential knowledge and skills needed to become a culinary professional.

***Culinary Essentials* will show you:**
- the value of quality customer service to the dining experience.
- the role of foodservice management, standards, regulations, and laws.
- why safety and sanitation must be controlled at all times.
- how to use the equipment found in the professional kitchen.
- how culinary nutrition will enable you to create successful menus.
- how to use standardized recipes to control costs.
- the cooking techniques used in quantity food preparation.

Johnson & Wales' philosophy is to learn by doing, so we hope you make good use of this learning tool and pursue a rewarding career in culinary arts. We invite you to visit **www.jwu.edu** to learn more about Johnson & Wales University and culinary arts careers.

JOHNSON & WALES
U N I V E R S I T Y

Karl Guggenmos M.B.A., GMC, AAC
WACS Global Master Chef
University Dean, Culinary Education

Paul J. McVety EdD
Dean, Culinary Academics

Johnson & Wales University Contributors

Dr. Manuel Pimentel, Jr.
Sr. Vice President Emeritus
University Relations

Bradley J. Ware Ph.D., CCE, CCC
Professor
College of Culinary Arts

Deb Bettencourt
Special Projects Coordinator
College of Culinary Arts

George O'Palenick CEC, CCE, AAC
Associate Professor
College of Culinary Arts

Marc DeMarchena M.A., WSET, FRDP, CWE
Associate Professor
College of Culinary Arts

Suzanne Vieira M.S., RD, LDN
Department Chair
Culinary Nutrition Program
College of Culinary Arts

Mitch Stamm CEPC
Associate Instructor
International Baking & Pastry Institute
College of Culinary Arts

Robert M. Nograd CMC
Dean Emeritus
Corporate Executive Chef

John Chiaro M.S., CEC, CCE, AAC
Associate Professor
College of Culinary Arts

Douglas Stuchel M.A.T.
Culinary Team Lead Co-op & Employment
Career Development Office

Katrina Herold B.S., CSW
Instructor
College of Culinary Arts

Peter Vaillancourt B.S.
Instructor
College of Culinary Arts

Elaine Cwynar M.Ed.
Associate Professor
College of Culinary Arts

Rainer Heinerwadel M.A.T., GMC
WACS Global Master Chef
Department Chair
Culinary Baccalaureate Program
College of Culinary Arts

Gary Welling A.S.
Department Chair
International Baking & Pastry Institute
College of Culinary Arts

Contributors and Reviewers

Educational Reviewers

Allen B. Asch
Area Technical Trade Center
Las Vegas, Nevada

Arnell M. Currie
Welsh High School
Welsh, Louisiana

Joyce Glen
Nettleton High School
Jonesboro, Arizona

Marsha Miller
Fort Payne High School
Fort Payne, Alabama

Kimberley M. Myers M.Ed., NBPTS
Aynor High School
Aynor, South Carolina

Holly P. Nix
Blacksburg High School
Blacksburg, South Carolina

Shirley Rauh
Lutheran High School South
St. Louis, Missouri

Amanda Riggen
Walker Career Center
Indianapolis, Indiana

Denise Schaefer CEC, CCE, AAC
Penta Career Center
Perrysburg, Ohio

Marilyn J. Schoolmeester
Edgerton High School
Edgerton, Minnesota

Wealthy Slattery
Crenshaw High School
Los Angeles, California

Kim Smith
Cary High School
Cary, North Carolina

Beverly J. Swisher
Wichita High School West
Wichita, Kansas

Susan Teelin
Camden Middle School
Camden, New York

Linda Larsen Valiga M.Ed.
Waukesha South High School
Waukesha, Wisconsin

Technical Reviewers

Stephanie Anagnoson
Math Expert
Santa Clarita, California

Chef Billie DeNunzio CCE
Institute of Culinary Arts
Eastside High School
Gainesville, Florida

Emily L. Kimbrough
Lead Chef Instructor
Charleston, South Carolina

Dr. Keith Mandabach CEC, AAC
Assistant Professor
New Mexico State University
School of Hotel, Restaurant,
and Tourism Management
Las Cruces, New Mexico

Jeff Nelken M.S., RD
Food Safety/HACCP Expert
Woodland Hills, California

Chef Erik Oberholtzer
Tender Greens
Culver City, California

Sally Porter
Hinds Community College
Jackson, Mississippi

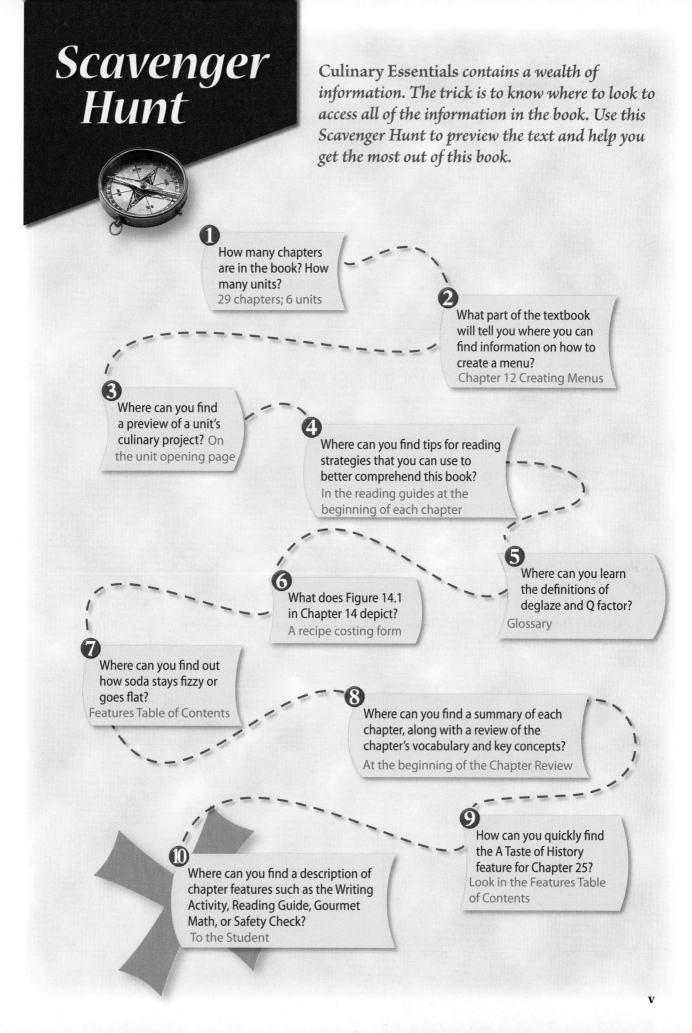

Scavenger Hunt

Culinary Essentials contains a wealth of information. The trick is to know where to look to access all of the information in the book. Use this Scavenger Hunt to preview the text and help you get the most out of this book.

1 How many chapters are in the book? How many units?
29 chapters; 6 units

2 What part of the textbook will tell you where you can find information on how to create a menu?
Chapter 12 Creating Menus

3 Where can you find a preview of a unit's culinary project? On the unit opening page

4 Where can you find tips for reading strategies that you can use to better comprehend this book?
In the reading guides at the beginning of each chapter

5 Where can you learn the definitions of deglaze and Q factor?
Glossary

6 What does Figure 14.1 in Chapter 14 depict?
A recipe costing form

7 Where can you find out how soda stays fizzy or goes flat?
Features Table of Contents

8 Where can you find a summary of each chapter, along with a review of the chapter's vocabulary and key concepts?
At the beginning of the Chapter Review

9 How can you quickly find the A Taste of History feature for Chapter 25?
Look in the Features Table of Contents

10 Where can you find a description of chapter features such as the Writing Activity, Reading Guide, Gourmet Math, or Safety Check?
To the Student

Table of Contents

To the Student xviii
National Academic Standards.................................... xxx
Reading Skills Handbook xxxii
How to Use Technology xlii
Student Organizations: SkillsUSA and FCCLA xliv
Johnson & Wales University
  High School Chef of the Year................................ xlvi

UNIT 1 — *Culinary Safety* — xlviii

CHAPTER 1 Safety and Sanitation Principles   2
  SECTION 1.1 Safety Basics..3
  SECTION 1.2 Sanitation Challenges 12
  Chapter 1 Review and Applications 21

CHAPTER 2 HACCP Applications   24
  SECTION 2.1 The Safe Foodhandler.............................. 25
  SECTION 2.2 The HACCP System................................. 30
  SECTION 2.3 The Flow of Food.................................... 37
  Chapter 2 Review and Applications 47

Chapter 9 LE

Unit 1 Culinary Career Spotlight
  Research and Development.. 50
Unit 1 Culinary Project ***Restaurant Inspections*** 52

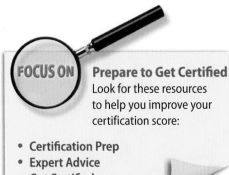

FOCUS ON **Prepare to Get Certified**
Look for these resources
to help you improve your
certification score:

• Certification Prep
• Expert Advice
• Get Certified
• Career Skills Handbook

Table of Contents

UNIT 2 The Foodservice Industry 54

CHAPTER 3 Foodservice Career Options 56
SECTION 3.1 Careers in Foodservice 57
SECTION 3.2 Foodservice Trends 67
SECTION 3.3 Entrepreneurship Opportunities 73
Chapter 3 Review and Applications 79

? LE chap 1

CHAPTER 4 Becoming a Culinary Professional 82
SECTION 4.1 Employability Skills 83
SECTION 4.2 Seeking Employment 93
SECTION 4.3 On the Job 103
Chapter 4 Review and Applications 111

CHAPTER 5 Customer Service 114
SECTION 5.1 Service Basics 115
SECTION 5.2 Serving Customers 126
Chapter 5 Review and Applications 137

CHAPTER 6 The Dining Experience 140 *move to unit*
SECTION 6.1 Dining Today 141
SECTION 6.2 The Dining Room Environment .... 150 *LE Chapt 7*
Chapter 6 Review and Applications 159

Unit 2 Culinary Career Spotlight **Media and Mentoring** 162
Unit 2 Culinary Project **Your Career in Foodservice** 164

UNIT 3 Quality Foodservice Practices 166

CHAPTER 7 Foodservice Management 168
SECTION 7.1 Management Basics 169
SECTION 7.2 Managing People and Facilities 178
SECTION 7.3 Foodservice Marketing 187
Chapter 7 Review and Applications 193

CHAPTER 8 Standards, Regulations, and Laws 196
SECTION 8.1 Foodservice Standards and Regulations 197
SECTION 8.2 Employment Laws 204
Chapter 8 Review and Applications 209

Unit 3 Culinary Career Spotlight
Management and Supervision 212
Unit 3 Culinary Project **Successful Foodservice Managers** 214

Table of Contents

UNIT 4 The Professional Kitchen 216

CHAPTER 9 Equipment and Technology 218

SECTION 9.1 The Commercial Kitchen 219
SECTION 9.2 Receiving and Storage Equipment 224
SECTION 9.3 Preparation and Cooking Equipment 230
SECTION 9.4 Holding and Service Equipment 241
Chapter 9 Review and Applications 247

CHAPTER 10 Knives and Smallwares 250

SECTION 10.1 Knives 251
SECTION 10.2 Smallwares 261
Chapter 10 Review and Applications 275

CHAPTER 11 Culinary Nutrition 278

SECTION 11.1 Nutrition Basics 279
SECTION 11.2 Meal Planning Guidelines 288
SECTION 11.3 Keep Food Nutritious 297
Chapter 11 Review and Applications 303

CHAPTER 12 Creating Menus 306

SECTION 12.1 The Menu 307
SECTION 12.2 Menu Planning and Design 313
SECTION 12.3 Pricing Menu Items 320
Chapter 12 Review and Applications 325

CHAPTER 13 Using Standardized Recipes 328

SECTION 13.1 Standardized Recipe Basics 329
SECTION 13.2 Recipe Measurement and Conversion 334
Chapter 13 Review and Applications 343

CHAPTER 14 Cost Control Techniques 346

SECTION 14.1 Calculate Food Costs 347
SECTION 14.2 Manage Food Cost Factors 356
Chapter 14 Review and Applications 365

Unit 4 Culinary Career Spotlight
Banquets and Catering 368

Unit 4 Culinary Project **Standardized Recipes** 370

UNIT **5** *Culinary Applications* 372

5-1

CHAPTER 15 **Cooking Techniques** 374

SECTION 15.1 How Cooking Alters Food 375
SECTION 15.2 Dry Cooking Techniques 381
SECTION 15.3 Moist Cooking Techniques 388
Chapter 15 Review and Applications 395

CHAPTER 16 **Seasonings and Flavorings** 398

SECTION 16.1 Enhancing Food 399
SECTION 16.2 Herbs and Spices 405
SECTION 16.3 Condiments, Nuts, and Seeds 415
SECTION 16.4 Sensory Perception 420
Chapter 16 Review and Applications 427

No **CHAPTER 17** **Breakfast Cookery** 430

SECTION 17.1 Meat and Egg Preparation 431
SECTION 17.2 Breakfast Breads and Cereals 442
Chapter 17 Review and Applications 451

No **CHAPTER 18** **Garde Manger Basics** 454

SECTION 18.1 What Is Garde Manger? 455
SECTION 18.2 Salads and Salad Dressings 462
SECTION 18.3 Cheese 470
SECTION 18.4 Cold Platters 476
Chapter 18 Review and Applications 483

5·1 *Project*

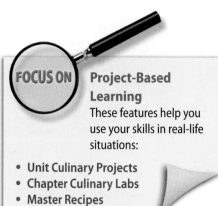

FOCUS ON **Project-Based Learning**
These features help you use your skills in real-life situations:

- Unit Culinary Projects
- Chapter Culinary Labs
- Master Recipes

Table of Contents

CHAPTER 19 **Sandwiches and Appetizers** **486**

SECTION 19.1 Sandwich-Making Basics..487
SECTION 19.2 Sandwiches...495
SECTION 19.3 Hot Appetizers...501
Chapter 19 Review and Applications...505

CHAPTER 20 **Stocks, Sauces, and Soups** **508**

SECTION 20.1 Stocks...509
SECTION 20.2 Sauces..516
SECTION 20.3 Soups...526
Chapter 20 Review and Applications...537

CHAPTER 21 **Fish and Shellfish** **540**

SECTION 21.1 Fish Basics...541
SECTION 21.2 Shellfish Basics..548
SECTION 21.3 Cooking Fish and Shellfish...558
Chapter 21 Review and Applications...565

CHAPTER 22 **Poultry Cookery** **568**

SECTION 22.1 Poultry Basics..569
SECTION 22.2 Cooking Poultry..576
Chapter 22 Review and Applications...583

FOCUS ON **Academic Success**
To help you succeed in your classes and on tests, look for these academic skills:

- Writing Tips
- Gourmet Math
- Science à la Carte
- A Taste of History
- Vocabulary Development

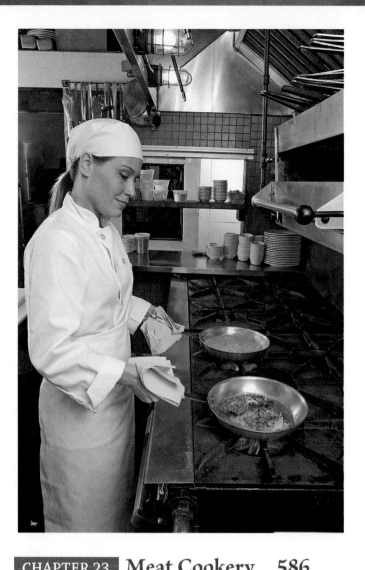

Table of Contents

FOCUS ON **Unit Culinary Projects**
Elements in these projects can build your culinary and academic skills:

- **Applied Culinary Skills**
- **Academics Behind the Project**
- **Evaluation Rubrics**

CHAPTER 23 **Meat Cookery** **586**

SECTION 23.1 Meat Basics 587
SECTION 23.2 Meat Cuts 594
SECTION 23.3 Principles of Cooking Meat 604
Chapter 23 Review and Applications...611

CHAPTER 24 **Pasta and Grains** **614**

SECTION 24.1 Pasta...615
SECTION 24.2 Rice and Other Grains 623
Chapter 24 Review and Applications...633

CHAPTER 25 **Fruits, Vegetables, and Legumes** **636**

SECTION 25.1 Fruits 637
SECTION 25.2 Vegetables 646
SECTION 25.3 Legumes 659
Chapter 25 Review and Applications...667

Unit 5 Culinary Career Spotlight *Chefs and Cooks* 670
Unit 5 Culinary Project *Local and Seasonal Foods*....................672

Table of Contents

UNIT 6 *Baking and Pastry Applications* **674**

CHAPTER 26 Baking Techniques **676**
- SECTION 26.1 Bakeshop Formulas and Equipment 677
- SECTION 26.2 Bakeshop Ingredients 687
- Chapter 26 Review and Applications 701

CHAPTER 27 Yeast Breads and Rolls **704**
- SECTION 27.1 Yeast Dough Basics 705
- SECTION 27.2 Yeast Dough Production 712
- Chapter 27 Review and Applications 725

CHAPTER 28 Quick Breads **728**
- SECTION 28.1 Making Biscuits 729
- SECTION 28.2 Making Muffins 736
- Chapter 28 Review and Applications 743

CHAPTER 29 Desserts **746**
- SECTION 29.1 Cookies 747
- SECTION 29.2 Cakes 754
- SECTION 29.3 Pies 764
- SECTION 29.4 Specialty Desserts 770
- Chapter 29 Review and Applications 775

Unit 6 Culinary Career Spotlight **Baking and Pastry** 778
Unit 6 Culinary Project **Creative Desserts** 780

Career Appendix **782**
Math Appendix **790**
Glossary **812**
Index **834**
Photo Credits **848**

 Assessment
Look for review questions and activities to help you remember important topics:

- Reading Checks
- Section and Chapter Reviews
- Chapter Lab Activities

Features Table of Contents

Culinary Math, Science, and History

Can you determine overtime pay for kitchen staff? Do you know how to form a permanent emulsion to make mayonnaise? The answers rest with your technical and academic knowledge. These academic features will help you succeed in school and in the workplace.

Gourmet Math

Cool Foods Safely 39
Splitting Profits in a Partnership....74
Overtime Pay 108
Geometry and Napkin Folding 154
Sales vs. Profit..........................176
Design to Scale 220
Drawing and Cutting Angles 253
Working with Percents 323
Unit Prices 338
Calculate Inventory Value 353
Calculate Food Orders.................491
Bulk Discounts 551
The Baker's Percentage 679
Use the 240 Factor 715
Adjust for Altitude......................761

Science à la Carte

Extinguish a Grease Fire.................9
Flat or Fizzy? 123
The pH Scale............................203
What Is Fat? 282
Color Fade 379
Taste Sensations 424
Green Eggs 437
Emulsions 466
The Science of Thickening.............518
Salmonella Bacteria 575
The Maillard Reactions.................607
Investigate Starch......................622
Moisture and Mold in Legumes 663
Baking Soda or Baking Powder? ...739

A TASTE OF HISTORY

Keep Food Cool 17
Battle Against Bacteria 36
The Emperor of Chefs 63
On-the-Job Training 95
Tipping Point 135
Eating in Style 142
Protecting Workers......................182
Food and Drug Watchdogs 200
Heating Things Up 234
A Most Useful Tool 254
Nutrition Pioneers 294
The À La Carte Menu....................309
The History of the Recipe 330
Weigh the Options......................358
Cooking Through Time 383
The Spice of Life 410
The Waffle Iron..........................446
The Big Cheese..........................474
The History of the Sandwich.........497
You Say Tomato 515
Oysters Rockefeller......................561
Cutting the Fat 580
The History of the Butcher 589
Pass the Pasta 619
Potato Promoter 651
Chocolate 693
The Origins of Yeast Dough...........709
Biscuits and Scones 735
Desserts, Colonial Style................765

Features Table of Contents

Safety, Sanitation, and Nutrition

Keeping a professional kitchen safe and sanitary is vital. And nutrition is a priority for foodservice businesses and customers. These features will show you the most important topics.

Safety Check

✓ Do Not Mix! 5
Use Ladders Safety 6
Egg Safety 40
Serving Safety........................... 120
Hot Plates 133
Keep Buffet Foods Safe 143
Safe Food Handling 201
Maintenance and Care 239
Internal Temperatures............. 380
Burned by Steam 394
Hot Pepper Safety..................... 401
Prevent Salmonella 435
Cold Platters.............................. 480
Guard Against
  Bacteria Growth..................... 488
Maintain Temperature............. 534
Frying Fat 562
Thawing Poultry 573
Wear Protective Clothes.......... 595
Green Potatoes 651
Canned Vegetables................... 653
Prevent Foodborne Illness 771

Sanitation Check

✓ Hepatitis A.................................. 16
Personal Hygiene....................... 18
The Kitchen Glow Test 39
Sanitary Tableware.................. 152
Handle Cheese 494
Serve Raw Fish
  and Shellfish........................... 559
Giblets 574
Prevent
  Cross-Contamination 592
Meat Temperatures.................. 609
Sanitize Pastry Bags 686
Avoid Contamination 722

❈ Nutrition Notes ❈

Nutrient Storage....................... 363
Nuts About Nutrition! 419
Nutrients in Salad Greens 464
Sandwich Nutrition 489
Soup's Effect on Appetite........ 528
Fish and Shellfish Nutrition 564
Poultry Nutrition 571
Choose Lean Meat 588
Nutrients in Pasta 616
Nutrients in Grains 627
Nutrients in Fruits.................... 638
Nutrients in Legumes 660
Nutrients in Quick Breads 741

Recipes and Tools

Do you know how to make an omelet? Can you choose the correct omelet pan? These features will improve your culinary preparation skills.

✳ MASTER RECIPE

Green Beans in Garlic Sauce 332

Southern Vegetable Soup.............340

Omelet with Cheese 436

Pancakes with Maple Syrup 447

American Grinder 493

Monte Cristo Sandwich 498

Béchamel Sauce...........................522

Beef Consommé............................533

Polenta 628

Sweet and Spicy Broccoli 656

Lentil Stuffed Zucchini 665

Apple Wheat Germ Cake 692

Soft Rolls 720

Banana Nut Bread..........................745

Vanilla Chiffon Genoise.................757

Basic Pie Dough 768

◤ Find More Recipes Online!

You can choose from more than 150 additional recipes through this book's Online Learning Center at **glencoe.com**.

✳ CULINARY SHOWCASE

Storage Equipment 227

Preparation Equipment.................232

Cooking Equipment......................235

Holding Equipment 243

Service Equipment 244

Hand Tools...................................263

Measuring Equipment...................268

Cookware 270

Herbs 407

Spices..411

Nuts and Seeds 417

Garnishing Tools 460

Common Pasta Shapes..................617

Popular Specialty Rices 626

Wheat Grains...............................629

Fruits...640

Vegetables 648

Common Legumes........................661

Baking and Pastry Tools 685

Features Table of Contents

Culinary Tips

Knowing important details makes a difference in a professional kitchen. This feature will give you information on everything from choosing utensils to determining the freshness of eggs.

⌢ Small Bites ⌢

Sanitary Jewelry?........................26

Bacteria and pH 38

Life Plans 60

Special Certification 62

Seasonal American Food...........68

Global Food Supplies 70

Thinking Skills 88

Common Job Interview
   Questions 100

Ending Employment................108

Special Needs...........................116

Adjust Utensils.........................133

Crumb the Table.......................134

Use the Correct Hand 145

Foodservice Management
   Professional Credentials 171

Facility Maintenance 186

Market Pricing..........................189

Glass and Aluminum
   Containers 226

Aluminum Warnings.................262

Complete Combinations 281

Dietary Details 293

Life Cycle of a Dish 314

Ingredient Preparation 331

Use the Q Factor? 353

Receiving Tools
   and Equipment........................360

Taking Inventory......................363

Something for Nothing 364

Pan-Frying Tip..........................384

Seasonings 387

Tomato Peeling 390

MSG Allergies...........................403

Egg Size and Storage...............434

Prevent Lumpy Cereal 449

Using Edible Flowers 466

Hors d'Oeuvres Guidelines 477

Sandwich Accompaniments ...490

Cut for Appeal 491

Sandwich-Making
   Techniques 496

Remove Salt 531

Cook Vegetable Soup 532

Soup Accompaniment
   Suggestions 534

Fat Quality 562

Find the Label 572

Storing Stuffing 582

Tenderize Meat 589

Kobe Beef 591

Aging of Pork 597

What Is in a Burger?.................603

Legumes for Livestock 666

Oil for Shortening? 691

Egg Freshness 694

Carryover Baking......................700

Use Compressed Yeast.............706

Enriched Hard Lean Doughs ...708

Overmixing 716

Altitude.....................................723

Cut Biscuits...............................734

Use Liners 737

Add Eggs Seperately 750

Use Basic Cookie Mixes 753

Creaming and Temperature....759

Altitude Adjustments..............761

Step-by-Step Procedures

Can you properly knead dough or prepare a white stock? These step-by-step photo features will show you how to apply your culinary knowledge.

HOW TO

Wash Your Hands 28

Change a Tablecloth 157

Grip a Knife.............................. 255

Safely Cut Food 256

Make a Chiffonade Cut 257

Make a Rondelle Cut................ 257

Make a Diagonal Cut 257

Dice Food.................................. 258

Mince Food............................... 258

Sharpen and True Knives 259

Dredge and Bread Food 385

Braise Food............................... 393

Make a Sachet 406

Scramble Eggs........................... 439

Make a French Omelet............. 440

Build a Salad 467

Make a Vinaigrette Dressing... 468

Prepare Quantities
  of Sandwiches 492

Prepare White Stock 512

Prepare a Glaze 514

Make a Roux 524

Peel and Devein Shrimp 554

Steam Fish en Papillote............ 560

Cut Up Poultry......................... 572

Truss Whole Birds 574

Carve Roasted Turkey.............. 578

Broil or Grill Poultry................ 579

Sauté Poultry 581

Braise Poultry........................... 581

Boil Pasta................................. 620

Stuff Pasta 621

Make Risotto 631

Grill Fruit 643

Whisk Mixtures 695

Use the Modified
  Straight-Dough Method........ 714

Use the Sponge Method.......... 716

Knead Yeast Dough 717

Create a Braided Loaf 719

Use the Biscuit Method 732

Cut and Form Biscuits.............. 733

Blend Muffins........................... 737

Use the Creaming Method 738

Prepare a Loaf Bread 740

Mix Creamed Cookie Dough ... 750

Make Biscotti............................ 751

Make Rolled Cookies 752

Prepare an Angel Food Cake... 756

Use the Blending Method
  for Cakes............................. 758

Prepare a Sponge Cake 759

Prepare a Chiffon Cake............ 760

Make Baked Custard................ 772

Make Crème Anglaise.............. 773

To the Student

☞ Begin the Unit

Discover the World
of Culinary Arts

Successful readers first set a purpose for reading. *Culinary Essentials* teaches you the culinary techniques you will need to make plans for your future. Think about why you are reading this book. Consider how you might be able to use what you learn as you plan for certification, and the workforce.

Preview the Project at the beginning of each unit. A preview lets you know what is to come. Use the preview to think about how what you are learning applies to the project.

Read the Chapter Titles to see the culinary topics you will learn.

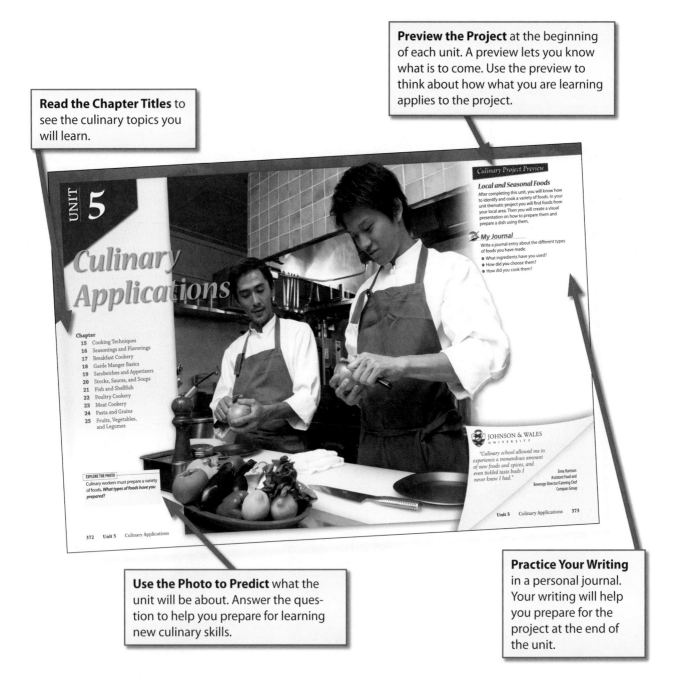

Use the Photo to Predict what the unit will be about. Answer the question to help you prepare for learning new culinary skills.

Practice Your Writing in a personal journal. Your writing will help you prepare for the project at the end of the unit.

☞ Close the Unit

What Did You Learn in Culinary Arts?

Every unit ends with a Culinary Project that lets you apply an important skill from the unit. To complete each project, you will perform research, connect to your community, create a report, and share what you have learned.

Read the Project Assignment The assignment explains what you will need to do.

Follow the Project Checklist to make sure that you have done everything you need to complete your culinary project.

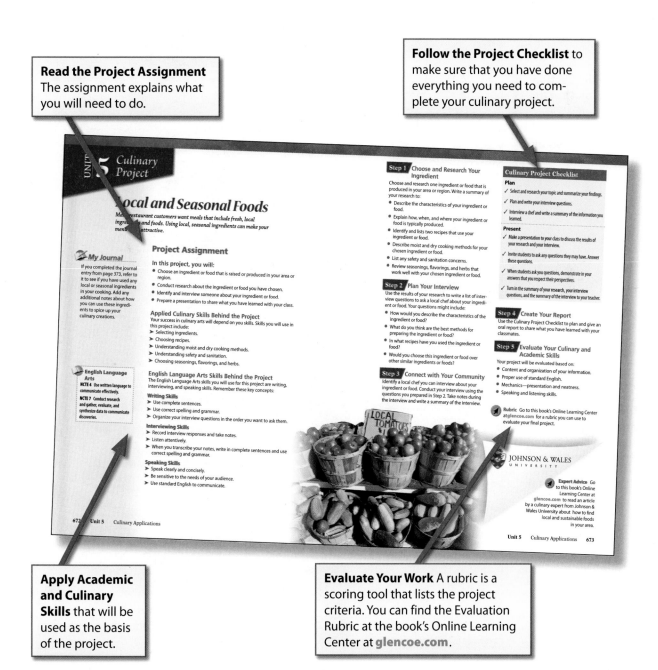

Apply Academic and Culinary Skills that will be used as the basis of the project.

Evaluate Your Work A rubric is a scoring tool that lists the project criteria. You can find the Evaluation Rubric at the book's Online Learning Center at **glencoe.com**.

To the Student

☞ Begin the Chapter

What Is the Chapter All About?

Use the information in the chapter opener to help you connect what you already know to chapter topics. Think about the culinary experiences you have had in your own life. Are there any similarities with those in your textbook?

Review the Section Titles to preview the key ideas you will learn. Keep these in mind as you read the chapter.

Use These Writing Tips to improve your writing and express your ideas.

CHAPTER 15

Cooking Techniques

SECTIONS

15.1 How Cooking Alters Food

15.2 Dry Cooking Techniques

15.3 Moist Cooking Techniques

WRITING ACTIVITY

Cause-and-Effect Paragraph

Cause-and-effect paragraphs explain the reasons for something, or the results of something. Write a cause-and-effect paragraph about how an egg changes when it is cooked.

Writing Tips

1 Use focusing sentences to help readers anticipate organization.

2 Use conjunctions such as "as a result," "due to," or "because."

3 End with a concluding sentence.

EXPLORE THE PHOTO

Different cooking methods affect the flavor, texture, appearance, and nutritional content of food. *How many different cooking techniques can you name?*

374

Explore the Photo to jumpstart your thinking about the chapter's main topics.

☞ Review the Chapter

Know and Understand the Concepts

Review what you learned in the chapter and see how this learning applies to your other subjects and real-world situations.

Read the Chapter Summary to review the most important ideas that you should have learned in the chapter.

Critical Thinking takes your knowledge of the chapter further. If you have difficulty answering these questions, reread the related parts of the chapter.

Practice Academic Skills and connect what you learned to your knowledge of language arts, math, science, and social studies.

Review Vocabulary and Key Concepts to check your recall of important ideas and terms.

Apply Real-World Skills to situations that you might find in a professional culinary setting.

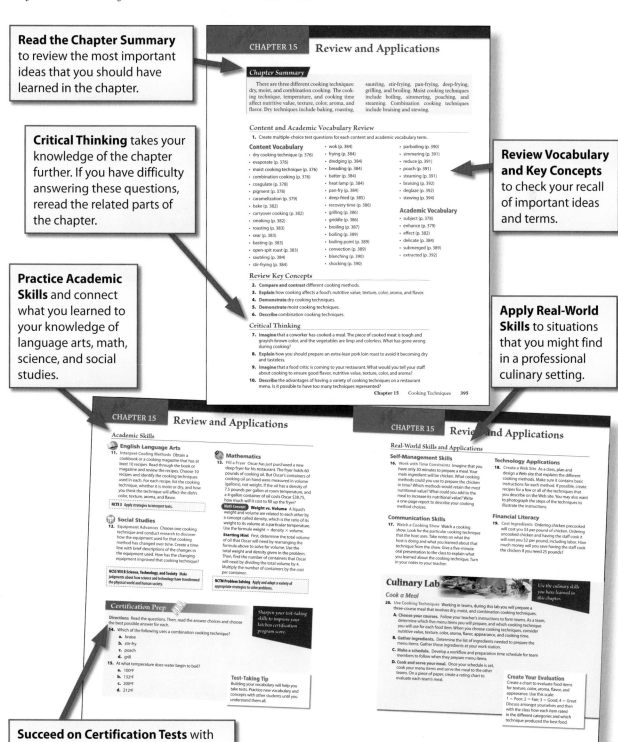

Succeed on Certification Tests with test-taking tips and practice questions.

☞ Begin the Section

Prepare with Reading Guides and Study Tools

Use the reading guide at the beginning of each section to preview what you will learn in the section. See if you can predict the information and skills in the section by using clues and information that you already know.

Predict Before You Read what the section will be about.

Check Vocabulary lists for words you do not know. You can look them up in the glossary before you read the section.

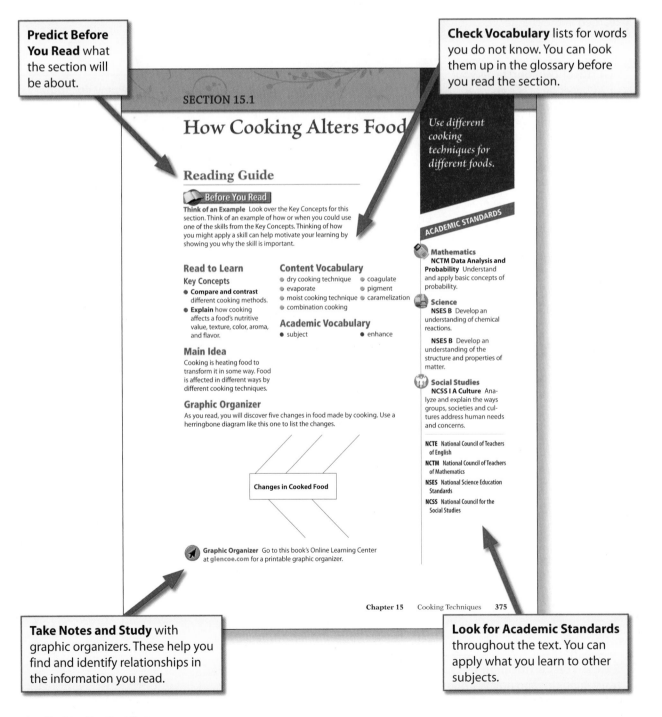

SECTION 15.1

How Cooking Alters Food

Use different cooking techniques for different foods.

Reading Guide

Before You Read

Think of an Example Look over the Key Concepts for this section. Think of an example of how or when you could use one of the skills from the Key Concepts. Thinking of how you might apply a skill can help motivate your learning by showing you why the skill is important.

Read to Learn

Key Concepts
- **Compare and contrast** different cooking methods.
- **Explain** how cooking affects a food's nutritive value, texture, color, aroma, and flavor.

Main Idea

Cooking is heating food to transform it in some way. Food is affected in different ways by different cooking techniques.

Graphic Organizer

As you read, you will discover five changes in food made by cooking. Use a herringbone diagram like this one to list the changes.

Changes in Cooked Food

Graphic Organizer Go to this book's Online Learning Center at **glencoe.com** for a printable graphic organizer.

Content Vocabulary
- dry cooking technique
- evaporate
- moist cooking technique
- combination cooking
- coagulate
- pigment
- caramelization

Academic Vocabulary
- subject
- enhance

ACADEMIC STANDARDS

Mathematics
NCTM Data Analysis and Probability Understand and apply basic concepts of probability.

Science
NSES B Develop an understanding of chemical reactions.

NSES B Develop an understanding of the structure and properties of matter.

Social Studies
NCSS I A Culture Analyze and explain the ways groups, societies and cultures address human needs and concerns.

NCTE National Council of Teachers of English

NCTM National Council of Teachers of Mathematics

NSES National Science Education Standards

NCSS National Council for the Social Studies

Chapter 15   Cooking Techniques   **375**

Take Notes and Study with graphic organizers. These help you find and identify relationships in the information you read.

Look for Academic Standards throughout the text. You can apply what you learn to other subjects.

⤳ Review the Section

Check Your Comprehension with Self-Assessments

After you read, use the section closer to check your understanding. Make sure that you can answer the questions in your own words before moving on in the text.

Maintenance and Repairs

All equipment must be regularly and properly maintained. This will ensure that the equipment stays in top operating condition. If equipment needs to be fixed, repairs must be made promptly. This will keep the foodservice operation running smoothly. The equipment must not be used until repairs are made to maintain kitchen safety.

It is important to follow proper maintenance procedures. This is true whether you are using a deep fat fryer or a manual can opener. Managers usually create an equipment maintenance and cleaning schedule. This schedule should be followed exactly for safety.

Insurance

Owners of foodservice operations buy insurance to protect their business operations, facility, employees, and customers. There are many different types of insurance that are available. Insurance can be purchased

⤳ Small Bites ⤳

Facility Maintenance Many foodservice operations sign maintenance contracts with repair companies. Under these contracts, repair companies regularly visit the facility and perform routine maintenance.

to cover damage from fire, injury to customers, damage to equipment, employee disability, employee health, loss of life, theft, and loss of the business.

Insurance can be costly, however. Properly training employees in safety techniques and maintaining proper equipment maintenance schedules can help reduce the cost of insurance. These precautions help make the foodservice workplace a safer environment for workers and customers.

Reading Check Describe How can managers improve the safety of their facilities?

SECTION 7.2 **After You Read**

Review Key Concepts

1. **Analyze** why positive reinforcement and mentoring are good methods of employee training.
2. **Describe** the qualities of an effective work area.
3. **Explain** a manager's responsibility for equipment handling.

Practice Culinary Academics

English Language Arts

4. Read articles in trade publications about management issues such as scheduling conflicts, handling delayed orders, and equipment breakdowns. Briefly summarize each article and your thoughts in response to the article. Discuss the articles you read and your thoughts about them as a class. Attach copies of the article to your summary page and turn them in.

> **NCTE 7** Conduct research and gather, evaluate, and synthesize data to communicate discoveries.

Mathematics

5. A small deli requires four employees: two sandwich makers (who earn $10.25/hour), a cashier (who earns $9.75/hour), and a manager (who earns $850/week). If the deli is open 40 hours in a week, what are its total weekly labor costs? What is its average hourly cost?

> **Math Concept** **Calculating Labor Costs** Calculate a company's total direct labor cost for a time period by adding all salaries and wages paid to employees over that period. Labor costs may also be averaged per hour.
>
> **Starting Hint** Calculate the weekly wages paid to the three hourly employees by multiplying each pay rate ($10.25/hour, $9.75/hour) by the number of hours worked per week (40). Add these amounts to the manager's weekly salary to find the total labor costs. Divide this sum by 40 to find the average hourly cost.

> **NCTM Number and Operations** Compute fluently and make reasonable estimates.

 Check your answers at this book's Online Learning Center at **glencoe.com**.

186 **Unit 3** Quality Foodservice Practices

Verify Your Understanding of key concepts and skills in the section.

Practice Culinary Academics related to the culinary world with these cross-curricular activities.

Check Your Answers online at this book's Online Learning Center at **glencoe.com**.

⌐ As You Read

Use Reading Strategies and Visuals to Study Effectively

In addition to the reading guide at the beginning of each section, there are a lot of reading strategies that can help you comprehend the text.

> **Skim the Headings** to help identify the main idea and supporting details.

> **Keep a Vocabulary Journal** Write down vocabulary words, and then find definitions in the text and in the glossary at the back of the book.

Quick-Service Breakfasts

Breakfast foods are very popular. In the United States, many people eat breakfast foods at any meal. The standard breakfast menu includes eggs, meat, potatoes, breads, pancakes, waffles, cereals, fruit, and yogurt. Some restaurants offer customers more unusual choices, such as a special pizza or breakfast burritos. In short, anything goes!

Most restaurants that serve breakfast offer a variety of options and combinations. Eggs are often served either scrambled, overeasy, hard, basted, poached, or as omelets. Eggs usually come with some form of breakfast bread. This could include toast, biscuits, or an English muffin. It could also include potatoes that have been sautéed or fried. Egg dishes may also be accompanied by meat, such as bacon, ham, or sausage.

Breads such as pancakes, French toast, and waffles can be ordered in combination with eggs and a meat choice, or alone. An example would be a stack of three to five pancakes with butter and syrup or fruit toppings. A small stack of two pancakes may accompany an egg dish.

Potatoes such as home fries, hash browns, and cottage fries are a common side dish for breakfast. **Home fries** are usually diced or sliced. **Hash browns** are shredded and may include onions and seasonings. For **cottage fries**, the potatoes are cut into ½-inch thick circles, and then baked or broiled.

More often than not, breakfast items may be ordered á la carte so that the customers can create their own combination of foods. This can also be profitable for the restaurant. But foodservice workers must know how to prepare a wide variety of breakfast proteins and breads. They also must learn to prepare breakfast items quickly and with skill. Most restaurant customers want their breakfast to be ready quickly.

Reading Check Determine What types of food items might be served with eggs?

Breakfast Breads and Cereals

Bread may be an even more popular breakfast item than eggs. Toast, muffins, biscuits, scones, and bagels are some of the many choices. Nearly every customer who orders an egg item will want some kind of bread with it. Many customers choose a bread item, such as pancakes, French toast, waffles, or cereal, as the [...] or main part, of their favorite breakfa[...]

Cereals appear on all breakfast m[...] are served either hot or cold. Cereals [...] from grains such as wheat, corn, [...] oats, and are a good source of carbo[...] Breakfast cereals should be stored i[...] containers to keep them from becom[...] or being infested by pests.

Quality Breakfast Breads [...] Cereals

Once breads are baked, they bec[...] quickly. Stale breads taste unappe[...] may become hard and dry. To avoid [...] it is necessary to consider how far in [...] you will be able to prepare and ba[...] before they are served.

Ready-Made Breads

Bread that is made in advance a[...] and delivered to foodservice establis[...] called **ready-made bread**. The choic[...] ity pre-prepared breads on a breakfas[...] almost unlimited. Bagels, scones, do[...] muffins, croissants, and English m[...] just a few examples. The only breakf[...] items that are routinely prepared to [...] toast, pancakes, French toast, and w[...]

Hot Cereals

Hot cereals typically fall into two [...]
- Granular cereals, such as grits, b[...] farina.
- Whole, cracked, or flaked cereals[...] oatmeal and cracked wheat.

Chapter 17 Breakfast Cooke[...]

> **Reading Checks** let you pause to respond to what you have read.

Hot cereals are served with milk or cream and white or brown sugar. Sometimes small ceramic bowls called ramekins filled with raisins, fresh fruit, brown sugar, or nuts are served with hot cereal. Hot cereals are a welcome menu choice for many healthconscious people.

Cold Cereals

Many cold cereals are purchased ready to eat. Some restaurants make their own special blend of granola (grə-ˈnō-lə). **Granola** is a blend of grains, nuts, and dried fruits. Like hot cereals, cold cereals are served with milk or cream, sugar, and sometimes fresh fruit, such as sliced strawberries or bananas. Cold cereals are a favorite breakfast choice for both children and adults. They are available in quantity portioning machines and as individual portions.

Ready-Made Breads

Breads and cereals are an essential component of breakfast menus. Rarely is an order of eggs sold without a breakfast bread. Quick

breads, such as pancakes and waffles, and breakfast items like toast and French toast are generally cooked to order. Many operations purchase ready-made pastries, muffins, and doughnuts. This section will introduce you to common breakfast breads and cereals.

Ready-made or convenience (kən-ˈvēn-yən(t)s) breads include pastries, doughnuts, and many kinds of quick breads, such as muffins. Ready-made breads can save a restaurant time during a busy breakfast rush.

Pastries

Pastries, also known as Danishes, are popular breakfast treats. They are made from yeasted, sweetened dough with butter, which gives pastries the rich flavor that makes them so appetizing. Egg is added to the dough of some kinds of pastries.

Many pastries are filled with almond paste, fruit, cream cheese, or nuts. Bear claws and strudel are two of the more wellknown types of pastries. Pastries can be made from scratch, from frozen doughs, or can be purchased ready-made.

◀ **Breakfast Breads** Many different types of breakfast breads are available. *What kinds of specialty breakfast breads and pastries are available in your area?*

444 **Unit 5** Culinary Applications

> **Examine Visuals** to reinforce content. Answer the questions so that you can better discuss topics in the section.

☞ Study with Features

Skills You Can Use at School and in the Workplace

As you read, look for feature boxes throughout each chapter. These features build skills that relate to other academic subjects and prepare you for the foodservice industry.

Gourmet Math You can solve math problems related to culinary skills and techniques. Each math concept is described for you, as well as a starting hint to help you solve each problem.

Science à la Carte You can connect the information in the chapter with the science content you have learned or are learning. Each of these features include a scientific procedure and how to analyze the information you find.

Gourmet Math

Unit Prices

Unit price is the cost per unit of measure. This may be per item, per pound, per quart, or any other unit measure. When you buy food packaged in two different quantities, it is wise to know which is the better buy. To find the better buy, you need to know the unit price.
Which breadcrumbs package is the better buy: ½ pound for 75¢, or 3 pounds for $5.65? Which orange juice is the better buy: 3 quarts for $7.45, or 10 quarts for $20.25?

Math Concept **Calculating Unit Rates** A unit rate is a ratio showing how much of one quantity is needed to match 1 unit of another quantity. Unit price, a type of unit rate, is calculated by dividing the price by the quantity.
Starting Hint To find which item is the better buy, you need to calculate the unit price for each item. Do so by dividing the item's price by its quantity. The unit price of the first breadcrumbs package, for example, equals $0.75 ÷ ½, or $1.50. This means that you pay $1.50 per pound of breadcrumbs.

> **NCTM Number and Operations** Understand numbers, ways of representing numbers, relationships among numbers, and number systems.

Science à la Carte

Color Fade

Do you know what gives green vegetables their color? Green vegetables, such as broccoli and spinach, contain two types of the pigment chlorophyll. One type of chlorophyll is a bright bluish-green color. The other type is a yellowish-green color. Green vegetables have about four times more of the blue-green type than the yellow-green type.
To maintain the color of a green vegetable, do not overcook it. Heat from cooking damages the vegetable's cells. This allows the acids that were in the once-living cells of the vegetable to be released. Once exposed to this acid, the chlorophyll changes to a brownish-yellow color.

Procedure

To complete the following experiment, you will need four broccoli stalks, a pot with a lid, and a second pot without a lid. Bring 3 cups of water to a boil in each uncovered pot. Separate the florets, or flowers, of the broccoli. Place half of the broccoli in one pot and cover it with the lid. Place the rest of the broccoli in the other pot without a lid. Cook both pots of broccoli for 7 minutes. After 7 minutes, drain each pot and place the broccoli into two separate bowls.

Analysis

Determine which style of cooking provided a greener vegetable. Examine each bowl. Describe the color and the texture of the broccoli in each bowl. Which dish has the greener broccoli? Explain in a short summary why you think one method of cooking had a greater impact on the color change than the other.

> **NSES B** Develop an understanding of chemical reactions.

A Taste of History These features help you to learn the local, national, and international impact of history on the foodservice industry. Each feature has a time line to show you how important culinary dates connect with world events.

A TASTE OF HISTORY

2004	2007
The Spirit rover leaves Cape Canaveral, Florida, for the planet Mars	Mandatory pasteurization of all California almonds begins

Battle Against Bacteria

French scientist Louis Pasteur was a pioneer in the study of microbiology. He was the first person to understand that bacteria can cause disease, and his experiments led to a process known as pasteurization. During pasteurization, controlled heat is applied to food to kill microorganisms that could cause disease or spoilage. Pasteurization had a major impact on the food industry. Today, pasteurization is commonly used for milk and other dairy products.

History Application

Research Pasteur's discovery of how bacteria and disease are linked and how pasteurization works. Write a paragraph discussing how you believe milk and milk products have been improved because of its use.

> **NCSS VIII B Science, Technology, and Society** Make judgments about how science and technology have transformed our understanding of human-environment interactions.

☞ Study with Features (continued)

How To These step-by-step photo features help you understand the basics of different culinary skills.

☆ HOW TO ☆

Braise
Food

1 Begin by searing the food in a frying or roasting pan. When using meats, a mixture of carrots, celery, and onions is usually added to the pan when the meat is seared.

2 Remove the food from the pan, and deglaze the pan.

3 Return the seared food to the deglazed pan and add liquid, such as stock or sauce. Add enough liquid to cover no more than two-thirds of the food.

4 Place the pan in a 350°F (177°C) oven, and cook the food slowly until it is tender when pulled apart with a fork. Turn the food every 20 to 30 minutes. Often, braised items are covered while cooking. Braising can also be done on the rangetop over low heat.

Safety Check Learn how to be safe in a professional kitchen with these tips.

Sanitation Check Sanitation is vital in the foodservice industry. These features will help you make sure that food is safe to eat.

Safety Check

✔ Egg Safety

Take the following extra precautions when you prepare eggs:

- Always store eggs and foods that contain eggs separately from raw foods. Also, store eggs away from foods that may have an undesirable odor. Eggs absorb odors easily.
- Always wash your hands before and after working with eggs and foods that contain eggs.
- Wash, rinse, and sanitize utensils, equipment, and work surfaces after you prepare eggs or products that contain eggs.
- Make sure cooked eggs do not sit out for more than a very short period of time.

CRITICAL THINKING *Why do foodservice professionals need to be extra cautious when they work with eggs?*

Sanitation Check

✔ Serve Raw Fish and Shellfish

Many restaurants offer raw fish or shellfish on the menu, such as sushi or raw oysters. Many health officials advise against serving raw fish or shellfish because of the danger of parasites and contamination from polluted water. However, if you do serve these items, follow these guidelines:

- Buy fish from reputable vendors.
- Choose only the highest quality fish because it will not be cooked.
- Handle the fish as little as possible.
- Follow state-mandated guidelines concerning the serving of raw fish and shellfish.

Critical Thinking *Why do you think you should handle the fish as little as possible?*

☞ Study with Features (continued)

Master Recipes These recipes from Johnson & Wales University are made for the professional kitchen. In each recipe, you will find international alternatives, solid nutritional information, and cooking techniques.

Culinary Showcase Full-color photos with descriptions show you the tools, equipment, and types of ingredients that you will use in the professional foodservice industry.

▥ MASTER RECIPE

Omelet with Cheese

YIELD: 10 SERVINGS
SERVING SIZE: 8 OZ.

Ingredients

30	Eggs, cracked into a bowl
	Salt and ground white pepper, to taste
8 oz.	Milk
5 oz.	Clarified butter, melted
1 lb.	Cheese, julienne
3 oz.	Fresh parsley, washed, excess moisture removed, and chopped

Method of Preparation

1. Season the eggs with salt and pepper. Add the milk, and whisk until the eggs are well combined.
2. Heat an omelet pan with ½ oz. of butter.
3. When hot, add a 6-oz. ladle of egg mixture.
4. Shake the pan, and mix the eggs until they begin to firm, lifting the edges to allow liquid egg to run underneath (see Chef Notes).
5. When the omelet is almost firm, or 145°F (63°C), turn it over.
6. Place about 1 oz. of cheese in the center of the omelet, fold, and roll onto a preheated dinner plate. Serve immediately, or hold at 135°F (57°C) or above.
7. Repeat the procedure until all of the eggs are cooked.
8. Garnish with chopped parsley.

Cooking Technique

Shallow-Fry
1. Heat the cooking medium to the proper temperature.
2. Cook the food product throughout.
3. Season, and serve hot.

Chef Notes

When the eggs have set in the sauté pan, place the pan under a broiler for 10-15 seconds to finish cooking the eggs. This creates a fluffier presentation and ensures that the eggs are well done.

Substitutions

- To lower the fat, use low-fat milk, or half the amount of cheese in each omelet.
- Add fresh herbs to the omelet to increase flavor without adding salt.
- To lower cholesterol, use egg whites, or an egg substitute.

International Flavor

The classic omelet recipe originated in France, but egg dishes are popular in many countries. Use the Internet or library to research these international omelet recipes, and write a half-page report on your findings:
- Frittata (Italy)
- Datemaki (Japan)
- Tortilla de patatas (Spain)

Glossary

Whisk to aerate with a whip
Julienne matchstick strips

HACCP

- Cook to 145°F (63°C)
- Hold cooked eggs at 135°F (57°C) or above
- Hold uncooked egg mixture below 41°F (5°C)

Hazardous Foods

- Eggs
- Milk

Nutrition

Calories 480	Calories from Fat 320
Total Fat 35g	
Saturated Fat 17g	
Trans Fat 0g	
Cholesterol 790mg	
Sodium 720mg	
Total Carbohydrate 4g	
Fiber 0g	
Sugars 3g	
Protein 34g	
· Vitamin A 35%	· Vitamin C 6%
· Calcium 30%	· Iron 20%

436   Unit 5   Culinary Applications

▥ CULINARY SHOWCASE

Service Equipment

Insulated Carriers Insulated carriers are large boxes that can hold hotel pans and sheet pans filled with cooked food. Insulated carriers keep hot foods hot and cold foods cold. Some insulated carriers have wheels. If the carrier has a spigot, warm or cold beverages can be stored inside.

Chafing Dishes Chafing dishes are typically stainless steel pans used to keep food hot during service. Hotel pans of food can be inserted into the chafing dish. Chafing dishes are available in a variety of sizes.

Canned Fuel Canned fuel is used to heat food [in] chafing dishes. [These...]

Nutrition Notes Do you know how nutritional poultry is? These features can offer you advice on the nutrition in food and how to enhance its value.

◈ Nutrition Notes ◈

Poultry Nutrition
Poultry is packed with protein. A 3½-ounce roasted chicken breast with skin has about 197 calories, 30 grams of protein, 84 milligrams of cholesterol, and 7.8 grams of fat.

CRITICAL THINKING *How does poultry fit into a well-rounded diet?*

☞ Small Bites ☜

Using Edible Flowers When you add flower petals to a salad, be sure to clean them well. Dirt and insects can hide deep down in the petals and slip unnoticed into the salad.

Small Bites Have you ever wanted to know how to crumb a table, or how to create a new dish for a menu? These handy features offer extra information on cooking techniques, the foodservice industry, equipment and tools, and more.

To the Student

✍ Online Learning Center

Use the Internet to
Extend Your Learning

Follow these steps to access the textbook resources at *Culinary Essentials'* Online Learning Center.

Online Learning Center Icon Look for this icon throughout the text that directs you to the book's Online Learning Center for more activities and information.

 Graphic Organizer Go to this book's Online Learning Center at **glencoe.com** for a printable graphic organizer.

Step 1 Go to **glencoe.com**.

Step 2 Select **your state** from the pull-down menu.

Step 3 Select **student/parent**

Step 4 Select **Family & Consumer Sciences**.

Step 5 Select **ENTER**.

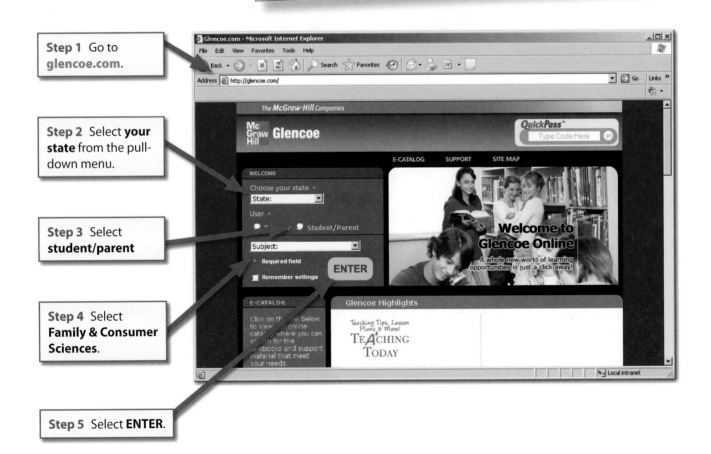

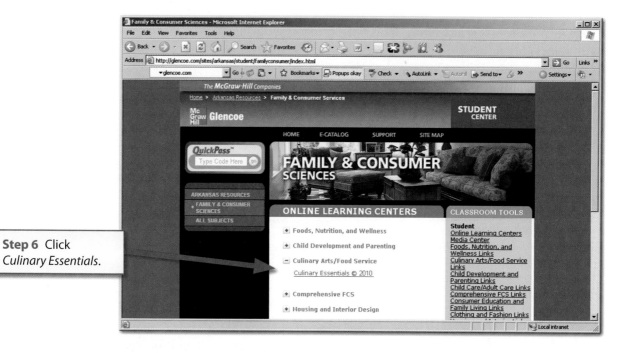

Step 6 Click *Culinary Essentials.*

Step 7 Click **Student Center** to access student resources.

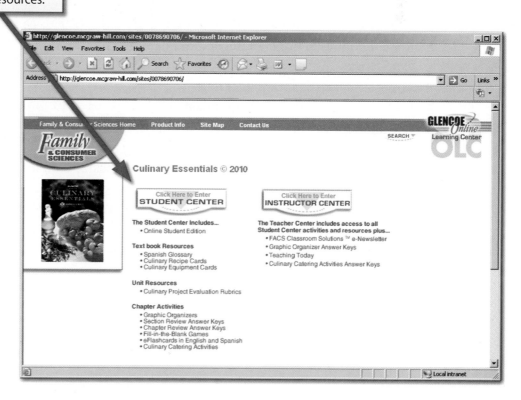

Prepare for Academic Success!

By improving your academic skills, you improve your ability to learn and achieve success now and in the future. It also improves your chances of landing a high-skill, high-wage job. The features and assessments in *Culinary Essentials* provide many opportunities for you to strengthen your academic skills.

Academic Standards Look for this box throughout the text to know what academic skills you are learning.

NCTM Number and Operations Understand numbers, ways of representing numbers, relationships among numbers, and number systems.

National English Language Arts Standards

To help incorporate literacy skills (reading, writing, listening, and speaking) into *Culinary Essentials,* each section contains a listing of the language arts skills covered. These skills have been developed into standards by the *National Council of Teachers of English and International Reading Association.*

- Read texts to acquire new information.
- Read literature to build an understanding of the human experience.
- Apply strategies to interpret texts.
- Use written language to communicate effectively.
- Use different writing process elements to communicate effectively.
- Conduct research and gather, evaluate, and synthesize data to communicate discoveries.
- Use information resources to gather information and create and communicate knowledge.
- Develop an understanding of diversity in language use across cultures.
- Participate as members of literacy communities.
- Use language to accomplish individual purposes.

National Math Standards

You also have opportunities to practice math skills indicated by standards developed by the *National Council of Teachers of Mathematics.* *

- Algebra
- Data Analysis and Probability
- Geometry
- Measurement
- Number and Operations
- Problem Solving

* Standards are listed with the permission of the National Council of Teachers of Mathematics (NCTM). NCTM *does not endorse the content or validity of these alignments.*

National Science Standards

The *National Science Education Standards* outline these science skills that you can practice in this text.

- Science as Inquiry
- Physical Science
- Life Science
- Earth and Space Science
- Science and Technology
- Science in Personal and Social Perspectives
- History and Nature of Science

National Social Studies Standards

The *National Council for the Social Studies* is another organization that provides standards to help guide your studies. Activities in this text relate to these standards.

- Culture
- Time, Continuity, and Change
- People, Places, and Environments
- Individual Development and Identity
- Individuals, Groups, and Institutions
- Power, Authority, and Governance
- Production, Distribution, and Consumption
- Science, Technology, and Society
- Global Connections
- Civic Ideals and Practices

Reading Skills Handbook

▶ Reading: What's in It for You?

What role does reading play in your life? The possibilities are countless. Are you on a sports team? Perhaps you like to read about the latest news and statistics in sports or find out about new training techniques. Are you looking for a part-time job? You might be looking for advice about résumé writing, interview techniques, or information about a company. Are you enrolled in an English class, an algebra class, or a business class? Then your assignments require a lot of reading.

Improving or Fine-Tuning Your Reading Skills Will:

- ◆ Improve your grades.
- ◆ Allow you to read faster and more efficiently.
- ◆ Improve your study skills.
- ◆ Help you remember more information accurately.
- ◆ Improve your writing.

▶ The Reading Process

Good reading skills build on one another, overlap, and spiral around in much the same way that a winding staircase goes around and around while leading you to a higher place. This handbook is designed to help you find and use the tools you will need **before, during,** and **after** reading.

Strategies You Can Use

- ◆ Identify, understand, and learn new words.
- ◆ Understand why you read.
- ◆ Take a quick look at the whole text.
- ◆ Try to predict what you are about to read.

- ◆ Take breaks while you read and ask yourself questions about the text.
- ◆ Take notes.
- ◆ Keep thinking about what will come next.
- ◆ Summarize.

▶ Vocabulary Development

Word identification and vocabulary skills are the building blocks of the reading and the writing process. By learning to use a variety of strategies to build your word skills and vocabulary, you will become a stronger reader.

Use Context to Determine Meaning

The best way to expand and extend your vocabulary is to read widely, listen carefully, and participate in a rich variety of discussions. When reading on your own, though, you can often figure out the meanings of new words by looking at their **context,** the other words and sentences that surround them.

> ## Tips for Using Context
>
> **Look for clues like these:**
>
> ◆ A synonym or an explanation of the unknown word in the sentence:
> *Elise's shop specialized in millinery, or hats for women.*
> ◆ A reference to what the word is or is not like:
> *An archaeologist, like a historian, deals with the past.*
> ◆ A general topic associated with the word:
> *The cooking teacher discussed the best way to braise meat.*
> ◆ A description or action associated with the word:
> *He used the shovel to dig up the garden.*

Predict a Possible Meaning

Another way to determine the meaning of a word is to take the word apart. If you understand the meaning of the **base,** or **root,** part of a word, and also know the meanings of key syllables added either to the beginning or end of the base word, you can usually figure out what the word means.

Word Origins Since Latin, Greek, and Anglo-Saxon roots are the basis for much of our English vocabulary, having some background in languages can be a useful vocabulary tool. For example, *astronomy* comes from the Greek root *astro,* which means "relating to the stars." *Stellar* also has a meaning referring to stars, but its origin is Latin. Knowing root words in other languages can help you determine meanings, derivations, and spellings in English.

Prefixes and Suffixes A prefix is a word part that can be added to the beginning of a word. For example, the prefix *semi* means "half" or "partial," so *semicircle* means "half a circle." A suffix is a word part that can be added to the end of a word. Adding a suffix often changes a word from one part of speech to another.

Using Dictionaries A dictionary provides the meaning or meanings of a word. Look at the sample dictionary entry on the next page to see what other information it provides.

Thesauruses and Specialized Reference Books A thesaurus provides synonyms and often antonyms. It is a useful tool to expand your vocabulary. Remember to check the exact definition of the listed words in a dictionary before you use a thesaurus. Specialized dictionaries such as *Barron's Dictionary of Business Terms* or *Black's Law Dictionary* list terms and expressions that are not commonly included in a general dictionary. You can also use online dictionaries.

Glossaries Many textbooks and technical works contain condensed dictionaries that provide an alphabetical listing of words used in the text and their specific definitions.

Dictionary Entry

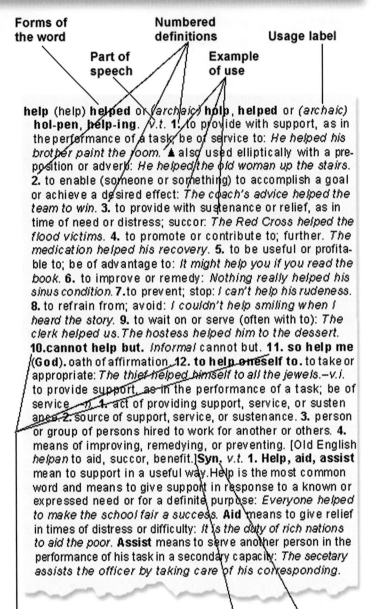

Forms of the word
Numbered definitions
Usage label
Part of speech
Example of use
Idioms
Origin (etymology)
Synonyms

help (help) **helped** or *(archaic)* **holp**, **helped** or *(archaic)* **hol·pen**, **help·ing**. *v.t.* **1.** to provide with support, as in the performance of a task; be of service to: *He helped his brother paint the room.* ▲ also used elliptically with a preposition or adverb: *He helped the old woman up the stairs.* **2.** to enable (someone or something) to accomplish a goal or achieve a desired effect: *The coach's advice helped the team to win.* **3.** to provide with sustenance or relief, as in time of need or distress; succor: *The Red Cross helped the flood victims.* **4.** to promote or contribute to; further. *The medication helped his recovery.* **5.** to be useful or profitable to; be of advantage to: *It might help you if you read the book.* **6.** to improve or remedy: *Nothing really helped his sinus condition.* **7.** to prevent; stop: *I can't help his rudeness.* **8.** to refrain from; avoid: *I couldn't help smiling when I heard the story.* **9.** to wait on or serve (often with to): *The clerk helped us. The hostess helped him to the dessert.* **10. cannot help but.** *Informal* cannot but. **11. so help me (God).** oath of affirmation. **12. to help oneself to.** to take or appropriate: *The thief helped himself to all the jewels.* –*v.i.* to provide support, as in the performance of a task; be of service. –*n.* **1.** act of providing support, service, or sustenance. **2.** source of support, service, or sustenance. **3.** person or group of persons hired to work for another or others. **4.** means of improving, remedying, or preventing. [Old English *helpan* to aid, succor, benefit.] **Syn.** *v.t.* **1.** Help, aid, assist mean to support in a useful way. Help is the most common word and means to give support in response to a known or expressed need or for a definite purpose: *Everyone helped to make the school fair a success.* **Aid** means to give relief in times of distress or difficulty: *It is the duty of rich nations to aid the poor.* **Assist** means to serve another person in the performance of his task in a secondary capacity: *The secretary assists the officer by taking care of his corresponding.*

Recognize Word Meanings Across Subjects Have you learned a new word in one class and then noticed it in your reading for other subjects? The word might not mean exactly the same thing in each class, but you can use the meaning you already know to help you understand what it means in another subject area. For example:

Math Each digit represents a different place **value**.

Health Your **values** can guide you in making healthful decisions.

Economics The **value** of a product is measured in its cost.

▶ Understanding What You Read

Reading comprehension means understanding—deriving meaning from—what you have read. Using a variety of strategies can help you improve your comprehension and make reading more interesting and more fun.

Read for a Reason

To get the greatest benefit from your reading, **establish a purpose for reading.** In school, you have many reasons for reading, such as:

- to learn and understand new information.
- to find specific information.
- to review before a test.
- to complete an assignment.
- to prepare (research) before you write.

As your reading skills improve, you will notice that you apply different strategies to fit the different purposes for reading. For example, if you are reading for entertainment, you might read quickly, but if you read to gather information or follow directions, you might read more slowly, take notes, construct a graphic organizer, or reread sections of text.

Draw on Personal Background

Drawing on personal background may also be called activating prior knowledge. Before you start reading a text, ask yourself questions like these:

- What have I heard or read about this topic?
- Do I have any personal experience relating to this topic?

Using a K-W-L Chart A K-W-L chart is a good device for organizing information you gather before, during, and after reading. In the first column, list what you already **know,** then list what you **want** to know in the middle column. Use the third column when you review and assess what you **learned.** You can also add more columns to record places where you found information and places where you can look for more information.

K (What I already know)	W (What I want to know)	L (What I have learned)

Adjust Your Reading Speed Your reading speed is a key factor in how well you understand what you are reading. You will need to adjust your speed depending on your reading purpose.

Scanning means running your eyes quickly over the material to look for words or phrases. Scan when you need a specific piece of information.

Skimming means reading a passage quickly to find its main idea or to get an overview. Skim a text when you preview to determine what the material is about.

Reading for detail involves careful reading while paying attention to text structure and monitoring your understanding. Read for detail when you are learning concepts, following complicated directions, or preparing to analyze a text.

▶ Techniques to Understand and Remember What You Read

Preview

Before beginning a selection, it is helpful to **preview** what you are about to read.

Previewing Strategies

- ◆ Read the title, headings, and subheadings of the selection.
- ◆ Look at the illustrations and notice how the text is organized.
- ◆ Skim the selection: Take a glance at the whole thing.
- ◆ Decide what the main idea might be.
- ◆ Predict what a selection will be about.

Predict

Have you ever read a mystery, decided who committed the crime, and then changed your mind as more clues were revealed? You were adjusting your predictions. Did you smile when you found out that you guessed who committed the crime? You were verifying your predictions.

As you read, take educated guesses about story events and outcomes; that is, **make predictions** before and during reading. This will help you focus your attention on the text and it will improve your understanding.

Determine the Main Idea

When you look for the **main idea**, you are looking for the most important statement in a text. Depending on what kind of text you are reading, the main idea can be located at the very beginning (news stories in newspaper or a magazine) or at the end (scientific research document). Ask yourself the following questions:

- What is each sentence about?
- Is there one sentence that is more important than all the others?
- What idea do details support or point out?

Taking Notes

Cornell Note-Taking System There are many methods for note taking. The **Cornell Note-Taking System** is a well-known method that can help you organize what you read. To the right is a note-taking activity based on the Cornell Note-Taking System.

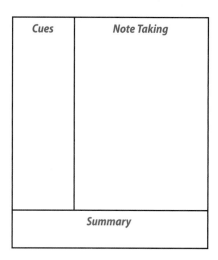

Graphic Organizers Using a graphic organizer to retell content in a visual representation will help you remember and retain content. You might make a **chart** or **diagram,** organizing what you have read. Here are some examples of graphic organizers:

Venn diagrams When mapping out a compare-and-contrast text structure, you can use a Venn diagram. The outer portions of the circles will show how two characters, ideas, or items contrast, or are different, and the overlapping part will compare two things, or show how they are similar.

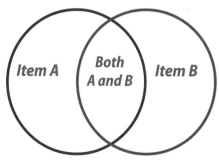

Flow charts To help you track the sequence of events, or cause and effect, use a flow chart. Arrange ideas or events in their logical, sequential order. Then, draw arrows between your ideas to indicate how one idea or event flows into another.

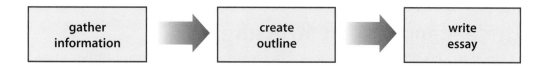

Visualize

Try to form a mental picture of scenes, characters, and events as you read. Use the details and descriptions the author gives you. If you can **visualize** what you read, it will be more interesting and you will remember it better.

Question

Ask yourself questions about the text while you read. Ask yourself about the importance of the sentences, how they relate to one another, if you understand what you just read, and what you think is going to come next.

Clarify

If you feel you do not understand meaning (through questioning), try these techniques:

> **What to Do When You Do Not Understand**
>
> ◆ Reread confusing parts of the text.
> ◆ Diagram (chart) relationships between chunks of text, ideas, and sentences.
> ◆ Look up unfamiliar words.
> ◆ Talk out the text to yourself.
> ◆ Read the passage once more.

Review

Take time to stop and review what you have read. Use your note-taking tools (graphic organizers or Cornell notes charts). Also, review and consider your K-W-L chart.

Monitor Your Comprehension

Continue to check your understanding by using the following two strategies:

Summarize Pause and tell yourself the main ideas of the text and the key supporting details. Try to answer the following questions: Who? What? When? Where? Why? How?

Paraphrase Pause, close the book, and try to retell what you have just read in your own words. It might help to pretend you are explaining the text to someone who has not read it and does not know the material.

▶ Understanding Text Structure

Good writers do not just put together sentences and paragraphs, they organize their writing with a specific purpose in mind. That organization is called text structure. When you understand and follow the structure of a text, it is easier to remember the information you are reading. There are many ways text may be structured. Watch for **signal words**. They will help you follow the text's organization (also, remember to use these techniques when you write).

Compare and Contrast

This structure shows similarities and differences between people, things, and ideas. This is often used to demonstrate that things that seem alike are really different, or vice versa.

> **Signal words:** similarly, more, less, on the one hand / on the other hand, in contrast, but, however

Cause and Effect

Writers use the cause-and-effect structure to explore the reasons for something happening and to examine the results or consequences of events.

Signal words: so, because, as a result, therefore, for the following reasons

Problem and Solution

When they organize text around the question "how?" writers state a problem and suggest solutions.

Signal words: how, help, problem, obstruction, overcome, difficulty, need, attempt, have to, must

Sequence

Sequencing tells you in which order to consider thoughts or facts. Examples of sequencing are:

Chronological order refers to the order in which events take place.

Signal words: first, next, then, finally

Spatial order describes the organization of things in space (to describe a room, for example).

Signal words: above, below, behind, next to

Order of importance lists things or thoughts from the most important to the least important (or the other way around).

Signal words: principal, central, main, important, fundamental

▶ Reading for Meaning

It is important to think about what you are reading to get the most information out of a text, to understand the consequences of what the text says, to remember the content, and to form your own opinion about what the content means.

Interpret

Interpreting is asking yourself, "What is the writer really saying?" and then using what you already know to answer that question.

Infer

Writers do not always state exactly everything they want you to understand. By providing clues and details, they sometimes imply certain information. An **inference** involves using your reason and experience to develop the idea on your own, based on what an author implies or suggests. What is most important when drawing inferences is to be sure that you have accurately based your guesses on supporting details from the text. If you cannot point to a place in the selection to help back up your inference, you may need to rethink your guess.

Draw Conclusions

A conclusion is a general statement you can make and explain with reasoning, or with supporting details from a text. If you read a story describing a sport where five players bounce a ball and throw it through a high hoop, you may conclude that the sport is basketball.

Analyze

To understand persuasive nonfiction (a text that discusses facts and opinions to arrive at a conclusion), you need to analyze statements and examples to see if they support the main idea. To understand an informational text (a text, such as a textbook, that gives you information, not opinions), you need to keep track of how the ideas are organized to find the main points.

Hint: Use your graphic organizers and notes charts.

Distinguish Facts from Opinions

This is one of the most important reading skills you can learn. A fact is a statement that can be proven. An opinion is what the writer believes. A writer may support opinions with facts, but an opinion cannot be proven. For example:

Fact: California produces fruit and other agricultural products.

Opinion: California produces the best fruit and other agricultural products.

Evaluate

Would you take seriously an article on nuclear fission if you knew it was written by a comedic actor? If you need to rely on accurate information, you need to find out who wrote what you are reading and why. Where did the writer get information? Is the information one-sided? Can you verify the information?

▶ Reading for Research

You will need to **read actively** in order to research a topic. You might also need to generate an interesting, relevant, and researchable **question** on your own and locate appropriate print and nonprint information from a wide variety of sources. Then, you will need to **categorize** that information, evaluate it, and **organize** it in a new way in order to produce a research project for a specific audience. Finally, **draw conclusions** about your original research question. These conclusions may lead you to other areas for further inquiry.

Locate Appropriate Print and Nonprint Information

In your research, try to use a variety of sources. Because different sources present information in different ways, your research project will be more interesting and balanced when you read a variety of sources.

Literature and Textbooks These texts include any book used as a basis for instruction or a source of information.

Book Indices A book index, or a bibliography, is an alphabetical listing of books. Some book indices list books on specific subjects; others are more general. Other indices list a variety of topics or resources.

Periodicals Magazines and journals are issued at regular intervals, such as weekly or monthly. One way to locate information in magazines is to use the *Readers' Guide to Periodical Literature*. This guide is available in print form in most libraries.

Technical Manuals A manual is a guide or handbook intended to give instruction on how to perform a task or operate something. A vehicle owner's manual might give information on how to operate and service a car.

Reference Books Reference books include encyclopedias and almanacs, and are used to locate specific pieces of information.

Electronic Encyclopedias, Databases, and the Internet There are many ways to locate extensive information using your computer. Infotrac, for instance, acts as an online reader's guide. CD encyclopedias can provide easy access to all subjects.

Organize and Convert Information

As you gather information from different sources, taking careful notes, you will need to think about how to **synthesize** the information, that is, convert it into a unified whole, as well as how to change it into a form your audience will easily understand and that will meet your assignment guidelines.

1. First, ask yourself what you want your audience to know.
2. Then, think about a pattern of organization, a structure that will best show your main ideas. You might ask yourself the following questions:
   - When comparing items or ideas, what graphic aids can I use?
   - When showing the reasons something happened and the effects of certain actions, what text structure would be best?
   - How can I briefly and clearly show important information to my audience?
   - Would an illustration or even a cartoon help to make a certain point?

Introduction

Computers are a path to the libraries of the world. You can find the answers to many of your questions on the Internet, often as quickly as the click of your mouse. However, they can also be misused. Knowing some simple guidelines will help you use technology in a safe and secure way.

Practice Safe Surfing!

Before you sign on to any site or visit a chat room, there are several things to consider:

- **Know to whom you are giving the information.** Check that the URL in your browser matches the domain you intended to visit.

- **Never give personal information of any sort** to someone you meet on a Web site or in a chat room, including your name, gender, age, or contact information.

- **Think about why you are giving the information.** If a parent orders something online to be delivered, he or she will need to give an address. But you should never give out your Social Security number, your birth date, or your mother's maiden name without adult consent.

- **Check with a parent or other trusted adult** if you are still unsure whether it is safe to give the information.

Tips for Using the Internet for Research

Here are some ways to get better search results:

- **Place quotes around your topic,** for example, "sports medicine." This will allow you to find the sites where that exact phrase appears.

- **Use NEAR.** Typing "sports NEAR medicine" will return sites that contain both words and have the two words close to each other.

- **Exclude unwanted results.** Simply use a minus sign to indicate the words you do not want, for example, "sports medicine" – baseball.

- **Watch out for advertisements.** Know which links are paid links. They may or may not be worth exploring.

- **Check for relevance.** Google displays few lines of text from each page and shows your search phrase in bold. Check to see if it is appropriate for your work.

- **Look for news.** After you have entered your search phrase and have looked at the results, click on a *News* link on the page. This will show you recent stories about your topic.

- **Try again!** If you have made an extensive search and not found what you want, start a new search with a different set of words.

- **Check other sources.** Combine your Internet search with traditional research methods.

How to Evaluate Web Sites

Learning to evaluate Web sites will make you a more savvy surfer and enable you to gather the information you need quickly and easily. When you are trying to decide whether a Web site provides trustworthy information, consider the following:

◆ **First, ask, "Who is the author?"** Do a quick Web search to see what else the author has written. Search online for books he or she has written and consider whether the person is credible.

◆ **Look at the group offering the information.** Be wary if they are trying to sell a product or service. Look for impartial organizations to provide unbiased information.

◆ **Look for Web sites that provide sources for each fact,** just as you do when you write a term paper. Look for clues that the information was written by someone knowledgeable. Spelling and grammatical errors are signs that the information may not be accurate.

◆ **Check for the date the article was written and when it was last updated.** The more recent the article, the more likely it will be accurate.

◆ **Finally, when using information from a Web site, treat it as you would treat print information.** Anyone can post information on a Web site. Never use information that you cannot verify with another source.

Plagiarism

Plagiarism is the act of taking someone else's ideas and passing them off as your own. It does not matter if it is just one or two phrases or an entire paper. Be on guard against falling into the trap of cutting and pasting. This makes plagiarism all too easy.

If you quote sources in your work, identify those sources and give them proper credit.

Copyright

A copyright protects someone who creates an original work. This can be a single sentence, a book, a play, a piece of music. If you create it, you are the owner. Copyright protection is provided by the Copyright Act of 1976, a federal statute.

Once a work's copyright has expired, it is considered to be in the public domain and anyone can reprint it as he or she pleases. Remember the following tips:

◆ **What is copyrighted?** All forms of original expression published in the U.S. since 1923.

◆ **Can I copy from the Internet?** Copying information from the Internet is a serious breach of copyright. Check the site's *Terms of Use* to see what you can and cannot do.

◆ **Can I edit copyrighted work?** You cannot change copyrighted material, that is, make "derivative works" based on existing material, without permission from the copyright holder.

What Is a Student Organization?

A student organization is a group or association of students that is formed around activities, such as:

- Family and Consumer Sciences
- Student government
- Community service
- Social clubs
- Honor societies
- Multicultural alliances
- Technology education
- Artists and performers
- Politics
- Sports teams
- Professional career development

A student organization is usually required to follow a set of rules and regulations that apply equally to all student organizations at a particular school.

What's in It for You?

Participation in student organizations can contribute to a more enriching learning experience. Here are some ways you can benefit:

- Gain leadership qualities and skills that make you more marketable to employers and universities.
- Demonstrate the ability to appreciate someone else's point of view.
- Interact with professionals to learn about their different industries.
- Explore your creative interests, share ideas, and collaborate with others.
- Take risks, build confidence, and grow creatively.
- Learn valuable skills while speaking or performing in front of an audience.
- Make a difference in your life and the lives of those around you.
- Learn the importance of civic responsibility and involvement.
- Build relationships with instructors, advisors, students, and other members of the community who share similar backgrounds/world views.

Find and Join a Student Organization!

Take a close look at the organizations offered at your school or within your community. Are there any organizations that interest you? Talk to your teachers, guidance counselors, or a parent or guardian. Usually posters or flyers for a variety of clubs and groups can be found on your school's Message Board or Web site. Try to locate more information about the organizations that meet your needs. Then think about how these organizations can help you gain valuable skills you can use at school, at work, and in your community.

SkillsUSA

SkillsUSA is a national organization serving teachers and students who are preparing for careers in technical, skilled, and service occupations. More than 285,000 students and instructors join SkillsUSA annually.

One of the most visible programs of SkillsUSA is the annual SkillsUSA Championships. You can compete in over 70 occupational and leadership skill areas. This competition also serves as a showcase for some of the best culinary students in the nation. Competing against the clock and each other, participants can prove their expertise in foodservice-related areas.

The championships are planned by technical committees made up of industry representatives from around the country. Along with technical skills, you must demonstrate your knowledge of kitchen safety practices and procedures. You may participate in the SkillsUSA Championships in the following skill areas:

- Culinary Arts
- Food and Beverage Service
- Commercial Baking
- Customer Service
- Total Quality Management
- Community Service
- Job Skill Demonstration

No matter how you place in these competitions, participating allows you to learn more about these skill areas and often make future job contacts.

FCCLA

Family, Career and Community Leaders of America is a nonprofit national career and technical student organization for young men and women in Family and Consumer Sciences education in public and private schools through grade 12. Everyone is part of a family, and FCCLA is the only national Career and Technical Student Organization with the family as its central focus. Since 1945, FCCLA members have been making a difference in their families, careers, and communities by addressing important personal, work, and societal issues through Family and Consumer Sciences education.

STAR Events Program

STAR Events (Students Taking Action with Recognition) are competitive events in which members are recognized for proficiency and achievement in chapter and individual projects, leadership skills, and career preparation. FCCLA provides opportunities for you to participate at local, state, and national levels.

JOHNSON & WALES
U N I V E R S I T Y

High School seniors can compete for college scholarships!

National High School Chef of the Year Contest

Have you created your own recipes? Are you considering a culinary arts career?

In the fall of each year since 1989, Johnson & Wales University, the world's largest foodservice educator, has invited high school seniors to submit their own original recipes into competition for thousands of dollars in Johnson & Wales tuition scholarships.

- Regional experts and celebrity judges from all areas of food service evaluate contest entries and bring excitement to the competition.
- Scholarships are awarded in amounts up to full tuition in the College of Culinary Arts at Johnson & Wales University. All scholarships apply to full-time, day-school study and are renewable for up to four years. Actual receipt of a scholarship is subject to the student being otherwise qualified and accepted for admission to Johnson & Wales University.
- The National Competition will be held at one of Johnson & Wales University's four campuses. The University arranges free transportation and accommodations for each student finalist whose entry is selected for national competition.

GENERAL JUDGING CRITERIA

CRITERIA	MAXIMUM POINTS
Overall Quality, Flavor, Taste, Texture, Doneness	40
Presentation	20
Creativity	20
Nutritional Value	100
Kitchen Score: Mise en Place; Sanitation/Cooking Techniques	100
TOTAL SCORE	**280**

For the current year's contest details, entry form, deadlines, judging criteria, contest guidelines, and competition dates, log on to: **www.jwu.edu/culinarycompetitions.aspx**

The Johnson & Wales University National High School Chef of the Year Contest is held in cooperation with the American Cancer Society and the American Heart Association. Because it is important to develop good dietary habits early in life to reduce cancer risks and heart disease, the American Cancer Society and the American Heart Association have published the following nutritional and dietary guidelines based on scientific research. You are encouraged to make healthful menu choices and take these guidelines into consideration when planning your entry to the Johnson & Wales University National High School Chef of the Year Contest.

American Heart Association®

- Some vegetables and fruits, such as mushrooms, tomatoes, chili peppers, cherries, cranberries and currants, have a more intense flavor when dried than when fresh. Use them when you want a burst of flavor. Plus, there is an added bonus: When they are soaked in water and reconstituted, you can use the flavored water in cooking.

- Shrimp, lobster, crab, crayfish and most other shellfish are very low in fat. But ounce for ounce, some varieties contain more sodium and cholesterol than do poultry, meat, or other fish.

- Some fish have omega-3 fatty acids, which may help lower the level of lipids (blood fats). Some fish high in omega-3 fatty acids are: Atlantic and Coho salmon, albacore tuna, mackerel, carp, lake whitefish, sweet smelt, and lake and brook trout.

- Some wild game, such as venison, rabbit, squirrel, and pheasant are very lean; duck and goose are not.

- Oils that stay liquid at room temperature are high in unsaturated fats. They include corn, safflower, soybean, sunflower, olive, and canola (rapeseed) oils. All are low in saturated fatty acids and can be used to help lower blood cholesterol in a diet low in saturated fatty acids.

- Use egg whites in place of whole eggs. In most recipes, one egg white and a little acceptable vegetable oil will substitute nicely for a whole egg.

American Cancer Society®

- Add fresh or dried fruits such as chopped apples, raisins, prunes, kiwi or orange sections to green leafy salads.

- Substitute applesauce for oil in muffins, quick breads and cakes. Use puréed prunes or baby food prunes instead of oil in brownies or chocolate cake.

- Substitute whole-wheat flour for up to half of the white flour called for in a recipe.

- Use evaporated skim milk instead of whole milk or cream in baked goods, sauces and soups.

- Use low-fat or nonfat yogurt to replace all or part of the sour cream or mayonnaise in a recipe. Replace all or part of the ricotta cheese with low-fat cottage cheese. Use a purée of cooked potatoes, onions, and celery as a creamy base for soups instead of dairy cream or half-and-half.

- Use low-fat cooking methods such as roasting, baking, broiling, steaming or poaching. Use either a cooking spray, broth, water, or a well-seasoned cast iron pan to sauté meats. If you must use oil or margarine, cut the amount in half.

Culinary Safety

Chapter

1 Safety and Sanitation Principles

2 HACCP Applications

EXPLORE THE PHOTO

Safety and sanitation rules should be followed in the kitchen at all times. *Can you list some ways to help keep a kitchen safe and clean?*

EXPLORE THE PHOTO ANSWER Answers will vary, but may include clearing walkways and cleaning up spills to avoid slips and falls, training on first aid, cleaning up preparation areas after use, and thoroughly cleaning and sanitizing equipment and tools.

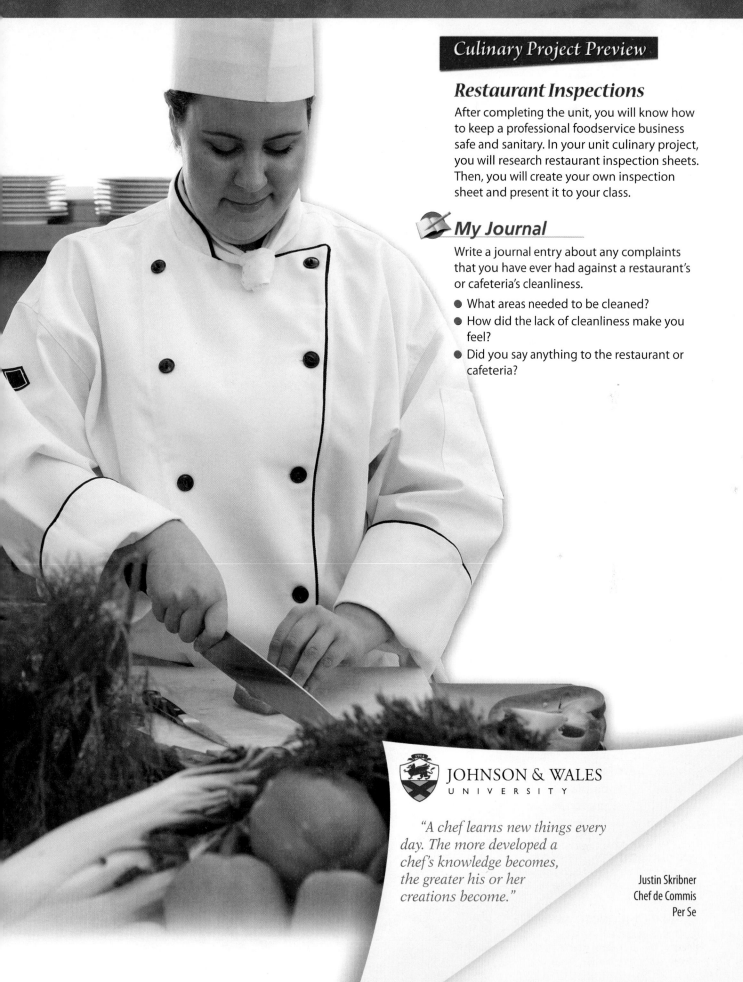

Restaurant Inspections

After completing the unit, you will know how to keep a professional foodservice business safe and sanitary. In your unit culinary project, you will research restaurant inspection sheets. Then, you will create your own inspection sheet and present it to your class.

My Journal

Write a journal entry about any complaints that you have ever had against a restaurant's or cafeteria's cleanliness.

- What areas needed to be cleaned?
- How did the lack of cleanliness make you feel?
- Did you say anything to the restaurant or cafeteria?

JOHNSON & WALES
UNIVERSITY

"A chef learns new things every day. The more developed a chef's knowledge becomes, the greater his or her creations become."

Justin Skribner
Chef de Commis
Per Se

Safety and Sanitation Principles

SECTIONS

1.1 Safety Basics

1.2 Sanitation Challenges

WRITING ACTIVITY

Freewriting

Visualize a commercial restaurant. Then, freewrite for five minutes about how you might prevent injuries in a commercial kitchen. Identify hazardous areas and what might be done to prevent accidents in those areas.

Writing Tips

1 Write the topic at the top of the paper to keep you focused.

2 Do not worry about form or structure.

3 Circle key ideas and phrases you can use later.

> **EXPLORE THE PHOTO**
>
> Safety and sanitation items help keep you safe in the workplace. *Why is an apron an important item?*

WRITING ACTIVITY ANSWER
Answers will vary, but writing should be clear, and contain proper spelling and grammar.

EXPLORE THE PHOTO ANSWER
Aprons help protect the wearer and prevent the spread of germs and physical contaminants.

Safety Basics

Reading Guide

 Before You Read

Preview Read the key concepts below. Write one or two sentences that predict what the section is about.

Read to Learn

Key Concepts

- **Identify** possible culinary workplace safety issues.
- **Explain** fire safety equipment and emergency procedures.
- **Describe** first aid measures for burns, wounds, and choking.

Main Idea

Burns and injuries can easily occur in a foodservice workplace. Establish fire safety procedures and know first aid measures to prevent or minimize damage.

Content Vocabulary

- occupational back support
- flammable
- lockout/tagout
- emergency
- first aid
- shock
- abrasion
- laceration
- avulsion
- puncture wound
- Heimlich maneuver
- cardio-pulmonary resuscitation (CPR)
- general safety audit

Academic Vocabulary

- routine
- document

Graphic Organizer

As you read, you will discover information about four types of kitchen protective gear. Use a web diagram like the one shown to list them.

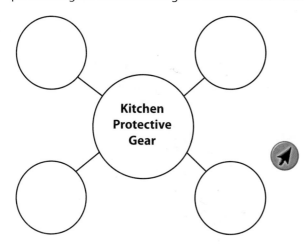

Graphic Organizer
Go to this book's Online Learning Center at **glencoe.com** for a printable graphic organizer.

ACADEMIC STANDARDS

English Language Arts
NCTE 7 Conduct research and gather, evaluate, and synthesize data to communicate discoveries.

Mathematics
NCTM Measurement Understand measurable attributes of objects and the units, systems, and processes of measurement.

Science
NSES B Develop an understanding of chemical reactions.

NCTE National Council of Teachers of English

NCTM National Council of Teachers of Mathematics

NSES National Science Education Standards

NCSS National Council for the Social Studies

GRAPHIC ORGANIZER ANSWER Aprons, gloves, shoes, and back braces.

Safe Working Conditions

Accidents can easily occur in a busy kitchen. The government has written laws and codes to help protect workers on the job. But it is the personal responsibility of each worker to practice safety in the kitchen at all times. Safety is an ongoing process.

Many foodservice workplace accidents can be prevented. Government agencies help. The Occupational Safety and Health Administration (OSHA) helps keep the workplace safe by writing workplace safety and health standards. Employers must post OSHA standards in their facilities.

The Environmental Protection Agency (EPA) also plays a role in promoting workplace safety. The EPA requires foodservice operations to track how they handle and dispose of hazardous materials such as cleaning products and pesticides.

Personal Protective Clothing

Personal protective clothing, such as uniforms, aprons, and gloves, can help you practice safety in the workplace.

Aprons

Aprons are an important piece of protective clothing. Use these apron guidelines:
- Make sure aprons are clean. Bacteria can quickly grow on dirty aprons.
- Change aprons when yours gets dirty.
- Always remove your apron if you leave the food preparation area.
- Always remove your apron to take out the garbage.

Gloves

Gloves should be worn to protect your hands from injury. Gloves also help protect against food contamination by bacteria and physical hazards.

Wash your hands thoroughly with soap and water before you put on gloves. Follow a proper hand-washing **routine**, or regular set of actions, to make sure hands are completely clean.

The type of gloves you should wear depends on the task you need to do. For example, you should use heavy-duty plastic gloves to clean pots. Gloves are available in light, medium, and heavy weights. Workers with latex allergies may try nitrile ('nī-trəl) latex-free gloves.

Foodservice gloves are for a single use only. For example, the gloves you wear to crack and mix eggs should not be reused to make a sandwich. You should change your gloves when they become soiled or torn, after at least every four hours of single-use, and immediately after you handle any raw food.

Shoes

Shoes are also a form of protective clothing. Shoes should be sturdy and have slip-resistant soles for safety. All shoes must have closed toes.

Back Braces

Foodservice workers may wear a special back brace to help them lift heavy items. An **occupational back support** is a type of back brace with suspenders. It is designed to support the lower back while lifting.

Personal Injuries

Foodservice workers are responsible to help prevent slips and falls, cuts, burns and scalds, and other personal injuries in the kitchen. For example, call out, "Hot cart coming through!" when you transport large pots full of hot liquids. This can warn others in the kitchen and help prevent accidents.

Slips and Falls

Slips and falls are common work-related injuries. Yet most slips and falls can be avoided.

Prevent Injury Follow these rules to help prevent slips and falls in the kitchen:
- Walk, never run, in the kitchen.

Burn Protection Always use dry pot holders or oven mitts to handle hot items. *Why would you not want to use moist pot holders or oven mitts to handle hot items?*

Wipe up spills immediately. Grease on a floor can cause you to slip or could cause equipment to slide.

- Use slip-resistant floor mats and make sure floors are in good repair.
- Wear shoes with slip-resistant soles. Never wear open-toed shoes.
- Use safe ladders or stools to reach high shelves. Never stand on a chair or a box.
- Always close cabinet drawers and doors.
- Ask for help or use a cart to move heavy objects.
- Keep traffic paths, especially around exits, aisles, and stairs, clutter free at all times.

Floors that are still wet from cleaning can be dangerous. Many slips and falls happen on wet floors because they are slick with water and cleaning products. Always post appropriate warning signs for safety.

Cuts

There are many sharp tools in a commercial kitchen. This means the risk of being cut in a commercial kitchen is high.

Sharp Tool Safety Guidelines Use these guidelines when you work with sharp tools to lower the risk of injury:

- Always use knives for their intended purpose only. Never use them to open plastic wrap or boxes, for example.
- Always cut away from your body, not toward your body. Cutting toward your body may cause an accident if your hand slips.
- Always carry a knife down at your side with the blade tip pointed toward the floor and the sharp edge facing behind you.

Safety Check

✓ Do Not Mix!

Although bleach and ammonia are both powerful cleaners, they should never be mixed. Mixing cleaners with these ingredients can cause chemical reactions that can create toxic, and even explosive, gasses.

CRITICAL THINKING *What can you do to ensure that bleach and ammonia cleaners are never mixed?*

PHOTO CAPTION ANSWER Moist pot holders or oven mitts create steam that can transmit heat, and may cause a burn.

SAFETY CHECK ANSWER Keep cleaning products with their original labels; follow all safety precautions listed on labels; store products separately.

- Look where you place your hands when you reach for a knife.
- Never wave your hands while holding a knife.
- If you drop a knife, do not try to grab for it as it falls. Pick up the knife after it falls to the table or floor.
- Hold knives with a firm grip on the handle when you use them or carry them.
- Never leave a knife handle hanging over the edge of a work surface.
- Keep knife handles and hands dry when you use knives.
- Keep knives sharp. Dull knives require you to apply more pressure. This may cause your hand to slip.
- Use a cutting board. Cutting on a regular counter surface could cause your hand to slip. It could also damage the knife.
- Wear protective gloves and cuff guards to clean commercial slicers.
- Wash sharp tools separately from other tools and dishes. Never leave knives soaking in a sink.
- Throw away broken knives or knives with loose blades.
- Store knives in a knife kit or a knife rack.

Burns and Scalds

Commercial kitchens have many types of heat-producing equipment. There also are many different ways a foodservice worker can get burned.

Prevent Burns You can keep burns from happening. These safety tips can help keep you safe when you work in a professional kitchen:

- Tilt pot lids away from your body to let the steam escape.
- Use dry pot holders or oven mitts. Wet cloth forms scalding steam when it touches hot pots and pans.
- Turn pot and pan handles away from the front of the range.
- Step aside when you open an oven door to avoid the rush of heat.
- Get help to move large hot containers. This also can save strain on your back.

- Follow manufacturer's directions to operate hot beverage machines. Read the instruction manual before operating them.
- Be careful when you filter or change the oil in fryers. Always wear gloves and aprons for protection.
- Always wear appropriate safety clothing when you use chemicals for cleaning. Some of these chemicals can cause burns.
- Keep oven doors closed. This will also help food cook more quickly and evenly.
- Clean ovens when they have cooled. Otherwise, you may burn yourself.
- Keep cooking areas, vent hoods, and other surfaces grease free to prevent fires.
- Always keep paper, plastic, and other flammable materials away from hot cooking areas to prevent fires. **Flammable** materials are those that are quick to burn.
- Unplug electrical appliances with frayed cords to prevent burns and electrical shocks. Inform your supervisor of the problem immediately

Back Injuries and Strains

Back injuries from improper lifting and bending are one of the most common types of workplace injuries. Many back injuries could be prevented if employees take the proper precautions. For example, pushing and pulling puts less strain on your back than lifting.

Safety Check

✓ **Use Ladders Safely**
Follow these guidelines to use a ladder safely:
- Only one person should use a ladder at one time.
- Always face the ladder. Do not stand on the top step. Climb only on the step side.
- Stay centered on the ladder so you do not tip over to the side.
- Do not carry objects that could make you lose your balance.

CRITICAL THINKING *What do you think could happen if you carried a large box up a ladder?*

SAFETY CHECK ANSWER The box would block your view of the ladder steps, and may cause you to lose your balance and fall.

Heavy Lifting Before lifting a heavy object, ask yourself these questions:

- Can I lift this object by myself?
- Is the object too heavy or too awkward to lift easily?
- Do I need help to move or lift the object?
- Is the path I must take free of clutter?

Follow these steps to safely lift heavy objects:

1. Bend at your knees.
2. Keep your back straight.
3. Keep your feet close to the object.
4. Center your body over the load.
5. Lift straight up and do not jerk your body.
6. Do not twist your body as you pick up or move the object.
7. Set the load down slowly. Keep your back straight.

Lifting tools can also be helpful. Use rollers under an object. A pulley or lever can help you move heavy objects more easily.

Kitchen Equipment Safety

Each kitchen is different in its design and the equipment used. You should be familiar with each piece of equipment before you operate it. If a piece of equipment is malfunctioning, be sure to follow the lockout/tagout procedure. **Lockout/tagout** means that all necessary switches on malfunctioning electrical equipment are tagged and locked from use.

Be familiar with equipment safety features, such as guards and safety devices. For example, a slicer has a hand guard that must be in place to operate the machine.

Cleaning and Maintenance

You will also need to clean and maintain equipment. Always follow these safety measures when you clean kitchen equipment:

- Turn all switches to the off position.
- Unplug the equipment.
- Follow the manufacturer's instructions and the food establishment's directions for cleaning.

 **Reading Check** Identify What type of shoes should you wear to work in a kitchen?

Avoid Back Injuries If you decide to lift an object by yourself, it is important to use the correct lifting technique. *How is this employee using a correct lifting technique?*

Fire Safety

Fires in the workplace cause substantial property and equipment damage each year. They also cause injuries, and even death. The flames and high heat sources used in foodservice workplaces can cause fires. A burn can be a very serious injury. Burns can be prevented by preventing fires. Fires are classified according to the type of material that catches fire. (See **Figure 1.1** on page 8.)

Fire Prevention

You can prevent and control fires. Practice good work habits and be prepared for emergencies. Keep the workplace clean, especially of built-up grease.

Here are some other tips to prevent fires and help keep your workplace safe:

- Be sure ashtray contents are completely out before you empty them into the trash.
- Be careful around gas appliances. Built-up gasses can explode if a match is lit nearby.

FIGURE 1.1 Fire Extinguisher Types

Fire Safety The universal picture symbols shown here are found on fire extinguisher labels. *What information do these symbols tell you?*

Class of Fire	Type of Flammable Material	Type of Fire Extinguisher to Use
Class A	 Wood, paper, cloth, plastic	Class A / Class A:B  
Class B	 Grease, oil, chemicals	Class A:B / Class A:B:C  
Class C	 Electrical cords, switches, wiring	Class A:C / Class B:C  
Class D	 Combustible switches, wiring, metals, iron	Class D 
Class K	 Fires in cooking appliances involving combustible vegetable or animal oils and fats	Class K 

- Store oily rags in closed metal containers so they do not start a fire.
- Make sure all smoke alarms work properly.
- Store flammable materials away from heat sources.
- Keep water away from electrical outlets.
- Clean the range and oven hoods and filters regularly to remove grease that can catch on fire.
- Keep all exits unlocked and accessible from the inside. Exits should also be clearly marked.

Fire Protection Equipment

Prevention is your best course of action when it comes to fires. But even with the right preventive steps, fires can still happen in a professional kitchen. It is essential to have the proper fire protection equipment on hand at all times.

Fire Extinguishers

Fire extinguishers are the most common type of fire protection equipment used in foodservice operations. The type, number, and location of fire extinguishers that are needed can vary. A fire extinguisher should be located within each work area.

Fire extinguishers use several types of chemicals to fight different kinds of fires. To fight a fire properly, you must use the right type, or class, of extinguisher.

Fire extinguishers are inspected and tagged on a regular basis. To use a fire extinguisher properly, hold the extinguisher upright and remove the safety pin. Point the nozzle at the bottom of the fire and push down the handle.

Hood and Sprinkler Systems

A hood system that is well vented can help remove excess smoke, heat, and vapors. Make sure hoods are cleaned regularly and are

FIGURE CAPTION ANSWER These symbols tell you the types of fires on which the fire extinguisher can and cannot be used.

working properly. If your kitchen has a sprinkler system, keep products and supplies at the regulated distance from the sprinkler equipment.

Fire Emergency Procedures

Every foodservice business has fire emergency procedures. Employees must be familiar with these procedures. Employers must post fire exit signs in plain view above exits. Employees should know where to meet outside the business for a head count in case of a fire. They should also know how to direct customers out of the building.

It is the foodservice staff's responsibility to keep customers calm during emergencies. If you discover a fire, call the fire department right away, even if the fire is small. Fires can grow large very quickly. Then, communicate clearly and help customers and coworkers leave the building quickly and calmly.

Reading Check Explain What should you do if you discover a fire in the workplace?

Emergency Procedures

Fires are not the only emergencies that can happen in a kitchen. An **emergency** is a potentially life-threatening situation that usually occurs suddenly and unexpectedly. You must know how to respond and who to contact during an emergency.

Post the telephone numbers of emergency services, such as poison control and the health department, near the phone. You should also learn basic first aid and life-saving techniques. It is your responsibility to know your employer's emergency policies.

First Aid

The immediate response to an emergency often involves first aid. **First aid** involves assisting an injured person until professional medical help can be provided. The American Red Cross offers courses that teach hands-on information about first aid in the workplace.

Science à la Carte

Extinguish a Grease Fire

The best way to extinguish an oil or grease fire is to use sodium bicarbonate ($NaHCO_3$). Sodium bicarbonate is also called baking soda. When it is heated, baking soda breaks down and forms carbon dioxide gas (CO_2), which smothers the fire.

Procedure

Perform research to find out why carbon dioxide gas smothers a grease or oil fire. You can perform your research at the library or interview a firefighter at your local fire department.

Analysis

Create a poster to explain why carbon dioxide gas smothers a grease or oil fire, based on your research. Keep track of the sources you use, and turn them in to your teacher.

NSES B Develop an understanding of chemical reactions.

Fire Protection This professional kitchen has several pieces of fire protection equipment. *How might the sprinkler system be used?*

FIGURE 1.2 Types of Burns

Bad Burns There are three types of burns, each one more severe than the last. *How would you treat a first-degree burn?*

Types of Burns		Characteristics of Burns
First-Degree Burns	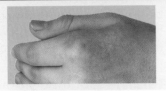	The skin becomes red, sensitive, and sometimes swollen. These are the least severe of all burns.
Second-Degree Burns	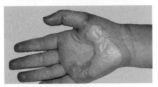	These burns cause deeper, painful damage, and blisters form on the skin. The blisters ooze and are painful.
Third-Degree Burns	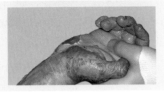	The skin may be white and soft or black, charred, and leathery. Sometimes third-degree burns are not painful because the nerves in the skin have been destroyed. These are the worst kinds of burns. Third-degree burns must be treated immediately at a hospital.

Emergency Action Tips

These general action tips should be followed during an emergency. They do not replace the need to be trained in first aid!

- Check the scene and stay calm.
- Check the victim. Keep him or her comfortable and calm.
- Call the local emergency number for professional medical help.
- Use proper first aid techniques.
- Keep people who are not needed away from the victim.
- Complete an accident report. Write the victim's name, the date and time of the accident, the type of injury or illness, the treatment, and when help arrived.

First Aid for Burns

Any type of burn requires immediate treatment. (See **Figure 1.2**.) If you or someone in the workplace is burned, call your local emergency number for medical assistance.

Follow these general guidelines for minor burns until help arrives:

- Remove the source of the heat.
- Cool the burned skin to stop the burning. Apply cold water on the affected area for at least five minutes. Use water from a faucet or soaked towels. Do not use ice or ice water. This can cause damage to the skin.
- Never apply ointments, sprays, antiseptics, or remedies to the burned skin unless instructed to do so by a medical professional.
- Bandage the burn as directed in your first aid manual.

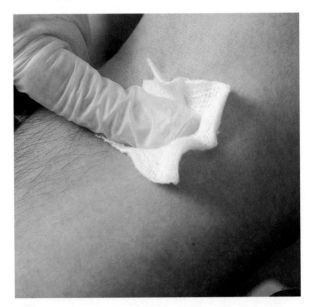

Wound Care Apply pressure to a wound to stop any bleeding. *What other steps should be taken to treat a minor wound?*

FIGURE CAPTION ANSWER Remove the the source of heat, cool the burned skin, bandage the burn, and have the victim rest to avoid shock.

PHOTO CAPTION ANSWER Wear gloves, clean with soap and water, place a bandage over the wound, apply direct pressure, hold limb above the heart.

- Minimize the risk of shock. **Shock** is a serious medical condition in which not enough oxygen reaches tissues. Elevate the victim's feet over his or her head. Keep the victim from getting chilled or overheated. Have the victim rest.

First Aid for Wounds

There are four types of open wounds:
- An **abrasion** is a scrape or minor cut. A rug burn is an abrasion.
- A **laceration** (ˌla-sə-ˈrā-shən) is a cut or tear in the skin that can be quite deep. A knife wound is a type of laceration.
- An **avulsion** (ˌə-ˈvəl-shən) happens when a portion of the skin is partially or completely torn off. A severed finger is an avulsion.
- A **puncture wound** happens when the skin is pierced with a pointed object, such as an ice pick, making a deep hole in the skin. Puncture wounds can be deep.

Treat Minor Wounds Follow these guidelines to treat a person with a minor cut.
- Wear disposable gloves to protect yourself and the victim from infection.
- Clean the cut with soap water.
- Place sterile gauze over the cut.
- Apply direct pressure over the sterile gauze or bandage to stop any bleeding.
- If bleeding does not stop, raise the limb above the heart.

Treat Serious Wounds Call for emergency help. Then, follow these guidelines:
- Wear disposable gloves to protect yourself and the victim from infection.
- Control the bleeding by applying pressure with sterile gauze or a clean cloth towel. Do not waste time by washing the wound first. Elevate the area while applying pressure.
- Cover the wound with clean bandages.
- Wash your hands thoroughly after emergency help has arrived.

First Aid for Choking

Choking is often caused by food that blocks a person's airway. This will cause difficulty speaking and breathing.

The **Heimlich maneuver** is a series of thrusts to the abdomen that can help dislodge something that is stuck in a person's airway. You should be formally trained to use the Heimlich maneuver. Use it only on someone who is conscious and choking. You can even use it on yourself. Never perform the Heimlich maneuver on someone who is pregnant. This could harm the baby.

The basic Heimlich maneuver steps are:
1. Stand behind the victim. Wrap your arms around the victim's waist. Locate the victim's navel.
2. Make a fist with one hand. Place the thumb side of your fist against the middle of the abdomen just above the navel and below the bottom of the breast bone.
3. Place your other hand on top of your fist.
4. Press your hands to the victim's abdomen. Use inward and upward thrusts.
5. Repeat this motion as many times as it takes to dislodge the object or food.

🅐 **Heimlich Maneuver** The Heimlich maneuver can be performed on a choking, conscious adult. *When would you not perform the Heimlich maneuver?*

PHOTO CAPTION ANSWER You would not perform the Heimlich maneuver on someone who is unconscious, or someone who is pregnant.

CPR

CPR, or **cardiopulmonary resuscitation** (ˌkär-dē-ō-ˈpu̇l-mə-ner-ē ri-ˌsə-sə-ˈtā-shən), is emergency care that is performed on people who are unresponsive. This includes those who are unconscious because of choking, cardiac arrest, stroke, or heart attack.

The sooner CPR is performed, the greater the victim's chance of survival. CPR helps keep oxygen flowing to the brain and heart. This is done until advanced care can have a chance to restore normal heart function. Contact your local chapter of the American Heart Association or the American Red Cross for training and information on how to perform cardiopulmonary resuscitation correctly.

Reports and Audits

As soon as possible after an emergency is over, you should **document**, or write down, the details of the emergency. Detailed emergency reports can help prevent future emergencies. They also can help limit a restaurant's liability in the event of an accident. Make sure that the information in the report is accurate. Your supervisor may want to discuss the information with you.

A **general safety audit** is a review and inspection of all safety procedures and equipment. The audit should be managed by foodservice employers, but carried out by foodservice workers. It should be performed at least once a year. Let a supervisor know if you find any of the following:

- Missing or low-charge fire extinguishers
- Blocked hallways or exits
- Missing safety information
- Frayed electrical cords

 **Reading Check** Determine How often should a general safety audit be performed?

 SECTION 1.1 **After You Read**

Review Key Concepts

1. **Identify** four types of personal injuries that foodservice workers must help prevent.
2. **Explain** how to use a fire extinguisher properly.
3. **Describe** the three types of burns.

Practice Culinary Academics

 English Language Arts

4. Choose one of the common sources of injury in the kitchen. Conduct research about the topic. Find an example of a situation where someone was injured in a professional kitchen setting. Write a short report to explain the injury, the cause of the injury, the consequences of the injury, and how the injury might have been prevented. Include your sources in your report, and turn them in to your teacher.

> **NCTE 7** Conduct research and gather, evaluate, and synthesize data to communicate discoveries.

Mathematics

5. Hot water can be dangerous even before it begins to boil. A two-second exposure to water at a temperature of 150°F can cause a burn. What is this temperature in degrees Celsius?

Math Concept **Converting Temperatures** In the metric system, temperatures are measured in degrees Celsius. To convert temperatures from Fahrenheit (F) to Celsius (C), use this equation: $C = (F - 32) \times \frac{5}{9}$.

Starting Hint To convert 150°F into a Celsius temperature, first subtract 32 from the Fahrenheit amount. Multiply the result by the fraction $\frac{5}{9}$. To do so, first multiply the result by 5, then divide that product by 9.

> **NCTM Measurement** Understand measurable attributes of objects and the units, systems, and processes of measurement.

 Check your answers at this book's Online Learning Center at **glencoe.com**.

READING CHECK ANSWER At least once per year.

Sanitation Challenges

Learn how to keep food safe to eat.

 Before You Read

Predict Before starting the section, read headings, bold terms, and photo captions to browse the content. Think about how they can help you predict the information in the section.

Read to Learn

Key Concepts
- **Describe** the sources of food contamination.
- **Identify** sources of chemical food contamination.
- **Illustrate** how to manage pests in a kitchen setting.

Main Idea

Food becomes contaminated by exposure to harmful microorganisms or chemical substances. Insects and rodents can also physically contaminate food.

Graphic Organizer

There are three types of hazards that can cause contamination in a kitchen. Use this problem-solution chart to identify each type of hazard, and then list the sources of contamination for each type of hazard. Finally, provide solutions to prevent that contamination.

Problem	Sources	Solutions

 Graphic Organizer Go to this book's Online Learning Center at **glencoe.com** for a printable graphic organizer.

Content Vocabulary

- sanitary
- contaminated
- direct contamination
- cross-contamination
- sanitation
- hazard
- toxin
- pathogens
- bacteria
- viruses
- parasite
- fungi
- mold
- cleaning
- sanitizing

Academic Vocabulary

- result
- transmit

ACADEMIC STANDARDS

Mathematics
NCTM Number and Operations Understand numbers, ways of representing numbers, relationships among numbers, and number systems.

Science
NSES C Develop an understanding of the behavior of organisms.

Social Studies
NCSS II B Time, Continuity, and Change Explain, analyze, and show connections among patterns of historical change and continuity.

....

NCTE National Council of Teachers of English

NCTM National Council of Teachers of Mathematics

NSES National Science Education Standards

NCSS National Council for the Social Studies

GRAPHIC ORGANIZER ANSWER: Biological: bacteria, viruses, parasites, fungi, molds, yeast; personal hygiene, sanitation, food handling. Chemical: cleaning products, pesticides; store and use properly. Physical: particles, foreign matter, pests; safety and sanitation.

Contamination Basics

Foodborne illnesses kill thousands of people each year and make many more people sick. For this reason, foodservice professionals need to know how to create a clean, safe, disease-free place that can be used for food preparation. They also need to know how to prevent and properly respond to foodborne illness outbreaks.

When consumers eat out, they expect the food to be prepared and served in a sanitary environment. **Sanitary** means clean. When harmful microorganisms or substances are present in food, the food is contaminated. **Contaminated** food is food that is unfit to be eaten. Eating contaminated food can make you sick and may even cause death.

Food can be directly contaminated or cross-contaminated:

- **Direct contamination** happens when raw foods, or the plants or animals from which they come, are exposed to harmful microorganisms. For example, harmful microorganisms found in soil that is used to grow grains could contaminate the grain and any products produced from the grain.
- **Cross-contamination** is the movement of harmful microorganisms from one place to another. People cause most cases of cross-contamination. For example, food handlers can transfer organisms or substances when they prepare or serve foods.

Foodservice workers must consider direct contamination and cross-contamination. They must practice proper sanitation techniques. The word **sanitation** means healthy or clean and whole. In the workplace, sanitation means healthy and sanitary conditions. Foodservice workers have a responsibility to prepare food in a sanitary environment. Federal, state, and local health departments have created regulations to protect consumers from foodborne diseases.

In the foodservice industry, workers need to know the different types of food hazards.

A **hazard** is a source of danger. These hazards are biological, chemical, and physical. Any of these hazards can **result**, or have an outcome, in contaminated food.

Biological Hazards

Biological hazards come from microorganisms such as bacteria. Other types of biological hazards include viruses, parasites, and fungi. Certain plants and fish can also carry harmful toxins. A **toxin** is a harmful organism or substance. However, disease-causing microorganisms called **pathogens** cause the majority of foodborne illnesses. For detailed information on specific foodborne illnesses, see **Figure 1.3** on page 15.

Foodborne Illness

Microorganisms can grow in and on food when it is not handled properly. Other conditions that can lead to foodborne illness outbreaks are cross-contamination, poor personal hygiene, and food handler illness. For example, uncooked meats that are stored above cooked meats in the refrigerator can cause cross-contamination because the uncooked meat may drip onto the cooked meat.

Each year the number of incidents of foodborne illness grows. Children, the elderly, and pregnant women have the highest risk to catch a foodborne illness. People who are chronically ill or who have weakened immune systems also are at risk. The good news is, conditions that cause foodborne illness can be prevented. Follow industry safety standards to help lower the threat of foodborne illness.

Bacteria Tiny, single-celled microorganisms are called **bacteria** (bak-'tir-ē-ə). Some forms of bacteria can make people very sick if they are eaten. People who have a bacterial illness may have symptoms such as nausea, abdominal pain, and vomiting. Other symptoms include dizziness, chills, and headache.

Bacteria multiply very quickly under the right conditions. The acronym FATTOM can help you remember these conditions:

Food Contamination There are several forms of bacteria, viruses, and parasites that can cause customers to become sick. *How can you prevent foodborne illnesses?*

Illness—Cause	Symptoms	Foods Involved
Salmonellosis— Bacteria	Cramps, nausea, headache, fever, diarrhea, vomiting.	Poultry and poultry products, eggs, meat and meat products, fish, dairy products, protein foods, fresh produce.
Campylobacter jejuni—Bacteria	Nausea, vomiting, fever, diarrhea, abdominal pain, headache, and muscle pain	Meats and poultry, unpasteurized milk and dairy products
Hepatitis A— Virus	Fatigue, discomfort, fever, headache, nausea, loss of appetite, vomiting, jaundice	Water, ice, salads, cold cuts, sandwiches, shellfish, fruit, fruit juices, milk and milk products, vegetables
Norwalk— Virus	Cramps, nausea, headache, fever, vomiting	Water, raw vegetables, fresh fruit, salads, shellfish
Trichinosis— Parasite	Abdominal pain, nausea, diarrhea, fever, swelling around eyes, thirst, sweating, chills, fatigue, hemorrhaging	Pork, nonpork sausages, wild game
Shigellosis— Bacteria	Abdominal pain, diarrhea, vomiting, fever, dehydration	Protein salads, lettuce, raw vegetables, poultry, shrimp, milk and milk products
Listeriosis— Bacteria	Headache, fever, chills, nausea, vomiting, diarrhea, backache, meningitis, encephalitis	Ice cream, frozen yogurt, unpasteurized milk and cheese, raw vegetables, poultry, meat, seafood
Rotavirus— Virus	Abdominal pain, diarrhea, vomiting, mild fever	Water, ice, salads, fruit, hors d'oeuvres
Anisakiasis— Parasite	Tingling in throat, abdominal pain, coughing up worms, cramping, vomiting, nausea	Fish, seafood
Giardiasis— Parasite	Cramps, nausea, intestinal gas, fatigue, loss of weight	Water, ice, salads
Botulism— Bacteria	Constipation and diarrhea, vomiting, fatigue, vertigo, double vision, dry mouth, paralysis, death	Underprocessed foods, canned low-acid foods, sautéed onions in butter sauce, baked potatoes, untreated garlic and oil products
E. Coli— Bacteria	Severe abdominal cramps, diarrhea, vomiting, mild fever, kidney failure	Raw ground beef, undercooked meat, unpasteurized milk and apple cider or juice, mayonnaise, lettuce, melons, fish from contaminated water
Staphylococcus aureus—Bacteria	Nausea, vomiting, stomach cramps, diarrhea	Handmade items that do not require cooking, such as sliced meats, puddings, and sandwiches

- **F=Food** Bacteria need food for energy to grow.
- **A=Acidity** Bacteria generally do not grow well in acidic environments.
- **T=Temperature** Bacteria can thrive in temperatures between 41°F (5°C) and 135°F (57°C). Some bacteria can survive freezing and cooking.
- **T=Time** Although some bacteria multiply more quickly than others, it does take time for them to grow.
- **O=Oxygen** Many bacteria need oxygen to live. However, some bacteria do not need oxygen to grow.
- **M=Moisture** Bacteria prefer foods that are high in protein and moisture.

FIGURE CAPTION ANSWER Refrigerate and heat foods to the proper temperatures, avoid contact between raw and cooked foods, and properly sanitize work surfaces.

Viruses Simple organisms that cause many food-related illnesses are called **viruses**. Viruses need a host, or another living cell, to grow. A host can be a person, animal, or plant. Once inside the host, the virus can multiply. Like bacteria, viruses can survive freezing and cooking. It is easy to **transmit**, or spread, viruses from person to person. They usually contaminate food when a foodservice worker uses poor hygiene. Poor hygiene may include sneezing on food or not washing your hands after going to the bathroom. Salads, sandwiches, milk, and other unheated foods are especially susceptible to viruses.

Parasites A **parasite** ('pär-ə-sīt) is an organism that must live in or on a host to survive. Parasites are larger than bacteria and viruses. Parasites are often found in poultry, fish, and meats. Some common parasites found in food include protozoa, roundworms, and flatworms.

Parasites can be eliminated from food by following proper cooking methods. Freezing the food product for a number of days also can destroy parasites. Poultry, fish, and meat should be cooked until the minimum internal temperature is reached. These foods, when uncooked, should not come into contact with other foods. Carefully check the food in several different spots to be sure that the safe temperature has been reached throughout the food. If the parasites are not eliminated, they can infect anyone who eats the contaminated food.

Fungi Spore-producing organisms found in soil, plants, animals, water, and in the air are called **fungi** ('fən-gī). Fungi also are naturally present in some foods. Some fungi can be large, such as mushrooms. Some fungi can be eaten, while others cannot. Eating some fungi can cause stomach problems, or even death.

Molds A **mold** is a form of fungus. The fuzzy-looking spores produced by molds can be seen with the naked eye. Molds can grow at nearly any temperature. Even if only part of a food has mold, the whole thing should be thrown away, although some cheeses can be saved.

Yeast Another form of fungus is yeast. Yeast is most often associated with bread and the baking process. In this case, yeast is helpful. However, if yeast is present in other foods, such as sauerkraut, honey, and jelly, it can cause those foods to spoil.

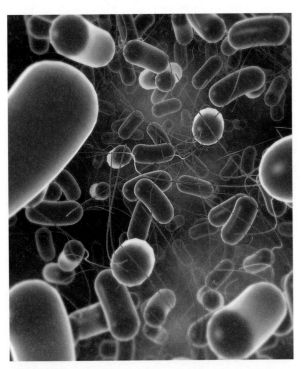

Bacterial Illness Salmonella bacteria is one of the leading causes of foodborne illness. *How could you help prevent the spread of salmonella in a foodservice operation?*

Sanitation Check

✓ Hepatitis A

Hepatitis A is a disease that causes inflammation, or swelling, of the liver. Foodservice workers with the disease can transmit the virus to food. It also can be transmitted by contact with contaminated water, or eating shellfish that has been raised in contaminated water. The symptoms of hepatitis A are similar to the flu. Hepatitis A can be prevented. You should wash your hands thoroughly after restroom use. In addition, a vaccination for hepatitis A can help protect you from infection.

CRITICAL THINKING *If you get a hepatitis A vaccination, can you forgo hand-washing procedures? Why or why not?*

PHOTO CAPTION ANSWER Thoroughly sanitize surfaces, keep foods at the proper temperatures, and avoid cross-contamination.

SANITATION CHECK ANSWER No. You could still spread hepatitis A to another person, or pick up other harmful microorganisms on your hands.

1941

Breakfast cereal Cheerios is introduced as CheeriOats by General Mills

1947

First two-door refrigerator/freezer is produced

Keep Food Cool

Until the early twentieth century, people in cities who needed ice to keep their food cold purchased ice from local ice houses. The ice houses stored ice that was collected in the winter months.

The first electric refrigerators were in use by the late 1800s, but there were no mass-produced modern refrigerators until after World War II. Today, food-service operations can choose from a large variety of refrigerators to keep food cold and fresh.

History Application

The evolution of the refrigerator/freezer had a direct connection to the frozen food industry. Create a time line about the frozen food industry that traces how the storage and shipping of frozen food has changed over time.

> **NCSS II B Time, Continuity, and Change** Explain, analyze, and show connections among patterns of historical change and continuity.

Forms of Fungus Mold is a type of fungus. *Why are some types of fungi safe to eat, but others are not?*

A TASTE OF HISTORY ANSWER The time line should include early methods of freezing food by the Greeks and Romans, the days of ice cellars, and Clarence Birdseye's quick-freezing methods. Events may also include

Outbreak Response

If you have ever felt queasy several hours after eating, you may have been a victim of a foodborne illness. An outbreak of foodborne illness happens when several people become sick after eating the same food.

Any outbreak of foodborne illness must be reported to the local health department. If you think there has been an outbreak at your facility, a quick response is essential. An outbreak could cost the business thousands of dollars in legal fees, insurance costs, and loss of customers. It also could force the foodservice establishment out of business.

A laboratory analysis can tell which food made customers sick. In most areas, the public health department will investigate any outbreak of foodborne illness to protect public health. The department's job is to learn how the illness was spread and how its spread can be prevented in the future.

If you suspect a foodborne illness outbreak, take these steps:

- Tell the manager or supervisor of your suspicions immediately. It is your supervisor's responsibility to contact the appropriate authorities for an investigation.
- Avoid panic. There are many reasons why people become ill, so it is best to let the health authorities check the situation.
- Save any food you suspect may be contaminated. Wrap food in its original container or in a plastic bag. Clearly label the bag or container Do Not Use.

Reading Check **Define** What is the difference between direct contamination and cross-contamination?

the introduction of TV dinners and other microwavable frozen foods.
PHOTO CAPTION ANSWER Many types of fungi, such as edible mushrooms and the veins in cheeses such as Stilton or Roquefort, are safe to eat. However, some fungi are toxic to humans, and can cause serious illness or death.
READING CHECK ANSWER Direct contamination happens when food is exposed directly to harmful microorganisms. Cross-contamination means harmful microorganisms are moved from one food to another.

Chemical Hazards

Chemical hazards include cleaning supplies, pesticides, food additives, and metals.

To help prevent chemical accidents, Material Safety Data Sheets (MSDS) must be kept on file. A material safety data sheet is a form that shows information about a substance and how to use it safely. The Occupational Safety and Health Administration's Right to Know law requires that employers post information about dangerous substances in the workplace and how to work with them safely.

Cleaning Products

Cleaning products used in the foodservice industry include:

- **Detergents** Used to clean walls, floors, prep surfaces, equipment, and utensils. Heavy-duty detergents cut through grease.
- **Hygiene Detergents** Used to clean, deodorize, and disinfect floors, walls, and table tops.

- **Degreasers** Solvent cleaners used on range hoods, oven doors, and backsplashes to remove grease.
- **Abrasive Cleaners** Used to scrub off dirt or grime that can be difficult to remove. Abrasive cleaners are used on floors and pots and pans to remove burned-on food.
- **Acid Cleaners** Used to remove mineral deposits in equipment such as dishwashers and steam tables. However, acid cleaners should not be used on aluminum. They can eat through the metal. Follow product directions and use with care.

To avoid possible contamination, each cleaning product should be used and stored properly. Cleaning products should not be stored near food. The storage area should be kept neat and well organized to avoid confusion or spills.

Cleaning products should always be kept in their original labeled containers. Confusing a cleaning product with a cooking ingredient can cause illness, or even death. Check the labels to make sure you know how to use each product safely. Follow directions to dilute them properly. Labels usually have antidotes for accidental swallowing, and signal words such as caution, warning, danger, and poison. Report any unlabeled products to a supervisor.

You must follow local regulations to throw away cleaning products. Local health departments should have suggestions for environmentally friendly disposal.

Kitchen Cleanliness

Keep the facilities clean and sanitary to help lower the risk of contamination. **Cleaning** means removing food and other soil from a surface. You should always clean as you work. Do not wait until all the work is done before cleaning or sanitizing. **Sanitizing** ('sa-nə-ˌtīz-iŋ) means reducing the number of microorganisms on the surface. You must do both to eliminate contamination.

Sanitation Check

✓ Personal Hygiene

Foodservice professionals must have excellent personal hygiene. Microorganisms can spread from tools, equipment, and cooking surfaces to food on the hands of foodservice workers. This can lead to food contamination, disease, or food poisoning. To lower the chance of spreading microorganisms in the kitchen, you should:

- Use proper hand-washing techniques.
- Practice good grooming and cleanliness.
- Wear gloves and other protective clothing when required.
- Maintain good health and stay home when you are sick.
- Immediately report any illnesses or injuries to your supervisor.

CRITICAL THINKING *How does good grooming prevent contamination?*

SANITATION CHECK ANSWER Good grooming keeps your body and clothes cleaner so you do not bring in harmful microorganisms from outside.

Industrial Cleaning
Here are some examples of industrial cleaning products. *How do you think industrial cleaning products differ from those used at home?*

Cleaning and Sanitizing

Everything in a foodservice operation should be kept clean and sanitary at all times. All pots, pans, and dishes, and all food contact surfaces, should be thoroughly cleaned each time they are used. For example, clean and sanitize a work surface before you use it to prepare another food product. Clean and sanitize tools at four-hour intervals. You should also clean them if they become contaminated by another food product.

In addition, you can use color-coded cutting boards and containers for each type of food product. This can help prevent cross-contamination. For example, you might use a green cutting board to cut raw vegetables. But you would never use that same cutting board to cut raw meat or chicken. Raw meat and chicken are more likely to carry bacteria that can cause illness if transferred to foods that will be eaten raw. You should take extra care with these foods. Be sure to sanitize all cutting boards thoroughly.

Kitchen tools and surfaces should be cleaned and sanitized with soapy hot water and a sanitizer. Notice the warning labels associated with using that product.

Pesticides

There are many pesticides ('pes-tə-ˌsīds) that are used in food storage and preparation areas to control pests like bugs or rats. If they are used carelessly or in large amounts, pesticides may contaminate food. Pesticides can make people who eat the contaminated food very sick. They can even cause death in large amounts.

Pesticides must be used according to directions. They should be stored away from food and in a locked or secure area. Be sure all pesticides are labeled correctly. They should always be kept in their original containers. Some jurisdictions require a special permit to use pesticides, while others do not allow their use.

Empty pesticide containers should never be reused for any purpose. Because pesticides are hazardous materials, they cannot just be thrown away. Check local regulations for disposing of hazardous waste before you throw away pesticides or pesticide containers.

Reading Check **Summarize** What are the potential dangers of using pesticides in a commercial kitchen?

PHOTO CAPTION ANSWER Generally, industrial cleaning products are stronger than home cleaning products, and are designed to kill a variety of bacteria.

READING CHECK ANSWER If used carelessly or in large amounts, pesticides can contaminate the food with toxic chemicals.

Physical Hazards

Physical hazards are caused by particles, such as glass chips, metal shavings, hair, bits of wood, or other foreign matter, that could get into food. Some physical hazards are found in food itself, such as bone shards or chips. However, most contamination occurs when foodhandlers do not follow proper safety and sanitation practices. Always use care when you prepare, cook, and serve food.

Pest Management

Wherever there is food, there may be insects and rodents. These pests can pose a serious threat to the safety of food products. Flies, roaches, and mice, for example, can carry harmful bacteria and spread disease. Once a facility is infested, it can be difficult to get rid of all pests. It is very important to create an effective pest management program.

Most pests need water, food, and shelter. A clean and sanitary environment is not attractive to most pests. Pests seek out damp, dark, and dirty places. Make sure garbage is disposed of quickly and in the appropriate containers.

To help keep pests out of storage areas:
- Keep storage areas clean, sanitary, and dry.
- Dispose of any garbage quickly.
- Keep food stored at least 6 in. (15 cm) off the floor and 6 in. (15 cm) away from walls.
- Remove as many items as possible from cardboard boxes before you store them.
- Maintain appropriate temperatures in storage areas.

A workplace may become infested even if you carefully follow a good pest management program. If you see signs of insects or rodents, report the problem to your supervisor. The supervisor can call a professional exterminator.

 **Reading Check** Explain What do pests need to live?

 SECTION 1.2 After You Read

Review Key Concepts

1. **Describe** the biological sources of food contamination.
2. **Identify** cleaning products commonly used in the foodservice industry.
3. **Explain** what to do if you suspect the workplace has become infested with pests.

Practice Culinary Academics

Science

4. **Procedure** Slice three pieces of bread in half, and expose each half to different conditions: 1) one dry and one wet; 2) one in the dark and one in the light; 3) one cold and one warm. Examine them every day for a week. Record any changes.

   Analysis Based on observation, what is the best way to store bread? Write a paragraph to explain.

   NSES C Develop an understanding of the behavior of organisms.

Mathematics

5. You are asked to make a batch of sanitizing solution by combining 4 gallons (512 ounces) of water with ½ ounce of liquid bleach. What is the ratio of bleach to water in this solution?

   Math Concept **Forming Ratios** A ratio is a comparison of two quantities, and is typically written as a fraction. Like other fractions, a ratio should be reduced to its lowest terms.

   Starting Hint Write a fraction with the amount of bleach (½ ounce as the numerator and the amount of water (512 ounces) as the denominator. Reduce the fraction to its lowest terms by dividing the numerator and denominator by their greatest common factor.

   NCTM Number and Operations Understand numbers, ways of representing numbers, relationships among numbers, and number systems.

 Check your answers at this book's Online Learning Center at **glencoe.com**.

READING CHECK ANSWER Pests need water, food, and shelter.

Chapter Summary

Safety rules and equipment help keep food-service workers safe. Use caution around gas appliances, store oily rags properly, and keep the workplace free of built-up grease to avoid fire danger. Employees should know first aid to treat emergencies, including CPR and the Heimlich maneuver.

Harmful microorganisms that cause illness can contaminate food. There are three types of hazards in the kitchen: biological, chemical, and physical. If an outbreak of foodborne illness occurs, follow company procedures and report it to your supervisor. Use cleaning products carefully, and according to directions.

Content and Academic Vocabulary Review

1. Use each of these vocabulary words in a sentence.

Content Vocabulary

- occupational back support (p. 4)
- flammable (p. 6)
- lockout/tagout (p. 7)
- emergency (p. 9)
- first aid (p. 9)
- shock (p. 11)
- abrasion (p. 11)
- laceration (p. 11)
- avulsion (p. 11)
- puncture wound (p. 11)
- Heimlich maneuver (p. 11)

- cardiopulmonary resuscitation (CPR) (p. 12)
- general safety audit (p. 12)
- sanitary (p. 14)
- contaminated (p. 14)
- direct contamination (p. 14)
- cross-contamination (p. 14)
- sanitation (p. 14)
- hazard (p. 14)
- toxin (p. 14)
- pathogens (p. 14)
- bacteria (p. 14)

- viruses (p. 16)
- parasite (p. 16)
- fungi (p. 16)
- mold (p. 16)
- cleaning (p. 18)
- sanitizing (p. 18)

Academic Vocabulary

- routine (p. 4)
- document (p. 12)
- result (p. 14)
- transmit (p. 16)

Review Key Concepts

2. Identify possible culinary workplace safety issues.

3. Explain fire safety equipment and emergency procedures.

4. Describe first aid measures for burns, wounds, and choking.

5. Describe the sources of food contamination.

6. Identify sources of chemical food contamination.

7. Illustrate how to manage pests in a kitchen setting.

Critical Thinking

8. Consider: Why are the type of shoes you wear in a kitchen important? What are the possible consequences of wearing inappropriate footwear in a kitchen?

9. Analyze response times. If foodborne illness breaks out at a restaurant, why are a quick response and notification of the local health department important?

10. Suggest outbreak solutions. Find a newspaper article about a foodborne illness outbreak. What methods would you suggest to help prevent a similar outbreak?

Review and Applications

Academic Skills

 English Language Arts

11. Kitchen Safety Training Imagine that you are responsible for training new kitchen employees in a restaurant. Write an outline for a five-minute oral presentation that you would give to employees on their first day on the job to teach them the kitchen safety procedures of your restaurant. Create any visual aids you believe would be helpful in training new employees. Give your presentation to the class and give your presentation outline to your teacher.

> **NCTE 4** Use written language to communicate effectively.

 Science

12. Hand Washing It is vital to have clean hands.

Procedure Form into groups as directed by your teacher. Have two group members cover their hands with washable paint. Then, wash off the paint, with one student using water only, and the other using soap and water.

Analysis Record how long it takes to wash off all of the paint using both methods. Create a procedure based on your results. Explain how it can be used at work and at home.

> **NSES F** Develop an understanding of personal and community health.

 Mathematics

13. Cleaning Product Proportions One common method for cleaning surfaces that can hold on to grease, such as countertops, is to use a solution of 3 tablespoons of vinegar and 1 gallon of water. You have been asked to make up a larger batch of this cleaning solution for use in your restaurant kitchen. How much vinegar should you add to 2.5 gallons of water so that the final solution has the same proportion of ingredients as the one described above?

Math Concept **Using Ratios to Solve for an Unknown** When proportions are equal, you can set up two equal ratios to relate what you already know to what you are solving for. Use x to represent the unknown amount in the second ratio.

Starting Hint Write two fractions representing the ratio of tablespoons of vinergar to gallons of water: first, using the original quantities (3/1), and second, representing the larger batch ($x/2.5$). Because the larger batch has the same proportions as the original formula, the two ratios are equal: $3/1 = x/2.5$. Solve for x by multiplying both sides of the equation by 2.5.

> **NCTM Algebra** Understand patterns, relations, and functions.

Certification Prep

Sharpen your test-taking skills to improve your kitchen certification program score.

Directions Read the questions. Then, read the answer choices and choose the best possible answer for each.

14. Which of the following is a virus?

    a. salmonella   **c.** hepatitis A

    b. listeriosis   **d.** trichinosis

15. If you feel ill and have flu-like symptoms, you should:

    a. Go to work and warn your co-workers to be careful around you.

    b. Call your boss and tell him or her that you are sick.

    c. Take medicine for your symptoms and go to work.

    d. Do not tell anyone and continue to work.

Test-Taking Tip

In a multiple-choice test, the answers should be specific and precise. Read the question first, and then read all the answer choices. Eliminate answers that you know are incorrect.

Real-World Skills and Applications

Management Skills

16. Design a Foodborne Illness Plan Imagine that you are the manager of a restaurant, and that recent outbreaks of foodborne illness around the country have you concerned. Design a system to document, investigate, and report incidents of foodborne illness. Write out a description of your plan.

Critical Thinking Skills

17. Use Detergents Effectively Split up into groups as directed by your teacher. Place two small spots of kitchen grease on a counter surface. Use a small amount of detergent and try to remove the first grease spot. Then, dilute the detergent with water and try to remove the second grease spot. Write a description of the results, and your group's observations on using detergent.

Financial Literacy

18. Purchase an Emergency Kit You have been given $500 to create an emergency kit for your restaurant. You may spend no more than 25% of your budget on a fire extinguisher. How much money do you have to spend on the fire extinguisher, and how much for other supplies?

Technology Applications

19. Create a Disaster Plan Imagine that you own a banquet facility. Your facility employs a host, servers, dishwashers, cooks, and an executive chef. Use a word-processing program to create a poster to show plans to deal with the following emergencies: a fire in the kitchen, a minor cut, and a customer having a heart attack. Include responsibilities for the employees, a general procedure, and key locations for emergency procedures.

Culinary Lab

Use the culinary skills you have learned in this chapter.

Develop a Safety Manual

20. Create a Manual In this culinary lab activity, you will work as part of a team to create a complete safety manual for a foodservice operation.

A. Plan the contents. Your manual should include the following information:

- Table of contents
- Short paragraph on the importance of workplace safety
- How OSHA and the EPA ensure workplace safety
- Employer and employee workplace safety responsibilities
- Kitchen safety guidelines
- First aid guidelines and a list of local emergency numbers
- Cross-contamination prevention guidelines
- Safe cleaning supply, chemical, and pesticide disposal
- Protective clothing checklist
- Personal hygiene tips

B. Prepare your manual. Discuss how you can present each item in your manual, and assign topics to each team member to research.

C. Conduct research. First, review the material in the chapter for information. Then, conduct additional research in your school library or on the Internet. Select pictures to include in your manual to illustrate the topics.

D. Write the manual. As a team, put together the results of your research in a word processing document. Insert the information and pictures in the proper order.

E. Share your work. Share your team's safety manual with the class and display it in the classroom.

Create Your Evaluation

Create a sheet that contains the following categories: Completeness, Organization, Appearance, Writing Quality, and Clarity. Rate the manuals from 1 to 10 for each of the qualities. Provide a short summary of what each manual did well, and how each could be improved.

HACCP Applications

SECTIONS

2.1 The Safe Foodhandler

2.2 The HACCP System

2.3 The Flow of Food

WRITING ACTIVITY

Outline

An outline shows the order of topics that will be discussed, how important each of those topics is, and the relationship between the topics. Create an outline for an essay about how to keep a kitchen sanitary.

Writing Tips

1 Outlines are divided into main points and subpoints.

2 Indent main points and subpoints of the same level equally. Subtopics are indented farther than main topics.

3 Points of equal importance should be at the same level.

WRITING ACTIVITY ANSWER
Outlines should be logical and well organized, and have a clear system of numbers, letters, or bullets.

EXPLORE THE PHOTO ANSWER
It kills harmful microorganisms that may live in the raw food.

EXPLORE THE PHOTO
Check the internal temperature of cooked foods to avoid foodborne illness. *Why does this help prevent foodborne illness?*

The Safe Foodhandler

Reading Guide

 Before You Read

Stay Engaged One way to stay engaged when reading is to turn each of the headings into a question, and then read the section to find the answers. For example, "Clothes" might be, "What types of clothes are worn in a professional kitchen?"

Read to Learn

Key Concepts
- **Demonstrate** appropriate personal hygiene for the workplace.
- **Illustrate** proper personal health practices to avoid the spread of foodborne illness.

Main Idea

Foodhandlers must help prevent the spread of foodborne illness. They must practice good personal hygiene, properly wash their hands, wear protective clothing, and report if they are sick.

Content Vocabulary
- foodhandler
- hygiene
- chef's coat
- protective clothing
- hair restraint
- hand sanitizer

Academic Vocabulary
- provide
- technique

Graphic Organizer

As you read, use a chart like this one to illustrate the proper hand-washing procedure. Describe each step.

Hand-Washing Technique
Step 1:
Step 2:
Step 3:
Step 4:
Step 5:
Step 6:

 Graphic Organizer
Go to this book's Online Learning Center at **glencoe.com** for a printable graphic organizer.

GRAPHIC ORGANIZER ANSWER 1) Wet hands and forearms; 2) lather with soap; 3) rub hands for 15 seconds; 4) rinse soap; 5) turn off faucet with paper towels; 6) dry hands.

Personal Hygiene

Cross-contamination can cause foodborne illnesses. Foodhandlers usually are the cause of cross-contamination. A **foodhandler** is a worker who is in direct contact with food. You can help prevent foodborne illnesses by practicing good hygiene. **Hygiene** is using good grooming habits to maintain health. You also must know how to properly wash your hands, wear protective clothing, and report illnesses.

Tiny microorganisms can be spread to food by foodhandlers in many ways. Good hygiene is the best defense. Good grooming means that you should arrive at work clean. Bathe daily with soap and water, and wash your hair regularly. Always wear deodorant to work. Your fingernails should be clean, short, and trimmed neatly. It is never appropriate to wear acrylic fingernails or nail polish while working in a commercial kitchen. Acrylic fingernails can fall off into food and become a physical hazard. Nail polish can chip off and fall into food, becoming a chemical hazard.

Clothes

Hands are not the only way microorganisms can spread. Clothes can also spread bacteria to the food you handle. Dirt can be tracked into the workplace on your shoes and clothes.

Always wear clean clothes to work. Most foodservice establishments will **provide**, or make available, a uniform for you to wear. Uniforms help protect you from spills and cuts, and also make you look more professional on the job. Kitchen foodservice workers often wear a chef's coat. A **chef's coat** is a working coat that traditionally has two rows of buttons down the front, long sleeves, and turned-up cuffs. If you wear your uniform home, wash it before wearing it again.

Your shoes also should be appropriate for the workplace. Make sure they are comfortable. You will be on your feet for many hours at a time. Choose shoes with slip-resistant soles. These will help you avoid accidents. Never wear open-toed shoes at work.

Protective Clothing

In addition to the clean clothes or uniform you wear to work, you will wear protective clothing. **Protective clothing** is clothing that is worn to help lower the chances of food contamination. For example, if you work in food preparation or clean-up areas, you will need to wear an apron. Always make sure your apron is clean. Remove it whenever you leave the food preparation area.

Foodhandlers often wear gloves to help prevent cross-contamination. Gloves act as a wall between your hands and the food you handle. This helps prevent cross-contamination. Wash your hands thoroughly before putting on gloves. Never use soiled or torn gloves. You must change gloves after each separate task. Change gloves every four hours if you perform the same task. Always change gloves immediately after handling any raw food.

Hair

Many microorganisms live in human hair and can be easily transmitted to food. When you brush hair away from your face, microorganisms move to your hands from your hair. When your hands touch food, the microorganisms move to the food. These microorganisms can cause foodborne illness.

Make it a habit to always have clean hair when you arrive at work. Microorganisms can easily grow in dirty, oily hair. Tie back longer hair in a hair restraint. A **hair restraint** is any barrier that holds back head or facial hair to keep it from contaminating food. Some establishments have regulations about

Some establishments have regulations about the type of hair restraints to be used. In general, a good hair restraint, such as a hairnet, will keep your hair away from food. It also will keep you from having to touch your hair while on the job. Some foodhandlers wear a chef's hat. These hats can come in a variety of shapes and sizes, but they all keep hair away from food and off of the face. Foodhandlers with beards should wear beard restraints.

Reading Check **Explain** What should you do with your hair when working in a kitchen?

Personal Health

Foodservice professionals need to be in good physical health when they work with food. Otherwise, harmful bacteria could be spread from the foodhandler to the food that will be served. A foodborne illness outbreak could be the result.

Proper Hand-Washing

You may think that wearing gloves can replace hand-washing. However, proper hand sanitation is very important in the foodservice industry. This is true even if you wear gloves for most tasks. Hand-washing is the most important thing you can do to prevent the spread of foodborne bacteria.

At first, it may seem silly to think that you need to learn how to wash your hands. However, a proper hand-washing **technique**, or method, can make the difference between a safe workplace and a potentially deadly one. This is because harmful bacteria are so easy to spread by hand.

To clean your hands and arms properly, thoroughly scrub any exposed surfaces with soap and warm water. You should wash your hands every two hours to help prevent cross-contamination. Always remember to wash your hands:

- Before you start work.

Hair Restraint Hairnets help keep hair from falling into your face or onto food. *Why is this important?*

- After any work breaks, including those to eat, smoke, drink, or chew gum.
- Before and after you handle raw foods such as meat, fish, and poultry.
- After you touch your hair, face, or body.
- After you sneeze, cough, or use a tissue.
- After you use the restroom.
- After you use any cleaning or sanitizing product.
- After you take out the garbage.
- After you clean dirty dishes and tables.
- After you touch anything that might contaminate food, such as a phone, money, door handles, or dirty tablecloths.

Hand sanitizers can be used after hand-washing. A **hand sanitizer** is a special liquid that kills bacteria on your skin. It is often used without water. While these products can reduce bacteria on your hands, you should never use a hand sanitizer instead of proper hand-washing techniques on the job.

Wash
Your Hands

1 Wet hands and forearms with hot water.

2 Apply enough soap to build up a good lather.

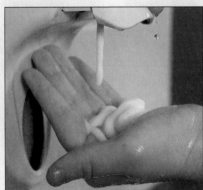

3 Rub hands and arms for at least 15 seconds. Be sure to remove soil from underneath fingernails.

4 Rinse off soap thoroughly under running hot water.

5 Dry hands and arms using a separate paper towel or a warm-air hand dryer.

6 Turn off the water faucet using a paper towel.

Illness

If you have symptoms of a disease that can be spread to others, such as fever, sneezing, coughing, vomiting, or diarrhea, call your employer immediately. You should not come to work sick. You may spread germs and bacteria to other workers or to customers.

If you feel sick while you are at work, it is your responsibility to tell your supervisor immediately. This is the only way to prevent contamination of the foods and work surfaces you will touch. Your supervisor will most likely send you home to recover. This will not only help prevent the spread of illness, but will help you recover more quickly. You cannot do your best work if you are sick.

Wounds

If you have a wound that may be infected, or a cut, burn, boil, or other sore, you might not feel sick. However, any bacteria that might be in the wound could easily spread to any of the food that you handle. This could cause a foodborne illness outbreak. Because of this, it is very important that you wash your hands and the wound area thoroughly. Keep cuts completely covered. Make sure the bandage is kept clean and dry. Change the bandage several times throughout the day.

If the wound is on your hand, wear gloves whenever possible as you perform your duties. Make sure your gloves do not become ripped or torn.

If you have a wound on your hand, even if it is covered by a bandage, you may be reassigned to a work area where you will not come into direct contact with food. This might include washing dishes, running the cash register, or cleaning kitchen or dining room areas.

 Reading Check **Summarize** What is the most important thing you can do to prevent the spread of bacteria?

 SECTION 2.1 **After You Read**

Review Key Concepts

1. **Explain** the proper use of gloves.
2. **Describe** what to do if you have a wound.

Practice Culinary Academics

 Social Studies

3. In addition to hair restraints, chefs also wear a hat. One type of chef's hat is called a toque-blanche, and it has a very distinctive shape. Research the history of the toque-blanche and write a paragraph explaining its history.

> **NCSS IV B Individual Development and Identity** Identify, describe, and express appreciation for the influences of various historical and contemporary cultures on an individual's daily life.

English Language Arts

4. Choose a partner and take turns demonstrating proper hand-washing techniques to each other. Have your partner evaluate your hand-washing technique. Then, evaluate your partner's hand-washing technique.

> **NCTE 12** Use language to accomplish individual purposes.

Mathematics

5. Recent research suggests that foodservice workers should trim their fingernails to $\frac{1}{16}$ inches or shorter. Imagine you work at a restaurant, and you want to comply with this standard. If one of your fingernails is currently 0.11 inches long, how much, if any, must be trimmed?

Math Concept **Working with Fractions and Decimals** To perform a calculation involving both a fraction and a decimal, first convert all numbers to decimals. To convert a fraction to a decimal, divide the numerator by the denominator.

Starting Hint To convert $\frac{1}{16}$ into a decimal, divide 1 by 16. Subtract this number from 0.11 to determine how much of your fingernail, if any, will need to be trimmed.

> **NCTM Number and Operations** Understand numbers, ways of representing numbers, relationships among numbers, and number systems.

 Check your answers at this book's Online Learning Center at **glencoe.com**.

READING CHECK ANSWER It is most important to wash your hands.

The HACCP System

Reading Guide

 Before You Read

Get a Notepad It is normal to have questions when you read. Write down questions while reading. Many of them will be answered if you continue. If they are not, you will have a list ready for your teacher when you finish.

Read to Learn

Key Concepts
- **Explain** the purpose of the HACCP system.
- **Outline** the processes of monitoring, corrective action, record keeping, and verification.

Main Idea

HACCP is a system developed to monitor the flow of food. The system helps foodservice workers control hazards and lower risks.

Content Vocabulary
- flow of food
- HACCP
- critical control point
- minimum internal temperature
- food thermometer
- calibrate
- record-keeping system
- log

Academic Vocabulary
- improved
- verify

 ACADEMIC STANDARDS

 English Language Arts
NCTE 8 Use information resources to gather information and create and communicate knowledge.

 Mathematics
NCTM Measurement Understand measurable attributes of objects and the units, systems, and processes of measurement.

 Science
NSES 1 Develop an understanding of systems, order, and organization.

Social Studies
NCSS VIII B Science, Technology, and Society Make judgments about how science and technology have transformed our understanding of human-environment interactions.

NCTE National Council of Teachers of English

NCTM National Council of Teachers of Mathematics

NSES National Science Education Standards

NCSS National Council for the Social Studies

Graphic Organizer

As you read, use a sequence chart like the one below to display the steps in the HACCP system. Write out each step in the rows below in the order in which you would perform them.

HACCP System
First Step:
Next Step:
Next Step:
Next Step:
Next Step:
Next Step:
Last Step:

 Graphic Organizer Go to this book's Online Learning Center at **glencoe.com** for a printable graphic organizer.

GRAPHIC ORGANIZER ANSWER 1) Identify and evaluate answers; 2) analyze critical control points; 3) follow standards; 4) monitor the system; 5) take corrective action; 6) verify the system; 7) document procedures.

HACCP Basics

As food moves through a foodservice operation, it is important to be able to spot potential hazards. By using a time-tested system called HACCP, the flow of food can be monitored. The **flow of food** is the path food takes from when it is received by an establishment to when it is disposed of as waste. Along this path, any hazards can be controlled and risks lowered.

Local health departments regularly inspect foodservice establishments. Your workplace should also inspect the kitchen to keep conditions sanitary. **HACCP**, or Hazard Analysis Critical Control Point, is the system used to keep food safe on its journey from the kitchen to the table. HACCP shows workers how to properly handle food, how to monitor food safety, and how to keep accurate records.

The HACCP system was developed by the Pillsbury Company for the National Aeronautics and Space Administration (NASA) in the early 1960s. The system was originally created to keep food safe in outer space. The HACCP system worked so well that it was used by many parts of the food industry. Over the years, HACCP has been **improved**, or made better. HACCP is now a standard food safety system used worldwide. The HACCP system looks at the flow of food through the foodservice establishment at several critical points. It helps foodservice employees:

- Identify foods and procedures that are likely to cause foodborne illness.
- Develop cleaning and sanitation procedures that will reduce the risk of foodborne illness.
- Monitor procedures to keep food safe.
- Keep records of how well the system works. (See **Figure 2.1**.)

▼ FIGURE 2.1 The HACCP System

Safety System The Hazard Analysis Critical Control Point system creates a structure to help ensure food safety. *Why do you think having a structure is important?*

Determine where food safety hazards might happen. For example, you might start by listing the areas and equipment that food comes in contact with while it is in the kitchen.

↓

Find the critical control points where contamination could happen.

↓

Set standards that are necessary for food to be considered safe. For example, set temperature limits for foods to be safe in storage areas.

↓

Create a procedure to monitor the standards. For example, you might use a thermometer to check the temperatures of all foods and keep a record of these temperatures.

↓

Take corrective action. For example, if a food does not meet an internal temperature standard, you may decide to change the cooking time.

↓

Evaluate your procedures regularly. You may need to modify your procedures to keep food safe.

↓

Develop a record-keeping system that identifies:
- Who documents the procedures.
- How documentation should be performed.
- When documentation should be performed.

FIGURE CAPTION ANSWER A structure will help ensure food safety so that all foodservice employees know their responsibilities and can track their actions.

FIGURE 2.2 **HACCP Analysis—The Flow of Food**

Handling Hazards These critical control points show the steps in the flow of food where contamination can happen. *Whose responsibility is it to make sure that these control points are monitored?*

Potential Hazard	Control Point	Corrective Action
Identifying hazardous items; improper food preparation	Menu items and recipes	Proper training
Receipt and acceptance of contaminated food products	Receiving	Inspect each delivery; reject contaminated goods
Cross-contamination; improper storage resulting in spoilage; bacteria	Storing	Follow storing procedures; maintain proper storage temperatures; discard old items
Cross-contamination; bacteria	Food preparation	Good personal hygiene; gloves; hand-washing; clean and sanitize utensils and work surfaces
Bacteria not killed; physical and chemical contaminants	Cooking	Achieve the minimum internal temperature; be aware of potentially hazardous foods, such as raw meats and eggs
Bacteria; physical contaminants	Food holding and serving	Maintain proper temperatures; use clean serving equipment
Bacteria	Cooling	Apply rapid cooling methods; store food properly
Bacteria	Reheating	Heat food rapidly; do not mix old food with new food

Food-Handling Hazards

The first step of the HACCP system is to identify and evaluate hazards. These hazards could cause illness or injury if they are not controlled. The most frequently found hazards include:

- Poor personal hygiene
- Contaminated raw foods
- Cross-contamination
- Improper cooking
- Improper holding
- Improper cooling
- Improper reheating
- Improper cleaning and sanitizing of equipment

Any of these hazards can lead to an outbreak of foodborne illness at a foodservice establishment. Because of this, it is critical that all foodservice workers follow the established HACCP system.

FIGURE CAPTION ANSWER Although owners and managers make the policies for each workplace, it is the responsibility of all foodservice employees to make sure that the HACCP system is followed.

Critical Control Points

The next step in the HACCP system is to carefully look at each critical control point. (**Figure 2.2** and **Figure 2.3** show the critical control points, and how a HACCP kitchen is set up.) A **critical control point** is a step in the flow of food where contamination can be prevented, reduced, or eliminated. For example, harmful bacteria and other microorganisms can grow in improperly cooked food. Microorganisms may survive cooking and contaminate the food. This could make diners very sick.

Cool Food Safely Cooling food must be done safely. If food is cooled improperly, harmful bacteria can grow. Cooling food quickly prevents bacterial growth. According to the U.S. Centers for Disease Control and Prevention, food that was not cooled properly is the most common cause of all reported foodborne illnesses.

This is one technique you can use to cool food safely:

1. Place food in a shallow pan.
2. Place the pan of food into a large pan filled with ice. Do not stack more than one pan of food on top of the large pan of ice.
3. Use a thermometer to check the internal temperature of the food often. Foods that have an internal temperature of 135°F (57°C) should drop to 70°F (21°C) within two hours and to 41°F (5°C) or below within four hours. Add ice as needed.
4. When the chilled temperature has been reached, remove the pan of food from the pan of ice. Dry the bottom of the pan of food and place a lid on it.
5. Label the pan of food with the date the food was prepared and its temperature at the time of storage.
6. Place the pan on the top shelf of the refrigerator.

Hazard Control After you have identified the critical control points, it is important to take steps to lower risks. For example, temperature and time are two important measurements that impact food safety. The HACCP system has standards for the temperatures of cooked foods.

The high temperatures you use when you cook food kill most of the food's harmful bacteria. The **minimum internal temperature** is the lowest temperature at which foods can be safely cooked. Microorganisms cannot be destroyed below this temperature. The minimum internal temperature is different from food to food. It is important to learn the correct temperature for each food you prepare. (See **Figure 2.4** on page 34.)

Temperature Danger Zone The temperature danger zone for holding foods is 41°F to 135°F (5°C to 57°C). (See **Figure 2.5** on page 34.) Hot foods must be thrown away after four hours if they are not held at 135°F (57°C) or above. If the temperature of food being held at 135°F (57°C) or above falls below 135°F (57°C), it should be reheated to at least 165°F (74°C). If the temperature drops below 135°F (57°C) again, the food should be discarded.

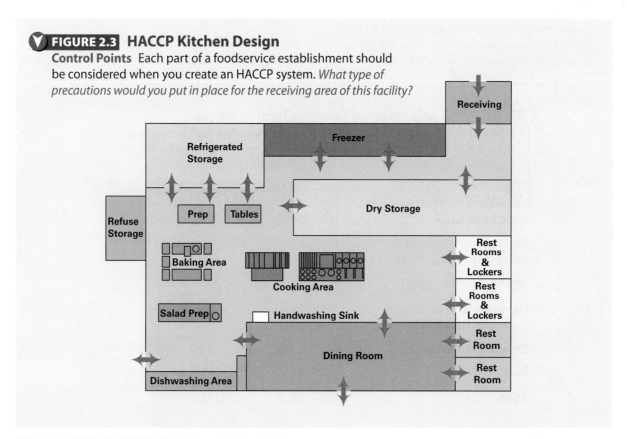

FIGURE 2.3 HACCP Kitchen Design
Control Points Each part of a foodservice establishment should be considered when you create an HACCP system. *What type of precautions would you put in place for the receiving area of this facility?*

FIGURE CAPTION ANSWER Employees who receive food should be carefully trained on how to check incoming food for quality, how to record incoming food, and how to reject contaminated food.

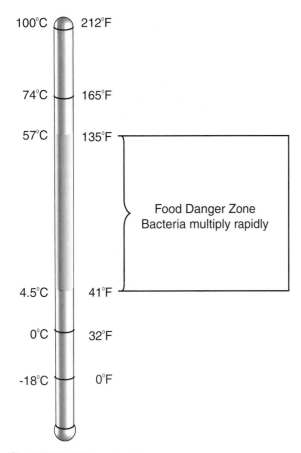

FIGURE 2.5 Food Danger Zone

Safe Food Temperatures The temperature danger zone for food is 41°F to 135°F (5°C to 57°C). *What should you do with food that has been in the danger zone for more than four hours?*

Food Danger Zone
Bacteria multiply rapidly

Food Thermometers There are many different types of food thermometers available. A **food thermometer** is a device used to check the temperatures of foods. The U.S. Food and Drug Administration (FDA) suggests these types for cooking:

- **Liquid-filled thermometers** are best used for casseroles and soups. They can break. They cannot measure thin foods.
- **Bimetal thermometers** are best used for roasts, casseroles, and soups. Some are safe to use in the oven, and some are not. They do not measure thin foods well.
- **Thermistor thermometers** are best used for foods such as hamburger patties and pork chops. They can measure the temperature of thin foods.
- **Thermocouple thermometers** are best used for foods hamburger patties and pork chops. They take readings very quickly, and can easily measure thin foods.
- **Infrared thermometers** can measure temperature quickly and accurately.

To measure the internal temperature of cooked food, place the thermometer in the thickest part of the food. Take at least two readings in different places. Do not place

FIGURE 2.4 Safe Internal Cooking Temperatures

Internal Temperatures Foods must be kept at specific internal temperatures to be considered fully cooked and safe to eat. *Why is it important for foods to be kept at a minimum internal temperature for a specific amount of time?*

Food Item	Temperature	Time
Pork, ham, bacon	145°F (63°C)	15 seconds
Poultry, stuffed meats and pasta, casseroles, stuffings	165°F (74°C)	15 seconds
Roasts (beef and pork)	145°F (63°C)	4 minutes
Hamburger, ground pork, sausages, flaked fish	155°F (68°C)	15 seconds
Steaks, veal, lamb	145°F (63°C)	15 seconds
Fish	145°F (63°C)	15 seconds
Eggs	145°F (63°C)	15 seconds

FIGURE CAPTION ANSWER Foods that have been in the temperature danger zone for more than four hours should be thrown away, as they can be unsafe to eat.

FIGURE CAPTION ANSWER Microorganisms cannot be destroyed below a minimum internal temperature. If foods hold that temperature for a specified amount of time, all parts of the food are safe to eat.

the thermometer too close to bone. Bone conducts heat quickly. This may give you a false temperature reading. Use thermometers to check the temperature of delivered foods, too. Fresh foods should be received at a temperature of 41°F (5°C) or below. Thermometers should be accurate to within 2 degrees.

Thoroughly clean, sanitize, and air dry the thermometer after each use. This will help you avoid cross-contamination. Thermometers should be calibrated ('ka-lə-brāt-əd) before each work shift or each food delivery. To **calibrate** a thermometer, you adjust it for accuracy. A thermometer should be recalibrated every day, and again if it is dropped.

Reading Check Identify What are the temperatures in the temperature danger zone, and the time limit for food?

System Monitoring

Foodservice workers are responsible for monitoring the food safety systems that are in place. This helps workers ensure that proper procedures are followed in the flow of food. They can also help spot potential problems.

For example, monitoring might include taking the temperature of turkey breast when it is received. You would make sure it is stored at 41°F (5°C) or below. You would also think about contamination that could happen when the turkey breast is stored. Raw turkey breast should be stored on the bottom shelf, below cooked foods in the refrigerator and any foods that are ready to eat. This will prevent raw turkey juices from contaminating any foods stored beneath the turkey breast.

Corrective Action

When you find a potential problem at a critical control point, you should take corrective action immediately. It is the responsibility of each foodservice worker to make sure that the kitchen and dining environments are safe places for customers to prepare food and eat.

For example, you see a foodhandler taking out the garbage, and then returning to the kitchen. You notice that the foodhandler has not washed his or her hands before entering the kitchen. What would you do? You should take immediate corrective action. Remind the foodhandler that garbage can be a breeding ground for harmful bacteria and other microorganisms. The foodhandler must wash his or her hands to avoid cross-contamination. Handling food with dirty hands could result in a foodborne illness.

Record Keeping

Record keeping is an important part of any safety and sanitation system. Most record-keeping systems are simple to use. A **record-keeping system** includes flow charts, policy and procedure manuals, written descriptions, and food temperature readings taken at different times.

Taking Temperatures Foodservice operations use a variety of food thermometers. *What types of thermometers work best with thin liquids?*

Logs are usually completed at the end of each work shift or meal period throughout the day. A **log** is a written record of day-to-day actions and procedures. Find out what record-keeping system is used at your food-service establishment, and what records your supervisor wishes to keep. Complete logs carefully.

Verification

A very important step in the HACCP system is to **verify**, or prove, that your system works correctly. You should be able to show standard operating procedures for a HACCP system. The flow of food should be traced at the end of each work shift by the chef or manager. He or she should read logs of temperature and time, spot any errors, and take corrective action if necessary.

 Reading Check **Explain** What should you do if you find a potential problem at a critical control point?

 **A TASTE OF HISTORY**

2004
└ The Spirit rover leaves Cape Canaveral, Florida, for the planet Mars

2007
└ Mandatory pasteurization of all California almonds begins

Battle Against Bacteria

French scientist Louis Pasteur was a pioneer in the study of microbiology. He was the first person to understand that bacteria can cause disease, and his experiments led to a process known as pasteurization. During pasteurization, controlled heat is applied to food to kill microorganisms that could cause disease or spoilage. Pasteurization had a major impact on the food industry. Today, pasteurization is commonly used for milk and other dairy products.

History Application

Research Pasteur's discovery of how bacteria and disease are linked and how pasteurization works. Write a paragraph discussing how you believe milk and milk products have been improved because of its use.

> **NCSS VIII B Science, Technology, and Society** Make judgments about how science and technology have transformed our understanding of human-environment interactions.

SECTION 2.2 After You Read

Review Key Concepts

1. **List** what HACCP shows foodservice employees.
2. **Explain** how to verify an HACCP system.

Practice Culinary Academics

Science

3. **Procedure** Choose a recipe. Identify the potential hazards you might find while creating it, and how they could be avoided.

   Analysis Choose one hazard you have identified, and create a step-by-step procedure to avoid it.

> **NSES 1** Develop an understanding of systems, order, and organization.

English Language Arts

4. Research the different types of food thermometers available and create a visual presentation with the three best options.

> **NCTE 8** Use information resources to gather information and create and communicate knowledge.

Mathematics

5. You are preparing a chicken dish. On the counter is poultry that has been left at a temperature of 17.5°C for 15 minutes. How many minutes remain in the poultry's temperature danger zone?

   Math Concept **Converting Temperature** Celsius temperatures (C) can be converted to Fahrenheit (F) using the following formula: $F = (\frac{9}{5} \times C) + 32$.

   Starting Hint Convert 17.5°C into °F by multiplying 17.5 by $\frac{9}{5}$ and adding 32 to the result. Check your answer against the danger zone temperatures.

> **NCTM Measurement** Understand measurable attributes of objects and the units, systems, and processes of measurement.

 Check your answers at this book's Online Learning Center at **glencoe.com**.

The Flow of Food

Reading Guide

 Before You Read

What You Want to Know Write a list of what you want to know about the flow of food. As you read, write down the heads in this section that provide the information.

Read to Learn

Key Concepts

- **Summarize** the steps in safely receiving and storing food.
- **Identify** safe holding, serving, cooling, and reheating guidelines.
- **Explain** how to properly clean, sanitize, and store dishes and glassware.

Main Idea

Foodservice workers need to be conscious of food safety and sanitation at each point in the flow of food, from receiving deliveries through serving.

Content Vocabulary

- receiving
- storage
- shelf life
- first in, first out
- shucked
- processing
- pasteurize
- produce
- perishable
- food preparation
- holding
- disposal point
- recycle
- manual dishwashing

Academic Vocabulary

- ideal
- affect

ACADEMIC STANDARDS

 Mathematics
NCTM Problem Solving Apply and adapt a variety of appropriate strategies to solve problems.

NCTM Data Analysis and Probability Select and use appropriate statistical methods to analyze data.

 Science
NSES F Develop an understanding of personal and community health.

NCTE National Council of Teachers of English

NCTM National Council of Teachers of Mathematics

NSES National Science Education Standards

NCSS National Council for the Social Studies

Graphic Organizer

As you read, use a flow chart like the one below to show the all of the points in the flow of food. Fill in each box with a point in the flow of food, starting with the first and ending with the last.

Flow of Food

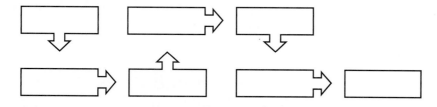

 Graphic Organizer Go to this book's Online Learning Center at **glencoe.com** for a printable graphic organizer.

GRAPHIC ORGANIZER ANSWER Receiving and storing food; preparation and cooking; holding; serving; cooling; reheating; disposal and cleanup.

Receive and Store Food

Critical control points are important in the flow of food. It is here that special attention is given to food products to prevent contamination. At each point in the flow of food, from receiving through serving, you need to be concerned with food safety and with sanitation.

Safety and sanitation procedures begin with receiving. **Receiving** is accepting deliveries of food and supplies. All food products must be carefully inspected for damage. You also should check that the food has been kept at the proper temperatures during delivery. As a foodservice professional, you need to look for these potential receiving problems:

- Foods that have been thawed and refrozen
- Foods that have an insect infestation
- Damaged foods or containers
- Items that have been repacked or mishandled
- Foods handled at incorrect temperatures

Storage Tips

Storage is another control point where improper handling can cause contamination. **Storage** means placing food in a location for later use. Always keep storage areas clean and dry. Make sure the temperature in storage areas is carefully monitored. Never store food in an unsanitary place, such as near sewage or in a bathroom.

There are three types of storage: dry, refrigerated, and frozen. The type of storage used depends on the type of food product being stored, and its shelf life. A product's **shelf life** is the period of time it can be stored and still be good to use.

Dry Storage

Foods that have a long shelf life are placed in dry storage. Flour, salt, dried beans, and canned foods are examples of items that should be kept in dry storage. The **ideal**, or perfect, temperature in a dry storage area is 50°F to 70°F (10°C to 21°C). All food products in dry storage should be kept at least 6 inches off the floor and at least 6 inches away from the wall. Clean and sanitize dry storage shelves and areas regularly.

Refrigerated Storage

Food products that need to be kept refrigerated should be stored at or below 41°F (5°C). Clearly label and date all containers when they are first stored. To prolong the shelf life of a refrigerated product, use the first in, first out (FIFO) inventory program. In the **first in, first out** program, food products that are oldest are used first, before newer products. This way, all products are fresh when they are used.

Store cooked foods and raw ingredients separately to prevent cross-contamination. If prepared or cooked and raw foods must be stored on the same side or shelving unit, always store cooked foods above raw foods. Frozen foods that are being thawed in the refrigerator should always be stored below prepared foods. Be sure to leave room around foods for air to circulate. Do not place hot foods in the refrigerator to cool.

Frozen Storage

Store frozen foods at 0°F (18°C) or below. Clearly label and date all containers when they are first stored. Never put a hot food product into a freezer, because this will **affect**, or act upon, the temperature of the storage area. It could cause foods in the freezer to thaw and remain in the temperature danger zone for too long.

⁓ Small Bites ⁓

Bacteria and pH The pH scale measures the acidity of a substance. The pH scale runs from 0 to 14. From 0 to 7 is acidic, from 7 to 14 is alkaline, and 7 is neutral. Neutral environments are the best for growing bacteria. The more acidic a food is, the less likely it is that bacteria will grow.

Storage by Food Type

Different foods are stored in different places. All foods should be stored properly. This will prevent contamination, spoilage, and the growth of harmful bacteria.

Seafood

Fish and shellfish are very sensitive to temperature changes. If the proper temperature for seafood is not maintained, microorganisms will grow rapidly.

Fresh, whole fish should be packed in ice at a temperature of 41°F (5°C) or lower. The fish should have bright, shiny skin. The texture should be firm and the flesh should spring back when touched.

The FDA closely oversees the shipping of shellfish. Shellfish must be purchased from an FDA-approved supplier. Shucked shellfish in packages of less than one-half gallon will have a sell-by date clearly shown on the label. **Shucked** shellfish have been removed from the shell. Packages with more than one-half gallon of shellfish will show the date the shellfish were shucked.

If you receive a container of live clams, oysters, or mussels, you must write the date they were delivered on the tag that is fastened to the container. These identification tags must remain attached until the last one is used, then kept for 90 days after the harvest date. This information is used to determine the source of possible contamination if a foodborne illness breaks out.

Sanitation Check

✓ The Kitchen Glow Test

Although work surfaces, equipment, walls, and floors may look clean, they may still be contaminated on a microscopic level. One way to uncover the presence of bacteria is through adenosine triphosphate bioluminescence (ə-'de-nə-ˌsēn (ˌ)trī-'fäs-ˌfāt ˌbī-ō-ˌlü-mə'ne-sən(t)s), or the glow test. Adenosine triphosphate, or ATP, is an energy molecule found in all living cells. Bacteria contains ATP molecules.

SANITATION CHECK ANSWER The glow test can help you thoroughly spot and clean more contaminated areas. It can also show you the areas that may be missed during routine cleaning.

Gourmet Math

Cool Foods Safely

You would like to use a two-stage cooling process to bring a pot of minestrone soup from 170°F down to a safe temperature for storage (41°F). The soup sits at room temperature for 15 minutes while you divide it into smaller containers. Next, you leave the containers in an ice bath for 1 hour and 45 minutes. Finally, you move the soup containers into the refrigerator for 2 hours. If hot soup cools at 16°F per hour at room temperature, at 56°F per hour in an ice bath, and at 15°F per hour in the refrigerator, will your soup cool safely?

Math Concept **Applying Rates** If you know the rate at which a value changes per hour, multiply that rate by the amount of time (in hours) to find the total change during that time period.
Starting Hint Convert each time period into hours (since the cooling rates are also given in hours). There are 60 minutes in an hour, so the 15 minutes at room temperature converts to $^{15}/_{60}$ = 0.25 hours. Multiply 0.25 hours by the cooling rate of 16°F per hour to find the total decrease during that period. Repeat this process for the ice bath and the refrigerator.

NCTM Problem Solving Apply and adapt a variety of appropriate strategies to solve problems.

Fresh Meat and Poultry

Government agencies inspect fresh meat and poultry to make sure it is free from disease. Meat and poultry also must be purchased

To test for the presence of ATP, an enzyme called luciferase (lü-'si-fə-ˌrās) is placed on the area to be tested. Luciferase is the enzyme found in the tails of fireflies. If luciferase comes into contact with ATP, it glows with light, called bioluminescence. A machine called a luminometer tests the amount of light. The stronger the light, the more contaminated the area.

CRITICAL THINKING *How can the glow test help you make the kitchen safer?*

GOURMET MATH ANSWER Room temperature: 0.25 × 16°F = 4°F; ice bath: 1.75 × 56°F = 98°F; refrigeration: 2 × 15°F = 30°F. Soup temperature after two hours: 170°F − 4°F − 98°F = 68°F; after four hours: 68°F − 30°F = 38°F. The soup will reach the safe temperature of 41°F in four hours.

from processing plants approved by the United States Department of Agriculture (USDA). Products that have been inspected have a seal of approval. (See **Figure 2.6.**) The USDA has strict quality standards and regulations that must be followed to earn these stamps.

However, microorganisms can still grow on foods even during processing. **Processing** means that food has been cleaned and prepared so that it can be cooked and eaten. These microorganisms can grow rapidly and contaminate the food. Look for these signs to make sure your meat and poultry are fresh:

Temperature The product should be delivered at 41°F (5°C) or below.

Color Beef and lamb should be red; pork should be light pink. Poultry should not have a purple or green color. It should not have dark wing tips.

Odor Meat and poultry should not have an offensive or sour odor.

Texture Meat should not feel slimy. Poultry should not be sticky under the wings or around joints.

Packaging Check for broken cartons, soiled wrappers, and leaks.

V FIGURE 2.6 **Inspected Meat and Poultry Seal of Approval** Foods that have been inspected by the USDA have a seal of approval. *What types of foods must be inspected by the USDA?*

U.S. INSPECTED AND PASSED BY DEPARTMENT OF AGRICULTURE

INSPECTED FOR WHOLESOMENESS BY U.S. DEPARTMENT OF AGRICULTURE

FIGURE CAPTION ANSWER The USDA inspects poultry, meats, and processed egg products. All other foods are inspected by the FDA.

Eggs

Like meat and poultry, eggs must be purchased from USDA-approved processing plants. Make sure the eggs you receive and store have the USDA inspection stamp. This stamp shows that the eggs have been purchased from a government-approved supplier.

When the eggs arrive at a foodservice establishment, they must be checked. Eggs should be received by the establishment within a few days of the packing date at the processing plant. Eggs should be delivered clean, dry, and uncracked. Store eggs immediately in a properly refrigerated storage area.

Dairy Products

Foodservice establishments should purchase and serve pasteurized dairy products. To **pasteurize** is to heat a product at high enough temperatures to kill harmful bacteria. Unpasteurized products can contain harmful microorganisms that can cause foodborne illness. Milk and milk products labeled Grade A are best used for cooking. Dairy products, such as cheese, sour cream, yogurt, and butter, should be received at 41°F (5°C) or below.

SAFETY CHECK ANSWER Bacteria can grow inside eggs, and there is no way to tell if they are there. Proper handling reduces the risk of foodborne illness.

Refrigerated and Frozen Foods

Many foodservice establishments use some foods that have already been prepared before they are received. Refrigerated processed foods should be delivered at 41°F (5°C) or below. Always closely inspect packages to check for damage.

All frozen foods should be completely frozen when they arrive at your facility. Check for signs that the food product has thawed and then been refrozen. The food may look discolored or dry, or ice crystals may be present. Another sign of thawing is liquid at the bottom of a product's container.

Dry and Canned Goods

Dry and canned goods have a longer shelf life than fresh meat, poultry, eggs, or fresh fruits and vegetables. But that does not mean you should not be concerned about food safety. Follow these guidelines to store dried foods:

- Inspect packages for damage.
- Keep dried foods in tightly sealed containers.
- Keep containers in a dry place.
- Watch for signs of insects and rodents.
- Check regularly for signs of spoilage.

You must also pay close attention to commercial canned goods. Signs of potential contamination include bulges, leaks, dents, and rust. (See **Figure 2.7**.)

Fresh Produce

The right temperature for receiving and storing fresh produce depends on the product. **Produce** is fresh fruits and vegetables. Remember, however, fresh fruits and vegetables are perishable. **Perishable** ('per-i-shə-bəl) products are products that can spoil quickly, especially if they are not stored properly.

Follow these general guidelines to receive and store fresh produce:

- Do not wash produce before storing. Wash produce just prior to preparing it. Extra water can cause mold and bacteria to grow.
- Handle produce with care. Most fruits and vegetables bruise easily.
- Check produce for insects and insect eggs.
- Check produce for spoilage, such as mold, bruising, or wilting.

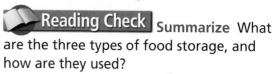 **Reading Check** Summarize What are the three types of food storage, and how are they used?

▼ **FIGURE 2.7** **Unsafe Canned Goods**

Cans to Avoid Cans with signs of bulging, dents, rust, or leaks should be immediately thrown away. *What advantage do commercially canned goods have over fresh foods?*

Bulges
Discard immediately. The can may have gas built up inside.

Leaks
Discard immediately. The can probably has a bad seal.

Rusty
Discard immediately. The can may be old.

Dents
Discard immediately. The can may have broken seams.

FIGURE CAPTION ANSWER Commercially canned goods have a longer shelf life than fresh meat, poultry, eggs, and produce.

READING CHECK ANSWER Dry storage, for foods with a long shelf life; refrigerated storage, for temporary storage of fresh foods; and frozen storage, for extended storage.

Preparation and Cooking

Now you know how to safely receive and store food. But there are still several points in the flow of food at which food could become unsafe. One of those points is food preparation. **Food preparation** means cooking and preparing foods to be eaten. Remember that you need to cook certain foods, such as poultry and meat, to specific internal temperatures for them to be safe to eat.

Another way to keep food safe is to prevent cross-contamination and microorganism growth. Salads with cold protein, such as chicken salad, can be the perfect place for microorganisms to grow. Because raw and cooked foods are combined in these dishes, not all of the microorganisms will be killed by heat.

To avoid contamination during food preparation, use tongs or spatulas instead of your hands. Hands can carry bacteria. Always make sure equipment, tools, cutting boards, and other surfaces are cleaned and sanitized often. Keep foods covered whenever possible.

To avoid cross-contamination, wash all fresh fruits and vegetables before you prepare them. Wash root vegetables and starches, such as potatoes, before and after you peel them. Never prepare uncooked meats in the same area you use to prepare fruits and vegetables.

Each type of food product you prepare is at risk for a different kind of contamination. Know the risks for individual foods to prepare them safely for customers. (See **Figure 2.8**.)

Hold Food Safely

In some foodservice establishments, foods may be cooked and served immediately. However, in other facilities, foods must be prepared ahead of time. Foods are then held on a steam table for service. The process of keeping foods warm or cold before serving them is called **holding**. For example, you might prepare a bean soup for lunch that will be served over a three-hour lunch period. The soup would need to be held at the right temperature for service.

Holding Guidelines

It is important to learn how to hold foods properly. Foods are at risk for microorganism growth during holding. These general guidelines can help you hold food safely:

- Keep foods covered to reduce the risk of contamination.
- Take the internal temperature of held food regularly. This should be done a minimum of every two hours.
- Hold cooked foods at 135°F (57°C) or above. If the temperature drops below 135°F (57°C), reheat the food to 165°F (74°C) for 15 seconds within two hours. Hold it again at 135°F (57°C). If the temperature drops below 135°F (57°C) for a second time, discard the food.
- Hold cold foods at 41°F (5°C) or below.
- Stir hot foods regularly.
- Do not warm up cold foods by placing them directly into a steam table. This can encourage bacteria to grow.
- Never mix a fresh batch of food with food that has been in holding. Discard food after it has been held for four hours.

Color Coding You can help prevent foodborne illness with color-coded cutting boards. *Why would color-coded cutting boards be useful to prevent foodborne illness?*

PHOTO CAPTION ANSWER Color-coded cutting boards can be used for specific food types (for instance, blue for fish, red for raw meat, and green for fruits and vegetables). This helps eliminate cross-contamination.

FIGURE 2.8 **Food Prep**

Prepare Foods Food preparation is a point in the flow of food at which food must be kept safe. *At what other points should food be kept safe?*

General Preparation and Cooking Guidelines

Use clean, sanitized cutting boards, knives, and tools.

Do not remove all the food from the refrigerator at one time. Work with only as much product as you will need for one hour.

Always prepare produce in a separate area from raw meats, poultry, eggs, or fish.

Clean and sanitize knives each time you prepare a different food product.

Do not let food sit on the counter. Prepare or cook it immediately, and then return what is left to storage.

Keep cold ingredients properly chilled in the refrigerator until you need them.

Fully cook protein foods, such as chicken, before you mix them with other food products.

Closely follow recipe directions when preparing foods.

Cook food to the proper minimum internal temperature.

Do not mix leftover foods with freshly prepared foods.

Reheat leftover sauces and gravies to 165°F (74°C) for 15 seconds before serving them.

Thoroughly cook foods that have been battered or breaded.

- Do not store cold foods directly on ice. Put the food in a storage container and then set the container into the ice until the food and the ice are at the same level in the container.

Serve Food Safely

You may remember that people are the main cause of cross-contamination in foods. When food is served, the chances of contamination are high. It is important to learn standard operating procedures about how foods should be served so that they remain safe.

Serving Guidelines

Every foodservice facility should have serving guidelines. All foodservice workers at the foodservice facility should follow these guidelines at this important step in the flow of food:

- Never touch ready-to-eat food with your bare hands.

- Never touch the surfaces of glasses, plates, or utensils that will come into contact with food or beverages. Instead, hold dishes by the bottom or an edge; hold cups by their handles; hold glasses by the lower third of the glass; and hold forks, knives, and spoons by their handles.
- Never allow one plate of food to overlap onto another plate of food.
- Use scoops to pick up ice. Never use your hands. Store scoops seperately from ice.
- Cleaning cloths should be used only for cleaning.

Cool Food Safely

The FDA recommends a two-stage method to cool food safely. In the first stage, cooked foods are cooled down to 70°F (21°C) within two hours. In the second stage, cooked foods are cooled down below 41°F (5°C) within four

FIGURE CAPTION ANSWER Food must be kept safe during receiving, storage, cooking, holding, serving, cooling, and reheating.

FIGURE 2.9 **Kitchen Sanitizers**

Sanitizers for Surfaces There are several sanitizers that can be safely used in the professional kitchen. Many are diluted, or mixed, with water before use. *Why do you think it is important to dilute these products properly?*

Type of Sanitizer	Amount to Use	How to Use
Chlorine	1 tsp. per gallon	Soft or hard water at 75°F (24°C)
Iodine	2 Tbsp. per 5 gallons	Hard water between 75°F–120°F (24°C–49°C)
Quaternary Ammonia	About 1 tsp. per gallon	Soft water at 75°F (24°C)

hours. This two-stage method takes six hours. Some facilities use a one-stage, four-hour method. In the one-stage method, foods are cooled down below 41°F (5°C). Check with local standards for cooling methods.

Refrigerators are not designed to cool hot foods. They are designed to hold cooled foods at cold temperatures. Remember that the more dense a food is, the slower it will cool. Shallow stainless steel pans allow food to cool quickly.

Reheat Foods Safely

Reheating cooked foods must be done carefully. Foods must be reheated so that they keep a minimum internal temperature of 165°F (74°C) for 15 seconds. Foods should be reheated within two hours of reaching 41°F (5°C). If you add a previously cooked food to another food, such as tomato sauce to spaghetti, the whole mixture must be reheated to a minimum internal temperature of 165°F (74°C).

Reading Check **Define** What is the definition of holding food?

Disposal Point

The last stop in the flow of food is the disposal point. The **disposal point** is the point at which food remaining after being eaten is disposed of properly. Cleaning and sanitizing are the key actions to take at the disposal point. Dishes, glasses, cups, utensils, and equipment must be cleaned and sanitized.

The first step is to scrape leftover food from dishes, equipment, tools, and glasses into the garbage can. Then, the dish or tool should be rinsed over the sink's garbage disposal unit before it is washed. Most foodservice operations use a combination of commercial sinks and dishwashers to clean and sanitize dishes, cookware, and utensils. Chemical sanitizers are used in both sinks and dishwashers to keep bacteria from growing. (See **Figure 2.9**.)

Waste Disposal

It is very important to throw away waste properly. Harmful bacteria can easily grow in garbage, and pests are attracted to it. Garbage should be disposed of in proper containers. It should never be left on counters. Garbage containers should be cleaned and sanitized every day. A fresh liner should be used every time garbage is taken out. Garbage should be taken out as soon as the container is full, and at the end of the day. Always wash your hands properly after taking out the garbage.

Recycling

A recycling program can help improve the environment. To **recycle** is to take a product at the end of its use and turn it into a raw material to make a different product. Some products that can be recycled include paper, glass, aluminum, steel, and some forms of plastic.

READING CHECK ANSWER Holding means keeping food that has been prepared in advance warm or cold between cooking and serving.

FIGURE CAPTION ANSWER A sanitizer that is undiluted can harm surfaces and skin. However, a sanitizer that is diluted too much may not be strong enough to kill bacteria.

To start a recycling program at a foodservice establishment, you must first decide what you will recycle. Then, set aside storage containers for different types of recyclable items, and separate items (glass, plastic, and aluminum, for example). Rinse all items to be recycled so they do not attract pests.

Manual Dishwashing

A three-compartment commercial sink is used for manual dishwashing. (See **Figure 2.10**.) **Manual dishwashing** is washing dishes, glasses, cookware, and utensils by hand. You must first scrape and prerinse dishes. Next, wash them in at least 110°F (43°C) water and detergent. Hold glasses upside down over the center brush in a dishwashing sink, and rotate the glass back and forth. Then, rinse the dishes with clear water at 110°F (43°C). Change the water as needed to keep it clear and hot. Sanitize items in at least 171°F (77°C) water for 30 seconds. Some health codes require 180°F (82°C) water for sanitizing. When sanitizing with chemical solutions, follow the manufacturer's directions for proper concentration and water temperature. Remove the items and allow them to air dry. Store the items in a clean, dry area.

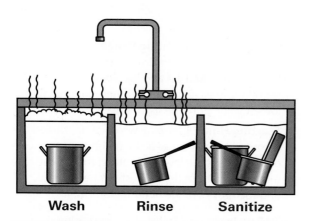

Wash   Rinse   Sanitize

▲ **FIGURE 2.10** **Three-Compartment Sinks**
Wash, Rinse, Sanitize A three-compartment sink is used to wash, rinse, and sanitize dishes. *What factors should you consider when you use a three-compartment sink?*

FIGURE CAPTION ANSWER You must use the proper proportion of sanitizer and water, and the correct water temperature.

Scrubbing and Scouring

To clean pots, pans, cooking tools, forks, knives, and spoons, follow the manual dishwashing procedures described above. Never use steel wool or metal scouring pads on small tools. This can cause nicks and scratches. Bacteria can hide and multiply in these scratches. In addition, steel wool fragments may remain on pots or pans, creating a physical hazard if they make their way into food. Sponges should not be used because they are great hiding places for harmful bacteria.

Commercial Dishwasher Use

Foodservice operations clean and sanitize a lot of dishes during a single day. Dishes can be cleaned by hand. However, this can take a large amount of time and resources. It is much more efficient for restaurants to use commercial dishwashers.

There are many types of commercial dishwashers:
- **Single-compartment** dishwashers have one compartment for all dishes and utensils.
- **Multi-compartment** dishwashers have more than one compartment.
- **Recirculating** dishwashers recycle prewash water through the dishes to save water and energy.
- **Conveyor** dishwashers clean dishes in racks on a belt that moves through the machine.
- **Door-model,** or stationary rack, dishwashers have a large front door to load dishes, and can wash many dishes at one time.

Dishwasher Guidelines

These general guidelines should be followed when using a commercial dishwasher:
- Scrape and rinse soiled dishes and presoak utensils and tools.
- Prerinse dishes to remove food and soil.
- Rack dishes, glasses, and utensils so that water will spray all of the surfaces. Glasses should be placed upside-down.

Dry and Store Items

How you dry and store dishes and glasses will determine whether they will stay clean and sanitary. You must follow a procedure to keep from contaminating the sanitized dishes and glasses.

Allow clean, sanitized dishes to air dry. Do not touch dish surfaces that will come in contact with food once they have been cleaned, sanitized, and dried. Wash your hands before you store items in a clean, dry area. All dishes should be completely dry before they are stacked and stored. Water that is left on dishes can become a breeding ground for bacteria, mold, and other disease-causing microorganisms. Do not stack dishes or glasses too high on storage shelves. This can create a safety hazard if they become unbalanced and fall.

 Reading Check **Determine** When should garbage be taken out?

 Doing Dishes Dishes should be thoroughly washed and sanitized each time they are used. *Why do you think that dishes should be air-dried instead of dried with a towel?*

SECTION 2.3 After You Read

Review Key Concepts

1. **Explain** how to receive and store dry and canned goods.
2. **Describe** how to reheat foods safely.
3. **Identify** the steps that must be taken before running a dishwasher.

Practice Culinary Academics

Science

4. **Procedure** Follow your teacher's instructions to form small groups. Prepare two servings of a cooked vegetable dish. Carefully follow the chapter's advice for storing one serving. Store the other serving in a way that would be unsafe. The next day, compare the two dishes by sight and smell, but do not eat them.

   Analysis Record your observations and make conclusions storing cooked vegetables.

> **NSES F** Develop an understanding of personal and community health.

Mathematics

5. You are holding a pot of gravy for service. At 6:00 p.m., its temperature measures 143.2°F. At 7:00 p.m., its temperature reads 136.1°F. At 8:00 p.m., its temperature reaches 141.6°F. What is the gravy's range of temperatures?

Math Concept **Calculating Range** Range is a statistical measure indicating the distance between the greatest and least numbers in a set of numbers. To calculate range, subtract the lowest value from the highest value.

Starting Hint Determine which of the three recorded temperatures is the highest, and which of the three is the lowest. Subtract the lowest temperature from the highest temperature to find the gravy's range of temperatures.

> **NCTM Data Analysis and Probability** Select and use appropriate statistical methods to analyze data.

Check your answers at this book's Online Learning Center at **glencoe.com**.

PHOTO CAPTION ANSWER A towel may spread bacteria to freshly washed dishes, contaminating them.

READING CHECK ANSWER As soon as the garbage container is full, and at the end of the day.

Review and Applications

Chapter Summary

To ensure food safety and quality, foodhandlers must follow procedures that promote a clean and healthy workplace. This starts when they get ready for work and lasts until their work shift is over. Foodhandlers must be in good physical health to work. They must practice good grooming habits. The HACCP system helps minimize hazards and ensure food safety in a professional kitchen. All food products must be inspected carefully, stored quickly and properly, monitored while in storage, prepared carefully, and disposed of properly.

Content and Academic Vocabulary Review

1. Create a fill-in-the-blank sentence for each term, with enough information to determine the missing word.

Content Vocabulary

- foodhandler (p. 26)
- hygiene (p. 26)
- chef's coat (p. 26)
- protective clothing (p. 26)
- hair restraint (p. 26)
- hand sanitizer (p. 27)
- flow of food (p. 31)
- HACCP (p. 31)
- critical control point (p. 32)
- minimum internal temperature (p. 33)
- food thermometer (p. 34)

- calibrate (p. 35)
- record-keeping system (p. 35)
- log (p. 36)
- receiving (p. 38)
- storage (p. 38)
- shelf life (p. 38)
- first in, first out (p. 38)
- shucked (p. 39)
- processing (p. 40)
- pasteurize (p. 40)
- produce (p. 41)
- perishable (p. 41)
- food preparation (p. 42)

- holding (p. 42)
- disposal point (p. 44)
- recycle (p. 44)
- manual dishwashing (p. 45)

Academic Vocabulary

- provide (p. 26)
- technique (p. 27)
- improved (p. 31)
- verify (p. 36)
- ideal (p. 38)
- affect (p. 38)

Review Key Concepts

2. Demonstrate appropriate personal hygiene for the workplace.

3. Illustrate proper personal health practices to avoid the spread of foodborne illness.

4. Explain the purpose of the HACCP system.

5. Outline the processes of monitoring, corrective action, record keeping, and verification.

6. Summarize the steps in safely receiving and storing food.

7. Identify safe holding, serving, cooling, and reheating guidelines.

8. Explain how to properly clean, sanitize, and store dishes and glassware.

Critical Thinking

9. Explain what you should do if you are preparing a sauce and you find that someone's hair has fallen in the sauce.

10. Evaluate record keeping. Why is detailed and accurate record keeping an important part of the HACCP system?

Review and Applications

Academic Skills

 English Language Arts

11. Develop a Disposal Procedure An effective workplace procedure must be clear enough for employees to understand so that they follow it correctly. Create a procedure for disposing of food and washing dishes, and write it out in a step-by-step or checklist form that employees could use to follow the procedure.

> **NCTE 12** Use language to accomplish individual purposes.

 Social Studies

12. Hygiene History Research the history and development of an aspect of food safety, for example, hand-washing, foodborne illness, or food storage. Write a report that details the development of your topic and that answers the following questions: How were the hazards discovered and solutions developed? How has human health improved as a result of these changes, both in the workplace and at home?

> **NCSS VIII B Science, Technology, and Society** Make judgments about how science and technology have transformed the physical world and human society and our understanding of human-environment interactions.

 Mathematics

13. Calculate Volume You have cooked a pot of soup for tomorrow's lunch. Following proper cooling guidelines, you would like to transfer the contents of the full 12-quart (693-cubic-inch) pot of hot soup into smaller containers for cooling. Each rectangular-shaped container is 12 inches long, 10 inches wide, and 2 inches deep. How many smaller containers will you need to hold all of the soup?

Math Concept **Calculating the Volume of a Box** Volume is the amount of space inside a solid object. The volume of a box (or a rectangular three-dimensional shape) is obtained by multiplying its length times its width times its height (or depth).

Starting Hint Calculate the volume in cubic inches of one container by multiplying its length (12 inches) by its width (10 inches) by its height (2 inches). Then, divide this number into the volume of soup (693 cubic inches) to determine the number of containers needed. Round up to the next whole number.

> **NCTM Geometry** Use visualization, spatial reasoning, and geometric modeling to solve problems.

Certification Prep

Sharpen your test-taking skills to improve your kitchen certification program score.

Directions Read the questions. Then, read the answer choices and choose the best possible answer for each.

14. The temperature danger zone is:

   a. 41°F to 135°F.

   b. 40°F to 140°F.

   c. 32°F to 212°F.

   d. 41°F to 70°F.

15. Food safety begins during:

   a. receiving

   b. storage

   c. preparation

   d. holding for service

Test-Taking Tip

Come up with the answer in your head before looking at the possible answers. You will be more confident in your answer, and avoid being tricked.

Real-World Skills and Applications

Time Management Skills

16. Get Ready for Work Imagine that you are a line cook in a restaurant. Your job requires you to be ready to begin work exactly at the start of your shift. You have one hour between school and work to get ready. Create a schedule to help you prepare for work. Include all activities for getting ready on your schedule.

Civic Responsibility

17. Customer Service Imagine that you are the manager of a restaurant that has had a recent outbreak of foodborne illness. One of your regular customers who has not been ill is concerned. Assume you have an HACCP system set up in your restaurant. How would you speak to the customer? Role-play your responses in class.

Technology Applications

18. Make a Spreadsheet Create a spreadsheet that could serve as a checklist for kitchen employees to check tasks as they work. Identify the critical control points, and underneath each create a list of the critical actions that will minimize the risk of food contamination.

Financial Literacy

19. Dishwashing Options Commercial dishwashers cost $4,000 and take one person to run. Dishwashing by hand requires three employees. Employee dishwashers earn a wage of $7.25 per hour. If employee dishwashers work 8 hours per day, how long will it take for a commercial dishwasher to become more cost-effective than manual dishwashing?

Culinary Lab

Your HACCP System

Use the culinary skills you have learned in this chapter.

20. Create an HACCP System In this lab, you will follow your teacher's instructions for forming teams. Working in teams, you will create an HACCP system for the commercial kitchen pictured on page 33, using the HACCP critical control points on page 31 as your guide.

A. Find the problems. As a team, determine the potential control point problems in each of the following areas on the diagram: receiving food, storing food, preparing and cooking food, holding food, and serving food. Create standard operating procedures for this kitchen.

B. Create a poster. Develop a poster that explains your team's solutions to the problems you have identified. Have your teacher approve the team's poster.

C. Check your foods lab. Inspect your foods lab using your team's HACCP inspection system poster. Note any areas that might need improvement.

D. Report to the class. Report your team's findings to the class.

E. Lead a discussion. Discuss each team's food lab inspection and poster recommendations. Analyze what they illustrated about the role of the HACCP system in keeping food safe.

Create Your Evaluation

Compare and contrast the systems and procedures of each team. Which systems and procedures were most effective? Thinking about each team's system and results, answer the following questions:

1. If you were designing a new system, would you change the way you look for critical control points? Why?
2. How can you be a better foodservice employee after this experience?

Research and Development

Have you ever wondered how the food products you eat are created?

Food manufacturers look for practiced chefs and foodservice workers to help develop new packaged, frozen, canned, semi-prepared foods and other food products. There are a variety of research and development careers that can be found in every part of the country.

To succeed in research and development, you will need a culinary degree and a basic understanding of food science. You will also need excellent oral and written communication skills and work experience.

Patrick Sullivan, RD, LDN, Metabolic Kitchen Nutritionist

Q **Describe your job.**

A I am a metabolic kitchen nutritionist for Johns Hopkins School of Medicine. I perform nutrition-related research studies that help form more effective diets for patients with nutritional complications. I am currently working on the first major American study of the Glycemic Index.

Q **Why did you choose your career?**

A I originally thought I would get a Culinary Arts degree, but I quickly changed to Culinary Nutrition after I took a class in Nutrition and Sensory Analysis. We had to take traditional recipes and modify them to meet a healthier diet. I loved how it was like solving a puzzle.

Q **Describe a typical work day.**

A Most of my days are spent performing day-to-day kitchen operations, such as cooking, purchasing, and receiving food. A large part of my job is quality control. Each participant's diet has been calculated and is carefully weighed to meet his or her needs. The diets that are created at this facility will one day be used as a model for hospitals around the country.

Q **What training and preparation did you receive?**

A I graduated with a bachelor's degree in Culinary Nutrition. I learned about cooking theory and techniques in my first two years. My last two years prepared me for nutrition from both a culinary and a clinical angle.

Q **How has your education helped you?**

A Every day I use the skills that I learned in school. Now I enjoy great job satisfaction. If you enjoy work and take pride in what you do, that positive outlook fills your personal life.

Q **What skills do you need for your job?**

A You need to be strong in recipe development and foodservice management. You have to be able to present food demonstrations and research study findings. As a nutrition expert, you may need to know how to interview with media reporters.

Career Ingredients

Education or Training	Most employers require a culinary dietetics or food science degree, business and marketing courses, and restaurant experience.
Academic Skills Required	English Language Arts, Mathematics, Science
Aptitudes, Abilities, and Skills	Commitment to professional standards, creativity, teamwork, communication skills, and marketing, sales, and organizational skills.
Workplace Safety	Basic kitchen safety, sanitation, and food-handling rules must be followed.
Career Outlook	Openings will be plentiful in the near future as the foodservice industry continues to expand.
Career Path	Advancement depends on skill, training, and work experience. Chefs with management experience may move into research positions.

Career Pathways

Nutritionists	Often help with the development of new food products. They identify the kinds and amounts of nutrients in foods. Some may help to develop consumer product statements.
Directors of recipe development	Create new recipes for a variety of menus. They must know many different food preparation techniques.
Food batchmakers	Set up food production equipment and modify recipes and formulas. They work to produce specific flavors or textures. They must have solid math and organizational skills.
Food scientists	Help produce, process, prepare, evaluate, and find different uses for food. They must have strong chemistry, biology, and psychology skills.
Packaging specialists	Develop packaging materials for specific food products. They must have strong skills in research, problem solving, and packaging equipment knowledge.
Product development specialists	Find ways to improve food products, such as better flavor or shelf life. They may also help develop new food products that meet quality standards.
Quality assurance specialists	Make sure foods meet quality, sanitation, and production standards.
Research chefs	Work with food scientists, manufacturers, and marketing departments to develop new food products.

Critical Thinking What classes have you taken in school that might help you prepare for a career in food research and development?

Culinary certification programs include menu development and nutrition. Develop a new recipe for a healthful, flavorful sandwich using a variety of ingredients. Your recipe should contain a balance of different types of ingredients.

COMPETITION PRACTICE

Imagine you are entering a sandwich-making competition. Prepare the sandwich recipe you created for the Get Certified practice, or a sandwich recipe of your teacher's choosing. You will be timed, and all food preparation must be done within that time. Evaluate your efforts based on the following rating scale:

1 = Poor; 2 = Fair; 3 = Good; 4 = Great

Judge your sandwich on:

- Whether you finished your recipe on time.
- The flavor and ingredients of the sandwich.
- The attractiveness of the plate, including any garnishes.

Restaurant Inspections

All restaurants undergo an inspection on a regular basis to ensure that food is being prepared in a safe and sanitized area. Using your research and interview, you will develop your own inspection sheet.

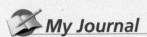

My Journal

If you completed the journal entry from page 1, refer to it to see if you have ever had a complaint against a restaurant's cleanliness. Add any additional notes about specific sanitation steps that the restaurant could improve upon.

English Language Arts

NCTE 6 Apply knowledge of language structure and conventions to discuss texts.

NCTE 7 Conduct research and gather, evaluate, and synthesize data to communicate discoveries.

Project Assignment

In this project, you will:

- Research restaurant inspection sheets to see what type of information appears on them.
- Identify and interview someone in the restaurant business who has gone through an inspection.
- Create your own inspection sheet.
- Prepare a presentation to share what you have learned with your class.

Applied Culinary Skills Behind the Project

Your success in culinary arts will depend on your skills. Skills you will use in this project include:

➤ Understanding workplace safety and sanitation guidelines.
➤ Identifying contamination and cross-contamination.
➤ Knowing the proper protective clothing for restaurant employees.
➤ Understanding the HACCP system.
➤ Determining the importance of safety measures when preparing, storing, and serving food.

English Language Arts Skills Behind the Project

The English Language Arts skills you will use for this project are writing, interviewing, and speaking skills. Remember these key concepts:

Writing Skills

➤ Use correct spelling, punctuation, and grammar.
➤ Use findings from research to communicate discoveries in writing.
➤ Organize the summary of your research in the order that leads you to your conclusion.

Interviewing Skills

➤ Listen attentively.
➤ Be aware of nonverbal communication.
➤ Ask additional questions to gain a better understanding.

Speaking Skills

➤ Speak clearly and concisely.
➤ Be sensitive to the needs of your audience.
➤ Speak slowly so that the audience can follow your presentation.

Step 1 Research Restaurant Inspections

Conduct research to find different restaurant inspection sheets. You may want to start by asking to see the inspection sheet for your state department of health. Write a summary of your research to:

- Explain how, when, and why inspections occur.
- Determine what the inspectors look for in an HACCP plan.
- Identify how restaurant personnel are inspected.
- List specific items regarding food storage, cleaning, and labeling.
- Describe the types of equipment and physical facilities that are inspected.
- Determine why a follow-up inspection may be required.

Step 2 Plan Your Interview

Use the results of your research to write a list of interview questions to ask a local restaurant worker who has been through an inspection. Your questions may include:

- How do you prepare for an inspection?
- What do you and the rest of the restaurant staff and patrons do during the inspection?
- Are you ever able to correct a violation while the inspector is still there?
- When do you hear the results of the inspection?
- How do those results impact your restaurant?

Step 3 Connect with Your Community

Identify a local restaurant employee you can interview about the inspection process. Conduct your interview using the questions you prepared in Step 2. Take notes during the interview and write a summary of the interview.

Culinary Project Checklist

Plan

- ✓ Research different inspection sheets and summarize your findings.
- ✓ Plan and write your interview questions.
- ✓ Interview a restaurant worker and write a summary of the information you learned.
- ✓ Create your own inspection sheet with a rating system.

Present

- ✓ Make a presentation to your class to discuss the results of your research, your interview, and your inspection sheet.
- ✓ Invite students to ask any questions they may have. Answer these questions.
- ✓ When students ask you questions, demonstrate in your answers that you respect their perspectives.
- ✓ Turn in the summary of your research, your interview questions, and the inspection sheet to your teacher.

Step 4 Create Your Inspection Sheet

Use the Culinary Project Checklist to plan and create a restaurant inspection sheet to share what you have learned with your classmates.

Step 5 Evaluate Your Culinary and Academic Skills

Your project will be evaluated based on:

- Content and organization of your information.
- Depth and detail of your inspection sheet.
- Speaking and listening skills.

 Rubric Go to this book's Online Learning Center at **glencoe.com** for a rubric you can use to evaluate your final project.

 JOHNSON & WALES
U N I V E R S I T Y

Expert Advice Go to this book's Online Learning Center at **glencoe.com** to read an article by a culinary expert from Johnson & Wales University about which areas health inspectors consider the most important in a kitchen.

The Foodservice Industry

Chapter

3 Foodservice Career Options
4 Becoming a Culinary Professional
5 Customer Service
6 The Dining Experience

EXPLORE THE PHOTO

Employees with the right training and job skills and an appealing dining atmosphere all help ensure that customers are satisfied. *Why do you think having satisfied customers is important?*

EXPLORE THE PHOTO ANSWER Customers who are satisfied will return to the restaurant. This will keep money flowing into the business.

Your Career in Foodservice

After completing this unit, you will know the jobs that are available in foodservice, and how customer service and the dining experience affect profits. In your unit culinary project, you will research the duties of a particular food-service job. Then, you will create a presentation scene for your classmates about what skills are needed in that job.

 My Journal

Write a journal entry about any foodservice careers that sound interesting to you.

- Why did you choose them?
- What do you think foodservice workers do in their daily routine?
- What skills do you think you will need to be successful?

JOHNSON & WALES
U N I V E R S I T Y

"The cross-training I received through a hotel internship was so helpful to understand the whole operation and be able to work in any department."

Brandon Marshall
Director of Catering
Quorum Hotel Tampa

Foodservice Career Options

SECTIONS

3.1 Careers in Foodservice

3.2 Foodservice Trends

3.3 Entrepreneurship
    Opportunities

WRITING ACTIVITY

Prewriting

Think about the different careers in the food industry. Write for five minutes about a job you would choose and why it appeals to you. Then, take five minutes to organize your topics into a logical order.

Writing Tips

1 Freewrite or collect ideas from other sources.

2 List ideas and see how they relate to each other.

3 Ask questions to clarify ideas.

EXPLORE THE PHOTO

Being a chef is just one of the many careers available in foodservice. *What other foodservice careers can you name?*

WRITING ACTIVITY ANSWER
Students should write continuously, rather than well. Materials should be organized into a coherent outline.

EXPLORE THE PHOTO ANSWER
Other careers may include management, food scientist, purchaser, or salesperson.

Careers in Foodservice

Explore the many career options open to you.

Reading Guide

 Before You Read

Use Notes When you read, keep a notepad handy. Whenever you come upon a section or term you are unfamiliar with, write the word or question on the paper. After you have finished the section, look up the terms or try to answer your questions based on what you have read.

Read to Learn

Key Concepts
- **Describe** different food production and service opportunities.
- **Examine** career opportunities related to food production and service.

Main Idea

There are a variety of job opportunities available in the food industry. In addition to food production, there are also jobs in service, management, and other areas.

Content Vocabulary

- kitchen brigade
- cross-train
- line cook/ station cook
- sous chef
- pastry chef
- prep cook
- garde manger
- executive chef
- research chef
- culinary scientist
- foodservice director
- catering director
- kitchen manager
- dining room supervisor
- restaurant manager
- purchaser
- vendor
- sales representative
- certification
- entry-level
- apprentice
- job rotation
- internship

Academic Vocabulary

- array
- evaluate

ACADEMIC STANDARDS

 English Language Arts
NCTE 4 Use written language to communicate effectively.

 Mathematics
NCTM Problem Solving Apply and adapt a variety of appropriate strategies to solve problems.

 Social Studies
NCSS II C Time, Continuity, and Change Identify and describe significant historical periods and patterns of change within and across cultures.

NCSS V C Individuals, Groups, and Institutions Describe the various forms institutions take, and explain how they develop and change over time.

NCTE National Council of Teachers of English

NCTM National Council of Teachers of Mathematics

NSES National Science Education Standards

NCSS National Council for the Social Studies

Graphic Organizer

As you read, use a wheel like this one to help you remember the five basic positions in the kitchen brigade. In each section of the wheel, name one position.

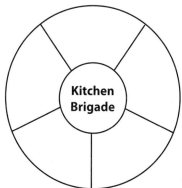

 Graphic Organizer
Go to this book's Online Learning Center at **glencoe.com** for a printable graphic organizer.

GRAPHIC ORGANIZER ANSWER Line cook/ station cook; sous chef; pastry chef; prep cook; garde manger chef.

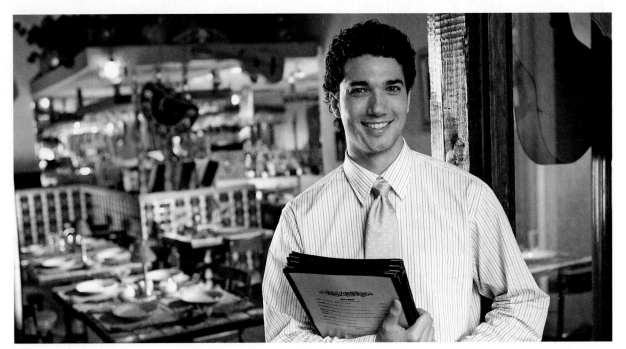

Calm Authority A restaurant host must remain calm, especially during peak dining times. *What other service staff opportunities are available in foodservice?*

Foodservice at a Glance

The foodservice industry is about people. This, of course, includes the customers who eat. However, it also includes the employees who cook and serve, and the managers who run the foodservice facilities. Foodservice continues to change and grow to meet the needs of its customers. This growth means that there are exciting job opportunities. Before you choose a career, you should explore all the job opportunities that are available to you.

According to the National Restaurant Association, there are more than 13.1 million people in the United States working in the foodservice industry. This makes it one of the largest employment segments in the country. Many people are interested in foodservice careers because of the number of jobs available.

The majority of foodservice jobs provide a service, such as cooking food or waiting on customers. Customers are willing to spend time and money for a pleasant dining experience. This means foodservice establishments want to hire well-trained employees.

You can choose from an **array**, or a wide selection, of foodservice career options. You can advance in your career if you are willing to work hard and get the proper training and education.

Service Opportunities

There are two general types of foodservice jobs. One type works directly with customers. The other type does actual food preparation. Individuals who are part of the service staff must be able to relate to all kinds of customers. It is emotionally and physically demanding to work directly with customers. No matter what happens, the service staff must keep a pleasant and helpful attitude. Four common types of service staff are host, cashier, server, and busser. These jobs and their duties are described in Chapter 5. Service jobs will always be available in the foodservice industry.

Production Opportunities

In the past, most foodservice operations used a traditional kitchen brigade system to divide responsibilities for preparing food.

In a **kitchen brigade**, specific preparation and cooking tasks are assigned to each member of the kitchen staff. **Figure 3.1** shows how these assignments match the person's job title. Many foodservice operations use a kitchen brigade to stay organized.

Today, however, many restaurants also **cross-train** their employees by giving them work experience in many different tasks. Cross-training reduces the restaurant's labor costs and results in fast service. The five basic positions in the kitchen brigade are line cook/station cook, sous chef, pastry chef, prep cook, and garde manger. These positions usually work separately in a restaurant or hotel kitchen. Cross-trained employees can work at more than one position.

Line Cook/Station Cook

Line cooks and **station cooks** work on the food production line. They cook foods and put them on plates for service staff to take to customers. They have experience preparing meals quickly. Work is usually divided into stations, such as the grill station and the fry station.

Sous Chef

The sous ('sü) chef, or "under" chef, reports to the executive chef. The **sous chef** supervises and sometime assists other chefs in the kitchen. The sous chef may also fill in for the executive chef when necessary.

Pastry Chef

The **pastry chef** is responsible for making baked items, such as breads, desserts, and pastries. Pastry chefs must be skilled in a variety of bread- and pastry-making techniques. Pastry chefs produce muffins, biscuits, cakes, pies, and other baked goods. Pastry chefs often start work very early in the morning.

Prep Cook

The **prep cook** prepares ingredients to be used by the line cooks. For example, a prep cook might wash and peel fresh fruits and vegetables. Prep cooks then properly store these foods to keep them fresh and easily available.

▼ FIGURE 3.1 Traditional Kitchen Brigade Professional Chefs Each type of chef has its own job title. *What types of chef jobs interest you the most?*

French Term	English Term
Sous ('sü) **Chef**	"Under" Chef
Chefs de Partie ('shef dœ-pär-'tē)	Line or Station Chef
Saucier (ˌsȯ-sē-'yā)	Sauce Cook
Poissonier (ˌpwä-sōn-'yā)	Fish Cook
Grillardin (ˌgrē-yär-'dän)	Grill Cook
Friturier (frē-ˌtü-rē-'yā)	Fry Cook
Rotisseur (ˌrō-tes'yœr)	Roast Cook
Entremetier (ˌän(n)-trə-mə-tē-'yā)	Vegetable Cook
Potager (ˌpȯ-tä-'zhā)	Soup Cook
Tournant (tür-'nän)	Swing Cook
Garde Manger (ˌgärd ˌmän-'zhā)	Pantry Chef
Patissier (pä-tis-'yā)	Pastry Chef
Boucher (bü-'sher)	Butcher

Garde Manger

The **garde manger** (ˌgärd ˌmän-'zhā), or pantry chef, is responsible for preparing cold food items. These items may include salads, cold meats and cheeses, cold appetizers, cold sauces, and garnishes to make plates of food look more attractive.

Management Opportunities

Management jobs in the foodservice industry are offered to people who have the right work experience, training, and education. Managers must be chosen carefully so that the operation will run efficiently and smoothly. You must work hard and have the right skills to become a manager.

FIGURE CAPTION ANSWER Answers will vary based on the students' personal interests, but should reflect their career goals.

Executive Chef

The **executive chef** manages all kitchen operations. The executive chef works together with the restaurant manager and the dining room supervisor as part of a management team. Executive chefs order supplies, create work schedules for the restaurant staff, and help develop menus and the types of foods that will be prepared by the restaurant. They also manage food preparation and service. Executive chefs must know the latest industry trends as soon as they become available. They must continue their education and attend conferences and seminars.

Research Chef

Large food manufacturers hire experienced research chefs to work in their labs or test kitchens. Many restaurant chains also hire research chefs. A **research chef** works closely with food scientists to produce new food products. Research chefs can turn favorite recipes into packaged foods that can be sold in supermarkets. They also help write nutrition information for nutrition labels.

Culinary Scientist

Culinary science combines culinary arts and food science. A **culinary scientist** uses culinary science to set new standards in food technology. A culinary scientist works together with research chefs to create new food products and to update cooking methods. To become a culinary scientist, you must know the basics of subjects such as culinary arts, nutrition, food science, and technology.

ᔕ Small Bites ᔕ

Life Plans When you decide on a career, you must also decide how that career will affect the rest of your life and your family. Create a life plan to help you decide how to fit everything in. Set realistic goals for yourself with small, doable steps, get support for your plans, and check your progress regularly.

Foodservice Director

The **foodservice director** manages the banquet operations of hotels, banquet facilities, hospitals, and universities. Foodservice directors coordinate events that require food and servers. In a large business, the foodservice director is in charge of all self-service or full-service dining operations. The foodservice director works closely with the executive chef.

Catering Director

The catering director reports to the foodservice director or manager. A large foodservice business usually has many special events going on at the same time, such as weddings and corporation banquets. The **catering director** coordinates the food for each function. Each special event must be carefully planned and coordinated so that there are enough servers and enough food.

Kitchen Manager

Most chain restaurants have a kitchen manager instead of an executive chef. The **kitchen manager** orders ingredients for menu dishes, and makes sure that they are prepared correctly. Kitchen managers also manage non-production kitchen employees, such as purchasers. Unlike an executive chef, a kitchen manager might not have the power to decide on the style of service and the style of food served at the business.

Dining Room Supervisor

A restaurant may or may not have a dining room supervisor. This depends on the size and the budget of the restaurant. The **dining room supervisor** coordinates and assigns duties to the serving staff, such as hosts, servers, and bussers. The dining room supervisor's goal is to make each customer's dining experience pleasant.

Restaurant Manager

The kitchen manager and dining room supervisor report directly to the restaurant manager. The **restaurant manager** oversees

Recipe Rewards Working in the foodservice industry can be a rewarding career choice. *What rewards do you think you can gain in the foodservice industry?*

the work of the entire restaurant. This includes the day-to-day work, such as record keeping, payroll, advertising, and hiring. The restaurant manager may do other work as well, such as cooking, especially if the restaurant's staff is short-handed or the restaurant's operating budget is limited.

Related Opportunities

As you can see, there are many foodservice opportunities for hard-working, experienced, and educated people. There are also other foodservice careers that can help a foodservice business run smoothly. These related careers include purchaser, vendor, and sales representative.

Purchaser

A **purchaser** buys food and supplies for restaurants according to his or her restaurant clients' current needs. A purchaser will search for the best prices and order the amount of each food needed to meet the demands of each restaurant's menu.

Sales Representative

A sales representative often works directly for a vendor. A **vendor** is a company that sells products and equipment to the foodservice industry. A **sales representative** helps chefs to select the food products and equipment that will best fit their needs and budgets. A successful sales representative will also allow customers to test new products and equipment.

Rewards and Demands

Working in the food industry has many rewards and demands. The type of business or level of employment will affect what those rewards and demands will be. For example, an executive chef has much more responsibility and demands on his or her time than a line cook or a prep cook does. But the rewards for an executive chef are also greater. The executive chef makes a much larger income and has more creative freedom than the line cook or prep cook.

Many foodservice employees work long hours, and sometimes work on holidays.

▲ **Teach Others** Teaching at a culinary school or university is an excellent career choice for an experienced chef. It can be fulfilling to help shape the future of others. *What other careers can experienced chefs choose?*

Working in the foodservice industry has many exciting and creative opportunities. But you must be willing to work hard and get training to gain the benefits. Careers can also offer you a bright future in the foodservice industry:

- Food researchers
- Food writers
- Food scientists
- Food processors
- Food stylists
- Food marketers
- Menu developers
- Recipe developers
- Foodservice trainers
- Registered dietitians and nutritionists
- Grocery and deli managers

After years of experience in the culinary field, chefs also may choose to teach at a culinary school or university.

Reading Check **Distinguish** What is the difference between a kitchen manager and an executive chef?

Education Opportunities

You can start to prepare for a foodservice career while you are still in high school. This section will help you learn how to get the right foodservice experience now. You will also learn about different educational and training programs that you can enter after you graduate from high school. These programs can help you get the skills and experience you need for a successful foodservice career.

PHOTO CAPTION ANSWER Answers may vary, but experienced chefs can choose management roles, such as executive chef, research chef, foodservice director, kitchen manager, or dining room supervisor.

READING CHECK ANSWER A kitchen manager might not have the power to decide on the style of food served at the business.

The Emperor of Chefs

Auguste Escoffier, one of the most innovative chefs in history, was born in France in 1846. He began his career at age 13 working for his uncle in Nice, and years later worked as head chef of the elegant Savoy Hotel in London. Escoffier simplifed classical French cuisine and service, and raised the reputation of culinary skills to an art. Escoffier restructured the kitchen so that it operated as a single unit called the brigade system, which is still in use today. Emperor Kaiser Wilhelm II called Escoffier the "emperor of chefs."

History Application

Research the major culinary contributions of the following French chefs:
- Marie-Antoine Carême
- Auguste Escoffier
- Fernand Point
- Michel Guerard

Create a time line to show the details of their accomplishments. Use photos when possible.

NCSS II C Time, Continuity, and Change Identify and describe significant historical periods and patterns of change within and across cultures.

Culinary Classroom Learning

There are many different ways you can prepare for a career in foodservice. You can begin in high school by taking a culinary arts or foodservice course. You can also look for part-time work at a foodservice business. After high school, you can enter an apprenticeship program, a certificate program, or an associate's or bachelor's degree program in foodservice or business. Once you work for a company, corporate training programs can also help you to gain valuable skills and experience.

You can work your way up to positions with more responsibility. The more education and training you have, the faster you will advance. Choose an education or training program that will best fit your career goals.

A TASTE OF HISTORY ANSWER Marie-Antoine Carême (1784–1833)–Codified French haute cuisine, identified mother sauces, standardized recipe terms. Auguste Escoffier (1846–1935)–Simplified French

A high school education is a solid base on which to build your foodservice career. Learning excellent reading, writing, listening, and speaking skills is vital. English and mathematics classes will teach you the basic skills you will need for any foodservice job. The academic knowledge you learn in science classes also applies to the foodservice industry. Many high schools, career centers, and vocational-technical schools offer special programs in foodservice techniques and the culinary arts.

Certification Programs

Many schools, colleges, and foodservice businesses offer certification programs. These programs usually require work experience, coursework, and a test. **Certification** is proof that you are an expert in a specific topic, such as culinary arts, baking, and pastry making. Getting certified in any culinary topic will make you more attractive to employers as a potential employee.

Before you enroll in a certification program, you must carefully **evaluate**, or study, the program. You should also evaluate the reputation of the school or operation that offers the certification. Find out what jobs are available for people who have received the certification. Remember, certification programs focus on specific skills. To advance in your career, you also may need a more formal education.

Associate's Degree Programs

Many colleges and universities offer associate's degree programs in culinary arts. These programs usually take two years to finish. Good associate's degree programs offer more than just classroom-based studies. They also offer hands-on practice so that you can use the culinary techniques you learn in class.

Choose a program that meets your needs and your career goals. Evaluate the culinary program and its teachers, the college or university itself, and find out how many graduates from the school's culinary program have been hired by the foodservice industry.

cuisine, increased reputation of culinary arts, introduced brigade system and Russian-style service. Fernand Point (1897–1955)–Created nouvelle cuisine. Michel Guerard (1933)–Introduced cuisine minceur.

🔺 **Higher Learning** Bachelor's degrees are offered at many colleges and universities. *What are some of the advantages to getting a bachelor's degree?*

Bachelor's Degree Programs

Bachelor's degree programs prepare you for management jobs in the foodservice industry. These programs usually take four years to finish. Bachelor's degree programs give in-depth training in one or more areas of study. For example, Johnson & Wales University offers several bachelor's degree programs. These include Culinary Arts, Baking and Pastry Arts, Culinary Nutrition, and Foodservice Management.

There are two types of bachelor's degrees that are best to have for success in a foodservice career. Foodservice-specific bachelor's degrees give students hands-on training in many types of food preparation techniques. They also teach specific foodservice information in the classroom. General bachelor's degrees teach students skills in related topics that they will need for management jobs. These topics include marketing, business, and management.

While they work toward a bachelor's degree, students may have the opportunity to participate in a cooperative education or work experience program. These programs match foodservice students with culinary businesses. Students can learn basic workplace skills working at these businesses while they earn class credit for their work.

Entry-Level Learning

Another way to learn about the foodservice industry is through a part-time, entry-level job in a foodservice operation. You do not need to have training or experience to hold an **entry-level** job, such as dishwasher and cashier. Instead, you learn the skills you will need while you are on the job. There are many entry-level jobs available in quick-service or full-service restaurants. Most foodservice businesses offer flexible hours. This will help you to schedule work around your school schedule. The work that you will do at an entry-level job will show you what it is really like to pursue a career in the foodservice industry. It will also help you to decide what type of culinary work you wish to pursue in your career.

Apprenticeships

An **apprentice** works under the guidance of a skilled worker to learn the skills of a particular trade or art. In the foodservice industry, an apprentice would learn food preparation techniques under an experienced chef or manager. An apprentice will learn through both hands-on skills and culinary classroom learning.

Professional foodservice organizations and foodservice industry associations usually offer apprenticeship programs. The American Culinary Federation sponsors apprenticeship programs across the United States. Different apprenticeships will take different amounts of time to finish.

Corporate Training Programs

Some corporations, such as large hotels and restaurants, offer special training programs for their employees. This training is sometimes for service jobs, but it is usually for kitchen jobs. For example, McDonald's® trains its managers at Hamburger University®, a training center in Oak Brook, Illinois. Managers are specially trained so that the style of management in all McDonald's® locations is the same. Large hotels, such as Marriott® and Hilton®, also provide corporate training programs for their employees.

Employees usually do not have to pay for corporate training programs. The corporation sponsors their training as part of the employees' formal orientation procedure. Some corporations will not allow employees to work in the kitchen until they have successfully completed a corporate training program. Corporate training programs give employees the opportunity to quickly advance within the corporation.

▲ **Professional Advice** Corporate training programs introduce new employees to the procedures they will follow and the equipment they will use on the job. *In what other ways can new employees learn about their jobs?*

PHOTO CAPTION ANSWER Employees can learn about their jobs by reading an employee handbook, participating in on-the-job training provided by their employ- ers, attending seminars on job skills, and asking their managers for additional training.

Military Training Programs

The branches of the military also can provide foodservice training. There are many entry-level foodservice jobs and management jobs available in all branches of the military. Most military foodservice workers leave the military with useful job skills to enter the foodservice workforce. This allows them to find foodservice jobs once they are out of the military.

On-the-Job Training Programs

On-the-job training is an option for many people who want to learn foodservice skills while working in the field. When training employees, some foodservice managers use a training method called job rotation. In the **job rotation** method, entry-level employees are rotated, or given specific amounts of time at one job, and then moved through a series of jobs. This method allows them to learn a variety of foodservice skills.

Internships are also a type of on-the-job training. During an **internship**, an advanced culinary student works at a foodservice business to get hands-on training. Sometimes interns are paid for their work, but many internships are not paid.

Culinary schools, and programs at high school, can help you find internships in the foodservice industry. Some school organizations, such as Family, Career and Community Leaders of America (FCCLA), offer internships to students.

 Reading Check **Distinguish** What is the difference between a certification program and an apprenticeship?

SECTION 3.1 After You Read

Review Key Concepts

1. **List** all of the positions in the traditional kitchen brigade.
2. **Describe** the different ways to prepare for a career in the foodservice industry.

Practice Culinary Academics

 English Language Arts

3. Imagine that you are a recruiter. Choose three jobs at different skill levels that are described in this section and write want-ad job listings for those jobs that describe the skills and any education you think that job candidates must have.

> **NCTE 4** Use written language to communicate effectively.

Social Studies

4. Research the history of the kitchen brigade. Write a one-page report about how the brigade system was developed and how it has changed over time.

> **NCSS V C Individuals, Groups, and Institutions** Describe the various forms institutions take, and explain how they develop and change over time.

 Mathematics

5. You are starting an apprenticeship for a local foodservice organization that requires the equivalent of 240 8-hour days of on-the-job training per year. If you currently work 120 hours per month at a local restaurant, will you meet the requirement of the apprenticeship, or will you fall short of the hours needed?

> **Math Concept** **Converting Units** To compare two measurements (such as days and hours), you must first convert the measurements to the same units of measure (such as hours per year).
>
> **Starting Hint** Calculate the total hours you worked per year by multiplying 120 hours times the months in a year (12). Is this greater than the required number of hours per year (240 days × 8 hours per day)?

> **NCTM Problem Solving** Apply and adapt a variety of appropriate strategies to solve problems.

Check your answers at this book's Online Learning Center at **glencoe.com**.

Foodservice Trends

What trends can you identify in the foodservice industry?

Reading Guide

 Before You Read

Prior Knowledge Look over the Key Concepts below. Write down what you already know about each concept and what you want to find out by reading the lesson. As you read, find examples for both categories.

Read to Learn

Key Concepts
- **Analyze** how foodservice trends affect service and food production operations.
- **Identify** commercial and noncommercial foodservice and food production operations.

Main Idea

Foodservice operations track and analyze industry trends to serve their customers. Foodservice trends may be affected by society, culture, ethnic trends, population trends, or the economy.

Content Vocabulary
- trend
- hospitality industry
- cuisine
- noncommercial operation
- commercial operation
- profit
- quick-service restaurant
- full-service restaurant
- fine-dining restaurant
- cafeteria
- on-site catering
- off-site catering

Academic Vocabulary
- analyze
- atmosphere

 ACADEMIC STANDARDS

 Mathematics
NCTM Number and Operations Understand numbers, ways of representing numbers, relationships among numbers, and number systems.

 Science
NSES A Develop abilities necessary to do scientific inquiry.

Social Studies
NCSS V C Individuals, Groups, and Institutions Describe the various forms institutions take, and explain how they develop and change over time.

NCTE National Council of Teachers of English

NCTM National Council of Teachers of Mathematics

NSES National Science Education Standards

NCSS National Council for the Social Studies

Graphic Organizer

Use a Venn diagram like the one below to organize the seven foodservice trends listed in this section into different categories according to the factors that influence those trends. When a trend fits into more than one category, write notes about it in the area of the diagram where the appropriate circles overlap.

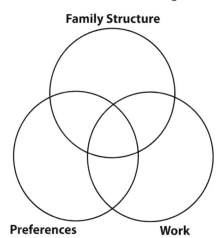

Family Structure

Preferences   **Work**

 Graphic Organizer
Go to this book's Online Learning Center at **glencoe.com** for a printable graphic organizer.

GRAPHIC ORGANIZER ANSWER
Answers will vary. Possible answers include theme and chain restaurants (family, preference); family-friendly atmosphere (family); catered events (work); and more.

The Hospitality Industry

To be successful, the foodservice industry must know how the people and communities it serves are changing. One way that foodservice operations can do this is to track and **analyze**, or study all the components of, industry trends. A **trend** is a general preference or dislike for something within an industry. These trends may be influenced by society, culture, ethnic diversity, population changes, or the economy. The foodservice industry has changed as the needs and wants of its customers have changed.

The **hospitality industry** supplies food and lodging to customers who are away from home. It includes businesses such as restaurants and hotels. As long ago as 3000 BCE, grain traders traveled all over the world to sell their products. The traders needed food and shelter on their journeys. When people began to offer these services, the hospitality industry was born. Today, the hospitality industry includes hundreds of thousands of businesses that stretch around the world. It employs millions of people and offers services to billions of customers worldwide.

Foodservice is a vital part of the hospitality industry. People who are away from home need snacks, meals, and drinks. Foodservice businesses serve people who are on vacation, too busy to cook, or meeting friends for dinner. Institutions such as schools and hospitals also provide food.

ꙮ Small Bites ꙮ

Seasonal American Food American cuisine took a new direction in 1971, when Alice Waters opened Chez Panisse. Dishes on the menu change every day. Waters believes in serving the freshest food when it is in season. Chez Panisse works together with local farmers and ranchers who believe in and use sound environmental practices. They supply the restaurant with its fresh meats and produce.

◀ **Family-Friendly Options** When parents work outside the home, little time may be left for meal preparation. *How does having a variety of foodservice options available benefit families?*

PHOTO CAPTION ANSWER Having a variety of foodservice options available, such as restaurants, and food take-out and delivery services, can save time.

Trend Forecasts

Foodservice operations must know how to best meet their customers' needs. Industry experts analyze how people think about food. They look at society, culture, population changes, and the economy. For example, as the population ages, more workers will be needed at places such as retirement centers and nursing homes. Both workers and customers are more ethnically and culturally diverse. Workers and customers often speak other languages besides English. This means there must be better communication between foodservice workers and their customers.

Foodservice managers have to understand these trends. This helps them develop ways to attract and keep employees. Trends in foodservice include:

- More theme and chain restaurants.
- Restaurants with a family-friendly atmosphere.
- An interest in ethnic foods.
- Foodservice operations expanding in sports facilities.
- Special events and private parties centered around food.
- A desire for more healthful food options and environmentally friendly restaurants.
- Supermarkets carrying prepared and packaged ready-to-eat meals.

Three society-based factors that affect customer needs are family structure, work, and preferences.

Family Structure

There are many different types of family structures. Some households contain both parents, while others are single-parent homes. Sometimes, more than two generations in a family live together under the same roof. Grandparents, aunts, or uncles may live in the same home. Depending on a family's structure and schedule, each household may prefer one type of restaurant over another. Often, families with children and teenagers have busy after-school schedules. Driving between sports practice, music lessons, or other activities may lessen the time that is available to prepare a meal at home.

Work

The number of people who work and the hours they spend working is another important economic trend. Men and women are both working more hours. This leaves them with little time to prepare meals. Restaurants and supermarkets offer take-out and delivery services that are quick and convenient.

Preferences

Customer preferences also are changing. Today's customers know more about food choices. They are more concerned about eating healthful foods. Many people want a wider variety of ethnic cuisines from which to choose. A **cuisine** is a style of cooking. Customers also expect to get value for the money they spend on food.

Trendsetting Foods The customer's wish for attractive, healthful, and flavorful food greatly affects foodservice trends. *What types of foods do you think today's restaurant customers want?*

Food Forecasting

As customer needs change, foodservice operations will find ways to meet those needs. Technology will affect the future of foodservice. Better computers and equipment are available every year. These will make food preparation and service faster and easier. However, technology cannot take the place of a helpful server's smile or a chef's artistic skill. The foodservice industry will always need people to give personal service to customers.

Reading Check **List** What trends do foodservice industry experts analyze?

Where Are the Opportunities?

The foodservice industry offers many types of jobs in different settings. These jobs range from entry-level jobs that require little or no experience, to jobs that require years of work experience and education.

The two main types of foodservice operations are noncommercial and commercial. A **noncommercial operation** works to pay for daily expenses, such as wages and food costs. Noncommercial operations include government facilities, schools, and hospitals. A **commercial operation** earns more than enough to pay for daily expenses. This creates a profit. A **profit** is the money a business makes after paying all of its expenses. Commercial operations include fast-food chains and fine-dining restaurants.

Restaurants

Jobs at restaurants are available across the country and throughout the world. (See **Figure 3.2.**) More people are eating away from home than ever before. Customers choose restaurants based on their needs. For example, one customer may decide on a fine-dining restaurant at which to celebrate a special occasion.

Quick-Service Restaurants

A restaurant that quickly provides a limited selection of food at low prices is called a **quick-service restaurant**. Fast-food chains are quick-service restaurants. Many quick-service restaurants offer take-out and delivery services. Entry-level jobs, such as a cook or cashier, are easy to find at quick-service restaurants. Many of these restaurants hire high school students on a part-time basis.

FIGURE 3.2 **Restaurant Job Opportunities**
Explore Careers There are many career opportunities in restaurants. *Do any of these jobs interest you?*

Restaurant	Job Opportunities
Quick-Service	Manager, Assistant Manager, Cashier, Prep Cook, Line Cook, Dishwasher, Cleaner
Full-Service	Dining Room Manager, Host, Cashier, Server, Busser, Dishwasher, Kitchen Manager, Line Cook, Prep Cook, Sauté Cook, Pantry Chef
Fine-Dining	Dining Room Manager, Maitre d', Head Server, Server, Captain, Busser, Dishwasher, Executive Chef, Sous Chef, Sauté Cook, Pastry Chef, Pantry Chef

READING CHECK ANSWER Industry experts analyze foodservice trends that are affected by society, culture, population changes, and the economy.

FIGURE CAPTION ANSWER Answers will vary depending on students' interests.

Full-Service Restaurants

Servers take customer orders and then bring the food to the table in a **full-service restaurant**. Customers who want service at medium prices in a relaxed mood will choose a casual restaurant. Casual, full-service restaurants may have themes, such as a sports bar and grill or a family restaurant.

Fine-Dining Restaurants

A **fine-dining restaurant** has an upscale **atmosphere**, or overall mood, excellent food and service, and higher menu prices. All employees at a fine-dining restaurant are very skilled in their jobs. Most jobs in fine-dining restaurants require both work experience and training.

Cafeterias

A **cafeteria** is a restaurant where customers serve themselves. They may also be served at a counter. Then, they take the food to tables to eat. Foodservice job opportunities at cafeterias include managers, cooks, servers, cashiers, and bussers.

Hotels and Resorts

Hotels and resorts provide their customers with food and beverages. Many lodging facilities have a variety of foodservice operations where customers can eat meals and snacks. This can include casual-dining restaurants, fine-dining restaurants, and room service. This range of foodservice means that there is a wide variety of jobs that are available.

Banquet Facilities

Banquet facilities are usually booked months in advance for weddings and other special occasions. Most banquet facilities are open only for catered events or meetings. They have large kitchens. They usually offer both full- and part-time jobs. Jobs include banquet manager, banquet captain, server, executive chef, sous chef, sauté cook, pantry chef, and catering manager.

Catering

Chefs, cooks, servers, bussers, and managers can all work for on-site catering operations. **On-site catering** means that food for special occasions is made at a customer's location. Many schools, hospitals, nursing homes, and government facilities have on-site catering. Some supermarkets also cater.

With **off-site catering**, a caterer prepares and delivers food from a central kitchen to different locations. Catering companies have an advantage over restaurants. They know in advance how many guests will attend and how much food is needed. Job opportunities are available for chefs, cooks, and servers.

Baking Skills Bakeries and pastry shops have many opportunities for pastry chefs and bakers. *What are the skills you must have to become a pastry chef?*

PHOTO CAPTION ANSWER Answers may include baking knowledge, ingredient knowledge, math and measurement skills, and science skills.

Bakeries and Pastry Shops

Commercial kitchens often purchase baked goods from bakeries and pastry shops. This method often costs less than making the food in house. There are also more customers who want homestyle baked goods. As a result, the number of jobs available at bakeries and pastry shops is growing.

Some bakeries and pastry shops are catering to people who may have special dietary needs. For example, some people may have allergies to common foods used in baking, such as wheat, cane sugar, yeast, eggs, and nuts. Specialty bake shops can make breads and pastries without some or all of these ingredients.

Bakeries and pastry shops offer more than bread for sandwiches and dinner rolls. Pastry chefs and bakers may be able to supply a commercial kitchen with dessert items for special occasions that require special tools or space that a kitchen is unable to provide.

Ethnic bakeries can also add special flavor to the commercial kitchen through the cultural baked goods they provide. Ethnic bakeries offer traditional fare for cultural holidays throughout the year that can help spice up the everyday menu.

 Reading Check Define What is a profit?

SECTION 3.2 After You Read

Review Key Concepts

1. **Explain** how changes in family structure influence food trends.
2. **Describe** the types of job opportunities available at hotels and resorts.

Practice Culinary Academics

 Social Studies

3. Research the history of a type of restaurant. Create a five-minute oral presentation that traces the development of the restaurant from its invention through modern times. If possible, use pictures to illustrate your presentation.

> **NCSS V C Individuals, Groups, and Institutions** Describe the various forms institutions take, and explain how they develop and change over time.

Science

4. **Procedure** Develop a survey to determine what the food preferences of high school students are. Conduct the survey on campus. Draw conclusions.

   Analysis Write a paragraph to explain what type of foodservice establishment you would open near your school.

> **NSES A** Develop abilities necessary to do scientific inquiry.

Mathematics

5. A new forecast predicts that average annual spending on supermarket ready-to-eat meals will increase from $1,000 per person today to $1,750 per person in five years. What is the percentage increase over the five-year period?

Math Concept **Percentage Increase** Find the percentage increase by first finding the total increase. Subtract the original amount from the new amount. Divide this result by the original amount, and then convert it to a percentage.

Starting Hint The total spending increase equals the new amount minus the original amount: $1,750 − $1,000. Divide the difference by the original amount, and convert the answer to a percentage by multiplying it by 100 and adding the percent symbol.

> **NCTM Number and Operations** Understand numbers, ways of representing numbers, relationships among numbers, and number systems.

 Check your answers at this book's Online Learning Center at **glencoe.com**.

READING CHECK ANSWER A profit is the money left over after all expenses are paid.

Entrepreneurship Opportunities

Reading Guide

 Before You Read

Be Organized A messy environment can be distracting. To lessen distractions, organize an area where you can read this section comfortably.

Read to Learn

Key Concepts
- **Identify** small-business opportunities available in foodservice.
- **Describe** the function of a business plan.

Main Idea

An entrepreneur is someone who creates and runs a business. Entrepreneurs in the foodservice industry open their own businesses, such as caterers, bakeries, or restaurants.

Content Vocabulary
- entrepreneur
- independent restaurant
- chain restaurant
- franchise
- overhead cost
- foodservice consultant
- employee recruiter
- business plan
- sole proprietorship
- partnership
- corporation
- free enterprise
- zoning
- license
- insurance

Academic Vocabulary
- guideline
- accurate

Graphic Organizer

Owning your own restaurant has both advantages and disadvantages. Use a pro-con chart like the one below to list the three pros and the three cons of owning a restaurant.

Restaurant Ownership

Pros	Cons

 Graphic Organizer Go to this book's Online Learning Center at **glencoe.com** for a printable graphic organizer.

You could own your own foodservice business!

ACADEMIC STANDARDS

 English Language Arts
NCTE 12 Use language to accomplish individual purposes.

 Mathematics
NCTM Number and Operations Understand the meanings of operations and how they relate to one another.

NCTM Number and Operations Understand numbers, ways of representing numbers, relationships among numbers, and number systems.

 Social Studies
NCSS VII B Analyze the role supply and demand play in determining what is produced.

NCTE National Council of Teachers of English

NCTM National Council of Teachers of Mathematics

NSES National Science Education Standards

NCSS National Council for the Social Studies

Small-Business Opportunities

Imagine being the boss. An **entrepreneur** (ˌän-trə-p(r)ə-ˈn(y) u̇r) is a self-motivated person who creates and runs a business. Entrepreneurs take personal and financial risks. They are hoping for personal satisfaction and financial rewards. Opening a business may be risky, but the rewards can be high. Food-service entrepreneurs usually begin by opening a small business such as a deli, bakery, or small restaurant.

A small business starts with an entrepreneur's dream. Through a lot of hard work and commitment, an entrepreneur can turn that dream into a reality. Small businesses that have fewer than 100 employees are a vital part of the U.S. economy. Small businesses produce a wide range of goods and services. They also employ many people in this country. In fact, more than 53% of the U.S. workforce is made up of people who work for small businesses.

Food Production Businesses

The changing world creates a strong need for new food products. Imagine taking your family's secret recipe and mass-producing it. Does this appeal to you? Do you think that the rewards of food-production entrepreneurship outweigh the costs?

Opening a food-production business has many advantages:

- **Ownership** You decide what to produce and how to produce it.
- **Job satisfaction** With the help of food-processing facilities, your secret recipe can make its way to supermarket shelves.
- **Earning potential** Entrepreneurs can make a lot of money if their product is popular among customers.

Opening a food-production business also has disadvantages:

- **Financial risk** Taking a product from an idea to the market takes a lot of money. You could lose all the money you invest, or even more.
- **Competition** You are not the only one trying to create a new food product. You will have many competitors in the marketplace. For this reason you will need to thoroughly evaluate your competitors before starting your business.
- **No guarantees** New products have a high rate of failure, no matter what industry they are from. There is no guarantee that your food product will be successful. Your food product must also meet strict government regulations. If it does not meet these regulations, you may not sell it.

Gourmet Math

Splitting Profits in a Partnership

Partnerships are a common way to raise enough money to put business ideas into motion. A partnership involves splitting profits and losses, or money you make or lose. Profits and losses are often distributed in proportion to each partner's investment.

Michelle and Alonzo have opened a new deli together as partners. Michelle invested $15,000 and Alonzo invested $25,000 in their new deli. Their net profit for the first year was $30,000. Their partnership agreement states that they will distribute the net profit or loss in proportion to their investments. What is each partner's share of the profit?

Math Concept **Multiplying Simplified Fractions** To multiply fractions, multiply the numerators and multiply the denominators. If the numerators and denominators have common factors, they can be simplified before multiplication.

Starting Hint Calculate the total amount invested, then write the amount each person invested as fractions, with the total amount invested as the denominator. Simplify the fraction. Multiply the simplified fractions by the total net profit to find each partner's share in the deli profits. Write the total net profit as a simple fraction using the amount as the numerator and 1 as the denominator.

NCTM Number and Operations Understand the meanings of operations and how they relate to one another.

Foodservice Businesses

Entrepreneurs can also choose to open a restaurant. There are several options from which to choose. There are three patterns of restaurant ownership: independent, chain, and franchise.

Independent Restaurants

An **independent restaurant** has one or more owners and is not part of a national restaurant business. The concept, theme, or style of the restaurant and its food is a personal choice. The owner is in control of every part of the business operation. The independent owner creates all of the company policies and sets menu prices. The owner makes all of the profit, but also is responsible for all of the expenses.

Chain Restaurants

A restaurant that has two or more locations that sell the same products and are operated by the same company is called a **chain restaurant**. Restaurants in the same chain have the same atmosphere, service, menu, and quality of food. Chain operations are run by a manager-employee in each location. The manager-employee does not make policy decisions for the chain. He or she reports to the person or company that owns the chain operation. Chain restaurants usually have lower expenses. Food and equipment can be bought in bulk by the parent company. This saves the chain money.

Franchise Restaurants

A franchise is a common type of ownership used by chain restaurants. In a **franchise**, a franchise company sells an individual business owner the right to use the company's name, logo, concept, and products. In return, the business owner agrees to run the foodservice business as outlined by the franchise company. There are some ways that business owners can customize their restaurants, but certain franchise **guidelines**, or rules, for how things are done, must be met. Quick-service restaurants are often operated as franchises.

Franchises can be expensive to own and operate. You need to have a large amount of money to buy a franchise business. A franchise business owner also usually pays an annual fee to the franchise company. This fee allows the business owner to keep using the company's name, logo, and products. In return, the business owner gets a business idea that is well developed, and strong support from the parent company.

Opening a restaurant business has many advantages:

- **Ownership** You can decide what type of restaurant to open.
- **Job satisfaction** You have a lot of creativity and flexibility to make decisions when you own a restaurant.
- **Earning potential** Some restaurant owners can make good money as their businesses grow.

Owning a restaurant also has several disadvantages:

- **Financial risk** Most restaurants have annual sales of less than $500,000. Expenses and overhead costs can be high. An **overhead cost** is an expense other than food and wages.
- **Competition** The restaurant business is a very competitive segment of the retail world. You will have many competitors in your market.
- **No guarantees** Nearly half of all individually owned restaurants fail within 12 months. About 85% of individually owned restaurants close within the first five years. You must work hard to overcome these odds.

Foodservice Management

There are many opportunities in foodservice management for entrepreneurs. A **foodservice consultant** offers advice and information to other foodservice business owners and managers. This advice might be on anything from menu design, to kitchen operations, pricing and cost control, to marketing.

⬆ **Experience Counts** An experienced executive chef can help restaurants with product and menu development. *What type of experience and skills do you think you need to develop food products?*

For example, an experienced chef might help a corporation opening a new chain of restaurants. Large corporations might hire a culinary expert to work with the corporation's marketing team to develop a new food product or service style.

Entrepreneurs might also be interested in becoming an employee recruiter. An **employee recruiter** helps businesses to find the right employees. Good employees can be hard for foodservice businesses to find. Many companies hire outside agencies and recruiters to locate and hire employees for their foodservice businesses.

Reading Check **List** What are the three patterns of restaurant ownership?

Business Plan Development

One of the main reasons new businesses fail is that the owner did not write and follow a business plan. A **business plan** is a document that describes a new business and a strategy to launch that business. All businesses should have a business plan. Your aim is to emphasize the key points that will persuade the reader of the value of the business concept. Parts of a business plan include:

- **Executive Summary** A brief recounting of all of the points in the business plan.
- **Management Team Plan** Presents your management team's qualifications.
- **Company Description** Outlines the company's basic background information, business concept, and goals and objectives.
- **Product and Service Plan** Describes the features and benefits of the business's products and services.
- **Vision and Mission Statement** Sets forth the guiding principles by which a company functions.
- **Industry Overview** Addresses the basic trends and growth within companies that provide similar or complementary products and services.
- **Market Analysis** Presents your market research and features a customer demographic profile that defines the traits of the company's target market.
- **Competitive Analysis** Demonstrates that the proposed business has an advantage over its competitors.

- **Marketing Analysis** Describes how a company plans to market, promote, and sell its products or services.
- **Operational Plan** Includes information about all the processes that take place in the business.
- **Organizational Plan** Offers information about the business's legal structure, record keeping, and legal and insurance issues.
- **Financial Plan** Presents finances and financial forecasts, and explains the reasoning behind the forecasts.
- **Growth Plan** Looks at how the business will expand in the future.
- **Contingency Plan** Suggests plans to minimize the risks in the business.
- **Cover Page, Title Page, Table of Contents, and Supporting Documents** Basic information about the company, the business plan, and any items or documents relating to the business plan.

Types of Business Ownership

There are three common types of legal business ownership (**See Figure 3.3**).

Sole Proprietorship

A **sole proprietorship** (prə-'prī-ə-tər-ˌship) is a business that has only one owner. About 75% of U.S. businesses are sole proprietorships. Sole proprietors earn all profits and are responsible for all expenses.

Partnership

A **partnership** is a legal association of two or more people who share the ownership of the business. Control of the business and profits from the business are divided between partners according to the terms of a partnership agreement.

Corporation

A **corporation** is created when a state grants an individual or a group of people a charter with legal rights to form a business. The owners buy shares, or parts of the company. These owners are called shareholders. They earn a profit based on the number of shares in the company that they own. If the business fails, the owners lose only the amount of money that they have invested in the business. There are several different types of corporations.

FIGURE 3.3 **Business Ownership Types**
Business Basics Each type of entrepreneurship business has advantages and disadvantages. *What type of business would you most like to own?*

Business Ownership	Advantages	Disadvantages
Sole Proprietorship	• Owner makes all decisions. • Easiest form of business to set up. • Least regulated form of business.	• Limited by the skills, abilities, and financial resources of one person. • Difficult to raise funds to finance business. • Owner has sole financial responsibility for company; personal assets sometimes at risk.
Partnership	• Can draw on the skills, abilities, and financial resources of more than one person. • Easier to raise funds than in sole proprietorship.	• More complicated than sole proprietorship. • Tensions and conflicts may develop among partners. • Owners liable for all business losses; personal property sometimes at risk.
Corporation	• Easier to finance than other forms of business. • Financial liability of shareholders limited.	• Expensive to set up. • Record keeping often time-consuming and costly. • Often pays more taxes than other forms of business.

FIGURE CAPTION ANSWER Answers will vary, based on students' interests.

Government Requirements

The U.S. economic system is known as the free enterprise system. **Free enterprise** means that businesses or individuals may buy and sell products, and set prices with little government control. Businesses however, are still subject to some government controls. The government passes laws that set workplace safety standards, price controls, and fair wages. These laws are meant to protect everyone who buys and uses goods and services.

Zoning and Licensing

Although the United States has a free enterprise system, government can still make rules about how businesses are run. Health codes, regulations, and zoning requirements must be met if you prepare food for sale. **Zoning** divides land into sections that can be used for different purposes, including residential (housing), business, and manufacturing. Only certain activities are allowed within these defined zones.

Before you set up a foodservice business, you will need to get a license that grants you permission to open a business. A **license** is a written permission to participate in a business activity. Business licenses are issued by local governments. You will also need special liability insurance. **Insurance** is a contract between a business and an insurance company. It provides financial protection against losses. Insurance policies are issued by insurance companies.

Record Keeping

You must keep **accurate**, or correct and updated, financial records to run a successful business. These records will include a detailed account of all income and spending for the business. These types of records are normally kept by the business owner or an accountant. Many people like to use record-keeping software to store an electronic copy of important information.

 Reading Check **List** Name the three types of business ownership.

 SECTION 3.3 **After You Read**

Review Key Concepts

1. **Describe** foodservice management entrepreneurship opportunities.
2. **List** the components of a business plan.

Practice Culinary Academics

Social Studies

3. Write a one-page essay on how the concept of supply and demand can be used by a restaurant to develop a business plan.

> **NCSS VII B** Analyze the role supply and demand play in determining what is produced.

English Language Arts

4. Imagine that you are opening your own foodservice business. Develop a company description and industry overview for your business plan. Outline the company's business concept and goals and objectives.

> **NCTE 12** Use language to accomplish individual purposes.

 Mathematics

5. It costs $4 to make a cupcake, for ingredients, labor, and overhead costs. If each cupcake sells for $5, what is your profit margin?

Math Concept **Calculating Profit Margin** Profit margin means the percentage of the price that is profit. Calculate profit margin by dividing the profit amount (price minus cost) by the price, and then converting the answer to a percentage.

Starting Hint Determine your profit per cupcake by subtracting the cost ($4) from the price ($5). Divide the profit amount by the price, and convert the answer to a percentage by multiplying it by 100 and adding the percent symbol.

> **NCTM Number and Operations** Understand numbers, ways of representing numbers, relationships among numbers, and number systems.

Check your answers at this book's Online Learning Center at **glencoe.com**.

READING CHECK ANSWER Sole proprietorship, partnership, and corporation.

Review and Applications

Foodservice careers include management opportunities, including research chef, food scientist, catering director, kitchen manager, and executive chef. Nonmanagement jobs include cashiers, cooks, servers, sous chefs, and hosts.

To prepare for a foodservice career, you will need a solid high school education and experience in a part-time, entry-level foodservice job. There are also opportunities for entrepreneurs to own businesses.

Content and Academic Vocabulary Review

1. Use these vocabulary terms to create a crossword puzzle on graph paper. Use the definitions as clues.

Content Vocabulary

- kitchen brigade (p. 59)
- cross-train (p. 59)
- line cooks/station cooks (p. 59)
- sous chef (p. 59)
- pastry chef (p. 59)
- prep cook (p. 59)
- garde manger (p. 59)
- executive chef (p. 60)
- research chef (p. 60)
- culinary scientist (p. 60)
- foodservice director (p. 60)
- catering director (p. 60)
- kitchen manager (p. 60)
- dining room supervisor (p. 60)
- restaurant manager (p. 60)

- purchaser (p. 61)
- vendor (p. 61)
- sales representative (p. 61)
- certification (p. 63)
- entry-level (p. 64)
- apprentice (p. 65)
- job rotation (p. 66)
- internship (p. 66)
- trend (p. 68)
- hospitality industry (p. 68)
- cuisine (p. 69)
- noncommercial operation (p. 70)
- commercial operation (p. 70)
- profit (p. 70)
- quick-service restaurant (p. 70)

- full-service restaurant (p. 71)
- fine-dining restaurant (p. 71)
- cafeteria (p. 71)
- on-site catering (p. 71)
- off-site catering (p. 71)
- entrepreneur (p. 74)
- independent restaurant (p. 75)
- chain restaurant (p. 75)
- franchise (p. 75)
- overhead cost (p. 75)
- foodservice consultant (p. 75)
- employee recruiter (p. 76)
- business plan (p. 76)
- sole proprietorship (p. 77)

- partnership (p. 77)
- corporation (p. 77)
- free enterprise (p. 78)
- zoning (p. 78)
- license (p. 78)
- insurance (p. 78)

Academic Vocabulary

- array (p. 58)
- evaluate (p. 63)
- analyze (p. 68)
- atmosphere (p. 71)
- guidelines (p. 75)
- accurate (p. 78)

Review Key Concepts

2. Describe different food production and service opportunities.

3. Examine education opportunities related to food production and service.

4. Analyze how foodservice trends affect service and food production operations.

5. Identify commercial and noncommercial foodservice and food production operations.

6. Identify small-business opportunities available in foodservice.

7. Describe the function of a business plan.

Critical Thinking

8. Debate why management jobs are often more demanding than employee jobs.

9. Predict future trends for serving customers and for restaurant types.

10. Discuss what purpose zoning laws might serve.

Review and Applications

Academic Skills

English Language Arts

11. Explore Jobs Choose three foodservice jobs that interest you. Use print and Internet resources to explore them further. Make a list of the education and training, work experience, and key skills needed for each job. Create a presentation to share your findings with the class. Describe what the job is and why you are interested in the job.

> **NCTE 8** Use information resources to gather information and create and communicate knowledge.

Science

12. Kitchen Brigade Experiment In the chapter you learned about the traditional kitchen brigade, where each person performs one specific task.

Procedure Break up into teams as directed by your teacher and select two simple meals to prepare. Prepare the first meal in a kitchen brigade style. Prepare the second meal without assigning tasks, just working as a group on everything.

Analysis Compare and contrast the processes. Write a paragraph to explain.

> **NSES 1** Develop an understanding of science unifying concepts and processes: systems, order, and organization.

Mathematics

13. Compare Trends Over the past year, the number of bakeries in your city has increased from 240 to 270. During that same period, the number of fast-food restaurants has risen from 5,000 to 5,125, and the number of frozen yogurt stores has increased from 32 to 48. Which one of these restaurant types had the largest total increase in number of locations? Which one of these restaurant types was the fastest-growing?

Math Concept **Percent Increase vs. Amount of Increase** When examining trends, you can determine the fastest-growing item by finding the item with the largest percentage increase. This may or may not be identical to the item with the largest total amount of increase.

Starting Hint For each restaurant type, calculate the total increase by subtracting the original amount from the new amount. Next, calculate the percentage increase for each restaurant type by dividing the total increase by the original amount. Convert the total to a percentage by multiplying it by 100 and adding the percent symbol. Finally, determine which of the three total and percentage increases are the highest.

> **NCTM Number and Operations** Understand numbers, ways of representing numbers, relationships among numbers, and number systems.

Certification Prep

Directions Read the questions. Then, read the answer choices and choose the best possible answer for each.

14. What type of foodservice career does a bachelor's degree prepare you for?

    a. line cook

    b. baker

    c. restaurant manager

    d. hostess

15. What type of restaurant is not part of a national name or brand?

    a. chain restaurant

    b. independent restaurant

    c. fast-food restaurant

    d. franchise

Sharpen your test-taking skills to improve your kitchen certification program score.

Test-Taking Tip
In a multiple-choice test, read the questions carefully. Look for negative words (not, never, except, unless), which can affect how you answer the problem.

Real-World Skills and Applications

Information Literacy

16. Research Future Trends Using print and Internet resources, analyze the societal, cultural, ethnic, population, and economic factors that affect the foodservice industry today. What are the different factors in each category, and how will they affect the food industry in the future? Discuss your findings as a class.

Research Skills

17. Locate Culinary Training Resources Using print and Internet resources, locate information on culinary training programs in your state. Look for information on apprenticeship programs, certificate programs, associate's degree programs, and bachelor's degree programs. Make a list with the name and contact information as well as the basic requirements for each program.

Technology Applications

18. Write an E-mail Imagine that you are responding to a job listing for a line cook that requires you to respond by e-mail. Write an e-mail requesting an interview and giving a short explanation of why you would be suitable for the job. List the skills you think will be important to have to be successful in the job. Keep your tone professional, since this is a business e-mail.

Financial Literacy

19. Determine Financial Needs Imagine that you are creating a business plan and you need to figure out your estimated budget. You have $10,000 to spend. You need to allocate 30% of your budget to food and supplies, 50% to wages, 15% to overhead costs, and 5% to insurance. How much money will be in each category?

Culinary Lab

Foodservice Careers

Use the culinary skills you have learned in this chapter.

20. Career Report In this lab, you will research jobs that interest you and present information about them in a report to the class.

A. Choose job titles. Identify at least five different job titles from the ones listed in this chapter that are of interest to you.

B. Research job skills. Use print and Internet resources to research the job titles you selected. Your research should include: a description of the job, a list of other titles the job may be known as, key skills needed, education and training requirements, average salary, list of resources used for research, and the pros and cons of your chosen jobs.

C. Interview a foodservice worker. If possible, interview someone who holds each position. Ask what role personal priorities and family responsibilities played in his or her career choice.

D. Create your report. Once you have completed your research, organize the job title information into a report.

E. Present your report. Present your report to the class.

Create Your Evaluation

Evaluate the reports of your classmates. Create an evaluation sheet that has the names of each presenter, along with your comments about their report. Include praise and constructive criticism, as well as further questions you might have for the presenter about the jobs. Also note whether the jobs they described sounded appealing to you or not.

Becoming a Culinary Professional

SECTIONS

4.1 Employability Skills

4.2 Seeking Employment

4.3 On the Job

WRITING ACTIVITY

Cover Letter

Choose a job in the foodservice industry that you believe you are qualified for and write a cover letter as if you were applying for that job. Use proper grammar and punctuation, and explain why you are qualified for the position.

Writing Tips

1 Explain your employment goal clearly.

2 Edit carefully for spelling and punctuation mistakes.

3 Reflect your attitude and communication skills.

EXPLORE THE PHOTO

Working in the foodservice industry requires many skills. *What are some other skills a chef must have besides cooking skills?*

WRITING ACTIVITY ANSWER
Letters should be written in an appropriate tone, and have an introduction, qualifications listing, and closing.

EXPLORE THE PHOTO ANSWER
A chef needs to have communication, listening, reading, thinking, and teamwork skills.

Employability Skills

Develop the skills you will need for success in the foodservice industry.

Reading Guide

 Before You Read

Preview Read the Key Concepts. Write one or two sentences predicting what the section will be about.

Read to Learn

Key Concepts
- **Demonstrate** basic employability skills in foodservice.
- **Evaluate** the characteristics of a positive work ethic.
- **Identify** the leadership skills necessary for foodservice employment.

Main Idea
To be employed in the foodservice industry, you must draw on skills that help you find and keep a job.

Graphic Organizer
Use a fishbone chart like the one below to list the five basic employment skills foodservice employees need to have to be successful.

Content Vocabulary
- calculate
- make change
- active listening
- distraction
- work ethic
- responsibility
- flexibility
- honesty
- reliable
- teamwork
- commitment
- leadership
- resource
- prioritize

Academic Vocabulary
- quality
- compensate

ACADEMIC STANDARDS

English Language Arts
NCTE 12 Use language to accomplish individual purposes.

Mathematics
NCTM Number and Operations Compute fluently and make reasonable estimates.

NCTE National Council of Teachers of English

NCTM National Council of Teachers of Mathematics

NSES National Science Education Standards

NCSS National Council for the Social Studies

Basic Employment Skills

 Graphic Organizer Go to this book's Online Learning Center at **glencoe.com** for a printable graphic organizer.

GRAPHIC ORGANIZER ANSWER Mathematics, listening skills, speaking skills, writing skills, and reading skills.

Sharpen Your Basic Skills

Congratulations! You have decided to pursue a career in foodservice! Whether you see yourself as a pastry chef or a restaurant manager, your next step is to make your goal a reality. The skills you will need to have to find and keep a job in foodservice are the same skills that you need to find and keep a job in any other field. You may already have many of these basic skills. However, you may need to work on certain skills. This section will help you polish the abilities you have and develop the skills you need to be successful in the foodservice industry.

Imagine that you are a foodservice employer looking to fill a job. What skills would you look for in a new employee? What attitude would you look for in an employee? The skills and attitude you want would depend on the job you were trying to fill. You might look for someone with a particular type of education, training, and work experience. For example, you would want a dining room manager to have experience managing facilities and employees.

Beyond any foodservice knowledge and experience, however, every employer expects you to have certain basic skills. To work toward a successful career in foodservice, improve your basic skills. These skills include the ability to calculate, communicate, think, negotiate, and work as a member of a team. Basic skills will help you get the knowledge and experience you will need for your career. They will also help you make a good impression during a job interview. First impressions are very important because they can last for a long time.

Math Skills

The ability to calculate and perform other math skills is a basic part of every foodservice job. To **calculate** means to work with numbers. You will add, subtract, multiply, and divide numbers in a foodservice career.

For example:

- Cooks, chefs, and bakers must use math skills to adjust recipe yields, weigh ingredients, and adjust cooking times and temperatures for different foods.
- Servers use math skills to calculate customers' bills, calculate sales tax, make change, and keep track of tips.
- Foodservice managers use math skills to order supplies, schedule deliveries, set up employee work schedules, complete payroll and tax forms, set portion sizes, and estimate profits for the business.
- All foodservice employees use basic math skills to keep track of their work hours and pay rates.

Some situations where math skills are used include weighing and measuring, working with percentages, and making change.

Weighing and Measuring

Ingredients must be accurately weighed and measured for recipes. This ensures that the food will be of a high quality. It also ensures that the recipe will turn out the same way every time it is made. You will also need to understand simple fractions to read and follow most recipes. Fractions may need to be multiplied or divided for recipes as well. They also may need to be converted to percentages like these:

$$\frac{1}{4} = .25 = 25\% \qquad \frac{1}{3} = .33 = 33\%$$

$$\frac{1}{2} = .50 = 50\% \qquad \frac{2}{3} = .66 = 66\%$$

$$\frac{3}{4} = .75 = 75\%$$

Working with Percentages

Foodservice workers must often work with percentages in recipes. For example, a recipe might read, "The fat should make up 40% of the dough." To make the recipe, you must know how to calculate using percentages. Percentages are also used to calculate the sales tax on the cost of a food item or a meal. A tax of 8%, for example, means adding 8 cents for every dollar to the total bill. Converting the percent to a decimal may make working with percentages easier.

Making Change

Servers, cashiers, and hosts need to know how to make change for customers. To **make change** means to count back the correct amount of change to a customer from the money he or she has paid for a check. This means you must be able to use math skills without using a pencil and paper. When making change at a table or cash register that does not automatically calculate the change amount for you, count up from the total of the check to the amount of money the customer gave you. Begin with the smallest coin and count up to the largest bill. For example, imagine that a customer pays for a $15.25 check with a $20 bill. You would count back the change of $4.75 as, "Seventy-five cents makes $16, and four dollar bills make $20."

When using a point-of-sale computer system that shows the amount of change that is due to the customer, count out the change from the largest bill to the smallest coin. For example, the $4.75 change from the example above would be counted back to the customer as, "Four dollars and seventy-five cents."

Listening and Speaking Skills

You will be listening and speaking almost constantly while at work. The kinds of listening and speaking skills you will need as part of a foodservice job are meant to help promote understanding. Listening does not mean that you simply appear to hear what is being said by a customer or a coworker. Listening means hearing the message and then responding to it in an appropriate way. To listen properly, you need to avoid distractions.

Active Listening

Whether you take a customer's order in a restaurant or carry out a chef's instructions, you will need to practice active listening. **Active listening** is the skill of paying attention and interacting with the speaker. Active listening shows that you have understood what a speaker has said.

These are the key steps in active listening. Practice them to become a good listener:

- Think about the purpose of the message. Why are you listening?
- Show your understanding of the message with eye contact and body language, such as nodding your head.
- Ask the speaker questions to help clarify points of the message that you do not understand.
- Listen for the speaker's inflections. Inflections are the rising and falling tones of the voice that communicate emotional content. For example, a speaker's tone usually rises when he or she is angry.
- Look at the speaker's body language. What is he or she saying with posture, gestures, and facial expressions?
- Select the most important points of the message as you listen.
- Take notes on the message. This is especially important if you are on the telephone.
- Listen for the end of the message.

Try to avoid distractions when you listen. A **distraction** is something that turns your attention away from the speaker and toward something else. Focus on what is being said. Even if you disagree with the speaker, listen carefully. Do not let your feelings about the speaker get in the way of your understanding of the message. Wait until the speaker has finished before you respond. Think carefully about how you will respond before you respond.

Speaking Skills

How well you are understood depends on how clearly you speak. These tips can help you to speak more clearly:

Pronounce Words Clearly and Correctly If you are unsure of how to pronounce a word or a name, check a dictionary or ask someone. Apologize if you are incorrect. Speak each syllable of a word. Do not slur your words together or drop the endings of words. This will make it difficult for people to understand what you are saying.

Do Not Use Slang Slang is not appropriate for use in the workplace.

Speak at a Medium Pace Your message will be missed by your listener if you speak too quickly. Your listener may also become distracted if you speak too slowly. You must speak at a medium pace for most people to understand you. If you are not sure, ask your listener if he or she understands what you are saying. If not, repeat yourself.

Regulate Your Volume If you speak too softly, people will not hear you. If you speak too loudly, you will annoy your listeners and distract others.

Telephone Skills

When you use the telephone, speak calmly, clearly, and at a medium volume. Even though you cannot be seen, smile while you speak. The person on the other end of the phone can sense your mood and attitude.

▼ **Phone Communication** Using the telephone correctly is an important communication skill. *Why is it important to have good manners when you speak over the phone?*

Your voice on the telephone may be a customer's first or only impression of your business. You should be polite and helpful at all times.

Follow these steps to properly answer a telephone in a foodservice business:

- Thank the caller for calling. Say "Good morning," "Good afternoon," or "Good evening," depending on the time of day. Identify the name of the business, and give your name.
- Ask the caller, "How may I help you?"
- If the call is for another employee, take a message or route the call to the correct person, depending on the restaurant's policy.
- If the call is for another customer, place the caller on hold and find the customer.
- If the call is for a request for a special occasion, such as a birthday or anniversary, write down the information and give it to the appropriate person.
- If the call is from someone wanting to make a reservation to eat, check to make sure the date is available. Then, enter the date into the reservations book. Write down other information, such as the customer's name, the number of people who will eat, any special requests, such as seating or dietary needs, and whether they prefer a smoking or non-smoking section. Offer any special information to the caller, such as the restaurant's dress code. Confirm the reservation information with the customer. Ask the customer to check in when he or she arrives at the restaurant, and thank the caller for calling.

Body Language

You can also speak without saying a word. Body language, or how you physically respond, also speaks for you. The way you sit, stand, move your hands, look, and smile or frown sends a clear message to the listener. Be aware of the body language you use as you speak to customers, coworkers, and supervisors. For example, if you stand with your arms folded across your chest, you may signal that you are not listening to the speaker.

 **FIGURE 4.1** **Business Letters**

Letter-Writing Skills Follow grammar and punctuation rules when you write business letters. *To whom might you write letters as a foodservice worker?*

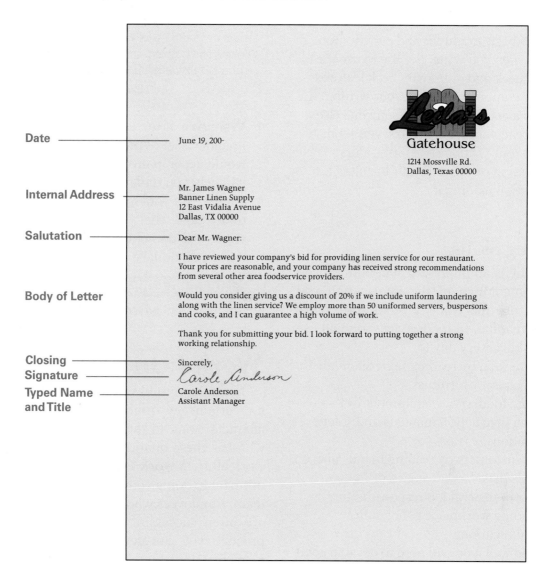

Date — June 19, 200-

Leila's Gatehouse
1214 Mossville Rd.
Dallas, Texas 00000

Internal Address —
Mr. James Wagner
Banner Linen Supply
12 East Vidalia Avenue
Dallas, TX 00000

Salutation —
Dear Mr. Wagner:

I have reviewed your company's bid for providing linen service for our restaurant. Your prices are reasonable, and your company has received strong recommendations from several other area foodservice providers.

Body of Letter —
Would you consider giving us a discount of 20% if we include uniform laundering along with the linen service? We employ more than 50 uniformed servers, buspersons and cooks, and I can guarantee a high volume of work.

Thank you for submitting your bid. I look forward to putting together a strong working relationship.

Closing — Sincerely,
Signature — *Carole Anderson*
Typed Name — Carole Anderson
and Title Assistant Manager

Writing Skills

Your ability to communicate in writing will help you find a job and perform well on the job. You will need to use writing skills every day on the job for business letters, work orders, menus, and more. Your writing skills will improve if you pay attention to your writing and reading skills. When you must write on the job, think about:

- **Your Audience** Before you write, picture the person or group who will be reading it. Tailor your writing to the reader's needs.

- **Your Purpose** Choose language that matches the purpose of your writing. Read what you have written and decide if your writing fulfills its purpose. Most business communications give information or instructions, ask for information or a decision, persuade a reader to agree with or act upon something, or to complain.

- **Style** The style of your communication includes your choice of language and tone. Business communications are written in a direct style with a professional tone.

FIGURE CAPTION ANSWER Answers will vary, but may include suppliers and vendors, employees and employers, and local and state government officials.

- **Form** The two most common forms of business writing are memos and business letters. (See **Figure 4.1** on page 87 for an example of a well-written business letter.) Follow basic grammar and punctuation rules when you write. Be sure to use the spell check and grammar check features on the computer to check your writing. It is also a good idea to have someone else proofread your letters before you send them. Your writing style forms a first impression of you and your business for the person reading it.

Reading Skills

Reading is an important skill both on and off the job. Much of the information you receive from the world around you comes through reading. In foodservice, you will use reading skills every day to:

- Prepare food by reading ingredient labels and recipes or formulas.
- Operate foodservice equipment by reading instruction manuals and safety precautions.
- Serve customers by reading menus and specials lists.
- Carry out general job responsibilities by reading workplace policies and communications.

To read well, you will need to develop good reading skills. You will use these basic reading skills on the job:

- **Preview** Before you read anything, read any headlines and subheads to get an overview. This will give you an idea of the topics that are to come.
- **Skim** Always look for key points when you read. This is called skimming.
- **Focus** After you have previewed or skimmed material, give your full attention to what you read. Think about what you are reading. See if you can answer questions that you have as you read.

⤙ Small Bites ⤚

Thinking Skills Foodservice employees also need analytical thinking skills. Decision-making skills are necessary to successfully face new situations. Critical thinking and problem solving skills will help you to respond to accidents and prevent emergencies.

- **Visualize** If the text is not illustrated, imagine a set of pictures or charts that would accompany what you read. This will help you understand the content.
- **Check** Ask yourself how well you understand what you read. If there are words you do not understand, look them up in a dictionary.

Reading Check **Give Examples** What are some ways in which cooks use math skills?

Work Ethic

In addition to basic skills, employers look for certain key **qualities**, or distinguishing characteristics, in their employees. A person who has these qualities usually has a strong work ethic. A **work ethic** is a personal commitment to doing your very best as part of the team. Employees who have a good work ethic are often successful in their careers. With practice, you can develop the qualities that help create a strong work ethic.

Responsibility

Being responsible is one of the most important qualities you can have for success in any job. **Responsibility** is your ability to be aware of what a particular situation demands of you. Responsible employees show up for work on time and work diligently to become familiar with job duties and do them correctly. When you are responsible, you accept the consequences of your choices and actions instead of blaming others for any mistakes you make.

READING CHECK ANSWER Cooks use math skills to adjust recipe yields, weigh ingredients, and adjust cooking times and temperatures.

Flexibility

In today's rapidly changing work environment, flexibility is very important. **Flexibility** is the ability to adapt willingly to changing circumstances. Being flexible means that you adjust to changes without complaining. It also means that you are willing to learn new techniques and skills. You will find it easier to be flexible if you are confident in your skills.

Honesty

Honesty is another important part of a strong work ethic. You practice **honesty** on the job when you are truthful and loyal in your words and actions. For example, if you make a mistake on the job, do not cover it up or blame someone else. Instead, admit to your mistake and find out how to prevent making the same mistake in the future. This quality is always appreciated by employers.

Reliability

Reliability (ri-ˌlī-ə-ˈbi-lə-ˈtē) is an extension of responsibility. You are **reliable** when other people can count on you to do what you say that you will do. When you show reliability on the job, you help the business to succeed.

Reliable people are more likely to advance on the job. A reliable employee is someone who:

- Arrives at work on time.
- Keeps personal matters separate from business matters.
- Works a full shift.
- Carries out a variety of assigned tasks without constant prompting.
- Takes on extra work when necessary without complaint.
- Gets enough rest to work effectively.
- Maintains good personal physical and mental health.

Teamwork

As a foodservice worker, you will often be part of a large team. A winning team, however, is more than just a collection of talented people. If you have ever played a team sport, you know how important it is that every member participates, no matter what their skill level is. When you learn to effectively communicate, resolve conflicts, and develop negotiation skills, it is called **teamwork**. A star player must support his or her teammates throughout the game. You can practice teamwork on the job when you work to support the efforts of your coworkers.

Work Together Teamwork is part of every job. *How might you demonstrate teamwork in a foodservice setting?*

PHOTO CAPTION ANSWER Answers will vary, but may include helping each other at preparation and cooking stations, serving customers as a team, helping cover empty shifts, and sharing information.

Commitment

Commitment is the dedication that you show to doing something. Commitment is the quality that supports all your abilities and skills to build a strong work ethic. Demonstrating commitment will set you apart as a valuable employee. You show a commitment to excellence when you display good business etiquette and always do your best.

Quality

A commitment to quality means that you always do work you are proud of. In foodservice, a commitment to quality means that you use quality ingredients, prepare and serve them in the most pleasing way and you serve customers to the best of your ability. You strive for the highest standards.

Excellence

Employees who are committed to excellence strive to do their very best at all times, no matter what job they are doing. They make the most of opportunities to improve their abilities and learn new skills. People who are committed to excellence are not willing to settle for work that is simply good enough.

Reading Check Explain What does it mean to have a commitment to quality?

Leadership Skills

Besides basic skills and a strong work ethic, employers also look for employees who have leadership skills. **Leadership** is the ability to motivate others to cooperate in doing a common task. Leadership is a quality every employee should practice.

Leadership Organizations

You do not need to wait until you are employed to develop leadership skills. Many organizations and programs help students develop leadership skills. Two such organizations are FCCLA and SkillsUSA. (See **Figure 4.2**.)

FIGURE 4.2 **Leadership Organizations**
Professional Programs Many student organizations, such as FCCLA and SkillsUSA, can help culinary students develop leadership skills. *How do you think they help develop leadership skills?*

Family, Career and Community Leaders of America (FCCLA)

FCCLA is a national organization of middle and high school students who take family and consumer sciences courses. FCCLA activities and skill events provide opportunities to develop leadership skills. One FCCLA program, Leaders at Work, is for students who work in food production and services or hospitality and tourism. Students can create projects to strengthen their communication, interpersonal, management, and entrepreneurship skills.

Students also can participate in challenging competitions such as the STAR (Students Taking Action with Recognition) events. Members may compete in areas such as culinary arts, entrepreneurship, and interpersonal communications.

SkillsUSA

SkillsUSA is a national organization of high school and college students who are enrolled in training programs for technical, skilled, and service occupations. SkillsUSA programs team up students with industry professionals to provide the SkillsUSA Championships.

Foodservice students can compete in contests for culinary arts and commercial baking.

Students are judged on technical skills, sanitation and food safety practices, food quality, and their creative presentation. Students can also compete in food and beverage service. Competitors demonstrate skills in table setting, greeting guests, taking reservations, menu presentations, and meal service.

Professional Organizations

Professional foodservice organizations can help foodservice employees sharpen their skills. Employees can also learn about new foodservice trends. Many professional organizations sponsor conventions and classes. There are organizations for all parts of the foodservice industry, including cooking, baking, and management. Some professional organizations include:

- International Association of Culinary Professionals
- American Culinary Federation
- American Institute of Baking
- National Restaurant Association
- U.S. Pastry Alliance
- Research Chefs Association

Use Resources Effectively

A **resource** is a raw material with which you do your work. It is up to you to make the best use of these resources and to avoid wasting them. The key resources are time, energy, money, things, and people.

You can use time effectively if you perform activities quickly and carefully. You can also learn to **prioritize**, or put things in order of importance. The world of food service is fast-paced. Time is your most limited resource. It is important to use your time well.

Use personal energy resources effectively. Get the right amount of rest, nutrition, and health care to do your job well.

Whenever you do a job that costs or earns money for your employer, you have an opportunity to practice leadership. If you are responsible for making purchases, look for good value for the money. If you receive money in payment, be careful and honest.

The materials, equipment, and tools used during your job are resources. Use supplies properly and carefully. Immediately report any damage to equipment and supplies. Always take care of your uniform, tools, supplies, and work area.

The foodservice industry has rushed service times preceded by slower preparation periods. You waste people resources when you perform your job so poorly that someone else has to redo the work.

Use Information Effectively

Information comes at you from countless sources. On the job, you will need to gather, use, and share information. You will also need to decide which resources are best for the job you must do.

Gather Information

Information that is useful for your job is everywhere. You can get information from newspaper headlines, radio and TV news bulletins, and the Internet. Learn the difference between useful information and idle chatter, false statements, and misleading opinions. Be careful when you gather information from the Internet. Some Web sites contain false information. Reliable information comes from known sources, such as government agencies or businesses.

Use and Share Information

Information by itself is worthless until you use it. You show leadership when you can gather, understand, evaluate and use information in a way that benefits your business and does not harm others.

Do not keep important information to yourself. The whole team benefits when you share knowledge that you have learned. Effective leaders share information with their team members and with other managers. They also recognize the difference between sharing useful information and spreading negative information, such as gossip, that can hurt others.

Use Technology Effectively

You will encounter and use computer technology in foodservice. However, technology is a resource. It is not a replacement for a skilled employee. You can learn to use technology effectively as a resource. This can mean knowing how to operate a point-of-sales computer system or an entire automated production line. The technology you will operate depends on your job. All kinds of cooking equipment, such as thermometers and convection ovens, use improved technology.

Here are some tips to keep in mind:

- **Apply Basic Computer Skills** You can adapt your knowledge of standard computer software to use foodservice computer technology. Computer use ranges from entering restaurant orders and tracking inventory to running automated food production equipment and converting recipes.

- **Respect Computer Resources** If your employer provides you with access to a computer, use it for business purposes only. Personal e-mail, Web surfing, online chatting, and computer games are inappropriate at work.

- **Use Your Own Skills** Computers can help with many aspects of work and running a business. But do not expect computers to do your job. Computer technology can help you, but a computer cannot think or solve problems. Be sure your basic skills are strong enough to **compensate**, or make up for the lack of something, when the computer system goes down. Commit yourself to learn and maintain the technological processes that apply to your job.

 Reading Check **Explain** What are some sources where you can gather information?

 SECTION 4.1 **After You Read**

Review Key Concepts

1. **Describe** three important math skills needed to work in the foodservice industry.
2. **List** the characteristics of a reliable employee.
3. **Identify** key resources a leader must use to be successful.

Practice Culinary Academics

English Language Arts

4. Imagine that you have been asked to lead a foodservice team that will prepare and serve refreshments for an upcoming school event. Create a flyer to attract volunteers for your team. The flyer should list the qualities you want in team members to help you carry out your task. It should also contain information about the event, and the food that will be prepared. Use graphics on your flyer, if possible, to make it more attractive.

> **NCTE 12** Use language to accomplish individual purposes.

Mathematics

5. One of your customers asks for her check. If she ordered $86.25 worth of food and drinks, and the local sales tax is 8¼ percent, what is the amount of sales tax due?

Math Concept **Converting Percentages to Decimals** Find the percent of a number by converting the percentage to a decimal and multiplying by that number. If the percentage includes a fraction, convert the fraction to a decimal first.

Starting Hint Rewrite 8¼ percent as 8.25%. Convert 8.25% to a decimal by removing the percent sign and moving the decimal point two places to the left (0.0825). Multiply 0.0825 by $86.25 to determine the tax due.

> **NCTM Number and Operations** Compute fluently and make reasonable estimates.

 Check your answers at this book's Online Learning Center at **glencoe.com**.

READING CHECK ANSWER Information can come from newspaper headlines, radio and TV news bulletins, and the Internet.

Seeking Employment

Sharpen your skills to find the right foodservice job for you.

Reading Guide

 Before You Read

Create an Outline Use this section's heading titles to create an outline. Turn the titles into Level 1 main ideas. Add supporting information to create Level 2, 3, and 4 details. Use the outline to predict what you are about to learn.

Read to Learn

Key Concepts
- **Identify** sources for foodservice job leads.
- **Illustrate** the proper skills to apply for a foodservice job.

Main Idea

Getting a job in the foodservice industry means sorting through many different options. This section will make you familiar with how to seek and apply for a job.

Content Vocabulary
- networking
- trade publication
- employment agency
- job lead
- résumé
- job application
- job portfolio
- job interview
- keyword

Academic Vocabulary
- suitable
- nature

ACADEMIC STANDARDS

 English Language Arts
NCTE 12 Use language to accomplish individual purposes.

 Mathematics
NCTM Number and Operations Understand numbers, ways of representing numbers, relationships among numbers, and number systems.

 Social Studies
NCSS V A Individuals, Groups, and Institutions Apply concepts such as role, status, and social class in describing the connections and interactions of individuals, groups, and institutions in society.

NCSS VI E Production, Distribution, and Consumption Analyze the role of specialization and exchange in economic processes.

NCTE National Council of Teachers of English

NCTM National Council of Teachers of Mathematics

NSES National Science Education Standards

NCSS National Council for the Social Studies

Graphic Organizer

As you read, use a web diagram like the one below to list the six actions you should take during an interview for a job.

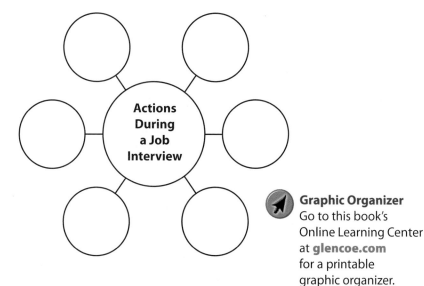

Actions During a Job Interview

Graphic Organizer Go to this book's Online Learning Center at **glencoe.com** for a printable graphic organizer.

GRAPHIC ORGANIZER ANSWER Shake hands, make eye contact, speak clearly, use good office manners, answer thoughtfully and completely, and ask questions.

Find Foodservice Employment

Your culinary career begins with your first foodservice job. Finding your first foodservice job will involve sorting through options, however. You may enter foodservice as a server in a restaurant or a counter worker in a bakery. This section will help you understand how to seek and apply for a job in the foodservice industry.

Employment in the foodservice industry is growing. The foodservice industry employs more people than any other private employment segment in the country. According to the National Restaurant Association, more than 13.1 million people in the United States prepare and serve food for a living. Total U.S. sales in foodservice are more than $558 billion annually. The foodservice industry continues to grow at a steady rate. Dining out is more popular than ever. All of this makes foodservice an ideal career choice. There are many entry-level jobs available. Opportunities for advancement are almost unlimited.

Where can you find out about foodservice job openings? Many first-time job seekers may believe that newspaper classified ads are the only place where they can search for a job. It is true that foodservice jobs are frequently listed in the newspaper. However, there are many other resources that also list foodservice job opportunities.

Job Sources

There are many resources available where you can find information about foodservice job openings. Successful job seekers will use all available resources in their communities. This broadens the opportunities they can find for successful employment.

Networking

If you have ever followed up on a job tip that you received from a family member or a friend, you have practiced networking.

Job Support Culinary experts can give you advice and support as you learn new skills. *From what other sources can you receive advice and support in your career?*

Networking means making use of all of your personal connections to reach your career goals. When you ask for job information from people you know, you will be more informed and confident when you apply for those jobs. Networking is the most direct way to find a job. Besides networking with your family members and relatives, there are other people with whom you can network.

Your network can also include:

- **Friends and Classmates** Other people who are interested in culinary arts also will be doing research to find foodservice jobs. They may be willing to share some of their information with you.
- **Teachers and Mentors** Teachers and mentors are adults who already know you. They are familiar with your strengths. They can give you advice on how to make use of those strengths on the job.

PHOTO CAPTION ANSWER You can receive advice and support from friends and classmates, teachers, employers, coworkers, school and professional organizations, and trade publications and books.

- **Employers and Coworkers** If you already have a job, your workplace also may be a source of information about job openings. Many companies list internal job opportunities and advancement opportunities before they tell the general public. Your coworkers may also know about job openings.
- **Organizations** School organizations, such as FCCLA and SkillsUSA, can help put you in contact with other members. These members may know about foodservice job openings that are available in your area. Community organizations also can provide networking information. Collect business cards as you network so that you can contact them in the future.

When you network, be courteous. Do not pressure people for information. Every reference you receive through networking is a personal gift. Treat it with respect. If you are given a job lead by someone you know, follow up on the lead in a responsible manner. Be on time for job interviews. Return phone calls and always present yourself professionally. Your dress, communication skills, and behavior reflect not only on you, but also on the person who recommended you. If you become aware of job information, share it with the members of your network.

Professional Organizations

You can find foodservice job openings through professional organizations. These organizations are made up of people employed in a field. They network on a state, national, or international level. Professional culinary organizations focus on the industry in general or on specialized areas such as baking.

Usually, you must pay a membership fee to join a professional organization. The benefits of being a member can outweigh the money you spend on the fee. Professional organizations offer publications, job listings, job placement services, scholarships, and network opportunities.

Foodservice jobs listed with professional organizations are usually higher paying jobs that require more skill than those listed in the local newspaper.

Trade Publications

You can extend your foodservice job search resources if you read culinary trade publications. A **trade publication** is a magazine or newsletter produced by and for members of the foodservice industry. They contain helpful articles on all parts of the industry. Most of them also have sections where employers can list job openings. Subscriptions to many trade publications are often included as part of a membership in professional organizations. Some of these trade publications can also be found in public libraries or on the Internet.

A TASTE OF HISTORY ANSWER Answers should include the proper age, details of the skills to be learned, and room and board arrangements.

Employment Agencies

One option is to use an employment agency to help with your job search. An **employment agency** is a business that puts employers in touch with potential employees. Employment agencies keep lists of foodservice job openings. You may be able to place your résumé with an employment agency. Most employment agencies charge fees for their services.

The Internet

You can use the Internet to access employment resources and look for foodservice jobs. You can also:
- Network with others.
- Contact professional foodservice organizations.
- Check out online versions of trade publications.
- Register your résumé with online employment agencies.

Keep your foodservice job search notes in a job file. Use a computer file or a set of index cards to record and review job information you receive. An entry in your job file is a **job lead** or possible employment opportunity. Keep a record of each source where you found job leads. (See **Figure 4.3** on page 97.)

Telephone Leads

Your job leads may include listings that give phone numbers and ask you to call for more information. When you make a phone call for a foodservice job lead, follow these guidelines:
- Call the number you have been given.
- Tell the person who answers the phone that you are calling in response to a job opening. He or she will direct your call to the contact person.
- When you are connected to the contact person, greet him or her politely and give your name and the name of the job opening you are interested in. If you were referred by someone, mention that person's name when you first introduce yourself.

- The contact person will tell you about the next steps in the application process. Write notes about the application process. These may include asking you to send a letter of application and a résumé (ˈre-zə-ˌmā). A **résumé** is a summary of your career objectives, work experience, job qualifications, education, and training. The contact person may offer to send you a job application or set up an appointment to meet. A **job application** is a form that employers use to collect personal information and previous work experience from job applicants.
- Write down all steps you are given. Repeat it back to the contact person to make sure you understand everything. Ask questions if necessary.
- Ask any questions you may have about the application process for the company. Answer any questions the contact person asks you.
- Thank the contact person for his or her time.

Apply for a Job

If you have found several good job leads, rank the possible jobs in order of your preference. Apply for the job you want most first.

The first step is usually to request, complete, and return a job application. Some job leads may require you to begin the application process with a telephone call. Other job leads will ask you to contact the employer by mail. If this is the case, you will send a letter of application and a résumé.

You will also want to create a job portfolio. A **job portfolio** is a collection of papers and samples that can be given to a potential employer. Your foodservice job portfolio should include:
- A résumé
- A letter of application
- A letter of reference
- A list of references that employers can call for more information about you
- A health record
- A copy of your Social Security card

Job Lead

Job: *Kitchen Worker*

Key Details: *35 hours per week, mostly evenings and weekends, on-the-job training provided*

Employer: *The Limberlost Restaurant*

Contact Person: *Maria Smith, Kitchen Manager*

Source of Lead: *Mike Smith, neighbor*

Next Steps: *Complete and return job application by October 25*

◀ **FIGURE 4.3 Job Leads**
Finding Work Job leads are usually specific about whom to contact and what skills are needed for the position. *What steps would you take to apply for this job?*

The second step to getting the job you want will be to secure a job interview. A **job interview** is a formal meeting between you and your potential employer. It is important to perform each step of the job application process in a polite and professional manner.

Job Applications

Make a good professional first impression. Do not walk into a potential workplace, even to ask for an application, unless your clothing is neat and appropriate and you are clean and well groomed. Remember that first impressions are usually lasting.

Filling out an application form is usually the first step. You need to know how to fill out a job application form correctly and completely.

Job application forms vary, but they all ask for the same kinds of information. Keep these tips in mind when you fill out a job application:
- Print neatly, and use blue or black ink. Use cursive handwriting for your signature only.
- Read the instructions to complete each blank space on the application before you respond. Try not to make errors. If you need to correct something, draw a neat line through what you need to correct and write the correct response.

- Carry important information with you. This includes your Social Security number, your driver's license number, and the names, addresses, and phone numbers of previous employers. It can create a poor impression to leave incomplete information in this portion of the application.
- Do not leave any part of the application form blank unless you are asked to do so. If a question does not apply to you, write "NA" or "not applicable" in the space provided. Employers will not consider applications that are not complete.
- Always tell the truth on an application. Submitting false information on a job application is illegal. You can be fired, and even prosecuted, for submitting false information.

Prepare Your Résumé

Your résumé is a very important tool for job seeking. It gives a prospective employer the information he or she needs to decide if you are **suitable**, or have the right qualifications, for a particular job. Choose the work experience, skills, and education or training that shows you are the best candidate for the job. Always be truthful and accurate.

FIGURE CAPTION ANSWER You would prepare a résumé with your skills and experience, write a cover letter, complete the job application, and return all the items to the contact person by the deadline of October 25.

Use these guidelines to prepare your résumé:

- Keep your résumé short.
- Stress foodservice education, training, work experience, and basic key skills, if you have any.
- Include your career objective. This is a short sentence that describes what you hope to do as a career.
- Use correct spelling and grammar. Use spell check and grammar check on your computer to check your work.
- Present your résumé on good-quality paper.
- Do not use decorative graphics and pictures.
- Include the right contact information.
- Use keywords to describe your work experience. A **keyword** is a word that makes it easier for employers to search for important information. Your résumé should contain keywords such as foodservice, restaurant, or baking. This makes is easier for employers with foodservice opportunities to find your résumé during an electronic search.

Write Letters

When you respond to a job lead in writing, you must write an effective letter of request or a cover letter to go along with your résumé. Use spell check and grammar check on your computer before you send a letter.

Letter of Request Write a letter of request when you need to ask a potential employer for an application form or for an interview. Include a brief summary of your education, and experience in the letter. A letter of request can also be written to networking contacts to request a reference. Always be polite, and keep your tone professional.

Cover Letter Write a cover letter when a job lead asks you to send a written response. Your cover letter should introduce you to the prospective employer without repeating the information that is already on your résumé. (See **Figure 4.4** on page 99.)

Reading Check Determine When should you write a cover letter to a potential employer?

READING CHECK ANSWER Write a cover letter when a job lead asks you to send a written response.

The Interview Process

Once you have completed the application process and have been asked to come in for an interview, you will need to prepare for your job interview. At an interview, you will have the chance to convince an employer that you are the right person for the job that is available. An employer will evaluate you by your appearance, attitude, and the answers you give to his or her questions. Sometimes the interview also includes having a meal with the employer. Remember to demonstrate good table manners. How you present yourself during the interview shows how you will behave in different situations.

Before the Interview

The interview process begins when an employer sets an appointment for your interview. Write down the date, time, and place of the interview. Double-check the information.

Do Your Homework

The more you know about the potential employer and the job opportunity, the better you will do during the interview. Check community business publications, local newspapers, Internet directories, or professional organizations for information about the business. Find out how large the business is, how profitable it has been, and what its plans for the future may be. Make notes about what you learn.

Choose Appropriate Clothing

A potential employer's first impression of you will be based on your appearance. Choose clothing that is appropriate for the workplace, that fits properly and is clean, pressed, and in good condition. Your personal grooming habits can make or break a job interview. You and your clothes should be clean, your hair should be well trimmed and conservatively styled, and your fingernails should be clean and neatly trimmed.

FIGURE 4.4 Cover Letters

Introduce Yourself Writing a professional letter to a prospective employer can make you more marketable. *What elements make this letter professional, rather than casual?*

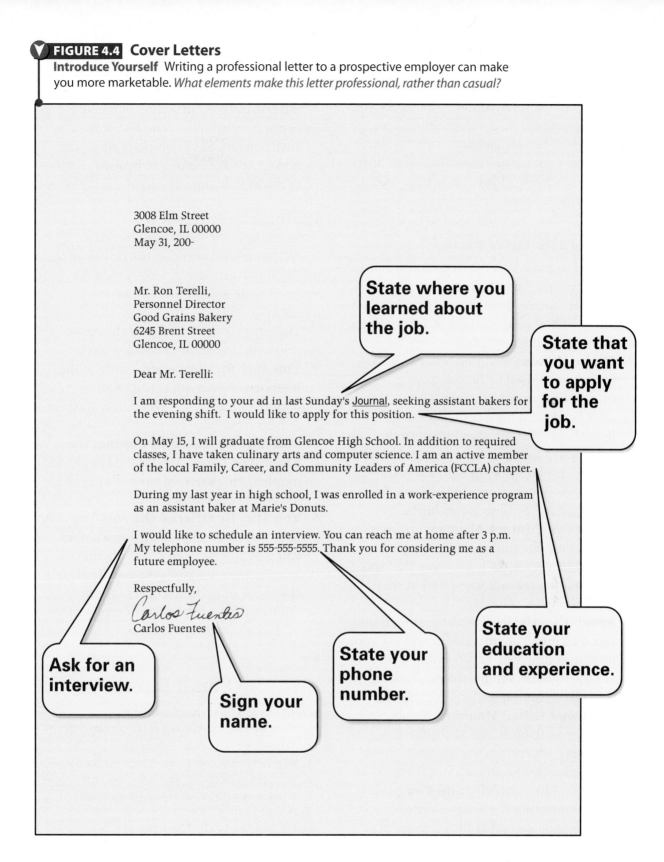

3008 Elm Street
Glencoe, IL 00000
May 31, 200-

Mr. Ron Terelli,
Personnel Director
Good Grains Bakery
6245 Brent Street
Glencoe, IL 00000

Dear Mr. Terelli:

I am responding to your ad in last Sunday's Journal, seeking assistant bakers for the evening shift. I would like to apply for this position.

On May 15, I will graduate from Glencoe High School. In addition to required classes, I have taken culinary arts and computer science. I am an active member of the local Family, Career, and Community Leaders of America (FCCLA) chapter.

During my last year in high school, I was enrolled in a work-experience program as an assistant baker at Marie's Donuts.

I would like to schedule an interview. You can reach me at home after 3 p.m. My telephone number is 555-555-5555. Thank you for considering me as a future employee.

Respectfully,

Carlos Fuentes
Carlos Fuentes

State where you learned about the job.

State that you want to apply for the job.

State your education and experience.

State your phone number.

Sign your name.

Ask for an interview.

FIGURE CAPTION ANSWER Answers may include using the greeting "Dear Mr. Terelli," proper grammar and spelling, using a space between each paragraph, use of the formal ending, and a full signature.

Be Prompt and Courteous

On the day of the interview, allow yourself plenty of time to locate the interview place. It is best to arrive a few minutes early. As you introduce yourself to a receptionist, host, or other person before meeting with the interviewer, be polite and respectful. The interviewer may check with these people later to see how you behaved.

During the Interview

The interview is very important. You will do well if you are prepared, positive, and relaxed. Remember, business etiquette is like the good manners that should be used at home. Keep the following points in mind:

- **Shake Hands** The interviewer will introduce himself or herself to you. Introduce yourself in return, and offer your hand for a firm, confident handshake. Remain standing until the interviewer asks you to be seated. He or she will probably begin with a few simple questions or comments to help you feel more at ease. Smiling never hurts.

- **Make Eye Contact** Maintain eye contact throughout the interview. Eye contact with the interviewer helps show that you are listening and are interested in what the interviewer is saying.

- **Speak Clearly** Use correct grammar and speak clearly. The interviewer will ask you questions designed to determine if you are the right person for the job. Answer the interviewer's questions completely.

- **Use Good Office Manners** Sit up straight, with both feet on the floor. Avoid nervous gestures, such as tapping. Never chew gum during an interview.

- **Answer Thoughtfully and Completely** Do not interrupt the interviewer or become sidetracked as the interviewer speaks. If you do not understand a question, ask the interviewer for clarification. If you do not know the answer, say so politely.

- **Ask Questions** The interview process is meant to help you get information, too. Ask the interviewer about the **nature**, or basic structure, of the job, your responsibilities, and the work environment. Save questions about the rate of pay and employee benefits, such as vacation time, for the end of the interview.

Ending the Interview

Regardless of how the interview ends, thank the interviewer for his or her time. A professional attitude accompanied by good manners will always be remembered. Shake hands as you leave.

The interviewer will signal the end of the interview in one of the following ways:

- **You May Be Contacted Later** If the interviewer does not specify a time period, politely ask, "When may I expect to hear from you?"

- **You May Be Asked to Contact the Employer Later** Ask for the telephone number, the preferred time to call, and the contact person's name.

- **You May Be Offered the Job** You may be asked to decide right away whether you will take the job. If you are unsure, ask the interviewer if you may think about the offer. If this option is offered, follow up by responding promptly.

⌒ Small Bites ⌒

Common Job Interview Questions
Some questions you can expect to be asked in a job interview include:

1. Why would you like to work for this company?
2. What are your qualifications for this job?
3. What are your strengths and weaknesses?
4. Why did you leave your last job?
5. Tell me about a challenge you met or a problem you solved in school or on the job.

Prepare answers to these common questions ahead of time so you can make a good impression during an interview.

Interview Skills The job interview is your chance to make a good impression. *How can your manners affect an employer's decision to hire you?*

- **You May Not Be Offered the Job** Do not be discouraged if you are turned down for a job. You may not have the right skills, or the employer may have found another applicant who is more suited to the job. The interviewer is under no obligation to tell you why you are not being offered the job. Accept the decision gracefully.

After the Interview

The interview process does not end when the interview is over. After each job interview, you have the following responsibilities to the potential employer:

- **Send a Thank-You Letter** The day after the interview, send the interviewer a letter to thank him or her for the interview. Do this even if you have been turned down for the job. Be sure the employer's correct address and the right amount of postage are on the envelope. This is good business etiquette.

- **Follow Up** If you have been asked to contact the employer, do so at the specified time. Send or deliver any information, such as references, that you have agreed to supply. If the employer has promised to contact you, wait the specified amount of time. If this time passes, telephone the employer and politely request information about the status of your application. You may be asked to provide more information.

- **Review the Session** As soon as possible after the interview, go over the session in your mind. Think about the first impression that you made. Make notes on anything you think you might do to improve during your next job interview. List any key information, such as employer expectations and job responsibilities, for this job. Write out any unanswered questions you have about the job. You may be able to ask these questions at a later time during a second interview.

PHOTO CAPTION ANSWER If your manners are poor, the employer may assume that you will act improperly, or will not fit into a team environment.

Job Offer Responses

When you receive a job offer from a potential employer, you have three options available to you as a response:

- **Accept the Offer** The employer will give you information on when you can begin work. You may be asked to participate in employee orientation or a training session before formally beginning your job. The employer will usually set up another interview. At this second interview, you will be given specific details on pay, benefits, schedules, and other job expectations. This is a good time for you to ask specific details about your work.

- **Ask for Time to Consider** This is the time to ask any unanswered questions that might affect your decision. With the employer, come to an agreement on when you will notify him or her of your decision. Do not put off responding to the employer.

- **Turn Down the Job Offer** You may decide that the job is not right for you. Or, perhaps you have been offered a better job in the meantime. If you do not intend to take the position that has been offered, say so. You do not need to give reasons for turning down a job offer. Simply say to the contact person, "Thank you for considering me, but I am not interested in taking the position." Always remain polite. There may come a time when you will meet the contact person again.

 Reading Check List What are the steps that you should take after a job interview?

SECTION 4.2 After You Read

Review Key Concepts

1. **Identify** potential networking sources.
2. **Describe** the proper way to fill out an application.

Practice Culinary Academics

 English Language Arts

3. Follow your teacher's instructions to form pairs. Role-play a job interview between an employer and a prospective employee. Then, switch roles. Give a short presentation on what behaviors made the most difference from each perspective.

> **NCTE 12** Use language to accomplish individual purposes.

Social Studies

4. Re-read "A Taste of History: On-the-Job Training" from this section. As a class, discuss the impact of apprenticeship on the foodservice industry and how apprenticeships are used today to benefit individuals in the foodservice industry.

> **NCSS VI E Production, Distribution, and Consumption**
> Analyze the role of specialization and exchange in economic processes.

Mathematics

5. You receive a job through an employment agency that charges a fee equal to 10% of your first month's wages. If you make $12.50 per hour, and work 160 hours your first month, what is the total fee?

Math Concept **Converting Percentages to Fractions** Since a percentage represents a ratio of a number to 100, every percentage can be rewritten as a fraction with 100 as the denominator and the percentage as the numerator.

Starting Hint Rewrite 10% as a fraction ($\frac{10}{100}$) and simplify to $\frac{1}{10}$. Multiply this fraction by the total first month's wages earned ($12.50 per hour × 160 hours) to determine the total fee due.

> **NCTM Number and Operations** Understand numbers, ways of representing numbers, relationships among numbers, and number systems.

 Check your answers at this book's Online Learning Center at **glencoe.com**.

On the Job

Reading Guide

Before You Read

Prepare with a Partner Before you read, work with a partner. Read the titles of the heads and ask each other questions about the topics that will be discussed. Write down the questions you both have about each section. As you read, answer the questions you have identified.

Read to Learn
Key Concepts
- **Summarize** the rights and responsibilities of employees and employers.
- **Explain** the differences between tips, deductions, and benefits.

Main Idea
Employees have certain rights guaranteed to them. They also have responsibilities to their employer. If you work well, you may gain opportunities for advancement.

Graphic Organizer
Use a KWL chart like the one below to keep track of your knowledge of working in the foodservice industry. Fill out what you already know in the first column. Read the section headings and write down what you want to know more about in the second column. After you have read the section, write down what you have learned in the third column.

Content Vocabulary
- evaluation
- initiative
- workers' compensation
- repetitive stress injury
- minimum wage
- compensatory time
- labor union
- discrimination
- probation
- empathy
- ethics
- gross pay
- deduction
- net pay
- tip
- benefits

Academic Vocabulary
- outline
- field

ACADEMIC STANDARDS

English Language Arts
NCTE 4 Use written language to communicate effectively.

Mathematics
NCTM Number and Operations Compute fluently and make reasonable estimates.

NCTM Problem Solving Solve problems that arise in mathematics and in other contexts.

Social Studies
NCSS X B Civic Ideals and Practices Identify, analyze, interpret, and evaluate sources and examples of citizens' rights and responsibilities.

NCTE National Council of Teachers of English

NCTM National Council of Teachers of Mathematics

NSES National Science Education Standards

NCSS National Council for the Social Studies

Employee Responsibilities on the Job

What I Know	What I Want to Know	What I Have Learned

Graphic Organizer Go to this book's Online Learning Center at **glencoe.com** for a printable graphic organizer.

GRAPHIC ORGANIZER ANSWER Students' charts will vary based on their previous experience and knowledge.

Rights and Responsibilities

It does not matter whether a job makes you part of a large workforce or of a small business. When you accept a job, you enter into a relationship. As an employee, you must maintain a good relationship between yourself and your employer. Both you and your employer have rights and responsibilities. Specific expectations and work rules will be explained to you by your employer when you begin your job.

In this section, you will learn about your rights as an employee and your responsibilities to your employer. You will learn about wages, taxes, and benefits. You will practice the skills you need to get along with coworkers on the job. You will also identify some of the qualities that you will need to advance in the foodservice industry.

Employee Responsibilities

As an employee, your main responsibility is to do the very best job possible for your employer. This means that you must be responsible, reliable, flexible, and honest. It also means that you must use job resources correctly and efficiently.

There are several ways for you to carry out your responsibilities:

- Show up for work when you are scheduled, and be on time for work. Stay at work for your full shift, or the specified hours of employment. Return promptly from designated breaks and meal periods.
- Use your work time responsibly. Keep busy on the job. Do not waste time chatting with coworkers. Never use company time or resources for personal business.
- Respect the business by learning and following your employer's rules, regulations, and policies. You will probably be given an employee handbook. Once you review the policies, you may be asked to sign a statement that says

▼ FIGURE 4.5 Culinary Advancement Opportunities

Move Up There are many job advancement opportunities in a professional kitchen. *Which of the jobs listed in the table are service-related?*

From	To
Server	Head server
Busser	Server
Dishwasher	Kitchen helper
Counter worker	Assistant manager
Host	Server
Dining room supervisor	Banquet captain
Cafeteria attendant	Cafeteria supervisor
Short-order cook	Line cook
Kitchen worker	Pantry supervisor
Baker's assistant	Baker
Cook	Sous chef
Caterer or chef	Restaurant owner
Prep cook	Line cook
Garde manger	Caterer
Pastry cook	Pastry chef
Line cook	Sous chef
Sous chef	Executive chef
Executive chef	Corporate chef

that you understand them. If you are in doubt about a company policy, ask your employer any questions.

- Work safely and familiarize yourself with the safety requirements of your job. Learn how to operate and maintain equipment safely. Report any unsafe conditions or practices to your supervisor immediately.
- Maintain a positive, enthusiastic attitude. Be polite and respectful to supervisors, other employees, and customers. Follow directions that you are given. Accept constructive criticism, and try to work your best without constant supervision.
- Complete each task that you are assigned. Keep your work area neat and well organized. Use company resources efficiently and responsibly.

FIGURE CAPTION ANSWER Service-related: Server, head server, busser, counter worker, assistant manager, dining room supervisor, banquet captain.

🔺 **Safety First** Performing your work safely protects you and your employer. *What other responsibilities do employees have on the job?*

Advance on the Job

Foodservice jobs offer many ways to advance. Advancement may come as a job promotion. Advancement also may include getting more responsibilities at the same job level. Sometimes, advancement may involve leaving your current workplace for a better job elsewhere, or beginning your own business. (See **Figure 4.5**.)

You will know how well you perform your job through evaluations that you receive from your employer. An **evaluation** is a written report of how well you have performed your duties, and what you can do to improve. You can use this information to make yourself ready for advancement.

Two qualities that will help you advance in your career are initiative and the desire to learn. The willingness to take on new tasks and levels of responsibility shows initiative (i-ˌni-shə-tiv). **Initiative** is the energy required to begin new tasks and see them through to completion. Workers with initiative do not wait to be told by their employers what to do

next. They seek ways to improve their on-the-job performance.

The desire to learn is also important. Continue your education or training through formal classes, workshops, or independent study. Be excited about the opportunity to learn and practice new workplace skills.

Employer Responsibilities

The employer-employee relationship goes both ways. Your employer has responsibilities to you, too. Your employer's main responsibility is to make sure that you are paid fairly for the work that you do. Your employer is also responsible to:

● Supply what you need to do your job.
● Provide you with safe working conditions.
● Make sure that you are treated fairly.

Your employer will **outline**, or describe in a basic way, what your job responsibilities and expectations are. You also may be offered on-the-job training. If you have any questions about your job duties, ask your supervisor.

PHOTO CAPTION ANSWER Answers may vary, but should include using time responsibly by showing up on time for a shift and staying busy on the job, learning and following an employer's rules and policies, and completing tasks as assigned.

Safe Working Conditions

Federal, state, and local regulations require your employer to provide you with safe working conditions. Your employer must:

- Eliminate any known health and safety hazards in the workplace.
- Provide you with the equipment and materials that are necessary for you to do your job safely.
- Let you know when job conditions or hazardous materials create a danger to your health and safety.
- Keep accurate records of job-related illnesses and injuries.
- Comply with environmental protection policies to safely dispose of waste materials.

Workers' Compensation

If you are injured on the job and cannot work, your employer has a legal responsibility to provide financial help. **Workers' compensation** is insurance that pays for medical expenses and lost wages if you are injured on the job. Your employer is required to pay for this insurance.

Preventing injuries is another important responsibility for your employer. For example, employers have supported research into common workplace injuries. One of these injuries is a **repetitive stress injury**, which can happen to employees who must perform the same motions over and over. Repetitive stress injuries can potentially disable an employee. Your employer should periodically evaluate the workplace to make sure that it is as safe as possible from injury. Some employers also offer information and classes on avoiding injury in the workplace.

Fair Labor Practices

Your employer has a legal responsibility to protect you from unfair treatment on the job. The federal government has passed laws to protect workers. U.S. labor laws are meant to protect the following rights of employees as they work at their jobs:

- To have an equal opportunity to find and keep employment, regardless of age, gender, race, ethnicity, religion, physical appearance, disability, or other factors.
- To be paid a fair wage.
- To be considered fairly for promotion, based on your skills and past performance.
- To be protected in times of personal and economic change.

Employers must pay their employees at least the federal minimum wage. The **minimum wage** is the lowest hourly amount a worker can earn. Some states have their own minimum wages. An employer must pay employees whichever minimum wage rate is higher. Some businesses pay employees a higher minimum wage than the federal government requires. Employers must compensate employees who work overtime with extra pay or time off. Paid time off to reimburse workers for overtime is called **compensatory time**.

American workers are guaranteed the right to join a labor union. A **labor union** is an organization of workers in a similar **field**, or line of work. Labor unions act as the voice of their members in collective bargaining. Collective bargaining includes negotiating safe working conditions, employment contracts, and other job benefits. About 15% of American workers belong to labor unions.

Employers must also protect their employees from discrimination in the workplace. **Discrimination** is unfair treatment based on age, gender, race, ethnicity, religion, physical appearance, disability, or other factors. For example, sexual harassment, or any unwelcome behavior of a sexual nature, is forbidden in the workplace. If you think that you have been a victim of discrimination, report the incident to your supervisor immediately so that he or she can take action.

Performance Evaluations

Your employer must provide you with feedback on your job performance. Some employers consider the first few months of your time working on a new job to be an employee probation (prō-'bā-shən) period. **Probation** is a short period of time when you first start work that gives your employer a chance to monitor your job performance closely. Your employer will use your probation time to confirm that you can do the job. Most probation periods last for three months.

Teamwork

You also enter into a relationship with your coworkers when you take a job. Many workplaces focus only on individual skills. Foodservice workplaces also focus on working as a team. Every worker is an individual, with his or her own personality traits, strengths, and weaknesses. To bring individuals together to create an effective team, each employee must practice good teamwork skills.

Keep a positive attitude. An upbeat, positive outlook contributes to the team spirit of the group. Complaining can bring down the attitude of the whole team and affect your job performance.

Respect yourself and others while on the job. You demonstrate self-respect when you accept responsibility for your actions, learn from your mistakes, and take care of your appearance. Being disrespectful can result in being fired from your job. Learn to practice empathy ('em-pə-thē) to better understand your coworkers. **Empathy** is the skill of thinking about what it would be like in another's place.

Resolve Conflicts

No matter how well you and your coworkers get along, you will not always agree. Disputes and conflicts are an inevitable part of being part of a team. While conflict can be unpleasant, you can learn something from the process of working to resolve conflicts respectfully. There must be give and take. Learn to negotiate.

You may find that there are some conflicts that cannot be resolved. Remember to focus on the problem. Do not focus on the personalities involved. Try to concentrate on performing your work to the best of your ability. If you are unable to work because of a conflict, discuss the issue with a manager. A manager may have a different view of the situation.

Workplace Diversity Your coworkers may have different backgrounds and opinions. *How can you demonstrate positive interpersonal skills with coworkers?*

PHOTO CAPTION ANSWER By actively listening to and valuing coworkers' opinions, encouraging coworkers to improve their own skills, speaking in a respectful manner, and respecting coworkers' individual customs and backgrounds.

~ Small Bites ~

Ending Employment There may come a time when you must terminate your employment. Always try to leave on good terms. Give at least two weeks' notice before leaving to give your employer time to find your replacement. Work as hard during those weeks as you did before you gave notice.

Ethical Behavior

Ethical behavior means doing what is right. Your **ethics** ('e-thiks) are your internal guidelines to distinguish right from wrong. Much of the time, it is easy to recognize the ethical course of action. When two choices appear equally right or equally wrong, ask yourself the following questions:

- Does the choice comply with the law?
- Is the choice fair to those involved?
- Has the choice been communicated to me honestly?
- Will I feel embarrassed or guilty about the choice?

Behaving ethically also means taking responsibility. If you make a mistake, you should admit it. Responsible employees learn from their mistakes and change their behavior to make better choices.

Reading Check **Explain** What are some responsibilities that a worker owes to his or her employer?

Wages and Benefits

When you agree to take a job, you trade your skills and efforts for pay. Your pay is determined by a number of factors, including your level of experience, the difficulty of the work, and the number of people competing for the same job. Employers pay weekly, every two weeks, or once a month.

If you are paid an hourly wage, your employer will pay you a certain amount for each hour that you work. Your pay will vary depending on how many hours you work. If you receive a salary, your employer will pay you a set amount of money regardless of how many hours you work.

Gourmet Math

Overtime Pay

Some employers would rather have an employee work overtime than hire additional help. The cost to hire and train new employees and the added cost of employee benefits are higher than the amount the employer would pay in overtime. Overtime pay may be paid at time-and-a-half or two times your hourly wage. Garrett is paid time-and-a-half overtime for any time he works over 40 hours in one week at Mason's Cafeteria. Last week, Garrett worked 44 hours. If Garrett's hourly rate is $10.40, how much was his gross pay for last week?

Math Concept **Rate Increases** To calculate an increased rate, multiply the original rate by the increase. For example, to calculate time-and-a-half pay, multiply the normal hourly rate by 1.5.

Starting Hint Determine the number of regular hours and the number of overtime hours Garrett worked. Multiply the number of regular hours times his normal hourly rate to determine his base pay. Multiply the number of overtime hours times his overtime pay rate (1.5 × $10.40) to find his overtime pay. Add the overtime pay to the base pay to determine Garrett's gross pay.

NCTM Number and Operations Compute fluently and make reasonable estimates.

READING CHECK ANSWER A worker must use his or her time responsibly, respect the rules, work safely, and earn his or her pay.

GOURMET MATH ANSWER 40 regular hours: 40 × $10.40 = $416. Overtime pay rate: 1.5 × $10.40/hour = $15.60/hour. 4 overtime hours: 4 × $15.60 = $62.40. Gross pay for the week: $416 + $62.40 = $478.40.

FIGURE 4.6 Paycheck Deductions

Pay Stub Elements A pay stub shows you the amount of each deduction taken from your paycheck. *What types of deductions may be withheld from your gross pay?*

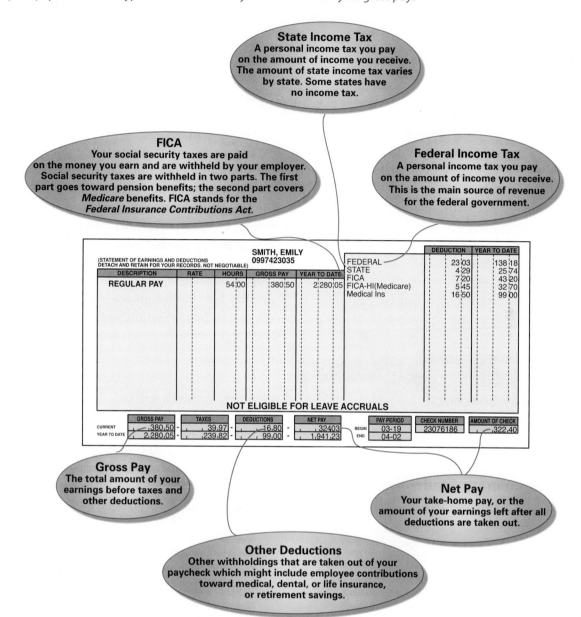

State Income Tax
A personal income tax you pay on the amount of income you receive. The amount of state income tax varies by state. Some states have no income tax.

FICA
Your social security taxes are paid on the money you earn and are withheld by your employer. Social security taxes are withheld in two parts. The first part goes toward pension benefits; the second part covers *Medicare* benefits. FICA stands for the *Federal Insurance Contributions Act.*

Federal Income Tax
A personal income tax you pay on the amount of income you receive. This is the main source of revenue for the federal government.

Gross Pay
The total amount of your earnings before taxes and other deductions.

Other Deductions
Other withholdings that are taken out of your paycheck which might include employee contributions toward medical, dental, or life insurance, or retirement savings.

Net Pay
Your take-home pay, or the amount of your earnings left after all deductions are taken out.

SMITH, EMILY
0997423035

(STATEMENT OF EARNINGS AND DEDUCTIONS DETACH AND RETAIN FOR YOUR RECORDS. NOT NEGOTIABLE)

DESCRIPTION	RATE	HOURS	GROSS PAY	YEAR TO DATE
REGULAR PAY		54:00	380:50	2,280:05

	DEDUCTION	YEAR TO DATE
FEDERAL	23:03	138:18
STATE	4:29	25:74
FICA	7:20	43:20
FICA-HI(Medicare)	5:45	32:70
Medical Ins	16:50	99:00

NOT ELIGIBLE FOR LEAVE ACCRUALS

	GROSS PAY	TAXES	DEDUCTIONS	NET PAY	PAY PERIOD	CHECK NUMBER	AMOUNT OF CHECK
CURRENT	380,50	39,97	16,80	32403	BEGIN 03-19	23076186	322,40
YEAR TO DATE	2,280,05	239,82	99,00	1,941,23	END 04-02		

Deductions

The total amount of money you are paid from working is called your **gross pay**. A **deduction** is money that is withheld from your gross pay for taxes, insurance, and other fees. The amount of money you actually receive after deductions is called your **net pay**, or take-home pay. (See **Figure 4.6**.) Ask your employer to explain any deductions.

FIGURE CAPTION ANSWER Social Security, personal state income, and personal federal income taxes, contributions for insurance, retirement savings, and withholdings for court judgments may all be withheld.

Tips

Some foodservice workers earn tips amounting to between 10% and 20% of the customer's check. A **tip** is a small bonus payment from a customer as a reward for excellent service. Because employers are allowed to count tip money as part of a worker's minimum wage, some foodservice workers may actually earn more in tips than they do in wages.

If you earn tips as part of your job, it is your responsibility to keep a record of the money you earn. You will need to report your tips as income when you file federal and state tax returns.

Benefits

In addition to your salary, your employer may offer benefits. **Benefits** are services or payments provided by an employer in addition to wages. Common benefits that employers give to employees include:

- Health and accident insurance. Sometimes employers will allow employees to pay for health insurance to cover dependents.
- Paid vacation days.
- Discounts on meals or company products for employees.

- Life insurance.
- Disability insurance, a policy that helps pay your expenses if you become disabled and can no longer work.
- Tuition reimbursement, or full or partial repayment of fees you pay for education courses that are related to your career.
- Savings and investment plans, such as a 401K, to help you earn money for retirement.

Figure in any benefits when you calculate your job compensation. A high wage may make up for few benefits. A good range of benefits, on the other hand, can make up for a lower wage. Carefully consider what benefits are important to you before you accept the job.

 Reading Check **Summarize** What are the two ways that an employer can choose to pay an employee?

SECTION 4.3 After You Read

Review Key Concepts

1. **Explain** the concept of worker's compensation.
2. **List** the different types of benefits an employer may offer.

Practice Culinary Academics

 English Language Arts

3. Follow your teacher's instructions to work with another student. Role-play a restaurant manager and a line cook discussing the line cook's duties. Then, switch roles. How did you communicate as an employer and as an employee? Write a short summary of your experience.

> **NCTE 4** Use written language to communicate effectively.

Social Studies

4. Choose an aspect of fair labor practices, such as minimum wage or discrimination, and research the development of the practice throughout history. Write a short report on the subject you have chosen. Be sure to list your sources.

> **NCSS X B Civic Ideals and Practices** Identify, analyze, interpret, and evaluate sources and examples of citizens' rights and responsibilities.

Mathematics

5. You worked 38 hours waiting tables at a restaurant last week, earning $8.75 per hour. In addition, you received $326.86 in tips for the week. How much money did you make per hour, including tips?

Math Concept **Multiplying Decimals** Multiply decimals the same way you would multiply whole numbers. Add the number of decimal places in each factor, and use that total number of decimal places in the product.

Starting Hint Determine your total wages for the week by multiplying your hours worked (38) by your hourly wage ($8.75 per hour). Add this amount to your tip income, then divide by the number of hours worked.

> **NCTM Problem Solving** Solve problems that arise in mathematics and in other contexts.

 Check your answers at this book's Online Learning Center at **glencoe.com**.

READING CHECK ANSWER An employer can pay an employee by the hour worked, or a set amount of pay as a salary.

Review and Applications

Chapter Summary

Basic employment skills for the foodservice industry include math, reading, writing, speaking, and listening skills. To find a job at a foodservice establishment, you can network with other professionals, join professional organizations, and read trade publications. You should also prepare a résumé as part of a job portfolio. Both employers and employees have certain rights and responsibilities in the workplace. If you work well, then there will be opportunities for you to advance to positions with better pay and more responsibility.

Content and Academic Vocabulary Review

1. Label each of these vocabulary terms as a noun, verb, or adjective.

Content Vocabulary

- calculate (p. 84)
- make change (p. 85)
- active listening (p. 85)
- distraction (p. 85)
- work ethic (p. 88)
- responsibility (p. 88)
- flexibility (p. 89)
- honesty (p. 89)
- reliable (p. 89)
- teamwork (p. 89)
- commitment (p. 90)
- leadership (p. 90)
- resource (p. 91)
- prioritize (p. 91)
- networking (p. 94)
- trade publication (p. 95)
- employment agency (p. 96)
- job lead (p. 96)
- résumé (p. 96)
- job application (p. 96)
- job portfolio (p. 96)
- job interview (p. 97)
- keyword (p. 98)
- evaluation (p. 105)
- initiative (p. 105)
- workers' compensation (p. 106)
- repetitive stress injury (p. 106)
- minimum wage (p. 106)
- compensatory time (p. 106)
- labor union (p. 106)
- discrimination (p. 106)
- probation (p. 107)
- empathy (p. 107)
- ethics (p. 108)
- gross pay (p. 109)
- deduction (p. 109)
- net pay (p. 109)
- tip (p. 109)
- benefits (p. 110)

Academic Vocabulary

- qualities (p. 88)
- compensate (p. 92)
- suitable (p. 97)
- nature (p. 100)
- outline (p. 105)
- field (p. 106)

Review Key Concepts

2. **Demonstrate** basic employability skills in foodservice.

3. **Evaluate** the characteristics of a positive work ethic.

4. **Identify** the leadership skills necessary for foodservice employment.

5. **Identify** sources for foodservice job leads.

6. **Illustrate** the proper skills to apply for a foodservice job.

7. **Summarize** the rights and responsibilities of employees and employers.

8. **Explain** the differences between tips, deductions, and benefits.

Critical Thinking

9. **Imagine** that you are working as the host in a restaurant. You overslept and you are running late. What should you do, and why?

10. **Offer** advice to your friend Carla. She wants to apply for a job as a server at a nearby restaurant. You know that she is friendly and outgoing, but that sometimes she does not finish her school assignments on time. What tips can you give her to get and keep the job?

Review and Applications

Academic Skills

 English Language Arts

11. Telephone Techniques Follow your teacher's instructions to form pairs. Role-play answering the telephone for foodservice businesses. Scenarios may include taking a reservation, transferring calls, and taking customer special requests. Use your best speaking and listening skills, as well as your customer service skills. Then, switch roles. As a class, evaluate how employee phone manners can affect customer service.

> **NCTE 4** Use written language to communicate effectively.

 Science

12. Create a Safety Assessment Employee safety is an employer's responsibility. Employers should take the time to assess whether working conditions are safe for all employees.

Procedure Assess your foods lab for safety, as if you were an employer. Pay attention to areas around cooking appliances and chemical storage.

Analysis Create a list of the areas that you think should be checked regularly for safety. Using the list, write a short summary of the current safety of your foods lab and how it might be improved.

> **NSES F** Develop an understanding of personal and community health.

 Mathematics

13. Find a Percentage You are waiting on three tables at a high-end restaurant during dinner service. Customer A leaves a tip of $35 on a $245 check. At another table, Customer B's meal costs $112.50, and she leaves you a tip of $17.50. Finally, Customer C leaves you a tip of $40 on a $260 check. Out of the three, which customer was the best tipper, on a percentage basis?

Math Concept **Solving Percentage Problems with Proportions** When you know two of three values (part, base, percentage) in a percentage problem and need to determine the third, set up a proportion and solve for the missing value: $\dfrac{\text{Part}}{\text{Base}} = \dfrac{\text{Percent}}{100}$

Starting Hint Determine the tip percentage for each customer using the formula above, substituting the tip amount for Part, the check amount for Base, and the variable p for Percent. For Customer A: $\dfrac{\$35}{\$245} = \dfrac{p}{100}$

Cross-multiply the proportion to get $\$35 \times 100 = 245 \times p$, or $3,500 = 245p$. Divide both sides by 245 to solve for p, which represents Customer A's tip percentage.

> **NCTM Number and Operations** Compute fluently and make reasonable estimates.

Certification Prep

Sharpen your test-taking skills to improve your kitchen certification program score.

Directions Read the questions. Then, read the answer choices and choose the best possible answer for each.

14. What position can you advance to if you start as a host?

    a. sous chef   **c.** kitchen helper

    b. server   **d.** caterer

15. How might a server use math skills?

    a. to weigh ingredients

    b. to estimate profits

    c. to adjust recipe yields

    d. to make change

Test-Taking Tip
In a multiple-choice test, the answers should be specific and precise. Read the questions first, and then read all the answer choices before you choose. Eliminate answers that you know are incorrect.

Review and Applications

Real-World Skills and Applications

Communication Skills

16. Interview a Restaurant Employee Interview a restaurant employee about how he or she got their job. Ask what the employee considers the most important skills used on the job. After you have completed your interview, give a five-minute oral report to the class on what you have learned, and relate it back to the information in the chapter.

Interpersonal and Collaborative Skills

17. Overcome Prejudice Follow your teacher's directions to divide into pairs or small groups. Role-play ways in which stereotypes and prejudices might negatively effect employee relations. Also role-play possible solutions to the situations you portray. Try to use good management and problem-solving skills to resolve the situation.

Technology Applications

18. Explore Job Search Resources Get your teacher's or parents' permission to go online and search for Internet job search resources, such as networking sites, professional organizations, and online job listing services. Choose one resource from the list and write a one-page summary of how to use it to look for foodservice jobs.

Financial Literacy

19. Determine Your Financial Situation Imagine that you are starting a job as a prep cook at a restaurant, making $7.25 per hour. You will work a full 40 hours per week at your new job, with no overtime. You will be paid every two weeks, and 15% of your pay will be deducted from each paycheck for taxes and fees for insurance. How much money will you take home per month?

Culinary Lab

Use the culinary skills you have learned in this chapter.

Interview Practice

20. Participate in Mock Interviews In this lab, you will invite a local foodservice manager, such as a chef, restaurant manager, or deli manager, to conduct mock interviews with the class. Then, you will evaluate the interviews.

A. Research background information. Research background information about the operations for which the guest interviewer works. Prepare any questions you have for the interviewer about his or her place of business.

B. Prepare your résumé. Write your résumé and complete a sample employment application.

C. Interview for a job. Participate in mock interviews with the guest interviewer. Videotape the interviews, if possible.

D. Create an evaluation chart. Use the following rating scale: Poor = 1; Fair = 2; Good = 3; Great = 4.

E. Evaluate the interviews. Evaluate the videotaped interviews using the evaluation charts. List strengths and offer suggestions for improvement.

Create Your Evaluation

Review your evaluation chart and the evaluations given to you by the teacher and other students. Create a plan for your next interview that includes the strengths that you will try to repeat and also includes your weaknesses and how you will try to improve on them so you can do a better interview.

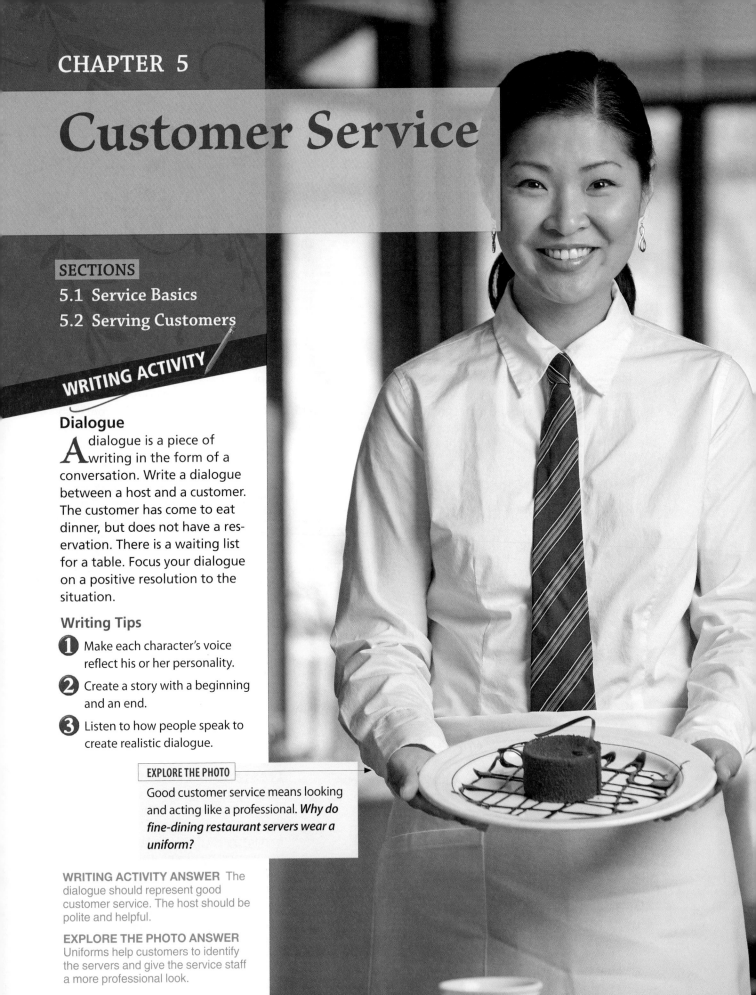

Customer Service

SECTIONS

5.1 Service Basics
5.2 Serving Customers

WRITING ACTIVITY

Dialogue

A dialogue is a piece of writing in the form of a conversation. Write a dialogue between a host and a customer. The customer has come to eat dinner, but does not have a reservation. There is a waiting list for a table. Focus your dialogue on a positive resolution to the situation.

Writing Tips

1 Make each character's voice reflect his or her personality.

2 Create a story with a beginning and an end.

3 Listen to how people speak to create realistic dialogue.

EXPLORE THE PHOTO

Good customer service means looking and acting like a professional. *Why do fine-dining restaurant servers wear a uniform?*

WRITING ACTIVITY ANSWER The dialogue should represent good customer service. The host should be polite and helpful.

EXPLORE THE PHOTO ANSWER Uniforms help customers to identify the servers and give the service staff a more professional look.

114

Service Basics

Reading Guide

 Before You Read

Adjust Reading Speed Improve your comprehension by adjusting your reading speed to match the difficulty of the text. Slow down and, if needed, reread each paragraph. Reading more slowly may take longer, but you will understand and remember more.

Read to Learn

Key Concepts
- **Outline** the duties of each member of the service staff.
- **Summarize** the traits servers need to have to provide excellent customer service.
- **Compare and contrast** the different types of beverage service.

Main Idea

It is important to know how to provide quality customer service. Quality customer service can bring back satisfied customers to a foodservice business.

Graphic Organizer

Use a tree diagram like the one below to help identify the role and duties of the four members of the service staff. In each box, write the title and duties of one member of the service staff.

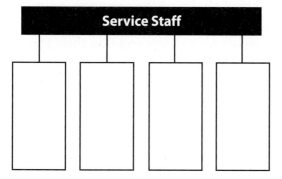

Service Staff

Content Vocabulary
- reputation
- host
- reservation
- server
- section/station
- busser
- service station
- course
- cashier
- patronage
- client base
- uniform
- bag-in-the-box system
- tank system
- espresso
- cappuccino
- demitasse
- infuse

Academic Vocabulary
- offset
- interact

 Graphic Organizer
Go to this book's Online Learning Center at **glencoe.com** for a printable graphic organizer.

ACADEMIC STANDARDS

 English Language Arts
NCTE 7 Conduct research and gather, evaluate, and synthesize data to communicate discoveries.

 Mathematics
NCTM Measurement Understand measurable attributes of objects and the units, systems, and processes of measurement.

 Science
NSES B Develop an understanding of chemical reactions.

NCTE National Council of Teachers of English

NCTM National Council of Teachers of Mathematics

NSES National Science Education Standards

NCSS National Council for the Social Studies

GRAPHIC ORGANIZER ANSWER Host: Greet customers, keep waiting list, track tables, seat guests. Server: Represent business, sell the menu, serve food, receive payment. Busser: Set up and clear tables, serve water and bread. Cashier: Process payments, make change.

The Service Staff

Quality customer service is very important to a restaurant business. It is one of the things that keep customers satisfied. Satisfied customers will come back to the restaurant. Well-prepared meals and a charming atmosphere will not **offset**, or compensate for, slow or inefficient service. You must know how to provide quality customer service to be a successful part of the service team.

Customers expect skilled and friendly service, consistency in the quality of the food, and a clean, comfortable environment. Customers who are greeted with a smile feel welcome. Customers will feel more relaxed if they can make eye contact with servers. Going beyond what customers expect gives a business a good reputation. A **reputation** is the overall quality or character of a person or business. A good reputation improves the chance of repeat business because customers will return.

No employee can afford to be rude or unskilled when serving customers or resolving their complaints. If there is a problem with an order, the food, or the service, the server should bring the problem to the manager's attention. The manager should then recognize the issue and resolve the complaint quickly and positively. The host, server, busser, and cashier are all members of a restaurant's service team. Each member of the service team plays a key role to ensure the success of the foodservice operation. The service staff is also sometimes called the front-of-the-house staff, because they work outside of the kitchen.

Host

The **host** is the employee who greets the customers by smiling warmly and welcoming them. The host should make an effort to recognize customers who visit frequently. The host also is in charge of the reservation system. A **reservation** is an arrangement to have a table held for a customer at a specific time.

～ Small Bites ～

Special Needs A host can accommodate customers who have special needs:

- **Sight Impairment** Offer Braille menus, if available, provide check information, offer help when the customer is ready to leave.
- **Hearing Impairment** Speak directly to the customer.
- **Obesity** Offer more comfortable seating, such as an armless chair.
- **Wheelchair** Keep aisles clear, make appropriate accommodations at tables.
- **Language Barrier** Determine customer's language, locate an employee who speaks the language, if possible, offer a menu in the customer's language.
- **Children** Be alert to the child's actions, offer special seating, get parent's permission to offer crackers or crayons to keep the child occupied.

When customers arrive, the host should ask them if they have made a reservation, and in what name.

Keeping track of waiting lists is another responsibility of the host. Hosts often track empty and busy tables on a printed or computerized chart. Use these guidelines to track and seat customers using a waiting list:

- Ask how many people will be dining. Review the waiting list and seating chart for empty tables that will fit.
- If there is no empty table available, apologize to the customer and ask if he or she would like to be placed on the waiting list.
- Tell the customer about how long the wait will be. Call the customer's name when the table is ready. Many restaurants use pagers to alert customers that their seats are available.
- Cross off the customer's name from the waiting list once he or she is seated. If you do not do this, you may become confused.

The host also leads the way to the table. The host should always walk slowly so that the customers can easily follow. The host then seats the customers and presents them with

Conserve Energy Every server should look for ways to save time, energy, and motion. *What are some ways that servers can conserve time, energy, and motion?*

their menus. Hosts in fine-dining restaurants should pull out chairs to seat customers. Each customer should receive a menu. If the customers have any special needs, such as a child's booster chair, the host will either provide the need or inform a server of the need. If the customer wishes to change seating, the host should inform the server of the change, and make sure the new seating is suitable. None of the services provided by the host should be rushed. A sense of being rushed will make customers feel uncomfortable.

Server

The **server** is the service staff member who has the most contact with the customers. Servers perform four tasks:

- Represent the foodservice operation
- Sell the menu
- Serve menu items skillfully

- Receive the correct payment from the customer

Servers must have good communication and interpersonal skills. They help set the tone of the dining experience. Servers are the sales staff of every foodservice operation. They help customers make beverage and food decisions by recommending menu items. A server must know the ingredients and preparation methods of all beverage and food items.

Use of Time and Motion

Service staff members are often responsible for serving a group of tables. This group of tables is called a **section** or **station**. The server should always look for ways to save time and energy when serving a section. Servers must be well organized and know how to set priorities, using as few steps as possible. For example, avoid unnecessary trips to the kitchen to increase your time management.

Cross-Training During training, chefs also learn basic money-handling skills.
Why is this important training for chefs?

Also, when pouring water at a table, the server should check his or her other tables to see if anyone else needs water.

There are other ways to save time and motion during service. You may set more than one table at a time, deliver food items for more than one table at a time, and clear dishes from more than one table at a time. Always be aware of customers at all the tables in a station. This allows you to be more effective and efficient.

Busser

The **busser** helps maintain an inviting table and keeps the service station stocked with supplies. The **service station** is where supplies are kept for the service staff to reset tables between customers. Bussers sometimes serve water and bread to customers as soon as they are seated. Then, as customers finish eating, the busser clears the table. The busser

also cleans and resets the table prior to seating the next customer, and notifies the host when the table is ready.

In some restaurants, the server or busser will clear the table between courses of a meal. A **course** is a part of a meal that is served at one time. Remember, dishes should not be removed from the table until all the customers have finished eating. When in doubt, you should ask the customers whether you may clear their dishes. Bussers also keep the dining room tidy.

Cashier

Some busy, informal, or family-style restaurants have a cashier. A **cashier** is the employee who correctly reads the amount of the bill, processes the payment, and makes change. Other restaurants may have servers process customer payments and bring change to the table.

PHOTO CAPTION ANSWER This training builds customer service skills, builds math skills, and teaches chefs about how money is made in the restaurant business.

The cashier should always thank customers for their support. Spending money at a business is called **patronage** ('pa-trə-nij). Some establishments also offer items for sale at the cash register. These may include cakes, pies, bottled dressings, sauces, or syrups. The cashier sells these items to customers as they pay their bills.

Reading Check Determine When should dishes be removed from the table?

Service Skills

All foodservice employees, especially those who **interact**, or talk and work together, with customers, must possess the following qualities. Each of these qualities is important to a successful career as part of the service staff:
- A positive attitude
- A neat and clean appearance
- Good communication and teamwork skills
- Thorough job knowledge and the ability to manage time wisely
- An ability to resolve customer complaints by positive means

Positive Attitude

It is critical to have a positive attitude at all times when you deal directly with customers. You cannot allow one difficult customer to affect your attitude. For example, a server may have just dealt with a difficult customer. That same server must be able to serve other customers without being visibly upset. It is important for service staff members to be able to manage stress well.

The proper attitude for a server is a willingness to please the customer. Without this willingness, you cannot succeed, despite any other skills you may have. This is also a way to build and maintain a client base. A **client base** consists of the customers who come regularly to your business. These behaviors show a willingness to please customers:

- Take pride in your work, regardless of your job assignment.
- Be cheerful. Friendliness matters to everyone around you.
- Try to resolve complaints and problems in a positive way.
- Show courtesy to customers and coworkers alike. This includes helping your coworkers if they need it.
- Never argue with customers. People prefer a relaxed, pleasant setting when dining out. Arguments create tension.
- Remember that the customer is never "wrong." Your role is to find solutions that will keep customers happy.
- Do not hold conversations with coworkers in the dining area. Customers need to know that they are your only priority.

Personal Attire

The service staff's appearance is key to giving customers a good first impression of both the staff members and the foodservice operation. Most foodservice operations have their own policies regarding proper attire, or clothing. Foodservice businesses usually require a uniform for serving staff. A **uniform** is clothing that is worn by a particular group to help identify workers. Here are some general grooming guidelines for service staff:
- Be sure your uniform fits properly and that it is clean and pressed.
- Keep your work shoes clean and polished.
- Remove any nail polish before going to work.
- Keep jewelry to a minimum.
- Wear proper underwear.

Personal Health

The energy and skills demanded in foodservice can be best achieved when you are in good physical and mental health. Foodservice careers often involve long hours on your feet. Getting enough sleep is key. Too little sleep weakens the body's immune system and puts the body at risk for illness. A lack of sleep does not promote good physical or mental health. Getting enough sleep also will help you handle stress, making you more successful at your job.

Foodservice employees often have to lift heavy objects, such as loaded serving trays. Exercise regularly to increase your strength.

In the foodservice industry, disease can spread easily to coworkers and customers. If you have a fever, a cold, or are vomiting, do not go to work and try to wait it out. Call your supervisor and see a doctor. Return to work only when you are completely well.

Personal Hygiene

When you work directly with the public, personal hygiene is very important. Follow these guidelines for personal hygiene:

- Keep your hair pulled back and out of the way.
- Keep your hands clean. Wash them frequently, including after handling food, clearing tables, coughing, or sneezing. Washing your hands after using the restroom is required.
- Keep your fingernails trimmed and clean.
- Be sure that your teeth are clean and your breath is fresh.
- Use body deodorant daily.
- Do not wear heavy colognes or perfumes.

Communication and Teamwork Skills

Service staff members must be able to communicate well with both customers and with coworkers. They also must be able to work as part of a coordinated team. Teamwork between service staff members is shown through verbal and nonverbal communication skills.

Verbal Communication

Verbal communication involves speaking to another person. It is important to speak clearly and loudly enough to be heard when talking.

▼ FIGURE 5.1 Clear Communication Check, Please Servers must be able to communicate clearly when writing out orders. *What does the shorthand used here tell you about this order?*

Safety Check

✓ Serving Safety

Many restaurants serve alcohol to guests. Servers who are old enough to serve alcohol have a responsibility to make sure that customers are old enough to drink, and use alcohol in a safe manner.

- Servers should check the identification of everyone in the party who is of questionable age. Verify the photo, name, and date of birth. If a server has questions about the identification, it should be compared to an ID guidebook.
- Assess the intoxication level of a customer. If the customer is intoxicated, the server is legally required to stop serving the customer alcohol. Servers should assess attitude changes, body language, speech, and disruptive behavior, and ask a manager for a final decision.
- If the identification is valid and the customer is not intoxicated, the server would take the order and place it with the bartender.

CRITICAL THINKING *Why do you think the law requires servers to stop serving an intoxicated customer?*

FIGURE CAPTION ANSWER This order calls for one egg special dish, cooked over easy, with sausage links; one order of French toast; one iced tea; and one hot tea.

SAFETY CHECK ANSWER Customers who are intoxicated may act in an unsafe manner, and may cause harm to other people.

Ice Makers Ice makers should be used only to make and store ice. *What should you do with the scoop after you are finished using it?*

Do not speak so rapidly that your words run together. Also, make sure that you face customers when you speak to them. Otherwise, customers may have to ask you to repeat yourself. Your tone of voice should always be professional, pleasant, and friendly.

Nonverbal Communication

One form of nonverbal communication includes body language, or expressing your thoughts through physical action. For example, stand attentively when you take orders. This shows customers that you are listening carefully.

Here are some general guidelines:
- Do not chew gum, eat, or drink while you serve customers.
- Do not lean, slouch, or stand around with your hands in your pockets.
- Do not touch your mouth, nose, or hair while you serve customers.

Writing is a form of nonverbal communication. Service employees use writing every day on the job. For example, when you write out an order, you are using nonverbal communication. (See **Figure 5.1**.) Or, you may need to leave a note for a coworker or write out an accident report. It is always important to write clearly and concisely so that your message is understood.

Reading Check **List** Describe the guidelines for professional body language.

Beverage Service

Good customer service includes offering a full range of well-prepared beverages. Whether it is juice, milk, coffee, tea, or soft drinks, customers expect a refreshing beverage that is safe to drink. To do this, each member of the service staff must know how to operate cold and hot beverage equipment.

Cold Beverage Equipment

Cold beverages range from bottled water to soft drinks, milk, iced tea, and juice. Each is dispensed from a special machine. Dispensers for tea, milk, or juice should be taken apart, cleaned, and sanitized daily. The U.S. Food and Drug Administration (FDA) recommends this practice to keep harmful bacteria from multiplying in the machine's tubing.

Ice Makers

Because ice can be contaminated easily, always use a plastic or metal scoop. Never use your hands or a glass to scoop ice. A glass is too fragile and could easily be broken by the ice. After you remove ice from the ice maker, place the scoop on a hook or in a holder on the outside of the ice maker. The ice maker should not be used for chilling any food or objects. Always close the ice maker and put away the ice scoop when it is not in use. Keep the floor around the ice maker dry to prevent slips and falls.

PHOTO CAPTION ANSWER The scoop should be placed on a hook or inside a holder after use. This is to keep it handy and clean, and to keep foodservice workers from having to dredge through the ice to find the scoop.

READING CHECK ANSWER Stand attentively; do not chew gum, drink or eat; do not lean or slouch; do not touch your mouth, nose, or hair while serving customers.

▲ **Fresh Brew** Foodservice coffee makers are often rented from the same company that provides coffee for the establishment. *How do foodservice coffee makers differ from home coffee makers?*

Soft Drink Machines

Soft drinks are often dispensed from a system that consists of a container of concentrated soda syrup, a tank of carbon dioxide (CO_2), and a soda gun dispenser. Two types of systems are the bag-in-the-box system and the tank system. The **bag-in-the-box system** is a cardboard box with a bag of concentrated soda syrup inside. Tubes are attached to air-tight pegs in the boxes.

In the **tank system**, two plastic lines are connected to each carbon dioxide tank. One line leads to the CO_2 tank and allows it to pressurize the soda syrup. The other line permits the soda to pass to the dispensing gun.

You must clean the nozzle and rubber holster on a soft drink machine daily. Place the nozzle in a pitcher of warm water with a sanitizer for 15 minutes and then allow it to air dry. The soda lines should be maintained by the soda supplier according to state sanitation laws.

Hot Beverage Equipment

Many customers order hot beverages with or following their meals. With the exception of water, tea is the most popular beverage in the world. Tea comes in the form of loose tea leaves or tea bags. Coffee has long been a favorite beverage as well. Coffee is also very popular internationally and can be prepared in a variety of ways. The equipment used to prepare coffee is as varied as are the forms of the beverage.

Coffee Makers

Most restaurants lease coffee makers from the company that supplies their coffee. This reduces expenses. Also, the coffee company provides regular maintenance for the machines. Some coffee machines make regular grind coffee only. Others make only espresso and cappuccino. **Espresso** (e-'spre-(ˌ)sō) is a beverage made by forcing

PHOTO CAPTION Differences include the amount of coffee that can be made, the speed of the brewing cycle, and the foodservice coffee maker's ability to boil water at the same time for hot tea.

Flat or Fizzy?

Have you ever wondered what makes a soft drink fizz, or what makes a soft drink go flat? The fizz in soft drinks is caused by carbonation. Carbon dioxide (CO_2), a clear, colorless gas, is dissolved into the soda mixture under pressure. In a container of soda, there is CO_2 in the soda and in the space between the soda and the top of the container. When the CO_2 in that space is lower than the CO_2 in the soda, more of the CO_2 comes out of the soda than returns to the soda. In other words, the CO_2 moves from the soda to the empty space. This causes the soda to become flat.

Procedure Create an experiment to see how carbonated beverages go flat. Get a soft drink bottle with a replaceable lid. Let the bottle sit open without its cap at room temperature overnight. The next day, replace the cap tightly and shake the container. Remove the cap and pour some of the liquid into a glass.

Analysis Taste the liquid you have poured into the glass. Record your observations on the taste and texture of the beverage. Draw conclusions on how this affects customer service.

NSES B Develop an understanding of chemical reactions.

---

hot water and steam through finely ground, dark-roasted coffee beans. **Cappuccino** (ˌka-pə-ˈchē-(ˌ)nō) is a beverage made from espresso and steamed and foamed milk.

To make coffee, first put the coffee pot on the burner. Check the filter basket to make sure it is clean. Then, line the filter basket with a coffee filter and add the correct amount of coffee. Note that the amount of coffee used will vary depending on the type of coffee maker. Return the filter basket to the coffee maker. Press the on switch and then the start switch.

Here are some general guidelines for using foodservice coffee makers:

- Turn on the hot plates and set the adjustable plates to high so that water will boil for tea.
- Do not place empty or near-empty glass pots on warming plates. They may break.

- Always ensure that the brew cycle has finished completely before you remove the pot. Interrupting the brew cycle by removing a pot too early will result in the first pot being too strong and incorrectly balanced, while the second pot will be too weak and bitter.
- Be sure to use coffee within 15 minutes if it is kept on a direct heat source such as a warming plate. After one hour, coffee will begin to lose flavor.
- If the coffee is kept in a vacuum or insulated container, it will maintain its quality and temperature for more than an hour.

Coffee-to-Water Proportion The proportion of coffee to water affects the strength of coffee. This preference varies with customers. In general, the recommended proportion is 1 pound of coffee to 1¾ to 2½ gallons of water. Do not try to brew more coffee than the machine can make at one time. For the best flavor, use good quality water.

Many commercial coffee makers use premeasured, vacuum-sealed packets of coffee. The packets are available in a wide variety of sizes. Follow the manufacturer's instructions to use this type of coffee. Some restaurants use fresh coffee beans. A coffee filter is placed under a coffee grinder to catch the coffee as the beans are ground.

Always match the grind of coffee to the coffee machine's brew cycle. Coffee beans can be ground from coarse to fine. Using the wrong grind for a particular coffee maker can produce results that are too weak, or that have coffee grounds in the coffee. It may also clog the coffee maker. A coarse grind takes longer to brew than a fine grind.

Espresso Machines

Espresso and espresso-based coffee drinks are a fast-growing segment of the hot beverage market. Espresso machines produce only one or two cups at a time, but each ounce of espresso takes only 17 to 23 seconds to run through the machine. Most machines require

Specialty Coffee Espresso is the basis for many different hot beverages. *In what kind of cup would you serve a single espresso?*

a grinder to finely grind the espresso coffee beans. This is done immediately prior to dispensing a designated portion into the filter. For convenience and freshness, vacuum-packed single and double doses of espresso, called pods, are available.

Traditionally, espresso is served in a half-size cup called a **demitasse** ('de-mi-ˌtas) cup. The cup should be filled about one-third of the way full. Double espressos may be served in regular coffee cups. A shot of espresso is the basis for other beverages. Cappuccino is an example of a beverage prepared from espresso. One shot of espresso is equal to 1 ounce. A quality serving of espresso should be covered with an amber-colored thin layer of froth called a crema ('krā-mə). A crema will form only if the coffee beans are fresh, the grind is correct, the water temperature was sufficiently hot and pressurized, the brew cycle was correct, and the equipment was clean. Always leave an espresso machine turned on.

PHOTO CAPTION ANSWER A single espresso would be served in a demitasse cup.

Tea-Making Equipment

Tea can be made in a variety of equipment. Pottery, china, stoneware, porcelain, and glass are all used to make strainers, kettles, teapots, and teacups. These may be simple or decorative in design. Like coffee, tea made in metallic equipment will give the liquid a metallic taste. Humidity, temperature, oxygen, and light all affect tea leaves. Store tea in a sealed container in a cool, dry place. Do not use the same service container for tea and coffee.

The final taste of tea is determined by the proportion of tea to water. Depending on the type and quality of tea leaves, use 6 ounces of water with 1 rounded teaspoon of loose tea or one tea bag.

Infusing Tea To **infuse** a substance means to extract its flavors by placing it in a hot liquid. When you infuse tea in fresh water, consider the water temperature and the length of time that the leaves and water are in contact. Infusion usually lasts from two to four minutes.

The water that you use to infuse tea should be at or near the boiling point to release the flavors and aromas of most teas. Color should not be used to determine how long to infuse tea. Tea will often turn a dark, rich color long before it is ready to be drunk. A good cup of tea depends on its flavor and aroma.

Clean Hot Beverage Equipment

In order to continue to provide your customers with flavorful and sanitary hot beverages, you must thoroughly clean hot beverage equipment, such as coffee makers, espresso machines, and tea containers, every day.

Coffee Makers Turn off or unplug the coffee machine, and remove the used filter and grounds from the filter basket. Remove the water spray fixture and clean it. Be sure to clean and replace the filter basket. Clean coffee pots at the end of each shift with a brush and commercial cleaner.

Espresso Machines The filter from an espresso machine should be removed immediately after serving the beverage. After each use, knock out the spent grounds into a special box, called a knock box. Empty the knock box when it is full, or at the end of the shift. Rinse the filter by running a cycle of hot water through it without coffee grounds. Place the filter upside down on top of the machine to air dry. Use an approved cleaner to clean the machine. Dispense the recommended amount of the cleaner into a filter that has a blind screen, or a screen with no holes in it. Run the brew cycle up to eight times once the blind filter with the cleaner has been inserted into the machine. Leave the cleaner in the system for 15 minutes, or according to the manufacturer's instructions. Remove the blind filter. Flush out the machine by running at least two brew cycles with clear water.

Tea Containers Tea-making equipment must be kept free of any mineral deposits that build up from both the water and the tea. This buildup can give the tea an unpleasant flavor and aroma. Boil tea-making equipment in a solution of one part white vinegar and one part water to clean the parts and remove mineral deposits.

 Reading Check Describe What is the correct coffee-to-water ratio?

SECTION 5.1 After You Read

Review Key Concepts

1. **Describe** the duties of the busser.
2. **Summarize** the general guidelines for a server's personal attire.
3. **Explain** how to clean and maintain a soda machine.

Practice Culinary Academics

English Language Arts

4. Find some trade magazine articles about how excellent customer service positively affects a restaurant's profits. Read each article carefully, and summarize the main points of each article. Using your summary, as a class discuss the advantages of developing professional service skills for the server and owner. Use points from your summary to support your arguments.

> **NCTE 7** Conduct research and gather, evaluate, and synthesize data to communicate discoveries.

Mathematics

5. Your restaurant's coffee maker brews half a gallon of coffee at a time. If you wish to transfer this coffee into 32-ounce thermal carafes for service, how many carafes will you need?

Math Concept **Converting Volume Units** One gallon is the equivalent of 128 ounces. To convert gallons to ounces, multiply the number of gallons by 128. To convert ounces to gallons, divide the number of ounces by 128.

Starting Hint Convert ½ gallon (0.5 gallon) into ounces by multiplying 0.5 by 128. The result is the total amount of brewed coffee in ounces. Divide this remainder by 32 to determine the number of carafes needed.

> **NCTM Measurement** Understand measurable attributes of objects and the units, systems, and processes of measurement.

 Check your answers at this book's Online Learning Center at **glencoe.com**.

Serving Customers

Reading Guide

 Before You Read

Look It Up As you read this section, keep a dictionary nearby in addition to the glossary at the back of this book. If you read a word that you do not know, look it up in the glossary or the dictionary.

Read to Learn

Key Concepts
- **Describe** the server's role in greeting customers and taking orders.
- **List** the order of service for a meal.
- **Demonstrate** how to total a check and accept different forms of payment.

Main Idea
The servers have a key role in how the customer rates his or her dining experience. This section will teach you about the role of servers and how their duties should be performed.

Graphic Organizer
Use a sequence chart like this one to show the 10 steps in serving a customer.

Serving Customers

First Step:
Next Step:
Next Step:
Next Step:
Next Step:
Next Step:
Next Step:
Next Step:
Next Step:
Last Step:

 Graphic Organizer Go to this book's Online Learning Center at **glencoe.com** for a printable graphic organizer.

Content Vocabulary
- cover
- highlighting
- upselling
- point-of-sale system
- hand service
- tray service
- tray stand
- preset
- appetizer
- underliner

Academic Vocabulary
- objective
- anticipate

Superior customer service skills make customers want to return.

ACADEMIC STANDARDS

 English Language Arts
NCTE 9 Develop an understanding of diversity in language use across cultures.

 Mathematics
NCTM Number and Operations Compute fluently and make reasonable estimates.

 Social Studies
NCSS V B Culture Analyze group and institutional influences on people, events, and elements of culture in both historical and contemporary settings.

....

NCTE National Council of Teachers of English

NCTM National Council of Teachers of Mathematics

NSES National Science Education Standards

NCSS National Council for the Social Studies

GRAPHIC ORGANIZER ANSWER Greet customers; take beverage orders and serve beverages; sell the menu and take food orders; transmit order to kitchen; serve food; check with customer, clear table; calculate and present check; collect payment and make change; reset table.

Opening Service

Customers have the most contact with servers when they dine out. From taking orders to presenting checks, the server plays a key role in how the customer rates his or her dining experience. In this section, you will learn about the role of servers and how their duties should be performed.

The host or busser may serve bread and water before the server arrives at the table. However, the server is the main caretaker of customers' needs throughout the meal. The server's job is to greet customers, take the order, serve the meal, and present the check. The server must make sure that the cover is clean, with all of the proper equipment necessary for the meal. A **cover** is an individual place setting that includes utensils, glasses, and dishes. The server should do everything possible to make the total dining experience enjoyable and relaxing.

Greet Customers

Give the customer a moment to adjust to his or her surroundings before approaching the table. Be sure to smile and maintain good eye contact with each customer. Say, "good morning," "good afternoon," or "good evening." If your customers are gathered to celebrate a special event, try to find out who the guest of honor is. Your **objective**, or goal, is to make customers comfortable. Let them know that you are a caring and attentive server.

Take the Beverage Order

The first point of service is to take the beverage order from customers. Repeat the beverage order to the customer to confirm it. You can use position numbers to make sure the right beverage is served to each customer. (See **Figure 5.2**.) This can be done if you take the beverage order in a clockwise direction around the table. It can also be done by numbering each customer at a table by his or her seat position.

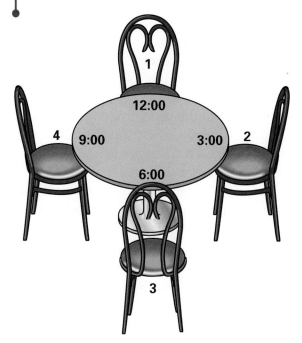

FIGURE 5.2 **Numbered Seating**
Table Positions In this illustration, the seats have been numbered clockwise. *How do you think this helps the service staff give customers the correct order?*

If the restaurant has a wine list, ask customers if they wish to order wine with their meals. If so, present the wine list. Explain any wine policies, such as whether customers can take home unfinished bottles.

Serve Cold Beverages

Beverages are either cold or hot. They are served on a small, handheld tray called a beverage tray. Cold beverages include milk, iced tea, soft drinks, juice, and water.

When you serve cold beverages:
- Be sure that the tray is clean and dry before you use it at a table.
- Use beverage napkins for each beverage if the table surface is not covered with a cloth.
- A server who will serve alcohol should check the bar to see when beverages are ready, and add appropriate garnishes.
- Arrange the glasses so that the beverage served first is closest to the rim of the tray. However, the tallest and heaviest

FIGURE CAPTION ANSWER Servers take orders clockwise beginning at 12:00, and then deliver them in the same order.

glasses should be in the center of the tray for balance. Adjust the positions of the glasses on the tray as they are served.

- Carry trays at waist level and with your left hand under the center of the tray. Use your right hand to place the beverage on the customer's right.
- When possible, beverages should be served from the right side. Do not reach across the customer.
- Do not hold the tray between you and the customer or you and the table.
- Do not allow a customer to remove beverages from the tray.
- Keep your fingers as far as possible from the rim of the glass. Handle a stemmed glass by the stem and other glasses at the base.
- When about two-thirds of a beverage has been consumed, ask whether the customer wants another one.
- Remove the empty glass before serving a fresh beverage to a customer. Unless the glass is empty, ask the customer whether you may remove it.

Water Service

Some foodservice operations serve water to customers as soon as they are seated. Customers may want only water with their meals, or in addition to another beverage.

When serving water, place water glasses above the entrée knife and in line with its tip. Do not allow a serving pitcher to touch the rim of a customer's glass. Do not fill a glass more than ½ inch from the rim. Overfilling is a sign of sloppy service and causes spilling.

Refill water glasses whenever needed during the meal. Do not allow customers' glasses to be less than ⅓ full.

Serve Hot Beverages

Many customers have coffee or hot tea with their meals. A hot beverage may be the customer's last impression of the meal and the service. To ensure quality service, warm the cups or mugs before presetting the table or placing them in front of the customer. A customer who receives hot coffee in a cold cup or mug will have lukewarm coffee, especially if he or she adds milk.

The setup for coffee or hot tea must be completed before the beverage is served. The setup for coffee consists of cream, sugar, a cup and saucer or a mug, and a teaspoon. Coffee is poured from the customer's right side with your right hand. Hot water for tea is often served in a separate container. Offer to bring more hot water as needed.

Sell the Menu

Servers represent the menu to customers. Servers must know the descriptions, ingredients, and prices of all regular and special menu items. Many customers have dietary requirements or allergies. Servers can suggest alternatives, or can check with the chef if the customer has questions.

Some restaurants allow servers to participate in taste panels. This allows them to try dishes that they will recommend to customers. Servers should be able to identify seasonings and cooking methods of special menu items.

An effective server encourages customers to try different items. You can use highlighting, open-ended questions, and upselling. When servers use these selling techniques, customers may be more inclined to try something new or order more items. It is part of the server's role to increase sales and enhance the customer's dining experience.

Highlighting

Servers can use highlighting to promote specials of the day or regular menu items. **Highlighting** means emphasizing a particular menu item. It is important for servers to have favorite items on the menu. It is easier to recommend items that you personally like. The enthusiasm shown by a server for a food item will be clear through his or her description. Remember, however, that the customer should make the final decision.

Listening Skills Listen carefully to each customer when you take food orders. *How can servers ensure that they have taken food orders correctly?*

Open-Ended Questions

Ask questions that require a specific answer. Open-ended questions cannot be answered with yes or no. For example, rather than asking, "Would you like something to start with?" you might ask, "What would you like to start with?" This suggests that the customer is expected to order something right away after sitting.

Upselling

The technique to suggest a larger size or better quality than the customer's original order is called **upselling**. For example, if the prime rib is offered in 10-ounce and 16-ounce servings, you might ask the customer, "Would you like the 16-ounce size?"

Take the Order

Servers use the same position numbers that were used for taking beverage orders to take food orders. Always ask if customers have any questions, or if they are ready to order. According to the restaurant's policy, ask if separate checks are needed. Also, ask about any dietary needs.

Servers should follow these general guidelines to take orders:
- Smile, maintain eye contact, and use a pleasant tone of voice.
- Listen carefully to each customer.
- Take one customer's complete order, and then confirm the order before you move to the next customer.
- Take the menu from each customer after you have taken his or her order.

Write the Order

Usually, the server takes orders on a customer check or transfers them directly into a computerized system. You need to write quickly and clearly when you take an order. You must learn the shortened forms of words, or abbreviations (ə-ˌbrē-vē-ˈa-shənz), that are understood by the kitchen staff.

PHOTO CAPTION ANSWER Servers can repeat orders back to customers to ensure that they have copied down the information correctly.

When you use an order pad, write down the table number and the customer's position number next to each item ordered. If a customer orders the same item as another customer, add the second customer's seat number next to the item. Place the quantity of each item in front of it. This technique will make it easier for the kitchen to fill the order. You may also need to write down additional information (for example, the degree of doneness for red meat or dressing on the side).

Transmit the Order

The three ways to place an order in the kitchen are to write out a customer check, recite the order from memory, or use a computerized point-of-sales system. Using a **point-of-sale system** involves a computer that has either a number or a button code for each item on the menu. By simply pressing a button or entering a code, the order is sent to the kitchen.

A verbal ordering system is sometimes used in very elegant restaurants. Most foodservice operations use a computerized point-of-sale system. A handwritten system of customer checks is used if the computer system breaks down. Servers must be able to clearly write an order in an organized way. Each course should be listed in the correct order.

Electronic Ordering

Nearly every foodservice establishment uses a computer to help communication and service flow smoothly. There are many benefits to using point-of-sale computer technology:

- **Fewer Errors** The computer sends orders to a printer in the proper workstations. For example, cold food orders are sent to the pantry and hot food orders are sent to the hot line. The computer also tracks each menu item and may be programmed to tell the server how many portions are available to sell.
- **Increased Efficiency** Using a touch pad computer to send orders also cuts down on steps for the server and increases accuracy in ordering. Orders are organized and easy to read, and the system prints accurate customer checks. Customers receive itemized checks with clearly marked totals.
- **Better Marketing** Management can also add messages to checks, such as "Make Your Reservations Early."
- **Theft Reduction** Item printouts help reduce employee theft. Each server's sales output is available for the manager to check during the server's shift.

To prevent misuse of the computer, each server receives an identity code or key. The computer prompts the server to enter information such as the check number, the number of customers, and the table number. After this information is entered, the server enters the order into the computer.

Reading Check Explain What is a server's objective when greeting customers?

Serve the Order

The technical aspects of service refer to the way items are physically placed before a customer. You should check to make sure that all dishes are complete and properly garnished before you serve them.

More important to customers, however, is the manner in which they are served. Most customers care about the following:

- When delivering dishes, did the server keep his or her fingers on the edge of the plate, away from the food?
- Did the server use his or her left hand to serve the food products from the customer's left side?
- Did the server anticipate customer needs instead of waiting to be asked?

Hand Service

Many restaurants use hand service instead of tray service. **Hand service** is bringing dishes to the table without using a tray. Hand service works well if the distance from the service line in the kitchen to all points of the dining room is short.

A server should be able to carry three soup cups or soup plates on the left arm and hand, with a fourth in the right hand. A server should be able to carry plates on the right arm, with the last plate in the left hand when serving the appetizer, salad, dinner, or dessert courses. You must develop the skill to carry plates, cups, or bowls without tipping or angling them. This will ruin the presentation, and soup or sauces will run onto the rim of the bowl or plate. If soup does spill along the rim of the bowl, wipe it clean using a server napkin or towel.

Hand service often requires more teamwork between service staff members. The size of a party may prevent one server from carrying all the plates to a table at one time. No matter what type of service is used, everyone at a table should be served at approximately the same time.

Tray Service

Tray service involves bringing dishes to the table at the same time on a large tray. Tray service allows the server to carry more cups, bowls, and plates without worrying as much about the presentation.

Tray service is almost universally used in banquet service. A single server can carry a course for 10 to 12 guests at a time. Dinner plates are covered with plate covers to allow dinners to be stacked one on top of another. For banquet service, portion foods onto trays, and prepare menu slips or tray cards to identify the dishes on the tray.

Service Trays and Stands

A **tray stand**, or tray jack, has metal, wood, or plastic leg frames that will fold. The leg frames are usually connected by two fiber or cloth support straps that hold the legs steady when the tray stand is set up. Some frames include a low-level shelf to use as a small side stand. Follow these general guidelines when you use service trays and tray stands:

- To prevent plate slippage and accidents, service trays are usually lined with rubber or cork. If the service tray is not already lined, use a wet service napkin to line the inside of the tray.
- Arrange items on the tray so it is as evenly balanced as possible.
- Pick up and carry the heaviest part of the tray closest to your body.
- Always carry a service tray in the left hand when going through a door. This allows you to go through a doorway without the door swinging back and hitting the tray.
- Carry the tray on your fingertips or palm, depending on the tray's weight.
- Use your left shoulder to help balance the tray if necessary.
- Carry the folded tray stand on your right while you walk in the dining room.
- Try not to place the tray stand right next to the customer's table when you set it up. Leave a little space instead.

Tray Service Carrying a service tray in one hand allows you to set up and take down a tray stand with the other hand. *Why is it important to have a procedure to set up and take down a tray stand?*

- After clearing a customer's table, use a service napkin to cover the tray before you carry it from the dining room.
- Remove the tray and tray stand as soon as the table is cleared.
- To prevent accidents, tray stands should always be folded and placed out of busy traffic lanes when they are not being used. Follow these steps when you unfold a tray stand at a table:
- Extend the arm holding the tray stand and flick your wrist. The support legs will separate, bringing the tray stand to an open position. Place the tray stand so that one set of legs faces your side. This will ensure that as you place the tray on the stand, the top cross bar will not obstruct your movements. The frame legs should be parallel to your body.
- Turn, bend your knees, and lower the tray horizontally until it sits directly on the tray stand.

- Carefully slide the tray across the top of the tray stand to distribute the tray weight evenly.
- Keep your back straight. Bend and lift with your knees and legs when you pick up or put down a loaded tray.
- Reverse the process when you remove the tray. While you hold the tray level, collapse the tray stand against your hip. Then, remove both the tray stand and the tray.

Course Service

In addition to following procedures for using trays and stands, servers must follow procedures for serving each course. There are separate guidelines for serving bread, appetizers, soup, salad, entrées, and desserts.

Food is always served from the customer's left with your left hand. Dishes are cleared from the customer's right with your right hand whenever possible.

PHOTO CAPTION ANSWER Procedures for using trays and tray stands help lower the possibility that the server might drop hot or heavy items from the tray.

✓ **Hot Plates**

Always use a clean, folded service towel when you handle hot plates. This will prevent hot plates from burning or hurting you or the customer. Be sure to warn customers when their plates are hot.

CRITICAL THINKING *Why is food sometimes served on a hot plate?*

Bread Service

Bread is usually served once the beverage order has been taken and served. Preset butter or olive oil. To **preset** items means to set them on the table before food is served. Place the bread or rolls in the center of the table. Do not touch the bread or rolls with your hands. Serve enough bread or rolls initially for each customer to have one-and-a-half servings.

Appetizer Service

Appetizers are frequently offered on a menu. An **appetizer** is a small portion of hot or cold food meant to stimulate the appetite that is served as the first course of a meal.

If a customer orders a cold and a hot appetizer, serve the cold appetizer first, unless asked to do otherwise. If two or more customers will share an appetizer, divide and plate equal, attractive portions. Or, place the appetizer between the customers. Offer serving utensils and a clean plate for each customer who will share the appetizer.

Soup Service

If the customer orders a cup or bowl of soup or chowder, you will serve it from the customer's left in a cup or bowl placed on a saucer or an underliner. An **underliner** is a dish placed under another dish to protect the table from spills. If the underliner does not have an insert for the bowl to sit in, use a paper doily to keep the bowl from slipping. Place the soup spoon on the saucer or underliner before you clear the soup to prevent accidents and spills.

Salad Service

The salad can be presented before or after the entrée. In the United States, a salad is usually served before the entrée. In other countries, a salad is often served after the entrée. Become familiar with any particular dining customs associated with ethnic cuisine.

Serve cold salads on chilled plates from the customer's left. Preset a salad fork and knife. Salad forks are generally smaller than dinner forks.

Entrée Service

When you hand-carry plates or use food trays, be sure the plates stay level. Carefully placed food items can shift, affecting presentation. Sauces can flow together if a plate is tipped. When you place the plate in front of the customer, allow about 1 inch between the edge of the plate and the table edge. Use your left hand to place the plate from the customer's left side.

Dessert Service

Dessert is usually the last chance to impress customers. Showing desserts is a very effective way of merchandising, or selling, them. Many foodservice operations display their desserts on trays or on rolling carts.

Ask customers if they would like milk, coffee, water, tea or a cordial, a sweet alcoholic beverage, with their desserts. When you preset the dessert course, set the appropriate utensil at the customer's place before you serve dessert. A dessert fork should be placed to the left for cake and pie. A dessert spoon is placed to the right for ice cream and pudding. Serve all desserts from the customer's left.

⌒ Small Bites ⌒

Adjust Utensils Forks, knives, and spoons should always suit the food order. Whichever utensil will be used first should be placed on the outside. If the customer has used an incorrect utensil, clear it from the table and preset the correct utensil for the next course.

Carry-Out Orders

Some customers may want to order food to carry out of the restaurant. Use these steps to prepare carry-out orders for customers:

- Place the customer's order with the kitchen. Specify that the order is for carry-out.
- Prepare any items that the kitchen would not, such as rolls.
- Assemble the order once it is ready, and double-check it to make sure it is correct.
- Place the order in a bag. Add any necessary condiments.
- Bring the order to the customer.

During and After the Meal

Servers should check back with their customers during the meal to see whether they are satisfied. However, be careful not to interrupt the customer too often. You can check back with customers by sight as well as sound. Check back with the customers once they have been given a minute or two to taste the food. Watch their reactions as they taste the food. If they appear content, no further action is required. If a customer's facial expression shows disappointment or displeasure, however, ask whether the dish is prepared to his or her liking.

Clear the Table

Use a tray to make clearing and carrying soiled dishes and service items safer, easier, and more efficient. Watch tables regularly to decide whether all customers have finished eating before clearing any dish. Customers might push the dish away, place their napkins on the table, or lay the utensils side by side across the dish to show that they have finished with a course.

If you clear a customer's dish before all of the customers are finished, you may make him or her feel rushed. Clear the dishes from the right side using your right hand. Do not reach across the table or in front of customers unless absolutely necessary. Keep cleared plates in your left hand away from the customer and table. Move around the table clockwise. Do not overstack dishes on your arm or on the tray, and do not stack dishes on top of food. Do not scrape leftover food from one plate onto another plate when you stack dishes.

Although many foodservice operations are smoke-free, some have separate smoking areas. Ashtrays should be changed by placing a clean ashtray over the dirty one. Remove both from the table, and then place the clean one back on the table.

Assess Customer Satisfaction

There are many ways to assess how satisfied customers are with their meals and service:

- Use a survey or feedback cards. Ask customers, "How was your meal?"
- Listen for customer comments throughout the meal.
- Share comments with your manager. File any written comments for later use.
- Work to improve your service based on customer comments.

Reading Check **Explain** When is the salad course usually served in the United States?

Calculate Customer Checks

Every restaurant has its own policy about customer checks. In some places, the server or cashier calculates the check. Other operations use a computer. Regardless of the method, you must accurately list charges on the check.

ᔡ Small Bites ᔡ

Crumb the Table Crumbing is the process of removing crumbs that may have accumulated during the meal. The proper way to crumb a table is to fold a service towel into a small square and use it to brush the particles onto a small plate. Some manufacturers make crumbing sets with a scraper.

READING CHECK ANSWER In the United States, the salad course is usually served before the entrée course.

It is expensive to operate a foodservice business. If servers do not accurately charge customers, profit will be lost. Managers generally double-check the accuracy of checks.

Hand-Calculated Checks

There are still a few foodservice operations where servers need to calculate the check by hand. Do this away from the customers' table and use a calculator. To prepare the check, list all of the charges and double-check that the prices are correct. Next, add the prices of all the food and beverage items. This is the subtotal. Then, add the sales tax to the subtotal. This gives you the grand total.

A TASTE OF HISTORY

2004
SpaceShipOne, the first privately funded spacecraft, launches

2005
Chef Thomas Keller replaces tipping in his restaurant with a fixed service charge

Tipping Point

The practice of tipping can be traced back to the coffeehouses of sixteenth-century Europe, and perhaps even further. English sources believe that the word "tip" was originally medieval street talk for "hand it over." Many historians believe that the first tips were gold that was thrown to peasants by feudal lords riding horses, as payment for safe passage. However, tipping did not become widespread in America until the middle of the nineteenth century.

For many years, the standard tip in America was 10%. This rose to 15% in the 1970s, and today, many foodservice workers receive a tip of 20% or more for a job well done. Internationally, tipping practices are varied. In some countries, the tip amount is automatically added to the check. In other countries, it is considered rude to tip a server. For some larger parties, a tip in the form of a service charge is added to the total of the check.

History Application

Write a dialogue between two people discussing the pros and cons of tipping and the effects it has on service employees.

NCSS V B Culture Analyze group and institutional influences on people, events, and elements of culture in both historical and contemporary settings.

Computer-Calculated Checks

Most foodservice operations use computers that perform every calculation. The server puts the order into the computer. That information then appears on the computerized check. Computer-calculated checks are convenient and reliable. Totals are accurate, and each item's price, the subtotal, the tax, and the grand total all appear on the check.

Check Errors

Errors are always possible. Errors are fairly simple to correct if you catch them early enough. If you make an error, simply draw a line through the error and begin again. Most foodservice operations use numbered checks. If a computerized check is printed before the error is noticed, or if a written check is beyond fixing, ask your supervisor what to do.

Present the Check

Prepare the customer check once you are certain the customer has finished ordering. A good server will **anticipate**, or predict, the request for the check. Make sure that all items and the check total are accurate. The check should be legible and clean.

Before you present the check, all unnecessary plates, glasses, and utensils should have been cleared from the table. Give the check to the host of the party, or place it in the center of the table. When the server collects the payment, the check is placed on a check tray, a small plate, or in a check folder. Check back often to see if payment is ready.

Cash

In many foodservice operations, the customers pay the server directly. Be sensitive to whether customers seem to want to sit and talk or pay the bill immediately. If the customer pays with cash, be sure that the correct payment is received. Never ask customers if they want change. Always give them the change and thank them for their business.

After you present the check, return to the table within five minutes, or when you see the customer has placed money or a credit card with the bill. Take the money to the cash register. Be sure the change is correct before you return it to the table. Place the money to the left of the person who paid the bill. Thank your customers and invite them to return.

Credit Cards

Many customers pay by credit card. Credit cards are easier to carry than cash, and they provide customers with an expense record.

Most restaurants today use an electronic credit card machine that may be part of a point-of-sale computer system. The card will need to be swiped through the machine correctly. The correct total must be entered into the computer. It should be double-checked before the total is transmitted.

Use these steps:
- Check the expiration date and the customer's signature.

- Make sure the customer signs the credit slip. Compare the signatures.
- Immediately return the credit card to the correct customer.
- If the card is declined, return it to the customer and ask for another form of payment.

Service Tips

Customers show their appreciation for good service by tipping. A tip is usually based on a percentage of the check amount, depending on the type of establishment. A good tipping guide is a minimum of 15% of the total of the check. Outstanding service at a restaurant might call for a tip of 20% to 30% of the check total. Although the federal government sets a minimum wage, servers are often paid less than the minimum wage by employers because money from tips is expected to make up the difference.

 Reading Check Describe How do you prepare a hand-calculated check?

SECTION 5.2 **After You Read**

Review Key Concepts

1. **Describe** how to transmit an order.
2. **List** the guidelines for serving bread.
3. **Demonstrate** how to handle credit cards.

Practice Culinary Academics
English Language Arts

4. Review the information on tipping in this section's A Taste of History feature. Research the practice of tipping in other countries. Take notes on your research, and organize it either by country or by tipping practice. Discuss as a class how tipping customs differ in other countries and what elements of different cultures might influence tipping practices. Use your notes to support your arguments.

NCTE 9 Develop an understanding of diversity in language use across cultures.

 Mathematics

5. You present a check of $86.43 to one of your customers, who then pays with a $100 bill. How much change is due to the customer? What bills and coins can you use to provide the change?

Math Concept **Calculating Change** The amount of change due is calculated by subtracting the amount due from the amount actually paid. Count out change beginning with pennies and moving up to larger coins and bills.

Starting Hint Subtract the amount due ($86.43) from the amount paid ($100) to determine the change. Count out the coins and bills you need to get from $86.43 to $100, starting with pennies.

NCTM Number and Operations Compute fluently and make reasonable estimates.

Check your answers at this book's Online Learning Center at **glencoe.com**.

READING CHECK ANSWER List all charges; double-check prices; add all food and beverage prices; add sales tax; present the check with the grand total listed.

Review and Applications

Chapter Summary

Customer service positions include hosts, servers, bussers, and cashiers. Service employees should have a positive attitude, a neat and clean appearance, good communication and teamwork skills, job knowledge, and the ability to use time wisely. Servers must greet customers, assist them with their questions, take their orders, transmit them to the kitchen, serve the food, and tabulate and present the check. Excellent service can help boost restaurant profits.

Content and Academic Vocabulary Review

1. Arrange the vocabulary terms below into groups of related words. Explain why you put the words together.

Content Vocabulary

- reputation (p. 116)
- host (p. 116)
- reservation (p. 116)
- server (p. 117)
- section/station (p. 117)
- busser (p. 118)
- service station (p. 118)
- course (p. 118)
- cashier (p. 118)
- patronage (p. 119)
- client base (p. 119)
- uniform (p. 119)
- bag-in-the-box system (p. 122)
- tank system (p. 122)
- espresso (p. 122)
- cappuccino (p. 123)
- demitasse (p. 124)
- infuse (p. 124)
- cover (p. 127)
- highlighting (p. 128)
- upselling (p. 129)
- point-of-sale system (p. 130)
- hand service (p. 131)
- tray service (p. 131)
- tray stand (p. 131)
- preset (p. 133)
- appetizer (p. 133)
- underliner (p. 133)

Academic Vocabulary

- offset (p. 116)
- interact (p. 119)
- objective (p. 127)
- anticipate (p. 135)

Review Key Concepts

2. **Outline** the duties of each member of the service staff.

3. **Summarize** the traits servers need to have to provide excellent customer service.

4. **Compare** and contrast the different types of beverage service.

5. **Describe** the server's role in greeting customers and taking orders.

6. **List** the order of service for a meal.

7. **Demonstrate** how to total a check and accept different forms of payment.

Critical Thinking

8. **Analyze** various companies' practices regarding customer satisfaction. How can this help you improve your service to customers?

9. **Describe** how good teamwork benefits the customer. How do the host, server, busser, and cashier work together as a team?

10. **Imagine** you are a restaurant manager hiring for server positions. What qualities would you look for in a potential employee? Why?

Academic Skills

 English Language Arts

11. Effective Communication Imagine you are a host and service is running behind. You are unable to seat a customer with a reservation. She has been waiting for 20 minutes. She is angry and asks to be seated immediately, but her table will not be ready for another 10 minutes. Write out two ways of handling the situation: One that demonstrates good customer service, and one that demonstrates poor customer service.

> **NCTE 12** Use language to accomplish individual purposes.

 Social Studies

12. Development of Utensils Research the development of eating utensils. How were the knife, spoon, and fork invented? How did people eat before they were invented? What other types of eating utensils do people use around the world? Choose one type of utensil and write a report about its invention and development, how it is used, and which cultures use that utensil. Cite your information sources.

> **NCSS VIII A Science, Technology, and Society** Identify and describe both current and historical examples of the interaction and interdependence of science, technology, and society in a variety of cultural settings.

 Mathematics

13. Probability During bread service, you bring a basket of rolls to a table. The basket contains 4 sourdough rolls and 3 wheat rolls, and is covered by a napkin. When you present the basket to your customer, he reaches into the basket without looking and selects a roll. What is the probability that he selected a sourdough roll, rather than a wheat roll?

Math Concept **Finding Theoretical Probability** The probability of an event is a number between 0 and 1 that measures the chance of the event occurring. To find an event's probability, write a fraction with the total number of possible outcomes as the denominator and the number of ways the event can occur as the numerator.

Starting Hint Determine the number of ways that the event of selecting a sourdough roll can occur. Because there are 4 different sourdough rolls in the basket, there are 4 ways that the customer can select a sourdough roll. This number becomes the numerator. The denominator equals all possible outcomes, which here is the total number of rolls that are in the basket.

> **NCTM Data Analysis and Probability** Understand and apply basic concepts of probability.

Certification Prep

Directions Read the questions. Then, read the answer choices and choose the best possible answer for each.

14. What piece of equipment is best used for removing ice from the ice maker?

    a. hand   **c.** water glass

    b. metal or plastic scoop   **d.** spoon

15. How much space should be allowed between the edge of the plate and the table edge when placing a plate in front of a customer?

    a. 1 foot   **c.** about 1 inch

    b. 3 inches   **d.** 18 centimeters

Sharpen your test-taking skills to improve your kitchen certification program score.

Test-Taking Tip
Be sure to read all answers, paying attention to words like correct and best. If you are asked to choose the best answer, there may be more than one correct answer from which to choose.

Real-World Skills and Applications

Communication Skills

16. Sell the Menu Get a menu from a local restaurant and review the items on the menu and their prices. Imagine that you work as a server in a restaurant. Follow your teacher's directions to form pairs. With your partner, practice suggesting items from the menu, and guiding the customer through the menu. Then, switch places.

Critical Thinking Skills

17. Good Customer Service Examine the relationship between skillful servers and customer satisfaction. How do well-trained servers contribute to customer satisfaction? How can poorly trained servers take away from customer satisfaction? How important do you think servers are to how a customer views his or her restaurant experience? Discuss these topics as a class.

Technology Applications

18. Create a Chart Using word processing or desktop publishing software, create a chart that illustrates the skills that you will need to have to provide good customer service at a restaurant. Your chart can take whatever form you like, but it must be easy for new foodservice employees to understand. It must also be a useful tool for anyone who wants to be reminded of good customer service skills. Display your finished charts in class.

Financial Literacy

19. Calculate Change It is important for a server to know how to quickly and accurately calculate change from a check for a customer. Calculate the change for the following restaurant payments: A $100 bill for a check total of $39.77; a $50 bill for a check total of $42.50; and a $20 bill for a check total of $11.23.

Culinary Lab

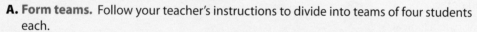

Use the culinary skills you have learned in this chapter.

Practice Table Service

20. Practice Serving In this project you will divide into teams of four and practice being the server to a table set for three people.

A. Form teams. Follow your teacher's instructions to divide into teams of four students each.

B. Gather supplies. Gather the following supplies: linen; beverage tray; serving tray and tray stand; glasses, cups, and saucers; bread plates; salad plates; soup bowls; dinner plates; dessert plates; flatware for each course; blank check and writing instrument; check tray or folder.

C. Assign duties. Determine the role each person will play and then enact a meal, from greeting the customer through payment and making change.

D. Prepare for service. Number a sheet of paper for as many students as will be servers. After each participant serves, write down what you thought of his or her service.

E. Evaluate service. Watch and listen closely as each server takes his or her turn and answer the questions listed in the evaluation section.

Create Your Evaluation

Fill out an evaluation page for each server answering the following questions:

- How does the server talk to the customer?
- How does the server move around the table?
- Does the server place and clear from the correct position?
- Does the server place and remove the tableware and glassware properly?

Make a list of the areas with which people had the most problems.

The Dining Experience

SECTIONS

6.1 Dining Today

6.2 The Dining Room
Environment

WRITING ACTIVITY

Write About an Event

Write a descriptive paragraph about a special dining event. Use sensory details to describe the atmosphere and decor, the type of service, and the food.

Writing Tips

1 Use meaningful sensory descriptions and details.

2 Organize your story in a logical manner.

3 Use language that is appropriate for your audience.

EXPLORE THE PHOTO

Fine-dining establishments feature an elegant atmosphere. *To what does the atmosphere of a restaurant refer?*

WRITING ACTIVITY ANSWER Paragraphs should use descriptive language, and correct spelling, grammar, and punctuation. The paragraph structure should be logical.

EXPLORE THE PHOTO ANSWER The atmosphere can include the decor, the lighting, the staff uniforms, and more.

Dining Today

Different dining styles attract different customers.

Reading Guide

 Before You Read

Vocabulary To gain a better understanding of vocabulary, create a Vocabulary Journal. Divide a piece of paper into three columns. Label the first column Vocabulary. Then, label the other columns What Is It? and What Else Is It Like? Write down each term and its definition as you read.

Read to Learn

Key Concepts
- **Categorize** the five main types of dining environments.
- **Distinguish** between different styles of meal service.

Main Idea

There are five different types of dining establishments: fine-dining, theme restaurants, casual dining, quick-service, and catering. There are also several different styles of meal service.

Content Vocabulary

- fine-dining restaurant
- theme restaurant
- casual-dining establishment
- trayline service
- counter service
- food court
- room service
- modern American plated service
- booth
- focal point
- family service
- banquette
- classical French service
- tableside
- flambé
- Russian/English service
- butler service
- hors d'oeuvre
- buffet
- chafing dish

Academic Vocabulary

- promote
- device

ACADEMIC STANDARDS

 English Language Arts
NCTE 1 Read texts to acquire new information.

 Mathematics
NCTM Geometry Use visualization, spatial reasoning, and geometric modeling to solve problems.

 Social Studies
NCSS IV E Individual Development and Identity Examine the interaction of ethnic, natural, or cultural influences in specific situations or events.

NCSS II D Time, Continuity, and Change Systematically employ processes of critical historical inquiry to reconstruct and reinterpret the past.

NCTE National Council of Teachers of English

NCTM National Council of Teachers of Mathematics

NSES National Science Education Standards

NCSS National Council for the Social Studies

Graphic Organizer

As you read, use a table like the one below to help you describe the five different types of dining.

Types of Dining

Dining Style	Description

 Graphic Organizer
Go to this book's Online Learning Center at **glencoe.com** for a printable graphic organizer.

GRAPHIC ORGANIZER ANSWER Fine-dining: high-quality food, service, decor; high prices. Theme: atmosphere creates another place or time. Casual dining: relaxed dining; mid-range prices. Quick-service: Limited menus; low prices; speedy service. Catering: food prepared at client location.

Types of Dining

Each type of dining environment has unique challenges for the foodservice professional. The type of establishment and its meal service strongly influence a customer's dining experience. Learn about these factors so that you can better serve customers. This will help you build a rewarding foodservice career.

Different types of dining appeal to different customers. The five most common types of dining are fine-dining restaurants, theme restaurants, casual-dining establishments, quick-service restaurants, and catering services. These types differ in menu prices, decor, the type of food served, and the way food is served.

Some restaurants **promote**, or advertise, themes and special events, such as special birthday dinners, holiday buffets, or seasonal specialties. Themes and events like these can bring in a strong customer base.

Fine-Dining Restaurants

A **fine-dining restaurant** has an environment with excellent food, elegant decor, and superior service. Customers are willing to pay top prices for a meal in fine-dining establishments. Some of these restaurants are famous for their chef's exceptional culinary skills. Others are known for their specific location.

Theme Restaurants

A **theme restaurant** often tries to recreate another place or time. Customers enjoy seeing sports memorabilia or an indoor waterfall in the middle of a simulated rain forest. They are attracted to the fun and unique atmosphere. The food can often be less important than the decor. Or, the food may be related to the theme, as in a table-top grill restaurant. Most theme restaurants have a moderately priced menu.

Casual-Dining Establishments

A **casual-dining establishment** attracts people who like to eat out, but are not interested in a formal atmosphere or high prices. Instead, they enjoy the relaxed environment and mid-range prices of casual dining.

Sometimes casual-dining restaurants have a theme. The Hard Rock Cafe® has a music theme, for example. Other common casual-dining establishments include family-style restaurants, neighborhood restaurants, grills and buffets, and vending machines.

Family-Style Restaurants

The menu is more limited in a casual, family-style restaurant. Traditional, child-friendly favorites, such as fried chicken and macaroni and cheese, are served. Family-style restaurants have mid-range prices.

Neighborhood Establishments

Two popular types of casual neighborhood establishments are lunch counters and coffee shops. The food is usually simple, inexpensive, and comes in generous portions. Coffee houses are a popular type of neighborhood establishment. Customers like neighborhood establishments because they are convenient and friendly.

Grills and Buffets

Casual grills and buffet restaurants offer self-service meals at budget prices. Buffet restaurants often offer all-you-can-eat specials that appeal to families and senior citizens. Many buffets and cafeterias offer trayline and counter service. **Trayline service** consists of customers going through a food line and placing items on their own trays. **Counter service** consists of customers sitting at a counter, rather than at a booth, banquette, or table.

Vending Machines

Vending machines offer a wide variety of foods and beverages. Vending machines operate 24 hours a day. They are popular with college students and factory workers. Many companies save money by using vending machines rather than running a full-service dining room or cafeteria.

Quick-Service Restaurants

Quick-service restaurants, also known as fast food, make up the largest section of the foodservice industry. A quick-service restaurant has limited menus, low prices, and speedy service. Food is prepared using exact standards and factory-like production.

Malls and shopping centers often place many quick-service restaurants into a single area. This area is called a **food court**. Food courts give shoppers convenient access to a variety of quick meals, snacks and beverages. Small food courts that offer three or four options can also be found in many hospitals, colleges, and supermarkets.

Catering Services

Catering is a growing segment of the foodservice industry. A caterer purchases, receives stores, prepares, cooks, delivers, and serves food to a customer in another location. Catered meals vary in size.

In an attempt to increase sales, many institutions have begun to provide catering services. For example, some supermarkets, schools, and hospitals use their kitchens to cater to outside customers.

Contract Foodservice

For a management fee, a foodservice contractor will provide food and beverage service for organizations such as schools, businesses, hospitals, and nursing homes. This can save money for an organization. Meals may still be prepared on-site. However, management of the foodservice is not run by the organization.

Airline Meals

Food catered for airlines is limited by storage needs and transportation. Airline customers may be offered one or more full meals, or just snacks and beverages. Meals for travelers are prepared in a commissary ('kä-mə-ˌser-ē), or a place where food is purchased and prepared. Then, it is delivered to airplanes and loaded onboard for people to eat. Special meals, such as vegetarian or low-fat requests, can be ordered in advance.

School Meals Foodservice in schools may be provided by a foodservice contractor. *How would this save money for a school?*

Hotel and Motel Restaurants

Hotel and motel restaurants offer longer service hours. Most of these restaurants serve three meals a day, seven days a week. Labor costs are high, especially with room service. **Room service** involves having servers bring specially ordered meals to a customer's room.

Cruise Ship Dining

For many people, one of the highlights of taking a cruise is the excellent food. There is no limit on the amount of food, and the cost is included in the price of the cruise. Food on a cruise ship is usually offered in different settings. Special dietary needs can also be met.

Reading Check **Apply** Why are vending machines popular with college students and factory workers?

Types of Meal Service

There is a style of serving meals to match every dining establishment's customers and goals. Different elements of each style can also be mixed. These include modern American plated, booth, family style, banquette, classical French, Russian/English, butler, and buffet service.

Modern American Plated Service

Modern American plated service began in the United States. It is now used worldwide. It is popular because it requires fewer and less extensively trained service staff than other types of meal service. It also gives the chef complete control over the preparation, portioning, and presentation of the food.

In **modern American plated service**, the food is completely prepared, portioned, plated, and garnished in the kitchen. The servers carry the plated food from the kitchen and place the prepared dishes in front of the customer. The server must be able to serve from both the left and the right side of each customer.

Follow these general guidelines for modern American plated service:

- Serve beverages and soup from the customer's right side, with your right hand and right foot forward. Move clockwise to the next customer.
- Serve solid foods from the customer's left side, with your left hand and left foot forward. Move counterclockwise to the next customer.
- Clear dishes from the customer's right side, with your right hand and right foot forward. You may clear some items that are on the customer's left from the left side, such as forks or bread plates.
- Completely serve and clear one guest before moving on to the next.
- Never break the order of service.

This type of service is more efficient than many other styles of service. The savings can be passed on to the customer through reasonable menu prices.

Booth Service

Booth service has different service guidelines because the server cannot go to the customer's left or right side. A **booth** table rests against, or is attached to, a wall. All customers must be served from a single focal point. A **focal point** is a service point. (See **Figure 6.1**.) The customers on the right side of the booth will be served from the left with the server's left hand. The customers on the left side will be served from the right with the server's right hand.

Use these general service guidelines to serve at a booth:

- Serve the customers in the back of the booth first.
- Using the correct hand procedures, clear soiled tableware first from the customers seated closest to the back.
- For beverage service, do not switch hands. Keep the tray in your left hand and serve beverages with the right. Try not to get in the way of the guest.
- Always keep your hands as close to table level as possible.
- Avoid handing items to customers whenever possible. Instead, place the item on the table.

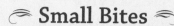
Family Service

Family service is used in a casual-dining atmosphere. In **family service**, food is delivered on a large platter or dish to an individual table. Customers serve themselves and pass the food around the table. This type of service creates an atmosphere of eating dinner at home. Foods are prepared completely in the kitchen and placed on platters or in casserole dishes. Then, they are placed in the center of the customers' table with the correct serving utensils and a service plate for each customer.

One advantage of family service is that it allows customers to choose their own portion sizes. Customers are also free to take second servings of a food if they want more. On the other hand, this service style can result in a large amount of food waste. It also lacks personalized service.

▼ FIGURE 6.1 Booth Seating

Booth Service In booth service, all customers are served from a single focal point.

Why would you serve the customers in the back of the booth first?

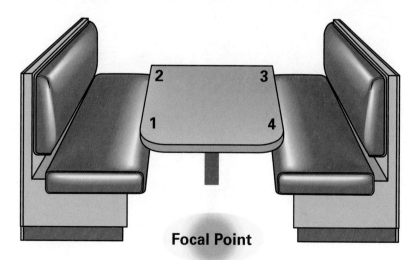

Focal Point

FIGURE CAPTION ANSWER Customers in the back of the booth should be served first so that the server does not accidentally brush against food already served to customers in the front of the booth.

Banquette Service

Banquette (ban-'ket) is a type of seating arrangement in which customers are seated facing the server with their backs against the wall. (See **Figure 6.2**.) Use the following guidelines when you serve at a banquette:

- Treat both ends of the banquette as focal points. Serve one side of the table at a time.
- When you serve a banquette with more than four people, serve each end of the table as you would a booth.
- Hold the beverage tray in your left hand. Serve with the right hand. Stand with your right hip close to the table.

Classical French Service

The most elegant and elaborate style of service is **classical French service**. It is used internationally when a formal style of service is desired. An important element of classical French service is that some foods are fully or partially presented or prepared tableside.

Tableside means at the table, in full view of the customer. This means that classical French service requires more time and labor than modern American plated service.

Servers of this style must be highly skilled. Successful classical French service uses a team system. The typical French brigade consists of a four-member team. Each member of the team has a specific duty:

- **Captain** The captain is responsible for supervising and organizing all aspects of classical French service in his or her station.
- **Front Waiter** The front waiter assists the captain when serving food and should be able to perform the duties of the captain in his or her absence.
- **Back Waiter/Runner** The back waiter or runner brings all of the food from the kitchen area to the service area.
- **Busser** The busser serves bread, butter, and water. He or she also clears the dishes and cleans the table after the customers have left.

▼ FIGURE 6.2 **Banquette Service**

Banquette Service In banquette service, both ends of the banquette are focal points.
How should you serve a banquette table that has more than four customers?

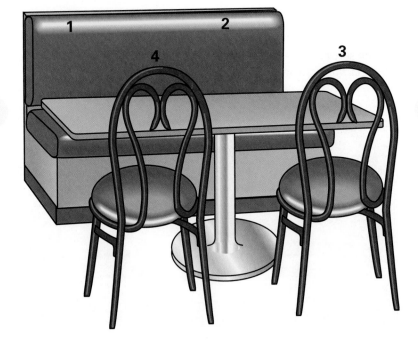

Focal Point   Focal Point

Tableside Service Preparing foods tableside is an elegant part of classical French service. *What other elements characterize classical French service?*

Tableside Preparation

Tableside food preparation is an important part of classical French service. However, it also can be used with other services. Tableside preparations are made on a cart called a guéridon (gā-rē-'dōⁿ) using a cooking unit called a réchaud (rā-shō). These preparations are classified into four categories:

Assembling This includes salads or dishes such as Caesar salad that must be assembled.

Saucing and Garnishing This category includes dishes that are precooked in the kitchen and need finishing touches, such as sauces and garnishes.

Sautéing or Flambéing Items in this category are sautéed or flambéed quickly in the dining room. To **flambé** (fläm-'bā) an item is to cook it tableside using flames as part of the preparation. Examples include shrimp with garlic or bananas foster.

Carving and Deboning Fish, meat, and poultry dishes are often carved or deboned, or have bones removed, tableside. This category also includes slicing cheese and peeling fruit. Peeling, coring, pitting, and slicing fruit allows customers to eat the fruit easily without using their fingers.

Russian/English Service

Russian service is another elegant, formal service that is used internationally. It is ideal for banquets where everyone is eating the same meal. In **Russian service**, also called **English service**, each course is completely prepared, cooked, portioned, and garnished in the kitchen and then placed on a service plate or platters. Each customer is served a portion of the product from large platters. It is served from the left, using utensils that are held in the server's right hand. Two different servers usually perform Russian service. One server delivers the entrée. The other server brings the rest of the meal.

Service guidelines for Russian/English service include:

- Servers have a clean service napkin or towel draped over their left forearm. Platters are held in the left hand.
- Service always moves counterclockwise.
- Empty plates and soup bowls are placed in front of the customer from the right side.
- Items are served with the right hand from the customer's left side. The server is standing with his or her left foot forward.
- A serving set is used to transfer food from the platter to the customer's plate.
- All items are removed from the table with the server's right hand from the customer's right side.

Russian Service Russian service is often used at formal banquets where everyone is eating the same meal. *What other types of service might be used at a formal banquet?*

Butler Service

In **butler service**, the server carries the prepared food on a silver tray to standing or seated customers. Customers serve themselves from the trays. This is an efficient and cost-effective way to serve bite-size foods to a large number of people. Butler service is often used to serve an **hors d'oeuvre** (ȯr-'dərv), or a very small portion of food served before a meal.

At a butler-served meal, each course is presented on a platter from the left side of each customer. Customers serve themselves while the server or butler holds the platter. Butler service is cost-effective; but there is no control over how much food is eaten or how it is presented on the plate. Butler service can be a very formal style of service. It also requires patience on the part of the server, since the server must wait until each customer is finished before moving on.

PHOTO CAPTION ANSWER Other types of service that would be appropriate for a banquet include modern American plated service and butler service.

Buffet Service

A **buffet** is a style of service in which all the food is attractively displayed on a table. In a buffet, customers are free to move among the displays of food. Some items are served to customers in a buffet line, while others are not. In most buffets, customers may return to get more food as many times as they wish. Hot foods are placed in chafing ('chā-fiŋ) dishes. A **chafing dish** is a device designed to hold a large pan of food over a canned heat source. A **device** is an item that serves a function. Customers choose what they want, and serve themselves. Customers must get a new plate or bowl each time they return to a buffet line for more food. Warmed or chilled plates and bowls are kept at one end of a buffet line. These plates and bowls must be restocked regularly. Customers may help themselves to food and beverages in buffet service. They may also be served certain foods. Because buffets are mostly self-service, servers can attend many customers.

Three types of buffet service include:

- **Self-Service** Customers serve themselves. This includes appetizers, entrées, salads, desserts, and beverages.
- **Staff-Service** Customers point out their choice, but are served by a member of the service staff. Some items, such as omelets, are prepared to order. Many quick-service restaurants also use this type of service. Prepared trays of foods are kept filled.
- **Mixed Service** Some stations along the buffet line offer self-service for customers, such as salads, accompaniments, or desserts. Other stations, such as a carving station for turkey, offer staff-service.

There are several advantages to a buffet setup. These advantages can include low labor costs and a wide selection of food for customers to choose. Buffets are usually a cost-effective choice for customers as well, allowing them to try many different types of food products.

There are some disadvantages, however. There may be large amounts of wasted food. If servers are careless, tables may not be properly cleared and guests may not receive timely beverage service.

 Reading Check **List** What are the four preparations that can be done at the table?

SECTION 6.1 After You Read

Review Key Concepts

1. **Describe** the four types of casual dining establishments.
2. **Compare and contrast** classical French service and Russian/English service.

Practice Culinary Academics

 Social Studies

3. Conduct research to find a historical restaurant in your community. Use at least two sources. You may look through your community's news archives, or interview restaurant owners and older members of the community. Write a report about the historical restaurant. Describe the establishment and its history.

> **NCSS II D Time, Continuity, and Change** Systematically employ processes of critical historical inquiry to reconstruct and reinterpret the past.

English Language Arts

4. Collect menus from five different types of dining establishments either from the restaurant or by searching on the Internet with your teacher's directions. Compare the offerings on each menu and write a description of what type of customers each restaurant might attract.

> **NCTE 1** Read texts to acquire new information.

READING CHECK ANSWER The four tableside preparations are assembling; saucing and garnishing; sautéing or flambéing; and carving and deboning.

 Mathematics

5. A banquette table at your restaurant measures 30 inches wide and 42 inches long. What is the perimeter of this table? What is the perimeter if two tables are pushed together to form a double-length table?

Math Concept **Calculating a Perimeter** Perimeter refers to the distance around a polygon. Because opposite sides of a rectangle have equal lengths, the perimeter of a rectangle with length l and width w equals $2l + 2w$.

Starting Hint Each table has two sides measuring 30 inches and 2 sides measuring 42 inches. One table's perimeter equals 30 inches + 30 inches + 42 inches + 42 inches, or (2×30 inches) + (2×42 inches).

> **NCTM Geometry** Use visualization, spatial reasoning, and geometric modeling to solve problems.

Check your answers at this book's Online Learning Center at **glencoe.com**.

The Dining Room Environment

Reading Guide

 Before You Read

Preview Choose a Content or Academic Vocabulary word that is new to you. When you find it in the text, write down the definition.

Read to Learn

Key Concepts
- **Describe** the side work that must be done before a service.
- **Contrast** the different types of glassware, dishware, and flatware.
- **Illustrate** how to properly set a table for different situations.
- **Describe** different types of centerpieces.

Main Idea

Maintaining the dining room environment means keeping stations stocked and setting tables appropriately. A well-set table includes napkins, settings, and centerpieces.

Graphic Organizer

As you read, use a main idea chart like the one below to list the four types of centerpieces. Write the centerpiece types in the first-level boxes, and details about each type in the second-level boxes.

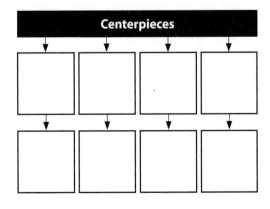

Centerpieces

 Graphic Organizer
Go to this book's Online Learning Center at **glencoe.com** for a printable graphic organizer.

Content Vocabulary
- side work
- condiment
- nonperishable
- glassware
- heat treated
- tableware
- flatware
- serviette
- table setting
- preset menu
- centerpiece

Academic Vocabulary
- elements
- perpendicular

> An organized dining room sets the right tone for any meal.

ACADEMIC STANDARDS

Mathematics
NCTM Geometry
Analyze characteristics of two- and three-dimensional geometric shapes and develop mathematical arguments about geometric relationships.

NCTM Geometry Use visualization, spatial reasoning, and geometric modeling to solve problems.

NCTE National Council of Teachers of English

NCTM National Council of Teachers of Mathematics

NSES National Science Education Standards

NCSS National Council for the Social Studies

GRAPHIC ORGANIZER ANSWER Lighting: Soothing, most common type, uses candles or electric lights. Floral: fresh, dried, or artificial flowers and plants, requires care. Edible: fruit or carved vegetables, sugar creations. Sculpted: ice, butter, beeswax, or chocolate, ice not practical for small tables.

Create a Dining Environment

Every member of the service staff should make sure that customers dine in an inviting atmosphere. An inviting atmosphere that includes good customer service can help restaurants to be more profitable. In this section, you will learn about some of the **elements**, or parts, that help to make a pleasant dining experience. From folding napkins to choosing centerpieces, there are many things you can do to make customers feel welcome.

The atmosphere of a restaurant refers to the textures, colors, aromas, lighting, and sounds that make up a dining environment. This can mean everything from the type of tableware used to the background music played. All of these elements work together to create a pleasing atmosphere. Elements of an atmosphere should be chosen carefully. This atmosphere helps determine the type of service and menu used.

Service is another important element in the dining environment. To be able to provide good service, the service staff must understand and properly use all dining room equipment. Managers must carefully train service staff on the restaurant's perferences.

Side Work

The first step to provide quality service is to prepare and place all necessary equipment before customers arrive. All service staff members have duties to perform before the dining room is open to customers. This is called **side work**. Side work may include cleaning and refilling salt and pepper shakers, sugar containers, and condiment containers. Service employees help stock bus stations with all the materials needed for service and perform routine cleaning duties, including cleaning the seats, table, table base, and floor, folding napkins, and setting tables.

PHOTO CAPTION ANSWER Salt and pepper shakers should be refilled before each shift begins.

Table Preparation Learning to set tables properly is an important skill. *When should salt and pepper shakers be refilled?*

Refill Salt and Pepper Shakers

Refill salt and pepper shakers before each shift. Be sure they are clean and not greasy. Empty and clean them regularly.

Here are some guidelines:

- Use a tray to collect the salt and pepper shakers. Take them to the kitchen and empty them.
- Wash the inside and outside of each shaker. Use a bottle brush to clean the inside.
- Wash the shaker tops to unplug them.
- Be sure the tops and shakers are completely dry before refilling. Otherwise, the salt and pepper will not flow properly.
- Fill the shakers. Use the right-size grain of salt and pepper.
- After you fill the shakers with fresh salt and pepper, tap them to clear out air pockets. Place the shakers on a tray and return them to the tables.

Sanitation Check

✓ **Sanitary Tableware**

Check that all tableware is clean before you use it. To prevent food contamination, handle plates by the rim. Do not use tableware that has clearly visible cracks or chips. Bacteria can settle into these cracks and contaminate a customer's food.

CRITICAL THINKING *How does handling a plate by the rim help prevent food contamination?*

Refill Sugar Bowls

Some state laws ban the use of sugar bowls because loose sugar is not sanitary. Instead, restaurants often use individual sugar packets. If sugar bowls are used, however, clean the bowls daily. Check for lumps, and remove them with a dry spoon. Always check and refill sugar containers before they become empty.

Refill Condiments

A **condiment**, such as mustard, pickle relish, and ketchup, is traditionally served as an accompaniment to food. Clean condiment containers daily, especially the grooves around the cap. Never use a paper towel to dry or wipe off a condiment container. Safety and sanitation regulations state that original condiment containers, such as a ketchup bottle, should not be refilled. Condiment containers can be grouped together into a caddy.

Some sauces and most salad dressings are perishable. Refrigerate these items when they are not being served to customers.

Nearly all condiments served in individual packets are nonperishable. **Nonperishable** items will not spoil quickly when stored correctly. Nonperishable condiments include ketchup and steak sauces, mustard, syrups, jams, and preserves. Keep frequently used condiments such as ketchup and steak sauce on tables or within easy reach.

Paper product supplies also need to be constantly refilled. For example, if straws and paper napkin dispensers are used, restock the supply frequently.

Bus Station

The bus station is where supplies for meal service are kept in the dining room. Check with your employer to see what should be stocked at the bus station.

Before each shift, check the bus station to make sure that the correct server tools, such as spoons, spatulas, and carving knives, are clean and ready. Restock beverage areas with cups, glasses, coffee, and tea. Bring dishware and flatware to the bus station from the kitchen or dish room as needed. At the end of the day, clean and close the bus station. Return any perishable and nonperishable items to their appropriate places.

Fold Napkins for Service

The restaurant owner or manager decides how napkins are to be folded. (See **Figure 6.3**.) Use these guidelines when you fold napkins:

- Place linen on a clean surface.
- Be sure that your hands are clean before handling linen.
- Handle customer napkins as little as possible.

Reading Check **Determine** Why do some state laws ban the use of sugar bowls?

Dish, Glass, and Utensil Choices

Foodservice establishments have a variety of dishes, glasses, and dining utensils in stock for customers to use during different dining situations. The types of dishware, glassware, and flatware you will choose for a table setting will depend on the types of foods and beverages you will serve during the meal. The choice will also depend on the type of restaurant in which you work. A fine-dining restaurant may have more types of dishes, glasses and utensils than a casual dining establishment. The fine-dining restaurant may also have a higher quality of dishware, glassware, and flatware from which to choose.

SANITATION CHECK ANSWER Handling a plate by the rim keeps servers' hands away from the food to prevent cross-contamination.

READING CHECK ANSWER Some state laws ban the use of sugar bowls because loose sugar is not sanitary.

FIGURE 6.3 **Napkin Folds**

Interesting Shapes Folding napkins into various shapes is an important part of side work. *Why do you think restaurants fold napkins into shapes?*

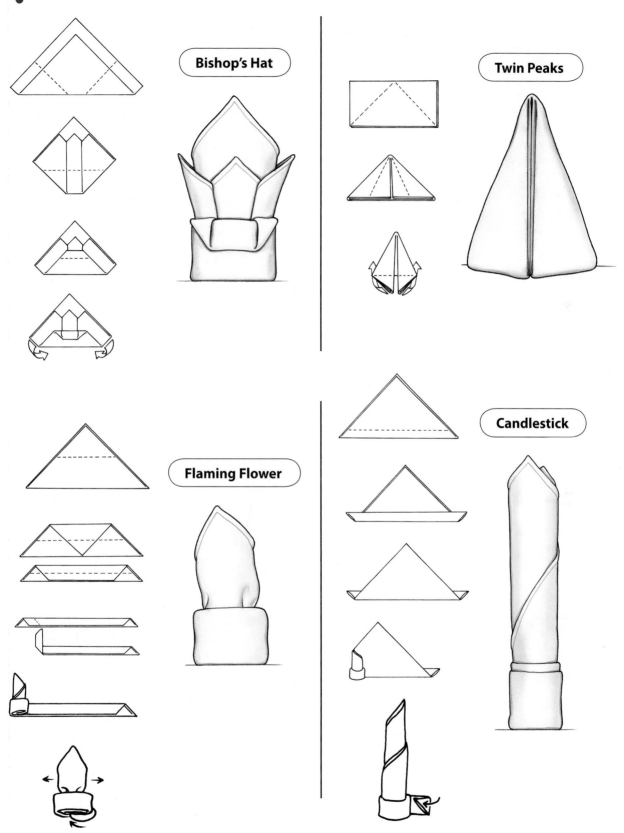

Bishop's Hat

Twin Peaks

Flaming Flower

Candlestick

FIGURE CAPTION ANSWER Restaurants fold napkins into interesting shapes to distinguish themselves from their competition and to capture customers' interest.

Chapter 6   The Dining Experience   **153**

Geometry and Napkin Folding

A square is made up of two large congruent triangles. For triangles to be congruent, all of the corresponding angles and sides must be the same. In this case, the two large congruent triangles are classified as isosceles triangles. Isosceles triangles have at least two congruent sides. These two isosceles triangles can also be classified as right triangles because each triangle contains a 90° angle.

Most restaurant napkins are in the shape of a square. A square has four right angles (90°) and four equal sides. These directions will allow you to fold a square napkin into a water lily design. As you fold, determine the number and types of triangles you encounter in each fold of the napkin.

STEP 1

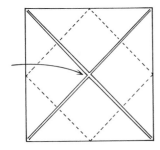

STEP 2

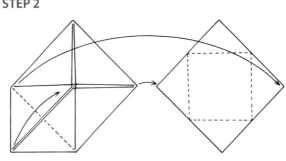

STEP 3

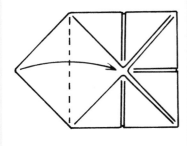

STEP 4

STEP 5

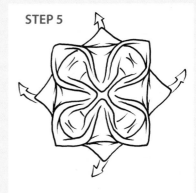

Math Concept **Triangles** Triangles can be classified by their angles. An acute triangle contains all acute angles (less than 90°). An obtuse triangle has one obtuse angle (more than 90°, but less than 180°). A right triangle has one right angle (90°). Triangles can also be classified by their sides. In an equilateral triangle, all sides are congruent (the same size). An isosceles triangle has at least two congruent sides. A scalene triangle has no congruent sides.

Starting Hint Look at the napkin in Step 1. How many triangles do you see? Classify each triangle in each step of the napkin folding and tally. Identify any patterns that you notice.

NCTM Geometry Analyze characteristics of two- and three-dimensional geometric shapes and develop mathematical arguments about geometric relationships.

GOURMET MATH ANSWER Step 1: 16 right triangles. Step 2: 4 right triangles. Step 3: 12 right triangles. Step 4: no true triangles, as shapes are obscured. Step 5: 4 right triangles. Students should notice that all triangles are right triangles.

FIGURE 6.4 **Glassware Types**
Glassware Basics The two categories of glassware are lead crystal and heat treated. *How do these two types of glassware differ?*

Juice	Water	Beverage	Stemware

Glassware

Restaurants use glassware for beverages such as juice, water, and iced tea. (See **Figure 6.4**.) Although there are many styles and patterns to choose, **glassware** can be divided into two categories: lead crystal and heat-treated glass.

- Lead crystal glassware is very hard, clear, and bright. Because this glassware is expensive and easily chipped, it is not practical for busy, casual restaurants. It is generally used in formal fine-dining restaurants.
- Glass that is heated and then cooled rapidly is called **heat treated**. It is strong and resists breaking and chipping. Most foodservice operations use heat-treated glassware.

Glassware should be carefully handled to stay unscratched. Use the following guidelines to handle all types of glassware:

- Store glassware upside down in a glass rack or on air mats on a shelf.
- Hold glassware by the base or stem.
- Never use chipped or cracked glassware.
- Always use a beverage tray to carry glassware in the dining room.

Tableware

Restaurants use a variety of tableware. **Tableware** is any kind of dish, from dinner plates to soup bowls to coffee cups.

Choose the correct tableware to set a visually pleasing table. For a formal presentation, you might use porcelain or fine china. For a casual look, you might use ceramic tableware.

Flatware

Flatware refers to dining utensils, such as spoons, forks, and knives. Flatware can also be referred to as cutlery. Flatware can be made of different quality grades of stainless steel or silver. Like glassware and tableware, flatware is available in many different styles. (See **Figure 6.5**.)

Flatware is carried through a dining room on a serviette. A **serviette** is a napkin-lined plate. Handle flatware by the waist, or midsection of the handle. This keeps your fingers from coming into contact with the end of the utensil that will go into the customer's mouth. It also prevents fingerprints on the handles.

Reading Check Explain Why is lead crystal not used in busy, casual restaurants?

FIGURE 6.5 **Tableware and Flatware**
Dish Options Foodservice operations use many types of tableware and flatware. *How should a server handle flatware in a dining room setting?*

Tableware

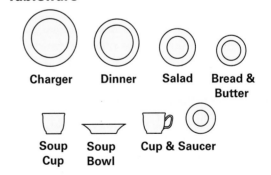

Charger	Dinner	Salad	Bread & Butter
Soup Cup	Soup Bowl	Cup & Saucer	

Flatware

Dinner Fork	Dinner Knife	Tea/Coffee Spoon
Dessert/Salad Fork	Butter Knife	Soup Spoon

FIGURE CAPTION ANSWER Lead crystal is hard, clear, and bright, expensive, and can be easily chipped. Heat-treated glassware is strong and resists chipping.

READING CHECK ANSWER Lead crystal is expensive and easily chipped, so is not practical.
FIGURE CAPTION ANSWER Flatware should be carried on a serviette, and be handled by the waist.

FIGURE 6.6 **Place Settings**
Setting Tables Table settings are different depending upon the type of meal being served. *What are the main differences you see here between the dinner and formal dinner place settings?*

Table Setting

Restaurant management determines the type and style of table setting that is used. A **table setting** is the specific arrangement of tableware, glassware, and flatware for a meal. (See **Figure 6.6**.) Customer comfort, cleanliness, and consistency are important:

- Place chairs around the table in front of the space for each place setting.
- Place centerpieces, salt and pepper shakers, and condiment holders at the same location on each table.
- To center each place setting, first place the napkin. If a place mat is used, center it in the place setting about 1 inch from the edge of the table. Place a napkin to the left of the place mat or in the center.
- Set forks to the left and knives and spoons to the right of each place setting.
- Always set knives with the cutting edge toward the center of the place setting.
- Flatware should not hang over the edge of the place mat or table. Place flatware 1 inch from the edge of either.
- Place all flatware from the outside in, following the order of use. Make sure there is room for the dinner plate.
- If you will preset dessert spoons or forks, place them at the top of the place setting, **perpendicular** (ˌpər'pən-'di-kyə-lər), or standing at right angles, to the other flatware. The spoon is placed above the fork. Point the spoon's handle to the right and the fork's handle to the left.

- Place the bread plate on the left, above the fork(s).
- Place a butter knife on the top of the bread plate with the cutting edge facing down toward the plate.
- Place the water glass above the tip of the dinner knife.
- Preset coffee cups to the right of the knives and spoons, with handles at the 4 o'clock position.

Table Preparation

The server must be sure that the tabletop, benches, chairs, and the floor area around the table are clean. This should be done before the shift begins, and between customer seatings. Check the table setup according to the restaurant plan. Make any accommodations for large groups. Make sure the spacing between tables is comfortable.

Check the underside of tabletops for any chewing gum. Wipe chairs and booth seats clean. Constantly inspect tables and the floor below them, especially when the tables are being reset. Clean food or spills off of menus. Check the ashtrays at smoking tables.

There are many different styles, types, and colors of linen napkins and tablecloths. Servers must set each tablecloth with the seam toward the table and make sure it is even on all sides. Using linen, however, is expensive. Many foodservice establishments use place mats, paper or vinyl tablecloths, or glass tabletops instead.

FIGURE CAPTION ANSWER The main differences are the placement of the napkin, the addition of the dessert fork and spoon, and the size of the plate.

Change
a Tablecloth

1 Remove all glassware and dishes from the table.

2 Place standard accessories, such as candles or flowers, on a tray. Never use a chair to hold such items.

3 Fold the soiled cloth back about one fourth of its length. Fold it onto the table, but do not show any of the surface underneath.

4 Bring out the clean tablecloth and place it over the folded portion of the soiled cloth.

5 With the seam down, drop the end of the new cloth so that it is opened one fold and hangs over the end of the table.

6 Using both hands, hold the two corners of both the clean and soiled cloths. Pull them toward the other end of the table.

7 When you reach the other end of the table, let go of the cloth corners.

8 Grasp the hanging corners of the soiled cloth and bring them to the other corners of the folded cloth.

9 Hold all corners and drop the top edge of the new cloth over the table. Do not let go of the corners of the soiled cloth.

10 Neatly fold the soiled cloth again, making sure that the trapped crumbs do not fall onto the floor.

11 Place the cloth on the tray.

12 Before placing the soiled linen in a linen bag, empty the crumbs in a lined trash can in the back of the foodservice operation.

Table Setting for Preset Menus

A **preset menu** is a meal served to a group of customers who have decided in advance on the menu and the time of service. The particular menu determines the table setting. An à la carte table setting is placed on the table in advance. Flatware is brought to the table after customers place their orders.

 Reading Check **Describe** How do you set the table for a preset menu?

Centerpieces

A **centerpiece** is a decorative object placed on tables to add beauty and interest. Centerpieces should not block the customer's view. Properly maintain and clean centerpieces.

Lighting Centerpieces

Lighting centerpieces, such as candles, are the most common centerpieces. Generally, they are used during the evening hours.

Floral Centerpieces

Floral centerpieces can be made from fresh, dried, or artificial flowers, leaves, and branches. Fresh flowers require extra care and are not always available.

Edible Centerpieces

Edible centerpieces are made from items that can be eaten, such as fruit or carved vegetables. They also can be spun sugar creations. Handle spun sugar centerpieces carefully. They are very delicate and will break easily.

Sculpted Centerpieces

Ice, butter, chocolate, and beeswax can all be carved into centerpieces. Large ice sculptures are often used on buffet tables. Ice sculptures are not practical as regular table centerpieces.

Reading Check **Determine** What materials are used to make floral centerpieces?

SECTION 6.2 **After You Read**

Review Key Concepts

1. **Explain** the correct technique for refilling salt and pepper shakers.
2. **Compare and contrast** the different categories of glassware.
3. **Illustrate** the correct way to change a table linen.
4. **Describe** the materials that are used in an edible centerpiece.

Practice Culinary Academics
Mathematics

5. Your restaurant chooses to use place mats at each table setting instead of tablecloths on each table. Each rectangular place mat that your restaurant uses measures 20 inches long and 14 inches wide. What is the area of this place mat in square inches?

Math Concept **Area of a Rectangle** The area (A) of a rectangle is equal to its length (l) times its width (w): $A = lw$. If necessary, convert the length and the width to the same units before you multiply the correct figures.

Starting Hint Following the formula for finding the area of a rectangle, the area of the place mat equals 20 inches × 14 inches. Because each measurement is already in inches, no conversion is necessary to find the correct answer.

NCTM Geometry Use visualization, spatial reasoning, and geometric modeling to solve problems.

Check your answers at this book's Online Learning Center at **glencoe.com**.

READING CHECK ANSWER The table setting is placed on the table in advance based on the meal ordered.

READING CHECK ANSWER Floral centerpieces are made from fresh, dried, or artificial flowers, leaves, and branches.

Review and Applications

Chapter Summary

There are five different types of dining environments: fine-dining, theme restaurants, casual-dining, quick-service, and catering services. There are also different styles of meal service, including modern American plated, booth, banquette, family style, classical French, Russian/English, butler, and buffet service. Bus stations should be stocked at all times with supplies. Cleanliness, uniformity, and customer comfort should be stressed when preparing table settings. Centerpieces bring beauty and interest to table settings.

Content and Academic Vocabulary Review

1. Create multiple-choice test questions for each content and academic vocabulary term.

Content Vocabulary

- fine-dining restaurant (p. 142)
- theme restaurant (p. 142)
- casual-dining establishment (p. 142)
- trayline service (p. 143)
- counter service (p. 143)
- food court (p. 143)
- room service (p. 144)
- modern American plated service (p. 144)
- booth (p. 145)
- focal point (p. 145)
- family service (p. 145)
- banquette (p. 146)
- classical French service (p. 146)
- tableside (p. 146)

- flambé (p. 147)
- Russian/English service (p. 147)
- butler service (p. 148)
- hors d'oeuvre (p. 148)
- buffet (p. 148)
- chafing dish (p. 148)
- side work (p. 151)
- condiment (p. 152)
- nonperishable (p. 152)
- glassware (p. 155)
- heat treated (p. 155)
- tableware (p. 155)
- flatware (p. 155)
- serviette (p. 155)
- table setting (p. 156)
- preset menu (p. 158)
- centerpiece (p. 158)

Academic Vocabulary

- promote (p. 142)
- device (p. 148)
- elements (p. 151)
- perpendicular (p. 156)

Review Key Concepts

2. Categorize the five main types of dining environments.

3. Distinguish between different styles of meal service.

4. Describe the side work that must be done before a service.

5. Contrast the different types of glassware, dishware, and flatware.

6. Illustrate how to properly set a table for different situations.

7. Describe different types of centerpieces.

Critical Thinking

8. Evaluate dishware. How might the tableware, glassware, and flatware used in a fine-dining restaurant differ from those used in a quick-service restaurant? Why?

9. Judge the importance of side work in customer service.

10. Analyze the benefits of a centerpiece. Why are centerpieces used when they serve no practical function?

Review and Applications

Academic Skills

English Language Arts

11. Table Setting Guide Imagine that you are the head server in a fine-dining restaurant, and you have just hired new servers. Create a guide to table setting for each meal. Include illustrations or diagrams if you wish. Make sure that someone who is a new hire would be able to understand your instructions. Explain each step clearly and completely, and label illustrations and diagrams as necessary.

> **NCTE 5** Use different writing process elements to communicate effectively.

Science

12. Test Serving Styles Systems of serving were developed by restaurants over time by observing what was most efficient and least likely to cause problems.

Procedure Compare the modern American plated service style with a service that is not based on any procedure. What do you observe about the difference between following a procedure and not following a procedure?

Analysis Make a list of your observations. As a class, discuss the importance of testing and creating procedures for table service.

> **NSES A** Develop abilities necessary to do scientific inquiry.

Mathematics

13. Calculate the Perimeter of a Triangle You work at a restaurant that uses cloth napkins. Each napkin is in the shape of a square measuring 20 inches on each side. It is your job to fold each napkin in a decorative design. You begin by folding the square napkin in half diagonally, creating a right triangle with two equal sides and one longer side. What is the perimeter of this triangle?

Math Concept **Using the Pythagorean Theorem** If you know the lengths of two sides of a right triangle, you can determine the third length using the Pythagorean Theorem. This states that $a^2 + b^2 = c^2$ (where c is the length of the hypotenuse, or side opposite the right angle, and a and b are the other two sides).

Starting Hint The perimeter is the sum of the lengths of the triangle's three sides. Because the two shorter sides of the folded napkin are identical to two of the sides of the original square, the length of each of those sides is 20 inches. Find the length of the longer side (the hypotenuse) of the triangle by solving for c in the Pythagorean Theorem: $c = \sqrt{a^2 + b^2}$, or $c = \sqrt{20^2 + 20^2}$.

> **NCTM Geometry** Analyze characteristics and properties of two- and three-dimensional geometric shapes and develop mathematical arguments about geometric relationships.

Certification Prep

Sharpen your test-taking skills to improve your kitchen certification program score.

Directions Read the questions. Then, read the answer choices and choose the best possible answer for each.

14. What is the cart used in French tableside service called?

   a. garçon

   b. guéridon

   c. wagon

   d. charrette

15. How often should condiment containers be cleaned?

   a. daily

   b. two times per week

   c. weekly

   d. monthly

Test-Taking Tip

Right after you read the question, try to predict the answer before looking at the choices. Then, if an option matches your prediction, choose that option.

Review and Applications

Real-World Skills and Applications

Interpersonal and Collaborative Skills

16. Practice Service Styles Follow your teacher's instructions to form teams. Practice each style of service until each team member has been the server. All team members should help do the side work. Rotate styles until each team has practiced all styles of service. Discuss with the class how the experience changed the more you worked with the same team.

Time-Management Skills

17. Fold Napkins Practice folding napkins like those shown on page 153. You should be able to make each of these napkin folds easily, and the napkin should retain its shape. Practicing skills like these will make you more efficient. The faster you can fold napkins, the more time you will have to set up.

Technology Applications

18. Create a Checklist Imagine that you are the front of the house manager for a restaurant. Choose the style of restaurant and type of service. Then, use a word-processing program to create a checklist for your employees. The checklist should have the steps to follow to create the appropriate dining atmosphere for your customers. Add as many details as possible from the chapter.

Financial Literacy

19. Purchase Glassware Imagine that you are in charge of purchasing glassware for a family-style restaurant. Lead crystal glasses cost $10.50 each, and heat-treated glasses cost $3.15 each. You need to purchase 100 glasses for your restaurant. How much money will you save by purchasing the heat-treated glasses?

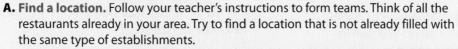

Culinary Lab

Use the culinary skills you have learned in this chapter.

Plan a New Restaurant

20. Plan with a Team Working in teams, plan a new restaurant for your area, and then present your plan to the rest of the class.

A. Find a location. Follow your teacher's instructions to form teams. Think of all the restaurants already in your area. Try to find a location that is not already filled with the same type of establishments.

B. Choose restaurant categories. Use the information in the chapter about types of restaurant and types of service to determine which categories your restaurant will fit. Consider the needs and abilities of the community when you make this decision.

C. Decide on the details. After selecting the type of operation and meal service, decide on the price range, environment, menu, and decor.

D. Make a poster. Create a poster showing the location, type, and meal service of your restaurant.

E. Present your plans. Share your team's plans for a new restaurant with the class.

Create Your Evaluation
When you listen to other teams describe their restaurant, think about why their plans sound like they could succeed. Make a list of the restaurants in the order that you would visit them. Explain after each why you placed it in the order that you did. Include what attracted you to it, or what made you less interested.

Media and Mentoring

The food industry needs people who inform and support others in the field.

As the general public expresses more interest in foods and cooking, the roles of foodservice professionals in the media expand. Food photographers, writers, and stylists all help spark public interest in good food. Consultants help foodservice businesses become more professional and successful.

To succeed in media and mentoring positions, you may need a culinary degree. Excellent communication skills and creativity will help you advance.

Alejandro Luna, Executive Pastry Chef and Consultant

Q Describe your job.

A I am a self-employed pastry chef and consultant. I have created a database of companies and colleagues who contact me to help them improve their operations.

Q Describe a typical work day.

A I keep long hours and am always on my feet. I prepare for the day's events and plan for upcoming events throughout the week. I spend a lot of time on the telephone and the computer doing research about my clients.

Q Why did you choose your career?

A I love the thrill of the day-to-day execution of my job and the satisfaction of instant reward. From the moment you cook or prepare a dish for a person, it is only a matter of minutes before you get a reaction from that person.

Q How did your career path lead to your current job?

A I worked really hard for years to get the knowledge I needed to take on different jobs. As a chef, you must be honest with yourself when you accept challenges. I felt I was at a point where I was in charge of my knowledge and could present my experience so that companies would realize I could help them.

Q Who or what has been your biggest career influence?

A Traveling has been my greatest influence. Every place has different customs and different ways of cooking food. Exposure to different cultures has taught me about new ingredients and new techniques. The mentors who have influenced me shared their time and knowledge to teach me not only about the field, but also how to be a better professional and person.

Q What skills are most important?

A The basic skills for becoming a pastry chef are learned with years of school and work. However, the patience, respect, and humility that you need come only with realizing that no one is below you. Your experience does not make you better as a person than anyone else.

Career Ingredients

Education or Training	Most consultants have a culinary degree and experience in the culinary workforce. Food journalists and photographers have bachelor's degrees in journalism or photography and experience in culinary arts.
Academic Skills Required	English Language Arts, Science
Aptitudes, Abilities, and Skills	Clear communication skills, ability to lead and work with others, creativity, marketing skills, and commitment to professional standards.
Workplace Safety	Workplace safety must be followed by all. In addition, food safety must be followed by chefs and cooking instructors.
Career Outlook	Openings will be plentiful in the near future as the foodservice industry continues to expand.
Career Path	Advancement depends on creativity and ability to communicate ideas clearly to others.

Career Pathways

Food journalists	Interviews others and writes articles for magazines, newspapers, and Web sites about restaurants and food trends. Food journalists must have excellent English Language Arts skills.
Food photographers	Takes photos of food and kitchen preparation for magazines, newspapers, books, and Web sites. They must be creative and have excellent photography skills.
Food stylists	Prepares foods for display and for food-related photography shoots. Food stylists must understand food science and preparation to make food look its best
Consultants	Helps foodservice businesses with organizing the business, creating menus, advertising, facility design, and more. Consultants must have knowledge of every part of the foodservice business. Personal experience is also recommended.
Cooking instructors	Teaches culinary students basic and advanced culinary skills. They usually have at least a bachelor's degree in Culinary Arts.

Critical Thinking What classes have you taken in school that might help you prepare for a career in food media and mentoring?

Many certification programs focus on menu creation. Think of a favorite dish and describe that dish in an advertisement for a restaurant that prepares the dish. Include information about the dish, but make sure that all information is accurate.

COMPETITION
★ ★ ★ ★ ★
PRACTICE

Competitors must deliver products that are good enough to be sold to the public. Create a version of the dish from your ad from the Get Certified practice, or one of your teacher's choosing. Once the dish is completed, take photographs of it from different angles. Evaluate your efforts based on the following rating scale:

1 = Poor; 2 = Fair; 3 = Good; 4 = Great

Judge your dish on:

● The attractiveness of the plate.
● The flavor of the food.
● Whether the food was photogenic from all angles.

Your Career in Foodservice

There are many types of foodservice careers that are needed to run a restaurant. Using your research and observation of a career you may enjoy, you will act out a scene from a restaurant in which you play the role of your chosen career.

My Journal

If you completed the journal entry from page 55, refer to it to see which careers in foodservice you have considered. Add any additional notes about these or other foodservice careers that you may be interested in after reading this unit.

English Language Arts

NCTE 8 Use information resources to gather information and create and communicate knowledge.

NCTE 9 Develop an understanding of diversity in language use across cultures.

Project Assignment

In this project, you will:

- Research foodservice careers to see which career you might enjoy the most.
- Identify and observe someone in the restaurant business who has the career you have chosen.
- Act the role of your chosen career in a restaurant scene with your fellow classmates.
- Present the scene to your class to share what you have learned.

Applied Culinary Skills Behind the Project

Your success in culinary arts will depend on your skills. Skills you will use in this project include:

➤ Identifying career opportunities in foodservice.
➤ Describing education and training for foodservice careers.
➤ Knowing basic skills needed for foodservice careers.
➤ Understanding the roles and responsibilities of different jobs in a restaurant.
➤ Determining how job duties may change during different meal times.

English Language Arts Skills Behind the Project

The English Language Arts skills you will use for this project are writing, interviewing, and speaking skills. Remember these key concepts:

Research Skills

➤ Perform research using a variety of resources.
➤ Discriminate between sources.
➤ Use the information you gathered to narrow down your choices.

Observation Skills

➤ Use positive body language.
➤ Take notes during the observation.
➤ Ask questions afterward to make sure you understand.

Speaking Skills

➤ Demonstrate understanding of your chosen career.
➤ Use creativity in your acting.
➤ Be aware of nonverbal communication.

Step 1 — Choose and Research Foodservice Careers

Choose and research careers in foodservice. Consider all of the jobs needed to run a restaurant. Write a summary of your research to:

- Identify career opportunities in foodservice.
- Describe what is involved in restaurant customer service opportunities.
- Explain careers in restaurant production, such as line cooks and sous chefs.
- Determine the management opportunities in foodservice.
- List the careers that interest you the most.
- Choose one career to research further.

Step 2 — Plan Your Observation

Use the results of your research to write a list of questions you would like answered should you observe someone in this career. Your questions may include:

- What type of training and education is needed for this career?
- What duties are required for this career?
- What tasks about this career are the most interesting to you?
- How did the tasks of this career vary during different dining times?
- How do you think you can prepare for this career now?

Step 3 — Connect with Your Community

Identify a person with your chosen career and ask him or her when would be a good time for you to observe them at work. Conduct your observation using the questions you prepared in Step 2. Take notes during the observation and write a summary of your findings.

Culinary Project Checklist

Plan

- ✓ Research foodservice careers and summarize your findings.
- ✓ Plan an observation with a person who has your chosen career.
- ✓ Write a summary about your observation.
- ✓ Create a real restaurant scene and play the part of your career

Present

- ✓ Make a presentation to your class to display a real restaurant scene.
- ✓ Invite students to ask any questions they may have. Answer these questions.
- ✓ When students ask you questions, demonstrate in your answers that you respect their perspectives.
- ✓ Turn in the summary of your research, your observation questions, and the observation summary to your teacher.

Step 4 — Create Your Inspection Sheet

Use the Culinary Project Checklist to plan and create a restaurant inspection sheet to share what you have learned with your classmates.

Step 5 — Evaluate Your Culinary and Academic Skills

Your project will be evaluated based on:

- Content and organization of your information.
- Depth and detail of your inspection sheet.
- Speaking and listening skills.

 Rubric Go to this book's Online Learning Center at **glencoe.com** for a rubric you can use to evaluate your final project.

 JOHNSON & WALES
U N I V E R S I T Y

Expert Advice Go to this book's Online Learning Center at **glencoe.com** to read an article by a culinary expert from Johnson & Wales University about how to gain experience in the foodservice industry.

Quality Foodservice Practices

Chapter

7 Foodservice Management

8 Standards, Regulations, and Laws

Foodservice standards, regulations, and laws ensure that food is safe to eat. *What responsibilities do you think foodservice managers have in ensuring that a business follows standards, regulations, and laws?*

EXPLORE THE PHOTO ANSWER Answers will vary, but may include training employees to understand the law, posting notices, and inspecting the facility to make sure that all standards and regulations are followed.

Successful Foodservice Managers

After completing this unit, you will know how foodservice managers function, and the laws, rules, and regulations that affect foodservice. In your unit culinary project, you will research the responsibilities of a foodservice manager. Then, you will create a visual presentation on what skills are needed to be a successful manager.

My Journal

Write a journal entry about how you use leadership skills in your daily life.

- What skills do leaders need to have?
- How do you use your skills to lead other people?
- How do you treat the people you lead?

JOHNSON & WALES
U N I V E R S I T Y

"I am always working on new food concepts. I find it exhilarating to think that food I helped design could be bought and eaten all across the United States."

David Horrocks
Research Chef
International Flavors &
Fragrances

CHAPTER 7

Foodservice Management

SECTIONS

7.1 Management Basics

7.2 Managing People and Facilities

7.3 Foodservice Marketing

WRITING ACTIVITY

Advertisement

Imagine that you are in charge of marketing for a restaurant. Create either a script for a broadcast advertisement or a visual representation of a print advertisement to attract customers.

Writing Tips

1 Focus on adverbs, adjectives, and nouns.

2 Use active verbs.

3 Diagram key words to help organize your thoughts.

EXPLORE THE PHOTO

A manager must effectively communicate with all employees. *Why should managers be problem solvers?*

WRITING ACTIVITY ANSWER
The ad's tone should reflect the restaurant style. It should also be appropriate to its target customers.

EXPLORE THE PHOTO ANSWER
A manager must deal with setbacks quickly and effectively to keep business running smoothly.

Management Basics

Do you know the duties of a foodservice manager?

Reading Guide

 Before You Read

Be Organized A messy environment can be distracting. To lessen distractions, organize an area where you can read this section comfortably.

Read to Learn

Key Concepts
- **List** the qualities and duties of an effective manager.
- **Explain** the foodservice manager's role in maintaining profitability.

Main Idea

An effective manager can manage both time and human resources within a foodservice operation. A manager is also responsible for applying cost control techniques.

Content Vocabulary
- overstaffing
- human resources
- orientation
- delegate
- autocratic
- democratic
- standardized accounting practices
- double-entry bookkeeping
- food cost percentage
- direct labor cost
- indirect labor cost
- income
- expense
- profit and loss statement
- forecasting
- break even
- inventory

Academic Vocabulary
- lapse
- adhere

ACADEMIC STANDARDS

English Language Arts
NCTE 5 Use different writing process elements to communicate effectively.

Mathematics
NCTM Problem Solving Apply and adapt a variety of appropriate strategies to solve problems.

NCTM Problem Solving Build new mathematical knowledge through problem solving.

Social Studies
NCSS VII B Production, Distribution, and Consumption Analyze the role that supply and demand plays in determining what is produced and distributed in a competitive market system.

NCTE National Council of Teachers of English

NCTM National Council of Teachers of Mathematics

NSES National Science Education Standards

NCSS National Council for the Social Studies

Graphic Organizer

As you read, use a puzzle organizer like the one below to list the four qualities of an effective manager.

Effective Management Qualities

 Graphic Organizer
Go to this book's Online Learning Center at **glencoe.com** for a printable graphic organizer.

GRAPHIC ORGANIZER ANSWER Communication, time management, resource management, and leadership.

Management Structures

Each foodservice business has its own management structure. Some smaller businesses may have an owner who also acts as the restaurant manager and supervisor. Most foodservice operations have several managers who are responsible for different resources. Larger businesses may have many layers of management. Several managers or supervisors may oversee different segments of food production and service.

Foodservice business structures usually have these layers:

- **Employees** work at jobs such as cook, server, and cleaning staff. Employees make up the largest group of people in a foodservice structure.
- **First-line managers**, or supervisors, are directly responsible for managing kitchen and service employees. Some facilities might have different first-line managers who oversee food production, service, and cleaning.
- **Middle managers** usually manage the first-line managers rather than the employees. They coordinate the business and make sure all rules are followed. These managers help first-line managers and top managers communicate.
- **Top managers**, or administrators, control the business. Top managers create policies and procedures. They also make the major decisions about sales, personnel, and finance.

Effective Management

It is a great challenge today to manage a foodservice operation. The success of a foodservice operation often depends on the manager's ability to do his or her job well. Good managers understand business and facility needs. They also understand the needs of their staff. To be an effective manager, you must understand how a business runs and how to lead people. Being a manager may seem a long way off if you are in your first foodservice job. However, you will be a better employee if you know how managers do their jobs.

Management Skills Good managers spot problems in the workplace and then act swiftly to solve them. *How would you solve the problem of an employee showing up late for his or her shift?*

PHOTO CAPTION ANSWER Answers will vary, but students might try discussing calmly with the employee why his or her tardiness affects the rest of the staff and the ability of the establishment to provide service to its customers. Students might also suggest warning him or her about the consequences of being late again.

To be a foodservice manager, you will need to know how to effectively manage people and facilities. You will also need to successfully advertise and market a foodservice operation to the public. You might have an idea for a restaurant and want to start a new business of your own. To accomplish any of these goals, you will need to become an effective manager. Effective managers are skilled in communication, time management, resource management, and leadership.

Communication

Managers need to encourage good on-the-job communication. This includes communication between employees and managers, and between customers and staff members. No matter where a communication **lapse**, or problem due to inattention, occurs, it can severely affect a foodservice operation's success.

Good managers also have an open-door policy for employees. This means that they always make time for employees to talk about ideas and problems. Good managers also listen carefully to what employees and customers have to say, and make changes based on those conversations.

Customer Complaints Foodservice operations often have their own rules for dealing with customer complaints. Often, the manager handles customer complaints. Managers must be good at politely speaking with people.

Keep these guidelines in mind if you must handle a customer complaint:
- Listen attentively to the customer's concerns.
- Show that you understand the customer's frustration.
- Address the customer's concern as quickly as possible and offer compensation if necessary. For example, you might not charge a customer for a poor-quality meal.
- Reassure the customer that the problem will not happen again.
- Find the cause of the problem and take the steps needed to prevent it from happening again.

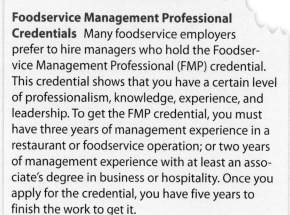

Small Bites

Foodservice Management Professional Credentials Many foodservice employers prefer to hire managers who hold the Foodservice Management Professional (FMP) credential. This credential shows that you have a certain level of professionalism, knowledge, experience, and leadership. To get the FMP credential, you must have three years of management experience in a restaurant or foodservice operation; or two years of management experience with at least an associate's degree in business or hospitality. Once you apply for the credential, you have five years to finish the work to get it.

Time Management

Time management is important for managers. Managers must know how to balance employee work schedules so that each shift is covered by the right number of employees. For example, to schedule servers for a day, a service manager might:
- Find out which servers are available to work on that day.
- Choose the right seating chart for the tables, based on the number of servers who will work.
- Assign a server to each section.
- Stop seating customers in a section when a server will be going off shift soon.
- Coordinate with the host to balance the number of customers in each section.

However, if too many employees are scheduled, they will be bored and the restaurant will lose money. Scheduling too many people to work on a given shift is called **overstaffing**.

Managers also look for ways that employees can save time. In other words, good managers find out how time is wasted. They also discover how work can be done more efficiently. Managers who look for ways to improve time management often make changes that make a business more profitable. A manager might refine the way a task is done, reorganize storage space, change staff or schedules, and add employee training.

Resource Management

The success of a foodservice business always depends on how its resources are managed. It is challenging and important to hire the right people for the job. Managing staff, or **human resources**, involves knowing the strengths and weaknesses of each employee.

It is vital to hold employee orientation. **Orientation** is a training session that is held for new employees to help them better understand the business. Orientation generally includes training on policies and procedures, quality standards, and business practices.

A good foodservice manager also manages the facility. This means making sure the building is safe, clean, and properly equipped.

Foodservice managers need to **adhere** to, or follow, many laws and regulations. Chapter 8 covers these items in detail. There are rules for every part of the operation. This includes hiring and firing employees, and the safety of the food that is served to customers. Managers have legal responsibilities to customers, employees, and the business. It is the manager's responsibility to know and follow all of the rules and regulations. The manager also must make sure that employees understand and follow the rules.

Public policy also affects the food production and service industry. These policies are usually posted in a foodservice business. They most often relate to smoking, wearing shoes and shirts, and the ability to refuse service.

Leadership

One of the most important qualities of a successful manager is his or her leadership style. Their staff must look to them for guidance and feel confident that their manager's decisions are best for the business. The best foodservice managers coach, delegate, direct, and support their staff. To **delegate** is to give responsibility to another person. Employees should feel that they are part of a team, and that they have responsibility for the success of the business.

Some managers use an **autocratic** leadership style, in which information and policies move from the top down. Other managers have a **democratic** style, in which everyone is involved in the decision-making process. There is no one correct style.

Reading Check Define What does overstaffing mean?

⬆ **Success Through Teamwork** Being part of a team helps employees feel that they are part of the success of the foodservice operation. *How does a good leader foster teamwork?*

PHOTO CAPTION ANSWER Generally, good leaders delegate tasks to employees, ask for employees' opinions on workplace policies and issues, and coach employees in developing their skills.

READING CHECK ANSWER Overstaffing means scheduling too many people to work on a given shift.

Maintain Profitability

If a commercial foodservice operation does not make money, it will not survive. Money is needed to purchase food, hire staff, and market the business. This takes careful planning. Although you can use credit, it is best to make more than enough profit.

Profitability, or the ability to make a profit, is not just a concern for managers. The actions of every foodservice employee affect an operation's profitability. For example, if a busser is careless and breaks dishes, he or she has caused the operation to lose money. In contrast, if a chef is so skilled that customers return just to sample more of his or her food, then that chef has helped the operation make money.

Managing time as profitably and efficiently as possible is essential to success. Here are some guidelines to manage time:

- Prepare daily and weekly plans. What needs to be done that day or that week?
- Make lists and mark off tasks as they are completed.
- Delegate responsibility. Let employees have the opportunity to prove themselves as good workers.
- Limit meetings. Invite only the employees that need to be there. Keep meetings to a specific time limit.
- Take time to plan for emergencies. Prepare a plan of action for problems such as employee illness and overdue food deliveries.

Effective Record-Keeping Systems

Businesses use standardized accounting practices when they keep financial records. **Standardized accounting practices** involve reporting figures in a way that can be easily compared to the figures from other businesses. Part of accounting by hand involves double-entry bookkeeping. In **double-entry bookkeeping**, transactions are recorded in at least two places so that records are balanced.

Accounting software can help you keep track of financial information. You also may wish to hire a professional bookkeeper.

Although many foodservice businesses keep handwritten records, many businesses now keep records on a computerized point-of-sale system. These systems have advantages. They track every menu item ordered. This way, managers can see what foods are most and least popular. Computer software can also help managers track:

- Profits.
- Expenses, such as marketing, advertising, and facility costs.
- Purchases, price lists, and inventory.
- Reservations.
- Recipes and food costs.
- Work schedules, and employee hours and wages.

Food, Beverage, and Labor Costs

Computerized systems also allow managers to look at the three elements that make up most of an operation's cost: food, beverages, and labor. A facility's **food cost percentage** is the ratio of the cost of food served to the sales of food served. For example, say the cost of food served during the month of June was $14,800. The income received from sales of food in June was $37,000. To find the food cost percentage, divide the food cost by the food sales cost. Then, multiply by 100 to convert the total into a percentage:

$14,800 \div $37,000 = 0.40
0.40 \times 100 = 40\%$ food cost percentage

For every dollar received in sales, 40 cents was spent toward payment for the food.

An operation's third major cost is labor. This involves the direct and indirect labor costs of running a facility. Wages paid to employees are a **direct labor cost**. An operation's costs for employee health insurance, taxes, and vacations are considered an **indirect labor cost**. The more that food is processed in-house, the higher the direct labor costs will be.

Perfect Portions Portion control techniques minimize waste by standardizing food quantities. *How do you think two customers would react if they received different-size portions of the same dish?*

The amount of money that goes out of a foodservice business cannot exceed the amount of money that comes into that foodservice business. If it does, the business will soon close because of a lack of money.

Income is the money that comes into a business. It generally includes food and beverage sales. An **expense** is money that goes out of a business. Expenses include:

- Food costs.
- Beverage costs.
- Nonedible supplies, such as paper napkins.
- Rent and insurance.
- Employee salaries and wages.
- Benefits.
- Marketing and advertising.
- Operating expenses, such as uniforms.
- Utility costs, such as water, gas, electricity, and waste removal.
- Sales tax and taxes on tips, which must be reported to the government.

Portion Control

If two customers order the same menu item, such as a slice of pie, they expect both slices to be the same size. Foodservice operations should follow strict portion control guidelines. This will control costs and keep customers happy. Recipes specify how many servings or portions will be created from each batch. By following portion control guidelines:

- No one has to guess about whether a serving size is too big or too small.
- The right amount of each menu item will be prepared.
- Food waste is minimized and cost is kept in line.
- Customers will be satisfied.

Waste Control

Managers must check every day for wasted food and supplies. They also must develop policies like these to minimize waste:

- Follow strict inventory procedures to identify product needs.
- Order only the supplies and food you need.
- Minimize waste during production.
- Train employees how to properly prepare food.
- Train employees how to properly use nonedible supplies.

PHOTO CAPTION ANSWER Answers may vary, but the customer who received the smaller portion would probably feel cheated.

Profit and Loss Statements

As a manager, you will want to know how money is being spent and how much profit is being made. A **profit and loss statement**, sometimes called an income statement, is a financial statement that shows exactly how money flows into and out of a business. Profit and loss statements usually show money flow over a specific period of time, such as one month, one quarter, or one year.

A profit and loss statement lists all the expenses and shows a total of those expenses for a specific period. It also lists the total sales for that same period. To find the net profit, left over after expenses are paid, you would subtract the total expenses from the total sales.

Managers are often asked to anticipate what things will cost, how many employees will be needed, and how much profit a business will make. Anticipating future trends is called **forecasting**. When costs for a business equal its income, the business is said to **break even**. To make a profit you will need to carefully manage your money and the food and other supplies that your business purchases.

Inventory Control

Follow standard inventory procedures to help ensure that food is stored correctly and that you will never run out of important items. **Inventory** is the amount of supplies a business has on hand. Food that is ordered but has not yet arrived at the facility is not considered part of the inventory.

Food and supplies are usually purchased in large quantities. This strategy can bring down the per-item cost for most food items. For example, if a manager buys a dozen eggs, it might cost $2. However, if the manager buys 30 dozen eggs, the cost per dozen might be lowered to $1.

Most facilities have an inventory tracking system to keep track of how much of a product is in inventory. Managers must make sure their employees know how to properly use an inventory tracking system. Otherwise, money will be wasted in extra inventory, or the business will run out of supplies. (See Chapter 14 for more information on inventory systems.)

◀ **Inventory Tracking** An important step in inventory is tracking product use. *Why is tracking product use important?*

PHOTO CAPTION ANSWER Tracking product use is important so that restaurant management does not order too much food, or run out of food at a critical time. Ordering too much food wastes money. Not having enough food on hand could cause customers to complain.

You must properly store food and supplies to maintain enough inventory. For example, food products should be labeled with the date they were first stored. They should also be stored in the proper areas, and the first-in, first-out system should be used.

In addition to food products, you also must track the use of nonedible supplies, such as cleaning products, paper goods, and office supplies. These should be kept in their assigned storage area away from food.

Purchasing Procedures

Making wise purchasing decisions is an important first step toward making a food-service business profitable. You will produce waste if you purchase more food than the restaurant uses. This will cost the food-service business money. If you do not purchase enough food, however, the restaurant will quickly run out of items. Customers will not be able to get the food they want, and they will leave the business unhappy. They may not return. Both of these problems can quickly lead to lost profits.

Good managers will always ask questions about the restaurant's menu selections before they make purchasing decisions. If the manager knows the answers to these questions before placing an order, it will lower the chances that money and food will be wasted on supplies that are not needed:

- How much food do we need to prepare the items on our menu?
- How long will the food last in storage?
- How much food do we already have in stock? How long have these food items been in our storage?
- How far ahead of time must the food be ordered so that it will be on hand when it is needed?
- How much room in each type of storage (dry, refrigerated, and frozen) do we have? Will we have room to store new items properly as they come in?

Gourmet Math

Sales vs. Profit

Businesses use many financial measurements to analyze how well or how poorly they are doing. A business will track its sales and calculate its average sales per customer to see how much the typical customer purchases. But sales alone do not show the health of a company. Subtracting expenses (such as the costs of materials, rent, and labor) from the sales amount shows the business's net profit (or, if negative, net loss).

In March, a coffee shop collected $36,000 from 2,900 customers, with expenses of $30,000. Determine the total sales, average sales per customer, and net profit for the month of March.

Math Concept **Average Sales and Net Profit** Calculate average sales per customer by dividing the total sales by the number of customers. Calculate net profit by subtracting expenses from total sales.

Starting Hint Determine the coffee shop's total sales for the month by identifying how much money the business received selling products to customers. Then, divide that amount by the number of customers to find the average sales per customer, rounding to the nearest cent. To calculate the total net profit for the month, subtract total expenses from total sales.

NCTM Problem Solving Apply and adapt a variety of appropriate strategies to solve problems.

Food Inspections

Whenever food is received at a foodservice facility, it must be inspected closely to make sure that the food is what was ordered. It should also be inspected for damage during transport. This should be done before the food or supplies are accepted into a restaurant's inventory. Any food or supplies that do not meet proper standards for quality, quantity, and packaging should be returned to the supplier immediately, and a supervisor should be notified.

Look for signs of damage to food during the transport process. For example, check meat, poultry, and fish packaging for signs that the product was not kept at the proper temperature. This includes leaking or foul-

GOURMET MATH ANSWER The coffee shop had $36,000 in sales. Average sale per customer: $36,000 ÷ 2,900 = $12.41. Net profit: $36,000 − $30,000 = $6,000.

smelling packages. Produce should not be wilted, bruised, or over-ripe.

When a manager inspects food that has been received, he or she should check to make sure that:

- The product's quality matches the specification, or description, for the product. For example, Grade A poultry should have a Grade A quality stamp on the packaging.
- The product is what was ordered, in the correct quantity. Check the amount received against the ordering and shipping paperwork.
- The product's unit size is what was ordered. Large oranges should be large, not medium-size.
- The product price the restaurant paid matches the product price on the order form. Mistakes can happen. If you do not check the price, you may end up paying more for a product than you had planned.
- The product was not damaged during shipment. Cans should not be dented, bulging, or leaking. Boxes should not be torn open. Any damaged product should be rejected.
- The product was shipped under the proper conditions. For example, frozen food should be thoroughly checked for evidence of thawing, such as standing water or ice crystals. Any frozen food that shows signs of thawing should be rejected.
- The product shows no signs of insect or pest damage, such as open packaging, bite marks or pest droppings. Any products that show signs of insect infestation should be rejected.

 Reading Check Explain What does a profit and loss statement show?

 SECTION 7.1 **After You Read**

Review Key Concepts

1. **List** changes that can make a business more profitable.
2. **Explain** what a manager should look for when inspecting food.

Practice Culinary Academics

Social Studies

3. Research supply and demand. Think about how a foodservice manager might consider supply and demand when making decisions. Discuss your thoughts with the class.

> **NCSS VII B Production, Distribution, and Consumption** Analyze the role that supply and demand plays in determining what is produced and distributed in a competitive market system.

English Language Arts

4. Imagine that you own a restaurant. You receive a complaint from a customer that her meal was below her expectations. Write a letter to respond.

> **NCTE 5** Use different writing process elements to communicate effectively.

Mathematics

5. On November 1, your restaurant has $25,000 worth of food in inventory. Another $10,000 worth of food is purchased every day of the month. On November 30, $20,000 of food remains. What is your cost of sales for November?

> **Math Concept** **Cost of Sales** Before profit can be determined, a business must know its costs. One measure, cost of sales, equals the opening inventory amount plus any additional purchases minus the closing inventory amount.
>
> **Starting Hint** Add the opening inventory amount ($25,000) to the amount of purchases made during the month ($10,000/day × 30 days), and subtract the closing inventory amount ($20,000).

> **NCTM Problem Solving** Build new mathematical knowledge through problem solving.

 Check your answers at this book's Online Learning Center at **glencoe.com**.

 READING CHECK ANSWER A profit and loss statement shows how money flows into and out of a business.

Managing People and Facilities

Reading Guide

 Before You Read

What You Want to Know Write a list of what you want to know about managing people and facilities. As you read, write down the heads in this section that provide that information.

Read to Learn

Key Concepts
- **Analyze** the manager's role in employee selection, training, and supervision.
- **Examine** the design issues that contribute to a profitable facility.
- **Give examples** of what foodservice facilities can do to manage loss prevention.

Main Idea

Managers must select employees, evaluate their progress, train and mentor them, and supervise them on the job. Managers must also create an efficient facility design and use loss prevention techniques.

Content Vocabulary
- job description
- open-ended question
- positive reinforcement
- mentor
- master work schedule
- design
- balance
- turnover rate
- traffic path
- bypassing
- loss prevention
- risk management

Academic Vocabulary
- obvious
- factor

Graphic Organizer

As you read, use an outline like the one shown to show how a manager can train an employee. In the center rectangle, write down the actions a manager can take to reach the goal. In the bottom rectangle, write the outcome of the manager's actions.

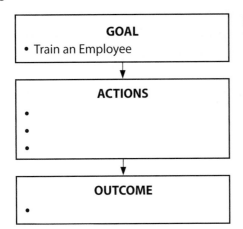

GOAL
- Train an Employee

ACTIONS
-
-
-

OUTCOME
-

 Graphic Organizer Go to this book's Online Learning Center at **glencoe.com** for a printable graphic organizer.

GRAPHIC ORGANIZER ANSWER Actions: Positive reinforcement, mentoring, orientation. Outcome: The employee learns to do the job properly.

ACADEMIC STANDARDS

 English Language Arts
NCTE 7 Conduct research and gather, evaluate, and synthesize data to communicate discoveries.

 Mathematics
NCTM Number and Operations Compute fluently and make reasonable estimates.

 Social Studies
NCSS VI I Power, Authority, and Governance Evaluate the extent to which governments achieve their stated ideals and policies at home and abroad.

NCTE National Council of Teachers of English

NCTM National Council of Teachers of Mathematics

NSES National Science Education Standards

NCSS National Council for the Social Studies

You must have the right skills to manage both people and places.

The Manager's Role

It can be exciting to be in charge! However, a management position also means a lot of responsibility. Managers make sure that all employees are properly trained and that they complete their tasks efficiently. To do this, managers must be good problem-solvers and decision-makers. Managers are often promoted to their positions after they work in lower level positions.

Successful managers are respected by the employees they supervise. They encourage and train employees. They also encourage employees to work as a team and to meet challenges with a positive attitude.

Employee Selection

It is part of a manager's job to find and interview new employees. What should managers look for when interviewing prospective employees? All the qualities an interviewer looks for are not **obvious**, or easily spotted. Most managers look for qualities such as honesty and teamwork. They also look for an employee with past education and work experience that fits the job opening.

Job Descriptions

Each job has its own set of duties and responsibilities. These specific duties are listed in a **job description**. Many job descriptions also list the skills needed for a position.

A job description has several different uses. First, it can be shared with prospective employees during an interview. A manager can use the job description to explain what the job will involve. Job descriptions also can be used to evaluate job performance. Employees who do not meet a job description requirement may need more training to improve their skills.

Job Applications

It can be difficult to choose the right employee for a job. The first step a manager takes is to review job applications. They should be neat and completely filled out.

The following items signal a warning to managers when they review job applications:

- Reasons for leaving a job may show poor interpersonal skills, such as "problems with coworkers."
- Reasons for time spent between jobs may show serious conflicts with a former employer. On the other hand, the person may have taken time off to have children or to go to college.

Interviewing Skills

The next and perhaps most important step in the hiring process is the interview. During an interview, a manager looks for a person who is:

- Clean and well groomed.
- A good communicator.
- Self-confident.
- A team player.
- Honest.
- Organized.
- Willing to learn new things.

Interview Questions During an interview, the manager must get an idea of whether or not the potential employee is right for the job. The best way to do this is to ask questions that can reveal a person's work ethic and attitude. Some of these questions are:

- What were the customers like in the last place you worked?
- If you could have changed anything about your last job, what would it have been?
- What was a difficult challenge you had on the job? How did you overcome it?
- Why should we hire you?

Illegal Interview Questions There are some questions that a manager may not ask during an interview. These include questions about race, gender, religion, national origin, birthplace, age, disability, or marital status. If you are asked any of these questions, you may politely decline to answer.

Open-Ended Questions Effective managers ask open-ended interview questions. An **open-ended question** is a question that requires more than a one- or two-word answer.

For example, instead of asking, "When did you leave your last job?" they will ask, "Why did you leave your last job?" They also listen carefully to a person's answers and note his or her body language.

Employee Training

Most new employees need to be trained to do their jobs. Managers usually train new employees during orientation. Orientation is the process of making a new employee familiar with his or her job. Orientation can last several hours or several weeks, depending on the job.

Some things that employees must learn during orientation include:
- Front-of-the-house and back-of-the-house duties, depending on their job
- Safety, security, and sanitation procedures
- Clerical duties, government regulations, and service guidelines

Positive Reinforcement

People learn better when they feel they are able to do a job correctly. People also act in ways that they feel will be rewarded. It is important for managers to build an employee's confidence during training. Managers use a technique called positive reinforcement. **Positive reinforcement** includes praising an employee when a job or task is done correctly.

Mentorship

When a new employee is hired, the manager may assign him or her to work with another employee. A **mentor** is an experienced employee who has a solid understanding of his or her job. New employees can ask their mentors questions about job duties and receive immediate answers.

Mentoring is an excellent way to train new employees on the procedures of a particular foodservice business. It is also a quick way to train employees who have changed jobs or been given new duties. Mentorships can help foodservice employees form teams.

Experienced Help Mentors introduce new employees to the procedures they will follow and the equipment they will use on the job. *Who should be a mentor?*

Employee Supervision

Managers have many duties when they supervise employees. Managers must:
- Set salary schedules.
- Explain benefits, policies, and procedures.
- Make sure employees follow all workplace laws and rules.
- Hold staff meetings.
- Resolve problems between employees.
- Negotiate contracts with labor unions.

Standards of Conduct

Most employees want to do a good job. Having established standards of conduct can help guide employees in a variety of situations. Standards should be changed when needed, and posted for all employees to see. Different employees may have different standards of conduct. For example, servers will have their own set of customer service standards.

PHOTO CAPTION ANSWER Mentors should be experienced foodservice workers who are able to teach and work well with others.

Standards may include information such as:

- The customer is always right. Never argue with a customer. Assume that you made the error and continue to offer service with a smile.
- Suggest alternatives. If a customer is dissatisfied with a food item, suggest an alternative menu choice.
- Avoid public arguments. Never argue with other employees in front of customers.
- Help out coworkers without being asked.
- Take appropriate breaks. Never take a break during peak hours without permission.

Drugs and Alcohol

Using drugs and alcohol can impair workers' reactions and decision-making skills. This can be very dangerous in a professional foodservice business. There are strict laws and rules that prohibit drug and alcohol use. It is the manager's job to ensure a safe facility for employees and customers. An employee who arrives at his or her workplace under the influence of drugs or alcohol could lose his or her job.

Work Schedules

Most foodservice operations have rules about schedules and work assignments. The manager must juggle each employee's sched-ule with a **master work schedule**. This shows the work shifts of all employees of a business. (See **Figure 7.1**.)

When developing schedules, managers rely on their past experience to predict how many employees they will need. They must also know who is available to work at different times. Managers should have a balance of new and experienced workers on each shift.

Employee Evaluation

Foodservice employees are evaluated on how well they do their work. Usually, the manager will evaluate the employee's skill level, overall work attendance and attitude, and teamwork skills.

During an evaluation, the manager identifies an employee's strengths and weaknesses. The employee will be able to ask questions. The manager will then fill out evaluation forms. The results of the performance evaluation are often used to determine any promotions and raises. Sometimes, they are used to terminate employees who are not able to do their jobs.

 **Reading Check** Define What is a job description?

FIGURE 7.1 Production Schedule

Work Schedules Developing an employee work schedule is an important part of a manager's job. *What should managers consider when scheduling employees?*

Employee	Item/Activity	Portions	Station
LH and FZ	Country Fried Steak with Gravy	25	Fry Station
TG	New Potatoes	25	Hot Station
CS	Green Beans	25	Hot Station
AP	Cloverleaf Rolls	50	Bake Station
JH	Strawberry Shortcake	25	Bake Station
CI and LM	Mixed Greens with Ranch Dressing	25	Garde Manger Station
PS and CF	Coffee & Iced Tea	50	Beverage Station & Servers
BW and RN	Kitchen Clean-up		Dishwashing Station
MD	Floater		As Needed

FIGURE CAPTION ANSWER Managers should consider the amount of work to be done, peak customer times, employee availability, and employee experience.

READING CHECK ANSWER A job description is a list of duties and responsibilities for a specific job.

Facilities Management

You might be surprised at the amount of work that goes into managing a foodservice facility. The design of a facility can affect how productive and successful the business is. A facility's **design** includes how the dining room, kitchen, and storage areas are laid out. A good design should help employees be efficient in their work.

How a facility and its contents are maintained is also important. A dirty or neglected restaurant will drive off customers. A clean, attractive restaurant will bring customers back.

General Layout

A foodservice operation's design is important to customers. As an employee, you will also be affected by the design of the workplace, or the space in which you will perform your job. A foodservice operation must be designed so that employees can do their tasks efficiently. The business facility also must be designed so that customers can enjoy their dining experience without distraction.

Balance

Dividing space to meet customer and preparation staff needs is called **balance**. For example, suppose a manager decides to squeeze the maximum number of customers into the dining area as allowed by law. The space that is left over is where the kitchen is built. It is important to consider how different areas will work together. Although more customers can fit into the restaurant, the kitchen may not be able to handle large numbers of orders efficiently.

Menu

One of the most important factors in design is the menu. The equipment, storage space, and work surfaces that are needed to make the menu items will all affect how a facility is designed.

Turnover Rate

Another factor in facility design is the turnover rate. A **turnover rate** is the average number of times a seat will be occupied during a block of time. For example, if customers stay an average of 20 minutes for breakfast, the potential turnover rate is 2½ times per hour. It may seem as if an average of 20 minutes for breakfast would equal a turnover rate of three customers per hour. But there must be enough time to set up between customers.

A facility's design can help create a certain turnover rate. If you want a high turnover rate, for example, tables can be placed closer together and more staff can be hired to provide quick and efficient service.

A TASTE OF HISTORY ANSWER Time lines should show the major developments in OSHA safety rules in chronological order. Students' answers may vary, but their paragraphs should generally conclude that OSHA's rules have made the foodservice industry a safer place for employees.

Traffic Paths

How people and materials move within a foodservice operation creates a certain **traffic path**. Managers must find the best way to allow movement along traffic paths. However, the space for traffic paths must be kept to a minimum. For example, if carts will be pushed or carried down a traffic path that contains a hot table, the path must be wide enough for both.

Bypassing

Work stations should be laid out in a logical sequence. This keeps bypassing to a minimum. **Bypassing** happens when people or materials must walk or be moved past unrelated stations during foodservice. For example, after vegetables have been cleaned and cut for grilling, they must be passed from the pantry station to the grill station. If the baking station is between the two areas, it will interrupt the workflow.

Production Space

The total amount of space to allow for food production depends upon the type and size of the facility. Managers must divide production space between all of the work areas, such as storage, food preparation, and dishwashing. (See **Figure 7.2**.)

FIGURE 7.2 **Restaurant Workspace Allocation**

Enough Space Make sure that each kitchen work area has enough space. *Why do you think creating space for traffic patterns is important?*

Work Area	Space
Receiving and storage	25%
Food preparation	42%
Dishwashing	8%
Traffic paths	15%
Employee facilities	10%
Total	100%

FIGURE CAPTION ANSWER If foot traffic is not efficient, employees will be unable to reach all areas, and will waste time getting out of each other's way.

Layout of Work Areas

When laying out work areas, managers will try to limit the necessary movement of people and goods. This will save time and energy. The first step of layout is to arrange the pieces of equipment into a work area. Then, the work area must fit into the entire facility. An effective work area layout will:

- Allow for easy maintenance and inventory access.
- Provide a safe and productive environment for employees.
- Make the work process flexible.
- Protect equipment from damage.

Opening and Closing

Managers are usually responsible for opening and closing a restaurant on a daily basis. A good manager has standard procedures for both. Opening a restaurant at the beginning of the day might include:

- Unlocking the front door and any storage areas.
- Turning on the lights and equipment.
- Inspecting the facility for cleanliness.
- Making sure all work stations are manned.

Closing procedures are important for a restaurant. Closing a restaurant at the end of the day might include:

- Locking the door and storage areas.
- Locking the safe.
- Supervising the cleaning of the restaurant.
- Filling out and filing daily paperwork, including guest checks, balancing the cash drawer, writing the bank deposit, and writing equipment and service records.
- Setting any security measures in place after all employees have left.
- Turning off lights and equipment before leaving for the day.

Reading Check **Define** What are traffic paths in a foodservice operation?

READING CHECK ANSWER Traffic paths are the movement of people and materials within the foodservice operation.

Loss Prevention Factors

A foodservice operation must focus on loss prevention to stay profitable. **Loss prevention** is the steps a business takes to eliminate waste and theft. If you make sure that each loss prevention **factor**, or issue, is covered, you will save a foodservice operation both time and money.

Safety

All foodservice facilities must be safe places to work. Unfortunately, foodservice employees are at risk for on-the-job injuries. The most common kitchen injuries include slips and falls, burns, and cuts. Chapter 1 covers these safety issues.

Managers can improve safety by properly training employees. This is especially important when employees first learn about their job duties. Safety precautions must always be followed. See **Figure 7.3** below for some of the safety standards that inspectors look for in a facility.

Kitchen Cleanliness Maintaining a clean kitchen is vital for a successful restaurant. *What cleanliness standards do you see in this picture?*

▼ FIGURE 7.3 **Inspection Points**

Safety Standards Inspectors look for these common safety standards in foodservice facilities. *Whose job is it to uphold these safety standards?*

Area	Sample Inspection Points	Frequency
Hot Station	• Clean the surfaces of all cooking and baking equipment according to the manufacturer's directions	Daily
Work Surfaces	• Clean and sanitize all work surfaces	Every 4 hours or before use of each raw food or when changing from raw to ready-to-eat food
Ice Machine	• Top clean and free of objects; rim of door free of mold; ice scoop properly stored	Daily
	• Floor is clean under machine; vent hood is clean; side and back walls next to the machine are clean	Daily
Dishwashing	• Spray hose is leak-free; prevents backflow	Daily
	• Glass-rack shelf is neat and clean	Monthly
	• Walls next to the dish machine are clean	Monthly
	• Dish machine is lime- and crust-free	Daily
	• Water temperature and sanitizer at proper levels	Daily

FIGURE CAPTION ANSWER It is the job of every employee to uphold safety standards.

PHOTO CAPTION ANSWER The floors and counters are clean and free of debris; all cooking tools are stored properly; the stove is clean; all food is put away.

Risk Management

Some large businesses might have a risk management supervisor on staff to create and manage safety procedures. **Risk management** means taking steps to prevent accidents from happening.

Smaller foodservice businesses may contact insurance companies about risk management. Some insurance companies give free or low-cost advice to businesses on how to keep employees and customers safe.

The American Red Cross and some local fire departments also offer free or low-cost risk management training programs. For example, all foodservice employees should be trained in basic first aid, cardiopulmonary resuscitation, and how to extinguish fires. Employees should also receive refresher training so that they remember how to stay calm and react appropriately during an emergency.

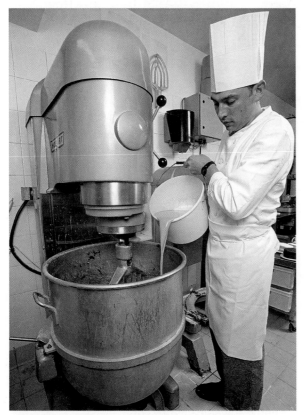

▲ **Prevent Injuries** Managers must enforce safety rules for using equipment to prevent injury. *What could happen if an employee incorrectly operates the equipment you see here?*

PHOTO CAPTION ANSWER An employee's clothing, fingers or hands could get caught in the equipment if safety precautions are not followed.

Sanitation

Foodborne illness is a major health concern. There are many different kinds of food and many different people handling it. If a facility is not kept clean, the chances of contamination are high. Managers must properly train employees about sanitation. Employees must follow strict rules about personal hygiene. Chapters 1 and 2 talk about sanitation and how it should be applied on the job.

Food Handling

Federal, state, and local governments make rules about the safe handling of food. Also, many trade associations, such as the National Turkey Federation, have their own standards and guidelines for safe food handling and storage. Improper food handling can result in contamination. Chapter 2 talks about safe food handling.

Foodservice operations are inspected regularly. Inspectors make sure that the operation follows government regulations for food handling. Health and safety inspectors will look for:

- A clean facility.
- Food preparation processes.
- Clean food storage areas.
- Proper worker sanitation practices.

Equipment Handling

Foodservice operations spend thousands of dollars on purchasing foodservice equipment and tools. If you do not handle, operate, or clean a piece of equipment correctly, you can damage it. You may also hurt yourself or others.

Managers must train all foodservice employees on how to use and clean equipment safely and correctly. Some laws require that operators of some equipment be at least 18 years old. Do not hesitate to ask questions of your manager or your mentor if you are unsure of how to use equipment safely. It is better to ask questions than to be harmed through misuse.

Maintenance and Repairs

All equipment must be regularly and properly maintained. This will ensure that the equipment stays in top operating condition. If equipment needs to be fixed, repairs must be made promptly. This will keep the foodservice operation running smoothly. The equipment must not be used until repairs are made to maintain kitchen safety.

It is important to follow proper maintenance procedures. This is true whether you are using a deep fat fryer or a manual can opener. Managers usually create an equipment maintenance and cleaning schedule. This schedule should be followed exactly for safety.

Insurance

Owners of foodservice operations buy insurance to protect their business operations, facility, employees, and customers. There are many different types of insurance that are available. Insurance can be purchased

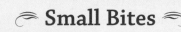

Small Bites

Facility Maintenance Many foodservice operations sign maintenance contracts with repair companies. Under these contracts, repair companies regularly visit the facility and perform routine maintenance.

to cover damage from fire, injury to customers, damage to equipment, employee disability, employee health, loss of life, theft, and loss of the business.

Insurance can be costly, however. Properly training employees in safety techniques and maintaining proper equipment maintenance schedules can help reduce the cost of insurance. These precautions help make the foodservice workplace a safer environment for workers and customers.

Reading Check Describe How can managers improve the safety of their facilities?

 SECTION 7.2 **After You Read**

Review Key Concepts

1. **Analyze** why positive reinforcement and mentoring are good methods of employee training.
2. **Describe** the qualities of an effective work area.
3. **Explain** a manager's responsibility for equipment handling.

Practice Culinary Academics
English Language Arts

4. Read articles in trade publications about management issues such as scheduling conflicts, handling delayed orders, and equipment breakdowns. Briefly summarize each article and your thoughts in response to the article. Discuss the articles you read and your thoughts about them as a class. Attach copies of the article to your summary page and turn them in.

> **NCTE 7** Conduct research and gather, evaluate, and synthesize data to communicate discoveries.

Mathematics

5. A small deli requires four employees: two sandwich makers (who earn $10.25/hour), a cashier (who earns $9.75/hour), and a manager (who earns $850/week). If the deli is open 40 hours in a week, what are its total weekly labor costs? What is its average hourly cost?

Math Concept **Calculating Labor Costs** Calculate a company's total direct labor cost for a time period by adding all salaries and wages paid to employees over that period. Labor costs may also be averaged per hour.

Starting Hint Calculate the weekly wages paid to the three hourly employees by multiplying each pay rate ($10.25/hour, $9.75/hour) by the number of hours worked per week (40). Add these amounts to the manager's weekly salary to find the total labor costs. Divide this sum by 40 to find the average hourly cost.

> **NCTM Number and Operations** Compute fluently and make reasonable estimates.

 Check your answers at this book's Online Learning Center at **glencoe.com**.

Foodservice Marketing

Learn how to successfully market a foodservice business.

Reading Guide

 Before You Read

Get a Note Pad It is normal to have questions when you read. Write down questions while reading. Many of them will be answered as you continue. If they are not, you will have a list ready for your teacher when you finish.

Read to Learn
Key Concepts
- **Demonstrate** how to analyze a marketplace for a foodservice business.
- **Identify** promotion and public relations techniques.

Main Idea
To successfully market a restaurant, you must study the location, customer base, competition, and trends to develop a marketing strategy.

Graphic Organizer
Use a network tree like this one to show how to analyze the marketplace. Fill in the second level with the four factors that you must analyze for a good marketing strategy.

Content Vocabulary
- marketplace
- clientele
- market segment
- mass marketing
- target market
- competitor
- positioning
- marketing plan
- promotion
- public relations
- publicity
- advertising
- direct marketing

Academic Vocabulary
- strategy
- adequate

ACADEMIC STANDARDS

 English Language Arts
  NCTE 4 Use written language to communicate effectively.

 Mathematics
  NCTM Number and Operations Understand the meanings of operations and how they relate to one another.

 Science
  NSES F Develop an understanding of population growth.

NCTE National Council of Teachers of English

NCTM National Council of Teachers of Mathematics

NSES National Science Education Standards

NCSS National Council for the Social Studies

Marketing Strategies

 Graphic Organizer Go to this book's Online Learning Center at **glencoe.com** for a printable graphic organizer.

GRAPHIC ORGANIZER ANSWER Location, customer base, competition, and trends.

Analyze the Marketplace

A foodservice business must do more than offer good food and service to survive. A successful business must make marketing a top priority. The right marketing can help a foodservice business keep current customers and attract new customers. A business must plan and research locations, menus, customers, competitors, and trends. Managers spend hours planning the marketing for a business, even before the doors are opened to its first customers. This section will tell you how this is done.

Marketing begins when you create a new business. You must analyze the marketplace as you plan the business. The **marketplace** includes the location, the people, and the atmosphere of a particular geographic area. New business owners must research each of these factors to predict whether a new business will succeed.

For example, suppose that you wanted to open a pastry shop. To analyze the marketplace, you would look at several different areas where you think the shop could be located.

When you consider possible locations, you might ask yourself:

- How busy is this location at mealtimes?
- Is this location convenient and accessible to a large number of people?
- What products and services will I offer?
- Does this area have a need for this type of foodservice facility? Is this service already being provided in the area?
- How much does it cost to rent or purchase space at this location versus other locations?
- Is this area showing signs of growth?
- Does this area draw from a multicultural population?

Marketing Strategies

Marketing affects the location of the foodservice operation, what food products are offered, how items are promoted, and who presents the product. Many foodservice operations go out of business within one to five years because they fail to take all of these factors into consideration. A marketing **strategy** or plan of action, lets you know how your area will respond to your business.

Market Research Investigating the marketplace is an important step for new business owners. *What marketing information does this picture show?*

PHOTO CAPTION ANSWER Answers will vary, but may include the cups and the customers' dress, which is casual, and the outdoor setting.

However, marketing strategies must be well planned, or you may get incorrect information.

Several basic marketing strategies can give you key information that you will need to operate your business. This can give you the best possible start toward profitability. To be successful, you must analyze the location, the customer base and its diversity, the competition, and trends.

Location

The location you choose for a new business is one of the most important choices you will make. It does not matter whether you choose an existing building that you will update or simply an empty lot. You should carefully look at the location before any construction or renovation begins.

Many businesses fail because they do not think about traffic patterns. Customers want easy, convenient access to their food choices. What if a new highway is built, or an existing highway is closed or rerouted? If it is difficult to get to a location, chances are customers will find another restaurant.

Questions to Ask Business owners can start by asking questions about the location, such as:

- What physical locations or structures can I afford?
- How much money do I need to spend on the physical structure?
- Should a new structure be built, or should an existing structure be renovated?
- Why did the last owner leave?

Customer Base

Next, business owners must analyze their clientele and their target market. The **clientele** are the people who will be the business's main customers. This strategy involves examining what type of people you want to attract as customers. Are they, for example, businesspeople, young and health-conscious, or families? Perhaps they are looking for familiar foods and flavors from their cultural heritage. A specific type of clientele is called a **market segment**.

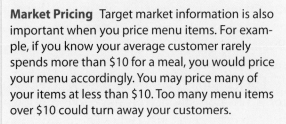

ᕕ Small Bites ᕗ

Market Pricing Target market information is also important when you price menu items. For example, if you know your average customer rarely spends more than $10 for a meal, you would price your menu accordingly. You may price many of your items at less than $10. Too many menu items over $10 could turn away your customers.

Market segments have different characteristics, or demographics. When you market to all possible segments at once, it is called **mass marketing**. The market segment that you most want to attract is called your **target market**. It is important to know your potential clientele and your target market when you market and advertise for a foodservice operation.

Competition

It is not enough to find the perfect location and create an inviting foodservice business. You may have a hard time getting new customers if you have many competitors. A **competitor** is a business that offers customers similar products or services to the ones that you offer. There may be several other businesses in your area that offer similar foods to yours at similar prices.

Business owners should always know who their competitors are. As a business owner, you must first decide how to market a business and where it will be located. Then, you must check out the competition.

Questions to Ask Foodservice business owners who want to understand their competition need to answer these questions:

- Will my business have competition, or is it one of a kind? How many competitors will it have?
- If there are competitors, how close are they to my chosen location?
- How will my operation be different and more attractive than what is offered by the competition?

Trends

Just because a business idea seems perfect now does not necessarily mean it will be a great idea next year or 10 years from now. Business owners always need to keep the future in mind.

For example, you might have a great idea for a hot dog stand. You have found a location, and it seems just right. There are many potential customers and no current competition. However, did you know that plans are being drawn up for a new baseball field one block away from your chosen location? How will the new ballpark affect your business a year from now? Will your business increase, or will the baseball field have its own hot dog stand?

Questions to Ask To investigate trends in the marketplace, foodservice business owners should ask:

- Is the location in an established area with other thriving businesses?
- Will customers have easy access to my business?

- Is there **adequate**, or enough, parking?
- Are other businesses nearby that might offer a steady supply of hungry customers?
- What is planned for the future of my chosen location?

Reading Check Explain Why is menu pricing an important factor in marketing?

Positioning and Public Relations

Strong positioning for a foodservice establishment can help attract new customers. It also can keep current customers coming back again and again. Positioning affects what potential customers will think about your establishment, and whether they will decide to visit. It helps them to know what your restaurant will offer in service and in food. Without strong positioning, your restaurant may not succeed.

◀ **Customer Preferences**
These customers are celebrating a special event. *What type of menu items would appeal to them?*

PHOTO CAPTION ANSWER Special menu items such as appetizers and desserts would be appealing to customers celebrating a special occasion.

READING CHECK ANSWER Menu items must be priced appropriately for the customers you wish to attract.

Positioning

Positioning is the way a foodservice business presents itself to the community. Many foodservice operations develop a position statement. This statement helps guide a business owner's decision-making and marketing efforts. A position statement explains what the business stands for and what its main goals are. A brief position statement for a restaurant might read: "The Healthy Alternative Café serves healthful food choices at affordable prices."

Marketing Plan

A **marketing plan** is a specific plan to market a business. A marketing plan includes items such as advertising, public relations, and promotions. Marketing plans usually include a calendar of when promotions and advertisements will happen, how much the business plans to spend, and what marketing and advertising it will choose. Most businesses want a diverse marketing mix.

A **promotion** is a specific effort to market a particular item or special. Promotions should focus on what the business does best. Always make sure that you have the food and supplies on hand to run a promotion. Consider your customers' needs before you create a promotion.

To develop a marketing plan, you must find out your objectives, or what you want to get from marketing. Be specific with your goals. You will want to check to see how well past marketing efforts have worked. Employees should know what the marketing plan is, so that they can support it.

At the end of a marketing plan, examine your records to see if it increased your business's profits. A good marketing plan should increase profits, not cost the restaurant money.

Atmosphere

Have you ever noticed how every foodservice facility has its own unique atmosphere? A facility's atmosphere is the feeling that customers get from the interior and exterior. The way a facility is designed helps shape its atmosphere. This includes details like the type of carpet, the wall coverings, the music, and even the staff uniforms. Make sure that your business's atmosphere fits the style and theme of your foodservice operation.

Business owners must thoroughly study their customer's needs and wants before they create an atmosphere. Studying customer needs and preferences is not something that happens only before a business opens. It is an ongoing process. Foodservice operations often use customer comment cards or surveys to gather information. This feedback is used to find out whether the business is on track. Management may need to alter the food choices, hours, or atmosphere to better meet customer needs.

Public Relations

Having good public relations is critical to the success of a foodservice facility. **Public relations** includes publicity and advertising that a foodservice operation uses to enhance its image. **Publicity** is the free or low-cost efforts of a facility to improve its image.

Publicity can be both negative and positive. Negative publicity, such as news of an outbreak of foodborne illness, may take months or even years to overcome. Positive publicity can include the use of special events and promotions. Charity events, fundraisers, and school food seminars all can create positive publicity.

Advertising

Foodservice businesses must advertise to become and stay successful. **Advertising** is a paid form of promotion that persuades and informs the public about what a business has to offer. Newspapers, television, radio, and the Internet are some advertising options. Business owners can write their own advertising, or can hire a professional writer. Ads should have correct spelling and grammar.

Compare costs among different forms of advertising to see which is the most affordable and reaches the right customers for your business. Once they have decided on certain types of advertising, business owners can create advertising schedules. An advertising schedule is a calendar that shows when each form of advertising will run. Chain restaurants usually coordinate their advertising for all locations.

Businesses can also improve their image in the community. This can be done by sponsoring events their customers care about. Imagine that you work at a pizza parlor. Your managers might donate pizzas to a charity bike-a-thon. Sponsorships and donations like this enhance a business's image in the community.

Direct Marketing

Direct marketing is a form of advertising in which promotional materials, such as letters, flyers, and advertisements, are mailed directly to customers within a certain distance from the foodservice business. Direct marketing can be carefully targeted to reach potential customers who are nearby. It can also be targeted to reach customers who have a certain income, or who have certain interests.

However, direct marketing has its disadvantages. People often do not read every piece of mail they receive. It can also be expensive to write, design, print, and mail direct marketing materials.

 **Reading Check** Identify What is a position statement?

SECTION 7.3 After You Read

Review Key Concepts

1. **Demonstrate** how to analyze a location for a foodservice business.
2. **Describe** direct marketing.

Practice Culinary Academics

 English Language Arts

3. Imagine that you opened a new restaurant one month ago in the neighborhood where you live. You are not yet getting very many customers. Create a position statement and a direct-marketing piece for a promotion to introduce your restaurant. You may choose any type of promotion.

> **NCTE 4** Use written language to communicate effectively.

 Science

4. **Procedure** Examine the types of restaurants in your area. Write down information on the foods they serve and how close they are to each other. Using this information, predict what types of restaurants might become popular in your area.

   Analysis Write a short report that details your predictions. Consider product, distribution, price, unmet needs, and competitors.

> **NSES F** Develop an understanding of population growth.

Mathematics

5. You are considering opening a coffee house in an office complex that has limited hours. You estimate that a second location, in a residential neighborhood, would offer 30% more customers, but that each customer would spend 20% less. Which location is better?

Math Concept **Thinking About Percentages** In this case, potential revenue for each location equals the number of customers times the amount each customer spends. Think about how increasing or decreasing the two factors would affect the result.

Starting Hint When there are two factors in an equation, and you wish to increase one factor and decrease the other, if the percentage increase is greater than the percentage decrease, the product will increase. Form a hypothesis about what would happen if one factor is increased by a larger amount than the other factor is decreased. Test this hypothesis by using sample numbers in the equation, and then increase one number by 30% and decrease the other by 20%. Does total revenue go up or down?

> **NCTM Number and Operations** Understand the meanings of operations and how they relate to one another.

 Check your answers at this book's Online Learning Center at **glencoe.com**.

READING CHECK ANSWER A position statement explains what a business stands for and what its main goals are.

Review and Applications

Chapter Summary

An effective manager is skilled in the areas of communication, time management, resource management, and leadership. Managers must train employees and make sure that they understand all of the operation's policies. To protect the operation and the employees, managers must also consider loss prevention factors. Marketing and public relations can help a foodservice operation maintain its customer base and attract new customers.

Content and Academic Vocabulary Review

1. Write a memo explaining good management. Use at least 12 of the following terms in your memo.

Content Vocabulary

- overstaffing (p. 171)
- human resources (p. 172)
- orientation (p. 172)
- delegate (p. 172)
- autocratic (p. 172)
- democratic (p. 172)
- standardized accounting practices (p. 173)
- double-entry bookkeeping (p. 173)
- food cost percentage (p. 173)
- direct labor cost (p. 173)
- indirect labor cost (p. 173)
- income (p. 174)
- expense (p. 174)
- profit and loss statement (p. 175)
- forecasting (p. 175)

- break even (p. 175)
- inventory (p. 175)
- job description (p. 179)
- open-ended question (p. 179)
- positive reinforcement (p. 180)
- mentor (p. 180)
- master work schedule (p. 181)
- design (p. 182)
- balance (p. 182)
- turnover rate (p. 182)
- traffic path (p. 183)
- bypassing (p. 183)
- loss prevention (p. 184)
- risk management (p. 185)
- marketplace (p. 188)
- clientele (p. 189)
- market segment (p. 189)
- mass marketing (p. 189)

- target market (p. 189)
- competitor (p. 189)
- positioning (p. 191)
- marketing plan (p. 191)
- promotion (p. 191)
- public relations (p. 191)
- publicity (p. 191)
- advertising (p. 191)
- direct marketing (p. 192)

Academic Vocabulary

- lapse (p. 171)
- adhere (p. 172)
- obvious (p. 179)
- factor (p. 184)
- strategy (p. 188)
- adequate (p. 190)

Review Key Concepts

2. List the qualities and duties of an effective manager.

3. Explain the foodservice manager's role in maintaining profitability.

4. Analyze the manager's role in employee selection, training, and supervision.

5. Examine the design issues that contribute to a profitable facility.

6. Give examples of what foodservice facilities can do to manage loss prevention.

7. Demonstrate how to analyze a marketplace for a foodservice business.

8. Identify promotion and public relations techniques.

Critical Thinking

9. Apply leadership skills. You have been hired as a quick-serve restaurant manager. The employees are college students. What style of leadership would you use? Why?

10. Develop a schedule. You have just been hired at a restaurant. Your manager is determining your work schedule and asks for input. Which factors would you consider?

Review and Applications

Academic Skills

 English Language Arts

11. Satisfied Customers Research a company known for its satisfied customers. This company does not need to be a foodservice business. Find examples of its advertising and marketing that point to customer satisfaction. Write a summary of how the advertising and marketing suggests to customers that the business has excellent customer service. Do you think it works? Why or why not? How could the advertising and marketing be more effective?

> **NCTE 1** Read texts to acquire new information.

 Social Studies

12. Safety Checklist Maintaining a safe environment is an important part of a manager's job. Each state has different safety guidelines. It is important that a restaurant be in compliance with these guidelines. Investigate the safety guidelines for foodservice kitchens in your state. Then, write a report on why these guidelines were chosen for inspection. List as many of the actual guidelines as possible in your report. Explain any management duties for inspections that are outlined in the state guidelines.

> **NCSS VI A Power, Authority, and Governance** Examine persistent issues involving the rights, roles, and status of the individual in relation to the general welfare.

 Mathematics

13. Understand Balance Sheets A balance sheet provides a snapshot of a company's financial position at a particular time. Your restaurant's balance sheet for December 31 indicates that on that date you had $10,000 in cash, $20,000 in food and supplies, and that the building and land owned by the restaurant was valued at $150,000. The restaurant owed its food supplier $30,000 and had a $70,000 bank loan outstanding. What is the value for owner's equity displayed on the balance sheet?

Math Concept **Basic Balance Sheet Equations**
A balance sheet is split into three sections: assets (things of value the company owns), liabilities (amounts the company owes), and owner's equity. The total assets must always equal the sum of liabilities and owner's equity: $A = L + O$.

Starting Hint Since the question asks for the amount of owner's equity, start by rearranging the balance sheet equation to solve for owner's equity: $O = A - L$. Add the dollar amounts of all items on the balance sheet owned by the company. These are the restaurant's assets (A). Any amounts owed to others are the restaurant's liabilities (L).

> **NCTM Problem Solving** Solve problems that arise in mathematics and in other contexts.

Certification Prep

Directions Read the questions. Then, read the answer choices and choose the best possible answer for each.

14. What does FMP stand for?

   a. Food Managing Partner

   b. First Management Person

   c. Foodservice Managing Program

   d. Foodservice Management Professional

15. Who regulates the safe handling of food?

   a. the restaurant owner

   b. federal, state, and local governments

   c. the President of the United States

   d. the customers

Sharpen your test-taking skills to improve your kitchen certification program score.

Test-Taking Tip
Look for key words in the answer choices that also appeared in the chapter you just studied. You may be able to eliminate those that did not.

Review and Applications

Real-World Skills and Applications

Communication Skills

16. Customer Service After finishing his meal, a customer complains to you that the food he ate was unsatisfactory. Describe two possible ways that you could handle this customer's complaint. Write a summary of each. Then, follow your teacher's instructions to form small groups, and hold a debate in class over how these ways might resolve or worsen the situation, and which way is best. Discuss group findings as a class.

Management Skills

17. Conduct an Interview Imagine that you are a restaurant manager interviewing potential employees for these service positions: server, cashier, busser, and host. Choose one of these positions and make a list of five to 10 questions that you would ask potential employees during the interview. Exchange lists with other students and discuss the questions with each other. Do the questions ask for the right information? Are there any that you would change?

Financial Literacy

18. Calculate Beverage Costs Imagine that you manage a restaurant and must calculate your beverage cost percentage for the last six months. The beverage cost for the months was as follows: Month 1: $15,000; Month 2: $13,500; Month 3: $14,000; Month 4: $15,000; Month 5: $13,700; Month 6: 14,500. The income received was: Month 1: $50,000; Month 2: $45,000; Month 3: $47,000; Month 4: $52,000; Month 5: $49,000; Month 6: $50,000.

Technology Applications

19. Create a Flyer Imagine that you are promoting a new restaurant in the area of your school. Use a desktop publishing program to create a flyer that promotes the restaurant. Decide on what type of food the restaurant will serve and what kind of atmosphere it will have. Also, decide on your target market. Include illustrations and whatever information you believe would be important to prospective customers when they decide on a restaurant.

Culinary Lab

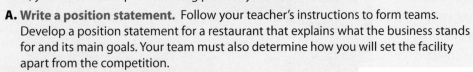

Use the culinary skills you have learned in this chapter.

Market a Foodservice Operation

20. Develop a Marketing Plan Suppose you have an idea for a new restaurant. Now, you must develop a marketing plan for your new restaurant.

A. Write a position statement. Follow your teacher's instructions to form teams. Develop a position statement for a restaurant that explains what the business stands for and its main goals. Your team must also determine how you will set the facility apart from the competition.

B. Determine the atmosphere. Describe the atmosphere of the facility, and its customers. Think of the design of the interior and the exterior, and the people who would eat there.

C. Choose advertising. Name three ways that you could advertise the restaurant. Consider the cost of each method and what types of customers it might reach.

D. Create an ad. Design an ad for the restaurant using one of the methods you have chosen. Incorporate the look and feel of the restaurant's atmosphere into the design of the ad.

E. Present the results. Share your restaurant ad, as well as your other advertising choices, with the class.

Create Your Evaluation

For each advertisement, give a review of how well it conveyed information. Create a mini-review as if you were a critic for each presentation. Answer these questions:

- What parts of the ad made you want to go to the restaurant? What parts did not?
- Would you want to eat at this restaurant?
- Is there any information that was left out?

Standards, Regulations, and Laws

SECTIONS

8.1 Foodservice Standards and Regulations

8.2 Employment Laws

WRITING ACTIVITY

Write an Explanation

An explanation is a description of how or why something happens. Write a paragraph explaining why the government regulates the food-service industry.

Writing Tips

1 First, plan the points you want to make in an outline or list.

2 Use helper words and phrases, such as because or since.

3 Organize the paragraph by addressing each subject, one at a time.

EXPLORE THE PHOTO

Food inspectors check foodservice operations to make sure they follow standards and regulations. *What do food inspectors check?*

WRITING ACTIVITY ANSWER
Explanations should focus on food quality, customer safety, and employee safety and workplace rights.

EXPLORE THE PHOTO ANSWER
Food inspections check to ensure that food is prepared in a sanitary way and labeled correctly.

Foodservice Standards and Regulations

Reading Guide

 Before You Read

What You Want to Know Write a list of what you want to know about foodservice standards and regulations. As you read, write down the heads in this section that provide the information.

Read to Learn

Key Concepts
- **List** the industry standards of quality used to evaluate food.
- **Summarize** the roles of various government agencies in the foodservice industry.
- **Explain** how facilities maintenance can help uphold foodservice standards.

Main Idea
Foodservice standards provide standard quality levels that a business should provide to its customers. Government laws and regulations increase the safety of food products.

Content Vocabulary
- standard
- violation
- regulation
- grading
- inspection
- genetically engineered food
- irradiated food
- Food Code
- solid waste
- environmental impact statement
- material safety data sheet (MSDS)
- accident report log

Academic Vocabulary
- performance
- enforce

Graphic Organizer

Use a table like this one to list the 10 standards of quality used in the foodservice industry to evaluate food. List one standard in each box.

Standards of Quality

 Graphic Organizer
Go to this book's Online Learning Center at **glencoe.com** for a printable graphic organizer.

GRAPHIC ORGANIZER ANSWER Safety, Nutritional Value, Appearance, Consistency, Flavor, Texture, Convenience, Ease of Handling, Packaging, and Storage.

 Mathematics
NCTM Data Analysis and Probability Formulate questions that can be addressed with data and collect, organize, and display relevant data to answer them.

Science
NSES B Develop an understanding of chemical reactions.

 Social Studies
NCSS VI I Power, Authority, and Governance Evaluate the extent to which government achieves its stated ideals and policies at home and abroad.

NCSS VI H Power, Authority, and Governance Explain and apply ideas, theories, and modes of inquiry drawn from political science to the examination of persistent ideas and social problems.

NCTE National Council of Teachers of English

NCTM National Council of Teachers of Mathematics

NSES National Science Education Standards

NCSS National Council for the Social Studies

Industry Standards

Imagine that you have just received a shipment of eggs from a supplier. How would you know if the eggs were safe or of good quality? Foodservice industry standards let you know for sure. Government laws and regulations increase the safety of food products. They also regulate safety in the workplace.

A **standard** is an established model or example used to compare quality. With standards in place, managers and food safety professionals can judge a business's **performance**, or the way a foodservice business operates. If a standard is not met, the foodservice operation is written up as being in violation. A **violation** means not following a rule. The operation may pay a fine. It could even be closed down if the violation is serious.

The main goal of the foodservice industry is to provide good quality food and service to customers. To do this, all of these quality standards must be considered: safety, nutritional value, appearance, consistency, flavor, texture, convenience, ease of handling, packaging, and storage.

Reading Check Explain What happens if a foodservice standard is not met?

Governmental Regulations

The foodservice industry is governed by regulations. A **regulation** is a rule by which government agencies enforce minimum standards of quality. Federal, state, and local governments **enforce** these regulations. To enforce means to ensure that laws and regulations are followed.

USDA Regulations

The U.S. Department of Agriculture (USDA) grades and inspects poultry and poultry products, eggs and egg products, and meat and meat products. The USDA also controls food grading, processing plant inspections, and the use of pesticides, preservatives, and food additives.

Food Grading

When the USDA inspects food and food products, they apply grades to them. (See **Figure 8.1**.) **Grading** food products involves applying specific quality standards to those products. Some products must be graded. Others are graded on a voluntary basis.

A product receives a grade based on its quality when it is packaged. The package is then stamped with the grading seal. Changes in the product may occur during handling and storing that can affect the food's quality. There are different grades for different kinds of products. For example, there are three grades of chicken and eight grades of beef.

Food Inspections

Inspections are conducted to ensure that food is sanitary and labeled correctly. An **inspection** is a test of a business's practices against standards. These inspections are conducted by the Food Safety and Inspection Service (FSIS). The FSIS is a public health

FIGURE 8.1 Food Grading Stamps

Make the Grade The USDA has many grades that show quality in a variety of foods. *Why do you think grading foods is important?*

agency that is part of the USDA. The FSIS checks that egg, poultry, and meat products are wholesome, safe, and correctly packaged and labeled. Inspected food is stamped to show it meets safety standards. (See **Figure 8.2**.)

FDA Regulations

The Food and Drug Administration (FDA) is part of the U.S. Department of Health and Human Services. The FDA enforces the Food, Drug, and Cosmetic Act of 1938. This law covers food and the packaging of foods other than fish, poultry, and meat.

In 1992, the FDA stated that food would be judged by its characteristics, not by the process used to make it. This also applies to genetically engineered and irradiated foods.

Genetically (jə-ˈne-ti-k(ə-)lē) **engineered food** is food that is made by recombining genes. Genes can be omitted or held back, or new genes can be spliced into a food. These foods may become new varieties, such as the combination of broccoli and cauliflower to create broccoflower. Genes may also be combined to improve foods, packing them with more nutrients than they would have naturally.

Irradiated (i-ˈrā-dē-ˌāt-ed) **food** is food that has been exposed to radiation to kill harmful bacteria. Beef, lamb, and pork are the three foods most commonly exposed to radiation. Other food products that may be irradiated include spices and some fruits and vegetables.

FIGURE 8.2 **Food Safety and Inspection Service Stamps**

Safe Food The Food Safety and Inspection Service checks to ensure that food is wholesome and safe to eat. *What is the difference between grading and inspection?*

FIGURE 8.3 **Irradiated Foods**

Radiation and Food Beef, lamb, pork, spices, and some fruits and vegetables are sometimes irradiated to kill harmful bacteria. *Why do you think irradiation is necessary for some foods?*

The FDA oversees irradiation to ensure that the foods are safe. (See **Figure 8.3**.) Irradiated foods must have a label to show they have been irradiated.

Labels

The FDA also requires that nutrition labels be placed on food packages. This is a result of the 1990 Nutrition Labeling and Education Act. The nutrition label shows the percent of daily dietary value in the food. This is usually based on a daily 2,000- or 2,500-calorie intake. (See **Figure 8.4** on page 200.) The nutrition label also shows the number of calories per serving, the total calories, and the amount of vitamins and minerals, fat, cholesterol, sodium, carbohydrates, and protein in the food.

Menus

Since 1997, the FDA has regulated health claims made by restaurants, such as low-fat menu items. These claims must meet FDA standards as listed in the Nutrition Labeling and Education Act. For example, the FDA standard for low fat is 3 grams or fewer per serving. A foodservice business must be able to provide nutritional information to any customer who asks for it. If the menu does not make any special claims, this information is not needed.

Nutrition Facts Nutrition labels provide valuable information. *What does this nutrition label tell you about the food it represents?*

Nutrition Facts

Serving Size 1/2 cup (114 g)
Servings Per Container 4

Amount Per Serving

Calories 90   Calories from Fat 30

	% Daily Value*
Total Fat 3 g	**5%**
Saturated Fat 0 g	**0%**
Trans Fat 0 mg	
Cholesterol 0 mg	**0%**
Sodium 300 mg	**13%**
Total Carbohydrate 13 g	**4%**
Dietary Fiber 3 g	**12%**
Sugars 3 g	
Protein 3 g	

Vitamin A	80%	Vitamin C	60%
Calcium	4%	Iron	4%

* Percent Daily Values are based on a 2,000 calorie diet. Your daily values may be higher or lower depending on your calorie needs:

	Calories	2,000	2,500
Total Fat	Less than	65 g	80 g
Sat Fat	Less than	20 g	25g
Cholesterol	Less than	300 mg	300 mg
Sodium	Less than	2,400 mg	2,400 mg
Total Carbohydrate		300 g	375 g
Fiber		25 g	30 g

Calories per gram:
Fat 9 • Carbohydrates 4 • Protein 4

Food Code

The FDA also recommends foodservice standards in the Food Code. The **Food Code** gives guidelines for handling food safely. It is updated every two years. It is not a law, so states can choose to use it or write their own code, using the Food Code as a guide.

FIGURE CAPTION ANSWER This label tells you that the food has no saturated or *trans* fat, no cholesterol, not too much sodium, and some fiber. It also shows that the food is high in vitamins A and C.

A TASTE OF HISTORY

1906	1908
The Pure Food and Drug Act is passed	Supreme Court Justice Thurgood Marshall is born

Food and Drug Watchdogs

In 1883, Dr. Harvey W. Wiley was appointed chief of the U.S. Department of Chemistry. This department was a predecessor to the Food and Drug Administration. Wiley recognized the need for food and drug scrutiny. He set out to put a stop to inferior food products and false medical remedies. He and his staff performed many investigations and made their findings public. Their determination led to the original Pure Food and Drug Act, passed on June 30, 1906.

History Application

Research the Pure Food and Drug Act of 1906. Write a paragraph that describes how this Act affected the food and drug industry, and the public.

> **NCSS VI I Power, Authority, and Governance** Evaluate the extent to which government achieves its stated ideals and policies at home and abroad.

Environmental Regulations

The Environmental Protection Agency (EPA) decides how solid waste is managed in the United States. **Solid waste** includes packaging material, containers, and recyclables. These regulations are enforced by federal, state, and local agencies. The EPA recommends that businesses reduce solid waste. This can be done by eliminating packaging where possible. It also recommends that reusable food containers be cleaned and sanitized before reusing them. Dispose of containers that hold chemicals. Never reuse them for food products.

The National Environmental Policy Act (NEPA) of 1969 protects the environment from damage caused by building development. Whenever a new restaurant is planned, an environmental impact statement (EIS) must be completed. An **environmental impact statement** describes the impact of the proposed facility and any negative effects it might have on the environment.

A TASTE OF HISTORY ANSWER The Act made it illegal to sell adulterated, or contaminated, foods and poisonous medicines. Students may note that it was a good first step to ensure the safety of foods and medicines.

OSHA Regulations

The Occupational Safety and Health Administration (OSHA) has two main responsibilities. It sets standards and inspects workplaces to make sure that employers provide safe and healthful environments. Many standards, such as these three, are the same in all types of workplaces:

- Employers must provide personal protective equipment, such as gloves.
- Manufacturers of hazardous materials must label their products for danger. OSHA also requires that employers have a material safety data sheet (MSDS) for each hazardous material. A **material safety data sheet** identifies any hazardous chemicals and their components. Employers must tell employees where these sheets are located.
- Employers must give employees access to any records of exposure to toxic materials.

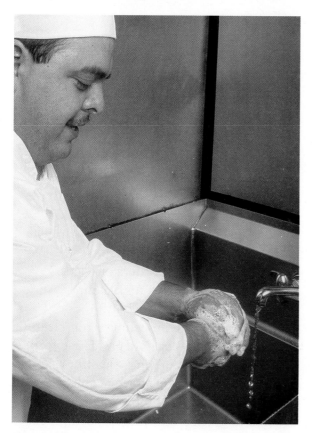

Keep Clean Built-in sanitation features include this hand-washing station. *What other kitchen rules can you think of that will help ensure sanitation?*

PHOTO CAPTION ANSWER Answers might include frequent hand washing, using separate cutting boards for meat and vegetables, wearing protective clothing during cooking, cleaning and sanitizing floors and countertops, and properly storing food.

OSHA also oversees record keeping of job-related illness and injury. One required form is an accident report log. An **accident report log** shows the details of any accident that happens in a business. If an accident causes three or more employees to be hospitalized, or one or more people to die, that accident must be reported to a local OSHA office within eight hours. OSHA will then investigate to see if any standards were violated.

State and Local Regulations

Many of the health regulations that affect foodservice operations are written by the state. Local health departments then enforce state regulations. A large city may also have its own health department that enforces regulations within city limits. The county health department enforces regulations in rural areas and small cities. Most national and statewide companies also have standards that are maintained by their own inspectors.

Reading Check Describe What is the difference between food grading and food inspection?

READING CHECK ANSWER USDA grades food according to specific standards of quality. Food inspections are conducted by the FSIS to make sure that food is sanitary and labeled correctly.
SAFETY CHECK ANSWER Trained managers can spot and correct violations before they cause problems.

Facilities Maintenance

There are also standards and regulations about how a facility should be maintained. Foodservice operations must have facilities that are designed so that they can be thoroughly cleaned. Any facility that cannot be thoroughly cleaned would not provide a safe environment for food. Floors, walls, and ceilings, equipment, and facility design are the main areas of a facility that must meet industry standards.

Floors, Walls, and Ceilings

Industry standards state that floors, walls, and ceilings should be constructed to be durable. They must also meet health and safety regulations. The FDA Food Code recommends that floors should be slip-resistant. They should not be able to absorb materials that are spilled on them.

Walls and ceilings should be light in color. This is especially true in food preparation areas. Light-colored walls and ceilings allow soil to be easily seen. This makes these areas easier to clean. All floors, walls, and ceilings should be kept in good condition. They should not have any holes, cracks, or peeling paint. They should be kept clean and sanitized at all times.

Equipment

The National Sanitation Foundation (NSF) International maintains sanitation standards for kitchen equipment and tools. In addition, Underwriters Laboratories (UL) classifies electrical equipment that meets NSF International standards. The equipment used in commercial kitchens must have the NSF International and UL stamps. Without these stamps, you may not be able to ensure the safety and quality of the equipment.

Make Accommodations Certain accommodations need to be made for those with disabilities. *What types of accommodations can be made in the workplace?*

When equipment is purchased for a professional kitchen, it should:
- Be easy to clean.
- Have smooth, nontoxic, food-contact surfaces that will not absorb bacteria.
- Have surfaces that resist corrosion, and that are nontoxic and chip resistant.
- Be free of surface pits and crevices. Bolts and rivets should be flush with the surface of the equipment, not sticking out. This prevents bacteria from growing in crevices in the equipment.
- Have rounded-off corners or edges.
- Be easy to take apart for cleaning.
- Be for commercial use only.

OSHA also has procedures for cleaning and maintaining equipment. These procedures cover disassembling, cleaning, sanitizing, reassembling, and storing equipment. All foodservice employees must follow these procedures to ensure that kitchen equipment is clean and sanitary. This protects the health of the customers and the employees.

PHOTO CAPTION ANSWER Answers might include placing access ramps near stairs, adapting bathrooms, creating more space in aisles, providing adaptive equipment for employees, modifying certain tasks or job descriptions, and providing support handles and equipment.

Facility Design

There are many different industry standards and state and local regulations that cover all aspects of foodservice business design. These standards generally cover:

- Having an efficient work flow in kitchen and dining room areas.
- Maintaining a low risk of contamination
- Maintaining easy access to safety and emergency equipment.

Facility maintenance standards also apply to the design of restrooms, sinks, ventilation, hand-washing stations, lighting, and waste disposal systems. All of these areas must be able to be cleaned and sanitized thoroughly. Areas that cannot be cleaned well may encourage the growth of bacteria and infestation by pests. Check with local and state agencies to find design standards before you design any foodservice business space.

 Reading Check **Determine** What government agency oversees workplace safety?

SECTION 8.1 — After You Read

Review Key Concepts

1. **Explain** why standards of quality have been developed to evaluate food.
2. **Summarize** FDA regulations on nutrition labels.
3. **List** the three main areas that must meet industry standards of facilities maintenance.

Practice Culinary Academics

Social Studies

4. Research one foodservice standard, law, or regulation at each of the local, state, and federal levels. Summarize the standard, law, or regulation and its purpose. How is it different at the local, state, and federal levels? How is it the same? Write a summary of your findings and present it to the class. List your sources.

> **NCSS VI H Power, Authority, and Governance** Explain and apply ideas, theories, and modes of inquiry drawn from political science to the examination of persistent ideas and social problems.

 Mathematics

5. A restaurant's OSHA-mandated accident report log lists 2 injuries in January, 5 in February, 0 in March, 3 in April, 1 in May, and 6 in June. Display this information in a bar graph.

   Math Concept **Bar Graphs** A bar graph uses vertical bars to display information. When creating a bar graph, you must decide which information to place along the horizontal scale, and which to place on the vertical scale.

   Starting Hint Use the horizontal scale to list the months, and the vertical scale to list the number of injuries. Draw a vertical bar above each month's name to show the number of injuries.

> **NCTM Data Analysis and Probability** Formulate questions that can be addressed with data and collect, organize, and display relevant data to answer them.

 Check your answers at this book's Online Learning Center at **glencoe.com**.

SCIENCE À LA CARTE ANSWER Charts should reflect that the baking soda, and dish detergent are bases. The vinegar, milk, orange juice, pickle juice are acids.

READING CHECK ANSWER OSHA is responsible for setting standards and inspecting facilities to ensure safety.

Employment Laws

Federal, state, and local laws help keep foodservice employees safe.

Reading Guide

Before You Read

Use Diagrams As you read through this section, write down the main idea. Write down any facts, explanations, or examples you find in the text. Start at the main idea and draw arrows to the information that directly supports it. Then, draw arrows from these examples to any information that supports them.

Read to Learn

Key Concepts

- **Identify** laws related to equal employment.
- **Describe** laws meant to protect workers.
- **Distinguish** between management and employee responsibilities for the working environment.

Main Idea

Employment laws protect workers' rights and safety. Laws also protect groups of people from discrimination.

Content Vocabulary

- law
- interstate commerce
- affirmative action
- sexual harassment
- disability
- musculoskeletal disorder
- ergonomics

Academic Vocabulary

- adapting
- determine

ACADEMIC STANDARDS

 Mathematics
NCTM Number and Operations Understand numbers, ways of representing numbers, relationships among numbers, and number systems.

Social Studies
NCSS V F Individuals, Groups, and Institutions Evaluate the role of institutions in furthering both continuity and change.

NCTE National Council of Teachers of English

NCTM National Council of Teachers of Mathematics

NSES National Science Education Standards

NCSS National Council for the Social Studies

Graphic Organizer

Use a concept map to organize the different types of laws that fall under the subheading of Employment Law. Look at the main headings of the section to determine the five different types of laws.

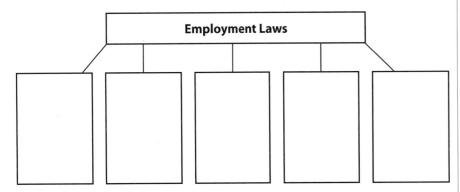

Employment Laws

 Graphic Organizer Go to this book's Online Learning Center at **glencoe.com** for a printable graphic organizer.

GRAPHIC ORGANIZER ANSWER Equal Employment Opportunity/Discrimination Law, Wage and Labor Law, Immigration Law, Workers' Compensation Laws, and Workplace Injury and Death.

Equal Employment Opportunities

Laws protect different groups of people from discrimination and make sure that workers are treated fairly. A **law** is an established rule. These include right-to-know laws. These laws require that employers tell employees about their rights in the workplace. Foodservice professionals should know the laws that protect them and follow them responsibly.

There are federal, state, and local laws that make sure that everyone has a chance to get a job. The Equal Employment Opportunities Act, passed in 1972, expanded some of the laws in the 1964 Civil Rights Act. It requires businesses to have affirmative action programs with the goal of preventing discrimination. This applies to all public and private employers involved in interstate commerce. **Interstate commerce** is business that happens over two or more states. This law also applies to restaurants with at least 15 employees who work at least 20 weeks per year. (See **Figure 8.5**.)

Affirmative Action

After the 1964 Civil Rights Act, employers created programs to locate, hire, train, and promote women and minorities. The goal of these programs is to prevent discrimination. Discrimination might prevent qualified people from getting jobs because of their race or gender. Programs like these are called **affirmative action** plans.

Employers with federal contracts of more than $50,000 must have affirmative action programs. This might include, for example, a foodservice company that supplies meals to a U.S. military base.

Age Discrimination

The Age Discrimination in Employment Act of 1967 protects people age 40 and older from being discriminated against in hiring, promotion, and wages. This law helps prevent people from not being hired based solely on their age. Experts predict that by 2030, one in three persons will be age 55 or older. Working beyond a standard retirement age is now more common.

▼ FIGURE 8.5 Employment Laws

Workers' Rights The United States has many laws that protect the rights of workers. *Why do you think these laws are important?*

Employment Laws	Provisions
Civil Rights Act	Employers may not discriminate based on race, color, national origin, sex, or religion; protects U.S. citizens working for U.S. companies overseas.
Equal Employment Opportunities Act	Requires businesses to have affirmative action programs. This includes restaurants with at least 15 employees who work at least 20 weeks per year.
Age Discrimination in Employment Act	Protects people 40 years of age and older from being discriminated against in any aspect of employment.
Americans with Disabilities Act	Prevents employers from refusing to hire or promote disabled persons, and ensures that all employees are treated equally. This law also requires public facilities make "reasonable accommodations" for the disabled.
Immigration Reform and Control Act	Only U.S. citizens and people who are authorized to work in the United States may be legally hired.
Immigration and Nationality Act	Prevents employers from hiring immigrants for low-skill, low-paying jobs without providing them with pension or insurance benefits.
Federal Employment Compensation Act	Protects employees who are injured or disabled due to work-related accidents.

FIGURE CAPTION ANSWER They ensure that workers are not discriminated against in the workplace. Workers should be able to perform the basic functions required of a job, but should not be penalized for their ethnicity, age, disability, or sex.

Skilled Workers Workers over age 60 can make a positive impact in the workplace. *How do you think older workers can positively impact a foodservice workplace?*

Sexual Harassment

The Equal Employment Opportunity Commission (EOC) defines **sexual harassment** as unwelcome advances, requests for sexual favors, and other verbal or physical conduct of a sexual nature. Such behavior includes jokes, gestures, and repeated requests for dates. If behavior like this affects an employee's work or creates an intimidating, hostile, or offensive workplace environment, it violates Title VII of the Civil Rights Act of 1964.

Create a Policy

Employees need to know what type of behavior is considered sexual harassment. An employer is responsible for the harassment if he or she does not take action. Sexual harassment policies should cover:

- Communication of the policy to all employees.

- Supervisor training in harassment cases.
- A formal system for complaints and how they will be investigated and solved.
- A plan for action on any complaints received. Businesses must protect the person who brought the complaint.
- Disciplinary action for any person guilty of harassment.
- Follow up on all harassment cases.

Americans With Disabilities

The Americans With Disabilities Act (ADA) became law in 1990. This law makes it illegal to put a person with a disability in a lower-paying job only because of the disability. It is also illegal to offer different pay to a person with a disability doing the same job as a person without disabilities. The ADA also prevents employers from refusing to hire or promote disabled persons.

The ADA defines **disability** as a physical or mental impairment that substantially limits one or more major life activities. The law requires public facilities to provide a reasonable accommodation or adjustments to the workplace for employees and customers with disabilities. This might mean adding access ramps near stairs, or **adapting**, or positively changing, customer bathrooms to accommodate wheelchairs. Reasonable accommodation allows employees with disabilities to enjoy the same benefits and privileges of employment that employees without disabilities enjoy.

Reading Check **Explain** Why are anti-discrimination laws established for the workplace?

Employee Protection Laws

The workplace is also subject to laws that govern wages, the right to work in this country, and injuries and death in the workplace. These laws ensure that employees can earn a fair wage, work legally, and be compensated in case of injury on the job.

PHOTO CAPTION ANSWER Older workers are often more experienced and can benefit a foodservice establishment by sharing that experience with their coworkers.

READING CHECK ANSWER Laws are established to ensure that everyone has a chance for equal employment.

Wage and Labor Laws

The hourly minimum wage is determined by the federal government. The U.S. Department of Labor does issue certificates for a lower rate for some employees, such as apprentices, student learners, and full-time college students. Most states also have an hourly minimum wage. Some state minimum wages may be higher than the federal minimum wage. Employers must pay their employees whichever is higher.

Immigration Laws

Before immigrants can be hired in the United States, they must receive special work permits from the government. Immigrants are also protected by workplace laws. It is against the law to hire immigrants for low-skill, low-paying jobs without giving them pension or insurance benefits.

The Immigration Reform and Control Act (IRCA) of 1986 states that only U.S. citizens and people who are authorized to work in the United States may be legally hired. All employers also must follow the Immigration and Nationality Act (INA) of 1952. This law states that employers must fill out an Employment Eligibility Verification Form, also called an I-9, for each person they hire. These forms may be checked by the U.S. Immigration and Naturalization Service to **determine**, or find out, an employee's immigration status.

Workers' Compensation

Workers' compensation laws make sure that injured or disabled workers can still have an income while they are unable to work. Federal employees are covered under the Federal Employment Compensation Act, passed in 1993. Money is awarded in cases of death or disability that happen on the job. If an employee is killed on the job, benefits are paid to the surviving family. Workers' compensation insurance is part of an employee's benefits. State and federal rules and regulations govern workers' compensation.

Workplace Injuries and Deaths

Since the Occupational Safety and Health Administration's (OSHA) beginning in 1971, workplace injury and illness rates have dropped by 40%. Deaths have dropped by 50%. OSHA's mission is to ensure employee safety and health by setting and enforcing standards, providing training and education, and working with employers to improve workplace safety and health. OSHA also provides posters and information supplements to employers and employees to make sure that workers know their rights.

One of the most common types of workplace injury is musculoskeletal disorders. A **musculoskeletal** (ˌməs-kyə-lō-ˈske-lə-təl) **disorder** is caused by repeated trauma to muscles or bones. These disorders include carpal (ˈkär-pəl) tunnel syndrome, which causes pain in the wrists and hands; lower back pain, which can affect movement and lifting; and tendinitis (ˌten-də-ˈnī-təs), which happens when a tendon in the body is overused. Tendinitis can cause swelling and pain.

Ergonomics

Because of the high rate of musculoskeletal disorders among workers, OSHA studies ergonomics. **Ergonomics** (ˌər-gə-ˈnä-miks) is the science of efficient and safe interaction between people and the things in their environment. An ergonomic workplace is arranged so that you can use equipment safely and efficiently. Kitchen equipment and tools can be arranged so that they are easy to use, and work tables can be placed at a height that makes them comfortable to use.

The study of ergonomics also helps manufacturers create tools that conform to the shape and movement of the human body. Kitchen tools that have been created with a focus on ergonomics may include special handles or grips. These features may help you complete a task more quickly.

Reading Check Determine Who decides the minimum wage that employers can pay employees?

READING CHECK ANSWER The federal government determines the hourly minimum wage that employers can pay employees. Some states also have minimum wage laws.

Who Is Responsible?

Each of the laws discussed in this section affects a foodservice worker on the job every day. Knowing these laws helps employees and employers understand their rights and responsibilities under the law. This means a safer workplace.

- **Employee Responsibilities** Employees must be aware of their rights under the law. You must follow laws and provide correct information about yourself and your job.

- **Managerial Responsibilities** Managers are required to post certain notices, such as the minimum wage laws and annual injury/accident reports. Managers must keep accurate records. They are responsible for knowing the law and enforcing it. They must also train employees to understand and follow laws.

 Safety Equipment Workers may be able to prevent injuries by wearing safety equipment. *What safety equipment is this employee using, and what is its function?*

Reading Check **List** What are the responsibilities of management when it comes to employment laws?

SECTION 8.2 After You Read

Review Key Concepts

1. **Describe** the provisions of the Equal Employment Opportunities Act.
2. **Distinguish** between the Immigration Reform and Control Act (IRCA) of 1986 and the Immigration and Nationality Act (INA) of 1952.
3. **Identify** employee responsibilities in the working environment.

Practice Culinary Academics

Social Studies

4. Choose one of the laws presented in this section. Think about how that law affects foodservice operations in your area. For example, the Americans With Disabilities Act may have required changes in construction. Write a list of your conclusions, and share your findings with the class.

> **NCSS V F Individuals, Groups, and Institutions** Evaluate the role of institutions in furthering both continuity and change.

Mathematics

5. The Americans With Disabilities Act requires your restaurant's bathrooms to have a wheelchair-accessible stall that is at least 4⅔ feet deep. If your bathroom stalls are currently 4½ feet deep, how much must they be extended?

Math Concept **Subtracting Mixed Numbers** Before subtracting fractions or mixed numbers with unlike denominators, you must convert them to equivalent fractions with common denominators. Find the lowest common denominator of all fractions in the problem.

Starting Hint Rewrite 4⅔ and 4½ as equivalent fractions with a common denominator. In this case, their lowest common denominator is 6. Then, subtract to get the answer.

> **NCTM Number and Operations** Understand numbers, ways of representing numbers, relationships among numbers, and number systems.

 Check your answers at this book's Online Learning Center at **glencoe.com**.

PHOTO CAPTION ANSWER This employee is wearing a back brace, designed to help him/her lift heavy items without straining the back.

READING CHECK ANSWER Post notices, keep accurate records, know and enforce laws, and train employees on laws.

Review and Applications

Chapter Summary

The USDA and the FDA recommend regulations for the foodservice industry. Foods inspected by the USDA receive a grade, stamp, or approval that shows that the product meets safety standards. Foodservice professionals must evaluate the quality of the food they serve and follow strict standards for safe food handling. Laws protect workers from discrimination and give employees the right to work in a safe and healthful environment.

Content and Academic Vocabulary Review

1. Use each of these vocabulary words in a sentence.

Content Vocabulary

- standard (p. 198)
- violation (p. 198)
- regulation (p. 198)
- grading (p. 198
- inspection (p. 198)
- genetically engineered food (p. 199)
- irradiated food (p. 199)
- Food Code (p. 200)
- solid waste (p. 200)
- environmental impact statement (p. 200)
- material safety data sheet (MSDS) (p. 201)
- accident report log (p. 201)
- law (p. 205)
- interstate commerce (p. 205)
- affirmative action (p. 205)
- sexual harassment (p. 206)
- disability (p. 206)
- musculoskeletal disorder (p. 207)
- ergonomics (p. 207)

Academic Vocabulary

- performance (p. 198)
- enforce (p. 198)
- adapting (p. 206)
- determine (p. 207)

Review Key Concepts

2. List the industry standards of quality used to evaluate food.

3. Summarize the roles of various government agencies in the foodservice industry.

4. Explain how facilities maintenance can help uphold foodservice standards.

5. Identify laws related to equal employment.

6. Describe laws meant to protect workers.

7. Distinguish between management and employee responsibilities for the working environment.

Critical Thinking

8. Debate the pros and cons of genetically engineered or irradiated foods as a class. How can these processes affect the foodservice industry?

9. Analyze the importance of the foodservice industry's strict standards concerning the temperature of foods. Why is this important? What are the consequences of not following these standards?

10. Understand USDA grading. Certain food products are graded by the USDA. If a food product is graded, can you go without inspecting it yourself? Why or why not?

Academic Skills

English Language Arts

11. **Write a Memo** Imagine you are employed as a legal consultant to the owner of a foodservice operation. The owner is hiring some new employees and wants a summary of the laws he will have to remember when making his decision of whom to hire. Write a memo summarizing the laws that would affect hiring decisions in a foodservice establishment.

> **NCTE 5** Use different writing process elements to communicate effectively.

Science

12. **Genetic Engineering** Genetically engineered foods are appearing in every grocery store and food supplier.

Procedure Research one genetically engineered food product. Discover how the food was modified, and for what purpose. Discover what the genetically engineered food is used for, and what has been the result of its use. Also, find any controversies surrounding the use of the product and what the international reaction has been to the product.

Analysis Write a short essay to explain your findings. Cite your sources.

> **NSES C** Develop an understanding of the molecular basis of heredity.

Mathematics

13. **Determine Egg Weights** The USDA assigns different classifications to eggs based on their size. The USDA assigns a size classification of jumbo when the net weight of a dozen eggs is 30 ounces. The phrase net weight means the weight of the eggs only (total weight minus the weight of the container). Write an algebraic equation showing the relationship between the total weight, the net weight of the eggs, and the container weight for a package of a dozen jumbo eggs. If the total weight is 31.5 ounces, what is the weight of the container?

Math Concept **Writing Expressions Involving Subtraction** When writing any algebraic expression, use variables, such as x and y, to represent any unknown values. For expressions involving subtraction, pay particular attention to the order of terms.

Starting Hint The equation should contain three values: total weight, container weight, and net weight of the eggs. Determine which two of those values are unknown, and represent those unknown amounts with variables in the equation. Determine which of those values is known, and use that actual value in the equation.

> **NCTM Algebra** Represent and analyze mathematical situations and structures using algebraic symbols.

Certification Prep

Sharpen your test-taking skills to improve your kitchen certification program score.

Directions Read the questions. Then, read the answer choices and choose the best possible answer for each.

14. Who is covered under the Federal Employment Compensation Act of 1993?

   a. veterans

   b. people with disabilities

   c. federal employees

   d. minors

15. Who oversees the conducting of food inspections?

   a. the restaurant owner

   b. the Food and Drug Administration

   c. the county government

   d. the Food Safety and Inspection Service

Test-Taking Tip

When answering multiple-choice questions, ask yourself if each option is true or false. This may help you find the best answer.

Review and Applications

Real-World Skills and Applications

Civic Responsibility

16. Interview a Foodservice Worker Research local, state, or federal standards for the foodservice industry. Write down 10 regulations that local foodservice operations must follow. Then, find a foodservice employee or manager, and interview him or her on how restaurants can follow these regulations. Take notes during your interview. When you have finished the interview, transcribe your notes. Write a short summary of the foodservice employee's or manager's recommendations, and turn in the summary and your interview notes to your teacher.

Critical Thinking Skills

17. Evaluate Your Home Kitchen Follow your teacher's instructions to go online and search for a restaurant inspection checklist. Choose one and print it out. Then, go through your home kitchen and use the checklist to evaluate it. Note for each item whether your kitchen passes, fails, or whether that item does not apply to a home kitchen.

Technology Applications

18. Make a Slide Presentation Follow your teacher's instructions to form teams. Work as a team to develop a slide presentation on one of the following topics: ergonomics in foodservice operations, workers' compensation, or wage and labor laws. Use slide presentation software to create your presentation. Display your presentation to the class. As a class, discuss the information that was presented in each presentation, and evaluate each.

Financial Literacy

19. Calculate Minimum Wage Imagine that you have been assigned to a committee responsible for examining your state's minimum wage. You have been asked to give a recommendation for the next federal minimum wage increase. Your state's current minimum wage is $5.85 per hour. You have gathered information that shows that during the past three years, the average cost of living has risen by 10%. Figure out what the new state minimum wage should be.

Culinary Lab

Use the culinary skills you have learned in this chapter.

Know the Law

20. Create a Chart Work as a team to research and then create a chart listing and explaining the laws presented in this chapter.

A. Make a chart. Follow your teacher's instructions to form teams. Working in teams, make a chart listing the titles of the various laws and regulations presented in this chapter.

B. Perform research. Use print and Internet resources to research the items on your team's chart.

C. List employment laws. List each law and regulation by name and explain how each one impacts employees in the workplace.

D. Create a poster. Select one law or regulation from the chart and create an educational poster that would inform foodservice employees about this law or regulation. Display the posters in class.

Create Your Evaluation

Look at each team's poster and write a brief evaluation of how well the poster conveys information about the law or regulation that it is meant to portray. Assess how quickly you can tell which law is being displayed and how helpful the poster would be in a work environment. Answer these questions:

● Would it raise the awareness of someone unfamiliar with the law?

● Does it contain enough information to be helpful?

Management and Supervision

Overseeing the operations of a foodservice business is vital.

People in foodservice management are responsible for overseeing the proper handling of food in commercial kitchens, storerooms, hotels, and restaurants. These managers and supervisors have strong backgrounds in business math, accounting, and record-keeping, along with basic computer skills. Being multilingual is often an asset, as managers must be able to communicate effectively with diverse groups of employees and customers.

Along with training staff and managing budgets, foodservice managers and supervisors are responsible for maintaining a safe and sanitary work environment, so an understanding of food and workplace safety is essential.

Herman Schumacher, Food and Beverage Manager

Q **What is your current position?**

A I am a food and beverage manager with Wyndham Hotels®.

Q **What education and training did you receive?**

A After high school graduation in my home country of the Netherlands, I worked in many restaurants trying to gain as much culinary knowledge and experience as I could. Like other food and beverage managers, I started in the business by attending culinary school. Afterward, I decided to work on a cruise ship because I wanted to see the world while honing my culinary skills. To become a manager, I realized that I would need to return to school and earn another degree in Hospitality Management.

Q **How do your past experiences help you on the job today?**

A I believe that each job experience helps to prepare me for the next one. For example, working aboard a cruise ship taught me speed and dexterity in cooking and also how to multi-task. I feel that the sum total of my life experience has prepared me for my future success.

Q **Are you still learning?**

A Yes. I believe that a successful chef is one who approaches each day as an opportunity to learn and improve his or her skills. I learn something new every day. That is one of the reasons I love my job so much.

Q **Where do you see yourself in five years?**

A My goal is to eventually become the general manager of a hotel.

Q **What advice would you offer new managers?**

A Focus on the fundamentals. Communication and strong interpersonal skills are valuable assets in becoming a food and beverage manager.

Career Ingredients

Education or Training	Most employers require a culinary degree and restaurant experience. Completion of business, accounting, and management courses are helpful.
Academic Skills Required	English Language Arts, Mathematics
Aptitudes, Abilities, and Skills	A background in foodservice, business math, and computer basics, along with strong interpersonal, communication, and leadership skills. Also, the ability to organize and solve problems. Multilingual skills are an asset.
Workplace Safety	Basic kitchen and dining room safety, sanitation, and food handling rules must be followed and enforced.
Career Outlook	Openings will be plentiful in the near future as the foodservice industry continues to expand.
Career Path	Advancement depends on skills, training, and work experience.

Career Pathways

Food and beverage managers	Responsible for a foodservice operation's entire food and beverage department. They coordinate the daily operations of all kitchen services and are also responsible for tracking costs, profits, and losses.
Assistant managers	Oversee the dining room and the kitchen staff under the guidance of the manager.
Dining room managers	Responsible for supervising and scheduling staff, as well as managing the dining room during meal service. Dining room managers must be outgoing and customer focused. A dining room manager is sometimes be called a maitre d'.
Executive chefs	Responsible for menu development, food orders, and supervising the cooking staff. Executive chefs must have many years of experience.
Production managers	Responsible for supervising the kitchen staff and all food preparation. Knowledge of cost control and quality food preparation is essential.
Purchasing agents	In charge of buying all the food and equipment necessary for food production. Effective communication and negotiation skills are important.
Storeroom supervisors	Responsible for receiving, issuing, and properly storing all food products. Attention to detail and accurate record-keeping skills help them maintain inventory control.

Critical Thinking What classes have you taken in school that might help you prepare for a career in foodservice management and supervision?

Culinary certification programs often incorporate management skills. To demonstrate an understanding of education, training, experience, and personality requirements, write a job posting for a dining room manager or maitre d', including all necessary skills.

COMPETITION
★ ★ ★ ★ ★
PRACTICE

Imagine that you are applying for the maitre d' position from the Get Certified practice. The interviewer wants you to role-play with another student who will pose as a customer with a complaint. Respond professionally, offering a solution that will satisfy everyone.

Evaluate your efforts based on the following rating scale:

1 = Poor; 2 = Fair; 3 = Good; 4 = Great

Judge your role-play on:

- The words you chose and the way you spoke to the customer.
- How well you maintained a professional demeanor.
- The solution you offered.

Successful Foodservice Managers

Foodservice managers are responsible for many aspects of a food organization. Using your research and interview with a foodservice manager, you will create a visual to share what you have learned with your class.

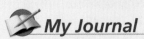

My Journal

If you completed the journal entry from page 167, refer to it to see how you use leadership skills in your daily life. Add any additional notes about how you think those leadership skills can help you succeed in foodservice management.

English Language Arts

NCTE 4 Use written language to communicate effectively.

NCTE 12 Use language to accomplish individual purposes.

Project Assignment

In this project, you will:

- Research the job responsibilities of a foodservice manager.
- Identify and interview a person who is a foodservice manager.
- Create a visual to display the skills needed to be a foodservice manager.
- Present the visual to your class to share what you have learned.

Applied Culinary Skills Behind the Project

Your success in culinary arts will depend on your skills. Skills you will use in this project include:

➤ Listing the leadership qualities an effective manager needs.
➤ Describing how a foodservice manager uses time and human resources.
➤ Understanding the basic and complex job responsibilities of a foodservice manager.
➤ Explaining how a manager can help market the business.
➤ Determining how the manager is involved with foodservice regulations and laws.

English Language Arts Skills Behind the Project

The English Language Arts skills you will use for this project are writing, interviewing, and speaking skills. Remember these key concepts:

Writing Skills

➤ Use correct spelling and grammar.
➤ Consider your audience.
➤ Organize your questions in the order you want to ask them.

Interview Skills

➤ During the interview, record responses and take notes.
➤ Listen attentively.
➤ Use standard English to communicate.

Speaking Skills

➤ Communicate effectively.
➤ Adapt and modify language to suit different purposes.
➤ Thoughtfully express your ideas.

Step 1 Research Job Tasks of Foodservice Managers

Research the job responsibilities of a foodservice manager. Write a summary of your research to:

- Describe the skills needed to be a manager in the foodservice industry.
- Identify the training and experience a manger needs.
- Explain how the skills of a leader and a manager are similar.
- Determine how managers use human resources.
- List the ways a manager helps with marketing.
- Identify why it is important for a manager to know foodservice regulations.

Step 2 Plan Your Interview

Use the results of your research to write a list of questions to ask a local foodservice manager. Your questions may include:

- What types of leadership skills do you feel are necessary for your job?
- What are some of your basic and complex job responsibilities?
- How do you manage people successfully?
- How do you successfully manage your and your coworkers' time in the business?
- How is management structured in your business?

Step 3 Connect with Your Community

Identify a person in your community who is a foodservice manager. Consider that managers may be found at restaurants, hotels, arenas, and theaters. Conduct your interview using the questions you prepared in Step 2. Take notes during the interview and write a summary of the interview.

Culinary Project Checklist

Plan

✓ Research the skills of a foodservice manager and summarize your findings.

✓ Plan an interview with a foodservice manager.

✓ Write a summary about your interview.

✓ Create a visual to display the skills needed to be a successful foodservice manager.

Present

✓ Make a presentation to your class to discuss the results of your research and interview.

✓ Invite students to ask any questions they may have. Answer these questions.

✓ When students ask you questions, demonstrate in your answers that you respect their perspectives.

✓ Turn in the summary of your research, your interview questions, and the interview summary to your teacher.

Step 4 Create Your Visual

Use the Culinary Project Checklist to plan and create your visual. Make a poster, video, slide show, or other visual that illustrates how to be a successful foodservice manager.

Step 5 Evaluate Your Culinary and Academic Skills

Your project will be evaluated based on:

- Depth of interview questions.
- Content of your visual presentation.
- Mechanics—presentation and neatness.

 Rubric Go to this book's Online Learning Center at **glencoe.com** for a rubric you can use to evaluate your final project.

JOHNSON & WALES
U N I V E R S I T Y

 Expert Advice Go to this book's Online Learning Center at **glencoe.com** to read an article by a culinary expert from Johnson & Wales University about the documents and systems used by foodservice managers.

The Professional Kitchen

Chapter

9 Equipment and Technology

10 Knives and Smallwares

11 Culinary Nutrition

12 Creating Menus

13 Using Standardized Recipes

14 Cost Control Techniques

EXPLORE THE PHOTO

A professional kitchen uses a variety of tools and equipment. *Can you name any of the tools and equipment you see here?*

EXPLORE THE PHOTO ANSWER Answers will include stock pots, sauce pots, sauté pans, range top, spatulas, spoons, and more.

Standardized Recipe Creation

After completing this unit, you will know the setup and equipment used in a professional kitchen, and understand how to control costs with recipes and portion sizes. In your unit culinary project, you will research and create your own standardized recipe. Then, you will give a report on the setup, equipment, and cost measures that affect your recipe.

My Journal

Write a journal entry about recipes you have used in the past.

- What kinds of recipes did you use?
- How did you choose them?
- Did you need any special skills to make the dishes from the recipes?

JOHNSON & WALES
UNIVERSITY

"Before I worry about whether I have a great food idea, I have to make sure it fits my cost structure, will interest customers, and matches my concept."

Will Gilson
Chef/Owner
Garden at the Cellar

Equipment and Technology

SECTIONS

9.1 The Commercial Kitchen

9.2 Receiving and Storage Equipment

9.3 Preparation and Cooking Equipment

9.4 Holding and Service Equipment

WRITING ACTIVITY

Topic Sentence

A topic sentence states the main idea of a paragraph. Write a topic sentence for a paragraph about cooking equipment found in a kitchen.

Writing Tips

1 The sentence should present only one topic.

2 The sentence should not be general or vague.

3 The sentence should give strong direction.

WRITING ACTIVITY ANSWER Topics should be broad enough to be filled in with details. Topic sentences should tell readers what is coming.

EXPLORE THE PHOTO ANSWER A professional kitchen includes receiving and storage equipment, and preparation and cooking equipment.

EXPLORE THE PHOTO

A foodservice employee should know how all of the equipment works. *What types of equipment might you find in a professional kitchen?*

The Commercial Kitchen

Efficient work flow and preparation are the keys to an organized professional kitchen.

Reading Guide

Before You Read

Predict Before starting the section, browse the content by reading headings, bold terms, and photo captions. Do they help you predict the information in the section?

Read to Learn

Key Concepts
- **Explain** the roles of the different stations in a professional kitchen.

Main Idea

A commercial kitchen is divided into work stations. Once the work stations have been identified, the cooking line is set up. The set up will determine the workflow.

Content Vocabulary
- work station
- work section
- work flow
- cooking line
- island
- mise en place
- work simplification
- range of motion

Academic Vocabulary
- efficient
- mode

Graphic Organizer

Use a cluster like this one to show the sections and stations within a professional kitchen. Fill in each rectangle with the station within each station in the bubble branching off of them.

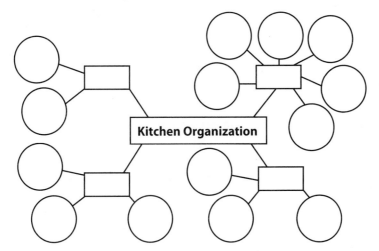

Kitchen Organization

Graphic Organizer Go to this book's Online Learning Center at **glencoe.com** for a printable graphic organizer.

GRAPHIC ORGANIZER ANSWER Beverage station (hot beverage, cold beverage); Garde manger section (salad, cold platter, sandwich); Short-order section (broiler, griddle, fry); Hot foods section (broiler, fry, griddle, sauté, dry heat, steam).

ACADEMIC STANDARDS

English Language Arts
NCTE 5 Use different writing process elements to communicate effectively.

Mathematics
NCTM Measurement Apply appropriate techniques, tools, and formulas to determine measurements.

NCTM Problem Solving Build new mathematical knowledge through problem solving.

Science
NSES 1 Develop an understanding of science unifying concepts and processes.

Social Studies
NCSS I A Culture Analyze and explain the way groups, societies, and cultures address human needs and concerns.

NCTE National Council of Teachers of English

NCTM National Council of Teachers of Mathematics

NSES National Science Education Standards

NCSS National Council for the Social Studies

Professional Kitchen Work Flow

Working as a foodservice professional means more than just cooking food. It involves teamwork and cooperation among kitchen staff. This creates an efficient work space. Before you begin to create all types of interesting dishes, you must become familiar with a commercial kitchen. A commercial kitchen layout is based on:

- The type of foodservice establishment.
- The amount of available space.
- The menu items to be prepared and the number of meals to be served.

Gourmet Math

Design to Scale

To determine which kitchen layout will work best, it is helpful to use a scale drawing. The ratio that compares a drawing to the actual object is called the scale. If the scale is given as ½ inches = 2 feet, then every ½ inch in the drawing represents 2 actual feet.

You would like to include a freezer that measures 45 inches wide and 21 inches deep on a scale drawing of a kitchen. If the drawing's scale is 1 inches = 5 feet, what are the scaled dimensions of the freezer?

Math Concept **Using Proportions with Scale Factors** To draw items to scale, write a proportion using the scale as one ratio. In the other ratio, use s to represent the item's scale size. Solve for s.

Starting Hint Since the original dimensions are given in inches, convert the 5 feet in the scale into inches by multiplying it by 12. Write a proportion with two ratios of new width over old width. One of the ratios should be the scale; the other should be s over 45. Solve for s. Then, repeat the entire process for the freezer's depth.

NCTM Measurement Apply appropriate techniques, tools, and formulas to determine measurements.

GOURMET MATH ANSWER The freezer's scaled width is 0.75 inches, and the scaled depth is 0.35 inches. Note that the scale of 1 inch = 5 feet is the equivalent to 1 inch = 60 inches. To determine the new width, set up a proportion where $1/60 = s/45$. Cross-multiply to get $60s = 45$, or $s = 45/60 = 0.75$. To determine the new depth, set up a proportion where $1/60 = s/21$. Cross-multiply to get $60s = 21$, or $s = 21/60 = 0.35$.

Stations, Sections, and Flow

The commercial kitchen is divided into work stations. A **work station** is a work area that contains the necessary tools and equipment to prepare certain types of foods. For example, onion rings are fried in a deep fryer. The work station where this takes place is called the fry station. Tongs and fry baskets would also be found at the fry station. Sometimes professional kitchens make changes to the traditional brigade system. The changes depend on the kitchen's size and arrangement.

Each work station is arranged so that kitchen employees do not have to leave their stations to perform their tasks. Work stations should have all necessary equipment, tools, work space, and power sources. They also should have their own storage facilities.

Similar work stations are grouped into larger work areas. This larger area is called a **work section**. Sometimes work stations can belong to more than one work section. For example, a fry station and a griddle station would be part of the short-order section and the hot foods section. (See **Figure 9.1**.)

FIGURE 9.1 **Kitchen Work Stations**
Section Divisions Different work stations are placed under the control of each work section. *What is the difference between a work station and work section?*

Sections	Stations
Beverage Section	• Hot Beverage Station • Cold Beverage Station
Garde Manger Section	• Salad Station • Cold Platter Station • Sandwich Station
Short Order Section	• Broiler Station • Griddle Station • Fry Station
Hot Foods Section	• Broiler Station • Fry Station • Griddle Station • Sauté Station • Dry Heat Station • Steam Station

FIGURE CAPTION ANSWER Work stations contain the tools and equipment necessary to prepare certain types of foods. Work sections are groupings of similar work stations.

▼ FIGURE 9.2 Cooking Lines

Multiple Choice There are several different ways to set up a cooking line. *What factors determine how a kitchen will set up its cooking line?*

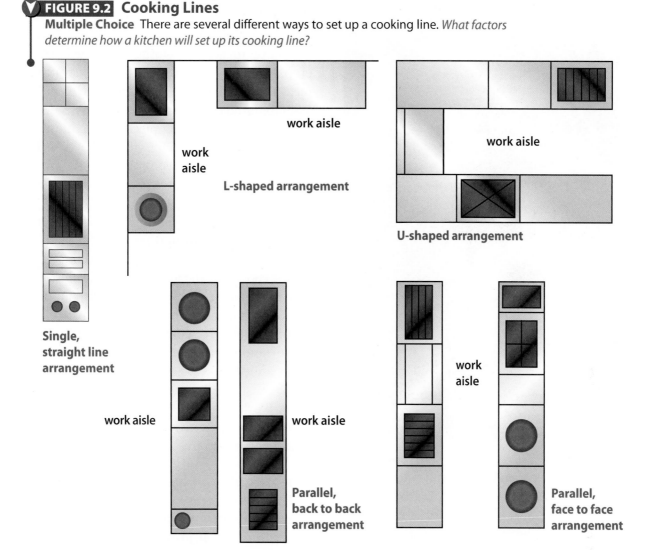

Single, straight line arrangement

L-shaped arrangement

U-shaped arrangement

Parallel, back to back arrangement

Parallel, face to face arrangement

work aisle

The layout of the kitchen has a direct effect on the work flow. **Work flow** is the orderly movement of food and staff through the kitchen. A good work flow helps reduce preparation and serving time. In addition to a well-designed kitchen, teamwork among staff and between work stations is essential for a good work flow. Having ingredients and equipment ready to use helps simplify tasks.

The Cooking Line

Once there are work stations and work sections, the cooking line is set up. The **cooking line** is the arrangement of the kitchen equipment. The cooking line arrangement determines what equipment and storage

areas can be placed above, below, or across from the equipment. You may also want to form an island. An **island** is a kitchen counter or equipment arrangement that can be approached from all sides. There are several different cooking line arrangements from which to choose.

Single, Straight-Line Arrangement A single, straight line allows equipment to be placed along a wall. This arrangement is used in larger kitchens.

L-Shaped Arrangement The L-shape separates equipment into two major work areas. One side of the line may be used for food preparation. The other side is used for cooking.

Equipment Sanitation It is important to keep equipment clean and running efficiently. *What are the consequences of not cleaning equipment properly?*

U-Shaped Arrangement This type of arrangement is often used by kitchens with limited space. It is also used in the dishwashing area of many commercial kitchens.

Parallel, Back-to-Back Arrangement Parallel, back-to-back consists of two lines of equipment, sometimes divided by a wall. This arrangement is often used on ships and in hotels.

Parallel, Face-to-Face Arrangement This arrangement consists of two lines of equipment facing each other, separated by a work aisle. It is used in larger kitchens where constant communication between stations is necessary.

PHOTO CAPTION ANSWER The consequences would be that bacteria may grow and transfer to food, or physical hazards may get into food. This could cause foodborne illness.

Mise en Place

Before you can prepare and cook the food, you have to get everything organized. Mise en place (ˌmē-ˌzän-ˈpləs) is a French term that means "to put in place." **Mise en place** includes assembling all the necessary ingredients, equipment, tools, and serving pieces needed to prepare food in the order in which they will be used. It can also involve preheating the oven, cleaning and chopping vegetables, measuring spices, and trimming meats. For example, if grilled salmon and vegetables are on the menu, you will need to cut and portion the salmon, prepare the vegetables and herbs, and assemble the cookware ahead of time. This helps save time by allowing the chef to cook without having to stop and assemble items.

To effectively perform mise en place, work simplification techniques are used. **Work simplification** means to perform a task in the most **efficient**, or productive, way possible. Work simplification in the foodservice industry involves the efficient use of food, time, energy, and personnel.

Personnel

Hiring temporary or part-time employees gives restaurants the extra help they need during peak times. It also helps lower expenses because restaurants do not have to pay too many employees during non-peak times.

Food

Food can be prepared and cooked in a variety of ways, but not every method is efficient. For instance, you can chop an onion by hand, but using a food processor will be quicker.

Time

Time management in the kitchen results in prompt service. Different foods have different cooking times. By reviewing recipes before cooking, you can determine how much time is needed. When you make food for a large group, arrange food or plan set-up time to efficiently work in a production **mode**, or functioning arrangement.

Energy

Arrange your work station effectively so that you do not expend any more energy than is necessary during food preparation. Hand tools and ingredients should be within easy reach. This allows for efficient range of motion. **Range of motion** means using the fewest body movements without unnecessary stress or strain. When your equipment, tools, and ingredients are close, you eliminate unnecessary stops and starts.

An efficient range of motion saves time and energy. It may also help prevent some accidents. Having equipment and tools neatly organized and in range can help prevent dropping items or injuring yourself on equipment. It will also keep you from straining back, arm, and leg muscles.

 Reading Check List When designing a kitchen, what factors should be kept in mind?

SECTION 9.1 After You Read

Review Key Concepts

1. **Explain** how efficient range of motion makes work easier.

Practice Culinary Academics

 Science

2. **Procedure** Study the process of cutting vegetables in your foods lab, starting with fetching the vegetables and ending with waste disposal. Take notes on the steps that are efficient, and those that are not.

   Analysis Look at your notes, and analyze them. Then, try to come up with a more efficient method of cutting vegetables, and test it.

   NSES 1 **Develop an understanding of science unifying concepts and processes.**

Social Studies

3. The concept of work flow is an important concept in many industries. Research a pioneer of work flow, such as Frederick Winslow Taylor, Henry Gantt, or David Siegel. Write a biography of the person you choose. Include information on the person's contributions, the early development of his or her ideas, and any modern work flow theories that have been developed since then.

   NCSS I A Culture **Analyze and explain the way groups, societies, and cultures address human needs and concerns.**

 English Language Arts

4. Imagine that you are an expert employed by your school to make the foods lab more efficient. Examine the arrangement of the equipment in the foods lab, and then write a report containing your analysis. Offer recommendations for improving its efficiency.

   NCTE 5 **Use different writing process elements to communicate effectively.**

 Mathematics

5. A dessert soufflé requires 10 minutes of preparation, 25 minutes to cook, and 2 minutes for plating. If a customer arrives at 6:15, and takes 49 minutes to get through dinner, when should you begin preparing his soufflé?

   Math Concept Adding and Subtracting Time When adding and subtracting time, calculate the minutes and hours separately. Remember that there are 60 minutes in one hour, so you may need to adjust your hour total accordingly.

   Starting Hint Determine the time dessert should be served by adding 49 minutes to 6:15. Then, subtract the time needed for the three cooking steps to find when preparation should begin.

   NCTM Problem Solving **Build new mathematical knowledge through problem solving.**

   Check your answers at this book's Online Learning Center at **glencoe.com**.

READING CHECK ANSWER When designing a kitchen, you should consider the type of establishment, the available space, and the menu items and number of meals that will be served.

Receiving and Storage Equipment

Reading Guide

 Before You Read

Check for Understanding If you have questions as you are reading, that means you are checking your understanding of the material. To get the most out of the text, try to answer these questions.

Read to Learn

Key Concepts
- **Categorize** the different types of professional receiving and storage equipment.

Main Idea

Receiving equipment helps foodservice professionals check and enter received food and supplies. Storage equipment provides space and temperature control to store food.

Content Vocabulary
- purchase order
- invoice
- receiving record
- platform scale
- counter scale
- portion scale
- dolly
- lowboy

Academic Vocabulary
- quantity
- note

Graphic Organizer

As you read, use a sequence chart like this one to describe the five steps involved in receiving shipments of food.

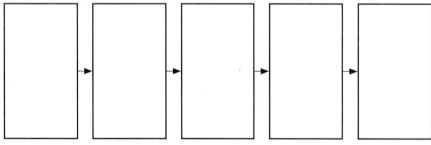

 Graphic Organizer Go to this book's Online Learning Center at **glencoe.com** for a printable graphic organizer.

ACADEMIC STANDARDS

How will you store food that comes into your foodservice operation?

 English Language Arts
NCTE 3 Apply strategies to interpret texts.

 Mathematics
NCTM Problem Solving Solve problems that arise in mathematics and in other contexts.

 Science
NSES B Develop an understanding of chemical reactions.

 Social Studies
NCSS VIII A Science, Technology, and Society Identify and describe both current and historical examples of the interaction and interdependence of science, technology, and society in a variety of cultural settings.

NCTE National Council of Teachers of English

NCTM National Council of Teachers of Mathematics

NSES National Science Education Standards

NCSS National Council for the Social Studies

GRAPHIC ORGANIZER ANSWER 1) Check purchase order against shipment. 2) Verify invoice for accuracy. 3) Inspect food items for quality. 4) Complete a receiving record. 5) Move the food items to the appropriate storage area.

The Receiving Area

Now that you know why a commercial kitchen is designed the way it is, you are ready to examine how food flows through a commercial kitchen. All products in the food flow begin with the receiving area. After they are received, they are stored.

Receiving involves more than just getting in an order of food or supplies. Receiving means checking that the food and supplies that were ordered were received in the right **quantity**, or amount, at the right price. Foodservice professionals need to know what to check for when they receive orders. Many times, problems happen when food and supplies are received. This is a big responsibility that should not be overlooked.

When you receive shipments of food, you should follow these steps:

- Check the purchase order against the actual shipment. A **purchase order** is a document asking a supplier to ship food or supplies at a predetermined price. Ensure that the order is correct and complete. **Note**, or make a record of, any missing items.
- Check the invoice to make sure it is accurate. An **invoice** is a bill from a supplier for providing goods or services. Make sure that the food prices are correct, and that you were invoiced only for the items you ordered. Note anything that is incorrect.
- Inspect the food items for quality. Reject any that do not meet quality standards.
- Complete a receiving record. A **receiving record** is a numbered record of everything that was received at a business during a particular day. The receiving record should include the quantity of each item received, the item price, the date delivered, and the supplier's name.
- Move the food items to the appropriate storage area. Each form of food, for example, frozen, fresh, packaged, canned, and dry, must be handled and stored differently.

Receiving Equipment

The type of receiving equipment you will use is determined by the size of the foodservice operation. Most operations have scales, thermometers, and dollies.

Scales

Receiving areas should have two types of scales: a platform scale and a counter scale. A **platform scale** has a platform to hold large or heavy items to be weighed. A **counter scale** usually has a platform, too, but it is small enough to be placed on a counter. Both can be used to weigh boxes. Some foodservice operations also have portion scales. A **portion scale** is a scale used to weigh cuts of meat.

Thermometers

Thermometers are used in the receiving area to check the temperature of frozen and fresh foods. These thermometers use infrared technology to check the temperature of food. They do not make direct contact with food products. Frozen foods should have a minimum internal temperature of 0°F (18°C) or below. Fresh foods should be kept at 41°F (5°C) or below. Food items that do not meet these safety standards should not be accepted.

Dollies

Dollies are used to move items from the receiving area to the storage area. A **dolly** is a small wheeled cart that can help move heavy boxes from place to place. Dollies help foodservice professionals work more efficiently.

In addition, a good receiving area should have a table large enough to hold boxes for inspection. Keep a box cutter handy to open the packages and boxes.

Food Storage

Food can be stored in refrigerators or freezers, on shelving units, or in storage bins and containers. The storage equipment you use depends on the type and amount of food to be stored, the space available, and the type of foodservice operation.

Food must be stored properly to prevent it from spoiling and causing foodborne illness. When you store food items, follow the first in, first out (FIFO) rule. This means that all food items should be used in the order in which they were received. Mark each item with the delivery date. Older items should be moved to the front of the storage area. Newer items are placed at the back.

Foods that will be stored in the freezer must be covered well in airtight wrapping to avoid freezer burn. Freezer burn, light-colored spots on frozen food where surface drying has occurred, can ruin foods. As with all food products, frozen foods should also be labeled and dated.

Refrigerators and Freezers

Fresh and frozen foods are stored in refrigerators and freezers. Commercial refrigerators

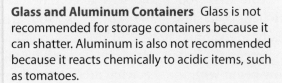

Small Bites

Glass and Aluminum Containers Glass is not recommended for storage containers because it can shatter. Aluminum is also not recommended because it reacts chemically to acidic items, such as tomatoes.

and freezers are used to keep fresh and frozen foods, such as vegetables, fruits, dairy products, fish, and meats, at the right temperature until they are used. There are three main types of commercial refrigerators: walk-in, roll-in, or reach-in units. There are also lowboy refrigerators and freezers. A **lowboy** is a half-size refrigerator that fits under the counter in a work station.

Equipment Selection

When a business needs to buy equipment, the first step is to identify the types of equipment that are needed for an efficient kitchen. Things to consider include type of restaurant, budget, space available, and menu items. Once the types of equipment have been identified, the features of that equipment should be decided upon. Smart business owners and managers compare prices, features, and maintenance service contracts before buying.

Equipment is expensive. Business owners must consider long-term business needs, and regulations and codes related to food storage before purchasing equipment. A purchase must provide the business with value over the long term.

Equipment Cleaning and Maintenance

It is important to keep storage equipment clean. Clean equipment protects against bacteria growth. When you clean storage equipment, there are general guidelines that you must follow.

Receiving Strategies Receiving involves more than simply getting in an order from a supplier. *What do you think are some other considerations when receiving food?*

PHOTO CAPTION ANSWER Other considerations include the quantity of food received compared to the invoice and the quality of the food received.

Walk-In Refrigerator Walk-in refrigerators are basically refrigerated rooms.

Roll-In Refrigerator Roll-in refrigerators have a rolling rack of sheet pans that can be rolled up a ramp and into the unit.

Reach-In Refrigerator Reach-in refrigerators are not as large as walk-in refrigerators. Reach-in refrigerators are typically one, two- or three-door units with sliding shelves.

Lowboy Refrigerator Food products that will be used often are stored in a lowboy. It can fit under the counter of a service station.

Freezer Freezers are units that can store foods for long periods of time. At temperatures of 0°F (18°C) or below, foods can be kept from one to six months, depending on the type of food and kind of packaging used.

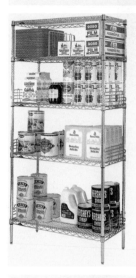 

Shelving Unit Shelving units are used to store various dry goods prior to use. There are several types of shelving units used in a commercial kitchen. Some shelves fit into corners to maximize space. Overhead shelves are located in each individual work station. There are also shelves designed to hold canned goods.

Storage Bins and Racks Storage bins are available in a variety of styles. Some storage bins are large, heavy plastic or polyurethane (ˌpä-lē-ˈyùr-ə-ˌthān) bins with lids. These storage bins are on wheels so they can be moved from one work area to another. Storage bins can also be open wire bins that hold packaged items or canned goods.

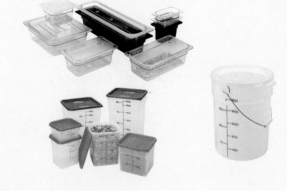

Storage Containers Smaller quantities of food are often placed in storage containers made of a sturdy, durable plastic. Labels identifying the contents and date of storage should always be clearly visible. Storage containers should always have well-fitting, air-tight lids.

Equipment Safety

When you operate equipment:
- Report missing warning labels and safety attachments to your supervisor.
- Report any improperly working equipment to your supervisor.

Refrigerators and Freezers

For cleaning and maintenance:
- Maintain a regular cleaning schedule.
- Turn off the appliance and move all food to a cold storage area.
- Wash the inside of reach-in and roll-in refrigerators and freezers with a solution of baking soda and water.

- Clean the walk-in refrigerator as instructed by your supervisor.
- Turn on the appliance and refill it with food.

Shelving Units and Storage Bins

When you clean storage equipment:
- Use hot, soapy water to thoroughly clean shelves and storage bins.
- Rinse with clean water and then sanitize.
- Dry the storage unit thoroughly.
- Put back foods only when the units are completely dry.

 **Reading Check** **Summarize** What is the FIFO process?

SECTION 9.2 After You Read

Review Key Concepts

1. **Categorize** the different types of refrigerators and freezers.

Practice Culinary Academics

 Science

2. **Procedure** Cook tomato sauce in an aluminum pot. At the same time, cook tomato sauce in a non-aluminum pot. Observe the differences between the two samples. How do the two samples look? Do they have a different odor? How have the pots been affected?

    Analysis Create a chart to show the results of your observations. Write a summary to draw conclusions on your findings.

    > **NSES B** Develop an understanding of chemical reactions.

 English Language Arts

3. Find and examine a sample invoice for any type of business. Review all of the abbreviations and information on the form. Discuss the information as a class until you have a basic understanding of how to read and interpret an invoice.

    > **NCTE 3** Apply strategies to interpret texts.

 Social Studies

4. Investigate the origins of the first in, first out process. How do you think that this concept came to be used by several different industries, and why? Write a short report to show your answer. Cite your sources.

    > **NCSS VIII A Science, Technology, and Society** Identify and describe both current and historical examples of the interaction and interdependence of science, technology, and society in a variety of cultural settings.

 Mathematics

5. You purchase a walk-in refrigerator for your restaurant for $2,100, and expect it to have a useful life of 7 years. What is its book value after 2 years if you use straight-line depreciation?

    Math Concept **Straight-Line Depreciation** Depreciation is an accounting concept that tracks the decline in value of an asset over time. In straight-line depreciation, the book value of the asset decreases an equal amount each year over its useful life.

    Starting Hint Divide $2,100 by the number of years in the refrigerator's useful life. In 2 years, the book value will be $2,100 minus 2 times the yearly depreciation amount.

    > **NCTM Problem Solving** Solve problems that arise in mathematics and in other contexts.

 Check your answers at this book's Online Learning Center at **glencoe.com**.

READING CHECK ANSWER FIFO means first in, first out. All food items should be used in the order in which they were received.

Preparation and Cooking Equipment

Reading Guide

 Before You Read

Create an Outline Use the section's heading titles to create an outline. Make the titles into Level 1 main ideas. Add supporting information to create Level 2, 3, and 4 details. Use the outline to predict what you are about to learn.

Read to Learn

Key Concepts

- **Explain** the maintenance and sanitation for preparation equipment.
- **Compare** the different heat sources used in cooking.
- **Categorize** the uses of different types of clean-up equipment.

Main Idea

Food preparation equipment is equipment used to process or prepare food. Food preparation equipment may be used in cooking or as part of cleanup.

Graphic Organizer

Use a step-by-step chart like the one below to show the seven steps you would take when cleaning a slicer.

Cleaning a Slicer

First
Then
Then
Then
Then
Then
Last

Content Vocabulary

- conduction
- convection
- induction
- radiation
- microwave
- pilot light
- recondition

Academic Vocabulary

- volume
- refer

Many different types of equipment are used to create delicious dishes.

 Graphic Organizer
Go to this book's Online Learning Center at **glencoe.com** for a printable graphic organizer.

GRAPHIC ORGANIZER ANSWER 1) Make sure slicer is unplugged. 2) Set blade control indicator to 0. 3) Take apart slicer. 4) Wash food carriage and blade in hot, soapy water. 5) Wipe rest of slicer with a damp cloth. 6) Rinse with a damp cloth, sanitize, dry, and reassemble slicer. 7) Oil the slicer.

Preparation Equipment

Have you ever thought about how much equipment it takes to prepare and cook food for a simple meal at home? Now, imagine what you would need to prepare and cook food in a school cafeteria where hundreds of students eat every day. The preparation is time consuming, and special equipment is necessary to do the job well.

The equipment used to prepare food can cut preparation time. Preparation equipment can be used to mix, chop, grind, grate, and slice a large **volume**, or amount, of food. This equipment processes food and prepares it for cooking. Mixers, food processors, and slicers are common pieces of preparation equipment used in a commercial kitchen.

Preparation Equipment Sanitation

You must follow safety precautions when you clean professional equipment. Never place your hand or another object in a machine when it is running. Always turn it off first and unplug it. **Refer** to, or reread briefly, the instruction manual before you clean any equipment.

These are general guidelines to clean preparation equipment. However, these guidelines do not replace instruction manuals or the guidance of your supervisor.

Mixer and Food Processor

To clean a mixer or food processor, refer to the instruction manual and follow these general steps:

- Make sure that the equipment has been turned off and unplugged.
- Remove the attachment and the bowl. Wash them in hot, soapy water. Rinse and sanitize each piece. Let them air-dry.
- Store attachments in an appropriate location.
- Wipe the machine clean with a damp cloth.

Slicer

When you clean a slicer, always follow safety precautions. The slicer is a dangerous piece of equipment. Refer to the instruction manual and follow these general steps:

- Be sure the machine is turned off and unplugged.
- Set the blade control indicator to zero.
- Follow the instruction manual to take the slicer apart.
- Wash the food carriage and blade in hot, soapy water. Use extra caution when cleaning the sharp blade. Rinse all pieces and let them air dry.
- Wipe off the rest of the machine with a damp, soapy cloth.
- Wipe the machine with a damp cloth, sanitize it, and dry it. Reassemble the slicer. Immediately put the blade guard back in place.
- Oil the slicer with nonedible oil as directed in the instruction manual.

Reading Check **List** Name three common pieces of food preparation equipment.

Cooking Equipment

Today's commercial kitchen uses a wide variety of equipment to cook food quickly and efficiently. Ranges, broilers, and ovens are just a few pieces of cooking equipment you will find in a commercial kitchen. Before you operate this equipment, you need to learn what it looks like and how it operates.

Heat Sources

Food is cooked by heat that is generated through a number of sources: gas, electricity, radiation, microwaves, and light. Cooking equipment can use any one of these sources, or sometimes a number of these sources at one time to generate heat that will cook food properly.

READING CHECK ANSWER Students may name any three: mixers, food processors, slicers, blenders, commercial juicers, work tables, or table-mounted can openers.

Preparation Equipment

Slicer A slicer has a 10-inch or 12-inch circular blade that rotates at high speed. It can be either automatic or manual. Slicers are used to slice foods into uniform sizes.

Bench Mixer A bench mixer has a removable stainless steel bowl and dough hook, paddle, and whip attachments. Counter models are available in 5-, 12-, and 20-quart sizes. Floor models come in 30-, 40-, 60-, 80-, and 140-quart sizes. The bench mixer is used to mix or whip doughs and batters. It can be used to slice, chop, shred, or grate foods by using different attachments.

Food Processor A food processor has a removable bowl and an S-shaped blade. Food processors are used to grind, purée, emulsify, crush, and knead foods. Special disks can be added to slice, julienne, and shred foods.

Table-Mounted Can Opener Professional kitchens use heavy-duty can openers that are mounted on the edge of a table. Clean and sanitize can openers daily to prevent contamination. Replace worn blades immediately, as they can shed metal shavings into food.

Blender Blenders have stainless steel blades that can be used to blend and mix a variety of ingredients. They can also crush ice. Commercial blenders have removable thermoplastic or stainless steel containers.

Commercial Juicer Commercial juicers separate the pulp from the juice automatically. They have stainless steel blades and removable bowls.

Work Tables Stainless steel and butcher block work tables are used in food production areas. Stainless steel tables are commonly used for food preparation. Butcher block tables are used more often at the bake station.

Gas

Gas is a natural heat source that produces intense heat with a flame. It cooks food evenly. Ranges, ovens, and broilers can be gas operated. Gas can cook through conduction or convection. **Conduction** heats food by direct contact between a hot surface and the food, such as cooking in a pan. **Convection** heats food by the circulation of heated molecules of hot liquid or air.

Electricity

Like gas, electricity cooks food with intense heat, but depending on the type of metal the pot is made from, food may not cook evenly. Electricity can also cook through conduction or convection.

Induction

Induction uses electricity to heat cookware by magnetic energy generated by coils under the stovetop. Pots and pans must be magnetic for induction cooking to take place. Stainless steel and cast iron pots and pans work best.

Radiation

Radiation cooks food by transferring energy from the cooking equipment to the food. The energy waves do not contain heat. Instead, these waves change to heat when they make contact with the food.

Microwave

Another heat source used is a type of radiation called microwaves. A **microwave** is an invisible wave of energy that causes water molecules to rub against each other and produce the heat that cooks food. Microwave ovens are an example of equipment that uses this heat source.

Light

Infrared lamps and FlashBake ovens use light waves as a heat source. The light waves do not contain heat, but heat is generated when

the energy contacts the food. Infrared lamps are used to keep food hot until it is ordered by customers. FlashBake ovens are used to prepare small or individual servings quickly.

Cooking Equipment Sanitation

When you clean cooking equipment, always follow the instruction manual for disassembling and reassembling equipment safely. The equipment manufacturer can do general maintenance and repairs on this equipment. These are some general guidelines for cleaning certain types of equipment.

Flat-Top Range

To clean a flat-top range, loosen any burned food with a scraper. Then, clean the rangetop with a damp, soapy cloth. Rinse it and wipe it dry.

A TASTE OF HISTORY ANSWER Answers will vary, but might include something like a platypus, which might be a spatula resembling a duck-billed platypus.

Cooking Equipment

Deep-Fat Fryer A deep-fat fryer cooks food at a constant temperature, which is controlled by a thermostat. Automatic or computerized fryers lower and raise food baskets in and out of hot fat at a preset time. Filtering allows the oil to be reused. Fryers are vital pieces of equipment in quick-service operations.

Open-Burner Range An open-burner range has four to six burner units, each with individual controls. Each burner has its own heat source. This allows for more efficient use of heat than with a flat-top range.

Griddle Griddles can be flat or ridged. They can be a part of the range top, or a separate unit. Food is cooked directly on the surface of the griddle.

Flat-Top Range Also known as a French-top range, the burners of a flat-top range are arranged under a solid top that produces even heat over a large surface area. Flat-top ranges cannot be used as a griddle.

Cooking Equipment *continued*

Microwave Oven A microwave oven uses invisible waves of energy called microwaves to heat, reheat, defrost, and cook foods.

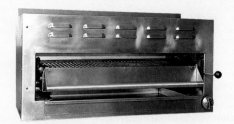

Broiler Broilers cook food quickly from start to finish using intense, direct heat located above the food. They can be combined with a conventional oven as shown here, or stand alone as a separate unit.

Tilting Skillet The tilting skillet is the most flexible piece of equipment in a commercial kitchen. It is a large, flat cooking surface with sides to hold liquids. The skillet can be tilted to pour out liquid. It can be used as a griddle, fry pan, brazing pan, stockpot, bain marie, or steamer.

Steamer A steamer cooks food quickly and nutritiously because it places the food in direct contact with hot water vapor.

Pressure Steamer A steam pressure cooker works like a regular steamer except that the steam is under pressure. A pressurized door and a steam valve control the desired amount of pressurized steam.

Steam-Jacketed Kettle A steam-jacketed kettle also uses steam to cook foods quickly, but the steam does not come into direct contact with food. The steam is pumped between two stainless steel containers. The steam heats the inner kettle and cooks food quickly and evenly.

Trunnion Kettle A trunnion (ˈtrən-yən) kettle is a type of steam-jacketed kettle that can be tilted to empty contents by turning a wheel or pulling a lever.

Combination Steamer/Oven This steamer/oven uses a combination of cooking methods. It can use a fan to circulate air around the food like a convection oven. It can also use steam to cook food. Finally, it can combine convection and steam cooking. Combination steamer/ovens are used to bake, poach, grill, roast, braise, and steam foods.

Deck Oven A deck oven is also known as a stack oven. Electric deck ovens have separate baking controls for the lower deck and for the upper deck. Deck ovens are used for baking, roasting, and braising.

Convection Oven A convection oven has a fan that circulates the oven's heated air. This fan allows you to cook foods in about 30% less time and at temperatures approximately 50° lower than a conventional oven. Convection ovens are used for baking, roasting, and braising.

Salamander A salamander is a small gas or electric broiler that is often attached to an open-burner range. Its heat source is also located above the food. Unlike a standard broiler, a salamander is used for browning, glazing, and melting foods.

FlashBake Oven A FlashBake, or infrared, oven uses both infrared and visible light waves above and below the food. Because the heat is so intense, foods cook very quickly without losing flavor and moisture. The FlashBake is used to bake smaller portions of food. It needs no preheating or venting.

Open-Burner Range

To clean an open burner, remove the grids and the drip pan. Soak them in hot, soapy water. While they are soaking, wash, rinse, and dry the rest of the range. Then, wash, rinse, dry, and replace the grids and drip pan. Gas ranges have pilot lights. A **pilot light** is a continuously burning flame that lights the burner when you turn on the range. Check to see that all the pilot lights are burning after you have cleaned the range. The flame should be blue, not yellow. Always tell a supervisor if you suspect a range has a gas leak.

Griddle

To clean a griddle, polish the top with a special griddle cloth or stone. Polish in the same direction as the grain of the metal. Using a circular motion will scratch the surface of the griddle. Wash the remaining area with warm, soapy water. Rinse and dry. Then, recondition the top by coating it with a thin layer of oil. To **recondition** a griddle means to coat in oil so that foods will not stick to it. Heat the griddle to 400°F (204°C) and wipe it clean. Repeat until the griddle is smooth and shiny.

Broiler

To clean a broiler, take out the grids and soak them in hot, soapy water. Remove caked-on food with a wire brush. Rinse, dry, and lightly oil. Scrape grease and burned food from the inside of the broiler. Wash the drip pans and put them back in place. Empty the grease trap, wash it, and replace it.

Conventional and Convection Ovens

When you clean an oven, make sure the oven has cooled completely first. Take out the shelves and wash them in hot, soapy water. Then, rinse them and let them air dry. Wash the inside of the oven with warm, soapy water and dry it with a soft cloth. Wipe the outside of the oven with warm, soapy water. Rinse it with a soft, wet cloth and polish it with another soft cloth.

READING CHECK ANSWER Heat sources include gas, electricity, microwaves, radiation, and light.

Microwave Oven

Let the microwave oven cool completely before you clean it. Wipe the inside and outside of the oven with a damp cloth and warm, soapy water. Then, rinse and wipe dry. Make sure the microwave oven door seals tightly. If the door is loose or damaged, do not use the oven.

Reading Check Identify Name five sources of heat for cooking food.

Clean-Up Equipment

Foodservice operations have a constant flow of customers everyday. Customers expect operations to be clean and efficient as well as having good food.

Commercial Sinks

Foodservice operations use several different types of commercial sinks. The most common type is the three-compartment sink. It is used to rinse, wash, and sanitize dishes.

Garbage Disposal

Garbage disposals are mounted on sink drains. They are used to eliminate scraps of food leftover from preparation or scraped from plates. However, a garbage disposal does not replace the need for a garbage can.

SAFETY CHECK ANSWER Poorly maintained equipment and tools can lead to contamination by physical hazards. It also can lead to poorly prepared food.

 Single-Tank Dishwasher Single-tank dishwashers are used by some restaurants. *What are the main features of a single-tank dishwasher?*

Commercial Dishwashers

A multi-tank, or carousel, dishwasher is common in large operations. Dishes are placed directly into racks on the conveyor belt. Hand-scraped, dirty dishes are rinsed and then manually loaded at one end of the machine, where they travel in a circle through areas that prewash, wash, rinse, sanitize, and dry them.

A single-tank dishwasher has only one compartment. Dishes that have been scraped by hand and rinsed can be loaded into its raised doors. As the doors are lowered, the washing cycle begins. Single-tank dishwashers are used to wash small loads of dishes.

 Reading Check **Name** List the main types of clean-up equipment used in professional kitchens.

SECTION 9.3 **After You Read**

Review Key Concepts

1. **Explain** how to clean a mixer or food processor.
2. **Describe** cooking with radiation.
3. **Compare** commercial sinks and commercial dishwashers.

Practice Culinary Academics

Social Studies

4. Read the A Taste of History feature about salamanders. There are many types of cooking equipment used through history around the world. Research one type of cooking equipment used in a different region of the world. Create a visual report on the equipment and how it is used. What dishes are prepared with this equipment? Explain how the culture of the region contributed to the development of this equipment.

> **NCSS IV E Individual Development and Identity** Examine the interaction of ethnic, national, or cultural influences in specific situations or events.

Mathematics

5. You have determined that a certain cake will bake in 20 minutes in your deck oven, 7 minutes in a FlashBake oven, and 14 minutes in your convection oven. What is the median baking time?

Math Concept **Finding the Median** The statistical term median refers to the middle number in an ordered set of numbers. If you have an even number of numbers, take the mean (average) of the two middle numbers.

Starting Hint Place the baking times in order from lowest to highest. The median will be the middle time in this list. Since you have an odd number of times, you do not need to worry about averaging.

> **NCTM Data Analysis and Probability** Select and use appropriate statistical methods to analyze data.

 Check your answers at this book's Online Learning Center at **glencoe.com**.

PHOTO CAPTION ANSWER Single-tank dishwashers have one compartment, are best for small loads, and dishes must be rinsed prior to loading them.

READING CHECK ANSWER The types of clean-up equipment are: commercial sinks, garbage disposal, and commercial dishwashers.

Holding and Service Equipment

Reading Guide

 Before You Read

Two-Column Notes Two-column notes are a useful way to study and organize what you have read. Divide a piece of paper into two columns. In the left column, write down main ideas. In the right column, list supporting ideas.

Read to Learn

Key Concepts
- **Identify** the uses of hot food holding equipment.
- **Evaluate** the uses of service equipment.

Main Idea

Holding equipment holds hot foods and maintains their temperature. Service equipment consists of all types of equipment for serving food to customers.

Content Vocabulary
- steam table
- bain marie
- proofing/holding cabinet

Academic Vocabulary
- replenish
- function

Graphic Organizer

As you read, use this table to organize a list of holding equipment and a list of service equipment.

Holding Equipment	Service Equipment

 Graphic Organizer Go to this book's Online Learning Center at **glencoe.com** for a printable graphic organizer.

Food must stay safe on its journey from the kitchen to the customer.

ACADEMIC STANDARDS

 English Language Arts
NCTE 5 Use different writing process elements to communicate effectively.

 Mathematics
NCTM Number and Operations Understand numbers, ways of representing numbers, relationships among numbers, and number systems.

 Science
NSES F Develop an understanding of personal and community health.

NCTE National Council of Teachers of English

NCTM National Council of Teachers of Mathematics

NSES National Science Education Standards

NCSS National Council for the Social Studies

Holding Equipment

Many times, foodservice operations cater meals or serve them buffet style. Keeping pre-prepared food hot requires special equipment designed to keep foods either hot or cold.

Steam tables, a bain marie, overhead warmers, and proofing/holding cabinets are used to hold hot foods. A **steam table**, or food warmer, keeps prepared foods warm in serving lines. A **bain marie** (ˌban-mə-ˈrē), or water bath, is used to keep foods such as sauces and soups warm. A **proofing/holding cabinet** is an enclosed, air-tight metal container with wheels that can hold sheet pans of food. The purpose of this equipment is to keep foods at a temperature of at least 135°F (57°C) until the food is served. The high temperature prevents bacteria from growing.

When food is being kept warm at high temperatures, the texture and color are likely to change. To prevent this, you should **replenish**, or restock, foods frequently.

Reading Check Explain When would a steam table be used instead of a bain marie?

Service Equipment

Foodservice operations need to have a variety of service equipment. Service equipment can be used in the dining room, at a buffet, or at a catered **function**, or event. Service equipment includes anything used to serve the customer, including hotel pans. (See **Figure 9.3** and **Figure 9.4**.)

Reading Check List Name at least five pieces of service equipment.

▼ FIGURE 9.3 Hotel Pan Capacity

Storage Variety Hotel pans come in a number of different sizes. *What are the advantages of using hotel pans to cook and serve food?*

Hotel Pan Size	Approximate Capacity	Hotel Pan Size	Approximate Capacity
Full Size 20¾ in. × 12¾ in.	• 2½ in. deep = 8.3 qts. • 4 in. deep = 13 qts. • 6 in. deep = 20 quarts	One-Third Size 6⅞ in. × 12¾ in.	• 2½ in. deep = 2.6 qts. • 4 in. deep = 4.1 qts. • 6 in. deep = 6.1 qts.
Half-Size Long 20¾ in. × 6⁷⁄₁₆ in.	• 2½ in. deep = 3.7 qts. • 4 in. deep = 5.7 qts.	One-Fourth Size 6⅜ in. × 10⅜ in.	• 2½ in. deep = 1.8 qts. • 4 in. deep = 3 qts. • 6 in. deep = 4.5 qts.
Two-Third Size 13¾ in. × 12¾ in.	• 2½ in. deep = 5.6 qts. • 4 in. deep = 9.3 qts. • 6 in. deep = 14 qts.	One-Sixth Size 6⅞ in. × 6¼ in.	• 2½ in. deep = 1.2 qts. • 4 in. deep = 1.8 qts. • 6 in. deep = 2.7 qts.
Half Size 10⅜ in. × 12¾ in.	• 2½ in. deep = 4 qts. • 4 in. deep = 6.7 qts. • 6 in. deep = 10 qts.	One-Ninth Size 6⅞ in. × 4¼ in.	• 2½ in. deep = .6 qts. • 4 in. deep = 1.1 qts.

FIGURE CAPTION ANSWER Food cooked and served in hotel pans can be quickly and easily used in buffet lines. Empty pans can be quickly changed for full ones.

READING CHECK ANSWER A steam table: used in a service area. A bain marie: used in the production area.
READING CHECK ANSWER Insulated carriers, chafing dishes, canned fuel, coffee systems, scoops, airpot brewing systems, utility carts, or hotel pans.

Holding Equipment

Steam Table Foods are placed in hotel pans and placed into steam tables filled with steaming hot water. The pans are covered with either flat or domed lids. The temperature of the water is kept hot enough to keep foods warm while they are being served.

Bain Marie Foods are placed in bain-marie inserts, which are then placed into a bain marie that is filled with hot water. A bain marie also can be used to melt ingredients that will be used in other dishes. A bain marie can also be used to bake certain products.

Overhead Warmers Overhead warmers are used in the service area to keep foods hot until they are picked up by the serving staff and delivered to the customer. Food should be kept under an overhead warmer for a short time. The heat can cause foods to dry out quickly.

Proofing/Holding Cabinet Temperature and humidity levels are controlled inside the cabinet. The internal climate of proofing/holding cabinets is ideal for proofing yeast-dough products. They are also used to keep food at 135°F (57°C) or above during service.

Service Equipment

Insulated Carriers Insulated carriers are large boxes that can hold hotel pans and sheet pans filled with cooked food. Insulated carriers keep hot foods hot and cold foods cold. Some insulated carriers have wheels. If the carrier has a spigot, warm or cold beverages can be stored inside.

Chafing Dishes Chafing dishes are typically stainless steel pans used to keep food hot during service. Hotel pans of food can be inserted into the chafing dish. Chafing dishes are available in a variety of sizes.

Canned Fuel Canned fuel is used to keep food warm in chafing dishes. These small containers of solid fuel are ignited and placed beneath the chafing dish.

Coffee Systems Coffee systems can brew coffee and keep it warm during serving time. A variety of models are available. Coffee systems consist of a water tank, thermostat, warming plate, and coffee server. Systems with a hot water spigot can also be used to make hot chocolate.

Scoops Scoops are used to measure equal amounts of food. They have a lever to mechanically release the food and are numbered according to size. The number indicates how many level scoops it takes to fill a quart. The higher the number, the smaller the amount of food the scoop holds.

Airpot Brewing Systems Airpot brewers are used to make hot beverages such as coffee. Airpots are tall, stainless steel containers with plastic lids and pump dispensers. They keep liquids hot for up to 10 hours.

Utility Carts Utility carts are made of heavy-duty plastic or stainless steel. They are on wheels that allow them to be moved easily. Utility carts also have handles that allow them to be pulled or pushed. They are used to display or hold food, to bus tables, or to move heavy items from one location to another.

Hotel Pans Hotel pans are stainless steel containers that are used to cook, serve, and store food. They come in many different sizes. Hotel pans fit in steam tables and other holding equipment.

▼ FIGURE 9.4 Hotel Pan Configurations

The Right Fit These are some of the most common configurations of hotel pans.
What other combinations can you suggest?

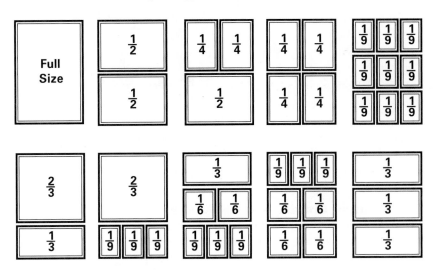

SECTION 9.4 — After You Read

Review Key Concepts

1. **Describe** the use of proofing/holding cabinets.
2. **Explain** how to use a scoop.

Practice Culinary Academics

Science

3. **Procedure** Cook soup in your foods lab. Once the soup is done, turn off the heat, and remove it from the stove burner. Use a thermometer to measure its temperature, both in Fahrenheit and Celsius. Take the temperature of the soup every five minutes. Record the temperature.

   Analysis Use your temperature recordings to draw conclusions about why proper holding is important. Write a brief summary, using your measured temperatures as proof.

   NSES F Develop an understanding of personal and community health.

English Language Arts

4. Imagine that you are conducting training at a foodservice establishment on holding foods for service. Create a guide to all the equipment.

Describe each piece of equipment and explain when each should be used. You may illustrate your guide if you wish.

NCTE 5 Use different writing process elements to communicate effectively.

Mathematics

5. Locate the full-size hotel pans in Figure 9.4 (Hotel Pan Configurations). What is the ratio of capacity to depth for the 4-inch deep pan? What about the 6-inch deep pan? Are the two ratios equal?

   Math Concept **Use Cross Products to Compare Ratios** Remember, a ratio is a comparison of two numbers that is written as a fraction. Two ratios are equal (or proportional) if their cross-products are equal.

   Starting Hint Write each ratio as a fraction with capacity as the numerator and depth as the denominator. Cross-multiply the denominator of one fraction by the numerator of the other, and vice versa. Are the products equal?

   NCTM Number and Operations Understand numbers, ways of representing numbers, relationships among numbers, and number systems.

    Check your answers at this book's Online Learning Center at **glencoe.com**.

FIGURE CAPTION ANSWER Answers will vary, but should remain equal in area to the full-size hotel pan. Configurations that are not equal to the full-size pan will not fit properly in warming or holding equipment.

Review and Applications

Chapter Summary

Effective work flow allows the orderly movement of food through the kitchen. An efficient kitchen will include well-organized work stations and work sections. Storage equipment should be used to keep foods fresh and organized until they are ready for use. Preparation equipment is used to perform a variety of tasks including shredding, grating, grinding, and slicing. Cooking equipment includes ranges, ovens, and steamers. Equipment used for clean-up includes commercial sinks and dishwashers. Holding equipment keeps foods hot until they are used. Service equipment is used to serve customers in the dining room, at the buffet, or at a catered function.

Content and Academic Vocabulary Review

1. Use each of these vocabulary words in a sentence.

Content Vocabulary

- work station (p. 220)
- work section (p. 220)
- work flow (p. 221)
- cooking line (p. 221)
- island (p. 221)
- mise en place (p. 222)
- work simplification (p. 222)
- range of motion (p. 223)
- purchase order (p. 225)
- invoice (p. 225)
- receiving record (p. 225)
- platform scale (p. 225)
- counter scale (p. 225)
- portion scale (p. 225)
- dolly (p. 225)
- lowboy (p. 226)
- conduction (p. 234)
- convection (p. 234)
- induction (p. 234)
- radiation (p. 234)
- microwave (p. 234)
- pilot light (p. 239)
- recondition (p. 239)
- steam table (p. 242)
- bain marie (p. 242)
- proofing/holding cabinet (p. 242)

Academic Vocabulary

- efficient (p. 222)
- mode (p. 222)
- quantity (p. 225)
- note (p. 225)
- volume (p. 231)
- refer (p. 231)
- replenish (p. 242)
- function (p. 242)

Review Key Concepts

2. **Explain** the roles of the different stations in a professional kitchen.
3. **Categorize** the different types of professional receiving and storage equipment.
4. **Explain** the maintenance and sanitation for preparation equipment.
5. **Compare** the different heat sources used in cooking.
6. **Categorize** the uses of different types of clean-up equipment.
7. **Identify** the uses of hot food holding equipment.
8. **Evaluate** the uses of service equipment.

Critical Thinking

9. **Explain** how the layout of a commercial kitchen affects work flow.
10. **Imagine** that the manager of your foodservice operation does not follow FIFO because of the small amount of business the establishment handles. Why is it important to follow FIFO anyway regardless of business size?

Academic Skills

English Language Arts

11. **Consumer Research** Conduct research on three different brands of microwave ovens. You may follow your teacher's instructions to look on the Internet or in consumer and trade magazines to gather information about products. Write an evaluation that compares the brands that you researched, then write a recommendation as to which would be best for a commercial kitchen.

> **NCTE 7** Conduct research and gather, evaluate, and synthesize data to communicate discoveries.

Social Studies

12. **Technology in the Kitchen** In this chapter, you have learned about the different types of equipment found in a professional kitchen. You have also learned about work flow and efficient kitchen setup. New technology is constantly being invented to change the flow of kitchen procedure. Research new kitchen technologies and do a report on one new technology and how it might effect workflow in a professional kitchen. Include visuals in your report.

> **NCSS VIII B Science, Technology, and Society** Make judgments about how science and technology have transformed the physical world and human society and our understanding of time, space, place, and human-environment interactions.

Mathematics

13. **Compare Refrigerator Sizes** You need to purchase a new refrigerator for your foodservice business. A reach-in refrigerator measures 68 inches in height, 25 inches wide, and 25 inches deep on the outside. A lowboy refrigerator's exterior dimensions are 44 inches tall, 55 inches wide, and 25 inches deep. For both refrigerators, the sides, front doors, and top are 2.5 inches thick, while the bottom is 5.5 inches thick. What is the ratio of the capacity of the lowboy to the capacity of the reach-in?

Math Concept **Capacity** Capacity measures the volume of interior space. It is calculated like volume, but the term capacity is only used for hollow objects. Remember, the volume of a rectangular object equals width × depth × height.

Starting Hint Find the interior width of the reach-in by subtracting 2.5 inches for the left wall and 2.5 inches for the right wall from the exterior width (interior width $= 25 - 2.5 - 2.5 = 20$ inches). Repeat for the depth and height to find the interior dimensions, and multiply all three interior dimensions to find the capacity. Repeat for the other refrigerator, and place the two capacities in a ratio.

> **NCTM Geometry** Use visualization, spatial reasoning, and geometric modeling to solve problems.

Certification Prep

Sharpen your test-taking skills to improve your kitchen certification program score.

Directions Read the questions. Then, read the answer choices and choose the best possible answer for each.

14. Which piece of receiving equipment would be used to ensure that food products meet safety standards?

  a. thermometers   **c.** work tables

  b. chafing dishes   **d.** scales

15. Which pieces of preparation equipment use attachments?

  a. roll-in refrigerator and lowboy refrigerator

  b. mixer and food processor

  c. table-mounted can opener and commercial juicer

  d. slicer and mixer

Test-Taking Tip
Come up with the answer in your head before looking at the possible answers. You will be more confident in your answer, and avoid being tricked.

Review and Applications

Real-World Skills and Applications

Interpersonal and Collaborative Skills

16. **Coordinate Jobs** As a class, choose a simple meal to prepare. Your teacher will assign you to work stations. As a group, coordinate responsibilities with those of the other work stations before beginning preparation. Then, prepare your meal, working together while manning each separate work station.

Critical Thinking Skills

17. **Make a List** List the characteristics of a well-designed professional foodservice kitchen and give reasons for each characteristic you choose. What makes that a feature of a well-designed kitchen? What benefit does that characteristic provide? Discuss your answers as a class.

Technology Applications

18. **Design a Kitchen** Use a graphic design or desktop publishing program to design the cooking line of a professional kitchen. Decide which setup you will use according to the information in this chapter, and then use the program to place and label the cooking equipment.

Financial Literacy

19. **Calculate Depreciation** Depreciation is a loss of value of a piece of equipment. Foodservice equipment has a useful life of seven years. Useful life means the length of time it can depreciate before it has no value. If a stove costs $5,000 when it is purchased new, how much value will it lose each year?

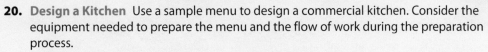

Culinary Lab

Use the culinary skills you have learned in this chapter.

Commercial Kitchen Design

20. **Design a Kitchen** Use a sample menu to design a commercial kitchen. Consider the equipment needed to prepare the menu and the flow of work during the preparation process.

A. Create your menu. Create a simple breakfast menu with three dishes. Determine the type of tasks that will need to be performed, the type of equipment needed, and the work stations needed to complete the dishes on the menu.

B. Choose your equipment. Select the appropriate commercial equipment from the features in this chapter.

C. Make your sketch. Create a sketch of the kitchen, showing work stations and the cooking line. You may use the cooking line you created for question number 18.

D. Label equipment. Label each piece of equipment on your sketch.

E. Adjust your design. Review your design and make any adjustments needed. Check that it is complete.

Create Your Evaluation

Evaluate each restaurant design by answering the following questions and explaining your answers:

- Was the right amount of equipment selected?
- Did the designer allow enough work space?
- How did the cooking line affect work flow?

CHAPTER 10

Knives and Smallwares

SECTIONS

Section 10.1 Knives

Section 10.2 Smallwares

WRITING ACTIVITY

Paragraph

A paragraph is a group of sentences that develop one central idea. Write a paragraph describing one type of knife and its main uses. Include a topic sentence, supporting sentences, and an ending sentence.

Writing Tips

1 Focus on the main idea of your paragraph.

2 Write clear and simple sentences to express your meaning.

3 Use the dictionary to help you find additional words.

EXPLORE THE PHOTO

Knives and smallwares are important tools in any professional kitchen. *Why is it important to know how to choose, care for, and use knives?*

WRITING ACTIVITY ANSWER Paragraphs should be clear and concise. Each should follow the instructions. Make sure capitalization and punctuation are used correctly.

EXPLORE THE PHOTO ANSWER
Knives are the tools that chefs will probably use the most as they work.

Knives

Learn to use, clean, and sharpen knives safely.

Reading Guide

 Before You Read

Stay Engaged One way to stay engaged when reading is to turn each of the headings into a question, and then read the section to find the answers. For example, Knife Safety and Care might be, "How can I use knives safely?"

Read to Learn

Key Concepts
- **Categorize** knives by their specific tasks.
- **Demonstrate** basic knife skills.
- **Explain** proper knife safety and storage.

Main Idea

Knives are the most commonly used kitchen tools. Therefore, it is important for a chef to know the construction, use, and maintenance of knives.

Content Vocabulary
- stainless steel
- tang
- rivet
- bolster
- serrated
- pare
- chiffonade
- rondelle
- diagonal
- roll cut
- julienne
- batonnet
- brunoise
- whetstone
- trueing

Academic Vocabulary
- transfer
- uniform

 ACADEMIC STANDARDS

 Mathematics
NCTM Geometry Use visualization, spatial reasoning, and geometric modeling to solve problems.

NCTM Number and Operations Understand the meanings of operations and how they relate to one another.

Science
NSES F Students should develop an understanding of personal and community health.

Social Studies
NCSS II B Time, Continuity, and Change Apply key concepts such as chronology and change to explain, analyze, and show connections among patterns of historical change and continuity.

NCTE National Council of Teachers of English

NCTM National Council of Teachers of Mathematics

NSES National Science Education Standards

NCSS National Council for the Social Studies

Graphic Organizer

Use a spider map like the one below to list the five parts of a knife. Fill in each branch with details about that part of a knife.

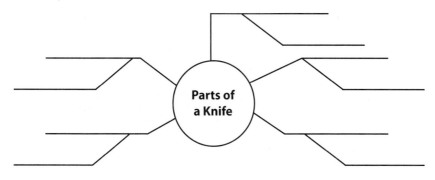

Parts of a Knife

 Graphic Organizer Go to this book's Online Learning Center at **glencoe.com** for a printable graphic organizer.

GRAPHIC ORGANIZER ANSWER 1) Blade: flat, cutting part; 2) Tang: part of the blade that continues into the handle; 3) Handle: the part held with the hand; 4) Rivets: metal pieces that fasten the handle to the tang; 5) Bolster: keeps food out of connection between handle and tang.

Knife Construction

Knives are the most commonly used kitchen tools. They are an important part of any chef's tool kit. A kitchen tool is an implement that is used in the kitchen. Accomplished chefs can perform countless valuable tasks with a sharp knife. To perform these tasks, however, chefs must be familiar with knife construction and type. They must also use proper cutting techniques and knife safety. Finally, chefs must know how to care for knives properly so that they will last.

To know which knife to use for a specific task, you must have a working knowledge of the different parts of a knife.

Blade

The blade of a high-quality, professional knife is made of a single piece of metal. The metal has been cut, stamped, or forged into the desired shape. The metals most often used for the knife blade are stainless steel and high-carbon stainless steel.

Stainless steel is a hard, durable metal made of chromium and carbon steel. It does not rust or discolor. Stainless steel also will not **transfer**, or pass to foods, a metallic taste. The main drawback is that it is hard to sharpen.

High-carbon stainless steel is a mix of iron, carbon, chromium, and other metals. This metal combines the best features of stainless steel and carbon steel, but it is expensive.

High-carbon stainless steel does not rust or discolor and can be sharpened easily. This is the most common metal used for knives in the professional kitchen.

Tang

The **tang** is the part of the blade that continues into the knife's handle. Some knives have full tangs, while others have partial tangs. A full tang is as long as the whole knife handle. Knives used for heavy work, such as chef's knives and cleavers, should have a full tang. Knives used for lighter work, such as paring knives and utility knives, may have a partial tang.

Handle

Knife handles can be made of several types of material, including plastic, vinyl, and hard woods such as rosewood and walnut. Because you will hold the knife for long periods of time, the handle should feel comfortable in your hand. Your hand may cramp from using a handle that is either too small or too large. Manufacturers make various sizes of handles. Try different sizes to find one that fits.

Rivet

The tang is attached to the knife handle with rivets. A **rivet** is a metal fastener. For comfort and sanitation, the rivets should be smooth and lie flush with the handle's surface.

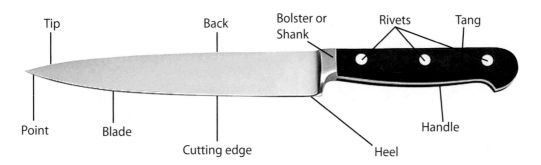

Tip   Back   Bolster or Shank   Rivets   Tang

Point   Blade   Cutting edge   Heel   Handle

▲ Parts of a Knife Knives used for heavy work should have a tang that runs the entire length of the handle. *Why do you think this is?*

PHOTO CAPTION ANSWER It will give the knife more strength and keep it from breaking at the handle when used for heavy kitchen work.

Boning · **Tournée** · **Paring** · **Fillet** · **Slicer** · **Serrated Slicer** · **Butcher** · **Chef's**

Types of Knives Chefs use a variety of knives in the kitchen for different tasks. *Which knife would you choose to cut bread slices?*

Bolster

Some knives have a shank, or bolster, in the spot where the blade and handle come together. Knives with a bolster are very strong and durable. The **bolster** helps prevent food particles from entering the space between the tang and the handle.

Types of Knives

A chef chooses knives according to the type of food that she or he is preparing. For example, chopping onions requires a different knife than one used for slicing bread.

Chef's Knife

The chef's knife, also called a French knife, is the most important knife in the chef's tool kit. This all-purpose knife has an 8- to 14-inch triangular blade. It can be used for peeling, trimming, chopping, slicing, and dicing. The 10-inch chef's knife is used for general work in a commercial kitchen. A skilled chef can also use this knife to cut large foods, such as meat, poultry, and fish, into smaller pieces. A smaller knife, but similar in shape to a chef's knife, is the utility knife. A utility knife is an all-purpose knife with a 5- to 7-inch blade. It is used mainly for peeling and slicing fruits and vegetables.

Gourmet Math

Drawing and Cutting Angles
When two straight lines have the same endpoint, they form an angle. The size of an angle is measured in degrees, and written as a number between 0 and 360 followed by the degree (°) symbol. Common reference angles are 0°, 45°, 90°, and 180°. Angles measuring 0° and 180° are straight lines. A 90° angle is a right angle, and a 45° angle is halfway between a straight line and a right angle.

In cooking, angle measures are often used to help you visualize how to hold a knife. Sketch a 10° angle and a 60° angle on a piece of paper, and practice cutting each of these angles on a raw potato.

Math Concept **Measuring Angles** Use a protractor to measure angles. If you do not have a protractor, you can estimate the degrees by picturing the common reference angles.

Starting Hint If you have a protractor, use it to draw exact 10° and 60° angles. You can also estimate the appearance of these angles without a protractor. A 10° angle is very small, while a 60° angle is two-thirds of the way between a straight line and a right (90°) angle.

NCTM Geometry Use visualization, spatial reasoning, and geometric modeling to solve problems.

PHOTO CAPTION ANSWER You would choose a serrated slicer knife, which would cut the bread without crushing it.

GOURMET MATH ANSWER Students should draw a 10° angle (which is very small) and a 60° angle (which is larger, but not as large as a right angle).

A Most Useful Tool

Knives are some of man's oldest tools. The earliest knives, used approximately 2 million years ago, were made of flint. Much later in history, man began to make knives from copper and bronze. In the early 1900s, advancements in steel manufacturing led to the development of the knives that are used in professional kitchens today.

Historical Application

Create a time line that traces the history of the knife, starting with a picture of an early knife. Finish with a picture of a modern chef's knife and label its parts.

> **NCSS II B Time, Continuity, and Change** Apply key concepts such as chronology and change to explain, analyze, and show connections among patterns of historical change and continuity.

Slicer

The slicer has a long, thin blade that is ideal for cutting large foods such as meat and poultry. The tip of this knife may be pointed or rounded. The blade may be rigid or flexible. The slicer's blade may also be **serrated** (sə-'rāt-ed), meaning that it is toothed like a saw. You can use a serrated slicer to slice coarse foods without crushing or tearing them.

Boning Knife

A small knife with a thin, angled 5- to 7-inch blade, the boning knife is used to remove bones from meat, fish, and poultry and trim fat from meat. The blade may be rigid or flexible. Rigid blades are used for heavier work. Flexible blades are used for lighter work.

Paring Knife

The paring knife has a rigid blade that is only 2 to 4 inches long. You can use this knife to pare a thin outer layer or peel from fruits and vegetables. To **pare** means to trim off.

Tournée Knife

Similar in size to the paring knife, the tournée (tür-'nā) knife has a curved blade that looks like a bird's beak. It is used to trim potatoes and vegetables into shapes that look like footballs.

Fillet Knife

The fillet knife has an 8- to 9-inch blade with a pointed tip. The blade may be rigid or flexible. It is mainly used to fillet fish.

Butcher Knife

The butcher knife has a 6- to 14-inch rigid blade whose tip curves up at a 25-degree angle. It is sometimes called a scimitar ('si-mə-,tär) because its curved blade resembles a saber by that name. You can use the butcher knife to cut meat, poultry, and fish.

 **Reading Check** **Define** What is a paring knife?

Knife Skills

One of the most important skills you will learn is how to use a knife properly. You will use a knife to perform many different tasks, from boning fish to paring fruits, slicing bread, and dicing or mincing vegetables. The more you practice, the more efficient you will become.

You can grip a knife in several different ways. Comfort and the task at hand will help you determine which grip to use. As a general rule, grip the knife firmly but not so tightly that your hand gets tired. Avoid placing your index finger on the top of the blade.

To make safe, even cuts, you need to guide the knife with one hand while you hold the food firmly in place with the other hand. Curl the fingertips on the hand that holds the food. This will help you avoid accidental cuts. Use the sharp edge of the blade to do the cutting. A sharp knife is the safest knife to use. Use smooth, even strokes, and never force the blade through the food. Report dull knives to a supervisor for sharpening.

A TASTE OF HISTORY ANSWER Time lines should include the first flint knives and continue through time showing copper, bronze, steel, and high-carbon steel and ceramic knives.

READING CHECK ANSWER A paring knife has a short, rigid blade. It is used to trim off the peel of fruits and vegetables.

Grip
a Knife

A Grip the knife by placing four fingers on the bottom of the handle and the thumb firmly against back of the blade.

B Grip the knife by placing four fingers on the bottom of the handle and the thumb against the side of the blade.

C Grip the knife by placing three fingers on the bottom of the handle, the index finger flat against the blade on one side, and the thumb on the other side. This grip offers extra control and stability.

Knife Cuts

It is important to cut foods into **uniform** pieces, or pieces that are even in shape and size, so that they cook evenly. Uniform sizes also make the finished product more visually appealing. When you use a properly sharpened knife, you can avoid bruising foods such as onions and tomatoes. The basic cutting techniques include slicing, mincing, and dicing. You can also roughly chop foods when visual appeal is not important, such as for stock vegtables. A rough chopped item, often vegetables, is called concassé.

Slicing

When you slice food, you will use a chef's knife to cut it into large, thin pieces. To slice safely, make sure the flat side of the food is down so that it will not slip. If necessary, cut a piece of the food to create a flat surface. You can make many different specialty slices

Chiffonade To **chiffonade** (ˌshi-fə-ˈnäd) means to finely slice or shred leafy vegetables or herbs. This cut is often used to make certain garnishes.

Rondelle A **rondelle** (rän-ˈdel), or round, is a disk-shaped slice. Rondelles are made from cylindrical fruits or vegetables, such as cucumbers or carrots.

Diagonal A **diagonal** cut results in an oval or elongated slice of a cylindrical fruit or vegetable. The technique used to slice a diagonal is similar to the one used for a rondelle except that you must hold the knife at an angle to get an oval-shaped slice.

Roll Cut A **roll cut**, or oblique cut, is done by first cutting a cylindrical fruit or vegetable as for a diagonal cut, rolling the fruit or vegetable by 180 degrees, and then doing another diagonal cut. This exposes more of the surface of the vegetable to decrease cooking time.

Safely
Cut Food

METHOD A

1 With your fingertips curled back, grip the food to be cut with your thumb and three fingertips. Holding the knife in your other hand, keep the tip of the knife on the cutting board, and lift the knife's heel.

2 Use the second joint of your index finger as a guide as you slice with a smooth, even, downward motion. To make slices of equal size, adjust your index finger as you work. As you slice, move your thumb and fingertips down the length of the food, using the tip of the knife as the support.

METHOD B

1 Use the same grip as described in Method A. Slice the food into the desired thickness by using the second joint of your index finger to guide you. Lift the tip of the knife and cut by moving the knife slightly toward you and down through the food.

2 Use your wrist, not your elbow, to move the knife. Do not apply too much downward pressure. Your wrist serves as the support for this slicing method. The weight of the knife should be doing most of the work.

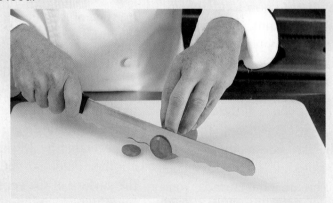

HOW TO

Make a
Chiffonade Cut

1 Wash and de-stem the vegetable's leaves as needed. Stack several leaves on top of one another and roll them tightly.

2 Holding the rolled leaves tightly, finely slice them.

HOW TO

Make a
Rondelle Cut

1 Peel the food if desired.

2 On a cutting board, hold the knife perpendicular to the food and make even slices.

HOW TO

Make a
Diagonal Cut

1 Peel the food if desired.

2 On a cutting board, hold the knife at the desired angle to the food being cut and make even slices.

Dice
Food

1 Peel the food if desired and square off the sides. Trim the food to the proper length for the slices you will make. Cut slices of the desired thickness.

2 Stack the slices and cut them into uniform sticks. These sticks should be of the same thickness as the slices.

3 To make a small dice, make a ¼-inch cut perpendicular to the length of a batonnet. A ⅜-inch cut from a ⅜-inch stick makes a medium dice. A ⅝-inch cut from a ⅝-inch stick creates a large dice. Making a ⅛-inch cut from a julienne makes a cube called a brunoise.

Mince
Food

1 Dice food using the same technique shown above.

2 Hold the tip of the knife on the cutting board with a flat hand. Use a rocking motion to mince the diced food with the knife's heel.

Sharpen
and True Knives

1 Using four fingers to guide the knife, hold the knife at a 20-degree angle against the whetstone. If you use a three-sided whetstone, start with the coarsest surface and end with the finest.

2 Press down on the blade, keeping it at the 20-degree angle. Gently draw the knife forward across the stone.

3 Gently bring the knife off the stone.

4 Turn the knife over and repeat steps 1–4, using strokes of equal number and pressure.

5 Hold the steel with the hand that you do not write with. Place your arm in front of you at a 60-degree angle.

6 Hold the knife in the hand that you write with. Rest the blade against the inner side of the steel at a 20-degree angle.

7 Keeping the knife at a 20-degree angle, slowly draw the blade along the entire length of the steel.

8 Repeat step 7 several times on each side of the blade until the knife edge is straightened.

9 After you use the steel, carefully wipe the blade to remove any particles of metal.

Mincing

Food that is cut into very small pieces is minced (ˈmin(t)sd). This technique is used most often on items such as shallots and garlic. To dice a food, use a chef's knife to cut julienne and batonnet sticks into ⅛- to ⅝-inch cubes.

Julienne Julienne (jü-lē-ˈen) cuts are ⅛-inch thick matchstick-shaped cuts. Carrots are often cut julienne.

Batonnet Batonnet (ˈbä-tō-ˌnä) cuts are ¼-inch thick matchstick-shaped cuts. Some restaurants serve batonnet-cut fried potatoes.

Brunoise Brunoise (brün-ˈwäz) cuts are ⅛-inch thick cubes often cut from julienne cuts.

 **Reading Check** Describe How do you mince food?

Knife Safety and Care

Now that you know how to select and use knives safely, you need to know how to care for them properly. Sanitize knives after each use and always store knives properly. To keep your knives in good condition, keep them sharp and clean. You will use a sharpening stone to keep your knives sharp. A **whetstone** is a sharpening stone made of either silicon carbide or stone. It may have up to three sides, with grains ranging from coarse to fine. After you have sharpened your knife, a steel is used to keep the blade straight and to smooth out irregularities. This process is called **trueing**. A steel can be used daily to keep knives sharp.

READING CHECK ANSWER First, dice the food, then hold the tip of the knife on the board with a flat hand and use a rocking motion to mince.

Use these knife safety guidelines:

- Always use the correct knife for the task.
- Always use a sharp knife. You will need to use more force with a dull knife.
- Always cut with the blade facing away from your body.
- Always use a cutting board.
- Never let the knife's blade or handle hang over the edge of a cutting board or a table.
- Carry a knife by the handle with the point of the blade straight down at your side. The sharp edge should face behind you.
- Do not try to catch a falling knife.
- When you pass a knife to someone, lay the knife down on the work surface, or carefully hold the dull side of the blade with the handle facing out.
- Never use a knife to open a can or pry something apart.
- Never leave a knife in a sink filled with water. Someone could reach into the sink and be cut.
- Carefully wipe the blade from its dull side so you do not cut yourself.

Knife Sanitation

When you keep your knives clean, you can protect the dish you are making from cross-contamination. The temperature and drying process in dishwashers causes knife handles to dry out and crack. Always wash the knife you have used by hand. Wash knives in hot, soapy water after every cutting task and before you store them. Let knives air dry thoroughly after you wash, rinse, and sanitize them.

Knife Storage

To prevent damage to blades or to people, knives must be stored safely. A convenient way to store knives is in a slotted knife holder. A slotted knife holder should be hung on a wall, not on the side of a table.

A knife kit is a safe, handy storage unit for a large knife collection. Individual slots keep each knife safely in place. Custom-built drawers are another storage option. Special slots hold each knife in place.

 **Reading Check** **Explain** Why is knife sanitation important?

SECTION 10.1 After You Read

Review Key Concepts

1. **Explain** the use of a boning knife.
2. **Categorize** the different types of cuts involved in dicing food.
3. **Demonstrate** proper knife storage.

Practice Culinary Academics

 Science

4. **Procedure** Coat a small piece of cheese with cinnamon. Cut the coated cheese with your knife, and then cut an uncoated piece of cheese with the same knife.

   Analysis What happens to the knife and the clean piece of food? What does this tell you about cross-contamination? Write a paragraph to explain.

   > **NSES F** Develop an understanding of personal and community health.

Mathematics

5. Julio dices a potato into equal-size cubes using a medium dice. If he stacks six of the potato cubes on top of one another, how tall will the stack be?

   Math Concept **Multiplying Fractions** To multiply when a fraction is involved, convert any mixed or whole numbers to improper fractions. Multiply the numerators to get the new numerator, then multiply the denominators to get the new denominator.

   Starting Hint Determine the number of inches in a medium dice. Multiply this number by 6, which you should rewrite as $\frac{6}{1}$. Reduce the result to lowest terms if necessary.

   > **NCTM Number and Operations** Understand the meanings of operations and how they relate to one another.

    Check your answers at this book's Online Learning Center at **glencoe.com**.

READING CHECK ANSWER Because it prevents the danger of cross-contamination.

Smallwares

Reading Guide

 Before You Read

Buddy Up for Success One advantage to sharing your notes with a buddy is that you can fill in gaps in each other's information. You can also compare notes before you start quizzing each other.

Read to Learn

Key Concepts
- **Select** appropriate tools and smallwares for specific tasks.
- **Illustrate** proper smallwares cleaning and sanitation.

Main Idea

Smallwares are hand tools, pots, and pans used for cooking. It is important for a chef to know the proper use and care of smallwares.

Graphic Organizer

Use a series of events chain like the one below to show the five steps to use when you clean and sanitize smallwares. Fill in one step of the process in each rectangle.

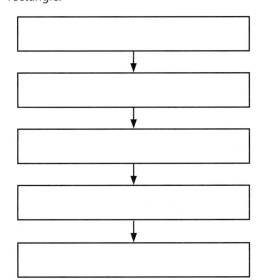

Content Vocabulary
- smallwares
- hand tools
- weight
- volume
- cookware
- heat transfer

Academic Vocabulary
- withstand
- gauge

How many different tools do you use in the kitchen?

 ACADEMIC STANDARDS

 English Language Arts
NCTE 12 Use language to accomplish individual purposes.

 Mathematics
NCTM Number and Operations Understand the meanings of operations and how they relate to one another.

Social Studies
NCSS V B Individuals, Groups, and Institutions Analyze group and institutional influences on people, events, and elements of culture in both historical and contemporary settings.

NCTE National Council of Teachers of English

NCTM National Council of Teachers of Mathematics

NSES National Science Education Standards

NCSS National Council for the Social Studies

 Graphic Organizer
Go to this book's Online Learning Center at **glencoe.com** for a printable graphic organizer.

GRAPHIC ORGANIZER ANSWER 1) Scrape and prerinse; 2) Fill sink with water and detergent; wash thoroughly; 3) Fill second sink with water or use running water to rinse; 4) Fill third sink with water, add sanitizing agent; submerge for 30 seconds; 5) Remove and air dry.

Smallwares Selection

Every restaurant has a supply of hand tools, pots, and pans used for cooking called **smallwares**. Stainless steel and wooden hand tools, aluminum pots, and copper-bottomed pans are some smallwares.

Handheld items used to cook, serve, and prepare food are known as **hand tools**. Hand tools are often used to cut and prepare fruit and vegetables. Hand tools include slicers, peelers, corers, cutters, and melon ballers. The majority of hand tools are made of stainless steel, aluminum, or plastic.

Choose Appropriate Tools

The tools in a professional kitchen may look similar to home tools. However, most home kitchen tools cannot **withstand**, or hold up to, the heavy use of a foodservice kitchen.

NSF International, previously known as the National Sanitation Foundation, tests tools for construction, comfort, and safety:

- Tools, equipment, and their coatings must be nontoxic and should not affect the taste, odor, or color of food.
- Surfaces that come into contact with food must be smooth.
- Tools and equipment must be easily cleaned.
- External corners and angles must be smooth and sealed.
- Internal corners and edges must be smooth and rounded.
- Waste must be easily removed from tools, equipment, and their coatings.
- Coatings and exposed surfaces must resist chipping and cracking.

> ### ☞ Small Bites ☜
>
> **Aluminum Warnings** Be careful not to use stainless steel utensils with aluminum cookware. Stainless steel utensils can scrape off a thin layer of aluminum and cause certain foods to become discolored. Tomatoes and other foods that are high in acid will chemically react with the aluminum.

Measuring Equipment

Accurate volume measures are essential to the success of recipes. They also help control portion size and costs.

Measurements are usually needed for an item's weight or volume. **Weight** is the heaviness of a substance, while **volume** is the space occupied by a substance.

Choose Cookware

Cookware plays an essential role in the professional kitchen. **Cookware** in any well-equipped kitchen includes pots, pans, and baking dishes. Pots and pans may be made of stainless steel, aluminum, copper, cast iron, or ceramics.

Heat Transfer

When you select cookware, you must consider **heat transfer**. Heat transfer is a measure of how efficiently heat passes from one object to another. The **gauge**, or type and thickness of the material, determines how well it transfers heat.

Copper has a high heat transfer rating. However, it is expensive and difficult to clean. That is why many professional kitchens choose to use aluminum-covered or stainless steel-covered pots and pans. Some kitchens also use cookware with copper-lined bottoms or cast-iron cookware.

Aluminum Aluminum is a common metal used for commercial cookware because it is lightweight, inexpensive, and rust free. It is also fairly heat efficient. However, aluminum may react chemically with some foods.

Stainless Steel Stainless steel is virtually rust free. However, it is a poor and uneven heat conductor. Stainless steel pots often have an added layer of aluminum or copper on the bottom for better heat transfer.

Reading Check Explain Why are the bottoms of stainless steel pots and pans usually lined with another type of metal?

READING CHECK ANSWER Stainless steel is a poor and uneven heat conductor, so stainless steel pots often are lined for better heat transfer.

Vegetable Peeler A vegetable peeler is commonly used to shave the skin of fruits and vegetables. It can also be used to make delicate garnishes, such as carrot curls and chocolate curls.

Apple/Fruit Corers Push the corer through the center of the fruit so that the core comes out in one long, round piece. Small corers can be used on fruits such as apples and pears, while large corers are used on fruits such as pineapples and grapefruits.

Tomato Corer A tomato corer is used to core and remove tomato stems. It can also remove vegetable markings, apple seeds, and potato eyes.

Kitchen Shears Kitchen shears are used to tackle a variety of cutting chores, such as snipping string and butcher's twine, trimming artichoke leaves, and dividing taffy.

Cutting Board Cutting boards are made from wood, plastic, or composite materials. They should have a smooth surface free of any deep scratches, nicks, gouges, or scars.

Cheese Slicer A cheese slicer is used to cut slices from hard or semihard cheeses.

Butter Curler The surfaces of a butter curler produce garnishes ranging from curls to grooves to marble-sized balls. Make sure the butter is cold and the blade has been warmed in hot water.

Egg Slicer An egg slicer works by placing a peeled, hard-cooked egg in the hollow of the slicer. Push the tool down and the wires will slice the egg or cut it into wedges. There are two kinds of egg slicers. One makes round shapes and the other makes wedge shapes.

Pizza Cutter A pizza cutter cleanly slices baked pizza into serving pieces.

Zester A zester is used to remove tiny strips from the outer surface of citrus peels, which add visual interest and flavor to foods. It can also be used on vegetables, such as carrots and radishes, to add shavings to salads. Zesters work best on fresh, firm fruits and vegetables.

Melon Baller A melon baller or Parisienne scoop is used to scoop out smooth balls from many foods, such as cheese, butter, and melons. The scoops range in size and shape, and sometimes have scalloped edges.

Whisks Balloon whisks are light and bouncy with a rounded end. They are ideal for beating egg whites or light batters. Rigid whisks are longer and have heavier, thicker wires. Rigid whisks can mix thick sauces and batters.

Solid, Perforated, and Slotted Spoons

Spoons are used to scoop, skim, mix, and serve. Perforated and slotted spoons are used to lift and drain foods from the liquid in which the food cooks.

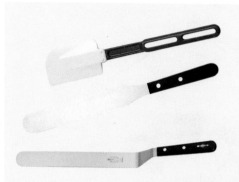

Rubber, Straight, and Offset Spatulas

A rubber spatula has a broad, flexible rubber or plastic tip on a long handle. It is used to scrape food from the inside of bowls and pans, or fold in whipped cream or egg whites. A straight spatula, or palette knife, has a long, flexible blade with a rounded end. It is used to scrape bowls and spread icing on cakes. An offset spatula, or turner, has a broad, bent stainless steel blade. It is used to lift and turn foods such as pancakes.

Chef's Fork A chef's fork, also known as a braising fork, is used to lift and turn large cuts of meats and other items. It is also used to hold heavy pieces of food during carving.

Tongs Tongs are spring-action or scissor-type tools used to pick up items such as meats, vegetables, or ice cubes.

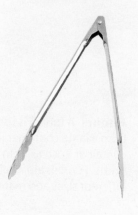

Skimmer A skimmer has a flat, perforated surface to remove food from stocks and soups. It is also used to skim impurities from the tops of liquids.

Meat Tenderizer Each side of a meat tenderizer has different-size tooth-like points that are made of aluminum or steel. These points tenderize meat by breaking up and bruising muscle fibers.

Strainers Strainers have a cup-shaped body made of perforated mesh. The holes range from extra-fine to coarse. Strainers can be used to drain pasta, vegetables, and stocks after cooking.

Chinois or China Cap A chinois (shēn-ˈwäz), or China cap, is a cone-shaped metal strainer used for straining sauces and stocks. A pestle (ˈpe-səl), or a round, bat-like instrument, can be used to press very soft food through the China cap.

Colander A colander is a large, perforated bowl used to rapidly drain water from cooked foods. It is also used to rinse food items before cooking.

Food Mill A food mill is a bowl-like container with disks used to purée and strain food. Disks are available in varying degrees of coarseness or fineness.

Box Grater Four-sided graters are the most common. Each side has different-size holes that determine the size of the grated food pieces, from slices to shreds to crumbs.

Funnel A funnel is used to pour liquid from a large container into a smaller container, such as from a pot into a bottle. Funnels are available in several different sizes and materials.

Pie Dividers Pie dividers are circular tools that contain six openings, each the size of a piece of pie. Pressing the tool over the pie marks the dish into the designated number of slices.

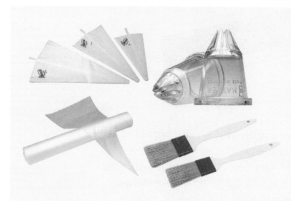

Pastry Tools Pastry bags are filled with icing or other soft foods for hand-squeezed pastry decorating and assembly. They can be made of nylon, plastic-lined cotton, or disposable paper. Pastry tips fit onto the pastry bags and shape the flow of food as it is squeezed out of the bag. A pastry brush is used to brush liquid onto dough before, during, or just after baking.

Rolling Pins A rolling pin is used to stretch and roll dough. Most rolling pins are made of hardwood, but marble may also be used. Rolling pins with grooves that add patterns or fancy designs to dough are also available. French rolling pins do not have handles.

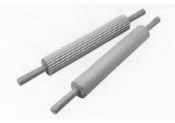

Bench Scraper This hand-held rectangular tool has a stainless steel blade and a sturdy handle. It is used to scrape surfaces and cut dough into equal pieces.

Food Molds Food molds can turn foods such as gelatins, custards, and puddings into eye-catching shapes. Food in liquid form is poured into the mold and allowed to set.

Vegetable Brush With their short, tough bristles, vegetable brushes are used to clean dirt off of vegetables.

Measuring Equipment

Portion Scale A portion scale is a type of spring scale used to determine the weight of an ingredient or portion of food. It can be reset to zero so that you can measure individual ingredients.

Electronic Scale An electronic, or digital, scale weighs an item when it is placed on its tray. The weight is displayed in numbers on a digital readout rather than by a needle. This readout is more accurate than a portion scale.

Balance Scale A balance scale is used to measure most baking ingredients. The ingredients being weighed are placed on one side while weights are placed on the other side. When the two sides are balanced, the ingredients weigh the same as the weights.

Volume Measures Volume is measured in 8-, 16-, 32-, 64-, and 128-ounce quantities. Volume measures are made of metal, which can withstand heavy use.

Liquid Measures Liquid measures also measure volume, and come in 1 cup, 1 pint, and 1-, 2-, and 4-quart sizes. The lip or spout of the measure helps prevent spills and makes pouring easier.

Measuring Spoons Measuring spoons are available in sets and usually include measurements of ¼, ½, 1 teaspoon, and 1 tablespoon for volume. Stainless steel is recommended because it is less likely to warp or change shape.

Ladle A ladle is used to portion liquids such as sauces and soups. Its long handle enables you to reach to the bottom of a deep pot or pan. The capacity, ranging from 1 to 16 ounces, is marked on the handle.

Stockpot A stockpot has straight sides and is taller than it is wide. A stockpot is used to cook large quantities of liquid on the range, such as stocks or soups. Some stockpots have a spigot at the bottom so that liquid can be drained off without lifting the pot.

Saucepan A saucepan has a long handle and straight sides. It is primarily used for heating and cooking food in liquid. Saucepans come in many sizes.

Saucepot The saucepot is similar in shape to a stockpot, only not as deep. The saucepot is used for rangetop cooking.

Sauté Pans There are two types of sauté pans: a pan with straight sides and a pan with sloped sides. Both are used to sauté and fry foods. The sloped pan allows the chef to flip items without using a spatula.

Wok A wok is useful for fast rangetop cooking. The wok's height and sloped sides are well suited for tossing ingredients, an essential step in stir-frying. Once food has been cooked, it can be pushed to the side of the pan, leaving the hot center free for new ingredients.

Cast-Iron Skillet A cast-iron skillet is a heavy pan that can withstand high heat. It is useful for frying and sautéing a variety of items when steady, even heat is desired.

Hotel Pans The cooked foods in a steam table are held in hotel pans. Hotel pans are often used to store refrigerated food and hold casseroles during baking. They come in many different sizes.

Roasting Pan A roasting pan is used to roast various types of meat and poultry. A lift-out rack that fits in the bottom of the pan allows fat and juices to drain off the food.

Sheet Pan Sheet pans come in half and full sizes. They can be used to bake biscuits, cookies, sheet cakes, rolls, and meats such as bacon and sausage.

Stainless Steel Mixing Bowls A well-equipped kitchen has several different-size stainless steel mixing bowls. These are used to combine, mix, and whip ingredients.

Springform Pan A springform pan is used to bake soft, sticky mixes, such as cheesecake. It has an insert that rests in the bottom of the pan, and the sides are closed with clasps. Opening the clasps gently releases the cake.

Pie Pan Traditional pies are baked in pie pans. Deep pie pans are slightly wider to accommodate deep-dish fruit and meat pies.

Loaf Pan A loaf pan, also known as a bread pan, is used to bake loaf-shaped foods, such as pound cake, meat loaf, and some breads.

Muffin Pan Different kinds of muffins and cupcakes can be baked in muffin pans. Muffin pans come in various sizes.

Tart Pan A tart pan is used to bake items with delicate crusts, such as tarts and quiches. The sizes range from 4.5 to 12.5 inches in diameter, and from 0.75 to 1.25 inches high. It has either fluted or smooth sides.

Tube Pan An aluminum tube pan is used to bake tube-shaped desserts, such as angel food cake. It may have a removable bottom.

Cleaning and Sanitation

You must thoroughly clean and sanitize tools and utensils to destroy bacteria.

Follow these steps to hand-wash and sanitize smallwares in a three-compartment sink:

1. Scrape and prerinse smallwares.

2. Fill the first sink with 110°F (43°C) water and detergent. Wash smallware thoroughly with a brush. Drain and refill the water as needed.

3. Fill the second sink with water at about 110°F (43°C) or use running water with an overflow. Rinse the smallwares to remove all traces of detergent.

4. Fill the third sink with 171°F (77°C) water. Some health codes require foodservice facilities to use 180°F (82°C) water. Sanitizers require specific temperature water to work correctly. Add the sanitizing agent in the amount and temperature of water that is listed on the container. Submerge smallwares for about 30 seconds.

5. Remove and air dry smallwares in a clean area. Do not dry smallwares with a towel. Towel drying can recontaminate them by spreading bacteria.

 Reading Check **Summarize** Explain how to sanitize smallwares.

SECTION 10.2 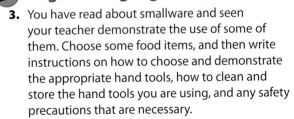 After You Read

Review Key Concepts

1. **Explain** how to select appropriate kitchen tools.
2. **Compare** aluminum and stainless steel cookware.

Practice Culinary Academics

English Language Arts

3. You have read about smallware and seen your teacher demonstrate the use of some of them. Choose some food items, and then write instructions on how to choose and demonstrate the appropriate hand tools, how to clean and store the hand tools you are using, and any safety precautions that are necessary.

> **NCTE 12** Use language to accomplish individual purposes.

Social Studies

4. Research the activities of NSF International. Choose one of its programs and write a short report describing the activities of that program. What does that program do and how does it affect the foodservice industry?

> **NCSS V B Individuals, Groups, and Institutions** Analyze group and institutional influences on people, events, and elements of culture in both historical and contemporary settings.

Mathematics

5. Imagine that you own a sandwich shop. You need slices of Cheddar cheese to make sandwiches for your customers. A 1-pound block of cheddar cheese from your supplier is 6 inches long. If you use a cheese slicer to cut the entire block into equal ³⁄₁₆-inch slices, how many slices of cheese will you have?

Math Concept **Dividing Fractions** To divide when a fraction is involved, convert any mixed or whole numbers to improper fractions. An improper fraction has a numerator that is equal to or larger than its denominator. Multiply the first fraction by the reciprocal of the second fraction. Reduce to lowest terms.

Starting Hint You must divide 6 inches (or $\frac{6}{1}$) by ³⁄₁₆ inch. Replace the second fraction with its reciprocal by reversing the numerator and denominator: $\frac{16}{3}$. Multiply the two fractions to find the number of Cheddar cheese slices.

> **NCTM Number and Operations** Understand the meanings of operations and how they relate to one another.

 Check your answers at this book's Online Learning Center at **glencoe.com**.

READING CHECK ANSWER Fill a sink with 171–180°F (77–82°C) water, add sanitizing agent, and submerge for 30 seconds, or use a chemical sanitizer in the proper concentration and recommended water temperature.

Review and Applications

Chapter Summary

Chefs use many types of knives to prepare food. The parts of a knife are the blade, tang, handle, rivet, and bolster. Basic cutting techniques include slicing, dicing, and mincing. When using a knife, be sure to use the correct type of knife. Make sure the knife you use is sharp. After using the knife, wash, rinse, and sanitize it, then put it away. Smallwares include hand tools, cookware, and measuring tools. Smallwares must be made of nontoxic materials, be easily cleaned, and be resistant to chipping and cracking. Properly clean and sanitize smallwares after each use.

Content and Academic Vocabulary Review

1. Write your own definition for each content and academic vocabulary term.

Content Vocabulary

- stainless steel (p. 252)
- tang (p. 252)
- rivet (p. 252)
- bolster (p. 253)
- serrated (p. 254)
- pare (p. 254)
- chiffonade (p. 255)
- rondelle (p. 255)
- diagonal (p. 255)
- roll cut (p. 255)
- julienne (p. 259)
- batonnet (p. 259)
- brunoise (p. 259)

- whetstone (p. 259)
- trueing (p. 259)
- smallwares (p. 262)
- hand tools (p. 262)
- weight (p. 262)
- volume (p. 262)
- cookware (p. 262)
- heat transfer (p. 262)

Academic Vocabulary

- transfer (p. 252)
- uniform (p. 255)
- withstand (p. 262)
- gauge (p. 262)

Review Key Concepts

2. **Categorize** knives by their specific tasks.
3. **Demonstrate** basic knife skills.
4. **Explain** proper knife safety and storage.
5. **Select** appropriate tools and smallwares for specific tasks.
6. **Illustrate** proper smallwares cleaning and sanitation.

Critical Thinking

7. **Imagine** that you work for a catering company. You are creating vegetable appetizers for a party. Which knives will you need and why?
8. **Analyze** measuring techniques. Why might you use a portion scale to measure ingredients for a cake?
9. **Evaluate** knife quality. If you have a limited budget but want to purchase some quality knives, which two knives would you purchase first? Why?
10. **Imagine** that a coworker at a restaurant needs to scald milk for a recipe. There is an aluminum pot and a stainless steel pot available. Which should he use, and why?

Review and Applications

Academic Skills

English Language Arts

11. Create a Radio Ad Choose one piece of equipment from this chapter, either a knife or smallwares. Create a radio script to advertise the knife or smallwares you chose. The script should contain dialogue that mentions the most useful features of your equipment. Use language that is likely to sell the product to a professional chef.

> **NCTE 12** Use language to accomplish individual purposes.

Science

12. Heat Conduction The way that metal conducts heat is very important to how well it cooks food.

Procedure Choose a few pans made out of different types of metals and heat the same food item in each pan. Use a thermometer to measure how quickly the food item heats in each pan.

Analysis Note your observations and then make conclusions about the heat conductivity of each material. Compare your results with the class.

> **NSES B** Develop an understanding of the structure and properties of matter.

Mathematics

13. Use a Balance Scale Paris recently purchased two large, identical-weight blocks of cheese, but has since discarded the wrapper that shows how much they weigh. She has also used exactly one-third of one of the blocks. If she places the full block of cheese on the left side of a balance scale, and the partial (two-thirds) block of cheese on the right side along with a 2-pound weight, causing the scale to be in balance, how much does the full block weigh?

Math Concept **Solving Equations with Like Terms** In an algebraic equation, like terms are those that contain the same variable (for example, $2x$ and $3x$). Simplify equations with like terms by using addition or subtraction to combine all like terms.

Starting Hint Use x to represent the weight of a full block of cheese. Write an algebraic equation with the contents of the left side of the balance scale on the left side of the equation, and the contents of the right side of the balance scale on the right side of the equation. Combine all terms containing x and solve for x.

> **NCTM Algebra** Represent and analyze mathematical situations and structures using algebraic symbols.

Certification Prep

Sharpen your test-taking skills to improve your kitchen certification program score.

Directions Read the questions. Then, read the answer choices and choose the best possible answer for each.

14. What angle should you use to sharpen a chef's knife?

- **a.** 20 degrees
- **b.** 25 degrees
- **c.** 60 degrees
- **d.** 90 degrees

15. What utensil should you use to serve spaghetti from a steam table?

- **a.** offset spatula
- **b.** tongs
- **c.** ladle
- **d.** spoon with holes

Test-Taking Tip

In a multiple-choice test, the answers should be specific and precise. Read the questions first, and then read all the answer choices before you choose. Eliminate answers that you know are incorrect.

Review and Applications

Real-World Skills and Applications

Self-Management Skills

16. Plan Ahead Imagine that you have been asked to prepare a three-course meal that includes a garden salad, beef stew, and strawberry shortcake. Find recipes for these dishes. Using the recipes, determine which types of knives and pieces of smallwares you will need to prepare the dishes.

Interpersonal and Collaborative Skills

17. Make Purchasing Decisions Divide into groups of two or three as directed by your teacher. Imagine that you are chefs for a restaurant and you must purchase new knives for the kitchen. Research knives together and come to a decision about which will be the best purchase for your restaurant. Why did you choose the knives you did?

Technology Applications

18. Make a Chart Use a word processing or desktop publishing program to make a chart to illustrate one of the following: types of knives, types of measuring equipment, or types of cookware. Include illustrations of each piece of equipment along with a short description of the item and its uses. Share your chart.

Financial Literacy

19. Sharpen Knives Sharpening knives regularly can help extend the life of your knives. Assume that a good knife-sharpening kit including a whetstone costs $50. A knife-sharpening service charges you $15 to sharpen your knives. If you sharpen your knives yourself once per week, how many times will you need to sharpen your knives before the knife-sharpening kit is the more cost-effective choice?

Culinary Lab

Use the culinary skills you have learned in this chapter.

Choose Knives and Smallwares

20. Choose Equipment for a Restaurant In this lab, you will determine the appropriate equipment to be purchased for a small restaurant. You will consider various factors and then make your choice.

A. Create your menu. Create a basic menu for a sandwich shop that serves simple lunches and dinners.

B. Consider your equipment. Consider the equipment you would need for your menu. You do not have much kitchen space, so try to determine which knives and smallwares could be used for more than one task.

C. Consider your preparation needs. Decide whether you will prepare most of your food or if you will have some food prepared and delivered.

D. List your choices. Make your final determination of which knives and smallwares you will choose for the sandwich shop and make a list of your choices.

E. Support your choices. Discuss your choices with the class. Answer the following questions: 1) Why do you believe you need the equipment you chose? 2) What equipment would you need to care for your knives and smallwares?

Create Your Evaluation

After the class discussion, write down any revisions you would make to your list. Why did you choose the revisions you did? Was it because of something a classmate said? Describe what took place in the discussion that made you change your mind. Also describe anything that took place in the discussion that you disagreed with and explain why you continue to disagree.

CHAPTER 11

Culinary Nutrition

SECTIONS

11.1 Nutrition Basics

11.2 Meal Planning Guidelines

11.3 Keep Food Nutritious

WRITING ACTIVITY

Write Using Details

Use sense detail to help your reader see, hear, taste, and touch your subject. Write a paragraph about a meal that tastes good, but is also healthful. Use adjectives that describe the food's look, taste, and texture.

Writing Tips

1 Start by writing down adjectives that you can use to describe your subject.

2 Do not get too caught up in the details.

3 Do not use too many adjectives. This will confuse the reader.

WRITING ACTIVITY ANSWER Paragraphs should convey sensory details, but be clear. General paragraph structure should be followed.

EXPLORE THE PHOTO ANSWER By understanding the nutritional content of the menu, you can help diners choose a healthful meal.

EXPLORE THE PHOTO

A nutritious meal contains a variety of nutrients to keep your body functioning properly. *How could you help create a nutritious menu?*

278

Nutrition Basics

Discover the building blocks of good nutrition.

Reading Guide

 Before You Read

Think of an Example Look over the Key Concepts for this section. Think of an example of how or when you could use one of the skills from the Key Concepts. Thinking of how you might apply a skill can help motivate your learning by showing you why the skill is important.

Read to Learn

Key Concepts
- **Summarize** the six categories of nutrients.
- **List** the types and uses of food additives.

Main Idea
Foodservice employees must understand the basics of nutrition to help them create healthful menus or make healthful ordering suggestions to diners.

Content Vocabulary
- nutrient
- carbohydrate
- legume
- glucose
- fiber
- protein
- amino acid
- complete protein
- incomplete protein
- fat
- hydrogenation
- trans fatty acid
- cholesterol
- lipoprotein
- cardiovascular
- saturated fat
- monounsaturated fat
- polyunsaturated fat
- vitamin
- minerals
- additive

Academic Vocabulary
- role
- regulate

ACADEMIC STANDARDS

 English Language Arts
NCTE 6 Apply knowledge of language structure and conventions to discuss texts.

 Mathematics
NCTM Measurement
Understand measurable attributes of objects and the units, systems, and processes of measurement.

 Science
NSES B Develop an understanding of the structure and properties of matter.

NSES B Develop an understanding of chemical reactions.

NCTE National Council of Teachers of English

NCTM National Council of Teachers of Mathematics

NSES National Science Education Standards

NCSS National Council for the Social Studies

Graphic Organizer

As you read, use a fishbone like the one below to list the six categories of nutrients.

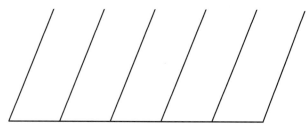

Nutrients

 Graphic Organizer Go to this book's Online Learning Center at **glencoe.com** for a printable graphic organizer.

GRAPHIC ORGANIZER ANSWER Carbohydrates, proteins, fats, vitamins, minerals, and water.

The Nutrients

Imagine that your cafeteria does not offer enough healthful choices on its menu. How will you make suggestions? You must first understand the basics of nutrition. You can then make more healthful suggestions.

The human body needs food for growth and to maintain life. An important factor in meeting this need is a food's nutrient content. A **nutrient** is a chemical compound that helps the body to carry out its functions. There are more than 40 nutrients in food. They are grouped into six categories: carbohydrates, proteins, fats, vitamins, minerals, and water.

Carbohydrates

A **carbohydrate** is the nutrient that is the body's main source of energy. Simple carbohydrates, or sugars, include both natural sugars and refined sugars. Natural sugars are part of many foods like fruits, vegetables, and milk. Foods with natural sugars also have other impor-

tant nutrients. Refined sugars are processed. These sugars provide little more than calories.

Complex carbohydrates are starches, such as pasta, grains, cereals, and legumes. A **legume** is the seeds and pods from certain plants. Beans, lentils, and peas are examples of legumes. Foods that are high in complex carbohydrates contain many other nutrients your body needs, such as vitamins and minerals. Your body breaks down simple and complex carbohydrates into a usable energy source known as **glucose**. Glucose gives your body the energy it needs to work properly.

Fiber

A unique form of a complex carbohydrate that does not provide energy is **fiber**. There are two types of fiber. Soluble fiber dissolves in water. Insoluble fiber absorbs water. Fiber helps the body's digestive system and waste elimination system function. Its main advantage is that it cannot be digested. As it passes through the body, fiber helps remove wastes.

◄ **Nutrient Variety**
Create dishes with a wide variety of nutrients. *Do you see sources of carbohydrates present in this salad?*

PHOTO CAPTION ANSWER There are carbohydrates and fiber present in the vegetables.

Simple Sugars Refined sugars are simple carbohydrates. *What is the difference between natural sugar and refined sugar?*

Insoluble fiber is found in the outer coating of whole grains. Soluble fiber is found in foods such as oat bran and grains. Soluble fiber has been linked with the prevention of heart disease and some cancers.

Proteins

Protein is a nutrient that builds, maintains, and repairs body tissues. It is essential for healthy muscles, skin, bones, eyes, and hair. It also plays an important role in fighting disease. If a person does not eat enough carbohydrate and fat, the body will use protein for energy.

Through digestion, protein is broken down into small units that can be combined in certain ways to produce complete proteins. These units are called **amino acids**. There are 22 amino acids. Some amino acids can be created by the body, while others cannot and must be gotten from food.

Animal foods, such as fish, meats, poultry, eggs, milk and milk products, provide all of the essential amino acids. A protein source that provides all of the amino acids is called a **complete protein**. Most plant foods lack some of the essential amino acids. A protein source that does not provide all of the amino acids is called an **incomplete protein**. However, by combining nuts or dry beans and grains, a person can eat all of the essential amino acids. This is especially important for those who do not eat animal products.

PHOTO CAPTION ANSWER Natural sugars are found within foods, such as fruits, vegetables, and milk. Refined sugars are processed and are used primarily as sweeteners.

Fats and Cholesterol

Fat and cholesterol play an essential **role**, or function performed, in keeping the body healthy. **Fat** regulates bodily functions and helps carry some vitamins through the system. It is a source of stored energy and a cushion for body organs. Fat adds flavor to foods. Popular types of cooking fat are lard and shortening, which are 100% fat. Butter and margarine are about 80% fat. There is strong evidence that shows that a diet higher than 30% in fat and cholesterol can put you at risk for heart disease and cancer.

Many fats, such as those in margarine and shortening, have gone through a hydrogenation process. **Hydrogenation** (hī-ˌdrä-jə-ˈnā-shən) is a process in which hydrogen is added under pressure to polyunsaturated fats, such as soybean oil. Hydrogenation changes liquid oil into a solid fat. An unsaturated fat that goes through the hydrogenation process becomes a **trans fatty acid**, or trans fat. Stick margarine and vegetable shortening are examples of hydrogenated fat.

Cholesterol

Cholesterol (kə-ˈles-tə-ˌrōl) is a fatlike substance that is found in all body cells and in all animal foods, such as meat, egg yolks, and dairy products. The body makes its own cholesterol to produce cell membranes, hormones, vitamin D, and bile acids, which help digest fats. Some cholesterol circulates through the bloodstream in a chemical package called a **lipoprotein** (ˌlī-pə-ˈprō-ˌtēn). There are two types of lipoproteins. They are low-density lipoproteins (LDL) and high-density lipoproteins (HDL).

Too much LDL, or bad cholesterol, can contribute to **cardiovascular** (ˌkär-dē-ō-ˈvas-kyə-lər), or heart-related, problems. LDL can build up on artery walls. This buildup slows or prevents the flow of blood to the heart and other vital organs. Higher HDL, or good cholesterol, helps lower the amount of total cholesterol in the blood. Make wise food choices to help reduce the amount of harmful cholesterol in the blood.

SCIENCE À LA CARTE ANSWER The cooking oil, peanut butter, and mayonnaise will all make the paper turn transparent. They all contain fat. The apple and flour do not have fat.

Science à la Carte

What Is Fat?
Fat is a compound that contains a chain of carbon and hydrogen atoms. All carbon atoms have four bonds, or links, to other atoms. Some of the bonds are single bonds and some are double bonds. Single bonds are formed when two atoms share one pair of electrons. Double bonds are formed when hydrogen bonds are missing. Without hydrogen, carbon cannot form single bonds. To make up for a missing hydrogen atom, a carbon atom will form a double bond with another carbon atom.

Fats are characterized by their chemical structure. All saturated fats have single bonds. Unsaturated fats are classified by the number of double bonds that form. For example, mono-unsaturated fat is missing two hydrogen atoms, and so has one double bond. Polyunsaturated fat has more than one double bond.

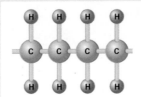

Saturated Fat
(Single Bonding)

Unsaturated Fat
(Double Bonding)

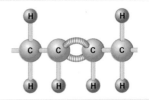

Procedure
Gather a brown paper lunch bag, cooking oil, an apple, peanut butter, mayonnaise, and flour. Cut the lunch bag into five sections. Label each section with the name of one of the ingredients listed and place it on a table or countertop. Use your finger to rub a small amount of cooking oil on one of the bag sections. Repeat the process with each of the other ingredients listed. When you are finished, lift each section of paper up to a light source. Which foods caused the paper to become transparent?

Analysis
Make a chart of each substance you test and record your observations. Which substances appear to contain fat? Which substances do not?

NSES B Develop an understanding of the structure and properties of matter.

Saturated Fats

A fat that tends to increase the amount of cholesterol in the blood and is solid at room temperature is called a **saturated** ('sa-chə-ˌrāt-əd) **fat**. Saturated fats can be found in lard, butter, whole-milk products, the visible fat on meat, and tropical (coconut, palm, and palm kernel) oils. Saturated fats have been linked to an increased risk of heart disease and other cardiovascular problems. Studies show that trans fatty acids may have the same, or even worse, effect on cholesterol as saturated fats.

Monounsaturated Fats

A **monounsaturated** (ˌmä-nō-ˌən-'sa-chə-ˌrā-təd) **fat** is usually liquid at room temperature. Olive oil and peanut oil are both examples of monounsaturated fat. Unsaturated fats are considered more healthful than saturated fats because they generally do not raise cholesterol levels. Monounsaturated fats are also present in foods such as avocados. Foods that contain monounsaturated fat can help lower the total cholesterol in your body as well as lower the risk of heart disease.

▼ FIGURE 11.1 Water-Soluble Vitamins

Daily Vitamins Water-soluble vitamins must be eaten every day. *What water-soluble vitamins can be found in eggs?*

Vitamin	Function in the Body	Food Sources
Thiamin ('thī-ə-mən) **(Vitamin B$_1$)**	• Helps use carbohydrates for energy • Promotes normal appetites	Dry beans; pork and other meats; whole and fortified grains
Riboflavin (ˌrī-bə-'flā-vən) **(Vitamin B$_2$)**	• Keeps skin and eyes healthy • Helps use carbohydrates, fats, and proteins for energy	Dairy products; meat, poultry, and fish; whole and fortified grains; eggs
Niacin ('nī-ə-sən) **(Vitamin B$_3$)**	• Keeps skin and nervous system healthy • Enables normal digestion • Helps use nutrients for energy	Meat, poultry, and fish; liver; shellfish; dry beans; nuts; whole and fortified grains
Vitamin B$_6$	• Assists in building red blood cells • Helps use carbohydrates and proteins • Keeps nervous system healthy	Meat, poultry, and fish; liver; shellfish; dry beans; potatoes; whole grains; some fruits and vegetables
Vitamin B$_{12}$	• Assists in building red blood cells • Keeps nervous system healthy • Helps use carbohydrates, fats, and proteins	Eggs; meat, poultry, and fish; dairy products; shellfish; some fortified foods
Folate ('fō-ˌlāt) **(Folic Acid)**	• Helps prevent birth defects • Assists in building red blood cells • Helps use proteins	Dark green, leafy vegetables; dry beans; orange juice; seeds; whole and fortified grains; fruits
Vitamin C (Ascorbic (ə-'skȯr-bik) **Acid)**	• Strengthens immune system • Keeps teeth, gums, blood vessels, and bones healthy • Helps heal wounds and absorb iron	Citrus fruits such as oranges and grapefruits; kiwi; cabbage; strawberries; broccoli; tomatoes; cantaloupes; green peppers; potatoes
Biotin ('bī-ə-tən)	• Helps use carbohydrates, fats, and proteins	Dark green, leafy vegetables; liver; egg yolks; whole grains
Pantothenic (ˌpan-tə-'the-nik) **Acid**	• Helps use carbohydrates, fats, and proteins for energy • Promotes growth and development • Helps produce cholesterol	Dry beans; meat, poultry, and fish; eggs; milk; whole grains; fruits and vegetables

FIGURE CAPTION ANSWER Riboflavin, vitamin B$_{12}$, biotin, and pantothenic acid can be found in eggs.

FIGURE 11.2 Fat-Soluble Vitamins

Stored Vitamins Fat-soluble vitamins are stored in fat cells in the body. *What fat-soluble vitamins can be found in dark green, leafy vegetables?*

Vitamin	Function in the Body	Food Sources
Vitamin A	• Keeps skin and hair healthy and strengthens immune system • Protects eyes and enables night vision	Dark green, leafy vegetables such as spinach; yellow-orange fruits and vegetables such as carrots, pumpkin, and apricots; dairy products; liver; egg yolks
Vitamin D	• Helps body absorb and regulate calcium and phosphorus for strong bones, teeth, and muscles	Fortified milk; fatty fish such as salmon, liver, egg yolks; exposure to sunlight causes the body to produce vitamin D
Vitamin E	• Protects other nutrients • Helps create muscles and red blood cells	Dark green, leafy vegetables such as spinach; vegetable oils; nuts; seeds; whole grains; wheat germ
Vitamin K	• Assists in blood clotting	Egg yolks; dark green, leafy vegetables such as spinach; liver; wheat germ and wheat bran

FIGURE 11.3 Major Minerals

Mineral Power Major minerals help the body to build strong bones and teeth, and maintain blood pressure. *What major minerals can be found in dairy products?*

Mineral	Function in the Body	Food Sources
Calcium	• Builds and renews bones and teeth • Needed for muscle contraction • Assists in blood clotting • Regulates nervous system and other processes	Dairy products; dry beans; fortified juices and cereals; dark green, leafy vegetables such as kale; turnips; canned sardines and salmon
Magnesium (mag-ˈnē-zē-əm)	• Builds and renews bones • Helps nervous system and muscles work	Whole grains; dry beans; dark green, leafy vegetables; nuts; seeds; fish; shellfish
Phosphorus (ˈfäs-f(ə-)rəs)	• Builds and renews bones and teeth • Helps use nutrients for energy	Dairy products; nuts; dry beans; whole grains; meat, poultry, and fish; egg yolks
Potassium (pə-ˈta-sē-əm)	• Helps maintain blood pressure and heartbeat • Maintains fluid balance in body	Fruits such as bananas, oranges, and cantaloupes; meat, poultry, and fish; dry beans; vegetables; dairy products
Sodium	• Helps regulate blood pressure • Maintains fluid balance in body	Salt; foods that contain salt; soy sauce; MSG

FIGURE CAPTION ANSWER Vitamins A, E, and K can be found in dark green, leafy vegetables.

FIGURE CAPTION ANSWER Calcium, phosphorus, and potassium can be found in dairy products.

FIGURE 11.4 **Trace Minerals**

Minor Minerals Trace minerals help the body with functions like using energy and healing wounds. *What trace minerals can be found in fish and shellfish?*

Mineral	Function in the Body	Food Sources
Chloride ('klȯr-ˌīd)	• Works with sodium to balance fluids • Helps nerve transmittal	Salt; foods that contain salt; soy sauce; meats; milk
Iron	• Helps cells use oxygen • Helps the blood carry oxygen	Meat, fish; shellfish; dry beans; egg yolks; dried fruit; whole and fortified grains; dark green, leafy vegetables
Iodine	• Helps use energy	Iodized salt; saltwater fish; shellfish; breads
Zinc	• Assists in growth and maintenance of tissues • Helps heal wounds and form blood • Helps use carbohydrates, fats, and proteins • Affects taste and smell	Whole grains; poultry, fish; shellfish products; legumes; dairy products; eggs
Copper	• Assists iron in building red blood cells • Keeps nervous system, bones, and blood vessels healthy	Meat, fish; shellfish; whole grains; nuts; seeds; dry beans
Fluoride ('flȯr-īd)	• Strengthens teeth and prevents decay	Fish; shellfish; fluoride is often added to drinking water
Selenium (sə-'lē-nē-əm)	• Helps heart function normally	Fish; shellfish; eggs; liver; whole grains

Polyunsaturated Fats

A **polyunsaturated** (ˌpä-lē-ˌən-'sa-chə-ˌrā-təd) **fat** is also usually liquid at room temperature. Corn oil, sunflower oil, and soybean oil are all polyunsaturated fats. Nuts, seeds, and fish also contain some polyunsaturated fats.

Vitamins

A **vitamin** is a substance that helps **regulate**, or control, many bodily functions. Vitamins are grouped by how they function with a letter. For example, there are many different types of B vitamins. Vitamins also help other nutrients to do their jobs. Vitamins are divided into two types: water-soluble and fat-soluble. Both types are vital to have in a diet for normal growth and bodily function.

Water-Soluble Vitamins

Water-soluble vitamins dissolve in water. They must be eaten every day because the body loses them in waste fluids. Water-soluble vitamins include vitamin C and all the B vitamins. (See **Figure 11.1** on page 283.)

Fat-Soluble Vitamins

Unlike water-soluble vitamins, fat-soluble vitamins are stored in the liver. Vitamins A, D, E, and K are fat-soluble vitamins. Fat-soluble vitamins can build up in the body if they are taken in very large quantities for a long period of time. This can cause disease or even death. (See **Figure 11.2** on page 284.) These vitamins are sometimes added to food. Milk is fortified with vitamin D. Vitamin D helps the body absorb the calcium already in the milk.

FIGURE CAPTION ANSWER Iron, iodine, zinc, copper, fluoride, and selenium can be found in fish and shellfish.

Improve Food Additives help to improve a food's shelf life, flavor, texture, or appearance. *Why might you choose to use a fat or sugar substitute?*

Type of Additive	Name of Additive	Foods with Additive
Thickeners and Stabilizers	• Modified food starches • Cornstarch • Flour	• Fruit fillings; pie fillings; puddings • Sauces; instant foods • Sauces
Gelling Agents	• Gelatin • Pectin	• Baked desserts; fillings • Sherbets; fruit jellies, preserves, jams; glazes
Nutrients	• Iron, vitamin C, thiamin, Riboflavin	• Enriched foods, such as breads, cereals, flour, juices, and flavored beverages
Coloring Agents	• Annato (ə-ˈnä-(ˌ)tō) • Citrus Red No. 2, Red No. 3, Green No. 3, Yellow No. 6	• Cheese • Soft drinks; baked items; cereals; candy
Flavoring Agents	• Vanilla, almond, lemon • MSG	• Baked items; ice cream; candy • Asian foods; soups
Fat Substitutes	• Olestra (ō-ˈles-trə) • Simplesse (sim-ˈples)	• Snack foods, such as potato chips • Frozen desserts, such as ice cream; sour cream; margarine; salad dressings
Sugar Substitutes	• Aspartame (ˈas-pər-tām) • Saccharin (ˈsa-k(ə-)rən) • Acesulfame-K (ˈā-sē-ˌsəl-ˌfām) • Sucralose (ˈsü-krə-ˌlōs)	• All-purpose sweetener used in all foods and beverages • Used as a table-top sweetener and in a variety of foods and beverages • Gelatin; pudding; candy; chewing gum; as a table-top sweetener • Dairy products; carbonated beverages; jams and jellies; chewing gum; syrup; as a table-top sweetener

Minerals

Minerals are an essential part of your bones and teeth. They also regulate body processes, such as nerve function. Minerals are needed in very small quantities. Not having enough of a particular mineral in a diet is called a mineral deficiency.

Minerals are divided into two categories: major and trace. The body needs more of the major minerals than it does of the trace minerals. However, both types are equally important for good health. **Figure 11.3** on page 284 lists the major minerals, their functions, and sources. **Figure 11.4** on page 285 lists the trace minerals.

FIGURE CAPTION ANSWER You might choose a fat or sugar substitute to lower the total calories or amount of harmful fats in a dish.

Water

Water is essential to sustain life. Water makes up about 60% of an adult's body weight. It cleans toxins from the body, cushions joints, and increases the body's ability to transport nutrients. Healthy adults need to drink 64 to 80 ounces of water each day. This water can come from any substance that is mostly water, such as juice, gelatin, soup, milk, and ice. However, water-based beverages that contain caffeine cause the body to eliminate water.

 **Reading Check** **Identify** How many different nutrients can be found in food?

READING CHECK ANSWER There are more than 40 different nutrients in food.

Food Additives

An **additive** is a substance added to a food to improve it in some way. Additives are used to:

- Allow food products to maintain their consistency.
- Improve the nutritional value of food products.
- Keep food products from spoiling, or losing their quality, too quickly.
- Provide rising for baked goods, or to control the acidity or alkalinity of foods.
- Improve the flavor or color of food products.

Direct food additives are added to a food product specifically to enhance or change it. Indirect food additives become part of a food product because of the way it is processed.

Some additives, such as vinegar and salt, have been used for centuries. Some additives are natural, while others are chemically produced. See **Figure 11.5** for additives that are commonly used in the foodservice industry.

The FDA is responsible for regulating additives that are put into foods to make sure that they are safe to eat. In some cases, the approval of additives may take many years. Food manufacturers must test an additive for its effectiveness, how it is measured, and its overall safety. The test results are submitted to the FDA for approval. Additives are evaluated regularly by the FDA. No additive has permanent FDA approval.

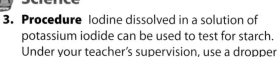 **Reading Check** List Which additives have permanent FDA approval?

 SECTION 11.1 **After You Read**

Review Key Concepts

1. **Compare** water-soluble vitamins and fat-soluble vitamins.
2. **List** the products in which coloring agents may be found.

Practice Culinary Academics

Science

3. **Procedure** Iodine dissolved in a solution of potassium iodide can be used to test for starch. Under your teacher's supervision, use a dropper to add iodine solution to a slice of potato, a slice of apple, and a piece of cheese.

    Analysis Make note of any color changes in the food. Write a paragraph theorizing what the color change means.

    > **NSES B** Develop an understanding of chemical reactions.

English Language Arts

4. Create a poster to illustrate nutrient functions, and sources of nutrients. Be creative when you choose how to present your information. Use photos, illustrations, and diagrams to help show important information.

    > **NCTE 6** Apply knowledge of language structure and conventions to discuss texts.

Mathematics

5. A can of cola has 41 grams of sugar in each 12-ounce can. If you drink nine cans over the span of a week, how many pounds of sugar have you consumed during that week from the soda?

    Math Concept **Converting Metric Weights** Metric weights are measured in grams. There are approximately 454 grams in one pound. To convert grams to pounds, divide the grams amount by 454. To convert pounds to grams, multiply the pounds amount by 454.

    Starting Hint Determine how many total grams of sugar you will consume by multiplying the number of cans times the sugar grams per can. Then, convert grams to pounds by dividing the total grams by 454.

    > **NCTM Measurement** Understand measurable attributes of objects and the units, systems, and processes of measurement.

 Check your answers at this book's Online Learning Center at **glencoe.com**.

READING CHECK ANSWER There is no additive that has permanent FDA approval.

Meal Planning Guidelines

Reading Guide

 Before You Read

Get Your Rest The more well rested and alert you are when you sit down to study, the more likely you will be to remember the information later. Studying in the same state of mind as when you are likely to take a test (fully rested and mentally sharp) will help to ensure your best performance.

Read to Learn

Key Concepts

- **Explain** the purpose of the Dietary Guidelines for Americans, nutrition labels, and MyPyramid.
- **Analyze** how age, activity level, lifestyle, and health influence dietary needs.

Main Idea

Government guidelines and dietary recommendations can help a professional chef create well-balanced meals. A well-planned menu should take into account different lifestyles and health needs.

Content Vocabulary

- Recommended Dietary Allowance (RDA)
- nutrition label
- daily value
- Dietary Guidelines for Americans
- nutrient-dense food
- glycogen
- dehydration
- vegetarian
- lacto-vegetarian
- ovo-vegetarian
- lacto-ovo-vegetarian
- vegan
- raw vegan
- macrobiotics
- food allergy
- diabetes
- cancer
- phytochemical

Academic Vocabulary

- duration
- impact

Graphic Organizer

Use a table like this one to illustrate the four factors that influence dietary needs and how they affect those dietary needs.

Dietary Needs

Factor	Influence

 Graphic Organizer Go to this book's Online Learning Center at **glencoe.com** for a printable graphic organizer.

GRAPHIC ORGANIZER ANSWER Age: Amount of nutrients needed. Activity Level: Amount of calories and hydration needed. Lifestyle: Foods someone will or will not eat. Health: Types of foods eaten, nutrients needed.

Today's customers want nutritious, tasty meals.

ACADEMIC STANDARDS

 English Language Arts
NCTE 5 Use different writing process elements to communicate effectively.

 Mathematics
NCTM Problem Solving Apply and adapt a variety of appropriate strategies to solve problems.

 Social Studies
NCSS VIII B Science, Technology, and Society Make judgments about how science and technology have transformed the physical world and human society.

NCSS II F Time, Continuity, and Change Apply ideas, theories, and modes of historical inquiry to analyze historical and contemporary developments.

NCTE National Council of Teachers of English

NCTM National Council of Teachers of Mathematics

NSES National Science Education Standards

NCSS National Council for the Social Studies

Government Guidelines

For almost 100 years, the U. S. government has provided dietary guidelines and recommendations to help consumers make healthful food choices. It is important for foodservice professionals to know these guidelines. They can help you create well-balanced meals. In addition, you must be aware of the factors that influence a person's dietary needs. These factors include age, activity level, lifestyle, and health.

Recommended Dietary Allowances

The **Recommended Dietary Allowances** (RDAs) are developed by the Food and Nutrition Board of the National Academy of Sciences. The RDA shows the amount of each essential nutrient that will meet the nutritional needs of the majority of healthy Americans for a day. RDAs are updated about every five years.

Nutrition Labels

The Nutrition Labeling and Education Act of 1990 required that most foods have

▼ FIGURE 11.6 Nutrition Label Sections

Read the Label The top section of a nutrition label contains information that varies with each food product. *What does the bottom part of the label contain?*

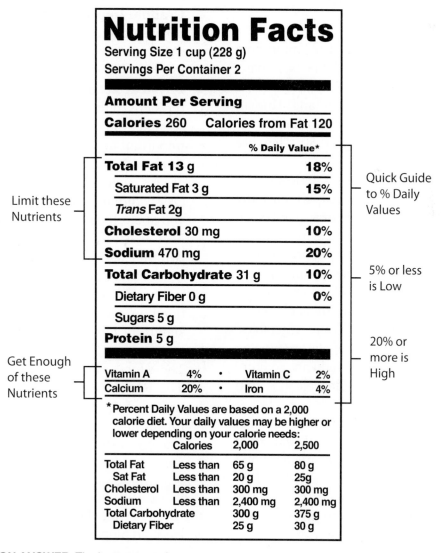

Nutrition Facts

Serving Size 1 cup (228 g)
Servings Per Container 2

Amount Per Serving

Calories 260   Calories from Fat 120

	% Daily Value*
Total Fat 13 g	**18%**
Saturated Fat 3 g	**15%**
Trans Fat 2g	
Cholesterol 30 mg	**10%**
Sodium 470 mg	**20%**
Total Carbohydrate 31 g	**10%**
Dietary Fiber 0 g	**0%**
Sugars 5 g	
Protein 5 g	

Vitamin A	4%	Vitamin C	2%
Calcium	20%	Iron	4%

*Percent Daily Values are based on a 2,000 calorie diet. Your daily values may be higher or lower depending on your calorie needs:

	Calories	2,000	2,500
Total Fat	Less than	65 g	80 g
Sat Fat	Less than	20 g	25g
Cholesterol	Less than	300 mg	300 mg
Sodium	Less than	2,400 mg	2,400 mg
Total Carbohydrate		300 g	375 g
Dietary Fiber		25 g	30 g

Limit these Nutrients

Get Enough of these Nutrients

Quick Guide to % Daily Values

5% or less is Low

20% or more is High

FIGURE CAPTION ANSWER The bottom part of a nutrition label provides general dietary information about nutrients.

nutrition labels. A **nutrition label** gives information on serving size, calories, and nutrients in the food. Nutrients are measured in grams and in daily value percentages.

The **daily value** of a nutrient is the amount of that nutrient that a person needs every day. This value is based on a 2,000-calorie diet. This number is only a guide, because each person's calorie needs are different. These daily values would be higher or lower if you eat more or less than 2,000 calories a day.

The nutrients that are listed first on a nutrition label are the ones that most people eat in adequate amounts. The nutrients at the bottom of the label are the nutrients that many people lack in their diets.

Dietary Guidelines for Americans

The **Dietary Guidelines for Americans** are published by the United States Department of Agriculture (USDA) and the United States Department of Health and Human Services. The Dietary Guidelines for Americans were first published in 1980. They are updated periodically.

The Dietary Guidelines for Americans offer information on proper eating habits for healthy Americans who are two years of age and older. The guidelines are based on scientific knowledge about diet, nutrition, and physical activity. They cover nine general topics: getting enough nutrients within calorie needs; maintaining a healthy weight; being physically active every day; choosing whole grains, fruits, vegetables, and milk; limiting fats and cholesterol; being choosy about carbohydrates; reducing sodium/increasing potassium; avoiding alcohol; and keeping food safe.

Federal nutrition assistance programs, such as the USDA's School Meal and Food Stamp Programs and the Supplemental Food Program for Women, Infants, and Children (WIC), are built off of the Dietary Guidelines. The Guidelines also form the basis for the MyPyramid food guidance system.

MyPyramid

The MyPyramid food guidance system was created in 2005, using the 2005 Dietary Guidelines for Americans. It was created to replace the original Food Guide Pyramid. MyPyramid is a visual tool that reminds people age two and older to eat nutritiously and exercise for better health. (See **Figure 11.7**.) The MyPyramid symbol shows the recommended proportion of foods from each food group. These groups are Grains, Vegetables, Fruits, Milk, and Meat & Beans. Oils are also represented in MyPyramid.

MyPyramid shows the importance of:

- **Personalization** MyPyramid can give specific recommendations for individual people about the kinds and amounts of foods they eat every day.
- **Gradual Improvement** Small changes to behavior and eating habits can make a big difference in your health. The slogan, "Steps to a Healthier You" suggests this theme.
- **Physical Activity** The person climbing the steps in the MyPyramid diagram reminds you that everyday activity is important to good nutrition.
- **Variety** You need foods from all of the groups each day for good health. There are six different color bands to remind you about the importance of variety.
- **Moderation** The wide base of the pyramid stands for foods with little or no solid fats, added sugars or caloric sweeteners. These should be chosen more often for good health. The narrow top stands for foods with more solid fats, added sugars, or caloric sweeteners. These foods should be selected less often.
- **The Right Proportions** The different widths of the bands in MyPyramid stand for the amount of food from each food group you should choose. These widths are a general guide, not exact proportions.

Reading Check Describe How can the Dietary Guidelines, nutrition labels, and MyPyramid help you plan nutritious menus?

READING CHECK ANSWER They can help you plan nutritious menu items by giving you guidelines for nutrient allowances, serving sizes and balanced meals.

Meet Dietary Needs

The Dietary Guidelines for Americans are a tool for foodservice professionals who want to plan balanced menus for healthy adults. However, foodservice professionals need to know that these guidelines do not apply evenly to everyone. Many factors can influence a person's dietary needs including age, activity level, lifestyle, and health. Religious and cultural factors can also influence dietary needs.

Age

Nutritional needs will change over a person's entire life span. Diffrerent times in that life span, including infancy, childhood, adolescence, and pregnancy, are all periods of growth that require extra nutrients. As people become adults and become elderly, their dietary needs change again.

At each stage of life, it is important to eat nutrient-dense foods, such as fruits and vegetables. A **nutrient-dense food** is a food that is low in calories, but rich in nutrients. Broccoli, carrots, sunflower seeds, and whole-wheat bread are examples of nutrient-dense foods.

Pregnant Women

A woman's eating habits before and during pregnancy influence her health and the health of her baby. Pregnant women and mothers of young infants should follow the dietary advice of MyPyramid for Pregnancy and Breastfeeding. MyPyramid for Moms offers the nutritional advice new moms need to stay healthy and provide enough nutrients to their child.

Infants

Infants grow more during their first year than at any other time of their lives. They need enough nutrients to fuel that growth.

▼ FIGURE 11.7 MyPyramid

Eating Plans MyPyramid offers personalized eating plans that are right for each individual. *What other nutritional help can you get from MyPyramid?*

FIGURE CAPTION ANSWER MyPyramid can help you make smart choices from every food group, find a balance between food and physical activity, get the most nutrition, and stay within your daily calorie needs.

Generally, the only food babies need for the first four to six months of their lives is breast milk or formula. Infants then move to iron-fortified cereals, strained vegetables and fruits, and eventually cut-up table foods. New foods are introduced slowly.

Children

Children over the age of two need a wide variety of foods served in small portions. Because their stomachs cannot hold much food at once, they need frequent snacks and meals to supply all the nutrients their growing bodies need. Nutritious snacks may include fresh fruit, half of a sandwich, or yogurt. It is normal for a child's appetite to vary, and for children to be picky about what they want to eat. Children may eat more than usual during growth spurts. They may eat less than usual during periods of low growth.

Teenagers

There are many psychological and physical changes that happen during adolescence. Teens grow more quickly than at any other time of life except infancy. This means that teens need an increase in almost all nutrients.

Teenagers are more susceptible to eating disorders, emotional, complex illnesses that are dangerous to a person's health. Anorexia nervosa, bulimia nervosa, and binge-eating disorder are examples.

Adults and the Elderly

People lose muscle and bone mass as they age. The function of body organs also drops, and the metabolism moves more slowly. This influences the amount of food and individual nutrients an elderly person needs.

Other factors that can influence the nutritional needs of the elderly include health problems, loss of teeth, a decreased appetite, and an inability to prepare nutritious meals.

Activity Level

Physical activity requires energy. The type of activity and its **duration**, or the amount of time it lasts, its frequency, and its intensity affect how much energy is needed.

▲ **Life Stages** Nutritional needs change many times over the course of a person's life. *What nutritional changes are needed for each of the stages of life shown here?*

PHOTO CAPTION ANSWER Pregnant women should follow MyPyramid for Moms advice. Infants need plenty of nutrients for growth. Children need a wide variety of foods in small portions. Teenagers need all nutrients.

Adults and the elderly need nutrients to support body functions and slow muscle and bone loss.

The nutrition that an athlete needs is different from the nutrition that a less-active person needs. Each person uses a different amount of energy to fuel his or her body. Your body breaks down carbohydrates into glucose for energy. It changes extra carbohydrates into **glycogen** (ˈglī-kə-jən), a storage form of glucose. When you exercise for long periods of time, your body uses part of its glycogen supply for energy. If you eat plenty of complex carbohydrates, your body will have a steady supply of glycogen when it needs it.

It is also important to drink plenty of water before, during, and after exercise. A large amount of water is lost from the body through perspiration. If you do not replace this water, it can lead to dehydration. **Dehydration** (ˌdē-ˌhī-ˈdrā-shən) is a serious fluid imbalance in the body. Dehydration can cause heat stroke or heat exhaustion.

Lifestyle

Many Americans are trying a vegetarian lifestyle, both as a social statement and for nutrition. Generally, a **vegetarian** (ˌve-jə-ˈter-ē-ən) does not eat meat or other animal-based foods. Vegetarians eat plant-based foods, such as vegetables, grains, fruits, and beans. Vegetarian diets are generally lower in fat, saturated fat, and cholesterol than typical American diets. Most vegetarian diets have enough nutrients if they include a variety of foods. Vegetarians must be careful to combine foods so that they get enough protein.

There are several types of vegetarians:

- A **lacto-vegetarian** eats or drinks some dairy products, such as cheese and milk, but does not eat eggs.
- An **ovo-vegetarian** eats eggs in addition to foods from plant sources.
- A **lacto-ovo-vegetarian** eats both dairy products (lacto) and eggs (ovo).
- A **vegan** (ˈvē-gən) does not eat any meat or animal products.
- A **raw vegan** eats only unprocessed vegan foods that have not been heated above 115°F (46°C).
- **Macrobiotics** is a diet that includes unprocessed foods, and organically grown fruits and vegetables. Some macrobiotics occasionally consume small amounts of fish.

There are many religions and cultures that have special dietary needs as well. For example, Buddhists tend to eat vegetarian diets, while some Jewish people eat only kosher foods.

Health

Proper nutrition is vital for good health. The right diet can help prevent and treat many health conditions. Some of these conditions include cardiovascular disease, food allergies, diabetes, and cancer.

Cardiovascular Disease

Over time, cholesterol in the system can block arteries that carry blood. This can cause a stroke or a heart attack. High blood pressure can also **impact**, or have a direct effect upon, the development of cardiovascular disease. Large amounts of salt or sodium over time can increase blood pressure.

The first step in treating high cholesterol or high blood pressure is to modify the person's diet and increase the amount of exercise the person gets. People who have high cholesterol should reduce their fat, saturated fat, and cholesterol intake, and increase their soluble fiber intake. People with high blood pressure need to limit the salt and the number of processed foods they eat. Processed foods tend to be very high in salt.

1929   **1931**

Christiaan Eijkman wins the Nobel Prize in Medicine

Fiberglass is introduced

Nutrition Pioneers

The connection between diet and health has been studied for many years. In 1757, Scottish physician James Lind found that eating citrus fruit helped prevent scurvy, a disease commonly contracted by sailors. Scurvy was later discovered to be a lack of vitamin C in the sailors' diets. The vitamin C in the citrus fruit prevented the disease.

In the early 1900s, Dutch scientist Christiaan Eijkman found that the inflammatory disease beriberi is also caused by poor diet. He discovered that vitamin B (thiamine) helped prevent and treat beriberi.

Historical Application

Visit a pharmacy and look at the label on any brand of multivitamin. Research the individual nutrients that are included in one of the multivitamins. Create a three-column chart listing at least five of the nutrients, the nutritional attributes for which they are known, and in which foods they can be found.

NCSS VIII B Science, Technology, and Society Make judgments about how science and technology have transformed the physical world and human society.

There are many ways a foodservice operation can help people with high cholesterol and high blood pressure meet their dietary goals. For example, you might plan meals around dishes rich in complex carbohydrates and fiber, such as dry beans and whole grains.

There are other ways to plan nutritious, tasty menu items as well. Use many different types of fruits and vegetables that are cooked with little or no fat or salt in your dishes. Offer moderate portions of lean meats and fish on your menu. Limit the use of fats, especially saturated fats, in your cooking. Use more healthful fat and oil alternatives such as olive oil instead of butter and skim milk instead of whole milk to reduce fat and cholesterol in your dishes. Use seasonings other than salt, such as herbs and spices, that are rich in flavor but low in sodium.

A TASTE OF HISTORY ANSWER Answers will vary, but might include vitamin A (helps regulate the immune system; found in liver, carrots, and sweet potatoes) or

Food Allergies and Food Intolerances

Foodservice operations need to give information to customers about foods that may cause allergic reactions. A **food allergy** is an allergic reaction triggered by the immune system in response to a particular food. The immune system mistakenly believes that the food is harmful. It produces antibodies to protect itself against the food. The next time a person with a food allergy eats a specific food, the immune system releases the antibodies, and allergic symptoms will occur.

Food allergies can be mild or severe. Severe food allergies can even cause death. The only way to prevent an allergic reaction to a food is to avoid the allergy-causing food.

Symptoms of an allergic reaction can include headaches, hives, difficulty breathing, nasal congestion, facial swelling and/or numbness, and gastrointestinal problems. Symptoms usually show up within minutes to a few hours after the food has been eaten. The most common foods that people are allergic to include fish, shellfish, milk products, eggs, wheat, soy products, tree nuts (such as walnuts and pecans), and peanuts.

A food intolerance is not the same thing as a food allergy. A food intolerance is a reaction to a particular food that does not involve the immune system. Lactose intolerance is an example of a food intolerance.

Diabetes

Almost 16 million Americans have diabetes. **Diabetes** is an illness that affects the body's ability to convert blood sugar into energy. There are two types of diabetes. Children and young adults usually have Type 1 diabetes. Type 1 diabetics do not produce insulin in their bodies. Insulin is a hormone that converts blood sugar and starches into energy. Type 2 diabetes is the most common type of diabetes. Type 2 diabetics either do not produce enough insulin, or their bodies' cells ignore the insulin.

vitamin D (promotes bone formation; found in salmon, mushrooms, eggs, and fortified dairy products).

Cancer-Fighting Chemicals Phytochemicals are thought to have anti-cancer properties. *What phytochemicals are found in citrus fruits?*

Phytochemical	Function in the Body	Food Sources
Flavonoids ('flā-və-nȯids)	• May function as an antioxidant • Lowers the risk of cancer	• Apples and grapefruit
Resveratrol (rez-'vir-ə-ˌtrȯl)	• Can prevent some types of cancer • May lower cholesterol	• Grapes
Limonene ('li-mə-ˌnēn)	• Releases detoxification enzymes in the liver	• Citrus fruits such as oranges, limes, and lemons
Ellagic Acid (ə-'la-jik)	• Triggers the production of enzymes that fight carcinogens	• Blackberries, cranberries, and strawberries
Lycopene ('lī-kə-ˌpēn)	• Can function as an antioxidant • May lower the risk of heart disease and cancer	• Tomatoes and watermelon
Capsaicin (kap-'sā-ə-sən)	• May prevent certain types of cancer • Diminishes blood clotting	• Hot peppers
Allyl Sulfide ('a-ləl 'səl-ˌfīd)	• Facilitates the production of enzymes that combat carcinogens	• Onions, garlic, leeks, and shallots
Isothiocyanates and Indoles (ˌī-sō-ˌthī-ō-'sī-ə-ˌnāts) ('in-ˌdōls)	• May increase the creation of enzymes that keep carcinogens from harming DNA	• Broccoli, cauliflower, brussels sprouts, and cabbage

Diabetes can cause long-term problems with healing, eyesight, and circulation. People with diabetes must balance food, portion sizes, exercise, and medication to avoid health problems and keep a healthful lifestyle.

Cancer

Cancer is the uncontrolled division and growth of cells that interferes with normal body functions. It is the second-leading cause of death in the United States.

Research shows that a low-fat diet that is rich in fruits, vegetables, and fiber should be part of people's daily eating habits. This kind of diet may decrease the risk of cancer in some people. Eating too much fat and saturated fat can increase the risk of cancer. Some foods, such as alcohol, may actually increase the risk

of cancer. Obesity is also linked to a higher cancer rate. Irradiated foods, however, have not been shown to increase cancer risk.

Phytochemicals Natural chemicals such as those found in plants, fruits, vegetables, grains, and dry beans are called **phytochemicals** (ˌfī-tō-'ke-mi-kəls). Many phytochemicals seem to have anti-cancer properties. Each type of food seems to have a different mix of phytochemicals. These substances are not vitamins or minerals. Plants produce them to protect themselves against illness and harmful effects of the sun. They are also partially responsible for the color, aroma, and flavor of plant foods. Phytochemicals may help protect the body against some cancers, heart disease, stroke, high blood pressure, and other chronic health conditions. (See **Figure 11.8.**)

FIGURE CAPTION ANSWER Flavonoids are found in grapefruits, and limonene is found in citrus fruits such as oranges, limes, and lemons.

Dieting and Weight Issues

Part of good nutrition is maintaining a healthy weight.

- Being underweight means having too little body fat. Being underweight can cause a person to be tired, and possibly more open to infections.
- Being overweight means having too much body fat. Being overweight can cause health risks for diseases such as diabetes, cardiovascular disease, and some forms of cancer.
- Being obese means that a person is substantially overweight. Obesity can cause many serious health risks, including osteoarthritis, diabetes, cardiovascular disease, and some forms of cancer. As a foodservice professional, you can create menus that will help customers plan their dietary needs in a smart way.

Offering your customers healthful choices can help them maintain a healthy weight. Foodservice professionals should not plan menus by following the latest fad diets. A fad diet is a weight-loss plan that is based on misinformation. Fad diets, especially those that involve eating an excess of a single type of food, do not provide the nutrients and food energy most people need.

The best way to plan a menu is based on choosing cooking techniques and food products that will produce healthful, tasty dishes. It is a smart business plan to allow for substitutions in menu items for people who may have heatlh concerns. Doing this will allow more customers to eat at a foodservice business, and will keep customers coming back.

Reading Check Explain How can age, activity level, and lifestyle affect a person's dietary needs?

SECTION 11.2 After You Read

Review Key Concepts

1. **Summarize** the contents of nutrition labels.
2. **Distinguish** between the types of vegetarians.

Practice Culinary Academics

Social Studies

3. Research the history of the Food Guide Pyramid and MyPyramid. Gather information on when they were introduced, how they were developed, and what information they provide. Make a poster that points out differences between the two.

> **NCSS II F Time, Continuity, and Change** Apply ideas, theories, and modes of historical inquiry to analyze historical and contemporary developments.

English Language Arts

4. Choose a menu from a local foodservice establishment. Write a column for your school newspaper critiquing the menu based on MyPyramid and the Dietary Guidelines. Make recommendations for more nutritious choices.

> **NCTE 5** Use different writing process elements to communicate effectively.

Mathematics

5. Fat has 9 calories per gram. Wesley, a teen male, consumes 2,800 calories per day. If Wesley wants no more than 30% of his calories to come from fat, how many fat grams can he eat per day?

> **Math Concept** **Finding the Percent of a Number** To find a percent of a number, change the percent to a decimal by removing the percent sign and moving the decimal point two places to the left. Multiply this decimal by the number.
>
> **Starting Hint** This is a multi-step problem. First, determine Wesley's total fat calories per day by multiplying 2,800 by 30%. Then, divide that total by 9 to find the total number of fat grams Wesley can eat per day.

> **NCTM Problem Solving** Apply and adapt a variety of appropriate strategies to solve problems.

 Check your answers at this book's Online Learning Center at **glencoe.com**.

READING CHECK ANSWER Age affects the amount of nutrients needed and portion sizes; activity level affects the need for nutrient-dense foods; lifestyles can affect the need for supplements and fortified foods.

Keep Food Nutritious

Reading Guide

 Before You Read

Use Color As you read this section, try using different colored pens to take notes. This can help you learn new material and study for tests. You could use red for vocabulary words, blue for explanations, and green for examples.

Read to Learn
Key Concepts
- **Evaluate** cooking methods to prevent nutrient loss.
- **Outline** ways to reduce the amount of fat, cholesterol, and sodium in recipes.

Main Idea
Knowing what nutrients are contained in food is just one part of nutritional knowledge. A chef should also know the effect of cooking on the nutrient content of food.

Content Vocabulary
- leach
- batch cooking
- smoking point
- purée

Academic Vocabulary
- process
- lessen

ACADEMIC STANDARDS

 English Language Arts
NCTE 12 Use language to accomplish individual purposes.

 Mathematics
NCTM Number and Operations Compute fluently and make reasonable estimates.

 Science
NSES E Develop understandings about science and technology.

NCTE National Council of Teachers of English

NCTM National Council of Teachers of Mathematics

NSES National Science Education Standards

NCSS National Council for the Social Studies

Graphic Organizer
Use a spider map like this one to illustrate ways to prevent nutrient loss. Fill in tips to prevent nutrient loss on the branches of each line.

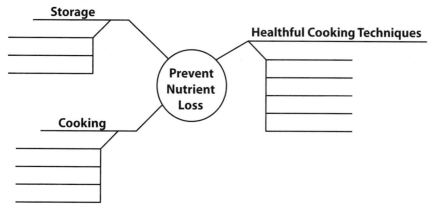

Storage

Healthful Cooking Techniques

Prevent Nutrient Loss

Cooking

 Graphic Organizer Go to this book's Online Learning Center at **glencoe.com** for a printable graphic organizer.

GRAPHIC ORGANIZER ANSWER Cooking: Use the right temperature, do not over-cook, use ingredients quickly, do not soak vegetables. Healthful Cooking Techniques: Steaming, grilling, poaching, stir-frying, microwaving. Storage: Cool temperatures, lessen holding time, make small batches.

Nutrient Loss Prevention

Suppose a pregnant woman dining at a restaurant orders red beans and rice. She knows that beans are an excellent source of iron, which is essential for a healthy pregnancy. What she may not know, however, is that the nutritional value of the beans could vary depending on how they are prepared.

From the time a food product is separated from the land or water, the possibility for nutrient loss begins. However, the way a food is prepared can speed up or slow down this **process**, or series of events or actions. A food's nutrients can be lost through improper preparation, cooking, and storage. The techniques that destroy nutrients can also destroy a food's color, texture, and flavor. You must know how to retain the maximum amount of nutrients in the foods that you cook.

PHOTO CAPTION ANSWER The food here is being stir-fried, which is an excellent cooking method for keeping most nutrients.

Cooking

The same elements that can harm food during preparation can harm it as it is being cooked. Follow these general guidelines while cooking to keep more nutrients in food:

- High temperatures can destroy vitamins in foods, such as deep-fried potatoes. Cook foods at the specified temperature.
- Prolonged cooking also causes nutrient loss. Do not overcook food items, such as boiled vegetables.
- Foods lose nutrients with age, so use them as soon as possible. Most foodservice operations use fresh produce and meats within three to four days and fresh ground meats within one to two days of receiving them.
- Nutrients, especially water-soluble vitamins B and C, will leach into the water. To **leach** means to dissolve. For this reason, do not let vegetables rest in water before or after cooking. When you clean produce, do not soak items in water for longer than necessary.

Healthful Cooking Techniques

It is the responsibility of foodservice operations to provide the public with tasty, healthful food choices. Menus should offer a variety of foods to fit different dietary needs. For example, you might cook using fresh, high-quality foods to provide customers with flavorful, healthful dishes.

Certain cooking techniques are better than others at keeping a food's full nutritional value. These techniques include steaming, grilling, poaching, stir-frying, and microwaving.

- **Steaming** This technique uses steam to cook food. Steaming can be done in a commercial steamer, a steam jacketed kettle or in pots with special steamer inserts.

Keep Nutrients How well foods maintain their nutrients depends on how the foods are prepared. *Will the food being prepared in this photo keep most of its nutrients?*

Keep Cool Once food is received, it should be stored properly. Fresh foods should be kept cool. *How else can cool temperatures be used in cooking?*

Methods such as boiling can cause food to quickly lose vitamins into the liquid. Few nutrients are lost, however, when steaming.

- **Grilling** Foods that are grilled are cooked on a grid-like surface above a heat source. Grilling requires little or no fat and, if done correctly, results in tender foods with a charbroiled flavor.

- **Poaching** Poaching involves gently simmering food in just enough liquid to cover the item. No fat is added, and the small amount of liquid minimizes the effects of leaching. The liquid can also be made into a sauce or soup.

- **Stir-Frying** Stir-frying is a technique that quickly cooks food in a minimum amount of oil. It results in crisp, colorful vegetables with minimal nutrient loss.

- **Microwaving** Microwaving is often used in foodservice operations to reheat foods quickly. Foods can be prepared, stored, and then reheated in a microwave as they are needed. This retains a food's nutrients by eliminating the need to keep the food hot for a long period of time. It is also healthful because no fat is added.

PHOTO CAPTION ANSWER Cool temperatures can be used to keep food from spoiling and to slow or stop the cooking process.

Storage

When serving food, it is important to remember how to keep foods from losing flavor and nutrients before they are eaten. Nutrients can still be lost after food is cooked. Storage exposes food to the harmful effects of water, light, air, and time. Use cool temperatures, **lessen**, or reduce, holding time, and cook in smaller batches to minimize these effects.

Temperature

Cool temperatures can slow down the processes that destroy a food's nutrients. One way to do this is to plunge cooked vegetables into cold water to stop the cooking process. Do not leave items in the water because the nutrients will leach out. Also, store covered foods in the refrigerator to slow down nutrient loss.

Holding

Food should not be held in a steam table for a long period of time. Exposure to heat and water will eventually remove some of the food's nutrients. If possible, continue to move the food around in the pan to avoid overcooking the food on the bottom.

Batching

One way to lessen food storage problems is to use batch cooking. **Batch cooking** is the process of preparing small amounts of food several times throughout a foodservice period. This decreases the amount of food that will have to be kept warm. It also allows the kitchen to turn out freshly prepared meals for customers to enjoy.

Reading Check Describe How do time and water impact food nutritionally?

Fats and Oils

Fat plays an important role as both a nutrient and a food. As a nutrient, it helps the body perform many important functions. Fat adds flavor, which is the first concern of most diners. Most vegetable oils have an average smoking point of 400°F (204°C). A **smoking point** is the temperature at which an oil will smoke in a pan. **Figure 11.9** lists the most common cooking oils and their uses.

Reduce Fat

Reduce fat and cholesterol with these suggestions:

- **Reduce Fat** Choose lean cuts of meat, and trim the fat, and remove skin from poultry. Use nonstick or cast-iron pans so that food can be cooked in less fat.
- **Reduce Total Fat** The total amount of fat and oil in many recipes can be reduced with little effect on flavor.
- **Reduce Saturated Fat** Oils rich in flavor, such as olive oil, can be substituted in smaller amounts for saturated animal fats. Replace part of the butter in a recipe with oil, low-fat sour cream, or yogurt.
- **Replace Fat** Where possible, replace part or all of the whole eggs in a recipe with egg whites or egg substitutes. Use high-quality, reduced-fat dairy products. Replace part of the fat in baking with puréed fruits. A **purée** is a food in which one or more of the ingredients have been ground in a food processor or blender.

▲ **Cut the Fat** Trimming the fat from cuts of meat is one way to reduce the amount of fat in a recipe. *In what other ways can you reduce fat in a recipe?*

▼ FIGURE 11.9 Common Cooking Oils

Nutrient and Food Oils play a role in nutrition as both a nutrient and a food. *What body functions do you think these oils helps perform?*

Cooking Oils	Description	Uses
Canola (kə-ˈnō-lə)	• High in monounsaturated fat • Neutral, light-colored oil with little flavor • Also known as rapeseed oil because it comes from the rape plant	All types of cooking, especially frying and baking
Coconut	• High in saturated fat • Little color	Used in blended oils and shortenings
Corn	• High in polyunsaturated fat • Light, amber-colored oil • Slight cornmeal flavor • Sometimes marketed as salad oil	Frying, salad dressing
Cottonseed	• High in polyunsaturated fat • Pale yellow oil with sweet flavor • Extracted from cotton plant seeds • Quality depends on the season, type of fertilizer used, and the way it was extracted	Shortening, salad dressing
Olive	• High in monounsaturated fat • Quality depends on soil, growing conditions, olive type, and the way it was extracted • Extra-virgin olive oil, meaning it was made from the first pressing of olives, is the highest quality • Ranges in color from deep green to pale yellow	All types of cooking, salad dressing
Peanut	• High in monounsaturated fat • Amber-colored oil with a very mild to nutty flavor	Frying, deep-frying, salad dressing
Safflower	• Very high in polyunsaturated fat • Golden-colored oil	Margarine, mayonnaise, salad dressing
Sesame Seed	• High in polyunsaturated fat • Two types: Middle Eastern, which is light with a mild flavor, and Asian, which is dark with a distinct, nutty flavor	All types of cooking
Soybean	• High in polyunsaturated fat • Yellow oil • Quality affected by season, climate, soil, and the way it was extracted	Margarine, salad dressing, shortening
Sunflower	• Very high in polyunsaturated fat • Pale yellow oil with little flavor or odor	All types of cooking, salad dressing, margarine, shortening
Vegetable	• Polyunsaturated fat • Products labeled vegetable oil are blended from many sources • Other types of vegetable oil are corn, soybean, and cottonseed	All types of cooking, salad dressing

FIGURE CAPTION ANSWER Oils contain essential fatty acids that help reduce inflammation in the body, affect the mood, and keep cells healthy. Oils are the major source of vitamin E in the body.

Other Low-Fat Options

Try these other options to cook with less fat:

- **Offer Plant-Based Foods** In addition to lean meats, offer menu items based on pasta, rice, grains, and legumes. Also, increase the amounts of fruits and vegetables served with or included as part of an entrée. Plant-based foods appeal to vegetarians and people who want low-fat, high-fiber meals.
- **Change Cooking Techniques** Roasting, steaming, and baking require little or no added fat. They are more healthful than methods like deep-frying and pan-frying.
- **Use Seasonings and Flavorings** Season foods with herbs and spices instead of butter. Use low-fat marinades with meats and seafood. Replace high-fat sauces with salsas or relishes.
- **Use Special Equipment** Specially made equipment can make low-fat cooking easier. For example, nonstick pans and cast-iron pans allow food to be browned in a minimal amount of fat.
- **Reduce Portion Size** Limit portion sizes of meat, poultry, and seafood to three to four ounces (precooked weight). Three ounces of meat is about the size of a deck of cards. Increase portion sizes of vegetables, grains, beans, and pasta.

Reading Check **List** What are three ways that you can reduce the amount of fat in a recipe?

SECTION 11.3 After You Read

Review Key Concepts

1. **Outline** healthful cooking techniques.
2. **Explain** how to replace fat in a dish.

Practice Culinary Academics

Science

3. **Procedure** Research one food product that was created using science and technology to meet special health needs, such as artificial sweeteners and fat substitutes.

   Analysis Write an analysis of the product and its benefits and drawbacks. Use scientific language to compare it to the food product for which it is a substitute.

   > **NSES E** Develop understandings about science and technology.

English Language Arts

4. Imagine that you are a nutrition expert hired to demonstrate to cooks how to prepare foods to conserve nutrients. Prepare a five-minute oral presentation, and give it to your class.

   > **NCTE 12** Use language to accomplish individual purposes.

Mathematics

5. An oat cereal has 3.5 grams of fat per ¾ cup serving, while a puffed cereal has 5 grams of fat per 1 ¼ cup serving. Given identical-size portions of each cereal, which one has more fat?

   Math Concept **Comparing Fat Content** To compare nutritional values of products with unequal serving sizes on their labels, use proportions to recalculate the values based on equal serving sizes, such as 1 cup.

   Starting Hint Convert the serving sizes to decimals. For each cereal, find out how many fat grams are in 1 cup by setting up a proportion (for example, 3.5 grams / 0.75 cups = x / 1 cup) and solving for x.

   > **NCTM Number and Operations** Compute fluently and make reasonable estimates.

Check your answers at this book's Online Learning Center at **glencoe.com**.

READING CHECK ANSWER Replace fat, offer plant-based foods, change cooking techniques, use seasonings and flavorings, use special equipment, or reduce portion size.

Review and Applications

Chapter Summary

There are six categories of nutrients: carbohydrates, proteins, fats, vitamins, minerals, and water. Each are essential to the body in different ways. Foodservice operations have many options to offer healthful meals, such as cooking with less saturated fat. Age, activity level, lifestyle, and health can all affect a person's dietary needs. How foods are prepared, cooked, and stored affects nutritional content. Use the proper techniques to preserve nutrients.

Content and Academic Vocabulary Review

1. Use at least 10 of these vocabulary terms in a brochure about personal nutrition.

Content Vocabulary

- nutrient (p. 280)
- carbohydrate (p. 280)
- legume (p. 280)
- glucose (p. 280)
- fiber (p. 280)
- protein (p. 281)
- amino acids (p. 281)
- complete protein (p. 281)
- incomplete protein (p. 281)
- fat (p. 282)
- hydrogenation (p. 282)
- trans fatty acid (p.282)
- cholesterol (p. 282)
- lipoprotein (p. 282)
- cardiovascular (p. 282)
- saturated fat (p. 283)
- monounsaturated fat (p. 283)
- polyunsaturated fat (p. 285)
- vitamin (p. 285)
- minerals (p. 286)
- additive (p. 287)
- Recommended Dietary Allowances (RDA) (p. 289)
- nutrition label (p. 290)
- daily value (p. 290)
- Dietary Guidelines for Americans (p. 290)
- nutrient-dense food (p. 291)
- glycogen (p. 293)
- dehydration (p. 293)
- vegetarian (p. 293)
- lacto-vegetarian (p. 293)
- ovo-vegetarian (p. 293)
- lacto-ovo-vegetarian (p. 293)
- vegan (p. 293)
- raw vegan (p. 293)
- macrobiotics (p. 293)
- food allergy (p. 294)
- diabetes (p. 294)
- cancer (p. 295)
- phytochemicals (p. 295)
- leach (p. 298)
- batch cooking (p. 300)
- smoking point (p. 300)
- purée (p. 300)

Academic Vocabulary

- role (p. 282)
- regulate (p. 285)
- duration (p. 292)
- impact (p. 293)
- process (p. 298)
- lessen (p. 299)

Review Key Concepts

2. **Summarize** the six categories of nutrients.

3. **List** the types and uses of food additives.

4. **Explain** the purpose of the Dietary Guidelines for Americans, nutrition labels, and MyPyramid.

5. **Analyze** how age, activity level, lifestyle, and health influence dietary needs.

6. **Evaluate** cooking methods to prevent nutrient loss.

7. **Outline** ways to reduce the amount of fat, cholesterol, and sodium in recipes.

Critical Thinking

8. **Evaluate** menu nutrition. Why should the dietary needs of people with health problems be considered when planning a restaurant menu?

9. **Explain** how you think requiring nutrition labeling on foods has affected consumers.

10. **Analyze** nutrition for customers. What are four questions a restaurant customer might ask about nutrition? How would you instruct servers to answer these questions?

Review and Applications

Academic Skills

English Language Arts

11. Create a Life Plan Imagine that you are a nutritionist working with a healthy adult who has a history of heart disease in his or her family. Create a life plan for the adult that includes nutritional advice for both adulthood and elder years. Organize and write the life plan so that your client can understand and use the plan. Create your plan in the form of a booklet for your client to read. Once you have written the life plan, give it to another student. Did the student find the information useful?

> **NCTE 5** Use different writing process elements to communicate effectively.

Social Studies

12. Nutritional Technology There are many ways for people to keep track of the nutrients and calories that they eat throughout the day to stay healthy. Investigate the types of technology, such as computer programs, that are available to help consumers and professionals locate food and nutrition information. How do these technologies help people to lead more healthy lifestyles? Write a short summary of your research.

> **NCSS VIII C Science, Technology, and Society** Analyze how science and technology influence the core values, beliefs, and attitudes of society.

Mathematics

13. Work with Large Numbers The amount of the phytochemical capsaicin found in a chili pepper is measured in heat units on the Scoville scale. Items with no capsaicin rate a 0 on the scale, while pure capsaicin rates about 16 million Scoville heat units. Chili peppers fall somewhere in between that range, but higher numbers indicate spicier peppers. A habanero pepper can rate up to 580,000 Scoville heat units. Write this number in scientific notation.

Math Concept **Scientific Notation** Scientific notation uses powers of 10 as shorthand for writing very large numbers. Start by moving the decimal point so that just one digit is to the left of the decimal. Count the number of places you moved the decimal. Remove all of the ending zeros, and write the number multiplied by 10 to the power of the number of decimal places moved.

Starting Hint For example, to write 6,250,000 in scientific notation, move the decimal point so that just one digit is to its left, resulting in 6.250000. Remove all trailing zeros to get 6.25. Since we moved the decimal point six places to the left, we rewrite the number as 6.25×10^6. Perform the same process for 580,000.

> **NCTM Number and Operations** Understand numbers, ways of representing numbers, relationships among numbers, and number systems.

Certification Prep

Sharpen your test-taking skills to improve your kitchen certification program score.

Directions Read the questions. Then, read the answer choices and choose the best possible answer for each.

14. What does RDA mean?
   a. Registered Dieticians of America
   b. Rational Dietary Advice
   c. Recommended Dietary Allowances
   d. Restricted Diet Allowances

15. What is the nationally recognized method for selecting foods that promote health?
   a. Government Food Handbook
   b. Dietary Guidelines
   c. President's Nutrition Checklist
   d. MyPyramid

Test-Taking Tip
In a multiple-choice test, the answers should be specific and precise. Read the questions first, and then read all the answer choices before you choose. Eliminate answers that you know are incorrect.

Real-World Skills and Applications

Research Skills

16. **Farm to Kitchen** It is important to understand where your food comes from. Choose one protein food and research the process of how it got from the farm to your table. Determine how scientific and technical advances have impacted its nutrition, safety, and availability. Create a poster to show your research.

Critical Thinking Skills

17. **Nutritious Substitutions** Substitutions must be made carefully when creating baked goods. Imagine you have a recipe for a pie crust that calls for solid shortening as the fat. What do you think would be the result of the recipe if you made it with liquid oil, rather than solid fat? Write a paragraph explaining your theory.

Technology Applications

18. **Design a Spreadsheet** Find a recipe that you like. Create a spreadsheet to show the original ingredients and cooking techniques for the recipe, alongside suggestions for making the recipe lower in fat and sodium. Give suggestions for ingredients and cooking techniques that you have learned from this chapter.

Financial Literacy

19. **Calculate Percentage of Costs** Imagine that you will be making a chicken salad for a catered picnic. The ingredients that you need for a healthful recipe for chicken salad cost $6.75 total. The chicken for the recipe costs $3.50. What percentage of the total cost of the ingredients is the cost of the chicken?

Culinary Lab

Use the culinary skills you have learned in this chapter.

Plan Nutritious Meals

20. **Plan a Daily Menu** Working in teams, you will plan a daily menu for an average, healthy adult that meets MyPyramid recommendations.

A. Plan a healthful meal. Divide into teams at the direction of your teacher. Working with your team, plan a nutritious breakfast, lunch, dinner, and two snacks for an average healthy adult.

B. Understand food servings. Assume the adult does an average amount of physical activity and requires a 2,000 calorie diet. Describe the serving size for each item, using the chart below as a guide.

Grain Group	3 oz to 8 oz
Fruit Group	1 c to 2 c
Vegetable Group	1 c to 3 c
Milk Group	2 c to 3 c
Meat and Bean Group	2 oz to 6 oz

C. Make the food appealing. Describe the overall appeal of each meal and snack, including the variety of colors, textures, and flavors.

D. Describe cooking techniques. Describe the ways that you would prepare, cook, and store each meal and snack so that nutrients are retained.

E. Make modifications. Describe what modifications you will make to cooking methods or ingredients to help you keep nutritional content high and fat and sodium low.

Create Your Evaluation

When you have finished your meal plan, trade menus with another team. Create an evaluation form with the following categories: nutritional value, variety, and appeal. Evaluate the other team's menu in each of those categories. Discuss your evaluation with the other team and suggest additional foods that could be substituted or modified to help reduce the amount of fat and cholesterol.

CHAPTER 12

Creating Menus

SECTIONS

12.1 The Menu

12.2 Menu Planning and Design

12.3 Pricing Menu Items

WRITING ACTIVITY

Purpose and Audience

The purpose of a piece of writing is the reason why it was written. The audience is the people the article was written for. Read several articles on the same topic, and then write a summary identifying the purpose and audience for each piece.

Writing Tips

1 Ask yourself what the author wants to happen.

2 Common purposes are to express ideas or to inform.

3 Imagine the kind of person that would use or enjoy the text.

EXPLORE THE PHOTO

Menu planning is an important step in defining a foodservice operation. *Why must a chef think carefully about which menu items to offer?*

The Menu

Reading Guide

 Before You Read

How Can You Improve? Before starting this section, think about the last exam you took on material you had to read. What reading strategies helped you on the test? Make a list of ways to improve your strategies to succeed on your next exam.

Read to Learn
Key Concepts
- **Categorize** the factors that influence a menu.
- **Describe** the types of menus used by foodservice establishments.

Main Idea
There are several factors to consider when developing a menu. In addition to considering the necessary factors, a chef must choose from among different menu types.

Content Vocabulary
- menu
- entrée
- fixed menu
- cycle menu
- du jour menu
- à la carte menu
- semi-à la carte menu
- table d'hôte menu
- prix fixe menu
- meal-based menu
- California menu
- continental menu
- accompaniment
- ethnic menu

Academic Vocabulary
- dictate
- complex

Graphic Organizer
As you read, use a line chart like the one below to list the seven factors that influence menu planning.

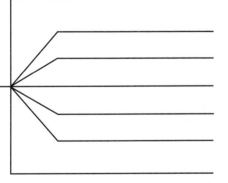

Menu Planning

 Graphic Organizer Go to this book's Online Learning Center at **glencoe.com** for a printable graphic organizer.

GRAPHIC ORGANIZER ANSWER Target customers, price, food served, equipment, worker skill, geography and culture, and eating trends.

ACADEMIC STANDARDS

 English Language Arts
NCTE 12 Use language to accomplish individual purposes.

 Mathematics
NCTM Number and Operations Understand numbers, ways of representing numbers, relationships among numbers, and number systems.

 Social Studies
NCSS V B Individuals, Groups, and Institutions Analyze group and institutional influences on people, events, and elements of culture in both historical and contemporary settings.

NCSS V C Individuals, Groups, and Institutions Describe the various forms institutions take, and explain how they develop and change over time.

NCTE National Council of Teachers of English

NCTM National Council of Teachers of Mathematics

NSES National Science Education Standards

NCSS National Council for the Social Studies

The Importance of the Menu

Whether you crave shrimp or cheeseburgers, you go to a restaurant because you like the type of food it serves. You can find out what kinds of food items a restaurant serves on the restaurant's menu.

A **menu** is a listing of the food choices the restaurant offers for each meal. The menu, however, is more than just a list that you look over before you place an order with the kitchen. It has a much larger role in the running of a foodservice operation. In fact, it impacts every step of a foodservice operation.

A menu determines:

- The type of customers the establishment will attract.
- The layout and type of equipment the restaurant will need.
- The foodservice workers that are needed and the skills they must have.
- The type and number of supplies to be ordered.

Influences on the Menu

If you were planning the menu for a restaurant, what items would you choose to include? How would you decide what types of foods to offer? What items would you choose to leave off? Menu planning is not as simple as listing items that you like to eat. There are many other factors that you must consider when you develop a menu.

Target Customers

You must think of the needs and lifestyles of the people that your restaurant will serve. You must know what types of foods are most desired by your target customers, and what prices they will be willing to pay.

The menu is a restaurant's main marketing tool. For example, a lunch deli serves food that can be prepared quickly. A school cafeteria needs to serve inviting and nutritious meals that will appeal to students. In both cases, foods need to be served in the most efficient and profitable way possible.

Meaningful Menus The style and design of a menu influence how a customer views the foodservice establishment. *What can you tell about this restaurant by looking at the style of its menu?*

PHOTO CAPTION ANSWER Answers will vary, but may include an Italian or Mediterranean cuisine, a casual dining establishment, and a focus on fresh ingredients.

Price

People expect different types of foodservice establishments to offer food that is within a certain price range. Food items that are above or below this price range will look out of place on the menu. Customers will tend to avoid menu items that look out of place. For example, a $25 entrée would be out of place at a family-style diner where most entrées cost around $8.95. An **entrée** ('än-trā) is any type of main dish. Entrées may include meat, poultry, or fish, casseroles, or even hot vegetarian items.

Type of Food Served

A foodservice establishment's menu should be planned to reflect the type of food that is served in that particular establishment. For example, customers expect to find French food items on the menu at a French restaurant. They do not expect to find Spanish dishes on the same menu.

Equipment

The type of equipment that is available in a restaurant's kitchen will **dictate**, or determine through necessity, what dishes can be listed on the restaurant's menu. For example, a specialty restaurant that has a broiler in its kitchen is able to serve steak as part of its menu, while a cafeteria that has no broiler would not.

Skill of Workers

Consider the skill level of your kitchen staff when you select items for a menu. The skill and training of the foodservice workers at a restaurant will determine what food items can be placed on a menu. Employees at a quick-service restaurant will not be able to make the **complex**, or involved and possibly difficult, dishes that a four-star restaurant staff has been trained to prepare.

Geography and Culture

The location of a foodservice operation also can dictate what dishes are on its menu. Some food ingredients are more readily available in certain areas. For example, most coastal restaurants serve seafood. Beef and pork are common in Midwest eateries. The culture of various regions and ethnic neighborhoods can also impact the food choices available in restaurants.

Eating Trends

One of the main food trends of today is the desire of consumers to eat more healthful foods prepared in healthful ways. Restaurant owners and managers watch trends like this carefully. This particular trend means that many restaurants now offer dishes that have more fruits, vegetables, whole grains, and legumes on their menus.

Reading Check Describe What aspects of a restaurant does the menu determine?

A TASTE OF HISTORY

1762 — Catherine the Great becomes ruler of Russia

1765 — Boulanger opens what is believed to be the first restaurant in Paris

The À La Carte Menu

The earliest cafes and inns had no menus in the sense that we know them today. Most of them served dishes that were chosen by the chef or owner. Patrons were charged a flat fee, and ate whatever was presented at the table.

A French soup vendor named Boulanger is believed to have been the first restaurant owner to use a menu. The dishes available were listed on a slate, or poste, along with the prices. This menu allowed Boulanger's patrons to choose only the dishes they preferred to eat. Dining out became more commonplace after the French Revolution.

Historical Application

Research French cuisine, from any time period. Create a menu from a French restaurant. Include at least one dish, with its description, cooking method, and main ingredients from each of these categories: appetizer, soup, salad, entrée, and dessert.

NCSS V B Individuals, Groups, and Institutions Analyze group and institutional influences on people, events, and elements of culture in both historical and contemporary settings.

A TASTE OF HISTORY ANSWER Students will need to research French food to complete their menus. Menus should include different courses and dishes that will fall into each category. Their menu descriptions should be clearly and creatively written. Spelling should be accurate.
READING CHECK ANSWER The menu determines the type of customer, the layout and equipment, the workers and their skill level, and the supplies a restaurant will have.

Chapter 12 Creating Menus **309**

Menu Types

You can find just as many different kinds of menus as there are different kinds of food-service operations. Every restaurant has a unique personality. The menu can help new customers understand the other clientele and atmosphere of a restaurant and the food it serves. (See **Figure 12.1**.) Some restaurants have the same patrons nearly every day, or a specific serving style.

A menu could be a printed card that the server or host hands to customers. It could be a hardcover booklet that lists a variety of items for all meals. It also could be a large sign behind a counter or a chalkboard menu that changes daily. The most popular types of menus include fixed and cycle menus; à la carte, semi-à la carte, and table d'hôte menus; prix fixe menus; and meal-based menus.

Fixed and Cycle Menus

A **fixed menu** offers the same dishes every day for a long period of time. You will generally find fixed menus in dining establishments that serve different people every day, such as hotels, ethnic restaurants, and fast-food operations. Many restaurants use this type of menu.

A **cycle menu** is used for a set period of time, such as a week, a month, or even longer. At the end of this time period, the menu repeats daily dishes in the same order. For example, if a cycle menu is used weekly, it repeats the cycle, offering the same dishes again on each Monday. You will usually find cycle menus used in institutions that serve the same people day after day, such as schools, universities and colleges, hospitals, factories, and military foodservice facilities.

Many different types of restaurants use du jour menus. A **du jour menu** lists dishes that are available on that particular day. It is a useful menu for restaurants that offer many specialty items, or for listing daily specials at any type of restaurant. A du jour menu may or may not have prices listed on it.

À la Carte, Semi-à la Carte, and Table d'Hôte Menus

In family-style and fine-dining restaurants, you will most often find foods listed three different ways on the menu:

- An **à la carte** (ˌä-lə-ˈkärt) **menu** offers each food and beverage item priced and served separately.
- On a **semi-à la carte menu**, you usually will find the appetizers and desserts priced separately. The entrée will probably include a salad or soup, potato or rice, vegetable, and possibly a beverage, at a single price.
- A **table d'hôte** (ˌtä-bəl-ˈdōt) **menu** lists complete meals, from appetizers to desserts and sometimes beverages, for one set price. A set banquet menu is also an example of a table d'hôte menu. However, in a set banquet menu, everyone is served the same meal for a set price.

Prix Fixe Menus

A **prix fixe** (ˈprē-ˈfēks) **menu** is similar to a table d'hôte menu in that it offers a complete meal for a set price. With a prix fixe menu, however, the customer chooses one selection from each course offered by the restaurant. Prix fixe menus are sometimes used at elegant restaurants. Some banquets also use prix fixe menus.

Meal-Based Menus

Other types of menus include breakfast, lunch, dinner, and ethnic. A menu that shows dishes available for a single meal is called a **meal-based menu**. Many foodservice operations have separate menus for breakfast, lunch, and dinner.

If a restaurant offers breakfast, lunch, and dinner meals all day, it will sometimes list them together on the same menu. This type of menu is called a **California menu**. Breakfast, lunch, and dinner menus may be listed as à la carte, semi-à la carte, table d'hôte, or as prix fixe offerings.

FIGURE 12.1 Menu Types

On the Menu This restaurant serves every meal of the day as shown by the menu.
What type of menu is it?

Breakfast

Juices & Fruits

Orange or Grapefruit Juice . . . $1.25	Apple or Pineapple Juice . . . $1.25
Chilled Grapefruit Sections . . . $1.75	Seasonal Fruit Cup . . . $1.75

Breakfast Entrées

Huevos Rancheros $4.95
Two fried eggs served on top of fried corn tortilla strips and a layer of salsa with hashbrown potatoes.

Two Eggs with Ham, Bacon or Sausage $4.95
Eggs cooked to order served with your choice of hashbrown potatoes or grits, toast, biscuit, or English muffin.

Sunrise Skillet Omelet $4.95
Our fluffy skillet omelet filled with your choice of three of the following: Cheddar or Swiss cheese, green peppers, onions, mushrooms or ham; served with your choice of toast, biscuit or English muffin.

French Toast with Maple Syrup $4.50
Three slices of golden-brown French toast and maple syrup served with your choice of ham, bacon or link sausage.

Blueberry Pancakes $3.95
Three light and fluffy pancakes topped with plump blueberries and maple syrup.

Hot Oatmeal $2.95
Served with milk, plump raisins and brown sugar.

Sides

One Egg	$.75	Toast	$.75
Ham, Bacon or Sausage	$2.50	Bagel or English Muffin	$1.50
Grits	$1.25	Hashbrown Potatoes	$1.25

Beverages

Coffee or Hot Tea (free refills)	$1.25
Milk	$1.25

Stafford's Diner

Lunch

Soups

Old-Fashioned Chicken Noodle Soup	Cup	$1.25
	Bowl	$2.25
Soup of the Day	Cup	$1.25
	Bowl	$2.25

Salads

Tossed Green Salad	$1.50	Grilled Chicken Caesar Salad	$4.95
Tuna Salad or Mixed Greens	$3.95	Chef Salad	$4.95

Sandwiches

Turkey Club $4.50
Tender roasted turkey with bacon, lettuce, tomato and Cheddar cheese, layered between three slices of fresh-baked bread.

California Burger $3.50
Quarter pound of choice grilled beef served with lettuce, tomato and onion.

Tuna or Chicken Salad Sandwich $3.25
A generous portion of tuna or chicken salad served on your choice of bread.

Sides

French Fries	$1.50	Mashed Potatoes with Gravy	$1.25
Creamy Coleslaw	$1.25	Seasonal Fresh Fruit	$1.75

Entrées

Fish & Chips $5.95
A generous portion of deep-fried cod and chips served with french fries and coleslaw.

Home-Style Swiss Steak $6.95
Tender beef Swiss steak, mashed potatoes with beef gravy, vegetable of the day, roll and butter.

Chicken Pot Pie $5.95
Chunks of chicken breast, peas, carrots and potatoes in savory white gravy topped with a flaky pastry, served with a side of baked cinnamon apples.

Beverages

Coffee or Hot Tea (free refills)	$1.25
Assorted Soft Drinks (free refills)	$1.35
Iced Tea (free refills)	$1.25
Milk	$1.25

Desserts

Assorted Fruit Pies	$2.25
Cheesecake	$2.50
Vanilla Ice Cream	$1.50
Carrot Cake	$1.75

Stafford's Diner

Dinner

Appetizers & Soups

Volcanic Potato Skins		$3.95
Crunchy Chicken Tenders		$4.95
Tomato-Basil Soup	Cup	$1.25
	Bowl	$2.25
Old-Fashioned Chicken Noodle Soup	Cup	$1.25
	Bowl	$2.25

Salads

Mixed Green Salad	$1.75	Caesar Salad	$2.95
Spinach Salad with Hot Bacon Dressing		Seasonal Fruit Salad with Mixed Greens	
	$2.95		$2.50

Entrées

Fried Chicken Dinner $6.95
Three pieces of crispy fried chicken served with a dinner roll and your choice of two sides.

Broiled Fillet of Sole $8.95
A 6 oz. broiled fillet of sole served with a dinner roll and your choice of two sides.

Home-Style Meatloaf $6.95
Two slices of home-style meatloaf served with mashed potatoes and gravy, a dinner roll and your choice of one side.

Stir-Fried Vegetables and Rice $5.95
A blend of fresh stir-fried vegetables served on brown rice with dinner roll and your choice of two sides.

Sides

Baked Potato	Macaroni & Cheese
Mashed Potatoes with Gravy	Baked Butternut Squash
Coleslaw	Glazed Baby Carrots
Steamed Broccoli	California-Blend Vegetable Mix

Additional side orders or separate side orders are $1.50 each.

Beverages

Coffee or Hot Tea (free refills)	$1.25	Iced Tea (free refills)	$1.25
Assorted Soft Drinks (free refills)	$1.35	Milk	$1.25

Desserts

Assorted Fruit & Cream Pies (An additional $.75 with ice cream)	$3.50
Cheesecake with Strawberries	$3.95
Brownie with Vanilla Ice Cream and Fudge Sauce	$2.75

Stafford's Diner

Breakfast

Most breakfast menus are made up of inexpensive food items that are cooked to order. This means that the dishes are not cooked until the customer places his or her order with the server. The variety of foods available means that customers can create their own specialized breakfasts.

Breakfast menus may be à la carte or continental. À la carte menus price and serve each item separately. A **continental menu** provides mostly a selection of juices, beverages, and baked goods. Continental menus are usually used only for breakfasts.

Breakfast menus usually include juices, fruits, cereals, eggs, French toast, pancakes, waffles, baked goods, beverages, and side items. Side items listed on breakfast menus often include toast, potatoes, grits, or various breakfast meats.

FIGURE CAPTION ANSWER This menu shows semi-à la carte pricing, in which appetizers and desserts are priced separately from entrées. It is also a series of meal-based menus.

Lunch

Lunch menus usually provide a wide selection of à la carte items. They also offer table d'hôte combinations, such as a soup and salad, or a soup and a sandwich.

Lunch portions are usually smaller than dinner portions, so they are usually lower priced. Some foodservice facilities offer daily lunch specials.

Lunch menus generally include appetizers, soups, salads, entrées, sandwiches, accompaniments, and desserts. An **accompaniment** is an item that comes with an entrée. Accompaniments might include a choice of potato, rice, or pasta, vegetable, or a small salad.

Dinner

Dinner menus usually include the same food categories as lunch menus. However, dinner menus are more complex to prepare and generally require more equipment and better-trained staff. Dinner menus have more selections, offer larger portions, and have higher prices.

Dinner is the most unhurried meal of the day. Customers often have limited time for breakfast and lunch. They often like to eat more slowly and spend time visiting during dinner.

Ethnic

An **ethnic menu** represents food choices from a specific country, such as China, Italy, Mexico, or France. Most people enjoy trying different ethnic foods for breakfast, lunch, or dinner.

You may find that ethnic food preferences are different in various regions of the United States. Even different areas of a city or town may have different ethnic food preferences.

 **Reading Check** **Define** What is a prix fixe menu?

SECTION 12.1  After You Read

Review Key Concepts

1. **Explain** how geography and culture can influence a menu.
2. **Describe** a cycle menu.

Practice Culinary Academics
Social Studies

3. Evaluate the types of restaurants and their menus in a neighborhood of your community. What does this tell you about the local culture? If possible, interview long-term residents of the area about how the local businesses have changed while they have lived there. What does this tell you about how the culture has changed?

> **NCSS V C Individuals, Groups, and Institutions** Describe the various forms institutions take, and explain how they develop and change over time.

English Language Arts

4. Imagine that you are opening a restaurant and getting ready to plan the menu. The restaurant can be any type you like, and will be located in the neighborhood where you live. Create a plan that evaluates each of the factors that affect menu choice, based on the type of restaurant you imagine you will open and your neighborhood.

> **NCTE 12** Use language to accomplish individual purposes.

Mathematics

5. During dinner service last month, 500 customers ordered from your prix fixe menu, while 3,500 customers ordered à la carte. What is the ratio of prix fixe to à la carte customers? What fraction of all customers ordered prix fixe?

> **Math Concept** **Ratios and Fractions** A ratio, which can be written in fractional notation, compares one number to a second number. A fraction compares a part of a whole to the whole amount. Reduce both to lowest terms.

Starting Hint For the ratio, write a fraction with prix fixe dinners over à la carte dinners, and reduce. The second question asks you to compare prix fixe dinners to total dinners served.

> **NCTM Number and Operations** Understand numbers, ways of representing numbers, relationships among numbers, and number systems.

 Check your answers at this book's Online Learning Center at **glencoe.com**.

 READING CHECK ANSWER A prix fixe menu offers a complete menu for a set price. The customer chooses one selection from each course.

Menu Planning and Design

Reading Guide

 Before You Read

Two-Column Notes Two-column notes are a useful way to study and organize what you have read. Divide a piece of paper into two columns. In the left column, write down main ideas. In the right column, list supporting details.

Read to Learn

Key Concepts

- **Evaluate** basic menu planning principles.
- **Define** menu styles and design guidelines.
- **Explain** different menu categories and how they are typically listed.

Main Idea

Foodservice professionals have developed several principles to plan successful menus. Once the menu is planned it needs to be organized to appeal to the customer.

Content Vocabulary

- garnish
- plating
- proportion
- truth-in-menu guideline
- printed menu
- clip-on
- table tents
- menu board
- spoken menu
- extender

Academic Vocabulary

- appeal
- entice

Graphic Organizer

Fill in each of the five menu planning principles in the five rectangles of a concept map like this one, along with a brief description of each principle.

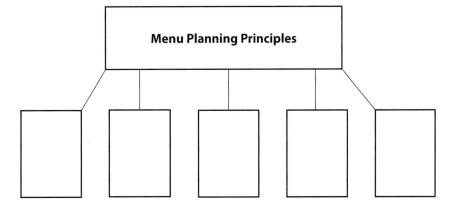

Menu Planning Principles

 Graphic Organizer Go to this book's Online Learning Center at **glencoe.com** for a printable graphic organizer.

GRAPHIC ORGANIZER ANSWER Variety: the amount of different foods offered. Balance: including foods from each food group. Truthfulness: menu statements must be accurate. Nutrition: healthful food choices. Flexibility: menus must be able to change from time to time.

Careful planning can make a menu a success.

ACADEMIC STANDARDS

 English Language Arts
NCTE 4 Use written language to communicate effectively.

 Mathematics
NCTM Number and Operations Understand numbers, ways of representing numbers, relationships among numbers, and number systems.

NCTE National Council of Teachers of English

NCTM National Council of Teachers of Mathematics

NSES National Science Education Standards

NCSS National Council for the Social Studies

Menu Basics

Imagine that you must plan and write a menu for a foodservice operation. You will want to write a clear and accurate menu that is easy to read. Foodservice professionals have created a set of principles that will guide you in planning a unique and appealing menu. Your menu will help your operation sell its food and meet customers' expectations.

The person who is responsible for planning the menu depends on the type of facility. In many foodservice facilities, the management staff plans the menu. In a large foodservice facility, such as a hotel, the executive chef works with management to plan the menu. Registered dietitians (RDs), foodservice directors, and chefs write menus for hospitals, schools, nursing homes, and other institutions. The main office usually plans the menu for chain restaurants.

Menu Planning Principles

You have already learned about various factors that influence menu planning. Foodservice professionals have developed some additional principles that will help you plan successful menus.

Variety

Some foodservice operations have limited menus. For example, a restaurant might offer only gourmet pizzas, or a school cafeteria might have a cycle menu. However, most customers expect to see a variety of dishes on a menu.

You can vary the types of food that you will offer. You also can vary the way the food is prepared. For example, for appetizers, you might have deep-fried vegetables and a cold shrimp cocktail. Entrées may include chicken, beef, and pork that are available roasted, baked, or broiled.

The visual **appeal**, or attraction, of a finished meal is also important. A meal without a variety of colors, shapes, sizes, temperatures, flavors, textures, number of items, and

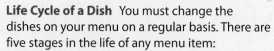

Small Bites

Life Cycle of a Dish You must change the dishes on your menu on a regular basis. There are five stages in the life of any menu item:

- Development, when the dish and its ingredients are planned.
- Introduction, when the dish is first placed on the menu.
- Growth, when the dish begins to be popular among customers.
- Maturity, when the dish has gained its highest popularity.
- Decline, when the dish begins to lose popularity.

It is important to remove a dish from a menu either before or just as it begins to go into decline.

different arrangements lacks appeal. Imagine a plate that contains barbecued chicken, a baked potato sprinkled with chives, and crisp carrots. This meal is colorful and has many textures and shapes.

Another way to add visual interest to meals is with garnishes. A **garnish** is an edible food, such as a sprig of parsley or an orange slice, that is placed on or around food to add color or flavor. A simple lettuce leaf and tomato slice can brighten up an ordinary chicken sandwich.

Balance

Fruits, vegetables, starches, meats and other protein foods, and dairy products are all essential parts of a healthful diet. A menu should include foods from each of these groups.

When a menu offers meal options, think about how foods will look on the plate. You will add to the visual appeal and flavor interest by varying the flavors, shapes, colors, and sizes of foods.

Placement Visualize how the foods will look on the plate and how the plate will be placed in front of the customer. **Plating** is the arrangement of food and garnishes on a plate.

Good plating is key to visual appeal. Attractively plated food leads to enhanced customer satisfaction.

Serving Size Do the portions of food look too small or too large on the plate? Will customers think they are getting their money's worth?

Proportion The **proportion** of a dish is the ratio of one food to another and to the plate. Is the proportion pleasing to the eye? For example, if you offer a smaller portions of food for children, the portions should be balanced in size to each other and to the size of the plate.

Number of Foods on a Plate As a general rule, an odd number of foods on a plate is more visually pleasing than an even number of foods on a plate.

Truthfulness

FDA guidelines require that certain menu statements are accurate. A guideline that shows truthfulness in statements about nutrition, quantity, quality, grade, and freshness is called a **truth-in-menu guideline**. (See **Figure 12.2**.) Restaurants that do not follow these guidelines can be required to pay a penalty.

For example, "homestyle pies" must be baked in the establishment's kitchen, not purchased already prepared. "Louisiana frog legs" must have come from Louisiana. However, some geographic names are accepted as generic descriptions, such as French fries or New England clam chowder.

Federal law also requires that nutritional statements like "low fat" or "light" be truthful. Restaurants must be able to prove any nutritional claims that are made in advertising. Heart patients on restricted diets may order a meal based on its nutritional claim. What might happen if a dish labeled "cholesterol free" on a restaurant menu is not really cholesterol free?

Nutrition

Regardless of the type of foodservice business, menus should offer healthful food choices. A menu planner at an institution has a special responsibility to provide nutritious, appealing, and well-prepared meals. People who eat at institutions usually cannot go somewhere else if they do not like the food. Nursing homes and hospitals must also offer a variety of foods for patients who need special diets, such as those following low-fat diets and people with diabetes or food allergies.

Low-Fat Diets People follow low-fat diets for many reasons, such as heart disease, cancer, weight control, or just to maintain a healthful lifestyle. These people need foods high in fiber and low in fat and cholesterol.

▲ **Proper Balance** Color, proportion, serving size and placement are all important components of a visually appealing meal. *Do you think one of these plates of food is more visually appealing?*

PHOTO CAPTION ANSWER Students should notice that the color, portion sizes, and mix of foods on the left plate are more appealing than those on the right plate.

FIGURE 12.2 Truth-in-Menu Guidelines

Accurate Menus Federal law requires that certain statements on menus be accurate. *Why is this important?*

Guideline	Examples
1. Brand names must be represented accurately.	Examples of brand names of products on a menu are: Hunt's Ketchup, Hellmann's Mayonnaise, Green Giant Frozen Vegetables, and Butterball Turkey.
2. Dietary and nutritional claims must be accurate.	To protect customers from potential health hazards, the dietary structure of food must be correctly stated. For example, low-sodium or fat-free foods must be correctly prepared to ensure the protection of customers. All nutritional claims must be supported with statistical data.
3. The preservation of food must be accurate.	The preservation of food is as follows: frozen; chilling; dehydration; drying, such as sun or smoking; bottled; and canned. If a menu planner wishes to use the previous terms, the terms must be used correctly on the menu. For example, fresh fish is not frozen.
4. Quantity must be accurate.	If a sirloin is 16 ounces, it must be stated on the menu that this is the weight prior to cooking.
5. Location of ingredients must be accurate.	If Dover Sole is on the menu, it must actually be from Dover, England. Pancakes with Vermont maple syrup must be served with syrup from Vermont, not New Hampshire.
6. Quality or grade must be accurate.	When listing quality or grade for meats, dairy products, poultry, and vegetables or fruits, accuracy is critical. For example, if you state that a steak is "prime sirloin," it must be exactly that. You cannot use choice-grade meats and say that they are prime on the menu.
7. Cooking techniques must be accurate.	If broiled swordfish is on your menu, it must be cooked exactly that way. You cannot serve the swordfish baked.
8. Pictures must be accurate.	For example, apple pie à la mode must be apple pie with ice cream.
9. Descriptions of food products must be accurate.	If shrimp cocktail is described on the menu as "four jumbo shrimp on a bed of crushed ice with a zesty cocktail sauce and lemon wedge," and the shrimp cocktail comes with medium-size shrimp, the description is incorrect.

Examples of low-fat, high-fiber foods include fruits, vegetables, and whole-grain breads and cereals.

Diabetes People with diabetes must balance food, portion sizes, exercise, and medication to stay healthy. Menu items that are appropriate for people with diabetes include fruits and vegetables; lean meats, poultry, and fish; low-fat and sugar-free products; and whole grains. It is also helpful to list information about the carbohydrate content of menu items.

Food Allergies You must provide detailed information to customers about common foods and ingredients that may cause allergic reactions. For example, a sauce that has peanuts should be listed on the menu. This way, customers who are allergic to peanuts can avoid the dish.

Flexibility

Menus need to change from time to time for many reasons. The target market or the cost of various ingredients may change.

FIGURE CAPTION ANSWER Many customers, especially those on restricted diets, make food choices based on these statements. False statements may affect a customer's enjoyment and health.

Food Allergies Menus should include detailed descriptions of the ingredients in dishes for customers with common food allergies. *How can customers prevent allergic reactions to foods?*

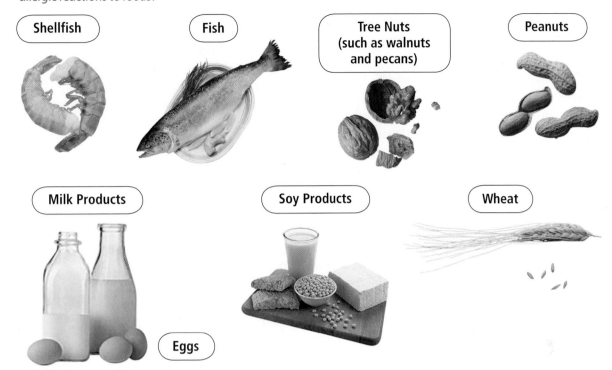

Shellfish

Fish

Tree Nuts (such as walnuts and pecans)

Peanuts

Milk Products

Soy Products

Wheat

Eggs

Write Menu Descriptions

Often, the basic menu list is a description of each item in the most appealing language possible. Because of limited space, each description should be as short as possible.

If customers do not understand what a dish is, they will not order it. Descriptions need to be clear and specific. For example, "fish" is too general. What kind of fish? How big is it? How is it cooked? How is it seasoned? "8-ounce charbroiled salmon with dill sauce" is a much better menu description.

It is also important that the actual food matches the printed menu description. The fish described above should indeed be salmon, weigh 8 ounces before cooking, be charbroiled, and come with dill sauce. **Entice**, or attract, customers with honest descriptions. If the meal they select from your menu does not meet their expectations, they will be disappointed.

Reading Check **Determine** Who is responsible for planning the menu at a nursing home?

PHOTO CAPTION ANSWER The only way for customers to prevent allergic reactions to foods is to avoid allergy-causing foods.

Menu Style and Design

You are given menus from two different restaurants. One is a thin piece of paper that doubles as a place mat. It features meals on the front and children's activities on the back. The other menu has a padded cover with the restaurant's name embossed in gold. The menu items are written in elegant letters on thick, cream-colored paper. Without even looking at the menu items, what are your impressions of these two restaurants? What kind of atmosphere would you expect at each?

The menu style and design reflect the personality of a restaurant and the customers who frequent it. Menus can also be a creative way to market a restaurant. Some menus feature the history of the building or the person who founded the eatery. Others display the daily menu in elegant calligraphy. Some display the day's menu casually on a chalkboard.

READING CHECK ANSWER A registered dietician or foodservice director plans the menu for a nursing home.

The menu is the main way in which a food-service operation communicates with its customers. The factors that have the most impact on menu style and design are the same influences on the menu that were discussed in Section 12.1.

Once you know what types of food to include on a menu, you need to organize it in a way that is most appealing to the customer. Dishes that are grouped in categories are easier for customers to find. The look and feel of the menu will also influence what customers think about the food.

The menu's cover design, color, style of lettering, weight of the paper, and the way descriptions are worded influence how customers feel about the restaurant. There are three common formats of menus. Each sets a different tone for a meal.

Printed Menu Format

A **printed menu** is any form of printed menu list that is handed to customers as soon as they sit down. These menus often contain a list of specials. A special list that is fastened directly to the menu is called a **clip-on**. Daily specials can also be written on folded cards that stand on the table. This is called a **table tent**. A table tent can also be inserted in a stand that sits on the table. Printed menus can be changed daily using a computer and printer. There are also computer programs that can help you design and print specialized menus.

Menu Board Format

A **menu board** contains a handwritten or printed menu on a board on a wall or easel. It can easily reflect daily menu changes. For example, a chalkboard can be erased and a board with printed inserts can be changed. Its informality and flexibility make it perfect for use in cafeterias and fast-food restaurants. The chalkboard menu also can be used in an upscale restaurant to emphasize freshness and creativity.

Spoken Menu Format

In some restaurants, after a customer is seated, a server states what foods are available and the prices of each. This is a **spoken menu**. It is often limited to a few items. Other restaurants present only the daily specials as a spoken menu.

Some foodservice professionals believe that a spoken menu is friendly and increases conversation between customers and servers. Others think that a spoken menu does not allow the customer time to study the menu and make a decision. Many guests view spoken menus as a sign of well-trained servers.

 **Reading Check** Summarize
Describe the menu board format.

Menu Categories

Regardless of size and style, all printed menus are broken down into categories. The type of restaurant determines the categories and the order in which they are listed. Some restaurants use all of the menu categories but change the names to reflect a menu theme. For example, a restaurant with a sports theme might label its appetizers as "First Inning." Other restaurants add and delete categories based on the type of meal they serve. For example, a breakfast menu would not include appetizers, but it might include a section of "skillet items." Generally, categories are listed in the order in which they are consumed.

- **Appetizers** Appetizers can be hot or cold, and can range from nachos to fruit salad to crab cakes. (See Chapter 19 for more information on appetizers.)
- **Soups** On some menus, soups and appetizers appear in the same category. Cold and hot soup choices range from thin, savory broths to thick, creamy chowders. See Chapter 20 for more information on soups.
- **Salads** This category refers to salads made with fresh, crisp vegetables and

sometimes fruit or nuts. Some house salads come with a choice of dressings that are created by the restaurant.

- **Cold Entrées** These entrées include salads topped with poultry, ham, or seafood, as well as cold meat, fruit, and cheese platters.
- **Hot Entrées** The ingredients and cooking methods for hot entrées vary greatly. Hot entrées usually include meat, poultry, fish, or seafood. They also can include casserole items, or extenders. An **extender** is an item made from leftover, low-cost ingredients. Vegetarian dishes such as vegetable lasagna are also popular hot entrées.
- **Sandwiches** Sandwiches, such as hamburgers and grilled cheese, are often shown only on lunch menus. They can be served either hot or cold and can be made from many different ingredients. Sandwiches often come with various breads, condiments, and spreads. See Chapter 19 for more information on sandwiches.

- **Accompaniments** Vegetables and starches that serve as side dishes fall into this category. Vegetables provide a healthful, low-cost, colorful addition to meals. Starches include pasta, potatoes, rice, and other grains.
- **Desserts** Desserts often are displayed on separate menus or on dessert trays. Because many customers do not eat dessert at every meal, servers may need to spend extra time selling desserts. Desserts can include ice creams, puddings, and pastries.
- **Cheeses and Fruits** Cheeses such as brie (brē) and Gouda ('gü-də) are often listed with fresh fruits as an alternative to an appetizer or dessert.
- **Beverages** This category lists beverage selections and prices. This usually includes juices, milk, coffee, tea, and soft drinks.

 Reading Check Identify What food items might be found in the accompaniments category?

SECTION 12.2 After You Read

Review Key Concepts

1. **Summarize** the items to think about when you plan a balanced meal.
2. **Describe** the spoken menu format.
3. **Summarize** the hot entrée category of a menu.

Practice Culinary Academics
English Language Arts

4. You have been asked to design a menu for a new upscale restaurant. Think of a theme for the restaurant, and describe how you would incorporate that theme into the menu design. List menu items for each category.

> **NCTE 4** Use written language to communicate effectively.

Mathematics

5. When you plan your menu, you determine that 40% of your entrées should be vegetarian. What fraction of entrées will be vegetarian? If 62½% of your appetizers are vegetarian, what fraction of appetizers are vegetarian?

Math Concept **Converting Percents to Fractions** Change percents into fractions by writing the percent as the numerator and 100 as the denominator. If the percent has a mixed number, change it to an improper fraction, then multiply by $\frac{1}{100}$.

Starting Hint Convert 40% into $\frac{40}{100}$, and reduce to lowest terms. 62½% should first be converted to an improper fraction, then multiplied by $\frac{1}{100}$, and finally reduced to lowest terms.

> **NCTM Number and Operations** Understand numbers, ways of representing numbers, relationships among numbers, and number systems.

Check your answers at this book's Online Learning Center at **glencoe.com**.

Pricing Menu Items

Menu items must be priced correctly to make a profit.

Reading Guide

 Before You Read

Look It Up As you read this section, keep a dictionary nearby in addition to the glossary at the back of the book. If you hear or read a word that you do not know, look it up in the glossary or the dictionary. Before long, the practice will become a habit. You will be amazed at how many new words you learn.

Read to Learn

Key Concepts
- **Identify** the influences that impact menu prices.
- **Compare and contrast** various menu pricing methods.

Main Idea

The final step in creating a menu is setting the prices. Choose the correct pricing to help make your business a success.

Content Vocabulary
- operating cost
- disposable income
- factor method
- markup-on-cost method
- contribution markup method
- covers
- average check method
- competitors' pricing method
- psychological pricing method

Academic Vocabulary
- guide
- upscale

Graphic Organizer

Use a describing wheel like this one to identify the influences that impact menu prices.

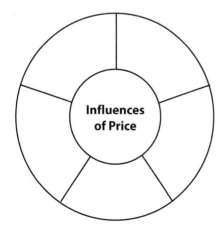

Influences of Price

 Graphic Organizer Go to this book's Online Learning Center at **glencoe.com** for a printable graphic organizer.

GRAPHIC ORGANIZER ANSWER Labor, competition, customers, atmosphere, and location.

 ACADEMIC STANDARDS

 English Language Arts
  NCTE 4 Use written language to communicate effectively.

Mathematics
  NCTM Number and Operations Compute fluently and make reasonable estimates.

  NCTM Problem Solving Apply and adapt a variety of appropriate strategies to solve problems.

 Social Studies
  NCSS VII B Production, Distribution, and Consumption Analyze the role that supply and demand, prices, incentives, and profits play in determining what is produced and distributed in a competitive market system.

NCTE National Council of Teachers of English

NCTM National Council of Teachers of Mathematics

NSES National Science Education Standards

NCSS National Council for the Social Studies

Menu Pricing

You have chosen your menu items, written enticing descriptions, and designed your menu to impress even the most experienced diner. Now you must set prices. If prices are too high, you will not attract customers and lose sales. If prices are too low, you will lose money or not meet your operating costs. An **operating cost** is anything that is a cost of doing business.

Menu prices must cover operating costs. They must also be fair to the customer. Menu prices are often influenced by labor, competition, customers, atmosphere, food and facility costs, and location.

- **Labor** Menu items that need more time, care, and skill in preparation are often set at a higher price. In general, a menu prepared by an experienced kitchen staff takes more labor. These menu items tend to be more expensive.
- **Competition** Review competitors' menus to see what they charge for similar items. Use your competition as a **guide**, or something that provides information, only, since details like portion size and ingredient quality may be different.
- **Customers** The types of customers your foodservice operation attracts will influence your menu prices. For example, you may charge less if your main customers are families rather than business professionals.
- **Atmosphere** The style of your foodservice operation helps determine prices. Customers expect fine-dining restaurants to have higher prices than casual, family-style restaurants.
- **Location** Restaurants in cities often serve people with a higher disposable income. **Disposable income** is money that people have left over for extras after paying all their bills. Because of this, restaurants in cities can have higher menu prices than restaurants in small towns.

Reading Check Describe How does competition influence menu pricing?

Pricing Methods

Setting and tracking the price of menu items enables the restaurant owner to stay in business and enjoy a profit. Some restaurants choose to set menu prices based on the cost of food and other costs associated with running the business. Other menus are priced according to competitor prices and the customer psychology of prices. Each pricing method has its pros and cons. Considering each method can help restaurant owners and managers understand how they can earn the highest profit for the food options and location of the restaurant.

Factor Method

The **factor method** uses a pricing scale based on a percentage of the food costs needed to operate the restaurant successfully. To use the factor method, you must first determine what the food cost percent should be. To determine the food cost percentage, you divide the total cost of food by the total food sales. Then, take that food cost percent

LE INSALATE

CAESAR Anchovies upon request...10.95
DI FUNGHI Endive and radicchio with grilled Shitake mushrooms.....................10.50
BELLA Arugola, pears, sun-dried cherries, goat cheese, shaved parmesan........9.95
TRI COLORI Arugola, endive, red radicchio and parmesan..............................9.25
FANTASIA Beets, grilled peppers, tomatoes, mozzarella and basil....................9.95
BURRATA Soft mozzarella, red and yellow tomatoes and basil.........................12.50
SPINACH SALAD
Baby spinach, garbanzo beans, goat cheese, walnuts, bacon bits and green apples.....10.95

GLI ANTIPASTI

MARINATED WHITE ANCHOVIES With Bottarga and micro green, Puglia olive oil and lemon juice.......12.95
CERTIFIED ORGANIC SALMON CARPACCIO Pounded thin with celery, capers, lemon and ponzu..12.50
TUNA CARPACCIO Thin sliced with lemon and miso sauce. Micro green and cherry tomato............13.50
CALAMARI FRITTI Rings only and served with arrabiata sauce 9.95
BRESAOLA Cured beef, sliced thin with arugola and Parmesan 14.50
PROSCIUTTO E MELONE Parma certified with melon 14.50
BEEF CARPACCIO Served with arugola and Parmesan 14.50
PORTOBELLO UBRIACO Grilled mushrooms with honey-orange sauce and Ubriaco cheese........12.50
CRESPELLE SCAMPI Crêpes sautéed with shrimp and pesto sauce 12.50
MELANZANE ALLA PARMIGGIANA Eggplant topped with burrata and basil 13.95

Set Prices Menu pricing must cover the cost of food, labor, and facility expenses, and a profit for the restaurant. *What other factors affect menu pricing?*

and divide it into 100%, which will result in your factor. Multiply the factor by the cost of the menu item. This will give you the menu selling price.

For example, if your food cost is $5,000 and your total sales are $20,000, this formula can help you determine your food cost percentage:

$$\begin{array}{r} .25 \text{ (food cost percent)} \\ \$20000.00\overline{)\$5000.00.} \\ \underline{400000.} \\ 100000 \\ \underline{100000} \\ 0 \end{array}$$

Your food cost percentage is 25%. If a hamburger and French fries cost $1.50 to make, you would calculate the menu price as follows:

1.
$$\begin{array}{r} 4 \text{ (factor)} \\ .25\overline{)1.00.} \end{array}$$

2. $1.50 (item cost)
$$\underline{\times\ 4\ \text{(factor)}}$$
$6.00 (selling price)

You would sell the hamburger and French fries for $6.00.

Markup-on-Cost Method

Another common way to determine prices is by using the **markup-on-cost method**. To find the selling price, take the food cost of an item and divide it by the desired food cost percentage.

For example, if you want the food cost percentage to be 25%, and a grilled cheese sandwich and cup of tomato soup cost $1.25 to make, you would calculate the price as follows:

$$\begin{array}{r} \$5.00 \text{ (selling price)} \\ .25\overline{)\$1.25.\ \text{(item cost)}} \end{array}$$

You would price the grilled cheese sandwich and tomato soup at $5.

Contribution Margin Method

The **contribution margin method** is a pricing method that uses a general contribution of customers to costs besides food for running a kitchen. You would add the average contribution margin per guest to the item's standard food cost.

For example, say you want to sell a turkey sandwich. The nonfood costs plus a profit for a month for the restaurant come to $4,000. The restaurant will serve approximately 30 **covers**, or expected meals, per day, averaging 900 a month. The base food cost for the turkey sandwich is $3. You would calculate the price as follows:

1.
$$\begin{array}{r} 4.44 \text{ (contribution margin)} \\ 900\overline{)4,000} \end{array}$$

2. $4.44
$$\underline{+\ \$3.00\ \text{(food cost)}}$$
$7.44 (selling price)

Average Check Method

The **average check method** prices items near an average check that you would like each customer to spend. This amount should be based on the profits you hope to get for a particular breakfast, lunch, or dinner check. For example, if you want an average check total of $12 per customer for lunch, your menu prices should be set so that most customers will automatically order food and beverages that come out to that total.

Competitors' Pricing Method

The **competitors' pricing method** charges approximately what the competition charges for similar menu items. Some places charge slightly less in an attempt to attract more customers. Other places may charge slightly more in an attempt to appear more **upscale**, or for more affluent customers. This method is risky because overhead costs such as rent, labor, food costs, and profit are different at every restaurant.

Gourmet Math

Working with Percents

People involved in foodservice use percents in daily decision making, but may not have time to perform full calculations. You can estimate a percent of a number by using compatible numbers and mental math.

For example, 28% of $19.85 is close to 30% of $20. Multiply 30% by $20 to get an estimate. The estimation process is easier if you remember these equivalent percents, decimals, and fractions:

Percent	Decimal	Fraction
10%	0.10	1/10
20%	0.20	1/5
25%	0.25	1/4
33 1/3	0.33	1/3
40%	0.40	2/5
50%	0.50	1/2
66 2/3%	0.66	2/3
75%	0.75	3/4
80%	0.80	4/5

If you want to make a 32% profit on a $17.80 entree, estimate how much profit that amounts to.

Math Concept **Estimating Percents** To estimate the percent of a number, replace the percent with its closest compatible percent (or its equivalent fraction) and replace the number with its closest compatible number, then multiply.

Starting Hint Replace $17.80 with its closest compatible number by rounding up to the nearest dollar. Find the percent in the table closest to 32%, and then find that percent's equivalent fraction. Multiply this fraction by the number to determine the estimated profit. You can then calculate the actual amount (by multiplying $17.80 $\times$ 0.32) to see how close your estimate is.

> **NCTM Number and Operations** Compute fluently and make reasonable estimates.

Psychological Pricing Method

Once the selling price is determined using other methods, the psychological pricing method can be used. The **psychological pricing method** is based on how a customer reacts to menu prices. For example, a customer may be more willing to order a $6.00 hamburger and French fries if you lower the price to $5.95.

Moving from one dollar category to another influences how customers view the value they get for their money. A price of $12.95 raised to $13.25 seems like a bigger increase than $13.25 raised to $13.75. However, the first increase is 30 cents, while the second increase is 50 cents.

Most restaurants start menu prices at the low end of a dollar category so that they can adjust the prices several times without entering the next dollar category. For example, an item at $13.25 can be raised to $13.50, and then to $13.75 before moving into the $14 range.

Restaurants that emphasize quality food at low prices, such as diners and quick-service restaurants, often use psychological pricing methods. Few fine-dining establishments use this type of pricing because it does not fit their image of luxury and elegance.

Tracking Results

There are many ways to track how well menu items are selling at your restaurant:

- Review your records to see how well certain menu items sold. Point-of-sale ordering software can help you easily track specific menu items. You can also use sales tax figures to track monthly sales.
- Decide which items will stay on the menu and which will come off. You may wish to modify the price or ingredients of some menu items, depending on what is popular among your customers.

Reading Check Pricing Methods Which factors are taken into account when using the psychological pricing method?

GOURMET MATH ANSWER $17.80 can be rounded up to $18.00, while 32% is close to 33 1/3%, which is equivalent to 1/3. Students can estimate the profit by taking 1/3 of $18.00, which equals $6.00. The actual profit amount is $17.80 $\times$ 0.32 = $5.696 $\approx$ $5.70.

READING CHECK ANSWER The factors include how customers react to menu prices, and how they view the value for their money.

Relative Risk There is a level of risk involved with every pricing method. *Why would some restaurants choose not to use the factor method of pricing?*

SECTION 12.3 After You Read

Review Key Concepts

1. **Explain** how location influences menu prices.

2. **Describe** how to find a selling price using the markup-on-cost method.

Practice Culinary Academics

 English Language Arts

3. Imagine that you are a consultant who has been hired to help a restaurant set menu prices. The restaurant will be located in the area where your school is located. Create a business report for the restaurant that analyzes the customers and location for the purpose of determining a good price range for the restaurant.

> **NCTE 4** Use written language to communicate effectively.

 Social Studies

4. Research the news for articles about factors that influence the price of different food items. Summarize the stories you find, and then explain how the situation described in the article might influence a restaurant owner who has dishes containing these foods on the menu.

> **NCSS VII B Production, Distribution, and Consumption** Analyze the role that supply and demand, prices, incentives, and profits play in determining what is produced and distributed in a competitive market system.

Mathematics

5. You would like to add whole-grain pancakes to your breakfast menu. If you want the food cost percentage to be 35%, and the pancakes cost $2.09 to make, use the markup-on-cost method to determine your selling price.

Math Concept **Markup-on-Cost Pricing** Divide the food cost of an item by the desired food cost percentage. Convert the food cost percentage to a decimal by moving the decimal point two places to the left.

Starting Hint Convert 35% into a decimal by removing the percent sign and shifting the decimal point two places to the left. Divide the food cost by this decimal to get the selling price.

> **NCTM Problem Solving** Apply and adapt a variety of appropriate strategies to solve problems.

 Check your answers at this book's Online Learning Center at **glencoe.com**.

FIGURE CAPTION ANSWER Student answers may vary. Although the factor method of pricing has the lowest risk level, a new restaurant may not have a past performance record with which to evaluate prices. Another reason might be that a restaurant has nearby competition for business.

Chapter Summary

Consider your target customers, cost, the type of food served, the type of equipment, operational skills required, geography and culture, and eating trends when you plan a menu. Menus should be varied and balanced, and descriptions of menu items should be accurate.

Menu categories include appetizers, soups, salads, cold entrées, hot entrées, sandwiches, accompaniments, desserts, cheeses and fruits, and beverages. Menu item categories are usually listed in the order that they are consumed.

Menu prices must cover the operating costs of the establishment. Pricing methods include the factor method, the markup-on-cost method, the contribution margin method, the average check method, the competitors' pricing method, and the psychological pricing method. Choose a method carefully.

Content and Academic Vocabulary Review

1. Arrange the vocabulary terms below into groups of related words. Explain your groupings.

Content Vocabulary

- menu (p. 308)
- entrée (p. 309)
- fixed menu (p. 310)
- cycle menu (p. 310)
- du jour menu (p. 310)
- à la carte menu (p. 310)
- semi-à la carte menu (p. 310)
- table d'hôte menu (p. 310)
- prix fixe menu (p. 310)
- meal-based menu (p. 310)
- California menu (p. 310)
- continental menu (p. 311)
- accompaniment (p. 312)
- ethnic menu (p. 312)

- garnish (p. 314)
- plating (p. 314)
- proportion (p. 315)
- truth-in-menu guideline (p. 315)
- printed menu (p. 318)
- clip-on (p. 318)
- table tents (p. 318)
- menu board (p. 318)
- spoken menu (p. 318)
- extender (p. 319)
- operating cost (p. 321)
- disposable income (p. 321)
- factor method (p. 321)
- markup-on-cost method (p. 322)

- contribution margin method (p. 322)
- covers (p. 322)
- average check method (p. 322)
- competitors' pricing method (p. 322)
- psychological pricing method (p. 323)

Academic Vocabulary

- dictate (p. 309)
- complex (p. 309)
- appeal (p. 314)
- entice (p. 317)
- guide (p. 321)
- upscale (p. 322)

Review Key Concepts

2. Categorize the factors that influence a menu.

3. Describe the types of menus used by foodservice establishments.

4. Evaluate basic menu planning principles.

5. Define menu styles and design guidelines.

6. Explain different menu categories and how they are typically listed.

7. Identify the influences that impact menu prices.

8. Compare and contrast various menu pricing methods.

Critical Thinking

9. Imagine that you are opening a restaurant. Which type of menu would you choose for your establishment? Give five reasons for your choice.

10. Describe what could happen if a foodservice establishment fails to consider food allergies in menu planning. How might this impact the customer?

Academic Skills

English Language Arts

11. Modify a Menu Pretend you are a menu consultant. Get three menus from local foodservice operations. Review each menu and modify them to accommodate one of the following dietary needs: vegan, lactose intolerance, and shellfish allergy. The entire menu need not be changed. Write a letter to each establishment explaining how they can modify their menus to accommodate the need.

> **NCTE 5** Use different writing process elements to communicate effectively.

Science

12. Analyze Menu Prices It is always useful to compile information for analysis in a scientific way before making a pricing decision.

Procedure Create three simple menus of three to five dishes each, and then price each dish using the pricing methods described in the chapter. Vary the menu design and meal descriptions. Then, show fellow students one menu each and have them explain what they would order and why.

Analysis Compile data on which dishes were chosen the most from each menu and why. Show your data, and in a short summary analyze how this information might help you plan a menu in the future.

> **NSES A** Develop abilities necessary to do scientific inquiry.

Mathematics

13. Calculate Menu Profitability Last month, your restaurant featured three different dinner specials. You would like to add one to the permanent menu. You sold 750 steak specials at $26 each, 600 salmon specials at $34 each, and 400 pasta specials at $22.50 each. If the food and preparation costs were $16 for the steak, $22 for the salmon, and $13.50 for the pasta, which item brought in the most revenue? Which generated the most profit? Which had the highest profit margin?

Math Concept **Revenue, Profit, and Profit Margin** The term revenue refers to the total amount of income generated by sales, and generally equals price times quantity sold. Profit equals revenue minus costs. Calculate the profit margin percentage by dividing profit by revenue.

Starting Hint Determine the revenue for each item by multiplying its sales price by the quantity sold. Calculate the total profit for each item by first determining total costs for each item (the cost of each item times the quantity sold), and subtracting that from the revenue amount. Divide the total profit by the total revenue for each item and convert the answer to a percentage to find the profit margin.

> **NCTM Number and Operations** Compute fluently and make reasonable estimates.

Certification Prep

> *Sharpen your test-taking skills to improve your kitchen certification program score.*

Directions Read the questions. Then, read the answer choices and choose the best possible answer for each.

14. In what type of establishment would you find a fixed menu?

    a. coffee shop   **c.** cafeteria

    b. hotel   **d.** cruise ship

15. What course is sometimes displayed on a separate menu?

    a. appetizers   **c.** salads

    b. sandwiches   **d.** dessert

Test-Taking Tip
In a multiple-choice test, read the questions carefully. Look for negative words (not, never, except, unless), which can affect how you answer the problem.

Review and Applications

Real-World Skills and Applications

Interpersonal and Collaborative Skills

16. Plan a Truthful Menu Follow your teacher's instructions to divide into small groups. Work together to plan a menu based on the truth-in-menu guidelines. Choose the courses you will offer and create three to five dishes for each course. Then, work together to agree on descriptions that meet the guidelines.

Communication Skills

17. Revise the Cafeteria Menu Survey fellow students and ask them to rate menu items in your school's cafeteria. Also, ask them for suggestions on how to improve the menu. Write a letter to the cafeteria manager with suggestions for revising the menu based on the information you gathered.

Technology Applications

18. Design a Menu Technology can be used to plan and organize the look of a restaurant. Use a graphic design program or word processing program to design a menu for a small café. Be sure to consider the potential customers as well as the atmosphere and type of food served when you design the menu. Share your menu with your classmates.

Financial Literacy

19. Determine Selling Price Use the factor method to determine the selling price of a slice of pepperoni pizza and an iced tea. Your food cost percentage is 50%. The item cost for the pizza is $3, and the item cost for the iced tea is 50 cents.

Culinary Lab

Use the culinary skills you have learned in this chapter.

Create a Menu

20. Work in Teams Working as a team, you will create a menu for a new foodservice operation. Consider all of the influences on menus as you plan.

A. Decide on the menu. Determine the type of menu and which meal of the day your menu will be for.

B. Add menu items. Your menu should have 10 items total. Determine the dishes that will be on the menu and create your descriptions. Be clear and concise, and think about nutrition and special dietary needs. Use the menu characteristics below to help organize the menu.

Menu influences	Target customers, cost, type of food, equipment, worker skill, culture/location, trends
Menu type	Fixed, cycle, à la carte, semi-à la carte, table d'hôte, prix fixe
Menu categories	appetizers, soups, salads, entrées sandwiches, accompaniments, desserts, cheeses/fruits, beverages

C. Price the menu. Determine the selling price. Use one of the pricing methods described in the chapter.

D. Design the menu. Develop the menu layout, and the display it for the class.

Create Your Evaluation

Create a rating sheet with spaces for rating design, price, and taste. Rate the design both on appearance and also on organization and ease of reading. Evaluate price on how well the price matches what the dishes seem to be worth. Finally, evaluate the dishes by how they would appeal to different types of customers.

Using Standardized Recipes

SECTIONS

13.1 Standardized Recipe Basics

13.2 Recipe Measurement and Conversion

WRITING ACTIVITY

Recipe

Choose a simple dish with few ingredients that you know how to prepare. Write a recipe for the dish. Before you begin, look at existing recipes as a guide.

Writing Tips

1 List any ingredients in the order that they will be used.

2 Include a list of the equipment and tools you will need.

3 Make each instruction brief and easy to follow.

EXPLORE THE PHOTO

Using a recipe helps ensure that the quality of your food is consistent. *Why would consistency be important in a foodservice operation?*

WRITING ACTIVITY ANSWER Recipes should follow a recognizable recipe format. There should be a dish title, ingredients, and clear instructions.

EXPLORE THE PHOTO ANSWER Consistency ensures that every customer gets the same high-quality food.

Standardized Recipe Basics

Reading Guide

 Before You Read

Check for Understanding If you have questions as you are reading, that means you are checking your understanding of the material. To get the most out of the text, try to answer these questions.

Read to Learn

Key Concepts

● **Explain** how standardized recipes help to maintain product consistency.

Main Idea

Recipes provide specific instructions to prepare food items. A recipe includes details on how to use ingredients, procedures, and cooking instructions.

Graphic Organizer

As you read, use a web diagram like this one to list the seven different parts of a recipe.

Content Vocabulary

● recipe
● quantity
● standardized recipe
● quality control
● product name
● yield
● portion size
● preparation procedure
● formula
● ingredient list
● baker's percentage

Academic Vocabulary

● consistent
● hallmark

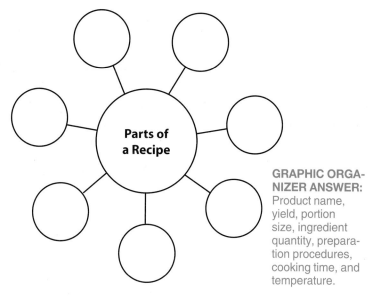

Parts of a Recipe

GRAPHIC ORGA-NIZER ANSWER: Product name, yield, portion size, ingredient quantity, preparation procedures, cooking time, and temperature.

 Graphic Organizer Go to this book's Online Learning Center at **glencoe.com** for a printable graphic organizer.

Standardized recipes produce good food every time.

ACADEMIC STANDARDS

 English Language Arts
NCTE 12 Use language to accomplish individual purposes.

 Mathematics
NCTM Measurement Understand measurable attributes of objects and the units, systems, and processes of measurement.

 Science
NSES B Develop an understanding of the structure and properties of matter.

Social Studies
NCSS VIII A Science, Technology, and Society Identify and describe both current and historical examples of the interaction and interdependence of science, technology, and society in a variety of cultural settings.

NCSS IX A Global Connections Explain how language can facilitate global understanding or cause misunderstanding.

NCTE National Council of Teachers of English

NCTM National Council of Teachers of Mathematics

NSES National Science Education Standards

NCSS National Council for the Social Studies

1545

The English cookbook
*A Proper Newe Booke of
Cokerye* is written

1558

Elizabeth I, queen of
England, is crowned

The History of the Recipe

The written history of the recipe can be traced back to 1400 BCE. Ancient Egyptians used painted hieroglyphics to show the preparation of food. However, it was not until Roman times that recipes were written down using words. In 1896, American Fannie Merritt Farmer is credited with creating the model for how we write recipes today. By standardizing measurements, she made sure that recipe results were more reliable.

History Application

Conduct research to find a written recipe that is at least 100 years old. Does the writing and recipe differ from recipes you can find in today's cookbooks? Does it provide enough information for you to follow? Rewrite the recipe to follow today's recipe style.

NCSS IX A Global Connections Explain how language can facilitate global understanding or cause misunderstanding.

Standardized Recipes

Recipes are important tools in the foodservice industry. A recipe is not just a general set of instructions. Instead, a **recipe** is an exact set of directions on how to use ingredients, equipment, and preparation and cooking techniques for a certain dish.

To get the result you want from a recipe, you must carefully follow the specific directions that are listed on the recipe. If you do, the food will be a **consistent** quality, or will be free from variations, every time you prepare it. You will also end up with the same quantity of food every time you prepare the dish. **Quantity** is the total amount a recipe makes.

A **standardized** ('stan-dər-ˌdīzd) **recipe** is a set of written instructions that is used to consistently prepare a known quantity and quality of a certain food. Standardized recipes are often changed to meet the needs of a particular user. Standardized recipes are also changed based on the type of equipment that a foodservice establishment has.

Each standardized recipe must go through quality control. **Quality control** is a system that ensures that everything will meet the foodservice establishment's standards. Recipes are tested many times to make sure that they work the same way every time before they are used for customers. To do this, directions on a standardized recipe must be clear and easy to follow, and ingredients must be listed correctly and accurately, in the order in which they will be used.

There are many benefits to using a standardized recipe:

- The quality of the food will be consistent each time the recipe is made.
- The quantity of the food will be consistent each time the recipe is made.
- You can control the portion size and cost of the recipe.
- Movement in the kitchen by foodservice workers will be more efficient because of clear, exact instructions.
- You will have fewer errors in food orders.
- You will eliminate waste by not overproducing food.
- You will meet customers' expectations of quality each time the food is prepared.

Standardized recipes offer many benefits to foodservice operations. However, they cannot solve problems caused by purchasing or receiving poor-quality items, or purchasing too much food. If you make a substitution in the ingredients in a recipe, you must retest the recipe to make sure that the dish still has the same quality. A recipe that is specific and that produces the same product each time is the **hallmark**, or distinguishing feature, of a successful foodservice organization.

The success of any standardized recipe depends upon the experience of the person who uses it. If the person who uses the recipe does not understand basic cooking techniques, for example, he or she will not get the right results from the dish.

A TASTE OF HISTORY ANSWER The rewritten recipe should be easy to understand and include ingredients and amounts, pre-preparation steps, directions, equipment, temperature and time, and yield.

An experienced cook may be able to make slight changes to recipes without changing the outcome. This is because an experienced cook has learned to apply sound judgment and past experience to the techniques and instructions in each recipe.

Parts of a Recipe

These parts are always the same for any standardized recipe (See the recipe on page 332):

- **Product Name** Customers expect to receive what they order from a menu. The **product name**, or name given to the recipe, should be consistent with the name of the dish listed on the menu. Both of these should accurately describe the same product. This helps eliminate confusion between the kitchen and service staff.
- **Yield** The number of servings, or portions, that a recipe produces is its **yield**. The yield of a recipe is an important factor that is used to calculate the cost per serving of the recipe.
- **Portion Size** The **portion size** is the amount or size of an individual serving. Standardized recipes always show a portion size. This allows you to plan enough food for your customers.
- **Ingredient Quantity** Standardized recipes give directions on how to measure each ingredient to help control quantity. Use the right quantity of each ingredient during preparation.
- **Preparation Procedures** A **preparation procedure** is a step that you must take to prepare the dish. Preparation procedures are the result of careful testing of the recipes by experienced culinary professionals. To consistently produce a high-quality product, you must follow any preparation procedures carefully in the order in which they are listed. Environment, such as altitude, may affect preparation procedures.
- **Cooking Temperatures** You can ruin a dish if you use too high or too low of a temperature for cooking. Range-top cooking temperatures are listed in a recipe as low, medium, or high. Temperatures for ovens and other appliances that have a thermostat to control cooking temperature are listed as exact degrees Fahrenheit or Celsius. Many recipes require that the oven be preheated to a specific temperature before any food is placed inside for cooking. The time that you will need for preheating will vary with the type of oven.
- **Cooking Time** Standardized recipes list the required cooking time for the dish. It is important to cook the food for the recommended time, using the specified equipment at the specified temperature. Using different equipment, a different size or type of cookware, or changing the cooking time can change the results. The dish may not come out the way you had expected.

Formula or Recipe?

A **formula** is a special type of recipe that is used in the bakeshop. Baking is different from cooking in many ways. One of the most important differences involves the chemistry of baking. Because baking involves chemical reactions, baked goods require precise formulas to work correctly. Small variations in the ingredients or measurements can affect the quality of the baked good item noticeably.

Although formulas and recipes are similar in the way in which they are written, there are three major differences between the two.

> ### ⤳ Small Bites ⤳
>
> **Ingredient Preparation** Ingredient quantity and preparation steps must be listed accurately on a recipe. Important preparation steps are usually written just before or after the mention of an ingredient. For many foods, chopping, slicing, or other preparation is done before you measure the ingredients.

※ MASTER RECIPE

Green Beans in Garlic Sauce

YIELD: 20 SERVINGS ⌐ **YIELD**
SERVING SIZE: 4 OZ. ⌐ **PORTION SIZE**

Ingredients

INGREDIENT QUANTITY		
3 lbs.	Fresh green beans, washed, ends trimmed, and cut in half
3 oz.	Butter
8 cloves	Garlic, peeled and minced
1 lb.	Canned crushed tomatoes
1 pt.	White chicken stock, heated to a boil
	Salt and freshly ground black pepper, to taste

Method of Preparation

1. In a saucepan, place the fresh green beans in boiling, salted water. Cook until done. Drain beans and shock in an ice bath. When beans are cold, remove and drain them.
2. In a sauté pan, melt the butter and sauté the garlic. Add the crushed tomatoes, and sauté for 5 minutes.
3. Add the green beans and chicken stock to the tomatoes, butter, and garlic.
4. Simmer at 180°F (82°C) until done. Season with salt and pepper to taste and serve, or hold at 135°F (57°C) or above.

PREPARATION PROCEDURES,

COOKING PROCEDURES,

COOKING TIME

Cooking Technique

Sauté

1. Preheat the cooking medium on high heat.
2. Add fat oil or oil. When fat or oil is almost smoking, add food.
3. Do not overcrowd the pan.

International Flavor

Green beans are used in many different cultures as a side dish. Use the Internet or library to research these or other international variations, and write a half-page report on your findings:

● Masaledar sem (India)

● Fagiolini di Sant' Anna (Italy)

Chef Notes

Fresh green beans should snap apart when bent. Green beans that bend but do not break are not fresh.

Substitutions

● To lower saturated fat, use olive oil rather than butter for sautéing.

● Use herbs or spices to add flavor without adding salt.

Glossary

Simmer to cook slowly and steadily in hot water
Shock to drop simmered or boiled food into cold water or ice to stop cooking

HACCP

● Hold at 135°F (57°C) or higher

Hazardous Foods

● Butter

Nutrition

Calories 284   Calories from Fat 41
Total Fat 5g
   Saturated Fat 3g
Cholesterol 10mg
Sodium 99mg
Total Carbohydrate 46g
   Fiber 12g
   Sugars 5g
Protein 17g
• Vitamin A 6%   • Vitamin C 10%
• Calcium 10%   • Iron 30%

- **Ingredient List Order** Recipes and formulas both contain an **ingredient list**. This list includes all ingredients that will be used in the dish. In recipes, ingredients are listed in the order that they will be used. This list will be followed by procedures to use those ingredients for successful results. In formulas, however, ingredients are typically listed in order by decreasing weight. These are often given as percentages.
- **Baker's Percentage** Precise weight measurements are used in formulas to prepare food. This type of measurement, often called a **baker's percentage**, includes the percentage of each ingredient in relation to the weight of flour in the final baked product. Baker's percentages make it easy to increase or decrease the quantity of individual ingredients. (Chapter 26 explains how to increase and decrease ingredients in detail.)
- **Preparation Instructions** Baking formulas may not always include the instructions that are needed to prepare the baked product.

 Reading Check **List** What are the three differences between recipes and formulas?

SECTION 13.1 After You Read

Review Key Concepts

1. **Explain** how quality control works.

Practice Culinary Academics

 Science

2. **Procedure** Locate a muffin recipe or formula and prepare it using the specified flour type. Then, prepare the recipe again using a different flour type.

   Analysis What are the differences in the two muffins? What do you think causes this difference? Form a hypothesis, and research to find if your hypothesis was correct. Write a summary of your findings.

   NSES B Develop an understanding of the structure and properties of matter.

 English Language Arts

3. Locate a recipe that you like and create a recipe card for it. Place each recipe element in the appropriate place and make sure that all elements are included. Make any appropriate changes to the recipe language to make it clearer and easier to follow.

   NCTE 12 Use language to accomplish individual purposes.

 Social Studies

4. Technology can help foodservice establishments improve the way they use standardized recipes. Find one example of how technology has improved the use of standardized recipes and present it to the class in a five-minute oral presentation. Use images if possible.

   NCSS VIII A Science, Technology, and Society Identify and describe both current and historical examples of the interaction and interdependence of science, technology, and society in a variety of cultural settings.

 Mathematics

5. The recipe for Green Beans in Garlic Sauce in this chapter yields 20 4-ounce servings. What is the total yield of the recipe in ounces? What is the total yield in pounds?

   Math Concept **Converting Ounces to Pounds** There are 16 ounces in 1 pound. When converting from a smaller unit to a bigger unit, the number will always be smaller. Therefore, you must divide by the conversion factor (16).

   Starting Hint Multiply the number of servings by the serving size to get the total number of ounces. To convert to the larger unit (pounds), divide the total ounces by 16.

   NCTM Measurement Understand measurable attributes of objects and the units, systems, and processes of measurement.

   Check your answers at this book's Online Learning Center at **glencoe.com**.

Recipe Measurement and Conversion

Reading Guide

 Before You Read

Use Diagrams As you read through this section, write down the main idea. Write down any facts, explanations, or examples you find in the text. Start at the main idea and draw arrows to the information that directly supports it. Then, draw arrows from these examples to any information that supports them.

Read to Learn

Key Concepts

- **List** different recipe measurements and when each is used.
- **Give examples** of the factors that affect recipe conversion.

Main Idea

Sometimes, foodservice professionals need to adjust recipes to meet their needs. Adjusted recipes should be tested before preparation, as many factors can affect conversion.

Content Vocabulary

- convert
- metric system
- balance scale
- electronic scale
- volume measurement
- count
- recipe conversion
- conversion factor
- shrinkage

Academic Vocabulary

- precise
- alter

Graphic Organizer

Use a sequence chart like this one to list the steps in converting the portion size of a recipe. Write one step in each box.

Converting Portion Size

First:
Next:
Next:
Last:

 Graphic Organizer Go to this book's Online Learning Center at **glencoe.com** for a printable graphic organizer.

Do you know how to adjust recipes to fit your needs?

 ACADEMIC STANDARDS

 English Language Arts
NCTE 5 Use different writing process elements to communicate effectively.

Mathematics
NCTM Number and Operations Understand numbers, ways of representing numbers, relationships among numbers, and number systems.

NCTM Number and Operations Compute fluently and make reasonable estimates.

Science
NSES 1 Develop an understanding of change, constancy, and measurement.

NCTE National Council of Teachers of English

NCTM National Council of Teachers of Mathematics

NSES National Science Education Standards

NCSS National Council for the Social Studies

GRAPHIC ORGANIZER ANSWER 1) Existing portions x existing portion size = existing yield. 2) Desired portions x desired portion size = desired yield. 3) Existing yield [division sign] existing yield = conversion factor. 4) Each ingredient amount x conversion factor = new ingredient amounts.

Standardized Recipe Measurements

Recipes are designed and written to yield a certain number of servings each time they are made. Sometimes, it is necessary to convert recipes to make more or less of a dish. To **convert** a recipe means to adjust ingredient quantities up or down. This can help meet the changing needs of the foodservice establishment. If you must change the yield or portion sizes, you must convert the recipe before you begin any ingredient preparation.

No recipe can be successful if you are careless about measuring ingredients. Careful measuring helps give you a consistent quantity each time a recipe is prepared and served. For a successful end product, each ingredient in the recipe must be measured precisely.

Measuring Tools Measuring tools come in many shapes and sizes. *Why is it important to have a variety of tools on hand?*

Standardized recipe measurements can make it quicker and easier to increase or decrease the amount that a recipe makes when needed. Ingredients are measured by weight (pounds, ounces), volume (cups, teaspoons), or count (2 eggs, 1 ear of corn).

Some measurements are done using the metric system. The **metric system** is a measurement system that uses powers of 10 to measure things. For example, 1 gram = 10 decagrams = 100 miligrams = 1,000 kilograms. It is easy to convert measurements from one unit to another by simply moving the decimal place.

Although the metric system is not used often in recipes from the United States, some measurement units, such as grams, may be found. Metric system measurements are often used in recipes from other countries where the metric system is the standard system for measurement.

Weight

In commercial foodservice establishments, most ingredients are measured by weight. Weight is a measurement that tells how heavy a substance is. Measuring by weight is the quickest, easiest, and most accurate way of measuring foods such as flour, sugar, meats, and cheeses. Ounces and pounds are examples of common weight measurements.

Scales for measuring weight come in many different types, sizes, and price ranges. The types of scales used in foodservice are balance, portion or spring, and electronic.

Balance Scale

A **balance scale**, also called a baker's scale, has two platforms. One platform holds the item that is being weighed. The other platform holds weights in predetermined amounts. These weights are added or removed until the two platforms are balanced. Counting the weights shows the weight of the food item. Balance scales are used when **precise**, or exact, measurement is important, such as in baking.

On the Scale Scales come in different types and models. *What is this type of scale, and what is it used for?*

Portion Scale

A portion, or spring, scale is similar to a bathroom scale. It weighs items by measuring how much the spring is depressed when an item is placed on its platform. A needle on a dial shows the weight of the item. Spring scales are often used as portion scales. For example, you might use a spring scale to measure meats in a deli.

Electronic Scale

An **electronic**, or digital, **scale** is similar to a spring scale. It, too, has a spring that is depressed when an item is placed on its platform. The amount that the spring is depressed measures the weight of the item displayed on a digital readout. This readout is more accurate than the readout from a needle guide, but digital scales are more expensive than spring scales. Electronic scales and spring scales can be used as a portion scale.

Volume

The term volume refers to the amount of space that a substance occupies. Volume measures are used most often to measure liquids in a foodservice setting. A **volume measurement** is a form of measurement that is expressed in cups, quarts, gallons, and fluid ounces.

Figure 13.1 and Figure 13.2 show common cooking abbreviations and equivalents, including volume measurements.

FIGURE 13.1 Measurement Abbreviations
Measurement Labels Standardized recipes use abbreviations for common measurements. *Why do standardized recipes use abbreviations instead of the full spelling of measurements?*

Measurement	Abbreviation
Teaspoon	tsp. or t.
Tablespoon	tbsp. or T.
Ounce	oz.
Fluid ounce	fl. oz.
Pound	lb. or #
Cup	c.
Pint	pt.
Quart	qt.
Gallon	gal. or G.
Barrel	bbl.
Dozen	doz.
Bunch	bch. or bu.
Case	cs.

FIGURE CAPTION ANSWER Standardized recipes use abbreviations to save space and to ensure that measurement notations are the same between recipes.

FIGURE 13.2 Measurement Equivalents

Equal Amounts This table shows you equivalents, or measurements that are equal to other measurements. *Why would it be important to know measurement equivalents?*

Measurement	Equivalent
3 tsp.	= 1 tbsp. = ½ fluid oz. = 15 mL
16 Tbsp.	= 1 c. = 8 oz. = 237 mL
2 c.	= 1 pt. = 16 oz. = 473 mL
2 pt.	= 1 qt. = 32 oz. = 946 mL
4 qts.	= 1 gal. = 128 oz. = 3.8 L
1 lb.	= 16 oz. = 454 g

Liquids are added to a recipe after they are measured by volume. The volume measure should always be placed on a level surface. If you hold the measure rather than placing it down on a level surface, you may get a false reading from the measure. This can affect the outcome of your recipe. Liquid should be filled to the correct line. Metal volume measures have measurement lines on both the outside and the inside.

Accurate Measurement It is important to measure liquids accurately when using volume measurements. *Why should volume measures always be placed on a level surface?*

Count

The number of individual ingredient items that are used in a recipe is called the **count**. You will measure ingredients by count when a particular food ingredient comes in standard sizes.

For example, most recipes list eggs by count instead of by weight or by volume. Volume measures for standard egg sizes are given only per dozen eggs. A cake recipe may ask for three large eggs. (Most recipes call for large-size eggs.) A cobb salad might ask for one hard-cooked egg. The same cobb salad recipe may also call for one small tomato, quartered, or three black olives, sliced.

In contrast, shrimp is often sold by the pound. In this case, the size of the shrimp will determine the count of the shrimp. The smaller the count per pound, the larger the individual shrimp size will be. The larger the count per pound, the smaller the individual shrimp size will be.

Reading Check Determine Which is most accurate: weight, volume, or count measurement?

Recipe Conversion

Sometimes you will need to **alter**, or change, a standardized recipe to produce more or less of a product. You may have more people coming to a restaurant for a special dinner, and need more food. Or, you may have fewer people coming to a banquet, and need less food.

When you change a recipe to produce a new amount or yield, you are practicing **recipe conversion**. You must have the proper math skills to correctly convert recipes. This is a skill that you will use a lot during your career as a foodservice worker. If you learn how to properly convert recipes, you can save money by preparing exactly the right amount of food. You will not have to waste food, time, or supplies to make the proper dishes.

Unit Prices

Unit price is the cost per unit of measure. This may be per item, per pound, per quart, or any other unit measure. When you buy food packaged in two different quantities, it is wise to know which is the better buy. To find the better buy, you need to know the unit price. Which breadcrumbs package is the better buy: ½ pound for 75¢, or 3 pounds for $5.65? Which orange juice is the better buy: 3 quarts for $7.45, or 10 quarts for $20.25?

Math Concept **Calculating Unit Rates** A unit rate is a ratio showing how much of one quantity is needed to match 1 unit of another quantity. Unit price, a type of unit rate, is calculated by dividing the price by the quantity. **Starting Hint** To find which item is the better buy, you need to calculate the unit price for each item. Do so by dividing the item's price by its quantity. The unit price of the first breadcrumbs package, for example, equals $0.75 ÷ ½, or $1.50. This means that you pay $1.50 per pound of breadcrumbs.

NCTM Number and Operations Understand numbers, ways of representing numbers, relationships among numbers, and number systems.

Total Yield Conversion Method

Before you increase or decrease the yield of a standardized recipe, you must determine a conversion factor for all of the ingredients. The **conversion factor** is the number that comes from dividing the yield you want by the existing yield in a recipe:

$$\text{existing yield } \overline{)\text{desired yield}}^{\text{conversion factor}}$$

For example, if the existing recipe yield is 40 portions, but the yield you need is 80 portions, the formula will look like this:

$$\text{(existing yield) } 40 \overline{)80 \text{ (desired yield)}}^{2 \text{ (conversion factor)}}$$
$$\frac{80}{0}$$

If you decrease a recipe, the conversion factor will be less than one. If you increase a recipe, the conversion factor will be more than one.

You will use the recipe conversion factor to increase or decrease a standardized recipe. To get the new food quantity, multiply each individual ingredient quantity by the conversion factor.

For example, say your restaurant has a recipe for chicken teriyaki that has a yield of 10 portions. The recipe calls for 3 pounds of boneless chicken and 20 fluid ounces of teriyaki sauce. You find that you will need more for tonight's dinner service, so you need to convert the yield to 15 portions. You would use the following steps to convert the recipe to make more:

1. Determine the conversion factor.
   15 (desired yield) ÷ 10 (existing yield) = 1.5 (conversion factor)
2. Multiply the existing quantity by the conversion factor to find the new quantity.

$$\frac{\begin{array}{r}\text{existing quantity}\\ \times \text{ conversion factor}\end{array}}{\text{desired quantity}}$$

$$\frac{\begin{array}{r}3.0 \text{ (pounds of chicken)}\\ \times 1.5 \text{ (conversion factor)}\end{array}}{4.5 \text{ (pounds of chicken)}}$$

$$\frac{\begin{array}{r}20.0 \text{ (fluid ounces of teriyaki sauce)}\\ \times 1.5 \text{ (conversion factor)}\end{array}}{30.0 \text{ (fluid ounces of teriyaki sauce)}}$$

You will likely be asked to convert recipes to different yields and different portion sizes. You must be accurate and consistent.

Portion Size Conversion

A foodservice establishment may need to increase or decrease the portion size of a recipe. This is an important skill. Perhaps customers are complaining that the portion size of a dish is too small for the cost. Or, perhaps the portion is so large that it results in little or no profit left over for the establishment.

1. To find the total existing yield, multiply the number of existing portions by the existing size of each portion.

existing portions
× existing portion size
total existing yield

Using the chicken teriyaki recipe example:

10 (portions)
× 5 ounces (portion size)
50 ounces (existing yield)

2. To find a new yield, multiply the desired portions by the desired portion size.

desired portions
× desired portion size
new yield

15 (desired portions)
× 8 ounces (desired portion size)
120 ounces (new yield)

3. Divide the new yield by the existing yield to get the conversion factor.

2.4 (conversion factor)
(existing yield) 50)120.00 (new yield)

4. Multiply each ingredient by the conversion factor to get the new ingredient yield.

existing yield
× conversion factor
new yield

3.0 pounds (existing yield, chicken)
× 2.4 (conversion factor)
7.20 pounds (new yield, chicken)

(The new chicken quantity can be rounded down or rounded up, as desired.)

20.0 fluid ounces (existing yield, teriyaki sauce)
× 2.4 (conversion factor)
48.9 fluid ounces (new yield, teriyaki sauce)

(See **Figure 13.3** on page 341 for an example.)

Factors that can Impact Conversion

These conversion calculations do not take into account problems that may arise when you alter standardized recipes. These problems could include adjustments to equipment size, cooking times, cooking temperatures, and recipe errors. When you make adjustments to deal with these problems, be sure to write them down on your recipe card. This will help you create the same quality dish every time.

Equipment

Recipes usually specify the size of equipment and size and type of cookware that you will need to use to prepare the food. If you increase or decrease a recipe's yield, you may need to change the size of the equipment. If you use the wrong-size equipment for a recipe, it can affect the outcome of a recipe. The dish may lack the quality that you expect.

Mixing and Cooking Time

Time is another important factor to consider when you convert recipes. In general, the mixing time and cooking time do not increase when a recipe is converted. Some changes, however, will affect mixing or cooking times. For example, a baking formula that has been decreased could be affected by overmixing. A baking formula that has been increased could be affected by undermixing.

Changes in one part of a recipe will create changes in other parts of a recipe. Preparation times may also be affected by changes in cookware.

For example, you will need a large stockpot to prepare the existing yield of the Southern Vegetable Soup recipe on page 340. If you decrease the soup recipe, you will need a smaller pot to cook the new yield of soup. This smaller volume will also likely decrease the cooking time. If you increase the recipe, you will need a larger pot to cook the new yield of soup. This will likely increase the cooking time.

Southern Vegetable Soup

YIELD: 10 SERVINGS
SERVING SIZE: 8 OZ.

Method of Preparation

1. Place the salt pork in a large marmite and render the fat, stirring frequently until browned. Add the beef and sauté until browned.
2. Add the tomatoes, and sauté for another 2 minutes.
3. Add the boiling stock, and simmer until the meat is slightly firm in texture.
4. Add all other ingredients, and continue to simmer until the vegetables are tender.
5. Season to taste and serve immediately in preheated cups, or hold at 135°F (57°C) or above. Reheat to 165°F (74°C) for 15 seconds.

Ingredients

2 oz.	Salt pork, cut into a small dice
10 oz.	Beef, bottom round, cut into small cubes
8 oz.	Canned peeled tomatoes, drained, seeded, and chopped
3½ qts.	Beef stock, heated to a boil
2 oz.	Frozen green beans
2 oz.	Red beans, cooked
4 oz.	Onions, peeled and diced brunoise
3 oz.	Celery stalks, washed, trimmed, and diced brunoise
6 oz.	Green cabbage, washed, cored, and chiffonade
3 oz.	Carrots, washed, peeled, and diced brunoise
2 oz.	Frozen corn kernels
2 oz.	Frozen okra, sliced
2 oz.	Zucchini, washed, trimmed, and cut in a ½-in. dice
	Salt and freshly ground black pepper, to taste

Cooking Technique

Boil (at sea level)

1. Bring the cooking liquid to a rapid boil.
2. Stir the contents, and cook the food throughout.
3. Serve hot.

Chef Notes

Season the soup near the end of the cooking time. Flavors get stronger as they cook together.

Substitutions

● To lower fat, drain excess fat from the pork and beef before adding other ingredients.

International Flavor

Use the Internet or library to research these international soup recipes, and write a report on your findings.

● Gazpacho (Spain)
● Ful Nabed (Egypt)
● Botvinia (Russia)

Glossary

Brunoise ⅛-inch dice
Chiffonade ribbons of leafy greens
Marmite stockpot
Render to melt fat over low heat to separate it from the meat tissue

HACCP

● Hold at 135°F (57°C) or above
● Reheat to 165°F (74°C) for 15 seconds

Hazardous Foods

● Beef

Nutrition

Calories 210 Calories from Fat 90
Total Fat 10g
  Saturated Fat 4g
  Trans Fat 0g
Cholesterol 30mg
Sodium 910mg
Total Carbohydrate 11g
  Fiber 2g
  Sugars 4g
Protein 17g
• Vitamin A 30% • Vitamin C 25%
• Calcium 6% • Iron 15%

FIGURE 13.3 Total Recipe Conversion Method

Increase Recipes Use a recipe conversion formula to ensure that recipes will taste the same, even when made in larger amounts. *What mathematics skills will you use to convert recipes?*

Ingredient	Amount	Conversion Factor	New Yield
Salt Pork	2 oz.	3.5	7 oz.
Bottom Round	10 oz.	3.5	35 oz.
Peeled Tomatoes	8 oz.	3.5	28 oz.
Beef Stock	3½ qts.	3.5	12.25 qts.
Green Beans	2 oz.	3.5	7 oz.
Red Beans	2 oz.	3.5	7 oz.
Onions	4 oz.	3.5	14 oz.
Celery	3 oz.	3.5	10.5 oz.
Green Cabbage	6 oz.	3.5	21 oz.
Carrots	3 oz.	3.5	10.5 oz.
Corn	2 oz.	3.5	7 oz.
Okra	2 oz.	3.5	7 oz.
Zucchini	2 oz.	3.5	7 oz.

Southern Vegetable Soup

Existing Yield: 10 servings

Existing Portion Size: 8 oz.

New Yield: 35 servings

New Portion Size: 8 oz.

Determine the Conversion Factor:

$$\frac{\text{Conversion Factor}}{\text{Existing Yield)New Yield}}$$

$$10\overline{)35.0}^{\,3.5}$$

Cooking Temperatures

Cooking temperatures can also be affected by a change in cooking equipment. For example, imagine that the restaurant where you work has just bought a new convection oven. However, the recipe that you are following was developed using a conventional oven. Because convection ovens bake foods much more quickly than standard ovens, the cooking time for the recipe must be adjusted.

Shrinkage

Shrinkage is the percentage of food that is lost during its storage and preparation. Shrinkage is often caused by moisture loss. The amount of shrinkage affects not only the cost of the ingredient, but also the portion sizes that are served to customers. You must know ahead of time how much shrinkage will affect a particular food product. If you do not, you may not purchase the correct amount for your establishment's needs.

Corned beef, for example, shrinks when you cook it. You must consider this shrinkage when you purchase the beef. You will have to start with a larger amount to end up with an adequate portion. As a general rule, corned beef shrinks by about 50%. after it has been cooked. If you need 10 pounds of cooked corned beef, you will need to purchase about 20 pounds of uncooked corned beef.

Recipe Errors

Sometimes, you may make an error in measuring an item, or there may be a mistake in a printed recipe. Very often, recipe errors are so minor that they do not affect the results of the dishes. However, even minor errors can become major problems if the recipe is increased or decreased. To avoid this type of problem, recipes that have been increased or decreased need to be tested before being made for customers.

FIGURE CAPTION ANSWER Students will use division and multiplication to convert recipes.

For example, a recipe may have mistakenly listed 2 ounces of cornstarch instead of 1 ounce. This mistake is so small that the extra cornstarch may not affect the taste or appearance of the dish. The mistake may go unnoticed until the recipe is tripled. The amount of cornstarch would then affect both the appearance and taste of the product.

Become familiar with a recipe before you attempt to recreate it. You can often find an error by reading through it carefully.

Reading Check Describe What problems might arise when converting recipes?

 Food Loss Remember to consider shrinkage when you purchase food. *What causes shrinkage?*

SECTION 13.2 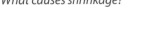 After You Read

Review Key Concepts

1. **Describe** the different instruments used for measuring weight.
2. **Explain** how shrinkage can affect recipe conversion.

Practice Culinary Academics

English Language Arts

3. Write a guide on how to convert the total yield of a recipe and the total portion size of a recipe. Include factors that could impact the conversion.

> **NCTE 5** Use different writing process elements to communicate effectively.

Science

4. **Procedure** A solid object placed in water will displace an amount of water equal to its volume. Measure various solid objects by placing them in a full container of water and then measuring the water that spills out in a volume measure.

   Analysis Write down the volumes of the objects you measured, a summary of displacement, and why your measurements are accurate.

   > **NSES 1** Develop an understanding of change, constancy, and measurement.

Mathematics

5. A recipe for potato skins yields 4 portions and requires 6 potatoes, 5 strips of bacon, and 4 ounces of Cheddar cheese. Using the total yield conversion method, change the recipe to yield 18 portions.

   Math Concept **Multiplying with Decimals** Perform the multiplication as you would with whole numbers. Add the number of total decimal places in all factors, and move the decimal point a corresponding number of places in the product.

   Starting Hint Calculate a conversion factor by dividing the desired yield (18 portions) by the original yield (4 portions). Multiply this conversion factor by each of the original quantities to find the new quantities.

   > **NCTM Number and Operations** Compute fluently and make reasonable estimates.

    Check your answers at this book's Online Learning Center at **glencoe.com**.

Review and Applications

Chapter Summary

A standardized recipe helps ensure consistency in quality, quantity, and portion size. Every standardized recipe provides information for foodservice to plan, prepare, and use the food product. Recipes list ingredient amounts by weight, volume, or count. You must use a formula to adjust a standardized recipe's total yield or portion size. Baking formulas may list ingredients in a different order, use a baker's percentage, and may lack specific instructions.

Content and Academic Vocabulary Review

1. Write each of the terms below on an index card, with definitions on the back. Use the cards to review.

Content Vocabulary

- recipe (p. 330)
- quantity (p. 330)
- standardized recipe (p. 330)
- quality control (p. 330)
- product name (p. 331)
- yield (p. 331)
- portion size (p. 331)
- preparation procedure (p. 331)
- formula (p. 331)
- ingredient list (p. 333)

- baker's percentage (p. 333)
- convert (p. 335)
- metric system (p. 335)
- balance scale (p. 335)
- electronic scale (p. 336)
- volume measurement (p. 336)
- count (p. 337)
- recipe conversion (p. 337)
- conversion factor (p. 338)
- shrinkage (p. 341)

Academic Vocabulary

- consistent (p. 330)
- hallmark (p. 330)
- precise (p. 335)
- alter (p. 337)

Review Key Concepts

2. **Explain** how standardized recipes help to maintain product consistency.
3. **List** different recipe measurements and when each is used.
4. **Give examples** of the factors that affect recipe conversion.

Critical Thinking

5. **Explain** retesting of standardized recipes. When would a chef need to retest a recipe?
6. **Discuss** some situations in which a recipe might need to be converted.
7. **Evaluate** if yield conversions are necessary. A coworker wants to simply double all ingredients to increase the yield of a recipe. Is this a good idea? Why or why not?
8. **Imagine** that severe winter weather has raised the cost of local produce. You may lose customers if you raise your prices. What can you do?
9. **Consider** what would happen if you replaced your conventional oven with a new model of conventional oven. Would you need to retest your standardized recipes? Why or why not?
10. **Explain** why weight is a better method of measurement to use than count for solid ingredients.

Review and Applications

Academic Skills

 ### English Language Arts

11. Create a Plan Imagine that you will prepare a standardized recipe for a catered event. Choose a recipe and write out the steps necessary, from purchasing the ingredients you will need to delivering the food to the event. Also, create supplemental information you will need, such as shopping and equipment lists. Write your plan in such a way that other members of your staff could follow it.

> **NCTE 12** Use language to accomplish individual purposes.

 ### Social Studies

12. Development of the Recipe Research the history of recipes, and choose one person who contributed to the development of modern recipes. Find out details about the person's life and their contributions to recipe development. Bring your details to class. As a class, discuss how modern cooking has been improved because of these developments. Turn in your notes to your teacher.

> **NCSS IV B Individual Development and Identity** Identify, describe, and express appreciation for the influence of various historical and contemporary cultures on an individual's daily life.

 ### Mathematics

13. Change Portion Size You currently have a bowl of asparagus soup on your menu, but have found that customers are reluctant to order such a large portion. You have decided to serve smaller cups instead. The current recipe yields eight 20-ounce servings and requires 4 pounds of asparagus, 12 cups of chicken broth, 2 onions, 1 cup of cream, and ¾ teaspoon of lemon juice. Convert this recipe so that it yields 20 11.5-ounce servings instead.

Math Concept **Rounding Decimals** To round a decimal to the nearest whole number, discard the decimal portion of the number. Increase the whole number portion by one if the number to the right of the decimal point was five or greater.

Starting Hint Determine the total yield of the old recipe by multiplying portion size by number of portions. Repeat for the new recipe. Calculate a conversion factor by dividing the new total yield by the old total yield. Multiply this conversion factor by each of the ingredient quantities to get the new quantities. Round to the nearest whole number (but round smaller quantities like the cream and lemon juice to the nearest 0.5 instead).

> **NCTM Number and Operations** Compute fluently and make reasonable estimates.

Certification Prep

Sharpen your test-taking skills to improve your kitchen certification program score.

Directions Read the questions. Then, read the answer choices and choose the best possible answer for each.

14. What measurement is preferred for liquid ingredients in recipes?

  a. volume measurement

  b. weight measurement

  c. count measurement

  d. height measurement

15. How many 5-ounce portions of soup can you make from a recipe yielding 24 8-ounce portions?

  a. 19   **c.** 28.4

  b. 38.4   **d.** 40

Test-Taking Tip

Read the directions carefully to figure out how many correct answers there are, whether you are penalized for guessing, and how much time is allowed for the test.

Review and Applications

Real-World Skills and Applications

Critical Thinking Skills

16. Convert a Recipe Find a recipe that is not standardized. Convert the recipe to a standardized recipe. Convert all solid ingredient measurements to weight measurements. Change any vague or nonspecific instructions. Test the changes you made to ensure that the recipe comes out properly.

Self-Management Skills

17. Create a Shopping List Imagine that you are opening a breakfast restaurant. Locate five standardized recipes that will be on your main breakfast menu. If you anticipate that you will serve 50 people each morning, create a list of the ingredients you will need to prepare enough breakfasts for two days.

Technology Applications

18. Create a Recipe Card Template Use a word processing or desktop publishing program to create a template to use as a recipe card. Make a space for each part of the recipe and use any guidelines or labels that will be helpful. Create five recipes using your template, and turn them in to your teacher.

Financial Literacy

19. Determine a Recipe Item Cost You have a turkey sandwich recipe that yields 12 sandwiches. It calls for 12 ounces of mayonnaise ($2.25), six 8-ounce turkey thighs ($5), 24 slices of pumpernickel bread ($7), three large tomatoes ($3), and 2 heads of romaine lettuce ($3). What is the item cost per sandwich?

Culinary Lab

Use the culinary skills you have learned in this chapter.

Convert Recipes

20. Make Corn Bread In this lab, you will lower the yield on a corn bread formula. Then, you will make the corn bread, and evaluate the finished product.

A. Calculate portion size. You need the following ingredients to make one full sheet pan of corn bread (yield: 9 lbs., 5 ¾ oz.; portions: 25):

- 1 lb., 12 oz. Bread flour, sifted
- 12 oz. Pastry flour, sifted
- 2¾ oz. Baking Powder
- 1 oz. Salt
- 6 oz. Dry milk solids
- 1 lb. Cornmeal
- 1 lb., 10 oz. Sugar, granulated
- 1 lb., 14 oz. Water
- 1 lb. Eggs, whole
- 12 oz. Oil, vegetable

Divide the existing yield by the existing portions to find the existing portion size.

B. Calculate the conversion factor. Calculate the conversion factor needed for a half-sheet pan of corn bread, to make 13 portions. Divide the desired yield by the existing yield. Then, multiply the existing quantity of each ingredient by the conversion factor to find the new quantity.

C. Bake the corn bread. Gather the new amounts of the ingredients, and bake the half-sheet pan of cornbread in a 400°F (204°C) oven for 30 to 40 minutes.

Create Your Evaluation

Evaluate the recipe and the final product. Write an evaluation of the corn bread's texture, appearance, and flavor. What are the pros and cons of using a different yield? In addition, evaluate your own performance on the lab. Did you have difficulty with any portion of it? Did you make any mistakes that you later needed to correct?

Cost Control Techniques

SECTIONS

14.1 Calculate Food Costs

14.2 Manage Food Cost Factors

WRITING ACTIVITY

Freewriting

Think about the different ways you can save money. Then, think about what a restaurant can do most often to save money. Freewrite about money-saving techniques for restaurants.

Writing Tips

1 Continue writing for the entire time period.

2 If you cannot think of the correct word, just draw a blank line in that spot and keep going.

3 Do not edit your writing or fix mistakes. That can be done later.

EXPLORE THE PHOTO

Controlling costs will help ensure a successful business operation. *What would happen if a business did not control its costs?*

WRITING ACTIVITY ANSWER
Answers should show fairly continuous writing that is related to the topic.

EXPLORE THE PHOTO ANSWER It will soon run out of money and go out of business.

Calculate Food Costs

Reading Guide

 Before You Read

Pace Yourself Short blocks of concentrated reading repeated frequently are more effective than one long session. Focus on reading for 10 minutes. Take a short break. Then, read for another 10 minutes.

Read to Learn

Key Concepts

- **Explain** how foodservice establishments manage portion control.
- **Describe** how to calculate unit cost.
- **Examine** the factors that affect yield percentages.
- **Summarize** how to cost a recipe.

Main Idea

It is important to calculate and control food costs to keep a business running smoothly. Several factors can influence the cost to prepare menu items.

Content Vocabulary

- specification
- scoop
- bulk
- flat
- as-purchased (AP) price
- unit cost
- trim
- debone
- product yield
- as-served (AS) portion
- edible portion (EP)
- yield test
- yield percentage
- by-products
- AP weight
- trim loss
- yield weight
- total weight as served
- Q factor
- cost per portion

Academic Vocabulary

- implement
- aspect

ACADEMIC STANDARDS

 Mathematics
NCTM Number and Operations Compute fluently and make reasonable estimates.

NCTM Number and Operations Understand numbers, ways of representing numbers, relationships among numbers, and number systems.

NCTE National Council of Teachers of English

NCTM National Council of Teachers of Mathematics

NSES National Science Education Standards

NCSS National Council for the Social Studies

Graphic Organizer

As you read, use a sequence chart like this one to list the four steps of the raw yield test. Write one step in each box.

Steps in a Raw Yield Test

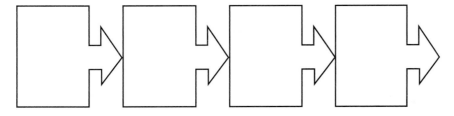

 Graphic Organizer Go to this book's Online Learning Center at **glencoe.com** for a printable graphic organizer.

GRAPHIC ORGANIZER ANSWER 1) Weigh the product to get the AP weight. 2) After trimming, weigh the by-product trimmed from the product to get the trim loss. 3) Subtract the trim loss from the AP weight. 4) Divide the yield weight by the AP weight to get the weight percentage.

Portion Control

A foodservice facility is more likely to cover its operating expenses if it monitors food costs. In this section, you will learn about factors that influence the cost of preparing menu items, such as portion size. You will also learn how to calculate and control food costs.

Customers expect their food to be uniform in size and quality. They are concerned not only with how the food looks and tastes, but also the value they receive at their meal for their food dollars.

You must serve consistent portions to have a successful foodservice operation. These guidelines can help you control portions:

- Purchase items according to standard specifications.
- Follow standardized recipes.
- Use standardized portioning tools and equipment.

Purchase by Specifications

A foodservice operation must develop and **implement**, or put into practice, standards to control food costs. These standards must be followed to be consistent in daily operations.

One way to maintain those standards is to purchase food according to specifications. A **specification**, or spec, is a written description of the products a foodservice operation needs to purchase.

One way to purchase by spec is to purchase products by count or number. The kitchen can then expect to create a definite number of food items from that amount. For example, whole cheesecakes can be purchased and then cut into a set number of individual servings.

A second way to purchase by spec is to order products already divided into individual servings. For example, most facilities purchase single-serving pats of butter or packets of sugar or ketchup.

Follow Standardized Recipes

Standardized recipes also help maintain fixed portions. A standardized recipe includes the portion size and the total number of portions you will make when you prepare a recipe.

The Right Amount This cheesecake was ordered so that an exact number of portions could be created. *Why is portion control so important to a foodservice operation?*

PHOTO CAPTION ANSWER Portion control allows restaurants to control food costs and keep customers happy.

For example, if you prepare sauerkraut based on your facility's standardized recipe, you will end up with a specific number of servings. If you cook Polish sausage for too long or at too high of a temperature, the meat could shrink. This would create smaller portions. It is important to use the cooking time and temperature that is specified in the standardized recipe.

Portioning Tools and Equipment

If you use different-size ladles to fill soup bowls, you will serve different amounts of soup. You must use the same-size ladle each time you serve to ensure that portions are consistent. Selecting the correct tools and equipment for each dish your facility prepares is an important **aspect**, or part of a problem or challenge, of portion size control.

A **scoop**, or a disher, is a commonly used tool to control portions during food preparation and serving. Use scoops to measure quantities of food such as cookie dough, mashed potatoes, or corn bread stuffing.

Scoops are available in a variety of sizes with color-coded handles. This helps foodservice employees match the appropriate scoop with a particular portion size. For example, for a recipe for boneless stuffed chicken breasts, you may need one No. 12 scoop of stuffing for each breast. However, this may apply only to your particular foodservice operation. Another operation's version of this recipe may use one No. 8 scoop of stuffing for each chicken breast.

Other portion control tools and equipment include ladles, spoons, balance and portion scales, slicers, and volume measures. Using these tools and equipment helps you more accurately control cost per portion. It also allows customers to know what size portion they can expect.

Reading Check **Explain** How can a foodservice operation control portion sizes?

READING CHECK ANSWER Follow standardized recipes, and portion food with the right tools and equipment.

Calculate Unit Cost

Most foodservice facilities purchase food in **bulk**, or in large quantities of a single food product. Buying in bulk is effective if storage space is available and no food is wasted. Examples of bulk packages include a case of canned tomatoes, a flat of strawberries, or a 50-pound bag of flour. A **flat** is a shallow box or container used to hold foods. Bulk items are divided into smaller quantities to use in individual recipes.

To find how much it costs to make one recipe, you must first find out how much the ingredients cost. To do this, convert the bulk price, called the **as-purchased (AP) price**, to the unit cost. The **unit cost** is the cost of each individual item.

For example, suppose a 50-pound bag of granulated sugar costs $22. A marinated mushroom salad recipe calls for 3 ounces of sugar. The unit for the sugar is ounces. To find the unit cost of each ounce of sugar, first convert pounds to ounces by multiplying 50 by 16. (There are 16 ounces in 1 pound.) To find how much each ounce costs, divide the total cost by the total number of units (in this case, ounces).

50 lb. × 16 oz. = 800 oz.

```
                  .0275
(units) 800.00. )22.00. (AP price)
                 1600
                  6000
                  5600
                   4000
                   4000

                      0
```

$0.0275 rounded up = $0.03 (unit cost)

The unit cost is $0.03 per ounce of sugar.

The AP price is the cost of a food product when it is first purchased, usually in a large quantity. Some foods, such as deli meats, are used completely after they are purchased. There is no food waste. Other foods need

The Right Weight The difference between AP and EP weight can be significant. *What are the consequences of underestimating a food's EP weight?*

some type of preparation, such as trimming or deboning, which results in waste. To **trim** food means to cut off excess fat or to cut food to a desired shape or size. To **debone** means to remove bones from meat, poultry, or fish.

Product Yields

Product yield is the amount of food product left after preparation. Many times, foods lose volume or weight as they are prepared.

A lot can happen to food to make the portion served to a customer smaller than the original product. For example, a roast can shrink up to one-third of its original size when it is cooked. The **as-served (AS) portion** is the actual weight of the food product that is served to customers.

Edible Portion

Many foods are reduced in size and weight during preparation and cooking. For example, carrots must be prepared before cooking by being peeled. After preparation, the consumable food product that remains is called the **edible portion (EP)**.

You can see that what you buy is not always what you serve. Foodservice buyers must consider the AP cost, EP cost, and AS portion when they decide how much of a food product to purchase.

Reading Check Explain What must foodservice buyers consider when they determine how much of a product to purchase?

Yield Percentages

Product yield is the usable portion of a food product. A **yield test** is a process by which AP food is broken down into EP and waste. The **yield percentage** is the ratio of the edible portion of food to the amount of food purchased.

Yields for various foods vary depending on many factors. For example, how much a foodservice operation typically trims its meat products and whether or not these trimmings are used in other recipes will affect the yield.

PHOTO CAPTION ANSWER Underestimating the EP weight for a particular food may cause you to run out of it too soon.

READING CHECK ANSWER Foodservice buyers must consider the AP cost, EP cost, and AS portion.

Calculate Inventory Value

Every foodservice establishment keeps food products and ingredients that will eventually be sold to customers, called inventory. Calculating inventory value can be as simple as counting the quantity of each item, and multiplying that quantity by the item's unit cost. More complicated situations arise when an item is purchased at different times at different costs. For this, an accounting method such as first in, first out (FIFO) can be used.

On Monday, 100 grapefruit were purchased for $250. On Wednesday, 50 grapefruit were purchased for $150. On Friday, 50 grapefruit were purchased for $115. What is the value of your closing grapefruit inventory (using FIFO) if you started the week with no grapefruit and ended with 64 grapefruit?

Math Concept **FIFO Calculations** To calculate inventory value using FIFO, assume that the items remaining in inventory were purchased last. Use the unit cost of the newest batch. If there are more items on hand than were in the newest batch, continue to the next-newest batch, and so on.

Starting Hint Assume the 64 remaining grapefruit come from the most recently purchased batches. There are only 50 items in the newest (Friday) batch, so the remaining 14 items should come from the Wednesday batch. Calculate the unit cost of each batch (cost ÷ quantity), and multiply by the quantity coming from that batch.

> **NCTM Number and Operations** Compute fluently and make reasonable estimates.

Raw Yield Tests

Raw yield tests are used on food products that do not have any usable leftover parts, or **by-products**. For example, the outermost leaves of a head of lettuce are trimmed and discarded when the lettuce is cleaned. The trimmings are never used for other dishes. For foods like this that have no by-products, you must keep this loss in mind when you determine the yield.

To conduct a raw yield test for products without by-products, follow these steps:

1. Weigh the product before trimming. This number is called the **AP weight**.
2. Weigh the waste material that was trimmed from the purchased product. This number is called the **trim loss**.
3. Subtract the trim loss from the AP weight. This number is the **yield weight**.
4. Divide the yield weight by the AP weight. This results in the yield percentage.

For example, say you take two whole red bell peppers from the refrigerator to prepare marinated mushroom salad. The two peppers weigh a total of 11 ounces. After trimming the peppers, you have 3 ounces of trim loss, or unusable waste. To find the yield percentage, subtract the trim loss (3 ounces) from the AP weight (11 ounces). Then, divide the yield weight by the AP weight.

$$
\begin{array}{r}
11 \text{ (AP weight)} \\
- 3 \text{ (trim loss)} \\
\hline
8 \text{ (yield weight)}
\end{array}
$$

$$
\begin{array}{r}
.727 \\
11 \text{ (AP weight)} \overline{)8.00} \text{ (yield weight)} \\
\underline{77} \\
30 \\
\underline{22} \\
80 \\
\underline{77} \\
3
\end{array}
$$

.727 rounded up = .73 or 73% (yield percentage)

The yield percentage of 11 ounces of fresh red bell peppers is 73%.

Each foodservice operation has its own standards for how workers should trim products. This means that yield percentages will differ in different foodservice operations.

Cooking Loss Test

To determine how cooking affects yield percentage, follow the steps on the next page.

1. Identify the net cost and yield weight of the raw food product.
2. Count how many portions are produced from the product after cooking.
3. Multiply the number of portions by the portion weight when the food is served. This gives you the **total weight as served**.

For example, the net cost of 20 pounds of boneless turkey breast is $62. When cooked, the turkey breast results in 46 portions, each weighing 6 ounces. To determine the total weight as served, multiply the number of portions (46) by the portion weight when served (6 ounces).

$$
\begin{array}{r}
46 \text{ (number of portions)} \\
\times\ 6 \text{ (portion weight)} \\
\hline
276 \text{ oz.}
\end{array}
$$

$$
\begin{array}{r}
17.25 \\
16 \text{ (oz.) } \overline{)\ 276 \text{ (oz.)}} \\
\underline{16} \\
116 \\
\underline{112} \\
40 \\
\underline{32} \\
80 \\
\underline{80} \\
0
\end{array}
$$

17.25 lbs. = total weight as served

The total weight of 20 pounds of boneless turkey breast when served is 17.25 pounds.

Shrinkage

Shrinkage may account for the weight loss that happens when food is cooked. Shrinkage is the difference between the AP weight and the AS weight.

By finding the percent of shrinkage, you will know how much shrinkage affects the cost per pound of a food product. To calculate this percentage, divide the shrinkage by the AP weight.

$$
\text{AP weight } \overline{)\text{ shrinkage}}^{\text{percent of shrinkage}}
$$

For example, you may want to determine the shrinkage percent of a hamburger patty. The AP weight of a hamburger patty is 4 ounces, while the AS weight of a cooked hamburger patty is 3.5 ounces. The difference of 0.5 ounces is the shrinkage. Divide the shrinkage (0.5 ounces) by the AP weight (4 ounces).

$$
\begin{array}{r}
.125 \\
4 \text{ (AP weight) } \overline{)\ 0.5 \text{ (shrinkage)}} \\
\underline{4} \\
10 \\
\underline{8} \\
20 \\
\underline{20} \\
0
\end{array}
$$

.125 = 12.5% (percent of shrinkage)

The percent of shrinkage is 12.5%.

Reading Check **Describe** How is shrinkage involved in food cost calculations?

Costing Recipes

Once you have calculated the total recipe cost, you can figure out how much each portion costs. Chefs determine the selling price of one portion based upon the cost of that portion. You can also adjust a selling price based on what your competition charges or what you think customers will pay. Once you know portion cost and decide on a selling price, you can determine an ideal food cost based on how many items you sell.

Recipe Costing Forms

A recipe costing form helps manage food purchasing and preparation. (See **Figures 14.1** and **14.2** on pages 354 and 355.) There are several parts of a recipe costing form:

Recipe Name The recipe name should be the same as the one listed on the menu.

Portion Size The standard amount of the food item that is served to each customer.

READING CHECK ANSWER The percent of shrinkage affects the cost per pound of a food product.

Yield The number of servings that one preparation of the recipe yields.

Menu Category The menu category in which the food appears. See Chapter 12 for traditional menu categories.

Ingredients The list of each ingredient used in the recipe.

Edible Portion (EP) The amount of an ingredient left after by-products or waste products have been removed from the as-purchased amount.

As-Purchased (AP) Amount The amount of the product that is purchased.

Unit Purchase Price The price paid for each individual item in a bulk purchase. An item is measured in units such as pounds, gallons, or cans.

Cost per Unit To determine the cost per unit, divide the unit purchase cost by the number of purchase units, or quantity. For example, the mushrooms in the form on page 354 cost $12.20 for 10 pounds. Therefore, $12.20 ÷ 10 pounds = $1.22.

For some ingredients, you may need to convert the purchase unit to the type of unit used in the recipe. For example, although sugar is purchased in 50-pound bags, the recipe amount is in ounces. To determine the cost of each ounce, first convert pounds to ounces as follows: 50 pounds × 16 ounces = 800 ounces. Then, you can determine the cost per unit.

Ingredient Cost To determine the cost for each ingredient used in the recipe, multiply the cost per unit by the AP amount. For example, the mushroom cost per unit is $1.22. Therefore, $1.22 × 2 pounds = $2.44, or the ingredient cost for the mushrooms.

Ingredient Total Cost Add together the cost of each ingredient to get the ingredient cost total. For the marinated mushroom salad, the ingredient total cost is $6.86.

Q Factor (1%-5%) The **Q factor**, or the questionable ingredient factor, is the cost of an ingredient that is difficult to measure. Most foodservice operations have a preset Q factor percentage, such as 5%. That percentage is multiplied by the total cost of ingredients to find the Q factor dollar amount.

Total Recipe Cost To calculate this cost, add the ingredient total cost and the Q factor.

Portion Cost To calculate the portion cost, divide the total recipe cost by the total number of portions that the recipe yields.

Cost per Portion

Once you have completed a recipe costing form, you will want to find the cost of individual portions of that recipe. The **cost per portion** represents the amount you would serve to an individual customer. To find this cost, divide the recipe cost by the number of portions or servings.

The standardized recipe for marinated mushroom salad makes 10 portions. You have added up the ingredient costs and found that the recipe cost is $7.20. To find the cost per portion, divide $7.20 by 10.

$$
\begin{array}{r}
.72 \\
10 \text{ (portions) } \overline{)7.20} \text{ (recipe cost)} \\
\underline{70} \\
20 \\
\underline{20} \\
0
\end{array}
$$

.72 = $0.72 (cost per portion)

The cost per portion is $0.72.

Reading Check **Describe** What situations would require you to use the Q factor?

FIGURE 14.1 Recipe Costing Form

Cost Estimates A recipe costing form can help restaurants determine the individual price of each portion. *Why is this important?*

Recipe Name: Marinated Mushroom Salad

Portion Size: 5 oz.

Yield: 10 servings

Menu Category: Salad

Ingredients		EP%	AP Amount	Unit Purchase Price		Cost Per Unit	Ingredient Cost
Quantity	Item		Quantity	Cost	Unit		
2 lb.	Button mushrooms, whole	100%	2.00 lb.	$12.20	10 lbs.	$1.22	$2.44
8 oz.	Diced red bell pepper	73%	10.96 oz.	$25.85	22 lbs.	$0.07	$0.77
1 oz.	Lemon juice	100%	1.00 oz.	$13.32	12 qt.	$0.03	$0.03
8 oz.	Olive oil	100%	8.00 oz.	$14.95	1 gal.	$0.12	$0.96
2 oz.	Granulated sugar	100%	2.00 oz.	$20.50	50 lbs.	$0.03	$0.06
1.5 oz.	Fresh basil, chopped	100%	1.50 oz.	$18.75	2.25 lbs.	$0.52	$0.78
1.5 oz.	Fresh oregano, chopped	100%	1.50 oz.	$4.70	12-oz. bag	$0.39	$0.59
1 head	Romaine lettuce, shredded	100%	1.00 head	$17.95	24 heads	$0.75	$0.75
8 oz.	Green peas	100%	8.00 oz.	$0.89	1 lb.	$0.06	$0.48
	Salt & pepper to taste						
	Ingredient Cost Total						$6.86
	Q Factor (5%)						$0.34
	Total Recipe Cost						$7.20
	Portion Cost						$0.72

FIGURE CAPTION ANSWER Knowing the price of each portion is important for determining the sale price.

▼ FIGURE 14.2 Recipe Costing Form

Do the Math With the right information, you can determine the cost per serving of any recipe. *Can you determine the cost per unit and individual ingredient costs for this form?*

Recipe Name: Grilled Chicken Sandwich

Portion Size: 5 oz.

Yield: 4 Sandwiches

	Ingredients	AP Amount	Unit Purchase Price	Cost Per Unit	Ingredient Cost
4 oz.	Boneless, skinless chicken breast	1 lb.	$2.67		
6 oz.	Provolone cheese	1 lb.	$2.39		
3 oz.	Mushrooms, sliced	1 lb.	$2.25		
8 slices	Tomato (each tomato = 8 slices)	2 tomatoes = 1 lb.	$0.53		
4 leaves	Lettuce	1 head = 16 leaves	$0.77		
4 oz.	Low-fat avocado dressing	1 gal.	$7.85		
8 slices	Bread, 7-grain	1 loaf = 24 oz./2 slices	$1.54		
4 oz.	Pickles, sliced, drained	6 oz.	$0.25		

SECTION 14.1  After You Read

Review Key Concepts

1. **Explain** how standardized recipes can help foodservice establishments manage portion control.
2. **Describe** how product yield affects unit cost.
3. **Summarize** how the cooking loss test is performed.
4. **Explain** how to find the cost per portion of a recipe.

Practice Culinary Academics

Mathematics

5. If 12 ounces of raw bacon weighs just 4.5 ounces after cooking, what is the shrinkage percentage? If the bacon cost $3.95 last week but costs $3.50 this week, what is the percent of decrease in price?

Math Concept **Percent of Decrease** Calculate the amount of decrease by subtracting the new number from the original number. Divide this amount by the original number to find the percent of decrease.

Starting Hint Shrinkage is really another name for a percent of decrease problem. Shrinkage deals with food weights. Calculate both problems the same way, using this formula: (original number − new number) ÷ original number.

> **NCTM Number and Operations** Understand numbers, ways of representing numbers, relationships among numbers, and number systems.

 Check your answers at this book's Online Learning Center at **glencoe.com**.

FIGURE CAPTION ANSWER Chicken: $0.17/oz., $0.68. Cheese: $0.15/oz., $0.90. Mushrooms: $0.14/oz., $0.42. Tomato: $0.27/tomato, $0.27. Lettuce: $0.05/leaf, $0.20. Dressing: $0.06/oz.; $0.24. Bread: $0.13/slice, $1.04. Pickles: $0.04/oz., $0.16.

Manage Food Cost Factors

Reading Guide

 Before You Read

Prior Knowledge Look over the Key Concepts at the beginning of the section. Write down what you already know about each concept and what you want to find out by reading the lesson. As you read, find examples for both categories.

Read to Learn

Key Concepts
- **Evaluate** the factors involved in purchasing.
- **Describe** the procedure for receiving goods.
- **Outline** how foodservice businesses control inventory and minimize waste.

Main Idea

Management and control of food cost factors is essential to run a foodservice operation. These factors include purchasing, receiving, storage and issuing.

Content Vocabulary
- issuing
- semiperishable
- inhibitor
- nonedible
- sales cycle
- open-market buying
- bid
- single-source buying
- physical inventory
- perpetual inventory
- parstock
- periodic-ordering
- bar code
- rotate stock
- requisition
- Daily Production Report

Academic Vocabulary
- confirm
- deteriorate

Graphic Organizer

There are six steps in foodservice purchasing. Use a chain of events diagram like the one below to list those steps.

Purchasing Steps

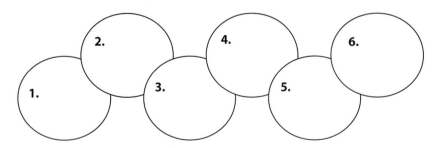

Manage expenses to make your restaurant successful.

ACADEMIC STANDARDS

 English Language Arts
NCTE 12 Use language to accomplish individual purposes.

 Mathematics
NCTM Data Analysis and Probability Select and use appropriate statistical methods to analyze data.

 Social Studies
NCSS V B Individuals, Groups, and Institutions Analyze group and institutional influences on people, events, and elements of culture in both historical and environmental settings.

NCTE National Council of Teachers of English

NCTM National Council of Teachers of Mathematics

NSES National Science Education Standards

NCSS National Council for the Social Studies

 Graphic Organizer Go to this book's Online Learning Center at **glencoe.com** for a printable graphic organizer.

GRAPHIC ORGANIZER ANSWER 1) Develop the order. 2) Get price quotes from vendors. 3) Choose a vendor and place the order. 4) Receive and store the order. 5) Follow up on any errors. 6) Issue products to the kitchen team.

Cost Control and Purchasing Goods

How can you keep costs under control in a foodservice operation? You might be surprised by how many factors affect cost control. Menu pricing is important. But purchasing, receiving, issuing, and storing methods are just as important. **Issuing** is the process of delivering foods from storage to the kitchen as needed for use. Kitchen waste and customer service can also impact an operation's profits. You must know how to properly manage and control each of these factors to be successful in the foodservice industry.

Purchasing involves more than buying products for a foodservice operation. It also involves elements that can directly affect a business's cost control. To make smart purchases, you must:

- Develop written specs for all items purchased.
- Determine the quantity of products needed.
- Assess inventory levels.

- Decide how much of each item to buy based on your current inventory and your projected needs.

Once you have done this, you can begin the purchasing process. Foodservice purchasing involves six steps:

1. Develop the order.
2. Get price quotes from vendors.
3. Select the vendor and place the order.
4. Receive and store the order.
5. Evaluate and follow up on any errors, if necessary.
6. Issue products to the production team in the kitchen.

Consistent purchasing procedures can help a foodservice operation in several ways. They allow a facility to keep enough products on hand at the lowest possible cost. This can improve customer service, as menu items will be available when customers ask for them. Purchasing procedures also ensure that high-quality products are purchased at the best price. For example, a purchaser might use USDA grading systems to ensure that the food that is purchased is of the right quality.

Product Storage Foodservice operations purchase many types of food products. *How should semiperishable items be stored?*

PHOTO CAPTION ANSWER Semiperishable products can be stored in the refrigerator, freezer or pantry, depending on the type of food and whether it has been opened.

Weigh the Options

Foodservice operators know that it is essential to have consistent portion sizes to maximize customer satisfaction and profits. Quite often, and especially in the baker's kitchen, this would be impossible to do without the use of a scale.

The oldest type of scale is the balance scale. Balance scales measure an object's weight and mass (how much material the object contains). Balance scales were first used in ancient Egypt around 7000 BC. A stick hung by a cord tied around its middle. Objects to be weighed were hung on cords tied to either end of the stick. If the weights were equal, the stick stayed parallel to the ground. The baker's scale that is used today is an example of a balance scale.

History Application

Research international measuring standards, such as the International System of Units. Create a chart to show the advantages of having such an organization with regard to trade and commerce.

> **NCSS V B Individuals, Groups, and Institutions** Analyze group and institutional influences on people, events, and elements of culture in both historical and environmental settings.

Using the grading system can help the purchaser compare foods from different suppliers.

Types of Products Purchased

In the foodservice industry, there are four types of products that a foodservice business can purchase: perishable foods, semi-perishable foods, nonperishable foods, and nonedibles.

Perishable items have a relatively short shelf life. These include products such as fresh fruits, vegetables, meat, poultry, and seafood. Perishable foods spoil easily. They should be purchased in quantities that will be used quickly, and stored properly as soon as they are received. Perishable items vary in price.

Semiperishable products are perishable food items that contain an inhibitor (in-ˈhi-bə-tər) An **inhibitor** is a substance that slows down the chemical breakdown of the food. This increases the products' shelf life. Semiperishable products include smoked fish, processed meats, and pickled vegetables.

Nonperishable foods, such as canned goods and flour, have a long shelf life. The quality of these items is unchanged when they are stored for up to one year.

A **nonedible** is a nonfood product. Nonedibles include cleaning materials and paper goods.

Food Specifications

A specification, or spec, is a written, detailed description of the products and supplies that a foodservice operation needs to purchase. (See **Figure 14.3**.) A spec acts as a quality control tool. It helps a commercial kitchen purchase exactly what is needed. Specs also tell vendors exactly what a foodservice operation expects to receive, both in quantity and in quality.

Foodservice operations usually have a spec sheet for nonperishable products as well. The specs usually include the following information:

- Name of the supplier
- Package size, quantity, or item count
- Form of the item to purchase
- Costs and quality limitations

Determine Purchase Quantities

There are several methods that can help you determine exactly how much of a product to purchase. First, you must know how much of each product the chef expects to use to prepare menu items for a given sales cycle. The **sales cycle** is the period of time between supply deliveries. The sales cycle varies for different foodservice operations.

The amount of available storage space and factors such as how perishable the food ordered is, how it will be used, and the cost of

A TASTE OF HISTORY ANSWER Weights and measures is often a subject of governmental regulation, to ensure fairness. Without oversight to ensure worldwide uniformity of weights and measurements, trading with other countries would be impossible.

Receiving List A food spec tells vendors exactly what the foodservice operation expects to receive. *What is this foodservice establishment expecting to receive?*

Food Purchasing Specification Order	
Exact Product Name:	Oranges
Packer Name:	N/A
Intended Use:	N/A
U.S. Grade:	Fancy
Product Size:	88 count
Type of Packaging:	Bulk
Package Size:	35-lbs. box
Form:	Fresh
Degree of Ripeness:	N/A
Additional Notes:	Firm and heavy in hand
Receiving Indicator:	No mold or chalk-white coating
Acceptable Substitute:	Navel for Valencia or Valencia for Navel
Point of Origin:	CA or FL
Price Per Unit:	
Comments:	

the food influence how much of a food product to purchase. Remember that perishable and semiperishable items are relatively expensive. Be careful when you order larger quantities. They may not be used before they spoil.

Common Purchasing Practices

Purchasers may buy food and supplies from vendors directly, or from distributing companies that sell products and equipment from many different vendors. Foodservice operations may use several purchasing methods. Two of the most common are:

- **Open-market buying** is the most common purchasing method. A foodservice operation gets price quotes for identical items from several vendors, and then chooses the vendor based on price and delivery history. A formal price quote from a vendor is often called a **bid**. Open-market buying is often used for purchasing perishable foods.
- In **single-source buying**, a foodservice operation purchases most of its products from a single vendor. A discount is usually given to a foodservice purchaser when a large amount of goods or supplies are purchased at one time.

Yield Tests

In Section 14.1, you learned how to calculate yield percentage (the ratio of the edible portion of food to the amount of food that was purchased). The results of yield testing will have an impact on your purchasing

FIGURE CAPTION ANSWER The foodservice establishment is expecting to receive a 35-pound box of 88 fresh, Fancy-grade oranges. The vendor may send either navel or Valencia oranges.

Take a Count It is important that employees frequently help managers take inventory. *Why is this important?*

decisions. They tell how much food you should purchase to end up with the right serving of food on each customer's plate. Yield tests must be performed accurately to help you plan correctly.

Vendor Relationships

Good relationships with vendors are very important. The relationship between a foodservice operation and its vendors must be based on mutual trust, honesty, and good business ethics. A foodservice operation must choose vendors that it trusts will not inflate prices or reduce the quality of the products delivered. Foodservice operations also must choose vendors that have a good record of delivering supplies on time, and based on the operation's specifications.

To maintain a good relationship with vendors, foodservice operators must schedule regular meetings with vendors and carefully study their supply catalogs. It is also a good idea to visit vendor showrooms, arrange for occasional on-site visits from vendors, and attend foodservice industry trade shows to view new products and equipment.

Reading Check **List** What are the four types of products a foodservice operation purchases?

Receiving Goods

After products have been purchased, the next important function in a foodservice business is receiving.

⌒ Small Bites ⌒

Receiving Tools and Equipment Make sure that the proper tools and equipment are available for receiving. You will waste time if you must go looking for them. Proper tools and equipment include:

- Heavy-duty gloves with nonslip fingertips
- Scales of the proper size; check that the scales are properly calibrated before use
- A calculator to check total costs or add up total weights
- Cutting devices for opening containers, packages, and boxes
- Thermometer

PHOTO CAPTION ANSWER Taking a regular inventory keeps foodservice businesses from ordering too much or too little.

READING CHECK ANSWER The four types of products purchased are: perishable, semiperishable, nonperishable, and nonedible.

Many foodservice establishments have formal guidelines for receiving goods. These guidelines help ensure that the products received are sanitary and that they are correct as ordered.

Check Purchase Orders and Invoices

One of the most important steps during the receiving process is to make sure that the items that have been received are the ones that appear on the purchase order. The purchase order lists the products the purchasing agent ordered. A purchase order should include:

- The type of product ordered
- The amount of product ordered and/or its weight
- Sometimes the unit price and total costs

In addition, you should **confirm**, or make sure, that the items that are listed on the invoice are the same ones that have actually been delivered. Immediately report any differences to a supervisor or manager.

Physical Inspection of Goods

Just because products show up on the receiving dock, it does not mean that they should be automatically accepted by the foodservice establishment.

First, you must visually inspect products. Check each package for quality, freshness, and signs of damage:

- Packages should be intact and clean, and have no evidence of stains or water damage.
- Packages should not have a strange odor.
- Foods such as raw meat should be checked for cross-contamination.
- Temperatures of foods should be checked by placing a thermometer between or underneath packages. Perishables must be received at 41°F (5°C) or below. Frozen foods must be received at 0°F (18°C) or below. If these temperatures are not met, bacteria may have a chance to grow. Depending on the product, you might also need to check for:

◄ Formal Guidelines Restaurants usually have formal guidelines set in place for how they want inventory figures kept. *Why is this important?*

PHOTO CAPTION ANSWER Formal guidelines help ensure that records are accurate and the restaurant receives the proper items.

- Product tampering or mishandling.
- Improper storage practices. For example, look for evidence that packages have thawed and been refrozen, such as ice crystals or stains.
- Pest or rodent infestation.
- Dented, leaking, or misshapen cans.

Next, weigh the products that have been received to make sure their weights match what was ordered. Notify a manager immediately if you find errors.

Reading Check **Explain** What is included on the purchase order?

Inventory Control

A foodservice establishment must control inventory to control costs. If an establishment fails to control costs, it will find itself out of business very soon. Inventory should include everything that is needed to operate the business. For example, items such as food products, tableware, and equipment should all be monitored in inventory. A **physical inventory** is a list of everything that an operation has on hand at one time.

As soon as items are received, you must update the inventory control system. Many facilities use a perpetual inventory to track inventory. A **perpetual inventory** is a continuously updated record of what a business has on hand for each item. Many facilities have their perpetual inventories stored on a computer. Some use perpetual inventory cards, although computerized systems are more common. (See **Figure 14.4**.)

Computerized point-of-sale systems help update food inventories as food items are sold. At a glance you can see what products you have plenty of and what products need to be reordered. Remember to always keep a backup copy of all computerized records off site, for safe keeping.

There is a delicate balance between having too much of a product in stock and too little. The amount of stock that will cover a facility's needs from one supply delivery to the next is called **parstock**. Product shortages, delivery delays, and even the weather can affect when food and supplies will arrive, and how much they will cost. Staple products for foodservice establishments, such as coffee, sugar, and rice, must be kept on hand at all times.

FIGURE 14.4 **Perpetual Inventory Card**

Name *Rice (white long-grain)*   Brand *China Rose*
Supplier *Lee Import co.*   Size *5 lb. sacks*

Date Rec'd	Quantity Rec'd	Date Issued	Quantity Issued	On-Hand	New Balance
9/26	10 5-lb. sacks			7 5-lb. sacks	17 5-lb. sacks
		9/28	1 5-lb. sack		16 5-lb. sacks
		10/2	3 5-lb. sacks		13 5-lb. sacks
		10/9	2 5-lb. sacks		11 5-lb. sacks
		10/13	3 5-lb. sacks		8 5-lb. sacks

Inventory Control A perpetual inventory card can help keep track of inventory amounts on hand. *Do you think this foodservice establishment will need to order more rice soon?*

FIGURE CAPTION ANSWER In just over two weeks, the restaurant has used nine 5-pound sacks of rice. Students should guess that the foodservice establishment will need to order more rice soon.

READING CHECK ANSWER The purchase order should list the type of product ordered, the amount and/or weight, and the unit price and total cost.

One way to decide how much to purchase is to use the periodic-ordering method. With the **periodic-ordering method**, a purchaser decides how much product will be used in a given time period. The purchaser then reviews the amount of product that is on hand, what will be needed, and how much parstock of the product is needed. This helps the purchaser decide how much to purchase that specific time.

To use the periodic-ordering method, add the parstock to the production needs, and subtract the amount on hand. This will give you the order amount:

parstock + production needs – stock on hand = order amount

Storing and Issuing Goods

As soon as goods are received and the inventory control system is updated, perishable and semiperishable goods need to be properly and immediately stored. Label, date, and store perishable and semiperishable products.

Some facilities use a bar code and computer system to keep track of inventory. A **bar code** is a series of bars, spaces, and sometimes numbers that contain coded information and are designed to be scanned into a computer. With this method, all items are given a bar code sticker when they are received. This helps track the item through the inventory system.

Storeroom Controls

Food and supplies should always be kept in the proper storage areas to help prevent spoilage, waste, and contamination. In general, the longer a food product is stored, the more its quality may **deteriorate**, or become worse. To effectively manage the inventory and storage of food products, they must be rotated so that older items are used before newer ones.

The system of rotating stock is called first in, first out (FIFO). To **rotate stock** means to place stored items in an orderly way so that older items are used first. Items that are stored first should be used first. Foodservice facilities each have their own procedures for how to rotate food on storage shelves to ensure that the FIFO system is followed.

Issuing Controls

Some facilities follow an issuing system that uses a requisition. A **requisition** is an internal invoice that allows management to track the physical movement of inventory through a business. A foodservice employee fills out a requisition each time food or supplies need to be taken from storage. A requisition also helps calculate the cost of the food that is used each day.

You should fill out requisition forms carefully. Record each item that you remove from storage before you remove it. Accurate records are critical to maintaining profits and keeping enough food and supplies on hand.

For the most effective issuing control, limit the access to storage areas to as few people as possible. Theft is a problem for many foodservice operations. Keep the storage doors locked and issue keys only to authorized employees.

Minimize Waste

The more food that is thrown out unused, the more profit that is lost. A well-designed menu will allow chefs to use leftovers for a variety of food products. This reduces food waste.

Another way to reduce waste is to track the history of food products as they are prepared each day. Many commercial kitchens use a **Daily Production Report** form to show how much food product was used, how much was sold, and how much was unused, or left over. Knowing exactly what was unused or left over at the end of the day will allow you

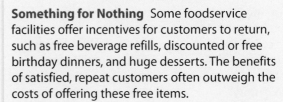

Small Bites

Something for Nothing Some foodservice facilities offer incentives for customers to return, such as free beverage refills, discounted or free birthday dinners, and huge desserts. The benefits of satisfied, repeat customers often outweigh the costs of offering these free items.

to prepare menus the following day that will use those foods.

Following the first in, first out (FIFO) inventory program will also help you to minimize waste. By clearly labeling and dating food, and properly storing it, you are able to use the food before its shelf life expires. Properly storing cooked foods and raw ingredients will eliminate the chances of cross-contamination. This will allow all of your food products to be used.

 Reading Check Describe What are two ways to minimize waste while foods are being stored?

SECTION 14.2 After You Read

Review Key Concepts

1. **Describe** the different methods of purchasing used by foodservice operations.
2. **List** the proper tools and equipment for receiving goods.
3. **Explain** how limiting storage access can help control costs.

Practice Culinary Academics

 English Language Arts

4. Examine your school's restaurant or cafeteria menu. Choose one dish from the menu, and list three ingredients used in that dish. Practice writing food purchasing specification sheets for those three ingredients. For this exercise, you will need to purchase enough of each ingredient for 100 servings total.

> **NCTE 12** Use language to accomplish individual purposes.

Mathematics

5. Your purchasing agent has gotten price quotes for a case of 40 frozen hamburger patties. One vendor quoted $35, a second vendor quoted $42, a third vendor quoted $46, and a fourth vendor quoted $39. What is the average price?

Math Concept **Finding the Mean** When you have a series of values, calculate the statistical measure mean, or average, by finding the sum of all of the values, and dividing that sum by the total number of values.

Starting Hint There are four different price quotes. Calculate the average by adding the four prices together, and dividing by the number of price quotes (4). If necessary, round to the nearest cent.

> **NCTM Data Analysis and Probability** Select and use appropriate statistical methods to analyze data.

 Check your answers at this book's Online Learning Center at **glencoe.com**.

READING CHECK ANSWER Ways to minimize waste include creating a menu that allows the chef to use leftovers, and tracking food products as they are prepared.

Review and Applications

Chapter Summary

One way for a foodservice operation to cover costs and improve customer satisfaction is through portion control. You can control portions by smart purchasing procedures. Follow specifications, follow standardized recipes, and use portioning tools and equipment. Proper receiving procedures and storeroom controls can control losses caused by damaged or spoiled products. Businesses should take inventory regularly. Controlled kitchen waste and excellent customer service also can help a foodservice operation control costs.

Content and Academic Vocabulary Review

1. Label each of these vocabulary terms as a noun, verb, or adjective.

Content Vocabulary

- specification (p. 348)
- scoop (p. 349)
- bulk (p. 349)
- flat (p. 349)
- as-purchased (AP) price (p. 349)
- unit cost (p. 349)
- trim (p. 350)
- debone (p. 350)
- product yield (p. 350)
- as-served (AS) portion (p. 350)
- edible portion (EP) (p. 350)
- yield test (p. 350)
- yield percentage (p. 350)
- by-products (p. 351)

- AP weight (p. 351)
- trim loss (p. 351)
- yield weight (p. 351)
- total weight as served (p. 352)
- Q factor (p. 353)
- cost per portion (p. 353)
- issuing (p. 357)
- semiperishable (p. 358)
- inhibitor (p. 358)
- nonedible (p. 358)
- sales cycle (p. 358)
- open-market buying (p. 359)
- bid (p. 359)
- single-source buying (p. 359)
- physical inventory (p. 362)

- perpetual inventory (p. 362)
- parstock (p. 362)
- periodic-ordering (p. 363)
- bar code (p. 363)
- rotate stock (p. 363)
- requisition (p. 363)
- Daily Production Report (p. 364)

Academic Vocabulary

- implement (p. 348)
- aspect (p. 349)
- confirm (p. 361)
- deteriorate (p. 363)

Review Key Concepts

2. Explain how foodservice establishments manage portion control.

3. Describe how to calculate unit cost.

4. Examine the factors that affect yield percentages.

5. Summarize how to cost a recipe.

6. Evaluate the factors involved in purchasing.

7. Describe the procedure for receiving goods.

8. Outline how foodservice businesses control inventory and minimize waste.

Critical Thinking

9. Decide how ignoring portions could impact a foodservice operation. What might happen if a cook decided to ignore portion control guidelines?

10. Describe the elements of a good vendor relationship. What are some ways that a new vendor could gain the trust of a foodservice operation?

Review and Applications

Academic Skills

English Language Arts

11. Create a Procedure Create a procedure to keep track of inventory in a small restaurant. The procedure should attempt to minimize waste and loss of profits. Once you have created your procedure, create a training manual that outlines your procedure for other employees. Write your procedure as if you were explaining it to first-time foodservice employees. Make sure it is easy to follow and organized logically.

> **NCTE 4** Use written language to communicate effectively.

Science

12. Determine Cooking Yield Cooking yield can affect how much you will need to purchase of certain foods.

Procedure Shape 4 ounces of ground beef into a ½-inch thick patty. Cook the patty to a minimum internal temperature of 165°F (74°C). Weigh the cooked patty. Repeat, but replace 1 ounce of the meat with cooked wild rice.

Analysis Compare the weight of the two cooked patties, the weight of the drippings from the patties, the yield percentage, and the tenderness. Write a summary of your findings.

> **NSES B** Develop an understanding of the structure and properties of matter.

Mathematics

13. Calculate Food Costs On a typical night, your restaurant serves 27 9-ounce (AS) portions of roast beef. Assume that the roast beef loses 25% of its weight while cooking, and that before it is cooked you trim and discard fat equal to 10% of its AP weight. If you are able to purchase the beef at $4.50 per pound, what is your daily roast beef food cost? If the restaurant serves dinner an average of 24 nights each month, what is your monthly food cost?

Math Concept **Undoing Percent Calculations** If you know that a value was decreased by a certain percentage, and you know the ending value but not the original value, you can determine the original value by dividing the ending value by 1 minus the percentage.

Starting Hint Work backwards to determine the total weight of beef that you need to purchase each day. Since the AS weight of 9 ounces represents the precooking weight decreased by 25%, find the precooking weight by dividing 9 ounces by $(1-25\%)$, or $9 \div 0.75$. Perform a similar calculation to get from the precooking weight to the AP weight. Divide the total ounces by 16 to convert to pounds.

> **NCTM Number and Operations** Understand numbers, ways of representing numbers, relationships among numbers, and number systems.

Certification Prep

Directions Read the questions. Then, read the answer choices and choose the best possible answer for each.

14. What is the ratio of edible food to the amount purchased called?

   a. product yield

   b. edible portion

   c. unit cost

   d. trim loss

15. What is the amount of stock needed to cover between deliveries called?

   a. requisition   **c.** parstock

   b. perpetual inventory   **d.** physical inventory

Sharpen your test-taking skills to improve your kitchen certification program score.

Test-Taking Tip
Try taking a few breaks during the exam by stopping for a moment, shutting your eyes, and taking some deep breaths. This can help you relax and focus.

Review and Applications

Real-World Skills and Applications

Interpersonal and Collaborative Skills

16. Develop Systems Follow your teacher's instructions to divide into groups and work together to develop systems for purchasing, receiving, storing, and inventory. Once you have finalized each system as a group, create a checklist for foodservice employees.

Communication Skills

17. Customer Service Divide into pairs at the direction of your teacher and take turns playing the role of a vendor and a foodservice purchaser. The vendor should try to convince the purchaser to become a customer by explaining the benefits of the company's products and services.

Technology Applications

18. Use Recipe Software Visit this book's Online Learning Center **glencoe.com** for links to recipe software. Use the software to create a recipe and then use it to increase the yield to double the amount produced. Then, determine the cost per portion of the original recipe, and analyze the nutritional value of the recipe if possible.

Financial Literacy

19. Calculate Costs Calculate the following:
1) A facility pays $25.50 for a 30-dozen case of eggs. Find the unit cost of each egg.
2) The total recipe cost for pecan pie, which yields 8 servings, is $4.67. Find the cost per portion for pecan pie.

Culinary Lab

Use the culinary skills you have learned in this chapter.

Conduct a Yield Test

20. Test Foods in Teams Working in groups as directed by your teacher, you will conduct a yield test on 10 carrots, 4 apples, 1 bunch of celery, 4 oranges, 1 head cabbage, 4 bananas, 4 onions, and 1 coconut.

A. Weigh your foods. Weigh each food product on a food scale. This is the AP weight. Record this number on a sheet of paper.

B. Trim your foods. Clean and trim the food product of unusable parts and weigh those parts. This is the trim loss. Record this number.

C. Calculate yield weight. Subtract the trim loss from the AP weight. This is the yield weight. Record the yield weight, then divide it by the AP weight. This is the yield percentage. Record this number.

D. Create menu items. Follow your teacher's instructions to form two teams: a vegetable team and a fruit team. Create a menu item based on the fruits or vegetables as prepared. Prepare a single portion of the menu item and serve it to the other team.

E. Calculate portions. Use the yield weights of the combined food products to figure out how much of each ingredient you would need to purchase to make two servings.

Create Your Evaluation

Create a chart that contains the results from each team. Compare and evaluate the results. Notice how the results differ and how they are the same. Discuss possible reasons for results that differ from team to team. Write an analysis under the chart that explains possible reasons for the differing results in the chart.

Banquets and Catering

These professionals make sure that the food, setting, and service for special events go off without a hitch.

Careers in banquets and catering require strict attention to detail and the ability to transform a customer's wishes into an event to remember. A culinary background is helpful in understanding customer needs and communicating those needs to the kitchen staff. Being multilingual is often helpful.

Strong interpersonal and listening skills are keys to successful catering operations. The ability to work diplomatically alongside different personalities is crucial. Maintaining excellent customer service is a top priority in this business.

Brandon Marshall, Catering Director

Q What is your current position?

A I am the Director of Catering for the Quorum Hotel Tampa.

Q Describe your job.

A My team and I are responsible for the food and beverage sales and marketing. I oversee two full-time catering sales/convention servicepeople, do administrative work, and work closely with the Director of Sales Marketing on marketing and advertising campaigns.

Q How did you find your current job?

A I came up through the food and beverage ranks, from washing dishes, to cooking, to kitchen management, to front of the house, to operations management, to sales, and now to director.

Q What education did you receive?

A I majored in Hospitality Management at Johnson & Wales University and received a Bachelor of Science in Hospitality Sales and Meeting Management. My education gave me real-world experience that has been the basis for my career.

Q Describe your on-the-job training.

A My first experience working in a hotel was at the Radisson Airport Hotel. It was fast-paced. I worked directly with clients, and we had a really fun, hard-working team. My experience there helped prepare me for my current position.

Q Describe a typical work day.

A I meet with our sales team daily to discuss sales initiatives, but otherwise, no two days are alike. I meet with clients, attend networking events, and work with our chef and operations team to design creative menus, decor, and set-ups. I also forecast and budget food and beverage sales.

Q What job skills are important?

A My job affects the entire hotel, so understanding how all of the other departments work is incredibly important.

Career Ingredients

Education or Training	Most employers require a culinary degree and completion of business, accounting, and management courses. Restaurant experience is a plus.
Academic Skills Required	English Language Arts, Mathematics
Aptitudes, Abilities, and Skills	Knowledge of the foodservice industry; excellent interpersonal, leadership, planning, organizational, and computer skills; background in business math, accounting, and marketing.
Workplace Safety	Basic kitchen and dining room safety, sanitation, and food handling rules must be followed and enforced.
Career Outlook	Openings will be plentiful in years to come as the foodservice industry continues to expand.
Career Path	Advancement depends on skill, training, and work experience.

Career Pathways

Banquet captains	Often host catered events and greet guests. Maintain contact with clients to make sure they are pleased before, during, and after the event. Other duties include overseeing table set-up and service.
Banquet managers	Responsible for arranging and carrying out the foodservice plan. They help prepare menus, order equipment, coordinate room set-up, and schedule staff.
Chefs	Oversee food preparation activities and the kitchen staff for banquets and large catered events.
Catering directors	Ensure that all aspects of a catered event are carried out in a timely and orderly manner, making sure that all departments perform on schedule.
Catering sales managers	Work with customers in planning all aspects of an event, such as menus, table arrangements, and decorations.
Head servers	Coordinate all of the dining room activities for an event. They also supervise the service staff and assist with executing banquet plans.
Menu planners	Work closely with the executive chef to select the menu items that will be offered. A working knowledge of cost control, food preparation, and customer needs is essential.

Critical Thinking What classes have you taken in school that might help you prepare for a career in banquets and catering?

Many culinary certification programs focus on menu design and presentation. Develop a main dish for a menu that is appropriate for a 100-guest wedding. Be sure the dish is healthful, balanced, and sutiable for the occasion.

COMPETITION
★ ★ ★ ★ ★
PRACTICE

Further develop your menu idea for a 100-guest wedding from the Get Certified practice. Create a three-course menu, considering all aspects, including the menu items, decorations, table set-up, design, and presentation. Evaluate your efforts based on the following rating scale:

1 = Poor; 2 = Fair; 3 = Good; 4 = Great

Judge your menu on:

● The appearance of the menu and its design.

● Menu items selected and menu balance.

● Appropriateness for the occasion and number of guests.

Standardized Recipes

One crucial tool used in the foodservice industry is the standardized recipe. Using your research and interview with a chef or cook, you will create a standardized recipe and share what you have learned with your class.

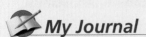

My Journal

If you completed the journal entry from page 217, refer to it to see what recipes you have used in the past. Add any additional notes about other recipes you think might be interesting to try.

English Language Arts

NCTE 4 Use written language to communicate effectively.

NCTE 7 Conduct research and gather, evaluate, and synthesize data to communicate discoveries.

Project Assignment

In this project, you will:

- Research standardized recipes and come up with an idea for your own.
- Identify and interview a chef or cook who is familiar with standardized recipes.
- Create your own standardized recipe from scratch, including details on the setup, equipment, and cost measures that affect your recipe.
- Present your recipe to your class to share what you have learned.

Applied Culinary Skills Behind the Project

Your success in culinary arts will depend on your skills. Skills you will use in this project include:

➤ Identifying the different parts of a recipe.

➤ Distinguishing between a formula and a recipe.

➤ Understanding how standardized recipes help maintain product consistency.

➤ Knowing the different parts of a standardized recipe, including how to use ingredients, procedures, cooking instructions, setup, and equipment.

➤ Determining how to develop a standardized recipe.

English Language Arts Skills Behind the Project

The English Language Arts skills you will use for this project are writing, interviewing, and speaking skills. Remember these key concepts:

Writing Skills

➤ Use correct spelling, grammar, and punctuation.

➤ Organize your questions in the order you want to ask them.

➤ Write in the format appropriate for the assignment.

Interviewing Skills

➤ During the interview, record responses and/or take notes.

➤ Listen actively and attentively.

➤ Ask additional questions to gain a better understanding.

Speaking Skills

➤ Speak clearly, slowly, and concisely.

➤ Adapt and modify language to suit different purposes.

➤ Speak in an organized manner that clearly communicates your points.

Step 1 Research Standardized Recipes

Research standardized recipes and their importance and structure. Write a summary of your research to:

- Understand why standardized recipes are important in the foodservice industry.
- Explain how standardized recipes help to control the quantity, quality, and portion size of the food.
- Determine how standardized recipes can prevent waste and decrease errors.
- List the parts of a standardized recipe.
- Identify facts you need to know before creating a standardized recipe, including setup, necessary equipment, and ingredients.

Step 2 Plan Your Interview

Use the results of your research to write a list of questions to ask a chef or cook. Your questions may include:

- How can standardized recipes prevent excess waste and decrease errors in the kitchen?
- How do standardized recipes help you control quantity, quality, and portion size?
- What factors do you need to consider before creating a standardized recipe?
- How do you create a standardized recipe?
- What determines how you adjust standardized recipes?

Step 3 Connect with Your Community

Identify a person in your community who is a chef or a cook at a restaurant, hotel, or cafeteria. Conduct your interview using the questions you prepared in Step 2. Take notes during the interview, and write a summary of the interview.

Culinary Project Checklist

Plan

✓ Research standardized recipes, and summarize your findings.

✓ Plan an interview with a chef or cook.

✓ Interview a chef or cook, and write a summary about your interview.

✓ Create a standardized recipe, including details on setup, equipment, and ingredients.

Present

✓ Make a presentation to your class to share your standardized recipe and discuss the results of your research and interview.

✓ Invite students to ask any questions they may have. Answer these questions.

✓ When students ask you questions, demonstrate in your answers that you respect their perspectives.

✓ Turn in the summary of your research, your interview questions, the interview summary, and your standardized recipe to your teacher.

Step 4 Create Your Standardized Recipe

Use the Culinary Project Checklist to plan and create your standardized recipe. Share what you have learned with your classmates.

Step 5 Evaluate Your Culinary and Academic Skills

Your project will be evaluated based on:

- Extent of your research on standardized recipes.
- Depth of interview questions.
- Content, detail, and correctness of your standardized recipe.
- Speaking and listening skills.

 Rubric Go to this book's Online Learning Center at **glencoe.com** for a rubric you can use to evaluate your final project.

 JOHNSON & WALES
U N I V E R S I T Y

 Expert Advice Go to this book's Online Learning Center at **glencoe.com** to read an article by a culinary expert from Johnson & Wales University about the economic and food safety aspects of a standardized recipe.

Culinary Applications

Chapter

15 Cooking Techniques

16 Seasonings and Flavorings

17 Breakfast Cookery

18 Garde Manger Basics

19 Sandwiches and Appetizers

20 Stocks, Sauces, and Soups

21 Fish and Shellfish

22 Poultry Cookery

23 Meat Cookery

24 Pasta and Grains

25 Fruits, Vegetables, and Legumes

EXPLORE THE PHOTO

Culinary workers must prepare a variety of foods. *What types of foods have you prepared?*

EXPLORE THE PHOTO ANSWER Answers will vary based on student experiences.

Local and Seasonal Foods

After completing this unit, you will know how to identify and cook a variety of foods. In your unit thematic project you will find foods from your local area. Then you will create a visual presentation on how to prepare them and prepare a dish using them.

My Journal

Write a journal entry about the different types of foods you have made.

- What ingredients have you used?
- How did you choose them?
- How did you cook them?

JOHNSON & WALES
UNIVERSITY

"Culinary school allowed me to experience a tremendous amount of new foods and spices, and even tickled taste buds I never knew I had."

Zena Harrison
Assistant Food and
Beverage Director/Catering Chef
Compass Group

CHAPTER 15

Cooking Techniques

SECTIONS

15.1 How Cooking Alters Food

15.2 Dry Cooking Techniques

15.3 Moist Cooking Techniques

WRITING ACTIVITY

Cause-and-Effect Paragraph

Cause-and-effect paragraphs explain the reasons for something, or the results of something. Write a cause-and-effect paragraph about how an egg changes when it is cooked.

Writing Tips

1️⃣ Use focusing sentences to help readers anticipate organization.

2️⃣ Use conjunctions such as "as a result," "due to," or "because."

3️⃣ End with a concluding sentence.

WRITING ACTIVITY ANSWER Paragraphs should follow a basic paragraph structure, with a topic sentence and supporting details.

EXPLORE THE PHOTO ANSWER Answers will vary depending on student knowledge.

EXPLORE THE PHOTO

Different cooking methods affect the flavor, texture, appearance, and nutritional content of food. *How many different cooking techniques can you name?*

How Cooking Alters Food

Use different cooking techniques for different foods.

Reading Guide

 Before You Read

Think of an Example Look over the Key Concepts for this section. Think of an example of how or when you could use one of the skills from the Key Concepts. Thinking of how you might apply a skill can help motivate your learning by showing you why the skill is important.

Read to Learn

Key Concepts
- **Compare and contrast** different cooking methods.
- **Explain** how cooking affects a food's nutritive value, texture, color, aroma, and flavor.

Main Idea

Cooking is heating food to transform it in some way. Food is affected in different ways by different cooking techniques.

Graphic Organizer

As you read, you will discover five changes in food made by cooking. Use a herringbone diagram like this one to list the changes.

Content Vocabulary
- dry cooking technique
- evaporate
- moist cooking technique
- combination cooking
- coagulate
- pigment
- caramelization

Academic Vocabulary
- subject
- enhance

Changes in Cooked Food

 Graphic Organizer Go to this book's Online Learning Center at **glencoe.com** for a printable graphic organizer.

GRAPHIC ORGANIZER ANSWER Nutritive value, texture, color, aroma, and flavor.

Cooking Techniques

Suppose the restaurant where you work offers chicken for dinner. There can be many different results, depending on how you choose to cook the chicken. You use very different cooking techniques to cook an egg, grill a steak, or stew tomatoes. Although each technique involves heating the food, they all use a different process to transfer heat to the food.

The degree of change that occurs during the cooking process depends on the length of cooking time, the temperature, and the cooking technique you use. Some methods will produce a great deal of change, while others will not produce very much change. The three cooking techniques are dry, moist, and a combination of both.

Dry Cooking

A **dry cooking technique** uses oil, fat, the radiation of hot air, or metal to transfer heat. No moisture is used in this cooking process. Any moisture that comes from the food evaporates into the air. To **evaporate** means that a liquid escapes from a pan as a vapor. Baking and sautéing are good examples of dry cooking techniques. You will learn more about using dry cooking techniques in Section 15.2.

Moist Cooking

A **moist cooking technique** uses liquid instead of oil to create the heat energy that is needed to cook the food. Boiling and simmering are good examples of moist cooking techniques. You will learn more about how to use moist cooking techniques in Section 15.3.

Combination Cooking

Combination cooking uses both moist and dry cooking techniques. This kind of cooking is a two-step process. You start by using one technique and finishing with the other. For example, for stew, you brown the meat, a dry cooking technique. Then, you simmer the meat and vegetables with seasonings, a moist technique. The objective of combination cooking is to build upon food flavors.

Method Knowledge You must know many different cooking methods to work in a professional kitchen. *Why is it important to understand how different cooking methods work?*

PHOTO CAPTION ANSWER Different foods require different cooking methods. You must know a variety of cooking methods to understand how to choose the correct one.

▲ **Perfect Timing** Perfectly cooked vegetables should be colorful and flavorful. *What happens to vegetables that have been overcooked?*

If you understand each type of cooking technique, you can combine them in ways that create great-tasting food. You will learn more about how to use combination cooking techniques in Section 15.3.

📖 **Reading Check** Distinguish What are the key differences between the dry, moist, and combination cooking techniques?

Changes in Cooked Food

A food's nutritive value, texture, color, aroma, flavor, and appearance do not stay the same after cooking. The cooking technique you choose can affect all of these factors. It is important to know how food will change after it is cooked.

Nutritive Value

The length of time food is cooked and the cooking technique you use determine how much nutrition a food will retain. Raw foods lose more nutritive value the longer they cook. In fact, certain cooking techniques can actually speed up nutrient loss. For example, boiling green beans extracts nutrients in two ways. Nutrients are destroyed simply because the green beans are exposed to heat. Nutrients also are lost during boiling because they are diluted in the liquid.

You might think that if you steam the green beans, you will maintain all of the nutrients. Although steaming is one of the best ways to minimize nutrient loss, exposure to heat will still extract some nutrients from the green beans. However, because the vegetables are cooked by the steam, and not in water, they will not lose nearly as many nutrients as if they had been boiled.

Texture

If you have ever overcooked vegetables, you have seen how cooking can change the texture of food. During cooking, moisture is lost, food tissue breaks down, and proteins coagulate. All of these factors change the texture of cooked food.

READING CHECK ANSWER Dry cooking uses metal, radiation, oil or fat to transfer heat. Moist cooking uses liquid. Combination cooking uses both dry and moist cooking methods.

PHOTO CAPTION ANSWER Vegetables that have been overcooked have a dull color, and are mushy in texture when compared to perfectly cooked vegetables.

When heat is applied, the proteins in food **coagulate**. This means that they change from a liquid or semiliquid state to a drier, solid state. The longer that you **subject**, or expose, the proteins to heat the firmer and more solid they will become. For example, compare the difference in texture between a soft-cooked egg and a hard-cooked egg. If you simmer an egg for three to five minutes, you will produce a soft-cooked egg with a partly solid white and a semiliquid yolk. To produce a hard-cooked egg with both a solid white and yolk, the egg must be simmered for 8 to 10 minutes. The length of time cooked will affect the texture of the egg white and yolk.

Coagulation also occurs in meat proteins as heat is applied during cooking. Meat proteins lose some moisture as the protein becomes more solid during cooking. Long, slow cooking techniques and moderate heat will make some meats tender, flavorful, and juicy. However, using too much heat can toughen the protein in those same meats. This happens because too much moisture is lost.

Color

The cooking process also affects the color of food. For example, certain ingredients that are commonly used to cook vegetables, such as lemon juice, vinegar and baking soda, can change the color of vegetables. There are cooking techniques, such as blanching, that can help keep the color of vegetables. (You will learn about blanching in Section 15.3)

Fruits and vegetables get their unique colors from naturally occurring pigments. A **pigment** is the matter in cells and tissue that gives them their color. Common pigments in foods include chlorophyll (green vegetables), flavonoids (red, purple, and blue vegetables), and carotenoids (yellow, orange, and red vegetables). Many foods have more than one type of pigment. Remember that the longer that fruits and vegetables are cooked, the more their color will change.

Likewise, as meat cooks for extended periods of time, moisture is extracted. The meat will lose its deep-red color as it cooks. These color changes happen at different temperatures.

Texture Changes When high-protein foods are cooked, their texture changes. *How can you tell which egg has been cooked longer?*

PHOTO CAPTION ANSWER The egg that has the yolk that appears more dry has been cooked for a longer period of time.

As the internal temperature of meat reaches between 140°F and 160°F (60°C and 71°C), the redness decreases significantly. The same thing happens when the meat reaches an internal temperature between 168°F and 176°F (76°C and 80°C). That is why the inside of a rare steak is red, a medium rare steak is pink, and a well done steak is brownish gray. Remember, however, that using a thermometer to measure internal temperature is the only safe way to determine if meat is done.

Aroma

The aroma created from cooking food can be as appealing as the flavor and presentation of the final dish. Cooking techniques that use fat as an ingredient or as a way to transfer heat create an appealing aroma. **Caramelization** ('ker-ə-məl-ə-ˌzā-shən), or the process of cooking sugar to high temperatures, is what creates these pleasing aromas. As the sugar in the food turns brown, a rich aroma is produced. Caramelization can also affect the color and flavor of food.

Flavor

The cooking process also affects the flavor of food. If you have ever eaten overcooked meat or vegetables, you know that over-cooking can ruin the flavor. However, if you use the correct cooking technique, you can actually **enhance**, or increase the quality of, the flavor of food. For example, if you grill meats over charcoal or woods such as hickory and mesquite, it will give them an appealing, smoky flavor. Foods that are cooked with dry-heat methods taste rich because of the caramelization that occurs. Moist cooking techniques help bring out a food's natural flavor.

The flavor of foods can also be changed during cooking by using seasonings and flavorings at different times during the cooking process. Cooking methods that use liquids rather than fats to cook can bring out

flavors in a food. Slow roasting foods will bring out rich flavors. Deep-frying foods creates a unique flavor that is enhanced by the crispness of the food.

It is important to enhance the flavor of food because it increases the appeal of the food to the customer. Appealing food is one of the main factors that will bring back customers to a restaurant. If you do not choose the right cooking method for a food, all other methods to enhance flavor will be wasted.

SCIENCE À LA CARTE ANSWER Students will find that the broccoli from the pot without the lid is greener. Cooking with the lid on keeps steam trapped in the pot, causing a faster acid reaction with the chlorophyll.

Another way to enhance the flavor of food is to add seasonings and flavorings before, during, or after the cooking process. These seasonings and flavorings, including herbs, spices, and condiments, will be discussed in more detail in Chapter 16. Not all seasonings and flavorings are used in the same way. Knowing which seasoning to add, and when to add it, is an important part of your culinary training.

 Reading Check Explain Why does the texture of foods toughen after prolonged exposure to heat?

 **Safety Check**

✓ **Internal Temperatures**
Although you should be careful not to overcook food, it must be cooked to a minimum internal temperature to be safe. A thermometer shows the minimum safe internal cooking temperatures for various foods.

CRITICAL THINKING *What might happen if food is not cooked to the minimum internal temperature?*

SECTION 15.1 After You Read

Review Key Concepts

1. **Describe** dry cooking techniques.
2. **Explain** how cooking can affect the texture of a food.

Practice Culinary Academics

 Science

3. **Procedure** Work in groups as directed by your teacher. Wash and peel several carrots and divide them into three even amounts. Cook each group using the following techniques: 1) steam, 2) roast, 3) sear and then braise.

   Analysis Sample each group of carrots and evaluate the differences in texture, color, aroma, and flavor. Why are there differences? Summarize your results.

   > **NSES Content Standard B** Develop an understanding of the structure and properties of matter.

 Social Studies

4. Choose a country and research common cooking techniques that are used in that country. What types of cooking methods are they? Can you predict how these techniques would affect nutritive value, texture, color, aroma, and flavor? Give a five-minute oral presentation on your findings. Use pictures to illustrate cooking techniques.

   > **NCSS I A Culture** Analyze and explain the ways groups, societies and cultures address human needs and concerns.

 Mathematics

5. Your sous chef prepared one dozen soft-cooked eggs and one dozen hard-cooked eggs. Unfortunately, he then mixed the two batches together in one container. What is the probability that if you grab two of the eggs, both will be hard-cooked?

   Math Concept **Probability of Dependent Events** When two events are dependent (the probability of a second event depends on the outcome of the first), find the probability of each event, and multiply those probabilities together.

   Starting Hint For the first selection, the probability that the egg is hard-cooked is 12/24 (or ½). However, when you select the next egg, remember that there will be one fewer hard-cooked egg, and one fewer egg overall.

   > **NCTM Data Analysis and Probability** Understand and apply basic concepts of probability.

   Check your answers at this book's Online Learning Center at **glencoe.com**.

READING CHECK ANSWER When heat is applied to food, the proteins in the food coagulate. The longer they are exposed to heat, the tougher the proteins become.

SAFETY CHECK ANSWER If there is any harmful bacteria in the food, it may not be destroyed and foodborne illness could be spread.

Dry Cooking Techniques

Bake, roast, or grill foods to give them a rich flavor.

Reading Guide

Before You Read

Study with a Buddy It can be difficult to review your own notes and quiz yourself on what you have just read. According to research, studying with a partner for just 12 minutes can help you study better.

Read to Learn

Key Concepts
● **Demonstrate** dry cooking techniques.

Main Idea

Dry cooking causes moisture in food to evaporate into the air. Dry cooking techniques include baking, roasting, sautéing, stir-frying, pan-frying, deep-frying, grilling, and broiling.

Content Vocabulary

- bake
- carryover cooking
- smoking
- roasting
- sear
- basting
- open-spit roast
- sautéing
- stir-frying
- wok
- frying
- dredging
- breading
- batter
- heat lamp
- pan-fry
- deep-fried
- recovery time
- grilling
- griddle
- broiling

Academic Vocabulary
● effect
● delicate

Graphic Organizer

Use a matrix like the one below to list the different dry cooking techniques, with a short description of each.

Dry Cooking Techniques

Technique	Description

 Graphic Organizer Go to this book's Online Learning Center at **glencoe.com** for a printable graphic organizer.

GRAPHIC ORGANIZER ANSWER Baking (dry heat in a closed space), roasting (like baking, long cooking times), sautéing (cooking in very little oil), stir-frying (quick cooking in a wok), frying (cooking in oil), pan-frying (in oil in a shallow pan), deep-frying (submerged in oil), grilling (over heat), and broiling (under heat).

 ACADEMIC STANDARDS

 English Language Arts
NCTE 5 Use different writing process elements to communicate effectively.

 Mathematics
NCTM Geometry Use visualization, spatial reasoning, and geometric modeling to solve problems.

 Science
NSES B Develop an understanding of the interactions of energy and matter.

Social Studies
NCSS V A Individuals, Groups, and Institutions Apply concepts such as role, status, and social class in describing the connections and interactions of individuals, groups, and institutions in society.

NCSS I B Culture Predict how data and experiences may be interpreted by people from diverse cultural perspectives and frames of reference.

NCTE National Council of Teachers of English

NCTM National Council of Teachers of Mathematics

NSES National Science Education Standards

NCSS National Council for the Social Studies

Dry Cooking

Dry cooking techniques include baking, roasting, sautéing, stir-frying, pan-frying, deep-frying, grilling, and broiling. Do not let the word dry fool you. It is called the dry cooking technique because no moisture is directly used in the cooking process. Any moisture that comes from the food evaporates into the air. Some dry cooking techniques use oil and fat to transfer heat. Others use metal and radiation of hot air to create heat. This section will introduce you to dry cooking techniques.

Baking

Baking is a very popular dry cooking technique. Bread and chicken are foods that are commonly baked. Fish, vegetables, fruits, breads, and pastry items also can be baked.

To **bake**, you use dry heat in a closed environment, usually an oven. No fat or liquid is added to the cooking process. Any moisture that comes from food is turned into steam and evaporates into the air. This is because the food is baked uncovered.

A large food product will continue to cook for 5 to 15 minutes after you remove it from the oven. This is called **carryover cooking**, or the cooking that takes place after you remove something from its heat source. This happens because the outside of the food is hotter than the inside of the food. This **effect**, or result, continues until the temperature throughout the food becomes stable. Carryover cooking can add 5 to 15 degrees to the food's final temperature. There is no way to stop the carryover cooking that happens at the end of dry heat cooking. You must keep this effect in mind when you plan cooking times.

Smoking

Smoking is usually done with meats, but also can be done with other foods, such as nuts, vegetables, and cheeses. **Smoking** is a form of cooking that uses low heat, long cooking times, and wood smoke for flavor. Commercial smokers are usually kept at a temperature of 225°F (107°C). Smoking is done with hot coals, to which smoking wood chunks of hickory, mesquite or just about any

Roasted Foods Roasting adds a rich flavor to meats and vegetables. *What other foods could be roasted?*

PHOTO CAPTION ANSWER Other foods that can be roasted include coffee beans, legumes such as soybeans, seeds, spices and grains.

hardwood or fruitwood is added. Foods are placed on the opposite side of the smoker as the coals and wood. This keeps the food from cooking too quickly.

Roasting

Like baking, **roasting** uses dry heat in a closed environment to cook food. Foods commonly roasted include meat and poultry. These foods are placed on top of a rack that is inside a pan. This allows air to circulate all the way around the food so that it cooks evenly. In general, roasting involves longer cooking times than baking.

Carryover cooking also applies to roasting. Remove roasted foods from the oven just before they reach the desired doneness. Remember to use a thermometer to check the internal temperature of foods for safety. The carryover heat that occurs will complete the cooking process.

Searing

Roasting differs from baking in that sometimes the outside of the food product is seared. To **sear** means to quickly brown the outside of food at the start of the cooking process. Searing enhances flavors and adds color. It also helps to build body in juice drippings that can later be used to make sauces. Searing can be done two different ways: in a pan on the rangetop or in the oven.

When you sear foods on the rangetop, heat the pan, then place the food in a pan that contains a small amount of heated oil. Brown the meat on one side, and then turn the meat until all of its surfaces are browned. After this is done, place the pan in a hot oven to finish the cooking process.

When searing in the oven, place the food, such as a roast, in a pan in a 450°F to 475°F (232°C to 246°C) oven. Cook the meat for about 15 to 20 minutes, or until the outside begins to turn golden brown. Then, reduce the heat to 325°F to 350°F (163°C to 177°C) to finish the cooking process.

A TASTE OF HISTORY

1960	1963
John F. Kennedy is elected President of the United States	Julia Child's cooking show *The French Chef* debuts on TV

Cooking Through Time

Cave drawings dating back to the Stone Age show that prehistoric life centered around the gathering and preparation of food. Prehistoric people had no choice but to grill or roast their food on small open fires. During the Middle Ages, the cauldron was the main cooking pot in the kitchen. Seventeenth- and 18th-century people cooked food over fire in kettles or on spits.

Chefs such as Elizabeth David and Julia Child have made an impact on cooking history by introducing both new and historic cooking methods to the masses through their cookbooks and television shows. Although some cooking methods have evolved, others remain the same today as they were in prehistoric times.

History Application

Imagine that you are a TV news reporter doing a story on Julia Child's life and career. Research Julia Child's career and write a short biography on her life. Explain how she revolutionized the cooking world.

> **NCSS V A Individuals, Groups, and Institutions** Apply concepts such as role, status, and social class in describing the connections and interactions of individuals, groups, and institutions in society.

Some meats should be basted during the cooking process to avoid dryness. **Basting** involves moistening foods with melted fats, pan drippings, or another liquid during the cooking time.

Open-Spit Roasting

Many cooks prefer to roast food over an open fire. This is called **open-spit roasting**. To open-spit roast, place the food, usually meat such as pork, on a metal rod or a long skewer. Then, slowly turn it over the heat source. Place a drip pan under the food to catch its juices. Many commercial roasters will automatically turn the spit during the long cooking time.

Check the internal temperature with a thermometer before you remove food from the spit. Remember that the food will continue to cook for another 5 to 15 minutes after you remove it from the heat source.

Sautéing and Stir-Frying

Sautéing (sȯ-'tā-iŋ) is a quick, dry cooking technique that uses a small amount of fat or oil in a shallow pan to cook foods. Sautéing is generally used with **delicate**, or fragile, foods that cook relatively quickly. These foods include fish fillets, scallops, tender cuts of meat, vegetables, and fruit. Most sautéed foods are served with a sauce.

During sautéing, you will want to seal the surface of the food. To do this, preheat a pan on high heat, then add a small amount of fat or oil. When the fat or oil is heated and nearly smoking, add the food. Do not overcrowd the pan. Doing so will lower the temperature of the food, and it will not cook properly. After the food is sealed, lower the temperature so that the food cooks evenly throughout. Foods may need to be turned in the pan while they are sautéing.

Stir-frying is a dry cooking technique that is similar to sautéing. When stir-frying, you use a wok. A **wok** is a large pan with sloping sides. Stir-fried foods require less cooking time than sautéed foods. Vegetables and tender, boneless meats are often stir-fried.

To stir-fry, place a wok over high heat, add a small amount of fat, and then add small pieces of food. Because of the wok's size and shape, it is important to constantly stir the food as it cooks.

Frying

It is hard for most people to resist crispy foods, such as fried chicken and French fries. Foods like these are prepared using a dry-heat cooking technique called **frying**. During frying, foods are cooked in larger amounts of hot fat or oil.

⌒ Small Bites ⌒

Pan-Frying Tip Chill cuts of meat before you pan-fry them. The outside of the meat will brown before the inside finishes cooking.

The outside of the food becomes sealed when it comes in contact with the hot oil during frying. The natural moisture that is in the food turns to steam, which bubbles up to the surface. Because the outside of the food is sealed, fried foods are often moist and juicy on the inside.

Foods are usually coated before frying. To do this, foods can be dredged, breaded, or battered.

Dredging One way to prepare foods for frying is to dredge them. **Dredging** means to coat foods with flour or finely ground crumbs.

Breading Another way to add texture and flavor to fried foods is to add a **breading**, or a coating made of eggs and crumbs.

Batter Another tasty way to prepare fried foods is to batter them before frying them. This adds texture and flavor. **Batter** is a semiliquid mixture that contains ingredients such as flour, milk, eggs, and seasonings. Dip the food into the batter immediately before frying.

Tips to Follow After Frying

After food has been fried, remove it from the oil and drain it well on an absorbent surface such as paper towels. You can also add seasoning at this time. Fried foods are best served and eaten immediately after being cooked. If you cannot serve fried foods right away, they can be temporarily stored under a heat lamp. A **heat lamp** uses light in the infrared spectrum to keep food warm during holding without becoming soggy.

Pan-Frying

One way to fry food is pan-frying. To **pan-fry**, heat a moderate amount of fat in a pan before adding food. Use enough fat to cover about one-half to three-quarters of

Dredge and Bread Food

1 Dredge the food product in seasoned, dry flour by dipping it into the flour and coating it evenly on all surfaces. Shake off any excess flour.

2 Immediately dip the food into an egg wash or other liquid. An egg wash is a mixture of beaten eggs and a liquid such as milk or water. Coat the food completely. Shake off any excess.

3 Quickly place the food into a container of dry crumbs and coat evenly. Crumbs can be made from bread, ground nuts, cereal, crackers, or shredded coconut.

the food. The fat should not be so hot that it smokes. Instead, it should be hot enough to sizzle when food is added, usually at 350°F to 375°F (177°C to 191°C).

Pan-frying does use more fat than sautéing, so it requires longer cooking times and lower heat. Because food is not completely covered by the oil during pan-frying, you will need to turn the food after one side is done to allow for even cooking throughout. Foods that are often pan-fried include chicken, potatoes, fish, and pork chops.

Deep-Frying

Another way to fry foods is to deep-fry them. **Deep-frying** means to cook foods by completely submerging them in heated fat or oil at temperatures between 350°F and 375°F (177°C to 191°C). Fried foods must be cooked until they are done on the inside. Temperature and timing on deep-fat fryers help you determine doneness. Deep-fried foods will be a golden brown color. Once deep-fried foods are done, remove them from the oil and briefly hold them up over the oil tank so that the excess fat can drip off. Oil must be changed frequently. Heat and use can cause oil to darken, break down, and give food an off flavor. Oil can also transfer strong flavors between foods.

The most popular types of deep-fried foods are potatoes, onions, fish, and poultry. Many foodservice operations purchase foods that are already breaded and are ready to be deep-fried. Commercial fryers with fry baskets that can sit directly in the oil are commonly used.

Commercial deep-fryers have some advantages over other frying equipment:

- There is less recovery time than with stove-top pots. **Recovery time** is the time it takes for the fat or oil to return to the preset temperature after the food has been submerged.
- The life of the fat or oil is maximized if correct temperatures are used.

Grilling

Many commercial kitchens use gas, electric, charcoal, or wood-fired grills. **Grilling** is often used for tender foods that cook relatively quickly. To grill foods properly, you must first preheat the grill. Depending on the type of food you wish to grill, brush the food lightly with oil, and then place it on the grill. Do not move the food after you place it initially. This will help create the distinctive markings of a grilled food product.

Griddle Use

Grilling can also be done on a griddle. A **griddle** is a flat, solid plate of metal with a gas or electric heat source. Griddles are commonly used to make sandwiches such as grilled cheese and breakfast items such as pancakes and eggs. Depending on the type of food that is cooked, you may want to add a little fat to the griddle to keep the food from sticking. The temperature of a griddle is about 350°F (177°C).

Food can also be grilled on a grooved griddle. This type of griddle has raised ridges. Although grooved griddles are similar in design to grills, they do not generate as much smoke as a grill. That is why food cooked on a griddle will not have the same smoky flavor as food cooked on a grill.

Colorful Cooking Cooking foods produces many changes in the food. *What changes occurred to this food as it cooked?*

PHOTO CAPTION ANSWER Answers include egg proteins coagulating, vegetables softening, flavors mixing, and nutrition changing.

Broiling

Broiling means to cook food directly under a primary heat source. When you broil food, the temperature is controlled by how close the food is to the heat source. Thicker foods should be placed farther from the heat source, and thinner foods should be placed closer to the heat source. This ensures that the inside and outside of the food will cook at the same rate.

Foods that are commonly broiled include vegetables, meats, and poultry. Tender foods lend themselves to being broiled. Foods are usually turned only once during cooking when they are broiled. The broiling rack may make grill marks on the food, or a heatproof

Small Bites

Seasonings Some cooks add seasonings to the meat before broiling. Do not add salt before broiling, however, because it draws out juices. This can dry out the meat.

platter may be used. Unlike a grill, broilers are heated only by gas or electricity. Additional flavors cannot be added to the food by burning charcoal or wood. Broiling uses no extra fat to cook food.

 Reading Check Compare and Contrast How do stir-frying and sautéing differ?

SECTION 15.2 After You Read

Review Key Concepts

1. **Explain** how to use a griddle.

Practice Culinary Academics

 English Language Arts

2. Imagine that you write an advice column for a local or school newspaper about cooking. Ask and answer two questions about using dry cooking techniques. Share your column with the class.

> **NCTE 5** Use different writing process elements to communicate effectively.

Science

3. **Procedure** Cook a piece of chicken and a potato. Record the temperature immediately after removing the food from the oven. Record the temperature again each minute until the food begins to cool.

   Analysis Create a chart of the cooling times for each item. What do you observe about carryover cooking times?

> **NSES B** Develop an understanding of the interactions of energy and matter.

 Social Studies

4. Choose a dry cooking technique and study its development. What were the first cultures to use the technique? How has it changed since then?

What cultures use the technique now? Create a two-page report to discuss your research.

> **NCSS I B Culture** Predict how data and experiences may be interpreted by people from diverse cultural perspectives and frames of reference.

Mathematics

5. To pan-fry some breaded chicken cutlets, Jody adds oil to her pan so that the oil is 1/2-inch deep. If the pan is 10 inches in diameter, how many fluid ounces of oil did Jody use?

> **Math Concept** **Volume of a Cylinder** Calculate the volume (V) of a cylinder as $V = \pi r^2 h$, where r = the radius of the circular base, and h is the height of the cylinder. Use 3.14 for π.

   Starting Hint Find the volume in cubic inches of the oil using the formula, with 0.5 inches as h and one-half the pan's diameter as r. One cubic inch = 0.554 fluid ounces, so multiply the volume by 0.554.

> **NCTM Geometry** Use visualization, spatial reasoning, and geometric modeling to solve problems.

 Check your answers at this book's Online Learning Center at **glencoe.com**.

Moist Cooking Techniques

Reading Guide

 Before You Read

Preview Understanding causes and effects can help clarify connections. A cause is an event or action that makes something happen. An effect is a result of a cause. Ask yourself, "Why does this happen?" to help you recognize cause-and-effect relationships in this section.

Read to Learn

Key Concepts
- **Demonstrate** moist cooking techniques.
- **Describe** combination cooking techniques.

Main Idea

Moist cooking involves heating food in a liquid. Sometimes moist cooking techniques are applied to food that has been partially cooked with a dry cooking technique.

Content Vocabulary
- boiling
- boiling point
- convection
- blanching
- shocking
- parboiling
- simmering
- reduce
- poach
- steaming
- braising
- deglaze
- stewing

Academic Vocabulary
- submerged
- extracted

Graphic Organizer

There are four steps in stewing foods. Use a sequence chart like this one as you read to list these steps.

Steps in Stewing Foods

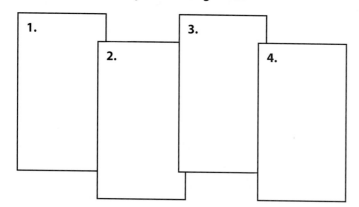

1.

2.

3.

4.

 Graphic Organizer Go to this book's Online Learning Center at **glencoe.com** for a printable graphic organizer.

GRAPHIC ORGANIZER ANSWER 1) Sear the food over high heat.
2) Completely cover food with liquid. 3) Bring to a simmer; cook until tender.
4) Add vegetables partway through cooking.

ACADEMIC STANDARDS

 English Language Arts
NCTE 12 Use language to accomplish individual purposes.

Mathematics
NCTM Problem Solving Build new mathematical knowledge through problem solving.

 Science
NSES B Develop an understanding of interactions of energy and matter.

NCTE National Council of Teachers of English

NCTM National Council of Teachers of Mathematics

NSES National Science Education Standards

NCSS National Council for the Social Studies

Cooking in Liquid

There is more than one way to cook eggs. Some people like them to be boiled so that they are hard-cooked, while others prefer their eggs lightly poached so that they are softer in texture. Boiling and poaching are both moist cooking techniques.

Cooking food using a moist technique involves heating food in a liquid other than oil. Moist cooking techniques include boiling, blanching, parboiling, simmering, poaching, and steaming. Sometimes, a moist cooking technique is applied to foods that have already been partially cooked using a dry cooking technique. This section will introduce you to moist and combination cooking techniques.

When you cook foods in water or other liquids, foods are completely **submerged**, or covered in liquid. Boiling, simmering, and poaching involve cooking in liquid. The doneness of food will depend on the type of food that is cooked and the specific method chosen.

Boiling

Boiling is a moist cooking technique in which you bring a liquid, such as water or stock, to the boiling point and keep it at that temperature while the food cooks. The **boiling point**, or temperature at which a liquid boils, of water is 212°F (100°C) at sea level. When liquid reaches the boiling point, food can be added and cooked.

When liquid boils, a process called convection occurs. During **convection**, the liquid closest to the bottom of the pan is heated and rises to the top. Meanwhile, the cooler liquid descends to the bottom of the pan. This sets off a circular motion in the pan that keeps the food in constant motion. This motion keeps food from sticking to the pan.

Boiling cooks food quickly. However, it can be harmful to some food. The rapid circular motion of the liquid does not harm pasta, but it can break apart a tender piece of fish. Because of this, very few food items are cooked completely by boiling.

🔺 **Bring to a Boil** Boiling is best used for foods that are not too tender or delicate. *Why should delicate foods not be boiled?*

PHOTO CAPTION ANSWER The action of boiling can be tough on delicate food, and may cause it to break apart during cooking.

🔺 **Cool Down** One way to cool food immediately after blanching is to plunge it into ice water. *What should be done with food after it has been blanched?*

Blanching

Using the boiling method to partially cook food is also known as **blanching**. It is a quick way to change the flavor and keep the color in foods. Blanching is usually a two-step process:

1. Completely submerge the food in a boiling liquid and blanch, or briefly cook, it.
2. Remove the blanched food from the liquid. To make sure the food stops cooking as soon as you remove it from the liquid, briefly plunge the food into ice water. This is called **shocking**. This will completely stop the cooking process.

Remember that a blanched food item is only partially cooked. You will need a second stage of cooking to complete the cooking process. For example, you might first blanch green beans and then sauté them in butter and herbs.

Blanching has many uses. Blanching is sometimes used to:

- Simplify peeling of vegetables and fruits.
- Precook foods before they are frozen.
- Soften herbs.
- Lock in the color of foods.

- Help preserve a food's nutrients.
- Remove excess salt from ham or pork.
- Remove blood from meats.
- Remove strong flavors from meats.
- Cook food partially to prepare it for faster service later.

Parboiling

Parboiling is a moist cooking technique that is similar to blanching. In **parboiling**, foods are put into boiling water and partially cooked. However, the cooking time for parboiling foods is longer than for blanching. Recipes that include parboiling will give you the exact timing for a particular food item. For example, ribs are often parboiled before they are grilled. This tenderizes the meat and reduces grilling time.

⌒ **Small Bites** ⌒

Tomato Peeling You can lightly blanch a fresh tomato to make it easier to peel. You must immediately plunge the tomato into ice water after blanching so that it does not continue to cook.

PHOTO CAPTION ANSWER Blanched food is only partially cooked, so it should be completely cooked using another cooking method.

Simmering

Simmering is the most commonly used moist cooking method. It can be used to cook food items, or blanch them. Foods should be simmered until they are moist and tender. Like boiling, simmering involves cooking food in liquid. However, during **simmering**, food cooks slowly and steadily in a slightly cooler liquid that is heated from 185°F to 200°F (85°C to 93°C). The bubbles in the liquid rise slowly to the surface of the liquid, but do not break the surface.

Because of the lower temperature, not as much convection action occurs during simmering. This makes simmering a much more gentle cooking process than boiling. Foods such as yellow squash and zucchini should be fully submerged in the liquid to simmer. The advantages of simmering include less shrinkage of the food, less evaporation and better control over evaporation, and less breakup of fragile food, such as fish.

Simmering is also used to **reduce**, or decrease the volume of, a liquid. For example, you might want to simmer spaghetti sauce to make it thicker.

Poaching

Poaching is an even gentler method of moist cooking than simmering. To **poach** means to cook food in a flavorful liquid between 150°F (66°C) and 185°F (85°C). Generally, tender or delicate foods such as fish and eggs are poached in just enough liquid to cover the food. You can poach food on the rangetop or in the oven. Sometimes the poaching liquid is used to make a sauce that accompanies the food when it is served.

Steaming

Steamed vegetables are both tasty and nutritious. **Steaming** means cooking vegetables or other foods in a closed environment filled with steam, such as in a pot with a tight-fitting lid. Steam is created inside the pot when water reaches the boiling point and turns into vapor. Although the food never touches the liquid, the temperature inside the closed environment rises high enough to cook the food. Steaming is generally faster than other moist cooking techniques.

▲ **Gentle Simmer** Simmering cooks foods slowly. *What are some of the advantages of simmering versus boiling?*

PHOTO CAPTION ANSWER Simmering produces less shrinkage in food, less evaporation in the pot, and less breakup of fragile food like fish than boiling does.

If pressure is added during steaming, the temperature inside the pot rises even higher. This cooks the food even faster. A pressure steamer holds steam under pressure. As the pressure increases, so does the temperature. For example, say you cook asparagus at 10 pounds of pressure per square inch (psi) at 240°F (116°C). If you increase the pressure to 15 psi, the temperature will rise to 250°F (121°C). Steamers cook foods, such as vegetables, without dissolving the nutrients.

Reading Check **Summarize** Why would you blanch a food?

Combination Cooking

Sometimes, great things happen when you combine the best of two techniques. This is the case with combination cooking. As the term suggests, combination cooking combines two techniques you have already learned: moist and dry. Two major combination techniques are braising and stewing. Braising and stewing involve both a dry and a moist cooking process. The first step for both cooking methods is usually to brown the food using dry heat. Then, the food is completely cooked by simmering the food in a liquid.

Cooking food using a combination technique is especially useful for tough, but flavorful, cuts of meat. The combination cooking process makes the meat more tender. It is also an excellent way to prepare large pieces of less-tender meat.

Braising

Braising is a long, slow cooking process. It can make tough cuts of meat more tender. Meat is first seared and the pan deglazed before the moist cooking technique is used. To **deglaze** means to add a small amount of liquid such as stock or water to a pan to loosen brown bits of food after searing or sautéing. An additional amount of stock, sauce, or water is added, and the food is cooked on top of the range or in the oven.

During cooking, braising produces a very flavorful liquid. The flavors **extracted**, or drawn out, from the food become highly concentrated.

Flavorful Liquid Braising liquid should be strained before it can be reused for sauces. *Why do you think this is?*

READING CHECK ANSWER Blanching is a quick way to change the flavor of food while retaining the color.

PHOTO CAPTION ANSWER Vegetables are added to a braising pan to add flavor to the dish. These vegetables should be strained out for sauces to stay liquid.

Imagine braising a pork loin. The juices from the pork are mixed with the braising liquid. The braising liquid takes on the flavor of the meat's juices.

Braised foods are always served with the cooking liquid. You will want to strain, thicken, and add salt, pepper, or other spices to the liquid before you serve it.

Braise
Food

1 Begin by searing the food in a frying or roasting pan.

2 Remove the food from the pan or push it to one side. Add mirepoix or vegetables that are appropriate to the preparation.

3 Cook the vegetables and deglaze by adding a small amount of liquid to the pan. Stir to dissolve the browned bits of food that stick to the pan. Return the seared food to the pan if you removed it.

4 Add enough liquid, such as stock or sauce, to cover no more than two-thirds of the food. Cover the pan, if desired. Place the pan in a 350°F (177°C) oven, and cook the food slowly until it is fork-tender. Turn the food every 20 to 30 minutes. Braising can also be done on the rangetop over low heat.

Stewing

Stewing is another combination cooking technique. However, stewed foods are completely covered with liquid during cooking. Cooking time for stewing is generally shorter than for braising. That is because the main food item in stew is cut into smaller pieces before cooking.

Follow these steps to stew foods:

1. First, sear the food in a pan over high heat. Tender cuts of meat should not be stewed or they will become tough.
2. Completely cover the food with liquid.
3. Bring the stew to a simmer and cook until tender.
4. Add vegetables, if desired, part of the way through simmering the main food.

This will ensure that the vegetables will not be overcooked when the main food in the stew is fully cooked.

 **Reading Check** Explain What are the differences between braising and stewing?

Safety Check

 Burned by Steam

Take special care when you remove the lids from pots or containers that may have steam trapped inside. Always tip the lid open by lifting it away from your hand and body. Steam is at least 212°F (100°C) and can cause severe burns.

CRITICAL THINKING *Why do you think the steam is so hot?*

 SECTION 15.3 **After You Read**

Review Key Concepts

1. **Explain** how to blanch foods.
2. **Describe** the braising process.

Practice Culinary Academics

 Science

3. **Procedure** Browning occurs in meat when it is cooked at high heat. Cook two pieces of meat. Sear one piece, and use another cooking technique on the second piece that does not involve searing.

   Analysis Compare the flavor of the seared meat with the other meat. Create a chart to record observations about the appearance and flavor. Write a short summary of why you think meat is browned before stewing or braising.

   > **NSES B** Develop an understanding of interactions of energy and matter.

 English Language Arts

4. Create a poster to illustrate the process of braising foods. Use drawings and text to display each step in the process. Display your posters in the classroom.

   > **NCTE 12** Use language to accomplish individual purposes.

Mathematics

5. Gina can cook basmati rice 3½ times faster in her pressure cooker than in a regular pot. If rice normally cooks in 20 minutes, what is the cooking time in the pressure cooker (to the nearest second)?

   Math Concept **Working with Time** To convert decimal minutes (such as 12.43) into minutes and seconds, keep the whole number portion (as minutes), and multiply the decimal portion by 60 (which represents the seconds).

   Starting Hint Find the new cooking time by dividing 20 minutes by 3½. Convert any decimal portion of your answer into seconds by multiplying it by 60. Round to the nearest second.

   > **NCTM Problem Solving** Build new mathematical knowledge through problem solving.

 Check your answers at this book's Online Learning Center at **glencoe.com**.

READING CHECK ANSWER In stewing, the food is completely covered by liquid. In braising, food is partially covered by liquid. Cooking time for stewing is shorter than for braising.

SAFETY CHECK ANSWER Water boils at 212°F (100°C). Steam is evaporated water, so it is the same temperature as boiling water.

Review and Applications

Chapter Summary

There are three different cooking techniques: dry, moist, and combination cooking. The cooking technique, temperature, and cooking time affect nutritive value, texture, color, aroma, and flavor. Dry techniques include baking, roasting, sautéing, stir-frying, pan-frying, deep-frying, grilling, and broiling. Moist cooking techniques include boiling, simmering, poaching, and steaming. Combination cooking techniques include braising and stewing.

Content and Academic Vocabulary Review

1. Create multiple-choice test questions for each content and academic vocabulary term.

Content Vocabulary

- dry cooking technique (p. 376)
- evaporate (p. 376)
- moist cooking technique (p. 376)
- combination cooking (p. 376)
- coagulate (p. 378)
- pigment (p. 378)
- caramelization (p. 379)
- bake (p. 382)
- carryover cooking (p. 382)
- smoking (p. 382)
- roasting (p. 383)
- sear (p. 383)
- basting (p. 383)
- open-spit roast (p. 383)
- sautéing (p. 384)
- stir-frying (p. 384)
- wok (p. 384)
- frying (p. 384)
- dredging (p. 384)
- breading (p. 384)
- batter (p. 384)
- heat lamp (p. 384)
- pan-fry (p. 384)
- deep-fried (p. 385)
- recovery time (p. 386)
- grilling (p. 386)
- griddle (p. 386)
- broiling (p. 387)
- boiling (p. 389)
- boiling point (p. 389)
- convection (p. 389)
- blanching (p. 390)
- shocking (p. 390)
- parboiling (p. 390)
- simmering (p. 391)
- reduce (p. 391)
- poach (p. 391)
- steaming (p. 391)
- braising (p. 392)
- deglaze (p. 392)
- stewing (p. 394)

Academic Vocabulary

- subject (p. 378)
- enhance (p. 379)
- effect (p. 382)
- delicate (p. 384)
- submerged (p. 389)
- extracted (p. 392)

Review Key Concepts

2. Compare and contrast different cooking methods.

3. Explain how cooking affects a food's nutritive value, texture, color, aroma, and flavor.

4. Demonstrate dry cooking techniques.

5. Demonstrate moist cooking techniques.

6. Describe combination cooking techniques.

Critical Thinking

7. Imagine that a coworker has cooked a meal. The piece of cooked meat is tough and grayish-brown color, and the vegetables are limp and colorless. What has gone wrong during cooking?

8. Explain how you should prepare an extra-lean pork loin roast to avoid it becoming dry and tasteless.

9. Imagine that a food critic is coming to your restaurant. What would you tell your staff about cooking to ensure good flavor, nutritive value, texture, color, and aroma?

10. Describe the advantages of having a variety of cooking techniques on a restaurant menu. Is it possible to have too many techniques represented?

Review and Applications

Academic Skills

English Language Arts

11. Interpret Cooling Methods Obtain a cookbook or a cooking magazine that has at least 10 recipes. Read through the book or magazine and review the recipes. Choose 10 recipes and identify the cooking techniques used in each. For each recipe, list the cooking technique, whether it is moist or dry, and how you think the technique will affect the dish's color, texture, aroma, and flavor.

> **NCTE 3** Apply strategies to interpret texts.

Social Studies

12. Equipment Advances Choose one cooking technique and conduct research to discover how the equipment used for that cooking method has changed over time. Create a time line with brief descriptions of the changes in the equipment used. How has the changing equipment improved that cooking technique?

> **NCSS VIII B Science, Technology, and Society** Make judgments about how science and technology have transformed the physical world and human society.

Mathematics

13. Fill a Fryer Oscar has just purchased a new deep fryer for his restaurant. The fryer holds 60 pounds of cooking oil. But Oscar's containers of cooking oil on hand were measured in volume (gallons), not weight. If the oil has a density of 7.5 pounds per gallon at room temperature, and a 4-gallon container of oil costs Oscar $38.75, how much will it cost to fill up the fryer?

Math Concept **Weight vs. Volume** A liquid's weight and volume are related to each other by a concept called density, which is the ratio of its weight to its volume at a particular temperature. Use the formula weight = density × volume.

Starting Hint First, determine the total volume of oil that Oscar will need by rearranging the formula above to solve for volume. Use the total weight and density given in the problem. Then, find the number of containers that Oscar will need by dividing the total volume by 4. Multiply the number of containers by the cost per container.

> **NCTM Problem Solving** Apply and adapt a variety of appropriate strategies to solve problems.

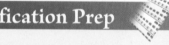

Certification Prep

Directions Read the questions. Then, read the answer choices and choose the best possible answer for each.

14. Which of the following uses a combination cooking technique?

    a. braise

    b. stir-fry

    c. poach

    d. grill

15. At what temperature does water begin to boil?

    a. 100°F

    b. 132°F

    c. 200°F

    d. 212°F

Sharpen your test-taking skills to improve your kitchen certification program score.

Test-Taking Tip
Building your vocabulary will help you take tests. Practice new vocabulary and concepts with other students until you understand them all.

Real-World Skills and Applications

Self-Management Skills

16. Work with Time Constraints Imagine that you have only 30 minutes to prepare a meal. Your main ingredient will be chicken. What cooking methods could you use to prepare the chicken in time? Which methods would retain the most nutritional value? What could you add to the meal to increase its nutritional value? Write a one-page report to describe your cooking method choices.

Communication Skills

17. Watch a Cooking Show Watch a cooking show. Look for the particular cooking technique that the host uses. Take notes on what the host is doing and what you learned about that technique from the show. Give a five-minute oral presentation to the class to explain what you learned about the cooking technique. Turn in your notes to your teacher.

Technology Applications

18. Create a Web Site As a class, plan and design a Web site that explains the different cooking methods. Make sure it contains basic instructions for each method. If possible, create recipes for a few or all of the techniques that you describe on the Web site. You may also want to photograph the steps of the techniques to illustrate the instructions.

Financial Literacy

19. Cost Ingredients Ordering chicken precooked will cost you $3 per pound of chicken. Ordering uncooked chicken and having the staff cook it will cost you $2 per pound, including labor. How much money will you save having the staff cook the chicken if you need 25 pounds?

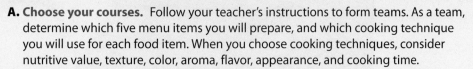

Culinary Lab

Cook a Meal

Use the culinary skills you have learned in this chapter.

20. Use Cooking Techniques Working in teams, during this lab you will prepare a three-course meal that involves dry, moist, and combination cooking techniques.

A. Choose your courses. Follow your teacher's instructions to form teams. As a team, determine which five menu items you will prepare, and which cooking technique you will use for each food item. When you choose cooking techniques, consider nutritive value, texture, color, aroma, flavor, appearance, and cooking time.

B. Gather ingredients. Determine the list of ingredients needed to prepare the menu items. Gather those ingredients at your work station.

C. Make a schedule. Develop a workflow and preparation time schedule for team members to follow when they prepare menu items.

D. Cook and serve your meal. Once your schedule is set, cook your menu items and serve the meal to the other teams. On a piece of paper, create a rating chart to evaluate each team's meal.

Create Your Evaluation

Create a chart to evaluate food items for texture, color, aroma, flavor, and appearance. Use this scale:
1 = Poor; 2 = Fair; 3 = Good; 4 = Great
Discuss amongst yourselves and then with the class how each item rated in the different categories and which technique produced the best food.

Seasonings and Flavorings

SECTIONS

16.1 Enhancing Food

16.2 Herbs and Spices

16.3 Condiments, Nuts, and Seeds

16.4 Sensory Perception

WRITING ACTIVITY

Essay Outline

Most writing assignments will require you to gather information. Choose one herb and research it in print resources and on the Internet. Highlight information that you feel is important. Then, create an outline for an essay.

Writing Tips

1. Use an Internet search engine, library catalog, or speak to a librarian to begin your search.

2. Evaluate each source to determine how reliable it is.

3. Choose information that will fit into your basic structure.

WRITING ACTIVITY ANSWER Discuss what makes sources reliable or questionable. Sudents should choose important information for outlines. Outlines should be in a logical order.

EXPLORE THE PHOTO ANSWER
Answers will vary based on personal knowledge. Students can look at the photo and choose from among the items pictured.

EXPLORE THE PHOTO

There are many different seasonings and flavorings you can use to enhance the flavor of food. *What seasonings and flavorings can you name?*

Enhancing Food

How do you like to season and flavor food?

Reading Guide

 Before You Read

Be Organized A messy environment can be distracting. To lessen distractions, organize an area where you can read this section comfortably.

Read to Learn

Key Concepts
- **Describe** the varieties and uses of seasonings and flavorings.

Main Idea
Seasonings and flavorings strengthen a food's natural flavor. Knowing which seasonings and flavorings work well with certain food items is an important cooking skill.

Content Vocabulary
- seasoning
- flavor enhancer
- flavoring
- extract
- spice
- zest
- pith
- monosodium glutamate
- blend

Academic Vocabulary
- distinct
- lend

Graphic Organizer
As you read, use a spider diagram like this one to list the four different types of pepper and their flavors.

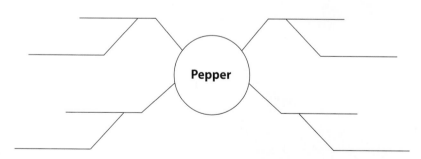

Pepper

 Graphic Organizer Go to this book's Online Learning Center at **glencoe.com** for a printable graphic organizer.

ACADEMIC STANDARDS

 English Language Arts
NCTE 12 Use language to accomplish individual purposes.

 Mathematics
NCTM Problem Solving
Solve problems that arise in mathematics and in other contexts.

 Science
NSES A Develop abilities necessary to do scientific inquiry.

 Social Studies
NCSS I E Culture
Demonstrate the value of cultural diversity, as well as cohesion, within and across groups.

NCTE National Council of Teachers of English

NCTM National Council of Teachers of Mathematics

NSES National Science Education Standards

NCSS National Council for the Social Studies

GRAPHIC ORGANIZER ANSWER Black pepper: Slightly hot, not bitter. White pepper: Slightly hotter than black pepper. Green peppercorn: Fresh flavor. Red pepper: Intense heat.

Seasonings and Flavorings

Imagine eating food without any flavor. Or, imagine that you ate several foods that all had the same flavor. This does not sound very appetizing, does it? Customers expect flavorful dishes when they visit a restaurant. Fortunately, foods have their own natural flavoring. Sometimes, however, these flavors need to be strengthened. Foodservice professionals use seasonings, flavorings, and flavor enhancers to help.

Enhancing the natural flavor of foods is part of the art of cooking. You need to understand how the flavor of food can be enhanced to work successfully in food production. Using seasonings and flavorings correctly is a skill that develops over time. Tasting foods throughout the cooking process will help you develop this skill.

Both seasonings and flavorings improve or strengthen the natural flavor of foods. A **seasoning** is an ingredient that intensifies or improves food without changing the food's natural flavor. If a seasoning is used correctly, the individual flavor of a seasoning cannot be tasted in the food product itself.

Some seasonings are called flavor enhancers. A **flavor enhancer** increases the way you perceive the food's flavor without changing the actual flavor of the prepared dish. They do not add flavor to a dish. Flavor enhancers do this by affecting your taste buds. Monosodium glutamate (ˌmä-nə-ˌsō-dē-əm ˈglü-tə-māt), or MSG, is an example of a flavor enhancer. It intensifies the flavor of savory foods.

A **flavoring**, on the other hand, is an ingredient that actually changes the natural flavor of the foods to which it is added. This enhances the experience of tasting the dish.

◀ **Season with Salt** Salt comes in many varieties. *What four kinds of salt are most often used in foodservice?*

PHOTO CAPTION ANSWER Table salt, rock salt, sea salt, and kosher salt are used most often in foodservice.

Flavorings have their own **distinct**, or separate and unique, flavors. An **extract**, or a concentrated flavor such as almond and vanilla, are flavorings.

A wide variety of ingredients can be used as seasonings, flavorings, and flavor enhancers. Salt and pepper are two of the most common seasonings that are used. A more detailed description of these ingredients follows.

Salt

Salt is the most commonly used food seasoning today. It can be added to most foods, even some sweet foods, to heighten flavor. Salt has a more distinctive taste on cool foods than on hot foods.

Table salt is the most common type of salt used in both food preparation and to season food at the table. There are other types of salt used in the foodservice industry as well. Rock salt usually is used as a bed during baking for foods such as clams, oysters, and potatoes. Sea salt is preferred by some chefs because it has a strong, distinctive flavor. Kosher salt is coarse and free of iodine or other additives. It has a milder flavor. Chefs also like to use kosher salt to season food during preparation.

The amount of salt that is added to food depends on the food that is being cooked. It also depends on the preference of the diner. Taste food before you add more salt to a dish. You can always add more salt, but you cannot remove it. Too much salt can ruin a dish.

Pepper

Pepper is the most widely used spice in the world. A **spice** is an aromatic vegetable product that blends with the natural flavor of foods. Pepper has been used since ancient times, in civilizations from Ancient Egypt to Ancient Rome to India. In the Middle Ages, pepper was widely traded and commonly used as a form of currency.

Pepper is usually used in its ground form rather than as whole peppercorns. Ground pepper brings out the flavor of many foods.

Whole or cracked pepper, however, is large enough to be detected on its own in the flavor of the food when it is added. A wide variety of peppers are used in the foodservice industry.

Black Pepper

Black pepper comes from the dried, unripe berries of the pepper plant. It is slightly hot, but not bitter. It is the most common pepper used. Black pepper stimulates juices in the stomach lining. This helps with digestion.

White Pepper

White pepper comes from the kernel of ripe pepper plant berries. It is an all-purpose seasoning that blends easily with most food, yet maintains a distinctive flavor. White pepper is a little hotter than black pepper.

Green Peppercorns

Green peppercorns come from unripened berries. They are preserved in brine until they darken, and have a fresh flavor. Green peppercorns are expensive. They are used only in special recipes, such as grilled veal tenderloin with a delicate brown sauce.

Red Pepper

Red pepper is not like black, white, or green pepper. Instead, it comes from the capsicum plant and is related more closely to the bell pepper family. Red pepper is used to add flavor to food, such as soups and sauces, without altering the food's natural flavor.

Popular Pepper There are several different types of pepper used in cooking. *Why do you think pepper is the most commonly used spice in the world?*

Hot red pepper, such as cayenne, can be difficult to use properly because of its intense heat. It is easy to add too much to food. Paprika (pə-'prē-kə) is a fine powder made from grinding sweet red pepper pods. Paprika can be sweet, mild, medium-hot, or hot. It is used in many ethnic cuisines.

Hot Pepper

Hot peppers are commonly referred to as chiles. They vary in their degree of hotness, color, and flavor. They can be used fresh, dried into flakes, or ground into powder. Hot peppers are often added to Indian and Asian foods for spice and flavor.

Onion

Onions are a flavoring that can be added to just about any food dish. The onion family also includes scallions, leeks, shallots, chives, and garlic. All of these flavorings have a strong aroma and flavor, especially when they are uncooked. Onions form part of the base for many stocks and soups. Onions are also used as part of a mirepoix, which can be used in braising meats as well as stocks and soups.

When you use foods from the onion family, keep in mind that, unlike herbs, fresh onions have a stronger flavor than dried ones. Depending on the form you use, you may need to adjust the amount of onion flavoring that you add to the food.

Lemon

The **zest**, or rind, of the lemon is another type of flavoring. The zest contains the flavorful oil of the lemon. It is usually peeled or scraped carefully off the top layer of the lemon. It is added to dishes such as fish, meats, vegetables, and desserts to give a citrus flavor.

When you cook with lemon, use only the juice or the zest. Do not use the **pith**, or the white membrane that is just underneath the zest. The pith is bitter. You can avoid the pith by not scraping too deeply through the zest.

PHOTO CAPTION ANSWER Answers may vary, but generally, pepper has been known to many cultures since ancient times. Pepper also goes well with a variety of foods, making it a good spice for most dishes.

Monosodium Glutamate

Monosodium glutamate, or MSG, is a type of salt that comes from seaweed. It intensifies the natural flavor of most of the foods to which it is added. It also provides a savory flavor to food. For example, MSG is often added to vegetables, poultry, and fish to bring out more flavor. However, MSG has no effect on the flavor of milk products or fruits. Some people are sensitive or allergic to MSG. Be sure to label its use in your recipes and on your menu to keep customers safe and healthy.

Onion Family The foods shown here belong to the onion family. *How are they used to flavor different foods?*

PHOTO CAPTION ANSWER Foods from the onion family have a strong flavor that can enhance other dishes. Fresh onions have a stronger flavor than dried or cooked onions, so care should be taken when you add them to recipes.

When to Season

As a general rule, you can season food at any time during the cooking process. However, certain forms of food **lend**, or adapt, themselves to adding seasoning at certain times. For example, when you cook a dish such as soup, in which the seasoning can mingle easily with the food, you can add seasonings during the entire cooking process. However, you should wait until the end of the cooking process before you add salt.

On the other hand, when you cook large pieces of food, such as a roast, you should add your seasonings at the beginning of the cooking process. If you add the seasonings early enough in the cooking process, it allows enough time for the seasonings to be absorbed effectively throughout the food. A roast has a long cooking time, so it will have plenty of time to absorb the seasonings.

You may choose to add your seasonings throughout the cooking process. However, you must be sure to taste the food and evaluate its flavor. Overseasoning can overpower and ruin the natural flavor of food. Dried seasonings should be added earlier in the cooking process than fresh seasonings.

Adding Flavor

Flavorings also can be added to food during the cooking process. However, the effects of flavorings on prepared food will depend on the length of the cooking time. You need to know how long the food must cook before you can decide when to add any flavorings.

Flavorings need heat to release their flavors. They also need time to blend with the natural flavors of the food to which they are added. For example, whole spices, such as ginger or whole peppercorns, take longer to be absorbed into food than ground spices. You will need to think about this timing when you add flavorings to foods during cooking. Flavorings should not be overcooked, however. Overcooked flavorings quickly lose their effect.

Some flavorings are considered blends. A **blend** is a combination of herbs, spices, and seeds. Chili powder, curry powder, and garlic salt are examples of blends. These are ready-made dried products that can be purchased from a supplier or created in a commercial kitchen. Blends can be created ahead of time, or on the spot. Some foodservice businesses have their own signature blends. Customers may sometimes purchase containers of these blends to take home for use in their own kitchens. When herbs are used together with spices in the form of a blend, they complement each other by enhancing the flavor of the food and of each other.

Enhancing food is a learned skill. It will take a great deal of practice to learn how to season and flavor food without overpowering the food. Practice combining flavors to see what effects you can achieve. Constantly taste food to determine the right level of seasoning for each dish.

 Reading Check Distinguish What is the difference between a seasoning and a flavoring?

SECTION 16.1 After You Read

Review Key Concepts

1. **Describe** the varieties of salt.

Practice Culinary Academics

 Science

2. **Procedure** Some cookbooks say that adding salt to water helps pasta cook faster, while others say it adds flavor. Cook two batches of pasta: one with salt and one without salt. As the water boils, create a hypothesis of what you think will happen.

   Analysis Record how long it takes the water to boil and the pasta to cook. Compare the flavor of each. What are your conclusions? Do they match your hypothesis? Write a summary explaining your findings.

   NSES A Develop abilities necessary to do scientific inquiry.

 English Language Arts

3. Conduct research to locate an older recipe that contains two or fewer seasonings. Rewrite the recipe, but add more seasonings and flavorings based on your knowledge of flavor from dishes you have tried before. Rewrite the recipe with the new seasonings and flavorings. If possible, test your recipe to see how the new seasonings and flavorings affect the dish.

   NCTE 12 Use language to accomplish individual purposes.

 Social Studies

4. Find a recipe from outside your culture. Make a note of the seasonings and flavorings that are used. Which are familiar to you, and why? Which are unfamiliar to you? Learn more about the unfamiliar seasonings and flavorings. Discuss your findings as a class.

   NCSS I E Culture Demonstrate the value of cultural diversity, as well as cohesion, within and across groups.

 Mathematics

5. A salt shaker weighs 152 grams when it is completely full. When you empty out exactly one-half of the salt, the shaker now weighs 116 grams. How much does an empty salt shaker weigh?

   Math Concept **Writing Algebraic Expressions** When you write an algebraic expression to solve a problem, pay particular attention to what the question is asking. Use variables, such as x and y, to represent any unknown values.

   Starting Hint If x = the weight of half of the salt (which you can calculate given the facts of the problem), and y = the weight of the shaker, then $x + y = 116$ grams.

   NCTM Problem Solving Solve problems that arise in mathematics and in other contexts.

   Check your answers at this book's Online Learning Center at **glencoe.com**.

READING CHECK ANSWER A seasoning enhances the flavor of food without changing it. A flavoring changes the natural flavor of food.

Herbs and Spices

Used correctly, herbs and spices can enhance a dish.

Reading Guide

 Before You Read

How Can You Improve? Before starting this section, think about the last exam you took on material you had to read. What reading strategies helped you on the test? Make a list of ways to improve your strategies to succeed on your next exam.

Read to Learn

Key Concepts
- **Compare and contrast** the uses and storage for different herbs.
- **Describe** the uses and storage for different spices.

Main Idea

A foodservice employee must be able to identify and use herbs and spices. Correctly used, they can enhance a dish. Incorrectly used, they can ruin a dish.

Content Vocabulary
- herb
- sachet
- bouquet garni
- aroma
- marinade
- paella
- risotto Milanese

Academic Vocabulary
- abundant
- opaque

 ACADEMIC STANDARDS

 English Language Arts
NCTE 8 Use information to gather information and create and communicate knowledge.

 Mathematics
NCTM Problem Solving Build new mathematical knowledge through problem solving.

Social Studies
NCSS I A Culture
Analyze and explain the ways groups, societies, and cultures address human needs and concerns.

NCSS III I People, Places, and Environments
Describe and assess ways that historical events have been influenced by, and have influenced, physical and human geographic factors in global settings.

NCTE National Council of Teachers of English

NCTM National Council of Teachers of Mathematics

NSES National Science Education Standards

NCSS National Council for the Social Studies

Graphic Organizer

Use a matrix like the one below to list how to use and store herbs and spices.

	Use	**Storage**
Herbs		
Spices		

 Graphic Organizer Go to this book's Online Learning Center at **glencoe.com** for a printable graphic organizer.

GRAPHIC ORGANIZER ANSWER Herbs: Fresh or dried; fresh should be kept damp and refrigerated, dried should be kept cool and dry. Spices: Whole, ground, or in chunks; should be stored in containers in dark storage.

Herb Varieties

Can you tell the difference between parsley and chervil? Do you know how to recognize nutmeg and allspice? Do you know how to properly store herbs and spices so that they remain fresh? Foodservice professionals need to know:

- What they look like.
- In what forms they are available.
- What their flavors and aromas are.
- How to correctly use them to enhance the flavor of food.

Herbs and spices enhance the flavor of food, but you must use them correctly. Incorrect use can ruin the flavor of foods.

Herbs are a flavoring that adds color and aroma to foods. An **herb** is a plant that grows in temperate climates. The parts of the plant that are harvested are the leaves and the stems. They can be used fresh or dried.

Basil, chives, oregano, and sage are examples of herbs. Fresh herbs should be used whenever possible. Fresh herbs are most **abundant**, or plentiful, in the summer. In the fall, fresh herbs can be dried or frozen for use during the winter. Knowing which herb to use, when to use it, and with what food is an important aspect of your job.

Herb Use

Herbs can be used with a variety of cold and hot dishes. Some herbs have a delicate flavor, while others have a bold flavor. Herbs can be purchased in two forms: fresh and dried. Fresh herbs are not as strong in flavor as dried herbs. When you use fresh herbs, you should use twice the amount of dried herbs that are called for in a recipe.

Fresh herbs should be minced or crushed as close to cooking or serving time as possible. They should be added at the end of the cooking process. You can add fresh herbs to uncooked foods, such as salads, several hours before serving time. Herbs often need plenty of time to release their flavor to cold foods. Dried herbs should be added at the beginning of or during the cooking process. Use a little and taste the food before you add more. Using too much can ruin the dish.

Some herbs and foods are natural combinations. For example, lamb is often flavored with rosemary. Basil seems to go hand-in-hand with tomato sauce. However, chefs often experiment with different combinations to create interesting dishes. You may also want to experiment with combining complementary herbs in a dish to see how they enhance flavor together.

HOW TO

Make
a Sachet

1 Place your herbs and spices in the center of a small square piece of cheesecloth.

2 Pull the four corners together and tie the bag with a long piece of twine. This makes removing the sachet easy.

Herbs

Basil Basil ('bā-zəl) is an herb from the mint family with tender, leafy stems. It is available in many varieties and has a mild, licorice-like flavor. Basil is available fresh or dried, as crushed leaves or ground. Basil is used in soups, tomato sauce, and salads. It is also used on pizza, vegetables, chicken, and pesto.

Bay Leaf Bay leaf is an herb that comes from the evergreen bay laurel tree. Bay leaves are commonly dried. They come whole, or broken into small flakes. They are used in soups, stews, vegetables, and meats. Whole bay leaves are generally removed from food before serving.

Chervil Chervil ('chər-vəl) is a slightly peppery herb that is shaped like parsley. It is available fresh or dried, as crushed leaves or ground. Chervil can be used in soups, sauces, salads, fish and shellfish dishes, and baked goods.

Chives Chives ('chīvs) are the long, toothpick-like leaves of a plant in the onion family. Chives have a delicate, onion flavor. Chives are available fresh, dried, or frozen. Chives can be used to flavor breads and soft rolls as well as soups, sauces, dips, and spreads. Chives can often be used in place of onions. They are commonly used to top off a baked potato with sour cream.

Cilantro Cilantro (si-'län-(ˌ)trō), from the coriander plant, has bright green leaves with longer stems. It has a distinct odor and a unique flavor. Cilantro is available fresh or chopped and frozen. Cilantro is used in sauces, salsa, and to add flavor to different dishes.

Dill Dill ('dil) is a feathery-leaved herb. It has a strong, distinct flavor that is commonly associated with pickles. Dill comes in fresh or dried leaves. Dill is used in many soups, salads, and breads. It also is used to flavor various vegetable and fish dishes.

Garlic Chives Garlic chives are flat stems. They have a mild, garlic flavor and are available fresh. Garlic chives can be used to flavor breads, soft rolls, soups, sauces, dips, and spreads.

Lemongrass Lemongrass is a tough, fibrous grass. The base has a lemony flavor. It comes in fresh stalks. Lemongrass is used in curries and in many southeast Asian dishes.

Marjoram Marjoram (ˈmär-jə-rəm) is a plant in the mint family. It has a warm, mild flavor. It is available as fresh or dried, as crushed leaves or ground. Marjoram is used to flavor soups, stews, gravies, sauces, and many poultry, fish, and meat dishes.

Mint Mint grows in many varieties, the most well known being peppermint and spearmint. Mint is available as fresh or dried leaves. Mint is used in sauces, sweet dishes, pastries, tea, and ice cream. It is often paired with chocolate. Mint is also used on lamb, peas, and in fruit beverages.

Oregano Oregano (ə-ˈreˈgə-ˌnō) is sometimes referred to as wild marjoram. It has a slightly bitter flavor. It is available as fresh or dried, as leaves or ground. Oregano is used in soups, sauces, tomato dishes, pizza, and meat and egg dishes.

Parsley Parsley (ˈpär-slē) is grown in many varieties. It has a soothing effect on your taste buds. It comes fresh or dried, as leaves or flakes. Parsley is widely used in soups, sauces, and dressings. It is often served as sprigs for a garnish, or chopped and used to add color to foods.

Rosemary Rosemary, an evergreen shrub with needlelike leaves, is a member of the mint family. It has a strong flavor and aroma. It is available fresh or dried, whole or ground. Rosemary is used in soups, stews, sauces, and baked goods.

Sage Sage is a member of the mint family. It has soft downy leaves that are fragrant and warm. It is available fresh or dried, whole or ground. Sage is often used in soups, stews, stuffings, and sausages. It is also used as a seasoning for poultry and pork.

Savory Savory ('sā-və-rē) is another member of the mint family. It has a spicy taste and comes fresh or dried, as crushed leaves. Savory is used with meat and fish dishes, chicken, eggs, stuffing, and in many baked goods.

Tarragon Tarragon ('ter-ə-gän) is an herb from the daisy family with a flavor that is a cross between mint and anise. It is what gives béarnaise sauce its flavor. It comes fresh or as dried, crushed leaves. Tarragon is used to flavor salad dressings, mustards, marinades, vinegar, sauces, and soups. It can also be used with chicken, veal, and fish.

Thyme Thyme ('tīm) is a shrub of the mint family. It has a sharp and spicy flavor. It is available fresh or dried, as crushed leaves or ground. Thyme is used in meat, poultry, and fish dishes, as well as in soups and baked goods.

Sachets

When you cook liquid dishes, such as soups, stocks, and sauces, fresh herbs can be added to the dish in a sachet or a bouquet garni. **Sachet** (sa-'shā) is French for bag. A **bouquet garni** (bü-'kā gär-'nē) is a combination of fresh herbs and vegetables tied in a bundle with butcher's twine. The bundle is simmered in the stock pot and removed before the dish is served. The most common ingredients in a bouquet garni are leeks, parsley, celery, and thyme.

Herb Storage

In general, fresh herbs should be wrapped loosely in damp paper towels and stored on sheet pans in a refrigerator. Store them at temperatures between 34°F (1°C) and 40°F (4°C). Dried herbs should be kept in containers that are **opaque**, or light-blocking, and airtight. Store dried herbs in a cool, dry place at temperatures between 50°F (10°C) and 70°F (21°C). Do not expose stored herbs to heat, light, and excess moisture. This can weaken their flavor. As dried herbs age, they naturally lose their flavor.

Reading Check Explain How should you properly store dried herbs?

Spice Varieties

Spices come from the bark, buds, fruits, roots, seeds, or stems of plants and trees. Unlike herbs, spices are commonly used only in their dried form. Spices come in two forms: whole or ground into powder. Spices can be sweet, spicy, or hot. The flavor and aroma of spices come from oils. Some plants provide both an herb and a spice. For example, dill leaves are an herb, and dill seeds are a spice. You should know each spice, its **aroma**, or distinctive pleasing smell, and its effect on food.

You can easily add spices to hot foods such as soups, sauces, and broths with the help of a sachet. A sachet allows you to add the flavor of spices to the food without leaving the actual spice in the dish to be served. Typical ingredients in a sachet include cloves, garlic, and crushed peppercorns.

Spice Use

Spices can be used in a variety of forms, such as whole, ground, sliced, or in chunks. The form you use partially depends on the length of cooking time. Whole spices take longer to release their flavor. This means that whole spices should be added as early as possible to the cooking process. A dish with a 10-minute cooking time would not give you enough time to use whole spices.

You can also use whole spices when you poach fruit or make a marinade. A **marinade** (ˌmer-ə-'nād) is an acidic liquid usually used to soak meat before it is cooked, to give the meat flavor and tenderness. Spices should be added to cold food several hours before serving time.

A TASTE OF HISTORY

1502
▼
└ Vasco de Gama claims a monopoly of pepper for the Portuguese

1509
▼
└ Ponce de Leon becomes governor of Puerto Rico

The Spice of Life

Spices today are plentiful and are used mostly as flavorings. However, throughout most of history, spices were a luxury. Pepper was once so expensive that it was sometimes used as currency to pay taxes. The search for better routes to spice-rich lands led to an era of great exploration and expansion. European countries even fought spice wars for control over these precious spices.

History Application

Research the European countries that dominated the spice trade and the routes their explorers took. Draw a map of the routes that the main spice traders took.

NCSS III I People, Places, and Environments Describe and assess ways that historical events have been influenced by, and have influenced, physical and human geographic factors in global settings.

Allspice Allspice is the dried, unripe berry of the pimiento (pəm-ˈyen-(ˌ)tō) tree, a tropical evergreen found in the West Indies and Latin America. The berries are dried and either left whole or ground. The flavor of allspice combines the flavors of nutmeg, clove, and cinnamon. It is available dry, whole, or ground. Whole allspice is used with pickles, meats, fish, sausages, and sauces. Ground allspice is used in pies, cakes, puddings, relishes, and preserves.

Anise Seeds Anise seeds are dried greenish-brown seeds with a strong, licorice-like aroma and flavor. They are dried and available whole or ground. Anise can be used to flavor a variety of dishes, including fish sauces, breads, cakes, cookies, and candies.

Cardamom Cardamom (ˈkär-də-məm) is the seed from the fruit of an herb in the ginger family. It has a sweet, almost pepper-like flavor and aroma. It is the third most-expensive spice in the world behind saffron and vanilla. It is available whole or ground. Cardamom is used in curries, sweet dishes, yogurt, and baked goods.

Cinnamon Cinnamon is the thin, dried inner bark of two related evergreen trees of the laurel family. It is used in baking more than any other spice. Cinnamon has a warm, spicy aroma and flavor. It is available dried in sticks or ground. Cinnamon is used in cakes, cookies, pies, curries, sweet potatoes, meat stuffing, and preserves.

Celery Seeds Celery seed is a tiny, seed-like fruit with a strong celery flavor. It is available whole, ground, or mixed with salt. In its whole form, celery seed is used in sauces, salads, cole slaw, and pickling. Ground celery seed is used in soups, stews, and salad dressings.

Chili Powder Chili powder is a dried, ground blend of cumin, garlic, onion, and chile peppers. It is used in chili, egg dishes, and meat dishes.

Cayenne Cayenne ((ˌ)kī-ˈən) comes from hot red peppers that are ground into powder. It has a strong flavor that gives food a "kick." It is dried and ground. Cayenne is used with meat, fish, eggs, and poultry. It is also used in soups, sauces, and salads.

Cumin Cumin (ˈkə-mən) seeds are the dried, ripened fruit of an herb in the parsley family. It looks like caraway seed, but has a much different flavor and aroma. Cumin is available whole or ground. It is the spice that lends chili its distinctive flavor. Cumin is also used to flavor chicken, fish, curries, couscous, sausages, and hard cheeses.

Chiles Chiles are peppers that grow in a variety of shapes and sizes from round to oblong. They range in color from red, yellow, and green to purple. Chiles can be mild, sweet, or extremely hot. They are available fresh and dried. Chiles are used in a variety of dishes including salads, pickles, sauces, vegetable dishes, salsas, and meat dishes.

Dill Seeds Dill seeds are the small, dark seeds of the dill plant. They have a slightly sharp taste and distinct odor. Dill seeds are used in soups and salads. They are also used with sauerkraut and fish.

Fennel Seeds Fennel (ˈfe-n'l) seeds come from a tall, hardy plant in the parsley family. In addition to fennel seeds, the fennel plant is used widely in cooking and pickling. Both have a mild, anise-like flavor. Whole fennel seeds are used in breads, crackers, and sausages. They are also used in tomato sauce, marinades, and with fish and shellfish.

Saffron Saffron (ˈsa-ˌfrän) is a yellow spice derived from the crocus plant. It has a sweet scent, but a bitter taste. Saffron is the most expensive spice in the world. It is available dried as whole threads or ground.

Pepper and Peppercorns The pepper plant is a smooth, woody vine that climbs tree trunks and produces grapelike clusters of small berries. The berries start green and then turn red as they ripen. There are three true varieties: green, black, and white. (Pink pepper is not derived from the pepper plant.) Each has its own unique flavor. Pepper is available whole, as peppercorns, or ground. Pepper is used in all sorts of dishes.

Nutmeg Nutmeg (ˈnət-ˌmeg) is the kernel of the fruit or seed of the evergreen nutmeg tree. Nutmeg is dried, removed from the shell, and either ground or kept whole for grating. Nutmeg has a sweet, warm, spicy flavor. Freshly grated nutmeg is superior in flavor to prepared ground nutmeg. Nutmeg lends itself to many baked items, soups, sauces, chicken, potatoes, and custards.

Mustard Seeds Mustard seeds are the small, round, smooth seeds of the watercress family. They have a tangy flavor. Mustard seeds are available whole, ground, or prepared as a condiment sauce. Mustard seeds are used in salads, salad dressings, and sauces. They are also used with meats, fish, cheese, and eggs.

Paprika Paprika is derived from dried, ripe, red sweet peppers. Its flavor is sweet. Hungarian paprika can be semi-hot or very hot. It is available fresh or dried, whole, canned, diced, or ground. Paprika is used in soups, stews, sauces, salad dressings, and tomato dishes. It is also used to accent fish and shellfish dishes.

Ginger Ginger is the underground stem of a plant native to Asia. It can be used fresh or dried. Dried ginger is most often used in baking to flavor cookies and cakes, or with fruits. Fresh ginger has a stronger flavor than the dried form and should be peeled before it is used. Ginger has a strong, sweet, peppery flavor. It is available whole, in pieces, in slices, or ground. Fresh ginger is used with fish, poultry, and curries.

Spices can also be used to add color to a dish. For example, saffron is used to give a soft yellow color to dishes such as **paella** (pä-'ā-yə), a Spanish rice dish with meat or shellfish, and **risotto Milanese** (ri-'sȯ-(ˌ)tō ˌmi-lə-'nəz), an Italian dish that includes rice that is sautéed in butter before stock is added. Ground cinnamon can be dusted over a dessert to make a beautiful topping.

Ground spices release their flavor immediately. In this case, it is best to add ground spices near the end of the cooking process.

Whenever you cook with spices, you must measure them accurately. Strong spices, such as clove, cayenne, or cumin, can overpower the food if you use too much. As a rule, spices should not dominate the food but complement it. The exceptions are curries or chilis.

Spice Storage

Spices should be stored in air-tight containers away from direct sunlight. Light can cause spices to deteriorate. This can rob spices of their flavor. Spices are best kept in a cool, dry place at temperatures of 50°F to 70°F (10°C to 21°C).

Many factors besides sunlight and heat can affect the flavor of spices. The age, type, and source of the spice play a role in how long a particular spice can be stored. Check spices often to make sure they have retained their strength. Discard spices that taste weak or strangely bitter.

 Reading Check **Determine** When should spices be added to foods?

SECTION 16.2 After You Read

Review Key Concepts

1. **Describe** how to properly store herbs.
2. **Explain** how to properly store spices.

Practice Culinary Academics

 Social Studies

3. The taste that defines a region's cuisine often comes from a particular blend of seasonings. Find a spice blend that is used in a region of the world. Prepare a short presentation on where and for what the blend is used. Include images in your presentation. You may also prepare a food with the spice blend as a demonstration.

> **NCSS I A Culture** Analyze and explain the ways groups, societies, and cultures address human needs and concerns.

English Language Arts

4. Conduct research on an herb that is not listed in this section, or conduct further research on an herb that is described in this section. Create a presentation on your chosen herb with visual aids. Present the information to your classmates, and turn in your notes to your teacher.

> **NCTE 8** Use information to gather information and create and communicate knowledge.

Mathematics

5. You would like to add freshly made mint ice cream to your restaurant's menu, and have decided to grow your own mint. Last month, your mint plant was 2 feet, 7 inches tall. You took care of the mint plant properly, and that care has paid off. This month, it is 4 feet, 1 inch tall. How much did it grow?

Math Concept **Subtracting Lengths** When you subtract measurements that are given in feet and inches, subtract the feet and inch amounts separately. If you wind up with a negative number of inches, add 12 to the inch amount, and subtract 1 foot.

Starting Hint Subtract 2 feet from 4 feet to get the new foot amount, and 7 inches from 1 inch to get the inch amount. Rewrite the answer to eliminate the negative number of inches.

> **NCTM Problem Solving** Build new mathematical knowledge through problem solving.

 Check your answers at this book's Online Learning Center at **glencoe.com**.

Condiments, Nuts, and Seeds

Reading Guide

 Before You Read

Use Color As you read this section, try using different colored pens to take notes. This can help you learn new material and study for tests. You could use red for vocabulary words, blue for explanations, and green for examples.

Read to Learn

Key Concepts
- **Describe** various condiments and the foods they can accompany.
- **Identify** a variety of nuts and seeds.

Main Idea

Condiments, nuts, and seeds can be served with food to enhance flavor. Condiments are added to prepared food, while nuts and seeds are used during cooking.

Content Vocabulary
- condiment
- salsa
- ketchup
- steak sauce
- prepared mustard
- fermented
- relish
- vinegar
- flavored oil
- seed
- nut

Academic Vocabulary
- accompaniment
- complement

Graphic Organizer

As you read, use a chart like the one below to help you describe the proper way to store condiments, nuts, and seeds.

Condiments	
Nuts and Seeds	

 Graphic Organizer Go to this book's Online Learning Center at **glencoe.com** for a printable graphic organizer.

What condiments do you use to season food?

ACADEMIC STANDARDS

 Mathematics
NCTM Data Analysis and Probability Understand and apply basic concepts of probability.

 Science
NSES C Develop an understanding of the cell.

 Social Studies
NCSS I E Culture
Demonstrate the value of cultural diversity, as well as cohesion, within and across groups.

NCTE National Council of Teachers of English

NCTM National Council of Teachers of Mathematics

NSES National Science Education Standards

NCSS National Council for the Social Studies

GRAPHIC ORGANIZER ANSWER Condiments: Unopened, in a cool, dry place; opened, in the refrigerator. Nuts and seeds: Fresh, in an air-tight container in a cool, dry, dark area.

Condiment Varieties

You have learned about herbs and spices and how they affect the flavor of foods, but what about the condiments, nuts, and seeds that can be served with food to enhance flavor? You will need to know which foods they enhance.

A **condiment** is traditionally served as an accompaniment to foods. An **accompaniment** is something that goes well with something else. Condiments' purpose is to **complement**, or go together well with, food flavors. They vary from sweet and tart to hot and spicy, or sour. Condiments can be purchased ready to use or can be created in the kitchen.

Sauces

Sauces can be used as a condiment for many foods. Many sauces can enhance foods:
- A **salsa** ('sȯl-sə) is a fresh or cooked mixture of chopped chiles, tomatoes, onions, and cilantro. Unopened, cooked salsas can be stored at room temperature for up to six months. Opened salsas should always be tightly covered and refrigerated. Fresh salsas can be refrigerated for seven days.
- **Ketchup** is a tomato-based sauce used throughout the world as a flavoring. Ketchup has a tangy, sweet-and-sour taste. Some ketchups have a flavoring added, such as jalapeño. As ketchup ages, it can taste stale.
- **Steak sauce** is a sauce that is tangier than ketchup. Steak sauce is used with grilled and broiled meats.

Prepared Mustards

A **prepared mustard** contains a combination of ground white, black, and brown mustard seeds, vinegar, salt, and spices. Prepared mustards have a variety of textures, from smooth to coarse to chunky. They also have a variety of flavors, from mild to hot. Prepared mustards are often served with pork, beef, vegetables, sandwiches, and salads. Prepared mustards can also be used in dips for vegetables, or as part of a sauce. As mustards age, they lose flavor.

Pickled Condiments

Some condiments have pickled ingredients. Pickles are made from vegetables that are **fermented** ((ˌ)fər-'men-ted), or chemically changed in brines or vinegars flavored and seasoned with dill, garlic, sugar, peppers, or salt. Cucumbers, tomatoes, and peppers are commonly pickled. A coarsely chopped or ground pickled item is called a **relish**. The most common flavors are sweet and dill.

Vinegars

Vinegar is a sour, acidic liquid used in cooking, marinades, and salad dressings. Some common vinegars are white vinegar, red wine vinegar, balsamic (bȯl-'sa-mik) vinegar, and cider vinegar. Discard vinegars three months after they are opened.

Flavored Oils

A **flavored oil** has been enhanced with ingredients such as herbs, spices, and garlic. The oils of these ingredients are extracted and then poured into olive or canola oil. Some flavored oils are created by simply adding the flavor enhancer itself, such as garlic, to olive or canola oil. Prepare only enough to use for one day to avoid foodborne illness.

Sometimes different vegetable oils are combined to create a unique taste. For example, Szechwan-flavored oil combines sunflower oil, canola oil, and sesame seed oil.

Condiment Storage

Unopened condiments should be stored in cool and dry areas. Temperatures should be between 50°F (10°C) and 70°F (21°C). Most opened condiments should be stored in the refrigerator.

Once opened, remove canned condiments from the cans and transfer them into airtight plastic containers. Store condiments in the refrigerator once they have been opened.

Reading Check Name With what kind of foods would you use hot sauce?

READING CHECK ANSWER Hot sauce is often used in soups and stews, and on vegetables and eggs.

Nuts and Seeds

Almonds A medium-brown nut that is white inside, almonds can be sweet or bitter. Sweet almonds are eaten; bitter almonds are used as a source for almond flavoring. Almonds are available whole in the shell, shelled, skinned, sliced, in pieces, or as a paste.

Brazils Brazils are not actually nuts, but the seeds of a fruit. Brazil nuts are available whole in the shell or shelled.

Cashews The cashew is the edible seed of a tropical evergreen tree. Most cashews are salted and roasted. They are available raw or toasted.

Chestnuts Chestnuts are sweet nuts that contain more starch and less fat than other nuts. They can be roasted, boiled, or steamed. Chestnuts are available whole in the shell, dried, and canned in water or syrup.

Hazelnuts Hazelnuts grow in clusters and are the nut of the hazelnut tree. They are sweet, rich, grape-size nuts and often are used in salads and main dishes.

Peanuts Although peanuts are considered nuts, they are actually small legumes that resemble peas. The two most common types are Virginia and Spanish peanuts. The Virginia peanut has larger kernels and more flavor than the Spanish variety. Many people are allergic to peanuts. Customers should be told which menu items include peanuts. Peanuts are available as dry roasted, granules, salted, unsalted, and in the shell.

Pecans Pecans are the nut of the pecan tree. They have a very thin shell. Pecans are available whole in the shell, chopped, and in halves.

Nuts and Seeds *continued*

Pine Nuts Pine nuts are the kernels of pine cones. They taste like almonds and are available raw, toasted, and frozen.

Pistachios Pistachios (pə-'sta-sh(ē-,)ōs) are pale green to creamy white in color and have a mild flavor. Pistachios are available in the shell, shelled, roasted and salted, and dyed red.

Walnuts Walnuts are the fruit of the walnut tree. Sizes vary from small to large. Walnuts are available whole in the shell, shelled as halves, and chopped.

Poppy Seeds Poppy seeds are the dark black, dried seeds of the poppy plant. Poppy seeds are available whole.

Pumpkin Seeds Pumpkin seeds come from pumpkins. They are available in the shell, toasted, and raw.

Sesame Seeds Sesame ('se-sə-mē) seeds are creamy-colored, flat, oval seeds that have a nutty flavor. They are available whole, roasted, and ground into paste.

Sunflower Seeds These seeds come from the sunflower. The whole seed can be eaten raw or cooked.

Nuts and Seeds

Nuts and seeds can be used to enhance natural flavor, or add color and texture to food. A **seed** is a plant grain. A **nut** is a hard-shelled dry fruit or seed. Nuts are available shelled and unshelled. Purchase nuts in small quantities because they can easily spoil. Use nuts carefully, as many people are allergic to them. Seeds can be used in many ways. Some seeds, such as cumin, are considered spices, and are used during cooking. Other seeds, such as poppy seeds, are used for baking.

Nut and Seed Storage

Store fresh nuts and seeds in an air-tight container in a cool, dry area with limited exposure to light. Nuts also can be refrigerated or frozen in airtight containers.

 **Reading Check** **Describe** What are the characteristics of a pistachio?

Nutrition Notes

Nuts About Nutrition!

Nuts are packed with essential nutrients. They are a good source of B vitamins, vitamin E, protein, and essential fatty acids. They are also high in calcium, folic acid, magnesium, potassium and fiber. Some scientific studies have concluded that a daily portion of just one ounce of nuts rich in monounsaturated fat can reduce the risk of heart disease by up to 10 percent. One ounce of nuts has about 180 calories and 17 grams of fat. Fifty to 80 percent of that fat is monounsaturated, the "good" fat that help the body reduce the level of LDL—the "bad" cholesterol.

CRITICAL THINKING *How could you add nuts to a dish?*

 SECTION 16.3 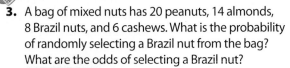 **After You Read**

Review Key Concepts

1. **Describe** pickles, and name the foods that are most commonly pickled.
2. **Identify** the nutritional benefits of nuts and seeds.

Practice Culinary Academics

Mathematics

3. A bag of mixed nuts has 20 peanuts, 14 almonds, 8 Brazil nuts, and 6 cashews. What is the probability of randomly selecting a Brazil nut from the bag? What are the odds of selecting a Brazil nut?

   Math Concept **Probability vs. Odds** Probability is the ratio of the number of chances an event can occur to the total number of possible outcomes. Odds are written as a ratio of the chances of an event not occurring to the chances of it occurring.

   Starting Hint For the probability, write a fraction with the number of Brazil nuts over the total number of nuts, and simplify. For the odds, count the number of nuts that are not Brazil nuts.

   NCTM Data Analysis and Probability Understand and apply basic concepts of probability.

Science

4. **Procedure** Water inside vegetables flows out into salty brine in a process called osmosis. Drain the juice from a jar of dill pickles. Cut the pickles in half. Mix a solution of water, sugar, and two fruit punch packets. Place the pickles in the jar and replace the brine with the fruit punch.

   Analysis Seal the jar and observe the pickles for a week. Keep a log of your observations. As a class, discuss what happened to the pickles, and why. Turn in your logs to your teacher.

   NSES C Develop an understanding of the cell.

Social Studies

5. Condiments in different cultures have similarities and differences. Compare and contrast three condiments used in different cultures. Create a chart to show your comparisons.

   NCSS I E Culture Demonstrate the value of cultural diversity, as well as cohesion, within and across groups.

 Check your answers at this book's Online Learning Center at **glencoe.com**.

NUTRITION NOTES ANSWER Student answers will vary, but could include using nuts as a topping, as an ingredient, or ground into powder as a flour substitute.

READING CHECK ANSWER Pistachios are pale green to creamy white in color and have a mild flavor. They are available in the shell, shelled, roasted and salted, and dyed red.

Sensory Perception

People use all five senses to enjoy food.

Reading Guide

 Before You Read

Create an Outline Use the section's heading titles to create an outline. Make the titles into Level 1 main ideas. Add supporting information to create Level 2, 3, and 4 details. Use the outline to predict what you are about to learn.

Read to Learn

Key Concepts
- **Summarize** the three sensory properties of food.
- **Illustrate** how sensory factors can affect a customer's enjoyment of food.

Main Idea

Using seasonings and flavorings requires foodservice professionals to understand sensory perception. This will improve your ability to taste and to create enjoyable dishes.

Content Vocabulary
- sensory perception
- sensory properties
- receptors
- stimuli
- translucent
- savory
- taste bud
- sensory evaluation
- blind taste test
- plate composition

Academic Vocabulary
- indication
- perception

ACADEMIC STANDARDS

 English Language Arts
NCTE 4 Use written language to communicate effectively.

 Mathematics
NCTM Geometry Use visualization, spatial reasoning, and geometric modeling to solve problems.

 Science
NSES C Develop an understanding of the behavior of organisms.

 Social Studies
NCSS I C Culture Apply an understanding of culture as an integrated whole that explains the functions and interactions of language, literature, the arts, traditions, beliefs and values, and behavior patterns.

NCTE National Council of Teachers of English

NCTM National Council of Teachers of Mathematics

NSES National Science Education Standards

NCSS National Council for the Social Studies

Graphic Organizer

Use a main idea chart like this one to list the three sensory properties of food. Then, list the senses that they stimulate.

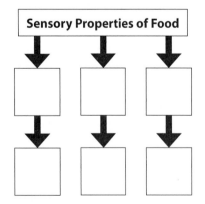

Sensory Properties of Food

 Graphic Organizer Go to this book's Online Learning Center at **glencoe.com** for a printable graphic organizer.

GRAPHIC ORGANIZER ANSWER Color and appearance: Sight. Flavor: Taste, smell, and touch. Texture: Touch and sound.

Sensory Properties of Food

To use seasonings and flavorings successfully, foodservice professionals must understand sensory perception. **Sensory perception** is how a person's eyes, nose, ears, mouth, and skin detect and evaluate the environment. Sensory perception will help you improve your ability to taste. Improved taste will help you to increase your customers' enjoyment of food.

Sensory properties of food affect how people perceive food. These sensory properties are color and appearance, flavor, and texture. Each one is detected by the five sense organs: the taste buds, nose, ears, skin, and eyes. (See **Figure 16.1**.)

When people eat, they use these sense organs to evaluate the food. This is done with special **receptors**, or groups of cells that receive stimuli. **Stimuli** are things that cause an activity or response. When a stimulus is detected, nerve impulses carry the signal to the brain, where it is processed.

When the stimulus is food, the sense organs of taste and smell cause a reaction that increases the production of saliva. Gastric secretions are also increased. These two fluids help with digestion and the distribution of nutrients to the body.

Color and Appearance

The appearance of food is usually the first **indication**, or sign, of how it will taste. The brighter and more colorful the food, the more visual appeal it has. Customers will prefer dishes that are colorful and are appealingly plated. The brain processes visual information about flavor and texture based on appearance alone. It then makes decisions about likes and dislikes. This happens because of people's highly developed sense of sight. In fact, our sense of sight is so highly developed that it may cause messages that are received from the other senses to be ignored. This means you must be absolutely sure that the color and appearance of food will be visually appealing to customers. Otherwise, it may not matter how good the food tastes.

Lighting

Different types of lighting affect how we see color. Foodservice professionals should be aware that the way that they see food in kitchen lighting may not be the way that the customer sees the food in dining room lighting. For example, when the color green is viewed under an incandescent light, it will appear more yellow than when it is viewed under fluorescent lighting. Warmer lighting tends to make food look more appetizing.

▼ FIGURE 16.1 **Sensory Perception of Food**

Sensing Quality Customers use their senses to determine the quality of a dish. *Why is it important that food look appealing on the plate?*

Sense	Receptor	Stimuli	Sensation
Taste Buds	Taste cells	Sugars, salts, acids, amino acids, and alkaloids	Taste
Nose	Olfactory cells	Odor chemicals	Smell
Skin	Free nerve endings; skin receptors	Chemicals; heat and pressure	Pain; touch
Eyes	Rods and cones	Light energy	Sight

FIGURE CAPTION ANSWER Our sense of sight is highly developed. Unappealing-looking food may cause a customer to reject a dish, regardless of its taste.

▲ **The Right Light** Lighting affects the color of food. *How does lighting affect this plate of food?*

Physical Structure

The physical structure of food affects color. For example, spinach is made of plant cells that contain a large amount of liquid. These plant cells are surrounded by air pockets. When raw spinach is cooked, air escapes from the pockets, and the plant cells burst. This causes the air pockets to fill with liquid, and the cooked spinach looks darker. Because light reflects off liquids differently than it does air, cooked onions appear **translucent**, or clear, rather than opaque, or cloudy.

Chemical Structure

The chemical structure of food also affects appearance. For example, the pigments, the chemicals that give vegetables their color, change during the cooking process. Pigments found in foods can be red (as in beets), white (as in cauliflower), green (as in broccoli), and yellow (as in squash). When properly cooked, pigments remain bright. When overcooked, pigments become dull. Foods with dull pigments are also often mushy in texture, and have lost nutritional value.

Flavor

The sensory property of flavor, or taste, is a combination of three sensory experiences: basic tastes, aromas, and touch, through nerve endings. People's perception of these three sensory experiences is chemical in nature. Salt, for instance, changes the chemistry of certain taste buds. This change in chemistry sends a signal to the brain that travels through nerve fibers. The brain translates this signal into the **perception**, or awareness, of saltiness.

Tastes

The basic tastes are: sweet, salty, sour, and bitter. Sometimes savory (ˈsā-və-rē) is included. **Savory** means stimulating and full of flavor.

Tastes are detected by taste buds. A **taste bud** is a specialized cell for tasting that is scattered over the surface of the tongue. In addition to taste buds, saliva plays an important role in taste perception. Without saliva, the sweeteners, salts, acids, and bitter components of food could not reach the taste cells.

PHOTO CAPTION ANSWER The colors look warm, vibrant, and inviting, and the textures are more easily seen.

Aroma

The perception of aroma is more complex than the perception of taste. Humans can detect hundreds, even thousands, of distinctly different aromas. The sense of smell allows people to differentiate between similar flavors, such as an orange and a tangerine. People can actually "taste" the different flavors.

Nerve Endings

Nerve endings that are just below the skin throughout the mouth and nose are responsible for detecting flavors. They allow you to feel the menthol in peppermint and the carbon dioxide in carbonated beverages. In fact, people who have lost their senses of taste and smell can often still detect the presence of certain flavors with these nerve endings.

Texture

The last sensory property of food that must be evaluated is texture. The characteristics of texture can vary greatly. For example, cooked rice can be rough or smooth, sticky or slick, hard or soft, moist or dry, chewy or crumbly.

The texture depends on the type of rice and how it was prepared.

Sound also plays a part. Taste can sometimes depend on crunch, such as for crisp vegetables or tortilla chips. Sometimes one characteristic stands out, but foodservice professionals should practice identifying food textures as completely as possible.

Texture Evaluation

Foodservice professionals must train themselves to pay attention to the texture of all foods. Ask these questions when you evaluate the texture of food:

- How does the food feel against the soft tissue in the mouth?
- How does the food react to being squeezed, pulled, bitten, or chewed? Is it hard? Does it bounce back like gelatin? Is it crumbly? When you evaluate texture, you will need to see how food reacts to being eaten.
- How does the food react to the warmth of the mouth? For example, the smoothness of ice cream and chocolate depend in part on how quickly and completely they melt in your mouth.

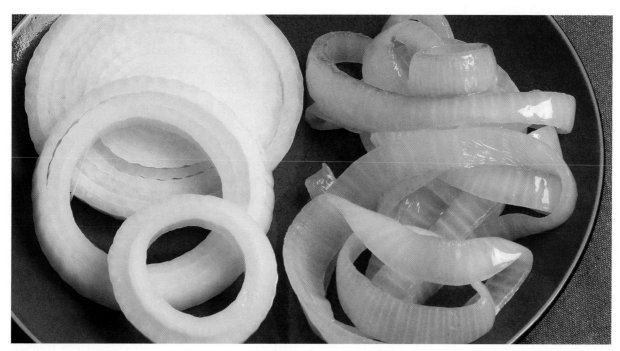

△ Translucent Onions Raw onions are opaque, while cooked onions are translucent. *Why does this happen?*

PHOTO CAPTION ANSWER When onions are cooked, air pockets between their cells burst, filling with liquid. Light reflects off of liquid differently than it does off of air, and so the onions appear translucent.

Taste Sensations

The tongue contains many tiny bumps called papillae (pə-'pi-(ˌ)lē). These bumps sense the basic tastes of bitterness, saltiness, sourness, and sweetness. Each bump contains more than 200 taste buds.

Procedure

Gather 4 coffee stirrers, 1 teaspoon salt, 1 teaspoon sugar, 1 teaspoon cocoa powder, one lemon, and a glass of water. Use the coffee stirrer to place a sample of salt on the tip of your tongue. Record whether it tastes sweet, sour, bitter, or salty. Repeat the procedure on each section of your tongue, and record the taste. After you complete the experiment with the salt, rinse your mouth with water and repeat the experiment with the sugar, cocoa powder, and lemon. Be sure to rinse between each sample.

Analysis

Examine your records. Did you notice any difference in taste between different parts of the tongue? Research to find out if taste on your tongue corresponds to different areas. Create a summary of your records and your research.

NSES C Develop an understanding of the behavior of organisms.

- Does the food leave a coating after swallowing? For example, shortenings, especially those with a high melting point, tend to leave a waxy coating in the mouth. Is the coating pleasant or unpleasant?
- How does the food sound when chewed? Potato chips are not crispy unless you can hear the crunch.

Reading Check List What are the sensory properties of food?

Sensory Evaluation

Sensory evaluation is the science of judging and evaluating the quality of a food by use of the senses. Many foodservice businesses conduct consumer taste tests to find out what their customers like and dislike. This helps food companies to design products that the customers will find tasty.

Customers test foods based on their likes and dislikes, but other food taste testers need to evaluate food objectively. Their job is to describe only the sensory characteristics. To increase the objectivity of the evaluations, blind taste tests are often done on food. A **blind taste test** means that the food samples are not labeled so that the testers will not know which product they are tasting.

You will need a lot of practice to successfully recognize and identify the many sensory characteristics of food. Culinary skills involve putting flavors together. The process of sensory evaluation, however, is one of taking flavors apart.

Product Factors

Different versions of the same type of food may taste or smell different from each other. For example, one vinaigrette (ˌvi-ni-'gret) dressing may taste more sour than another even though they both contain the same amount of acid. Several factors shape the characteristics of a food product.

Type of Ingredients

Vinaigrette dressings are made of oil, vinegar, and herbs. Different vinaigrettes may contain the same amount of acid. However, if they contain different types of acid, they will not taste the same. For example, if one vinaigrette is made from vinegar and the other is made from lemon juice, the vinaigrette with vinegar will seem more acidic.

Product Temperature and Consistency

Products that are warm usually have a stronger flavor and aroma than those that are cold. Thicker products may have less flavor than thinner ones. This is because flavor molecules take longer to dissolve or evaporate in saliva when food products are thicker.

SCIENCE À LA CARTE ANSWER Although it used to be thought that different areas of the tongue related to different basic tastes, new research has proven that we have taste receptors for all of the basic tastes on all areas of our tongue. Students should cite research sources, and should turn in complete summaries.

READING CHECK ANSWER The sensory properties of food are color and appearance, flavor, and texture.

Presence of Other Factors in Foods

You can suppress a person's ability to perceive flavor in foods when you combine flavors or aromas in those foods. For example, if you add a small amount of sugar to vinaigrette salad dressing, it will not taste as acidic. This is true even if the amount of sugar added is so small that sweetness from the sugar cannot be detected.

- Add acid to food to make the food taste less sweet.
- Add salt to food to make the food taste less sour.
- Add sugar to food to make the food taste less bitter.

Flavor Enhancers

Flavor enhancers change the natural flavor of food without adding a flavor of their own. They are able to do this through the chemistry that occurs between the enhancer and your body. It is believed that flavor enhancers interact with certain taste chemicals and receptors in your mouth. This produces a different perception of how foods taste with the enhancer than how they taste alone.

Amount of Oil and Water

The amount of oil or water in foods will affect the perception of taste and smell. A taste chemical that dissolves in oil will not fully dissolve in saliva. Because of this, little of it will reach the taste buds. When an odor chemical dissolves in water or oil, it will not evaporate to the olfactory cells where it can be smelled.

Plate Composition

The **plate composition**, or the way in which foods are arranged on a plate, should be carefully planned even before the food is cooked. Create contrasts in color and appearance, height, shape, texture, flavor, and temperature of foods.

Color and Appearance

The colors of food presented on a plate should be vibrant and contrasting. Carefully choose the foods and the plate on which the food will be served. However, the plate should not detract from the food presentation.

◀ **Varying Shapes** Plate food with varying shapes to make it interesting to the eye. *What other features do you see that make this plate of food visually appealing?*

PHOTO CAPTION ANSWER Answers will vary, but may include the sauce, the vibrant colors, and the varying textures.

Height

Often, one of the most difficult elements in plate composition is varying the heights of food on a plate. For example, mashed potatoes might be neatly piped onto the plate in a circular pinnacle. Grilled steak is then placed leaning slightly against the mashed potatoes. A cob of corn could be cut in half and stood on each side of the steak.

Shape

Vary the shape of foods in every presentation. Do not serve a round meatloaf patty with sautéed peas and boiled new potatoes. These are all round forms. Instead, try serving it with asparagus spears and diced, roasted potatoes.

Texture

Include a variety of textures on each plate. Choose foods that may have soft, hard, chewy, crunchy, creamy, or meaty textures.

Flavor

Each element of food in a plate presentation should contribute to the overall flavor, including any garnishes added. Flavor should be considered before cooking.

Temperature

Foods should be served at the appropriate temperatures. Properly use hot and cold serving plates.

Garnishing

A garnish makes food or drink items look more appealing. Not all food presentations need a garnish. However, garnishes should complement the food. Some dishes are so identified with a particular garnish that they may appear incomplete without it.

 **Reading Check** **Explain** What plating elements should be considered?

SECTION 16.4 After You Read

Review Key Concepts

1. **Explain** how lighting affects the perception of food.
2. **Illustrate** how product temperature can affect a customer's enjoyment of food.

Practice Culinary Academics

 English Language Arts

3. The next time you eat a meal, focus on the sensory properties of the meal: the color, appearance, flavor, and texture. Try to remember how you perceived each property when you ate the meal. Write a description of the meal using details to describe each of the sensory properties.

> **NCTE 4** Use written language to communicate effectively.

 Social Studies

4. To the Japanese, presentation and sensory properties are very important in a meal. Do some research or interview a chef of Japanese cuisine about how the sensory properties affect the preparation of various Japanese menu items.

How might you apply these practices to your own cooking? Write a one-page report of your research.

> **NCSS I C Culture** Apply an understanding of culture as an integrated whole that explains the functions and interactions of language, literature, the arts, traditions, beliefs and values, and behavior patterns.

Mathematics

5. You would like to place a circle of mashed potatoes in the center of an 11-inch dinner plate so that it covers one-half of the surface area of the plate. What is the diameter of the mashed potatoes?

> **Math Concept** **Area of a Circle** Calculate the area (A) of a circle as $A = \pi r^2$, where r indicates the radius (or ½ of the diameter) of the circle. Use 3.14 for π.
>
> **Starting Hint** Calculate the area of the plate as $A = (3.14)(5.5)(5.5)$. Take half of that amount (which is the area of the potatoes), and plug that into the formula as A, and solve for r.

> **NCTM Geometry** Use visualization, spatial reasoning, and geometric modeling to solve problems.

 Check your answers at this book's Online Learning Center at **glencoe.com**.

READING CHECK ANSWER Consider color, appearance, height, shape, texture, flavor, temperature, and garnishing.

426 **Unit 5** Culinary Applications

Review and Applications

Chapter Summary

Seasonings and flavorings are used to enhance the natural flavor of a food. Spices and flavorings can be added to foods at any time during the cooking process. The most common seasonings are herbs and spices. Other seasonings and flavorings include condiments and nuts. Condiments are flavored sauces that are served with food. Nuts add color, texture, and flavor to food. Evaluate color, appearance, flavor, and texture of food. Foodservice professionals taste a variety of food products to evaluate, or analyze, their characteristics.

Content and Academic Vocabulary Review

1. Arrange the vocabulary terms below into groups of related words. Explain your groupings.

Content Vocabulary

- seasoning (p. 400)
- flavor enhancer (p. 400)
- flavoring (p. 400)
- extract (p. 401)
- spice (p. 401)
- zest (p. 402)
- pith (p. 402)
- monosodium glutamate (p. 403)
- blend (p. 404)
- herb (p. 406)
- sachet (p. 410)
- bouquet garni (p. 410)
- aroma (p. 410)
- marinade (p. 410)
- paella (p. 414)
- risotto Milanese (p. 414)
- condiment (p. 416)
- salsa (p. 416)
- ketchup (p. 416)
- steak sauce (p. 416)
- prepared mustard (p. 416)
- fermented (p. 416)
- relish (p. 416)
- vinegar (p. 416)
- flavored oil (p. 416)
- seed (p. 419)
- nut (p. 419)
- sensory perception (p. 421)
- sensory properties (p. 421)
- receptors (p. 421)
- stimuli (p. 421)
- translucent (p. 422)
- savory (p. 422)
- taste bud (p. 422)
- sensory evaluation (p. 424)
- blind taste test (p. 424)
- plate composition (p. 425)

Academic Vocabulary

- distinct (p. 401)
- lend (p. 403)
- abundant (p. 406)
- opaque (p. 410)
- accompaniment (p. 416)
- complement (p. 416)
- indication (p. 421)
- perception (p. 422)

Review Key Concepts

2. Describe the varieties and uses of seasonings and flavorings.

3. Compare and contrast the uses and storage for different herbs.

4. Describe the uses and storage for different spices.

5. Describe various condiments and the foods they can accompany.

6. Identify a variety of nuts and seeds.

7. Summarize the three sensory properties of food.

8. Illustrate how sensory factors can affect a customer's enjoyment of food.

Critical Thinking

9. Choose three seasonings that you would use in the preparation of a lamb dish. Explain which three you would choose, and why.

10. Explain why you think some foodservice operations might choose to use dried herbs rather than fresh herbs.

Review and Applications

Academic Skills

 English Language Arts

11. Evaluate Magazine Articles Locate three magazine articles that focus on seasonings or flavorings. Evaluate each magazine article by answering these questions: what is the intended audience for this article? What is the focus of the article? What kind of information does the article give? What is the writing style of this article? If you were to write an article, what seasoning or flavoring would you choose and what would be the focus?

> **NCTE 3** Apply strategies to interpret texts.

 Science

12. Apples and Onions Your sense of smell plays an important role in how you perceive the flavor of food.

Procedure Get several pieces of cut up apple and onion and a blindfold. With a partner, take turns being blindfolded. While you are blindfolded, pinch your nose and have your partner give you a piece of each food, not revealing which you are getting. Can you tell which is which? Try it again but with your partner holding the food so you can smell it. Can you tell which is which now?

Analysis Write a short summary of your experience, and theorize why the sense of small is so important to the sense of taste.

> **NSES B** Develop an understanding of the structure and properties of matter.

 Mathematics

13. Calculate Salt Use You are in charge of refilling the salt and pepper shakers at your restaurant. On Monday, you fill an empty 2-ounce salt shaker completely full. The next day, you fill it up again when it is ¾ full. Wednesday, the shaker is ⅞ full when you refill it. On Thursday, you fill it again when it is ⅔ full. At the end of the week, you refill the shaker when it is ½ full. What is the total amount of salt that you put in the shaker during the week?

Math Concept **Order of Operations** If an expression contains multiple operations, you can save time and effort if you perform the operations in a certain order. Perform the operations in this order: **P**arentheses, **E**xponents, **M**ultiplication and **D**ivision, and finally **A**ddition and **S**ubtraction. Within each type of operation, work from left to right. Use the acronym PEMDAS to remember this mnemonic device for order of operations for evaluating math expressions.

Starting Hint Each day, you add a fraction of 2 ounces to the shaker. For example, if the shaker is ¾ full, you will add (¼ × 2 ounces) of salt to the shaker. Write an expression listing all of the amounts added to the shaker: 2 + (¼ × 2) + (⅛ × 2) and so on. Solve within the parentheses first, and convert any fractions to common denominators. Use the PEMDAS order to help you to solve the equations in the expression.

> **NCTM Number and Operations** Understand the meanings of operations and how they relate to one another.

 ## Certification Prep

Directions Read the questions. Then, read the answer choices and choose the best possible answer for each.

14. What is the shelf life of opened vinegar?

    a. 2 weeks   **c.** 3 months

    b. 1 month   **d.** 1 year

15. What is the first indication of how food will taste?

    a. appearance   **c.** texture

    b. aroma   **d.** flavor

Sharpen your test-taking skills to improve your kitchen certification program score.

Test-Taking Tip
If the test is timed, you may have a tendency to rush. If you go too fast, you may lose focus or miss something. Take your time, but keep an eye on the clock.

Real-World Skills and Applications

Critical Thinking Skills

16. Replace Salt Think of five dishes to which you normally add salt, either during or after preparation. Now, think of other seasonings, flavorings, or condiments that could be added to the dish instead of salt that would improve the flavor without adding sodium. Make a list of the dishes and substituting that you find. Discuss your possible answers as a class.

Interpersonal and Collaborative Skills

17. Create a Recipe Collection Gather five recipes that use different seasonings and flavorings. The seasonings and flavorings can be used during or after preparation. As a class, divide each recipe into categories of herbs, spices, condiments, and seeds and nuts. Some recipes may fit in more than one category. Write down the recipes in a standard format. Then, create a classroom recipe file for the recipes you have gathered.

Technology Applications

18. Make a Spreadsheet Using spreadsheet software, make a chart listing the different seasonings and flavorings in the chapter and some potential uses for each. Include columns for the type (seasoning or flavoring), how it works, what foods it might enhance, and the page number it is found on in this book. Divide the spreadsheet into categories so that you can easily locate the type of item you wish to use. Turn in a copy of your spreadsheet to your teacher. You may wish to combine the spreadsheets as a class.

Financial Literacy

19. Purchase Spices 20 ounces of Chinese 5 Spice Powder costs $20 from your supplier. The ingredients are: cinnamon ($5.00), star anise ($5.00), anise seed ($3.00), ginger ($5.00), and cloves ($6.00). How much money will you save by purchasing the blend rather than purchasing each ingredient individually?

Culinary Lab

Herbs and Spices in Action

Use the culinary skills you have learned in this chapter.

20. Create a Sauce Working in teams, you will use herbs and spices to create a unique sauce. Think about the food you will serve it with and the desired final outcome.

A. Choose seasonings and flavorings. Choose a basic sauce to prepare. Review the list of herbs and spices and investigate how they are used with various foods.

B. Decide on the details. Decide which spices or herbs will produce the unique flavor your team wants for its sauce. Also, decide on the best time to add your seasonings to produce the maximum flavor.

C. Prepare your sauce. Cook your sauce, adding the seasonings you have chosen. Write down the ingredients and amounts used, and the steps you took when you prepared the sauce. When you are satisfied with the sauce, write out the recipe for others to use.

D. Do a taste test. Taste every team's sauce. Evaluate each sauce, and keep a record of your evaluations.

Create Your Evaluation

Share your team's sauce with the class. Evaluate each team's sauce for flavor, color, and texture. Use the following rating scale to score each team's sauce: 1 = Poor; 2 = Fair; 3 = Good; 4 = Great. Discuss your ratings as a class and why you chose the ratings you did for each group. After hearing your ratings, think about ways to improve the sauce.

CHAPTER 17

Breakfast Cookery

SECTIONS

17.1 Meat and Egg Preparation

17.2 Breakfast Breads and Cereals

WRITING ACTIVITY

Write a First Draft

Many people make breakfast for a loved one. Create an outline, and write the first draft of an essay about how to make a special breakfast. Include details about foods, presentation and service.

Writing Tips

1 Organize your ideas in an outline.

2 Organize your outline into paragraphs.

3 Plan each paragraph around one main idea.

EXPLORE THE PHOTO

Breakfast is important because it refreshes you and provides energy for later in the day. *What might be some negative effects of skipping breakfast?*

WRITING ACTIVITY ANSWER The draft and outline should be organized logically, and contain details. Students should keep their draft to complete the Chapter 18 Writing Activity.

EXPLORE THE PHOTO ANSWER Skipping breakfast can leave you low in energy and missing nutrients that you may not be able to make up in your other meals.

Meat and Egg Preparation

Eggs and meats form a basis for many breakfast dishes.

Reading Guide

 Before You Read

Buddy Up for Success One advantage to sharing your notes with a buddy is that you can fill in gaps in each other's information. You can also compare notes before you start quizzing each other.

Read to Learn

Key Concepts
- **Give examples** of common breakfast protein choices and their characteristics.
- **Explain** how to prepare breakfast meats.
- **Describe** at least five ways to cook eggs.

Main Idea

Traditional breakfast foods usually include eggs, meat, potatoes, breads, pancakes, waffles, and cereals. There are many different ways to prepare eggs and breakfast meats.

Content Vocabulary
- breakfast meats
- bacon
- Canadian bacon
- sausage
- hash
- albumin
- porous
- egg substitutes
- pasteurized
- soufflé
- dehydrated
- curdle
- omelet
- season
- frittata
- quiche
- shirred
- ramekin

Academic Vocabulary
- designate
- alternative

ACADEMIC STANDARDS

Mathematics
NCTM Number and Operations Understand meanings of operations and how they relate to one another.

Science
NSES B Develop an understanding of chemical reactions.

Social Studies
NCSS I A Culture Analyze and explain the ways groups, societies, and cultures address human needs and concerns.

NCTE National Council of Teachers of English

NCTM National Council of Teachers of Mathematics

NSES National Science Education Standards

NCSS National Council for the Social Studies

Graphic Organizer

Use a web diagram like the one below to identify the six ways to cook eggs that are described in this section.

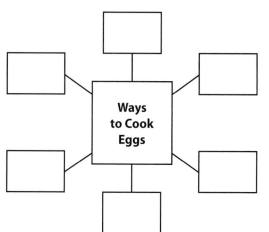

Ways to Cook Eggs

 Graphic Organizer
Go to this book's Online Learning Center at **glencoe.com** for a printable graphic organizer.

GRAPHIC ORGANIZER ANSWER Fried, poached, scrambled, omelet, shirred, and simmered in the shell.

Breakfast Proteins

Several breakfast protein foods are from the pork family, including ham, bacon, and sausage. Eggs are another common breakfast protein food. These protein foods are often served together. Frequently, breakfast protein foods are served with a bread or potato choice to round out the meal.

Types of Meats

Typical **breakfast meats** that are found on foodservice menus include ham, bacon, Canadian bacon, sausage, hash, and steak, although there are many other protein-based breakfast possibilities, such as smoked salmon, tofu, and turkey bacon. The best way to ensure a quality breakfast protein food is to use high-quality meats.

Ham and Bacon

Precooked ham is most often used as a breakfast meat. Slices of ham are either browned under a broiler or warmed on a griddle. When cooking breakfast ham in large quantities, it is often baked.

Bacon comes from the side of a pig, and is cured and often smoked for flavor. Most foodservice operations purchase pork bacon that is already sliced, although it is also available in whole slabs. In addition to pork bacon, turkey bacon is available in many restaurants for customers who want a breakfast meat with less fat. Smoky flavored bacons, such as hickory smoked, are available. Bacon may be served thin- or thick-sliced. The thickness is specified by the number of slices per pound. The average number of slices per pound is 18 to 22.

Canadian Bacon

Canadian bacon is a breakfast meat that comes from boneless pork loin. It is smoked and brined, and has a thin layer of fat on its surface. Canadian bacon is cut smaller than ham slices, but it is cooked and served in a similar way to ham.

Sausage

Sausage is usually made of ground pork that has been seasoned and stuffed into casings. Sausage is served in links or formed into patties. Links have a longer shelf life than patties because links have casings that keep the meat from drying out. Some sausages may be made from turkey or chicken.

Hash

Hash is chopped meat that is mixed with potatoes, onions, and seasonings that is usually fried together until lightly browned. Most hashes are made from corned beef, although some are made with roast beef. Hash is often served with eggs.

Steak

Steak is commonly paired with eggs for a hearty breakfast. Round tip steaks are often used for breakfast. This cut is from near the tenderloin so it is very tender.

Breakfast Combinations Breakfast meats accompany many standard breakfast menu items. *What combinations are most appealing to you?*

PHOTO CAPTION ANSWER Answers will vary, based on student preferences.

Egg Quality Egg grading is based on the quality of the yolk, white, and shell.
What are the differences between egg yolk and egg white?

Grade	Characteristics	Uses
AA	Yolk is firm, centered in the shell, holds its shape, and stands up high; white is clear and thick, so it does not spread out over a large area when broken in the pan; shell is clean, normal shape	Poaching, frying, hard- or soft-cooked
A	Thinner than AA, so it spreads slightly when broken in the pan; fairly firm yolk; clear white	Hard- or soft-cooked
B	Less firm yolk and white, so the egg does not hold its shape in the pan and spreads over a wide area; yolk is large and flat; shell may be slightly stained or an abnormal shape	Scrambled eggs; baking

Egg Composition

Eggs are an inexpensive source of protein. They can be prepared in many different ways to suit various tastes. An egg has three main parts: the shell, the yolk, and the white.

- **Shell** Like any shell, an eggshell protects the egg's content. Eggshells range in color from white to brown, and they vary in thickness and how porous they are. The color of the eggshell indicates the type of chicken that laid the egg. However, it does not affect the interior color of the egg or the taste.

- **Yolk** The yolk, almost one-third of the egg's weight, contains fat and protein, along with vitamins and iron. Most of an egg's calories and all of its cholesterol and fat are found in the yolk. The color of the yolk depends on the diet of the chicken.

- **White** Two-thirds of an egg is made of the clear white, or **albumin** (al-'byü-mən). The thickest part of the white surrounds the yolk. Riboflavin (,rī-bə-'flā-vən) (vitamin B$_2$) and more than half of the protein of the egg are found in the white. It is clear and soluble when the egg is uncooked, but becomes white and firm when cooked.

Eggs may look solid, but they are actually very porous ('pȯr-əs). **Porous** means that flavors and odors can be absorbed through the shell and that the egg can lose moisture even when the shell is unbroken. For this reason, eggs need to be stored carefully. They should be kept away from foods, such as onions, with a strong odor. Eggs will keep for several weeks if stored at 36°F (2°C).

Egg Grades and Quality

The U.S. Department of Agriculture is responsible for grading eggs according to three grades: Grade AA, Grade A, and Grade B. These grades **designate**, or are a sign of, several qualities, such as an egg's appearance when it is cracked into a pan, and the characteristics of the yolk, the white, and the shell. (See **Figure 17.1**.)

Size Size is part of the grading process. There are six categories: jumbo (30 ounces), extra large (27 ounces), large (24 ounces), medium (21 ounces), small (18 ounces), and peewee (15 ounces). The size is not determined per egg, but by the weight per dozen. (See **Figure 17.2** on page 434.)

FIGURE CAPTION ANSWER Egg yolk is yellow, is almost a third of the egg's weight, and has most of the egg's calories and all of the egg's cholesterol and fat. Egg white, or albumin, is clear and contains over half of the egg's protein.

FIGURE 17.2 Egg Size

Big or Small? The size range of eggs is determined by the weight per dozen. *Why would you use smaller eggs rather than larger ones?*

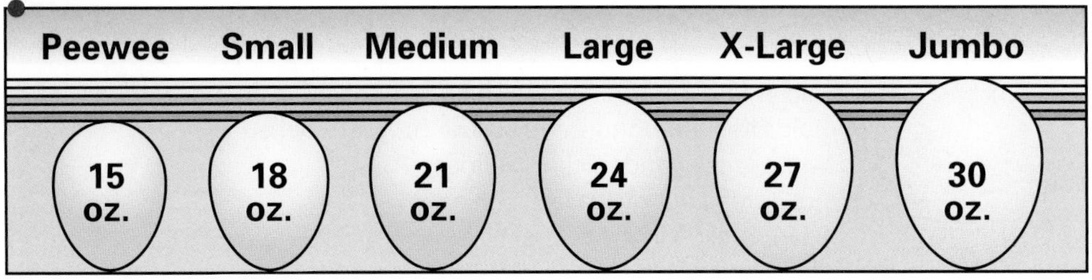

Peewee	Small	Medium	Large	X-Large	Jumbo
15 OZ.	18 OZ.	21 OZ.	24 OZ.	27 OZ.	30 OZ.

Forms of Eggs

Eggs are sold in three forms: fresh, frozen, and dried. Each form has particular uses. **Egg substitutes** are available for people with dietary concerns such as high cholesterol. One egg substitute is made with albumin and a vegetable substitute for the yolk. Eggs are used in many recipes to thicken, bind, and add moisture, color, and flavor.

Fresh Eggs Fresh eggs are used in commercial kitchens and for home use. The appearance of a poached egg is better when the egg is fresh because the yolk gets flatter as it ages.

Frozen Eggs Frozen eggs are high-quality fresh eggs that are pasteurized (ˈpas-chə-rīzd) and then frozen. **Pasteurized** egg products are heated at very high temperatures for a short time to destroy bacteria. They come in large containers and need to thaw for a couple of days in the refrigerator before they can be cooked. Frozen Grade A eggs are often used in commercial kitchens for scrambled eggs

and other recipes that call for beaten eggs. For example, a **soufflé** (sü-ˈflā), or puffed egg dish that is baked in the oven, can be made with frozen egg yolks and frozen egg whites.

Dried Eggs Dried eggs are **dehydrated** ((ˌ)dē-ˈhī-ˌdrāt-əd). This means that the water is removed. Dried eggs have a long shelf life. They are used in commercial foodservice operations.

Reading Check **Decide** What grade of egg would you use for scrambled eggs, poached eggs, and hard-cooked eggs?

Breakfast Meat Cookery

Most breakfast meat and egg dishes can be prepared quickly and do not require much advance preparation. The most common breakfast meats, including ham, bacon, and sausage, have relatively high levels of fat. Because bacon can be made of nearly 70% fat, it will shrink during cooking. You do not need to add more fat during cooking.

The best way to cook breakfast meats is at a low temperature. Do not overcook them. Meat becomes dry, tasteless, and tough if it is overcooked.

Ham and Bacon

Precooked ham slices just need to be warmed and browned slightly under the broiler or on the griddle before they are served.

~ Small Bites ~

Egg Size and Storage Most standardized recipes assume that large eggs will be used. Keep these storage tips in mind for eggs:

- Store eggs in their original containers or in covered containers.
- Store eggs away from foods with strong flavors or odors, such as onions.
- Thaw frozen eggs in the refrigerator and use them in baked dishes that will be thoroughly cooked.

FIGURE CAPTION ANSWER You might want a peewee egg to create an appropriate-size presentation for an appetizer or small entrée. You may also choose medium or small eggs based on cost, availability, or portion control.

READING CHECK ANSWER Scrambled: Grade B; poached: Grade AA; soufflés: Grade B; hard-cooked: Grade AA or A.

Most bacon served with breakfast is made from pork, but turkey bacon is an **alternative**, or substitute. To help reduce shrinkage, cook bacon at a low temperature. Use an oven when you cook bacon in large quantities.

Use these steps to cook bacon in the oven:

1. Arrange the bacon in single strips on a sheet pan lined with parchment paper.
2. Cook at 300°F to 350°F (149°C to 177°C) until the bacon is almost done.
3. Remove the bacon from the oven. Be very careful not to spill the hot grease.
4. Finish cooking the bacon on the griddle.
5. Blot excess grease, and serve.

Sausage

Sausage is generally made from fresh pork, although turkey and chicken sausage are also available. It comes in patties, links, and sometimes out of the casing. Sausage must be cooked until well done, but not dry and hard.

In most restaurants, sausage is cooked in bulk. It is often first cooked in the oven, and then finished to order on the griddle. It is easier to prevent sausage from drying out during cooking than it is to prevent sausage patties from drying out.

Hash

Hash can be purchased ready-made, or can be made fresh in the commercial kitchen. Roast beef or corned beef are chopped into small cubes, and then lightly sautéed with potatoes, onions, and sometimes other vegetables such as celery and bell pepper until the entire mixture is golden brown.

Steak

Steak is usually cooked to order for breakfast menus. Depending on customer preference, steaks can be cooked rare, medium-rare, medium, medium-well, or well done. It is usually served with some form of eggs.

Safety Check

✓ Prevent Salmonella

Salmonella bacteria are found in a chicken's intestinal tract. It is a serious health concern when you use raw or undercooked eggs. To avoid salmonella poisoning:

- Refrigerate eggs immediately.
- Use only pasteurized egg products.
- Do not use eggs that are broken or cracked.
- Be careful not to drop in any shell pieces with the liquid egg.
- Thoroughly wash work surfaces, tools, equipment, and your hands.

CRITICAL THINKING *Why should you not use eggs that are broken or cracked?*

Plate Cooked Meats

Most breakfast meats are served in combination with eggs and potatoes on the same plate. Sometimes, especially with large omelets, the meat may be served as a side dish on a separate plate. Either way, breakfast meats should be served hot, completely cooked, but not overcooked and dry. Be careful not to hold meat too long so it becomes dry.

Reading Check Explain List the steps of how to cook bacon in the oven.

Egg Cookery

Knowing how to cook eggs properly is also a health issue. Undercooked eggs pose a serious health threat because of salmonella bacteria. You must understand all of the different ways to cook eggs. Cooking eggs is one measure of a chef's skill.

It is important to cook eggs at a moderate temperature. If you overcook eggs at a high temperature, you will have a tough, rubbery, and discolored final product. In addition, the eggs' flavor may be affected. Likewise, eggs that are left in a steam table will turn green if they get too hot and begin to overcook. This will make the eggs unappealing to customers.

✳ MASTER RECIPE
Omelet with Cheese

YIELD: 10 SERVINGS
SERVING SIZE: 8 OZ.

Ingredients

30	Eggs, cracked into a bowl
	Salt and ground white pepper, to taste
8 oz.	Milk
5 oz.	Clarified butter, melted
1 lb.	Cheese, julienne
3 oz.	Fresh parsley, washed, excess moisture removed, and chopped

Method of Preparation

1. Season the eggs with salt and pepper. Add the milk, and whisk until the eggs are well combined.
2. Heat an omelet pan with ½ oz. of butter.
3. When hot, add a 6-oz. ladle of egg mixture.
4. Shake the pan, and mix the eggs until they begin to firm, lifting the edges to allow liquid egg to run underneath (see Chef Notes).
5. When the omelet is almost firm, or 145°F (63°C), turn it over.
6. Place about 1 oz. of cheese in the center of the omelet, fold, and roll onto a preheated dinner plate. Serve immediately, or hold at 135°F (57°C) or above.
7. Repeat the procedure until all of the eggs are cooked.
8. Garnish with chopped parsley.

Cooking Technique

Shallow-Fry

1. Heat the cooking medium to the proper temperature.
2. Cook the food product throughout.
3. Season, and serve hot.

Chef Notes

When the eggs have set in the sauté pan, place the pan under a broiler for 10-15 seconds to finish cooking the eggs. This creates a fluffier presentation and ensures that the eggs are well done.

Substitutions

- To lower the fat, use low-fat milk, or half the amount of cheese in each omelet.
- Add fresh herbs to the omelet to increase flavor without adding salt.
- To lower cholesterol, use egg whites, or an egg substitute.

International Flavor

The classic omelet recipe originated in France, but egg dishes are popular in many countries. Use the Internet or library to research these international omelet recipes, and write a half-page report on your findings:

- Frittata (Italy)
- Datemaki (Japan)
- Tortilla de patatas (Spain)

Glossary

Whisk to aerate with a whip
Julienne matchstick strips

HACCP

- Cook to 145°F (63°C)
- Hold cooked eggs at 135°F (57°C) or above
- Hold uncooked egg mixture below 41°F (5°C)

Hazardous Foods

- Eggs
- Milk

Nutrition

Calories 480   Calories from Fat 320
Total Fat 35g
  Saturated Fat 17g
  Trans Fat 0g
Cholesterol 790mg
Sodium 720mg
Total Carbohydrate 4g
  Fiber 0g
  Sugars 3g
Protein 34g
- Vitamin A 35%   • Vitamin C 6%
- Calcium 30%   • Iron 20%

Egg Cooking Concerns

It is important to understand that coagulation, or the temperature at which egg protein becomes solid, varies with different parts of the egg. In general, whole beaten eggs coagulate at about 156°F (69°C). Egg whites coagulate at a slightly lower temperature than yolks. Because of this, it is possible to make eggs that have soft yolks but cooked whites.

When you make scrambled eggs that are mixed with a liquid such as milk, the coagulation temperature increases to 180°F (82°C). Most burners set on high are much hotter than that, meaning that eggs can easily become overcooked at that setting. The eggs and solids may separate, or **curdle** ('kər-dəl).

Fried Eggs

Fried eggs are the most popular breakfast egg dish. For best results, use Grade AA eggs. Fried eggs must be cooked to order and served immediately. In some quick-service operations, fried eggs are cooked in egg rings to produce a uniform shape. However, most fried eggs are cooked in a pan on the range top or on the griddle. (See **Figure 17.3** on page 438.)

When you turn an egg on the griddle, flip the egg by sliding the spatula underneath it. Then, lift one side up and over, leaving one edge of the egg touching the griddle. This will keep the yolk from breaking.

Poached Eggs

It is best to use very fresh eggs for poaching since they hold their shape better. Break one egg at a time into a small dish. Then, add each egg to simmering water that contains 1 or 2 teaspoons of an acid such as vinegar. This will cause the egg to coagulate quickly. Do not use boiling water to poach eggs because it causes the eggs to separate and become tough.

Scrambled Eggs

Scrambled eggs are usually made with whole eggs. However, egg whites can be used for customers who prefer fewer calories and less fat and cholesterol.

Omelets

The **omelet** ('äm-lət) is an egg specialty dish made of beaten eggs that are cooked without stirring. Once the eggs are set, they are folded in half in the pan.

Science à la Carte

Green Eggs

When hard-cooked eggs are overcooked, a green ring may form around the egg yolks. The green color is the reaction between sulfur and iron compounds at the surface of the egg yolk. This is a harmless reaction, but it can make the eggs look unappealing. Green yolks in hard-cooked eggs can be avoided if you use the proper cooking time and heat level, and by rapidly cooling the cooked eggs. Scrambled eggs can also turn green with too much heat.

Procedure

Follow your teacher's instructions to divide into four teams. Each team should prepare a serving of eggs:

- **Team A** Prepare two hard-cooked eggs according to recipe directions for cooking and standing time.
- **Team B** Prepare two hard-cooked eggs following the recipe, but allow the eggs to stand for 5 minutes longer than the recipe directions.
- **Team C** Prepare two scrambled eggs according to recipe directions using medium heat.
- **Team D** Prepare two scrambled eggs according to recipe directions, but use high heat.

Analysis

Record your observations about cooking time, and the appearance and flavor of the eggs. Contrast the eggs prepared by each cooking method. What are the differences between the cooked eggs? Why did they occur? Discuss your findings as a class.

> **NSES B** Develop an understanding of chemical reactions.

SCIENCE À LA CARTE ANSWER Student results may vary, but overall eggs cooked by Teams B and D may have a slight green tint.

FIGURE 17.3 Fried Egg Cooking Methods

Fried Eggs The yolks of fried eggs can be prepared to different levels of doneness.
What should you do if you break the yolk while preparing a fried egg?

Type of Egg	Description	Method
Sunny-Side Up 	Egg is not flipped over during cooking, so the yellow yolk stands up. The yolk should be well-visible, highly mounded, and yellow.	Make sure you do not break the yolk when cracking the egg into the pan. Cook on medium heat for about 4 minutes, until the white is firm.
Basted 	A type of sunny-side up egg. The yolk will have a thin cover of white on it.	Egg is cooked in butter over low heat. The butter is spooned over the egg as it continues to cook, basting it. Variation: Instead of basting with butter, add 1-2 tsp. of water and cover the pan so the steam cooks the top of the egg.
Over-Easy 	Egg is turned over during frying and cooked so that the yolk is still liquid when served and cut.	Cook about 3 minutes on the first side over medium heat, then turn it and cook about 2 minutes on the other side.
Over-Medium 	The yolk is partly cooked.	Cook a little longer than for over-easy.
Over-Hard 	The yolk is firm and fully cooked.	Cook until the yolk is completely firm but not overcooked and rubbery.

A seasoned omelet pan and high heat can make a beautiful omelet. A nonstick coated omelet pan can also be used. Nonstick pans require no seasoning. When you **season**, or condition, a pan, you seal the surface with a layer of baked-on oil to prevent sticking. Seasoning must be done with cast-iron cookware.

Make sure that you care for omelet pans properly. Incorrect seasoning or misuse may cause omelets to stick.

FIGURE CAPTION ANSWER If you break the yolk of a fried egg, you must begin new with another egg. This is why care must be taken when turning a fried egg.

French and American Omelets

Both French and American omelets are folded omelets. This means that toppings are added in the center of the omelet, and then it is folded around the toppings. French omelets must be stirred and shaken simultaneously, which takes practice. French omelets have two advantages over American omelets:
- They are lighter and puffier in texture.
- They cook faster.

Scramble
Eggs

1 Break eggs into a bowl and whisk them until they are well blended. Stir in a little milk or cream if desired.

2 Heat butter in a sauté pan, or on a griddle if you are preparing many orders at once. Add the egg mixture.

3 Cook over low to medium heat, stirring slowly with a spatula by shifting portions of the egg mixture as it coagulates, allowing the uncooked egg to run underneath the cooked portion.

4 When eggs are set, but not overly hard, they are done. Scrambled eggs continue to cook a little after they are removed from the pan.

5 Remove the eggs from the heat. The eggs will still be soft, shiny, and moist. They should not be green or brown.

Soufflé Omelets

A soufflé omelet is a baked egg dish that puffs up. To make a soufflé omelet, separate the yolks from the whites. Whip the egg whites to full volume, then fold the egg white mixture into the beaten yolks. Pour into a buttered soufflé dish and bake until cooked and puffy.

Soufflés can also be made by blending egg yolks into a thick sauce base. Béchamel sauce is often used for this. A filling such as cheese or toasted almonds is added, and the egg whites are folded into the base mixture. The mixture is then baked in a buttered soufflé dish dusted with breadcrumbs, grated cheese, or sugar. Soufflés like this make excellent light entrées or desserts.

Frittatas

A **frittata** (frē-'tä-tə) is a flat, open-face omelet. They are not folded over. Instead, the eggs are beaten and mixed with the precooked filling ingredients, and then cooked over low heat without stirring. A frittata can either be turned over and cooked on the other side, or placed under the broiler until the top is set and slightly browned. Frittatas are usually cut in wedges and served warm or cold.

Quiche

A **quiche** ('kēsh) is a pie crust filled with a mixture of eggs, cream, cheese, and vegetables or meat. Quiche can be served for breakfast, lunch, or dinner.

Make a French Omelet

1. Crack eggs into a bowl and whip with a wire whisk.

2. Place the pan on the burner and turn the burner on high heat. When the pan is hot, add clarified butter and swirl it around to coat the entire inside of the pan.

3. After pouring the beaten eggs into the hot pan, allow them to coagulate for a brief moment and then stir the eggs. Allow the uncooked portion to run underneath the cooked portion. Shaking the pan gently while doing this can help.

4. Once the eggs are set but still soft, add the filling and then fold the omelet neatly. Cook the omelet until lightly firm.

5. Slide the omelet out of the pan and onto a plate.

Shirred Eggs

Shirred ('shərd) eggs are covered with cream or milk and sometimes bread crumbs. They are usually prepared in ramekins lined with a variety of ingredients, such as spinach, bread, ham, bacon slices, or artichoke hearts. A **ramekin** ('ra-mi-kən) is a small individual baking dish. The egg is cracked into the center of the cup and topped with grated cheese, onion, and herbs. Sauces may also be added after baking.

To make shirred eggs:

1. Butter the ramekins to keep ingredients from sticking.

2. Line the ramekins, if desired, with a slice of ham or other appropriate ingredient.

3. Carefully break an egg or two into the dish.

4. Sprinkle with salt and pepper, if desired.

5. Bake the eggs at 350°F (177°C) until they begin to set.

6. Add grated cheese, onion, or fresh herbs, such as minced fresh thyme, parsley, or basil, to the top and finish baking.

Serve Shirred Eggs

Shirred eggs can be beautiful with the proper plating. Arrange garnishes on one side of the plate. Spoon hot cream, mild green chili, mushroom, tomato, or brown sauces over the eggs. Or, place asparagus tips, sautéed mushrooms, or crumbled bacon on top.

Simmer Eggs in the Shell

Soft-, medium-, and hard-cooked eggs are all cooked in the shell in hot water. Boiling water can cause eggs to become tough and discolored. Instead, place the eggs in cold water. Then, simmer the eggs until they are done cooking.

Eggs prepared properly should have evenly cooked whites and yolks. The yolk should not be discolored, and the egg should not have an unpleasant taste.

To make simmered eggs in the shell:

1. Make sure the eggs have been at room temperature for an hour before cooking to prevent the shells from cracking as they cook.

2. Fill a saucepan with enough water to cover the eggs.

3. Simmer the eggs according to the level of doneness desired:
   - Soft-cooked: 3 minutes
   - Medium-cooked: 4 to 5 minutes
   - Hard-cooked 8 to 10 minutes

Egg Plating

Fried eggs and scrambled eggs are often served with toast, meat, potatoes, and a garnish. Presentation should be attractive and uncluttered. The garnish used most often is a twisted slice of orange or a slice of melon.

Shirred eggs are served in their individual baking dishes, which are then placed on a larger plate that holds the side dishes. The garnish will be placed on top of the eggs.

Omelets must be attractively plated, with a simple garnish, such as a sprig of parsley. Side dishes are usually not served with omelets. Often, only toast is served.

Soft- and medium-cooked simmered eggs are usually served in egg cups in the shell, accompanied by side dishes and garnishes. The customer uses a spoon to gently tap the top of the shell to break it and then scoops out the insides for eating. Hard-cooked eggs can be served in a variety of ways.

 Reading Check Describe How do you successfully fry an egg?

SECTION 17.1 — After You Read

Review Key Concepts

1. **Describe** the composition of an egg.
2. **Explain** how to prepare ham.
3. **Describe** how to scramble an egg.

Practice Culinary Academics

 Social Studies

4. Many different cultures have egg dishes that are both similar to and different from to dishes you may eat at home. Research some common dishes from other cultures that use eggs and write a report describing the country of origin, ingredients, and methods of preparation. Share what you learned with the class.

> **NCSS I A Culture** Analyze and explain the ways groups, societies, and cultures address human needs and concerns.

Mathematics

5. Neal has purchased a 1-foot slab of applewood-smoked bacon for his restaurant. If he slices the bacon ³⁄₁₆ of an inch thick, how many slices will he get out of the slab?

Math Concept **Dividing Fractions** To divide when a fraction is involved, convert any mixed or whole numbers to improper fractions. Multiply the first fraction by the reciprocal of the second fraction. Reduce to lowest terms.

Starting Hint You will need to divide 12 inches (which is the equivalent of 1 foot) by ³⁄₁₆ inch. To do so, multiply ¹²⁄₁ by ¹⁶⁄₃, and simplify the result.

> **NCTM Number and Operations** Understand meanings of operations and how they relate to one another.

 Check your answers at this book's Online Learning Center at **glencoe.com**.

READING CHECK ANSWER Use grade AA eggs, cook at a low temperature, and cook to order. Be careful not to break the yolk when you flip the egg.

Breakfast Breads and Cereals

Reading Guide

 Before You Read

Predict Before starting the section, browse the content by reading headings, bold terms, and photo captions. Do they help you predict the information in the section?

Read to Learn

Key Concepts

- **List** the food items commonly served in quick-service breakfasts.
- **Categorize** the different types of breakfast quick breads and cereals.

Main Idea

Some type of bread or cereal is usually found in any breakfast dish. Pancakes, French toast, and waffles are usually cooked to order, while pastries and other breads are often ready-made.

Content Vocabulary

- home fries
- hash browns
- cottage fries
- ready-made bread
- granola
- pastries
- doughnut
- quick breads
- muffin
- biscuit
- scone
- English muffin
- fold
- side order
- French toast

Academic Vocabulary

- mainstay
- function

Graphic Organizer

Use a sequence chart like this one to take notes about the four steps to prepare French toast.

Steps for Preparing French Toast

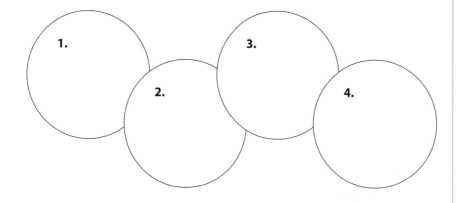

 Graphic Organizer Go to this book's Online Learning Center at **glencoe.com** for a printable graphic organizer.

GRAPHIC ORGANIZER ANSWER 1) Slightly beat eggs. 2) Add milk, sugar, cinnamon, nutmeg, and vanilla to the eggs and stir. 3) Dip each slice of bread in the batter, coating thoroughly. 4) Brown each side of the bread on the griddle.

ACADEMIC STANDARDS

 English Language Arts
NCTE 12 Use language to accomplish individual purposes.

 Mathematics
NCTM Measurement Apply appropriate techniques, tools, and formulas to determine measurements.

 Social Studies
NCSS VIII B Science, Technology, and Society Make judgments about how science and technology have transformed the physical world and human society.

NCSS IX A Global Connections Explain how cultural elements can facilitate global understanding.

NCTE National Council of Teachers of English

NCTM National Council of Teachers of Mathematics

NSES National Science Education Standards

NCSS National Council for the Social Studies

Create baked goods and cereals to round out a breakfast menu.

Quick-Service Breakfasts

Breakfast foods are very popular. In the United States, many people eat breakfast foods at any meal. The standard breakfast menu includes eggs, meat, potatoes, breads, pancakes, waffles, cereals, fruit, and yogurt. Some restaurants offer customers more unusual choices, such as a special pizza or breakfast burritos. In short, anything goes!

Most restaurants that serve breakfast offer a variety of similar options and combinations. Eggs are often served either scrambled, over-easy, hard, basted, poached, or as omelets. Eggs usually come with some form of breakfast bread. This could include toast, biscuits, or an English muffin. It could also include potatoes that have been sautéed or fried. Egg dishes may also be accompanied by meat, such as bacon, ham, or sausage.

Breads such as pancakes, French toast, and waffles can be ordered in combination with eggs and a meat choice, or alone. An example would be a stack of three to five pancakes with butter and syrup or fruit toppings. A small stack of two pancakes may accompany an egg dish.

Potatoes such as home fries, hash browns, and cottage fries are a common side dish for breakfast. **Home fries** are usually diced or sliced. **Hash browns** are shredded and may include onions and seasonings. For **cottage fries**, the potatoes are cut into ½-inch thick circles, and then baked or broiled.

More often than not, breakfast items may be ordered á la carte so that the customers can create their own combination of foods. This can also be profitable for the restaurant. But foodservice workers must know how to prepare a wide variety of breakfast proteins and breads. They also must learn to prepare breakfast items quickly and with skill. Most restaurant customers want their breakfast to be ready quickly.

 **Reading Check** **Determine** What types of food items might be served with eggs?

READING CHECK ANSWER Eggs might be served with toast, biscuits, English muffins, bacon, ham, or sausage.

Breakfast Breads and Cereals

Bread may be an even more popular breakfast item than eggs. Toast, muffins, biscuits, scones, and bagels are some of the many choices. Nearly every customer who orders an egg item will want some kind of bread with it. Many customers choose a bread item, such as pancakes, French toast, waffles, or cereal, as the **mainstay**, or main part, of their favorite breakfast.

Cereals appear on all breakfast menus and are served either hot or cold. Cereals are made from grains such as wheat, corn, rice, and oats, and are a good source of carbohydrates. Breakfast cereals should be stored in airtight containers to keep them from becoming stale, or being infested by pests.

Quality Breakfast Breads and Cereals

Once breads are baked, they become stale quickly. Stale breads taste unappealing and may become hard and dry. To avoid staleness, it is necessary to consider how far in advance you will be able to prepare and bake breads before they are served.

Ready-Made Breads

Bread that is made in advance at bakeries and delivered to foodservice establishments is called **ready-made bread**. The choice of quality pre-prepared breads on a breakfast menu is almost unlimited. Bagels, scones, doughnuts, muffins, croissants, and English muffins are just a few examples. The only breakfast bread items that are routinely prepared to order are toast, pancakes, French toast, and waffles.

Hot Cereals

Hot cereals typically fall into two categories:
- Granular cereals, such as grits, barley, or farina.
- Whole, cracked, or flaked cereals, such as oatmeal and cracked wheat.

Hot cereals are served with milk or cream and white or brown sugar. Sometimes small ceramic bowls called ramekins filled with raisins, fresh fruit, brown sugar, or nuts are served with hot cereal. Hot cereals are a welcome menu choice for many health-conscious people.

Cold Cereals

Many cold cereals are purchased ready to eat. Some restaurants make their own special blend of granola (grə-'nō-lə). **Granola** is a blend of grains, nuts, and dried fruits. Like hot cereals, cold cereals are served with milk or cream, sugar, and sometimes fresh fruit, such as sliced strawberries or bananas. Cold cereals are a favorite breakfast choice for both children and adults. They are available in quantity portioning machines and as individual portions.

Ready-Made Breads

Breads and cereals are an essential component of breakfast menus. Rarely is an order of eggs sold without a breakfast bread. Quick breads, such as pancakes and waffles, and breakfast items like toast and French toast are generally cooked to order. Many operations purchase ready-made pastries, muffins, and doughnuts. This section will introduce you to common breakfast breads and cereals.

Ready-made or convenience (kən-'vēn-yən(t)s) breads include pastries, doughnuts, and many kinds of quick breads, such as muffins. Ready-made breads can save a restaurant time during a busy breakfast rush.

Pastries

Pastries, also known as Danishes, are popular breakfast treats. They are made from yeasted, sweetened dough with butter, which gives pastries the rich flavor that makes them so appetizing. Egg is added to the dough of some kinds of pastries.

Many pastries are filled with almond paste, fruit, cream cheese, or nuts. Bear claws and strudel are two of the more well-known types of pastries. Pastries can be made from scratch, from frozen doughs, or can be purchased ready-made.

● **Breakfast Breads** Many different types of breakfast breads are available. *What kinds of specialty breakfast breads and pastries are available in your area?*

PHOTO CAPTION ANSWER Answers will vary based on the area.

Doughnuts

A **doughnut** is a sweetened, deep-fried pastry that is often ring-shaped, but may also be bar-shaped or round. There are two categories: cake and raised. Cake doughnuts use baking powder, while raised doughnuts get their rising power from yeast. Cake doughnuts are heavier than raised doughnuts, and they tend to have spices or chocolate added to the mix as well. Many doughnuts have a glaze made of sugar and other flavorings. Others, such as fritters, have bits of fruit such as apple mixed into the dough before frying.

Quick Breads

Many foodservice operations rely on **quick breads**, a type of bread made from quick-acting leavening agents such as baking powder. They are easy to make, even from scratch, because they do not need yeast to rise. This means quick breads take less time to mix and bake. Chapter 28 covers different types and baking methods for quick breads in depth.

In restaurants, quick breads complement the main entrée or serve as the main part of a continental breakfast. Muffins are especially useful because they are so versatile. A **muffin** is a quick bread made with egg and baked in a cupcake mold. Varieties from corn muffins to seasonal berry muffins can add interest and nutrition to any breakfast menu choice.

While muffins are popular, loaf-style quick breads fulfill the same **function**, or purpose, and are very tasty. Cranberry nut bread, banana bread, and zucchini bread are just a few of the quick breads that can add interest and pizzazz to a breakfast menu. A **biscuit** is a small, round quick bread. Biscuits are usually rich and savory, but can be sweet. Biscuits should have a light, tender, and flaky texture. A **scone** ('skōn) is a type of quick bread similar to biscuits that is often cut into triangle shapes.

Quick breads are enhanced by servings of flavored cream cheese, jellies, and jams alongside them. These toppings and spreads are usually served in small ramekins on the side or in pre-packaged, individual servings.

Breakfast Bread Some breakfast breads are purchased by restaurants as ready-made breads. *Why do some restaurants purchase their quick breads?*

PHOTO CAPTION ANSWER Some restaurants find it convenient to purchase quick breads rather than making fresh every day.

Toast, English Muffins, and Bagels

Toasted bread is a popular addition to most breakfast dishes. Be careful when you toast bread so that it does not burn. You may also toast English muffins. An **English muffin** is made from bread dough that is shaped into rounds and cooked on a griddle. English muffins are usually purchased pre-cooked. Bagels are also popular breakfast choices.

Pancakes and Waffles

Both pancakes and waffles are made from batters that can be mixed ahead of time and refrigerated. Wet and dry ingredients for these foods are mixed separately. The wet ingredients are then added to the dry ingredients and stirred until well moistened. Do not overmix. This can cause the pancakes to be tough and rubbery.

Pancake Preparation

Follow these steps whenever you prepare pancakes:

1. Ladle ¼-cup portions onto a 375°F (191°C) griddle that has been lightly buttered. To ensure round pancakes, leave enough room between each pancake for spreading.

2. When bubbles appear on the top of the pancakes, it is time to turn them. You should turn, or flip, a pancake only once. If you turn it more often, the pancake will get hard.

3. Cook pancakes until they are nicely browned on both sides.

Waffle Preparation

Follow these steps to prepare waffles:

1. Mix the wet ingredients in one bowl and the dry ingredients in another. Add the liquid ingredients to the dry ingredients.

2. Beat the egg whites into soft peaks, add sugar, and beat until the peaks are stiff.

3. Fold the egg whites into the batter. To **fold** means to use a rubber spatula to carefully mix the egg whites and batter so that you do not lose volume.

4. Pour the batter onto a preheated, lightly oiled waffle iron, and then close the top.

5. Cook until the signal on the waffle iron shows that the waffles are done.

Pancake and Waffle Plating

Pancakes and waffles are cooked to order and should be served piping hot. Pancakes become tough and waffles lose their crispness when they are held for too long. They may be served with a variety of condiments, including butter, hot syrup, cold flavored syrups, fruit toppings, whipped cream, or nuts.

Pancakes and waffles are often served with a side order of breakfast meats, eggs, or both. A **side order** is an order of food in addition to what is served as the main dish. Pancakes are not usually served with other breakfast breads.

✳ MASTER RECIPE
Pancakes with Maple Syrup

YIELD: 50 SERVINGS
SERVING SIZE: 4 EACH
COOKING TECHNIQUE: BAKE

Ingredients

1 qt.	Pasteurized eggs
3 qt.	Milk
2 tbsp.	Vanilla extract
6 lbs.	All-purpose flour
8 oz.	Sugar
6 oz.	Baking powder
1 lb.	Butter, melted
2 qt.	Maple syrup, heated and kept warm at 135°F (57°C) or above

Method of Preparation

1. In a mixing bowl, beat the eggs.
2. Add the milk and vanilla to the beaten eggs, and mix well. Set aside.
3. Mix all of the dry ingredients together. Add the egg mixture, and whisk to a smooth batter.
4. Stir the butter into the mixture.
5. Let the batter rest for 1 hour before using.
6. Preheat the griddle.
7. To cook, pour approximately 2 ounces of batter on a seasoned, lightly buttered griddle.
8. Cook until the bubbles appear on the top and the edges become dry.
9. Turn over, and cook the other side until done. Serve immediately, or hold at 135°F (57°C) or above.
10. Hold the unused batter at 41°F (5°C) or below if not used immediately.
11. Serve with warm syrup.
12. Repeat the procedure until all of the batter is used.

Cooking Technique

Griddling

1. Preheat the griddle.
2. Place the food product on the griddle when hot.

Chef Notes

For best results, make pancakes to order. Do not over mix the batter, or the pancakes will be tough.

Substitutions

- Use low-fat or nonfat milk to lower fat in the recipe.
- Reduce the sugar to reduce the calories in the recipe.

International Flavor

Pancakes can be either savory or sweet, and made with different ingredients. Many different cultures have pancakes as part of their cuisines. Use the Internet or library to research these, and write a summary of each recipe's ingredients and cooking method.

- Potato Pancakes (Germany)
- Pannekoeken (Holland)
- Ho Bac Jon (Korea)

Glossary

Beat to mix by stirring quickly
Whisk to aerate with a whip

HACCP

- Hold at 135°F (57°C) or above
- Hold unused batter at 41°F (5°C) or below
- Hold maple syrup at 135°F (57°C) or above

Hazardous Foods

- Milk
- Pasteurized eggs

Nutrition

Calories 480   Calories from Fat 110
Total Fat 12g
    Saturated Fat 6g
    Trans Fat 0g
Cholesterol 110mg
Sodium 420mg
Total Carbohydrate 84g
    Fiber 1g
    Sugars 38g
Protein 10g
- Vitamin A 8%   · Vitamin C 0%
- Calcium 30%   · Iron 20%

French Toast

French toast is bread that has been dipped in a batter and then sautéed. French toast is a favorite breakfast choice. French toast is technically not a quick bread. It is made from yeast leavened bread. However, it is quick to make, it is commonly served with breakfast and is usually made to order. It can be made with different types of bread, including sourdough. Fruit and powdered sugar can be added for a beautiful presentation. French toast is a good way for commercial kitchens to use day-old bread. Day-old bread is firmer and holds batter well when it is grilled.

Some establishments choose to serve crunchy French toast. After soaking the bread in the egg mixture, the bread is dipped in bran or corn cereal and then quickly fried. This leaves a crunchy, sweet coating on the surface of the French toast. Crunchy French toast is often served with sliced bananas and syrup as common accompaniments.

French Toast Preparation

Follow these steps to prepare and cook French toast:

1. Slightly beat eggs.
2. Add milk, sugar, cinnamon, nutmeg, and vanilla to the eggs and stir well.
3. Dip each slice of bread into the batter, being sure to thoroughly coat each side. For crunchy French toast, dip in crushed cereal after battering.
4. Brown each side of the bread slices on the griddle to preferred doneness.

French Toast Plating

When it is served, French toast is cut in half diagonally, and the halves are arranged attractively on a plate. French toast may be served with hot or cold syrup, fruit toppings, jam or preserves, powdered sugar, or a combination of these items. French toast may also be served with a side order of breakfast meat or with eggs.

Pretty Presentation Create an artful presentation for French toast with fresh berries. *What other ways can you creatively plate French toast?*

PHOTO CAPTION ANSWER Answers will vary, but may include sliced fruit, whipped cream, nuts over the toast, and serving it with different flavored syrups.

 Cereal Toppings An assortment of cereal toppings add visual interest and flavor to cereal. *What do you think are customers' favorites?*

Potatoes

Potatoes are a common accompaniment to all types of breakfast foods. Potatoes can be grilled or pan-fried, often with onions, bell pepper, and other vegetables. American fries are baked or fried. Cottage fries are either baked or broiled. Hash browns are made from boiled potatoes that are shredded or chopped fine, and then sautéed.

Hot and Cold Cereals

Cereals are a popular choice for many people who want a hearty, nutritious breakfast. Cereals come in many varieties, and can be served hot or cold. Cereals can be presented alone, or as an accompaniment.

Hot Cereal Preparation

Hot cereals are another popular breakfast choice. Whole, cracked, or flaked grains are the cereals that are most often served hot. To make hot cereal, follow the directions for each type of grain carefully.

PHOTO CAPTION ANSWER Answers will vary based on students' perceptions of customer likes and dislikes, but may include fresh and dried fruits, nuts, white or brown sugar, milk or cream, and honey.

Follow these steps to cook hot cereals:

1. Measure water in a pot and bring it to a boil. Milk or cream can be used instead of water. This will make the cereal creamier, but it is much more expensive.

2. Add a measured amount of cereal carefully, stirring it constantly.

3. As soon as the cereal thickens, stop stirring. If you continue to stir, the cereal will become gummy.

4. Cover the pot, reduce the heat, and cook the cereal until done.

5. Keep the cereal covered until ready to serve.

⌇ Small Bites ⌇

Prevent Lumpy Cereal To prevent lumps in hot cereals, add a small amount of cold water to the cereal before adding the cereal to boiling water. This keeps the grains separate. Be sure to factor in the amount of cold water to the total amount of water added during the cooking process.

Hot Cereal Plating

Hot cereals are served in a bowl that is usually placed on top of a plate. Many people like to add accompaniments to their cereal. Milk, half-and-half (half milk and half cream), or cream may be served along with small ramekins of raisins, nuts, or fruit slices. Toast, English muffins, or a quick bread may also be served with hot cereals.

Cold Cereal Preparation

Cold cereals require no preparation. They are served with milk or cream, fruit, nuts, or sugar. Some restaurants offer customers a wide variety of individual servings of boxed cold cereals. The customer gets to choose which cereal he or she wants to eat. Other restaurants may offer granola along with accompaniments, such as fruits, nuts, and yogurt. Granola can be purchased ready-made, or can be made at a restaurant. Granola may also be served already mixed with yogurt and fruit in a tall glass. Sometimes granola is served warm, with milk and brown sugar.

Cold Cereal Plating

Although cold cereals are thought of as a breakfast eaten at home, they are often served in restaurants as well. Cold cereals are served with milk, half-and-half, or cream, and are presented with sliced fruit such as bananas or berries. Milk is usually served in a small pitcher so that customers can add it themselves. Cold cereals are often accompanied by toast, English muffins, or quick breads. Usually, however, cold cereals are not served with eggs or breakfast meats.

 **Reading Check** Describe How are hot cereals plated?

 SECTION 17.2 **After You Read**

Review Key Concepts

1. **List** the different types of quick breads.
2. **Describe** the different types of cereals.

Practice Culinary Academics

 English Language Arts

3. Choose one type of quick bread and write a one-page essay about how to bake that type of quick bread. Create an outline, and write a rough draft before finalizing your essay. Explain the general procedure, tips and tricks, and any potential problems.

> **NCTE 12** Use language to accomplish individual purposes.

 Social Studies

4. Doughnuts are made by frying rings or balls of dough. Conduct research to find fried bread products from other cultures. Research their taste and their origins. Discuss your findings with the class. Also, discuss whether or not the items you found would make a good breakfast item in the United States.

> **NCSS IX A Global Connections** Explain how cultural elements can facilitate global understanding.

 Mathematics

5. Your cafe serves regular pancakes that are 8 inches in diameter, and silver dollar pancakes that are 2 ½ inches in diameter. You need to know how many pancakes should be served on a plate. This means you will need to know the area of each type of pancake. What is the area covered by each type of pancake, to the nearest square inch?

Math Concept **Calculating the Area of a Circle**
Calculate the area (A) of a circle as $A = \pi r^2$, where r indicates the radius (or ½ of the diameter) of the circle. Use 3.14 for π.

Starting Hint Multiply the diameter of each type of pancake by ½ to find the radius of each type of pancake. Plug those values into the area formula given above for r, and solve the formula for A. Round your results to eliminate the decimals.

> **NCTM Measurement** Apply appropriate techniques, tools, and formulas to determine measurements.

 Check your answers at this book's Online Learning Center at **glencoe.com**.

Review and Applications

Chapter Summary

Eggs are a basic ingredient in many breakfast dishes. Grading eggs allows foodservice operations to choose the right eggs for their needs. Types of cooked eggs include fried, poached, scrambled, omelet, shirred, and simmered. Meats such as bacon, ham, and sausage are common at breakfast.

Quick bread choices include muffins, biscuits, loaf breads, and scones. Pancakes, and waffles are also considered quick breads. French toast, although technically not a quick bread, is a popular breakfast item. Hot and cold cereals are also served at breakfast with a variety of sides.

Content and Academic Vocabulary Review

1. Use these vocabulary terms to create a crossword puzzle on graph paper. Use the definitions as clues.

Content Vocabulary

- breakfast meats (p. 432)
- bacon (p. 432)
- Canadian bacon (p. 432)
- sausage (p. 432)
- hash (p. 432)
- albumin (p. 433)
- porous (p. 433)
- egg substitutes (p. 434)
- pasteurized (p. 434)
- soufflé (p. 434)
- dehydrated (p. 434)
- curdle (p. 437)

- omelet (p. 437)
- season (p. 438)
- frittata (p. 439)
- quiche (p. 439)
- shirred (p. 440)
- ramekin (p. 440)
- home fries (p. 443)
- hash browns (p. 443)
- cottage fries (p. 443)
- ready-made bread (p. 443)
- granola (p. 444)
- pastries (p. 444)
- doughnut (p. 445)

- quick breads (p. 445)
- muffin (p. 445)
- biscuit (p. 445)
- scone (p. 445)
- English muffin (p. 446)
- fold (p. 446)
- side order (p. 446)
- French toast (p. 448)

Academic Vocabulary

- designate (p. 433)
- alternative (p. 435)
- mainstay (p. 443)
- function (p. 445)

Review Key Concepts

2. Give examples of common breakfast protein choices and their characteristics.

3. Explain how to prepare breakfast meats.

4. Describe at least five ways to cook eggs.

5. List the food items commonly served in quick-service breakfasts.

6. Categorize the different types of breakfast quick breads and cereals.

Critical Thinking

7. Analyze a typical breakfast for nutrition. What suggestions can you make for low-calorie, low-cholesterol, or low-fat alternatives?

8. Explain why you think that milk or cream is sometimes added to the preparation of scrambled eggs.

9. Imagine that you work at a restaurant and find that whole eggs have been left out on the prep station overnight. What would you do with the eggs, and why?

10. Examine the differences between cooked and uncooked ham. Why do you think ham is often purchased pre-cooked by restaurants?

Academic Skills

English Language Arts

11. Healthful Breakfasts Review the information in this chapter, and then review MyPyramid recommendations from Chapter 11. Using these recommendations and your knowledge of breakfast foods, create three healthful breakfast menus. Describe the ingredients and portion sizes for each dish, and explain how they fit into MyPyramid recommendations. Remember that breakfast is only one of three meals in the day.

> **NCTE 8** Use information resources to gather information and create and communicate knowledge.

Social Studies

12. Global Breakfast Create a list of common breakfast foods. Do you know where the ingredients in your list came from? Are there any ingredients that might have come from another country? Research the origins of different breakfast foods, and discuss as a class why some of the foods we eat come from different countries.

> **NCSS VII I Production, Distribution, and Consumption**
> Distinguish between the domestic and global economic systems, and explain how the two interact.

Mathematics

13. Make Bacon Leilani has purchased another slab of applewood-smoked bacon for her restaurant. This one is 8 inches long and cost her $40. At Leilani's restaurant, bacon is served as a breakfast side dish for $5, with four strips of bacon per order. She would like to make a 50% profit margin on this bacon. How thick should she cut each piece?

Math Concept **Profit Margin** The term profit margin indicates the percentage of the price that is profit. Subtract the profit margin from 100% to find the cost percentage. Calculate price by dividing total cost by the cost percentage.

Starting Hint If Leilani will make a 50% profit margin on the slab of bacon, she must also have a 100% − 50% = 50% cost percentage. Thus, Leilani needs to charge a total of $40 ÷ 50% = $80 for the entire slab. How many orders must she sell to collect $80? How many total slices of bacon are in those orders? Divide 8 inches by that total number of slices to find the per-slice thickness. (You may want to write this as a fraction, and simplify.)

> **NCTM Problem Solving** Apply and adapt a variety of appropriate strategies to solve problems.

Certification Prep

Sharpen your test-taking skills to improve your kitchen certification program score.

Directions Read the questions. Then, read the answer choices and choose the best possible answer for each.

14. Which part of the egg contains more than half of the protein?

    a. shell

    b. yolk

    c. white

    d. chicken

15. What grade eggs should you use for fried eggs?

    a. Grade AA

    b. Grade A

    c. Grade BB

    d. Grade B

Test-Taking Tip

If allowed, jot down on a scrap paper important facts that you want to remember. This way, you will not worry about forgetting them during the test.

Real-World Skills and Applications

Self-Management Skills

16. **Manage Resources** Imagine that you are a breakfast chef in a restaurant. The manager has informed you that costs need to be cut. What kind of trade-offs might you make to cut costs? Why is knowing how to make trade-offs important in good restaurant management? Write a one-page summary of your thoughts on cutting costs, along with examples of how restaurants might cut costs for breakfast menus. Discuss your ideas as a class.

Collaborative and Interpersonal Skills

17. **Plan and Make a Breakfast** As a class, plan and make a breakfast for the school maintenance workers or another group that must arrive early to the school. Work together to plan the menu, the quantities needed, and assigned tasks. Then, schedule a time with the group you will serve, and prepare the breakfast.

Technology Applications

18. **Menu Costs** Use a calculator to plan a breakfast menu for one of three levels of restaurant: a coffee house, a low-cost diner, or an upscale restaurant. Determine a five-item breakfast menu first. Then, make a list of each ingredient needed. Research ingredient costs and determine the item cost and the cost of the menu. Write up the menu and turn in your pricing notes to your teacher.

Financial Literacy

19. **Calculate Breakfast Cost** Imagine that your school offers a breakfast program where you can get breakfast in the cafeteria for $2. If you make your own breakfast instead of buying breakfast every day, the average cost is $1.10. How much money would you save during the five-day school week if you made your own breakfast each day?

Culinary Lab

Prepare an Omelet

> *Use the culinary skills you have learned in this chapter.*

20. **Work in Groups** For this lab, you will work in groups as directed by your teacher to create an American omelet. Then, you will plate the omelet, taste it, and evaluate your work.

  A. **Choose an omelet.** As a group, determine what kind of fillings will go in your omelet. Also, determine what kind of bread choices will be served with the omelet.

  B. **List pre-preparation tasks.** Determine whether you have any meat ingredients that will need to be cooked ahead of time, vegetables that will need to be diced, or cheese that will need to be grated. Prepare a list of these tasks.

  C. **Prepare your omelet.** Divide your task list among team members, and cook the omelet according to the method chosen. Add ingredients when appropriate. Once the omelet is finished, plate it along with the bread choice.

  D. **Evaluate omelets.** Each team should taste its own omelet and the other teams' omelets. Rate each omelet according to this scale: 1 = Poor; 2 = Fair; 3 = Good; 4 = Great.

Create Your Evaluation

On a separate piece of paper answer the following questions:

● How did the pre-preparation contribute to the omelet's preparation?

● Is there anything you would do differently next time? Why or why not?

Include the grades and comments from each team's omelet in your evaluation.

CHAPTER 18

Garde Manger Basics

SECTIONS

18.1 What Is Garde Manger?

18.2 Salads and Salad Dressings

18.3 Cheese

18.4 Cold Platters

WRITING ACTIVITY

Revise Your Draft

The first draft of an essay usually needs improvements. Examine the first draft you wrote for Chapter 17 and revise it for spelling and grammar. Add details you may have forgotten.

Writing Tips

1 Clarify your sentences.

2 Ask a friend to look for errors.

3 Review your paper a final time.

EXPLORE THE PHOTO

The garde manger chef plans, prepares, and plates cold foods. *What foods might a garde manger chef prepare?*

WRITING ACTIVITY ANSWER Papers should be grammatically correct and show improvement.

EXPLORE THE PHOTO ANSWER
Hors d'oeuvres, salads, canapés, fancy sandwiches, cold food trays, and garnishes.

What Is Garde Manger?

The garde manger chef is a vital part of the kitchen brigade.

Reading Guide

 Before You Read

Get Your Rest The more well rested and alert you are when you sit down to study, the more likely you will be to remember the information later. Studying in the same state of mind as when you are likely to take a test (fully rested and mentally sharp) will help to ensure your best performance.

Read to Learn

Key Concepts
- **Identify** the duties of the garde manger work station.

Main Idea
The garde manger chef is responsible for preparing cold foods, such as salads, salad dressings, cold hors d'oeuvres, fancy sandwiches, canapés, and cold platters.

Content Vocabulary
- canapé
- forcemeat
- dry cure
- wet cure
- garde manger brigade
- charcuterie
- quenelle
- score
- tournée

Academic Vocabulary
- artistic
- appropriate

Graphic Organizer
In this section, you will learn about different garnishing tools. Use a chart like this one to match the nine garnishing tools with the ingredients for which they are suited.

Garnishing Tool	Ingredients

Graphic Organizer Go to this book's Online Learning Center at **glencoe.com** for a printable graphic organizer.

GRAPHIC ORGANIZER ANSWER 1) Vegetable peeler: Vegetables, chocolate. 2) Butter curler: Butter. 3) Zester: Citrus, vegetables. 4) Melon baller: Cheese, potatoes, butter, melons. 5) Tournée knife: Vegetables. 6) Channel knife: Citrus, carrots, cucumbers. 7) Decorating spatula: Cream cheese, butter, frosting. 8) Paring knife: Fruits, vegetables. 9) Fluting knife: Any ingredient requiring detail work.

ACADEMIC STANDARDS

 English Language Arts
NCTE 12 Use language to accomplish individual purposes.

 Mathematics
NCTM Measurement Apply appropriate techniques, tools, and formulas to determine measurements.

 Science
NSES F Develop an understanding of science and technology in local, national, and global challenges.

 Social Studies
NCSS II D Time, Continuity, and Change Systematically employ processes of critical historical inquiry to reconstruct and reinterpret the past, such as using a variety of sources and checking their credibility.

NCTE National Council of Teachers of English

NCTM National Council of Teachers of Mathematics

NSES National Science Education Standards

NCSS National Council for the Social Studies

Garde Manger Basics

The garde manger chef, also known as the pantry chef, is the person who plans, prepares, and presents **artistic**, or creative, cold foods. These foods include salads and salad dressings, cold hors d'oeuvres, fancy sandwiches, canapés (ˈka-nə-ˌpās), and cold platters. A **canapé** is an appetizer that is served on a small piece of bread or toast.

The garde manger chef plans dishes using many fresh ingredients, including vegetables, fruits, prepared meats, fish, seafood, breads, and cheeses. Simple ingredients are used to create and artistically present hors d'oeuvres, salads, canapés, fancy sandwiches, garnishes for all types of dishes, and fruit, cheese, meat, relish, and combination trays. In addition, he or she may also prepare cold sauces, some hot hors d'oeuvres and hot appetizers, and artistic garnishes and ice sculptures.

Garde manger chefs also make forcemeats as part of their work. **Forcemeat** is a mixture of ground, raw meat or seafood that is emulsified with fat. The mixture can be ground fine or coarse. Forcemeats are used in many different items from charcuterie, such as sausages and pâtés. Pork fatback is often used as the fat for a forcemeat because it has a neutral flavor that will not interfere with other flavorings or seasonings.

There are four main types of forcemeats that are made at a garde manger workstation:

- **Straight forcemeats** usually have equal parts of pork, pork fat and another type of meat. The meats are cubed and then seasoned or cured, and ground.
- **Country-style forcemeats** are coarse in texture. They contain a combination of pork, pork fat, and liver and garnish ingredients.
- **Gratin forcemeats** have the main ingredient sautéed before being ground. The French word gratin means browned.
- **Mousseline forcemeats** have a light texture. Cream is added to light meats such as veal, poultry, fish, or shellfish.

Cured meats are also a specialty of the garde manger. Cured meat has a different flavor and texture from cooked meat, and is an interesting addition to many foods.

◀ **Hors d'Oeuvres Variety** The garde manger brigade is in charge of making cold hors d'oeuvres. *What occasions might call for an hors d'oeuvres tray like this one?*

PHOTO CAPTION ANSWER Cold hors d'oeuvres might be served at banquets, buffets, or special occasions.

There are two ways to cure foods. In a **dry cure**, the food is coated in salt, sweeteners, and flavorings, and then wrapped in paper or cheesecloth. Once it is cured, the meat is washed to remove the coating. Then, it is cooked, smoked, dried, or aged. Prosciutto, an Italian ham, is made by dry curing with salt. A **wet cure** is also called a brine. Food is submerged in a mixture of sea salt, some form of sweetener, spices, and herbs that are dissolved in water. Once it is cured, it is removed from the brine and rinsed. Then, the food is dried, smoked, aged, or cooked. Bacon, tongue, brisket, corned beef, and pastrami are all wet-cured meats.

Some large restaurants or hotels may ask the garde manger chef to create table arrangements and edible centerpieces for buffets. These centerpieces may be made from materials such as ice, cheese, butter, fruit, or salt dough.

The garde manger chef manages the garde-manger department in restaurants, large hotels, and many catering operations. He or she manages a team of people called a **garde manger brigade**. Each member of the garde manger brigade specializes in a particular type of cold food preparation. Although it is called a brigade, the garde manger brigade has a much looser structure than the traditional kitchen brigade. Some of the kitchen brigade positions that are under the management of the garde manger chef include:

- The Boucher, who butchers all meats and poultry.
- The Poissonnier, who cleans, prepares, and stores fish and shellfish.
- The Buffetier (bə-fe-'tyēr), who maintains the buffet.
- The Hors d'Oeuvrier, who makes all hors d'oeuvres.
- The Charcutier, who makes sausage and smoked items, such as meats, cheeses, and nuts.
- The Commis, an apprentice of the garde manger chef.

In planning this kind of food, the garde manger brigade considers:

- The cost of ingredients and the time required to prepare dishes.
- The use of many different food items so that the menu is interesting.

- The use of different colors and textures throughout the meal.
- The appeal of the food and the ability of the brigade.

Garde Manger History

The term garde manger means keeping to eat. Wealthy families in France in the 1700s had a household steward who would keep foods in the family's cold store room. This person was very important because much of the food kept in the cold room was butchered, pickled, salted, cured, or smoked during the fall season and stored for months. The steward had to keep the food safe and portion it out to last for the winter season.

During the Middle Ages, many of the food preparation techniques that were done by the garde manger chefs were performed and taught by guilds. **Charcutèrie** was the name of a guild that prepared and sold cooked items made from pigs. When the guild system was abolished during the French Revolution, garde manger chefs performed the tasks of the charcutières and went to work in restaurants.

Butchers originally worked under the garde manger station. But as the need for cuts of meat increased, more space was needed for butchering. Eventually, the butcher worked out of a separate butchery shop.

The work of the garde manger chef requires a high level of skill and artistry. However, in some modern restaurants, the term garde manger is used to identify the salad station, and the position is often filled by an entry-level cook.

Garde Manger Equipment

The garde manger chef uses many different tools to do his or her job. This means that the garde manger chef needs a well-planned and well-equipped work area. Usually, the garde manger work station will include:

- Walk-in and reach-in refrigerators and freezers.
- Several ranges to cook foods, such as roast beef and turkey, before they are served cold.
- A smoker.
- Ice-cube makers.
- A food slicer or mandoline.
- A food processor.

Garnish Making Garnishes can be made with everyday tools, as well as with specialized garnishing tools. *Can you guess how some of these garnishes were made by looking at the tools?*

PHOTO CAPTION ANSWER Shavings and strips were made with a peeler; shapes were made with different types of knives, and even scoops, to give texture to the surface of the carrot before cutting.

FIGURE 18.1 **Common Garnishes**

Vegetable Garnishes A variety of vegetables make up common garnishes to complement food. *Are all of these garnishes made by the garde manger brigade?*

Garnish	Pronunciation	Ingredients
Clamart	(kla-ˈmär)	Peas
Crécy	(krā-ˈsē)	Carrots
Doria	(ˈdȯ-rē-ä)	Cucumbers cooked in butter
Dubarry	(ˌdü-bə-ˈrē)	Cauliflower
Fermière	(fer-ˈmyer)	Carrots, turnips, onions, and celery
Florentine	(ˈflȯr-ən-ˌtēn)	Spinach
Judie	(jü-ˈdē)	Braised lettuce
Lyonnaise	(ˌlī-ə-ˈnāz)	Onions
Niçoise	(nē-ˈswäz)	Tomatoes cooked with garlic and black olives
Parmentier	(ˌpär-mən-ˈtyā)	Potatoes
Princesse	(prän-ˈses)	Asparagus
Provençale	(ˌprō-ˌvän-ˈsäl)	Tomatoes, garlic, parsley, and mushrooms or olives
Vichy	(ˈvi-shē)	Carrots cooked and glazed
Bouquetière	(ˌbü-kə-ˈtyēr)	Bouquet of vegetables
Jardinière	(ˌjär-də-ˈnyēr)	Garden vegetables
Primeurs	(pre-ˈmyür)	First spring vegetables
Printanière	(ˌprin-tə-ˈnyēr)	Spring vegetables

• Individual molds, pastry bags, a garnishing set that includes a variety of garnishing knives, offset spatulas, an egg wedger and slicer, and large cutters

Because the garde manger brigade will prepare a wide variety of foods, it is important that the garde manger work station be kept clean and well organized at all times.

Garnish Preparation

Many garnishes are created in the garde manger work station. The word garnish comes from the French word garnir, meaning to decorate or furnish. In the culinary world, it means to use food as an attractive decoration.

It is something that should add real value to the dish by increasing its nutritional value and visual appeal. A simple garnish, such as an asparagus tip or a wedge of fruit, can be used to add eye appeal in the form of color and balance.

Although many garnishes are made by the garde manger chef, some are not. Hot garnishes are made by chefs at other work stations and transferred to the plate. However, garnishing is still a traditional garde manger duty.

A garnish should complement the flavors and textures of the meal. Mushrooms, cucumbers, scallions, pickles, radishes, and lemons are good examples of garnishes. A **quenelle** (kə-nel), or a purée of chopped food formed into shapes, can also be used. (See **Figure 18.1**.)

FIGURE CAPTION ANSWER No, some garnishes are made by hot station chefs.

Garnishing Tools

Vegetable Peeler Although this tool is used mainly to shave the skin from fruits and vegetables, it is also an important garnishing tool. Use it to make decorative carrot curls and chocolate curls.

Butter Curler This tool has a curved, hook-like blade that can be used to make curls to grooves to marble-size balls. For best results, use ice-cold butter and a butter curler with a blade that has been warmed in hot water.

Zester To add eye appeal and flavor to your dish, use the zester to remove small strips of the colored part of citrus peels. You can also use this tool to shave pieces from colorful vegetables, such as carrots and radishes.

Decorating Spatula This spatula has a flat blade that is used to create attractive designs on soft foods, such as cream cheese, butter, and frosting.

Paring Knife The paring knife has a sharp, V-shaped blade. You can use this tool to carve fruits and vegetables.

Channel Knife This odd-shaped knife can be used to pare strips of peel from citrus fruits and thin grooves from carrots and cucumbers.

Melon Baller A melon baller or a Parisienne (pə-ˌrē-zē-ˈen) scoop can be used to scoop out balls of cheese, potatoes, butter, and melons.

Tournée Knife You can use this small knife with a curved blade to make tournéed vegetables that have an oblong shape with seven equal sides and blunt ends.

Fluting Knife Because this knife is small and very sharp, you can use it to do detail work that requires a lot of control. A fluting knife has a triangular blade that is about 2 inches long.

Having the **appropriate**, or correct, tools will allow you to create all sorts of garnishes. You can make some garnishes with everyday tools, such as forks, spoons, and paring knives. For example, use a fork to **score**, or make ridges in a diamond-shaped pattern, on pies and meats. Or use a tournée knife to **tournée** (tōr-ˈnə), or turn, vegetables. You can make quenelles by using two spoons to shape a purée. Fruits and vegetables can be cut into decorative shapes with a paring knife.

There are many tools that are commonly found at the garde manger station. These tools include:

- Vegetable peelers
- Butter curlers
- Zesters
- Melon ballers
- Tournée knives
- Fluting knives
- Decorating spatulas
- Paring knives
- Channel knives

Garde manger chefs may also be creative in their tool choices. Some garde manger chefs may use cookie cutters to create interesting garnishes, or graters to create new textures in food. Using unusual tools can create garnishes with a special appeal.

 **Define** What is a garnish?

SECTION 18.1 After You Read

Review Key Concepts

1. **Identify** the factors the garde manger chef considers when planning dishes.

Practice Culinary Academics

 Science

2. **Procedure** Garde manger chefs often work with preserved foods. Take apples, potatoes, or carrots, and slice them as thin as possible. Arrange them on a rack and quickly place them in a freezer. Keep them there for a week, observing the slices each day.

   Analysis Research freeze-drying during the week. Predict what will happen to the food. Write a paragraph of your prediction. Include your observations, and turn in the paragraph to your teacher.

   NSES F Develop an understanding of science and technology in local, national, and global challenges.

English Language Arts

3. Create a chart that names, describes, and illustrates the types of garnishes that a garde manger chef might prepare. Include pictures or drawings of each item as well as a short description next to its name.

   NCTE 12 Use language to accomplish individual purposes.

 Social Studies

4. Research the title of garde manger chef. What does the title mean? What are its origins? What was the task of the earliest garde manger chefs? Write a two-page report, and include your sources.

   NCSS II D Time, Continuity, and Change Systematically employ processes of critical historical inquiry to reconstruct and reinterpret the past, such as using a variety of sources and checking their credibility.

 Mathematics

5. At the garde manger station, Clancy uses a ¾-inch melon baller to form butter into spheres. If each table receives a plate with 4 butter spheres, how many tablespoons of butter does each table receive?

   Math Concept **Spherical Volume** The volume (V) of a sphere (or ball) is calculated using the formula $V = 4/3\ \pi r^3$, where r is the radius of the sphere. Use 3.14 for π.

   Starting Hint Multiply the width of the melon baller by ½ to find the radius (r), and plug that number into the volume formula. Multiply by 4 (since there are 4 spheres), and multiply again by 1.1 to convert to tablespoons.

   NCTM Measurement Apply appropriate techniques, tools, and formulas to determine measurements.

 Check your answers at this book's Online Learning Center at **glencoe.com**.

Salads and Salad Dressings

Reading Guide

 Before You Read

Stay Engaged One way to stay engaged when reading is to turn each of the headings into a question, then read the section to find the answers. For example, "Edible Flowers" might be, "Which edible flowers are used in salads?"

Read to Learn
Key Concepts
- **List** the main types of salads served during a meal.
- **Outline** the preparation techniques for salad greens.
- **Describe** the different types of salad dressings.

Main Idea
A salad is a mixture of ingredients with a dressing. In addition to greens and vegetables, salads can be made with meat, cheese, pasta, fruit, nuts, and grains.

Graphic Organizer
As you read, use a tree diagram like this one to list the four different types of salad dressings.

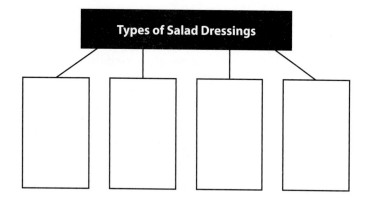

Graphic Organizer Go to this book's Online Learning Center at **glencoe.com** for a printable graphic organizer.

GRAPHIC ORGANIZER ANSWER Vinaigrette, fatty dressing, cooked dressing, and fruit dressing.

Content Vocabulary
- salad
- croutons
- spinach
- kale
- radicchio
- mesclun
- dressing
- vinaigrette
- scorch

Academic Vocabulary
- elaborate
- subtle

Salads are a popular side dish and entrée.

ACADEMIC STANDARDS

 Mathematics
NCTM Number and Operations Understand numbers, ways of representing numbers, relationships among numbers, and number systems.

 Science
NSES B Develop an understanding of the structure and properties of matter.

 Social Studies
NCSS III H People, Places and Environments Examine, interpret, and analyze physical and cultural patterns and their interactions.

NCTE National Council of Teachers of English

NCTM National Council of Teachers of Mathematics

NSES National Science Education Standards

NCSS National Council for the Social Studies

Types of Salads

What do you think of when you hear the word salad? Do you think of a bowl of lettuce with a few carrots and tomatoes mixed in? These ingredients may make up a common salad, but they are just the beginning. A **salad** is a mixture of one or several ingredients with a dressing. Vegetables, leafy greens, meat, fish, cheese, pasta, fruits, nuts, and grains can all be used in salads.

There are five main types of salads: appetizer salads, accompaniment salads, main-course salads, separate-course salads, and dessert salads. Each is served at a different time during the meal. Usually, however, only one salad will be served with a meal.

- **Appetizer Salads** An attractively arranged salad served before the main course is designed to sharpen the appetite. Depending on the meal and setting, it might be quite simple, such as a salad of all greens, a garnish, and a vinaigrette (ˌvi-ni-ˈgret) dressing. It might also be a more **elaborate**, or detailed, salad with poultry, fish, beans, or seafood as the main ingredient. Some restaurants charge extra for an appetizer salad, while others include it in the meal price.

- **Accompaniment Salads** An accompaniment salad is one that is served with, and complements, the main dish. If the main course is light, the accompaniment salad might be a heavier pasta, bean, or potato salad. If the main dish is heavy, a lighter tossed green salad is appropriate. The accompaniment salad should not include food items served with the main course.

- **Main-Course Salads** A main-course salad replaces the regular main course. This salad should function as a balanced meal, with a variety of vegetables and a protein serving, such as fish, chicken, beans, or a chicken or egg salad. Fruit can also be included. All ingredients should be attractively arranged.

- **Separate-Course Salads** A light salad served after the main course to refresh the appetite, a separate-course salad is served before dessert. This type of salad should be simple. For example, it may be a small portion of mixed greens with a light vinaigrette dressing, or a small salad of fresh citrus fruits or asparagus.

- **Dessert Salads** A dessert salad is made from fruits, nuts, or a combination of similar ingredients. These can be served with a sweetened dressing, or cooked and set into a gelatin mold. Sweetened dressings often have a whipped cream as their base.

Salad Structure and Arrangement

Salads can be served before, during, or after the main course. This means that salad-making can be a challenging, creative task. Salads must go well with the overall menu that has been planned, both in flavor and in ingredients used. To plan and prepare appealing salads that go with an overall menu, follow these guidelines:

- Combine colors, textures, and flavors that look and taste good together. Adding a garnish can add texture. **Croutons** (ˈkrü-tänz), or small pieces of bread that have been grilled, toasted, or fried and sometimes seasoned, are a popular garnish.

- Do not repeat ingredients in salads that appear in other dishes. For example, if chicken is the main dish, do not plan chicken salad as an appetizer.

- Match the type of dressing used with the salad ingredients. Select salad ingredients that complement the rest of the meal. For example, if the main course is heavy, you might end the meal with a light salad of seasonal fruit.

Reading Check Explain When is a separate-course salad served?

READING CHECK ANSWER A separate course salad is served after the main course.

Green Salads

Green salads use fresh greens as their base. These salads can be served as an appetizer, or as a main course. Green salads can include many different kinds of ingredients, from vegetables to meat. Chefs often add fresh herbs, nuts, or even edible flower petals. You can make a salad mild or spicy by using different leafy greens. When you mix different greens, you can make salads with interesting, unusual flavors and textures. Three main types of greens and leafy vegetables are used in tossed salads: traditional greens, flavor-adding greens, and herbs and other specialty items.

Traditional Greens

Greens are the traditional main ingredient in tossed salads. Because they have a mild flavor, they can be used by themselves or combined with other, more flavorful greens. The romaine and butterhead lettuces add flavor and texture. Iceberg lettuce has less flavor, but it stays crisp longer than other greens.

There are many different types of traditional greens that can be used:

- **Baby** lettuce consists of many types of lettuces, including baby green bibb, red sails, and baby red oak, that have a delicate flavor. They have wrinkled or wavy leaves.
- **Butterhead** lettuce has a soft texture. Its leaves form a loose rosette shape. It has a buttery, mild flavor.

- **Iceberg** lettuce has dense leaves that are a pale green color. Iceberg lettuce leaves stay crisp for a long time, but they are not as flavorful as other lettuce leaves.
- **Loose-Leaf** lettuce consists of red, green, and oak leaf lettuces. They have leaves that curl along the edges.
- **Mâche** has dark-green, delicate leaves that have a slightly nutty flavor.
- **Romaine** lettuce heads are not rounded. Instead, they form a cylinder shape. The leaves are ruffled and loosely packed.

Spinach is not a lettuce. This dark-green, leafy vegetable is full of calcium and adds color and flavor to salads. Try to select small, young leaves for a delicate, distinctive flavor and texture. Spinach must be thoroughly washed and have its stems removed before serving.

🅐 **Healthful Greens** Different salad greens not only add flavor, they can also add nutrition. *Why do you think darker greens add nutritional value to salads?*

Salad Greens Lettuce varieties add a wide range of textures and flavors to salads. *How does spinach differ from traditional salad greens?*

Flavor-Adding Greens

In recent years, many flavor-adding greens have been used in green salads. Some of these greens are spicy, some bitter, and some have a distinct yet delicate flavor. These greens include arugula (ə-ˈrü-gə-lə), mizuna (mi-ˈzü-nə), and chicory (ˈchi-k(ə-)rē). They are classified as greens, although they may be red, yellow, brown, or white. They add interesting new flavors, textures, and colors.

There are many different types of flavor-adding greens:

- **Arugula** has a spicy, peppery flavor. Arugula leaves look like dandelion leaves.
- **Curly Endive** leaves are curly and sharp, and have a bitter flavor. They are pale yellow-green or sometimes white in color.
- **Dandelion** leaves are long and narrow. Although we know dandelions as weeds that grow in a lawn, the leaves add a complex, bitter flavor to salads.
- **Endive** has short creamy white or pale yellow leaves. Endive leaves have a bitter flavor.
- **Escarole** leaves have a nutty, but bitter, flavor.

- **Frisée** leaves are very curly. They are also compact and delicate. They have a slightly bitter, but nutty, flavor.
- **Mizuna** leaves are long and spiky. Their flavor is slightly peppery.
- **Tat-Soi** leaves are spoon shaped and dark green. They add a spicy and sweet flavor to salads.
- **Radicchio** (ra-ˈdi-kē-ō) has bitter-tasting, crisp leaves. The leaves are compacted tightly together on the head.
- **Sorrel** leaves are small and green. Although they look like spinach leaves, they have a slightly lemony taste.
- **Watercress** leaves grow in running streams. The leaves are small and green, with a slightly bitter, peppery flavor.

As salads have become popular dishes for people wanting healthful foods, many other types of greens are being added to salads. Other greens that are more familiar as cooked vegetables are also being added to salads as raw leafy greens to give more flavor. These greens include kale, a cabbage with curly green or multicolored leaves, and Chinese cabbage.

PHOTO CAPTION ANSWER Spinach, a leafy green vegetable, is not a lettuce, and is full of calcium.

Herbs and Other Specialty Items

Sprigs of fresh herbs, such as oregano and basil, can be included in green salads to add flavor and complement other dishes. Parsley, dill, mint, sage, chives, and cilantro all make flavorful additions. Only a small amount of an herb is needed. Too much of any herb will overpower the other flavors and ruin the salad. Herbs should be as fresh as possible, since they will be eaten raw. Leaves can be either torn or chopped.

Science à la Carte

Emulsions

An emulsion is a mixture of two liquids that typically do not blend with each other. In food, an emulsion is a liquid fat and a water-based liquid that are held together. Vinaigrette, which is made from oil and vinegar, is an example of a short-lived emulsion. When first shaken together, they will emulsify. However, after a short time surface tension will make the oil pull away from the vinegar. This separates the two ingredients.

An emulsifier helps liquids, such as vinegar and oil, combine uniformly and remain combined without separating. Egg yolk is a natural emulsifier.

Procedure

For this experiment, you will need ⅓ cup vinegar; ⅔ cup cooking oil; 1 pasteurized egg yolk; and a small bowl or bottle with a lid. Record your findings at each step.

- Place the vinegar and oil into the bowl. Place the lid on the bowl and shake it for 10 seconds. Let the bowl sit for 10 minutes.
- Add the pasteurized egg yolk to the bowl. Replace the lid and shake the bowl again. Let the mixture sit for a few minutes.

Analysis

Review your recorded observations at each step of the procedure. Make a table with two columns. In the left column, record the action you took. In the right column, describe the appearance of the mixture, and whether it was a short-lived emulsion or a permanent emulsion.

NSES B Develop an understanding of the structure and properties of matter.

Small Bites

Using Edible Flowers When you add flower petals to a salad, be sure to clean them well. Dirt and insects can hide deep down in the petals and slip unnoticed into the salad.

There are two specialty items to consider when you make tossed salads. **Radicchio** is a cabbagelike plant with a slightly bitter, red leaf. In small quantities, radicchio adds color and flavor to fresh salads. **Mesclun** ('mes-klən) is a popular mix of baby leaves of lettuces and other more flavorful greens, such as arugula. The benefits of using mesclun are its tender texture and **subtle**, or understated, flavors.

Edible Flowers

It should not come as a surprise that some flowers are tailor-made for salads. They add unusual flavors, dashes of bright color, and interesting textures. Edible flowers should be purchased from a grower that does not use pesticides.

Nasturtiums (nə-'stər-shəmz), with their tangy blossoms, are one of the more popular floral additions. Pansy, primrose, rose, and violet petals are also popular. Flowering herbs, such as oregano, rosemary, chives, and thyme, can be used as well.

Green Salad Preparation Techniques

Selecting good, healthful greens for salads can make the difference between a flavorful salad with a lot of texture, and a limp, taste-less dish. Here are some things to keep in mind when you work with salad greens.

Choose Quality Greens

Whenever possible, purchase salad greens daily, and select ones that appear fresh and undamaged. Slightly wilted greens can be revived if they are submerged in ice water for

Build
a Salad

1 Build the foundation, or base, of the salad. This is the part upon which the rest of the salad is built. The foundation may be a bed of lettuce leaves or another type of vegetable or fruit.

2 Add the body of the salad, which features the salad's main ingredients. These ingredients might include lettuce, vegetables, pasta, meat, poultry, or fish. Some salads may have the body ingredients already mixed with a dressing.

3 Add the garnish. The salad garnish, like other garnishes, is a colorful element that adds eye appeal to the plate. Although a garnish such as an herb or a lemon wedge may be used, the garnish might also be hard-cooked egg wedges or black olives. Other common salad garnishes include fruit, cheese, and nuts.

4 If the salad requires a dressing to be added after composition, ladle the dressing over the salad.

30 to 60 minutes. Remove the greens from their packing cartons and wash them just before you prepare the salad.

Prepare Greens

Leafy greens, which grow close to the ground and easily pick up dirt, dust, insects, and sand, need to be thoroughly cleaned before preparation. To ensure proper cleaning of salad greens, separate the leaves and submerge them in cold water several times to rinse off all dirt and grit. Never clean greens under running water. You will bruise the greens. Change the water several times if

necessary. Lift the greens carefully out of the water. Do not drain the water from the bottom of the sink below the greens. Be sure to dry the leaves thoroughly with paper towels or use a salad spinner.

Once the greens have been well cleaned, cut or tear them into bite-size pieces. Many culinary experts believe greens are damaged less by tearing than by cutting. However, in a large foodservice setting, it may not be practical to tear all of the greens. Cutting is faster, and if done quickly with a well-sharpened blade, cutting will produce perfectly acceptable salad greens.

Make a
Vinaigrette Dressing

1 Combine the vinegar and herbs or spices in a bowl. Select an appropriate vinegar and add complementary herbs, spices, or mustard.

2 Slowly add the oil to the vinegar with a whisk. Blend well. Generally, the ratio of oil to vinegar is three to one.

3 If pasteurized eggs are added, whisk them thoroughly until the dressing is well-blended.

Store Greens

It is best to use up greens every day. Be sure to keep them in their original packaging. Store them three to four degrees above freezing and away from ripening fruits, such as tomatoes and apples.

Reading Check **Describe** What categories of leafy greens are used in tossed green salads?

Salad Dressings

A **dressing** is a sauce that is added to salads to give them flavor and to help hold the ingredients together. When you plan dressings, pick ones that go well with the flavors in the salad but do not overwhelm them. Check the greens to make sure they are dry.

Vinaigrette Dressings

Vinaigrette is a mixture of vinegar and oil. Most vinaigrette salad dressings have a ratio of three parts oil to one part vinegar. For interesting flavors, try different vinegars, such as balsamic or herbed, and different oils.

Olive oil and nut oils are especially flavorful. Also, you might add chopped fresh herbs if they complement the greens or other dishes in the menu. Pasteurized eggs can be added to any vinaigrette. When the eggs are well beaten with the other ingredients, the vinaigrette does not separate and clings well to the greens.

Make Vinaigrette Dressings

Vinaigrette dressings are easy to prepare. They should sit at room temperature for several hours before they are served. They also need to be stirred well right before use. Vinaigrette dressings made with pasteurized eggs should be kept refrigerated.

Fatty Dressings

Dressings made from mayonnaise or other dairy products can be used on green salads, fruit salads, and potato or pasta salads. Fatty dressings can also be used to bind together ingredients in chicken, tuna, and egg salad. As the name suggests, however, these fatty dressings have a high fat content and should be used in moderation. Some of the most common are creamy French, Thousand Island, Russian, ranch, bleu cheese, and creamy Italian.

READING CHECK ANSWER Traditional greens, flavor-adding greens, herbs, and other specialty items, such as edible flowers.

Make Fatty Dressings

Mayonnaise is often the key ingredient in a fatty dressing. Use these steps to make a fatty dressing:

1. Whisk together dairy products to make the base of the dressing. Mayonnaise and dairy products such as buttermilk provide a good dressing base.
2. Blend lemon juice into the creamy base.
3. Add herbs, spices, condiments, and chopped eggs or vegetables for variety.

Cooked Dressings

These dressings have a cooked ingredient as well as a thickening agent, such as cornstarch. Some cooked dressings use vinaigrette as a base. Others use little or no oil.

Make Cooked Dressings

Cooked dressings may be savory or sweet. Sweet cooked dressings may include fruit or fruit juice.

To prepare a cooked dressing:

1. Mix the sugar, starch, and flavorings in a stainless steel bowl.
2. Add the eggs as directed by the recipe and beat until smooth.
3. Place the milk or fruit juice in a saucepan and bring it to a simmer. Be careful not to scorch the milk. To **scorch** means to burn with too intense of a heat.
4. Gradually beat the milk or fruit juice into the egg mixture.
5. Cook the mixture until no starch flavor remains. Stir constantly.

Fruit Dressings

Fruit dressings may be sweet, tart, or spicy. They may be made with puréed fruit or fruit juice. They make an interesting accompaniment to green salads, and even with other fruits.

Reading Check Explain How are fatty dressings made?

 **SECTION 18.2**  **After You Read**

Review Key Concepts

1. **List** the components of a salad arrangement.
2. **Outline** how to store salad greens.
3. **Describe** fruit dressing.

Practice Culinary Academics

Social Studies

4. Rice vinegar is made from fermented rice or rice wine in China, Korea, and Japan. It comes in dark and light varieties. Find a recipe for a salad dressing that calls for rice vinegar. From where does the recipe originate? Write down the recipe and your research on its origins. As a class, discuss the recipes and their points of origin.

   NCSS III H People, Places, and Environments Examine, interpret, and analyze physical and cultural patterns and their interactions.

Mathematics

5. You observe that 40% of your first 50 customers ordered bleu cheese dressing, while 30% selected the vinaigrette and 30% selected the Thousand Island. If the next 10 customers choose the vinaigrette, what are the new percentages for each dressing?

   Math Concept **Finding the Percent of a Number** To find a percent of a given number, change the percent to a decimal by removing the percent sign and moving the decimal point two places to the left. Multiply this decimal by the number.

   Starting Hint Multiply each percent by 50 to determine the number of customers who ordered each dressing. Add 10 to the vinaigrette total, then divide each total by 60 to find the new percentages.

   NCTM Number and Operations Understand numbers, ways of representing numbers, relationships among numbers, and number systems.

 Check your answers at this book's Online Learning Center at **glencoe.com**.

READING CHECK ANSWER Fatty dressings are made by whisking together dairy products, then adding lemon juice and other ingredients.

Cheese

Reading Guide

 Before You Read

Two-Column Notes Two-column notes are a useful way to study and organize what you have read. Divide a piece of paper into two columns. In the left column, write down main ideas. In the right column, list supporting details.

Read to Learn

Key Concepts
- **Explain** how to identify and store cheeses.

Main Idea

There are many kinds of cheeses that each have their own unique flavor and texture. Cheese can be eaten as part of a main dish or on its own as part of a cheese plate.

Content Vocabulary
- cheddaring
- whey
- ripening
- veined cheese
- rind
- fresh cheese
- processed cheese
- emulsifier
- cold-pack cheese

Academic Vocabulary
- varied
- beneficial

Graphic Organizer

Before you read, use a KWL chart like this one to write down five things that you already know about cheese, and what you would like to learn about cheese. Use the last column to take notes about new information as you read.

Cheese

What I Know	What I Would Like to Know	What I Have Learned

 Graphic Organizer Go to this book's Online Learning Center at **glencoe.com** for a printable graphic organizer.

GRAPHIC ORGANIZER ANSWER This graphic organizer is to aid students in their note taking as they read, to organize new information that they learn, and to confirm information that they already know.

ACADEMIC STANDARDS

 English Language Arts
NCTE 4 Use written language to communicate effectively.

 Mathematics
NCTM Problem Solving Apply and adapt a variety of appropriate strategies to solve problems.

 Science
NSES A Develop abilities necessary to do scientific inquiry.

Social Studies
NCSS I B Culture Predict how data and experiences may be interpreted by people from diverse cultural perspectives and frames of reference.

NCSS I E Culture Demonstrate the value of cultural diversity, as well as cohesion, within and across groups

NCTE National Council of Teachers of English

NCTM National Council of Teachers of Mathematics

NSES National Science Education Standards

NCSS National Council for the Social Studies

Types of Cheese

Cheese is one of the most **varied**, or available in different kinds, of foods available today. There are hard cheeses, such as Cheddar and Colby (ˈkōl-bē) Jack, that can be sliced for sandwiches or grated and baked in hot dishes. There are soft cheeses that can be spread on bread and crackers. Crumbly cheeses taste great in salads. Cheese is also a popular addition to a cold platter tray or buffet platter.

Each type of cheese has its own distinct color, flavor and texture. Cheeses may be made from many different types of milk, such as cow's milk, goat's milk, and sheep's milk. Cheese is also nutritious, with plenty of protein and calcium.

Because there are so many different types of cheese, you can always find one that will go well with other foods that you serve. To select cheeses that will go well with the menu, it helps to be able to identify the different types of cheese.

Hard Cheeses

The hard cheeses include Cheddar and Colby. Some of these cheeses are made by a process called cheddaring. During **cheddaring**, slabs of cheese are stacked and turned. This process squeezes out the whey and gives the hard cheeses their special texture. **Whey** is the liquid portion of coagulated milk. Whey is also pressed out of the cheese during cheddaring.

Cheeses that have holes in them, including Gruyère (grü-ˈyer), Jarlsberg (ˈyärlz-bərg), and Swiss, are also hard cheeses. The holes in these cheeses come from healthful bacteria that grow inside the cheese. These bacteria release gases during the ripening process. Hard cheeses are excellent for cheese trays, fancy open-face sandwiches, or with fruits or desserts.

Ripening Cheese

The texture and flavor of most cheeses are affected by a process called ripening. During **ripening**, healthful bacteria and mold are at work in the cheese, changing its texture and flavor. As cheeses are ripened, they are stored in a temperature- and humidity-controlled environment. Ripening can occur from the surface of the cheese to the inside. Or, it can occur from the inside of the cheese outward.

Hard cheeses have been carefully ripened for a long time. The extra aging enhances their flavor and makes them dry and hard. Parmesan and Romano (rə-ˈmä-(ˌ)nō) are two other popular hard cheeses. Each has its own special flavor and is available in many market forms.

Hard Cheeses White Cheddar, Romano, and Swiss cheeses are hard cheeses. *How is Cheddar cheese made?*

PHOTO CAPTION ANSWER Cheddar cheese is made by cheddaring. This enhances its flavor and makes it dry and hard.

Try adding Parmesan, with its deep, spicy flavor, to pasta salads for a buffet luncheon. Romano and Asiago (ˌä-zhē-ˈä-(ˌ)gō) cheeses have a sharp flavor that goes well with many salads. Include small chunks in main-course salads to add flavor and to make them more filling. You can also sprinkle finely grated hard cheeses on one of the tossed green salads in a buffet line.

Firm Cheeses

Firm cheeses are not brittle, hard, or soft. Some are flaky and others are dense. Provolone (ˈprō-və-ˈlō-nē) is a firm cheese with a smooth texture and light ivory color. Provolone can have a very mild flavor, but aged versions can be quite sharp. Provolone is good on cold sandwiches as well as in cooked dishes, such as pizza and pasta.

When ripened for several months, Gouda (ˈgü-də), a Dutch cheese made from cow's milk, has a firm texture. It has a mild, nutty flavor that is popular for snacks and for dipping. Gouda is often sold in wheels of varying sizes that are covered with yellow or red wax. The wax is peeled off before the cheese is eaten.

Edam (ˈē-dəm) is another Dutch cheese made from cow's milk that is firm when aged. It is light yellow and has a slightly salty taste.

Semisoft Cheeses

Semisoft cheeses are smooth and easy to slice. They come in two types. One type is buttery cheeses that slice well. The other type includes softer, pungent cheeses. This type of semisoft cheese is often called a **veined cheese** because it has veins of mold running through it. The mold in these cheeses is put into the cheese during ripening. It is **beneficial**, or helpful, not harmful for people to eat. In fact, it is this mold that gives the cheese its unique flavor.

Buttery Semisoft Cheeses

The texture of the buttery semisoft cheeses comes from the way the rind is made. The **rind** is the outer surface of the cheese. These rinds vary in texture, color, and thickness. Cheeses such as Port du Salut (ˈpȯr-də-sə-ˈlü) and havarti (hə-ˈvär-tē) are sealed in wax before they are ripened. Other semisoft cheeses, including Bel Paese (ˌbel-pä-ˈā-ze), form their own rind as they ripen. All these cheeses are excellent for making canapés and serving on cheese trays. The king of pizza toppings, mozzarella cheese, is also a semisoft cheese.

Veined Semisoft Cheeses

The semisoft cheeses that have blue veins running through them have strong, distinctive flavors and aromas. Their intense flavor comes from the type of beneficial mold allowed to grow in each one. The aging process also affects the flavor. All of the veined semisoft cheeses are ripened in caves or in rooms that have the same moisture and temperature as caves.

▲ Firm Cheeses Provolone, Edam, and Gouda cheeses are examples of firm cheeses. *What are the differences between hard cheeses and firm cheeses?*

PHOTO CAPTION ANSWER Some hard cheeses are dry and hard throughout. Firm cheeses are neither brittle, hard, nor soft, but they can be flaky or dense.

Semisoft Cheeses Havarti, mozzarella, and Roquefort cheeses are semisoft cheeses.
Is mold in cheese harmful?

Gorgonzola (ˌgȯr-gən-ˈzō-lə), Roquefort (ˈrōk-fərt), and Stilton (ˈstil-tən) are some of the most popular veined cheeses. They are named after the places where they are made. They are excellent cheeses to spread on crackers for appetizers. They can also be crumbled and added to tossed salads and salad dressings.

Soft Cheeses

Soft cheeses have a thin skin and a creamy center. This category includes many different kinds of cheeses. Fresh, creamy ricotta (ri-ˈkä-tə) is a soft cheese. Runny, pungent Camembert (ˈka-məm-ˌbər) is also a soft cheese. Farmer's cheese is made from whole or partly skimmed cow's milk. It has a slightly tangy flavor and is milky white. Another soft cheese similar to cottage cheese is baker's cheese. It is used to make baked goods, such as pastries and cheesecakes.

The difference between these soft cheeses is that some have been ripened while others have not. During the ripening process, the bacteria and mold in an unripened cheese alter its flavor and texture. This gives ripened soft cheeses a distinctive flavor.

Fresh Soft Cheeses

Another word used to describe unripened soft cheese is fresh. A **fresh cheese** is not ripened, or aged, after it is formed into a final shape. Cream cheese, cottage cheese, and mascarpone (ˌmas-kär-ˈpō-(ˌ)nā) are popular unripened soft cheeses. Ricotta and mascarpone both have a sweet flavor and are often used in baking desserts. Cream cheese is also used in baking desserts, such as cheesecake.

Feta (ˈfe-tə) is another popular unripened soft cheese. It is a sharp-flavored cheese made from sheep's or cow's milk. Feta can be crumbled and added to tossed salads and breads.

Ripened Soft Cheeses

Ripened soft cheeses have very different flavors and textures from unripened cheeses. High in butterfat, they have richer flavors and are runny and creamy when completely ripe. They are surrounded by a rind that bulges out when the cheese is ripe and ready to be cut. If a ripened cheese is cut before it is ripe, it will have very little flavor and a dry texture. This type of cheese will not continue to ripen once it has been cut.

To test ripened soft cheeses for ripeness, press firmly and gently in the cheese's middle before you cut it. If it is ripe, you will feel some softness in the middle. If it is overripe, you will smell an ammonia odor. Overripe cheese should be discarded.

PHOTO CAPTION ANSWER Mold in some cheeses, such as Roquefort and Stilton, is not harmful to eat. Cheese is perishable, however, and mold that grows on cheese while stored in the refrigerator can be harmful.

▲ **Soft Cheeses** Ricotta, brie, and cream cheeses are examples of soft cheeses. *Are there differences between soft cheeses?*

Camembert and brie (brē) are the most well-known ripened soft cheeses. Served ripe and at room temperature, they make excellent appetizers or dessert cheeses. They go well with fruit.

A TASTE OF HISTORY ANSWER Charts might include semi-hard Manchego from Spain and Mexico (sheep), medium-hard Gouda from Holland (cow), or soft chévre from France (goat).

Specialty Cheeses

Specialty cheeses include pasteurized processed cheese and cold-pack cheese. **Processed cheese** is a combination of ripened and unripened cheese. These cheeses are pasteurized with flavorings and emulsifiers and poured into molds. An **emulsifier** is an additive, such as egg yolk, that allows unmixable liquids, such as oil and water, to combine uniformly. Once the cheeses have gone through this process, they do not continue to ripen. Their flavor and texture remain the same for a long time.

Cold-pack cheese is made from one or more varieties of cheese, especially Cheddar or Roquefort cheeses. The cheese is finely ground and mixed until it is spreadable. No heat is used to make cold-pack cheese.

Cook with Cheese

Cheese is a flavorful addition to most recipes. However, cheese must melt, not cook. Cheeses that are ripened or processed generally will melt well.

When you use cheese in a recipe, you must heat it at low temperatures for only a short time. Otherwise the cheese may burn. Generally, add cheese to sauces toward the end of the cooking process. Add cheese as a topping to a baked product at the end of the baking time.

PHOTO CAPTION ANSWER Some soft cheeses have been ripened, while others have not.

Serve and Store Cheese

All ripened cheeses should be served at room temperature. To bring out their full flavor, take them out of the refrigerator 30 to 60 minutes before serving. Unripened, fresh cheeses should always be refrigerated until just before they are served. If you prepare cheese boards or trays:

- Select cheeses with contrasting shapes and colors so that the tray will look appealing.
- Choose cheeses that are easy to cut.
- Include a different knife with each type of cheese.

- Do not pre-slice the cheese. This will cause it to dry out.
- Provide bread rounds, crackers, or sliced fruit.

Cheese needs special care. It should be well wrapped and stored in the refrigerator. Cheeses that are not properly wrapped will dry out and pick up flavors of other foods in the refrigerator. Loosely wrap soft cheeses with greaseproof or waxed paper.

 Reading Check Explain How does aging affect cheese?

SECTION 18.3 After You Read

Review Key Concepts

1. **Explain** how to identify soft cheeses.

Practice Culinary Academics

Science

2. **Procedure** Wrap standard amounts of four different types of cheese in wax paper and store them in the refrigerator. Monitor the cheese for mold growth each day for one or two weeks.

   Analysis Create a hypothesis about which cheese will show signs of mold first, and why. Record your observations along with your hypothesis.

   NSES A Develop abilities necessary to do scientific inquiry.

English Language Arts

3. Pair up at the direction of your teacher and write a script for a radio show about cheese. One partner should play the host, and the other should play a caller asking a question about cheese. Perform your script for the class.

   NCTE 4 Use written language to communicate effectively.

Social Studies

4. Cheese is made in many different ways around the world, and from many different dairy sources.

Choose one cheese processing source, and research how the cheese is made, and what dairy source it uses. Create a visual presentation using images of the cheesemaking process.

NCSS I B Culture Predict how data and experiences may be interpreted by people from diverse cultural perspectives and frames of reference.

Mathematics

5. An aged Cheddar costs $7.50 per pound; Stilton costs $8.99 per pound; and a French brie costs $13.99 per pound. If you serve a cheese plate with 4 ounces of Cheddar, 3 ounces of Stilton, and 2 ounces of brie, what is the total food cost?

   Math Concept **Equivalent Weights** There are 16 ounces in 1 pound. Divide ounces by 16 to convert to pounds. Divide per-pound rates by 16 to convert to per-ounce rates.

   Starting Hint Since each price is per pound, divide each price by 16 to find the per-ounce price. Multiply each per-ounce price by the number of ounces served, and add the amounts.

   NCTM Problem Solving Apply and adapt a variety of appropriate strategies to solve problems.

 Check your answers at this book's Online Learning Center at **glencoe.com**.

READING CHECK ANSWER Aging enhances the flavor of cheese and changes its texture.

Cold Platters

Create cold platters for banquets and special events.

Reading Guide

 Before You Read

Take Guilt-Free Days of Rest The reason for resting is to refresh oneself. However, if you feel guilty about resting ("I really should be reading"), then your precious rest period will only create more stress. The brain has a hard time absorbing new data when it is stressed. Your reading skills will be much more effective if you are relaxed and ready to learn.

Read to Learn

Key Concepts
- **Demonstrate** how to make canapés and rolled fancy sandwiches.
- **Summarize** the steps to make different types of cold platters.

Main Idea
Cold platters can be served in a variety of settings. They allow you to offer guests a variety of foods in small amounts.

Content Vocabulary
- single-food hors d'oeuvre
- hors d'oeuvre variés
- finger food
- liner
- hummus
- crudité
- prosciutto
- aspic
- antipasto
- relish tray
- marinated vegetable

Academic Vocabulary
- whet
- muted

Graphic Organizer
There are four steps to making canapés. As you read, use a sequence chart like the one below to list these steps.

Making Canapés

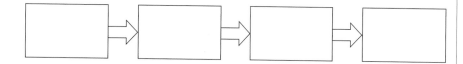

 Graphic Organizer Go to this book's Online Learning Center at **glencoe.com** for a printable graphic organizer.

ACADEMIC STANDARDS

 English Language Arts
NCTE 12 Use language to accomplish individual purposes.

 Mathematics
NCTM Geometry Use visualization, spatial reasoning, and geometric modeling to solve problems.

Social Studies
NCSS I A Culture Analyze and explain the ways groups, societies, and cultures address human needs and concerns.

NCTE National Council of Teachers of English

NCTM National Council of Teachers of Mathematics

NSES National Science Education Standards

NCSS National Council for the Social Studies

GRAPHIC ORGANIZER ANSWER 1) Cut bread and toast lightly. 2) Cover bread with spread. 3) Add toppings. 4) Add garnishes.

Cold Hors d'Oeuvres

Cold platters are an ideal way to offer guests many different kinds of interesting foods. They also work well in a variety of settings. Cold platters are very convenient at informal gatherings where people will come and go during the event. In more formal settings, a cold platter can bring people together and **whet**, or increase, the appetite before the meal is served.

An hors d'oeuvre is a bite-size, tasty food that is served before the meal. Hors d'oeuvres can be very simple. They might be a simple tray of olives, sliced vegetables, and dips. Or, they might be quite fancy, such as a tray of small seafood tarts.

There are three main types of hors d'oeuvres:

- **Single-Food Hors d'Oeuvre** Consisting of one item, a **single-food hors d'oeuvre** might be a jumbo shrimp.
- **Hors d'Oeuvre Varies** A combination of plated items with enough hors d'oeuvres for one person is called an **hors d'oeuvre variés**. This might include about 10 small food items.
- **Finger Foods** An hors d'oeuvre that is presented on a platter from which each guest serves him- or herself is called a **finger food**. Stuffed mushrooms, sliced vegetables, small tarts, and canapés are examples of common finger foods.

In recent years, exactly when and how hors d'oeuvres are served has changed. People have loosened up a bit and are looking for creative ways to make their meals and receptions interesting. Food magazines and television shows have introduced fancy hors d'oeuvres to a wider audience. They want interesting hors d'oeuvres, and eye-catching ways that they are presented.

There are many different kinds of cold hors d'oeuvres that are made by the garde manger chef. This section will focus on canapés and fancy sandwiches. (See Chapter 19 for information on hot hors d'oeuvres.)

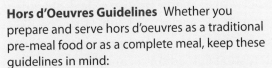

Small Bites

Hors d'Oeuvres Guidelines Whether you prepare and serve hors d'oeuvres as a traditional pre-meal food or as a complete meal, keep these guidelines in mind:

- Keep each food item small, at one to two bites.
- Prepare flavorful items that go well with the other foods being served.
- Make items attractive to the eye. That is, they should look good alone as well as with the other foods being served.

Canapés

Have you ever eaten tiny, open-face sandwiches at a party or reception? This type of flavorful, little sandwich is called a **canapé**. From the French word for sofa, a canapé appetizer consists of a platform, or base, and a cushion, or topping.

- **Base** The base can be a cracker, toasted crustless bread, a thin slice of fried or fresh bread, sliced vegetables, or small pastry shells.
- **Topping** The topping, sometimes called the nourishing element, can be anything from sliced meat, shrimp, and cheese to vegetable spreads. You can experiment with many different flavors for canapé toppings.
- **Spread** A spread, such as a flavored butter, mustard, cream cheese, or mayonnaise, adds flavor to a canapé and keeps the base from getting soggy.

In addition to the base, topping, and spread, a canapé might also have:

- A **liner**, or an ingredient that adds visual interest and texture, such as a small lettuce leaf.
- A garnish, such as an olive, a pimiento (pə-ˈmen-(ˌ)tō), a sweet red pepper, an onion slice, peas, or a parsley sprig, to add visual interest and flavor.

Creativity and canapés go together. All kinds of meats, seafood, cheeses, and vegetable spreads can be used alone or in combination.

When you select spreads, do not forget other options such as **hummus** ('hə-məs), a Middle-Eastern dish made from mashed chickpeas, lemon juice, garlic, and tahini (tə-'hē-nē), a sesame seed paste. Hummus can make an interesting spread for a canapé.

Do not believe that you must stick with traditional breads, such as white, rye, and wheat, to use as a canapé base. Although these breads can be used to make tasty canapés, try using less common herb breads and specialty breads that have chopped nuts or olives kneaded into the dough before they were baked.

If you use vegetables as the base for canapés, try tomatoes, sliced cucumbers, mushroom caps, sliced zucchini, small Romaine lettuce leaves from the heart, and endive leaves. These all make sturdy bases for toppings. Vegetable spreads make excellent toppings for these vegetable bases.

Make Canapés

Follow these steps to make canapés:
1. Cut bread into basic geometric shapes and toast lightly. Let it cool.
2. Cover each piece of bread with a spread, if desired, to prevent the bread from becoming soggy. Add a liner, such as a lettuce leaf.
3. Add toppings, from simple slices of meat to decorative vegetable spreads.
4. Add garnishes for flavor and visual interest.

Fancy Sandwiches

The garde manger brigade may be asked to prepare fancy sandwiches for many different occasions. These occasions may be as casual as a picnic or as formal as a reception. To prepare fancy sandwiches for more formal events, the garde manger brigade must consider not just the breads and fillings, but also the way the sandwiches are cut and presented to the guests.

One of the most visually appealing types of fancy sandwiches is a rolled sandwich.

Rolled sandwiches are filled with a spread and vegetables or cheese, and then rolled and cut to create a dramatic presentation.

Make Rolled Fancy Sandwiches

To prepare rolled fancy sandwiches, use these five steps:
1. Cut several day-old loaves of bread into slices lengthwise. White, wheat, rye, and herb breads work well. Breads that contain nuts are not a good choice because they will not flatten well. You will need to use a slicing machine for this step.
2. Cut the crust from all of the slices using a serrated bread knife, and roll each piece flat with a rolling pin. The bread should be less than ⅛-inch thick when you have finished rolling it.
3. Cover each piece of bread with a thin layer of a flavorful spread. Good fancy sandwich spreads include flavored butters, flavored and plain cream cheese, and vegetable or even fruit spreads. You may also use softened blue-veined cheeses. If the main spread does not have a lot of fat, spread the bread with soft butter before you add the flavored spread. This will keep the bread from getting soggy. All butters and spreads should be very soft to avoid tearing the bread.
4. Place the interior items at one end of the bread, and roll it up tightly. These items should be both tasty and colorful, such as cheese sticks, pimientos, green or black olives, pickles, or other pickled vegetables. Wrap the roll in plastic wrap and refrigerate it for several hours.
5. When the roll is quite cold, unwrap it and cut the log into ½-inch slices with a slicer. Arrange the slices artistically onto a serving platter and serve. Add garnishes to the platter that relate to the ingredients in the sandwiches.

 **Reading Check** Identify What is an hors d'oeuvre?

READING CHECK ANSWER Hors d'oeuvres are small, bite-size foods that are served before the main meal to whet the appetite.

Rolled Treat A rolled fancy sandwich is an eye-catching way to combine interesting spreads and vegetables. *How do you think this rolled sandwich was made?*

Cold Platter Preparation

Cold platters are a common product of the garde manger work station. Cold platters can be very simple or very complex. Here are some examples of typical foods that might be served on cold platters as part of a buffet, at a reception, or before a formal dinner:

- Platters of raw sliced vegetables served with dips. **Crudité** (ˌkrü-di-ˈtā) is the French word for raw, or in this case, raw vegetables.
- Platters of specially prepared food items, such as canapés, salads on croutons, pinwheel sandwiches, or melon slices and prosciutto (prō-ˈshü-(ˌ)tō). **Prosciutto**, the Italian word for "ham," is dry-cured, uncooked ham that is usually served in thin slices.
- Platters of cheese, meat, fruit, or a combination of all three can be served with different types of dips, breads, sliced fruit, and crackers. Items can be combined to fit individual tastes.

Cold platters are a convenient way to offer guests tasty, nutritious foods in an informal way. Guests are able to make their own individual choices from the tray. In addition, cheese and meat trays provide high-quality protein. The breads and crackers that accompany them are full of energy-producing carbohydrates. When whole-grain breads are included, fiber, minerals, and other nutrients are also present. Fruits, as a base for cheese or served alone, add vitamins and minerals.

Cold Platter Buffets

Cold platter buffets give culinary professionals the chance to use their creative culinary talents. A cold platter buffet has three main elements:

- **Centerpiece** This could be an uncut part of the main dish. The centerpiece for a cold meat platter, for example, may be a roast. It also could be a large, attractive bowl with a sauce or condiment. Not all centerpieces are meant to be eaten. They should, however, be made of food-based materials. For example, the centerpiece

PHOTO CAPTION ANSWER This sandwich was made by placing a spread and smoked salmon on a flat, thin bread and cutting the rolled sandwich diagonally. It could then be cut into bite-size pieces.

for a fruit platter could be a hollowed-out watermelon bowl filled with cantaloupe, honeydew, and watermelon balls.

- **Serving Portions** These portions come from the main dish, such as slices of meat from a roast or sliced cheese. Portion sizes for meats should average about 3 ounces. For cheeses, portion sizes should average about 1 ounce. Display these servings artistically on the platter.
- **Garnish** This item should add both appeal and nutritive value. A garnish for a meat platter, for example, might be flower-shaped vegetables cut in sizes that are in proportion to the meat and cheese slices that are on the platter.

Visual Appeal

Here are some other tips that you can use to prepare a visually appealing cold platter buffet:

- Be sure that the individual food items are easy to pick up. Guests should be able to take individual servings without ruining the overall presentation of the buffet.
- Keep it simple. No-frills displays hold up better over time than overdone ones. Displays should look just as good at the end of a buffet as they do at the beginning.
- Use attractive, durable platters that are suitable for the foods that you will be serving. Choices include mirrors, plastic, china, and silver or other metals. Because some metals discolor or leave a metallic taste in food, make sure they are covered with a liner or aspic ('as-pik) before foods are added to the platter. **Aspic** is a savory jelly made from meat or vegetable stock and gelatin.
- Do not remove a food item once you have placed it on a tray. If you rearrange items on silver or mirrored platters, the food will leave smudges. The food will also look less attractive the more you handle it. You must have a specific plan in mind before you begin arranging a platter. The best way to do this is to draw a plan on paper.

The plan should include shapes, sizes, color, number of items, and appropriate garnishes.

- The platter must complement the overall buffet display. It should also be visually appealing on its own.

Fruit and Cheese Trays

You may prepare fruit and cheese trays as a main course for a lunch buffet or as a dessert course for a dinner buffet. Fruit is often paired with cheese for two reasons. First, their flavors complement each other. Sweet, juicy fruits go well with earthy, rich cheeses. Second, cheese has more visual appeal when it is paired with fruit. The **muted**, or soft, colors of cheese are enhanced by the vibrant colors of fruits, such as grapes, melons, apples, and pears.

There are many ways to prepare fruit and cheese trays. These trays are not always arranged with individual portions the way that other buffet items are. Often, the trays are displayed with whole cheeses or large pieces of cheese. Utensils are included, and guests are expected to cut their own slices. This arrangement is done partly because cheese dries out after it has been cut. Cheese is also more attractive as a whole. Fruits, too, are not always displayed as individual portions on trays. Many fruits become discolored after they have been cut.

Choose cheeses based on their color, texture, shape, and flavor. Cheeses of different colors and shapes make an attractive visual display, especially when they are combined with colorful fruits.

Combination Trays

Combination trays may include meat with fruit, meat with cheese, or meat with fruit and cheese. Combination trays are excellent for buffets or parties because they give guests a wide variety of nutritious, tasty foods. Some combination trays also include raw or marinated vegetables.

An example of a combination tray is antipasto (ˌan-tē-ˈpas-(ˌ)tō). **Antipasto** is the Italian word for appetizer or before the meal. A typical antipasto tray includes cold meats, such as Genoa salami and various hams, assorted cheeses, olives, and marinated vegetables. Fruits, such as cantaloupe and other melons, may also appear on an antipasto tray.

Relish Trays

A **relish tray** is an attractive arrangement of raw, blanched, or marinated vegetables. Sometimes relishes are called crudités. The kinds of vegetables used and the way they are arranged is only as limited as the creativity of the chef.

You might arrange an assortment of carrots, cucumbers, mushrooms, radishes, zucchini, squash, peppers, jicama, cauliflower, broccoli, olives, cherry tomatoes, and endive with a special sauce for dipping. You can also use marinated vegetables. A **marinated vegetable** has been soaked in a liquid, typically made of vinegar, oil, herbs, and spices. Relish vegetables should be attractively cut and served on a platter.

Dips

Relish trays are usually served with a dip that complements the vegetables. Creamy dips, made from a base of mayonnaise, sour cream, or cream cheese, are an especially good choice. Dips can be flavored with herbs, spices, clams, garlic, or chopped hard-cooked eggs. Dips can be served inside hollowed-out vegetables or breads. This will give the relish tray visual appeal.

Cold Hors d'Oeuvre Platters

Mixed hors d'oeuvres or a single type of hors d'oeuvre can be served as a cold platter.

Vegetable Assortment Relish trays can be nutritious, tasty, and attractive. *Do relish trays always have only fresh, raw vegetables?*

PHOTO CAPTION ANSWER No. They can also include marinated or blanched vegetables, usually with some type of dip.

The arrangement should be artistic and it should also make it easy for people to pick up an individual hors d'oeuvre without having to touch or move others.

Here are some other important things to keep in mind when you prepare cold hors d'oeuvre platters:

- Season each hors d'oeuvre carefully. Because hors d'oeuvres are supposed to whet the appetite, seasonings and flavorings are especially important. Seasonings and flavorings should complement the hors d'oeuvre's flavor, not overpower it.
- Slice, shape, and portion the items carefully. The platter should offer a variety, but not an overwhelming number of choices that can confuse guests.

- Consider the overall color, shape, and look of the platter as well as the look of individual hors d'oeuvres. There should not be too much unused space, and the items should look good together. Garnishes should enhance the platter, not overwhelm it.
- Include the proper sauces and utensils with each type of hors d'oeuvres tray. Provide separate utensils for each item on a cold platter. For example, you would provide a spoon for a dip and small tongs for crudités. Change the utensils if they become dirty, or if the part of the utensil that touches food becomes compromised.

 Reading Check **Explain** What kinds of dips are usually served with relish trays?

SECTION 18.4 After You Read

Review Key Concepts

1. **Demonstrate** how to prepare the bread for a fancy sandwich.
2. **List** the typical items on an antipasto tray.

Practice Culinary Academics

 English Language Arts

3. Create a proposal for an original cold platter for a catering event. Describe the items on the platter, how they would be prepared, and how they would be presented. Include a diagram of how each food item would be arranged on the platter. Write the proposal as if you were presenting it to an employer.

   NCTE 12 Use language to accomplish individual purposes.

 Social Studies

4. Cold platters are a good choice for serving at parties. Perform research to find cold dishes from other cultures that could be adapted for an American cold platter. How are these items served in their culture of origin? How would you adapt them for a cold platter? Create a drawing of your new cold platter, including a description of the new food.

   NCSS I A Culture Analyze and explain the ways groups, societies, and cultures address human needs and concerns.

Mathematics

5. Armando works for a catering company that is preparing fancy sandwiches for a corporate event. Armando begins preparing fancy sandwiches by slicing herb bread into 2 ½-inch squares. He then cuts each square diagonally into two equal triangles. What is the area of each triangle?

   Math Concept **Calculating the Area of a Triangle** The area of a triangle equals $(\frac{1}{2})bh$, where b equals the base of a triangle, and h is the triangle's height. If b and h are in inches, area will be in square inches.

   Starting Hint Draw a square and label each side as 2 ½ inches. Draw a diagonal line that divides the square in half. Look at one of the triangles you just created, and use the formula described above to determine its base and height.

   NCTM Geometry Use visualization, spatial reasoning, and geometric modeling to solve problems.

   Check your answers at this book's Online Learning Center at **glencoe.com**.

READING CHECK ANSWER Creamy dips are usually served with relish trays because they cling well to vegetables.

Review and Applications

Chapter Summary

Garde manger chefs specialize in the preparation of cold foods. The garde manger chef must consider ingredient variety, color, texture, and cost to prepare and serve foods. Some dishes the garde manger brigade prepares include garnishes, salads, cheese plates, cold hors d'oeuvres, cold platters and relish trays.

A salad can be eaten before a meal, during a meal, or at the end of a meal. There are many varieties of cheese. Cold hors d'oeuvres include canapés and finger sandwiches. Cold platters feature cheese, meat, or fruit and may be simple or complex. Relish trays have vegetables and often a dip to enhance flavor.

Content and Academic Vocabulary Review

1. Create a fill-in-the-blank sentence for each term, with enough information to determine the missing word.

Content Vocabulary

- canapé (p. 456)
- forcemeat (p. 456)
- dry cure (p. 457)
- wet cure (p. 457)
- garde manger brigade (p. 457)
- charcuterie (p. 458)
- quenelle (p. 459)
- score (p. 461)
- tournée (p. 461)
- salad (p. 463)
- croutons (p. 463)
- spinach (p. 464)
- kale (p. 465)
- radicchio (p. 466)
- mesclun (p. 466)
- dressing (p. 468)

- vinaigrette (p. 468)
- scorch (p. 469)
- cheddaring (p. 471)
- whey (p. 471)
- ripening (p. 471)
- veined cheese (p. 472)
- rind (p. 472)
- fresh cheese (p. 473)
- processed cheese (p. 474)
- emulsifier (p. 474)
- cold-pack cheese (p. 474)
- single-food hors d'oeuvre (p. 477)
- hors d'oeuvre variés (p. 477)
- finger food (p. 477)
- liner (p. 477)

- hummus (p. 478)
- crudité (p. 479)
- prosciutto (p. 479)
- aspic (p. 480)
- antipasto (p. 481)
- relish tray (p. 481)
- marinated vegetable (p. 481)

Academic Vocabulary

- artistic (p. 456)
- appropriate (p. 461)
- elaborate (p. 463)
- subtle (p. 466)
- varied (p. 471)
- beneficial (p. 472)
- whet (p. 477)
- muted (p. 480)

Review Key Concepts

2. **Identify** the duties of the garde manger work station.

3. **List** the main types of salads served during a meal.

4. **Outline** the preparation techniques for salad greens.

5. **Describe** the different types of salad dressings.

6. **Explain** how to identify and store cheeses.

7. **Demonstrate** how to make canapés and rolled fancy sandwiches.

8. **Summarize** the steps to make different types of cold platters.

Critical Thinking

9. **Imagine** that you are preparing an hors d'oeuvre tray that will be served before a main meal. What factors will impact your hors d'oeuvres choice?

10. **Consider** accompaniment salads that go with a main course of baked fish. What type of salad would you prepare, and why?

Review and Applications

Academic Skills

English Language Arts

11. Languages Across Cultures Garde manger, hors d'oeuvre and canapé are examples of French words that are used in foodservice. What other French words can you think of that you might use as a garde manger chef? Create a vocabulary list, with definitions and a pronunciation guide.

> **NCTE 9** Develop an understanding of diversity in language use across cultures.

Science

12. Melting Point Different cheeses have different melting points.

Procedure Cut pieces of three different types of cheese and place each on a cracker. Put them in a toaster oven at 300°F (149°C) and watch them closely until each piece melts, or until the cracker starts to burn. Remove each slice from the oven after it has melted.

Analysis Keep track of how long it takes each piece of cheese to melt. Why do you think some cheeses have higher melting points? Do some cheeses not melt at all?

> **NSES B** Develop an understanding of the interactions of energy and matter

Mathematics

13. Work Rates Robyn and Antonio work at the garde manger station at a large hotel kitchen. They have been asked to prepare a cheese platter for a banquet later in the day. It typically takes Robyn 15 minutes to cut four large blocks of cheese into cubes, while it usually takes Antonio 20 minutes to do the same. If they work together, how long will it take them to cut four blocks of cheese into cubes?

Math Concept **Combining Rates of Work** In work-related problems, determine the rate of work for each worker. Write an algebraic equation with a variable that represents the total time needed to complete the job by both Robyn and Antonio.

Starting Hint If it takes Robyn 15 minutes to cut all the cubes, she can complete $\frac{1}{15}$ of the job in 1 minute. Similarly, Antonio can finish $\frac{1}{20}$ of the job in 1 minute. If x represents the total minutes needed for the pair to complete the job together, then $1/x$ represents their combined effort per minute. You know that $\frac{1}{15} + \frac{1}{20} = 1/x$. Solve for x.

> **NCTM Problem Solving** Solve problems that arise in mathematics and in other contexts.

Certification Prep

Directions Read the questions. Then, read the answer choices and choose the best possible answer for each.

14. Which type of salad should have a protein served with it so it can function as a balanced meal?
- **a.** appetizer salad
- **b.** accompaniment salad
- **c.** main-course salad
- **d.** separate-course salad

15. What type of cheese is made by the cheddaring process?
- **a.** hard cheese
- **b.** firm cheese
- **c.** semisoft cheese
- **d.** soft cheese

> *Sharpen your test-taking skills to improve your kitchen certification program score.*

Test-Taking Tip
When you study for a test, write your vocabulary words on flash cards with the definition of each on the back of the card. Quiz yourself each day until you know them all.

Real-World Skills and Applications

Self-Management Skills

16. Design a Salad Imagine that you are a menu planner for a restaurant. You decide to create a nutritious salad. Write down the factors you must consider. Describe your salad, and include an ingredient list. Explain what makes your salad nutritious. Describe the type of customers who might be interested in your salad.

Interpersonal and Collaborative Skills

17. Promote a Cheese Follow your teacher's instructions to break into teams. Imagine that your team is part of an ad agency that is developing a print ad for a particular type of cheese. Describe the cheese, its qualities, its uses, and any nutritional benefits in your ad. Display your ad in the classroom.

Technology Applications

18. Recipe Search Under your teacher's or parents' supervision, search the Internet for salad recipes. Locate one recipe for each main type of salad. Label each recipe with its type and the source. Bring your recipe to class. Compile the recipes to make a class recipe book, organized by salad type.

Financial Literacy

19. Purchase Cheese Imagine that you buy a 1-pound brick of Cheddar for $4.99 for your restaurant. You use ¾ of the cheese before it must be thrown away. The next time, you purchase a 16-ounce bag of shredded Cheddar for $5.99 and use it all. Which was a more cost-effective choice?

Culinary Lab

Use the culinary skills you have learned in this chapter.

Create Garnishes

20. Use Tools to Create Garnishes In this lab, you will practice using various tools to make different types of garnishes. Then, you and a partner will evaluate your work.

A. Choose garnishing tools. You will need to choose five tools that are listed in Section 18.1 to practice your garnish-making skills. You may use the food suggestions provided, or you may be creative about which foods you will use with which tool.

B. Make garnishes. Use the tools you chose as described in this chapter. If you use a tool on an ingredient that is not mentioned in Section 18.1, make sure that your choice makes sense.

C. Practice with garnishes. Practice each garnish a few times, and then choose your best effort to display for the class.

D. Match the garnishes with food. Determine the food item each garnish would best accompany and create a list to accompany your garnishes.

Create Your Evaluation

After you have finished making the garnishes and chosen your best examples, work with a partner at your teacher's direction to evaluate the garnishes. After reviewing all garnishes and discussing them with your partner, write a one-page evaluation. Evaluations should include:

- Things that might have been done differently.
- Other accompanying food possibilities that were not considered.
- Whether the right tool choices for each ingredient were made.

Sandwiches and Appetizers

SECTIONS

19.1 Sandwich-Making Basics

19.2 Sandwiches

19.3 Hot Appetizers

WRITING ACTIVITY

Step-By-Step Guide

Sandwiches are prepared in steps. Write a step-by-step guide for making your favorite type of sandwich. Be clear and concise with your directions.

Writing Tips

1 Explain any terms your reader may not know.

2 Write each step in chronological order.

3 Use appropriate transition words and verbs.

EXPLORE THE PHOTO

Sandwiches are a convenient meal choice for many occasions. *What makes sandwiches a convenient meal?*

WRITING ACTIVITY ANSWER
All Important steps should be in chronological order. Transition words should help the text flow smoothly.

EXPLORE THE PHOTO ANSWER
Sandwiches are easy to take on the go, combine several food groups into one meal, and have many possible ingredient combinations.

Sandwich-Making Basics

Learn the fundamentals of sandwich making.

Reading Guide

 Before You Read

Use Diagrams As you read through this section, write down the main idea. Write down any facts, explanations, or examples you find in the text. Start at the main idea and draw arrows to the information that directly supports it. Then, draw arrows from these examples to any information that supports them.

Read To Learn

Key Concepts
- **Identify** different types of sandwiches.
- **Distinguish** between various breads and spreads for sandwiches.
- **Select** appropriate sandwich fillings.

Main Idea

A sandwich consists of bread, a spread, and fillings. It takes skill to make sandwiches that are both delicious and nutritious.

Content Vocabulary
- Pullman loaf
- croissant
- focaccia
- kaiser roll
- torpedo roll
- pita
- tortilla
- chapatti
- phyllo
- crêpe
- mayonnaise
- pesto
- sauerkraut

Academic Vocabulary
- foundation
- maintain

 ACADEMIC STANDARDS

 English Language Arts

NCTE 7 Conduct research and gather, evaluate, and synthesize data to communicate discoveries.

Mathematics

NCTM Problem Solving Solve problems that arise in mathematics and in other contexts.

NCTM Measurement Understand measurable attributes of objects and the units, systems, and processes of measurement.

NCTE National Council of Teachers of English

NCTM National Council of Teachers of Mathematics

NSES National Science Education Standards

NCSS National Council for the Social Studies

Graphic Organizer

There are five different types of sandwiches. Use a diagram like this one to write notes about the five common sandwich types.

Closed Sandwiches	Open-Face Sandwiches	Triple-Decker Sandwiches	Finger Sandwiches	Wraps

 Graphic Organizer Go to this book's Online Learning Center at **glencoe.com** for a printable graphic organizer.

GRAPHIC ORGANIZER ANSWER Students' organizers should help them take notes as they read the section.

Sandwich Types

All it takes to make a sandwich is bread, a spread, and fillings. But from this simple set of ingredients, you can make a wide variety of tasty sandwiches. Depending on the ingredients that you choose, a sandwich can be a nutritional powerhouse or a high-fat meal. The vast array of ingredients also increases the skill level that is needed to prepare sandwiches by foodservice workers. Through organization and practice, you can learn to make fresh, flavorful sandwiches that will appeal to a wide variety of customers. Types of hot and cold sandwiches include closed, open-face, triple-decker, finger, and wraps.

- **Closed Sandwiches** These sandwiches have two slices of bread with the filling placed in between them.
- **Open-face Sandwiches** The spread and fillings of an open-face sandwich are added to the top of one or two pieces of bread. The bread slices are not closed together after the filling is put into place.
- **Triple-Decker Sandwiches** These sandwiches include three slices of bread that are stacked. Fillings are placed between each layer.

Safety Check

✓ Guard Against Bacteria Growth
Sandwiches often combine hot and cold items. This is a perfect environment for bacteria growth. Follow these guidelines to avoid cross-contamination:

- Keep hot foods hot and cold foods cold.
- Wash your hands with hot, soapy water before, during, and after handling different foods.
- Minimize the cross-use of utensils.
- Frequently clean and sanitize all work surfaces and utensils.

CRITICAL THINKING *How does keeping hot foods hot and cold foods cold help avoid cross-contamination?*

- **Finger Sandwiches** These small, fancy closed sandwiches often have their crusts removed, and are usually cut into various shapes. Finger sandwiches are also sometimes used as appetizers.
- **Wraps** These easy-to-eat sandwiches are made with soft, flat breads that are folded, or wrapped, around the fillings. A wide variety of fillings can be used in these sandwiches.

Reading Check Describe What does an open-face sandwich look like?

Breads and Spreads

Bread provides the base to a sandwich and adds to the appearance and flavor of the final product. If you choose a fresh and tasty bread, you will build a sandwich on a solid **foundation**, or starting point. It is important to keep the bread fresh and dry for a tasty, appealing sandwich.

Spreads act as a barrier between the fillings and the bread. They prevent moist fillings from soaking into the bread, making the sandwich difficult to pick up and unappealing.

Types of Bread

There is a vast array of tasty and nutritional sandwich breads from which to choose. These can range from bagels to buns to Pullman loaves. A **Pullman loaf** is a rectangular-shaped sandwich bread loaf with a flat top and an even texture. Croissants (krȯ-'sänts) and fruit breads also can be used to make flavorful sandwiches. A **croissant** is a flaky, crescent-shaped roll that makes an interesting sandwich. When you choose breads for sandwiches, choose ones that are not too hard or crusty, or that overpower the taste of the filling. Also, choose breads that are thick and firm enough to hold the filling without tearing when the sandwich is picked up. If a bread choice is soft, you may want to cut the sandwich in half to make it easier to pick up.

White, rye, sourdough and wheat bread are typical cold sandwich choices. Today, however, many types of flatbreads are also used to make sandwiches. One popular flatbread is focaccia (fō-'kä-ch(ē-)ə). **Focaccia** is an Italian flatbread that is flavored with olive oil and herbs. It has a hearty, robust flavor.

Small, rectangular loaves of white or rye bread are also used for finger sandwiches. These breads can be sliced thinly and still **maintain**, or keep, a circle, diamond, or triangle shape after they are cut. Some breads crumble easily when they are sliced. Avoid using these breads for sandwiches that are thinly sliced unless the bread has been frozen before being sliced. This will help the sandwiches hold their shapes.

Rolls

In addition to traditional hot dog and hamburger rolls, there are many other types of rolls that can be used for sandwiches. These rolls include hard, kaiser ('kī-zər), onion, and torpedo (tȯr-'pē-(ˌ)dō), a crusty, chewy Italian roll. A **kaiser roll** is a round, crusty roll that is often sprinkled with poppy or sesame seeds. A **torpedo roll** is a long, skinny sandwich roll. Local terms for sandwiches made with torpedo rolls vary as to region. They are called heroes in the New York City area, hoagies in Philadelphia, grinders in New England, poor boys in New Orleans, and submarine sandwiches or subs all over the country.

Other specialty breads can also be used for sandwiches. A **pita** ('pē-tə) is a round-shaped flatbread cut open to form a pocket. A **tortilla** (tȯr-'tē-yə) is a flattened, round bread baked on a griddle or deep-fried. It can be cut into pinwheel sections for open-face sandwiches, or used as a wrap for sandwich fillings. A **chapatti** (chə-pä-tē) is an Indian whole-wheat flatbread. **Phyllo** ('fē-(ˌ)lō) is a very thin, layered pastry dough. Both of these can also be used to create sandwich wraps. Another option is a crêpe ('krāp). A **crêpe** is a small, thin pancake made with egg batter. Crêpes make excellent wraps for sweet sandwiches.

Types of Spreads

There are three main types of sandwich spreads: butter, mayonnaise, and vegetable purées. Butter and mayonnaise keep wet fillings from soaking into the bread as well as from falling off of the bread. Mustards are also a popular sandwich spread, although they are usually combined with other spreads because they do not provide a barrier against moisture for the bread. There are many different types of mustards to use.

Butter

Butter adds a smooth, rich flavor to a sandwich. Flavored butters, such as red chili butter or garlic butter, can add zip to a fish or pork sandwich. Whip or soften the butter to increase its volume and softness for easy spreading. This way, the butter will not tear the bread when it is spread. Whipping the butter can also help cut food costs because you will use less butter overall on the bread.

Some people prefer to use margarine instead of butter. Both contain partially saturated fat. Butter has more essential fatty acids and vitamins than margarine. However, margarine has no cholesterol. The choice between butter and margarine for a sandwich spread is a matter of preference and taste. Some people prefer the taste of butter.

NUTRITION NOTES ANSWER Answers will vary, but may include using low-fat or nonfat cheese, using lower-fat spreads, and using lean meats as fillings.

Mayonnaise

Mayonnaise has been the spread of choice of sandwich makers for generations. **Mayonnaise** is a permanent suspension of egg yolks, oil, and vinegar or lemon juice. It is used as a spread on many different types of sandwiches. There are low-fat and nonfat versions of mayonnaise that are available. It is hard to imagine a bacon, lettuce, and tomato sandwich or a tuna salad sandwich without mayonnaise. Even mayonnaise, however, can be flavored with herbs, fruits, pesto, and condiments such as mustard to give it more flavor and make a sandwich more interesting. **Pesto** (pes-(ˌ)tō) is a sauce made by combining olive oil, pine nuts or walnuts, a hard cheese such as parmesan, and fresh basil, garlic, salt, and pepper.

Mayonnaise is usually purchased ready-made. However, mayonnaise can be made by hand. Even though most culinary professionals will not have to make mayonnaise, it is good to know how. Some specialty foodservice businesses make mayonnaise by hand every day. To make mayonnaise, you would combine the ingredients and whisk while slowly adding oil to create the emulsion.

Small Bites

Sandwich Accompaniments Sandwich accompaniments may include one or more of the following:

- Raw vegetables
- Salad or fruit
- Grilled, marinated vegetables
- Pickle spears, or green or black olives
- Chips or French fries

Vegetable Purées

Vegetable purées are often made with chopped olives, avocados, or eggplant. These purées make an interesting alternative spread to use on sandwiches. Purées add different flavors and textures to sandwiches, but they usually do not provide a moisture barrier.

If you use a vegetable purée, you may wish to add another spread or a lettuce leaf that will act as a barrier. You may also wish to apply the spread immediately before you serve the sandwich.

Reading Check List What types of rolls are used to make sandwiches?

▲ **Nutritional Fillings** Vegetables are a common pita sandwich filling. *What nutritional elements can you spot in this pita sandwich?*

PHOTO CAPTION ANSWER The pita bread provides carbohydrates and fiber, the vegetables provide vitamins and minerals, the cheese provides calcium and protein, and the meat provides protein.

READING CHECK ANSWER Hot dog and hamburger buns, hard, kaiser, onion, and torpedo.

Sandwich Fillings

Sandwich fillings may include hot or cold meats, poultry, fish, cheeses, vegetables, or a combination of all of these items. The only real limit to the filling of a sandwich is your imagination. The filling is the main attraction of a sandwich, so you must prepare each filling item carefully and make sure that it is of the highest quality. For example, a chicken breast that will be used as a filling must be carefully cooked and sliced. The lettuce for the sandwich must be crisp and completely rinsed and dried. Tomatoes and onions should be evenly sliced. This makes for a better presentation as well as a more appealing sandwich.

Vegetables that are grilled or marinated, such as red and yellow peppers, make elegant, colorful fillings. A pita sandwich that is filled with vegetables and a flavorful dressing is packed with zest and nutrition. Finger sandwiches often contain cream cheese that is topped with finely chopped vegetables that give color and texture to the cream cheese. Vegetarian sandwiches can be made with different vegetables and sprouts to add texture and flavor, as well as nutrition.

Meats, Poultry, Fish and Seafood

Most sandwiches feature some type of protein food as a filling. Chicken, turkey, beef, pork, ham, eggs, and tuna are common sandwich fillings. Fish is becoming a more common filling. Let your imagination be your guide when you choose a protein for a sandwich.

⌒ Small Bites ⌒

Cut for Appeal The way a sandwich is cut adds to its visual appeal. The arrangement of sandwich sections on a plate gives the customer a hint of the filling. Avoid pushing down on a sandwich before or during cutting. Cut sandwiches as close to serving time as possible.

Gourmet Math

Calculate Food Orders

When you plan a meal for a large number of people, you can prevent overbuying or underbuying of ingredients by using your knowledge of multiplication and division.

For example, imagine you need to purchase ingredients for chicken salad sandwiches for a luncheon buffet with 345 guests. Expect one-third of the guests to eat chicken salad sandwiches. Each sandwich consists of 3 ounces of chicken salad and two tomato slices on a croissant. Chicken salad comes in 32-ounce containers. Croissants are sold 12 in a package. One tomato can be cut into 8 slices. What quantity of each ingredient should you purchase?

Math Concept **Multi-Step Problems** When presented with a complex problem, identify the individual calculations required. If some steps depend on answers from other steps, perform the steps in the appropriate order.

Starting Hint First, determine how many sandwiches are needed by multiplying 345 guests by ⅓. Calculate the amount of chicken salad needed by multiplying 3 ounces times the number of sandwiches, then dividing by 32 (to find the number of containers). At each step, if your answer has a remainder, round up to the next whole number (because you cannot purchase fractional containers).

NCTM Problem Solving Solve problems that arise in mathematics and in other contexts.

These ingredients can also be combined with other fillings to create a hearty sandwich. Corned beef and sauerkraut ('saù(-ə)r-ˌkraút), spicy chicken sausage and red peppers, and broiled crab and cheese are good examples of combined fillings. **Sauerkraut** is finely sliced cabbage that has been fermented in brine.

The key to a flavorful sandwich is understanding which food flavors will work well together. You must also consider which breads, spreads, and vegetables will give the sandwich the correct texture. If flavors do not mix well together, customers will not order the sandwich again, and the restaurant will lose money.

Prepare
Quantities of Sandwiches

1 Set up your work station so that all necessary utensils and ingredients are close at hand. Items should be within your range of motion to avoid unnecessary movements that cause fatigue.

2 Arrange slices of bread or rolls in equal rows on the sheet pan.

3 Use a spatula to apply a spread to each slice of bread or portion of the roll. This seals the bread before the filling is added. It helps prevent sandwiches from getting soggy.

4 Arrange any base vegetables such as lettuce on top of the spread.

5 Add any other vegetables onto the spread. Add the filling.

6 Use a spatula to spread the filling evenly.

7 Add tomatoes. Using both hands, cover the two middle rows with the remaining slices of bread or half of the roll.

8 Either plate the sandwiches immediately or wrap them in plastic wrap and refrigerate until they are served.

American Grinder

YIELD: 50 SERVINGS
SERVING SIZE: 1 SANDWICH

Method of Preparation

1. Split the submarine roll, spread with mayonnaise, and fill with shredded lettuce and tomato slices.
2. Fill with meats, alternating ham, salami, and turkey.
3. Top with sliced cheeses, cut in half, and serve with a pickle.

Ingredients

50	Submarine rolls, split
1½ pts.	Mayonnaise
2 heads	Iceberg lettuce, cleaned and washed, cut chiffonade
7 lbs.	Tomatoes, washed, cored, and sliced
6 lbs.	Ham, sliced thin
3 lbs.	Salami, sliced thin
6 lbs.	Turkey, sliced thin
3 lbs.	Provolone cheese, sliced
3 lbs	American cheese, sliced
50	Pickle spears

International Flavor

In the southern United States, a sandwich served on an elongated roll is called poor boy. In New England, it is called a grinder. Research these other forms of sandwiches, and create a chart to show their similarities and differences.

- panino (Italy)
- gyro (Greece)
- schwarma (Middle East)

Chef Notes

Serve with crosscut, seasoned French fries and cole slaw. In quantity food production, the mayonnaise should be served on the side.

Substitutions

- To lower the fat, use low-fat or nonfat cheeses or vegetable slices, and lean cuts of meat.
- Use mustard instead of mayonnaise to lower cholesterol. Or, replace salami with lean roast beef.

Cooking Technique

There is no cooking required for this dish.

Glossary

Chiffonade ribbons of leafy greens
Crosscut sliced across the surface

HACCP

- Keep all ingredients chilled to 41°F (5°C) or below

Hazardous Foods

- Mayonnaise
- Ham
- Salami
- Turkey
- Provolone and American cheese

Nutrition

Calories 740   Calories from Fat 400
Total Fat 45g
　Saturated Fat 20g
　Trans Fat 0g
Cholesterol 115mg
Sodium 3070mg
Total Carbohydrate 43g
　Fiber 5g
　Sugars 5g
Protein 44g
- Vitamin A 25%   • Vitamin C 25%
- Calcium 45%   • Iron 20%

Sanitation Check

✓ Handle Cheese

Follow these guidelines when you handle cheese:

- Wash your hands well to avoid contaminating the cheese.
- Keep your workspace, cutting equipment, and other utensils clean and sanitized to prevent cross-contamination.
- Keep cheese tightly covered in plastic wrap in the refrigerator. Cheese dries out quickly when unwrapped and sliced.

CRITICAL THINKING *How does keeping cheese wrapped prevent it from drying?*

Cheese

Cheese plays an important part in many sandwiches. It is often used as the main source of protein in vegetarian sandwiches. Cheese is also full of important nutrients. It is high in protein, vitamin A, calcium, and phosphorus.

Cheese can also be high in fat, although low-fat and nonfat processed cheeses are available. Keep in mind, however, that low-fat and nonfat cheeses do not melt as easily as regular cheese. This could create a problem when these cheeses are used for hot sandwiches. Knowing the types and characteristics of cheeses will help you select the best cheese for any particular sandwich.

Types of Cheese

Many different types of soft, semisoft, semihard, and hard cheeses make good sandwich fillings. Sliced cheese may be added to closed sandwiches or melted on top of an open-face sandwich. Flavored, spreadable cream cheeses are often used for finger sandwiches made with fruit breads. (For more information on the different types of cheese, see Section 18.3.)

Reading Check Explain Why is cheese an important part of a sandwich?

SECTION 19.1 After You Read

Review Key Concepts

1. **Compare and contrast** open-face and closed sandwiches.
2. **List** the guidelines for choosing a sandwich bread.
3. **Select** appropriate sandwich accompaniments.

Practice Culinary Academics

English Language Arts

4. Perform research to learn the history of the sandwich. Find out about its origins and how it became a popular meal. Compare an American sandwich with a type of sandwich served in another country. Write an essay about the differences and similarities, using an opening paragraph, a body, and a closing paragraph.

NCTE 7 Conduct research and gather, evaluate, and synthesize data to communicate discoveries.

Mathematics

5. Marco is preparing a giant submarine-style sandwich for a luncheon. The entire sandwich is 7 feet long, and must be cut into 32 slices. How long in inches should each slice be?

Math Concept **Equivalent Lengths** There are 12 inches in 1 foot. Convert feet to inches by multiplying by 12. Convert inches to feet by dividing by 12.

Starting Hint The question asks for the length of each slice in inches, so begin by converting 7 feet into inches. Divide that amount by 32 to find the per-slice measurement. Reduce any fractions to lowest terms.

NCTM Measurement Understand measurable attributes of objects and the units, systems, and processes of measurement.

Check your answers at this book's Online Learning Center at **glencoe.com**.

SANITATION CHECK ANSWER Plastic wrap holds in the moisture and prevents it from escaping, keeping cheese moist.

READING CHECK ANSWER Cheese is often the main protein source in vegetarian sandwiches, and contains important nutrients.

Sandwiches

Reading Guide

 Before You Read

Adjust Reading Speed Improve your comprehension by adjusting reading speed to match the difficulty of the text. Slow down and, if needed, reread each paragraph. Reading more slowly may take longer, but you will understand and remember more.

Read to Learn
- **Outline** the steps in making and plating different types of hot sandwiches.
- **Explain** the procedure for making various types of cold sandwiches.

Main Idea
Sandwiches can be either hot or cold. Many of the same type of ingredients are used in hot or cold sandwiches.

Content Vocabulary
- grilled sandwich
- Monte Cristo
- au jus
- pastrami
- club sandwich
- salad sandwich

Academic Vocabulary
- variation
- obtain

Graphic Organizer
As you read, use a web diagram like the one below to list the four tips to keep in mind when you make hot open-face sandwiches.

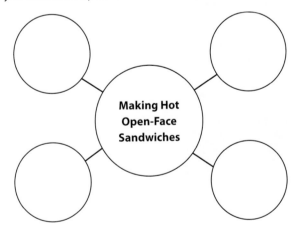

Making Hot Open-Face Sandwiches

 Graphic Organizer Go to this book's Online Learning Center at **glencoe.com** for a printable graphic organizer.

GRAPHIC ORGANIZER ANSWER Do not let the sauce run into any cold items on the plate; do not oversauce items; make sure sauces are not too thick or too thin; make a nest for the lettuce, or use a seashell for presentation.

ACADEMIC STANDARDS

 English
NCTE 8 Use information resources to gather information and create and communicate knowledge.

 Mathematics
NCTM Geometry
Analyze characteristics of two- and three-dimensional geometric shapes and develop mathematical arguments about geometric relationships.

 Science
NSES C Develop an understanding of the behavior of organisms.

 Social Studies
NCSS I E Culture
Demonstrate the value of cultural diversity, as well as cohesion, within and across groups.

NCTE National Council of Teachers of English

NCTM National Council of Teachers of Mathematics

NSES National Science Education Standards

NCSS National Council for the Social Studies

Hot Sandwich Basics

From the all-American hot dog to the elegant Monte Cristo, hot sandwiches are popular with customers of all ages. Cold sandwiches, such as tuna salad or bacon, lettuce, and tomato, are ordered by customers every day. Many of the same types of ingredients can be used in hot and cold sandwiches.

Types of Hot Sandwiches

Examples of closed hot sandwiches include grilled ham and cheese and hot barbecued chicken. Popular open-face hot sandwiches are hot turkey and hot beef sandwiches, usually served with mashed potatoes and gravy. Hot crab with cheese and avocado is another example of a hot open-face sandwich.

One of the most popular hot open-face sandwiches is pizza. Pizza can be made with either a thin or a thick crust. There are many pizza topping combinations, such as pepperoni and mushroom. Many restaurants regularly offer individual-size pizzas, and some restaurants offer unusual toppings, such as barbecued chicken.

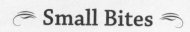

Small Bites

Sandwich-Making Techniques When you set up a sandwich work station, have these utensils close at hand: sharp knives, serving spoons, a spatula, a toaster, tongs, and a cutting board.

Basic Sandwiches

Basic sandwiches contain at least one hot filling. The filling may be sandwiched between two slices of bread as a closed sandwich or served open-face. Basic closed sandwiches include the hamburger and hot dog. Tortillas are used to make burritos or tacos, with a hot filling of chicken, beef, or seafood inside. These fillings are often combined with cold vegetables such as lettuce, tomatoes, onions, or avocado.

Grilled Sandwiches

Grilled cheese sandwiches are a traditional favorite. To make a **grilled sandwich**, you would butter and then brown the outside of each slice of bread on the griddle. You can create an interesting **variation**, or change, such as grilled cheese and avocado or grilled tuna and cheese.

Combination Fillings Hot fillings are often combined with cold vegetables such as avocado, lettuce, tomatoes, or onions. *What might you serve with this hot sandwich?*

PHOTO CAPTION ANSWER Answers will vary, but could include French fries, a side salad, fresh fruit, fresh vegetables, potato salad, a cup of soup, or pickles.

Fried Sandwiches

Have you ever heard of a Monte Cristo sandwich? There are many varieties of this classic sandwich. Some old, elegant hotel dining rooms built their reputations on their own special versions of the Monte Cristo.

A **Monte Cristo** is a closed, shallow-fried or deep-fried sandwich. Some chefs make Monte Cristos with thin slices of ham and Swiss cheese and Dijon mustard. Others include turkey or chicken breast and use butter or mayonnaise between the layers. Some chefs also add a layer of strawberry or raspberry jam. The sandwich is then dipped in egg batter and either shallow-fried or deep-fried.

Hot Sandwich Preparation

Here are some tips to keep in mind when you prepare hot sandwiches:

- When you grill sandwiches, the filling is only heated, not cooked. Make sure all hot meat fillings are thoroughly cooked before you grill them.

- Completely assemble the sandwiches before grilling. Because most of them contain cheese, they cannot be pulled apart to add other fillings after they are heated.
- Make sure that cold fillings, such as lettuce, are crisp and cold. If they are placed underneath hot fillings such as cheese, they may wilt.
- Some cooks place cold fillings on the side for the customer to add to the sandwich when it is served. This is almost always done with hamburgers. The lettuce, tomato, onion, and pickles are placed to the side.
- Do not overload hot wraps or they will become messy to eat. If one ingredient is too chunky, it can break the wrap or cause everything to fall out.
- Make sure that hot sandwiches are served on warm plates.

Hot Sandwich Plating

Hot sandwiches may be served either open-face or closed. Grilled cheese sandwiches, for example, are usually served closed. Hamburgers may be served either open or closed. Hot turkey or crab sandwiches are sometimes served open-face with gravy or sauce spooned on top.

Hot sandwiches are often served with a side salad or a cup of soup. Potatoes, such as French fries, are another popular side dish.

Tips for Hot Open-Face Sandwiches

Here are some tips to keep in mind when you serve hot open-face sandwiches:

- If the sandwich has gravy, sauce, or melted cheese on top, do not let the sauce run onto any cold items on the plate. No one wants to eat carrots covered in gravy, or lettuce drowning in barbecue sauce.
- Do not oversauce items.
- Make sure the sauce is not too thin or too thick.
- Make a nest for the lettuce or put cold relishes in a seashell for an elegant presentation.

A TASTE OF HISTORY ANSWER Answers might include the Club Sandwich from the United States (chicken breast, bacon, lettuce and tomato); falafel from the Middle East (garbanzo bean balls, cucumbers, tomatoes and tahini in a pita); or Gyro from Greece (lamb, chopped tomato, and cucumber-yogurt dressing in a pita).

✹ MASTER RECIPE
Monte Cristo Sandwich

YIELD: 50 SERVINGS
SERVING SIZE: 5 OZ.

Ingredients

6.25 lbs.	Turkey breast, cooked and sliced thin
6.25 lbs.	Virginia ham, sliced
50 oz.	Swiss cheese, sliced
150 slices	White bread
25 each	Whole eggs, slightly beaten
1 lb.	Butter or oil

Method of Preparation

1. Place a slice of bread on a sheet pan; place one slice of turkey on the bread, and then place a second slice of bread on the turkey.

2. Place one slice of ham and one slice of Swiss cheese on top of the second slice of bread. Cover with a third slice of bread.

3. Dip the sandwich in egg. Cook on both sides to a golden brown on a well-buttered griddle. Cut in half on the diagonal. Hold at 135°F (57°C).

Cooking Technique

Grill

1. Clean and heat the grill.
2. To prevent sticking, brush the food product with oil.

Chef Notes

In some regions, this sandwich is fried. Do not prepare the sandwiches too far in advance, because they will become soggy.

Substitutions

- To lower the fat, use low-fat or nonfat cheese, or vegetable slices.
- Use whole-grain bread to increase fiber content.
- Spread mustard on the inside of the sandwich to add flavor.

International Flavor

Grilled sandwiches are popular in many cultures. Research the history of these grilled sandwiches, and write a one-page paper on their similarities and differences.

- Reuben (United States)
- Croque monsieur (France)
- Panini (Italy)

Glossary

Assembly line system of organized steps to do a lot in little time

HACCP

- Hold at 135°F (57°C) or above

Hazardous Foods

- Ham
- Cheese
- Turkey
- Eggs

Nutrition

Calories 540	Calories from Fat 230

Total Fat 25g
  Saturated Fat 11g
  Trans Fat 0g
Cholesterol 200mg
Sodium 1790mg
Total Carbohydrate 44g
  Fiber 0g
  Sugars 10g
Protein 35g

- Vitamin A 10%
- Vitamin C 15%
- Calcium 35%
- Iron 20%

Garnishing Hot sandwich garnishes include lettuce, tomato, onion, and different condiments. Customers often appreciate sandwich garnishes being served on the side. That way, they can add the ones they want and leave the rest off.

Au Jus Open-face sandwiches are sometimes served **au jus** (ō-'zhü(s)), or accompanied by the juices that a chef will **obtain**, or get, from roasting meat. A barbecued chicken sandwich might be accompanied by a cup of barbecue sauce. A French dip sandwich is served with a cup of jus on the side of the plate. The sandwich is dipped into the jus before it is eaten.

Reading Check List What are three types of hot sandwiches?

▲ **Salad Sandwiches** Prepare salad sandwiches, such as this one, immediately before serving. *Why should this be done?*

Cold Sandwich Basics

Some cold sandwiches are made with precooked poultry, fish, or meat. Roast beef, pastrami (pə-'strä-mē), or turkey deli sandwiches, for example, are typically served cold. **Pastrami** is a seasoned smoked meat. The vegetables added to cold sandwiches, such as onions or pickles, are also served cold.

Some cold sandwiches are nutritionally balanced and need no accompaniment, such as a spicy lentil pita sandwich with yogurt sauce.

Cold sandwiches are rarely served open face. Usually, they are made from two or three pieces of bread, or a split soft or multigrain roll. A triple-decker sandwich that features cold, sliced cooked turkey and ham, or bacon, is called a **club sandwich**. Club sandwiches also contain cheese, tomato, and lettuce. The ingredients are layered between three slices of toasted bread and cut into four triangles.

Preparation and Plating

When you prepare cold sandwiches, there are several guidelines to keep in mind. Use the freshest bread possible. If the bread is toasted, you can use day-old bread. However, butter the bread quickly after toasting it to preserve moisture and keep it from drying out.

Do not prepare salad sandwiches in advance. A **salad sandwich** is a sandwich that has a salad made with a fatty dressing, such as mayonnaise, as the filling. The moisture from a salad such as chicken salad or egg salad will soak into the bread. If the sandwich is prepared ahead of time, it will be soggy by the time it is served. Use moisture barriers such as lettuce to help keep the bread dry.

Plate hot sandwiches on hot plates, and cold sandwiches on cold plates. Garnish the plates as appropriate for the type of sandwich. Many sandwiches are cut in half diagonally to show the fillings and to create a dramatic presentation. Frilled toothpicks are often used to keep sandwich halves from falling apart.

Cold Sandwich Plating

Cold sandwiches are usually cut into halves or thirds. Triple-decker sandwiches are often cut into fourths. Each section is held together by a frilled toothpick. Make sure that cold sandwiches are served on cold plates. Otherwise, the sandwich may become warm.

Sandwiches are often served with accompaniments such as potato chips, French fries, or soup. Salads such as cole slaw salad, fruit salad, green salad, potato salad, macaroni salad, and three-bean salad are also popular choices. Many restaurants offer a combination of a half of a sandwich with salad or soup as a daily special. Some restaurants offer only certain types of sandwiches as part of a soup or salad and sandwich combination.

Garnishing Garnishes for cold sandwiches should be selected carefully. They will impact the appearance of the plate and the texture and flavor of the sandwich. Choose garnishing items whose shape, color, and texture add interest to the sandwich. Some popular garnishes include fruit, radishes, celery and carrots, lettuce, and parsley. Some garnishes are meant to be eaten with the sandwich, such as the lettuce, tomato, and onion that are presented on the plate with a hamburger. Others, such as a beautifully carved radish, are meant to bring color and texture to the plate, although they are edible.

 Reading Check | **Identify** What are three accompaniments for cold sandwiches?

SECTION 19.2 | After You Read

Review Key Concepts

1. **Describe** how to plate hot sandwiches.
2. **Explain** how to choose a garnish for a cold sandwich.

Practice Culinary Academics

 English Language Arts

3. The word sandwich comes from the fourth Earl of Sandwich. Many words are derived from people's names. These words are called eponyms. Can you find other examples of eponyms? Write a list, and discuss your list with the class.

> **NCTE 8** Use information resources to gather information and create and communicate knowledge.

 Science

4. **Procedure** Obtain some mustard seeds or other sprouting seeds, and follow the directions on the package to grow the sprouts.

   Analysis Once the sprouts have grown, add them to a sandwich. Do they make a good sandwich ingredient? Write an evaluation of how the sprouts added interest to the sandwich.

> **NSES C** Develop an understanding of the behavior of organisms.

Mathematics

5. Liam slices a pizza into 10 equal slices. In degrees, what is the measure of the angle of each slice? If, on a second pizza, Liam makes his cuts at 45° angles, how many slices will he cut?

> **Math Concept** **Central Angles** In a circle, when two lines extend inward from the circle's outer edge and come together in the center, they form a central angle. The sum of all central angles in a circle is 360°.

> **Starting Hint** Think of the point of each pizza slice as a central angle. Because the first pizza was divided into 10 equal sections, the angle of each section must be 360° ÷ 10. The second pizza calculation would follow this equation: 360° ÷ 45° = the number of slices.

> **NCTM Geometry** Analyze characteristics of two- and three-dimensional geometric shapes and develop mathematical arguments about geometric relationships.

Check your answers at this book's Online Learning Center at **glencoe.com**.

READING CHECK ANSWER Possible answers include potato chips, French fries, soup, or various salads.

Hot Appetizers

Reading Guide

Before You Read

What You Want to Know Write a list of what you want to know about hot appetizers. As you read, write down the heads in this section that provide that information.

Read to Learn

Key Concepts
- **Give examples** of various types of hot appetizers.
- **Categorize** methods for serving hot appetizers.

Main Idea

Appetizers are designed to stimulate the appetite. A variety of advanced food preparation techniques are used to prepare and arrange hot appetizers.

Content Vocabulary
- brochette
- bouchée
- barquette
- Swedish meatball
- rumaki

Academic Vocabulary
- emphasize
- proportional

Enticing hot appetizers can make a meal special.

ACADEMIC STANDARDS

 English Language Arts
NCTE 12 Use language to accomplish individual purposes.

 Mathematics
NCTM Measurement Apply appropriate techniques, tools, and formulas to determine measurements.

 Science
NSES A Develop abilities necessary to do scientific inquiry.

NCTE National Council of Teachers of English

NCTM National Council of Teachers of Mathematics

NSES National Science Education Standards

NCSS National Council for the Social Studies

Graphic Organizer

There are three types of service for hot appetizers. Use a chart like this one to list the services, give the reason for using that type of service, and give an example of a setting where that type of service may be used.

Service	Reason	Example

Graphic Organizer Go to this book's Online Learning Center at **glencoe.com** for a printable graphic organizer.

GRAPHIC ORGANIZER ANSWER Table service: Used in a restaurant or at an event where everyone is seated; a dinner party or small wedding. Buffet service: Used at a large event with no set eating time; a large reception or party. Butler service: Used at a standing event or outdoor event; a cocktail party.

Make Hot Appetizers

Appetizers are served as the first course of a meal, while hors d'oeuvres are small bites of food served before the meal or at a separate reception. Many people use the word appetizer to mean a wide range of foods served before the main course. This could even include items such as soups and salads. Appetizers are designed to stimulate the appetite. Ingredients can come from every food group. This section will **emphasize**, or point out, how to prepare and arrange hot appetizers.

Appetizers can be passed, plated, or part of a buffet line, such as Swedish meatballs or cocktail sausages. It is important to include a variety of foods and flavors. Make sure that they complement the taste of the main dish.

Presentation is key in serving appetizers. If appetizers are served buffet-style, arrange them so that they seem to flow toward guests. If plated, use plates and trays with interesting shapes and sizes. Notice how the appetizers look on the plate. Do not pack them in. Be sure to leave some open space on the plate. Add a small garnish for presentation.

Types of Hot Appetizers

Appetizers are often served before the soup. At a classical dinner, hot appetizers are served after the soup. Hot appetizers can be created from almost any ingredient.

Brochettes

A combination of meat, poultry, fish, and vegetables served on a small skewer is called a **brochette** (brō-'shet). The items are marinated, then baked, broiled, or grilled. Brochettes, sometimes called kebabs (kə-'bäbs), often come with a dipping sauce, such as teriyaki or peanut.

To make brochettes, cut all items into consistent shapes and sizes so that they are **proportional**, or about the same size, when skewered. Before assembling, soak the bamboo skewers in water to help keep them from burning.

Filled Pastry Shells

This appetizer uses shells made from puff pastry, called a **bouchée** (bü-'shā). It may also use dough formed into a small boat-shaped shell, called a **barquette** (bär-ket) or tartlet.

Appetizer Presentation Appetizers such as shrimp can be presented in many attractive ways. *What other garnishes could be used to present this appetizer?*

PHOTO CAPTION ANSWER Answers will vary, but may include sprigs of fresh herbs, carrot curls, or cucumber strips.

The shells are baked ahead of time, then filled before serving so that they do not become soggy. Fillings can include cheeses, stews, meat, poultry, and vegetables.

Meatballs

Meatballs can be made from ground beef, poultry, veal, or pork. They are usually served with a sweet and sour, mushroom, tomato, or cream sauce. Swedish meatballs are always a crowd pleaser. A **Swedish meatball** is made with ground beef or pork and onions, and is served with a gravy.

Rumaki

Appetizers that are made of blanched bacon that is then wrapped around vegetables, seafood, chicken liver, meat, poultry, or fruits are called **rumaki** (rə-ˈmä-kē). Sometimes rumaki are brushed with a marinade or sauce before they are cooked. The rumaki are then fried, baked, or broiled.

Stuffed Potato Skins

Stuffed potato skins are made from hollowed out potatoes that are filled with a combination of ingredients such as cheese, bacon, and chives. They are then baked or broiled. Sour cream and onion are often added to stuffed potato skins before serving. Salsa is often served on the side.

Chicken Wings

Chicken wings are dipped in a spicy coating of seasonings and then deep-fried. Their spicy flavor ranges from mild to extra hot. Chicken wings can also be served sweet, baked, or roasted in a honey barbecue or deviled sauce.

Sometimes, only the meatier section of the wing is served in place of full chicken wings. These portions have more meat on them, but may still be called chicken wings on the menu.

 **Reading Check** Define What is a brochette?

Plate and Serve Hot Appetizers

Appetizers should be presented in an attractive, functional way. Appetizers served at the table, in a buffet, or at a cocktail party provide a chance for creative plating.

Table Service

The art of serving hot appetizers to each individual at the table depends on the appetizer. For example, brochettes could be served on a small plate, with a garnish to the side. When you serve appetizers at the table, take the opportunity to make each plate or bowl a special presentation.

A Hot Idea Hot appetizers can be arranged and served on attractive plates or trays and taken to individual tables. *What are two other ways that hot appetizers may be served?*

READING CHECK ANSWER A brochette is a combination of meat, poultry, fish and vegetables served on a skewer.

PHOTO CAPTION ANSWER Hot appetizers may also be served at a buffet on one or more tables, or through butler service passed on individual trays.

Buffet Service

For buffet service, food is presented all together on one or more tables. The individual presentation depends on how the appetizers are grouped on each serving plate. Place a garnish on each plate that holds appetizers. Arrange appetizers and garnishes in a manner that is visually pleasing. Allow space between each one so that they can be picked up easily.

Butler Service

Appetizers that are carried on a serving plate at a standing event, such as a party or reception, are passed according to what is called butler service. When appetizers are passed, people must be able to choose them and eat them easily while standing. Items on the plate should flow toward the customer. Be sure each item can be eaten in one or two bites and without a knife and fork. They should be given a napkin on which to hold the appetizer.

Holding and Storage

For hot appetizers to taste their best, they should be served hot. This often means cooking and assembling them just prior to serving.

Some appetizers, such as Swedish meatballs, may be baked and then kept warm for a short period of time. Other appetizers, such as bouchées, need to be assembled just before serving because they do not keep well. Chafing dishes are the best option for holding appetizers on a buffet line.

A polysulfone container can be used to hold appetizers on the steam table or to store appetizers in the refrigerator. These containers range in size from 6 inches by 12 inches, to 12 inches by 20 inches. They can be as deep as 6 inches. In other words, they can hold a large supply of food.

 Reading Check Describe How should you hold appetizers on a buffet line?

SECTION 19.3 After You Read

Review Key Concepts

1. **Describe** what a meatball is.
2. **Compare and contrast** table service and butler service.

Practice Culinary Academics

English Language Arts

3. Create a public service announcement to promote healthy appetizer choices. Include examples of healthy appetizers as suggestions. Present your announcement to the class.

> **NCTE 12** Use language to accomplish individual purposes.

Science

4. **Procedure** Make an appetizer before dinner for the next two to three days.

   Analysis Track the sensory qualities and how the appetizer affects your appetite. What do you observe about what makes a good appetizer? Create a chart that records your observations.

> **NSES A** Develop abilities necessary to do scientific inquiry.

 Mathematics

5. Carlo has been instructed to make 200 meatballs, each an inch in diameter. Approximately how many cups of meatball mixture (consisting of ground beef and other ingredients) must he prepare to form all 200 meatballs?

Math Concept **Spherical Volume** The volume (V) of a sphere (or ball) is calculated using the formula $V = 4/3\pi r^3$, where r is the radius of the sphere. Use 3.14 for π.

Starting Hint Find the volume in cubic inches of one meatball, and multiply by 200 to find the total volume needed for all meatballs. Convert to cups by dividing cubic inches by 14.4. Round to the nearest cup.

> **NCTM Measurement** Apply appropriate techniques, tools, and formulas to determine measurements.

 Check your answers at this book's Online Learning Center at **glencoe.com**.

READING CHECK ANSWER Appetizers should be held and kept warm in a chafing dish on a buffet table.

Review and Applications

Chapter Summary

There are five types of sandwiches: closed, open-face, triple-decker, finger, and wraps. Utensils needed at a sandwich work station include sharp knives, serving spoons or scoops, and a toaster. Guidelines for preparing hot sandwiches include completely assembling grilled sandwiches before cooking. Guidelines for preparing cold sandwiches include using the freshest bread possible.

Appetizers are served as the first course of a meal. They are often served before the soup. They are served after the soup in a classical dinner. Appetizers may be prepared ahead of time and assembled just before serving, or may be prepared and cooked just prior to serving. Appetizer service depends on what, where, and when the appetizers are being served. The type of appetizer and occasion determine the presentation.

Content and Academic Vocabulary Review

1. Use each of these vocabulary words in a sentence.

Content Vocabulary

- Pullman loaf (p. 488)
- croissant (p. 488)
- focaccia (p. 489)
- kaiser roll (p. 489)
- torpedo roll (p. 489)
- pita (p. 489)
- tortilla (p. 489)
- chapatti (p. 489)
- phyllo (p. 489)
- crêpe (p. 489)

- mayonnaise (p. 490)
- pesto (p. 490)
- sauerkraut (p. 491)
- grilled sandwich (p. 496)
- Monte Cristo (p. 497)
- au jus (p. 499)
- pastrami (p. 499)
- club sandwich (p. 499)
- salad sandwich (p. 499)
- brochette (p. 502)
- bouchée (p. 502)

- barquette (p. 502)
- Swedish meatball (p. 503)
- rumaki (p. 503)

Academic Vocabulary

- foundation (p. 488)
- maintain (p. 489)
- variation (p. 496)
- obtain (p. 499)
- emphasize (p. 502)
- proportional (p. 502)

Review Key Concepts

2. Identify different types of sandwiches.

3. Distinguish between various breads and spreads for sandwiches.

4. Select appropriate sandwich fillings.

5. Outline the steps in making and plating different types of hot sandwiches.

6. Explain the procedure for making various types of cold sandwiches.

7. Give examples of various types of hot appetizers.

8. Categorize methods for serving hot appetizers.

Critical Thinking

9. Explain how cost-control and portion-control techniques might be used when making sandwiches.

10. Imagine that you must provide appetizers. The items you have on hand are potatoes, fish, bacon, bell peppers, onions, and cheese. What would you make?

Academic Skills

English Language Arts

11. Give Directions As a class, think of names of sandwiches that you know. Write the names down on cards. Place all of the cards into a hat, and draw a card out of a container at the instruction of your teacher. Follow your teacher's instructions to pair up into partners. Take turns giving each other instructions on how to prepare your sandwich. Do research if necessary.

> **NCTE 4** Use written language to communicate effectively.

Social Studies

12. Global Appetizers Many cultures have traditional recipes that make small-size dishes that would be appropriate served as hot appetizers. Research and locate five dishes from different countries around the world that could also be prepared as a hot appetizer. Write a short summary of the ingredients and preparation for each dish. You may include photos or illustrations with your summaries, if you wish.

> **NCSS I E Culture** Demonstrate the value of cultural diversity, as well as cohesion, within and across groups.

Mathematics

13. Make Cheeseburgers The diner where Tak works purchases pre-sliced cheddar cheese for burgers, but Tak must form the ground beef patties by hand. The patties must be wide enough that the cheese does not overlap the edges. If each cheese slice is a uniform 3 inches by 4 inches, what is the minimum diameter of the hamburger patties that Tak must make?

Math Concept **Pythagorean Theorem** The Pythagorean Theorem states that, for right triangles, $a^2 + b^2 = c^2$ (where c is the length of the hypotenuse, or side opposite the right angle, and a and b represent the other two sides).

Starting Hint Draw a rectangle representing the cheese slice, labeling two opposing sides as 3 inches and the others as 4 inches. Draw a circle around (but bigger than) the rectangle, representing the hamburger patty. The smallest possible circle you can draw would just barely touch the four corners of the rectangle. If you were to draw a diagonal line connecting two of the corners, this line would also be the diameter of the circle. Use the Pythagorean Theorem to find the length of this line.

> **NCTM Geometry** Use visualization, spatial reasoning, and geometric modeling to solve problems.

Certification Prep

Directions Read the questions. Then, read the answer choices and choose the best possible answer for each.

14. What type of sandwich classification is pizza?

    a. closed sandwich

    b. open-face sandwich

    c. triple-decker sandwich

    d. finger sandwich

15. What is the consistent ingredient in all rumaki?

    a. blanched bacon

    b. vegetables

    c. meat

    d. fruit

> *Sharpen your test-taking skills to improve your kitchen certification program score.*

Test-Taking Tip
Start studying for tests early and review the material a little at a time. Do not wait until the night before and try to review everything at once.

Real-World Skills and Applications

Management Skills

16. Revamp a Menu Imagine that you have reviewed your establishment's lunch menu and determined that more items from the Milk, Vegetables, and Fruits Groups are needed. You decide to add some sandwiches to provide these groups. Write descriptions of five sandwiches that will provide items from these groups.

Interpersonal and Collaborative Skills

17. Reinvent an Appetizer Divide into groups at the direction of your teacher. Imagine that you are caterers who have been hired to cater an event for vegetarians. As a group, reinvent some of the appetizers described in the chapter so that they would be an appropriate choice for vegetarians.

Technology Applications

18. Design a Database Design a nutrition database for 10 sandwiches using a spreadsheet or database program. Make sure to include both sandwiches with meat and some without. Research and provide nutritional information for each sandwich as one of the columns in your spreadsheet or fields in your database.

Financial Literacy

19. Compare Costs You want to make a ham and cheese sandwich and are looking at your ingredient options. You need 4 ounces of cheese, 4 ounces of meat, and 2 slices of bread for each sandwich. Ham costs $5 per ½ pound. Cheese costs $4 per ½ pound. Bread costs $4.50 for 18 slices. How much will each sandwich cost to make?

Culinary Lab

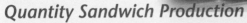

Use the culinary skills you have learned in this chapter.

Quantity Sandwich Production

20. Cater a Picnic Imagine that your class has received an order to cater an outdoor picnic. You will need to provide 25 cold meat sandwiches using whole-wheat, rye, sourdough, and white bread.

A. Choose a sandwich. Follow your teacher's instructions to form teams. As a team choose one type of sandwich to make. Create a chart to show the sandwich type, bread, filling, spread, cheese, garnish, and accompaniments.

B. Arrange your workspace. Draw a diagram of how you will arrange your workspace, with all ingredients and utensils in place.

C. List sandwich-making steps. Write out detailed guidelines for each step of the sandwich-making process.

D. Evaluate your processes. Share your team's sandwich production plan and work space guide with the other teams.

Create Your Evaluation

Evaluate each team's production plan as a group discussion. Discuss the advantages and disadvantages of using each plan to make the sandwiches. Then, as a group, decide on which team has created the most workable plan. Prepare all of the sandwiches according to the chosen plan. Then, discuss what you learned about sandwich production from the experience of planning and then making sandwiches in quantity.

Stocks, Sauces, and Soups

SECTIONS

20.1 Stocks

20.2 Sauces

20.3 Soups

WRITING ACTIVITY

Memo

Imagine that you work in a restaurant that is planning on adding a selection of pastas to the menu. Write a memo to the executive chef explaining what sauces you think might go well with pasta, and why.

Writing Tips

1 State the purpose of your memorandum.

2 Explain your subjects clearly.

3 Organize the paragraphs in a logical way.

> **EXPLORE THE PHOTO**
>
> The right herbs and spices add flavor to a stock. *What do you think stock is used for?*

WRITING ACTIVITY ANSWER
The memo should be in the correct format. Supporting paragraphs should explain sauce choices.

EXPLORE THE PHOTO ANSWER
Stocks are used as a base for sauces and soups.

Stocks

Reading Guide

 Before You Read

Preview Understanding causes and effects can help clarify connections. A cause is an event or action that makes something happen. An effect is a result of a cause. Ask yourself, "Why does this happen?" to help you recognize cause-and-effect relationships in this section.

Read to Learn

Key Concepts
- **Identify** the elements of a stock.
- **Explain** the preparation of different varieties of stock.

Main Idea
Stocks are the liquids that form the foundation of sauces and soups. Learning how to make stocks can help you create flavorful sauces and soups.

Graphic Organizer
As you read, use a problem-solution chart like this one to list the three potential problems that could happen when preparing white stock, and how to prevent those problems.

Content Vocabulary
- stock
- nourishing element
- mirepoix
- base
- white stock
- brown stock
- fish stock
- fumet
- vegetable stock
- glaze
- reduction

Academic Vocabulary
- supplement
- reserve

Preparing White Stock

Problem	Solution
1.	
2.	
3.	

 Graphic Organizer Go to this book's Online Learning Center at **glencoe.com** for a printable graphic organizer.

GRAPHIC ORGANIZER ANSWER 1) Impurities in the bones; rinse or blanch bones. 2) Cloudy stock; add cold water to stock before boiling, keep at a simmer, use a ladle to skim impurities. 3) Bones do not release flavor, bones darken; completely cover bones with liquid.

ACADEMIC STANDARDS

 English Language Arts
NCTE 2 Read literature to build an understanding of the human experience.

 Mathematics
NCTM Problem Solving
Build new mathematical knowledge through problem solving.

 Science
NSES B Develop an understanding of the interactions of energy and matter.

 Social Studies
NCSS IV B Individual Development and Identity
Identify, describe, and express appreciation for the influence of various historical and contemporary cultures on an individual's daily life.

NCTE National Council of Teachers of English

NCTM National Council of Teachers of Mathematics

NSES National Science Education Standards

NCSS National Council for the Social Studies

Stock Basics

The French word for stock is fond, meaning bottom, ground, or base. Since the 16th century, the quality of sauces and soups has depended upon the stocks that are used as their base. Learning the skill of making stocks will allow you to build sauces and soups on a strong foundation.

A **stock** is the liquid that forms the foundation of sauces and soups. Simmering various combinations of bones, vegetables, and herbs extracts their flavors to create this foundation.

Elements of a Stock

A stock is composed of four ingredients: the nourishing element, mirepoix, bouquet garni, and liquid. These ingredients are usually mixed in the following proportions to make most stocks:

- 5 parts nourishing element
- 1 part mirepoix
- bouquet garni
- 10 parts liquid

Nourishing Element

The most important ingredient in a stock is the nourishing element. A nourishing element includes any one or a combination of the following:

- Fresh bones (beef, lamb, chicken, fish, veal, or game)
- Meat trimmings
- Fish trimmings for fish stock
- Vegetables for vegetable stock

The **nourishing element** provides flavor, nutrients, and color. Some nourishing elements may bring other benefits to the stock, such as bones, which add gelatin.

Mirepoix

Mirepoix (mir-'pwä) is a mix of coarsely chopped vegetables that is used in a stock to add flavor, nutrients, and color. The ingredients vary with each recipe, but usually include two parts onions, one part celery, and one part carrots.

Bouquet Garni

French for garnished bouquet, a bouquet garni is a combination of fresh herbs and vegetables, such as carrots, leeks, celery, thyme, and parsley stems, that are tied in a bundle with butcher's twine. This bundle is added directly to the liquid and is allowed to simmer. The bouquet garni is removed before the stock is used in other foods.

Liquid

Liquid, almost always in the form of water, makes up the largest portion of stock. The liquid used to make stock should be cold when you begin to cook. This brings out the maximum flavor of the ingredients and prevents the stock from turning cloudy. When all the ingredients are prepared, the ratio of liquid to the nourishing element should be 2 to 1.

Commercial Stock Bases

Stocks can be purchased in a powdered or concentrated form, called a **base**. Using a commercial base saves time and money. However, what many bases add in convenience, they lose in flavor quality.

When you choose a commercial base, check the list of ingredients. Remember that the ingredients are listed in order from highest weight amount to lowest weight amount. A better-quality commercial stock base will list fish, meat, or poultry extracts rather than salt or sodium first. You can give commercial stock bases a fresher taste by simmering them for a few hours with bones and mirepoix. Then, strain the mixture and use it like a stock.

Some chefs use commercial stock bases to give sauces and soups a stronger flavor. Commercial stock bases can also be added as a **supplement**, or addition, when there is not enough stock available. Recipes must be adjusted when using bases because of the high amount of salt they contain.

 **Reading Check** List What are the four main ingredients of stocks?

READING CHECK ANSWER The four main ingredients of stocks are a nourishing element, a mirepoix, a bouquet garni, and a liquid.

Mirepoix in Stock A mirepoix adds flavor, color, and nutrients to stocks. *What vegetables would you use for a mirepoix?*

Types of Stocks

White, brown, fish, and vegetable stocks are the main types of stocks. They are sometimes referred to by their French names. (See **Figure 20.1**.)

White Stock

A **white stock** is made from chicken, beef, veal, or fish bones simmered with vegetables. White stock is generally colorless while it is cooking. To keep the stock as clear as possible, you may blanch the bones before adding them. However, some chefs think doing so causes flavor to be lost.

Brown Stock

Brown stock is made from either beef, veal, chicken, or game. It gets its color from roasting the ingredients without water, in a hot oven. The browned bones, mirepoix, and tomatoes or tomato product combine to give a brown stock its color. This mixture is then transferred to a stockpot and simmered along with water and herbs.

Brown Stock Preparation

The steps to make white stocks and brown stocks are mostly the same. (See How to Prepare White Stock on page 512.) The main difference is that for brown stocks, the bones and mirepoix are browned by roasting.

Follow these steps for brown stock:
1. Cut the beef or veal bones into 3- to 4-inch pieces.
2. Browning is slowed down by moisture, so do not wash or blanch the bones.
3. Place the bones one layer deep in a roasting pan.
4. Roast bones in the oven at 375°F (191°C) or higher for more than an hour, stirring occasionally. Some chefs lightly oil the bones before browning.

PHOTO CAPTION ANSWER A mirepoix usually contains onion, celery, and carrots.

FIGURE CAPTION ANSWER White stocks can be made from chicken, beef, veal, or fish bones that have not been roasted, that are simmered with vegetables.

Prepare
White Stock

1 Cut bones into 3- to 4-inch piecess. Chicken and fish bones do not need to be cut.

2 Rinse the bones in cold water to remove any impurities. You can blanch the bones, if desired. Place the bones in a stockpot.

3 Add cold water until the bones are completely covered. Cold water dissolves impurities ((ˌ)im'pyur-ə-tēs) and blood in the bones it covers. These impurities will clump and rise to the surface when the water heats, where they can be skimmed off the top. Using hot water will cause the impurities to clump too rapidly. This prevents them from rising to the top and results in a cloudy stock.

4 Bring water to a boil. Then, reduce it to a simmer to slowly release the full flavor of the ingredients.

5 To keep the stock clear, use a skimmer or ladle to remove any impurities and fat from the surface. Skim as needed.

6 Add the mirepoix. Boiling makes the stock cloudy, so keep the water at a simmer.

7 Make sure liquid is still completely covering the bones. Bones will not release their flavor unless they are under water, and will darken if exposed to air.

8 For the best flavor, simmer stock for the recommended amount of time:

- Fish bones: 30-45 minutes
- Chicken bones: 3-4 hours
- Beef or veal bones: 6-8 hours

9 Skim all of the impurities and fat from the stock.

10 Strain the stock through a china cap.

11 Cool the stock quickly, as discussed later in this section.

5. Place the browned bones in a stockpot and cover with water. Bring the water to a simmer.
6. **Reserve**, or keep, the excess fat from the roasting pan.
7. Deglaze the pan with water. To deglaze means to add a liquid and stir over heat until the drippings are dissolved.
8. Add the deglazed mixture to the stockpot.
9. Combine the mirepoix and reserved fat in a pan, while the bones are beginning to simmer. Brown in the oven or on top of the range.
10. Skim impurities and fat from the stock as it begins to simmer.
11. Add the tomatoes or tomato product and caramelized vegetables to the stockpot, up to three or four hours before the end of cooking. Do not stir the stock or it will become cloudy. Continue following the steps for making white stock.

Fish Stock

Fish stock is made by slowly cooking the bones of lean fish or shellfish. The procedure to make fish stock is the same as to make a white stock, although the cooking time for fish stock is shorter. If lemon juice or other acids are added to the water, the result is a flavorful liquid called a **fumet** (fyü-'mā). A fumet is more strongly flavored than regular fish stock since it is reduced by 50%.

Vegetable Stock

Vegetable stocks, which do not include meat products, are an important addition to many healthful dishes. In addition, vegetable stock forms the base for many vegetarian and vegan dishes. The basic ingredients of a **vegetable stock** are vegetables, herbs, spices, and water. Proportions and kinds of vegetables will vary with different recipes. Vegetable stock needs to be simmered only 30 to 45 minutes.

If you want a particular flavor of vegetable stock, use more of that vegetable. Then, add

Fish Dish A fish stock is made with the bones of lean fish or shellfish. *What other ingredients can be added to a fish stock?*

neutral-tasting vegetables such as celery and onions to round out the flavor. All-purpose vegetable stock does not include strongly flavored vegetables, such as artichokes, brussels sprouts, or cauliflower. These vegetables tend to overpower other flavors. Some dark-green, leafy vegetables, such as spinach, develop an unpleasant odor when they are cooked for too long.

Glazes

A **glaze** is a stock that is reduced and concentrated. This results in a flavorful, thick, and syrupy liquid that turns solid when it is refrigerated. Glazes are created through reduction. **Reduction** is the process of evaporating part of a stock's water through simmering or boiling. Small amounts of glaze can be used to flavor sauces, vegetables, meat, poultry, and fish.

PHOTO CAPTION ANSWER Mirepoix, a bouquet garni containing herbs, and lemon juice or other acids can be added to make a flavorful fish stock.

Prepare
a Glaze

1 Place a large quantity of stock in a heavy pan.

2 Bring the stock to a simmer.

3 Skim the surface as needed.

4 Clean the sides of the pan with a moistened, natural-bristle brush as the stock reduces and becomes syrupy.

5 Transfer the stock to a smaller pan when reduced by half to two-thirds.

6 Continue to reduce until the stock coats a spoon.

7 Strain the stock through a chinois, or china cap, and pour into containers.

8 Follow recommended procedures for cooling stock; then label, date, and refrigerate or freeze the containers.

Cooling and Storing Stocks

Always cool stock before you store it. There are three ways to cool stock. You can use Rapi-Kool®, which is a brand of container that can be filled with water and then frozen. This frozen container is then put into the stock to speed up the cooling process. Another method is to pour the stock into a container that is less than 4 inches deep and place it in the refrigerator. Stock should never be cooled in the refrigerator. A refrigerator is not meant to cool hot foods. The stock will cool too slowly in a refrigerator. This could allow bacteria to grow, making the stock unsafe to eat.

A third cooling method is explained below:

1. First, place the stockpot on a rack or on blocks in an empty sink. Make sure the stockpot is balanced and will not spill.

This is called venting. It will allow cold water to move beneath and around the pot as the sink fills with water.

2. Insert an overflow pipe over the drain to allow the water to circulate.

3. Next, turn on the cold water tap.

4. Continue to run cold water into the sink, forcing the extra water to drain out the overflow pipe as it becomes warm from the stockpot.

When the stock is cool, transfer it to a plastic container with a tight-fitting lid, and label and date it. Never place hot stock in a refrigerator to cool it. The steam and heat may damage other foods. It may also damage your refrigerator, and can raise the overall temperature inside the refrigerator. Stock can be stored for several days in a walk-in or reach-in refrigerator.

1847 — The canning of tomatoes is first documented

1848 — The first Women's Rights Convention takes place in Seneca Falls, New York

You Say Tomato

It is hard to imagine Italian sauces without tomatoes as a main ingredient. Yet, the tomato was not introduced to Italy until the 16th century. Tomatoes are native to Central America, and not to Europe. Cousin to the potato, the tomato was discovered by Spanish explorers during their travels to Mexico and Peru. Today, the United States is the world's leading producer of tomatoes.

History Application

In addition to being packed with taste, tomatoes are nutritionally loaded. Write a short ode to the tomato. In your ode, include nutritional information and some ways tomatoes can be enjoyed.

NCSS IV B Individual Development and Identity Identify, describe, and express appreciation for the influence of various historical and contemporary cultures on an individual's daily life.

Stock that has not been cooled correctly can spoil within six to eight hours. Discard stock if you are unsure of its freshness.

Remove the layer of fat before you use the stock. Fat rises to the surface and becomes solid when a stock chills. This fat layer acts as a preservative, keeping the stock below it fresh. However, the fat layer must be scraped or lifted off before you reheat the stock. The fat will not incorporate back into the stock when it is heated. Stock may also be strained through cheesecloth to remove additional fat.

Like other foods, stock should be reheated properly to help avoid foodborne illness. Reheat stock to a temperature of 165°F (74°C) for at least 15 seconds. Hold stock at a temperature of 135°F (57°C) or above when it is to be used for service.

Reading Check Explain What is the purpose of the fat layer in a cooled and stored stock?

SECTION 20.1 After You Read

Review Key Concepts

1. **Identify** items that can be nourishing elements.
2. **Explain** the preparation of fish stock

Practice Culinary Academics

English Language Arts

3. Do you remember the fable of Stone Soup? Find a version of the fable and read it. Compare the soup made in the story to the instructions given for making stocks. Write a paragraph to describe how you think the stone soup would compare to a stock.

NCTE 2 Read literature to build an understanding of the human experience.

Science

4. **Procedure** Try cooking a stock first by adding ingredients to boiling water, then by starting with ingredients in cold water and heating gradually.

   Analysis Does the stock started in boiling water become cloudy? Write a summary.

NSES B Develop an understanding of the interactions of energy and matter.

Mathematics

5. In a 12-inch diameter stockpot, you pour 10 quarts (577.5 cubic inches) of water over fish bones and trimmings. If the resulting mixture is 8 inches high in the pot, what was the volume of the fish parts?

Math Concept **Volume of a Cylinder** Calculate the volume (V) of a cylinder as $V = \pi r^2 h$, where r = the radius of the circular base, and h is the cylinder's height. Use 3.14 for π.

Starting Hint The volume of the fish parts equals the volume of the mixture (which you can calculate using the formula above, with r = 6 inches) minus the volume of the water alone (577.5 cubic inches).

NCTM Problem Solving Build new mathematical knowledge through problem solving.

Check your answers at this book's Online Learning Center at **glencoe.com**.

A TASTE OF HISTORY ANSWER Poems will vary, but should mention that tomatoes contain vitamins; are a good source of nutrients; are low in fat and sodium; and contain the antioxidant lycopene.

READING CHECK ANSWER The fat layer acts as a preservative.

Sauces

Reading Guide

 Before You Read

Look It Up As you read this section, keep a dictionary nearby in addition to the glossary at the back of the book. If you hear or read a word that you do not know, look it up in the glossary or the dictionary. Before long, the practice will become a habit. You will be amazed at how many new words you learn.

Read to Learn

Key Concepts
- **List** the main ingredients in a sauce.
- **Distinguish** between the five mother sauces.
- **Outline** the steps to prepare a roux.

Main Idea
Sauces are flavored, thickened liquids. They can add flavor and excitement to a dish that is otherwise bland.

Content Vocabulary
- sauce
- thickening agent
- Béchamel
- hollandaise sauce
- gelatinization
- coulis
- cheesecloth
- mother sauces
- sauce espagnole
- demi-glace
- tomato sauce
- roux
- velouté
- marinara sauce
- gravy
- compound butters
- clarified butter

Academic Vocabulary
- mediocre
- clarity

Graphic Organizer
As you read, use a category tier organizer like this one to list the three different types of sauce ingredients in the second-tier boxes. Then, list specific examples of those ingredients in the third-tier boxes.

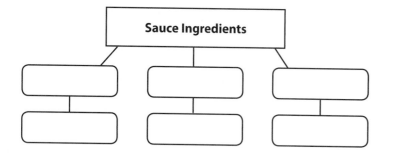

Sauce Ingredients

 Graphic Organizer Go to this book's Online Learning Center at **glencoe.com** for a printable graphic organizer.

GRAPHIC ORGANIZER ANSWER 1) Liquid ingredients: Stock, vinegar, tomato products, milk. 2) Seasonings and flavorings: Salt, pepper, mustard, spices, herbs. 3) Thickening agents: Flour, cornstarch, arrowroot, purées.

 Mathematics
NCTM Measurement Apply appropriate techniques, tools, and formulas to determine measurements.

 Science
NSES B Develop an understanding of the interactions of energy and matter.

 Social Studies
NCSS I B Culture Predict how data and experiences may be interpreted by people from diverse cultural perspectives and frames of reference.

NCTE National Council of Teachers of English

NCTM National Council of Teachers of Mathematics

NSES National Science Education Standards

NCSS National Council for the Social Studies

Sauce Basics

One of the best ways to add flavor and excitement to any dish is with a good sauce. In fact, a good sauce can turn a **mediocre**, or average, dish into a memorable one. People enjoy sauces with a variety of foods, from chicken to vegetable dishes. Learning to make a good sauce is a basic step toward becoming a great cook.

Generally, a **sauce** is a flavored, thickened liquid. It is usually formed by adding a thickening agent, seasonings, and flavorings to stock. A **thickening agent** is an ingredient, such as cornstarch, that adds body to the sauce. Two sauces that are not made with stock are **béchamel** (ˌbā-shə-ˈmel), a basic French white sauce made with milk and a thickener, and hollandaise sauce. **Hollandaise** (ˌhä-lən-ˈdāz) **sauce** is made from lemon juice, butter, and eggs.

Sauces are meant to complement the foods they accompany. They should never overpower or detract from the food. It takes a lot of time to make a good sauce. Many restaurants use condensed or powdered commercial bases mixed with water to create stocks. The stocks and sauces then do not need to be reduced, since there is no gelatin in these commercial bases. Although quality may be a concern, these bases do guarantee a consistent flavor and texture. Premade sauces are also available, but they may not have the flavor of freshly made sauces.

Sauce Ingredients

Sauces are made of liquid ingredients, thickening agents, and seasonings and flavorings. Classic sauces rely on combinations of a few basic ingredients.

Liquid Ingredients

The liquid ingredient in most sauces serves as the base, or body. You will commonly use some type of stock as the base for a sauce. You may use white stock made from chicken, veal, or fish. Other sauces call for brown stock.

Vinegar or tomato products may be added to sauces for acidity. Sometimes milk is used as a base. Clarified or drawn butter is another liquid ingredient in sauces.

Thickening Agents

A major difference between stocks and sauces is that a sauce must be thickened. Most thickening agents are forms of starch. Starch granules will absorb moisture when placed in a liquid, a process called **gelatinization** (jə-ˌla-tə-nə-ˈzā-shən). Most sauces use this process in thickening. A good sauce will have these four characteristics:

- No lumps
- A flavor that is not floury or pasty
- Sticks to the back of a spoon
- Will not break apart when it cooks down

Thickening agents include flour, cornstarch, arrowroot, instant starches, bread crumbs, and vegetable purées.

Flour Bread or all-purpose flour is most often used to thicken the fat from the pan in which the entrée has been sautéed. Flour may also be combined with butter that has just been melted as a quick way to thicken a sauce or soup.

Cornstarch Cornstarch is a powdery, dense flour with almost twice the thickening power of flour. It is often used in desserts and sweet sauces. A sauce made with cornstarch will be almost clear in appearance and have a glossy texture.

Arrowroot Arrowroot is similar to cornstarch, but more expensive. It is made from the roots of several tropical plants. Arrowroot creates a clearer sauce than cornstarch does. It is also used in frozen foods because the sauce will not break down when it is frozen and then reheated.

Instant Starches Instant starches have been dried after being cooked. They can thicken a liquid without being heated. They are used more commonly in baking than in sauce making.

Bread Crumbs Because they are cooked, bread crumbs can thicken a liquid quickly.

Keep in mind, however, that a sauce that is thickened with bread crumbs will not be smooth.

Vegetable Purées A purée is a food that has been mashed, strained, or finely chopped into a smooth pulp. Purées can be used to thicken sauces. A vegetable, such as potatoes, or a combination of vegetables may be cooked with herbs, spices, and other flavorings and then puréed. If you need to thin a purée, add water, cream, or stock. A **coulis** (kü-'lē) is a sauce made from a fruit or vegetable purée. Vegetable purées and coulis are healthful choices because they do not rely on the fat content of the heavier sauces.

Seasonings and Flavorings

The liquid ingredients may make up the basic flavor of most sauces, but the seasonings and flavorings you include will add the finishing touches. You can change the character of your sauce simply by changing an ingredient or two.

You already know that seasonings and flavorings can be used to enhance the flavors of a dish. Salt, pepper, mustard, vinegar, spices, and herbs can all change the flavor of a sauce.

Thickening by Reduction

Sauces are also thickened by reduction, the process of simmering down a liquid. A liquid can be cooked down to one-half or one-fourth of its original amount. This concentrates the flavor even more, because the amount of water is reduced.

Use several layers of cheesecloth and a china cap to strain the sauce for the greatest smoothness. **Cheesecloth** is a loose-woven cotton cloth used in cheesemaking and cooking. Straining will also remove the stems and leaves of any spices, herbs, or other seasonings. This will not remove the flavor.

Sauces will be judged by their quality in the following categories:
- Appearance, for shine and color
- Flavor
- Texture, or smoothness
- Thickness, as appropriate to the type of sauce
- **Clarity** ('kler-ə-tē), or how clear it is

Science à la Carte

The Science of Thickening

Starches, such as flour and cornstarch, are often used to thicken sauces. Starch is made up of many granules of glucose molecules that are bonded together. Because of the large structure of a starch molecule, it normally does not dissolve in cold water. As the water is heated, however, the molecules that make up the starch get more active. This weakens the bonds between the starch molecules, and they absorb the water. The hotter the water gets, the more the granules absorb, until they begin to swell. This is called gelatinization. Near the boiling point of the liquid, between 160°F to 180°F (71°C to 82°C), the granules have absorbed so much water that each granule finally pops. Starch rushes into the sauce and the sauce thickens.

Procedure

Follow your teacher's instructions to form Team One and Team Two. Each team will start with 1 pint of chicken broth, one small sauce pot and 2 tablespoons of bread flour. Team Two will also have a ½-cup container with a cover. Complete the following experiment.

- **Team One** Pour 1 pint of chicken broth into a pot and heat it until it becomes very hot. Add 2 tablespoons of bread flour to the broth. Stir and continue heating.
- **Team Two** Pour 1 pint of chicken broth into a pot and heat it until it becomes very hot. Place 2 tablespoons of bread flour into the ½-cup container and add ¼ cup of water. Cover and shake well. Pour this mixture into the broth, stir, and continue heating.

Analysis

Compare both teams' findings. What was different about each broth mixture? Share your ideas on why there were differences. See if you can come to one conclusion. Use this conclusion to write a cooking tip on the best way to thicken hot soup or sauce.

NSES B Develop an understanding of the interactions of energy and matter.

SCIENCE À LA CARTE ANSWER The broth in Team One's pot should have lumps, and the broth in Team Two's pot should not. By premixing the starch and water in a small cup before adding it to the hot liquid, the starch granules have a chance to scatter.

Storage

Sauces are generally prepared to be used the same day. If a sauce must be stored, pour melted butter on top or cover the sauce with oiled parchment paper before storing. This will reduce the amount of fat that will come to the surface of the sauce. Sauces should be labeled, dated, and kept refrigerated. Place the sauce in a plastic storage container with a tight-fitting lid.

Reading Check Explain What is the best way to store sauces?

Mother Sauces

The five basic sauces are known as **mother sauces**, or grand sauces. These sauces are all made by combining a liquid with a thickening agent. Compound sauces are made from these mother sauces. For example, a mother sauce such as béchamel forms the basis for an additional five sauces.

Sauce Espagnole

Made from thickened brown stock, **sauce espagnole** (ˌes-pan-'yól), which is French for Spanish sauce, also contains some type of tomato product. In general, this type of sauce has few added seasonings. **Demi-glace** ('de-mē-ˌglas) is made from sauce espagnole. It is half espagnole sauce and half brown stock that has been reduced by half. Demi-glace comes from the French for half-glaze. Demi-glace forms the basis for many compound brown sauces. Some chefs use demi-glace more often than they use espagnole sauce as an individual sauce.

Tomato Sauce

Tomato sauce is made by simmering a tomato product with flavorings, seasonings, and stock or another liquid. Although basic tomato sauce is made with vegetables only, some variations add meat. Tomato sauce is a very versatile sauce.

◀ **Thickened Sauces** Many sauces are thickened with a form of starch. *How can you tell if a sauce has been sitting too long?*

READING CHECK ANSWER Cover the sauce with melted butter or oiled parchment paper, put in a plastic container, label, date, and store in the refrigerator.

PHOTO CAPTION ANSWER Sauces that have been sitting too long appear lumpy, rather than smooth and creamy.

Béchamel Sauce

Also known as a cream sauce or a white sauce, this mother sauce is made by thickening milk with a white roux (rü), seasonings, and flavorings. A **roux** is a cooked mixture made from equal parts of fat and flour by weight.

Velouté

From the French word for velvety, **velouté** (və-ˌlü-ˈtā) sauce, also known as blond sauce, is made by thickening a light-colored stock with a light-colored roux. The sauce is named after the type of stock it contains.

Hollandaise Sauce

From the French word for Dutch, hollandaise sauce is made from emulsified egg yolks, clarified butter, seasonings, and often lemon juice. Emulsifying takes place when substances, such as water and oil, are mixed with an emulsifier like egg yolks. Once mixed, these substances will not separate.

Other Sauces

From the five basic mother sauces come hundreds of different compound sauces. For example, adding olive oil and herbs to a basic tomato sauce creates a **marinara sauce**.

Not all sauces, however, come from these mother sauces. Some sauces are made from a purée of fruits or vegetables. Other sauces are made from meat juices or butter.

Salsa Salsas can include a combination of raw vegetables or fruits, spices, onions, and chiles. They can be used for more than dipping vegetables or chips, however. Salsas can also be used as sauces for potatoes, poultry, meat, or fish entrées.

Relishes Relishes are another type of sauce. Often made with fruits or vegetables, this sauce may be used as a condiment or a sauce for meat, poultry, and fish. The sauce may be cooked or pickled, meaning preserved in a seasoned solution of vinegar or brine. Relishes may be sweet, savory, or spicy. They also vary in texture from smooth to chunky.

Colorful Salsa Salsa is a colorful and tasty addition to many foods. *What foods do you think salsa would complement?*

PHOTO CAPTION ANSWER Answers will vary, but could include chips, raw vegetables, meats, fish, or potatoes.

Gravy Gravy is a type of sauce made from meat or poultry juices; a liquid such as milk, cream, or broth; and a thickening agent such as a roux. Pan gravy is made from the deglazed pan drippings of roasted meat or poultry. The pan gravy is served with the meat. You may also serve gravy with a side dish such as mashed potatoes.

Compound Butters You can make a **compound butter** by adding seasonings to softened butter. You may have eaten at a restaurant where herbs, such as basil, chives, or parsley, have been blended into the butter served with the bread. Sometimes a compound butter is placed on top of a piece of fish or meat just before serving it. As the butter melts, it flavors the food. It also makes an elegant presentation.

Independent Sauces Applesauce, cocktail sauce, sweet and sour sauce, and barbecue sauce are four common examples of independent sauces. These sauces may be served hot or cold.

Reading Check Contrast What are the differences between béchamel and velouté sauces?

Roux Preparation

Many sauces are formed from a stock and roux. A roux is the most commonly used thickening agent. Many chefs use 60% flour and 40% fat to decrease the calories and fat in sauces. Being able to make a good roux is a very important skill.

Equal parts of fat and flour by weight form a paste when they are cooked together. Roux can be white, blond, or brown, depending in part on how long it is cooked.

Roux Ingredients

The following cooking fats can be used to make roux:

- **Clarified Butter** Also known as drawn butter, **clarified butter** is purified butterfat. This means that the butter is melted with the water and milk solids removed. Clarified butter is preferred for making roux because the water in unclarified butter changes the consistency of the roux. One pound of clarified butter results from 1¼ pounds of butter. Clarified butter must be made ahead of time.

▲ **Mother Sauces** The mother sauces pictured here are demi-glace (espagnole), tomato, and béchamel. *Why are they called mother sauces?*

READING CHECK ANSWER Béchamel is made by thickening milk with a white roux. Velouté is made by thickening light-colored stock with light-colored roux.

PHOTO CAPTION ANSWER The five basic sauces are called mother sauces because more complex sauces are formed from them.

Béchamel Sauce

YIELD: 1 GAL.
SERVING SIZE: 2 OZ.

Ingredients

4 qts.	Milk
1 each	Onion clouté, cut in half
6 oz.	Clarified butter
6 oz.	All-purpose flour, sifted
	Salt and ground white pepper, to taste
	Nutmeg, to taste

Method of Preparation

1. In a saucepan, heat the milk with the onion clouté, and simmer for 10 minutes.
2. In another saucepan, heat the clarified butter over moderate heat.
3. Gradually add flour to the butter to make a blonde roux. Using a spoon, mix the roux thoroughly, and cook it approximately 5 to 6 minutes. Remove from the heat, and cool slightly.
4. Remove the onion clouté from the milk.
5. Gradually add the hot milk to the roux, whisking constantly. Heat to a boil. Reduce to a simmer. Simmer for 20 minutes or until the proper flavor and consistency are achieved.
6. Season to taste.
7. Strain through a fine chinois into a suitable container. Hold at 135°F (57°C) or above, or cool to an internal temperature of 41°F (5°C) or below. Label, date, and refrigerate.
8. Reheat to 165°F (74°C) for 15 seconds.

International Flavor

It is believed that Béchamel sauce originated in France in the 18th century. Many countries use similar ingredients to create white sauce. Research these recipes, and create a chart showing the differences in ingredients and cooking techniques used.

- Alfredo sauce (Italy)
- White gravy (United States)
- Crema Mexicana (Mexico)

Cooking Technique

Simmer

1. Heat the cooking liquid to the proper temperature.
2. Submerge the food product completely.
3. Keep the cooked product moist and warm.

Chef Notes

The sauce is ready when the proper thickness has been achieved and the floury taste is cooked away. To prevent a dried surface (skin) from forming while holding the sauce in a bain marie, cover the surface with plastic wrap.

Substitutions

- To lower the fat content, use low-fat milk or nonfat half-and-half.
- Try adding lemon or cheese for additional flavor and interest.

Glossary

Clouté studded with cloves
Chinois cone-shaped strainer
Bain marie hot-water bath

HACCP

- Hold at 135°F (57°C) or above
- Cool to an internal temperature of 41°F (5°C) or below
- Reheat to 165°F (74°C) for 15 seconds

Hazardous Foods

- Milk
- Butter

Nutrition

Calories 90	Calories from fat 35

Total Fat 4g
  Saturated Fat 2.5g
  Trans Fat 0g
Cholesterol 10mg
Sodium 85mg
Total Carbohydrate 10g
  Fiber 0g
  Sugars 6g
Protein 4g

- Vitamin A 2% • Vitamin C 0%
- Calcium 15% • Iron 2%

- **Margarine** Because of its low cost, margarine is often used instead of butter. Although the quality of margarine varies, it does not generally make as good of a sauce as butter does.
- **Animal Fats** These fats include lard, butter, and the fats that come directly from an animal, such as chicken fat. Use these fats to flavor sauces. For example, use veal fat in veal velouté and chicken drippings in chicken gravy.
- **Vegetable Oil** These oils include those specific oils that come from plants as well as blends of different vegetable oils, including corn, safflower, and soybean. Because these oils do not add flavor to a sauce, they are not recommended for making sauces.
- **Shortening** This white, solid fat has no flavor and a high melting point. This makes shortening better for frying or baking than for sauce making.

Starch content plays an important role in the thickening power of flour. Because bread flour contains less starch than cake flour, 10 ounces of bread flour has the same thickening power as 8 ounces of cake flour.

Bread flour is used to thicken sauces in most commercial kitchens. That is why the recipes for most sauces are based on using bread flour or all-purpose flour, which has about the same thickening power as bread flour. If you use a different kind of flour, be sure to adjust the ratio of roux to liquid. For example, Cajun ('kā-jən) recipes may call for browned flour. This flour has been browned in an oven. Browned flour has less thickening power than unbrowned flour.

Proportions of Roux Ingredients

Remember that you must use equal parts of fat and flour to make a good roux. Test this by making sure that there is enough fat to coat all the granules of starch. If too much fat is used, the excess will rise to the top and must be skimmed off. The right consistency for a roux is stiff, not runny.

Roux Tips

Roux can be tricky to prepare well. Keep the following in mind when you prepare roux:
- Do not use aluminum cookware. It will give the roux a metallic taste and make light-colored sauces gray. Instead, use heavy stainless steel pots. They will keep the sauces from burning or scorching, or tasting metallic.

More Mother Sauces These mother sauces are velouté and hollandaise. *How is velouté named?*

PHOTO CAPTION ANSWER Velouté is named after the type of stock it contains.

Make
a Roux

1 Heat the fat, usually clarified butter, in a heavy saucepan so that the fat will not scorch.

2 Make a paste by adding all of the bread flour and stirring.

3 Using medium heat, cook the paste until it is the consistency of wet sand and the right color. Stir roux often to keep it from burning. Burnt roux will add an unpleasant flavor and dark spots to the liquid. It will not thicken properly. When finished, the roux should be stiff.

- Do not use very high or very low temperatures. A roux that is very hot can spatter and burn someone as it is mixed into a liquid. A roux that is colder than room temperature will cause the fat to solidify. An ice-cold roux will solidify.

- Do not over thicken. A sauce must almost reach the boiling point before the roux begins to thicken it. Add 1 pound of roux per gallon of sauce for a medium consistency.

The color of a sauce depends on the length of time a roux is cooked. To create a white, blond, or brown roux, use the cooking times in **Figure 20.2**.

To avoid creating lumps when you mix a roux and a liquid base together, use one of the following methods:

- Add cold stock to the hot roux. Use a whisk to stir briskly.

- Dissolve the cold roux with warm or hot liquid before you add it to a hot stock. This will prevent lumps from forming. Stir briskly.

Cook the sauce mixture for at least 20 minutes after it begins to boil. The final cooking will take away any floury taste.

Reading Check **Describe** How can you avoid lumps when you mix a roux and a liquid base together?

FIGURE 20.2 **Roux Cooking Times**
Roux Timetable Different types of roux require different cooking times. *How do you create a brown roux?*

Roux Color	Cooking Time
White	4 to 6 minutes
Blond	6 to 8 minutes
Brown	15 to 20 minutes

READING CHECK ANSWER Add cold stock to hot roux, stirring with a whisk, or dissolve cold roux with warm liquid before adding to the hot stock.

FIGURE CAPTION ANSWER By roasting the flour for the roux in the oven before preparation, and then cooking it for 15 to 20 minutes.

 Roux Consistency Stir a roux so that it will not scorch. *What consistency should a finished roux have?*

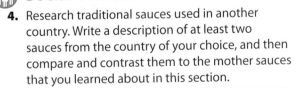

SECTION 20.2 — After You Read

Review Key Concepts

1. **List** the items that can be used as thickening agents.
2. **Describe** a sauce espagnole.
3. **Outline** the guidelines to remember when you prepare a roux.

Practice Culinary Academics

Social Studies

4. Research traditional sauces used in another country. Write a description of at least two sauces from the country of your choice, and then compare and contrast them to the mother sauces that you learned about in this section.

> **NCSS I B Culture** Predict how data and experiences may be interpreted by people from diverse cultural perspectives and frames of reference.

Mathematics

5. A restaurant offers French fries with a variety of dipping sauces served in paper cones. If the cones are 3 inches tall and 3 inches in diameter, how many fluid ounces of sauce can they hold?

> **Math Concept** **Volume of a Cone** The volume (V) of a cone or pyramid is ⅓ times base times height. Since the base of a cone is a circle, $V = (\frac{1}{3})(\pi r^2)(h)$. Use 3.14 for π.

Starting Hint Use the volume formula to find the volume of a cone, with h = the cone's height and r = half of the cone's diameter. Convert to fluid ounces by dividing by 1.8.

> **NCTM Measurement** Apply appropriate techniques, tools, and formulas to determine measurements.

 Check your answers at this book's Online Learning Center at **glencoe.com**.

PHOTO CAPTION ANSWER A finished roux should have a stiff consistency, but should not be scorched.

Soups

Reading Guide

 Before You Read

Use Color As you read this section, try using different colored pens to take notes. This can help you learn new material and study for tests. You could use red for vocabulary words, blue for explanations, and green for examples.

Read to Learn

Key Concepts

- **Give examples** of various types of soups.
- **Illustrate** proper soup presentation and storage.

Main Idea

Soups provide both flavor and nutrition. Once you understand the basic procedures for preparing soups, you can create a variety of classic and creative soups.

Graphic Organizer

There are five steps to making a clear soup. As you read, use a sequence chart like the one below to record these steps.

Content Vocabulary

- clear soup
- broth
- consommé
- sweating
- clarify
- raft
- thick soup
- cream soup
- specialty soup
- bisque
- chowder
- cold soup
- vichyssoise

Academic Vocabulary

- characteristic
- reflects

ACADEMIC STANDARDS

 English Language Arts
NCTE 1 Read texts to acquire new information.

 Mathematics
NCTM Measurement
Understand measurable attributes of objects and the units, systems, and processes of measurement.

 Science
NSES B Develop an understanding of the structure and properties of matter.

NCTE National Council of Teachers of English

NCTM National Council of Teachers of Mathematics

NSES National Science Education Standards

NCSS National Council for the Social Studies

Making a Clear Soup

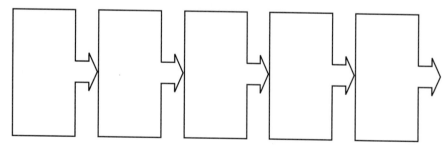

 Graphic Organizer Go to this book's Online Learning Center at **glencoe.com** for a printable graphic organizer.

GRAPHIC ORGANIZER ANSWER 1) Simmer or brown meats and sweat vegetables. 2) Add simmering stock to vegetables. 3) Continue to simmer the soup. 4) Skim off impurities and fats. 5) Season soup to taste.

Types of Soups

Soup is a popular menu choice as an appetizer or as a main course. Customers like the variety of flavors and nutrition that different soups provide. This section introduces you to the skills involved in making soups. Once you understand the basic procedures for preparing soups, you will be able to make a wide variety of nourishing meals. You may even create some interesting new soups.

Soups are frequently served at lunch and dinner. A lunch special may include a combination of soup and salad, soup and potato, or soup and sandwich. A hearty minestrone (ˌmi-nə-ˈstrō-nē) or French onion soup can satisfy your hunger at dinner when served with a chunk of crusty bread. Menus most often offer the choice of either a cup or a bowl of soup. A soup is sometimes served between a course of a multiple course meal. A simple soup will cleanse and recondition the palate. This means that it will have a neutral flavor.

Soups are as old as history. One of the first types of soups can be dated to about 6000 BCE.

By this time, waterproof and heatproof containers had been discovered. This made boiling foods possible. The word soup originates from sop, a dish consisting of a soup or thick stew that was soaked up with bread.

Commercial canning become possible in the 19th century. This made commercial soups available. Today, there are many canned and dried soups on the market. Most restaurants, however, prefer to make their own soups from scratch. Fresh soups made of high-quality ingredients have the best flavor.

Soups are usually classified as clear or unthickened soups, thick soups, and specialty soups. Most soups begin with a stock. (See Section 20.1.)

Clear Soups

A **clear soup** is made from clear stock or broth. Clear soups are not thickened. **Broth**, sometimes called a bouillon, is made from simmered meat and vegetables. Vegetable soup is made from a clear stock or broth that has been seasoned and may include meat,

◀ **Clear Combinations** Clear soups are fairly simple to prepare and, when garnished, are appealing to the eye. *What would you serve alongside this soup?*

PHOTO CAPTION ANSWER Answers will vary based on student preferences, but may include a salad, bread, a sandwich, or fruit.

vegetables, and a starch such as potatoes, rice, or noodles. A concentrated, clear soup that is made from a rich broth is called a **consommé** (ˌkän(t)-sə-ˈmā).

Clear soups are made primarily of broths that can stand alone as a dish. Broths are more flavorful than stocks because the meat, not merely the bone, is simmered along with the other ingredients. A broth will have even more flavor when stock, rather than water, is used as the liquid ingredient for the soup.

Clear soups are relatively simple to prepare. It is important that the ingredients are of the highest quality available.

Follow these steps to make a clear soup:
1. Simmer or brown the meats and sweat the vegetables that will flavor the soup. **Sweating**, or cooking vegetables in fat over low heat, is a process that allows the vegetables to release moisture. This helps vegetables release their flavors more quickly when they are combined with other ingredients. Do not let the vegetables brown. If you live at an altitude that is higher than 2,500 feet, you might have to extend the cooking time.
2. Add simmering stock to the vegetables.
3. Continue to simmer the soup on a medium heat.
4. Skim off the impurities and fats as they rise to the surface while the soup mixture is simmering.
5. Season the soup to taste before serving.

Consommé

Consommé is made from stock or broth. The broth is reduced to evaporate some of the water. This makes the liquid more concentrated. A consommé's strong flavor is its most important **characteristic**, or feature. Second to its richness, however, is the clarity of the consommé. To **clarify** a consommé means to remove the particles as they float to the top. This way the particles do not cloud the consommé, and it remains clear. Because a consommé must be completely clear, starting with the best broth is very important.

Consommé Preparation The steps below explain how to make a consommé:
1. Combine ground poultry or beef, lightly beaten egg white, and other ingredients such as a tomato product.
2. Add cold broth and stir. If the broth has a weak flavor, heat it in a separate pan and reduce it until it is concentrated. Chill it, then, add it to the other ingredients.
3. Stir the mixture occasionally as you bring it to a simmer over medium heat.
4. The egg white and meat proteins coagulate as they cook, forming a raft. The **raft** is a floating mass that forms from the mixture of meat and eggs. The raft traps the impurities that rise to the top of the broth. Do not stir the mixture after this point, and do not cover the soup. Mixing will redistribute the impurities into the soup.
5. Lower the heat and simmer slowly for 1 to 1½ hours to extract flavor and clarify.
6. Use several layers of cheesecloth or coffee filters and a china cap to strain the consommé. Taste and adjust seasonings as needed.
7. Cool, label, date, and refrigerate if the consommé will not be used immediately.

Soup Raft The raft has an important role in making consommé. *What are the main ingredients in a raft?*

8. Remove any fat from the surface when the consommé is completely cooled.
9. When you reheat the consommé, remove any dots of remaining fat on the surface by blotting the surface with a paper towel.

Vegetable Soups

Vegetable soup is one of the easiest clear soups to prepare, but you must still pay attention to details. Meat-based stock or broth is used most often. For vegetarian soup, use a vegetable-based stock or broth. Make sure you cut all the vegetables about the same size so that they will cook evenly. Pasta or grains, such as rice or barley, may be added to make the soup more hearty.

Thick Soups

A **thick soup** is not clear or transparent. Thick soups include a thickening agent, such as roux, cream, or a vegetable purée. Thick soups such as cream of chicken or cream of mushroom are examples.

Thick soups differ from clear soups because of the thickening agents that are added to them. Cream soups, which are the most common thick soups, are often thickened with roux and made with cream or milk. Milk thins the soup. Cream adds richness without thinning the soup. Cream soups can be made from leafy or soft vegetables such as broccoli, asparagus, or spinach. Hard vegetables, including squash or roasted red peppers, may also be used.

Purée Soups

Soups that are thickened by grinding the soup's main ingredient in a food processor or blender are called purées. Split pea, navy bean, and butternut squash soup are examples. These hearty soups are filling and are sometimes served as a main course. Purées may contain milk or cream.

Purée Soup Preparation Purée soups are also thick soups. Although cream is occasionally used to thicken a purée soup, the main ingredient of the soup itself is puréed for thickness. Purée soups have a coarser texture than cream soups. The coarse texture comes from legumes or starchy vegetables such as potatoes. These ingredients form the base of the soup. Because the soup is made from these ingredients, it is usually very thick and hearty.

PHOTO CAPTION ANSWER The main ingredients in a raft are the coagulated egg white and meat proteins. The raft traps impurities that rise to the top of the broth.

It often makes a good meal with bread. These are the steps to make a purée soup:

1. Cut up fresh vegetables and sweat them in fat over low heat.
2. Add the liquid, such as stock, that has been simmering in a separate pan.
3. Add starchy or dried vegetables.
4. Simmer the soup until all vegetables are cooked but not overcooked.
5. Purée the soup, using a food processor or blender.
6. Simmer again, and check that the soup has reached the desired thickness.
7. If the soup is too watery or too thick, add a thickening agent or more liquid to adjust the thickness.
8. Add final seasonings and serve.

Cream Soups

A **cream soup** is a velvety-smooth, thick soup. Cream soups are made with cooked vegetables that are sometimes puréed. Purée-ing soup requires the vegetables to be cooked to a tender consistency so that they are easily folded into the soup. To fold means to stir in gently. Cream soups may also be made with rich chicken broth.

Cream Soup Preparation Follow these steps to make a smooth cream soup:

1. Sweat hard vegetables, such as carrots or celery, in butter or oil by slowly cooking them over low heat.
2. Once the vegetables have sweated, thicken the soup by adding flour to make a roux.
3. Add hot stock or milk to the roux and vegetables. Simmer, but do not boil. Be careful that the soup does not brown.
4. Add a spice sachet or bouquet garni if you wish, along with any soft vegetables such as asparagus or broccoli. Cook the vegetables until they are just soft.
5. Skim impurities and fat from the soup as it simmers.
6. Purée the soup until it is very smooth.
7. Add hot Béchamel sauce or cream to finish the soup.
8. Taste the soup, and adjust the seasonings before serving.

◀ **Purée Base** Puréed soup is thick and hearty. *What ingredients would you use as a base for puréed soup?*

PHOTO CAPTION ANSWER You would use starchy, coarse textured vegetables, such as peas, legumes, or potatoes, as a base for puréed soup.

Specialty Soups

A **specialty soup** highlights the cuisine of a specific region, or **reflects**, or shows, the use of special ingredients or techniques. Some examples of specialty soups include bisques, chowders, cold soups, and international soups.

Bisques and Chowders

A specialty soup that is usually made from shellfish and contains cream is called a **bisque** ('bisk). For example, lobster bisque is prepared like a cream soup. A bisque is made with a concentrated stock of shellfish, such as lobster or shrimp, plus cream, and roux. Even the shells are added for flavor during cooking. The shells are removed before the bisque is strained.

A specialty soup made from fish, seafood, or vegetables is called a **chowder**. Chowders may be compared to stews because they are hearty, chunky soups. Most are based on vegetables, shellfish, or fish. Chowders are often thickened with roux. They usually include potatoes, and use cream or milk for the liquid ingredient.

Because bisques and chowders generally include milk or cream, it is best not to leave them on the serving line for too long. The milk may curdle or spoil the batch. Ideally, make small batches of these soups.

Cold Soups

A **cold soup** is a specialty soup that may be cooked or uncooked, and then chilled. This decision depends on the ingredients. Yogurt, cream, or puréed fruit is often used as a thickener for cold soups.

Cold soups are either cooked and then chilled, or not cooked. There are many ways to prepare a cold soup. It is also important to note that adding dairy products to cold soups reduces their shelf life.

Cooked Cold Soups Many hot soups may be chilled and served cold. One of the most popular cold cooked soups is **vichyssoise** (,vi-shē-'swäz), a cold version of potato-leek soup. Cold cream soups are different from hot cream soups in several different ways:

- Cream is added to a cold soup just before it is served, after it has already chilled. This process increases the soup's shelf life because the cold soup is not stored with the cream already added.
- Cold dulls the flavor of a soup, so taste a cold cream soup just before serving to ensure that it is flavorful enough.
- The consistency of the cold cream soup should be thinner than the hot cream soup. Use either less thickener or more liquid.

Uncooked Cold Soups Uncooked cold soups are easy to prepare. The majority of the work in preparing these soups comes from chopping the ingredients. Fresh fruit or vegetables are often puréed to make the soup thicker. Sometimes, cream or yogurt is added, too. It is best to make uncooked cold soups in small batches so that they stay fresh. Cold soups should be served as cold as possible in cold bowls.

International Soups

International soups are linked to different nations or cultures. For example, Borscht ('bȯrsh(t)) is a beet soup originally from Russia. There has been a steady increase in the number of ethnic restaurants in the United States. It is not uncommon to find authentic Indian and Thai soups offered as specialties. Soup is almost always offered on both lunch and dinner menus in ethnic restaurants. These soups use ingredients that are associated with a culture's cuisine.

Some international soups, such as French onion and gazpacho (gəz-'pä-(ˌ)chō), a cold Spanish soup, have become mainstream in the United States. These soups are often found in restaurants that have mostly American-style cuisine. They have also become popular in many areas of the world.

Some international soups are hearty enough to be meals. Minestrone is one of the many international soups that can easily stand alone as a meal. Minestrone is an Italian soup that can be served as an appetizer or as a meal. It includes not only a variety of vegetables, but pasta and beans, too. This gives it a hearty texture, and a good nutritional content. Minestrone is also low in fat.

There are many different types of soups from all different cultures:

- Ginataan is a soup from the Philippines made from coconut milk, milk, fruits and tapioca pearls. It is served hot or cold.
- Oshiruko is a Japanese bean soup.
- Egg drop soup from China features egg in a broth.
- Bouillabaisse is a French fish soup. It is also made in other parts of the world.

⌒ Small Bites ⌒

Cook Vegetable Soup When you make a vegetable soup, be sure to add the vegetables based on how long they will need to cook. For example, carrots take longer to soften than spinach does, so add the carrots first. If all of the vegetables are added at the same time, the softer vegetables will become overcooked.

In Catalonia it is called bullebesa.
- Gumbo is a Creole soup that comes from the American South. The soup is thickened with okra pods.
- Mulligatawny soup from India has curry as a flavoring.
- Menudo is a traditional Mexican soup that has tripe and hominy.
- Phọ is a Vietnamese beef noodle soup.

If you can learn to make a variety of interesting international soups, you can create an exotic, flavorful menu.

Reading Check Identify What are the different classifications of soup?

▲ **International Flavor** International soups such as gazpacho have become commonplace on many restaurant menus. *What are the main ingredients in gazpacho?*

PHOTO CAPTION ANSWER The main ingredients usually are garlic, onion, red and green peppers, tomatoes, olive oil, vinegar, bread, and salt and pepper.

READING CHECK ANSWER Clear or unthickened soups, thick soups, and specialty soups.

Beef Consommé

YIELD: 50 SERVINGS
SERVING SIZE: 8 OZ.

Method of Preparation

1. In a mixing bowl, combine the lean ground beef, mirepoix, tomato purée, herbs, spices, salt, and white pepper to taste. Mix the egg whites and meat mixture until blended. Refrigerate for one hour.

2. In a marmite, blend the cold beef stock with the above clarifying ingredients.

3. Place on moderate heat. Carefully watch the clarifying ingredients to make sure they do not scorch. Stir occasionally, until a raft forms. Then stop stirring.

4. Simmer the soup for 1½ hours or to the desired strength, making sure the raft does not break or sink. Remove the first cup of consommé through the spigot, and discard.

5. In a chinois lined with four to five layers of wet cheesecloth, slowly strain the liquid into a soup insert, separating the clarifying ingredients from the liquid. Hold at 135°F (57°C) or above.

6. Adjust the seasonings. Remove all of the fat from the consommé, and serve very hot with the appropriate garnish.

7. Cool to an internal temperature of 41°F (5°C) or below.

8. Reheat to 165°F (74°C) for at least 15 seconds.

Ingredients

3 lbs.	Ground beef, lean
2 pts.	Tomato purée
16 each	Black peppercorns
6 each	Bay leaves
3 oz.	Parsley stems
1½ tsp.	Thyme leaves
Salt and pepper to taste	
10 each	Egg whites, slightly whipped
5 gal.	Cold brown beef stock, or strong beef broth

Mirepoix:

12 oz.	Onion, peeled, cut brunoise
2 lbs.	Carrots, washed, peeled, cut brunoise
4 stalks	Celery, washed, trimmed, cut brunoise
2 pts.	Tomato purée

International Flavor

Many different cultures use consommé as a base for other recipes. Research these recipes, and list three more recipes with consommé bases.
- Markklösschen (Germany)
- Egg Drop Soup (China)

Chef Notes

If the stock is gelatinous, allow it to liquefy before using it.

Substitutions

- For chicken consommé, add ground chicken and use cold chicken stock.
- For vegetable consommé, use the vegetable stock, increase the egg whites, and replace the onions with leeks.

Glossary

Mirepoix roughly chopped vegetables
Brunoise ⅛-inch dice
Marmite stockpot
Chinois fine, cone-shaped strainer

HACCP

- Hold at 135°F (57°C) or above
- Cool to 41°F (5°C) or below
- Reheat to 165°F (74°C) for 15 seconds

Hazardous Foods

- Egg whites
- Ground beef

Nutrition

Calories 120   Calories from fat 30
Total Fat 3g
  Saturated Fat 1.5g
  Trans Fat 0g
Cholesterol 20mg
Sodium 880mg
Total Carbohydrate 9g
  Fiber 1g
  Sugars 4g
Protein 14g
- Vitamin A 60%   • Vitamin C 6%
- Calcium 4%   • Iron 10%

✓ Maintain Temperature

Because bacteria growth slows down only in cold food, it is important to reheat foods to safe temperatures at 165°F (74°C) or above. Before you place cream soups on a steam table, heat them to the proper temperature.

CRITICAL THINKING *What are the potential consequences of failing to reheat soup to 165°F (74°C) or above?*

Soup Presentation and Storage

Whether as an appetizer or a meal, a soup's presentation is important. The size and type of the cup or bowl is usually determined by the type of soup, the meal at which it is served, and when during the meal it will be eaten. The soup portion served as an appetizer should be between 6 and 8 ounces, and between 10 and 12 ounces for a main course portion.

The temperature of the bowl or cup will influence the presentation of the soup, too. The bowl should be warm for serving a hot soup, and cold for serving a cold soup. Most importantly, when you serve the soup, make sure the soup itself is the right temperature. Serve cold soups at 41°F (5°C) or below. Serve hot soups at 165°F (74°C) or above.

Soup Garnishes

Soups can look plain. This is why their presentation should be enhanced with a garnish. Each hot consommé is named according to its garnish. For example, consommé Célestine (sə-'les-tēn) is garnished with small, thin, savory pancakes cut into julienne strips. The soup was named after the chef to Napoleon III.

Garnishes such as parsley or sour cream often make the difference between an appetizing appearance and a dull one. Toppings, add contrast to a soup that is all one color, such as puréed soup. Garnishes must be applied just before the soup is served.

Garnish Guidelines

Use the following suggestions to garnish soups:
- Garnishes should be attractively arranged.
- Vegetables or meats for garnishes should be cut about the same size and shape.

▲ **Soup Presentation** Soups may be presented in interesting ways. *Can you identify each type of soup shown here?*

Purée of Potato Leek Soup

YIELD: 50 SERVINGS
SERVING SIZE: 8 OZ.

Method of Preparation

1. In a stockpot, heat the clarified butter or oil, and lightly sauté the leeks. Add the vegetable stock, garlic, and potatoes, and heat to the first boil. Reduce to a simmer.
2. Simmer the soup until the potatoes are tender.
3. When the potatoes are tender, strain, and pass the mixture through a food mill.
4. Place the soup in a stockpot. Heat to a boil. Simmer to the desired consistency. Adjust seasoning with salt, white pepper, and nutmeg. Hold at 135°F (57°C) or above.
5. In a separate saucepan, poach the julienne of leeks in the vegetable stock. Add to the soup as a garnish.
6. Cool to an internal temperature of 41°F (5°C) or below.
7. Reheat to 165°F (74°C) for at least 15 seconds.

Ingredients

6 oz.	Clarified butter
2 lbs.	Leeks (use only the white part), washed, trimmed, split, and rough chopped into small pieces
6 cloves	Garlic, peeled and minced
7 lbs.	Potatoes, peeled, washed, and rough chopped into small pieces
3 gal.	Vegetable stock
½ tsp.	Nutmeg
1 lb.	Leeks, whites (garnish), washed, trimmed, split, and cross-cut

International Flavor

Potatoes are used as a staple ingredient in many different countries. Research these recipes, and write a half-page paper on how potatoes are used in each.

● Aloo bhurta (India)
● Potato paprikash (Hungary)

Chef Notes

Trim leek roots, cut off the tops just where white turns to pale green, and remove the toughest outer layer of leaves.

Substitutions

● Use a small amount of oil for sautéeing instead of butter to reduce cholesterol.

Cooking Technique

Simmer and Poach

1. Heat the cooking liquid to the proper temperature.
2. Submerge the food product completely.

Glossary

Clarified butter purified butterfat
Food mill a tool for mashing foods

HACCP

● Hold at 135°F (57°C) or above.
● Cool to 41°F (5°C) or below internally.
● Reheat to 165°F (74°C) for at least 15 seconds.

Hazardous Foods

● Butter

Nutrition

Calories 100 Calories from Fat 30
Total Fat 3.5g
  Saturated Fat 2g
  Trans Fat 0g
Cholesterol 10mg
Sodium 3040mg
Total Carbohydrate 16g
  Fiber 2g
  Sugars 2g
Protein 4g
• Vitamin A 6% • Vitamin C 25%
• Calcium 2% • Iron 6%

This is especially important for garnishing a consommé, because the clear soup will highlight any uneven cuts.

- The flavor and texture of the garnish should complement the soup.
- If you use vegetables or starches as garnishes, cook them separately so they will not cloud the soup.
- Do not overcook garnishes. Vegetables should not be mushy. Meat or poultry should not fall apart. Rice and pasta should hold their shape. To keep from overcooking, prepare these garnishes separately and hold them on the side until just before serving.

Soup Storage

When you make large batches of thick soup, cool and refrigerate the soup before you add the milk or cream. It is best to heat only small batches of soup if you hold the soup in a steam table. Restock the soup when necessary. Soups will continue to thicken while they are set in holding in the steam table. Be sure to check the consistency before you serve them. Heat the base over low heat, then add the milk or cream to the base. To keep the soup from scorching, stir it often. Taste the soup to see if the seasonings need to be adjusted.

 **Reading Check** List What are some suggested accompaniments for soup?

SECTION 20.3 After You Read

Review Key Concepts

1. **Give examples** of specialty soups.
2. **Illustrate** proper soup garnishing.

Practice Culinary Academics

 English Language Arts

3. Locate an article in a food magazine that describes a soup or a recipe for soup. Identify the type of soup. Then, compare and contrast the steps for making the soup, or the information given about the soup, with the information you read in this section. Did you learn more about that type of soup? Write a half-page summary of what you learned.

> **NCTE 1** Read texts to acquire new information.

 Science

4. **Procedure** Make a clear soup with broth and vegetables. Use at least one starchy vegetable. Notice the texture and thickness of the soup. Now purée the soup to make a puréed soup.

   Analysis Notice the texture and thickness of the soup before and after adding the purée. Record any differences, and write a summary of why any differences exist.

> **NSES B** Develop an understanding of the structure and properties of matter.

 Mathematics

5. During an average dinner service, your restaurant serves 20 cup-size (6 fluid ounces) portions of asparagus soup, and 9 bowl-size (11 fluid ounces) portions. How many quarts of soup should be prepared for each evening?

Math Concept **Equivalent Volume Measurements** There are 32 fluid ounces in one quart. To convert fluid ounces into quarts, divide by 32. To convert quarts into fluid ounces, multiply by 32.

Starting Hint For each serving size, calculate the total volume of soup needed by multiplying number of servings by portion size. Add the two totals together, and convert to quarts. Round to the nearest quart.

> **NCTM Measurement** Understand measurable attributes of objects and the units, systems, and processes of measurement.

 Check your answers at this book's Online Learning Center at **glencoe.com**.

READING CHECK ANSWER Whole-grain wafers, corn chips, crackers, melba toast, or bread sticks.

Review and Applications

Chapter Summary

The four basic types of stock are white, brown, fish, and vegetable. Basic stocks are the base for many different types of sauces and soups. There are five basic sauces called mother, or grand sauces. Other sauces include compound sauces, independent sauces, and those made from purées, meat juices, and butter. Sauces can be adjusted by thickening them or adding seasonings and flavorings. The types of soups are clear, thick, and specialty. Presentation and garnishing of soups varies according to their type. Store soups in tightly sealed containers.

Content and Academic Vocabulary Review

1. Write a memo explaining the features of a good soup. Use at least 12 of the following terms in your memo.

Content Vocabulary

- stock (p. 510)
- nourishing element (p. 510)
- mirepoix (p. 510)
- base (p. 510)
- white stock (p. 511)
- brown stock (p. 511)
- fish stock (p. 513)
- fumet (p. 513)
- vegetable stock (p. 513)
- glaze (p. 513)
- reduction (p. 513)
- sauce (p. 517)
- thickening agent (p. 517)
- Béchamel (p. 517)
- hollandaise sauce (p. 517)
- gelatinization (p. 517)

- coulis (p. 518)
- cheesecloth (p. 518)
- mother sauces (p. 519)
- sauce espagnole (p. 519)
- demi-glace (p. 519)
- tomato sauce (p. 519)
- roux (p. 520)
- velouté (p. 520)
- marinara sauce (p. 520)
- gravy (p. 521)
- compound butters (p. 521)
- clarified butter (p. 521)
- clear soup (p. 527)
- broth (p. 527)
- consommé (p. 528)
- sweating (p. 528)
- clarify (p. 528)

- raft (p. 528)
- thick soup (p. 529)
- cream soup (p. 530)
- specialty soup (p. 531)
- bisque (p. 531)
- chowder (p. 531)
- cold soup (p. 531)
- vichyssoise (p. 531)

Academic Vocabulary

- supplement (p. 510)
- reserve (p. 513)
- mediocre (p. 517)
- clarity (p. 518)
- characteristic (p. 528)
- reflects (p. 531)

Review Key Concepts

2. **Identify** the elements of a stock.
3. **Explain** the preparation of different varieties of stock.
4. **List** the main ingredients in a sauce.
5. **Distinguish** between the five mother sauces.
6. **Outline** the steps to prepare a roux.
7. **Give examples** of various types of soups.
8. **Illustrate** proper soup presentation and storage.

Critical Thinking

9. **Analyze** what might happen if you reduce cooking times. Beef stock and veal stock take eight hours to cook. What could happen if you cut the cooking time in half?

10. **Determine** which type of soup you think has more nutritional value: hot vegetable soup, or gazpacho. Why?

Review and Applications

Academic Skills

English Language Arts

11. Research Regional Soups Many regions of the world have a traditional soup. Choose one regional soup and write a research essay on it. Write about the region the soup comes from, the ingredients of the soup, and how it is made. Discuss how the soup is served, and any variants of the soup, including variants found in other countries. Include your sources.

> **NCTE 7** Conduct research and gather, evaluate, and synthesize data to communicate discoveries.

Science

12. Choose Vegetables for Stock The freshness of the vegetables you use for a stock can make a difference.

Procedure Make a chicken or fish stock in two pots. In one pot, use vegetables that are barely fresh. In the other, use fresh vegetables.

Analysis Compare the flavor of the two stocks. What do you observe? Why do you think one is more flavorful than the other? Create a chart that shows your observations and a summary of those differences.

> **NSES B** Develop an understanding of the interactions of energy and matter.

Mathematics

13. Compare Stock Bases Teri's restaurant goes through 60 gallons of chicken stock each month. To reduce food costs, Teri would like to start using commercial stock base. One product she is considering comes in packages that yield 5 gallons of stock, costing $11.25 per package. A second product is a powder that comes in a package of four containers for $14.50. Each container claims to make 22 8-fluid-ounce servings. Which product will be less expensive on a monthly basis?

Math Concept **Equivalent Volume Measurements** There are 128 fluid ounces in 1 gallon. To convert fluid ounces into gallons, divide by 128. To convert gallons into fluid ounces, multiply by 128.

Starting Hint Find the cost to produce 60 gallons of stock using each product. For the concentrate, set up a proportion such as $11.25 / 5 gallons = x / 60 gallons, and solve for x. For the powder, use a similar proportion after calculating the total stock produced from each package by multiplying $4 \times 22 \times 8$, and then converting the result into gallons.

> **NCTM Problem Solving** Apply and adapt a variety of appropriate strategies to solve problems.

Certification Prep

Directions Read the questions. Then, read the answer choices and choose the best possible answer for each.

14. What is a mirepoix?

  a. the powdered, or concentrated form of a stock.

  b. the liquids that form the foundation of sauces and soups.

  c. a mix of coarsely chopped vegetables and herbs.

  d. a combination of fresh herbs and vegetables.

15. What is a roux?

  a. purified butterfat

  b. a thickened brown sauce.

  c. a sauce made from a fruit or vegetable purée.

  d. equal parts of fat and flour by weight.

Sharpen your test-taking skills to improve your kitchen certification program score.

Test-Taking Tip
Review the vocabulary list and the key concepts in each chapter to help you study for your test.

Review and Applications

Real-World Skills and Applications

Self-Management Skills

16. List Nutritious Soups Imagine that you are trying to plan a healthful menu for your restaurant. You want to add some soups to the menu, but you want them to be nutrient-dense. List three soups that are nutrient-dense and contain items from several food groups. Make a list of which ingredients come from which food groups.

Collaborative and Interpersonal Skills

17. Reinvent a Soup Imagine that your restaurant has decided to revamp its menu. The soups on the menu now are minestrone, clam chowder, and roasted red pepper purée. Follow your teacher's instructions to form groups and discuss ways to revise these standard soups to be more interesting to customers. Discuss your ideas with the class.

Technology Applications

18. Design a Menu Use a word processing or graphic design program to design a menu for a restaurant that features soups and main dishes made with sauces. The menu should fit onto one or two pages and should describe each item accurately in the space given. Use illustrations or photographs to make your menu exciting. Turn in your completed menu to your teacher.

Financial Literacy

19. Compare Sauce Costs You own an Italian restaurant. In your restaurant, you use about 80 ounces of tomato sauce per night. Purchasing canned tomato sauce would cost you about 8 cents per ounce. Making your own would cost 11 cents per ounce. What would be the price per night of making your own tomato sauce versus purchasing canned sauce?

Culinary Lab

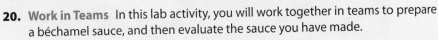

Use the culinary skills you have learned in this chapter.

Make a Béchamel Sauce

20. Work in Teams In this lab activity, you will work together in teams to prepare a béchamel sauce, and then evaluate the sauce you have made.

A. Plan your sauce. With your team, determine the fat and flour you will use and plan your procedures.

B. Review Béchamel basics. Discuss the characteristics of a good Béchamel so that your team knows its objectives. Review the guidelines in the section for making Béchamel sauce and make sure they are incorporated in your procedures.

C. Make your sauce. Prepare the Béchamel sauce recipe on page 522.

D. Taste your sauce. Present your sauce to the class for tasting and evaluation.

Create Your Evaluation

Create one comment card for each team's sauce. As you taste each sauce, evaluate its the taste, texture, and appearance on the comment card. Include comments about anything that could be done to improve the sauce. Once everyone has had a chance to taste and evaluate each sauce, discuss your comments with the class.

CHAPTER 21

Fish and Shellfish

SECTIONS

21.1 Fish Basics

21.2 Shellfish Basics

21.3 Cooking Fish and Shellfish

WRITING ACTIVITY

Classification

Classifications help to break down and explain the parts of something that make up a whole. Write a classification of different types of fish or shellfish that you know, as an introduction to the subject.

Writing Tips

1 Begin with an introduction that defines the broad topic.

2 Describe each category and provide supporting details.

3 Keep it simple. Do not use too many categories.

EXPLORE THE PHOTO

Fish and shellfish are healthful protein choices for a main dish or appetizer. *What types of shellfish can you name?*

WRITING ACTIVITY ANSWER
Classifications should briefly describe classes of fish or shellfish. They should have an introduction and conclusion.

EXPLORE THE PHOTO ANSWER
Answers will vary, but may include shrimp, lobster, clams, mussels, and snails.

Fish Basics

Fish is a popular choice in most restaurants.

Reading Guide

 Before You Read

Understanding It is normal to have questions when you read. Write down questions while reading. Many of them will be answered as you continue. If they are not, you will have a list ready for your teacher when you finish.

Read to Learn

Key Concepts
- **Describe** the composition and structure of fish.
- **Distinguish** between the different market forms of fish.

Main Idea
Fish is a low-fat, healthful protein that is popular with diners. Selecting high-quality fish is an important skill for foodservice professionals.

Content Vocabulary
- fatty fish
- lean fish
- flat fish
- round fish
- boneless fish
- drawn
- dressed
- fillets
- butterflied
- freezer burn
- drip loss
- vacuum packed

Academic Vocabulary
- classify
- keep

Graphic Organizer
As you read, use a web organizer like this one to list the eight different market forms of fresh fish.

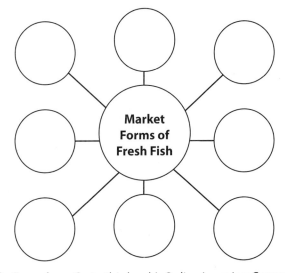

Market Forms of Fresh Fish

 Graphic Organizer Go to this book's Online Learning Center at **glencoe.com** for a printable graphic organizer.

GRAPHIC ORGANIZER ANSWER Whole, drawn, dressed, fillets, butterflied, steaks, cubes, sticks.

ACADEMIC STANDARDS

 English Language Arts
NCTE 7 Conduct research and gather, evaluate, and synthesize data to communicate discoveries.

 Mathematics
NCTM Data Analysis and Probability Select and use appropriate statistical methods to analyze data.

Social Studies
NCSS VII F Production, Distribution, and Consumption Compare how values and beliefs influence economic decisions in different societies.

NCTE National Council of Teachers of English

NCTM National Council of Teachers of Mathematics

NSES National Science Education Standards

NCSS National Council for the Social Studies

Structure of Fish

More than 30,000 species of fish live in oceans or freshwater sources. These cold-blooded animals are important to the food-service industry. Approximately 75% of all the fish eaten in the United States is eaten in restaurants. Customers looking for a tasty, low-fat, healthful alternative to meat often choose fish. Knowing how to select, purchase, and store fish will allow a foodservice operation to serve fish of the highest quality.

Like poultry and meat, fish is made up of protein, fat, water, and vitamins and minerals. Fish can be divided into two broad categories. Some fish are called fatty fish. **Fatty fish** have a relatively large amount of fat. Salmon is a popular type of fatty fish. Fish with little fat are known as **lean fish**. Haddock is a common example of lean fish. A major difference between fish and meat is that fish has very little connective tissue. Because of this, fish:

- Are naturally tender.
- Cook rapidly, requiring low heat.
- Can be cooked using moist cooking techniques to keep its natural moistness.
- Will fall apart when cooked, if not handled carefully.

Fish have backbones, an internal skeleton of cartilage and bones, gills for breathing, and fins for swimming. Fish may be divided into three categories, based on their skeleton type. (See **Figure 21.1**.)

- **Flat Fish** Flat fish have a backbone running horizontally through the center of the fish. They swim horizontally and have both eyes on the top of their heads. Flounder and halibut are examples of flat fish. Generally, flat fish swim along the bottom of the ocean. They have dark skin on the upper side of their bodies to hide from predators.
- **Round Fish** Round fish are fish that have a backbone on the upper edge of their bodies. They have an eye on each side of their heads, and they swim vertically. Trout, bass, and cod are common types of round fish.
- **Boneless Fish** Boneless fish are fish that have cartilage instead of bones. Sharks are boneless fish. Many boneless fish also have smooth skin instead of scales. Some chefs will **classify**, or sort, boneless fish with round fish.

Reading Check Compare What is the major difference between fish and meat?

▼ **FIGURE 21.1** **Flat and Round Fish**

Fish Structure Flat fish and round fish have slightly different bone structures. *What are the characteristicis of flat fish?*

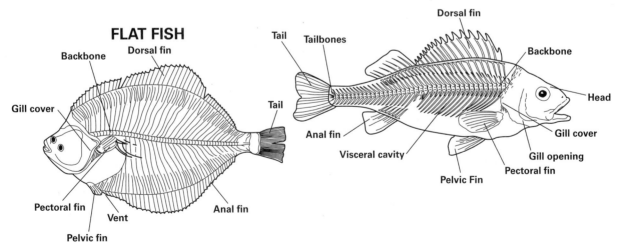

FLAT FISH

Backbone · Dorsal fin · Gill cover · Pectoral fin · Vent · Pelvic fin · Anal fin · Tail

ROUND FISH

Dorsal fin · Tail · Tailbones · Backbone · Head · Gill cover · Gill opening · Pectoral fin · Pelvic Fin · Visceral cavity · Anal fin · Tail

FIGURE CAPTION ANSWER Flat fish swim horizontally, have a backbone that runs horizontally through the center of their bodies, and have both eyes on top of their heads.

READING CHECK ANSWER Fish has very little connective tissue.

Sole

Red Snapper

Flounder

Mackerel

Halibut

Sea Bass

Tuna

Cod

Mahi-Mahi

Grouper

Salmon

Catfish

Perch

Pompano

Rainbow Trout

Tilapia

⚓ **An Ocean of Fish** Most foodservice operations serve only a portion of the types of fish that exist worldwide. *Which of these fish are flat fish?*

PHOTO CAPTION ANSWER The sole, halibut, and flounder are flat fish.

Market Forms of Fish

As the demand for fish has increased and the supply has decreased, fish have become more expensive. Fish were once available only to those living along the coasts or near fresh-water sources. Now, fish can be preserved and shipped to any location quickly and safely. However, the names used for different fish may vary from one region of the country to another. For example, bluefish are sometimes called blue snappers.

Fish may be purchased whole or in the form in which it will be cooked and served. (See **Figure 21.2**.) The available options may vary depending on whether the fish is purchased fresh, frozen, or canned. Generally, restaurant owners find it less expensive to buy fish that is already processed because of processing time that is required to prepare fish for cooking.

Inspection and grading of fish is not required by law like it is for meat and poultry. However, it generally is still inspected. See Section 21.2 for more information on inspection and grading of fish.

Fresh Fish

Before most fresh fish is made available for purchase, it is usually processed in some way. The unwanted parts of the fish, such as heads and fins, are often removed. There are eight forms of fish that can be purchased.

- **Whole** Whole fish refers to the entire fish as it comes out of the water. Because the internal organs are not removed, this form has the shortest shelf life.
- **Drawn** Fish that have had their gills and entrails removed are called **drawn** fish. This form has the longest shelf life. Whole fish are often purchased drawn.
- **Dressed** Drawn fish that have had their fins, scales, and sometimes their head removed are called **dressed** fish.
- **Fillets** The sides of fish are called **fillets**. These are the most common cut offered in restaurants. Fillets can be cut with or without bones and skin. Round fish produce two fillets, one from each side. Flat fish produce four fillets. Two large fillets are cut from the top and two are cut from the bottom of the fish.

▲ **A Popular Choice** Fish is a popular choice in restaurants today. *Why do you think fish is so popular?*

PHOTO CAPTION ANSWER Answers may vary, but should include that many kinds of fish are available, fish can be cooked a number of ways, and fish has a high nutritional value.

Fish Forms Fish is available either whole or in the form in which it will be cooked.

Why is it usually less expensive to purchase processed fish?

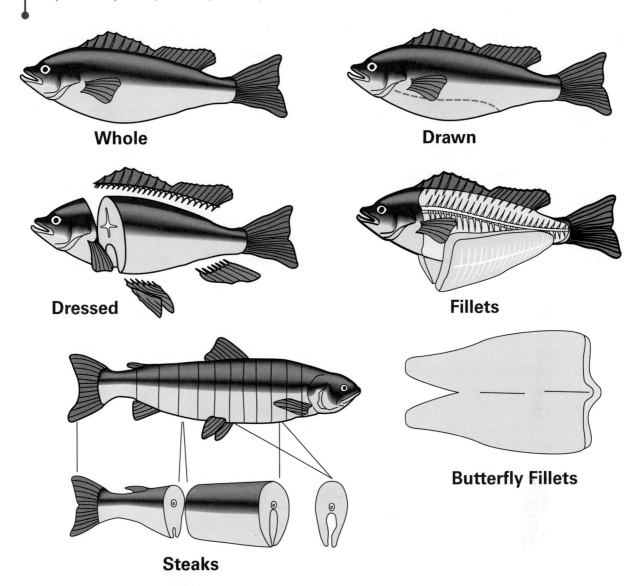

Whole

Drawn

Dressed

Fillets

Steaks

Butterfly Fillets

- **Butterflied** A **butterflied** fish resembles an open book. The fish is dressed, then cut so the two sides lie open, yet are attached by skin.
- **Steaks** Cross-section cuts of dressed fish are called steaks. The backbone and skin may still be attached. When the cuts are from a large fish, such as swordfish, they are boneless.
- **Cubes** Leftover pieces from large fish are called cubes. They are often used in stir-fries, stews, or kebabs.

- **Sticks** Small, leftover pieces of fish that are pressed together form fish sticks. They are breaded or battered and sold frozen.

Purchase and Store Fresh Fish

Because fresh fish is not usually graded, the person who receives a shipment of fish must check it for freshness. (See **Figure 21.3** on page 546.) Fresh fish spoils more quickly than fresh poultry or meat. Whole fish should be stored on ice. Fillets should be kept on ice in watertight containers.

FIGURE CAPTION ANSWER Because of the time it takes a chef to process a fish. Also, fresh, whole fish is the most perishable market form, and must be used as soon as possible.

From the time fish is caught to the time it is cooked and served, maintaining proper storage temperatures is critical to the quality and safety of the fish. The shelf life of fish decreases one day for every day it is stored above 32°F (0°C).

Frozen Fish

Some people believe that frozen fish is not as tasty as fresh fish. However, modern processing methods often mean that frozen fish is less likely to be contaminated. More frozen fish is served in restaurants today than fresh fish.

Quality Characteristics

Use the following quality checks when you purchase and receive frozen fish.

- Frozen fish should not be thawed.
- Fish should not have freezer burn. **Freezer burn** is the discoloration and dehydration caused by moisture loss as a food freezes. Fish also should be kept well-wrapped.
- Fish should have a thin layer of ice as a glaze. This glaze should not have evaporated or melted.
- Fish should not have a fishy smell. A fishy smell results from improper handling.

Thaw and Handle Frozen Fish

Frozen fish products are usually raw or battered and breaded. Follow these guidelines to handle it safely:

- Never thaw fish at room temperature. Always thaw fish in the refrigerator. Allow 18 to 36 hours for frozen fish to thaw in the refrigerator. If you are in a hurry, keep fish in its original packaging, and run it under cold water at 70°F (21°C) or lower.
- You can cook small pieces of fish while they are frozen. This makes for easier handling and less drip loss. **Drip loss** is the loss of moisture that occurs as fish thaws.
- Fish may be partially thawed, then prepped and cooked. Partially thawed fish will handle more easily than completely thawed fish.
- If frozen fish is already breaded or prepared in some way, be sure to follow the package directions for cooking.
- Do not refreeze fish.

Because fish spoils quickly, it is important to store and use it carefully. If a fish tastes strong, it has already begun to spoil. Always check for quality before you prepare fish.

FIGURE 21.3 Quality Tests for Fresh Fish

Fresh Fish Fresh fish is not usually graded, so foodservice workers must check it for freshness. *What happens to fresh fish if it is not stored at the correct temperature?*

Look	Feel	Smell
Does the meat separate when the fillet is bent? This is a sign of deteriorated connective tissue between the muscles.	When the fish is pressed, is there a fingerprint left? Fish should be firm. If a dent is visible after the fish is pressed, the fish has begun to decay.	Does the fish smell bad? Fresh fish should smell like seaweed or the ocean. If the fish smells like ammonia, it has gone bad and should not be used.
Are there blood spots in the flesh? Is the fish dry? Fish should be moist and free of blood.	Is the fish slimy? This can be a good sign in whole fish, but a bad sign in fillets.	
If the gills are still attached, are they pink or grayish brown? Fresh fish will have red gills.		
Are the eyes sunken or cloudy? Fresh fish generally have round, clear eyes.		

FIGURE CAPTION ANSWER Fresh fish that is not kept at the proper temperature rapidly spoils. The shelf life of fresh fish decreases one day for every day it is stored above 32°F (0°C).

Purchase and Store Frozen Fish

When you buy frozen fish, be wary of ice inside the fish. This shows that the fish was partially thawed and then refrozen. Be sure that there are no white spots or dry spots, which are signs of freezer burn.

Frozen fish can be kept safely frozen for up to six months, if stored at 0°F (18°C). To prevent freezer burn, keep fish vacuum packed or wrapped tightly in plastic. **Vacuum packed** fish are fish that have been placed in airtight containers from which the air has been removed to prevent the growth of bacteria.

Some fish is frozen and then vacuum packed prior to being sold. These fish are sometimes canned or sold in pouches. Fish sold in pouches are often packaged in individual servings.

Canned Fish

The most common varieties of canned fish are tuna and salmon. Tuna may be packed in oil or water.

Some canned salmon may contain skin and edible bones that add nutrients and flavor. The label should tell you if it is skinless and boneless. Canned salmon generally has no added liquid and comes in chunk style.

Do not purchase cans that are dented or damaged. As with other canned goods, store canned fish on shelves in a cool, dry place. When opened, transfer any unused fish to a covered container. Label and date the container and refrigerate. The fish will **keep**, or stay fresh, for two to three days.

 Reading Check Explain How should fresh fish be stored?

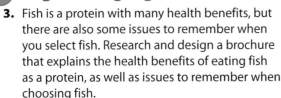 **SECTION 21.1** After You Read

Review Key Concepts

1. **Describe** the composition and structure of flat fish.
2. **Distinguish** between fish fillets and fish steaks.

Practice Culinary Academics

 English Language Arts

3. Fish is a protein with many health benefits, but there are also some issues to remember when you select fish. Research and design a brochure that explains the health benefits of eating fish as a protein, as well as issues to remember when choosing fish.

> **NCTE 7** Conduct research and gather, evaluate, and synthesize data to communicate discoveries.

 Social Studies

4. Research the different ways we get fish, including the issues of overfishing and sustainability in fishing, and the environmental and health issues associated with farming. Write a report on your findings, and decide whether these methods are sustainable for the future.

> **NCSS VII F Production, Distribution, and Consumption** Compare how values and beliefs influence economic decisions in different societies.

 **Mathematics**

5. Charlie is responsible for purchasing squid for appetizers for the restaurant where he works. Charlie has purchased 15 squid tubes ranging in size: 4, 8, 5, 6, 5, 6, 7, 5, 8, 6, 7, 6, 7, 4, and 6 inches. What is the median length of the tubes? What is the mode?

Math Concept **Finding the Median and Mode** Given a series of values, the mode is the value that occurs most frequently. The median is the middle number in the series, when the numbers are arranged in ascending order.

Starting Hint Arrange the lengths in order from lowest to highest. Identify the length in the middle of the range. This is the median. Count how many times each number appears. The one that appears most often is the mode.

> **NCTM Data Analysis and Probability** Select and use appropriate statistical methods to analyze data.

 Check your answers at this book's Online Learning Center at **glencoe.com**.

READING CHECK ANSWER Whole fish should be stored on ice. Fillets should be kept on ice in watertight containers. Fish should be kept at 32°F (0°C) or below.

Shellfish Basics

Reading Guide

 Before You Read

Think of an Example Look over the Key Concepts for this section. Think of an example of how or when you could use one of the skills from the Key Concepts. Thinking of how you might apply a skill can help motivate your learning by showing you why the skill is important.

Read to Learn

Key Concepts

- **Explain** the structure, composition, and grading of shellfish.
- **Differentiate** between types of mollusks.
- **Distinguish** between types of crustaceans.
- **Identify** other types of seafood.

Main Idea

Shellfish meat is expensive and often considered a luxury. Shellfish is versatile, however, and can be used in appetizers and soups as well as main courses.

Content Vocabulary

- PUFI mark
- mollusk
- univalve
- bivalve
- cephalopod
- barnacle
- IQF (individually quick frozen)
- crustacean
- sleeper
- devein
- calamari
- escargot
- surimi

Academic Vocabulary

- luxury
- mandatory

ACADEMIC STANDARDS

Mathematics
NCTM Number and Operations Understand numbers, ways of representing numbers, relationships among numbers, and number systems.

NCTM Problem Solving Apply and adapt a variety of appropriate strategies to solve problems.

NCTE National Council of Teachers of English

NCTM National Council of Teachers of Mathematics

NSES National Science Education Standards

NCSS National Council for the Social Studies

Graphic Organizer

As you read, use a category tree like the one shown to organize the categories of shellfish. In the first set of boxes, fill in the three types of shellfish. In the next set of boxes, fill in examples of each type.

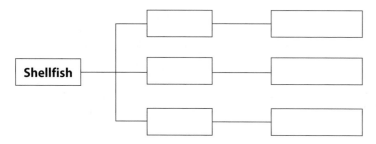

Shellfish

 Graphic Organizer Go to this book's Online Learning Center at **glencoe.com** for a printable graphic organizer.

GRAPHIC ORGANIZER ANSWER Mollusks: oysters, clams, mussels, scallops; Crustaceans: lobsters, shrimp, crab, crayfish; Other seafood: squid, frog legs, escargot, surimi, eel.

Shellfish Basics

Shellfish are often considered a **luxury**, or expensive and extravagant, food. Shellfish meat is expensive because much of the body of the animal is not used for special dishes. However, shellfish appear in many places on the menu. They can be found as appetizers, in soups, and as entrées. Every foodservice professional should know how to select and prepare shellfish.

Structure of Shellfish

Unlike fish, shellfish have no bones. They have hard shells that cover their bodies. Shellfish are found in both fresh water and salt water. Two types of shellfish are mollusks (ˈmä-ləsks) and crustaceans (ˌkrəs-ˈtā-shens).

People eat many different parts of shellfish. Muscles, legs, tails, claws, and tentacles are all used in various dishes. Sometimes shellfish are eaten whole, with or without the shell. Most shellfish are lean and composed primarily of water, vitamins, minerals, protein, and fats.

Learning to prepare shellfish takes time and practice. Each type has special physical characteristics that must be taken into account. For example, some need to be removed from the shell before cooking, while others are cooked in the shell.

Inspection and Grading

Fish and shellfish are inspected, just as meat and poultry are. Although grading is not required, the U.S. Department of Commerce (USDC) will inspect and grade fresh fish and shellfish for a fee. The inspection of frozen and canned fish is **mandatory**, or required.

Fish are inspected for accurate labeling, safety and cleanliness in preparation, and wholesomeness. Grading is done to be sure that the fish meet standards for flavor and appearance. Because there are so many kinds of fish, the USDC has set criteria for only the most common types of fish.

Inspection

The USDC inspects fish and shellfish in one of the following three ways:

- Type 1 inspection covers processing methods and the processing plant itself. The product receives a PUFI mark if it is safe, clean, accurately labeled, and has a good flavor and odor. A **PUFI mark** means Packed Under Federal Inspection. (See **Figure 21.4**.)
- Type 2 inspection covers things such as labeling, weight, and packaging.
- Type 3 inspection is for sanitary conditions only.

Grading

Fish are graded based on standards for flavor and appearance. Only fish inspected under Type 1 criteria can be graded. Fish may be judged as Grade A, B, or C. Processed or canned products are either B or C quality.

- **Grade A** Highest quality, no physical defects, good odor and flavor
- **Grade B** Good quality
- **Grade C** Fairly good quality

 **Reading Check** Describe What is Type 3 inspection of shellfish?

▼ **FIGURE 21.4** **Fish Inspection**
PUFI Mark The Packed Under Federal Inspection mark given by the USDC covers processing methods and the processing plant. *What does this mark mean when seen on a package of shellfish?*

PACKED UNDER FEDERAL INSPECTION
DEPARTMENT OF COMMERCE
UNITED STATES OF AMERICA

Mollusks

A **mollusk** is a shellfish that has no internal skeletal structure. Instead, it has a shell that covers its soft body. Mollusks are classified in three major groups. The groups are divided according to the kind of shell the mollusk has.

A **univalve** ('yü-ni-ˌvalv), such as conch, has a single shell. A **bivalve** ('bī-ˌvalv) has two shells that are hinged together. Common examples of bivalves include mussels, oysters, and clams. Instead of an outer shell, a **cephalopod** ('se-fə-lə-ˌpäd), such as squid or octopus, has a thin internal shell. Cephalopods have tentacles, or false legs, attached to the head near the mouth.

Oysters

Oysters can be purchased any time during the year, but they are best to eat in the fall, winter, and spring. Oyster meat is very delicate and has a high percentage of water. Because the salts, nutrients, and minerals of the water flavor the meat, oysters within the same species may taste different, depending on where each was harvested. Also, the flavor can be watery and bland during warmer months when oysters reproduce.

Market Forms

Oysters may be purchased live, shucked, or canned. A shucked oyster has had the meat removed from the shell. Shucked oysters can be purchased either fresh or frozen and range in size from very small to extra large. They are graded by size, as shown in **Figure 21.5**. Canned oysters are rarely used in commercial kitchens.

Handling and Storage

When you purchase live oysters, check that the shells are tightly closed or that they close quickly when they are tapped. If they do not move, they are dead and should be thrown away. Oysters should have a clear appearance and be plump. Both shucked and live oysters should have a sweet, mild odor.

Store live oysters in cardboard containers in the cooler. They should be draped with seaweed or damp towels. Check oysters daily, and throw out any dead ones. If the oysters have already been shucked, keep them in containers surrounded by ice on all sides, and keep the harvesting tag. Fresh oysters should keep for up to a week in the refrigerator.

Before you open oysters, scrub their shells. Then, place them on a sheet pan in a hot oven until the shells open. The oysters can then be removed from the shell. If a shell does not open, throw away the oyster. Oysters can also be removed raw from the shell but this can be dangerous and takes skill and practice.

Clams

Clams are harvested from both the West Coast and the East Coast. Types of clams from the West Coast include the razor clam, rock clam, and butter clam. Clams from the East Coast are known by their shells. They either have a soft shell or a hard shell. Soft-shell clams may be called steamers or longnecks. Hard-shell clams are also called quahogs ('kō-ˌhȯgs) and are classified according to size. Chowder clams are the largest clams. Cherrystone clams are the second largest. The smallest clams are called littlenecks.

▼ FIGURE 21.5 Oyster Grades

Purchase Oysters Oysters are graded by size, and are best eaten during the fall, winter, and spring. *Why do you think summer harvested oysters are not as popular?*

Grade of Oysters	Number per Gallon
Very Small	more than 500
Small or Standards	301-500
Medium or Selects	211-300
Large or Extra Selects	161-210
Extra Large or Counts	160 or fewer

FIGURE CAPTION ANSWER Oysters reproduce during warmer months, and their flavor when eaten raw during these months can be watery and bland.

Market Forms

Like oysters, clams should be purchased live for the greatest freshness. They should smell fresh and sweet. Clams may be purchased in three forms:

- Whole, in the shell
- Shucked, either frozen or fresh
- Canned, either chopped or whole

Handling and Storage

Treat clams carefully so that their shells do not break. Store live clams in cardboard containers or in their original containers in the refrigerator for up to one week. Do not store in a sealed environment. Like oysters, they must be kept damp.

Scrub hard-shell clams before you open or cook them. Soft-shell clams can be sandy inside. Some chefs like to soak soft-shell clams in water for a few hours with salt or cornmeal. The clams eat the salt or cornmeal and expel the sand. However, clams can die due to lack of oxygen so they must be kept in large amounts of water or the water must be changed every 30 minutes.

Gourmet Math

Bulk Discounts

Shellfish is typically sold in bulk. Many vendors offer quantity discounts.

Mai Ling's seafood supplier sells medium oysters at $75 per gallon. The supplier offers several quantity discounts: a discount of 5% off the total price for buying at least 10 gallons of oysters, 10% for at least 15 gallons, and 20% for at least 20 gallons. Mai Ling's restaurant needs 9 gallons of oysters per day. What is the average daily cost if she buys a one-day supply each day? If she buys a two-day supply every two days? If she buys a three-day supply every three days?

Math Concept **Calculate Discount Price**
Calculate the discount price by multiplying the original price by (100% minus the discount percentage).

Starting Hint When she buys a two-day supply, or $2 \times 9 = 18$ gallons, Mai Ling will receive a 10% discount. The new price will be $100\% - 10\% = 90\%$ of the regular price. Multiply $0.90 \times 18 \times \$75$ to find her two-day price, and divide by 2 for the average per day.

NCTM Number and Operations Understand numbers, ways of representing numbers, relationships among numbers, and number systems.

PHOTO CAPTION ANSWER Clams are classified by size.

Mollusk Varieties There are many different varieties of mollusks available. *How are clams classified?*

GOURMET MATH ANSWER One-day price: $9 \times \$75 = \$675$. 2-day: $\$1,350 \times (1 - 0.10) = \$1,215$, $\$1,215 \div 2 = \$607.50$. 3-day: $\$2,025 \times (1 - 0.2) = \$1,620$, $\$1,620 \div 3 = \$540$.

Mussels

Mussels come from around the world. Mussels look like small, dark blue or black clams. Their meat generally ranges from yellow to orange in color and is tender but firm when cooked.

Mussels from Southeast Asia and New Zealand have a green edge to their tan or light gray shells, and white or orange meat. Flavor is not affected by the color. These mussels are generally more expensive.

Market Forms

Mussels may be sold live, shucked, vacuum packed, or frozen in the shell. The shells of live mussels should be closed or should close when tapped lightly. Throw out any mussels that seem hollow or are very lightweight. If the mussels are too heavy, they are most likely filled with sand, and should also be thrown away. If mussels have been shucked, they are generally packed in brine to preserve them, or sold frozen. Live or fresh shucked mussels must be used quickly because they can become toxic after they die.

PHOTO CAPTION ANSWER Fresh mussels should be alive just before being cooked because they can quickly become toxic after they die, causing illness.

Handling and Storage

When you prepare mussels, scrub the shells under cold running water. Use a clam knife to scrape off any barnacles ('bär-ni-kəls) that have attached themselves to the shells. A **barnacle** is a crustacean that attaches itself to rocks, boats, or other sea life. Just before cooking, pull off the mussel's "beard," which sticks out between the two shells. If the mussel is sandy, soak it in water and cornmeal to get rid of the sand.

Keep mussels in the refrigerator and away from light. Store them in the paper sack or cardboard box they arrive in, and keep the container damp.

Scallops

Scallops are available year-round and are sweet in flavor and white in color. They generally are sold already shucked. The muscle that closes the shell is the only part of the scallop that is commonly eaten in the United States. If scallops smell fishy or strong, they have spoiled or aged.

Sea scallops and bay scallops are the two most common kinds of scallops. Sea scallops are the largest, with about 10 to 40 per pound. Bay scallops are small and more delicately flavored, and range from about 50 to more than 150 per pound.

Market Forms

Scallops are sold fresh and shucked by the pound or the gallon. They may also be sold frozen, in five-pound blocks, or IQF. **IQF (individually quick frozen)** fish or shellfish have been quickly frozen piece by piece. The freezing happens quickly, so few ice crystals form. This improves the quality.

Handling and Storage

Remove the little side muscle that is attached to the large adductor muscle on the sides of scallops. The adductor muscle opens and closes the valves on a bivalve mollusk. Although scallops can be prepared with the side muscle attached, this muscle tends to be very tough. Cover and refrigerate scallops. Do not place them directly on ice or they will become watery and lose their flavor. Sometimes large sea scallops are cut into smaller pieces before they are cooked.

Reading Check Summarize What is the proper way to store mussels?

Crustaceans

A **crustacean** has a hard outer shell and a jointed skeleton. Examples include lobster, shrimp, crab, and crayfish. Crustaceans tend to be expensive because so much work is needed to produce a small amount of meat. Restaurants often purchase crustaceans already processed to save preparation time. This will also save restaurant money in labor costs for chefs to prepare the meat. Crustaceans can be prepared in almost any way, as long as they are not overcooked. Overcooking makes them tough.

Lobsters

Northern lobsters may be considered the most valued seafood delicacy. This animal has two large claws, four pairs of legs, and a flexible, large tail. The lobster shell, which turns red when cooked, is actually bluish or dark green. Lobster meat from the tail, legs, and claws is sweet and white. Lobsters can weigh up to about 20 pounds. Rock, or spiny, lobsters are warm-water lobsters. They are sold only as IQF lobster tails.

Cooked lobster meat smells sweet and fresh. If a lobster is in the process of dying, it is called a **sleeper**. Sleepers should be cooked at once so that the meat will still be good. Once lobster meat has been cooked, cover and refrigerate it. The meat will keep only for a day or two.

Market Forms

Lobsters are sold live, frozen, or as fresh-cooked meat. Uncooked lobster tails are also available IQF.

Handling and Storage

The lobster must be split and cut for some preparations, such as broiling or cubing for use in stews or sautés. When you cook live lobster, plunge it head first into boiling water.

Live lobsters should be stored in special saltwater tanks. They can also be kept in a cool location, wrapped in seaweed or heavy, wet paper.

Shrimp

Shrimp are classified by the count per pound. The smaller the shrimp, the higher the count. It takes less work to peel and devein large shrimp, but they are more expensive. To **devein** ((ˌ)dē-ˈvān) a shrimp means to remove its intestinal tract, located along the back. Deveined shrimp cost more and are sold either raw or cooked. It takes about a pound of raw shrimp to make a half-pound of peeled and cooked shrimp.

Peel and Devein Shrimp

1 First, use your forefinger to remove the legs.

2 Use your fingertips to gently peel and remove the shell.

3 Leave the tail on if the shrimp will be broiled or deep-fried. Remove the tail for most other preparations.

4 Cut down the back of the shrimp with a paring knife and remove the vein just below the surface.

5 Make the cut deeper to butterfly the shrimp.

Market Forms

Shrimp may be purchased raw in the shell, either fresh or frozen. These are called green shrimp. They may also be purchased P/D. This is an abbreviation for peeled and deveined. The third form available is PDC. This is an abbreviation for peeled, deveined, and cooked. Both P/D and PDC shrimp are usually individually quick frozen and have a glaze of ice on them. Some shrimp may also be battered and breaded.

Handling and Storage

Keep frozen shrimp frozen until they need to be used. To thaw shrimp, place them in the refrigerator. Keep thawed or fresh shrimp wrapped and on crushed ice. Unwrapped shrimp will lose flavor and nutrients.

If serving shrimp cold, they can be peeled after they are cooked. If shrimp are to be served hot, they should be peeled and deveined before cooking. Shrimp can also be butterflied to reduce their thickness so that they cook faster.

Crab

Popular in casseroles, curries, and chowders, crab are plentiful along North America's coasts. Crab may be shipped canned, fresh, or frozen. The following types of crab are used in restaurants:

- **Blue Crab** A small, 4- to 6-ounce crab from the East Coast. Most frozen crabmeat comes from blue crabs.
- **Soft-Shell Crab** A blue crab that has just molted, or shed its shell. Because the shell has not had time to harden, it is eaten as well as the meat. Only the head and the gills must be removed before frying or sautéing the crab.
- **Alaskan King Crab** This is the largest type of crab. They can weigh between 6 and 20 pounds. Even though they are expensive, king crab are popular in restaurants because large chunks of meat can be easily removed.
- **Alaskan Snow Crab** Alaskan snow crabs are also called spider crabs. Snow crab can be used as a less expensive substitute for king crab.
- **Dungeness** (ˌdən-jə-ˌnes) **Crab** Found along the West Coast, they range from 1½ to 4 pounds and have very sweet meat.
- **Stone Crab** The claws of stone crab are popular in the Southeast. To protect the species, people fishing can harvest only one claw per stone crab. They twist off the claw and put the crab back in the sea. The crab will grow a new claw within 18 months.

Market Forms

Although crab taste best fresh, picking the meat is an involved and lengthy process. Most crab are purchased in the shell, already cooked and frozen. Soft-shell crab are sold whole, while king crab legs are sold both split and whole. Snow and stone crab claws are also sold whole.

Handling and Storage

Frozen crabmeat spoils rapidly when it is defrosted. It should be kept frozen until it is ready to be used. Keep live crab cool and packed in damp seaweed until it is ready to be cooked.

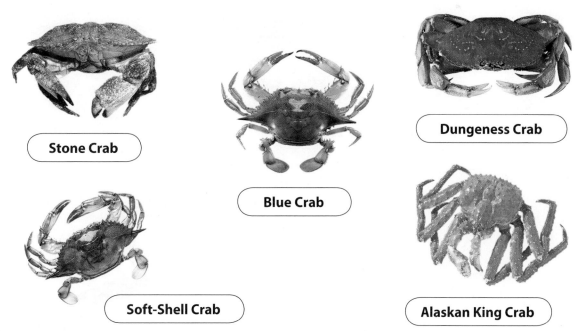

Stone Crab

Soft-Shell Crab

Blue Crab

Dungeness Crab

Alaskan King Crab

Types of Crab There are a variety of crabs available for cooking. *What type of nutrients can be found in crab meat?*

PHOTO CAPTION ANSWER All crab meat is high in protein and minerals, and low in fat.

Crayfish

Crayfish are freshwater crustaceans that look like miniature lobsters. They generally range from 3½ to 7 inches in length. Crayfish are sometimes called crawfish and crawdads in the southern United States. Their tail meat is lean, sweet, and tender. Whole crayfish and peeled tail meat are sold both live and frozen. They are available year-round.

As with lobsters and crabs, live crayfish should be kept in a cool location and wrapped in seaweed. If purchased live, keep them alive until ready to cook. Wash them several times in cool water before cooking. Frozen crayfish should be thawed in the refrigerator and cooked within a day.

Crayfish are served in French restaurants and used in Cajun and Creole cooking. Whole crayfish are often boiled and served on top of rice. Crayfish tail meat is usually deep-fried and used in soups and sauces.

Reading Check Give Examples
What types of crabs are used in restaurants?

Other Seafood

Some types of seafood, such as frogs and snails, spend part of their lives on land, but are still classified as seafood. These seafood products are often sold smoked, pickled, or in brine to preserve the seafood and add flavor. These products need to be refrigerated.

Squid

On some menus, squid goes by its Italian name, **calamari** (ˌkä-lə-ˈmär-ē). Squid have 10 tentacles and look somewhat like an octopus. It is the tentacles and the hollowed-out body that are eaten. Squid is cut into small pieces, which may be either simmered in a seasoned sauce or liquid, or quickly fried. Squid can be used as an appetizer, as a protein on salads, or as part of a main dish, such as pasta.

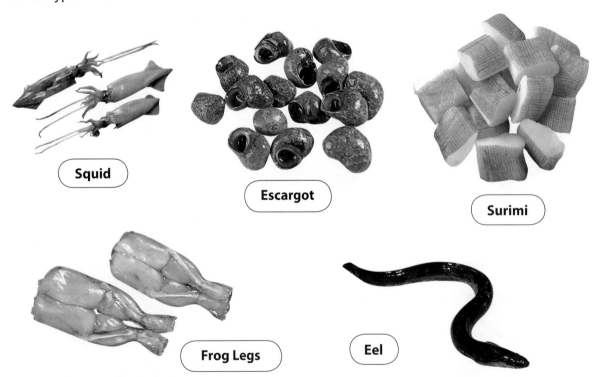

Squid

Escargot

Surimi

Frog Legs

Eel

▲ **Other Seafood** These seafood products are often found smoked, brined, or pickled.
Which of these seafood spend part of their lives out of the water?

READING CHECK ANSWER Blue crab, soft-shell crab, Alaskan king crab, Alaskan snow crab, Dungeness crab, and stone crab.

PHOTO CAPTION ANSWER Escargot (snails) and frogs spend part of their lives out of the water.

Frog Legs

Frog legs are from frogs that are farm raised. Frog legs are only sold in pairs. Foodservice operations use only the rear legs. They can be served poached with a sauce, deep-fried, or sautéed.

Escargot

Imported from France, where they are called **escargot** (ˌes-kär-ˈgō), snails are generally served as appetizers in the shell, with garlic butter. Snails are usually removed from the shells, prepared, and cooked before being poured back into the shells to serve. It takes about 32 snails to equal 1 pound of meat. Commercial farming of snails in the United States is becoming more popular, since fresh snails taste better than canned snails.

Surimi

Surimi (sù-ˈrē-mē) is a combination of different kinds of white fish and flavoring, minced and formed into different shapes.

While many types of white fish are used to make surimi, Alaska pollock is the most common. Two of the most popular forms of surimi are imitation crab and lobster. To make these imitations seem more real, color is added. Surimi is a widely used substitute for lobster and crab in North America because of its lower cost. Surimi is often used to make a cold imitation crab salad, with a mayonnaise-based dressing.

Eel

Eels are long, thin fish that have a sweet, mild flavor. They are very popular in Europe and Asia and in some ethnic communities in the United States. They are usually sold fresh, smoked, and pickled. Eels should be frozen only if they are first gutted and cleaned, and then quick-frozen. Eels also make a popular sushi dish, although they are used cooked, not raw.

 Reading Check Name What are two popular forms of surimi?

SECTION 21.2 After You Read

Review Key Concepts

1. **Explain** the meaning of the different grades of shellfish.
2. **Differentiate** between univalves, bivalves, and cephalopods.
3. **Describe** the characteristics of a crustacean.
4. **Identify** methods of cooking squid.

Practice Culinary Academics
Mathematics

5. You need to purchase five king crabs for your restaurant, and would like the crabs' average weight to be 15 pounds. If you have already selected four crabs weighing 12, 14, 16 ½, and 17 pounds, how much should the fifth crab weigh?

Math Concept **Calculating Mean** A mean is an average of a set of terms. When you have a series of values, calculate the mean by finding the sum of all of the values, and dividing that sum by the number of values.

Starting Hint You know that the sum of five values, divided by 5, equals 15. Write an algebraic equation to find the missing value: $(12 + 14 + 16\frac{1}{2} + 17 + x) \div 5 = 15$.

NCTM Problem Solving Apply and adapt a variety of appropriate strategies to solve problems.

 Check your answers at this book's Online Learning Center at **glencoe.com**.

Cooking Fish and Shellfish

Reading Guide

 Before You Read

Be Organized A messy environment can be distracting. To lessen distractions, organize an area where you can read this section comfortably.

Read to Learn

Key Concepts
- **Summarize** the methods for cooking fish and shellfish.

Main Idea

There are several methods for cooking fish and shellfish. These can include moist cooking, deep-frying, baking, and sautéing.

Content Vocabulary
- sushi
- flake
- moist baking
- en papillote
- tartar sauce
- caper

Academic Vocabulary
- discard
- sufficient

Graphic Organizer

As you read, use a matrix like the one shown to record the guidelines for determining the doneness of fish and shellfish for each cooking method.

Determining the Doneness of Fish and Shellfish

Baking	Broiling & Grilling	Sautéing & Pan-Frying	Deep-Frying

ACADEMIC STANDARDS

 English Language Arts
NCTE 4 Use written language to communicate effectively.

 Mathematics
NCTM Measurement Understand measurable attributes of objects and the units, systems, and processes of measurement.

 Science
NSES B Develop an understanding of chemical reactions.

 Social Studies
NCSS VIII B Science, Technology, and Society Make judgments about how science and technology have transformed human society.

NCTE National Council of Teachers of English

NCTM National Council of Teachers of Mathematics

NSES National Science Education Standards

NCSS National Council for the Social Studies

 Graphic Organizer Go to this book's Online Learning Center at **glencoe.com** for a printable graphic organizer.

GRAPHIC ORGANIZER ANSWER Baking: Internal temperature is 145°F (63°C) for 15 seconds, opaque flesh that flakes, pulls away, and springs back when pressed. Broiling: Outside browned and crispy, inside juicy and tender. Sautéing: Slightly brown and crispy, inside juicy and tender. Deep-Frying: Batter is golden brown.

Fish and Shellfish Cookery

You have many methods from which to choose when you cook fish and shellfish. Dishes may be simple or elaborate, low-fat or rich. Moist cooking methods and deep-frying, baking, and sautéing, offer a number of ways to prepare seafood. Fish and shellfish are also sometimes served raw. **Sushi** ('sü-shē) is a Japanese dish of raw or cooked fresh fish or seafood and rice. There are many different forms of sushi, from rolled, to topped on rice, to served scattered over rice.

Fish has little connective tissue, so a long cooking time is not needed to tenderize it. When you cook fish, you must pay attention to time, temperature, and the cooking process. Cook fish until its internal temperature is 145°F (63°C) or above for 15 seconds.

Fish is also usually low in fat. This means it can quickly dry out when it is overcooked. To prevent this, chefs sometimes use moist cooking techniques, such as steaming or poaching. Fish flesh will **flake**, or break away in small layers, when it is done. Remember that fish retains heat, even when removed from a heat source. Therefore, it continues to cook, and can easily overcook.

Like fish, shellfish can easily be overcooked. Overcooking and excessively high heat will cause shellfish to dry up and shrink or become rubbery and tough. Clams or mussels cooked in the shell will open as they cook. **Discard**, or throw away, any shells that do not open, because the meat will not be safe to eat. To prevent dryness, moist cooking methods are most often used.

Bake Fish and Shellfish

Fish steaks and fillets, as well as small fish and shellfish, can be baked in an oven. Combination cooking methods are sometimes used to bake fish. For example, fish may be initially browned in a small amount of oil in a sauté pan to give it color and flavor, then baked to finish cooking. When you bake lean fish, you should baste it frequently with oil or butter to prevent the fish from drying out.

Fish or shellfish may also be baked in a sauce, such as curry or tomato. Baking in a sauce also helps prevent the meat from becoming dry.

Baking Guidelines

Fatty fish, such as pompano or salmon, are not as likely to dry out. These types of fish are the best fish for baking. Generally, fish and shellfish are baked between 350°F (177°C) and 400°F (204°C). Large fish will bake more evenly at the lower temperature. Cook fish until its internal temperature at its thickest part is 145°F (63°C) or above for 15 seconds.

Moist Baking Adding vegetables and liquid to a large piece of fish or a whole fish is called **moist baking**. Other moist cooking techniques used for fish and shellfish include simmering, poaching, and steaming. Liquids from moist cooking are often used for sauces that go with the fish or shellfish. Wrapping fish or shellfish in parchment paper with vegetables, herbs, and sauces or butters is a type of steaming called **en papillote** (ən ˌpä-pē-'yō).

Sanitation Check

✓ Serve Raw Fish and Shellfish

Many restaurants offer raw fish or shellfish on the menu, such as sushi or raw oysters. Many health officials advise against serving raw fish or shellfish because of the danger of parasites and contamination from polluted water. However, if you do serve these items, follow these guidelines:

- Buy fish from reputable vendors.
- Choose only the highest quality fish because it will not be cooked.
- Handle the fish as little as possible.
- Follow state-mandated guidelines concerning the serving of raw fish and shellfish.

CRITICAL THINKING *Why do you think you should handle the fish as little as possible?*

SANITATION CHECK ANSWER The more you handle the fish, the greater the possibility of introducing contaminants from your hands or from the kitchen.

Steam

Fish en Papillote

1 Fold the parchment paper in half and crease the folded edge. Cut the parchment paper into the desired shape and size to prepare the fish.

2 Butter the parchment paper on both sides.

3 Add the fish, vegetables, and butter to one side of the parchment paper. Fold the other side of the parchment over the fish.

4 Seal the edges of the paper by crimping, or pinching and pressing them together around the entire paper.

5 Bake until the package is puffy and lightly browned. Cut the package and fold back the top to serve.

These cooking methods add little or no fat, keep the meat from drying, and preserve nutrients and natural flavors.

Broil and Grill Fish and Shellfish

Because of the high heat used, broiled, grilled, and barbequed seafood dishes can be prepared quickly. Many diners view broiled and grilled dishes as more healthful than dishes cooked with other methods.

The appearance of broiled or grilled fish or shellfish may be enhanced by a relish or side sauce. Grilled vegetables are also a natural accompaniment. Citrus garnishes, such as lemon, lime, or orange, are generally served with broiled or grilled seafood. Sometimes lemon and herb butters are served instead.

Broiling and Grilling Guidelines

The high heat of broiling or grilling gives fish and shellfish a smoky flavor. Brush butter or oil over the fish before broiling to keep the meat from sticking. This also keeps lean fish moist.

To cook a thicker cut of fish or shellfish evenly, turn it once during broiling. Thin pieces are broiled on one side only.

1896

The state of Utah enters the Union

1899

Oysters Rockefeller is created in New Orleans

Oysters Rockefeller

Oysters have been cultivated worldwide for more than 2,000 years. They have long been a popular food in the United States. Native Americans once considered oysters a staple in their diet. Early Colonial settlers ate oysters by the gross (144) instead of the dozen (12).

New Orleans, Louisiana, is the birthplace of several famous oyster dishes, including Oysters Rockefeller. Named after business tycoon John D. Rockefeller, the dish was created in 1899 when a shortage of snails from Europe prompted Jules Alciatore to substitute oysters as the main ingredient in a dish for Antoine's, his father's restaurant.

History Application

Research the history and problems of the oyster population in the United States. Write a short report about your findings.

NCSS VIII B Science, Technology, and Society Make judgments about how science and technology have transformed our understanding of human-environment interactions.

Fatty fish, such as swordfish or trout, are a good choice for broiling. Many types of shellfish are broiled on the half shell or on skewers to make them easier to handle.

Lean Versus Fat All varieties of fish may be broiled. However, fatty fish is the best choice. Lean fish can become dry very quickly. Before you broil either lean or fatty fish, you may wish to coat the fish with butter, oil, or a vegetable oil spray.

Use Fish Steaks or Fillets Fish steaks thicker than 1½ inch and whole fish are not the best choices for broiling. The high heat used in broiling will finish cooking the outside of thick fish before the inside is done. When grilling thicker steaks and fillets you may have to start cooking them over high heat and move them to a cooler part of the grill to finish cooking.

Avoid Overcooking Broiling and grilling require high temperatures, which cook fish and shellfish quickly. Overcooking will make fish dry and shellfish tough.

Sautéing and Pan-Frying

Sautéing and pan-frying are often mistaken as the same thing. Sautéing will add flavor to the food because the food's surface is lightly browned. Pan-frying uses more fat

Grilled Fish Grilled salmon is a popular dish in many restaurants. *Why is salmon a good choice for grilling?*

A TASTE OF HISTORY ANSWER Oysters clean the water they live in and their shells provide shelter for other animals. Over-harvesting is a problem, but so is disease caused by pollution.

PHOTO CAPTION ANSWER Salmon is a good choice for grilling because it is a fatty fish, and is less likely to dry out during cooking.

✓ Frying Fat

Always take special care when you work with hot fat. It can easily spatter and burn you. Drain and serve deep-fried foods immediately after cooking.

CRITICAL THINKING *What are some potential consequences of leaving the food sitting in the fat after frying?*

than sautéing does, and the food is coated with seasoned batters, flour, or breading before cooking. This creates a flavorful crust that protects the fish during cooking.

Be sure that the pan and the cooking fat are both hot before you add fish or shellfish. Because only a short cooking time is needed, use high heat to brown the surface when you sauté thin slices of fish or small pieces of shellfish. Thicker pieces may require lower heat so that they do not get too brown. Adding too much fish or shellfish to the pan at the same time causes the fat to cool. The food will then simmer in its own juices instead of sauté.

Sautéing and Pan-Frying Guidelines

Because both sautéing and pan-frying use oil or clarified butter, they work well for lean fish. Usually just enough fat to cover the bottom of the pan is **sufficient**, or enough, for sautéing. Pan-frying requires more fat.

To keep fish from sticking, use flour or breading to form a crust. For better appearance, brown the presentation side first. This is generally the thicker side of a fillet. Turn pan-fried fish or shellfish only once during cooking to help prevent fillets from breaking. Sautéed or pan-fried items will cook quickly over a high heat.

Dredging and Breading To dredge a food is to evenly coat it with a bit of flour or cornmeal. Make small batches if there are several pounds of fish to prepare. For a better crust, soak the fish in milk and drain it before breading. Dredge the fish or use large shakers with handles to sprinkle the breading onto the fish.

Deep-Frying

Deep-frying is the most common method used to fry fish in the United States. Although the foodservice industry often uses frozen, breaded fish for deep-frying, fresh fish or shellfish may also be deep-fried. To protect both the fat and the fish, coat the item with batter or breading before cooking. This will provide an attractive coating and a crispy texture. The best shellfish to deep-fry are scallops, oysters, shrimp, and clams. Lean fish, usually in sticks or small fillets, are also a good choice.

Deep-Frying Guidelines

When you prepare frozen breaded fish, cook the fish without first thawing it. If the portion thaws, the fish will be soggy. Review the guidelines for breading and frying in Chapter 15. Batter recipes for vegetables can also be used for fish or shellfish.

Determine Doneness

Because fish and shellfish are naturally tender, it is critical to avoid overcooking. Remember that overcooking results in dry fish and tough shellfish. Use the following guidelines to help you determine when fish and shellfish are done cooking:

- Fish starts flaking. Cooking fish causes the muscle fibers to begin separating from each other.
- Flesh pulls away from the bones or shell of the fish easily.
- Flesh springs back when pressed. Uncooked seafood is soft and mushy instead.
- Flesh becomes opaque. Light cannot be seen through the flesh.

Steamed Shellfish Shellfish such as clams will open when they are cooked in their shells. *What should you do with clams or mussels that do not open during cooking?*

In addition, use these guidelines with each specific cooking technique:

- **Baking** Bake fish until the internal temperature is 145°F (63°C) or above for 15 seconds. Also check that the flesh flakes, pulls away from the bones or shell, springs back when pressed, and is opaque.
- **Broiling and Grilling** When broiled or grilled, the outside of fish and shellfish should be slightly browned and crispy. The inside should be juicy and tender.
- **Sautéing and Pan-Frying** Sautéed and pan-fried fish and shellfish are done cooking when their surfaces are slightly browned or crispy. As in broiling and grilling, the insides should be juicy and tender.
- **Deep-Frying** If the oil has reached the proper temperature, deep-fried fish and shellfish are done when their batter is a rich golden brown. When you use prepackaged frozen items, follow the package guidelines. The package will generally give a range of times and temperatures for correctly cooking these items.

PHOTO CAPTION ANSWER Clams or mussels that do not open their shells during cooking should be discarded.

Plate Fish and Shellfish

Serving seafood attractively is an important part of preparation. Because seafood tends to be pale, adding colorful side dishes is a must. The contrasting color and texture make the overall meal appealing. For example:

- A mix of steamed carrots and broccoli brightens the plate and is low in fat.
- If shellfish is served chilled, a cocktail sauce and fresh lemon slices usually accompany it.
- Some seafood dishes are served on beds of sautéed leeks or seaweed.
- Colorful sauces can be plated underneath seafood to add color and flavor.

Garnish Fish and Shellfish

Tartar sauce may be the most familiar sauce that accompanies seafood. **Tartar sauce** is a sauce made of mayonnaise and chopped pickles. However, other sauces, such as hollandaise or a caper sauce, work just as well for steamed or poached items. A **caper** is a flower bud of a Mediterranean shrub, used for seasoning.

Citrus wedges, such as lemon or orange, often accompany grilled or broiled seafood items. If an item has been broiled with a seasoned butter, an additional serving of the butter may be used for garnish. Common garnishes such as parsley or chives may also be used.

 Reading Check Determine What garnishes are commonly used with different types of fish and shellfish?

SECTION 21.3 After You Read

Review Key Concepts

1. **Summarize** the methods for sautéing or pan-frying fish and shellfish.

Practice Culinary Academics

 Science

2. **Procedure** Find a recipe for a shrimp marinade that contains a citrus such as lemon, orange, or lime juice. Divide shrimp into three groups. Marinate one group of shrimp for a long period of time, at least an hour. Marinate another group for around 10 minutes. Do not marinate the third group at all. Prepare all of the shrimp.

   Analysis Compare the textures of the three groups. What do you observe about the textures of the different shrimp? Create a chart that shows the differences. Hypothesize what causes those differences.

   > **NSES B** Develop an understanding of chemical reactions.

English Language Arts

3. Follow your teacher's instructions to form into small groups. Each group should choose one method of cooking fish or shellfish and create a poster listing guidelines to remember when using that cooking method. Include artwork to illustrate each guideline. Share the posters with the class and display them in the foods lab.

   > **NCTE 4** Use written language to communicate effectively.

 Social Studies

4. Study how the industry of fishing has changed in modern times. What types of equipment do commercial fishermen use to help them catch large quantities of fish and to save time? How has this changed from traditional methods of fishing? Create a five minute presentation of your findings.

   > **NCSS VIII B Science, Technology, and Society** Make judgments about how science and technology have transformed human society.

Mathematics

5. To cook a red snapper en papillote, a restaurant uses a 24-inch-long sheet of parchment paper. If a roll of parchment paper is 40 yards long, how many sheets can the restaurant get from each roll?

   Math Concept **Equivalent Lengths** There are 3 feet in one yard, so multiply yards by 3 to convert to feet. There are 12 inches in one foot, so multiply feet by 12 to convert to inches.

   Starting Hint The question asks you to divide 40 yards by 24 inches. To do so, convert the yards into inches by first multiplying by 3 to convert yards to feet, then multiplying by 12 to convert feet to inches.

   > **NCTM Measurement** Understand measurable attributes of objects and the units, systems, and processes of measurement.

 Check your answers at this book's Online Learning Center at **glencoe.com**.

READING CHECK ANSWER Common garnishes include tartar sauce, hollandaise sauce, herb vinaigrette, citrus wedges, or seasoned butter.

NUTRITION NOTES ANSWER People with a risk of heart disease, or people who are trying to lose weight might eat fish.

Review and Applications

Chapter Summary

Fish is similar to poultry and meat in that it has protein, fats, and water. Fish have very little connective tissue. Fresh, frozen, or canned fish are available whole or in the form in which they will be cooked, such as fillets or cubes.

Inspect fresh fish closely for quality characteristics before purchasing. Fresh fish should be stored on ice and used quickly. Keep frozen fish well wrapped and in the freezer. You must know the different handling and storage methods for each type of shellfish.

There are many options for cooking fish and shellfish, including baking, grilling, and moist cooking techniques. Garnishes for fish and seafood might include sauce, citrus wedges, or seasoned butter.

Content and Academic Vocabulary Review

1. Arrange the vocabulary terms below into groups of related words. Explain why you put the words together.

Content Vocabulary

- fatty fish (p. 542)
- lean fish (p. 542)
- flat fish (p. 542)
- round fish (p. 542)
- boneless fish (p. 542)
- drawn (p. 544)
- dressed (p. 544)
- fillets (p. 544)
- butterflied (p. 545)
- freezer burn (p. 546)
- drip loss (p. 546)
- vacuum packed (p. 547)

- PUFI mark (p. 549)
- mollusk (p. 550)
- univalve (p. 550)
- bivalve (p. 550)
- cephalopod (p. 550)
- barnacle (p. 552)
- IQF (individually quick frozen) (p. 553)
- crustacean (p. 553)
- sleeper (p. 553)
- devein (p. 553)
- calamari (p. 556)
- escargot (p. 557)
- surimi (p. 557)

- sushi (p. 559)
- flake (p. 559)
- moist baking (p. 559)
- en papillote (p. 559)
- tartar sauce (p. 563)
- caper (p. 563)

Academic Vocabulary

- classify (p. 542)
- keep (p. 547)
- luxury (p. 549)
- mandatory (p. 549)
- discard (p. 559)
- sufficient (p. 562)

Review Key Concepts

2. Describe the composition and structure of fish.

3. Distinguish between the different market forms of fish.

4. Explain the structure, composition, and grading of shellfish.

5. Differentiate between types of mollusks.

6. Distinguish between types of crustaceans.

7. Identify other types of seafood.

8. Summarize the methods for cooking fish and shellfish.

Critical Thinking

9. Draw conclusions about how healthful cooking techniques for fish and shellfish can help people on a low-fat diet.

10. Imagine that you are a health inspector. Describe what you might do if you found that a sushi restaurant was not choosing the best quality fish.

Academic Skills

English Language Arts

11. Design a Menu Imagine that you are in charge of planning the menu for a foodservice operation. You want to plan creative dishes using both fish and shellfish. Create a clear, descriptive menu that includes at least two items made with fish or shellfish in each category: appetizers, soups, salads, sandwiches, and entrées. Be sure to describe the type of seafood used in each dish, as well as the cooking method.

> **NCTE 12** Use language to accomplish individual purposes.

Social Studies

12. Fish Around the World People in other countries eat fish dishes that are not as well known in the United States. For example, *gravlax* is a Scandinavian appetizer consisting of raw salmon cured in salt, sugar, and dill. Research a dish from a culture other than your own that contains fish or shellfish. Prepare a presentation that includes a recipe, the country or region of origin, a description, and an explanation of how it is served and eaten.

> **NCSS I A Culture** Analyze and explain the way groups, societies, and cultures address human needs and concerns.

Mathematics

13. Determine Fish Weight The largest wholesale fish and seafood market in the world is the Tsukiji fish market in Tokyo, Japan. Six days a week, freshly caught seafood products from around the world are brought into the market, auctioned to wholesalers, and then shipped to purchasers in dozens of countries. More than 2,000 metric tons of fish are handled every day in Tsukiji. How many pounds of fish does the market handle per day, to the nearest 1,000 pounds?

Math Concept **Converting Weights** A metric ton is not the same as a customary (U.S.) ton. A metric ton equals 1,000 kilograms, while a customary ton (also known as a short ton) equals 2,000 pounds. There are about 0.4536 kilograms in one pound.

Starting Hint First, you will need to convert the 2,000 metric tons into kilograms by multiplying by 1,000. Then, convert kilograms into pounds by dividing by 0.4536. Round your answer to the nearest thousand by changing all digits to the right of the thousands place to zeros. But if the digit to the right of the thousands place was 5 or greater, add one to the thousands place.

> **NCTM Number and Operations** Compute fluently and make reasonable estimates.

Certification Prep

Directions Read the questions. Then, read the answer choices and choose the best possible answer for each.

14. What are the sides of the fish called?
- **a.** fillets
- **b.** steaks
- **c.** cubes
- **d.** sticks

15. What is a mollusk that has two shells hinged together called?
- **a.** univalve
- **b.** bivalve
- **c.** cephalopod
- **d.** crustacean

Sharpen your test-taking skills to improve your kitchen certification program score.

Test-Taking Tip
When you learn a new vocabulary word, practice using it right away. Try to use it in conversation or in your writing with someone.

Review and Applications

Real-World Skills and Applications

Self-Management Skills

16. Quick and Nutritious Entrée Imagine that you work in a restaurant and your manager has asked you to develop a nutritious entrée using either fish or shellfish. The entrée must be prepared quickly during busy lunch and dinner shifts. What type of fish or shellfish would you choose? Which cooking methods would you use and why? What would you add to increase nutritional value?

Interpersonal and Collaborative Skills

17. Make a Cooking Show Follow your teacher's instructions to form into groups or work together as a class to create a cooking show. Your show should demonstrate how to prepare a fish or shellfish dish. Perform your group's show for the class, and film it if possible. If you worked as a class, try to present it to another class.

Technology Applications

18. Design a Web Site Design a Web site that shows readers simple and creative ways to prepare fish and shellfish. Include several recipes, descriptions of cooking methods, and photos. Recipes should be clear and easy to follow. Descriptions of cooking methods should show individual steps of that cooking method. As a class, choose the best design and post it on your school's Web site.

Financial Literacy

19. Choose a Market Form Imagine that you need 10 pounds of salmon to make it through your next dinner service. Whole salmon weigh 5 pounds each, and you can get a 50% yield from the whole fish. How many whole fish will you need to buy to get 10 pounds?

Culinary Lab

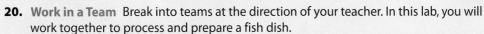
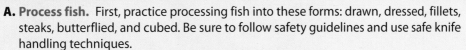

Use the culinary skills you have learned in this chapter.

Prepare Fish Dishes

20. Work in a Team Break into teams at the direction of your teacher. In this lab, you will work together to process and prepare a fish dish.

A. Process fish. First, practice processing fish into these forms: drawn, dressed, fillets, steaks, butterflied, and cubed. Be sure to follow safety guidelines and use safe knife handling techniques.

B. Prepare your fish. After processing the fish, choose one of the following techniques and prepare the fish: baking, broiling, grilling, sautéing, pan-frying, or deep-frying.

C. Determine doneness. Determine the doneness of your fish using tips from this chapter.

D. Present your fish. Plate and garnish your fish to make it appealing, and share your creation with other teams.

Create Your Evaluation

Taste each team's fish and answer the following questions:

- Was the form of each team's fish recognizable even after cooking? Why or why not?
- Was the cooking method for each team's fish appropriate to the market form? Why or why not?
- How would you rate the visual appeal and flavor of each team's fish on a scale of 1 to 5?

Poultry Cookery

SECTIONS

22.1 Poultry Basics

22.2 Cooking Poultry

Descriptive Writing

Many things affect whether customers enjoy a dish. Write a descriptive paragraph about a special meal where poultry is served. Include specific details about the setting and atmosphere.

Writing Tips

1 Decide what atmosphere or feeling you want to create.

2 Write a strong topic sentence.

3 Present details in a logical order.

EXPLORE THE PHOTO

Poultry can be cooked using a variety of methods. *Why do you think poultry is a popular choice to serve at restaurants?*

WRITING ACTIVITY ANSWER Paragraphs should include details in logical order, and should have correct spelling and grammar.

EXPLORE THE PHOTO ANSWER Answers will vary, but may include lower cost, customer preference, and versatility.

Poultry Basics

Discover the basics of this popular, versatile food.

Reading Guide

Before You Read

Preview Scan the section and choose a Content or Academic Vocabulary word that is new to you. When you find it in the text, write down the definition.

Read To Learn

Key Concepts
- **Identify** different kinds, classes, and market forms of poultry.
- **Explain** how poultry is inspected and graded.
- **Describe** how to handle, store, and prepare poultry for cooking.

Main Idea
Poultry products are available in a variety of forms and classes. They must be handled and stored properly to stay fresh.

Content Vocabulary
- poultry
- kind
- maturity
- connective tissue
- light meat
- dark meat
- giblets
- market form
- ready-to-cook
- trussing

Academic Vocabulary
- acceptable
- indicate

ACADEMIC STANDARDS

 Science
NSES C Develop an understanding of the behavior of organisms.

NSES F Develop an understanding of community health, and natural and human-induced hazards.

 Mathematics
NCTM Data Analysis and Probability Select and use appropriate statistical methods to analyze data.

NCTE National Council of Teachers of English

NCTM National Council of Teachers of Mathematics

NSES National Science Education Standards

NCSS National Council for the Social Studies

Graphic Organizer
As you read, you will find eight factors you must consider when choosing a poultry product. Use a diagram like this one to help organize your information.

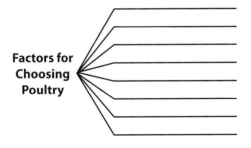

Factors for Choosing Poultry

 Graphic Organizer
Go to this book's Online Learning Center at **glencoe.com** for a printable Graphic Organizer.

GRAPHIC ORGANIZER ANSWER Kind, market form, class, style, color, odor, inspection, and grading.

What Is Poultry?

Birds that are raised for human consumption are called **poultry**. Poultry products are usually less expensive than many meat products and may be adapted to a wide variety of dishes. You may also use a wide variety of cooking techniques to cook poultry. Before you cook poultry, you will need to understand the eight factors for making the right choice: kind, market form, class, style, color, odor, inspection, and grading. You will also need to know how to safely handle and store poultry.

The United States Department of Agriculture (USDA) categorizes poultry according to species, or **kind**. The kinds of poultry include chicken, turkey, goose, duck, pigeon, and guinea. Each kind of poultry is divided into different classes based on the age and gender of the bird. (See **Figure 22.1**.)

Poultry is similar to meat in structure. Both poultry and meat are made up of muscle, connective tissue, fat, and bone. Poultry flesh is made up of protein, water, and fat. The fat in all types of poultry is found just underneath the skin.

▼ **FIGURE 22.1** **Poultry Classifications**

Poultry Choices There are many different kinds of poultry available. *What kinds of poultry would you choose for customers who prefer tender or very tender poutlry?*

Type of Poultry	Description
 **Chicken**	
Cornish hen	Young (5–6 weeks); very tender
Fryer or broiler	Young (9–12 weeks), male or female; tender
Roaster	Young (3–5 months), male or female; tender
Capon	Male, under 10 months; very tender
Stewer	Mature female, over 10 months; tough
 **Turkey**	
Fryer-roaster	Young bird, male (tom) or female (hen); tender
Young turkey	Hen or tom, with tender flesh but firmer cartilage
Yearling turkey	Fully mature, but tender
Mature or old turkey	Hen or tom with tough flesh and coarse skin
 **Goose**	
Young goose	Under 6 months; tender
Mature goose	Over 6 months; tough
 **Duck**	
Broiler or fryer duckling	Young, with soft windpipe; tender
Roasting duckling	Young, with hardening windpipe; tender
Mature duck	Old, with tough flesh
 **Pigeon**	
Squab	3–4 weeks; light, tender meat
Pigeon	Over 4 weeks; dark, tough meat
 **Guinea**	
Young guinea	Under 6 months; tender
Old guinea	Up to 12 months; tough

FIGURE CAPTION ANSWER Cornish hens, fryer/broiler chickens, roaster chickens, capons, fryer/roaster turkeys, young and yearling turkeys, young geese, broiler/fryer and roasting ducklings, squabs, and young guineas.

Maturity and Tenderness

A bird's age is commonly called its **maturity**. Older poultry is tough. If you want tender poultry, select a younger bird. Tenderness is also affected by the amount of exercise a bird gets. The more a bird exercises, the more connective tissue is created. **Connective tissue** holds muscle fiber together. A bird with more connective tissue will have tougher flesh.

Birds that rarely fly, such as turkeys and chickens, have lighter-colored wing and breast meat, commonly called **light meat**. The parts of a bird that have more muscle and connective tissue, such as the thighs and legs, are darker in color. This is commonly called **dark meat**. Light meat has less fat and cooks faster than dark meat. Dark meat has more fat and generally takes a longer time to cook. Duck and goose are composed of mostly dark meat. All poultry has **giblets**, the edible internal organs of the bird.

Reading Check **Summarize** What effect does exercise have on poultry's toughness?

Evaluating Poultry

Poultry is available in many market forms, classes, and styles. **Market form** is the form poultry is in when it is purchased. Fresh poultry works well when the poultry is to be cooked within one to two days. Frozen poultry may be kept for up to six months.

Many establishments find fully cooked poultry convenient to use in recipes for soups, salads, and casserole dishes. It can be purchased frozen and canned.

The two classes of poultry are maturity and gender, or whether a bird is male or female. Old birds are tougher than young birds and male birds are tougher than female birds.

Style refers to the state of the bird when it is received at a foodservice operation. It will also reflect, or demonstrate, the amount of processing that was done. Poultry is sold whole or in parts, bone-in or boneless, or ground.

Foodservice operations purchase poultry either whole or in parts. Poultry that has been prepared and packaged is called **ready-to-cook**, or RTC poultry. Whole, fresh poultry is usually less expensive than cut poultry and can be cut into pieces by foodservice professionals.

Light and Dark Different parts of poultry can be divided into light and dark meat. *Which parts pictured here are light meat, and which are dark meat?*

Judging Quality

As a foodservice professional, you need to be familiar with what makes a poultry product **acceptable**, or of good quality. There are two main ways to judge quality in poultry:

- **Color** Poultry color should vary from cream to yellow. It should not be purple or green from bruising or spoiling. Dark wing tips are also a sign of spoilage. Do not use poultry that is spoiled.
- **Odor** Poultry should not have a strong odor, or feel sticky under the wings or around the joints. A strong odor and sticky feel **indicate**, or show, that the poultry is spoiled. Discard any spoiled poultry immediately.

Inspection and Grading

All poultry must be federally inspected by the USDA to see that it is processed in sanitary conditions and is safe to eat. The poultry should also be free from visible signs of disease. Poultry that passes inspection earns the USDA Inspection Stamp of Approval. However, poultry must be properly handled and stored to stay fresh and safe.

⌒ Small Bites ⌒

Find the Label Grading and inspection stamps are attached to the wing of the bird by a tag. If the bird is processed and shipped in packaging, you will find the stamp on the product packaging.

✳ HOW TO ✳

Cut Up
Poultry

1 Place the bird on the cutting board, breast side down, and remove the wings at the joint.

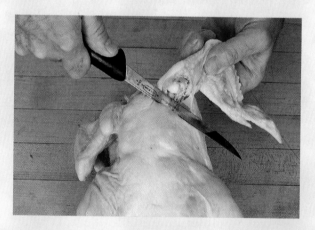

2 Turn the bird on its side, grasp the breast, and begin cutting between the breast and the leg. Turn the bird over and repeat.

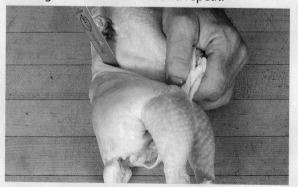

3 Pull the leg back and cut along the backbone to remove the leg. Turn the bird over and repeat. Set the legs aside.

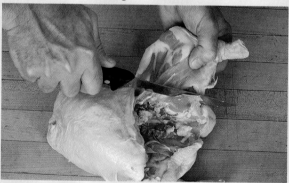

Most poultry should also be graded. USDA inspection is required for poultry, but grading is optional. The poultry grading system uses letters to show the level of quality. The highest grade poultry can receive is an A. Grade A poultry is higher quality and is a more consistent product. For a bird to earn Grade A, it must:

- Be plump and meaty.
- Have clean skin with no blemishes, tears, cuts, or bruises.
- Have no broken bones.
- Have all feathers plucked and removed, including pinfeathers.

Birds that do not meet these standards receive grades B or C. Lower-quality birds that receive these grades are used to make processed poultry products where the presentation is not as important, such as chicken fingers or turkey pot pies.

Reading Check Evaluate What are the differences between USDA inspection and USDA grading?

Safety Check

✓ Thawing Poultry

Never defrost any poultry product at room temperature. Always thaw poultry in the refrigerator. Allow 24 hours of defrosting time for every 5 pounds of poultry. Once raw poultry thaws, it should be used within two to three days.

CRITICAL THINKING *What could happen if you defrost poultry at room temperature?*

4 Cut along each side of the backbone toward the front of the breast. Then, remove the entire backbone.

5 Use the tip of the knife to expose the breastbones and ribs.

6 Grasp the back of the breast and remove the breast and keel bones.

7 Lay the boneless breast on the cutting board and split into two pieces.

8 To separate the drumstick from the thigh, cut between the joints.

READING CHECK ANSWER Inspection is mandatory, and indicates safety. Grading is optional, and indicates quality.

SAFETY CHECK ANSWER Bacteria may grow as the poultry defrosts, and could cause foodborne illness.

Truss
Whole Birds

1 Cut a piece of butcher's twine about three times the bird's length.

2 Tuck the wings behind the back.

3 Tie the twine loosely around the tail of the bird. Wrap the twine around the legs, and cross in front.

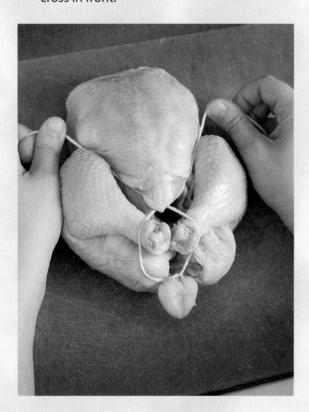

4 Flip the bird over, and tie a knot in the twine.

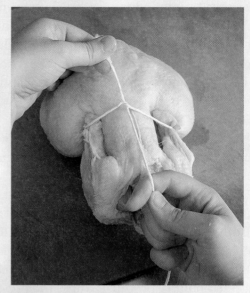

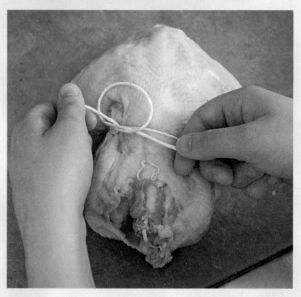

5 Tie a slip knot in the twine to secure.

Sanitation Check

✔ Giblets

Giblets are the edible internal organs of poultry. They include the liver, gizzard (stomach), and heart. Giblets are usually found in a package stuffed inside a whole, cleaned bird. The neck is usually packed with the giblets. Chicken livers and gizzards are also sold separately. Giblets are often used to flavor other dishes.

Giblets packaged separately from poultry should be kept cold to prevent bacteria from growing. Store giblets at 41°F (5°C) or below, and use within one to two days. You can also freeze them at 0°F (−18°C) or below. For the best quality, use giblets within three to four months of freezing.

CRITICAL THINKING *What dishes do you think might use giblets?*

SANITATION CHECK ANSWER Answers may include stuffings, broths, gravy, and casseroles.

Handling and Storage

Fresh and frozen poultry must be handled very carefully to avoid illness or spoilage. Fresh poultry is highly perishable, which means that it can quickly spoil if not handled properly. Once you receive fresh poultry, place it in cold storage or pack it in ice until you are ready to use it. If the poultry will not be used within two to three days, it should be frozen immediately.

You can store frozen poultry for up to six months at or below 0°F (−18°C). Make sure to keep frozen poultry in its original packaging. When you remove it from the freezer to thaw, keep it in its packaging until it is completely defrosted. Never refreeze poultry.

If you will be preparing and serving a whole bird, you will want to truss it. **Trussing** involves tying the legs and wings against the bird's body. It allows for even cooking and creates an attractive final product.

 Reading Check Explain What should you do once you receive fresh poultry?

SECTION 22.1  After You Read

Review Key Concepts

1. **Identify** the different market forms, classes, and styles of poultry.
2. **List** the characteristics of Grade A poultry.
3. **Explain** how fresh and frozen poultry should be safely stored and used.

Practice Culinary Academics

 Science

4. **Procedure** Imagine that your restaurant receives a shipment of whole chickens a week early.

   Analysis Describe the procedures you would follow to check the chickens for quality. Explain how you would store them to keep them fresh.

   NSES F Develop an understanding of community health, and natural and human-induced hazards.

 Mathematics

5. Supply prices can vary. You call three different wholesale poultry suppliers and are quoted the following prices for chicken breasts in bulk: $72, $85, and $93. What is the average price?

   Math Concept The mean, median, and mode are all measures of central tendency because they provide a summary of numerical data in one number. The mean is the same as the average.

   Starting Hint To find the mean, first add all of the values ($72, $85, and $93) together. Divide the total of the values by the number of values in the set of data (3).

   NCTM Data Analysis and Probability Select and use appropriate statistical methods to analyze data.

 Check your answers at this book's Online Learning Center at **glencoe.com**.

Cooking Poultry

Reading Guide

 Before You Read

Preview Scan the section and choose a Key Concept that is new to you. Write it on a piece of paper. When you find it in the text, write one or two sentences explaining the concept.

Read To Learn

Key Concepts
- **List** various dry and moist poultry cooking techniques.
- **Explain** the problems that can occur when stuffing poultry.
- **List** side dishes commonly served with poultry.

Main Idea

You can use a variety of dry and moist techniques to cook tender, well-done poultry.

Graphic Organizer

As you read, check off whether each cooking technique is a dry or moist method. Use a chart like the one shown to help organize your information.

Technique	Dry	Moist
Roasting/Baking		
Broiling/Grilling		
Frying		
Sautéing		
Simmering		
Poaching		
Braising		

Content Vocabulary
- render
- baste
- dredging
- crosshatch
- smoking point
- pressure-frying
- stuffing
- cavity

Academic Vocabulary
- process
- principle

ACADEMIC STANDARDS

 English Language Arts
NCTE 8 Use information resources to gather information and create and communicate knowledge.

 Mathematics
NCTM Algebra Represent and analyze mathematical situations and structures using algebraic symbols.

 Social Studies
NCSS V B Individuals, Groups, and Institutions Analyze group and institutional influences on people, events, and elements of culture.

NCTE National Council of Teachers of English

NCTM National Council of Teachers of Mathematics

NSES National Science Education Standards

NCSS National Council for the Social Studies

 Graphic Organizer
Go to this book's Online Learning Center at **glencoe.com** for a printable graphic organizer.

GRAPHIC ORGANIZER ANSWER Dry: Roasting/baking, broiling/grilling, frying, sautéing. Moist: Simmering, poaching. Dry and moist: Braising.

Poultry Cooking Principles

A variety of moist and dry methods can be used to prepare poultry. This makes poultry one of the most versatile food products served. Most poultry products are low in fat and can quickly become dry and overcooked. Learning how to best apply proper cooking methods will help you create a moist final product.

Using lower temperatures and longer cooking times can produce moist results. Cooking with low heat, however, has disadvantages. It does not brown the surface of poultry well. Cooking at high temperatures causes the fat in skin to **render**, or melt. This creates a well-browned and crispy skin that seals in juices.

The presence or absence of bones affects moisture and flavor during the cooking **process**, or series of actions. Bones actually help the bird retain some of its moisture.

Roasting and Baking

Roasting and baking poultry are essentially the same process. Many chefs use the term "roasting" when cooking whole birds and "baking" when cooking parts of a bird. Roasted or baked poultry should be golden brown on the outside and tender and juicy on the inside. Using the proper cooking temperature makes all the difference. (See **Figure 22.2**.) The goal is to make the skin crispy and brown without drying out the meat.

Cook Whole Birds Cooking whole birds using dry heat is called roasting. *How can you make sure a bird comes out juicy and flavorful?*

Often, a poultry recipe will direct you to start cooking using a high temperature. Then, you will be directed to lower the temperature to finish cooking. This technique promotes even cooking and seals in juices to prevent the meat from drying out.

To help whole poultry retain moisture during roasting, you should baste it during the last stage of the cooking process. To **baste**, spoon the fat drippings that have collected in the pan over the bird every 15 to 20 minutes. Baste only larger birds, like turkeys.

You do not have to baste a duck or a goose. Because these birds have a high fat content, basting will make them too juicy and may make them taste greasy. Roast them on a rack so the fat will drip into the pan, away from the bird. Some kinds of poultry, such as guineas and squabs, have very little fat. They can benefit from barding, or wrapping poultry in a layer of fat before cooking. This helps the bird retain moisture while it cooks.

Another way to keep poultry juicy during cooking is to oil the skin prior to the cooking process. This helps prevent the skin from drying out and locks in moisture.

FIGURE 22.2 **Variable Heat** Different kinds of poultry require different roasting temperatures. *Why do you think this is?*

Poultry	Roasting Temperature
Chicken	375°F–400°F (191°C–204°C)
Turkey	Start at 400°F–425°F (204°C–218°C) to brown skin; reduce to 325°F (163°C) to finish.
Duck/Goose	375°F–425°F (191°C–218°C)
Squab	400°F (204°C)
Game Hen	375°F–400°F (191°C–204°C)

FIGURE CAPTION ANSWER Answers may include the size of the bird and the amount of fat present.

PHOTO CAPTION ANSWER Begin cooking at a high temperature, then lower it, baste or bard as appropriate.

Carve
Roasted Turkey

1 Place the cooked turkey on a clean, sanitary cutting surface. Allow the turkey to stand for 20 minutes.

2 Remove the legs and thighs by pulling each leg away from the body with a fork. Use a boning knife to cut through the joint.

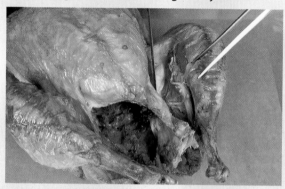

3 Separate the thigh from the leg and cut through the joint.

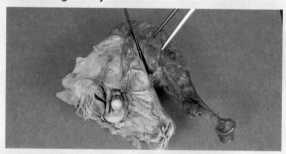

4 Slice the meat off the thigh parallel to the bone.

5 Carve the bird along one side of its breast-bone to remove a breast.

6 Cut the breast meat into slices at an angle across the grain, or direction of muscle fibers, of the flesh.

7 The breast can also be carved without removing it from the bird. Make a horizontal cut just above the wing toward the rib bones.

8 Slice the breast meat at an angle.

Searing

Your recipe may call for you to sear poultry before it is roasted or baked. Searing means to brown the poultry's surface quickly over high heat, usually in a hot pan. Searing is also done by **dredging**, or coating poultry parts in seasoned flour and then browning them in a skillet. Searing helps seal in juices. This is commonly done with chicken parts. For example, chicken is first cooked at 450°F (232°C) for 15 minutes. This allows the surface to brown. The heat is then reduced to 325°F (163°C). Then, the chicken finishes cooking in a 325°F to 350°F (163°C to 177°C) oven.

Broiling and Grilling

Broiled or grilled poultry can make a very attractive dinner plate. The food should have a well-browned surface and **crosshatch** grill marks, set at a 90-degree angle. Smaller birds or poultry pieces are ideal for broiling or grilling.

Frying Poultry

There are three ways to fry poultry: pan-frying, deep-frying, and pressure-frying. All three usually require that the food first be coated with a seasoned flour mixture or batter.

❊ HOW TO ❊

Broil or Grill
Poultry

1 Preheat the broiler or grill.

2 Prepare the poultry. It can be marinated, seasoned, or simply brushed lightly with oil.

3 Place the poultry with its presentation side down on a grid or rack in a broiler.

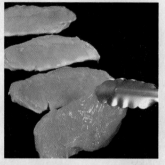

4 Turn the poultry 90 degrees midway through cooking to create crosshatch grill marks.

5 Periodically brush the poultry with oil or marinade to help keep it moist.

6 Carefully turn over the poultry using tongs so it can cook on the opposite side. If the poultry has skin, use a spatula and tongs to avoid breaking the skin while turning.

7 Poultry is done when it reaches an internal temperature of 165°F (74°C) or higher for 15 seconds.

Pan-Frying

In pan-frying, the poultry is dipped in a batter or seasoned flour mixture that will turn golden brown and crispy when the food is done. Poultry should be juicy and flavorful, not oily or greasy. When pan-frying, the temperature of the fat or oil should be below the 400°F (204°C) **smoking point**, when the oil is so hot that it smokes. Cooking at the proper temperature will help avoid an oily taste. Always brown the presentation side first.

Deep-Frying

Poultry, especially chicken, is often deep-fried in fat. The poultry pieces are coated prior to frying. Common coatings include batter, flour, egg, and cracker or cereal crumbs.

Deep-fried chicken should be cooked at 325°F to 350°F (163°C to 177°C). The cooking time will depend on the size of the chicken pieces and the meat color. Dark meat takes longer to fry than light meat, and should be cooked separately. There should never be more than one layer of chicken in a frying basket. Otherwise, the oil will cool and the product will be greasy.

Pressure-Frying

Pressure-frying uses the same frying **principle**, or rule, as other frying methods but uses a commercial pressure fryer. A pressure fryer cooks foods more quickly and at lower temperatures than other frying methods. Foods that are pressure-fried are extra crispy on the outside and juicy on the inside. This makes them less greasy than other fried foods. You can pressure-fry any food that you would deep-fry.

Sautéing

Sautéing is a method of cooking poultry in an open pan until it is brown and juicy. Sautéing requires little fat.

Simmering and Poaching

Poaching is commonly used to cook whole, young, tender birds. Simmering is used for older, tougher birds. For simmering, poultry is cut into pieces.

Because these two cooking methods do not create strong flavors, it is important that the poultry be seasoned when it is cooked. Use flavorful stock as the cooking liquid or add a mirepoix or bouquet garni.

In both simmering and poaching, the liquid should completely cover the poultry. The broth created during cooking can be especially flavorful. You can reserve some of the liquid for later use with other recipes such as gravies or sauces.

Braising

Braising is a cooking method that starts with dry-heat cooking and ends with moist-heat cooking. Braised poultry should always be accompanied by the liquid in which it was prepared.

Like poultry that is simmered or poached, braised poultry gets a boost of flavor during cooking from its cooking liquid. Seasonings can be added to the liquid during cooking. The liquid may be reserved for use in sauces.

A TASTE OF HISTORY

2000 — The human genome is deciphered

2006 — New York bans trans fats from restaurants

Cutting the Fat

Trans fats are a health concern for restaurant customers. Trans fats are created when oils are turned into solids, or hydrogenated.

This concern has not gone unnoticed. In December 2006, New York City banned the use of artificial trans fats at restaurants. Several fast-food restaurants also changed their recipes to remove trans fats from some fried foods, including fried chicken, French fries, and baked goods.

History Application

Research New York City's ban on trans fats at restaurants. Write a paragraph that describes how this ban will affect the health of New York City's residents.

> **NCSS V B Individuals, Groups, and Institutions** Analyze group and institutional influences on people, events, and elements of culture.

A TASTE OF HISTORY ANSWER Restaurant patrons may enjoy increased health benefits, as trans fats can increase the level of bad cholesterol in the blood.

Sauté
Poultry

1 Prepare the poultry by cutting it into thin slices. You may also flatten the poultry with a meat mallet prior to cooking.

2 Heat a small amount of fat in a pan. The fat must be hot before adding the poultry.

3 Dredge the poultry in seasoned flour if desired and lay it into the hot fat, presentation side down.

4 Cook until the presentation side is golden brown. Then, turn the poultry over and cook until the product is well done. Check the internal temperature.

5 You can finish some sautéed dishes by deglazing the pan with liquid to make a flavorful pan juice or sauce.

Braise
Poultry

1 Brown and sear the poultry in a small amount of fat in a rondeau, or braising pan.

2 Add liquid, and bring to a simmer. The liquid should cover two-thirds of the poultry.

3 Cover the pan and continue to simmer on the rangetop or in the oven until the poultry is done. To test for doneness, use a fork to see that the meat is tender and cuts easily without falling apart. The meat must hold an internal temperature of 165°F (74°C) for at least 15 seconds.

Determining Doneness

No matter how poultry is cooked, the meat must be well done to be safe. Any kind of poultry should be cooked to a minimum internal temperature of 165°F (74°C). The cooked poultry should hold this temperature for at least 15 seconds. To properly measure temperature, place a meat thermometer in the thigh of the bird at its thickest part, away from the bone.

Stuffings

A **stuffing**, or seasoned food mixture often made with bread, can be an excellent addition to a poultry dish. However, the FDA Model Food Code says that all parts of stuffed food must be cooked to 165°F (74°C), including the stuffing. Although the flesh of the bird may reach a safe temperature, the stuffing may not. Bacteria can quickly multiply in the stuffing inside the bird's **cavity**, or hollow interior. By the time the stuffing fully cooks, the poultry is often dry. To be safe, prepare the stuffing for whole poultry separately.

⌁ Small Bites ⌁

Storing Stuffing If you prepare wet and dry stuffing ingredients ahead of time, they should be kept refrigerated in a shallow baking pan. Never store stuffing in the same container as poultry because bacteria can grow.

Plating Poultry

How poultry is presented on the plate that you serve to a customer is important. Dishes can be garnished in the kitchen area, or poultry can be sliced and served at tableside.

Although many recipes suggest serving stuffing with poultry, there are other choices. Some side dishes include vegetables, casseroles, wild rice, potatoes, and pasta. Common garnishes for poultry include vegetables, fruits, and nuts.

Reading Check **Explain** Where can poultry be prepared for presentation?

SECTION 22.2 After You Read

Review Key Concepts

1. **Identify** the various methods that can be used to cook poultry.
2. **Explain** when you should use a dry or moist technique for cooking poultry.
3. **Describe** a typical stuffing.

Practice Culinary Academics
English Language Arts

4. You have been asked to select side dishes for the poultry dishes on a new menu. Use the Internet, library, and other resources to research appropriate side dishes for the following: roasted turkey, fried chicken, grilled chicken breast. Create a one-paragraph summary about the side dishes you chose, and why you chose them.

> **NCTE 8** Use information resources to gather information and create and communicate knowledge.

Mathematics

5. A poultry dinner at your restaurant sells for $8. The food cost to prepare the dinner is 30% of the selling price. If you prepare 245 poultry dinners for a banquet, what is the total cost of food for the poultry dinners?

Math Concept **Variables and Expressions** Translate verbal phrases into algebraic expressions by first defining a variable. In this way, algebraic expressions can be used to represent real-world situations.

Starting Hint Calculate how much money each dish will cost to make by solving for x: $8 \times 30\% = x$. Change 30% into a decimal (0.30), and multiply x by the total number of poultry dishes.

> **NCTM Algebra** Represent and analyze mathematical situations and structures using algebraic symbols.

 Check your answers at this book's Online Learning Center at **glencoe.com**.

READING CHECK ANSWER Either in the kitchen or carved at the tableside.

Review and Applications

Chapter Summary

All poultry must be inspected for safety by the USDA. The USDA first sorts poultry by species. Then, the birds are divided into classes by age and gender. Poultry flesh is made of three main components: water, protein, and fat. Fresh and frozen poultry are highly perishable and must be handled carefully. Fresh poultry should be used or frozen within 72 hours. Truss whole birds before cooking.

Follow cooking instructions for each type of bird so that well done poultry is tender and juicy. Roasting, baking, broiling, grilling, sautéing, pan-frying, deep-frying, and pressure-frying are all ways to cook poultry using dry heat. Simmering, poaching, and braising are moist-heat cooking methods that use liquids. Stuffing must be prepared properly and stored separately from the bird.

Content and Academic Vocabulary Review

1. Use each of these key terms and academic vocabulary words in a sentence.

Content Vocabulary

- poultry (p. 570)
- kind (p. 570)
- maturity (p. 571)
- connective tissue (p. 571)
- light meat (p. 571)
- dark meat (p. 571)
- giblets (p. 571)
- market form (p. 571)
- ready-to-cook (RTC) (p. 571)

- trussing (p. 575)
- render (p. 577)
- baste (p. 577)
- dredging (p. 579)
- crosshatch (p. 579)
- smoking point (p. 580)
- pressure-frying (p. 580)
- stuffing (p. 582)
- cavity (p. 582)

Academic Vocabulary

- acceptable (p. 572)
- indicate (p. 572)
- process (p. 577)
- principle (p. 580)

Review Key Concepts

2. Identify different kinds, classes, and market forms of poultry.

3. Explain how poultry is inspected and graded.

4. Describe how to handle, store, and prepare poultry for cooking.

5. List various dry and moist poultry cooking techniques.

6. Explain the problems that can occur when stuffing poultry.

7. List side dishes commonly served with poultry.

Critical Thinking

8. Contrast the differences between light meat and dark meat. What are some of the reasons you might choose one over the other?

9. Explain whether you agree that turkey and chicken are two of the most popular poultry choices in American culture. Why do you think this is or is not true?

10. Analyze why you think chefs might choose older, tougher birds for recipes if most customers prefer tender poultry meat.

Review and Applications

Academic Skills

Social Studies

11. Research International Cuisine You will be opening a new restaurant. Use the Internet, the library, or other sources to research the use of poultry in dishes from another culture. What cooking methods are used? What spices and seasonings are used? What side dishes are served? Use presentation software or other visual aids to create a five-minute oral report on your research.

> **NCSS I A Culture** Analyze and explain the way cultures address human needs.

English Language Arts

12. Design a Flyer Not long ago, you bought a neighborhood restaurant. The restaurant had been open for a long time but had been losing customers for a few years. The restaurant has been closed for two months while you remodeled it and designed a new menu. Design a flyer to let the neighborhood know the restaurant will reopen soon and that poultry will be a featured item on the new menu.

> **NCTE 5** Use different writing process elements to communicate effectively.

Mathematics

13. Calculate a Percentage You are planning the menu for a large, formal catering event for a local school. The menu will have a number of different choices from which to choose. The school has asked that 30% of the meals have poultry as the main entrée. You and your catering staff will be serving 500 meals. To meet the school's request, how many of the meals will include poultry?

Math Concept **Multiply Decimals by Whole Numbers** A percent is a ratio that compares a number to 100. To write a percent as a fraction, drop the percent sign and use the number as the numerator, with a denominator of 100. Convert it to a decimal by dividing the denominator by the numerator.

Starting Hint To calculate this percentage, rewrite the percent (30%) as a fraction with a denominator of 100 ($^{30}/_{100}$); convert the fraction to a decimal (.30). Then, multiply this decimal by the number of meals (500). Remember to put the decimal point in the correct place in your answer.

> **NCTM Number and Operations** Understand meanings of operations and how they relate to one another.

Certification Prep

Sharpen your test-taking skills to improve your kitchen certification program score.

Directions Read the questions. Then, read the answer choices and choose the best possible answer for each.

14. After using a cutting board to debone a chicken, the same cutting board is used to cut tomatoes. What is the proper procedure?

   a. wipe the cutting board and flip it to the clean side.

   b. use a section of the cutting board that was not previously used.

   c. clean and sanitize the cutting board

   d. spray the cutting board with sanitizer and wipe it off.

15. What is the most common ingredient in stuffing?

   a. breads   **c.** seafood

   b. meats   **d.** vegetables

Test-Taking Tip

In a multiple choice test, read the questions carefully. Look for negative words (not, never, except, unless) and positive words (always, sometimes), which can affect how you answer the problem.

Real-World Skills and Applications

Teamwork Skills

16. Create a Recipe Follow your teacher's instructions to form into teams. Create a turkey sandwich recipe for a health-focused restaurant. The recipe must be both healthy and flavorful. Once you have created your sandwich, work as a team to create a promotion to market your sandwich to customers.

Critical Thinking

17. Get Information You are being hired to cater poultry dishes for a dinner party for a large company. The company would like three different options. List five questions to ask the company about what kinds of poultry dishes would be appropriate. Then, list at least one possible answer to each question.

Technology Applications

18. Create a Spreadsheet You are in charge of teaching poultry cooking methods to new cooks at your restaurant. Use spreadsheet software to create a chart. List the different methods of cooking poultry, how to perform each method, and what class and style you might choose for each method.

Financial Literacy

19. Compare Ingredient Costs You need to order chicken for your busy chicken restaurant. Whole chicken costs less than chicken parts, but whole chicken must be cut up by a chef. Use the Internet or library resources to find the costs of each market form of chicken. Which form is the most cost-effective to order?

Culinary Lab

Use the culinary skills you have learned in this chapter.

Prepare Poultry

20. Cook a Poultry Dish Choose a cooking method and a recipe to prepare poultry in teams. Each team will judge the others' poultry dishes.

A. Choose from the following list:

- Roasted
- Baked
- Broiled
- Grilled
- Pan-fried
- Deep-fried
- Pressure-fried
- Poached
- Braised

B. Choose a recipe. Decide on a recipe that uses the cooking method your team chose.

C. List your materials. Make a list of the cooking items you will need to prepare your poultry dish. List oils, coatings, spices, and seasonings as well as equipment.

D. Prepare your dish. Prepare your poultry dish using the cooking method your team chose. Plate your poultry dish. The presentation of the dish is important.

E. Serve your dish. Serve your poultry dish to another team. Have that team evaluate it based on the following rating scale: 1 = Poor; 2 = Fair; 3 = Good; 4 = Great.

Create Your Evaluation

Write a one-page evaluation of another team's poultry dish. Use these categories for your evaluation:

- **Appearance** Is it cooked to the appropriate doneness? Does it appear burned or undercooked? Is it appropriately plated and garnished?

- **Flavor** Is the flavor consistent with the cooking method and food?

- **Texture** Is the poultry moist, tender, and juicy?

Meat Cookery

SECTIONS

23.1 Meat Basics

23.2 Meat Cuts

23.3 Principles of Cooking Meat

WRITING ACTIVITY

Letter to the Editor

Write a letter to the editor about your views on eating meat. Explain your choice. If you support eating meat, give tips for healthful meat eating. If you do not, give suggestions for a healthful diet without meat.

Writing Tips

❶ Write concise sentences that clearly state your thoughts.

❷ Link the sentences together clearly and logically.

❸ Support your position with facts, statistics, and citations.

EXPLORE THE PHOTO

Meat is the main component of many delicious entrees. *What are some commonly eaten types of meat?*

WRITING ACTIVITY ANSWER
Students should use a business letter format. Letters should have an introduction, supporting details, and a conclusion.

EXPLORE THE PHOTO ANSWER
The most common types of meat are beef, pork, veal, and lamb.

Meat Basics

Reading Guide

 Before You Read

How Can You Improve? Before starting this section, think about the last exam you took on material you had to read. What reading strategies helped you on the test? Make a list of ways to improve your strategies to succeed on your next exam.

Read to Learn
Key Concepts
- **Identify** the structure and cuts of meat.
- **Summarize** the details of meat inspection, grading, handling, and storage.

Main Idea
Meat is an essential part of most foodservice operations' menus. It is important to know how to purchase and safely store meat.

Content Vocabulary
- meat
- marbling
- fat cap
- barding
- larding
- muscle fibers
- collagen
- elastin
- primal cut
- fabricated cut
- carcass
- yield grade

Academic Vocabulary
- composed
- reveal

Graphic Organizer
Use a chart like the one below to list and describe the three components of meat found in this section.

Meat Component	Description

 Graphic Organizer Go to this book's Online Learning Center at **glencoe.com** for a printable graphic organizer.

GRAPHIC ORGANIZER ANSWER Muscle fibers: Fibers in lean meat that affect texture and flavor. Connective tissue: Connects muscle to bone, binds muscle fibers, breaks down into gelatin. Bones: Make up the skeleton.

You must know how to choose the right types of meat for a menu.

ACADEMIC STANDARDS

 English Language Arts
NCTE 12 Use language to accomplish individual purposes.

 Mathematics
NCTM Number and Operations Understand numbers, ways of representing numbers, relationships among numbers, and number systems.

 Social Studies
NCSS I B Culture Predict how experiences may be interpreted by people from diverse cultural perspectives and frames of reference.

NCSS V B Individuals, Groups, and Institutions Analyze group and institutional influences on people, events, and elements of culture in both historical and contemporary settings.

NCTE National Council of Teachers of English

NCTM National Council of Teachers of Mathematics

NSES National Science Education Standards

NCSS National Council for the Social Studies

Structure of Meat

Meat is an important part of many people's diets. It is also an essential part of most food-service establishment menu offerings. It is very important to learn about the different types of meats available. You will need to know how to purchase the best cuts of meat and how to safely store them.

Meat is the muscle of animals, such as found in cattle and hogs. In general, all meats contain the same three basic nutrients: water, protein, and fat.

Meat has the following amount of nutrients:
- About 75% of muscle is water
- About 20% of muscle is protein
- About 5% of muscle is fat

Water is a very important nutrient to keep in mind when preparing meat. Too much cooking will make meat dry. As meat cooks, it gets smaller due to shrinkage. Shrinkage happens when the meat loses water as it cooks. The longer you cook meat, the less it will weigh. Meats cooked at low temperatures do not lose as much water as meats cooked at high temperatures.

There are two types of fat in meat: marbling and fat cap. **Marbling** is fat within the muscle tissue. The amount of marbling affects the meat's tenderness, taste, and quality. In general, the more marbling there is in a piece of meat, the more tender and flavorful the meat will be.

The **fat cap** is the fat that surrounds muscle tissue. An animal uses this layer of fat as an energy source and to keep itself warm. This layer of fat is frequently left on the meat during cooking to keep meat moist and juicy. If there is not a fat cap, barding or larding is a proven alternative to keep meats from drying out during cooking.

With **barding**, you wrap a lean meat with fat, such as bacon, before roasting. A few minutes before doneness, you remove the meat from the oven, unwrap the fat, put the meat back in the oven, and allow the surface of the meat to brown.

With **larding**, long, thin strips of fat or vegetables are inserted into the center of the lean meat. This adds moisture and can make the final product visually appealing.

Components of Meat

Meat products have three components:
- **Muscle Fibers** You may have heard that leaner cuts of meat have fewer calories. That is because lean meat is almost completely **composed**, or made up, of muscle fibers with little fat. **Muscle fibers** determine meat's texture and contribute to its flavor. Coarsely textured meat such as ham has tough, large fibers. Smooth-textured meat such as beef tenderloin has tender, small fibers.
- **Connective Tissue** Connective tissue connects muscles to bones and binds muscle fibers together. Connective tissue is tough. To cook meats properly, you need to understand how connective tissue functions. Connective tissue is composed of either collagen or elastin. **Collagen** is soft, white tissue that breaks down into gelatin and water during slow, moist cooking processes. **Elastin** is a hard, yellow tissue that does not break down during cooking. Elastin is the tissue some people refer to as gristle. Older animals generally have a lot of elastin. To reduce the effects of elastin, cut it away from the meat.

- **Bones** Bones make up the skeleton of the animal. An older animal has whiter bones, while a younger one has redder bones. Learn the bone structure of an animal to help you identify the different cuts of meat and how they are carved.

Primal Cuts

A **primal cut**, sometimes called a wholesale cut, is a large, primary piece of meat separated from the animal. Primal cuts are the most popular forms of meat purchased by foodservice operations. Although primal cuts are large cuts of meat, they are easily handled and stored.

Fabricated Cuts

A **fabricated cut** is a smaller portion taken from primal cuts. It is a smaller, menu-sized portion of meat. You would likely purchase fabricated cuts if you were planning to serve roasts, stews, or steaks. Purchasing fabricated cuts as exact portions can limit waste. It is good to know how fabricated cuts are made to understand how these cuts should be cooked.

Whole Carcass

The **carcass** is what is left of the whole animal after it has been slaughtered. (See **Figure 23.1** on page 590.) The carcass does not usually include the head, feet, or hide. However, pork can be purchased with the feet and head still attached. Most foodservice establishments do not purchase meat in this form.

☞ Small Bites ☜

Tenderize Meat To tenderize meat that has a lot of connective tissue, try the following techniques:

- Sear and then braise the meat
- Slice it thinly against the grain
- Grind it
- Break down the collagen by adding a chemical tenderizer.

A TASTE OF HISTORY

1906	1909
The Federal Meat Inspection Act is put into effect	William Howard Taft is inaugurated President of the United States

The History of the Butcher

The history of the butcher and meat seller goes back to ancient Rome, where Roman butchers slaughtered and sold meat according to regulations that governed the type of meat each butcher sold. During the Middle Ages, butchers occupied open stalls from which they butchered and sold their wares. This is in sharp contrast to today's meat production, in which animals are slaughtered for meat at large-scale meat-packing operations. Today's butcher operates under a strict set of guidelines for training and operations. On-the-job training is common because simple meat-cutting techniques require only a few days to learn. Complicated tasks, such as eviscerating slaughtered animals, require several months of training.

History Application

The U.S. Department of Agriculture voluntarily grades meat. Write a listing the various grades, the characteristics that determine each grading, and why you feel grading is necessary.

> **NCSS V B Individuals, Groups, and Institutions** Analyze group and institutional influences on people, events, and elements of culture in both historical and contemporary settings.

The labor, equipment, and facilities needed to process a whole carcass are expensive. In addition, many foodservice establishments may not be able to use all parts of a carcass. This results in a waste of food and money.

Cutting the Carcass

Beef carcasses are split into two sides. Each side is divided into a hind and a quarter. In general, veal and lamb carcasses are divided between their last two ribs to create the foresaddle and hindsaddle.

Reading Check Explain How is the size of the muscle fibers related to the texture of the meat?

READING CHECK ANSWER Large muscle fibers in meat yield a coarse texture, while smooth-textured meat has thin, small fibers.

FIGURE 23.1 **Meat Carcasses**

Purchase Meat Beef, veal, and lamb carcasses are generally split into two main sections. *Why do most restaurants avoid purchasing whole carcasses for use?*

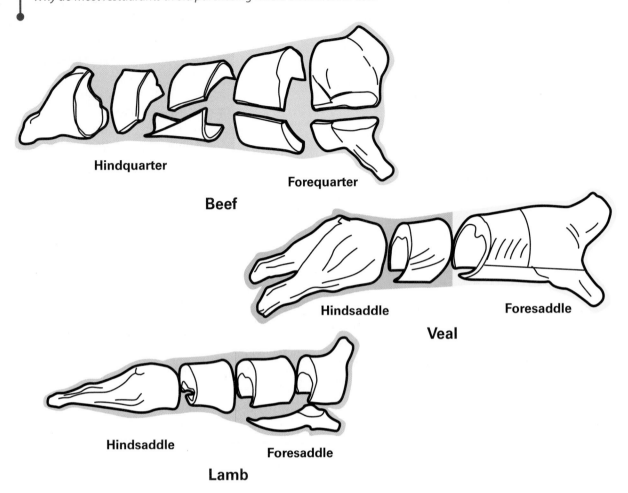

Hindquarter

Forequarter

Beef

Hindsaddle

Foresaddle

Veal

Hindsaddle

Foresaddle

Lamb

Purchasing Meats

Imagine that you have been given the job of buying meat for your foodservice operation. Where would you begin? What cuts would you ask for? How would you know the quality of the meats? There are several factors to consider when you purchase meat:

- The menu and the meats that will fit those recipes
- The cooking methods to be used
- The price (For example, how much can your customers afford, and how much is your foodservice operation willing to pay for top-quality meats?)
- Quality and value

To assist in making quality meat purchases, many foodservice operations use guides such as *The Meat Buyers Guide*, which is put out by the North American Meat Processors Association. This guide provides Institutional Meat Purchase Specifications (IMPS) for quality meats and photos of various meat cuts to help ensure that meats purchased are consistent in quality and cut. You must be sure to be specific when you place an order. All meats must be purchased from a USDA-approved processing plant.

The storage facilities, the cooking techniques that a facility uses, and the speed with which food must be prepared all affect the selection of types and sizes of meat.

FIGURE CAPTION ANSWER The facilities and equipment required to process a whole carcass are too expensive, and not all carcass parts may be used.

Meat Inspection and Grading

In 1906 under U.S. President Theodore Roosevelt, the U.S. federal government passed the Meat Inspection Act. This law requires the inspection of all meats that are transported across state lines. It also requires the federal government to inspect animals before slaughter and carcasses after slaughter, establishes sanitation standards for meat-processing plants, and allows the government to routinely monitor the activities of these plants. It guarantees that the meat is wholesome, and that the animal was not diseased.

The meat for foodservice operations must have a United States Department of Agriculture (USDA) Inspection Stamp. (See **Figure 23.2**.) The U.S. Food Safety and Inspection Service (FSIS), part of the USDA, is responsible for performing inspections. FSIS checks to make sure that meat is clean, safe to eat, and properly packaged. Meats that pass inspection are given a USDA stamp made from a harmless vegetable dye so it will not need to be cut off prior to cooking. The USDA stamp will not **reveal**, or make known, anything about the quality or tenderness of the meat. It reveals only that it is fit for human consumption. Since the inspection stamp appears in only a few places on the animal, it is generally only seen on retail cuts of meat.

As with poultry, meat is graded to indicate its quality. (See **Figure 23.3**.) The USDA's grading program is completely voluntary to the meat industry, which pays for the service. This grading is usually done within 24 hours of slaughtering and inspection. Some meat producers and processors use their own criteria to grade meats. This independent grading is often less consistent than the USDA's grading system.

The USDA grading shield stamp indicates how tender and flavorful the meat will be when it is prepared. Meat is graded for both quality and yield. Different types of meat have different criteria, however. A piece of beef is not evaluated for the same features as a piece of mutton. In general, however, USDA graders usually check for:

- Color
- Texture
- Firmness
- Marbling
- Age of the animal

FIGURE 23.2 Inspection Stamps

USDA Inspection All meats that are transported across state lines must be inspected by the USDA. *What do these inspection stamps say about the quality of the meat?*

FIGURE 23.3 Meat Grades

Quality Issues USDA grades indicate the quality of a piece of meat. *What are the differences between prime and choice meat?*

Meat	Quality Grades
Beef	USDA Prime, Choice, Select, Standard, Commercial, Utility, Cutter, Canner.
Pork	Pork is not quality graded because the quality is always uniform.
Veal	USDA Prime, Choice, Good, Standard, Utility.
Lamb	USDA Prime, Choice, Good, Utility.

FIGURE CAPTION ANSWER USDA stamps do not indicate anything about the quality of the meat. They indicate only that the meat is fit to be eaten, and that the animal was not diseased.

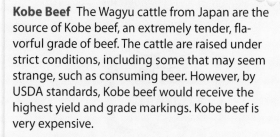

⤳ Small Bites ⤳

Kobe Beef The Wagyu cattle from Japan are the source of Kobe beef, an extremely tender, flavorful grade of beef. The cattle are raised under strict conditions, including some that may seem strange, such as consuming beer. However, by USDA standards, Kobe beef would receive the highest yield and grade markings. Kobe beef is very expensive.

FIGURE CAPTION ANSWER Prime grade meats have excellent marbling and a thick layer of fat cap. Choice meats have less marbling than prime meats, but still have a good flavor, tenderness, and juiciness.

✓ Prevent Cross-Contamination

When you prepare meats, practice these safety measures to help prevent cross-contamination:

- Store meats separately from other foods.
- Store raw meats below all other foods.
- Prepare meat products in areas separate from other foods.
- Sanitize knives and cutting boards after each use.
- Ground meats should be used more quickly because of possible bacterial contamination.

CRITICAL THINKING *Why are ground meats more susceptible to bacterial contamination?*

Quality Grades

Quality grading is a means to measure differences in the quality of the meat you purchase. This type of grading shows meat's tenderness, juiciness, and flavor. The quality grades are different for each type of meat.

USDA Prime meats are used in the very best foodservice establishments. These meats are also the most expensive. For a meat product to receive a USDA Prime grade, it must have excellent marbling and a thick layer of fat cap. (See **Figure 23.4**.)

The Choice grade is more widely accepted in the foodservice industry. It is the grade most preferred by consumers because of its flavor and tenderness. It is also a great value.

The Select grade has very little marbling. It is usually purchased by foodservice operations concerned about keeping costs down.

Below the Select grade are the Utility, Cutter, and Canner grades. These are used primarily for processed meat products, such as hamburger patties and luncheon meats.

Yield Grades

A **yield grade** measures the amount of usable meat on beef and lamb. (See **Figure 23.5**.) The best grade is Yield Grade 1, and the lowest is Yield Grade 5. This means that meat that has been marked Yield Grade 1 will contain a good amount of usable muscle. If you purchase a piece of beef that is marked Yield Grade 5, it probably has a large amount of fat and not much muscle.

Meat Handling and Storage

Meat storage requires careful attention. Meat can quickly spoil if it is not properly handled. This can cause food waste, or even possible foodborne illness if the spoiled meat is used.

- **Fresh Meat** Fresh meat should be stored in the refrigerator at 41°F (5°C) or below. Wet-aged meat should remain sealed until the meat is ready for use. Ground meat, such as hamburger, must be wrapped air-tight so that it stays fresh. Place meat on trays so that juices from the meat will not contaminate other foods or the storage unit floors. Store uncooked meats on the lower shelves of the refrigerator, with ground meats shelved below other meats. Raw meats should always be placed on the lowest shelf so that they will not drip.

▼ **FIGURE 23.4** **Meat Grading System**
Prime Cuts USDA Prime meats are the highest quality grade sold in the United States. *What grade of meat is the most commonly sold grade in the United States?*

▼ **FIGURE 23.5** **Yield Grades**
A Good Yield USDA Yield Grades indicate the amount of usable meat on cuts of beef and lamb. *What does this stamp indicate about meat?*

SANITATION CHECK ANSWER Only the outside of a whole cut of meat is susceptible to contamination. Grinding meat distributes any contamination throughout the meat.

FIGURE CAPTION ANSWER USDA Choice meats are the most commonly sold grade in the United States.
FIGURE CAPTION ANSWER It indicates a moderate amount of usable muscle meat and unusable fat.

FIGURE 23.6 Meat Storage

Meat Safety Meats can spoil quickly if they are not stored and handled properly. *Why do you think raw meats should be stored on the lowest shelf of the refrigerator?*

Meat Products	Refrigerator	Freezer
Beef, roasts and steaks	2-5 days	6-9 months
Lamb, roasts and steaks	2-5 days	6-9 months
Pork, roasts and chops	2-5 days	4-8 months
Beef and lamb, ground	1-2 days	3-4 months
Pork, sausage	1-2 days	2 months

- **Frozen Meats** To freeze fresh meat, place it in a freezer at 0°F (18°C) or below. Never freeze meat in containers. Always wrap the meat in air-tight, moisture-proof packaging to prevent freezer burn. Freezer burn causes meat to spoil. Labeling and dating packages and following first-in, first-out procedures help avoid food waste caused by spoilage. Meats should always be thawed under refrigeration and never on the counter left at room temperature. (See **Figure 23.6** for how long meats can be kept in storage.)

 Reading Check **Determine** Why does meat develop more flavor as it ages?

SECTION 23.1 After You Read

Review Key Concepts

1. **Explain** the purpose of barding and larding.
2. **List** the factors for purchasing meat.

Practice Culinary Academics

 English Language Arts

3. Imagine that you are training new employees in a foodservice operation. Create a guide to purchasing meat for them. Include tips, examples of cuts, and information about the structure and qualities of meat.

> **NCTE 12** Use language to accomplish individual purposes.

Social Studies

4. Many in our society have the luxury of being able to eat only the best cuts of meat. Traditionally, however, people in most cultures would use as much of the animal as possible. Research meat dishes in different cultures that are made from parts of the animal we normally would not often use. Create a visual presentation to show the recipe, and the meat cut it uses.

> **NCSS I B Culture** Predict how experiences may be interpreted by people from diverse cultural perspectives and frames of reference.

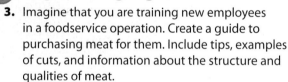 **Mathematics**

5. Shandra is preparing veal for the dinner service at the restaurant where she works. To tenderize veal cutlets that are ⅔-inch thick, Shandra pounds them to a thickness of ⅛ inch. What fraction is the new thickness of the original thickness? What percentage is the new thickness of the original thickness?

Math Concept **Convert Fractions to Percents**
To convert a fraction into a percent, divide the numerator by the denominator, multiply by 100, and add the percent symbol.

Starting Hint The pounded veal is (⅛) / (⅔) of the original thickness. Because it is improper to have fractions within a fraction, simplify the fraction by dividing ⅛ by ⅔ (which is the same as multiplying ⅛ by 3/2). Convert this fraction to a percent.

> **NCTM Number and Operations** Understand numbers, ways of representing numbers, relationships among numbers, and number systems.

 Check your answers at this book's Online Learning Center at **glencoe.com**.

FIGURE CAPTION ANSWER Raw meats should be stored on the lowest shelf of the refrigerator to avoid dripping onto other foods.

READING CHECK ANSWER As meat ages, connective tissue breaks down, tenderizing the meat and enhancing its flavor.

Meat Cuts

Reading Guide

 Before You Read

Take Guilt-Free Days of Rest The reason for resting is to refresh oneself. However, if you feel guilty about resting ("I really should be reading"), then your precious rest period will only create more stress. The brain has a hard time absorbing new data when it is stressed. Your reading skills will be much more effective if you are relaxed and ready to learn.

Read to Learn

Key Concepts

- **Identify** the quality characteristics and cuts of pork.
- **Describe** the quality characteristics and storage of lamb.
- **List** the quality characteristics of veal.
- **Explain** the quality characteristics of beef.

Main Idea

Before being shipped, meat is divided into primal cuts. Primal cuts are then further divided into fabricated cuts before they are prepared.

Content Vocabulary

- pork
- processing
- curing
- lamb
- mutton
- veal

Academic Vocabulary

- portion
- resist

ACADEMIC STANDARDS

 Mathematics
NCTM Problem Solving
Solve problems that arise in mathematics and in other contexts.

NCTE National Council of Teachers of English

NCTM National Council of Teachers of Mathematics

NSES National Science Education Standards

NCSS National Council for the Social Studies

Graphic Organizer

As you read, use a matrix like this one to list the primal cuts for each type of meat.

Primal Cuts

Pork	Lamb	Veal	Beef

 Graphic Organizer Go to this book's Online Learning Center at **glencoe.com** for a printable graphic organizer.

GRAPHIC ORGANIZER ANSWER Pork: Loin, picnic shoulder, Boston butt, belly, fresh ham. Lamb: Shoulder, shank/breast, rack or rib, loin, leg. Veal: Shoulder, shank/breast, rack, loin, leg. Beef: Chuck, brisket/plate/flank, rib, loin, round.

Cuts of Pork

Before being shipped to foodservice operations, a meat carcass is usually divided into primal cuts and portioned. (See **Figure 23.7** on page 596.) Primal cuts are easier for foodservice workers to handle. Standards have been established that specify how pork, lamb, veal, and beef should be divided into smaller fabricated cuts. These smaller pieces of meat can be prepared in many different ways. Learning the basic primal and fabricated cuts, the location and shape of the bones, and the characteristics and processes of each kind of meat will prepare you to handle and serve meat correctly.

Pork is the meat from hogs that are less than one year old. There are five different primal pork cuts: loin, picnic shoulder, Boston butt, belly, and fresh ham. The largest primal cut is the loin.

- **Loin** The loin can be divided into several fabricated cuts, such as pork tenderloin, pork chops, and pork back ribs. Pork tenderloin is the most tender cut of pork. The pork chop is a favorite of many customers. The best pork chops are those that are center cut. All loin cuts can be cooked using a variety of cooking methods.
- **Shoulder/Butt** The picnic shoulder is the lower part of the foreleg. It is sometimes called a picnic ham. This part of the shoulder has a higher fat content than other cuts, making it ideal for roasting. The picnic shoulder cut can be cooked using any method. It can be fabricated into fresh and smoked picnic hams. The picnic shoulder also may be boned and cut into smaller pieces, and then sautéed, braised, or stewed. Just above the picnic shoulder is the shoulder butt, or Boston butt. This cut has a high fat content but is very meaty. The Boston butt can be divided into steaks and chops. It can be boned and smoked like a ham.
- **Spareribs/Belly** The pork belly is a primal cut with a high percentage of fat and little

lean meat. The fabricated cut is spareribs. Any left over meat is cut for bacon.
- **Ham** The primal cut called the ham is actually a **portion**, or part, of the hind leg. This cut is very large and has lots of muscle and little connective tissue. Fresh ham can be cut with the bone in or boneless, or with the shank removed. The shank of the ham is sometimes called the ham hock.

Quality Characteristics of Pork

Today, pork is much leaner than it once was. Pork can be nearly as lean as skinless chicken. Three ounces of pork tenderloin, the leanest cut, has about 1.4 grams of fat, while a 3-ounce skinless chicken breast has about 0.9 grams of fat.

Uncooked pork should be light pink to red in color, and the fat should be white. There should be no odor. Discard pork that appears brown, green, or purple, or that has black, green, or white spots. This indicates that the pork is spoiled. A slimy feel or a bad odor also indicate spoilage.

Hogs are butchered before they are one year old. This means that they are more tender than older animals. There are many rules and regulations about how hogs are raised and slaughtered that protect both the animals and the public from disease, infection, and contamination.

Purchase Pork This poster shows the primal and fabricated cuts of pork available to restaurants. *What percentage of these pork cuts will most likely be processed before arriving at a foodservice establishment?*

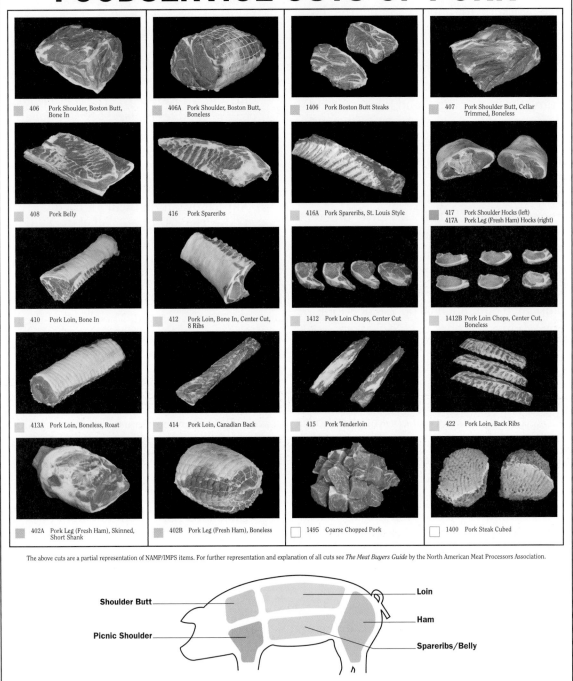

FOODSERVICE CUTS OF PORK

406   Pork Shoulder, Boston Butt, Bone In

406A   Pork Shoulder, Boston Butt, Boneless

1406   Pork Boston Butt Steaks

407   Pork Shoulder Butt, Cellar Trimmed, Boneless

408   Pork Belly

416   Pork Spareribs

416A   Pork Spareribs, St. Louis Style

417   Pork Shoulder Hocks (left)
417A   Pork Leg (Fresh Ham) Hocks (right)

410   Pork Loin, Bone In

412   Pork Loin, Bone In, Center Cut, 8 Ribs

1412   Pork Loin Chops, Center Cut

1412B   Pork Loin Chops, Center Cut, Boneless

413A   Pork Loin, Boneless, Roast

414   Pork Loin, Canadian Back

415   Pork Tenderloin

422   Pork Loin, Back Ribs

402A   Pork Leg (Fresh Ham), Skinned, Short Shank

402B   Pork Leg (Fresh Ham), Boneless

1495   Coarse Chopped Pork

1400   Pork Steak Cubed

The above cuts are a partial representation of NAMP/IMPS items. For further representation and explanation of all cuts see *The Meat Buyers Guide* by the North American Meat Processors Association.

Shoulder Butt —   Loin

Picnic Shoulder —   Ham

Spareribs/Belly

NAMP/IMPS Number (North American Meat Processors Association/Institutional Meat Purchase Specifications)

©2002 North American Meat Processors Association

American Meat Science Association

NAMP
North American
Meat Processors Association

National Pork Producers Council

FIGURE CAPTION ANSWER About 70% of pork cuts are processed in some way before arriving at foodservice establishments.

Processing Pork

While some pork is purchased fresh, such as pork chops, most pork is processed. **Processing** is the act of changing pork by artificial means. When pork is processed and cut to make ham and bacon, it usually is cured, aged, or smoked. Processing may also involve a combination of these three processes. About 70% of the carcass is processed before it ever arrives at a foodservice operation.

Curing and smoking are types of processing. Processing not only changes the flavor of the food, but it also greatly improves its preservation.

Curing Pork

Preserving pork with salt, sugar, spices, flavoring, and nitrites is called **curing**. Ham that has been cured, for example, has a pink color that makes it visually appealing. Cured pork will **resist**, or avoid, spoilage better than fresh pork. It also retains a fresher flavor for a longer period of time.

Curing changes the color and flavor of the pork. The oldest form of curing is dry curing. Seasonings, such as salt, are rubbed on the surface of the pork. Usually the entire surface of the pork is covered and then stored until the seasoning is absorbed into the meat. There are other common forms of curing:

Pickle Curing Pork is submerged in brine, or pickling liquid, until the mix completely penetrates the meat.

Injection Curing Brine is injected directly into the meat.

Sugar Curing Pork is covered with a seasoned, sweet brine that contains brown sugar or molasses.

Smoking

Aged hams are a popular variety of pork. These hams are cured and then smoked. Smoking means exposing the pork to the smoke of fragrant hardwoods, such as hickory.

Irradiation

Outbreaks of foodborne illnesses have made customers more aware about environmental issues and potential health risks. This has led to a change in how meat, particularly pork, is processed.

When pork is irradiated, it is exposed to medium doses of radiation. This process does not cook the meat, but it delays spoilage by destroying cells that cause it. It also greatly enhances food safety. However, irradiation should never replace proper food handling and sanitation techniques.

Reading Check Explain Why is irradiation used to process meat?

Cuts of Lamb

Lamb meat comes from sheep that are less than one year old. Meat from older sheep is called **mutton**, and it is usually tough. The carcass of a lamb is normally divided into the shoulder, shank/breast, rack or rib, loin, and leg. (See **Figure 23.8** on page 598.)

- **Shoulder** The shoulder is a large piece of primal-cut meat that contains rib bones, the arm, blade, neck bones, and muscles. It is difficult to divide the shoulder into fabricated cuts because of the large number of bones and muscles it contains. Either the shoulder is cut into pieces and used for stew, or the meat is ground.

- **Shank/Breast** This primal cut includes the breast and foreshank of the carcass. It is not used often in foodservice. If the breast is used, it is braised either as boneless or bone-in. The foreshank is meatier and can be served as an entrée.

READING CHECK ANSWER Irradiation eliminates potentially harmful microorganisms and enhances food safety.

Purchase Lamb This poster shows the most common cuts of lamb. *Which of the cuts pictured here are primal cuts?*

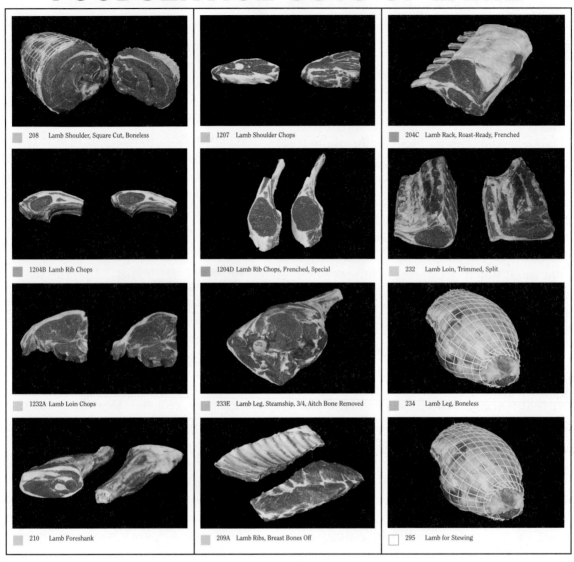

FOODSERVICE CUTS OF LAMB

208 Lamb Shoulder, Square Cut, Boneless	1207 Lamb Shoulder Chops
204C Lamb Rack, Roast-Ready, Frenched	
1204B Lamb Rib Chops	1204D Lamb Rib Chops, Frenched, Special
232 Lamb Loin, Trimmed, Split	
1232A Lamb Loin Chops	233E Lamb Leg, Steamship, 3/4, Aitch Bone Removed
234 Lamb Leg, Boneless	
210 Lamb Foreshank	209A Lamb Ribs, Breast Bones Off
295 Lamb for Stewing	

The above cuts are a partial representation of NAMP/IMPS items. For further representation and explanation of all cuts see *The Meat Buyers Guide* by the North American Meat Processors Association.

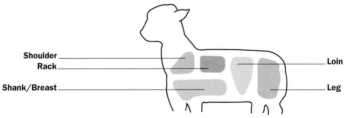

Shoulder — Loin
Rack —
Shank/Breast — Leg

NAMP/IMPS Number (North American Meat Processors Association/Institutional Meat Purchase Specifications)

©2000 North American Meat Processors Association

FIGURE CAPTION ANSWER The primal cuts pictured here are the shoulder, the foreshank, the loin, and the leg.

- **Rack** The rack is what results from cutting the rib tips in the breast. It is located between the shoulder and the loin and includes eight ribs and some of the backbone. The tender rib-eye muscle is a part of the rack. Fabricated cuts include the lamb rack and rib chops.
- **Loin** The primal cut that comes from the area between the rib and leg is called the loin. It includes a rib and some of the backbone, tenderloin, loin-eye muscle, and flank. Loin meat is generally very tender. Fabricated cuts include boneless roasts and bone-in or boneless chops.
- **Leg** The hind leg of the lamb contains some of the backbone, tail, hip, round, and shank bones. Usually the leg is split and boned before cooking. Sometimes a bone-in leg is roasted or braised. The fabricated cuts are steaks. The leg also can be diced and stewed or ground into patties.

Quality Characteristics of Lamb

The lamb meat purchased by a foodservice operation should have these characteristics:
- Pinkish to deep red color
- Firm and finely textured
- Some marbling in its lean areas

Spoiled lamb may look brown instead of pink, and may have a slimy feel or strange odor. Discard spoiled lamb.

Storing Lamb

Fresh lamb can spoil quickly even when kept in a cooler. Do not exceed these maximum refrigeration storage times:
- Two to five days in the refrigerator at 41°F (5°C) or below
- Six to nine months in the freezer at 0°F (−18°C) or below

 **Reading Check** Identify What are the quality characteristics of lamb?

Cuts of Veal

Veal is the meat from calves that are less than nine months old. Some veal is from calves that are only eight to sixteen weeks old. Veal primal cuts include the shoulder, foreshank/breast, rack, loin, and leg. (See **Figure 23.9** on page 600.)
- **Shoulder** The primal shoulder cut includes four rib bones and some of the backbone, blade, and arm bones. Fabricated cuts include steaks and chops, but they are not as tender as those from the loin. Meat from the shoulder is usually braised or stewed.
- **Foreshank/Breast** The shank and breast are one primal cut. It includes rib bones, cartilage, breastbones, and shank bones.
- **Rack** The double rib primal cut is very small, tender, and expensive. The rib cut consists of a double rack of ribs and part of the backbone. Fabricated cuts include whole or halved racks, rib-eye, and chops.
- **Loin** The primal loin cut is located behind the ribs. It consists of the loin eye, the top of the rib bones, and the tenderloin. Fabricated cuts include tenderloin, medallions, and chops.
- **Leg** The primal leg cut includes the leg and the sirloin. The leg is fabricated into scallops and cutlets. The leg also can be cooked whole.

Quality Characteristics of Veal

Veal is delicately flavored and tender. In general, veal should have the following characteristics:
- Firm texture
- Light pink color
- Little fat

Spoiled veal may be sticky or smell odd.

Reading Check Define What is veal?

Purchase Veal Primal cuts of veal include the shoulder, shank/breast, rack, loin, and leg.

Why do you think customers might choose veal over beef?

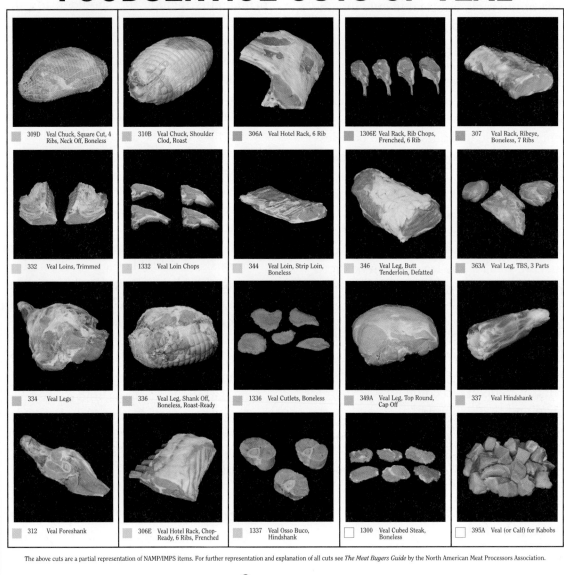

FOODSERVICE CUTS OF VEAL

309D Veal Chuck, Square Cut, 4 Ribs, Neck Off, Boneless	310B Veal Chuck, Shoulder Clod, Roast	306A Veal Hotel Rack, 6 Rib	1306E Veal Rack, Rib Chops, Frenched, 6 Rib	307 Veal Rack, Ribeye, Boneless, 7 Ribs
332 Veal Loins, Trimmed	1332 Veal Loin Chops	344 Veal Loin, Strip Loin, Boneless	346 Veal Leg, Butt Tenderloin, Defatted	363A Veal Leg, TBS, 3 Parts
334 Veal Legs	336 Veal Leg, Shank Off, Boneless, Roast-Ready	1336 Veal Cutlets, Boneless	349A Veal Leg, Top Round, Cap Off	337 Veal Hindshank
312 Veal Foreshank	306E Veal Hotel Rack, Chop-Ready, 6 Ribs, Frenched	1337 Veal Osso Buco, Hindshank	1300 Veal Cubed Steak, Boneless	395A Veal (or Calf) for Kabobs

The above cuts are a partial representation of NAMP/IMPS items. For further representation and explanation of all cuts see *The Meat Buyers Guide* by the North American Meat Processors Association.

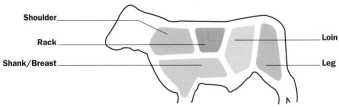

Shoulder
Rack
Shank/Breast
Loin
Leg

NAMP/IMPS Number (North American Meat Processors Association/Institutional Meat Purchase Specifications)

©2000 North American Meat Processors Association

American Meat Science Association

NAMP
North American
Meat Processors Association

BEEF
USA
National Cattlemen's
Beef Association

FIGURE CAPTION ANSWER Customers might choose veal over beef because of veal's tenderness and lower fat content.

Tender Cuts Some cuts of beef are tender and juicy. *Why might you serve a tender cut of meat with a sauce?*

Cuts of Beef

Americans eat more beef than any other kind of meat. The carcass is divided into five primal cuts. (See **Figure 23.10** on page 602.)

- **Chuck** The chuck comes from the shoulder. The chuck contains part of the backbone, rib bones, blade bones, and arm bones. It has quite a bit of flavor, but is tough. Fabricated cuts include ground chuck, stew meat, cube steak, short ribs, and rib pot roast. Chuck is best cooked using a moist heat or combination cooking method.

- **Brisket/Plate/Flank** Brisket is made up of the breast, breastbone, ribs, and arm. The brisket can be salt-cured to make corned beef. The brisket may also be cured to make pastrami. The shank is used in stocks, consommés, and other soups. The plate is located on the side of the beef. It contains rib bones and cartilage. Fabricated cuts include short ribs and skirt steak. Located along the edge of the rib and loin, the flank is a tough, but flavorful, cut of beef.

Fabricated cuts include London broil and flank steak. The flank can also be ground.

- **Rib** Rib is the primal cut of beef that consists of ribs and some of the backbone. Fabricated cuts include rib-eye roast, rib-eye steaks, rib roast, beef ribs, and beef short ribs.

- **Loin** The loin is the front portion of the beef loin that has a rib and some of the backbone. Short loin includes some of the most tender and expensive parts of the carcass. Fabricated cuts include club steaks, porterhouse steaks, T-bone steaks, filet mignon, and boneless strip loin. The sirloin contains the backbone and some of the hipbone. Fabricated cuts are sirloin roast and sirloin steaks.

- **Round** The round is the large, hind leg. Fabricated cuts include eye of round, outside round, top round, bottom round, knuckle, and shank. The bottom round includes the outside round and the eye of round. These tougher cuts are used for stew beef or braising. The top round is more tender than the bottom, and is usually prepared as a roast.

PHOTO CAPTION ANSWER Sauces can help enhance the flavor of tender meats.

FIGURE 23.10 Foodservice Beef Cuts

Purchase Beef Cuts of beef can be processed in different ways before it arrives at a restaurant. *How does aging beef under refrigeration change the texture of the meat?*

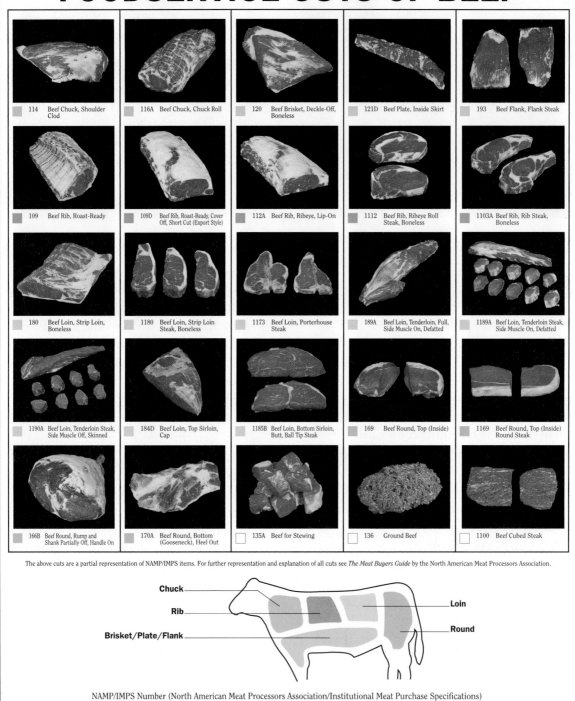

FOODSERVICE CUTS OF BEEF

114	Beef Chuck, Shoulder Clod
116A	Beef Chuck, Chuck Roll
120	Beef Brisket, Deckle-Off, Boneless
121D	Beef Plate, Inside Skirt
193	Beef Flank, Flank Steak

109	Beef Rib, Roast-Ready
109D	Beef Rib, Roast-Ready, Cover Off, Short Cut (Export Style)
112A	Beef Rib, Ribeye, Lip-On
1112	Beef Rib, Ribeye Roll Steak, Boneless
1103A	Beef Rib, Rib Steak, Boneless

180	Beef Loin, Strip Loin, Boneless
1180	Beef Loin, Strip Loin Steak, Boneless
1173	Beef Loin, Porterhouse Steak
189A	Beef Loin, Tenderloin, Full, Side Muscle On, Defatted
1189A	Beef Loin, Tenderloin Steak, Side Muscle On, Defatted

1190A	Beef Loin, Tenderloin Steak, Side Muscle Off, Skinned
184D	Beef Loin, Top Sirloin, Cap
1185B	Beef Loin, Bottom Sirloin, Butt, Ball Tip Steak
169	Beef Round, Top (Inside)
1169	Beef Round, Top (Inside) Round Steak

166B	Beef Round, Rump and Shank Partially Off, Handle On
170A	Beef Round, Bottom (Gooseneck), Heel Out
135A	Beef for Stewing
136	Ground Beef
1100	Beef Cubed Steak

The above cuts are a partial representation of NAMP/IMPS items. For further representation and explanation of all cuts see *The Meat Buyers Guide* by the North American Meat Processors Association.

Chuck
Rib
Brisket/Plate/Flank
Loin
Round

NAMP/IMPS Number (North American Meat Processors Association/Institutional Meat Purchase Specifications)

©2000 North American Meat Processors Association

American Meat Science Association

NAMP
North American
Meat Processors Association

BEEF
USA
National Cattlemen's
Beef Association

FIGURE CAPTION ANSWER Aging beef under refrigeration breaks down meat fibers, making the meat more tender and flavorful.

Quality Characteristics of Beef

When you purchase beef for a foodservice operation, always check for the grade and inspection stamps. The best quality beef will have a bright red color. The meat purchaser will also need to decide on the desired fat thickness for the meat. Fat marbling in beef ranges from slight to moderately abundant.

Processing Beef

Like pork, beef can be processed in several different ways before it arrives at a foodservice operation. The method of processing greatly affects how the beef will taste.

Curing

Beef, like pork, also can be cured and smoked. These processes help increase the shelf life of beef and greatly affect its flavor. Smoking meat will also decrease its surface moisture, helping to prevent bacterial growth.

Aging

Aging beef under refrigeration has long been known to increase its tenderness and enhance its flavor. Aging beef is hung in a controlled environment, such as a meat locker, with strict humidity and temperature conditions. Under these conditions, the meat fibers begin to break down, tenderizing and flavoring the meat.

Irradiation

Beef can also be irradiated to kill microorganisms. Although irradiated beef has far fewer microorganisms, such as *E. coli* bacteria, it still must be refrigerated and carefully stored to prevent cross-contamination. Irradiated beef also has a longer shelf life.

Reading Check Determine What is the purpose of aging beef?

SECTION 23.2 📖 After You Read

Review Key Concepts

1. **Describe** the different ways that pork can be processed.
2. **Identify** the primal cuts of lamb.
3. **List** the primal cuts of veal.
4. **Explain** what a chuck is and describe its characteristics.

Practice Culinary Academics
 Mathematics

5. The Big Steak Restaurant is offering a free steak to customers as a promotion, while supplies last. The restaurant has 72 ounces of steak to give away. If customers eat half the steak in the first 2 hours, ⅔ of what is remaining in the next 2 hours, and ⅓ of what is left in the next 2 hours, how much is left at the end of the night?

Math Concept **Multiplying Fractions** To multiply fractions, simply multiply all numerators to find the new numerator, then multiply all denominators to find the new denominator. Reduce the answer to lowest terms.

Starting Hint Subtract each fraction from 1 to find the fraction uneaten (rather than eaten) during each segment. Multiply the fractions together to find the total fraction uneaten, then multiply by 72 ounces to find the amount left.

NCTM Problem Solving Solve problems that arise in mathematics and in other contexts.

 Check your answers at this book's Online Learning Center at **glencoe.com**.

READING CHECK ANSWER Aging beef under refrigeration has long been known to increase its tenderness and enhance its flavor.

Principles of Cooking Meat

Reading Guide

 Before You Read

Two-Column Notes Two-column notes are a useful way to study and organize what you have read. Divide a piece of paper into two columns. In the left column, write down main ideas. In the right column, list supporting ideas.

There are a variety of different ways to cook meat.

Read to Learn

Key Concepts
- **Demonstrate** different cooking methods used for meats.

Main Idea

A foodservice employee must fully understand meat cooking techniques. Meat is expensive and the operation will lose money if it is improperly cooked.

Content Vocabulary
- high-heat cooking
- low-heat cooking
- rest
- grain
- spice rub
- trichinosis
- rare
- medium rare
- medium
- medium well
- well done

Academic Vocabulary
- satisfy
- content

Graphic Organizer

As you read, use a web diagram like this one to list the seven different methods used to cook meat.

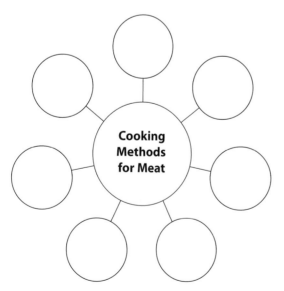

Cooking Methods for Meat

 Graphic Organizer Go to this book's Online Learning Center at **glencoe.com** for a printable graphic organizer.

GRAPHIC ORGANIZER ANSWER Roasting, broiling, grilling, sautéing, pan-frying, braising, and stewing.

 English Language Arts
NCTE 4 Use written language to communicate effectively.

 Mathematics
NCTM Measurement Understand measurable attributes of objects and the units, systems, and processes of measurement.

 Science
NSES B Develop an understanding of chemical reactions.

Social Studies
NCSS VIII B Science, Technology, and Society Make judgments about how science and technology have transformed the physical world and human society.

NCTE National Council of Teachers of English

NCTM National Council of Teachers of Mathematics

NSES National Science Education Standards

NCSS National Council for the Social Studies

Cooking for Tenderness

Meat is one of the highest expenses for foodservice operations. Selecting the right cuts of meat is just the first step. To get the most value for its money and to **satisfy**, or fill, customers' appetites, a foodservice operation must fully understand cooking techniques for meat. Tender cuts of meat become tough when they are cooked improperly. Likewise, tough cuts of meat can become tender when they are cooked correctly. Meat can be delicious and nutritious, but only when it is properly prepared.

If you have ever eaten a burned hamburger, you know what overcooking does to meat. Some dry cooking techniques will firm proteins without breaking down connective tissue. This makes meat tough. You would not want to use a dry cooking technique with a less-tender piece of meat that has a lot of connective tissue. A better choice would be a moist cooking technique. This exposes the meat to moisture and heat during cooking. Moist cooking helps to break down the connective tissue and tenderize the meat.

High-Heat and Low-Heat Cooking

The temperature of the heat source has an important effect on how meat is cooked and how the final product will taste. High-heat cooking can toughen proteins and dry out meat over extended periods of time. However, high heat, when used correctly, can result in an excellent final product. **High-heat cooking**, such as broiling and grilling, is used for tender cuts of meat like tenderloins and strip steaks.

Low-heat cooking is the best method for preparing large cuts of meat, such as top round. Low-heat cooking does not shrink the meat because moist heat, in the form of steam or liquid, penetrates the meat more quickly than dry heat. However, many restaurants use cuts of meat that do not require long cooking times.

Pay close attention to how much fat a cut of meat has prior to cooking. A meat's fat **content**, or amount, will affect the cooking technique. In general, if a meat is high in fat, do not add additional fat while you cook. Adding fat will make the final product oily or greasy.

Meat Cooking Methods Use the cooking technique that is right for the cut of meat you are preparing. *What would happen if you improperly cooked a tender piece of meat?*

PHOTO CAPTION ANSWER Improperly cooking tender meat would cause it to become dry and tasteless.

Barding Meat Barding involves wrapping meat with fat before cooking. *What cuts of meat would benefit most from barding?*

Fat can be added for meats that are low in fat, such as veal. Veal roasts could be barded or larded. Marinades can add fat to lower-fat meats. You can also add a small amount of fat to the cooking pan. This will help prevent the meat from drying out.

Roasting Meats

Remember that roasting is a dry technique that uses hot, dry air to cook the food. To roast meat, season it and then place it in a hot oven. Roasted meats do not use water or other liquids and are not generally covered during the cooking process. It is helpful to baste the meat with its natural juices or a flavorful seasoned stock. This keeps the meat from drying out.

Whether you use barding or the meat's own layer of fat, lay the meat fat side up for cooking. This way the fat will naturally baste the meat and keep it moist.

To help enhance the meat's flavor and retain moisture, chefs often bard the meat when they roast it. Barding involves wrapping meat with fat, such as bacon, prior to cooking. Tie the fat to the meat with butcher's twine. A few minutes before the meat is done, remove the fat and allow the surface of the meat to brown.

Seasoning meats that will be roasted can be tricky. Salt cannot simply be added to the meat before the meat is roasted because the salt will not penetrate the meat during cooking. To season meat that will be roasted, follow these tips:

- Trim any heavy fat covering, leaving a thin fat layer. This will help the seasoning penetrate the meat.
- Season the meat several hours prior to roasting. This may mean adding seasonings to the surface of the meat, larding the meat with strips of fat, or inserting seasonings, such as garlic or cloves.
- Season the meat again after it is done.
- Season the meat's juices and serve them with the meat.

Sauces and gravies add flavor and moisture to roasted meats. Sauces can be made from meat drippings. It is especially important to add sauce or gravy if the meat is well done. To make a rich gravy, deglaze the roasting pan and combine the drippings with a thickening agent and a demi-glace, or a concentrated brown stock that has been reduced. (For more on how to make and use stocks and sauces, see Chapter 20.)

PHOTO CAPTION ANSWER Cuts of meat that are low in fat, have no surrounding fat, or are tough can benefit from barding.

Carving Roasted Meats

Carving roasted meats correctly is an important final step to serving an appetizing roast meat dish. Incorrectly carving meat can cause well-roasted meat to taste dry and tough. Allow the meat to rest before carving. To **rest** means to allow meat to sit so that juices redistribute throughout the meat. This makes it easier to slice the meat, and keeps the meat moist.

Always carve against the grain. **Grain** is the direction of muscle fibers, or treads, in meat. This means to cut against the muscle fiber structure of the meat. If the meat is sliced along the muscle fiber structure, it will be tough and stringy. Cut across muscle fibers instead.

Science à la Carte

The Maillard Reactions

When meat is braised, it is often first grilled or pan fried in a skillet at a high temperature, above 285°F (141°C). Doing this allows the meat to undergo a series of reactions involving its sugars and proteins. These are called the Maillard reactions, named after Dr. L.C. Maillard, an early 20th-century chemist. The Maillard reactions help develop the flavor, outer texture, and color of meat.

There are three conditions necessary for a Maillard reaction:

● A nonacidic, or base, environment (pH higher than 7).

● Enough protein, and therefore enough amino acids, in the meat.

● Meat carbohydrates combined with the amino acid from a protein.

Procedure

Prepare two pork chops. Grill or pan-fry one pork chop to medium well, and braise the other to medium well. Compare the results.

Analysis

Which pork chop is crispier? Which pork chop has a darker color? Why did the cooking methods result in two different outcomes? Use your findings to write instructions for preparing a brown, crispy, and well-cooked pork chop.

NSES B Develop an understanding of chemical reactions.

Broiling and Grilling Meats

Two other dry cooking techniques, broiling and grilling, or barbequing, are popular ways to prepare meats. Broiling and grilling use high temperatures and relatively fast cooking times. Broiled and grilled meats are usually cooked to rare or medium with a browned, crusty surface and a tender, juicy interior. Barbequing uses low heat and slow cooking times. Restaurants that serve meat rare must have a warning on the menu about undercooked meat and the possibility of bacteria.

Remember these tips when you broil and grill:

● The shorter the cooking time, the higher the heat needed.

● The thicker the cut, the longer the cooking time needed.

● Set the grill controls for different temperatures across the surface of the commercial grill.

● Vary the cooking temperature by moving the meat to different areas of the grill, depending upon the heat needed.

● When you grill red meats, make sure the heat is high enough so that the surface becomes brown and crispy.

● To create cross-hatch grill marks, or grill lines, place the presentation side of the meat down on the grill. Cook long enough for the grill lines to show. Then, rotate the meat about 90 degrees to form the additional grill lines.

Seasoning

Seasoning meats that will be broiled or grilled rather than roasted is best done just prior to cooking them. Meats that tend to become dry when broiled or grilled, such as veal or pork, may be marinated or served with seasoned butter. Meats can be placed in marinades minutes or hours before cooking. Spice rubs can also be used to season meats. A **spice rub** is a mixture of ground spices that is rubbed on raw food before it is cooked.

Sauces and Accompaniments

Butter sauces, such as Béarnaise, and brown sauces, such as mushroom, are excellent additions to meat dishes. Sauces are usually served in a separate bowl, next to the meat, under the meat, or drizzled over the meat on a dinner plate. Most sauces are made before broiling or grilling and do not use juices from the meat itself.

Other accompaniments include vegetables, such as green beans and potatoes. These can be an excellent addition to the meal if they are grilled or broiled. However, you should remember that a meal could become less interesting when all the foods are cooked using the same technique.

Sautéing and Pan-Frying Meats

Tender cuts of meat and thin pieces of meat are usually sautéed. Meats that contain bones or breaded meats are pan-fried. Both cooking techniques require you to pay attention to the amount of heat and fat you use.

Follow these tips:
- Heat the pan before adding the fat.
- Use the correct amount of oil called for in the recipe. It should be enough to evenly cook all surfaces.
- Never overcrowd the pan.
- Turn or move the meat as little as possible.
- Avoid using unclarified butter because it burns easily.

Seasoning

The sauces that accompany sautéed or pan-fried meats will greatly enhance their flavor. A variety of sauces will bring out the flavors of meat cooked with these techniques.

You might also want to marinate the meat before cooking it. If so, make sure to thoroughly pat the meat dry before cooking it, or it will not brown correctly.

Use of Fat

The amount of fat used in sautéing and pan-frying differs. To sauté, use a small amount of fat and heat it until it is very hot before you add the meat. The amount of fat used depends on the amount of meat sautéed. The reason such a small amount is needed is that all surface areas of the meat will touch the pan.

◀ **Meat Accompaniments** Flavorful accompaniments are usually served with broiled or grilled meat, like this veal chop. *What accompaniments do you think could be served with broiled or grilled meats?*

PHOTO CAPTION ANSWER Answers will vary, but may include potatoes, fruit, vegetables, and grains.

To pan fry, use a moderate amount of fat in a pan, and heat it until it is hot before you add the meat. To evenly brown the meat, use enough fat to conduct heat to the meat's surfaces. Flat meats do not require as much fat as unevenly-shaped meats. You may have to lower the heat a bit to fully cook the product without burning the outside.

Braising and Stewing Meats

Braising and stewing are both combination techniques that begin by browning the food using dry heat. Braising involves partially covering the meat with liquid and cooking until tender. You may decide to cover the pan while the food cooks. During stewing, the liquid completely covers the meat. Both methods finish cooking by simmering in a liquid. The liquid used in both of these cooking methods is extremely important to the success of the final dish.

To begin the braising or stewing process, first season the meat. Avoid using large amounts of salt, because this will slow the browning process. Many chefs marinate meat for several hours or even a whole day before braising or stewing.

Use these tips to braise or stew meat:
- Pat the meat dry prior to browning, especially if it has been marinated.
- Dredge the meat in flour just before cooking to improve browning.
- Do not use more liquid than is necessary.
- When meat is done, it should be fork tender.

Determine Doneness

Most people are particular about how they like their meat cooked. The difference between meat that is well done and meat that is rare can be considerable.

A meat's doneness depends on:
- The cooking method
- The size and type of meat
- The internal temperature of the meat
- The color of the meat
- The amount of time the meat is cooked

Internal Temperature

The best way to test a meat's doneness is to test its internal temperature. Follow these rules:
- Insert the thermometer at an angle, into the thickest part of the meat.
- Avoid taking the temperature in fatty areas.
- Avoid touching or getting near bone with the thermometer.
- Meat is done when it reaches its proper internal temperature, and held at that temperature for at least 15 seconds.

Pork must be cooked to the correct internal temperature. To kill parasites, cook pork to an internal temperature of 145°F (63°C) for 15 seconds. If pork is not cooked correctly, your customers could contract trichinosis (ˌtri-kə-ˈnō-səs). **Trichinosis** is an infestation by a parasite that can cause muscular pain, stomach upset, fever, weakness, and swelling.

Although many people enjoy eating beef and lamb rare, there is a risk of foodborne illness when meat is cooked at low internal temperatures. Steaks/chops should be cooked to an internal temperature of 145°F (63°C) and held at this temperature for at least 15 seconds. Ground beef should be cooked to 155°F (68°C) and held at that temperature for 15 seconds.

Many states require restaurants to warn their customers of the danger of eating undercooked meats by including a disclaimer on the menu. Check with your local and state health departments for further guidelines.

Color

The color of meat changes when it is cooked. Learning what the colors indicate helps to determine when a particular type of meat product is done. Red meat starts red and changes to gray as the product cooks. Light meat turns pink and changes to white and then to tan as it cooks. Pork and veal become white to tan in color when cooked. It is important to remember that color is not the same as internal temperature.

- **Rare** meat is browned on the surface, with a red center. A thin outer layer of cooked meat appears gray.

- **Medium rare** meat is browned on the surface with a thicker outer layer of gray and a red to slightly pink center.
- **Medium** meat is browned on the surface with an even thicker outer layer of gray and a pink center.
- **Medium well** meat is browned on the surface with a thick outer layer of gray and a center that is barely pink.
- **Well done** meat is browned on the surface and gray on the inside.

 Reading Check Compare How do high-heat cooking and low-heat cooking affect meat?

SECTION 23.3 After You Read

Review Key Concepts

1. **Demonstrate** how to determine the doneness of meat.

Practice Culinary Academics

 English Language Arts

2. Create a cooking guide for meat. Include instructions and illustrations for cooking meat, including general tips and specific guidelines for different cooking methods.

> **NCTE 4** Use written language to communicate effectively.

 Social Studies

3. A method of cooking meat that is gaining popularity is sous vide. Sous vide involves placing meat in airtight bags and cooking for an extended period of time at relatively low temperatures. Research sous vide and explain its developments. Write a summary with the pros and cons of this method.

> **NCSS VIII B Science, Technology, and Society** Make judgments about how science and technology have transformed the physical world and human society.

 Science

4. **Procedure** Put a teaspoon of corn syrup in a nonstick skillet. Open an amino acid caplet from a health food store and smell the powder inside. Pour the amino acid in the skillet and turn the heat to high. Move the skillet back and forth to disperse the powder.

Analysis Notice the different odors and colors as the mixture heats. Write a paragraph describing them.

> **NSES B** Develop an understanding of chemical reactions.

 Mathematics

5. Marco finds an old recipe with temperatures given in degrees Celsius. To what internal temperature should he cook pork? If he cooks a hamburger to 70°C, is that a safe temperature?

Math Concept **Converting Temperatures**
Convert temperatures from Fahrenheit (F) to Celsius (C) using the formula $C = (F - 32) \times \frac{5}{9}$. To convert °C to °F, use the formula $F = (\frac{9}{5} \times C) + 32$.

Starting Hint Remember, pork should be cooked to an internal temperature of 145°F. Convert this temperature to °C using the correct formula. Convert 70°C to °F using the correct formula, and determine if it is the correct temperature for ground beef.

> **NCTM Measurement** Understand measurable attributes of objects and the units, systems, and processes of measurement.

Check your answers at this book's Online Learning Center at **glencoe.com**.

READING CHECK ANSWER High-heat cooking can dry out meat, but can be used with tender cuts. Low-heat cooking uses steam or liquid to penetrate large meat cuts.

Review and Applications

Chapter Summary

Meats can be purchased in the form of primal cuts or fabricated cuts. Primal cuts of pork, lamb, veal, and beef are then divided into fabricated cuts for ease of handling and preparation. To buy the highest quality of pork, lamb, veal, or beef, look for the quality characteristics for each type of meat.

Using the correct method to cook meat can enhance its flavor and tenderize it. The doneness of meat depends on the cooking method, the type and cut of meat, the internal color and temperature, and the customer's preferences. Meat may be rare, medium rare, medium, medium well, or well done.

Content and Academic Vocabulary Review

1. Create multiple-choice test questions for each content and academic vocabulary term.

Content Vocabulary

- meat (p. 588)
- marbling (p. 588)
- fat cap (p. 588)
- barding (p. 588)
- larding (p. 588)
- muscle fibers (p. 588)
- collagen (p. 588)
- elastin (p. 588)
- primal cut (p. 589)
- fabricated cut (p. 589)
- carcass (p. 589)
- yield grade (p. 592)
- pork (p. 595)

- processing (p. 597)
- curing (p. 597)
- lamb (p. 597)
- mutton (p. 597)
- veal (p. 599)
- high-heat cooking (p. 605)
- low-heat cooking (p. 605)
- rest (p. 607)
- grain (p. 607)
- spice rub (p. 607)
- trichinosis (p. 609)
- rare (p. 610)
- medium rare (p. 610)
- medium (p. 610)

- medium well (p. 610)
- well done (p. 610)

Academic Vocabulary

- composed (p. 588)
- reveal (p. 591)
- portion (p. 595)
- resist (p. 597)
- satisfy (p. 605)
- content (p. 605)

Review Key Concepts

2. Identify the structure and cuts of meat.

3. Summarize the details of meat inspection, grading, handling, and storage.

4. Identify the quality characteristics and cuts of pork.

5. Describe the quality characteristics and storage of lamb.

6. List the quality characteristics of veal.

7. Explain the quality characteristics of beef.

8. Demonstrate different cooking methods used for meats.

Critical Thinking

9. Imagine that you have purchased some fresh meat and are storing it in the refrigerator. You check on it and notice that it is discolored. What could be the cause of this?

10. Analyze meat cooking methods. A sirloin steak weighs 16 ounces before it is cooked, and 14 ounces after it is cooked. Which cooking method do you think was used and why?

Academic Skills

English Language Arts

11. Design a Menu Use the Internet to find creative menu items that feature meat, or create your own meat dishes using the cooking techniques described in this chapter. Then, design a menu that includes an appetizer, a soup, a salad, a sandwich, and an entrée. Choose a creative design for the menu that reflects the character of a restaurant that would serve the dishes you have chosen.

> **NCTE 12** Use language to accomplish individual purposes.

Social Studies

12. Humane Farming One of the dilemmas facing foodservice employees today is choosing meat that is humanely raised. Research national, regional, or local community organizations that deal with the issue of humane treatment of farm animals. Interview a person there about this issue. Take notes during your interview, and give a five-minute presentation on your notes. After the presentations have been given, discuss the issues as a class.

> **NCSS X J Civic Ideals and Practices** Participate in activities to strengthen the "common good," based upon careful evaluation of possible options for citizen action.

Mathematics

13. Source Beef Juan's restaurant sells ¼-pound hamburgers. He can buy pre-formed hamburger patties in a pack of 50 for $44.99. His supplier also offers a 10-pound package of ground beef for $32.99. As a third alternative, Juan can buy a 3-pound package of beef chuck for $8.99. Juan's employee makes $12 per hour. She can form 200 hamburger patties in an hour, and can grind 120 pounds of beef chuck in an hour. Which option is least expensive for Juan?

Math Concept **Comparing Costs** When comparing costs, all costs must represent the same unit of measurement. For example, it is not possible to make a direct comparison between $5 per pound and $3 per item. But if you know the weight of each item, it is possible to convert the prices to the same units, using ratios.

Starting Hint In each of the three cases, use the cost of producing one hamburger as your unit of comparison. Include labor costs if necessary. For the ground beef, since you know that $32.99 buys 10 pounds, set up a proportion to find the cost of ¼ pound: $32.99 / 10 = x / 0.25$. Add the cost of forming one hamburger patty (which you can find by setting up another proportion: $12 / 200 = x / 1$).

> **NCTM Number and Operations** Compute fluently and make reasonable estimates.

Certification Prep

Directions Read the questions. Then, read the answer choices and choose the best possible answer for each.

14. Which grade of beef is most commonly used in restaurants?

    a. prime   **c.** select

    b. choice   **d.** standard

15. What primal cut produces a filet mignon of beef?

    a. chuck   **c.** rib

    b. brisket   **d.** loin

Sharpen your test-taking skills to improve your kitchen certification program score.

Test-Taking Tip
Pay attention to the instructions given on the correct writing utensil to use. Some machine-graded tests can only be taken with a No. 2 pencil.

Review and Applications

Real-World Skills and Applications

Critical Thinking Skills

16. Work with Limited Resources Your normal dinner service includes an entrée that uses 5 pounds of beef loin on average per night. For tonight's service you have only 3 pounds of beef loin, and the new order will not arrive until tomorrow. What are your options? Write a paragraph to explain your choices, and why you made them.

Interpersonal and Collaborative Skills

17. Keep Meat Safe Divide into small groups at the instruction of your teacher. Imagine that you are caterers who are catering a dinner for 100 people. Your entrée will be a beef lasagna. Identify food safety issues for purchasing, storing, preparing, cooking, and serving the beef lasagna. Discuss each team's answers as a class.

Technology Applications

18. Make a Video Create a two- to five-minute video that shows viewers how to check the doneness of meat. In the audio, explain what you are doing and why, and the correct temperatures to check for. Remember to explain the tools you are using and show in detail how to use them.

Financial Literacy

19. Stretch the Food Dollar Pork loin is $7.99 per pound. You have 10 pounds of pork loin. Your pork loin entrée uses 8 ounces of pork. You have reservations for 80 people. You can either purchase 10 more pounds of pork, or reduce the serving size to 4 ounces and add extra rice and vegetables for $1.50 per plate. Compare the cost of each option.

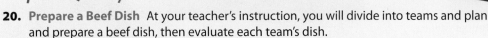

Culinary Lab

Use the culinary skills you have learned in this chapter.

Prepare Quality Meats

20. Prepare a Beef Dish At your teacher's instruction, you will divide into teams and plan and prepare a beef dish, then evaluate each team's dish.

A. Choose a recipe. Working with your team, choose a beef dish to prepare.

B. Choose a meat cut. Choose the best cut of meat by looking for marbling; small, tender fibers; and a red color.

C. Cook your dish. Choose a cooking method for your type of meat and prepare accordingly. Cook the beef and share your finished product with the class. Explain why you chose a particular cooking method.

D. Evaluate your dishes. Evaluate each team's meat dish according to the instructions below.

Create Your Evaluation

Use the following rating scale to judge the quality of each team's dish: 1=Poor; 2=Fair; 3=Good; 4=Great. Evaluate the meat on:

- **Appearance** (Is it cooked to appropriate doneness, and plated and garnished well?)
- **Flavor** (Is the flavor appropriate to the preparation method and food product?)
- **Texture** (Is the meat tender, moist, and juicy?)

Pasta and Grains

SECTIONS

24.1 Pasta

24.2 Rice and Other
Grains

WRITING ACTIVITY

Write Using Transitions

A transition is a word, phrase, or sentence that connects one part of a piece of writing to another. Write a description of the different types of pasta you know, focusing on the transitions.

Writing Tips

1 Think of how sentences fit into the whole.

2 Explain the relationship between different sentences and paragraphs.

3 Help the reader anticipate what is coming next.

EXPLORE THE PHOTO

Pasta allows you to combine different food groups into one hearty meal. *What types of ingredients do you like to add to pasta?*

WRITING ACTIVITY ANSWER
Transitional words should mostly be about sequence or time. Make sure transitions are used appropriately and that they improve the flow of the essay.

EXPLORE THE PHOTO ANSWER
Answers will vary. Tomato sauce, parmesan cheese, and various meats and vegetables are popular additions.

Pasta

Pasta is one of the most versatile food items available.

Reading Guide

 Before You Read

Study with a Buddy It can be difficult to review your own notes and quiz yourself on what you have just read. According to research, studying with a partner for just 12 minutes can help you study better.

Read to Learn

Key Concepts
- **Identify** the types, characteristics, and proper storage of pasta.
- **Outline** the best ways to cook pasta.
- **Explain** how to serve pasta.

Main Idea
Pasta is a staple in commercial kitchens and is a popular menu choice. To prepare it successfully, you must become familiar with the different varieties of pasta.

Content Vocabulary
- pasta
- semolina flour
- casserole
- al dente
- colander
- soup plate

Academic Vocabulary
- labor
- achieve

ACADEMIC STANDARDS

 English Language Arts
NCTE 6 Apply knowledge of language structure and conventions to discuss texts.

 Mathematics
NCTM Number and Operations Understand meanings of operations and how they relate to one another.

 Science
NSES B Develop an understanding of the structure and properties of matter.

 Social Studies
NCSS IV E Individual Development and Identity Examine the interaction of ethnic, national, or cultural influences in specific situations or events.

NCTE National Council of Teachers of English

NCTM National Council of Teachers of Mathematics

NSES National Science Education Standards

NCSS National Council for the Social Studies

Graphic Organizer
Use this sequence chart to list the seven steps of the general process for cooking pasta.

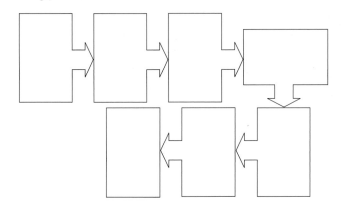

 Graphic Organizer Go to this book's Online Learning Center at **glencoe.com** for a printable graphic organizer.

GRAPHIC ORGANIZER ANSWER 1) Put 1 gallon of water for each pound of pasta in a pot; 2) Add 1 ounce of salt per gallon; 3) Bring the water to a boil and add pasta; 4) Stir pasta as it boils; 5) Test for doneness; 6) Drain pasta into a colander; 7) Serve.

Types of Pasta

Pasta is one of the easiest and most versatile food products used today. It is available in a variety of sizes, shapes, colors, and flavors. **Pasta** is a starchy food product that is made from grains. It is considered a staple in many commercial kitchens. Pasta increases in volume as it cooks and yields a high profit. Pasta is a very popular menu choice. To create successful pasta dishes, you need to become familiar with the varieties of pasta available and how to prepare them.

Pasta can be used in place of other starchy foods in a meal. One of the main ingredients of pasta is flour. Usually, wheat flour is used. The other main ingredient in pasta is a liquid, such as water or eggs. Oil is sometimes added to pasta dough to give it a richer texture.

Most commercial dried pastas are made from **semolina** (ˌse-mə-ˈlē-nə) **flour**, a hard-grain wheat flour that is high in the proteins that form gluten. Semolina flour produces a smooth dough and creamy yellow color.

There are more than 100 varieties of pasta available in a number of shapes, sizes, and flavors. A pasta's color reflects its flavor. You can buy pasta dried or fresh, but fresh pasta cooks faster.

The shape of some pastas makes them ideal for certain sauces. For example, a thinner, tomato-based sauce like marinara is ideal for angel hair pasta, while Alfredo sauce adheres well to fettuccini (ˌfe-tə-ˈchē-nē).

Quality Characteristics of Pasta

Imagine that a 20-pound case of pasta has been delivered to your establishment. Do you know if the pasta meets your restaurant's standards of quality? How can you tell? Here are two ways to determine the quality of the pasta used in foodservice operations:

- **Flour** Semolina, a high-protein flour, produces the best dry pasta. Dry pasta should contain 100% semolina flour.

- **Freshness** Dry pasta should be hard and brittle. It should snap cleanly instead of bending easily.

Purchasing and Storage

Both dried and fresh pasta usually are purchased by weight. Dried pasta is available in 1-, 5-, and 10-pound bags and boxes. Twenty-pound bulk cases are also common. Fresh pasta can be purchased in 1- to 2-pound boxes, or frozen in 10- to 20-pound cases. Fresh pasta is also available in bags or cartons.

Dried Pasta

Dried pastas, often purchased in bags or boxes, are available in tube, flat, and shaped forms. Tubes and shaped pastas are generally not available fresh. Dried pasta should be brittle and should break easily. The surface should look dull or be marked by small pits or scars. Sauces cannot soak into smooth, shiny, dried pasta.

Dried pasta comes in a variety of interesting and unusual flavors. Besides the typical spinach, tomato, and plain pastas, you can also get a variety of combination flavors, such as tomato-dill, spinach-herb, or carrot-ginger.

Dried pasta can be stored in a cool, dry place for several months. When storing dried pasta, temperatures in the storage area should be between 50°F to 70°F (10°C to 21°C).

❧ Nutrition Notes ❧

Nutrients in Pasta

All pasta products are high in carbohydrates and the B vitamins thiamin and riboflavin. The protein in pasta varies based on the amount of semolina it contains. Semolina is high in protein, so the more semolina that is used, the more protein the pasta provides. On average, one serving of pasta (2 ounces dry) contains 1 gram of fiber, 1 gram of fat, 3 grams of protein, and .65 milligrams of iron.

CRITICAL THINKING *Why might pasta that is higher in protein be more desirable to use than a pasta that is lower in protein?*

NUTRITION NOTES ANSWER Pasta that is higher in protein would be desirable to vegetarians who need alternative protein sources to meat in their diets.

Common Pasta Shapes

Elbow Macaroni Elbow macaroni are curved, narrow tubes that are short in length. They are used baked, for macaroni and cheese, macaroni salad, and casseroles.

Spaghetti This pasta consists of thin, round strands. Very thin spaghetti is called spaghettini. Spaghetti is boiled, and served with meat or tomato sauce, oil, butter, or thin sauces.

Egg noodles Egg noodles are long or short ribbons with spinach, tomato, or other flavorings that are added to the dough. Egg noodles are baked into casseroles, some sauces, and puddings.

Lasagne (lə-ˈzän-yə) These are wide, flat noodles that have rippled edges. They are used baked as a layered casserole with tomato sauce, cheese, and meat or seafood.

Capellini/Angel Hair (ˌka-pə-ˈlē-nē) Capellini is a fine, solid, strand-like pasta that is thinner than spaghetti. Capellini is boiled and used with thin sauces, seafood, tomatoes, garlic, or in soups.

Linguine (liŋ-ˈgwē-nē) Linguine is thin, flattened spaghetti that is about ⅛-inch wide. It is boiled, and often served with clam sauce, marinara sauce, and seafood.

Farfalle (fär-ˈfä-(ˌ)lā) Farfalle are flat, wide noodles that are squeezed in the center to resemble bow ties before they are dried. Farfalle are boiled, or baked with artichokes or seafood. With farfalle, you would use medium or rich sauces with meat or vegetables.

Common Pasta Shapes *continued*

Fettuccini (ˌfe-tə-ˈchē-nē) Fettuccini are flat, long, ¼-inch-wide noodles. They are best boiled and served with rich cream sauces, such as alfredo, or meat sauces that adhere well to these ribbon-like noodles.

Orzo (ˈȯrd-(ˌ)zō) Orzo are small, rice-shaped pasta. They are best in pilaf, salads, and soups.

Fusilli (fyü-ˈsi-lē) Fusilli are corkscrew-shaped twists. They are boiled, and baked in dishes with medium or thick, creamy sauces.

Manicotti (ˌma-nə-ˈkä-tē) Manicotti are medium-size hollow tubes, cut straight or angled. They are stuffed with cheese, meat, seafood, or vegetables, and baked.

Soba (ˈsō-bə) Soba are Japanese noodles that are similar in appearance to egg pasta. They are made from buckwheat flour. Soba are used in Asian foods, hot and cold dishes, and salads.

Penne (ˈpe(n)-(ˌ)nā) Penne are short- to medium-size hollow tubes that are cut diagonally. They are also called quills or pens. Penne are usually baked with hearty meat or tomato sauces and cheese.

Conchiglie (con-ˈkē-lyā) Conchiglie pasta are shaped like shells. They are usually stuffed, or used in salads. They are good with meat or seafood sauces, and are often filled with seafood, meat, or cheese, and baked.

Fresh Pasta

Fresh pasta can be made in the kitchen. However, it requires a great deal of **labor**, or hard work, to produce. It is also difficult to get a consistent product. Fresh pasta can be purchased fresh or frozen. Fresh pasta also comes in a variety of flavors, such as spinach, tomato-garlic, and whole-wheat.

Fresh pasta must be tightly wrapped and kept refrigerated to prevent its drying out. Even when refrigerated, fresh pasta should be used within a few days after it has been made. It can also be kept in the freezer to be used within a few weeks.

Reading Check **Determine** What standards of quality should you look for when evaluating pasta?

Cooking Pasta

Cooking pasta is a simple process. However, before you actually cook the pasta, you will need to complete the mise en place for everything you are going to use. You also will need to be familiar with the recipe. Some pasta dishes require the pasta to be fully cooked. Other recipes require pasta to be partially cooked and added to a casserole along with a variety of other ingredients. A **casserole** is a mixed food dish that is baked and served in a casserole dish.

Pasta can be boiled or baked. Boiling pasta is a simple process. Both fresh and dried pastas can be boiled. Baked pasta is usually one of the main ingredients of a casserole dish, such as stuffed manicotti or lasagne. When pasta is baked, the noodles are partly cooked first by boiling.

Boiling Pasta

When boiling pasta, you need to use enough water to cook it properly. Pasta can be cooked when a customer orders it. It also can be cooked in large amounts ahead of time. Dried pasta is sometimes cooked ahead

1793 ▼
Marie Antoinette, queen of France, is beheaded

1798 ▼
A Frenchman opens one of the first pasta factories, in Philadelphia

Pass the Pasta

Popular legend has it that Marco Polo introduced pasta to Italy following his exploration of the Far East. There, the Chinese were making a noodle-like food as early as 3000 BCE. However, Italians ate pasta dishes many years before Marco Polo's journey. Greek mythology suggests that the Greek god Hephaestus invented a device that made strings of dough, which may very well have been the first spaghetti! Regardless of its origins, today, pasta dishes can be found all over the world.

History Application

Pasta comes in many shapes and sizes, and every country has its own variety. Create a chart that describes at least five different types of pasta. Vary the countries from which these types originate.

NCSS IV E Individual Development and Identity Examine the interaction of ethnic, national, or cultural influences in specific situations or events.

of time. Fresh pasta is not because it cooks quickly and becomes too soft.

Baking Pasta

When pasta is baked with a filling and a sauce, or simply a sauce, the flavors blend during the baking process. You cannot **achieve**, or do, this simply by adding a sauce to the top of plain cooked pasta.

Some types of pasta, such as lasagne noodles, are cooked and then layered in a casserole with other ingredients such as cheese, meat, spinach, and tomato sauce for a hearty, baked dish. Manicotti and cannelloni are stuffed with a filling such as cheese and covered in sauce. Macaroni and cheese is also a baked pasta dish. It is a popular dish in the United States.

Boil
Pasta

1 Use at least 1 gallon of water for each pound of pasta in a large enough stockpot for the pasta to move around freely.

2 Add about 1 ounce of salt per gallon of water. The pasta will absorb the water and salt during the cooking process.

3 Bring the water to a full boil and add the pasta.

4 Stir the pasta with a large cooking spoon or braising fork occasionally as it continues to boil for the indicated time. The combination of rapid convection movement, the large amount of water, the small amount of pasta, and the stirring motion will keep the pasta from sticking together.

5 Test the pasta for doneness. The best way to tell if pasta is done is to taste it. Pasta that still has a white line through it is not done all the way.

6 Drain the cooked pasta into a colander.

7 If you will serve the pasta immediately, do not cool or rinse it. Just plate the pasta and serve it. If you will serve the pasta later, rinse it with cold, running tap water to halt the cooking process. Drain the pasta, add a small amount of oil, and toss it gently. This will help keep the pasta from sticking together. If you will serve pasta in a salad, let the pasta cool before you mix it in.

In most cases, the pasta is partially cooked before it is layered or stuffed. Then it is assembled with other ingredients and baked. In many foodservice operations, baked pasta dishes are served piping hot in individual baking dishes. They are usually accompanied by fresh bread and a cold, crispy salad on a separate plate.

Determine Doneness

When you cook Italian-style pasta, cook it **al dente** (äl-'den-(ˌ)tā), or "to the bite," meaning that the pasta is tender, but still firm. If pasta is cooked past the stage at which it is tender but still firm when bitten into, it quickly becomes soft and mushy. This can make pasta very unappetizing.

Each type of pasta has a different cooking time. If pasta is overcooked or undercooked, the dish being prepared could be ruined. The amount of water, the altitude, and various other factors can affect the cooking time, too. It is important to check pasta carefully to stop the cooking process at the al dente stage.

To check for doneness, you can bite into a piece of the pasta. If it is tender, but still firm, remove the pasta from the heat and drain it carefully over the sink in a colander.

A **colander** is a container with small holes in the bottom for rinsing and draining food. Another alternative is to cut through a piece of pasta with a fork. If it cuts easily, it is done.

Stuffing Pasta

Once cooked, some pasta can be stuffed with ingredients. Tubular pastas, such as manicotti or cannelloni, are usually stuffed. Ravioli are stuffed squares, rounds, or triangles. A variety of other pasta shapes can be stuffed, too. The filling ingredients may include cheese, meat, seafood, poultry, or vegetables.

The fillings, with the exception of meat, can be cooked or uncooked. Meat fillings, however, must be completely cooked before being stuffed into the pasta. This is because the time it takes the pasta to cook may not be sufficient to cook the meat safely.

Some large tubular pastas, such as cannelloni and manicotti, are often only partly cooked in boiling water. They are then stuffed with a filling and covered in a sauce. These dishes are baked as casseroles to finish the cooking process. When you partially cook pasta, make sure it does not become overcooked. It will continue to cook during baking. If it is too soft, it will not hold the stuffing well.

Reading Check Evaluate How do you determine the doneness of pasta?

⚜ **HOW TO** ⚜

Stuff
Pasta

1 Determine the pasta to be used.

2 Prepare the pasta by cooking it in boiling, salted water. You can use either dry or fresh pasta. The cooking time will depend on the form of pasta used. It will also depend on whether you will fully or partially cook the pasta.

3 Make the filling and chill in the refrigerator.

4 Drain the pasta. Shock it in cold water to stop the cooking process. Drain before continuing.

5 Remove the filling from the refrigerator.

6 Ladle a small amount of sauce into the bottom of the baking dish or hotel pan.

7 Use a pastry bag to pipe the filling into the cooked pasta. Roll pasta, if necessary.

8 Place the stuffed pasta into the baking dish and ladle a small amount of sauce over the filled pasta.

9 Bake as indicated on the standardized recipe.

READING CHECK ANSWER Taste the pasta. If it is tender but firm, it is done.

Chapter 24 Pasta and Grains **621**

Serving Pasta

The first important rule of serving pasta is to serve it at the correct level of doneness. If you have boiled the pasta for the proper amount of time, it will be firm to the bite, or al dente. Undercooked pasta will be too hard and pasta that is cooked for too long will end up mushy. When pasta is cooked to order, it is important to plate and serve it immediately. The sauce and other ingredients must be added, and any side vegetables and garnishes must be ready to plate and serve to the customer immediately.

Often, pasta with sauce is served alone on a plate. Some pasta dishes are served on soup plates. A **soup plate** is a shallow bowl-shaped plate. Others are served as side dishes in smaller portions. After serving, you can freeze leftover cooked pasta by itself, though it freezes best in a sauce. Freeze it in serving-size portions for later convenience.

 Reading Check Describe What are the different ways that pasta is served?

SECTION 24.1 After You Read

Review Key Concepts

1. **Name** the two types of pasta available to buy.
2. **Explain** how to stuff pasta.
3. **Describe** how to prepare a kitchen for serving pasta.

Practice Culinary Academics

English Language Arts

4. Create an advertisement about a new type of pasta. Identify the pasta product, the audience, and the advertising medium (print, television, radio, or Internet). Research the properties of pasta and then share the product's benefits.

> **NCTE 6** Apply knowledge of language structure and conventions to discuss texts.

Mathematics

5. Your restaurant serves spaghetti in 1¾-cup servings. If it takes 4 ounces of dry spaghetti to produce 2 cups of cooked spaghetti, how many full servings can you get from a 5-pound bag of dry spaghetti?

Math Concept **Dividing Fractions** To divide when a fraction is involved, convert any mixed or whole numbers to improper fractions. Multiply the first fraction by the reciprocal of the second fraction. Reduce to lowest terms.

Starting Hint If one pound is 16 ounces, then 5 pounds is 16×5 ounces. Set up a proportion to find the number of cups of cooked pasta produced by that many ounces of dry spaghetti. Then, divide by 1¾.

> **NCTM Number and Operations** Understand meanings of operations and how they relate to one another.

 Check your answers at this book's Online Learning Center at **glencoe.com**.

SCIENCE À LA CARTE ANSWER The ½ pound of pasta will have a better appearance, texture, and taste because it had more water proportionally in which to circulate.

READING CHECK ANSWER Pasta can be served alone on a plate, or in a soup plate.

Rice and Other Grains

Grains are a popular staple item in any foodservice business.

Reading Guide

 Before You Read

Prepare with a Partner Before you read, work with a partner. Read the titles of the heads and ask each other questions about the topics that will be discussed. Write down the questions you both have about each section. As you read, answer the questions you have identified.

Read to Learn

Key Concepts
- **Describe** different varieties of rice.
- **Identify** common grains.
- **Demonstrate** various cooking methods used for rice and other grains.

Main Idea

Grains have a high nutritional value and can be dried for storage for long periods of time. This makes them a popular diet staple.

Content Vocabulary
- grain
- rice
- risotto
- brown rice
- white rice
- enriched rice
- parboiled rice
- barley
- oat
- oat berry
- wheat
- couscous
- corn
- polenta
- hominy
- masa harina
- pilaf method
- risotto method

Academic Vocabulary
- option
- versatile

Graphic Organizer

As you read, use a herringbone organizer like this one to list the seven types and varieties of rice.

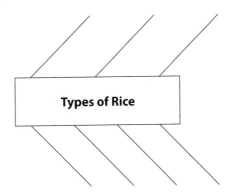

Types of Rice

 Graphic Organizer Go to this book's Online Learning Center at **glencoe.com** for a printable graphic organizer.

GRAPHIC ORGANIZER ANSWER Types of rice: Short-grain, medium-grain, and long-grain. Varieties: Brown rice, white rice, converted rice, and specialty rice.

ACADEMIC STANDARDS

 Mathematics
NCTM Number and Operations Understand numbers, ways of representing numbers, relationships among numbers, and number systems.

 Social Studies
NCSS IX C Global Connections Analyze and evaluate the effects of changing technologies on the global community.

NCTE National Council of Teachers of English

NCTM National Council of Teachers of Mathematics

NSES National Science Education Standards

NCSS National Council for the Social Studies

Types of Rice

Grains are a staple in the diets of people around the world. This is because of the variety of grains, and the fact that they store well and have high nutritional value. A **grain** is a single, small, hard seed. Grains are packed with nutrients. The main nutrients in grains are in the form of carbohydrates and fat. Grains are usually dried for storage. Cooking grains with liquid adds water back to the dried grains. This makes the grain tender and edible. There is a wide variety of grains to choose from. Rice, wheat, and corn are three of the most common grains. Others include barley, oats, cornmeal, and hominy. By learning how to prepare rice and other grains, you will be able to prepare a variety of dishes.

Rice, the starchy seeds of a cereal grass, is served around the world. Rice picks up the flavors of other foods so it is often served as part of a main dish. Rice increases in volume as it cooks and yields a high profit.

All varieties of rice come in different grain types: short-grain, long-grain, and medium-grain.

- **Short-Grain** Short-grain rice contains the most starch. It becomes sticky when cooked, but is the most tender type of rice. Short-grain rice is used in risotto, for example. **Risotto** is a rice dish in which the grain has been sautéed in butter, and then simmered in a flavored cooking liquid, which has been added gradually to the rice until it has finished cooking.

- **Medium-Grain** Medium-grain rice is firm when it is hot. It becomes sticky, like short-grain rice, when it cools.

- **Long-Grain** Like short-grain rice, long-grain rice remains slightly firm when cooked properly. However, it should not become sticky when cooked. The grains of rice separate easily after cooking. Long-grain rice can be used in just about any food dish.

Rice Grains Pictured here are different grain types of rice. *How do rice grain types differ?*

Processing Rice

All three types of rice can be processed. Processing rice removes the hull, or outer covering, from the grain. If the grain is left alone, the rice is brown. If the grain is polished, the rice is white. White rice can be processed even further, producing converted rice and instant rice. Rice varieties are helpful in selecting rice for different menus.

Brown Rice

Rice that has had the hull, or outer covering, removed but is unpolished, is called brown rice. **Brown rice** has a tan color, a chewy texture, and slightly nutty taste. Available in long-grain, short-grain, and medium-grain, brown rice takes longer to cook and needs more cooking liquid than white rice.

White Rice

White rice has had the outer layers of the grain removed. Without the outer layers, the rice grain is white and cooks more quickly with less water. White rice has a lighter texture, but is also lower in some vitamins and minerals. There are many varieties of white rice: long-grain rice, short-grain rice, hard rice, soft rice, and enriched rice. **Enriched rice** has a vitamin and mineral coating added to the grain. This makes up for nutrients lost when the outer coating is removed. All types of white rice can be enriched.

Converted Rice

Converted rice, sometimes referred to as **parboiled rice**, has been partially cooked with steam and then dried. This process removes some of the surface starch and increases the nutrient value by forcing nutrients from the outer layer into the grain. After it is steamed, the rice is polished and milled. This results in a light, white-grain rice that has more nutrients than regular white rice.

Converted rice can be used in the same way as regular white rice, except that converted rice takes longer to cook and requires slightly more liquid. It also becomes very fluffy. The grains do not clump together if they are served from a steam table.

Specialty Rice

Many interesting, flavorful types of rice have made their way into American menus from a variety of foreign foods. These rices, with their different textures and flavors, offer foodservice professionals an interesting **option**, or choice, for including rice in planning menus.

Rice Handling and Storage

Uncooked rice should be stored in airtight containers at room temperature in a dry, dark room. White rice has a long shelf life if properly stored because the sprouting portion of the grain, which contains oil, has been removed with the hull. Brown rice, even when properly stored, has a shorter shelf life because the grain contains oil, which causes the rice to spoil sooner.

After rice has been cooked, it should be used as soon as possible. Its high protein content and neutral pH mean it can spoil easily and be dangerous to eat if left too long at room temperature. Make sure to refrigerate any unused, cooked rice as soon as possible.

Reading Check Identify What are the three main types of rice grains?

Other Grains

Although rice is a very **versatile**, or adaptable, and popular grain, there are many other grains that can add variety and nutrition to the menu. The high carbohydrate and protein content of traditional grains, such as oats, wheat, and barley, can add nutritional value and flavor to any meal. In addition, specialty grains, such as kasha ('kä-shə), quinoa ('kēn-wä), and triticale ('tri-tə-'kā-lē), offer diverse flavors, textures, and colors.

Grains are also an important part of menu planning because they can be used from breakfast to dinner to prepare many different kinds of dishes. For example, kasha and oatmeal make excellent breakfast cereals. Cracked wheat can be used in cold salads.

READING CHECK ANSWER The three types of rice grains are short-grain, long-grain, and medium-grain.

Arborio (ˌär-bȯr-ē-ō) Arborio is a short-grain, white rice that becomes sticky when it is cooked. Use 3 cups of water for every cup of rice. It is the best rice to use for risotto-style preparation.

Basmati (ˌbäz-ˈmä-tē) Basmati has extra-long grains that are polished and cream-colored. It has a light, sweet flavor. Basmati is aged before it is used, so it should be well rinsed. Use 1½ cups of water for every cup of rice. Basmati has a delicate flavor that is best used in side dishes, including pilaf.

Jasmine (ˈjaz-mən) Jasmine is a long-grain white rice that is similar to basmati, but has a more delicate flavor. It is best as a side dish.

Wild Rice Wild rice is not a true rice, but a wild water grass. It is a brown and black grain that has a nutty flavor and chewy texture. There are three grades of wild rice, with the best having a very long grain. Cook wild rice in three times the amount of water as rice. Wild rice is served as a side dish and used in poultry stuffing. Lower grades are used in soups and baked goods.

Red Rice Red rice is also called Wehani (we-ˈhä-nē) rice. It has an aromatic, earthy flavor. It is served with meat and bean dishes.

Barley

Barley is a hardy, adaptable grain that can grow in both warm and cold climates. It is available unmilled, and in a form called pearled barley, which has been milled and polished.

Barley has a slightly sweet flavor and chewy texture. It is often added to soups and stews, giving them a hearty consistency and rich texture. Barley is also used as a poultry stuffing and as a pilaf side dish.

Because of its mild flavor, barley is a good candidate for cooking with onions, garlic, herbs, and other seasonings. Use a ratio of three parts liquid to one part barley to cook barley.

Oats

Oats are the berries of oat grass. They can be purchased as oatmeal and as a whole grain, called groats or oat berries. Oatmeal, a popular but plain hot cereal, can be dressed up with fruits, berries, cream, maple syrup, and other similar toppings to turn a simple breakfast into something special. Oatmeal also makes an excellent addition to bread and cookies. A ratio of two parts liquid to one part oats is used to cook oatmeal.

Oat berries, or groats, do not have the outer layer removed, so they are a whole grain, with all the texture and nutrients found in other whole grains. They can be cooked and served as a hot cereal, used to stuff poultry, and added to baked goods. A ratio of four parts liquid to one part oat groats is used.

Wheat Products

Wheat, in the form of flour, is a staple in bread-making and other kinds of baking. **Wheat** is actually a very versatile grain that is also milled into semolina and cracked wheat. These two wheat products can be served as side dishes, and used in stuffings and casseroles.

⚜ Nutrition Notes ⚜

Nutrients in Grains
Adding ingredients that have been removed during the milling process can increase the nutritional value of grains. For example, 4 ounces of toasted wheat germ adds 33 grams of protein, 56 grams of carbohydrates, 14 grams of fiber, 6 grams of niacin, and more than 1,000 milligrams each of potassium and phosphorus.

CRITICAL THINKING *How do you think the milling process removes ingredients?*

NUTRITION NOTES ANSWER Milling removes the outer part of the grain, which is nutrient-rich.

Couscous ('küs-ˌküs) is made from semolina that is milled from wheat.

Corn Products

Corn is different from the other grains discussed in this section because it can be eaten fresh. It also can be eaten as a dried grain. When eaten fresh, it is served as a vegetable. As a dried grain, it comes in two main forms: cornmeal, used to make breads and polenta; and hominy, a dried corn kernel.

Polenta

Polenta (pō-'len'tə) is made from cornmeal that is gradually sprinkled into simmering water or stock and cooked until it becomes a thick paste. It is the right consistency when it pulls away from the pot when stirred. Polenta can be served with butter, cheese, or various sauces. It also can be poured into shaped containers or spread on a baking sheet to cool. When cool, it can be sliced or cut into interesting shapes that can be baked, fried, grilled, or broiled. A very versatile food, polenta can be served as a breakfast food with maple syrup, as an appetizer, or as a side dish for dinner. Spices, dried tomatoes, cheese, herbs, and other ingredients can be added during the simmering process.

Hominy

Hominy is made by soaking dried corn in lye so that the kernels become swollen. As they swell, the outer layers loosen and are easily removed.

Hominy is often served as a side dish or added to soups. When cooking hominy, use 2 to 2½ times the amount of water as grain. Hominy also is made into other corn products, including grits, which are cracked hominy served as a side dish or as a cereal. Cook grits in four parts water to one part grits. **Masa harina** ('mä-sə ä-'rē-nä) is a finely ground hominy used in tortillas and breads.

Reading Check Name What are four different kinds of specialty grains?

READING CHECK ANSWER Answers include rice, barley, oats, wheat, and corn.

✳ MASTER RECIPE
Polenta

Ingredients

2 qts.	Water
1½ tsp.	Salt
1 lb.	Cornmeal, medium-ground

International Flavor

Cornmeal is used in many different recipes throughout the world. Research these recipes, and create a chart showing the differences in ingredients and cooking techniques used.

- Arepas (Mexico)
- Wasna (Midwestern United States)
- gali akpono (Africa)

Method of Preparation

1. In a medium saucepot, heat the water to a boil; add the salt, and gradually add the cornmeal, stirring continuously with a wooden spoon.

2. When mixture is blended without lumps, lower the heat, and simmer until thickened, approximately 30 minutes. When done, the polenta will pull away from the side of the pot.

3. Pour the polenta into an oiled pan, and spread to a ½-inch thickness.

4. Allow the polenta to rest a few minutes, then cut into portions. Hold at 135°F (57°C) or above.

Chef Notes

It is important to get all of the lumps out of the polenta before it simmers. Otherwise, the lumps will stay and make the polenta unappealing.

Substitutions

- Use herbs for flavor instead of salt to lower the sodium content.
- Add lemon for additional flavor and interest.

Cooking Technique

Simmer

1. Heat the cooking liquid to the proper temperature.
2. Submerge the food product completely.
3. Keep the cooked product moist and warm.

Glossary

Cornmeal ground corn used in cooking and baking
Rest off of heat, and unstirred

HACCP

- Hold at 135°F (57°C) or above

Hazardous Foods

None

Nutrition

Calories 170	Calories from Fat 5
Total Fat 1g	
Saturated Fat 0g	
Trans Fat 0g	
Cholesterol 0mg	
Sodium 300mg	
Total Carbohydrate 36g	
Fiber 2g	
Sugars 1g	
Protein 3g	

- Vitamin A 2%   • Vitamin C 0%
- Calcium 0%   • Iron 2%

Cracked Wheat The whole wheat berry is cracked into irregular pieces. These pieces cook more quickly than whole berries. Cracked wheat has a brown exterior and a white interior. This unmilled grain is high in nutrients. Cook it in twice as much water as wheat. It is best used in side dishes, and as a hot cereal.

Semolina Semolina is made when the bran and germ are removed from Durum wheat. It comes in cream-colored pellets that are partially cooked. To cook semolina, soak it briefly in water, drain, and steam until tender. It is best for side dishes, as a hot cereal, in dumplings, and for sweet pudding.

Couscous Couscous is a granular form of semolina. To cook it, soak it in water, drain, and then steam it. Packaged, precooked couscous is also available. Add precooked couscous to boiling water and let it stand about five minutes. Couscous is used for sweet and savory side dishes.

Kasha Kasha is hulled, roasted buckwheat groats that are sometimes ground or cracked. It has a strong nutty flavor. Cook kasha in 1 to 1½ times the water as groats. Kasha is used in side dishes and cold salads.

Quinoa Quinoa is a small, bead-shaped grain. It has an ivory color and a neutral flavor. Quinoa cooks quickly and is high in protein. Add it to side dishes and soups.

Triticale Triticale is a type of wheat and rye that has more protein, a nutty-sweet flavor, and a low gluten content. It comes as berries, flour, or flakes. Triticale is cooked similarly to cracked wheat and semolina. It is used in side dishes, casseroles, and as a cereal.

Kamut (kä-ˈmōōt) Kamut is brown and has a rice-like shape. It has an earthy, nutty flavor. Ground kamut is used in baked goods and pasta making.

Spelt (ˈspelt) Spelt is a wheat product that is available as a whole grain or ground. It can be boiled or simmered, and has a mild, nutty flavor. It is used in baked goods.

Amaranth Amaranth is a very small, round grain that is light brown in color. It is used in salads, baked goods, and in cooking.

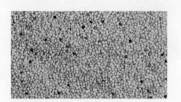

Cooking Rice and Other Grains

Cooking rice and grains involves adding enough water to make the grain moist and tender. Depending upon the length of the rice or grain, the proportion of water to rice or grain, and the cooking method, the product can be light and fluffy or sticky. The degree of tenderness may vary, depending on the grain and the way in which it will be served.

Boiling

To boil grains, the grain is added to slightly salted, boiling water and then simmered until tender. Boiling produces a good product that can be served as is or incorporated into other dishes such as salads or casseroles. The proportion of water to grain is about the same as for cooking pasta.

Steaming

Steaming grains is different from steaming vegetables. To steam grains, add the appropriate amount of boiling liquid to the grain.

Cover and cook the grain until the liquid is completely absorbed by the grain.

Grains can be steamed in a saucepan on the rangetop. They can also be steamed in the appropriate bakeware in the oven, or steamed in a convection steamer or rice cooker.

Braising

Braising, often called the **pilaf method**, involves sautéing the grain in oil or butter before adding the liquid. Often, onions, garlic, seasonings, and items such as red or green peppers may be added to the rice during the sautéing process. The coating of oil on each grain results in a fluffy product in which individual grains do not stick together.

Once the grain is sautéed, a seasoned liquid is added. The grain is then usually cooked on the range in a saucepan or baked in the oven in a hotel pan.

Generally, the grain is done when all the water has been absorbed and there are small, tube-like holes on the surface. Cooking can either be completed on the range, or the saucepan or stockpot can be removed from the heat for the last 5 or 10 minutes of cooking and left to stand tightly covered.

Cooking in the oven instead of on the range is the preferred method because the uniform heat results in a more flavorful product in which each grain remains separate from the others. Ethnic spices and a variety of chopped foods can be added after sautéing, before the liquid is added.

Risotto

The **risotto method** is a little like boiling and the pilaf method combined. First, the grain is sautéed, and then a small amount of hot liquid, often a soup stock, is added. The grain is stirred until most of the liquid is absorbed. This process of adding liquid and stirring the grain is continued until the grain is completely cooked. When the grain is done, it will still be firm. Seasonings and chopped mushrooms can be added to risotto after the sautéing stage.

Risotto Cooking Method

Grains cooked with the risotto method are creamy. Risotto should be served immediately after being cooked to maintain its texture and creamy consistency. Butter, olive oil, or cheese are often stirred in just before serving.

Serving Rice and Other Grains

All grains should be served as soon as possible after being cooked. They lose their texture quickly and can become either clumped or dried out if they are held for a long period of time. Any grains not used immediately after being cooked should be properly cooled, labeled, dated, and refrigerated in an air-tight container.

Reading Check Describe What are the four most common ways of cooking grains?

HOW TO

Make
Risotto

1. Simmer the seasoned liquid in a pot.

2. In a separate saucepan, heat the fat.

3. When the fat is melted, add onions, garlic, and seasonings. Sauté for two minutes.

4. Add the grains to the melted fat and other ingredients in the saucepan. Stir the grains into the fat so they are evenly coated. Do not scorch the grains.

5. Gradually add the simmering liquid to the grains in stages. Stir frequently to prevent scorching.

6. Test for doneness.

7. Remove saucepan from heat source.

8. Add butter, herbs, and cheese. Mix and serve.

READING CHECK ANSWER The four most common ways of cooking grains are boiling, steaming, braising, and the risotto method.

Steamed Rice Rice can be steamed in a rice cooker or in a pot with a lid. *How do you know that this rice is cooked?*

SECTION 24.2 After You Read

Review Key Concepts

1. **Explain** how to store rice properly.
2. **Describe** two corn products that can be made from hominy.
3. **Identify** the proper way to serve rice and other grains.

Practice Culinary Academics

 Social Studies

4. Rice and other grains are a diet staple in almost every country. Technology has been developed to genetically modify rice. Research genetically modified rice and write a report on what it is, how and why it is modified, and any pros and cons of using it. Cite your sources in your report and turn in your research notes with your paper to your teacher.

> **NCSS IX C Global Connections** Analyze and evaluate the effects of changing technologies on the global community.

Mathematics

5. Abigail can buy a 20-pound bag of rice from one supplier for $19.59. She can buy a 12-pound bag of rice from a second supplier for $12.99. She can also purchase 5-pound bags for $7.75 each. Which of the three options is the best buy?

Math Concept **Unit Price** To compare prices for differing amounts of an item, calculate a unit price for each item by dividing the price by the quantity. This tells you the price of one unit.

Starting Hint For each of the three products, divide the price for the entire package by the number of pounds in the package. This will tell you the price per pound for each item.

> **NCTM Number and Operations** Understand numbers, ways of representing numbers, relationships among numbers, and number systems.

 Check your answers at this book's Online Learning Center at **glencoe.com**.

PHOTO CAPTION ANSWER This rice is cooked because there are characteristic steam holes, or tunnels, on the surface of the rice.

Review and Applications

Chapter Summary

Pasta is a staple food in most commercial kitchens. Most pasta is made from semolina flour. It is available fresh or dried. Pasta can be boiled or baked. Pasta can also be stuffed.

Grains have a high nutritional value and can be dried for storage for long periods of time.

There are many different types of rice, wheat grains, and other grains. Grains can be steamed, braised, boiled, or cooked by the risotto method. Grains should be served as soon as possible after being cooked. They should be stored in an airtight container in the refrigerator.

Content and Academic Vocabulary Review

1. Write each of the terms below on an index card, with definitions on the back. Use them to review.

Content Vocabulary

- pasta (p. 616)
- semolina flour (p. 616)
- casserole (p. 619)
- al dente (p. 620)
- colander (p. 621)
- soup plate (p. 622)
- grain (p. 624)
- rice (p. 624)
- risotto (p. 624)
- brown rice (p. 625)

- white rice (p. 625)
- enriched rice (p. 625)
- parboiled rice (p. 625)
- barley (p. 626)
- oat (p. 627)
- oat berry (p. 627)
- wheat (p. 627)
- couscous (p. 627)
- corn (p. 627)
- polenta (p. 627)
- hominy (p. 627)

- masa harina (p. 627)
- pilaf method (p. 630)
- risotto method (p. 631)

Academic Vocabulary

- labor (p. 619)
- achieve (p. 619)
- option (p. 625)
- versatile (p. 625)

Review Key Concepts

2. Identify the types, quality characteristics, and proper storage of pasta.

3. Outline the best ways of cooking pasta.

4. Explain how to serve pasta.

5. Describe different varieties of rice.

6. Identify common grains.

7. Demonstrate various cooking methods used for rice and other grains.

Critical Thinking

8. Evaluate a cooking problem. Your cannelloni dish did not hold together during cooking. You partially cooked the pasta before stuffing. Why might the dish have fallen apart?

9. Analyze the different types of rice steamers. Compare the features and price and draw conclusions about their effectiveness and efficiency.

10. Imagine that you have been asked to prepare rice for 150 people at a banquet. What equipment would you use and how would you keep the rice hot?

Academic Skills

 ### English Language Arts

11. Create a Grain Chart Create a chart that shows the different types of grains, as well as some information about each grain, such as suggested uses and cooking times. Include an illustration, or glue an example grain to the chart as an illustration. Hang the charts around the room when they are complete and use them for reference as you create original dishes.

> **NCTE 4** Use written language to communicate effectively.

 ### Science

12. Design an Experiment When rice is cooked, the starches it contains will determine whether the rice becomes sticky or fluffy.

Procedure Design an experiment to determine the starch content of different types of rice using the scientific method. Begin by coming up with a hypothesis (educated guess) about the results and then create a procedure to test your results. Perform the experiment. Take notes during your experiment.

Analysis Examine your notes. Write up your results in a lab report. Was your hypothesis true or untrue? Is there anything you would change about your procedure?

> **NSES A** Develop abilities necessary to do scientific inquiry.

 ### Mathematics

13. Evaluate Logical Statements Antonio's Italian restaurant has a small menu, serving just 15 types of pasta, each priced at $12. In addition to the pasta, Antonio also serves two daily fish specials, priced at $18 each. Determine whether the following conditional statements are true or false: (a) "If a customer ordered spaghetti, he was charged $12." (b) "If a customer paid $18 for food, she ordered a fish special." Now, write the converse of each statement, and determine if the converse is true or false.

Math Concept **Converse of a Conditional Statement** A conditional statement is one that is written in if/then format, and can be either true or false. To take the converse of a conditional statement, switch the order of the hypothesis (the original "if" part of the statement) and the conclusion (the "then" part).

Starting Hint Imagine the statement, "If it is raining, then the sun is not shining." To find the converse of this statement, swap the "if" and "then" portions of the statement: "If the sun is not shining, then it is raining." Note that while the original statement is true, the converse is false (just because it is not sunny does not mean that it is raining). However, the converse does not always have the opposite truth value of the original statement.

> **NCTM Reasoning and Proof** Select and use various types of reasoning and methods of proof.

Certification Prep

Sharpen your test-taking skills to improve your kitchen certification program score.

Directions Read the questions. Then, read the answer choices and choose the best possible answer for each.

14. How much water should you use to cook one pound of pasta?
- **a.** 8 ounces
- **b.** 1 litre
- **c.** 1 gallon
- **d.** 1 cup

15. What rice is used to make risotto?
- **a.** arborio
- **b.** basmati
- **c.** jasmine
- **d.** wild rice

Test-Taking Tip
If you run up against a word you do not recognize, try to use the context to figure it out. Sometimes the way the word is used in a sentence can help you figure out its definition.

Review and Applications

Real-World Skills and Applications

Interpersonal and Collaborative Skills

16. Improve School Menus Divide into groups at your teacher's instruction. Imagine that your group has been hired as consultants by the school cafeteria. Suggest five healthful grain dishes that could be added to the menu. Present your suggestions in the form of a report to the school administration. Include the specific types of grain in your report.

Critical Thinking Skills

17. Liven Up Your Diet As a class, list all of the common grain foods people eat. Think up alternate grain foods that could be substituted for those you have listed, based on information from this chapter, for more variety. For example, instead of sandwich bread, perhaps you might try a flatbread or pita. Create a chart to show your substitutions.

Technology Applications

18. Online Research With guidance from your teacher or parents, use the Internet to research a grain that is new to you. Find out about the appearance of the grain, the processing, the taste and texture, and how it is cooked and prepared. Use a word processing program to write a report on your information. Include all of the information you have gathered.

Financial Literacy

19. Choose a Market Form Lee owns a restaurant that serves pasta dishes. Lee is deciding which market form of linguine to purchase at the market. Fresh linguine is $5.00 for 11 ounces. Frozen linguine is $9.00 for 24 ounces, and dried linguine is $2.00 for an 8-ounce box. Calculate the cost per ounce and determine which of the three options is the best bargain.

Culinary Lab

Use the culinary skills you have learned in this chapter.

Prepare Polenta

20. Work In Teams In this lab, you will divide into teams and prepare polenta using different versions of one recipe, then compare the results.

A. Form teams. Divide into four teams at the instruction of your teacher. Each team will prepare a variation of the polenta recipe on page 628.

B. Prepare your work station. Make a list of the equipment and smallwares your team will need to prepare its version of the recipe.

C. Cook your polenta. Team A will substitute 2 quarts vegetable stock for water. Team B will substitute 2 quarts chicken stock and 4 ounces butter in place of water. Team C will add 6 ounces diced and sautéed carrots, onions, and green pepper just before step 2. Team D will add lemon pepper seasoning and diced fresh red peppers just before step 3.

D. Evaluate the results. Plate one serving of your version of the polenta, divide it into four equal pieces, and serve one piece to each team.

Create Your Evaluation

After sampling each of the polenta dishes, answer each of the following questions on a piece of notebook paper:

- Which variation of the polenta recipe was the most time consuming to prepare? Why?
- Which variation of the polenta recipe was the most difficult to prepare? Why?
- Which variation of the polenta recipe made the best presentation? Why?
- Which variation of the polenta recipe tasted the best? Why?

CHAPTER 25

Fruits, Vegetables, and Legumes

SECTIONS

25.1 Fruits

25.2 Vegetables

25.3 Legumes

WRITING ACTIVITY

Freewrite About Yourself

Freewrite about your thoughts and feelings toward vegetables. Discuss whether you like or dislike vegetables, and why or why not. Also discuss your favorite and least favorite vegetables.

Writing Tips

1 Write whatever comes to mind.

2 Write without stopping to reread, rephrase, or rethink.

3 Do not be concerned about the quality of the writing.

EXPLORE THE PHOTO

There is a wide variety of fruits, vegetables, and legumes. *Do you think fruits, vegetables, and legumes are good sources of nutrition?*

WRITING ACTIVITY ANSWER
Students should let their thoughts come out in their writing, regardless of logical order.

EXPLORE THE PHOTO ANSWER
Fruits, vegetables, and legumes have a lot of nutrients relative to their calorie count.

Fruits

Fruits can be an exciting part of salads, meals, and desserts.

Reading Guide

 Before You Read

Use Diagrams As you read through this section, write down the main idea. Write down any facts, explanations, or examples you find in the text. Start at the main idea and draw arrows to the information that directly supports it. Then, draw arrows from these examples to any information that supports them.

Read To Learn

Key Concepts
- **Distinguish** between the different market forms of fruit.
- **Identify** dry and moist methods of cooking fruit.

Main Idea

Fruits add nutrition, flavor, color, and texture to a meal. A chef should understand the type and forms of fruit and how to serve and store each one.

Content Vocabulary
- drupe
- in season
- lug
- ripe
- ethylene gas
- compote
- chutney
- rehydrate
- cobbler
- compotier
- fondue

Academic Vocabulary
- lesser
- diminish

ACADEMIC STANDARDS

 English Language Arts
NCTE 12 Use language to accomplish individual purposes.

 Mathematics
NCTM Data Analysis and Probability Understand and apply basic concepts of probability.

 Science
NSES C Develop an understanding of the cell.

NCTE National Council of Teachers of English

NCTM National Council of Teachers of Mathematics

NSES National Science Education Standards

NCSS National Council for the Social Studies

Graphic Organizer

As you read, use a describing wheel like this one to list the eight types of fruit.

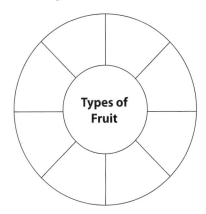

Types of Fruit

 Graphic Organizer Go to this book's Online Learning Center at **glencoe.com** for a printable graphic organizer.

GRAPHIC ORGANIZER ANSWER Citrus, melons, berries, drupes, pomes, grapes, tropical fruits, and exotic fruits.

Types of Fruit

From appetizers to desserts, fruits add texture, nutrition, color, and flavor to any meal. Fruits come from flowering plants. They contain at least one seed. Fruits are divided into eight categories: citrus fruits, melons, berries, drupes ('drōops), pomes, grapes, tropical fruits, and exotic fruits. A **drupe** has soft flesh, thin skin, and one pit, or stone. You need to understand the types and forms of fruits. You also need to know how to serve and store each of them.

Fresh Fruit

Fresh fruit, when in season, adds color and flavor to any meal. **In season** means during the fruit's main growing season. Fruits that are locally out of season can be shipped from other parts of the world where they are in season. Knowing what is in season in your area allows you to plan seasonal menus. This will also help keep costs down. Fresh fruit contains nutrients, such as vitamins and phytochemicals. A phytochemical is a natural chemical found in plants that may help reduce the risk of some types of cancer.

The type of fruit, its nutritional content, and the food product in which it will be used determine whether a foodservice operation purchases ripe or unripe fruit. These factors also determine the grade of fruit purchased.

Grading

The USDA has a voluntary grading program for fresh fruits. Grades are based on a variety of factors, including shape, size, texture, color, and defects. These grades are:

- U.S. Fancy: Premium quality
- U.S. No. 1: Good, average quality
- U.S. No. 2: Medium quality; represents most produce
- U.S. No. 3: Lowest grade quality

Most foodservice operations purchase U.S. Fancy grade products when they serve fresh fruit. **Lesser**, or lower, grades of fruits are typically made into jams, jellies, and sauces.

Purchase Fresh Fruit

Fresh fruits may be purchased ripe or unripe. They are sold by count or weight and packed in flats, lugs, or cartons. A **lug** is a box, crate, or basket in which produce is shipped to market. Lugs often hold 25 to 40 pounds of produce. Flats are shallow boxes, crates, or baskets that are used to ship pints and quarts of produce such as strawberries. States have different weight requirements for each type of packaging.

Some fruits, such as melons, berries, and pineapples, are purchased cleaned, peeled, or cut. They may be purchased in bulk with sugar and preservatives added or packed in large containers of water. Although purchasing prepared fresh fruit may save time in trimming and cutting, the price is often greater. Also, the taste and freshness may **diminish**, or decrease, as a result of the processing.

Ripen and Store Fresh Fruit

Fruits change in several ways as they ripen. To be **ripe** means that the fruit is fully grown and ready to eat. They grow into their full size, and the color deepens and changes. The flesh becomes soft, juicy, and less tart, and the flavor and aroma intensify. Fresh fruits should be used at the height of their ripeness, as judged by taste and appearance.

Ripening does not stop when a fruit is perfectly ripe. It is important to understand when a fruit is ripe and how much longer it will take until it spoils. Some fruits, such as bananas, are often purchased unripened, since they continue to ripen after harvesting. Other fruits, such as pineapples, ripen only on the plant and must be rushed to market.

Fresh fruits in season provide color and flavor to any meal. Fruits give off **ethylene** ('e-thə-ˌlēn) **gas**, an odorless, colorless gas that is emitted naturally as fruits ripen. Unripened fruits can be exposed to ethylene gas to encourage ripening. To stop fruits from ripening further, keep them chilled and isolated from other fruits.

Apples, melons, and bananas give off large amounts of ethylene gas. Store them separately from more delicate fruits and vegetables.

Canned Fruit

Commonly canned fruits include pears, peaches, and pineapples. Fruits can be canned in heavy or light syrup, in water or fruit juice, or in solid pack cans that contain little or no water.

Fruits are exposed to high temperatures during canning. The heat destroys microorganisms and eliminates oxidation, both of which cause fruit to spoil. This sealed environment also slows the spoiling of the fruit. The heat required in canning softens fruit, but it does not affect the nutritional content of the fruit.

Purchase and Store Canned Fruit

Canned fruits are available in different standard-size cans. Cooked fruit products, such as pie fillings, also come in cans. Store canned fruit on shelves in a cool, dry area. After opening any kind of canned fruit, transfer any leftover fruit to a storage container, label, date, and refrigerate.

Canned fruit has an extended shelf life as long as the can remains sealed and undamaged. Do not purchase dented cans. If a can has a bulge, throw it away immediately without opening it. Bulges are a sign that botulism, a foodborne illness, is present. People can become ill if they eat food from these damaged cans.

▲ **Beautiful Fruit** Fresh fruits can be a colorful and flavorful treat. *Will pineapple ripen once it has been picked?*

PHOTO CAPTION ANSWER No. Pineapple will ripen only when it is still on the plant.

Fruits

Citrus Fruits Citrus fruits have a thick, firm rind covered by a thin layer of colored skin, called the zest. The soft, white layer between the zest and the flesh of the fruit is called the pith. The pith is slightly bitter. The flesh of citrus fruits is segmented and acidic. They grow on trees and shrubs and are harvested when ripe. Quality citrus fruits are not blemished, or soft and puffy. Citrus fruits will not continue to ripen after they are picked.

Melons Sweet melons are fruits with a netted skin or a smooth rind that range in color from creamy to jade green. Sweet melons belong to the class of muskmelons (ˈməsk-ˌme-ləns). Quality melons are firm, heavy for their size, and have a good aroma. Watermelons are in a class of their own. Some melons are picked when they are ripe. Others ripen after being picked. Because they are 90% water, melons are usually served raw or puréed into soups or sorbets.

Berries Berries are juicy, thin-skinned fruits with tiny seeds. They grow on bushes and vines and are picked when fully ripened. Berries will not continue to ripen after they are picked. Quality berries are sweet, plump, and even in color.

Drupes Drupes, also known as stone fruit, have soft flesh, thin skin, and one pit, or stone. Drupes can be picked ripe or they can ripen after they are picked. Quality drupes are firm and plump, without bruises or blemishes. These fragile fruits grow on shrubs and trees.

Pomes Pomes are firm, thin-skinned fruits that grow on trees. They have a central core filled with tiny seeds. Pomes can be picked ripe or be ripened after they are picked. Quality pomes have smooth skin and no blemishes, bruises, or soft spots.

Grapes Grapes grow in clusters on vines. Their flavor and color are found mostly in their skin. Grapes are almost always eaten raw. They can be picked ripe or ripen after they are picked. Quality grapes are plump and juicy, with rich color.

Tropical Fruits Tropical fruits grow in hot, tropical regions of the world. These fruits ripen after they are picked. Because of quick transportation and distribution, these fruits are readily available in the United States. Quality tropical fruits are firm, plump, unblemished, and have good color.

Exotic Fruits The exotic fruit category contains many types of unusual fruits. These fruits can be picked ripe or ripen after they are picked. Quality exotic fruits are semisoft, slightly heavy, and have good color. The exotic fruits shown here are available in most areas of the United States.

Frozen Fruit

Fresh fruit can be effectively preserved through freezing. Freezing stops the growth of microorganisms that cause food to spoil. Freezing does not affect the fruit's nutritional value, but it does change the texture of the fruit. Freezing breaks down the cell structure of fruit when the water in the fruit expands during freezing. Then, as fruit thaws, it loses shape because part of the cell structure has been broken down. This leaves the fruit mushy.

Many fruits, such as pears and berries, are individually quick frozen (IQF). This reduces the number of ice crystals that form, keeping the quality of the frozen product higher. It also helps the fruit to retain its shape. You do not have to use, or thaw, the whole container at one time.

Grading

Frozen fruits are labeled U.S. Grade A—Fancy, U.S. Grade B—Choice or Extra Standard, or U.S. Grade C—Standard. The characteristics of each are as follows:

- U.S. Grade A: Premium quality
- U.S. Grade B: Above average quality
- U.S. Grade C: Medium quality

Purchase and Store Frozen Fruit

Frozen fruits are available sliced, packed in sugar syrup, whole, or pitted, peeled, and sliced. Frozen purées are also available. All forms of frozen fruits should be sealed in moisture-proof bags or other containers. Frozen canned fruits are also available. They come in cans or large plastic containers and usually contain a large amount of sugar and water.

After frozen fruit is purchased, immediately transfer fruit that will not be used to a freezer so it does not thaw. Keep the temperature at a constant 0°F (−18°C) or below. If the temperature is allowed to vary, the fruit may develop freezer burn.

Dried Fruits

Drying is another common technique for preserving fruits. Popular dried fruits include bananas, apples, apricots, grapes, plums, and figs. You can add dried fruits to biscuits, muffins, cakes, and pies.

Dried fruits are also used in compotes and chutneys. A **compote** is fresh or dried fruits that have been cooked in a sugar syrup. **Chutney** is a condiment made of fruit, vinegar, sugar, and spices. It can be smooth or chunky, hot or mild. Chutneys are served cold, warm, or hot. Compotes and chutneys often accompany poultry and meats.

Rehydrate ((ˌ)rē-ˈhī-ˌdrāt), or add water into, dried fruits before use. This is done by placing the fruit in boiling water for one-half to one minute. Fruit juices formed by soaking dried fruits in hot liquid until the liquid absorbs the flavor of the fruit can be used in fruit soups and smoothies.

Purchase and Store Dried Fruit

Dried fruits are vacuum packed, or shrink-wrapped, for purchasing and shipping. They are available in 1-pound packages. They also come in 30-pound bulk sizes.

Store dried fruits in labeled and dated airtight containers. Keep the containers in a cool place out of direct sunlight to prevent mold from forming. Dried fruits with low moisture, such as raisins, spoil more quickly than other types. Purchase amounts of dried fruits that will be used within a month.

Reading Check Explain How are canned fruits purchased and stored?

Cooking Fruit

Although fruits are usually served raw, they also can be cooked using a variety of methods. The most common cooking techniques include baking, poaching, simmering, deep-frying, sautéing, broiling, and grilling.

Grill
Fruit

1 Prepare fruit for grilling. Place fruit on a heated grill. Cook until grill marks develop.

2 To create crosshatch marks, carefully lift the fruit and turn it 90 degrees. Place the fruit back down on the grill.

3 When the grill marks are set, turn the fruit over and repeat the process. Cook until the fruit reaches the desired doneness.

When you cook fruits, take care not to overcook them. If you do, they will become mushy and lose their flavor. Add sugar or acid, such as lemon juice, to help prevent overcooking. The fruit takes the sugar or acid into its cells, which helps keep the fruit firm and retain its form.

Preparation of Fruit

Before you prepare and cook fruit, you need to gather your ingredients, smallwares, and utensils. You also need to complete the mise en place for the fruit. Each type of fruit will require different pre-preparation. For some fruits, such as bananas, mangoes, and papayas, your first step in pre-preparation would be to soften and ripen them at room temperature.

In general, you can follow these guidelines:

1. Wash the fruit in cold water. Drain well. Remove any stems. If the fruits have skin that needs to be peeled or pulled, do so now.
2. Cut the fruit into halves, quarters, slices, or chunks.
3. Remove any seeds and pits. Some fruit may also need to be cored.
4. To prevent enzymatic browning, dip the fruit in citrus juice. This step is not necessary for all fruit.

Cooking with Dry Heat

Dry cooking methods for fruit include broiling and grilling, baking, sautéing, and deep-frying. Take care not to dry out the fruit by overcooking.

Broiling and Grilling

Bananas, apples, peaches, and pineapples are often broiled or grilled. The fruits must be quickly cooked so that they do not become mushy and lose their shape. These fruits can be sliced or served as halves. Often, they are coated with honey or sugar, or sprinkled with lemon juice, cinnamon, or nutmeg.

Place fruits to be broiled on a sheet pan. For grilling, place large fruits directly on the grill or thread them onto skewers. Rotate thick slices to make sure they cook all the way through.

Baking

Many fruits can be baked into delicious desserts. For example, berries, peaches, and apples can be baked with a crust to make fruit cobblers. A **cobbler** is a deep-dish fruit dessert. These can be served with whipped cream or vanilla ice cream. You can also bake sweet and tart fruits together to provide an interesting contrast of flavors. Or, try stuffing whole, cored apples or peach halves with raisins; then drizzle them with honey and bake. The fruit skins help hold in moisture and flavor.

Some fruits are added to meats and then baked. For example, ham is often baked with pineapple. Other fruits, such as plums, can be cooked with poultry to make a flavorful sauce. Fruit juices and purées can also be used with baked meats to create sauces that bring out the flavor of the meat.

Sautéing

When fruits are sautéed in butter, sugar, and other spices, they develop a sweet, rich, and syrupy flavor. You can serve bananas, cherries, pears, and apples this way for a delicious dessert. To sauté fruits, first peel and core them and remove any seeds. Cut them into neat, even slices, place them in a sauté pan, and cook over high heat. Sautéed fruits can be used in a main course and as desserts served with ice cream. Sautéing will create a crispy crust on the outside of the fruit pieces.

Deep-Frying

A few fruits, such as bananas, pineapples, and apples, can be coated in batter and deep-fried. Peel, core, and slice the fruit into neat, even slices. If the fruit is too moist, dry it with a paper towel so that the batter will stick to it. Then, the fruit can be deep-fried, as described in Chapter 15.

Cooking with Moist Heat

Two moist cooking methods that are commonly used for cooking fruit are poaching and simmering. They can both maintain moisture in the fruit.

◀ **Fruit as Dessert** Poached fruit is often used in salads or desserts. *What types of fruit might be poached?*

PHOTO CAPTION ANSWER Apples, pears, peaches, plums, and apricots are all common fruits to poach.

Poaching

In poaching, fruits are submerged in various liquids, such as water or sugar syrup. Apples, apricots, peaches, pears, and plums are often poached. Poaching is done at very low temperatures, so it takes some time to cook fruits using this method. The slow cooking time helps the fruit retain its shape and flavor and soften gradually.

Simmering

Simmering is used to make fruit compotes and stewed fruits. Fresh, frozen, canned, or dried fruits can be simmered successfully. Serve stewed or simmered fruits hot or cold, as appetizers, side dishes, or desserts.

To simmer fruit, first peel, core, and slice the fruit. Place it in a pan with cooking liquid, such as water, sugar, syrup, honey, and spices. Bring the liquid to a simmer. Cook until the fruit is done, and add a sweetener if desired. Garnish the simmered fruit with some of the liquid from simmering. This will make an attractive plate.

Plate and Garnish Fruits

The fundamentals of plating apply to all fruits. Strive for an attractive plate that is colorful and well balanced. It is important to use a variety of different fruits. This will provide better plate composition. Do not allow drippings to touch the rim of the plate. Also, avoid leaving thumbprints on the rim.

Compotes are served in a glass or crystal **compotier** (ˌkäm-pōt-tē-ˈyā). A compotier is a deep, stemmed dish used to serve compotes, candies, and nuts.

Fondue

The term **fondue** (fän-ˈdü) refers to dipping foods into a central heated pot. In the case of fruit fondue, bite-size chunks of fresh fruits are often dipped into a chocolate sauce made of melted chocolate and cream.

 Reading Check Explain How would you decide which cooking method to use with fruit?

SECTION 25.1 After You Read

Review Key Concepts

1. **Identify** the uses of dried fruits.
2. **Explain** how to prepare fruit for cooking.

Practice Culinary Academics

 English Language Arts

3. Write a letter to a cooking magazine suggesting three new dishes that can be made with fruit. Describe each dish, the cooking method, and give any important information about each dish.

> **NCTE 12** Use language to accomplish individual purposes.

 Science

4. **Procedure** Cook fruit using different methods. Observe any changes.

   Analysis What causes fruit to change texture as it is cooked? Conduct research to discover the answer. Write a summary of your discovery.

> **NSES C** Develop an understanding of the cell.

 Mathematics

5. This summer, Alex's ice cream shop is offering six different fresh fruit sorbets: Raspberry, Strawberry, Orange, Pineapple, Lemon, and Mango. How many different ways can Alex arrange these names on the menu board?

   Math Concept **Arrangements and Factorials** When you have *n* items, you can arrange all of them *n*! ways. The "!" stands for "factorial," which is the product of all sequential integers between 1 and *n*.

   Starting Hint Alex has 6 total sorbet names, so he can arrange them in 6! ways. To compute factorials, perform the appropriate multiplication. For example, $3! = 3 \times 2 \times 1$, while $4! = 4 \times 3 \times 2 \times 1$.

> **NCTM Data Analysis and Probability** Understand and apply basic concepts of probability.

Check your answers at this book's Online Learning Center at **glencoe.com**.

READING CHECK ANSWER Dry methods should be used with sturdy fruits, while moist methods work well with soft fruits.

Vegetables

Reading Guide

 Before You Read

Take Guilt-Free Days of Rest The reason for resting is to refresh oneself. However, if you feel guilty about resting ("I really should be reading"), then your precious rest period will only create more stress. The brain has a hard time absorbing new data when it is stressed. Your reading skills will be much more effective if you are relaxed and ready to learn.

Read To Learn

Key Concepts
- **Identify** the purchasing and storage for fresh, canned, frozen, and dried vegetables.
- **Describe** dry and moist cooking methods for vegetables.

Main Idea
Vegetables are edible plants that grow in a variety of colors, flavors, and textures. Vegetables add variety and nutrition to a main course.

Content Vocabulary
- tuber
- floret
- solanine
- mealy potato
- waxy potato
- net weight
- drained weight
- packing medium
- mandoline
- bouquetière

Academic Vocabulary
- hasten
- mark

Graphic Organizer
Commercial kitchens usually classify vegetables into eight categories. Use this tree diagram to name them.

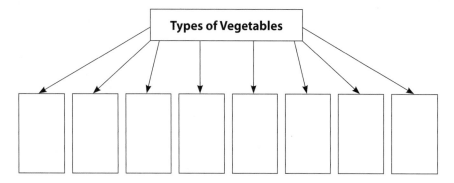

Types of Vegetables

 Graphic Organizer Go to this book's Online Learning Center at **glencoe.com** for a printable graphic organizer.

GRAPHIC ORGANIZER ANSWER Squash family, roots and tubers, seeds and pods, cabbage family, stems, stalks, and shoots, the onion family, fruit-vegetables, and leafy greens.

How many different ways can you use vegetables?

 ACADEMIC STANDARDS

English Language Arts
NCTE 8 Use information resources to gather information and create and communicate knowledge.

Mathematics
NCTM Algebra
Understand patterns, relations, and functions.

Social Studies
NCSS II D Time, Continuity, and Change
Employ processes of critical historical inquiry to validate and weigh evidence for claims.

NCSS VIII B Science, Technology, and Society
Make judgments about how science and technology have transformed the physical world and human society.

NCTE National Council of Teachers of English

NCTM National Council of Teachers of Mathematics

NSES National Science Education Standards

NCSS National Council for the Social Studies

Vegetable Basics

Like fruits, vegetables are versatile foods that add color, flavor, and texture to any meal. Many commercial kitchens offer vegetable-based entrées to meet the demands of health-conscious customers. Becoming familiar with the types and flavors of vegetables and the best ways to prepare and store them is important for every foodservice employee.

Vegetables are edible plants. Different parts of vegetables are eaten, including the flowers, seeds, stems, leaves, roots, and tubers. A **tuber** is the short, fleshy underground stems of plants. The potato is an example of a tuber. Certain types of fruit are classified as vegetables by commercial kitchens because they are savory rather than sweet. These fruits, such as eggplants and tomatoes, are prepared and served like vegetables.

Vegetable Classifications

Commercial kitchens usually classify vegetables into the following categories: the squash family; roots and tubers; seeds and pods; the cabbage family; stems, stalks, and shoots; the onion family; fruit-vegetables; and leafy greens. These categories group vegetables by how they are used in the kitchen. For example, kale and cauliflower are members of the cabbage family, but from a culinary perspective they are used quite differently. Kale is a leafy green and cauliflower is a vegetable floret ('flòr-ət). A **floret** is a small flower that makes up the head of some plants.

Purchase and Store Fresh Vegetables

The quality of the ingredients you use to prepare dishes directly affects the outcome of the finished product. Vegetables are no different. You must understand how to select fresh, high-quality vegetables and store them to maintain this quality. This will help ensure fresh, flavorful dishes.

Grading

The USDA provides a voluntary grading system for vegetables that is used by almost all wholesalers. Grades are based on the appearance, quality, and condition of vegetables when they arrive on the market. Vegetables are graded as:

- U.S. Extra Fancy
- U.S. Fancy
- U.S. Extra No. 1
- U.S. No. 1

Premium quality is classified as U.S. Extra Fancy. When you choose vegetables to use in a foodservice operation, look for the highest-quality product. Some recipes, however, allow a lesser-quality product to be used.

Some vegetables are graded differently for the retail market. Onions, potatoes, and carrots are graded by an alphabetical system, with Grade A being the best.

Ripening

Although many vegetables are fully ripe when purchased, they continue to ripen when exposed to oxygen in the air. The ripening rate depends on the type of vegetable and the way it is stored.

There are some vegetables you will want to continue to ripen. For example, tomatoes and other fruit-vegetables may be purchased unripe so they are damaged less in shipping. As with fruits, you can **hasten**, or speed up, ripening by exposing these fruit-vegetables to ethylene gas.

Storage

Different vegetables require different storage conditions. Starchy vegetables, such as potatoes, winter squash, and vegetables in the onion family, are best stored at 60°F to 70°F (16°C to 21°C) in a dry location. If they are stored in a refrigerator, they will lose flavor and texture. Most other vegetables should be stored at refrigerator temperatures of 41°F (5°C) or below. Store vegetables away from fruits that emit ethylene gas, such as bananas. The gas will cause the vegetables to continue to ripen, and possibly spoil.

Squash Family Members of the squash family have large root systems and trailing vines. Their flowers are often edible in addition to the main vegetable. Quality squash are firm, free of blemishes, and show no signs of mold.

Roots and Tubers Roots grow deep into the soil, while tubers are large, round, underground stems that grow just below the surface of the soil. Both store and provide food to their plants, making them rich in nutrients. Quality roots and tubers are firm, unwrinkled, unblemished, and have good color.

Seeds and Pods This category consists of vegetables with edible seeds. Some of the pods are also edible, but the seeds are more nutritious. Quality seeds and pods are firm, well shaped, and without blemishes.

Cabbage Family Vegetables in the cabbage family grow quickly in cool weather. Commercial kitchens use the flowers, leaves, and heads of these plants. They are served raw as well as cooked. Quality cauliflower, broccoli, and cabbage are firm, heavy for their size, and have good color.

Stems, Stalks and Shoots Vegetables in this category produce edible stems, stalks, and shoots. They are picked when they are young and tender. Quality stems, stalks, and shoots are firm, unblemished, and have no browning.

Onion Family Vegetables in the onion family are often used for seasoning and flavoring. Most have a strong taste and odor. Quality onions are firm, fresh-looking, and have good color.

Fruit-Vegetables Vegetables that are often called fruit-vegetables come from flowering plants and contain at least one seed. Therefore, they are technically the fruit of the plant. For the purpose of commercial kitchens, however, they are categorized as vegetables because they are savory rather than sweet. Quality fruit-vegetables have smooth, unblemished skin.

Leafy Greens Vegetables in this category can be served raw or cooked. They shrink when cooked because of their high water content. Flavors of leafy greens range from mild to spicy. Quality greens have crisp, bright leaves without any brown spots.

Purchase and Store Potatoes

Potatoes are a versatile vegetable. Foodservice operations use potatoes in some form at each meal. Most foodservice operations purchase potatoes in 50-pound cartons or bags. The number of potatoes in each carton varies depending on the size of the potatoes.

Store potatoes in a dry, dark area with temperatures of 45°F to 55°F (7°C to 10°C). Do not refrigerate potatoes. The cool temperature will convert some of the potato starch to sugar. This will make the potato too sweet. Do not eat green potatoes. Green potatoes contain a toxic substance known as solanine. Solanine can upset your stomach and interfere with nerve transmission.

Types of Potatoes

Potatoes are divided into two main types: mealy and waxy. A **mealy potato** has thick skin and starchy flesh. Mealy potatoes are best for deep-frying, baking, whipping, and purée-ing. A **waxy potato** has thin skin and contains less starch than mealy potatoes. They are best for boiling.

There are a wide variety of mealy and waxy potatoes:

Russet A mealy potato also known as Idaho. Russets are a popular choice for baking and frying.

Red A waxy, pink- to red-skinned potato. Red potatoes are good roasted and in salads, soups, and casseroles.

Yukon A buttery-flavored mealy potato with golden flesh. Yukon potatoes can be baked, puréed, and made into salads and casseroles.

Sweet This type comes in two varieties: white and red. White sweet potatoes have yellow flesh and a mealy texture. Red sweet potatoes have a darker orange flesh and a less mealy texture. Both types are used in soups and casseroles, and can be boiled, roasted, and puréed.

Quality Characteristics

Use the following characteristics when you select potatoes:

- All varieties of potatoes should be heavy and firm, without soft spots, green color, or sprouting eyes.
- Sweet potatoes should have dry-looking, orange and golden-orange skins.

Types of Potatoes Potatoes are a versatile vegetable that comes in mealy and waxy varieties. *How might potatoes be used at every meal at a restaurant?*

PHOTO CAPTION ANSWER Potatoes can be made into hash browns or potatoes O'Brien for breakfast, into French fries or potato salad for lunch, and mashed or baked to accompany a dinner.

- Avoid sweet potatoes with softened ends. This will **mark**, or show, the beginning of spoilage.
- Other potatoes should have dry, tight skins, without wrinkles.

Market Forms of Potatoes

Many market forms of potatoes can be used in the professional kitchen.

Fresh Fresh potatoes are readily available year-round. They can be baked, fried, boiled, whipped, or puréed and served with sour cream, nonfat yogurt, or butter.

Canned Most types of potatoes are available in cans, already cooked, whole or sliced. Use of canned potatoes eliminates the risk of spoilage and can result in a high-quality dish. Keep in mind, however, that most canned sweet potatoes are packed in a sugary or spicy sauce.

A TASTE OF HISTORY

1772	1775
Paris Faculty of Medicine declares potatoes to be edible	Paul Revere warns the American colonists of the British troops' arrival

Potato Promoter

Many Europeans, especially the Irish, considered the potato an ideal staple food. The French were slow to accept it, however. Many believed that the potato, a part of the nightshade family, was poisonous. A pharmacist named Antoine Parmentier saw the potato's merits and sought ways to change their minds. Parmentier believed potatoes could help ward off the starvation caused by famines that were plaguing France, and so he became a potato promoter. As a result of Parmentier's efforts, the potato became an important part of French cuisine.

History Application

Parmentier worked hard to convince the people of France about the benefits of the potato. Write a dialog between two people, where one is trying to convince the other about the health benefits of the potato.

> **NCSS II D Time, Continuity, and Change** Employ processes of critical historical inquiry to validate and weigh evidence for claims.

Safety Check

✔ Green Potatoes

Discard potatoes with green skin or green spots on the skin. These potatoes contain solanine. Solanine is caused by prolonged exposure to light. Solanine is not destroyed by heat and does not dissolve in water. This toxin can cause gastrointestinal (ˌgas-trō-in-ˈtes-tə-nəl) problems and central nervous system problems.

CRITICAL THINKING *How can you avoid the formation of solanine in your potatoes?*

Frozen Many foodservice operations purchase frozen potatoes that are precut for French fries. The French fries are blanched in deep-frying fat and then frozen. This product enables foodservice operations to quickly prepare French fries, without cleaning, peeling, and slicing fresh potatoes. Prepared potato dishes available frozen include hash browns and stuffed baked potatoes.

Dehydrated Dried potato flakes, dices, slices, and shreds can be mixed with milk or hot water to make mashed potatoes, hash browns, scalloped potatoes, and other popular dishes. Some dehydrated potatoes may need soaking before cooking.

Purchase and Store Preserved Vegetables

Techniques like canning, freezing, and drying are used to lengthen the shelf life of vegetables. Cooked vegetables can also be preserved through canning and freezing. These techniques may affect the flavor and texture of vegetables.

Canned Vegetables

Almost every variety of vegetable is available canned, which brings many advantages to the commercial kitchen. Canned vegetables are already cleaned, peeled, cut into pieces, and cooked. Combinations of vegetables combined with seasonings and flavorings are also available canned. Additionally, they have been heat-treated to kill microorganisms.

Canning effectively preserves the flavor and texture of vegetables such as beets, sweet potatoes, peas, corn, and beans. However, the heat used during canning softens most vegetables and can cause some nutrient loss. Use the liquid from the canned vegetables to retain some of these nutrients. Canning can also dull the color of green vegetables.

The USDA grading system for canned vegetables is:
- U.S. Grade A or Fancy
- U.S. Grade B or Extra-Select
- U.S. Grade C or Standard

The **net weight** of canned vegetables is the weight of the contents. The **drained weight** is the weight of the food product without the packing medium. A **packing medium** is a liquid used to protect the food product. It can be thin or thick. Canned vegetables come in a variety of commercial sizes. (See **Figure 25.1**.)

Frozen Vegetables

Frozen vegetables offer convenience similar to that found with canned vegetables, but the quality is higher. Most nutrients are retained during freezing. Vegetables also keep their bright colors and flavors because of the quickness with which they are precooked and frozen. As with fruits, some vegetables are individually quick frozen. This improves their texture and appearance.

▼ **FIGURE 25.1** **Canned Vegetable Sizes**
Use Canned Vegetables Almost every variety of vegetable can be found in canned form. *When might you choose to use canned vegetables rather than fresh vegetables?*

Can Size	Weight	Cans per Case
No. 2	20 oz.	24
No. 2½	28 oz.	24
No. 300	14–15 oz.	36
No. 303	16–17 oz.	36
No. 5	46–51 oz.	12
No. 10	6 lb., 10 oz.	6

FIGURE CAPTION ANSWER When a particular variety is out of season, or to create quick versions of stewed dishes or soups. Canned vegetables can also be used in purées.

Some frozen vegetables are frozen raw. Others are completely cooked and need only to be thawed and heated before serving. Some frozen vegetables are frozen with a sauce. Do not refreeze unused portions. Instead, store them in the refrigerator as you would fresh vegetables.

The same grading system used for canned vegetables is used for frozen vegetables. The most common pack for frozen vegetables is a 20-pound bulk bag in a cardboard case. Other packs include six 4-pound bags and 12 2.5-pound bags or boxes. Keep all packages in a freezer at a steady temperature of 0°F (–18°C) or below.

Dried Vegetables

Dried vegetables are not as common in foodservice operations as canned and frozen vegetables. The drying process affects the appearance, taste, and texture of vegetables. The advantage to using dehydrated vegetables is convenience. Essentially, everything is done in the processing plant instead of the commercial kitchen.

Reading Check Explain What are the advantages of using frozen vegetables in a foodservice operation?

Cooking Vegetables

Unlike fruits, most vegetables are served cooked. Cooking softens vegetables and intensifies their flavor. It also makes them easier to chew and digest. To maintain flavor and quality, cook vegetables in batches as close to serving time as possible. Improper cooking and holding techniques can cause vegetables to lose nutrients and can damage their texture, color, and flavor. For example, to help white and red vegetables retain their color, cook them in liquid that is slightly acidic. Learn how to apply the right cooking techniques so that you can serve tender vegetables packed with nutrition and flavor.

READING CHECK ANSWER Frozen vegetables are more convenient than fresh vegetables, and the nutrients and color are retained.

Pre-Preparation for Vegetables

Efficiently preparing and arranging vegetables is an important step in cooking vegetables. The number and types of vegetables you will need to prepare vary with each recipe.

Washing

Because vegetables grow outside and often close to the ground, they can pick up sand, dirt, grit, chemicals, and even insects. It is critical to clean them thoroughly just before preparation. Because water can leach nutrients from vegetables, clean the produce quickly under cold running water. Follow these other guidelines:

- Scrub root vegetables with a strong-bristled brush.
- Soak cabbage family vegetables, in salted water for a short amount of time. This will draw out any insects.
- Store cut vegetables, such as carrots, in the refrigerator until ready to be used.

Unlike other vegetables, leafy green vegetables are washed in a water bath. This allows debris and sand to settle to the bottom of the vegetable sink. To avoid further contact with debris, lift the greens out of the water.

Peeling, Cutting, and Shaping

The way you peel, cut, and shape vegetables will influence how they will cook and how they will look when they are served. Depending on how each vegetable will be used, its preparation will differ.

Always trim off and discard only inedible skins, leaves, stems, and stalks. You could use a vegetable peeler to remove a thin layer of vegetable skin. Cut vegetables into uniform pieces to ensure even cooking. Many foodservice operations use food processors to uniformly cut vegetables. Another hand-operated machine, called a **mandoline** (ˌman-də-ˈlin), is used for slicing vegetables and fruits, such as potatoes and apples. In using a mandoline, food is held in a metal carriage while slicing to protect the fingers. See **Figure 25.2** on page 654 for popular cuts and shapes that are used on vegetables and potatoes.

SAFETY CHECK ANSWER Bacteria growing in the food cause the can to swell. A dented can signals a possible leak in the can.

Cook Vegetables with Dry Heat

Cooking vegetables with dry heat preserves flavors and nutrients. Because vegetables are not submerged in water, there is no risk of nutrients leaching into liquid. Dry cooking techniques such as grilling can also give vegetables interesting flavors.

You can brush butter, seasonings, flavorings, or flavored oils on vegetables before cooking them for added flavor. Never use flavored oils for deep-frying. Evenly slice vegetables to ensure uniform cooking and add to the visual appeal of the final product.

Broiling and Grilling

Broiling and grilling both cook vegetables quickly with relatively high heat. The heat caramelizes the vegetables. This gives them a pleasing flavor. Many kinds of vegetables can be grilled or broiled, including potatoes, tomatoes, peppers, squash, eggplant, zucchini, and corn.

You can thread small sliced vegetables, such as mushrooms and tomatoes, onto wooden or metal skewers for grilling. Be sure to cut larger vegetables, such as eggplant and squash, into slices and place them directly on the grill. For broiling, arrange slices or chunks of vegetables on a sheet pan. Broiling can also be used to reheat a vegetable that has already been cooked. You can marinate vegetables before you broil or grill them for extra flavor.

Safety Check

✓ **Canned Vegetables**
The high heat used during the canning process kills microorganisms. However, occasionally cans are not properly sealed, processed, or handled. Throw away any swollen or dented cans and cans that contain discolored food. People can become seriously ill if they eat food from these cans.

CRITICAL THINKING *Why would a swollen or dented can signal the possible presence of microorganisms?*

Vegetable Shapes The shape of the vegetable cut will influence how vegetables cook and how they will look when served. *How are vegetables cut into a brunoise most commonly used?*

Vegetable Cuts		
 **French Fry** ½ × ½ × 3 inches	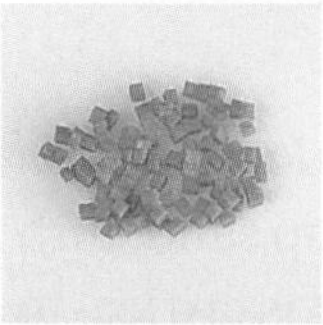	**Brunoise** ⅛ × ⅛ × ⅛ inch (small dice)
 **Stick** ⅜ × ⅜ × 2 inches		**Mirepoix** ½ inch average rough cut
 **Baton** ¼ × ¼ × 3 inches (small stick)		**Chips** ⅛ inch thick slice
 **Julienne** ⅛ × ⅛ × 2 inches (short, matchstick)		**Waffle** ⅛ inch thick slice; perforated
 **Fine Matchstick** 1/16 × 1/16 × 2 inches		**Tournée** 7-sided; 2 inch-long barrel
 **Large Dice** ¾ × ¾ × ¾ inch		**Round** Round disks of varying thickness
 **Medium Dice** ½ × ½ × ½ inch	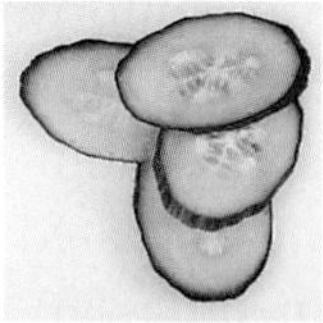	**Diagonal** Bias-cut slices of variable thickness
 **Small Dice** ¼ × ¼ × ¼ inch		**Chiffonade** Thin ribbons

FIGURE CAPTION ANSWER Carrots, celery, and leeks are commonly brunoised, and are often used as a garnish, or in soups such as gazpacho.

Baking

Baked vegetables are cooked at a lower temperature for a longer period of time than grilled or broiled vegetables. Squash, onions, potatoes, and other root vegetables are excellent baked. They should be well cleaned, peeled, and, unless they are baked whole, cut into uniform pieces. Baked vegetable casseroles are a good option for vegetarian customers or those wanting a healthful meal option.

Sautéing

Sautéing cooks vegetables in a small amount of butter or oil in a hot sauté pan. Sautéing happens quickly because the heat is high. This means that all vegetables must be cut and ready to cook before you begin.

Many different kinds of vegetables can be sautéed, including mushrooms, summer squash, and onions. Firm vegetables such as broccoli, brussels sprouts, carrots, beans, celery, and potatoes need to be blanched before sautéing. Otherwise, they will not get soft enough. Sautéed vegetables should look brightly colored and still be slightly crisp.

Deep-Frying

Deep-fried vegetables are usually coated in batter, and then submerged in hot oil. Potatoes are popular deep-fried as French fries or potato chips. Other vegetables that can be deep-fried include onions, mushrooms, cauliflower, okra, and eggplant. Be sure to cut vegetables into even pieces. Wipe off any excess moisture before deep-frying.

Cook Vegetables with Moist Heat

Moist cooking methods used in vegetable cookery include blanching, parboiling, steaming, simmering, poaching, and braising. Before you cook with these techniques, clean vegetables thoroughly and cut them into uniform pieces. Clean all surfaces and utensils that touch fresh vegetables with hot water and soap before and after preparation. Add bouillon, herbs, spices, or butter to the cooking liquid for extra flavor. To retain nutrients, cook vegetables for the minimum amount of time needed and in a small amount of liquid. If possible, you can reuse this flavored liquid in the dish you are preparing, or in soups or stocks.

Green vegetables need to be cooked without a cover to let the acid escape. Red vegetables need to be cooked covered to keep the acid inside. They also may need to have an acid such as vinegar added to the water to replace lost acid.

Blanching

Often used to loosen the skins of vegetables, blanching involves plunging foods briefly into boiling water and then plunging them into cold water to stop the cooking process. Blanching is also used to increase the color and flavor of vegetables before freezing them. Sometimes, blanching is a first step for a second cooking process such as sautéing. It can also make it easy to remove skins from tomatoes.

Parboiling

Parboiling is used to partially cook vegetables. Another method is then used to finish cooking the vegetables, such as grilling or sautéing. Parboiling is also used to remove strong flavors and loosen skins or peels. Winter squash, root vegetables such as potatoes, and members of the cabbage family such as kale are commonly parboiled.

Steaming and Simmering

Steamed vegetables are cooked by being placed above boiling water in a perforated container. Today, most commercial kitchens use combination or pressureless steamers. Simmered vegetables sit in a shallow layer of lightly boiling water. Use just enough water to cover the bottom of the pan, and cover with a lid. The end result of both techniques is the same: soft, colorful, flavorful vegetables.

Sweet and Spicy Broccoli

YIELD: 6 SERVINGS
SERVING SIZE: 10 OUNCES

Ingredients

2 heads	Broccoli, blanched slightly and shocked
1 c.	White raisins
1 tsp.	Garlic, minced
½ c.	Olive oil
2 tbsp.	Fresh ginger, very finely chopped
¼ c.	Vinegar
2 tbsp.	low-sodium soy sauce
1 tsp.	Crushed red pepper flakes
2 tbsp.	Mayonnaise
1 tsp.	Dijon mustard
1 tsp.	Honey
½ c.	Water

Method of Preparation

1. Cut the florets from the heads of broccoli and save 2 of the stems.
2. In a food processor, combine ¾ cup of the broccoli florets, the 2 stems, and all of the other ingredients. Process until smooth. If it is too pasty, add more water.
3. When consistency is smooth, pour contents of food processor over the remaining florets and stir mixture until the sauce is evenly distributed. It is ready to serve immediately.

Chef Notes

Broccoli has a stronger odor the older it is. Use fresh broccoli for the best flavor.

Substitutions

● Use low-fat or nonfat mayonnaise, or a soy substitute, to lower fat.

Cooking Technique

Blanching

1. Bring water to a boil.
2. Place food in the water, and boil for a short time.
3. Remove frood from water, and place it in cold water or an ice bath to stop the cooking process.

International Flavor

Broccoli can be added to many different types of dishes. Research how broccoli is used in these dishes, and suggest ways to add broccoli to two more dishes. Write your answer in a half-page report.

● Gado-gado (Indonesia)
● Beef with Broccoli (China)

Glossary

Shock to bathe cooked food in cold water or ice.
Floret a flowering part of a vegetable or plant.

HACCP

● Hold at 135°F (57°C) or above
● Store at 41°F (5°C)

Hazardous Foods

● Mayonnaise

Nutrition

Calories 360   Calories from Fat 210
Total Fat 23g
  Saturaded Fat 3g
  Trans Fat 0g
Cholestrol 0g
Sodium 290g
Total Carbohydrates 35g
  Fibers 6g
  Sugars 19g
Protein 7g
• Vitamin A 30%   • Vitamin C 300%
• Calcium 10%   • Iron 10%

Poaching and Braising

Poached vegetables cook in just enough simmering liquid to cover the food. Braising vegetables is done by simmering them in a seasoned liquid or sauce in the oven. Save this liquid and serve it with the vegetables for added flavor. Popular vegetables used for braising are cabbages, celery, leeks, onions, endive, Swiss chard, and fennel. See Chapter 15 for more information on poaching and braising.

Determine Doneness

Every vegetable has slightly different characteristics when it is properly cooked, so there is no one rule to follow for cooking time. However, most vegetables are done cooking when they are just tender enough to cut with a fork. Leafy vegetables should become brighter in color than when they are raw, and should be slightly wilted. Instead of relying on a specific cooking time, pay attention to how vegetables look, taste, smell, and feel.

◀ Moist Cooking Vegetables can be cooked by blanching, parboiling, steaming, simmering, poaching, and braising methods. *How do you retain the nutrients in moist-cooked vegetables?*

PHOTO CAPTION ANSWER Cook them for the minimum amount of time in the liquid.

Plate and Garnish Vegetables

As with any other food, an important factor in cooking vegetables is its visual appeal on the plate. Uniform-size pieces arranged in an attractive pattern make the entire plate look appealing. Plate vegetables using the following arrangements:

- Place the main entrée to the front of the plate, with the vegetables to the back.
- Place the main item in the center of the plate with vegetables placed randomly around the item. Vegetables could be arranged in a pattern instead.
- Place vegetables in the center of the plate with the main item leaning against it. The main item also could be sliced and placed around the vegetables.

- Put a **bouquetière** (ˌbo͞o-kə-ˈtyir), or bouquet of three or more vegetables, arranged on a plate surrounded by other foods.

You can use a lot of creativity when you plate vegetables. Simple garnishes, such as chopped scallions or minced lemon zest, add visual appeal, texture, and flavor. For example, to zest a lemon, you would pull the zester over the lemon to cut thin strips of the lemon zest.

 **Reading Check** **Summarize** How would you grill vegetables?

Review Key Concepts

1. **Identify** the market forms of potatoes.
2. **Describe** the pre-preparation process for vegetables.

Practice Culinary Academics

 ### English Language Arts

3. Choose one vegetable that grows in your region. Research its nutritional value, when it is in season, and how to prepare and store it. Describe the flavor and texture and create one main course or side dish using the vegetable. Write a one-page report with an illustration or photograph.

> **NCTE 8** Use information resources to gather information and create and communicate knowledge.

 ## Social Studies

4. Visit a local farmer's market or produce department. Speak with a farmer or produce manager about how they grow and store their vegetables. Ask them about any technology that helps them grow vegetables more easily, or improves their quality. Report back to the class about what you learned.

> **NCSS VIII B Science, Technology, and Society** Make judgments about how science and technology have transformed the physical world and human society.

Mathematics

5. A local organic farm sells your restaurant asparagus at $2 per pound, plus a flat $5 fee for delivery. Write an algebraic equation that shows the relationship between the total order price and the number of pounds ordered. Then, graph this equation.

Math Concept **Graphing Algebraic Equations** If an equation has two variables (x and y), rearrange the equation so that y is by itself on one side. Choose any five values for x, and calculate the corresponding values for y. Plot each of the five pairs on a graph, and connect them with a line.

Starting Hint Let y represent total order cost, and x stand for the number of pounds ordered. Write an equation beginning "$y =$". Remember that x is the horizontal measurement on the graph, and y the vertical.

> **NCTM Algebra** Understand patterns, relations, and functions.

 Check your answers at this book's Online Learning Center at **glencoe.com**.

READING CHECK ANSWER Brush them with a small amount of oil if desired, season and place on a hot grill. Smaller vegetables can be threaded on skewers.

Legumes

Legumes can make a hearty meal or a seasoned side dish.

Reading Guide

 Before You Read

Preview Choose a Content or Academic Vocabulary word that is new to you. When you find it in the text, write down the definition.

Read to Learn

Key Concepts

- **List** the various types and quality characteristics of legumes.
- **Describe** the process of preparing and cooking legumes.

Main Idea

Legumes are a group of plants that have pods that contain seeds. Legumes are nutritious, have a long shelf life, and are a healthful, flavorful addition to a meal.

Graphic Organizer

As you read, use a table like this one to list the three methods for cooling legumes quickly.

Legume Cooling Methods

 Graphic Organizer Go to this book's Online Learning Center at **glencoe.com** for a printable graphic organizer.

GRAPHIC ORGANIZER ANSWER 1) Divide into smaller quantities, place in pre-chilled shallow pans, refrigerate overnight. 2) Use an ice bath. 3) Use cold paddles.

Content Vocabulary

- legume
- pulse
- preprocessed legumes
- digestible
- quick soak

Academic Vocabulary

- withered
- accessible

ACADEMIC STANDARDS

 English Language Arts
NCTE 6 Apply knowledge of language structure and conventions to discuss texts.

Mathematics
NCTM Problem Solving Apply and adapt a variety of appropriate strategies to solve problems.

 Science
NSES C Develop an understanding of the interdependence of organisms.

 Social Studies
NCSS VII A Production, Distribution, and Consumption Examine how the scarcity of productive resources requires the development of economic systems to make decisions about how goods and services are to be produced and distributed.

NCTE National Council of Teachers of English

NCTM National Council of Teachers of Mathematics

NSES National Science Education Standards

NCSS National Council for the Social Studies

Types of Legumes

Legumes are considered vegetables, but are treated as a separate topic. A **legume** ('le-ˌgyüm) is a plant that has double-seamed pods that contain a single row of seeds. Examples include peas, beans, lentils ('len-təls), soybeans, and peanuts. Cultures around the world have used legumes as a staple food for thousands of years. Legumes are nutritious, have a long shelf life, and contribute flavor and texture to any meal. Customers demand healthful foods with flavor. Commercial kitchens are making legumes an important part of their menus.

Legumes are not picked as fresh beans and peas. They are left on the vine until the bean or pea is plump and beginning to dry. At this point, the pods are harvested from the vine and the legumes are removed. When a seed of a legume is dried, it is called a **pulse**. Lentils and dried peas are examples of pulses.

Legumes come in different shapes, sizes, and colors. There are dozens of different types of legumes, each with a different texture and flavor.

Legumes can be used in a variety of dishes and in many different ways. They are often added to soups and salads, and substituted for meat. Many vegetarian dishes feature legumes as a protein source. For example, when making tacos, you could use legumes instead of ground beef as the main ingredient. Legumes can also be made into dips and spreads. They can be eaten as a snack item, or served as the main entrée.

Quality Characteristics

When you select legumes, consider the following quality standards. Legumes should be brightly colored and uniformly sized. They should not be marked, shriveled, damaged, or broken. Legumes are graded as:

- U.S. No. 1: The highest quality
- U.S. No. 2: Above average quality
- U.S. No. 3: Medium quality

Purchasing and Storage

When you purchase legumes, look for uniformly sized pieces, which ensure even cooking. The legumes should have smooth skin and should not look **withered**, or shrunken and wrinkled. Withering is a sign that the legumes are old. Legumes continue to dry as they age, so purchase enough to last only one month. Older legumes require more cooking liquid and a longer cooking time.

Legumes can also be purchased in canned form. Although the canning process does destroy nutrients, some nutrients can be recovered by using the canning liquid.

Preprocessed legumes are also available. These legumes have already been soaked, which means they will take less time to cook.

As with other dry goods, legumes should be stored in a cool, dark, dry place with good ventilation. Keep opened packages of legumes in air-tight, moisture-proof containers. Do not store bags of legumes on the floor. Pests may infest them. You should never store dry legumes in the refrigerator or in a humid area. They will begin to absorb moisture immediately and spoil. Legumes need to be protected from heat and light. Vitamin B_6 is found in beans, and it is sensitive to light.

Reading Check List What are the quality characteristics of legumes?

Common Legumes

Baby Lima Beans Lima beans are a flat-shaped bean. They are pale, light green in color, and have a smooth texture and a sweet flavor.

Black-Eyed Peas This is a medium-size, oval-shaped pea. Black-eyed peas are dark beige in color, with a black dot on the skin. They have a smooth texture and a savory flavor.

Cannelini (ˌka-nə-ˈlē-nē) **Beans**
Cannellini beans are larger than American white beans. They have a creamy white color, a mild flavor, and a smooth texture.

Fava (ˌfä-və) **Beans** The fava is a large, flat, kidney-shaped bean. It is brown or white in color. Fava beans have a fine texture and are slightly firm.

Garbanzo (gär-ˈbän-(ˌ)zō) **Beans**
Garbanzo beans are medium-size and round. They are also called chick peas. Garbanzo beans are a beige color, and have a firm texture and a nutty flavor.

Great Northern Beans This is a medium-size, oval-shaped bean. It is creamy white color. Great Northern beans have a powdery texture and a mild flavor.

Green and Brown Lentils These lentils are disk-shaped, pea-size beans. They are green and brown in color.

Navy Beans Navy beans are small and oval in shape. They are white in color, have a powdery texture, and a mild flavor.

Peanuts Peanuts are oblong kernels. They are light brown in color, and have a firm texture.

Pinto Beans Pinto beans are medium-size, oval-shaped beans. They are beige and brown in color, and are typically mottled. They have a powdery texture and an earthy flavor.

Black Beans Black beans are medium-size and oval-shaped. They are also called turtle beans. Black beans have a creamy interior flesh with a black shell or skin, and a sweet flavor.

Red Kidney Beans As the name suggests, these are kidney-shaped beans. They are reddish-brown in color, and they have a soft texture and a robust flavor.

Soybeans Soybeans are a round bean. They are green, black, or yellow in color and have a bland flavor.

Yellow and Green Split Peas These whole peas have had the skin removed and are split in half. They are yellow and green in color. They have a soft, floury texture with a sweet taste.

Cooking Legumes

All legumes must be cooked to be digestible. **Digestible** means that the nutrients, such as protein, are more **accessible**, or available, to the body. Red kidney beans contain a natural toxin that is destroyed during cooking. The flavor of legumes varies with the product. Some are very flavorful by themselves. Others are quite bland and require seasoning. Great Northern beans and Navy beans are legumes that require seasoning. Soybeans can also be bland without seasoning.

Cooking legumes involves rehydration, the process of adding water back into the legume. Since the beans have been thoroughly dried, they need to become filled with water again. This usually is accomplished in two steps: soaking and simmering.

Check and Soak Legumes

Before you cook legumes, you must get everything ready for preparation. Dishes that use legumes must be carefully planned out to leave enough time for sorting, soaking, and cooking the legumes. Carefully sort through legumes before cooking. Remove any shriveled or discolored legumes. Also, check for objects such as pebbles or stems that might have slipped into the package. Items such as these can be a physical hazard to customers.

Next, rinse legumes in cold water repeatedly until the water is clear. Most legumes require soaking, but check the package to be sure. In general, the longer legumes soak, the less time they will take to cook. Remove any legumes that float. Insects may have eaten the insides of those legumes. The most efficient way to soak legumes is to leave them overnight in three times their volume of water in the refrigerator. An alternative method is to **quick soak** them. Put the beans in a pot and cover with water. Bring the water to a boil and cook for a few minutes. Turn off the heat, cover the beans, and let them sit for one hour. Discard the water.

All types of legumes are rich in iron, vitamins, protein, and starch. Legumes can also be made into substitute items. Soy milk, an emulsion made from ground soy beans and water, is used as a milk substitute. Legumes are sometimes ground into a flour and used as a substitute for wheat flour in baking recipes.

SCIENCE À LA CARTE ANSWER Students should note from the passage that a moisture content of 10% or less is desirable. Therefore, only if the cooked weight is 18 ounces or more are the legumes desirable for eating.

Simmer Legumes

After you prepare the legumes, you will simmer them. Simmering legumes allows the hard, dry legumes to slowly reabsorb water.

After soaking legumes, follow these general guidelines to cook legumes:

1. Simmer the legumes and cooking liquid for 30 minutes to three hours.
2. When legumes are tender, but not too soft, they are ready to be used.
3. Test for doneness by tasting a few beans. If their texture is not soft enough, they are not ready and must be simmered for longer. Legumes that will go into a hot dish can be added to the dish after simmering. Legumes that will be added to a cold dish must be properly cooled before they are added to the cold dish.

Cool Cooked Legumes

After legumes have been cooked, allow them to cool before using them. Keep the legumes in the cooking liquid while they cool. This will keep them moist. Use one of the following methods to cool legumes quickly:

- Divide the hot legumes into smaller quantities. Place them into pre-chilled shallow pans and refrigerate.
- Use an ice bath to bring down the temperature of the food. First, divide the food into small, shallow pans. Place the pans in ice water in a sink.
- Use cold paddles, such as Rapi-Kool®, that you fill with water and freeze. Stirring legumes with cold paddles will help cool them quickly. Sanitize the paddles every time you use them.

⬆ Sort and Soak Legumes should be sorted before use, and those below standards of quality should be discarded. *Why should legumes also be rinsed prior to soaking and use?*

Lentil Stuffed Zucchini

YIELD: 6 SERVINGS
SERVING SIZE: 11 OUNCES

Ingredients

⅓ c.	Brown lentils
½ c.	Water
1 large	Carrot, finely chopped
1 rib	Celery, finely chopped
½ c.	Onion, finely chopped
¼ ea.	Green bell pepper, finely chopped
¼ ea.	Red pepper, finely chopped
2 clv.	Garlic, minced
1 ea.	Bay leaf
6 med.	Zucchini
Dash, + ¼ tsp.	Salt
2 dashes + ¼ tsp.	Pepper
¼ c.	Tomato paste
¼ c.	Walnuts, finely chopped
2 tbsp.	Flat-leaf parsley, fresh, finely chopped
2 tsp.	Thyme, fresh, finely chopped
1 tsp.	Dill, snipped, fresh
1 tsp.	Tarragon, fresh, finely chopped
¼ c.	Parmesan cheese
¼ c.	Bread crumbs, dried

Method of Preparation

1. Combine the lentils, water, carrot, celery, onion, bell pepper, red pepper, garlic, and bay leaf in a large saucepan. Cover and simmer over medium-high heat until the lentils are tender and the liquid is absorbed, about 30 minutes.

3. Meanwhile, preheat the oven to 350°F (177°C). Lightly oil a 10-inch by 8-inch baking dish. Bring a large pot of water to a boil over high heat, add the zucchini, and cook until just tender, about 15 minutes. Drain and cool slightly.

4. Trim the ends and slice each zucchini in half lengthwise. Use a spoon to scoop out about half of the inside of the zucchini and discard, leaving a ¼-inch-thick shell. Arrange the zucchini shells in the prepared pan and sprinkle with salt and pepper.

5. When the lentils are cooked, remove the bay leaf. Stir in the remaining ¼ tsp. salt and ¼ tsp. pepper, tomato paste, walnuts, parsley, thyme, dill, and tarragon. Taste and adjust the seasoning.

6. Stir together the Parmesan, bread crumbs and a dash of pepper in a small bowl.

7. Spread about 2 Tbsp. of the lentil mixture into each zucchini half. Sprinkle with the Parmesan mixture.

8. Bake for 30 minutes, or until the zucchini are completely tender and the cheese is melted. Hold at 135°F (57°C) or above.

Chef Notes

This vegetarian entrée offers a meaty texture from the lentils, and provides high quantities of fiber and protein.

Cooking Technique

Baking

1. Preheat oven to desired temperature.
2. Place items to back on the correct rack in the oven.

International Flavor

Vegetables are ideal for stuffing because they hold up well in the oven. Research these recipes, and make a chart of their similarities and differences.

- Dolmades (Greece)
- Basic Stuffed Zucchini (Italy)

Glossary

Jalapeno a dark green chili pepper from Mexico

HACCP

- Hold at 135°F (57°C) or above.

Hazardous Foods

- none

Nutrition

Calories 160   Calories from Fat 45
Total Fat 5g
  Saturated Fat 1g
  Trans Fat 0g
Cholesterol 5mg
Sodium 300mg
Total Carbohydrate 24g
  Fiber 6g
  Sugars 8g
Protein 92g
- Vitamin A 60%   • Vitamin C 90%
- Calcium 10%   • Iron 20%

Cooked Legume Storage

Often, more legumes are prepared than will be used. In this case, cooked legumes can be labeled, dated, and stored in the refrigerator. Use them within three days. Legumes that will not be used within the three-day period can be frozen. Package the cooked legumes in an air-tight, moisture-proof container.

To keep them moist, add just enough cooking liquid to cover them. Label the container with the date and contents. Frozen legumes can be stored for six months.

Plate and Serve Legumes

Legumes can be used in salads, soups, stews, or casseroles. They also can be served alone or with rice. Legumes can also be used as a meat substitute in dishes such as lasagna or chili. For a change of pace, use legumes in place of common side dishes such as mashed potatoes.

 Reading Check Describe What is the mise en place for legumes?

SECTION 25.3 **After You Read**

Review Key Concepts

1. **List** the various types of legumes.
2. **Describe** the process of preparing and cooking legumes.

Practice Culinary Academics

 English Language Arts

3. Write an advertisement promoting legumes as a healthful protein alternative to meat. Describe the health benefits and the advantages of substituting legumes for some of the meat in your diet.

    NCTE 6 Apply knowledge of language structure and conventions to discuss texts.

Social Studies

4. Besides being nutritious and high in protein, legumes may also have the ability to fix nitrogen from the air. This means that they could help fertilize soil for growing. Research this process and create a visual presentation to evaluate how it can benefit farmers.

    NCSS VII A Production, Distribution, and Consumption Examine how the scarcity of productive resources requires the development of economic systems to make decisions about how goods and services are to be produced and distributed.

 Mathematics

5. Russell's restaurant serves a salad that requires 1.5 cups of cooked fava beans per serving. If a pound of dry fava beans is 2 cups by volume, and fava beans triple in volume when cooked, how many servings can he make from a 5-pound package of dry beans?

    Math Concept **Multi-Step Problems** Study the problem carefully and determine the individual calculations you will need to make. Determine the proper order for those calculations by identifying the steps that require answers from other steps.

    Starting Hint Start with the 5 pounds of dry beans, and determine how much volume (in cups) that weight represents. Then, determine the volume of those beans once cooked. How many 1.5-cup servings can you get from that total?

    NCTM Problem Solving Apply and adapt a variety of appropriate strategies to solve problems.

Check your answers at this book's Online Learning Center at **glencoe.com**.

READING CHECK ANSWER Carefully sort through the legumes and remove shriveled or discolored ones. Also, check for foreign objects. Rinse and soak legumes.

Review and Applications

Chapter Summary

There are eight categories of fruit. The quality characteristics of fruit vary with each type of fruit, its season, and its form. Fruits can be cooked using either dry or moist methods.

There are also eight classifications of vegetables. All vegetables are judged on their appearance and the condition they are in when they arrive on the market. By applying the appropriate cooking technique, tender vegetables that are packed with nutrition and taste can be served.

There are dozens of types of legumes. Legumes should be brightly colored and uniformly sized. They should not be marked, discolored, shriveled or broken.

Content and Academic Vocabulary Review

1. Label each of these vocabulary terms as a noun, verb, or adjective.

Content Vocabulary

- drupe (p. 638)
- in season (p. 638)
- lug (p. 638)
- ripe (p. 638)
- ethylene gas (p. 639)
- compote (p. 642)
- chutney (p. 642)
- rehydrate (p. 642)
- cobbler (p. 644)
- compotier (p. 645)
- fondue (p. 645)
- tuber (p. 647)
- floret (p. 647)
- solanine (p. 650)
- mealy potato (p. 650)
- waxy potato (p. 650)
- net weight (p. 652)
- drained weight (p. 652)
- packing medium (p. 652)
- mandoline (p. 653)
- bouquetière (p. 658)
- legume (p. 660)
- pulse (p. 660)
- preprocessed legumes (p. 660)
- digestible (p. 663)
- quick soak (p. 663)

Academic Vocabulary

- lesser (p. 638)
- diminish (p. 638)
- hasten (p. 647)
- mark (p. 651)
- withered (p. 660)
- accessible (p. 663)

Review Key Concepts

2. Distinguish between the different market forms of fruit.

3. Identify dry and moist methods of cooking fruit.

4. Identify the purchasing and storage for fresh, canned, frozen, and dried vegetables.

5. Describe dry and moist cooking methods for vegetables.

6. List the various types and quality characteristics of legumes.

7. Describe the process of preparing and cooking legumes.

Critical Thinking

8. Imagine that you are in charge of selecting and purchasing fruit for your foodservice operation. How do you determine which fruits to buy?

9. Evaluate holding procedures. You have made a mashed potato dish for a dinner party and the entrée is running late. How can you keep the potatoes hot?

10. Illustrate your knowledge of storage. You have just received a delivery of potatoes, bananas, oranges, tomatoes, leafy greens, frozen corn, and dried split peas. How will you store them?

Review and Applications

Academic Skills

English Language Arts

11. Write a Memorandum Imagine that you are a pastry chef in a foodservice operation. Write a memorandum to the executive chef and manager of the operation persuading them to use more fruit in the dessert menu. Use information from the chapter, but write in your own words and an appropriate business format and tone. Explain why fruit desserts are both delicious and more nutritious than other desserts.

> **NCTE 4 Use written language to communicate effectively.**

Social Studies

12. Fruit and Vegetable Pilot Program The government encourages schools to offer fruits and vegetables as snacks by providing them free to participating schools as part of the USDA Fruit and Vegetable Pilot Program. Conduct research to learn more about this program. Find out if your school participates. If your class does not participate, consider writing letters to the administration to ask them to participate, if possible.

> **NCSS VI B Power, Authority, and Governance** Explain the purpose of the government and analyze how its powers are acquired, used, and justified.

Mathematics

13. Make a Selection Peter is updating his restaurant's Web site, and would like to add some photographs to add visual appeal. At the moment, he is preparing to take a picture of some fruit. He has a bowl containing an apricot, peach, papaya, plum, orange, pear, mango, apple, and banana. Peter would like to select three of the fruits and line them up for a picture. What is the total number of possible ways he can line up three different fruits?

Math Concept **Permutations** A permutation is an ordered arrangement of a group of items. If there are n total items, and you select r of them, then the number of permutations is equal to $n! / [(n − r)!]$

Starting Hint There are nine total fruits, out of which Peter will select three. Use the permutation formula to determine the number of arrangements, which results in $9! / 6!$. If you write out the numerator and denominator in longhand (e.g., $9 \times 8 \times 7$ etc.), you will be able to cancel out many of the numbers, making your calculation easier.

> **NCTM Data Analysis and Probability** Understand and apply basic concepts of probability.

Certification Prep

Sharpen your test-taking skills to improve your kitchen certification program score.

Directions Read the questions. Then, read the answer choices and choose the best possible answer for each.

14. What grade of fruit is purchased for fresh fruit salad?

   a. U.S. Fancy   **c.** U.S. Extra Standard

   b. U.S. Choice   **d.** U.S. Standard

15. What type of potato is ideal for baking and deep frying?

   a. russet   **c.** yukon

   b. red   **d.** sweet

Test-Taking Tip
When you evaluate choices, locate the words you know right away and determine whether they fit with the question. If not, you can dismiss them right away.

Review and Applications

Real-World Skills and Applications

Interpersonal and Collaborative Skills

16. Global Cuisine Follow your teacher's instructions to break into teams. Imagine that you are the staff of a new restaurant. As a team, create five dishes featuring fruit, vegetables, or legumes from other cultures. Share your dishes.

Self-Management Skills

17. Estimate Juice Needs Imagine that your foodservice operation serves freshly squeezed orange juice at breakfast. Each glass is 6 ounces and you expect about 25 customers for breakfast. Find out how to make fresh-squeezed juice and estimate how many oranges you will need for one day's breakfast.

Technology Applications

18. Use the Internet Use the Internet to find information about legumes. Learn five interesting pieces of information that you did not know before about legumes. Share what you have learned with the class. List the Web sites where you found the information.

Financial Literacy

19. Cost per Ounce Often, package sizes of food vary and it is difficult to comparison shop for the best value. Most packages are labeled in ounces, however, so to comparison shop you must determine the cost per ounce. Which is a better bargain on pre-prepared fruit salad: an 8-ounce package for $1.50, a 12-ounce container for $1.75, or a 16-ounce container for $2?

Culinary Lab

Use the culinary skills you have learned in this chapter.

Cook Fruits or Vegetables

20. Compare Cooking Methods Working in teams, you will compare the results of cooking fruits or vegetables for different lengths of time.

A. Choose your fruit or vegetable. Choose a fruit or vegetable to use for the lab. Create a chart like the one shown below.

Cooking Time	Texture of Fruit or Vegetable	Color of Fruit or Vegetable	Flavor of Fruit or Vegetable
5 Minutes			
10 Minutes			
20 Minutes			

B. Begin cooking. Prepare the fruit or vegetable for cooking, and then simmer for 5 minutes. After 5 minutes, remove one serving of the fruit or vegetable to a plate.

C. Taste test. Examine this serving of your fruit or vegetable and record your responses on the chart. Taste the fruit or vegetable and record the flavor changes.

D. Continue cooking. Repeat steps B and C twice more, filling in the chart with your observations each time.

Create Your Evaluation

Answer the following questions as you review the observations on your chart:

- What conclusions can you draw about cooking times?
- Which stage of cooking did you prefer for the doneness of this fruit or vegetable?
- How does the length of cooking time and the cooking method impact a foodservice operation?

Chefs and Cooks

Chefs and cooks determine the fate of a restaurant's reputation.

Whether a restaurant prides itself on home-style cooking or international dishes, it relies on the talent and expertise of its chefs and cooks. Depending upon the type and size of the establishment, chefs usually supervise the work of cooks.

Chefs and cooks rely on their judgment and experience as they constantly taste, smell, and season food being prepared in their kitchens. They must be able to work independently, as members of a team, under extreme pressure, and in crowded spaces. They make sure the food tastes good and is visually appealing.

Ryan Marcoux, Sous Chef

Q **Describe your job.**

A I am sous chef for Sel de la Terre, but recently my job description has become a little confusing because I am helping Sel de la Terre open a new restaurant. So, right now, I cook 50% of the time, but once we open the new location, I will cook 80% of the time.

Q **What is your typical work day like?**

A I go in at noon and work with the invoices, recipes, and menus. I meet with the head chef for the new location. I also meet with the wait staff to talk about our menu changes and prix fix for the day. During service, I do back expo and swing, which means I call the tickets to the hot line and help whoever is in the weeds.

Q **Why did you choose your career?**

A First, I love food. Second, I think some people are born to be in the kitchen, and I am one of them. Being a chef is a lifestyle. It takes a certain breed to do what we do.

Q **What education did you receive?**

A I earned a degree in Culinary Arts. This helped me with my fundamental knowledge of cooking but more importantly, it helped me understand how to manage a kitchen.

Q **How did you find your current job?**

A The Nicas family, who owns The Castle Restaurant, gave me my start. I completed a four-year apprenticeship, working there 40-plus hours a week while in school. This enabled me to show my commitment to this industry and gave me a solid résumé and great recommendations.

Q **What skills are most important to your job?**

A I think time management and organization are the most important skills because these help you focus on details, and details are what make the difference.

Career Ingredients

Education or Training	Most employers require a culinary degree, and restaurant experience is usually a necessity.
Academic Skills Required	English Language Arts, Mathematics
Aptitudes, Abilities, and Skills	In-depth knowledge of the food industry, good eye-hand coordination, strong interpersonal and leadership skills, planning and organizational skills, ability to work independently and as a team, and ability to handle pressure.
Workplace Safety	Basic kitchen safety, sanitation, and food handling rules must be followed.
Career Outlook	Openings will be plentiful for years to come as the foodservice industry expands.
Career Path	Advancement depends on skill, training, and work experience. Chefs with supervisory experience may advance to executive chef.

Career Pathways

Executive chefs	Highly-skilled chefs with years of experience. Their duties include hiring and supervising cooking staff, planning menus, and ordering food.
Sous chefs	Also known as area chefs, they are in charge of running the kitchen. They assist the executive chef and make sure that the staff is cooking, portioning, and garnishing food properly.
Sauce chefs	Prepare fish, stews, sautéed dishes, braised or roasted entrees, and sauces.
Garde manger chefs	Cold-food chefs who prepare appetizers, salads, ice carvings, buffets, and cold meat preparations.
Roast cooks	Specialize in oven-roasted, baked, fried, and grilled items.
Vegetable cooks	Cooks who specialize in pastas, vegetables, and soups.
Pastry chefs	Trained in the art of making hot, cold, and frozen pastries and breads.
Restaurant chefs	Known as line cooks, they are responsible for à la carte dishes.
Tournants	Cooks who take the place of absent staff members.

In a very large foodservice operation, the following could also be present: **soup cook**, **legume cook**, **fish cook**, **hors d'oeuvre cook**, **buffet cook**, **butcher**, **preserver cook**, **grill cook**, **fry cook**, and **staff cook**.

Critical Thinking What classes have you taken in school that might help you prepare for a career as a chef or cook?

Culinary certification programs include cooking techniques. Develop a recipe for a pasta dish, making sure it is both creative and healthful. The dish should be visually appealing, taste good, and incorporate a variety of ingredients.

COMPETITION
★ ★ ★ ★ ★
PRACTICE

Imagine you have been hired as a new vegetable cook, and the executive chef has asked you to prepare a new pasta dish. Prepare the dish you developed for the Get Certified practice. All preparation must be done within a time period specified by your teacher. Evaluate your efforts based on the following rating scale:

1 = Poor; 2 = Fair; 3 = Good; 4 = Great

Judge your menu on:

- Whether you finished your dish on time.
- The flavor of your dish and the ingredients you included.
- The visual appeal of your dish.

Local and Seasonal Foods

Many restaurant customers want meals that include fresh, local ingredients and foods. Using local, seasonal ingredients can make your menu more attractive.

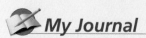

My Journal

If you completed the journal entry from page 373, refer to it to see if you have used any local or seasonal ingredients in your cooking. Add any additional notes about how you can use these ingredients to spice up your culinary creations.

English Language Arts

NCTE 4 Use written language to communicate effectively.

NCTE 7 Conduct research and gather, evaluate, and synthesize data to communicate discoveries.

Project Assignment

In this project, you will:

- Choose an ingredient or food that is raised or produced in your area or region.
- Conduct research about the ingredient or food you have chosen.
- Identify and interview someone about your ingredient or food.
- Prepare a presentation to share what you have learned with your class.

Applied Culinary Skills Behind the Project

Your success in culinary arts will depend on you skills. Skills you will use in this project include:

➤ Selecting ingredients.
➤ Choosing recipes.
➤ Understanding moist and dry cooking methods.
➤ Understanding safety and sanitation.
➤ Choosing seasonings, flavorings, and herbs.

English Language Arts Skills Behind the Project

The English Language Arts skills you will use for this project are writing, interviewing, and speaking skills. Remember these key concepts:

Writing Skills
➤ Use complete sentences.
➤ Use correct spelling and grammar.
➤ Organize your interview questions in the order you want to ask them.

Interviewing Skills
➤ Record interview responses and take notes.
➤ Listen attentively.
➤ When you transcribe your notes, write in complete sentences and use correct spelling and grammar.

Speaking Skills
➤ Speak clearly and concisely.
➤ Be sensitive to the needs of your audience.
➤ Use standard English to communicate.

Step 1 Choose and Research Your Ingredient

Choose and research one ingredient or food that is produced in your area or region. Write a summary of your research to:

- Describe the characteristics of your ingredient or food.
- Explain how, when, and where your ingredient or food is typically produced.
- Identify and lists two recipes that use your ingredient or food.
- Describe moist and dry cooking methods for your chosen ingredient or food.
- List any safety and sanitation concerns.
- Review seasonings, flavorings, and herbs that work well with your chosen ingredient or food.

Step 2 Plan Your Interview

Use the results of your research to write a list of interview questions to ask a local chef about your ingredient or food. Your questions might include:

- How would you describe the characteristics of the ingredient or food?
- What do you think are the best methods for preparing the ingredient or food?
- In what recipes have you used the ingredient or food?
- Would you choose this ingredient or food over other similar ingredients or foods?

Step 3 Connect with Your Community

Identify a local chef you can interview about your ingredient or food. Conduct your interview using the questions you prepared in Step 2. Take notes during the interview and write a summary of the interview.

Culinary Project Checklist

Plan

✓ Select and research your topic and summarize your findings.

✓ Plan and write your interview questions.

✓ Interview a chef and write a summary of the information you learned.

Present

✓ Make a presentation to your class to discuss the results of your research and your interview.

✓ Invite students to ask any questions they may have. Answer these questions.

✓ When students ask you questions, demonstrate in your answers that you respect their perspectives.

✓ Turn in the summary of your research, your interview questions, and the summary of the interview to your teacher.

Step 4 Create Your Report

Use the Culinary Project Checklist to plan and give an oral report to share what you have learned with your classmates.

Step 5 Evaluate Your Culinary and Academic Skills

Your project will be evaluated based on:

- Content and organization of your information.
- Proper use of standard English.
- Mechanics—presentation and neatness.
- Speaking and listening skills.

 Rubric Go to this book's Online Learning Center at **glencoe.com** for a rubric you can use to evaluate your final project.

JOHNSON & WALES
U N I V E R S I T Y

 Expert Advice Go to this book's Online Learning Center at **glencoe.com** to read an article by a culinary expert from Johnson & Wales University about how to find local and sustainable foods in your area.

Baking and Pastry Applications

Chapter

26 Baking Techniques

27 Yeast Breads and Rolls

28 Quick Breads

29 Desserts

EXPLORE THE PHOTO

Baking and pastry chefs can make many tasty treats. *What do you think are the differences between cooking and baking?*

EXPLORE THE PHOTO ANSWER Generally, it is easier to alter recipes slightly when cooking for a desired flavor, texture, or color. Baking formulas must be followed exactly, however, or the baked good may not turn out as expected.

Creative Desserts

After completing this unit, you will know how to prepare a variety of baked goods and desserts. In your unit culinary project, you will choose and research a dessert recipe. Then, you will create a visual presentation to show how to make a dramatic dessert presentation.

My Journal

Write a journal entry about special desserts that you have eaten.

● What desserts have you tried?
● What made the desserts special?
● Did the desserts enhance a special event?

JOHNSON & WALES
U N I V E R S I T Y

"I feel that any job can be taught given enough time. However, without drive and determination, you cannot grow your career."

Kendra Mellar
Assistant Chocolatier
Garrison Confections

Baking Techniques

SECTIONS

26.1 Bakeshop Formulas and Equipment

26.2 Bakeshop Ingredients

WRITING ACTIVITY

Brochure

A brochure is a persuasive document that advertises for something or conveys information in small amounts. Imagine that you are opening a bakery in a small community. Write a brochure introducing the local residents to your bakery.

Writing Tips

1 Keep your mind on the purpose of the brochure.

2 Develop the text first, then figure out the design.

3 Try to appeal to the customers' emotions as well as their logic.

EXPLORE THE PHOTO

Bakeshops have special equipment and ingredients. *Can you name some special bakeshop equipment?*

WRITING ACTIVITY ANSWER
Brochures should be persuasive, informative, and eye-catching.

EXPLORE THE PHOTO ANSWER
Students might name any equipment particular to bakeshops, such as bakeware, stand mixer, or spatulas.

Bakeshop Formulas and Equipment

Reading Guide

 Before You Read

Stay Engaged One way to stay engaged when reading is to turn each of the headings into a question, then read the section to find the answers. For example, "Use a Balance Scale" might be, "How do you properly use a balance scale?"

Read to Learn

Key Concepts
- **Explain** baking formulas.
- **Describe** the function of various bakeshop equipment.
- **Identify** bakeshop tools.

Main Idea
Baking requires precise measurement and accuracy to achieve a good result. It also requires special baking equipment to produce professional quality products.

Content Vocabulary
- scaling
- percentage
- sheeter
- stack oven
- convection oven
- reel oven
- springform pan
- tart pan
- sheet pan
- mold
- ring

Academic Vocabulary
- imprecise
- invaluable

Graphic Organizer
As you read, use this chart to list the three different types of ovens used in bakeshops and their characteristics.

Type of Oven	Characteristics

 Graphic Organizer Go to this book's Online Learning Center at **glencoe.com** for a printable graphic organizer.

ACADEMIC STANDARDS

 English Language Arts
NCTE 5 Use different writing process elements to communicate effectively.

 Mathematics
NCTM Number and Operations Compute fluently and make reasonable estimates.

NCTE National Council of Teachers of English

NCTM National Council of Teachers of Mathematics

NSES National Science Education Standards

NCSS National Council for the Social Studies

GRAPHIC ORGANIZER ANSWER Deck oven: Free-standing rectangular oven with stacked compartments. Convection oven: Oven with a fan to circulate hot air. Reel oven: Oven with shelves that rotate.

Bakeshop Formulas

Baking is an exact science that requires precise measuring and accuracy. Baking also requires the use of special baking equipment and smallwares to produce professional products. The type of equipment found in a bakeshop is customized for that particular operation. The size of the operation and how many baked goods it produces will determine the need for specific equipment and tools.

Although you may add a dash of this and a pinch of that when you make a pot of chili, you will never use such **imprecise**, or inexact, measurements in a commercial bakeshop. A baker uses a formula. This is a recipe that includes the exact amount of each ingredient. These amounts are often listed as percentages of the total formula. The success of a formula is determined in large part by accurate ingredient measurement and following instructions carefully.

Accuracy is crucial in baking because most baked products are made from the same basic ingredients: flour, liquids, fat, sugar and sweeteners, eggs, leavening agents, and flavorings. You will learn more about these ingredients in Section 26.2. The difference between two baked products is often the proportion of each ingredient in the formula. If the proportions are off, you will end up with a different product or an unacceptable product. That is why it is important to read through a formula several times to make certain you understand all of the instructions.

It is also important to add ingredients in the exact order specified in the formula. Remember, you cannot make adjustments once an item goes into the oven. A baked product's ingredients must be measured accurately from the start.

Bakeshop Measurements

Bakeshop ingredients are measured by weight or volume. Volume is the space an ingredient occupies. Weight measures the mass or heaviness of something. These two

Precise Baking You must use precise measurements to create beautiful baked products. *What is the difference between baked products?*

PHOTO CAPTION ANSWER Because most baked goods have the same basic ingredients, the difference is usually only the proportion of ingredients.

methods of measurement often produce very different results. For example, if a formula calls for 8 ounces of flour, you cannot substitute 1 cup of flour. Assuming that 8 ounces is the same as 1 cup can ruin the final product.

Because accurate and consistent measurement is so important, bakers tend to weigh most ingredients on a balance scale. Bakers refer to weighing as **scaling**. Many of the dry ingredients used in baking, such as flour, are easily and accurately weighed. Liquid ingredients, such as eggs and milk, can also be weighed, but are sometimes measured. Corn syrup, honey, and molasses are always weighed. Measuring ingredients by weight gives consistent, reliable results.

Use a Balance Scale

Professional bakers use a balance scale or a digital electronic scale to measure ingredients for a baked good formula. When you use a balance scale, it must balance before and again after you use it.

To properly use a balance scale, follow these steps:

1. Place the scale scoop or container on the left side of the scale. You can also use waxed paper if the ingredient amount is small.
2. It is important to compensate for the weight of the scoop or container. Do this by placing pound weights on the right side of the scale and adjusting the ounce weights on the horizontal bar until the left and right sides balance. Once this is done, you can measure ingredients.
3. To get a specific amount of an ingredient, add weights to the right side of the scale that equal the desired weight of the ingredient. You may have to make adjustments using the scale and the ounce weights on the horizontal bar.
4. Add the ingredient to the scoop, container, or waxed paper on the left side of the scale until the scale is balanced.

Gourmet Math

The Baker's Percentage

The baker's percentage allows you to change the yield of a formula without changing the quality of the final product. You first need to calculate the weight of flour for the new yield. Then, multiply each ingredient's baker's percentage by the new flour weight to find the new weights for each ingredient.

Convert the formula for Quick Coffee Cake below to yield a total of 10 pounds.

Ingredient	Amount	Baker's Percentage
Pastry flour	1 lb., 12 oz.	100%
Whole eggs	10 oz.	36%
Vegetable oil	12 oz.	43%
Water	1 lb., 8 oz.	86%
Baking powder	1 ¼ oz.	4%
Dried milk solids	3 oz.	11%
Salt	½ oz.	2%
Granulated sugar	1 lb., 8 oz.	86%
TOTAL	6 lbs., 6 ¾ oz.	368%

Math Concept **Equivalent Weights** There are 16 ounces in 1 pound. Convert pounds to ounces by multiplying by 16. Convert ounces to pounds by dividing by 16, writing the remainder as ounces. For example, 20 ounces equates to 1 pound, 4 ounces.

Starting Hint Convert the new yield to ounces: 10 pounds $\times$ 16 = 160 ounces. Because the baker's percentages remain the same, you know that in the new formula, 160 ounces is 368% of the weight of flour. Thus, you can calculate the new flour weight by dividing 160 ounces by 368% (160 $\div$ 3.68). Then, find the new weight of each of the other ingredients by multiplying their percentages by the new weight of the flour. Round all weights to the nearest one.

NCTM Number and Operations Compute fluently and make reasonable estimates.

Use Math Skills

Bakers often convert an entire formula to make the desired number of servings.

What if a cake formula makes five 8-inch cakes, but the bakeshop where you work needs to make 10 cakes?

Original Formula (Five 8-inch; Cakes)		New Formula (10 8-inch; Cakes)
2 lbs.	egg whites	4 lbs.
12 oz.	cake flour	1 lb., 8 oz.
12 oz.	confectioners' sugar	1 lb., 8 oz.
¼ oz.	cream of tartar	½ oz.
1 lb., 4 oz.	granulated sugar	2 lbs., 8 oz.
⅛ oz.	salt	¼ oz.
¼ oz.	vanilla extract	½ oz.
⅛ oz.	almond extract	¼ oz.

Notice that the new formula simply doubles each ingredient. That is because you are making 10 8-inch cakes instead of five.

Many professional bakers use formulas that contain percentages. A **percentage** is a rate or proportion of 100. In other words, if 5% of the eggs are cracked, this means that 5 out of 100 eggs are cracked. Formulas are often expressed in baker's percentages. A baker's percentage means that each ingredient is a certain percentage of the weight of the total flour in the formula. The weight of flour is important because it is the core ingredient of baked goods.

For example, if one kind of flour is used in a formula, its weight is 100%. If two kinds of flour are used in a formula, their total weight is 100%. To find the percentage of each ingredient used in a formula, all ingredients must be expressed in the same unit, such as pounds. Once all the units are the same, you can use this calculation:

$$\frac{\text{weight of ingredient}}{\text{weight of flour}} \times 100\% = \% \text{ of ingredient}$$

For example, imagine you are trying to find the percentage of water used in a formula for bread dough. The formula calls for 15 pounds of bread flour and 9 pounds of water. Calculate the percentage as follows:

$$\frac{9 \text{ lb. (weight of water)}}{15 \text{ lb. (weight of flour)}} \times 100\% = 60\% \text{ water}$$

So, the baker's percentage of water is 60%.

PHOTO CAPTION ANSWER The spiral dough hook replicates hand kneading and is used for kneading yeast doughs.

Baker's percentages allow you to compare the weight of each ingredient. What is especially convenient about baker's percentages is that one ingredient can be changed without recalculating percentages for each ingredient. Remember that the total percentages of all the ingredients will always add up to more than 100%.

Reading Check Explain Why is accurate measurement so important in baking?

Large Bakeshop Equipment

Bakeshop equipment is exposed to wet, sticky ingredients and extreme changes in temperature. It is important for bakeshop equipment to be durable, of good quality, and well maintained. You must keep all bakeshop equipment and tools clean and maintained. (See Chapter 9 for more information.)

Mixers

Mixers are essential to every bakeshop. They perform a variety of functions. They are used to mix, knead, or whip batters and doughs. The most common mixer in the bakeshop is the bench, or tabletop, mixer. It comes with three basic attachments: a spiral dough hook, a flat beater or paddle, and a whip.

There are bench mixers for small volumes and floor mixers for larger volumes. Mixer capacity ranges from 5 to 140 quarts. Commercial bakeshops typically use floor models with at least a 30-quart capacity. These mixers have adapter rings that allow you to use several different-size bowls on one machine.

Sheeter

A **sheeter** is a piece of equipment that rolls out large pieces of dough to a desired thickness. It is used mostly for rolling and folding doughs, such as puff pastries, croissants, and Danish pastries. It also can be used to flatten pie or pizza dough.

Climate Control Proofing cabinets keep dough at a consistent temperature while it rises prior to baking. *What two elements does a proofing cabinet control?*

Dough Sheeters Industrial sheeters are used to roll and fold doughs. *What else could a sheeter do?*

Proofing Cabinets

A proofing cabinet, also called a proofer, is a freestanding metal box on wheels that is temperature- and humidity-controlled. Proofing cabinets can be used to keep baked products warm or to proof yeast doughs. A proofing cabinet allows dough to rise slowly in a humidity controlled, low-heat environment before it is baked. This is vital to creating baked products of high quality.

Bakery Ovens

Commercial ovens are **invaluable**, or extremely helpful, pieces of equipment in the bakeshop. These ovens are used to produce a large variety of baked products. Both electric and gas models can be equipped with convection fans that circulate the oven's heated air. Some ovens even come with steam injection for proper volume and crust development in bread baking. Certain specialty bread bakers use old-world types of ovens that are brick-lined and fueled by wood.

Deck Oven

This freestanding rectangular oven, also known as a **stack oven**, has a series of well-insulated compartments stacked on top of one another. Because each of these shelves has a separate door and temperature control, you can bake a variety of items at once. Deck ovens are used to bake a variety of items. You will find the deck oven in most bakeries and pizza kitchens.

Deck ovens offer bakers a lot of flexibility. Bakers who use deck ovens can produce large or small amounts of baked goods because each deck has a separate control. Different products can be baked in each deck.

Convection Oven

A **convection oven** has a fan that circulates the oven's heated air. This fan allows you to cook foods in about 30% less time and at temperatures approximately 25° to 35° lower than temperatures in a conventional oven. Convection ovens range in size, and are available in either gas or electric models.

Dual Baking Deck ovens are used in high-volume baking to cook a variety of products at once. *Where would you most likely find deck ovens?*

PHOTO CAPTION ANSWER You would most likely find deck ovens in bakeries and pizza restaurants.

Sheet Pan

Soufflé Mold

Brioche Pan

Ramekin

Fluted, Oblong Tart Pan

Tube Pan

Muffin Pan

Springform Pan

Tart Pan

Rings

Cake Frames

Pans and Molds The type of mold or pan used will depend on the type of baked good that is being made. *What type of pan or mold would you commonly choose to bake a cheesecake?*

PHOTO CAPTION ANSWER You would choose a springform pan to bake a cheesecake.

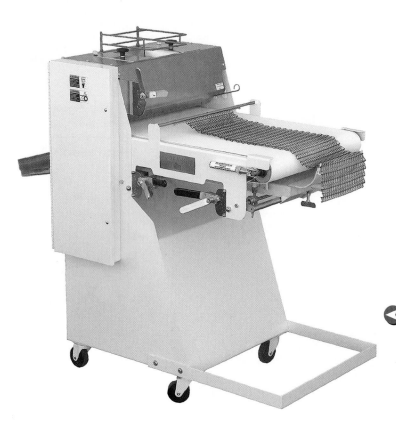

 **Bread Molder** This bread molder can mold bread products, and can produce rolls, buns, or specialty breads. *What type of establishment would be likely to use this machine?*

Reel Oven

With shelves that move or rotate like a Ferris wheel, a **reel oven** is used when all items need the same baking conditions. In other words, a reel oven bakes a quantity of similar items evenly. All items are exposed to the same temperature and humidity.

A reel oven is also called a rotating or revolving oven because its shelves rotate within the oven chamber. Also, the movement of the baked goods creates convection currents similar to those made by a convection fan. Reel ovens are easier to load and unload than deck ovens because you do not have to bend down or reach up.

Reading Check Define What is a sheeter?

Bakeshop Smallwares

A commercial bakeshop needs many different hand tools for cutting, molding, scooping, dividing, and finishing. Many tools are used to form, cut, glaze, and decorate different baked products. Depending on the function of a particular bakeshop, however, the equipment used may vary greatly.

Pans, Molds, and Rings

Bakeshop pans are available in many types, sizes, shapes, and thicknesses. Choosing the correct pan for the job is important because it can affect the final outcome of the product. The surface of a pan will affect the outcome of the product, too. A pan with a shiny surface will reflect some heat away during the baking process so there is less surface browning. A pan with a darker surface tends to retain the heat.

The correct size and shape of baking pan is important in obtaining good texture, height, and appearance. If you put too much batter in a cake pan, the cake will rise and spill over the top. The cake may also collapse. On the other hand, if the pan is too large or the sides too high, the sides will shield the batter from the heat of the oven and slow down the baking process. This results in an overbrowned cake with poor volume and texture.

READING CHECK ANSWER A sheeter is a piece of equipment that rolls out large pieces of dough to a desired thickness.

PHOTO CAPTION ANSWER A large bakery, or bread and roll manufacturer, would be most likely to use a bread molder.

Baking and Pastry Tools

Pastry Bags Pastry bags can be made of nylon, plastic-lined cotton, canvas, polyester, or plastic. They are cone-shaped with two open ends. The smaller end is pointed and can be fitted with decorator tips of different sizes and shapes. The larger end can be filled with doughs, fillings, icing, or whipped cream. When the bag is squeezed, the contents are forced through the decorator tip.

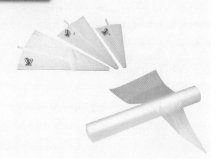

Pastry Brushes These flat-edged brushes are used to brush liquids such as butter on dough before, during, or after cooking.

Pastry Pattern Cutters Pastry pattern cutters are used to cut dough into specific shapes.

Bench Scraper Also called a dough cutter, this handheld rectangular tool has a stainless steel blade and a handle made of slip-resistant plastic or wood. The bench scraper can be used to clean and scrape surfaces and to cut and portion dough.

Rolling Pins These long, cylindrical tools are used to roll out bread and pastry doughs and shape cookies. The bakers' rolling pin is made from hardwood and has handles on each side. The French rolling pin is also made from hardwood, but does not have handles. Rolling pins should not be submerged in water for cleaning.

Sanitation Check

✓ Sanitize Pastry Bags

If you use a non-disposable pastry bag, wash the bag in warm, soapy water after each use. To do this, remove the decorator tip, and turn the bag inside out. Wash both the bag and tip thoroughly. Then, rinse and sanitize them. Stretch and hang the bag to let it air dry.

CRITICAL THINKING *What should you do if you want to use a pastry bag, but it has not been sanitized?*

Some pans have removable bottoms that make it easier to free the baked product. A **springform pan** has a clamp that is used to release the pan's bottom from its circular wall. These pans are used to bake cheesecakes.

Some tart pans also have removable bottoms. A **tart pan** is a shallow pan that ranges in diameter from 4½ to 12½ inches. They can be round, square, or rectangular and have fluted sides that slope slightly.

Sheet pans are another common bakeshop pan. A **sheet pan** is a shallow, rectangular pan that comes in full, half, and quarter sizes. Sheet pans are used to make a variety of baked goods, including rolls, biscuits, and cookies.

A **mold** is a pan with a distinctive shape. They range from small, round, ceramic pans to long, narrow molds used for breads. A **ring** is a type of container that has no bottom. They come in various heights and are usually round, but they can also be square.

 **Analyze** How does a pan's surface affect the outcome of the baked product?

SECTION 26.1 After You Read

Review Key Concepts

1. **Explain** how to use a balance scale.
2. **Describe** the function of a proofing cabinet.
3. **Identify** different types of pans used in a bakeshop.

Practice Culinary Academics

English Language Arts

4. Imagine that you are going to be a pastry chef in a shop that will make all different types of specialty cupcakes. Write a letter to your business partner detailing which equipment you want to be purchased for the shop, and why. Be sure to explain the purpose of each piece of equipment. Your letter should be in a standard business letter format. Check your grammar and spelling before turning in your letter.

> **NCTE 5** Use different writing process elements to communicate effectively.

Mathematics

5. Calculate the baker's percentages for the following bread formula: Bread flour, 3 kilograms; rye flour, 1 kilogram; water, 2.8 kilograms; yeast, 80 grams; salt, 120 grams. Total, 7 kilograms.

Math Concept **Metric Equivalents** In the metric system, the prefix kilo- indicates 1,000. Thus, 1 kilogram equals 1,000 grams. To convert kilograms to grams, multiply by 1,000. To convert grams to kilograms, divide by 1,000.

Starting Hint Remember, both types of flour added together will equal 100%. Thus, 100% = 3 kilograms + 1 kilogram = 4 kilograms. Divide each weight by 4 kilograms and multiply by 100%. You will need to convert grams to kilograms for the salt and yeast.

> **NCTM Number and Operations** Compute fluently and make reasonable estimates.

 Check your answers at this book's Online Learning Center at **glencoe.com**.

SANITATION CHECK ANSWER You should wash the bag in warm, soapy water, rinse it, and sanitize it.

READING CHECK ANSWER A pan with a shiny surface will reflect heat away and cause less surface browning. A pan with a darker surface will retain heat and cause a deeper color.

Bakeshop Ingredients

Reading Guide

 Before You Read

Preview Understanding causes and effects can help clarify connections. A cause is an event or action that makes something happen. An effect is a result of a cause. Ask yourself, "Why does this happen?" to help you recognize cause-and-effect relationships in this section.

Read to Learn

Key Concepts

- **Identify** the different categories of ingredients and their roles in the baking process.
- **Compare and contrast** different dough mixing methods.

Main Idea

The basic ingredients in baking are flour, liquids, fat, sugar and sweeteners, eggs, leavening agents, and flavorings. The ingredients determine the flavor, texture, and visual appeal of a baked good.

Content Vocabulary

- hard wheat flour
- gluten
- crumb
- soft wheat flour
- bread flour
- cake flour
- pastry flour
- staling
- dried milk solids
- shortening
- oil
- leavening agent
- baking soda
- baking powder
- yeast
- fermentation
- dough
- beat
- blend
- cream
- cut-in
- fold
- knead
- sift
- stir
- whip

Academic Vocabulary

- surround
- contribution

Graphic Organizer

Before you read, use a KWL chart to write down three things that you already know about bakeshop ingredients and three things you would like to learn. As you read, write what you have learned.

What I Know	What I Want to Know	What I Learned

 Graphic Organizer Go to this book's Online Learning Center at **glencoe.com** for a printable graphic organizer.

GRAPHIC ORGANIZER ANSWER This graphic organizer prompts students to write what they already know and note new information as they read.

Each basic baking ingredient has a specific function.

ACADEMIC STANDARDS

 English Language Arts
NCTE 4 Use written language to communicate effectively.

Mathematics
NCTM Algebra Use mathematical models to represent and understand quantitative relationships.

 Science
NSES F Develop an understanding of personal and community health.

 Social Studies
NCSS II D Time, Continuity, and Change Employ processes to validate and weigh evidence for claims.

....

NCTE National Council of Teachers of English

NCTM National Council of Teachers of Mathematics

NSES National Science Education Standards

NCSS National Council for the Social Studies

Basic Ingredients

From a simple list of ingredients such as flour, liquids, fat, sugar and sweeteners, eggs, leavening agents, and flavorings, you can make an endless variety of baked products. Ingredients are more than just parts of a baking formula. They add flavor, texture, and visual appeal to all types of baked products. In this section, you will learn about basic baking ingredients and mixing techniques.

Use Exact Ingredients

Baking, unlike cooking, leaves little margin for error. You cannot just substitute the same amount of cake flour for bread flour and expect to come up with the same end result. To become a successful baker, you must understand how key ingredients work together. Baking formulas have been developed using exact types of ingredients. If the formula is not followed precisely, the product's texture and taste will be affected.

Wheat Flour

Wheat flour is the main ingredient in many baked goods. The proteins and starch in flour give these products structure. The classification of flour is based on the type of wheat it comes from: soft or hard. **Hard wheat flour** comes from kernels that are firm, tough, and difficult to cut. Bread flour is one type of hard wheat flour.

Hard wheat has a high protein content. When wheat flour is mixed with water, certain proteins form gluten. **Gluten** is a firm, elastic substance that affects the texture of baked products. The higher a flour's protein content, the more potential it has to form gluten.

Gluten is the substance that makes bread dough strong and elastic. Without gluten, you could not stretch the dough and hold in the gases that make it rise. The dough would collapse, resulting in poor volume and a coarse crumb. **Crumb** is the internal texture of a baked product.

Soft wheat flour, such as cake flour and pastry flour, comes from a soft wheat kernel. This type of flour has a low protein content, making it ideal for tender baked products such as cookies and pastries. Bread flour, cake flour, and pastry flour are all types of wheat flour.

Bread Flour Breadmakers use **bread flour**. It has a high gluten-forming protein content. These proteins allow the bread to rise fully and develop a fine crumb. They also give the bread a chewier, firmer texture. Bread flour is used to make yeast breads, pizza, and bagels.

Cake Flour **Cake flour** is lower in protein than bread flour and pastry flour. Cake flour produces a softer and more tender product than bread flour. Cake flour is bleached with chlorine ('klȯr-ˌēn) to help produce a fine, white crumb in cakes.

Pastry Flour The protein content of **pastry flour** is between that of bread flour and cake flour. It is used in pie dough, cookies, muffins, and quick breads. It is used for cakes only if cake flour is unavailable.

Other types of flours used in the bakeshop are listed in **Figure 26.1** on page 689.

Liquids

Liquids are an essential part of baking. The most common liquids used in baking are water, milk, and cream. Liquids can also be found in eggs, sugar syrups, and butter, which contains about 15% water.

Accurate measurement of liquids is important because too much or too little can affect the outcome of the baked product. For example, adding too much water in pie dough will cause excess gluten formation, which may result in a tough texture.

Water Water is the most common liquid ingredient used in baking, especially for breads. It has many uses besides moistening dry ingredients. Water is necessary for gluten structure to form in flour. Also, water temperature is used to adjust temperatures in dough. This applies to bread dough in particular, where dough temperature is important. Because water is tasteless, odorless, and colorless, it does not affect the flavor or color of baked products. It also adds no fat or calories.

FIGURE 26.1 **Flour Characteristics**

Flour Choices Different types of flour are used for different types of baked goods.
Why might you want to choose a non-wheat flour for some baked goods?

Other Types of Flour	Characteristics
Whole-wheat flour	• Dark flour made from whole-wheat grains; only the outer hull is removed • Fine or coarse ground • May be combined with bread flour or all-purpose flour for better volume and milder flavor • High protein, but moderate gluten content • Often combined with bread flour for better gluten structure in breads
Cracked wheat flour	• Dark flour made from cut, not ground, whole-wheat grains • Usually soaked or partially cooked before adding to dough to soften the flour • Must be mixed with bread flour or whole-wheat flour when used in baked goods
Non-wheat flours	• Whole or milled flours made from corn, rye, barley, buckwheat, oat, and other grains as well as from potatoes and soybeans • Varying colors, textures, and gluten levels • Usually mixed with bread flour to provide a better gluten structure.

Milk and Cream Milk is another important liquid ingredient. Its protein, fat, and sugar content make it a valuable addition to baked products, ice creams, and custards. Milk also improves the flavor and texture of bread and other baked goods.

Some of the improvements milk can make include:

● Creating a soft, rather than crispy, crust on items such as cream puffs or éclairs (ā-'klers).

● Adding more color or flavor to crusts when it is applied to the surface of the baked product.

● Extending shelf life by delaying staling. **Staling** is the process by which moisture is lost, causing a change in the texture and aroma of food. Staling causes the crumb to be dry and the crust to become soft and moist.

Dried milk solids are also used in baked goods. Since milkfat can reduce milk's shelf life, dried milk solids are usually purchased as nonfat dry milk. Nonfat dry milk can be reconstituted with water or used dry. If kept dry, it is easier to use and can be stored without refrigeration. You can sift it with dry ingredients or mix it with shortening, before you add the water separately.

Dairy products such as buttermilk, yogurt, and sour cream are also used in the bakeshop. These products contain live bacteria that convert milk sugar into acid. The acid in buttermilk, for example, provides a whiter, more tender crumb in biscuits.

Another common dairy product, heavy cream, has a high fat content. This fat content allows it to tenderize baked goods. Cream is often whipped for toppings, chilled desserts, and fillings such as pastry cream. It is used as a liquid ingredient in custards, sauces, and ice creams. (You will learn more about desserts in Chapter 29.)

Fats

During the baking process, fats **surround**, or enclose, the flour particles and prevent long strands of gluten from forming. This tenderizes the baked good. Fats also add to the flavor, moistness, browning, flakiness, and leavening, depending on the type of fat. In baking, solid fats are referred to as **shortening**. Purified oils are made solid by a process called hydrogenation. In hydrogenation, the oils are made

FIGURE CAPTION ANSWER Some people are allergic to the gluten produced by wheat flours, but can safely eat baked goods made with non-wheat flours.

solid by adding hydrogen to the oil. The most common types of fat used in the bakeshop include all-purpose shortening, emulsified shortening, oil, butter, and margarine.

Vegetable Shortening When most people hear the word shortening, they think of a solid, white, flavorless fat used for baking. This type of shortening, known as vegetable shortening, is made from purified oils that have been hydrogenated to make them solid and less likely to become rancid. Vegetable shortening has a fairly high melting point, which makes it ideal for forming flaky pie doughs. It is also a good choice for frying and for making cookies and cakes.

Emulsified Shortening Some shortenings contain emulsifiers. Emulsified shortenings are also called high-ratio shortenings because they allow the baker to add a high ratio of water and sugar to a cake or icing. Some high-ratio shortenings look like all-purpose shortenings.

High-ratio liquid shortenings look like creamy oils. Some cake formulas are designed to use high-ratio liquid shortenings. These cakes will be extra moist, airy, and tender and will have a longer shelf life than cakes made with other fats. Other fats cannot replace high-ratio liquid shortenings because of their unique characteristics.

Trans fat-free shortenings are also widely available on the market. Hydrogenated fats are responsible for most of the trans fats that people consume. Trans fat-free shortenings can provide a more healthful alternative.

Oil An **oil** is a fat that is extracted from plants such as soybeans, corn, peanuts, and cottonseed. They are liquid at room temperature and neutral in flavor and color because they are highly refined. Because oil blends more easily throughout a mixture, it can coat more strands of gluten. Therefore, oil causes baked products to be more tender. Oil is used in quick breads, some pie crusts, deep-fried products like doughnuts, and rich sponge cakes like chiffon (shi-'fän).

Butter Have you ever tasted a frosting that seemed to melt in your mouth? That frosting was probably made with butter. Butter can be purchased with or without salt. Unsalted butter is used in baking because of its pleasant flavor. Because butter is soft at room

PHOTO ANSWER CAPTION Wheat gluten allows leavening, or rising, and gives chewiness to baked products like bagels.

temperature, however, doughs made with butter are sometimes hard to handle. Butter is only 80% fat, so it produces a less tender baked product than shortening.

Margarine Margarine is typically a hydrogenated vegetable oil that has color, flavor, and water added. Margarines have improved over the years. While they cannot match butter's superior flavor, they are less likely to spoil and are usually lower in saturated fat. Margarines can be purchased either salted or unsalted.

Sugars and Sweeteners

Sugars and sweeteners add a sweet, pleasant flavor to baked products. Flavor, however, is not their only **contribution** to, or role in, baking. The other functions of sugars and sweeteners include:

- Creating a golden-brown color.
- Stabilizing mixtures such as beaten egg whites for meringue (mə-'raŋ).
- Providing food for yeast in yeast breads.
- Retaining moisture for a longer shelf life.
- Tenderizing baked products by weakening the gluten strands and delaying the action of other structure builders such as egg protein.
- Serving as a base for making icings.

Sugar is produced from sugarcane or sugar beets. The cane or beet is crushed to extract the juice. The juice is then filtered and gently heated to evaporate the water. Through a series of heat-induced steps, the sugar is crystallized ('kris-tə-ˌlīzd), or turned into crystals, and separated from the dark, thick molasses that forms. It must be refined to produce sugar grains of different sizes. Various sugars and sweeteners are used in the bakeshop.

⌒ Small Bites ⌒

Oil for Shortening? In general, oil should never be substituted for a solid shortening in baking formulas. It will result in baked goods with lower volume and pie crusts that lack flakiness and crumble easily. It is better to make sure that you have the proper bakeshop ingredients on hand before you begin to bake.

Molasses Molasses is the thick, sweet, dark liquid made from sugarcane juice. There are many grades of molasses available. Premium grades have a golden-brown color and a mild, sweet flavor. Lower grades are typically darker in color with a less sweet, stronger flavor. This stronger color and flavor is often desirable in baked products.

Brown Sugar Brown sugar is a soft-textured mixture of white sugar and molasses. It can be light or dark in color. Store brown sugar in air-tight containers to prevent moisture absorption.

Turbinado Sugar Turbinado sugar is raw sugar that has been steam-cleaned. Its coarse crystals are blond colored and have a delicate molasses flavor. Turbinado sugar is used in some baked products and beverages.

Coarse Sugar Coarse sugar, also known as sanding sugar, consists of large, coarse crystals that do not dissolve easily. It is used to decorate items such as doughnuts or cakes.

Granulated Sugar Regular granulated sugar is often referred to as extrafine white sugar or table sugar. It is the most common sugar used in the bakeshop. Granulated sugar is used in cooked icings, candies, and other baked products.

Confectioners' Sugar Confectioners' sugar, also known as powdered sugar, is granulated sugar that has been crushed into a fine powder. Confectioners' sugar also contains about 3% cornstarch, which helps keep the sugar from clumping. It is often used in uncooked icings and glazes and as a decorative dusting on baked products.

Superfine Sugar Superfine sugar is more finely granulated than regular white sugar. As a result, it dissolves almost instantly. Superfine sugar is perfect for making sweetened cold liquids and egg white meringues less gritty. Meringues can be used for such items as toppings on pies.

Corn Syrup Corn syrup is produced from the starch in corn. The starch granules are removed from corn kernels and treated with acids or enzymes to create a thick, sweet syrup.

Apple Wheat Germ Cake

YIELD: 8 SERVINGS
SERVING SIZE: 9 OZ.

Ingredients

2 ¼ c.	Whole wheat pastry flour
¼ c.	Non-fat dry milk solids
4 tsp.	Baking powder
1 tsp.	Salt
3 tsp.	Ground cinnamon
¾ c.	Wheat germ
1 c.	Honey
½ c.	Peanut oil
4 each	Eggs
1 tsp.	Orange rind, grated
1 tsp.	Vanilla extract
6 small	Sweet apples, peeled, cored, and thinly sliced

Method of Preparation

1. Preheat oven to 350°F (177°C).

2. Sift together in a bowl the flour, milk solids, baking powder, salt, and cinnamon.

3. In another bowl, combine the wheat germ, honey, peanut oil, eggs, orange rind, and vanilla, and stir into the dry ingredients. The batter will be liquid.

4. Place ⅓ of the batter in an oiled, 3-qt. baking dish and spread ½ of the sliced apples over the batter.

5. Top with another ⅓ of the batter and spread remaining apples over batter.

6. Top with the remaining batter.

7. Bake 40 to 45 minutes. Cover with aluminum foil if the cake starts to brown before it is baked.

8. Cool slightly in the pan and serve warm.

Cooking Technique

Combining

1. Prepare the components to be combined.

2. Add one to the other, using the appropriate mixing method (if needed).

Chef Notes

Wheat germ contains vitamin E, a powerful antioxidant. It is the fatty part of the wheat kernel.

Substitutions

- Although MacIntosh apples are recommended for this recipe, any apple variety may be used in its place.

International Flavor

Research the following recipes to discover what types of apples they use. Then, research the apples and write a paragraph on each type.

- Scandinavian Apple Cake (Scandinavia)
- Irish Potato Apple Cake (Ireland)
- Apfeltorte (Germany)

Glossary

Antioxidant substance that works against the chemical reactions to oxygen

Staple an item that is used or needed frequently

HACCP

- Store shell eggs at 41°F (5°C) or lower

Hazardous Foods

- Eggs

Nutrition

Calories 540	Calories from Fat 160

Total Fat 19g
  Saturated Fat 3.5g
  Trans Fat 0g
Cholesterol 120mg
Sodium 590mg
Total Carbohydrate 83g
  Fiber 9g
  Sugars 47g
Protein 11g

- Vitamin A 4%
- Vitamin C 10%
- Calcium 20%
- Iron 20%

Light corn syrup has no color, while dark corn syrup has a molasses-like flavor. Corn syrup does not crystallize easily, so it is a popular ingredient to use in frostings, candies, jams, and jellies.

Maple Syrup Maple syrup adds a unique flavor to baked products. It is made from the sap of a maple tree. Syrups are graded according to their color and flavor. The lighter and milder the syrup, the higher grade it will receive.

Honey Honey is a thick, sweet liquid made by bees from flower nectar ('nek-tər). The type of flower affects the final flavor and color of the honey. Honey is widely used to give baked products a distinct, sweet flavor. It should be stored in a cool, dry place. Refrigerated honey will crystallize and form a gooey mass. If this happens, the honey can be heated in the microwave in small amounts or in a pan of hot water over low heat.

Eggs

Eggs are the second most important ingredient in baked products. Eggs come in a variety of sizes. Formulas listing the amount of eggs by number instead of weight have based the formula on large eggs, which weigh about 2 ounces each.

Commercial bakeshops use egg yolks instead of whole eggs when they want a richer, more tender product. They also use egg whites in place of whole eggs when they bake low-fat products. Eggs serve these functions during baking.

- **Structure** Because of their protein content, eggs give structure to baked products such as cakes. They also help thicken some products such as custard sauces.
- **Emulsification** Egg yolks have natural emulsifiers that help blend ingredients smoothly.
- **Aeration** (,er-'ā-shən) Beaten or whipped eggs assist in leavening because they trap air that expands when heated, causing baked products to rise.

A TASTE OF HISTORY

1840
The first postage stamp is introduced in England

1847
The first commercial chocolate bar is produced

Chocolate

Long before chocolate was a sweet candy, it was a spicy drink dating back to the ancient Mayans and Aztecs. Later, Christopher Columbus brought the seeds from the cacao tree back home to Spain, and eventually the drink's popularity spread throughout Europe. Since then, new technologies and innovations have changed the texture and taste of chocolate, but it still remains one of the world's favorite flavors.

History Application

Everyone has his or her favorite chocolate bar. Create a survey that will identify which chocolate bar is a favorite of your family and friends. In the survey, ask them why they prefer a particular type. Gather the results and discuss them as a class.

NCSS II D Time, Continuity, and Change Employ processes to validate and weigh evidence for claims.

- **Flavor** Eggs add a distinct flavor.
- **Color** Egg yolks add a rich, yellow color to baked products and crusts.

Shell eggs and egg products, such as liquid frozen eggs, dried eggs, and liquid refrigerated eggs, are used in baking.

Shell Eggs Shell eggs are eggs sold in their shells. They are often called fresh eggs. If stored properly at 41°F (5°C) or below, they will last up to four weeks beyond the packing date. Shell eggs are purchased in flats, each of which holds 2½ dozen, or 30 eggs. There are 12 flats in a case, meaning that one case contains 30 dozen, or 360, eggs. Shell eggs can be separated into yolks and whites by carefully cracking the egg and pouring off the white while leaving the yolk in the shell. You may also use an egg separator.

Egg Products Egg products have been removed from the shell, and pasteurized.

A TASTE OF HISTORY ANSWER Students' surveys should ask questions such as "Do you like you chocolate bar with or without nuts" and "Do you prefer milk chocolate or dark chocolate?"

The whites can be separated from the yolks, and additives included if necessary. For example, frozen egg yolks have 10% sugar added to prevent them from gelling. The egg products are then packaged and refrigerated, frozen, or dried and packed in pouches.

Egg products are popular because of their convenience. They can be substituted for shell eggs in many baked products. Frozen egg products must be thawed in the refrigerator, so plan ahead when using them. Do not let them sit at room temperature, as egg products are highly perishable. Dried eggs are often used in prepared mixes such as for cakes. High-quality, dried egg whites are often preferred for making meringues over liquid egg whites because they are more stable.

Leavening Agents

A **leavening agent** is a substance that causes a baked good to rise by introducing carbon dioxide (CO_2) or other gases into the mixture. The gases expand from the heat of the oven, stretching the cell walls in the baked product. The end result is a light, tender texture and good volume. The main leavening agents are air, steam, baking soda, baking powder, and yeast.

Air Air is an important leavening agent in all baked products since air is added during the mixing process. Angel food cake is a good example of a baked product that relies on air as a leavening agent. You can add air to a mixture by whipping egg whites.

Steam Steam is another important leavening agent. It is created during the baking process when water evaporates to steam and expands. Because water in one form or another is in all baked products, steam is an important leavening gas. It is especially important to items such as puff pastries and croissants.

Baking Soda Baking soda, or sodium bicarbonate (ˈsō-dē-ˌəm bī-ˈkär-bə-net), is a chemical leavening agent that must be used with acid to give off CO_2 gas. There are many sources of acid used in baking, such as buttermilk, sour cream, and yogurt; fruits and

⬿ Small Bites ⬾

Egg Freshness You can tell whether an egg is fresh by putting the whole egg in a glass of water. If it floats, the egg is old.

fruit juices; most syrups, including honey and molasses; and chocolate. The CO_2 gas is what causes the baked products to rise. Mix baking soda thoroughly, or it will leave an unpleasant aftertaste.

Baking Powder Baking powder is made up of baking soda, an acid such as cream of tartar, and a moisture-absorber such as corn starch. When mixed with a liquid, baking powder releases CO_2. The type used in the bakeshop is double-acting. This means that when it first comes in contact with moisture, it gives off CO_2. When it comes into contact with heat, it gives off more CO_2. Double-acting baking powder can be fast- or slow-acting. Fast-acting varieties react more quickly when mixed with liquids. The slow-acting varieties need more heat to release CO_2. Baking powder is used as a leavening agent in cakes, cookies, muffins, and quick breads.

Yeast Yeast is a living organism. During a process called **fermentation** (ˌfər-mən-ˈtā-shən), yeast breaks down sugars into carbon dioxide gas and alcohol, which are necessary for the rising process in products such as bread. Yeast products get their distinctive aroma and flavor from this process. The types of yeast most commonly used in bakeshops are compressed yeast, dry active yeast, and quick-rise dry yeast.

Sometimes called fresh or wet compressed yeast, compressed yeast is moist and must be refrigerated. Compressed yeast is available in 0.6-ounce cubes or 2-pound blocks. It should be creamy white, have a crumbly texture, and smell like freshly baked bread. To use compressed fresh yeast, crumble it into warm water. Do not use compressed yeast that looks brown, feels slimy, or smells sour.

Whisk
Mixtures

1 When you whisk light mixtures, hold the whisk like a pencil, with the balloon end pointing away from you.

2 When you whisk heavier mixtures, it is less tiring if you hold the whisk with the balloon end facing you, and slightly bend your wrist.

Compressed yeast rapidly deteriorates at room temperature.

Dry active yeast has had most of its moisture removed by hot air, which leaves granules of dormant yeast that are asleep. Dry yeast must be reactivated in liquid that is between 100°F and 110°F (38°C and 43°C) before being added to other ingredients. Dry active yeast is available in ¼-ounce packets, 4-ounce jars, or 1- to 2-pound vacuum-sealed bags. Unopened packages can be stored in a cool, dry place for several months. Once opened, containers of dry active yeast should be kept frozen. When you substitute active dry yeast for compressed yeast, use 50% less than called for in the formula.

Also called instant yeast, quick-rise dry yeast is similar in appearance to dry active yeast. However, its leavening action is much quicker, speeding the rising of dough. Quick-rise dry yeast provides closer results to compressed yeast. To use quick-rise dry yeast, first blend it with the dry ingredients.

Then, add water that is between 100°F and 110°F (38°C and 43°C) to activate the yeast. Quick-rise dry yeast lasts at least one year in unopened packages or when it is stored frozen.

Salt

Salt also has an important role in baking. It enhances the product through its own flavor as well as bringing out the flavor of other ingredients. Salt also acts on gluten and results in an acceptable texture. A certain amount of salt is also necessary to slow down or control fermentation in yeast products. However, salt can negatively react in baked goods if it is not measured accurately or if it is added at the wrong point in the mixing process.

Flavorings

Flavorings include extracts and spices. Although flavorings do not usually influence the baking process, they do enhance the flavor of the final baked product.

Extracts Extracts are liquid flavorings that contain alcohol. They are mostly concentrated, volatile oils or essences diluted with alcohol. Vanilla extract is the exception. It is made by passing alcohol through the vanilla bean, with little or no heat, to extract flavor.

Spices Spices add to the enhancement of food and baked goods by adding flavor, color, or aroma. Most spices come from the bark, roots, flower buds, berries, or seeds of aromatic plants or trees. Although they are not commonly thought of as spices, coffee beans and vanilla pods also fall into this category. Citrus zest, or the outer skin of oranges, lemons, and limes, is considered a spice, too.

Ground spices release their flavor quickly and are often purchased in quantities that can be used within three months. The flavor of whole spices comes out over long cooking periods such as those used in baking. Spices should be used carefully so that they do not overpower the food. Spices used frequently in baking are listed in **Figure 26.2**.

Chocolate and Cocoa

Chocolate and cocoa add body, bulk, and a unique color and flavor to a wide variety of baked products. Both items are made from the cacao (kə-'kā-ō) bean.

▼ **FIGURE 26.2** **Spices Used in Baking**

Spice of Life Spices are used to give interesting flavor to baked goods. *What baked goods do you think anise is used in?*

Spices	Uses in the Bakeshop
Allspice	Used in cakes and puddings; allspice is the dried, unripe berry of a tropical tree; available whole or ground; combines flavors of cinnamon, nutmeg, and cloves
Anise	Used in cakes, cookies, and candies; anise is the dried seed of a plant; available whole or ground; licorice-like flavor
Cardamom	Used in pastries and baked goods; cardamom is the seed of a native Indian herb; available whole or ground; sweet, peppery flavor
Cinnamon	Used in cakes, cookies, pies, breads, and desserts; cinnamon is the thin, dried inner bark of an evergreen tree; available ground or in sticks; warm, spicy flavor
Cloves	Used in baked goods such as breads and pies; cloves are the dried flower buds of an evergreen tree; available whole or ground; warm, spicy flavor
Ginger	Used in baked goods such as cookies and cakes; ginger is the underground stem of a tropical plant; available dried or fresh; sweet, peppery flavor
Nutmeg	Used in custards, pies, breads, and other baked goods; nutmeg is the kernel or seed of the fruit of an evergreen tree; available whole or ground; sweet, warm, spicy flavor
Poppy Seed	Used in breads, rolls, and other baked goods; poppy seed is the dried, ripened seed of a Middle-Eastern plant; nutty flavor

FIGURE CAPTION ANSWER Students' answers may vary, based on their experience, but may include rye breads, Italian pizzelles (a traditional waffle cookie), and pfeffernüsse.

NUTRITION NOTES ANSWER Those who are concerned with cardiovascular disease.

Chocolate and Cocoa All varieties of chocolate and cocoa come from the cacao bean. *What is the difference between cocoa powder and Dutch-process cocoa powder?*

The meat of the cacao bean is roasted and ground into a thick substance called chocolate liquor. Cocoa butter is a by-product of cocoa powder production. More steps are then taken to create a variety of chocolate or cocoa products. The most common varieties in the bakeshop are unsweetened chocolate, semi-sweet chocolate, white chocolate, cocoa powder, and Dutch-process cocoa powder.

Chocolate must be tempered when it is used. Tempering allows crystals in chocolate to be distributed evenly. This creates a creamy, shiny final product.

Unsweetened Chocolate This form of chocolate is also known as bitter or baking chocolate. It is the pure, hardened substance that results from roasted and ground cacao beans. Unsweetened chocolate has no added sugar or milk solids. It is bitter because it contains no sugar. Unsweetened chocolate gives baked products an especially rich taste because it still contains all of the cocoa butter from the bean.

Semi-sweet Chocolate Sugar, lecithin ('le-sə-thən), and vanilla are added to unsweetened chocolate to create semi-sweet or bittersweet chocolate. Semisweet chocolate is often used in chocolate chip cookies and glazes.

White Chocolate White chocolate is made from cocoa butter, sugar, vanilla, lecithin, and dried or condensed milk. There is no chocolate liquor in white chocolate.

Cocoa Powder Cocoa powder is the dry, brown powder that remains once the cocoa butter is removed from the chocolate liquor. It is used mostly in baking and has no added sweeteners or flavorings. Cocoa powder absorbs moisture and provides structure, the same way that flour does.

Dutch-Process Cocoa Powder Adding an alkali, or base, to cocoa powder makes Dutch-process cocoa powder. Dutch-process cocoa has a darker color and milder flavor than regular cocoa. It is less likely to lump and produces a milder, smoother chocolate flavor. Dutch-process cocoa can be substituted for unsweetened chocolate when adjustments are made to the amount of cocoa and shortening that is used.

PHOTO CAPTION ANSWER Adding an alkali, or base, creates Dutch-process cocoa powder, which is darker, lower in acidity, and milder in flavor.

Additives and Nuts

Additives are used in the bakeshop to color, thicken, provide texture in, and replace fat in baked products. (See **Figure 26.3** for a list of common additives that are used in the professional bakeshop.)

Nuts are often used to provide flavor, texture, and color in baked products. **Figure 26.4** on page 699 shows the nuts most commonly used in commercial bakeshops. (For more information on nuts, see Chapter 16.)

Reading Check Analyze Why is gluten so important in the baking process?

Mixing Batters and Doughs

Batters and doughs are formed when the dry and liquid ingredients are combined to create baked products. Batters contain almost equal parts of dry and liquid ingredients. Batters are usually easy to pour. Cakes and muffins are baked products made from batters.

A **dough** contains less liquid than a batter, making it easy to work doughs with your hands. Doughs may even be stiff enough to be cut into shapes. Many types of breads are made from dough.

▼ FIGURE 26.3 Dessert Additives

Helpful Additions Additives can help color, thicken, replace fat, and preserve moisture in baked goods and desserts. *What additive would you choose if you wanted to keep a wedding cake's icing smooth and moist?*

Additive	Food Items	Purpose
Thiamin Niacin Riboflavin Iron	• Flours, breads	• Nutrients
Beta carotene Red No. 3 Green No. 3 Yellow No. 6	• Margarine • Candies • Various baked products	• Coloring agents
Lecithin	• Chocolate, baked products, margarine	• Emulsifier
Carrageenan Pectin Modified starches	• Ice cream, cream cheese, sherbets, fruit fillings, puddings, pie fillings	• Thickeners and stabilizers
Glycerine	• Cake icings	• Humectant (used to retain moisture and keep foods soft)
Chlorine Potassium bromate Benzoyl peroxide Ascorbic acid	• Cake flour • Bread flour • All flour • Bread flour	• Bleaching and maturing agents
Sodium bicarbonate Potassium carbonate	• Baking powder • Dutch-processed cocoa powder	• Acids, alkalis, and buffers (used to adjust and control acidity or alkalinity)
Gum and starch derivatives	• Frozen desserts	• Fat replacers
Polydextrose	• Baked products, puddings	• Bulking agent (used to provide texture and body in reduced-fat goods)

FIGURE CAPTION ANSWER You would choose glycerin as an additive to keep a wedding cake's icing smooth and moist.

READING CHECK ANSWER Gluten makes dough or batter strong, elastic and able to rise.

Mixing Methods

There are many ways to mix batters and doughs. The mixing method that you choose will depend on the type of baked product you will make. Many baked goods require you to use more than one type of mixing method.

- **Beating** Agitating ('a-jə-ˌtāt-iŋ) ingredients vigorously to add air or develop gluten is called **beating**. You may use a spoon or a bench mixer with a paddle attachment for beating.

- **Blending** Mixing or folding two or more ingredients together until they are evenly combined is called **blending**. Use a spoon, whisk, rubber spatula, or bench mixer with a paddle attachment for blending.

- **Creaming** Vigorously combining softened fat and sugar to add air is called **creaming**. Use a bench mixer on medium speed with a paddle attachment.

- **Cut in** To **cut in**, mix solid fat with dry ingredients until lumps of the desired size remain. Use a pastry cutter, a bench mixer and paddle attachment, or two knives to cut in fat. You may also rub the fat and flour between your fingers.

- **Folding** Gently adding light, airy ingredients such as eggs to heavier ingredients by using a smooth circular movement is called **folding**. Folding is a good technique to use to keep mixtures from deflating.

FIGURE 26.4 **Common Baking Nuts**
Flavorful Texture Nuts provide flavor and texture to baked goods. *What nuts might you choose to bake into a banana bread?*

Nuts	Uses in Baking
Almonds	Used in breads, cakes, pastries, marzipan, and as decorations; sweet almonds are eaten, bitter almonds are used as a source of flavorings and extracts; available whole, slivered, ground, sliced, and in flour or meal form
Chestnuts	Used to flavor buttercreams and fillings, and as a decoration for cakes and cookies; sweet flavor; available dried, chopped, and canned as a paste
Coconuts	Used in cakes, cookies, pies, and desserts; available grated or flaked and may be sweetened or unsweetened; desiccated (ˌde-si-ˈkāt-əd) coconut is dried, unsweetened coconut that has been ground to a fine meal
Hazelnuts	Also known as filberts; used in candies, baked goods, and desserts; can be made into a paste for flavoring buttercreams and fillings; available whole in the shell, whole shelled, or chopped
Macadamia Nuts	Used in cakes, cookies, and ice creams; smooth, buttery flavor; available roasted and salted; very expensive
Peanuts	Used in pastries and candies, such as peanut brittle; often combined with chocolate creations; available raw, dry roasted, in granules
Pecans	Used in pies, breads, and desserts; mild and sweet flavor; available shelled in halves or pieces; expensive, but other nuts can easily be substituted
Pine Nuts	Used in breads, cookies, and pastry; available raw or toasted; resemble almonds in flavor
Pistachios	Used in cakes, pastries, and to flavor buttercreams and ice creams; mild flavor and fine texture; available shelled, roasted, and salted
Walnuts	Used in cookies, brownies, cakes, muffins, and ice creams; available in halves, which are mostly used for decoration, and pieces

FIGURE CAPTION ANSWER Answers will vary based on student preference, but common nut choices for banana bread are pecans or walnuts.

Small Bites

Carryover Baking Baked products continue to bake for a short time after being removed from a hot oven. This process is called carryover baking. The chemical and physical changes that occur during the baking process do not stop immediately. The product continues to bake because of the heat contained in the product. If you do not take carryover baking into account, you will end up with overbaked products.

- **Kneading** Working a dough by hand or in a bench mixer with a dough hook to develop gluten and evenly distribute ingredients is called **kneading**.

- **Sifting** Passing dry ingredients such as flour through a wire mesh to remove lumps, blend, and add air is called **sifting**. Use a rotary sifter or a mesh strainer for sifting.

- **Stirring** Gently blending ingredients until they are combined is called **stirring**. Use a spoon, rubber spatula, or whisk for stirring.

- **Whipping** Vigorously beating ingredients to add air is called **whipping**. Use a whisk or a bench mixer with a whip attachment for whipping.

 Reading Check Contrast What are the differences between batters and doughs?

SECTION 26.2 After You Read

Review Key Concepts

1. **Identify** the most common types of fat used in a bakeshop.
2. **Compare and contrast** folding with kneading.

Practice Culinary Academics

 English Language Arts

3. Choose one of the ingredient types described in the chapter, and write a dialogue in which an instructor introduces that ingredient type to a student. You may give general information about that ingredient type or distinguish between the different kinds of that ingredient.

> **NCTE 4** Use written language to communicate effectively.

Science

4. **Procedure** In addition to flavor and texture, nutrition is also a consideration when you bake. Obtain nutrition labels for unsweetened chocolate, semisweet chocolate, white chocolate, cocoa powder, and Dutch-process cocoa powder.

   Analysis Compare the nutrition information for each. Graph the data.

> **NSES F** Develop an understanding of personal and community health.

Mathematics

5. Erica needs 24 cups of 2% milk to prepare a cake formula. However, her kitchen only has reduced fat (1%) milk and whole (4%) milk available. How many cups of each type of milk should she use?

Math Concept **Writing Equivalent Equations** Performing the same operation to both sides of an algebraic equation will result in an equivalent equation. For example, to remove decimals from the equation $.06x + .2y = .54$, you can multiply both sides by 100 to get $6x + 20y = 54$.

Starting Hint Let x = cups of 1% milk and y = cups of 4% milk. You know that $x + y = 24$, and you also know that $0.01x + 0.04y = (0.02)(24)$, or $1x + 4y = 48$. Rewrite the first equation as $x = 24 - y$, and substitute $(24 - y)$ for x in the second equation.

> **NCTM Algebra** Use mathematical models to represent and understand quantitative relationships.

Check your answers at this book's Online Learning Center at **glencoe.com**.

READING CHECK ANSWER Batters contain almost equal parts of dry and liquid ingredients and are easy to pour. Doughs contain less liquid and are easy to work with your hands.

Review and Applications

Commercial bakers use formulas because their accuracy ensures a consistent final product. Commercial bakers prefer to use weight measurements for greater accuracy. Bakeshop equipment must be properly cared for.

Flour, liquids, fats, sugars and sweeteners, eggs, leavening agents, and flavorings are ingredients of baked goods. The main difference among baked products is the proportion of ingredients in the formulas.

Content and Academic Vocabulary Review

1. Write each of the terms below on an index card, with definitions on the back. Use them to review.

Content Vocabulary

- scaling (p. 679)
- percentage (p. 680)
- sheeter (p. 681)
- stack oven (p. 682)
- convection oven (p. 682)
- reel oven (p. 684)
- springform pan (p. 686)
- tart pan (p. 686)
- sheet pan (p. 686)
- mold (p. 686)
- ring (p. 686)
- hard wheat flour (p. 688)
- gluten (p. 688)
- crumb (p. 688)

- soft wheat flour (p. 688)
- bread flour (p. 688)
- cake flour (p. 688)
- pastry flour (p. 688)
- staling (p. 689)
- dried milk solids (p. 689)
- shortening (p. 689)
- oil (p. 690)
- leavening agent (p. 694)
- baking soda (p. 694)
- baking powder (p. 694)
- yeast (p. 694)
- fermentation (p. 694)
- dough (p. 698)
- beat (p. 699)

- blend (p. 699)
- cream (p. 699)
- cut in (p. 699)
- fold (p. 699)
- knead (p. 700)
- sift (p. 700)
- stir (p. 700)
- whip (p. 700)

Academic Vocabulary

- imprecise (p. 678)
- invaluable (p. 682)
- surround (p. 689)
- contribution (p. 691)

Review Key Concepts

2. Explain baking formulas.

3. Describe the function of various bakeshop equipment.

4. Identify bakeshop tools.

5. Identify the different categories of ingredients and their roles in the baking process.

6. Compare and contrast different dough mixing methods.

Critical Thinking

7. Analyze measuring techniques. What might happen if a baker measured dry ingredients in measuring cups instead of weighing them on a scale?

8. Imagine you are looking at different ovens to purchase for a new bakery. What factors would you consider?

9. Explain Why is it important for a baker to know the protein content of different types of flour?

10. Evaluate baking methods. If 10 cherry pies all have dry crusts that are too dark after being baked according to a formula, what could have happened, and how could it have been prevented?

Academic Skills

English Language Arts

11. Write Formula Procedures Find baking formulas for three different baked goods. Look at the formulas and see if you can figure out how to follow them. Write down the procedure you would follow in order to make the baked good. Make sure that each step of the procedure is easy to follow and clear, even to a new bakeshop employee.

> **NCTE 3** Apply strategies to comprehend texts.

Science

12. Gluten The gluten in flour affects the texture of a baked good. Gluten makes bread dough strong and elastic. The amount of gluten in the flour you use will change the texture of the final product.

Procedure Follow your teacher's directions to form groups. Choose a bakeshop formula as a group. As a group, make the same product using flours with two different gluten levels.

Analysis Compare the finished products. What are the differences? What can you conclude about the importance of gluten in baking? Write a summary of your answer.

> **NSES B** Develop an understanding of chemical reactions.

Mathematics

13. Use Baker's Percentages Danielle needs to make 100 pounds of bread using the formula listed below. Calculate the exact weight (to the nearest ounce) of each ingredient that Danielle will need: Bread flour, 100%. Water, 65%. Salt, 2%. Yeast, 2%. Shortening, 5%. Sugar, 4%. Dry milk solids, 7%. Total, 185%.

Math Concept **Decimal Weights** There are 16 ounces in 1 pound. To convert a decimal pound amount into pounds and ounces, take the amount to the right of the decimal point and multiply by 16, then round that product to the nearest whole number. The result becomes the ounce portion of the weight. For example, given a weight of 4.28 pounds, multiply 0.28 × 16 to get 4.48, which rounds to 4. The weight is thus 4 pounds, 4 ounces.

Starting Hint Divide the total pounds needed (100) by the total formula percentage (185%) to find the weight of the flour. To do so, first convert the percentage into a decimal by dividing by 100 (simply move the decimal point two places to the left). Multiply each ingredient's percentage by the weight of the flour to find the weight of each ingredient.

> **NCTM Number and Operations** Compute fluently and make reasonable estimates.

Certification Prep

Sharpen your test-taking skills to improve your kitchen certification program score.

Directions Read the questions. Then, read the answer choices and choose the best possible answer for each.

14. Which is an individual soufflé mold?
- **a.** brioche pan
- **b.** ramekin
- **c.** tart pan
- **d.** springform pan

15. What is the process in which oils become solid?
- **a.** staling
- **b.** hydrogenation
- **c.** leavening
- **d.** fermentation

Test-Taking Tip
If a new term is a compound phrase of two or more words, try to figure it out by looking at the meanings of the individual words before looking it up for yourself. This will help you remember the word's meaning.

Real-World Skills and Applications

Interpersonal and Collaborative Skills

16. Start a Bakeshop Follow your teacher's instructions to form a business team. Divide into chefs, marketers, and dieticians. Chefs will create five baked good product ideas. Marketers will create names and descriptions for the products. Dieticians will evaluate the nutrition content for each. Share your work with the class.

Information Literacy

17. Read Flour Labels Obtain and examine labels for different types of flours. What is their gluten content? What additives, if any, do they contain? How does the nutrition compare? Write your findings and conclusions in a chart and share it with the class.

Technology Applications

18. Baking Equipment PowerPoint Using the information in the chapter on different baking equipment, create a PowerPoint presentation that describes the various equipment used in a bakeshop. Use words, graphics, and/or photos. Share the presentation with the class.

Financial Literacy

19. Purchase Eggs You need to purchase egg products for use in your bakeshop. Shell eggs cost $7.50 per flat. Liquid egg products cost $6.00 per 32 ounces. There is the equivalent of half an egg per ounce in a package of liquid egg product. How much per egg does each option cost? Which option has the best price?

Culinary Lab

Use the culinary skills you have learned in this chapter.

Measure Ingredient Yields

20. Practice Measuring Working in teams, you will practice converting and measuring ingredients for baking using the appropriate equipment.

A. Review ingredients. Working in teams, review the ingredients for the formula of Chocolate Applesauce Cake, shown below. The formula yields six 9-inch cakes, or 8 pounds, 9½ ounces. You want to make 10 9-inch cakes, or 14 pounds, 5 ounces. Create a chart and determine the amount of ingredients needed to yield 10 9-inch cakes.

Cake flour, sifted, 1 lb., 11 oz., 100%
Cocoa powder, sifted, 1½ oz., 6%
Baking soda, sifted, ¾ oz., 3%
Baking powder, sifted, ¾ oz., 3%
Salt, ¾ oz., 3%
Cinnamon, ground, ¾ oz., 3%

Brown sugar, 2 lbs., 4 oz., 133%
Vegetable oil, 1 lb., 5 oz., 78%
Eggs, whole, 13 oz., 48%
Applesauce, 12 oz., 44%
Buttermilk, 1 lb., 8 oz., 89%
TOTAL 8 lbs., 9½ oz., 510%

B. Use the baker's percentage. Add the baker's percentage and change the total to a decimal. Convert the new yield to ounces by multiplying pounds by 16. Divide the new yield by the decimal figure to determine the weight of the flour. Change each ingredient's baker's percentage to a decimal. Multiply each of these numbers by the weight of the flour to determine the new ingredient amount. If needed, round the results to the next highest number.

C. Measure ingredients. After filling out your chart, practice measuring each ingredient with the appropriate tool: baker's or electronic scale, measuring cups or spoons, or volume measures.

Create Your Evaluation

Write out an evaluation of each ingredient and how difficult or easy it was to measure. What made some ingredients more difficult to measure? Discuss each ingredient as a class and share your observations with the other students. Compare your results. Did everyone have the same difficulties, or was it varied?

Yeast Breads and Rolls

SECTIONS

27.1 Yeast Dough Basics

27.2 Yeast Dough Production

WRITING ACTIVITY

Summary

A summary is a short explanation of the basic information in a larger text. Practice by writing a summary of the different types of ingredients you would use in baking.

Writing Tips

1 Skim the text and focus on any headings and subheadings.

2 Write a statement to summarize the main point.

3 Follow with statements that briefly explain the information.

EXPLORE THE PHOTO

Yeast breads can be made in different shapes, sizes, textures and flavors. *What do you think accounts for all of these differences in yeast breads?*

WRITING ACTIVITY ANSWER
Summaries should include short descriptions of ingredients and their functions in baking.

EXPLORE THE PHOTO ANSWER
The different combinations of other ingredients besides yeast, and the relative amounts of those ingredients.

Yeast Dough Basics

Quality yeast breads can be a substantial part of any meal.

Reading Guide

 Before You Read

Prior Knowledge Look over the Key Concepts at the beginning of the section. Write down what you already know about each concept and what you want to find out by reading the lesson. As you read, find examples for both categories.

Read to Learn

Key Concepts
- **List** yeast dough ingredients and their functions.
- **Distinguish** between the three different types of yeast doughs.
- **Summarize** the characteristics and uses of rolled-in-fat yeast doughs.

Main Idea
Breads are usually a part of every meal. Learn about the characteristics of quality yeast products to plan a variety of menu accompaniments.

Content Vocabulary
- leavens
- peel
- starter
- hard lean dough
- crust
- chemical dough conditioner
- soft medium dough
- sweet rich dough
- rolled-in fat yeast dough
- gipfels
- Danish pastry dough

Academic Vocabulary
- tempted
- notable

ACADEMIC STANDARDS

Mathematics
NCTM Algebra Use mathematical models to represent and understand quantitative relationships.

Science
NSES B Develop an understanding of chemical reactions.

Social Studies
NCSS II B Apply key concepts such as time, chronology, and change, and show connections among patterns of historical change and continuity.

NCTE National Council of Teachers of English

NCTM National Council of Teachers of Mathematics

NSES National Science Education Standards

NCSS National Council for the Social Studies

Graphic Organizer
Before you read the section, list the details of what you know already and what you wish to learn about yeast dough products in the first two columns. Fill in the last column after you have read this section.

What I Know	What I Want to Know	What I Learned

 Graphic Organizer Go to this book's Online Learning Center at **glencoe.com** for a printable graphic organizer.

GRAPHIC ORGANIZER ANSWER Answers will vary depending on students' knowledge and interests.

Yeast Dough Ingredients

From bagels to flaky croissants, breads are usually a part of every meal. Yeast breads appeal to your eyes, nose, and taste buds. Learning about the characteristics of quality yeast products is important to foodservice professionals. It will help you plan a variety of nutritious and flavorful menu accompaniments that delight customers.

Yeast breads and rolls are made from dough. Dough is basically flour or meal mixed with liquid that forms a paste. Yeast **leavens** ('le-vəns), or causes dough to rise as it fills with CO_2 bubbles. This process is called fermentation.

Quality yeast products are the result of a careful balancing act. (**Figure 27.1** on page 707 shows how these ingredients work together.) The leavening action of the yeast is balanced with the development of gluten. Gluten, along with wheat protein, gives bread texture. The formation of gluten is controlled by mixing water and wheat flour, and by the way dough is handled during preparation. Most yeast doughs are oven-baked in pans, on sheets, or pushed into the oven on peels. A **peel** is a wooden board that a baker uses to slide breads onto the oven floor or hearth ('härth).

Yeast

As described in Chapter 26, the three most commonly used yeasts in baking are compressed yeast, active dry yeast, and quick-rise dry yeast.

Be sure to check which form of yeast is called for in a formula. Dry yeast is about twice as strong as compressed yeast, but the two forms are similar in taste when the correct proportions are used. When you substitute compressed yeast for dry yeast, use double the amount of dry yeast called for in the formula. When you substitute dry yeast for compressed yeast, use half the amount. Too much or too little yeast will affect the yeast fermentation. Quick-rise dry yeast can be used in the same proportions as active dry yeast.

All yeast is sensitive to temperature. Yeast growth slows down at temperatures below 34°F (1°C). Temperatures above 138°F (59°C) kill yeast cells. The ideal temperature range for yeast fermentation is 78°F to 82°F (26°C to 28°C).

Because yeast loses its potency as it ages, all yeast is labeled with an expiration date. Yeast must be used before this date to produce the best quality yeast products.

Starters

The unique flavor and texture of some breads, such as sourdough, come from the use of a starter. A **starter** is a mixture of flour, yeast, and a warm liquid that begins the leavening action. A portion of the starter is then used to leaven dough. Sourdough starters are also available as active dry cultures and are used much like dry yeast.

Other Yeast Dough Ingredients

The variety of yeast products you see in a bakery display case all begin with flour, water, and yeast. The type and amount of additional ingredients, along with factors such as shaping and baking methods, determine the end product. Each ingredient in a yeast dough carries out a special function for the end product.

Choosing the appropriate flour is critical to the preparation of quality yeast breads and rolls. Different types of flour give the product different qualities. (For more information on flour, see Chapter 26.)

 **Reading Check** **Define** What is leavening?

> ### ⁀ Small Bites ⁀
>
> **Use Compressed Yeast** To blend compressed yeast with other ingredients, you must first soften the yeast. To soften compressed yeast, mix it with liquid that is about 85°F (29°C). Use a portion of the liquid to be used with the dough.

READING CHECK ANSWER Leavening is when yeast or steam causes the dough to rise.

Baking Yeasts Pictured here are two common types of yeast used in baking. *Why is temperature control important when you prepare yeast doughs?*

▼ FIGURE 27.1 Yeast Dough Ingredient Functions

Proper Functions Each ingredient in a baked good has several functions in a formula. *What ingredients add to a baked good's nutritional value?*

Ingredient Function	Flour	Salt	Sugar	Fat	Milk Solids	Water	Yeast
Binds ingredients	✓	✓				✓	
Absorbs liquids	✓	✓	✓		✓		
Adds to shelf life	✓	✓	✓	✓	✓	✓	✓
Adds structure	✓	✓	✓	✓		✓	
Affects eating quality	✓	✓	✓	✓	✓	✓	✓
Adds nutritional value	✓	✓	✓	✓	✓		✓
Affects flavor	✓	✓	✓	✓	✓		✓
Affects rising	✓	✓	✓			✓	✓
Affects gluten	✓	✓	✓	✓		✓	
Adds texture	✓	✓	✓	✓	✓		✓
Colors crust	✓	✓	✓	✓			
Affects shape	✓		✓		✓		
Affects volume	✓	✓			✓		✓
Adds tenderness			✓	✓	✓		

PHOTO CAPTION ANSWER A temperature that is too cold will put the yeast into hibernation, and a temperature that is too hot will kill the yeast.

FIGURE CAPTION ANSWER Flour, sugar, fat, milk solids, and yeast all contribute to a baked good's nutritional value.

Regular Yeast Doughs

Yeast products are generally classified according to the type of dough used to produce them. Regular yeast doughs are prepared by combining yeast with the other ingredients into one mixture. The three most common regular yeast doughs used in food-service operations are hard lean doughs, soft medium doughs, and sweet rich doughs.

Hard Lean Doughs

A hard lean dough consists of 0% to 1% fat and sugar. Hard lean doughs are the most basic yeast doughs. A **hard lean dough** is often made solely from flour, water, salt, and yeast. Hard lean doughs yield products with a relatively dry, chewy crumb and a hard crust. The crumb is the internal texture of a bread or roll. The **crust** is the outer surface of a bread or roll.

Fats make a hard lean dough easier to manipulate, but they also soften the crumb.

In commercial baking operations, **chemical dough conditioners** such as chlorine dioxide (ˈklȯr-ēn dī-ˈak-sīd) are sometimes used. These chemical dough conditioners may be added during the baking process to strengthen the glutens that give hard lean dough products their dense structure.

Similar to traditional hard lean doughs are whole-grain breads, rye breads, and sourdoughs. Their textures are much more dense because of the coarser, heavier flours and hotter baking methods used. The crumb is chewier and the crust is usually darker and crisper.

> ### ⤳ Small Bites ⤳
>
> **Enriched Hard Lean Doughs** Hard lean doughs are stiff, dry, and more difficult to work with than soft medium doughs. Some bakers add eggs or oil to hard lean doughs to make them richer. Whole eggs may be added for color, fat, or additional moisture.

▲ **Forms of Dough** Hard lean doughs are used for breads such as crusty rolls, while soft medium doughs are used for sandwich breads and buns. *What other types of breads are similar to traditional hard lean doughs?*

PHOTO CAPTION ANSWER Whole-grain breads, rye breads, and sourdoughs are similar to traditional hard lean doughs because of their dense texture after baking.

1928   **1929**

Rohwedder bread   Wall Street stock
slicing machine   market crash occurs
is introduced in
Chillicothe, Missouri

The Origins of Yeast Doughs

Yeast provides the leavening action in many of the baked goods produced in foodservice. The world's earliest breads were unleavened and made from mixtures of ground grain and water. Archaeological evidence suggests that the Egyptians were making leavened bread as early as 4,000 BCE, and probably began to do so by accident. Unbaked, flattened bread dough left in the open air probably picked up wild yeast spores, leavening the bread.

History Application

Document the effect yeast has on bread dough by photographing the different stages the dough goes through during the breadmaking process. Label the photos during each stage.

> **NCSS II B** Apply key concepts such as time, chronology, and change, and show connections among patterns of historical change and continuity.

Soft Medium Doughs

A **Soft medium dough** produces items with a soft crumb and crust. The percentage of fat and sugar in these doughs is 6% to 9%. Soft medium dough is elastic and tears easily.

Yeast products made from soft medium dough include Pullman bread. Pullman bread is white or wheat sandwich bread that is made into squared-off loaves. These loaves get their shape from baking in a 2-pound loaf pan that is enclosed on all sides. Other soft medium dough products include dinner rolls, such as cloverleaf and Parker House rolls.

Sweet Rich Doughs

At the other extreme from regular yeast doughs are sweet rich doughs. A **sweet rich dough** incorporates up to 25% of both fat and sugar. Because sweet rich doughs use such large amounts of fat and sugar, their structure is soft and heavy. The high gluten content of bread flour helps sweet rich doughs support the additional fat and sugar.

Most sweet rich doughs are moist and soft. When you work with a sweet rich dough, you may be **tempted**, or enticed, to add more flour to make the dough easier to handle. However, adding flour will toughen the final product. Use only a light dusting of flour on your hands and work surfaces when working with sweet rich doughs.

Many sweet rich dough products are famous for their golden yellow crumb and brown crust. The traditional means of achieving this golden color is to add many eggs to the dough. However, the egg can break down the gluten and make the dough too heavy. Many commercial bakeshops use yellow food coloring to enhance the color of dough. You can also add shortening to increase the dough's richness. Some examples of sweet rich dough products are yeast-raised coffee cakes, cinnamon buns, and doughnuts.

Reading Check Name What are three types of regular yeast doughs?

Rolled-In Fat Yeast Doughs

Bakers use rolled-in fat yeast doughs to make rolls and pastries. Rolled-in fat doughs differ from regular yeast dough.

When you make a **rolled-in fat yeast dough**, combine the fat into the dough through a rolling and folding action. This process yields a dough made of many thin, alternating layers of fat and dough. As the dough bakes, the heated fat layers release moisture in the form of steam. The steam becomes trapped between the layers of dough, pushing them apart and lifting them. The finished products are **notable**, or well known, for their rich, flaky texture. Two popular kinds of rolled-in fat yeast dough products are croissants and Danish pastries.

A TASTE OF HISTORY ANSWER Photos should include the bubbly stage, the stretchy stage, doubling in volume, puffy stage, and finished dough.

READING CHECK ANSWER The three types of regular yeast doughs are hard lean dough, soft medium dough, and sweet rich dough.

🔺 **Sweet Rolls** Sweet rich doughs can be used to create a vast array of taste-tempting bread products. *Why are sweet rich doughs so moist and soft?*

Rolled-in fat yeast doughs traditionally use butter for the fat layers. Butter adds a rich flavor and aroma, but it is difficult to handle while rolling and folding. Butter must be at the right temperature. Warm butter is too soft to roll, and cold butter cracks when folded. Instead, you may want to use other high-moisture fats, such as margarine or shortening. They may be substituted partially or completely for the butter. This will improve handling ability and lower costs.

Rolled-in fat yeast doughs also differ from regular yeast doughs in gluten development. Gluten develops during folding and rolling, so little kneading is required with rolled-in fat yeast doughs. Overdeveloping the gluten in a rolled-in fat yeast dough will make the finished product tough and chewy. Larger foodservice operations often use sheeters to ensure consistent rolled-in fat yeast dough production.

Croissants

Croissants are crescent-shaped, flaky rolls. They can be used appropriately for either sweet or savory dishes, including sandwiches. Croissant dough is a soft, wet mixture of bread flour, yeast, cold milk, salt, butter, and a little sugar. You can add dry milk solids and cold water to the dough instead of milk. The cold water or milk slows the leavening action of the yeast. Eggs are not part of the traditional formula, but can be added for additional richness. Butter or another high-moisture fat equal to 25% to 50% of the weight of the dough is rolled in.

A freshly baked croissant should be light golden brown. It should have a flaky, layered texture and an open grain or crumb. Croissant dough can be shaped into traditional crescents or the tighter half circles that Swiss and German bakers call **gipfels** ('gāp-fels).

Danish Pastry

Danish pastry dough is sweeter and richer than croissant dough. Danish pastry is usually eaten as a breakfast or dessert item. Unlike croissant dough, Danish pastry dough is rich in eggs. It can also include milk. Many different flavorings and additives, such as nuts, fruits, extracts, and sugar glazes, make these products tempting treats.

Danish pastry is also softer, flakier, and more tender than croissants. These characteristics, along with a more intense flavor, are because of the Danish pastry's higher percentage of rolled-in fat. This percentage can range from 10% to 50%.

Reading Check **Explain** What is the difference between croissant and Danish pastry dough?

 Balancing Act All ingredients in baked products must work together. *What will happen if they do not?*

Review Key Concepts

1. **Describe** the function of a starter.
2. **List** products that can be made from a soft medium dough.
3. **Summarize** the characteristics of a quality croissant.

Practice Culinary Academics

 Science

4. **Procedure** Make a yeast balloon. Take a balloon and stretch it out by blowing it up a few times. Add a packet of yeast and 2 tablespoons of sugar to 1 cup of very warm water. Once the yeast and sugar have dissolved, pour the mixture into a bottle and stretch the balloon over the mouth of the bottle.

    Analysis What happens to the balloon? Keep a log of any events, and write a summary of what happened, and why you think any changes occurred.

    NSES B Develop an understanding of chemical reactions.

 Mathematics

5. Christine has baked 80 croissants to sell at her bakery. Each croissant costs Christine $0.60 to make, and she sells each one for $1.25. How many croissants must Christine sell during the day to cover the cost of the products used to make the croissants?

    Math Concept **Calculating Profit** Calculate profit with the formula Profit = Income − Expenses. A positive result represents a profit, while a negative answer indicates a loss. The break-even point occurs when income = expenses.

    Starting Hint Christine's expenses will equal $80 \times \$0.60 = \$48$. Determine the break-even point by calculating the number of croissants (x) needed for income to equal expenses: $\$1.25(x) = \$48$. The next whole number higher than x will represent a profit.

    NCTM Algebra Use mathematical models to represent and understand quantitative relationships.

    Check your answers at this book's Online Learning Center at **glencoe.com.**

READING CHECK ANSWER Croissant dough is a soft, wet mixture of bread flour, yeast, cold milk, salt, butter, and sugar. Danish pastry dough is sweeter and richer.

PHOTO CAPTION ANSWER The baked product could turn out different than expected, or unacceptable.

Yeast Dough Production

> *You must carefully prepare yeast dough for it to rise correctly.*

Reading Guide

 Before You Read

Think of an Example Look over the Key Concepts for this section. Think of an example of how or when you could use one of the skills from the Key Concepts. Thinking of how you might apply a skill can help motivate your learning by showing you why the skill is important.

Read to Learn

Key Concepts
- **Describe** the mixing methods for yeast doughs.
- **Outline** the stages in properly preparing yeast doughs.
- **Demonstrate** the baking of quality yeast breads.
- **Illustrate** how to cool, store, and serve yeast breads.

Main Idea

Yeast dough production requires proper mixing and careful preparation. A baker must learn to avoid common causes of failure when preparing yeast doughs.

Content Vocabulary
- straight-dough method
- modified straight-dough method
- sponge method
- preferment
- let down
- continuous bread-making
- punch
- rounded
- bench box
- bench rest
- shape
- seams
- pan loaf
- free-form loaf
- pan
- proof
- wash
- slash
- dock
- oven spring

Academic Vocabulary
- critical
- correspond

ACADEMIC STANDARDS

Mathematics
NCTM Number and Operations Compute fluently and make reasonable estimates.

NCTM Measurement Understand measurable attributes of objects and the units, systems, and processes of measurement.

NCTE National Council of Teachers of English

NCTM National Council of Teachers of Mathematics

NSES National Science Education Standards

NCSS National Council for the Social Studies

Graphic Organizer

Use this sequence chart to list the four stages of baking in sequence.

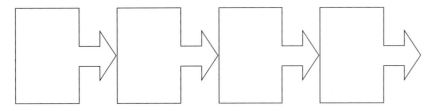

Graphic Organizer Go to this book's Online Learning Center at **glencoe.com** for a printable graphic organizer.

GRAPHIC ORGANIZER ANSWER 1) Oven spring. 2) Structure develops. 3) Crust forms. 4) Finished product.

Yeast Dough Preparation

The production of quality yeast breads and rolls requires good technique, patience, and creativity. To produce a good yeast product, you will need to learn dough mixing methods.

The steps involved in making yeast breads vary depending on the type of dough that is used and the item that is being produced. However, the same general stages apply to all yeast dough products:

1. Scaling ingredients
2. Mixing and kneading
3. Fermentation
4. Dividing dough
5. Rounding dough
6. Bench rest
7. Shaping dough
8. Panning dough
9. Final proofing
10. Baking dough
11. Cooling dough
12. Packaging dough

Keep these quality guidelines in mind:

- Maintain personal cleanliness at all times.
- Keep utensils, materials, and machinery clean and in good working order.
- Use the best quality ingredients.
- Read all formulas carefully and measure ingredients properly.
- Maintain the appropriate environmental temperatures.
- Regulate dough temperatures.
- Serve only freshly baked and properly stored yeast products.

Mixing Methods

There are three basic methods of mixing yeast dough ingredients: the straight-dough method, the modified straight-dough method, and the sponge method. Each of these methods gives its own characteristics to the finished product. Each method also affects the activity of the yeast and the formation of the gluten.

Straight-Dough Method

You will use the straight-dough method to mix the ingredients for most basic breads. The **straight-dough method** calls for mixing all the ingredients together in a single step. Ingredients may be mixed by hand or with a bench mixer. The straight-dough method is the method by which nearly all the bread in the world is made.

In doughs mixed by the straight-dough method, the yeast begins acting on all the ingredients immediately. As you continue mixing or working the dough, the gluten develops.

Modified Straight-Dough Method

The **modified straight-dough method** breaks the straight-dough method into steps. These steps allow for a more even distribution of sugars and fats throughout the dough. This modification is commonly used to prepare rich doughs.

Sponge Method

Some yeast products, such as crusty hearth breads or sweeter doughs, benefit from the sponge method. The **sponge method** allows the yeast to develop separately before it is mixed with the other ingredients. The sponge method mixes the dough in two stages to give yeast extra time to leaven the bread. This method results in a more intense flavor and a lighter, airy texture. The sponge method makes a very soft, moist, and absorbent dough.

Preferment One modification of the sponge method is sometimes called the preferment method. **Preferment** is the process of removing a portion of the dough. It is kept dormant for 8 to 24 hours and then added to the next day's bread products. This method enhances the fermentation, color, and taste of the final baked products.

Reading Check Examine What is the main benefit of using the sponge method?

READING CHECK ANSWER It allows the yeast to develop separately, resulting in a more intense flavor and a lighter, airy texture.

Use
the Modified
Straight-Dough Method

1 Combine the fat, sugar, salt, milk solids, and flavorings in the mixer. Mix well, but do not whip.

2 Add eggs one at a time, as they are absorbed into the mixture.

3 Add the rest of the liquids and mix briefly.

4 Add the flour and the yeast last.

5 Mix until a smooth dough forms.

Stages of Making Yeast Dough

Because each step in the process of making yeast dough is critical, it is important that you complete each step in the proper order. Skipping any steps or being unprepared for a step can lead to the failure of your product.

Scaling Ingredients

Accurate, or correct, measurement, or scaling, of all ingredients is **critical**, or necessary, in the preparation of yeast doughs. Successful formulas are based on proportional mixtures of ingredients. Too much or too little of an ingredient will affect yeast activity, gluten formation, and product quality.

Use a baker's scale to weigh all ingredients that are denser than milk or water. This includes flour, yeast, shortening, eggs, honey, molasses, malt, and oil. Milk and water may be measured with volume measures.

Scale each ingredient separately. Make sure the weight of each ingredient will **correspond** to, or match, the weights called for in the formula. Remember that weight and volume are not the same unit of measurement. Even a small error in measuring can cause a baked product to fail. This will waste time, and will cost extra money through wasted resources. In some formulas, ingredients are given as a percentage of the total weight of the flour. Foodservice operations usually post procedures for converting percentages to weights and weights to percentages.

Use the 240 Factor

The desired dough temperature for yeast dough is 80°F. Several factors affect dough temperature, including flour temperature, room temperature, friction temperature (which depends on the mixer speed), and water temperature. Of these, only the water temperature can be easily modified by the baker. Commercial bakers use a shortcut known as the 240 Factor to easily calculate desired water temperature. Simply add together the flour, room, and friction temperatures, and subtract that total from 240°F. The result is the target water temperature.

Find the ideal water temperature for yeast rolls given the following conditions: flour temperature = 62°F; room temperature = 25°C; and friction temperature = 30°F.

Math Concept **Converting Temperature**

Celsius temperatures (C) can be converted to Fahrenheit (F) using the following formula:

$F = (9/5 \times C) + 32$

Starting Hint Because the 240 Factor calculations utilize degrees Fahrenheit, start by converting the room temperature from Celsius to Fahrenheit using the conversion formula above. Then add the three temperatures (flour, room, and friction), and subtract that sum from 240 to get the desired water temperature.

> **NCTM Number and Operations** Compute fluently and make reasonable estimates.

Mixing and Kneading

When you mix dough ingredients thoroughly, it ensures even yeast distribution, gluten development, and a uniform mixture. Be careful not to overmix, as it can lead to let down. A **let down** is a condition in which the ingredients in a dough completely break down. Once the ingredients are mixed, the dough must be kneaded to further develop the gluten. Kneading means to work the dough until it is smooth and elastic.

In **continuous breadmaking** or commercial baking, mixing and kneading are done in a spiral mixer.

There are four stages to the continuous breadmaking process:

- **Pickup** Use a low speed to mix the water and yeast. If oil is used, add it immediately after the liquid ingredients. Then, incorporate the dry ingredients, and add solid fats or shortenings last. Once all ingredients have been added to the mixer, turn the speed to medium.
- **Cleanup** During this stage the ingredients come together into a ball around the dough hook. The bottom of the mixing bowl can be clearly seen. All liquid is absorbed into the flour.
- **Development** During this longest stage of mixing and kneading, oxygen is incorporated into the dough and gluten is developed. The dough will be uneven in color and will tear easily.
- **Final Clear** This stage is reached when proper gluten has developed. To verify gluten formation, cut off a small piece of dough and stretch it apart with your fingers. It should stretch to such a thinness that light can be seen through the dough. You should also be able to stretch the dough several times without it breaking. At this point, remove the dough from the mixer.

Fermentation

Once a regular yeast dough has been kneaded thoroughly by hand or has reached the final clear stage in a mixer, the dough is ready for fermentation. Fermentation is the process by which yeast converts the sugars in dough into alcohol and carbon dioxide. Gases that are trapped in the gluten cause the dough to rise.

For fermentation to take place, you must:
- Shape the kneaded dough into a ball.
- Coat it with a thin film of oil.
- Cover the dough to keep it from drying out. Avoid popping any bubbles that may appear beneath the dough surface.
- Place the dough in a proofing cabinet, or proofer.

GOURMET MATH ANSWER Converting the room temperature into °F results in $(9/5 \times 25) + 32 = (45) + 32 = 77°F$. Thus, the desired water temperature equals $240 - (62 + 77 + 30) = 240 - 169 = 71°F$.

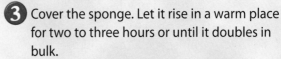

HOW TO

Use
the Sponge Method

1 Combine 50% water with 50% flour.

2 Add the yeast. Sugar or malt may also be added to this mixture to promote faster yeast growth.

3 Cover the sponge. Let it rise in a warm place for two to three hours or until it doubles in bulk.

4 Combine the sponge with the remaining ingredients either by hand or in a mixer.

Use a probe thermometer to measure the dough temperature before you place it in the proofer. If you are not using a proofer, regularly measure dough temperature throughout fermentation. Remember that allowing dough to become too cool will slow yeast action, while heat over 90°F (32°C) will cause fermentation to accelerate.

Fermentation is complete when the dough has approximately doubled in size. Although you will be able to see the increased volume of the dough, there is a way you can test to see if it is ready. You can test whether fermentation is complete by inserting two fingers into the dough up to the knuckles and then removing them. If the finger pressure leaves a slight impression around which the dough closes very slowly, fermentation is complete. The dough is then ready to be punched.

Punching Dough

The action of turning the sides of the dough into the middle and turning the dough over is called **punching**. This is done by pressing gently and firmly, not by hitting or kneading the dough.

> ### ☞ Small Bites ☜
>
> **Overmixing** If you overmix or over knead a regular yeast dough, you will cause the ingredients in the dough to let down. Once the ingredients have let down, they have broken down completely. Overmixed dough is warm and sticky and falls apart easily. Adding flour can help offset overmixing to a certain extent. However, it is better to avoid overmixing dough in the first place.

Punching accomplishes four important actions:

Maintains Dough Temperature By effectively turning the dough inside out, punching moves the cooler exterior surfaces to the middle. This evens the dough temperature.

Releases Carbon Dioxide If too much of the gas developed during this first stage of fermentation remains within the dough, it will become concentrated and slow the later stages of fermentation.

Introduces Oxygen Punching the dough incorporates oxygen from the air.

Develops Gluten Any handling of the dough strengthens the gluten.

Dividing Dough

Once the dough has been punched, it must be divided for baking. Commercial bread formulas give portions by weight. To divide dough, use a bench scraper to cut the dough into uniform pieces. Weigh the pieces on a baker's scale, as when scaling ingredients.

You will need to work quickly when you portion dough. Fermentation continues during this process. The last pieces portioned may become over fermented if there is any delay. Keep the large mass of dough covered as you work so that its surface does not dry out. If any small pieces of dough are left, divide them evenly and add them to the larger pieces. Tuck them under each portion so that they will be well incorporated. Otherwise, the smaller pieces will ferment too fast.

Rounding Dough

Divided dough must be **rounded**, or shaped into smooth balls. To do this, put the dough on the bench. With the palm of your hand, cup the dough with a circular motion, working the dough with your fingertips. This will cause the dough to form into a smooth, firm, round ball.

HOW TO
Knead
Yeast Dough

1 Grasp the dough and bring it toward you.

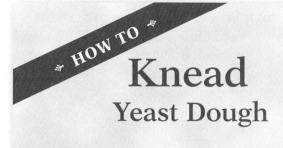

2 Flip the dough, then form a fist and push the dough away with your knuckles.

3 Repeat the process until the dough is smooth and elastic.

Rounding dough provides it with a skin to prevent the loss of too much carbon dioxide. Some formulas call for the dough to be folded over during rounding. This provides a kind of second punching after dividing. If the dough is not rounded, it will rise and bake unevenly, with a lumpy or rough surface.

When you round, perform each of the subsequent actions, such as shaping and panning, in the same order, so that the dough ferments consistently. The first portion rounded should also be the first piece to be shaped, and so on.

Bench Rest

Depending on the formula, at this time the rounded portions may need to be placed in bench boxes or left covered on the work bench. A **bench box** is a covered container in which dough can be placed before shaping. This short, intermediate proofing stage, called a **bench rest**, allows the gluten to relax. The dough becomes lighter, softer, and easier to shape.

Shaping Dough

Once the portions have been properly rounded and, if necessary, rested, they must be shaped. **Shaping** forms the dough into the distinctive shapes associated with yeast products.

Some general principles apply to the shaping process:
- **Work Quickly** Fermentation continues during shaping. Cover the portions you are not working with to prevent them from drying out.
- **Shape Pieces in Order** Start with the first piece you rounded. Keep the same order to ensure consistency.
- **Use Very Little Flour** A dusting of flour on your hands and the work surface will keep the dough from sticking. Too much will dry it out.
- **Place Any Seam at the Bottom Seams**, or the places where edges of the dough meet, should be straight and tight. The seam is the weakest part of the piece. Seams can open during baking and ruin the product's shape.

- **Shaping Loaves** Although bread loaves come in a wide variety of textures and tastes, there are essentially two ways to shape dough into loaves. **Pan loaves** are rolled and placed, seam down, into prepared loaf pans. In baking, loaves receive their characteristic shape from the support offered by the high sides of the loaf pans. **Free-form loaves**, such as braided loaves and artisan breads, are shaped by hand. They are baked, seam side down, on flat pans, and they can be baked directly on a hearth.
- **Shaping Rolls** Yeast rolls are like individually portioned loaves. Shape rolls with the same care used to shape loaves. This will produce items with an attractive, even surface and uniform size.

Depending on the formula, rolls may be shaped and baked on flat sheets, like free-form loaves. They may also be placed in special pans that offer additional structure during baking. Cloverleaf and butterflake rolls, for example, are baked in greased muffin pans. Brioche (brē-'ȯsh) rolls, like brioche loaves, are baked in special fluted tins. Pan rolls, Parker House rolls, and knots are baked on flat sheets or in shallow baking pans.

When you pan rolls, allow enough room between the rolls to ensure even browning. Avoid crowding. Most formulas indicate how many rolls will fit on a sheet and how they should be placed.

Panning Dough

Shaped dough is ready for **panning**, or placing in the correct type of pan. Pizza is sometimes shaped directly on the pan. Other breads are shaped on the bench. Each formula specifies the size and type of pan to be used and indicates how the pan should be prepared. In general, pans dusted with cornmeal are used for baking lean doughs. The cornmeal keeps the baked product from sticking to the pan. It does not change the flavor. Sheet pans that have been lined with parchment or lightly greased are used for soft medium doughs.

Final Proofing

The final fermentation stage for regular yeast dough items is called final proofing. **Proofing** allows the leavening action of yeast to achieve its final strength before yeast cells are killed by hot oven temperatures. Yeast dough items are proofed once they have been shaped and panned.

Final proofing requires higher temperatures and humidity levels than fermentation—temperatures of 85°F to 95°F (29°C to 35°C) and humidity levels of 80% to 90%. The use of a proofer is essential to maintain these conditions.

The length of the final proofing time depends on the type of dough. Most doughs are fully proofed when finger pressure leaves an indentation that closes slowly around the center but does not collapse. Fully proofed items are slightly less than double in size.

Proofing time is shortened for rich and sweet doughs. This is done to keep the weight of the heavier dough from collapsing during baking. Some other items, such as rye breads, are also deliberately underproofed. Underproofed dough is known as young dough. Overproofed dough, or dough that has more than doubled in size during final proofing, is called old dough.

Washing, Slashing, and Docking

Many yeast dough products require special additional preparations before baking. These preparations, called washing, slashing, and docking, affect the baking quality and eye appeal of the finished items.

Washing Applying a thin glaze of liquid to the dough's surface before baking is called **washing**. Depending on the type of item and the wash used, washing can lighten or darken the crust's color, and make the surface shiny and glossy. (See **Figure 27.2** on page 721 for different types of washes and how they affect baked goods.)

❈ HOW TO ❈

Create
a Braided Loaf

① Divide dough into three parts. Roll into three equal strips.

② Cross strip 3 over strip 2. Cross strip 1 over strip 2. Cross strip 2 over strip 1. Repeat until half the bread is braided.

③ Flip the bread over so the three unbraided strips are facing you. Repeat step 2 until the whole loaf is braided.

❋ MASTER RECIPE

Soft Rolls

YIELD: 26 LBS., 15 OZ. (18 DOZEN)
SERVING SIZE: ONE 2-OZ. ROLL

Ingredients

9 lbs.	Water
1 lb.	Dry milk solids
1 lb.	Sugar, granulated
8 oz.	Yeast, compressed
14 lbs.	Flour, bread
4½ oz.	Salt
1 lb.	Shortening, vegetable

International Flavor

Bread is a staple in many countries, especially in Europe, and the soft roll is a favorite. Research these rolls from other cultures, and create a visual presentation to show the differences in shape.

● Brioche (France)

● Baps (Scotland)

● Potato roll (Ireland)

Cooking Technique

Pastry Technique (See the Method of Preparation.)

Method of Preparation

1. Gather the equipment and ingredients.

2. Scale the ingredients.

3. Soften the compressed yeast in part of the water. The water temperature should be 78°F to 82°F (26°C to 28°C).

4. Use the straight-dough method for mixing the dough. Combine all of the ingredients in the bench mixing bowl.

5. Mix until proper gluten development occurs. To test the gluten development, cut a small piece of dough from the mass in the bowl. Stretch the dough to a thinness that allows light to clearly shine through. If the dough can be stretched a few times without tearing, it is ready for fermentation.

6. Lightly coat the dough with oil before putting it into the proof box.

7. Ferment the dough.

8. Punch the dough down when it is almost double in bulk. (See Chef Notes.)

9. Divide the dough using a bench scraper.

10. Round the dough.

11. Allow the dough to rest for a short time to relax the gluten.

12. Shape the rolls.

13. Place the rolls in parchment-lined or lightly-greased pans.

14. Put the panned rolls into the proofing cabinet to ferment prior to baking. (See Chef Notes.)

15. Bake the rolls at 375°F (191°C) for 20 minutes or until evenly browned.

Chef Notes

To test the dough for punching readiness, insert two fingers into the dough. If the indentation remains, the dough is ready for punching. The rolls are properly proofed when almost double in bulk, or when the dough closes around a finger indentation without collapsing.

Substitutions

● Use butter instead of shortening for a richer flavor.

● Add crumble topping for coffee rolls, cinnamon or pecans to transform the rolls into sweet treats.

Glossary

Gluten elastic protein substance that makes dough stay together
Fermentation break-down of a compound caused by an enzyme, such as yeast

HACCP

● Bake at 375°F (191°C)

Hazardous Foods

● Yeast

Nutrition

Calories 140   Calories from Fat 25
Total Fat 2.5g
  Saturated Fat 0.5g
  Trans Fat 0g
Cholesterol 0mg
Sodium 250mg
Total Carbohydrate 25g
  Fiber 1g
  Sugars 3g
Protein 5g
• Vitamin A 0%   • Vitamin C 0%
• Calcium 4%   • Iron 2%

FIGURE 27.2 Baking Washes

Wash Types A wash can give an enhanced color and gloss to baked yeast rolls. *With what other baked goods can you use a wash?*

Desired Effect	Type of Wash
A crisp crust	Water
A glossy, firm crust	Egg white and water
A deep-colored, glossy crust	Whole egg and water
A deep-colored, soft, glossy crust	Whole egg and milk
A deep-colored, soft crust	Milk

Apply the wash with a pastry brush, either before or after proofing. Check the formula for timing. If you apply the wash after proofing, be careful not to puncture the surface and deflate the dough. Avoid puddling or dripping egg washes, which cause uneven browning. Excess washing can burn or cause items to stick to the pan.

Slashing Making shallow cuts in the surface of the item, done just before baking, is called **slashing**. Slashing, also called stippling, helps gases escape from hard-crusted breads during baking. This allows for higher rising and the development of a more tender crumb. Improperly slashed breads will burst or break along the sides during baking. The patterns made by slashing, which leave a scarred or cross-hatched impression in the baked crust, also add visual appeal.

To slash dough, follow these guidelines:
1. Use both hands, steadying the item with one hand while you cut with the other.
2. Use a utility blade; a sharp, unserrated knife; or a clean, sharp razor. Blunt or serrated edges bruise or tear the surface of the dough.
3. Make shallow, slightly angled cuts, just under the surface of the dough.
4. Make all cuts of equal length, overlapping cuts by one-third of their length.
5. Make the slashes on the full surface of the dough in a symmetrical pattern.

Bread Slashes Use a utility blade or sharp knife to make slashes. *Why are many breads slashed before baking?*

FIGURE CAPTION ANSWER Washes can be used on pastries and pie crusts as well as rolls and breads.

PHOTO CAPTION ANSWER So that gasses can escape during baking, keeping the crust intact and helping the bread to rise higher.

Docking The process of making small holes in the surface of an item before baking is called **docking**. Used primarily with rich doughs or rolled-in doughs, docking allows steam to escape and promotes even baking. Docking also keeps rich doughs from rising too much during baking. Follow the formula's directions for docking. Use a sharp-tined fork or a skewer to dock the dough.

Reading Check Explain When does fermentation take place?

Baking Yeast Dough

Baking is the process that changes dough into breads or rolls through the application of heat. Oven temperature and baking time are determined by five factors.

- **Dough Type** Young, under fermented doughs require cooler oven temperatures, higher humidity, and longer baking times than fully proofed doughs. Old, over fermented doughs require higher oven temperatures, less humidity, and shorter baking times.
- **Dough Richness** Lean doughs require higher oven temperatures and shorter baking times. Rich doughs require lower oven temperatures and longer baking times.
- **Portion Size** Smaller items, such as rolls, require shorter baking times than larger items, such as loaves.
- **Desired Color** The desired color of the crust often depends on the tastes of the customer. Higher oven temperatures

Sanitation Check

✓ Avoid Contamination
Never apply an egg wash to a product that has already been baked. The egg will remain uncooked, presenting the risk of salmonella bacteria.

CRITICAL THINKING *When should you apply an egg wash to the product?*

SANITATION CHECK ANSWER Apply the egg wash after the product has been assembled, just before or after final proofing.

and longer baking times generally yield a darker crust color than lower temperatures and shorter baking times. An egg wash can add color to a crust that must be baked at a low temperature or for a short time. Egg washes should never be added to baked goods after baking. This can create a potential for foodborne illness, and will make the baked product soggy.

Formulas will list the ideal oven temperature and baking time. Slight adjustments may be necessary. Appropriate placement of pans in the oven is also important. Air and heat must be allowed to circulate freely around the pans. This can be accomplished by placing pans at the appropriate distance from the heating element. Crowding the oven slows baking time and results in unevenly baked items.

Baking with Steam

Breads with thin, crispy crusts, such as French and Italian loaves, benefit from the addition of steam to the oven during baking. The steam keeps the crumb soft while adding a glossy shine to the surface. As the sugars in the crust caramelize, a thin, crispy crust is formed.

Some bakery ovens are equipped to inject a desired amount of steam into the oven for several seconds depending on the type of bread and the formula. In ovens without steam injectors, a pan can be added with just enough water so the water evaporates during the early stages of baking.

Stages of Baking

As yeast dough products bake, their internal temperatures rise. Each of the four stages of the baking process contributes to the final product.

Oven Spring

During the first five minutes of baking, the dough suddenly rises and expands as the yeast reacts to the heat of the oven. This final leavening effort, occurring before internal temperatures become hot enough to kill the yeast cells, is called **oven spring**.

READING CHECK ANSWER In regular yeast doughs, fermentation occurs throughout the process, primarily during the fermentation and final proofing stages.

Steam injection helps achieve oven spring. Oven spring will not occur if there is too much salt or not enough yeast in the dough or if the dough was overproofed. At this early stage, the dough is very soft and will collapse if touched.

Structure Develops

As the internal temperature rises from 130°F (54°C), starch granules in the dough begin to absorb moisture and swell up. At 150°F (66°C), the starches gel and become the final structure of the bread. At 165°F (74°C), the gluten begins to dry out and coagulate as the starch gel replaces it. The crumb is formed during this stage.

Crust Forms

At 165°F (74°C), the crust begins to form as the starches and sugar on the surface of the dough brown and thicken. The product will appear done at this stage, but additional baking time is needed to evaporate the alcohol given off by the yeast. Yeast products removed from the oven too early will not taste right.

Finished Product

By the time the internal temperature has reached 176°F (80°C), the alcohol will have evaporated. Finished products have an internal temperature of approximately 220°F (104°C).

Test for Doneness

A gauge of whether a product is done is the thump test. Tap the top of the loaf. If the loaf gives off a hollow sound, indicating that it is filled with air and not moisture, it is done. Watch rolls and small loaves carefully, as their bottom surfaces may burn before the crust color develops fully.

Another way to test for doneness is to look at the crust. If it is evenly brown on top and bottom, it is done. **Figure 27.3** explains some common problems when baking yeast dough.

Reading Check Summarize What happens during oven spring?

Cooling, Storage, and Serving

Once a yeast dough product is removed from the oven, it must be cooled and stored properly to maintain the highest possible quality.

- Remove yeast products from their pans immediately.
- Place them on cooling racks or screens at room temperature. One exception is rolls baked on sheets. These may be left on the sheets to cool, if they are well spaced.
- Cool yeast products completely before slicing or wrapping.

Glazing

In some cases, you will brush melted butter or shortening or a glaze onto a hot yeast dough product immediately after removing it from the oven. Sweet dough products such as coffee cake and Danish pastry may be glazed with a mixture of water and sugar or corn syrup while they are still warm.

Staling Prevention

Yeast dough products begin the process of staling as soon as they are baked. Staling causes yeast dough products to lose their freshness. During staling, the crust becomes moist and tough, while the interior crumb of the bread becomes dry and crumbly. Staling also causes breads to lose flavor.

> ### ⤳ Small Bites ⤳
>
> **Altitude** The moisture in dough evaporates more slowly at higher altitudes, such as those found in mountainous areas. Oven temperatures may need to be increased slightly in high altitudes to prevent the dough from expanding too much and breaking down the cell structure in the bread.

READING CHECK ANSWER The dough suddenly rises and expands as the yeast reacts to the heat of the oven.

FIGURE 27.3 Yeast Bread Troubleshooting

Common Problems There are many problems that can go wrong when baking yeast bread. *How do you know if a loaf of yeast bread is baked properly?*

Product Failure	Possible Cause
Poor shape	• Too much liquid in dough • Improper shaping of dough • Incorrect proofing • Too much steam in oven
Blisters on crust	• Too much liquid in dough • Improper fermentation
Top crust separates from the loaf	• Loaf poorly shaped • Top not slashed • Dough dried out during proofing • Lack of moisture in oven
Large holes in crumb	• Too much yeast • Over kneaded dough • Inadequate punching of dough
Poor flavor	• Improper fermentation • Inferior, spoiled, or rancid ingredients

You can slow the staling process:

- **Additions to Dough** Depending on the formula, ingredients such as malt syrup may be added to the dough at the mixing process to help slow staling.
- **Adequate Proofing** Underproofed items stale more quickly than those that have received proper proofing.
- **Avoid Refrigeration** Refrigeration speeds up the staling process of yeast breads.

Proper Packaging and Storage

Do not wrap products while they are still warm. Most breads should not be kept for more than one day in a foodservice operation. If you will be keeping them longer than one day, wrap them tightly in moisture-proof wrapping and store them in a freezer to prevent staling. Items with thin crusts, such as French bread, should be wrapped in paper when they are stored. If thin-crust products are wrapped in plastic, they will become soggy.

 Reading Check Explain How do you prevent staling in yeast doughs?

SECTION 27.2 After You Read

Review Key Concepts

1. **Describe** the straight-dough mixing method.
2. **Outline** the stages in mixing and kneading yeast dough.
3. **List** the factors that determine oven temperature and baking time.
4. **Illustrate** how to properly pack a yeast bread.

Practice Culinary Academics

 Mathematics

5. Ryan has just finished baking two baguettes. One of them is 55 centimeters long; the other is 61 centimeters in length. What is the length of each baguette in millimeters? In meters? In kilometers?

Math Concept **Metric Length Equivalents**
The metric system of measurement is based on powers of 10. One millimeter is 1/1000 of a meter, or 0.001 meters. One centimeter is 1/100 of a meter, or 0.01 meter. One kilometer is 1,000 meters.

Starting Hint One millimeter is 1/10 smaller than one centimeter, so multiply centimeters by 10 to find millimeters. Divide centimeters by 100 to find meters. Divide that meter amount by 1,000 to find kilometers.

NCTM Measurement Understand measurable attributes of objects and the units, systems, and processes of measurement.

 Check your answers at this book's Online Learning Center at **glencoe.com**.

FIGURE CAPTION ANSWER A properly baked yeast bread loaf will sound hollow when lightly tapped, indicating that it is filled with air and not moisture.

READING CHECK ANSWER Some bakeries add chemicals to extend shelf life. You can also proof, wrap, and store the bread properly.

Review and Applications

Chapter Summary

Yeast breads are made from dough, a mixture of flour, water, salt, yeast and other ingredients. Yeast dough products are classified according to the type of dough used to produce them.

Regular yeast dough is first kneaded thoroughly, by machine or by hand, and then fermented. Lack of interaction between ingredients can cause failure.

Content and Academic Vocabulary Review

1. Use each of these vocabulary words in a sentence.

Content Vocabulary

- leavens (p. 706)
- peel (p. 706)
- starter (p. 706)
- hard lean dough (p. 708)
- crust (p. 708)
- chemical dough conditioners (p. 708)
- soft medium dough (p. 709)
- sweet rich dough (p. 709)
- rolled-in fat yeast dough (p. 709)
- gipfels (p. 710)
- Danish pastry dough (p. 711)
- straight-dough method (p. 713)

- modified straight-dough method (p. 713)
- sponge method (p. 713)
- preferment (p. 713)
- let down (p. 715)
- continuous breadmaking (p. 715)
- punch (p. 716)
- rounded (p. 717)
- bench box (p. 718)
- bench rest (p. 718)
- shape (p. 718)
- seams (p. 718)
- pan loaf (p. 718)
- free-form loaf (p. 718)

- pan (p. 718)
- proof (p. 719)
- wash (p. 719)
- slash (p. 721)
- dock (p. 722)
- oven spring (p. 722)

Academic Vocabulary

- tempted (p. 709)
- notable (p. 709)
- critical (p. 714)
- correspond (p. 714)

Review Key Concepts

2. List yeast dough ingredients and their functions.

3. Distinguish between the three different types of yeast doughs.

4. Summarize the characteristics and uses of rolled-in fat yeast doughs.

5. Describe the mixing methods for yeast doughs.

6. Outline the stages in properly preparing yeast doughs.

7. Demonstrate the baking of quality yeast breads.

8. Illustrate how to cool and store yeast breads.

Critical Thinking

9. Imagine you have a customer who is following a low-fat diet. Which would you recommend: Italian bread, Parkerhouse rolls, or croissants? Why?

10. Examine seasonings. You have a basic formula for white yeast bread. What could you do to make the final product more flavorful?

Review and Applications

Academic Skills

English Language Arts

11. Bread in Many Languages Find the names of different types of yeast breads from around the world. What are the names of the different bread products and what do they mean in the language of origin? Write a list of the names, their countries of origin, and their meanings in their native languages. Compare lists as a class.

> **NCTE 9** Develop an understanding diversity in language use across cultures.

Social Studies

12. Breads Around the World Study yeast breads from various countries. What are the similarities and what are the differences? Can you think of possible factors that may have contributed to these similarities and differences? What aspects of the culture contributed to the features of the yeast breads of that culture? Create a five-minute presentation that discusses three different examples of yeast breads, and how and why they differ.

> **NCSS IV E Individual Development and Identity** Examine the interaction of ethnic, national, or cultural influences in specific situations or events.

Mathematics

13. Donut Deal Bob recently began advertising his bakery in a local newspaper. The ad included a coupon for 25¢ off each donut purchased. On the first day of the new promotion, Bob sold 265 donuts, bringing in $238. However, Bob realized that his cashier was throwing away the coupons redeemed, and he does not know how many were used. If a regular donut sells for $0.95, and a discounted donut (with coupon) sells for $0.70, how many discounted donuts were sold?

Math Concept **Distributive Property of Multiplication** Multiplying a sum (or a difference) by a number is the equivalent of multiplying each addend by that same number, and then adding the two products. For example, $7(4 + 2)$ is the same as $(7 \times 4) + (7 \times 2)$.

Starting Hint The problem can be solved with an algebraic equation. Let d stand for the number of discounted donuts sold. Then $(265 - d)$ must equal the number of regular-price donuts sold. Multiply the price of each type of donut by the quantity of each type of donut to find total revenue: $(\$0.95)(265 - d) + (\$0.70)(d) = \$238$. Solve for d.

> **NCTM Algebra** Represent and analyze mathematical situations and structures using algebraic symbols.

Certification Prep

Sharpen your test-taking skills to improve your kitchen certification program score.

Directions Read the questions. Then, read the answer choices and choose the best possible answer for each.

14. What is the ideal temperature range for yeast fermentation?

    a. 78°–82°F

    b. 80°–90°F

    c. 85°–95°F

    d. 176°–220°F

15. What is a lean dough product often eaten at breakfast?

    a. croissant

    b. sourdough

    c. bagel

    d. cinnamon buns

Test-Taking Tip
Use familiar word parts, such as suffixes and prefixes, to help you remember new definitions.

Real-World Skills and Applications

Interpersonal and Collaborative Skills

16. Promote a Yeast Bread Follow your teacher's instructions to break into teams. Imagine that your team is an ad agency developing a print ad for a particular yeast bread product. Describe the product, its qualities, its nutritional benefit, and suggested uses in your ad. Use photographs or illustrations in your ad, if possible. Share your team's ad with the class. As a class, rate each ad's effectiveness.

Self-Management Skills

17. Trim the Fat Your doctor has recommended that you lower your fat intake. Examine your yeast bread product consumption and recommend ways you can change the types of bread products you eat to lower your fat intake. Make a list of the substitutions. List specific ingredients in the products that may increase fat intake.

Technology Applications

18. Internet Research With your teacher's permission, use the Internet to research one yeast bread product. Learn about the ingredients of that product and how it is made, as well as the texture, appearance, and flavor of the final product. Share your findings with the class through a five-minute oral presentation. Use slides, photographs, or illustrations with your presentation, if possible.

Financial Literacy

19. Purchase Yeast Samara bought 8 ounces of instant yeast for $3. She used about ¾ of it before it had to be thrown away. Anita bought an 8-ounce bag of active dry yeast for $5 and was able to use it all because it kept longer. Compare each person's usage. Who made the more cost-effective choice?

Culinary Lab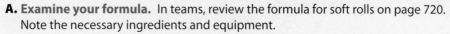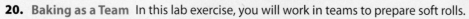

Use the culinary skills you have learned in this chapter.

Bake Soft Rolls

20. Baking as a Team In this lab exercise, you will work in teams to prepare soft rolls.

A. Examine your formula. In teams, review the formula for soft rolls on page 720. Note the necessary ingredients and equipment.

B. Make dough. Prepare the dough.

C. Observe the process. Make observations about the type of yeast used, the optimal temperature for the yeast, the texture and feel of the dough, which mixing method was used, what bread-baking stages were followed, how the team tested for doneness, and what the characteristics of the end product were.

D. Serve the rolls. Serve the rolls and have a contest to determine which team's soft rolls were the best.

Create Your Evaluation

Evaluate each team's bread by creating a scoring sheet and giving each team a score in the following categories: Shape, Volume, Crumb, Crust, Color, Tenderness, and Taste. Rate each category on a scale of one to four. 1 = Poor; 2 = Fair; 3 = Good; and 4 = Great.

CHAPTER 28

Quick Breads

SECTIONS

28.1 Making Biscuits

28.2 Making Muffins

WRITING ACTIVITY

Compare and Contrast Paper

Biscuits and muffins are two different types of quick breads, but they have similarities as well. Write a compare and contrast paper that identifies what you believe are the similarities and differences between biscuits and muffins.

Writing Tips

1 Use a graphic organizer to map your ideas.

2 Organize your comparison by subject or by features.

3 Use appropriate transition words and phrases.

EXPLORE THE PHOTO

Quick breads make a good breakfast choice, but can be served at any meal. *Why do you think quick breads make a good breakfast choice?*

WRITING ACTIVITY ANSWER The paper should describe each detail clearly and be organized logically.

EXPLORE THE PHOTO ANSWER Answers will vary. For example, quick breads can be made quickly or made the night before.

Making Biscuits

Reading Guide

 Before You Read

Create an Outline Use the section's heading titles to create an outline. Make the titles into Level 1 main ideas. Add supporting information to create Level 2, 3, and 4 details. Use the outline to predict what you are about to learn.

Read to Learn
Key Concepts
● **Compare and contrast** the biscuit, blending, and creaming methods of mixing.
● **Deconstruct** the steps required to make quality biscuits.

Main Idea
Quick breads are products with a bread- or cake-like texture that do not contain yeast. They do not require a lot of time or equipment to produce.

Graphic Organizer
As you read, use a web diagram like this one to show the seven different typical ingredients in a quick bread.

Content Vocabulary
● biscuit method
● blending method
● creaming method
● pour batter
● drop batter
● deflate

Academic Vocabulary
● consistency
● separation

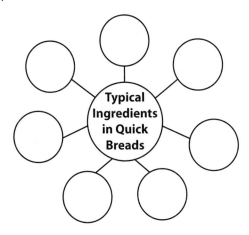

 Graphic Organizer Go to this book's Online Learning Center at **glencoe.com** for a printable graphic organizer.

GRAPHIC ORGANIZER ANSWER Flour, eggs, fat, sugar, salt, a chemical leavening agent, and a liquid.

Biscuits and other quick breads are a good choice for breakfast and other meals.

ACADEMIC STANDARDS

 English Language Arts
NCTE 12 Use language to accomplish individual purposes.

 Mathematics
NCTM Measurement Understand measurable attributes of objects and the units, systems, and processes of measurement.

 Social Studies
NCSS I A Culture Analyze and explain the ways groups, societies, and cultures address human needs and concerns.

NCSS II D Time, Continuity, and Change Employ processes to validate and weigh evidence for claims.

NCTE National Council of Teachers of English

NCTM National Council of Teachers of Mathematics

NSES National Science Education Standards

NCSS National Council for the Social Studies

Types of Quick Breads

Quick breads are baked goods that can be served at breakfast, at lunch, or with dinner. Some examples of quick breads are pancakes, biscuits, muffins, scones, waffles, and loaf breads.

Quick breads are those products that have a bread- or cake-like texture, but do not contain yeast. Therefore, quick breads do not need to rise or proof before baking. Instead of using yeast, quick breads use chemical leavening agents such as double-acting baking powder and baking soda.

Quick breads are typically baked on sheet pans or in loaf and muffin pans. Quick breads can be plain, lightly glazed, sprinkled with confectioner's sugar, or frosted. They can be served warm or cold. Quick breads can be part of a more complex dish, or can be served as a main dish of their own.

Typical ingredients in a quick bread product are flour, eggs, fat, sugar, salt, a chemical leavening agent, and a liquid. Flour is the foundation of quick breads. A combination of hard and soft wheat flours produces the best quick bread products. Eggs provide added volume and structure. They are a natural leavening agent. Fat is used to keep the baked product moist and tender. It also helps in creaming, or mixing. Sugar and other sweeteners, such as brown sugar or molasses, improve the flavor and color of quick breads. Sugar also helps in creaming. Salt strengthens gluten and adds flavor.

In addition, leavening agents, such as double-acting baking powder or baking soda, allow quick breads to leaven, or rise. The liquid, typically milk, adds moisture. It allows the dry ingredients to be blended into a batter or dough. Liquid also helps produce gluten.

The same ingredients are used in most quick breads. However, the proportion of these ingredients varies. The proportion of ingredients is determined by the product that is being made. Some specialty quick bread doughs, such as phyllo dough and pâte à choux can be used for both appetizers and desserts.

The flour used in quick breads ranges from wheat to oatmeal. Grains such as bran and cornmeal are often added for flavor and texture. Spices, nuts, fruits, and other ingredients may be added to create interesting flavors.

Types of Batter Pour batters and drop batters have different consistencies. *Why do you think there is a difference in consistency between the two batter types?*

PHOTO CAPTION ANSWER The difference in consistency between pour batters and drop batters is based on the amount of liquid in the formula.

FIGURE 28.1 **Quick Bread Ingredient Proportions**

Quick Breads Quick breads can be made from thick and thin batters and doughs.
Why do you think different quick breads require different forms of batter and dough?

Quick Bread Products	Amount of Flour	Amount of Liquid	Consistency
Biscuits (soft doughs)	Three parts	One part	Sticky, pliable
Pancakes (pour batters)	One part	One part	Thin, pours
Muffins and Fritters (drop batters)	Two parts	One part	Thick, forms in drops

Quick Bread Methods

Quick breads are produced by one of three methods: the biscuit method, the blending method, or the creaming method.

- The **biscuit method** requires cutting the fat into the dry ingredients. This is done until the fat and dry ingredients resemble cornmeal. Then, the liquid ingredients are added. This process produces flaky items such as biscuits.
- The **blending method** combines the liquid, sugar, liquid fat, and eggs at the same time. Then, the dry ingredients are added to the mixture. The liquid fat and sugar act as a tenderizer. The blending method is most commonly used to make muffins and fruit breads.
- The **creaming method** involves using solid shortening instead of liquid fat. In this method, the sugar and pre-softened shortening are creamed together with a mixer on low speed until the mixture is light and fluffy. The eggs are then added one at a time. After the eggs are added, the dry and liquid ingredients are alternately added. Muffins made by the creaming method are more cake-like in texture.

The type of quick bread and the **consistency**, or texture, of its dough or batter determine which method you should use.

Quick breads can be made from soft doughs or batters. (See **Figure 28.1**.) Soft doughs are thicker in consistency than batters. They can be rolled and cut into shapes prior to baking while batters cannot. Baking powder biscuits and scones are examples of soft dough quick breads.

Quick bread products, such as pancakes and muffins, are made from either a pour batter or drop batter. A **pour batter** will often vary in consistency. Some are so thin they can be poured from the mixing bowl to the cookware just like water. Others are almost as thick as drop batters. A **drop batter** is usually so thick it needs to be scraped or dropped from a portion or ice cream scoop to the cookware.

Reading Check Describe What are two characteristics of quick breads?

The Biscuit Method

Biscuits are a popular baked item in many foodservice operations. They are typically served at breakfast. Biscuits vary in shape, size, and filling, and are simple to make. Proper mixing is the key to producing quality biscuits. Overmixing will produce tough biscuits.

The basic ingredients in biscuits are flour, a leavening agent, shortening, sugar, salt, and milk. Sometimes eggs and butter are used to improve quality and flavor.

Eggs also build structure. They increase the volume of biscuits by acting as a natural leavening agent. If you decide to add eggs to your biscuit mixture, you will need to adjust the amount of other leavening agents.

The biscuit method is used most often when you make dough products such as biscuits and scones. As you have read, the biscuit method involves cutting in the fat with the dry ingredients. This method typically is performed by using a mixer on low speed. Be careful not to overmix.

FIGURE CAPTION ANSWER The type of quick bread, the method used to make it, and its final desired shape will determine whether a quick bread will have a batter or a dough.

READING CHECK ANSWER Quick breads have a cake-like texture, and use chemical leavening agents such as baking powder or baking soda.

Use the Biscuit Method

1 Prepare the sheet pan. Grease the sheet pan with a commercial pan grease or line the pan with parchment paper.

2 Scale, or measure, the ingredients. The measurements must be exact if the biscuits are to maintain quality.

3 Sift all the dry ingredients into the mixing bowl.

4 Cut or rub the shortening into the dry ingredients. This will result in a mixture containing small pieces of fat. This step can be performed using the mixer with either the paddle or pastry knife attachments.

5 Whisk the eggs and milk together in a separate stainless steel bowl.

6 Add the combined liquid ingredients to the flour mixture. Mix lightly. Be careful not to overmix. Overmixing will make the biscuits tough.

7 Take the mixed dough to a pre-floured bench and set it down. Flour the top of the dough by dusting it with bread flour.

8 Knead the dough lightly using your fingertips only. Then, fold it in half and rotate it 90 degrees. Continue this process about 5 to 10 times. Do not over knead. Over kneading will make the biscuits tough. The dough should be soft and elastic, but not sticky.

9 Allow the dough to rest 15 minutes before rolling.

Baking Biscuits

As soon as the biscuits are shaped and placed on the sheet pan, allow them to relax for 10 minutes before you bake them. This will allow the gluten to react and help the chemical reaction of the baking powder or baking soda. Place the sheet pans in a hot conventional oven. The oven temperature should be between 400°F (204°C) and 425°F (218°C). Bake the biscuits for approximately 8 to 10 minutes. The tops of the biscuits should be lightly browned.

Remove the sheet pans from the oven and allow the biscuits to cool on wire racks. Serve the biscuits immediately. Butter, jam, preserves, and honey can accompany the biscuits. Biscuits can also be served with gravy.

Quality Biscuits

When checking the quality standards for biscuits, you should first make sure the mixture is thoroughly blended. This must be achieved without overmixing. If the mixture is overmixed, the baked product will lack quality.

⚹ HOW TO ⚹

Cut and Form
Biscuits

1 Roll the prepared dough onto a pre-floured surface. The dough should be rolled out to about ½- to 1-inch in thickness.

2 Check the dough's depth. Make sure the dough is uniform in thickness. Biscuits double in height during baking.

3 Cut the dough into shapes using a round hand cutter or pastry knife. When using a hand cutter, be sure to cut straight into the dough. Do not twist the cutters. Twisting can prevent the dough from rising correctly.

4 Place the raw biscuits on a sheet pan lightly greased with commercial pan grease or lined with parchment paper. The sides of the dough should not be touching. Brush the tops of the raw biscuits with egg wash prior to baking. This will make the crust golden in color.

Rolled and cut biscuits should be light, tender, and flaky. Properly kneading and cutting the dough determines this quality. Over kneading or twisting the hand cutters can **deflate** the dough, or cause the dough to lose volume. Biscuits should have high volume.

There are several quality standards you should meet when you bake biscuits.

- **Appearance** Biscuits should be the same size with flat tops and straight sides.
- **Color** Biscuits should have a golden brown crust. The crumb should be creamy or flaky, depending on the type of biscuit.
- **Texture** Rolled and cut biscuits should be light, tender, and flaky. Flaky biscuits should easily separate into layers when they are broken apart. This **separation**, or dividing, is due to the fat that melts between the layers during baking. The fat separates the layers.
- **Flavor** Biscuits should have a pleasing, delicate flavor. A bitter flavor may indicate too much baking powder or baking soda. You may want to add different flavor ingredients to the mixture for variety. Such ingredients include herbs, chives, cheese, and bacon.

🔺 **Baked Biscuits** Quality biscuits are a favorite accompaniment to many meals. *What characteristics do quality biscuits have?*

PHOTO CAPTION ANSWER Quality biscuits should have flat tops and straight sides, a golden brown crust, should be tender and flaky, and should separate into layers when pulled apart.

Cooling and Serving Biscuits

Biscuits can be cooled on wire racks after baking. However, they are best served when hot. You can serve biscuits throughout the day. Most foodservice operations offer them at all meals.

There are many items that you can serve with biscuits to add flavor and variety for customers, including:

- honey
- butter
- honey butter
- jam
- preserves

 Reading Check Summarize How are biscuits cut and formed?

SECTION 28.1 After You Read

Review Key Concepts

1. **Explain** the biscuit method of mixing.
2. **Describe** the quality standards to aim for when making biscuits.

Practice Culinary Academics

 English Language Arts

3. Imagine that you are opening a small cafe that will serve coffee and quick breads. First, decide what type of quick breads you will offer, and find recipes for those quick breads. Then, create a menu listing to describe your quick bread offerings.

NCTE 12 Use language to accomplish individual purposes.

Social Studies

4. Quick breads are found in the cuisine of many cultures around the world. For example, in Ireland, soda bread became popular after bicarbonate of soda was introduced, because Irish wheat does not rise well with yeast. What other examples of quick breads from around the world can you find? Create a chart to show their characteristics.

NCSS I A Culture Analyze and explain the ways groups, societies, and cultures address human needs and concerns.

 Mathematics

5. Carrie is preparing biscuits that are each ⅝-inch tall before baking. If the biscuits double in height during baking, how tall will each finished biscuit be, in centimeters?

Math Concept **Converting Length Measurements** The closest metric distance measurement to the inch is the centimeter. One inch = 2.54 centimeters, while one centimeter = 0.3937 inch. To convert inches to centimeters, multiply inches by 2.54.

Starting Hint Multiply ⅝ by 2 to find the final height of a biscuit. Convert that fraction to a decimal by dividing the numerator by the denominator. Multiply that number by 2.54 to convert to centimeters.

NCTM Measurement Understand measurable attributes of objects and the units, systems, and processes of measurement.

 Check your answers at this book's Online Learning Center at **glencoe.com**.

A TASTE OF HISTORY ANSWER Students' charts will give specific reasons why one sample is more appealing than the other, and what bearing the different ingredients had on the results.

READING CHECK ANSWER Biscuits can be rolled and cut using round hand cutters or a pastry knife. They can also be formed by dropping the dough on a sheet pan.

Making Muffins

Quality muffins must be made carefully.

Reading Guide

 Before You Read

Use Diagrams As you read through this section, write down the main idea. Write down any facts, explanations, or examples you find in the text. Start at the main idea and draw arrows to the information that directly supports it. Then, draw arrows from these examples to any information that supports them.

Read to Learn

Key Concepts
- **Explain** the blending and creaming methods of mixing muffins.
- **Describe** how to make quality loaf quick breads.
- **Outline** the steps used to bake quality muffins.

Main Idea

Muffins use the blending or creaming mixing methods. Knowing how to prepare quality muffins is a useful skill for a foodservice employee.

Content Vocabulary
- baking cup
- elastic
- tunnels
- potency
- streusel
- walls
- aftertaste

Academic Vocabulary
- desired
- deteriorate

ACADEMIC STANDARDS

 English Language Arts
NCTE 5 Use different writing process elements to communicate.

 Mathematics
NCTM Number and Operations Compute fluently and make reasonable estimates.

 Science
NSES B Develop an understanding of chemical reactions.

NCTE National Council of Teachers of English

NCTM National Council of Teachers of Mathematics

NSES National Science Education Standards

NCSS National Council for the Social Studies

Graphic Organizer

As you read, use a tree diagram like this one to list the quality characteristics of muffins.

Quality Characteristics of Muffins

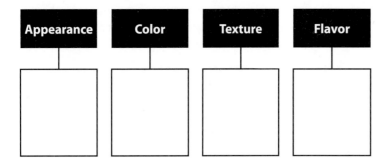

Appearance	Color	Texture	Flavor

 Graphic Organizer Go to this book's Online Learning Center at **glencoe.com** for a printable graphic organizer.

GRAPHIC ORGANIZER ANSWER Appearance: Round with dome-shaped top, uniform size. Color: Golden-brown surface. Texture: Even grain, tender and moist, no tunnels. Flavor: Sweet and pleasant, no bitter aftertaste.

Blending Method

Muffins can be bread- or cake-like in texture. This depends on the method that is used to mix the ingredients. Muffins can be different shapes and sizes. Muffins usually have fruit or nuts added to the mixture to add flavor and texture to the baked product.

The blending method is used to produce muffins, loaf breads, pancakes, and waffles. The blending method involves using oil or liquid fat to blend the ingredients. Batters for these baked goods are sometimes interchangeable. For example, bran muffin batter can be poured into a loaf pan instead of a muffin pan. The end result is bran loaf bread instead of bran muffins. You would need only to adjust the baking time.

The basic ingredients in muffins are flour, leavening agent, eggs, oil, sugar, salt, and a liquid. Flour blends may be used to increase the nutritional value of the product.

Muffins are made from a drop batter. They are leavened by a leavening agent, such as baking powder. The structure of the muffin is achieved when the flour, starches, gluten, and egg proteins coagulate during heating.

⌒ Small Bites ⌒

Use Liners To bake muffins that have a moist, tender exterior, line the muffin pans with paper cups. If you want muffins with a crust, omit the liners. Instead, grease the bottoms and sides of the muffin pans.

✳ HOW TO ✳

Blend
Muffins

1 Sift the dry ingredients into a separate mixing bowl. Add sifted, dry ingredients to the liquid and sugar mixture.

2 Combine and blend the liquid ingredients with the sugar until smooth.

3 Mix together until the dry ingredients are just moistened. Do not overmix. This will make the batter tough. The batter should look lumpy.

Creaming Method

When you prepare cake-like muffins made with solid shortening, you will need to use the creaming method of mixing. The creaming method involves combining the sugar and fat first until light and fluffy.

When you cream muffins, use these steps:

1. Scale the ingredients.
2. Sift the dry ingredients into a separate mixing bowl and set aside.
3. Combine the solid fat and the sugar in the mixing bowl until smooth, fluffy, and creamy. Use the paddle attachment on the mixer.
4. Add the eggs one at a time. Blend well after each addition.
5. Add the flour and liquid ingredients alternately in approximately three parts. Continue to mix until the batter is smooth.

Dividing Muffin Batter

Dividing the muffin batter involves transferring the batter from the bench mixing bowl into individual muffin pans. Use a portion scoop to divide, or pan up, the muffins, scraping up the side and upper edge of the mixing bowl to level off the scoop.

It is important to divide the batter evenly. Using a portion scoop can help achieve this. You also can drop the batter into the pan by hand. To do this well requires practice. Fill the pans ½ to ¾ full. Leave enough space for the muffins to rise as they bake.

You may want to line each muffin pan with baking cups. A **baking cup** is a paper lining that keeps the muffin from sticking to the muffin pan.

Reading Check Explain How should you portion muffin batter?

● **Uniform Sizes** Muffins should be uniform in size when they are baked. *How can you help ensure this?*

PHOTO CAPTION ANSWER Divide the batter evenly using a portion scoop.

READING CHECK ANSWER Transfer it from the mixing bowl into individual muffin tins. Do not stir, divide it evenly, and fill tins ½ to ¾ full.

Loaf Breads

Loaf breads are similar in preparation to muffins. Like other quick bread products, loaf breads are made from flour, leavening agents, eggs, fat, sugar, salt, and a liquid. Baking powder is the chemical leavening agent used in loaf breads.

Loaf breads are made from a drop batter or a very thick pour batter. The baked product should have a uniform texture. The crust should be lightly browned, but not thick. The crumb should be tender and moist, not tough or dry. Loaf breads also should have rounded tops with a split down the center.

The time spent mixing loaf bread batter is crucial. Undermixing will result in a lumpy batter with dry pockets of flour. Overmixing will overdevelop the gluten. The batter will be stringy or elastic. **Elastic** means stretchy and flexible. The end product will be tough and will have **tunnels**, or large, irregular holes, in the crumb. When you mix loaf bread batter, you should mix it lightly. Mix it long enough to only blend all the ingredients. Then scale the batter into the pan.

You can alter the flavor of loaf breads by substituting or adding ingredients. For example, fold in walnuts, cranberries, or zucchini to make walnut bread, cranberry bread, or zucchini bread. You can also use bananas or pumpkin to make banana bread or pumpkin bread.

Quick Breads and Gluten

Unlike yeast breads, very little gluten is developed in quick breads. This is a **desired**, or wanted, result. Quick breads should be tender, not chewy. Too much gluten will result in a less tender product.

Quick breads use chemical leavening agents, such as baking soda or baking powder, instead of yeast and fermentation to rise. They will not turn out as expected if there is too much gluten in the mixture. Too much gluten will make the mixture heavy instead of light. This will create an inferior-quality quick bread.

Leavening Quick Breads

Leavening agents allow quick breads to rise quickly without proofing. A leavening agent is a substance that causes dough or batter to rise. The two most common chemical leavening agents are double-acting baking powder and baking soda.

Purchase Leavening Agents Purchase leavening agents, such as baking powder, in the smallest amount possible that you need. It is true that you may receive better prices when you purchase them in larger quantities.

SCIENCE À LA CARTE ANSWER Students should find that bubbles form when baking powder is mixed with water, and when baking soda is mixed with vinegar.

Prepare
a Loaf Bread

1 Grease the bottom of deep pans, such as loaf pans.

2 Prepare the loaf bread batter using either the creaming or blending method. The choice will depend on the formula.

3 Heat a conventional oven to 400°F (204°C).

4 Scale the appropriate amount of loaf bread batter into the greased pans. Allow the batter to rest.

5 Place the loaf pans in the oven. Place a shallow trough of oil down the center of the top of the loaf bread batter. This will prevent uneven splits.

6 Bake at 400°F (204°C) for the length of time specified in the formula. Check for doneness. If the loaf is firm to the touch and springs back, or if a skewer is inserted and comes out clean, it is done.

However, if the leavening agents are not used within a short time, they will **deteriorate**, or go down in quality. This will result in low-quality baked products. The money saved buying bulk quantities is then wasted. Chemical leavening agents must maintain their freshness.

Store Leavening Agents Store leavening agents in air-tight containers. Keep the containers in a cool, dry place. Always keep the lids on the containers, even if you use the leavening agents frequently throughout the day. This will prevent contamination, moisture absorption, and spillage.

If cared for properly, baking soda and baking powder can have a shelf life of two to four months. Date your containers to note their freshness. They can lose approximately 10% of their **potency**, or strength, each month. This is why it is important to purchase only the amount you need.

Reading Check Describe How are quick breads leavened?

READING CHECK ANSWER Quick breads can be leavened by chemical leavening agents such as baking powder or baking soda.

Baking Muffins

When you bake muffins, dry and liquid ingredients can be mixed ahead of time. Once they are combined, however, you will need to bake the muffins immediately. Otherwise, your muffins could lose volume.

To bake muffins, follow these steps:

1. Set the conventional oven temperature at 385°F to 400°F (196°C to 204°C) and grease the muffin pan with commercial pan grease.
2. Using a portion scoop, lift the batter from the mixing bowl and drop or pour it into the prepared muffin pan. A portion scoop will provide equal-size muffins. Be careful not to mix the batter when scooping it out.
3. Garnish the muffin batter with sugar, cinnamon, nuts, or streusel (ˈstrü-səl) toppings. A **streusel** topping is a sweet crumbly topping for cakes and quick breads generally made of flour, brown sugar, and granulated sugar.
4. Place the muffin pans in the oven. Bake the muffins for the time listed on the formula. Test the muffins for doneness by pressing on the top of one of the muffins.

If it springs back, it is done. If it does not spring back, it needs to bake longer. If you need to leave the muffins in to bake longer, stay close by and watch them carefully to make sure they do not overcook. The tops also should be a golden brown color.

5. Remove the muffin pans from the oven and let the pans cool on wire racks until the muffins are warm.
6. Turn the muffins out of the pan onto the cooling rack. If muffins stick, tap the bottom of the pan to loosen them.

🔺 **One Scoop per Muffin** A portion scoop will help you maintain consistent-size muffins. *Why would you choose to use baking cups in a muffin pan?*

PHOTO CAPTION ANSWER Baking cups will help keep the sides of the muffins moist and soft. A crust will form if they are not used.

NUTRITION NOTES ANSWER Fruit products, such as citrus zest or juice, strawberries or dried papaya will add vitamin C.

Quality Muffins

Muffin tops should be golden brown, and the **walls**, or sides of the muffin, should not be too thick. Muffins should be tender and moist. The crumb should break apart without crumbling. Look for these characteristics:

- **Appearance** Muffins should be round in shape with dome-shaped tops. They should be uniform in size.
- **Color** Muffins should have a golden brown surface.
- **Texture** The grain should be even. The muffin should be tender and moist, not dry or brittle. Muffins should not be filled with tunnels.
- **Flavor** The flavor should be sweet and pleasant with no bitter aftertaste from too much leavening. An **aftertaste** is a secondary flavor that comes after the main flavor has subsided.

Cooling and Serving Muffins

Muffins are cooled in the pans until they are warm. The muffin pans should be placed on top of wire racks to allow air to circulate around the pans.

Muffins are better if they are made daily and served immediately. Muffin batter can be premade and refrigerated for three days prior to baking. The batter also can be frozen for two weeks. You can freeze muffin batter either before or after portioning.

To thaw the frozen batter, place it in the refrigerator. Allow it to thaw overnight. The batter will be ready to bake in the morning.

Muffins are served at breakfast, lunch, and sometimes dinner. They may be accompanied by jams and jellies.

 Reading Check **Summarize** How should muffins be cooled?

 SECTION 28.2  **After You Read**

Review Key Concepts

1. **Explain** how to divide muffin batter.
2. **Describe** how to check loaf breads for doneness.
3. **Outline** how to cool and serve muffins.

Practice Culinary Academics

 English Language Arts

4. Make a poster to hang in a bakeshop window advertising a muffin or loaf quick bread product. Illustrate the product and write up brief pieces of information to help sell the product. Be sure to list advantages of well-made quick breads. Posters should tempt others to purchase the quick bread. Hang your posters in the classroom.

> **NCTE 5** Use different writing process elements to communicate effectively.

Mathematics

5. It costs Ray $5.50 in ingredients and labor to make a loaf of zucchini bread that is 13 ¾ inches long. If Ray sells individual slices that are each 1 ¼-inch thick, what is his cost per slice?

Math Concept **Dividing Fractions** To divide when a fraction is involved, convert any mixed or whole numbers to improper fractions. Multiply the first fraction by the reciprocal of the second fraction. Reduce to lowest terms.

Starting Hint Determine how many slices are in one loaf by dividing 13 ¾ by 1 ¼, after first converting each mixed number to an improper fraction. Divide $5.50 by your result to find the cost per slice.

> **NCTM Number and Operations** Compute fluently and make reasonable estimates.

 Check your answers at this book's Online Learning Center at **glencoe.com**.

READING CHECK ANSWER Muffins are cooled in the pans until they are warm. The muffin pans should be placed on wire racks to allow air to circulate around them.

Review and Applications

Chapter Summary

Quick bread characteristics include a bread- or cake-like texture. There are basic ingredients in all quick breads; the proportion of ingredients to each other determines the product being made. Quick breads can be prepared using one of three methods: the biscuit method, the blending method, or the creaming method. The biscuit method is used to make dough products such as biscuits or scones. To meet the standards of quality, biscuits should be golden brown, flaky, and have a good flavor.

The blending method involves using oil or liquid fat to blend ingredients. The creaming method involves combining solid fat and sugar before adding the remaining ingredients. Muffins are usually made with these methods.

Content and Academic Vocabulary Review

1. Create a fill-in-the-blank sentence for each term, with enough information to determine the missing word.

Content Vocabulary

- biscuit method (p. 731)
- blending method (p. 731)
- creaming method (p. 731)
- pour batter (p. 731)
- drop batter (p. 731)
- deflate (p. 734)
- baking cup (p. 738)
- elastic (p. 739)
- tunnels (p. 739)
- potency (p. 740)
- streusel (p. 741)
- walls (p. 742)
- aftertaste (p. 742)

Academic Vocabulary

- consistency (p. 731)
- separation (p. 734)
- desired (p. 739)
- deteriorate (p. 740)

Review Key Concepts

2. Compare and contrast the biscuit, blending, and creaming methods of mixing.

3. Deconstruct the steps required to make quality biscuits.

4. Explain the blending and creaming methods of mixing muffins.

5. Describe how to make quality loaf quick breads.

6. Outline the steps used to bake quality muffins.

Critical Thinking

7. Understand consequences. While baking biscuits, you accidently add yeast to the formula in addition to baking powder. What should you do, and why?

8. Explain how to portion a batch of muffin batter evenly if you do not have a portion or ice cream scoop.

9. Imagine that you have a quick bread formula that is not labeled with the name of the product. How would you determine what the end product will be?

10. Imagine that you have a friend who says her grandmother never measures anything, and her muffins turn out great. How would you explain to her the importance of measuring?

Academic Skills

English Language Arts

11. Broaden Your Knowledge Find and read a text about quick breads. It could be a magazine article, an informational section of a cookbook, or part of a non-fiction text. Summarize anything new that you have learned that was not covered in this chapter. Cite specific examples.

> **NCTE 2** Read literature to build an understanding of the human experience.

Science

12. Quick Bread Leavening You must choose the right leavening agent in the right amount to make quick bread.

Procedure Choose a muffin recipe and make it according the directions. Then, make it again with the following substitutions: once with no baking powder, once with half the suggested amount of baking powder, and once with double the suggested amount of baking powder.

Analysis Compare the different batches in terms of height, weight, texture, and flavor. Note your observations in a chart that shows the difference between the batches.

> **NSES B** Develop an understanding of chemical reactions.

Mathematics

13. Bake Biscuits For the first time at her restaurant, Angela will serve biscuits with breakfast. She will bake the biscuits on a commercial baking sheet measuring 26 inches by 18 inches. Angela is familiar enough with the biscuit formula to know that the biscuits expand greatly during cooking, and she would like to leave a 2-inch gap on all sides of each biscuit. If each uncooked biscuit is 2 inches in diameter, how many can she fit on one baking sheet?

Math Concept **Distributive Property of Multiplication** Multiplying a sum by a number is the equivalent of multiplying each addend by that same number, and then adding the two products. For example, $6(3 + 1)$ is the same as $(6 \times 3) + (6 \times 1)$.

Starting Hint For the length of the sheet, if there are x biscuits, there will be $(x + 1)$ gaps between biscuits (including one at either end of the baking sheet). Thus, (2 in.)(x) + (2 in.) $(x + 1) = 26$ in. Solve for x to find how many biscuits will fit across the 26-inch length; then use a similar equation for the 18-inch width. Multiply the two totals together to get the total number of biscuits.

> **NCTM Algebra** Use mathematical models to represent and understand quantitative relationships.

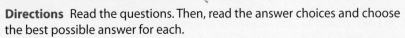

Certification Prep

Sharpen your test-taking skills to improve your kitchen certification program score.

Directions Read the questions. Then, read the answer choices and choose the best possible answer for each.

14. How long should biscuit or scone dough be allowed to rest before baking?

  a. 5 minutes

  b. 10 minutes

  c. 15 minutes

  d. 20 minutes

15. What is the ideal temperature for baking muffins?

  a. 325°F–350°F (163°C–177°C)

  b. 350°F–375°F (177°C–191°C)

  c. 385°F–400°F (196°C–204°C)

  d. 400°F–425°F (204°C–218°C)

Test-Taking Tip
Look for multiple choice options that say always, none, or never. They are usually not correct answers.

Review and Applications

Real-World Skills and Applications

Critical Thinking Skills

16. Stretch Ingredients You are baking muffins. You have ingredients to make a dozen muffins. Your friend calls you to say that there are more guests coming to the party. How can you make muffins with the ingredients you have and still have enough for everyone? Discuss as a class.

Interpersonal and Collaborative Skills

17. Food Safety Imagine that you are making biscuits to serve at a banquet. As a class, review the process of preparing biscuits. Identify food safety issues that may come up and how you would handle those issues.

Technology Applications

18. Make a Video Create a two- to five-minute video that shows viewers how to check the doneness of biscuits, muffins, and quick bread loaves. In the audio, explain what you are doing and what qualities you look for as you check. Videos should contain examples taken from this chapter.

Financial Literacy

19. What to Bake? You can make two dozen 4-ounce muffins for $3.60, and one quick bread scaled into a loaf pan at 2½ pounds, with a serving size of 3½ ounces, for $3.20. Which would you make, and why?

Culinary Lab

Use the culinary skills you have learned in this chapter.

Make Banana Nut Bread

20. Work as a Team Divide into teams at the instruction of your teacher and prepare different variations of the Banana Nut Bread formula below.

A. Choose team assignments. Divide into four teams. Bake the bread, with the following variations:

- Sugar, granulated, 1 lb., 4 oz.
- High-ratio shortening, 6 oz.
- Baking soda, sifted, ½ oz.
- Lemon powder, ½ oz.
- Salt, 1/8 oz.
- Bananas, fresh, or canned, mashed, 8 oz.
- Eggs, whole, 2 oz.
- Water, cold, 1 lb., 8 oz.
- Bread flour, sifted, 1 lb.
- Cake flour, sifted, 1 lb.
- Baking powder, sifted, ½ oz.
- Nuts, finely chopped, 4 oz.
- Banana compound, 2 oz.
- (Bake at 375°F, or 191°C)

- **Team A** will prepare the bread using canned bananas and no nuts.
- **Team B** will prepare the bread using canned bananas with nuts added.
- **Team C** will prepare the bread with fresh bananas and no nuts.
- **Team D** will prepare the bread with fresh bananas and nuts.

B. Evaluate each bread. Sample each team's variation and evaluate them. Rate each variation of the bread for texture, crust, crumb, and appearance.

Create Your Evaluation

After you have evaluated each bread, answer the following questions:

- How does the flavor and texture vary for each version?
- What factors contributed to the differences?
- How did the pre-preparation steps vary?
- How did this impact total preparation time?
- How did the total preparation time vary for each team?

Desserts

SECTIONS

Section 29.1 Cookies
Section 29.2 Cakes
Section 29.3 Pies
Section 29.4 Specialty Desserts

WRITING ACTIVITY

Personal Narrative

Have you ever seen a very special dessert? Write a short story about a memorable dessert. Describe the occasion, the type of dessert, and give sensory details about its appearance, flavor, and texture.

Writing Tips

1 Freewrite to gather ideas.

2 Ask yourself questions to help fill in details of the narrative.

3 Construct an outline to help organize your narrative.

EXPLORE THE PHOTO

Desserts are the sweet conclusion to a meal. *What types of desserts can you name?*

WRITING ACTIVITY ANSWER Narratives should describe the event and dessert in detail. Students should turn in their freewriting and outlines.

EXPLORE THE PHOTO ANSWER Answers will vary depending on the students' personal knowledge.

Cookies

Reading Guide

Before You Read

Pace Yourself Short blocks of concentrated reading repeated frequently are more effective than one long session. Focus on reading for 10 minutes. Take a short break. Then, read for another 10 minutes.

Read to Learn

Key Concepts
- **Distinguish** between crisp, soft, and chewy cookies.
- **Describe** types of cookies, and the methods for mixing, baking and storing them.

Main Idea

Cookies are small desserts that can be crisp, soft, or chewy and come in many shapes. Cookies are made using either a one-stage method, or a creaming method.

Graphic Organizer

Use a web diagram like this one to identify the six factors that determine the spread of a cookie.

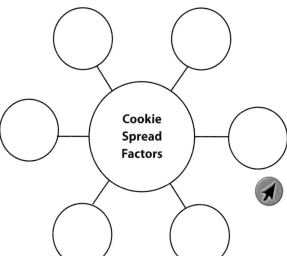

Graphic Organizer
Go to this book's Online Learning Center at **glencoe.com** for a printable graphic organizer.

GRAPHIC ORGANIZER ANSWER Flour type, sugar type, amount of liquid, baking soda, fat type, and baking temperature.

Content Vocabulary
- crisp cookie
- spread
- soft cookie
- chewy cookie
- one-stage method
- drop cookie
- tuile
- warped
- double pan

Academic Vocabulary
- turn
- deal

ACADEMIC STANDARDS

 English Language Arts
NCTE 12 Use language to accomplish individual purposes.

 Mathematics
NCTM Measurement Apply appropriate techniques, tools, and formulas to determine measurements.

Social Studies
NCSS I A Culture Analyze and explain the ways groups, societies, and cultures address human needs and concerns.

NCTE National Council of Teachers of English

NCTM National Council of Teachers of Mathematics

NCSS National Council for the Social Studies

NSES National Science Education Standards

Cookie Characteristics

It is nearly impossible to imagine a world without cookies. They are served in quick-service and family-style restaurants as well as in cafés where they may be served beside a dish of ice cream. It seems that almost any crunchy or flavorful ingredient, from candy to nuts to fruit, can turn basic cookie dough into a special dessert.

Cookies are classified according to their texture. They can be crisp, soft, or chewy. For example, biscotti (bē-'skä-tē) are hard and crispy, while a macaroon (ˌma-kə-'rün) is chewy and soft. Sometimes, the texture of a cookie, such as a chocolate chip cookie, is a matter of personal taste. Some people prefer them soft and chewy, while others prefer them crispy. It is important to know the various types of cookies so that you get the texture you want.

Crisp Cookies

A **crisp cookie** has very little moisture in the batter. Most are made from stiff dough, without much liquid in the mix. They also have a high ratio of sugar.

Cookie Texture Different cookie textures appeal to a variety of customers. *Why do cookie textures differ?*

PHOTO CAPTION ANSWER Cookie textures differ because of the ratio of ingredients present.

During the baking process, crisp cookies **spread**, or expand, more than other cookies because of the greater amount of sugar they contain. Crisp cookies dry fast during baking because of their thinness and must be stored in air-tight containers without refrigeration. If they absorb moisture, they will **turn**, or become, soft.

Soft Cookies

Soft cookies have a much different ratio of ingredients than crisp cookies do. A **soft cookie** has low amounts of fat and sugar in the batter, and a high proportion of liquid, such as eggs. Corn syrup, molasses, or honey is often used along with granulated sugar. Syrups retain moisture after the baking process, providing a soft texture.

Soft cookies are finished baking when their bottoms and edges turn a light golden brown. Soft cookies, like crispy cookies, must be stored in air-tight containers and not refrigerated. Soft cookie dough can be used in cookie-forming machines such as a spritz machine.

Chewy Cookies

All chewy cookies are soft, but not all soft cookies are chewy. A **chewy cookie** needs a high ratio of eggs, sugar, and liquid, but a low amount of fat.

For chewy cookies, the gluten in the flour must develop during the mixing stage. The amount of gluten in a particular kind of flour determines how much the cookie will expand. Gluten provides both stretch and flexibility to the cookie, which makes it chewy. Pastry flour is ideal for cookie production. However, a combination of cake flour and bread flour may be used for a chewier texture.

Cookie Spread

Some cookies require hand-labor to produce a particular molded shape. Although some cookies hold their shape while baking, most cookies will spread.

The spread of a cookie is determined by six factors:

- **Flour Type** Pastry flour is used in cookies for its medium gluten content. This creates the proper spread.
- **Sugar Type** Granulated sugar provides the right amount of spread. If a finer grain of sugar, such as confectioners' sugar, is used, the cookie will spread less.
- **Amount of Liquid** A cookie dough with a high amount of liquid, such as eggs, will have more spread. For reduced spread, decrease the amount of eggs in the recipe.
- **Baking Soda** In a cookie dough, the baking soda promotes the proper spread by relaxing the gluten. Baking soda is used as a leavening agent when it is combined with liquid and an acid.
- **Fat Type** The type of fat used in cookie dough also affects the spread of the cookie. When butter or margarine is used, more spread is created. When all-purpose shortening is used, less spread is created.
- **Baking Temperature** Oven temperatures that are too low cause excessive spread. Oven temperatures that are too high give little or no spread.

Reading Check Identify
What are the different textures of cookies?

Making Cookies

When making cookies, you must determine the appropriate mixing type. The type of cookie that you make determines the mixing method you will use.

Mixing Methods

Most cookie doughs contain the same ingredients. Sugar, fat, eggs, flour, baking soda, and leavening agents, such as baking powder, are mixed together in varying amounts. Additional ingredients such as chocolate, nuts, or fruits may also be added.

One-Stage Method

Some cookies are made using the **one-stage method**. All ingredients, including melted butter or oil, are mixed in a single stage. All ingredients should be at room temperature and accurately measured.

Follow these steps:

1. Put all the ingredients in a mixer.

2. Blend at low speed using the paddle attachment. It will usually take two to three minutes to blend the batter or dough.

3. Scrape down the sides of the bowl with a spatula as necessary to be sure all the ingredients are well blended.

Spread Space Be sure to leave enough space between cookies to allow for even spread. *What will happen to the cookies if you do not leave enough room?*

PHOTO CAPTION ANSWER If you do not leave enough room between drop cookies, the cookies will bake into each other and be misshapen at the edges.

READING CHECK ANSWER The textures of cookies are crisp, soft, or chewy.

Creaming Method

The creaming method is the most common method for mixing cookie dough. Creaming together sugar and fat, such as butter or shortening, makes a smooth mixture. It is smooth because air has been beaten into the fat and sugar cells. The air cells expand, lightening the texture of the cookies while they bake. A smooth mixture that is created by the creaming method will easily combine with other ingredients, such as fruit, nuts, chocolate chips, or seeds.

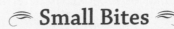
Cookie Types

Cookies may be classified not only by texture and mixing methods, but also by type.

HOW TO

Mix
Creamed Cookie Dough

1 With all the ingredients accurately measured and at room temperature (70°F, or 21°C), use the paddle attachment on the bench mixer to cream sugar, fat, flavorings, and salt together. The mixture will become lighter in volume, texture, and color. Cream only slightly for a chewy cookie. Careful consideration should be given to the lightness of a cookie batter. Excessive lightness will cause a cookie to spread too much while it bakes.

2 After creaming, add eggs in stages to allow for their proper absorption into the mixture. Blend them in at low speed.

3 In a separate bowl, sift flour and other dry ingredients together.

4 Then, add dry ingredients to the creamed mixture and continue to mix on low speed until the dry ingredients are incorporated. Be careful not to overmix the batter. Overmixing develops the gluten, preventing the cookie from spreading properly as it bakes.

Make
Biscotti

1 Divide the dough into equal portions, usually about 16 ounces each.

2 Roll the dough into logs approximately 1½ to 2 inches in diameter.

3 On each parchment-lined sheet pan, place three logs spaced a fair distance apart. Flatten the dough slightly, if desired.

4 Brush the dough with an egg wash if desired, then bake.

5 After the bars have cooled, slice them diagonally into cookies about ½-inch thick. Place the cookies on sheet pans and bake again at 375°F (191°C) until the cookies are dry and lightly browned.

The five basic types of cookies are drop, rolled, icebox, molded, and bar cookies.

It is easier to classify cookies by their type than by their mixing method. Mixing methods are relatively simple, but cookie types can vary a great **deal**, or amount. Regardless of the method used to make the cookie, it is important that all the cookies in a batch be of the same thickness and size.

Drop Cookies

Chocolate chip, peanut butter, and oatmeal are examples of a **drop cookie**. The soft batter or dough for drop cookies uses the creaming process.

Follow these steps to make drop cookies:

1. Choose a scoop for the size of cookie that is desired.

2. Drop the cookies onto parchment-lined baking sheets; if the recipe calls for greased baking sheets, be sure to follow directions.

3. Leave enough space between the cookies on the baking sheet to allow for even baking and spreading. Keep in mind how much a particular type of cookie will spread. Sometimes a recipe will recommend using a weight dipped in sugar to flatten each cookie. Most drop cookies will spread without being flattened.

Rolled Cookies

Sugar cookies are examples of rolled cookies. Rolled cookies have a stiff dough that is rolled out. Shapes are then cut out of the dough and baked. Rolled cookies can be cut by hand or by machine.

Icebox Cookies

Icebox cookies are perfect for making sure that freshly baked cookies are always on hand. Drop cookie dough and sugar cookie dough work well for icebox cookies. The dough can be rolled into logs, wrapped and stored in the refrigerator. Once the rolls of mixed dough have been placed in the refrigerator, the cookies can be sliced and baked as needed.

Molded Cookies

Crescents, almond lace, and tuile ('twēl) are examples of molded cookies. **Tuile** is a Belgian cookie that comes out of the oven soft. Tuile and almond lace cookies are shaped after baking.

Make
Rolled Cookies

1 Chill the dough for rolled cookies after mixing. Using as little flour as possible, roll out the dough to ⅛-inch thickness.

2 Use cookie cutters to cut out the cookies. To minimize the amount of wasted dough, cut the cookies as close together as possible. The dough can be rolled and cut twice. The scrap left over after the second cutting should be discarded because it will make tough cookies.

3 Place cookies on a parchment-lined baking sheet and bake.

▼ **FIGURE 29.1** **Cookie Dough Troubleshooting**

Cookie Problems Measurements for cookie ingredients must be as exact as measurements for other types of baked goods. *What might be the problem if your cookies do not spread properly?*

Cookie Dough Errors	Spreading	Crumbly	Hard	Dry	Lack of Spread
Poorly mixed	✓	✓			✓
Too little sugar					✓
Too much sugar	✓	✓			
Too little flour			✓	✓	✓
Too much flour				✓	
Too much leavening		✓			
Too much baking soda	✓				
Not enough eggs		✓			
Too much shortening		✓			

FIGURE CAPTION ANSWER Problems with cookie spread may be due to poor mixing of the ingredients, too little sugar in the dough, or too little flour in the dough.

Bar Cookies

These cookies are made from dough that has been shaped into long bars, baked, and then cut. Popular bar cookies are hermits, coconut bars, and fruit bars. Biscotti are bar cookies that are baked, sliced, and then baked again.

Baking and Cooling Cookies

Always use clean pans that are not warped for baking cookies. A **warped** pan has become slightly less flat because of excessive heat and use. Lining the pans with parchment paper keeps cookies from sticking to the pan. It also allows for even browning. (**Figure 29.1** on page 752 offers troubleshooting tips for baking cookies.)

The heat from the pan that continues to bake the cookies once they are removed from the oven is called carryover baking. It is better to slightly under bake cookies. To prevent burning the bottoms or edges of cookies before they are done, **double pan** them by

Small Bites

Use Basic Cookie Mixes It can be more cost-effective to use a basic cookie mix as the foundation for several types of cookies. Some mixes require the addition of liquid only. Others may require liquid, fat, and eggs.

placing the sheet pan inside a second pan of the same size. This double-pan technique is recommended for rich dough. When you bake two sheets at one time on separate oven racks, reverse them halfway through the baking process. This ensures even baking.

Cookies are done when the bottoms and edges turn light golden brown. Be sure not to remove cookies from the pans until they are firm enough to handle.

Reading Check Name What are the five different types of cookies?

SECTION 29.1 After You Read

Review Key Concepts

1. **Explain** what gives a chewy cookie its chewy texture.
2. **Describe** how to cool cookies.

Practice Culinary Academics

 English Language Arts

3. Imagine that you run a bakery and that you will offer five different kinds of cookies. Create a display card for each type of cookie. Give the name of the cookies, and describe them in a way that is informative and appealing to a potential customer.

> **NCTE 12** Use language to accomplish individual purposes.

Social Studies

4. Cookies have a varied history. Some have interesting origination stories. Research one type of cookie. Determine where the cookie originated from and how it was originally created. Write a report on your chosen cookie.

> **NCSS I A Culture** Analyze and explain the ways groups, societies, and cultures address human needs and concerns.

Mathematics

5. Serena is a baker at a local bakery. She is making rolled cookies for a party. Serena uses a circular cutter that is 2 ½ inches in diameter to cut cookies from rolled dough. After baking, each cookie's diameter is 3 inches. By what amount did the circumference of each cookie increase during baking?

> **Math Concept** **Circumference** The distance around a circle is known as the circle's circumference. Calculate circumference (C) as $C = \pi d$, where d = the circle's diameter and $\pi = 3.14$.
>
> **Starting Hint** Using $d = 2.5$ inches in the above formula, calculate the circumference of a raw cookie. Subtract that from the circumference of a baked cookie, using $d = 3$ inches.

> **NCTM Measurement** Apply appropriate techniques, tools, and formulas to determine measurements.

 Check your answers at this book's Online Learning Center at **glencoe.com**.

READING CHECK ANSWER The five different cookie types are drop cookies, rolled cookies, icebox cookies, molded cookies, and bar cookies.

Cakes

Reading Guide

 Before You Read

Use Color As you read this section, try using different colored pens to take notes. This can help you learn new material and study for tests. You could use red for vocabulary words, blue for explanations, and green for examples.

Read to Learn

Key Concepts
- **Differentiate** between different types of cakes and their ingredients.
- **Summarize** how to mix, prepare, bake, and ice cakes.

Main Idea

There are five types of layer cakes that are distinguished by their mixing methods. To make a successful cake, you must know how to scale and pan it properly.

Graphic Organizer

Use a herringbone organizer like the one here to list the five types of cakes.

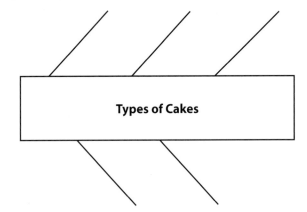

Types of Cakes

Content Vocabulary
- high-fat cake
- low-fat cake
- pound cake
- sponge cake
- emulsified shortening
- genoise
- angel food cake
- chiffon cake
- meringue
- high-ratio layer cake
- Italian meringue
- fondant
- Swiss meringue
- simple syrup

Academic Vocabulary
- stabilize
- collapsing

ACADEMIC STANDARDS

 English Language Arts
NCTE 5 Use different writing process elements to communicate effectively.

 Mathematics
NCTM Geometry
Analyze characteristics of two- and three-dimensional geometric shapes and develop mathematical arguments about geometric relationships.

NCTM Number and Operations Understand the meanings of operations and how they related to one another.

 Science
NSES B Develop an understanding of chemical reactions.

NCTE National Council of Teachers of English

NCTM National Council of Teachers of Mathematics

NSES National Science Education Standards

NCSS National Council for the Social Studies

 Graphic Organizer Go to this book's Online Learning Center at **glencoe.com** for a printable graphic organizer.

GRAPHIC ORGANIZER ANSWER Pound cakes, sponge or foam cakes, angel food cakes, chiffon cakes, and high-ratio layer cakes.

Types of Layer Cakes

Customers often look forward to something sweet, such as cake, for the end to a good meal. Cakes are made of eggs, flour, sugar, fat, leavening, and flavorings. They can be elaborate, like multi-layered tortes, or combined with other desserts, like ice cream cake. This section introduces different types of cakes and how to make them.

Cake Ingredients

Cake ingredients either weaken or strengthen a cake's structure and determine its texture, moisture, and sweetness. For example, sugar and fat, used in the right amounts, help weaken cake structure and give the cake tenderness. On the other hand, eggs and flour both have proteins that, when they are baked, join together to give the cake support.

The starch in flour also helps **stabilize**, or support, the cake by absorbing liquid when it is mixed. Liquid, such as milk or water, forms gluten when it combines with flour. When mixed, gluten gives structural support to the cake.

High-Fat Cakes

A **high-fat cake** generally uses baking powder as its leavening agent. High-fat cakes, such as butter cake, also require that air cells be creamed into the center of the fat cell. The air cells then pick up the leavening gases that the heat of the oven releases.

Low-Fat Cakes

A **low-fat cake**, such as sponge cake, is leavened from air that is whipped into the egg batter. These cakes have a light and springy texture. This makes them a good choice for desserts such as a torte that has many layers with cream and fruit between them. A torte is a cake that uses a large amount of eggs, and sometimes ground nuts or bread crumbs as well as flour.

Pound Cakes

The pound cake's origin can be traced back to England. A **pound cake** contains a pound each of butter, flour, sugar, and eggs. The butter pound cake is a familiar example, and is considered to be the basis for all layer cakes.

Cake Textures Cakes come in a variety of pleasing textures and flavors. *What do you notice about these cakes' textures?*

PHOTO CAPTION ANSWER Pound cake has a dense texture, while angel food cake has a lighter texture.

Prepare
an Angel Food Cake

1 Whip the egg whites with half the sugar, salt, and cream of tartar to full volume.

2 Sift the remaining half of the sugar with the flour. Fold the sugar and flour mixture into the egg-white foam just until it is absorbed.

Sponge or Foam Cakes

A **sponge cake**, which is also called a foam cake, has an airy, light texture because of large amounts of air whipped into the eggs. This type of cake does not rely on butter or modern types of fat such as all-purpose shortening or emulsified shortening. **Emulsified shortening** is a type of fat that helps create a smooth consistency throughout the mixture. Instead, sponge or foam cakes have a base of whipped, whole eggs.

European sponge cake, which is called **genoise** (zhā-'nwäz), is the most common example. Genoise can be the basis for special desserts with layers of jam, chocolate, or fruit filling. Because whole eggs are used in the batter, sponge cakes are richer than angel food cakes.

Angel Food Cakes

An **angel food cake** is a type of foam cake that is made with egg whites, but not egg yolks. The air whipped into the egg whites leavens the cake. Once the egg whites have been whipped, the cake batter must be finished quickly, or it will collapse when the air beaten into the egg whites escapes.

Usually angel food cakes are baked in tube pans. The pans are left ungreased so that as the batter rises it can attach to the sides of the pan. Turn the pan upside down as it cools, and leave the cake to cool inside the pan to keep the cake from **collapsing**, or falling. Angel food cake may be served plain, frosted, topped with a chocolate or fruit-flavored glaze, or served with whipped cream or fresh fruit. Because angel food cakes contain no egg yolks or other fat, they are a more healthful alternative to other cakes.

Chiffon Cakes

A **chiffon** (shi-'fän) **cake** is a variation of a genoise cake. Chiffon cakes are made by using whipped egg whites, or **meringue** (mə-'raŋ), to lighten the batter. The egg yolks and part of the sugar are whipped to full volume and then the flour is added to the yolk and sugar mixture. Finally, the egg whites and the remaining sugar are whipped and then folded in.

Chiffon cakes have less saturated fat and cholesterol than any cake except angel food cake, and about half the fat of a pound cake. Like angel food cakes, chiffon cakes are cooled upside down.

Vanilla Chiffon Genoise

YIELD: 10 LBS., 6 OZ. (7 9-IN. CAKES)
SERVINGS: 70

Ingredients

2 lbs.	Egg yolks
3 lbs.	Sugar, granulated
12 oz.	Oil, vegetable
2 lbs.	Egg whites
2 lbs., 4 oz.	Flour, cake, sifted
1 oz.	Baking powder
5 oz.	Water, room temperature
To taste	Extract, vanilla

International Flavor

This light and airy cake can be served simply or dressed up into something exotic. Choose one of these dishes or find your own unusual recipe and write it up in recipe form.

- Pantespani (Greek)
- Lamington (Australia)
- Biskvit (Russia)

Method of Preparation

1. Gather the equipment and scale the ingredients.
2. Properly grease the cake pans.
3. Place the egg yolks and half of the granulated sugar in a 5-qt. mixing bowl; whip to full volume.
4. Continue mixing on medium speed, and slowly incorporate the oil.
5. In another 5-qt. mixing bowl, whip the egg whites to a medium peak; slowly add the remaining granulated sugar to make a meringue.
6. Sift together the cake flour and baking powder.
7. Combine the water and vanilla extract.
8. Alternately add the flour and water mixtures into the yolk mixture by hand.
9. Fold the meringue into the batter.
10. Scale 1 lb., 8 oz. batter into each greased, paper-lined, 9-in. cake pan.
11. Bake at 360°F (182°C) until spongy in the center.

Cooking Technique

Whipping

1. Hold the whip at a 45° angle.
2. Create circles, using a circular motion.
3. The circular motion needs to be perpendicular to the bowl.

Combining

1. Prepare the components to be combined.
2. Add one to the other, using the appropriate mixing method (if needed).

Chef Notes

Fold the egg whites carefully into the other ingredients. If you stir too much, you will lose air in the mixture, and the cake will not rise properly.

Glossary

Perpendicular at right angles to a given line or plane

Components an ingredient, or part of a sum

HACCP

- Bake at 360°F (182°C)

Hazardous Foods

- Egg yolks
- Egg whites

Nutrition

Calories 220	Calories from Fat 80

Total Fat 8g
  Saturated Fat 1.5g
  Trans Fat 0g
Cholesterol 160mg
Sodium 70mg
Total Carbohydrate 31g
  Fiber 0g
  Sugars 20g
Protein

- Vitamin A 4%   • Vitamin C 0%
- Calcium 4%   • Iron 8%

High-Ratio Layer Cake

A **high-ratio layer cake** contains a high ratio of both liquids and sugar, giving the cake a very moist and tender texture. It is necessary to use a high-ratio shortening or emulsified shortening to help absorb the quantity of liquids. These cakes have a tight, firm grain because of the mixing method. The paddle attachment is used on the bench mixer to limit the amount of air that is mixed into the batter. Wedding cake is an example of a high-ratio layer cake.

Reading Check Identify What is a chiffon cake?

Baking Cakes

The process of baking a cake begins with the right mixing method. Once the cake is mixed, it must be carefully scaled and panned so that the cakes come out a consistent size.

Cake Mixing Methods

Each mixing method produces a certain kind of cake. (See **Figure 29.2** on page 759.) Bakers use the creaming method, the blending method, the sponge or foam method, the angel food method, and the chiffon method.

Creaming Method

The creaming method was once the standard method for mixing a cake. Ingredients should be at room temperature and accurately scaled.

Blending Method

The blending method is often called the two-stage method because the liquids are added in two stages. This method produces a smooth batter that makes a moist, tight, and firm-grained cake. It is used to make high-ratio cakes, which means using large amounts of liquids and sugar as well as emulsified shortenings to absorb the liquids and sugar.

✳ HOW TO ✳
Use
the Blending Method for Cakes

1 Blend the sifted flour, sugar, chemical leaveners, and other dry ingredients for 30 seconds on medium speed.

2 Add the emulsified shortening and half of the liquids.

3 Mix on low speed until the ingredients are moistened. Then, increase the speed to medium and mix for 5 minutes.

4 Scrape the sides of the bowl and add the remaining liquid.

5 Blend on low speed for 3 minutes.

READING CHECK ANSWER A chiffon cake is made by using whipped egg whites or meringue to lighten the batter.

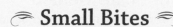

▼ FIGURE 29.2 Cake Mixing Methods

The Right Mix Different cake recipes require different mixing methods. *Why is the choice of mixing method so important in cake making?*

Type of Cake	Mixing Methods
High-fat or Shortened Cakes	• Creaming, Two-stage
Low-fat or Foam-type Cakes	• Sponge, Angel food, Chiffon method.

⟫ HOW TO ⟪

Prepare
a Sponge Cake

1 Once all ingredients are at room temperature, melt the butter and set it aside.

2 Heat sugar and eggs in a double boiler, stirring constantly, to about 110°F (43°C).

3 Beat the eggs at high speed for 10 to 15 minutes, until they are thick and light. When properly beaten, the foam will fall in a ribbon-like shape when you lift the beater.

4 Sift all of the dry ingredients. Then, carefully fold them into the foam. Because the foam can easily be deflated, most bakers do this step by hand.

5 Fold in the melted butter, but do not overmix.

6 Pan and bake the batter at once so that it does not lose volume.

FIGURE CAPTION ANSWER Using the incorrect mixing method for a particular type of cake will keep it from rising during baking, producing a flat, chewy cake.

Sponge or Foam Method

In the sponge mixing method, leavening is formed from air that is trapped in the beaten eggs. When the ingredients are warmed to room temperature, the foam has a greater volume, creating a sponge-like texture.

Angel Food Method

Angel food cakes have no fat and are based on egg-white foam. They do, however, contain a large amount of sugar. Do not add all of the sugar to them at once. Gradually add the sugar as you whip the egg whites to create high-volume foam.

Chiffon Method

The chiffon method is closely related to the angel food method. Both methods rely on whipped egg whites for volume and a light texture. Unlike the angel food method, the chiffon method involves folding whipped egg whites into whipped egg yolks and oil.

Preparation Methods

To keep cakes from sticking, baking pans are usually coated with fat and flour or lined with parchment paper. This allows the cake to release easily from the pan after baking is done. Commercial pan preparations are also available, such as spray pan release, which is a type of grease.

Pans should be filled one-half to two-thirds full. This will keep the batter from spilling over the sides of the pan as it rises. Spread the batter evenly with an offset spatula. Do not work the batter too much, or air cells will collapse and the cake will not rise properly. When you make multiple cakes or a multi-layer cake, always fill pans to the same level. If one pan has more batter, it will be larger and require longer to bake than the other cakes. For all but foam cakes, tap the filled pans firmly on a bench or counter to let large air bubbles escape before baking.

❊ HOW TO ❊
Prepare
a Chiffon Cake

1 Whip the egg yolks and half of the sugar to full volume. They will be pale yellow in color.

2 Fold in sifted flour and other dry ingredients.

3 Whip the egg whites and the remaining half of the sugar until a meringue with medium to stiff peaks forms.

4 Gently fold the meringue into the yolk mixture a small amount at a time.

Small Bites

Altitude Adjustments For high altitude areas, use these alterations for recipes that include a leavening ingredient:

- For altitudes of about 2,000 feet, decrease the amount of baking powder or other leavening agent called for in the recipe by 15%.

- For altitudes of about 5,000 feet, decrease the level of baking powder or other leavening agent called for in the recipe by 40%.

- For altitudes at about 8,000 feet, decrease the amount of leavening agent by 60%.

- Above 3,000 feet, the baking temperature for cakes should be increased by 25 degrees. This temperature will help prevent liquid evaporation.

Pan Preparation

It is important to have the pans prepared before the batter is mixed. Pans should be filled as soon as possible after mixing is complete so that air cells in the batter do not collapse. Then the cakes can go directly into the oven. This will help create a high-quality baked product.

Most pans are either sprayed with an oil and flour mixture or greased and dusted with a bit of flour. Extra flour should always be tapped out of the pan so that the bottom of the cake does not become doughy. Some baked items can be placed on pans lined with parchment paper. Parchment paper is easily pulled off of the bottom of the cake after it has cooled, and will help keep the cake from sticking.

Scaling Cake Batters

Because it is important that cakes are consistently the same size, the batter is scaled before it is panned. (See **Figure 29.3**.) How a batter is scaled is based on the amount of liquid in the batter and the amount of handling a batter can withstand. Creaming method cakes should be scaled by weight. Blending method cakes can be scaled by weight or volume.

FIGURE CAPTION ANSWER If the cake pan were too small, the cake would overflow and brown on the outside too quickly. If the cake pan were too large, the cake would not heat evenly or rise correctly.

Gourmet Math

Adjust for Altitude

The higher the altitude, the lower the air pressure. This means that a higher percentage of liquid evaporates at high altitudes than it does at low altitudes. Because liquid evaporates from cakes as they bake, they may end up tasteless and tough.

You are catering a family reunion in Denver. You plan to make a large sheet cake for the party. The sheet cake formula calls for 5 ounces of baking powder. Denver is 5,280 feet above sea level. For altitudes of about 5,000 feet, you must decrease the baking powder by 40%. What is the percentage of baking powder in the formula after adjusting for altitude?

Math Concept **Converting Fractions to Decimals** A fraction can be converted to a decimal by moving over the decimal to the left by two places.

Starting Hint Move over the decimal place in 40% two spaces to the left. Then, multiply that number by the number of ounces of baking powder to find out how much the baking powder will decrease. Subtract that number from the original number of ounces to get the new ounce total of baking powder.

> **NCTM Number and Operations** Understand the meanings of operations and how they relate to one another.

▼ **FIGURE 29.3** **Cake Pan Choices**

Pan Choices You must choose the correct-size pan for the type of cake you plan to bake. *What would happen if you were to choose the wrong-size cake pan?*

Pan Type and Size	Scaling Weight
High-fat Cakes	
• Round 8 in.	• 14-18 oz.
• Square 9 in. × 9 in.	• 24 oz.
• Loaf 2¼ in. × 3½ in. × 8 in.	• 16-18 oz.
Low-fat Cakes	
• Round 8 in.	• 10 oz.
• Sheet 18 in. × 26 in., ½-in. thick (for jelly roll or sponge roll).	• 2½ lb.
• Tube (angel food and chiffon) 10 in.	• 24-32 oz.

GOURMET MATH ANSWER 5 × .40 = 2. 5 − 2 = 3 ounces of baking powder.

Baking Techniques

Preheat the oven to the correct temperature. If the oven is too hot, the cake may set before it has risen fully, or it may set unevenly, causing the crusts to be too dark. A temperature that is too low creates poor texture and volume because the cake will not set fast enough. Cakes also may collapse if oven temperatures are too low.

Ovens and the shelves in them should be level. When pans are placed in the oven, they should not touch each other. Air needs to flow between the pans for even baking.

It is important to keep the oven door closed while they bake. Cakes may fall if they are disturbed before they finish rising or become partially browned.

Determine Doneness

A cake is done if:
- A pick or cake tester comes out clean when it is inserted into the center.
- The center of the cake's top springs back when it is lightly pressed.
- The cake pulls slightly away from the sides of the pan.

Cooling Cakes

Cakes may break if they are removed from the pan too early. Always cool cakes for at least 15 minutes before you remove them from the pan. When you remove sheet cakes, lightly sprinkle the top with granulated sugar. Place an empty sheet pan with the bottom side down on top of the cake. Turn both pans upside down and remove the top pan from the cake. If parchment paper has been used to line the pan, peel it off the cake.

To remove a chiffon or angel food cake from the pan, loosen the cooled cake using a spatula or knife. Put a cooling rack or tray on top of the cake pan. Turn over the cake pan and rack carefully holding on to both. Carefully remove the pan from the cake.

Icing and Storage

Icing improves a cake by forming a protective layer around the cake that seals in moisture. Icing also adds richness and flavor. Fudge-type icings hold up well on cakes and last longer in storage.

Buttercream is usually used to make cakes, tortes, and desserts taste better and look more attractive. These are five different types of buttercream icing:
- Simple buttercream is made by combining butter, shortening, confectioners' sugar, egg whites, and vanilla.
- French buttercream is made with beaten egg yolks and butter.
- Italian buttercream is made with Italian meringue and butter. **Italian meringue** is meringue that is made with a boiling sugar syrup instead of granular sugar. It is very stable. It makes a light buttercream.
- German buttercream is made with butter, emulsified shortening, and fondant. **Fondant** is a mixture of sugar, water, and flavorings that serves as a base for icings.
- Swiss buttercream is made with Swiss meringue and butter. **Swiss meringue** is a meringue that is made by dissolving sugar and egg whites together over simmering water, and then beating them. Swiss buttercream is light.

Royal icing is another type of icing that is used to frost cakes and cookies, and to pipe decorations on cakes. It has a smooth, hard matte finish.

Icing Cakes

When you decide what type of icing to use, be sure that the icing is not too heavy for the type of cake. Dense cakes pair well with fudge-type icings and simple or German buttercreams. However, lighter buttercreams such as Swiss and Italian, whipped cream, and fruit fillings go well with sponge cakes. Simple syrups can also be used. A **simple syrup** is made of sugar dissolved into hot water.

Before you spread the icing on a cake, tap off any loose crumbs that would interfere with a smooth appearance. Do not spread too much on the first layer. The iced cake should have a uniform appearance, with an even amount of icing on all surfaces. Icing should not ooze out of the side after the layers have been placed.

Before you begin icing, you must have all fillings in place on the cake. This may include fruit or mousse fillings between layers of a cake. It may also include ice cream, either as the top layer of the cake, or between cake layers. Ice cream cakes must be frozen first, before they are iced. Icing used on ice cream cakes must stand up to being frozen without cracking. You may use many different types of frosting for this purpose.

To ice the top layer, start from the center and work out to the edges. Then, spread the icing down the sides. Smooth the surface of the icing before you add decorations. You can use a pastry bag to pipe icing into shapes.

Storing and Serving Cakes

Cakes should be wrapped in air-tight containers or plastic wrap and stored in the refrigerator until they are needed. Frosted cakes should be stored in the refrigerator until they are served. Because frosting easily absorbs refrigerator odors, decorated cakes should be boxed or covered first. Always bring cakes to room temperature before you serve them.

 Reading Check Describe What is the process for icing a cake?

SECTION 29.2 After You Read

Review Key Concepts

1. **Differentiate** between a pound cake and a sponge cake.
2. **Summarize** how to prepare a cake pan.

Practice Culinary Academics

 English Language Arts

3. Create a brochure about cakes for special diets. Research for information about cakes that meet special diet needs, such as low-fat or low-sugar diets. Create a brochure that has both nutritional information and recipes.

> **NCTE 5** Use different writing process elements to communicate effectively.

 Science

4. **Procedure** Bake four small cake layers. For the first one, follow the recipe exactly. For the second one, leave out the fat. For the third one, leave out the egg, and for the fourth one, leave out the baking powder.

   Analysis What are the differences between the various cakes? Write a summary about the ingredients' roles.

> **NSES B** Develop an understanding of chemical reactions.

 Mathematics

5. A rectangular sheet cake measures 18 inches by 9 inches. If the cake is cut in half to form two square cakes, each square will occupy half the area and half the volume of the original cake. Will each square also have half the perimeter of the original cake?

   Math Concept **Perimeter** The distance around the outside of a closed shape is its perimeter. Calculate perimeter (P) by adding the lengths of all sides. For squares, $P = 4s$, where s is the length of one side.

   Starting Hint Calculate the perimeter of the 18- by 9-inch original cake and the 9- by 9-inch square cake. Write a fraction of new perimeter to old perimeter in lowest terms.

> **NCTM Geometry** Analyze characteristics of two- and three-dimensional geometric shapes and develop mathematical arguments about geometric relationships.

Check your answers at this book's Online Learning Center at **glencoe.com**.

READING CHECK ANSWER Tap off loose crumbs, do not spread too much icing on the first layer, start from the center and work outward.

Pies

Pies are a popular dessert in most restaurants.

Reading Guide

 Before You Read

Prepare with a Partner Before you read, work with a partner. Read the titles of the heads and ask each other questions about the topics that will be discussed. Write down the questions you both have about each section. As you read, answer the questions you have identified.

Read to Learn

Key Concepts
- **Identify** pie dough ingredients and types.
- **Describe** the process of making different types of pies.

Main Idea

Pie consists of a dough and a filling. Pie dough can be mealy or flaky. Once pies are prepared, they must be properly stored.

Content Vocabulary
- latticework
- basic pie dough
- flaky dough
- mealy dough
- dust
- fluting
- baking blind
- modified starch

Academic Vocabulary
- contrast
- slightly

ACADEMIC STANDARDS

 English Language Arts
NCTE 8 Use information resources to gather information and create and communicate knowledge.

 Mathematics
NCTM Geometry Use visualization, spatial reasoning, and geometric modeling to solve problems.

 Social Studies
NCSS II B Time, Continuity, and Change Apply key concepts such as time, chronology, and change to explain patterns of historical change and continuity.

NCSS III H People, Places, and Environments Examine, interpret, and analyze physical and cultural patterns and their interactions, such as cultural transmission of customs and ideas.

NCTE National Council of Teachers of English

NCTM National Council of Teachers of Mathematics

NSES National Science Education Standards

NCSS National Council for the Social Studies

Graphic Organizer

As you read, use a line chart like this one to list the five different types of pie fillings.

Types of Pie Filling

Graphic Organizer Go to this book's Online Learning Center at **glencoe.com** for a printable graphic organizer.

GRAPHIC ORGANIZER ANSWER Cooked fruit, flavored pastry cream, egg custard, soft pie filling, and chiffon pie filling.

Pie Dough Basics

A few ripe peaches sweetened and baked in a crust with a latticework top make an appetizing pie. **Latticework** is a grid pattern on a pie crust made with individual strips of crust. Fruit pies, cream pies, and custard pies have long been considered favorite American desserts. This section presents the basics of pie dough and pie fillings.

Basic pie dough is sometimes called 3-2-1 dough. This ratio refers to the weight of three parts flour, two parts fat, and one part water. Successful pie crusts are based on gluten development in the flour and the mixture of flour and fat.

Pie Dough Ingredients

Using proper technique is an important factor in making pie dough. It also helps to understand how the ingredients work together.

Pastry Flour

Pie dough is made from pastry flour because the high gluten content in bread flour absorbs most of the liquid. This makes the dough tough and rubbery. However, pastry flour has enough gluten to keep the dough together so it can be rolled out.

Vegetable Shortening

Butter or vegetable shortening is used to make dough. With a high melting point of 90°F to 100°F (32°C to 38°C) and consistent quality, vegetable shortening is the best fat for a pie dough. The shortening should be cut or rubbed into the flour. The size of the fat particles in the dough determines its flakiness.

Water

Water or milk at 40°F (4°C) or colder is added to the dough to form gluten as it is mixed with flour. It is important not to overmix pie dough or it will become tough. The cold temperature of the water is also important so that the fat in the dough firms up. The crust will fall apart if not enough liquid is added. In **contrast**, or as a comparison, the crust becomes tough if too much liquid is used, because too much gluten develops.

Salt

Salt tenderizes the gluten and enhances flavor. To be sure salt is distributed evenly, either dissolve it in the liquid before you add it to the dough, or sift the salt with the flour.

Types of Pie Dough

Two-crust pies have both a bottom and a top crust. The top crust may be partially open in a latticework pattern or decorated with dough cutouts. Single-crust pies are often filled with cream or custard mixtures.

A pie is frequently judged by its flaky and tender crust. The two types of pie dough are flaky and mealy.

A TASTE OF HISTORY

1773 ▼
Sugar and Molasses Act imposed a tax on molasses for non-British producers

1779 ▼
France and Spain attack the British fortress of Gibraltar

Desserts, Colonial Style

Although their food supplies were limited at first, American Colonial cooks were very resourceful and managed to make some tasty desserts. Corn, pumpkins, and beans were new to them, and they learned to incorporate them into their meals. Pies made with pumpkin and native berries were popular. So was Indian pudding, which was made with cornmeal. Sweeteners included molasses and maple syrup.

History Application

Research American Colonial food. Imagine that you live in Colonial times. Write a diary entry about the dinner you have just helped your family prepare. Include details about your colony, and the foods and the methods of food preparation involved.

NCSS III H People, Places, and Environments Examine, interpret, and analyze physical and cultural patterns and their interactions, such as cultural transmission of customs and ideas.

A TASTE OF HISTORY ANSWER Answers will vary, but should include the traditional foods of the time such as turkey, cornmeal mush, fruit pies, meat puddings, and cider.

Flaky Pie Dough

Flour is not completely blended with the fat for **flaky dough**. Flaky pie dough is either long-flake or short-flake. In long-flake, the fat is about the size of walnuts, which creates a very flaky crust. This is used for the top crust of pies. In short-flake, the fat is in pieces about the size of peas. The gluten develops after the water is added and the dough is mixed. Then, the moistened flour and fat form flaky layers when the dough is rolled out. This dough is often used for two-crust pies.

Mealy Pie Dough

The texture of **mealy dough** resembles coarse cornmeal. The fat is blended into the flour more completely than it is for flaky dough. Mealy dough also requires less water or milk. The flour particles in mealy dough are more highly coated with fat and will not absorb as much liquid. Because the baked dough is less likely to absorb moisture from the filling, the crust will not be soggy. Because of this, mealy dough is used for the crust in custard and fruit pies.

Elegant Desserts Pies and tarts make elegant, tasty desserts for all occasions. *What type of pie dough do you think was used for this pie?*

PHOTO CAPTION ANSWER Flaky pie dough was used for the top crust, and mealy pie dough was used for the bottom crust.

Shaping Pie Dough

It is important not to overmix pie dough. To keep the dough flaky, pie dough should normally be mixed by hand. Pastry flour should be sifted together with the salt before mixing to lessen clumping. Next, the fat is cut or rubbed into the flour until the fat is the size of peas. The cold liquid is then added, and all ingredients are mixed until the dough holds together.

Dough should be covered with plastic wrap and chilled before using it. Some chefs refrigerate the dough overnight so that the gluten can relax. This allows the dough and fat to firm for easy handling and rolling. Because pie dough should not be kept refrigerated longer than one week, the dough can also be frozen in 8- to 10-ounce portions. If you will freeze the dough, wrap it in air-tight packaging, label and date it, and defrost it overnight in the refrigerator before use.

The mixing method for both flaky and mealy dough varies only **slightly**, or a little bit. The fat is cut or rubbed into the sifted flour for both kinds of dough. However, the fat in flaky dough is left in pieces the size of walnuts or peas, while the fat in mealy dough is blended to a cornmeal-like consistency. The larger pieces of fat determine the flakiness of the dough.

After the dough has been chilled, it is ready to be shaped. If the dough is too cold, allow it to soften slightly before you work with it.

Scaling the Dough

For a 9-inch top crust, use 7 ounces of dough. For a 9-inch bottom crust, use 8 ounces of dough. Add 1 ounce of dough to the top crust and 2 ounces of dough to the bottom crust for each additional inch of crust diameter.

Dusting

Dust the bench and rolling pin with flour. To **dust** is to sprinkle very lightly with flour. Do not use too much flour when you dust the bench and rolling pin. Flour makes the dough tougher.

Rolling and Panning

Roll the dough to a round shape ⅛-inch thickness all over, after lightly flattening it. Roll the dough from the center to the outer edges in all directions. Check the dough occasionally to be sure it is not sticking.

Roll the dough tightly around the rolling pin to lift it without breaking. Unroll the dough into the pan. Without stretching the dough, press it into the sides of the pie pan. Avoid air bubbles between the pan and the dough.

Fluting Single-Crust Pies

Fluting the edges of the crust gives a nice finish to the pie. **Fluting** is a manner of decorating the crust by making uniform folds around the edge of the pie. Fold under the extra dough extending beyond the edge of the pan and bring it above the pan's rim, even with the edge. Press your thumbs together diagonally to make a ridge around the dough.

Sealing and Fluting Two-Crust Pies

Place the cold filling in the bottom crust, and then place the top crust on top of the filling. Use a small amount of water or egg wash to moisten the edge of the bottom crust, and seal the two crusts together. Tuck the edge of the top crust under the bottom crust. Flute the crust and apply an egg wash or a glaze to the top crust if desired.

Baking Pie Shells

Sometimes bakers bake pie shells in advance, which is known as **baking blind**. The dough is fitted into a pan and pierced with fork tines or a dough docker so that blisters will not form in the dough as it bakes. An empty pie pan is placed on top of the dough and turned upside down to bake. Another method is lining the shell with parchment paper and filling the shell with dried beans or pastry weights.

Reading Check Distinguish What are the two types of pie dough?

Making Pies

The pie dough is made not only to be the base of the pie, but also to create a shell to contain the filling. The filling is a sweet mixture of different ingredients that makes up the center of the pie and is covered by the pastry.

Pie Fillings

A variety of fruit, custard, and cream pie fillings can be used. Pie fillings can be topped with many food items, such as meringue, whipped cream, and marshmallows.

Cooked Fruit Fillings

Cooked fruit fillings can be purchased ahead of time, or made on the premises. Ready-made fillings are purchased in 10-pound cans or 20- to 45-pound pails for commercial use.

The fruit filling must cool before it is added to the unbaked shells. Fruit pies are baked between 400°F and 425°F (204°C and 218°C) until the crust has an even, golden brown color.

Types of Starches

Various starches are used to thicken pie fillings.
- Cornstarch sets up a gel that allows the filling to hold its shape when sliced.
- **Modified starch**, also called waxy maize, is a type of corn product that will not break down when frozen.
- Tapioca or flour starches are less often used because they cloud the pie filling.
- Pregelatinized starch is precooked, and can be used if the fruit does not need to be cooked before filling the pie shell.

Cream Pie Fillings

Cream pies are filled with flavored pastry cream, which is a cornstarch-thickened egg custard. The filling is cooked on the range and then placed in a pre-baked crust. Often, cream pies are topped with a meringue.

✳ MASTER RECIPE

Basic Pie Dough

Ingredients

12 oz.	Flour, pastry
8 oz.	Shortening, vegetable
¼ oz.	Salt
4 oz.	Water, ice-cold
0-1 oz.	Dried milk solids (optional)

International Flavor

Many different cultures use a form of pie dough to make savory dishes. Use the Internet to research these recipes, and write a half-page report on your findings.

- Steak and kidney pie (England)
- Tepsi boregi (Turkey)
- Kurnik (Russia)

Method of Preparation

1. Gather the equipment and scale the ingredients.
2. Sift the flour to aerate it, removing lumps and impurities.
3. Rub the shortening, by hand, into the flour.
4. Dissolve the salt in the cold water.
5. Incorporate the water into the flour until it is sticky. Do not overwork the dough.
6. Allow the dough to rest and chill properly, preferably overnight.
7. Divide the dough into 3 8-oz. portions.
8. Roll out the dough on a lightly floured pastry cloth. Roll the dough to about a ⅛-in. thickness in a circular form. The dough should be about 1 in. larger than the inverted pie pan.
9. Fold the rolled-out dough in half and carefully place the dough over half the pie pan. Unfold the dough to cover the entire rim of the pie pan. Gently pat the dough from the center of the pan out to work out any air bubbles under the crust.

Cooking Technique

Combine

1. Prepare the components to be combined.
2. Add one to the other, using the appropriate mixing method (if needed).

Chef Notes

The dry milk solids can be sifted at the beginning with the pastry flour. The process would be continued in the same manner.

Substitutions

- Add 1 oz. of sugar to slightly sweeten the taste of the dough.

Glossary

Aerate to add air to flour by agitating it
Cut or Rub to mix in fat with flour
Inverted upside down

HACCP

- Refrigerate pie dough no longer than one week

Hazardous Foods

- Vegetable shortening

Nutrition

Calories 140   Calories from Fat 80
Total Fat 9g
   Saturated Fat 2.5g
   Trans Fat 0g
Cholesterol 0mg
Sodium 120mg
Total Carbohydrate 11g
   Fiber 0g
   Sugars 0g
Protein 1g
- Vitamin A 0%   • Vitamin C 0%
- Calcium 0%   • Iron 6%

Custards

Custard pie fillings are made with eggs. For custard and soft pies, the unbaked crust is filled with uncooked filling, and then both are baked together. Sometimes a crumb crust is used. When the pie bakes, the egg protein firms the pie. Do not overcook the filling. Begin the baking process in a hot oven at 400°F to 425°F (204°C to 218°C) for the first 10 minutes. Then, reduce the oven temperature to between 325°F and 350°F (163°C and 177°C).

Soft Pies

Soft pies also have eggs in them that firm the pie when it bakes. Pecan is a type of soft pie.

Chiffon Pies

Chiffon pies are based on either cooked fruit or cream filling stabilized with gelatin. Then, a meringue is folded in. The filling is then placed in a prebaked shell and chilled.

Baking Pies

For the first 10 minutes, pies should be baked at 400°F to 425°F (204°C to 218°C). Fruit pies, however, are baked in high heat for the entire baking period. Reduce the temperature after the first 10 minutes for custard pies.

Determine Doneness

Custard or soft pies are done if no liquid shakes. The best way to judge if a fruit pie has finished baking is to follow formula guidelines.

Storing and Serving Pies

Custard pies and cream pies must be refrigerated. A baked fruit pie can be kept at room temperature for serving. Unbaked pie shells or unbaked fruit pies may be frozen for as long as two months.

 **Reading Check** Explain How do you know a pie is done?

 SECTION 29.3 After You Read

Review Key Concepts

1. **Identify** the basic ingredients of a pie dough.
2. **Describe** how to check for pie doneness.

Practice Culinary Academics

 English Language Arts

3. Imagine that you are compiling a food reference book, and you are working on the pie section. Research one type of pie and then use the information you find to write up a reference-style entry on that type of pie.

> **NCTE 8** Use information resources to gather information and create and communicate knowledge.

 Social Studies

4. Research the history of pie and create a time line of historical events that have to do with pie or its ingredients. Display your time lines in class and compare them and see which events each student has included.

> **NCSS II B Time, Continuity, and Change** Apply key concepts such as time, chronology, and change to explain patterns of historical change and continuity.

 Mathematics

5. A freshly baked cherry pie is exactly 9 ½ inches in diameter. If the pie is cut into eight perfectly equal slices, what is the perimeter of each slice?

> **Math Concept** **Circumference** Calculate the circumference (C) of a circle as $C = \pi d$, where d = the circle's diameter and $\pi = 3.14$.

> **Starting Hint** Picture a circle divided into eight equal wedges. Two of the sides (the straight ones, coming to a point in the circle's center) of each wedge will be equal to the radius of the circle, or ½ the diameter. The third, curved, side will equal ⅛ of the circle's circumference.

> **NCTM Geometry** Use visualization, spatial reasoning, and geometric modeling to solve problems.

 Check your answers at this book's Online Learning Center at **glencoe.com**.

READING CHECK ANSWER Custard/soft pies are done when no liquid shakes. Fruit pies should bake according to the formula.

Specialty Desserts

Reading Guide

 Before You Read

Get Your Rest The more well rested and alert you are when you sit down to study, the more likely you will be to remember the information later. Studying in the same state of mind as when you are likely to take a test (fully rested and mentally sharp) will help to ensure your best performance.

Read to Learn

Key Concepts

- **Compare and contrast** the methods for making and storing specialty desserts.

Main Idea

Specialty desserts include frozen desserts, custards, and puddings. A skilled chef can make desserts with a high-quality appearance, texture, and taste.

Content Vocabulary

- custard-style ice cream
- American-style ice cream
- frozen yogurt
- sherbet
- sorbet
- custard
- pudding
- stirred custard
- Bavarian
- mousse
- parfait
- sundae

Academic Vocabulary

- alternative
- substituted

Graphic Organizer

As you read, use a matrix like the one below to list the various specialty desserts in their proper category.

Frozen Desserts	Custards and Puddings	Bavarians, Chiffons, and Mousses
1.	1.	1.
2.	2.	2.
3.	3.	3.
	4.	

 Graphic Organizer Go to this book's Online Learning Center at **glencoe.com** for a printable graphic organizer.

GRAPHIC ORGANIZER ANSWER Frozen desserts: Ice cream, frozen yogurt, sherbet/sorbet. Custards and puddings: Baked custard, smooth custard, starch-thickened pudding, baked pudding. Bavarians, chiffons, and mousses: Bavarian cream, chiffon, mousse.

 English Language Arts
NCTE 7 Conduct research and gather, evaluate, and synthesize data to communicate discoveries.

 Mathematics
NCTM Data Analysis and Probability Formulate questions that can be addressed with data and collect, organize, and display relevant data to answer them.

 Science
NSES B Develop an understanding of the structure and properties of matter.

 Social Studies
NCSS IX A Global Connections Explain how cultural elements can facilitate global understanding.

NCTE National Council of Teachers of English

NCTM National Council of Teachers of Mathematics

NSES National Science Education Standards

NCSS National Council for the Social Studies

Specialty Dessert Types

Frozen desserts are a convenient **alternative**, or option, to pastry desserts. Frozen desserts do not require the strict measurements and ingredient ratios that baked goods do. They can be a simple dessert solution for foodservice operations that do not have an accomplished pastry chef on staff.

Frozen Desserts

Some desserts may not be baked goods, such as gelatin desserts, or even cooked items. They may use a combination of preparation methods, such as dessert crêpes and soufflés. Frozen desserts, puddings, custards, mousse ('müs), chiffons (shi-'fäns), and Bavarians (bə-'ver-ē-əns) are included in this section.

Dessert options include a variety of frozen dishes. Frozen desserts include ice cream, frozen yogurt, sherbet, and sorbet (sȯr-'bā).

Ice Cream

Ice cream is one of the most versatile and popular frozen desserts. It may be served plain in a cone or dish, or as the basis of a rich dessert with fruit or chocolate shavings. **Custard-style ice cream** is made with cooked vanilla custard that consists of cream, milk, eggs, sugar, and flavorings. **American-style ice cream** has no eggs, is uncooked, and is made with milk, cream, sugar, and flavorings. Gelato is an Italian-style ice cream that is more dense in texture.

Frozen Yogurt

Frozen yogurt includes the typical ingredients for American ice cream with the addition of yogurt. Starches or heavy creams are sometimes added to provide smoothness.

Fruits and other flavors, such as chocolate or vanilla, are the most common additions to yogurt. Nonfat frozen yogurt is made from nonfat yogurt. It is a common addition to menus.

Safety Check

✔ Prevent Foodborne Illness

Cream desserts, such as custard, can carry foodborne bacteria. Follow these safety guidelines:

- Store cream desserts in food-grade plastic or stainless steel.
- Do not serve leftover cream-filled products, such as éclairs or cream puffs.
- Keep cream desserts covered when cooling to prevent a skin from forming.
- Cool cream quickly in a shallow pan to avoid contamination.
- Use pasteurized egg products when preparing Bavarians, chiffons, and mousses.

CRITICAL THINKING *Why is it important to use food-grade plastic to store cream desserts?*

Sherbet and Sorbet

Sherbet combines fruit juices, sugar, water, and a small amount of cream or milk to increase smoothness and volume. If the milk or cream is omitted, the result is called **sorbet** in French. Sorbets are served as an intermezzo (ˌin-tər-'met-(ˌ)sō), or a brief interlude, between courses at a formal meal to cleanse the palate for the next course. It is also served as a light dessert to finish a meal. An ice is a dessert of shaved ice with a syrup poured over it.

Ice cream and sherbet are both mixed constantly in a churn as they freeze. Otherwise, they would freeze into solid blocks. The circulation of air increases the volume, and ice crystals remain small.

Custards and Puddings

A **custard** is made of eggs, milk or cream, flavorings, and sweeteners. Custards are baked or cooked in a double boiler on the range. Custard can be served alone; as the base for fruit pies, tarts, or ice cream; or for a dessert sauce.

Pudding is a dessert made from milk, sugar, eggs, flavorings, and cornstarch or cream for thickening.

Make
Baked Custard

1 Mix eggs, sugar, salt, and vanilla in a bowl until blended.

2 Scald milk in a double boiler by heating it to just below simmering. To scald means to heat just below the boiling point.

3 Slowly pour the milk into the egg mixture. Be sure to stir it constantly.

4 Skim off any bubbles that form on top of the custard. Pour the custard into cups that are arranged in a shallow hotel pan.

5 Pour water into the hotel pan, making sure that the level of water is halfway up the sides of the custard cups.

6 Bake the custard at 325°F (163°C) for the length of time indicated in the formula or until it is set. It should have the consistency of firm gelatin.

7 Remove the custard from the oven, being careful not to spill the hot water. Cool, label, date, and then store the custard covered in the refrigerator.

Stirred and Baked Custards

A **stirred custard** is made on the range in a double boiler or saucepan. To keep the custard from overcooking, it must be stirred constantly. These custards, therefore, do not set as firmly as baked custards do. Stirred or baked custard is used as a dessert sauce, or can become part of a more complex dessert.

Baked Custard Baked custards work on the same principle as stirred custards. The eggs must coagulate and the custard must become thick, not runny. Thickening occurs during the baking process. If over baked, the protein in the eggs coagulates too much. This leads to a curdled, broken, and watery custard. Custards should be taken from the oven when the center is still slightly fluid.

Smooth Custard Add small amounts of hot liquid gradually while beating the egg and liquid mixture to keep the custard from curdling. When custard curdles, the eggs separate from the solids, making it tough. A bain marie, or a water bath, is used to insulate the custard pan so that the custard does not bake too quickly. When baking, keep the oven at a low setting between 325°F and 350°F (163°C and 177°C). Double boilers should be kept at between 165°F and 170°F (74°C and 77°C).

Puddings

A good pudding results from careful preparation and a trusted recipe. The most common dessert puddings in foodservice operations are starch-thickened and baked.

Make
Crème Anglaise

1 Heat heavy cream and vanilla to scalding, when bubbles form around the edges of the pan.

2 In a separate bowl, whisk together egg yolks and sugar.

3 Slowly mix in ½ cup of the scalded milk mixture into the eggs, to warm, or temper, them so they do not scramble.

4 Gradually add the tempered egg yolk mixture to the remaining milk mixture on a double boiler. Whisk constantly while adding the egg yolk mixture.

5 Cook on the double boiler until the crème anglaise thickens, and can coat a spoon.

Starch-Thickened Puddings Starch-thickened puddings, also called boiled puddings, require starch as the thickening agent to make them firm up. To cook the starch, the pudding is boiled in a saucepan. Pastry cream is a good example of starch-thickened pudding. The resulting mixture can be poured into molds and chilled. To serve these puddings, unmold them and garnish them with chocolate shavings, fresh mint, or fruit such as raspberries.

Baked Puddings Two popular styles of baked puddings are rice pudding and bread pudding. Both of these desserts are made by adding a large amount of either rice or bread to the custard. They may have nuts or fruits added. Baked puddings are often topped with rich sauces to enhance their appearance and make them more flavorful.

Bavarians, Chiffons, and Mousses

Bavarians, chiffons, and mousses are all based on ingredients and techniques discussed earlier. Custard, whipped cream, and thick fruit fillings make these airy desserts.

A **Bavarian**, or Bavarian cream, is made of whipped cream, gelatin, and a flavored custard sauce. The gelatin is softened in cold water or another liquid. Then, it is dissolved in a hot custard sauce and cooled until it is nearly set. Next, whipped cream is folded in, and the entire mixture is put in a mold to set.

The amount of gelatin is key in a good Bavarian cream. While too much gelatin makes the Bavarian rubbery and overly firm, too little gelatin makes the dessert too soft to hold its shape. Be sure to measure accurately.

Chiffons can be served as chilled desserts, not only as pie fillings. The process of making a chiffon is similar to the method described above for Bavarians except that meringue is **substituted**, or switched, for the whipped cream. Other chiffon bases may be fruit fillings and pastry cream. Serving chiffons with interesting garnishes can create contrasting flavors, colors, and textures. The final effect should be pleasing to the eye.

Mousse is a light and airy dessert made with both meringue and whipped cream to enhance the lightness. Fresh fruit or melted chocolate often serves as a base for mousse. Mousse is often served in eye-catching containers, such as hollowed fruits or special molds. Mousse may be served with whipped topping.

Storing and Serving Desserts

Any dessert with eggs or cream must be kept refrigerated or frozen until it is served. Ice cream and sherbet should be kept at 0°F (–18°C) or below. Before serving a frozen dessert, it should be held at 8°F to 15°F (–13°C to –9°C) for 24 hours, so that it will be soft enough to serve.

Parfaits (pär-'fās) and sundaes are two popular desserts. A **parfait** is a frozen dessert flavored with heavy cream. A **sundae** contains one or more scoops of ice cream topped with garnishes, fruits, or syrups.

 Reading Check List What are the common ingredients in Bavarians, chiffons, and mousses?

SECTION 29.4 After You Read

Review Key Concepts

1. **Compare** Bavarians, chiffons, and mousses.

Practice Culinary Academics

 Science

2. **Procedure** Some fruit can affect the way gelatin sets. Make two gelatin dessert mixes: one as per the directions, and one with raw pineapple added.

   Analysis Observe the results. Research fruit enzymes, and create a hypothesis to explain any differences you observe.

   > **NSES B** Develop an understanding of the structure and properties of matter.

 English Language Arts

3. Conduct research, and then write an essay on the special skills that are needed to become a pastry chef. Why are desserts usually made by these specialized chefs rather than a generally trained chef?

   > **NCTE 7** Conduct research and gather, evaluate, and synthesize data to communicate discoveries.

 Social Studies

4. Conduct research to find three specialty desserts from other cultures that are not baked goods. Describe the desserts, how they are made, and their country and culture of origin.

   > **NCSS IX A Global Connections** Explain how cultural elements can facilitate global understanding.

 Mathematics

5. On Tuesday, Mr. Kim sold 90 scoops of chocolate, 45 scoops of vanilla, 27 scoops of pistachio, 9 scoops of peach, and 9 scoops of blackberry at his ice cream shop. Display this information in a circle graph.

   Math Concept **Circle Graphs** A circle graph (or pie chart) can be used to indicate percentages of a whole, which are shown as sections (wedges) of the circle. Because a full circle is 360 degrees, multiply each percent times 360 degrees to find the angles of each section.

   Starting Hint Convert each total into a percentage of all scoops sold, and multiply each percent by 360 degrees. Draw a circle, and use a protractor to divide the circle into sections with the correct angles. Label each section.

   > **NCTM Data Analysis and Probability** Formulate questions that can be addressed with data and collect, organize, and display relevant data to answer them.

Check your answers at this book's Online Learning Center at **glencoe.com**.

READING CHECK ANSWER Custard sauce, whipped cream, and gelatin are usually in all three products.

Review and Applications

Desserts include cookies, cakes, pies, frozen desserts, and puddings. Cookies vary in mixing and panning methods and baking time. The five types of cakes have two basic categories of batter, with different mixing methods.

Flaky and mealy pie doughs are chosen for different types of end products. Fruit, custard, and cream are all varieties of pie fillings.

Frozen desserts offer a wide range of variety, from ice cream to sherbet.

Content and Academic Vocabulary Review

1. Write a letter explaining the appeal of different desserts. Use at least 12 of the following terms in your letter.

Content Vocabulary

- crisp cookie (p. 748)
- spread (p. 748)
- soft cookie (p. 748)
- chewy cookie (p. 748)
- one-stage method (p. 749)
- drop cookie (p. 751)
- tuile (p. 751)
- warped (p. 753)
- double pan (p. 753)
- high-fat cake (p. 755)
- low-fat cake (p. 755)
- pound cake (p. 755)
- sponge cake (p. 756)
- emulsified shortening (p. 756)
- genoise (p. 756)
- angel food cake (p. 756)
- chiffon cake (p. 756)

- meringue (p. 756)
- high-ratio layer cake (p. 758)
- Italian meringue (p. 762)
- fondant (p. 762)
- Swiss meringue (p. 762)
- simple syrup (p. 762)
- latticework (p. 765)
- basic pie dough (p. 765)
- flaky dough (p. 766)
- mealy dough (p. 766)
- dust (p. 766)
- fluting (p. 767)
- baking blind (p. 767)
- modified starch (p. 767)
- custard-style ice cream (p. 771)
- American-style ice cream (p. 771)
- frozen yogurt (p. 771)
- sherbet (p. 771)

- sorbet (p. 771)
- custard (p. 771)
- pudding (p. 771)
- stirred custard (p. 772)
- Bavarian (p. 773)
- mousse (p. 774)
- parfait (p. 774)
- sundae (p. 774)

Academic Vocabulary

- turn (p. 748)
- deal (p. 751)
- stabilize (p. 755)
- collapsing (p. 756)
- contrast (p. 765)
- slightly (p. 766)
- alternative (p. 771)
- substituted (p. 774)

Review Key Concepts

2. Distinguish between crisp, soft, and chewy cookies.

3. Describe types of cookies, and the methods for mixing, and baking them.

4. Differentiate between different types of cakes and their ingredients.

5. Summarize how to mix, prepare, bake, and ice cakes.

6. Identify pie dough ingredients and types.

7. Describe the process of making different types of pies.

8. Compare and contrast the methods for making and storing specialty desserts.

Critical Thinking

9. Determine ingredients. If you wanted to increase the spread of a cookie and you had used all your milk and eggs, what would you add?

10. Analyze baking formulas. Why do high-ratio cakes require a high amount of emulsified shortening to absorb the liquids?

Academic Skills

English Language Arts

11. **Find an Article** Locate an in-depth cookbook or an instructional cooking magazine on making a dessert type that you have read about in this chapter. Read the text, and then write a short summary of what you have learned that has expanded on your knowledge from this chapter. Be sure to include any preparation or cooking techniques that are listed in your summary.

> **NCTE 1** Read texts to acquire new information.

Social Studies

12. **Dessert History** Choose one type of dessert that you have learned about in this chapter and research its history. Create a brief presentation on the history of your chosen dessert and present it to the class. Include any people who have contributed to the development of the dessert over time. Use illustrations or photos to show your dessert and its ingredients.

> **NCSS II D Time, Continuity, and Change** Systematically employ processes of critical historical inquiry to reconstruct and reinterpret the past, such as using a variety of sources and checking their credibility.

Mathematics

13. **Frost a Layer Cake** Debra is preparing a circular, three-layer yellow cake. Each layer of cake is 1½ inches tall and 8 inches in diameter. She would like to put a layer of chocolate frosting on top of each layer of cake, and would also like to cover the sides of the entire cake in the same chocolate frosting. For frosting that is ¼-inch thick in each location, what is the total surface area (in square inches) that Debra must cover in frosting?

Math Concept **Area and Circumference of Circles** Calculate circumference (C) as $C = \pi d$, where d = the circle's diameter and $\pi = 3.14$. Calculate the area (A) of a circle as $A = \pi r^2$, where the radius $r = (½)d$.

Starting Hint Calculate the area on the top of one circular layer of cake, and then multiply by 3 (since there are three layers). Find the surface area of the sides of the cake by multiplying the circumference of the cake times the total height (three cake layers + three frosting layers) of the cake.

> **NCTM Geometry** Use visualization, spatial reasoning, and geometric modeling to solve problems.

Certification Prep

Sharpen your test-taking skills to improve your kitchen certification program score.

Directions Read the questions. Then, read the answer choices and choose the best possible answer for each.

14. Which types of cakes are leavened with baking soda?

  a. high-fat cakes

  b. low-fat cakes

  c. chiffon cakes

  d. angel food cakes

15. Which dessert is often used as an intermezzo between courses at a formal meal?

  a. sorbet

  b. ice cream

  c. Bavarian

  d. smooth custard

Test-Taking Tip

If you do not know the answer to a question, make a note and move on to the next question. Come back to it later after you have answered the others.

Review and Applications

Real-World Skills and Applications

Interpersonal and Collaborative Skills

16. Create a Quiz Work together with a partner to create a quiz with five multiple-choice and five true/false questions about desserts. The questions should be based on information found in this chapter. Swap your test with another group and take each other's tests. Then, grade each other's work.

Decision Making Skills

17. Compare Nutritional Information Research the nutritional information for different types of cakes. Create a chart to compare the nutrition of these cakes. Write conclusions about each type of cake. Which are the healthiest in your opinion, and which are the least healthy?

Technology Applications

18. Dessert Blog Under your teacher's supervision, perform online research on a dessert. You may even try preparing the dessert, and taking pictures of your final product. Create a short blog entry with facts about the dessert.

Financial Literacy

19. Make Dessert Choices You are making desserts for a party of 50 people. The apple pie costs $0.84 per serving and the ice cream costs $0.75 per serving. You will need to buy a new ice cream scoop for $10. Or, you could make chocolate mousse with whipped cream. The mousse costs $1.39 per serving and the whipped cream costs $0.43 per serving. Which dessert is least expensive to serve?

Culinary Lab

Use the culinary skills you have learned in this chapter.

Make Cream Puffs

20. Work in Teams During this lab, you will work in teams to prepare and serve a basic cream puff recipe, and then evaluate the results.

A. Form teams and bake. Divide into teams at your teacher's direction and prepare the Basic Cream Puffs formula below. Prepare either a custard filling, a pudding, a sweetened fruit, or an ice cream filling.

- Unsalted butter or shortening, 8 oz.
- Salt, ¼ oz.
- Granulated sugar, ¼ oz.
- Water or whole milk, 1 lb.
- Bread flour, sifted, 10½ oz.
- Eggs, 1 lb.

(Yield: 25 cream puffs; serving size: 2 oz.)

B. Add fillings. Split the cream puffs almost all the way around, or cut in halves almost down to the bottom crust. Fill one half of the puff with the filling and put the halves together.

C. Add toppings and serve. Choose one of the following toppings: confectioners' sugar, frosting, hot fudge sauce, fresh fruit, nuts, or ice cream. Add your topping and plate your dessert. Share desserts with other teams, and create an evaluation.

Create Your Evaluation

After tasting your cream puff, write a brief explanation of why you chose the filling and topping you did and why they go well together. Then, evaluate your dessert using the following rating scale: 1 = Poor; 2 = Fair; 3 = Good; 4 = Great. Explain the reasons for your rating.

Baking and Pastry

The art of baking and pastry appeals to both the palate and the eye.

Baking and pastry employees use a variety of doughs and batters to produce breads, cakes, muffins, pies, biscuits, scones, pastries, and other elegant desserts. Attention to detail, excellent eye-hand coordination, and an artistic flair are key skills for those interested in baking and pastry.

Baking and pastry workers must be skilled in basic bread and pastry techniques and have in-depth knowledge of how different ingredients function together. These individuals can find work in a variety places, from small neighborhood bakeries to large hotel catering operations.

Casey Shiller, Executive Pastry Chef

Q Describe your job.

A I am the executive pastry chef for the Boeing® Leadership Center. I supervise the preparation of all cakes, pies, cookies, muffins, breakfast pastries, plated desserts, breads, and pastries. I am also a faculty member at St. Louis Community College, where I teach classes in baking, pastry, chocolates, wedding cakes, and confectionary art.

Q What kind education have you received?

A I graduated with honors with a Bachelor of Science in Pastry Arts and Baking from Johnson & Wales University. That was the foundation for my career and a necessary experience for me to have followed my career path.

Q What has been your career path?

A I have had a number of work experiences that have allowed me to continually develop my technical skills and gain valuable knowledge. Before coming to the Boeing® Leadership Center,

I worked at various hotels, including the Trump Plaza Hotel-Casino®, Trump Taj Mahal Hotel-Casino®, Trump Worlds Fair Hotel-Casino®, and The Ritz-Carlton® Amelia Island.

Q How do you maintain your enthusiasm for your work?

A I find that it is very important to stay involved. I am an active member of the American Culinary Federation (ACF), the U.S. Pastry Alliance, and the St. Louis Chefs de Cuisine Association. I also coach the Missouri State Junior Culinary Team.

Q What have been your most rewarding professional achievements?

A In the year 2000, I was named one of the Top 10 Rising Star Pastry Chefs 2000 by Chocolates a la Carte®. I have also earned several gold and silver medals for my chocolate sculptures and plated desserts at the New York Food Show.

Career Ingredients

Education or Training	Most employers require a culinary degree, plus at least two to four years of on-the-job training.
Academic Skills Required	English Language Arts, Mathematics, Science
Aptitudes, Abilities, and Skills	Creativity, artistic ability, good eye-hand coordination, a keen sense of taste and smell, good communication skills, ability to work under pressure, excellent organizational skills, and inventory control experience.
Workplace Safety	Basic kitchen safety, sanitations, and food handling rules must be followed.
Career Outlook	Openings will be plentiful for years to come as the foodservice industry continues to expand.
Career Path	Baking, pastry, and supervisory experience needed for advancement.

Career Pathways

Baker's helpers	Assist bakers in preparing non-dessert baked items, such as breads and rolls.
Baker and pastry apprentices	Work closely with the baker or pastry chef in preparing baked products and fancy desserts.
Pastry cooks	Work under a pastry chef. Prepare items, such as desserts and specialty cakes, for all occasions.
Pastry chefs	Responsible for the preparation of pastries and desserts. They supervise pastry cooks and bakers. May be responsible for creating new formulas.
Bakers	Prepare breads and rolls. In some operations, they also bake cakes and pies. In large operations, each baker may focus on one type of baked product.
Production bakers	Must be familiar with large retail baking systems, product development, bakery management, and sales.
Confectionery food technologists	Work with developing bakery and confectionery products and establish specifications for raw materials used in food products.
Restaurant chefs	Known as line cooks, they are responsible for á la carte dishes.
Chef instructors	Experienced chefs who choose, after many years of experience, to become instructors.

In large bakery and pastry operations, you may also find: **district sales managers**, **cake decorators**, **production supervisors**, **bakery/food scientists**, **executive pastry chefs**, and **flavorists**.

Critical Thinking What classes have you taken in school that might help you prepare for a career in baking and pastry?

Most culinary certification programs incorporate baking techniques. Develop a new or modified recipe for a sweet or savory pie. Determine the type of filling, dough, crust, and final appearance of the pie. Be creative.

COMPETITION PRACTICE

Imagine you have entered a pie-making competition. You will be timed, and you must complete the pie you developed in the Get Certified practice within that time. The finished product should be visually appealing, salable, and appetizing. Evaluate your efforts based on the following rating scale:

1 = Poor; 2 = Fair; 3 = Good; 4 = Great

Judge your menu on:

- The visual presentation of your finished pie.
- Whether you finished your pie on time.
- How the pie tastes.

Creative Desserts

Most desserts are cooked or baked, but most frozen desserts do not require this. These convenient desserts often accompany elegant meals and can be easily made at foodservice operations that do not have an accomplished pastry chef on staff.

My Journal

If you completed the journal entry from page 675, refer to it to see what special desserts you have tried in the past. Add any additional notes about other desserts, especially frozen desserts, that you are interested in tasting or trying to make.

Project Assignment

In this project, you will:

- Research different types of frozen desserts.
- Identify and observe a pastry chef or someone else who makes frozen desserts.
- Create your own frozen dessert, focusing on a dramatic finished appearance.
- Present a report to your class to share what you have learned.

Applied Culinary Skills Behind the Project

Your success in culinary arts will depend on your skills. Skills you will use in this project include:

➤ Identifying the different types of frozen desserts and how they are made.
➤ Explaining the possible benefits of frozen desserts over pastry desserts.
➤ Understanding the basic skills used to create various frozen desserts.
➤ Knowing how to make the presentations of frozen desserts dramatic and appealing.

English Language Arts Skills Behind the Project

The English Language Arts skills you will use for this project are research, observation, and speaking skills. Remember these key concepts:

Research Skills

➤ Gather and evaluate data using a variety of resources.
➤ Discriminate between sources.
➤ Use the information you gathered to narrow down your choices.

Observation Skills

➤ Listen actively and attentively.
➤ Take notes during your observation.
➤ Ask additional questions to gain a better understanding.

Speaking Skills

➤ Adapt and modify language to suit different purposes.
➤ Speak slowly and clearly so your audience can follow your presentation.
➤ Be aware of nonverbal communication.

English Language Arts

NCTE 8 Use a variety of resources to gather and synthesize information and to create and communicate knowledge.

NCTE 12 Use spoken, written, and visual language to accomplish individual purposes.

Step 1 / Research Frozen Desserts

Research the various types of frozen desserts and how they are made. Write a summary of your research to:

- List the different types of frozen desserts.
- Explain the basic skills behind the creation of the various types of frozen desserts.
- Describe the steps involved in making the different types of frozen desserts.
- Identify situations in which frozen desserts might be preferable to pastry desserts.
- Determine meals that frozen desserts would go well with and complement.
- Understand how to present finished frozen desserts in an appealing and dramatic fashion.

Step 2 / Plan Your Observation

Use the results of your research to write a list of questions you would like answered as you observe a professional making frozen desserts. Your questions may include:

- What are the various types of frozen desserts, and how are they made?
- What is your favorite frozen dessert recipe and why?
- Can you explain the basic skills behind making frozen desserts?
- What tips can you offer on how to make finished frozen desserts look appealing?

Step 3 / Connect with Your Community

Identify a person in your community who makes frozen desserts. This could be a pastry chef or any other culinary professional who makes frozen desserts. Conduct your observation using the questions you prepared in Step 2. Ask questions and take notes during the observation, and write a summary of your findings.

Culinary Project Checklist

Plan

- ✓ Research frozen desserts, and summarize your findingss.
- ✓ Plan an observation with a pastry chef or some other culinary professional who makes frozen desserts.
- ✓ Observe this person, and summarize what you learned during this observation.
- ✓ Make an oral presentation on your chosen frozen dessert.

Present

- ✓ Make a presentation to your class to share information on your frozen dessert and discuss the results of your research and observation.
- ✓ Invite students to ask any questions they may have. Answer these questions.
- ✓ When students ask you questions, demonstrate in your answers that you respect their perspectives.
- ✓ Turn in the summary of your research, your interview questions, and the summary of the interview to your teacher.

Step 4 / Make Your Frozen Dessert

Use the Culinary Project Checklist to plan, create, and present an oral report on how to make one type of frozen dessert. Present information from your observation, and share what you have learned with your classmates.

Step 5 / Evaluate Your Culinary and Academic Skills

Your project will be evaluated based on:

- Extent of your research on frozen desserts.
- Depth of observation questions.
- Speaking and listening skills.

 Rubric Go to this book's Online Learning Center at **glencoe.com** for a rubric you can use to evaluate your final project.

JOHNSON & WALES
U N I V E R S I T Y

Expert Advice Go to this book's Online Learning Center at **glencoe. com** to read an article by a culinary expert from Johnson & Wales University about the positive effects these desserts have on a restaurant's profit margin.

Career Appendix

 ## MAKING CAREER CHOICES

A career differs from a job in that it is a series of progressively more responsible jobs in one field or a related field. You will need to learn some special skills to choose a career and to help you in your job search. Choosing a career and identifying career opportunities require careful thought and preparation. To aid you in making important career choices, follow these steps:

STEPS TO MAKING A CAREER DECISION

1. Conduct a self-assessment to determine your:
   - values
   - lifestyle goals
   - interests
   - skills and aptitudes
   - personality
   - work environment preferences
   - relationship preferences

2. Identify possible career choices based on your self-assessment.

3. Gather information on each choice, including future trends.

4. Evaluate your choices based on your self-assessment.

5. Make your decision.

After you make your decision, plan how you will reach your goal. It is best to have short-term, medium-term, and long-term goals. In making your choices, explore the future opportunities in this field or fields over the next several years. What impact will new technology and automation have on job opportunities in the next few years? Remember, if you plan, you make your own career opportunities.

 ## PERSONAL CAREER PORTFOLIO

You will want to create and maintain a personal career portfolio. In it you will keep all the documents you create and receive in your job search:

- Contact list
- Résumé
- Letters of recommendation
- Employer evaluations
- Awards
- Evidence of participation in school, community, and volunteer activities
- Notes about your job search
- Notes made after your interviews

 ## CAREER RESEARCH RESOURCES

In order to gather information on various career opportunities, there are a variety of sources to research:

- **Libraries.** Your school or public library offers good career information resources. Here you will find books, magazines, pamphlets, films, videos, and special reference materials on careers.

In particular, the U.S. Department of Labor publishes three reference books that are especially helpful: the *Dictionary of Occupational Titles (DOT),* which describes about 20,000 jobs and their relationships with data, people, and things; the *Occupational Outlook Handbook (OOH),* with information on more than 200 occupations; and the *Guide for Occupational Exploration (GOE),* a reference that organizes the world of work into 12 interest areas that are subdivided into work groups and subgroups.

- **The Internet.** The Internet is becoming a primary source of research on any topic. It is especially helpful in researching careers.

- **Career Consultations.** Career consultation, an informational interview with a professional who works in a career that interests you, provides an opportunity to learn about the day-to-day realities of a career.

- **On-the-Job Experience.** On-the-job experience can be valuable in learning firsthand about a job or career. You can find out if your school has a work-experience program, or look into a company or organization's internship opportunities. Interning gives you direct work experience and often allows you to make valuable contacts for future full-time employment.

THE JOB SEARCH

To aid you in your actual job search, there are various sources to explore. You should contact and research all the sources that might produce a job lead, or information about a job. Keep a contact list as you proceed with your search. Some of these resources include:

- **Networking with family, friends, and acquaintances.** This means contacting people you know personally, including school counselors, former employers, and professional people.

- **Cooperative education and work-experience programs.** Many schools have such programs in which students work part-time on a job related to one of their classes. Many also offer work-experience programs that are not limited to just one career area, such as marketing.

- **Newspaper ads.** Reading the Help Wanted advertisements in your local papers will provide a source of job leads, as well as teach you about the local job market.

- **Employment agencies.** Most cities have two types of employment agencies, public and private. These employment agencies match workers with jobs. Some private agencies may charge a fee, so be sure to know who is expected to pay the fee and what the fee is.

- **Company personnel offices.** Large and medium-sized companies have personnel offices to handle employment matters, including the hiring of new workers. You can check on job openings by contacting the office by telephone or by scheduling a personal visit.

- **Searching the Internet.** Cyberspace offers multiple opportunities for your job search. Web sites, such as Hotjobs.com or Monster.com, provide lists of companies offering employment. There are tens of thousands of career-related Web sites, so the challenge is finding those that have jobs that interest you and that are up-to-date in their listings. Companies that interest you may have a Web site, which will provide valuable information on their benefits and opportunities for employment.

APPLYING FOR A JOB

When you have contacted the sources of job leads and found some jobs that interest you, the next step is to apply for them. You will need to complete application forms, write letters of application, and prepare your own résumé. Before you apply for a job, you will need to have a work permit if you are under the age of 18 in most states. Some state and federal labor laws designate certain jobs as too dangerous for young workers. Laws also limit the number of hours of work allowed during a day, a week, or the school year. You will also need to have proper documentation, such as a green card if you are not a U.S. citizen.

JOB APPLICATION

You can obtain the job application form directly at the place of business, by requesting it in writing, or over the Internet. It is best if you can fill the form out at home, but some businesses require that you fill it out at the place of work.

Fill out the job application forms neatly and accurately, using standard English, the formal style of speaking and writing you learned in school. You must be truthful and pay attention to detail in filling out the form.

PERSONAL FACT SHEET

To be sure that the answers you write on a job application form are accurate, make a personal fact sheet before filling out the application:

- Your name, home address, and phone number
- Your Social Security number
- The job you are applying for
- The date you can begin work
- The days and hours you can work
- The pay you want
- Whether or not you have been convicted of a crime
- Your education
- Your previous work experience
- Your birth date
- Your driver's license number if you have one
- Your interests and hobbies, and awards you have won
- Your previous work experience, including dates
- Schools you have attended
- Places you have lived
- Accommodations you may need from the employer
- A list of references—people who will tell an employer that you will do a good job, such as relatives, students, former employers, and the like

LETTERS OF RECOMMENDATION

Letters of recommendation are helpful. You can request teachers, counselors, relatives, and other acquaintances who know you well to write these letters. They should be short, to the point, and give a brief overview of your assets. A brief description of any of your important accomplishments or projects should follow. The letter should end with a brief description of your character and work ethic.

LETTER OF APPLICATION

Some employees prefer a letter of application, rather than an application form. This letter is like writing a sales pitch about yourself. You need to tell why you are the best person for the job, what special qualifications you have, and include all the information usually found on an application form. Write the letter in standard English, making certain that it is neat, accurate, and correct.

RESUMÉ

The purpose of a résumé is to make an employer want to interview you. A résumé tells prospective employers what you are like and what you can do for them. A good résumé summarizes you at your best in a one- or two-page outline. It should include the following information:

1. **Identification.** Include your name, address, telephone number, and e-mail address.

2. **Objective.** Indicate the type of job you are looking for.

3. **Experience.** List experience related to the specific job for which you are applying. List other work if you have not worked in a related field.

4. **Education.** Include schools attended from high school on, the dates of attendance, and diplomas or degrees earned. You may also include courses related to the job you are applying for.

5. **References.** Include up to three references or indicate that they are available. Always ask people ahead of time if they are willing to be listed as references for you.

A résumé that you put online or send by e-mail is called an *electronic résumé*. Some Web sites allow you to post them on their sites without charge. Employers access these sites to find new employees. Your electronic résumé should follow the guidelines for a regular one. It needs to be accurate. Stress your skills and sell yourself to prospective employers.

COVER LETTER

If you are going to get the job you want, you need to write a great cover letter to accompany your résumé. Think of a cover letter as an introduction: a piece of paper that conveys a smile, a confident hello, and a nice, firm handshake. The cover letter is the first thing a potential employer sees, and it can make a powerful impression. The following are some tips for creating a cover letter that is professional and gets the attention you want:

- **Keep it short.** Your cover letter should be one page, no more.
- **Make it look professional.** These days, you need to type your letter on a computer and print it on a laser printer. Do not use an inkjet printer unless it produces extremely crisp type. Use white or buff-colored paper; anything else will draw the wrong kind of attention. Type your name, address, phone number, and e-mail address at the top of the page.
- **Explain why you are writing.** Start your letter with one sentence describing where you heard of the opening. "Joan Wright suggested I contact you regarding a position in your marketing department," or "I am writing to apply for the position you advertised in the Sun City Journal."
- **Introduce yourself.** Give a short description of your professional abilities and background. Refer to your attached résumé: "As you will see in the attached résumé, I am an experienced editor with a background in newspapers, magazines, and textbooks." Then highlight one or two specific accomplishments.
- **Sell yourself.** Your cover letter should leave the reader thinking, "This person is exactly what we are looking for." Focus on what you can do for the company. Relate your skills to the skills and responsibilities mentioned in the job listing. If the ad mentions solving problems, relate a problem you solved at school or work. If the ad mentions specific skills or knowledge required, mention your mastery of these in your letter. (Also be sure these skills are included on your résumé.)
- **Provide all requested information.** If the Help Wanted ad asked for "salary requirements" or "salary history," include this information in your cover letter. However, you do not have to give specific numbers. It is okay to say, "My wage is in the range of $10 to $15 per hour." If the employer does not ask for salary information, do not offer any.

- **Ask for an interview.** You have sold yourself, now wrap it up. Be confident, but not pushy. "If you agree that I would be an asset to your company, please call me at [insert your phone number]. I am available for an interview at your convenience." Finally, thank the person. "Thank you for your consideration. I look forward to hearing from you soon." Always close with a "Sincerely," followed by your full name and signature.

- **Check for errors.** Read and re-read your letter to make sure each sentence is correctly worded and there are no errors in spelling, punctuation, or grammar. Do not rely on your computer's spell checker or grammar checker. A spell check will not detect if you typed "tot he" instead of "to the." It is a good idea to have someone else read your letter, too. He or she might notice an error you overlooked.

INTERVIEW

Understanding how to best prepare for and follow up on interviews is critical to your career success. At different times in your life, you may interview with a teacher or professor, a prospective employer, a supervisor, or a promotion or tenure committee. Just as having an excellent résumé is vital for opening the door, interview skills are critical for putting your best foot forward and seizing the opportunity to clearly articulate why you are the best person for the job.

RESEARCH THE COMPANY

Your ability to convince an employer that you understand and are interested in the field you are interviewing to enter is important. Show that you have knowledge about the company and the industry. What products or services does the company offer? How is it doing? What is the competition? Use your research to demonstrate your understanding of the company.

PREPARE QUESTIONS FOR THE INTERVIEWER

Prepare interview questions to ask the interviewer. Some examples include:

- "What would my responsibilities be?"
- "Could you describe my work environment?"
- "What are the chances to move up in the company?"
- "Do you offer training?"
- "What can you tell me about the people who work here?"

DRESS APPROPRIATELY

You will never get a second chance to make a good first impression. Nonverbal communication is 90 percent of communication, so dressing appropriately is of the utmost importance. Every job is different, and you should wear clothing that is appropriate for the job for which you are applying. In most situations, you will be safe if you wear clean, pressed, conservative business clothes in neutral colors. Pay special attention to grooming. Keep makeup light and wear very little jewelry. Make certain your nails and hair are clean, trimmed, and neat. Do not carry a large purse, backpack, books, or coat. Simply carry a pad of paper, a pen, and extra copies of your résumé and letters of reference in a small folder.

EXHIBIT GOOD BEHAVIOR

Conduct yourself properly during an interview. Go alone; be courteous and polite to everyone you meet. Relax and focus on your purpose: to make the best possible impression.

- Be on time.
- Be poised and relaxed.
- Avoid nervous habits.
- Avoid littering your speech with verbal clutter such as "you know," "um," and "like."
- Look your interviewer in the eye and speak with confidence.
- Use nonverbal techniques to reinforce your confidence, such as a firm handshake and poised demeanor.
- Convey maturity by exhibiting the ability to tolerate differences of opinion.
- Never call anyone by a first name unless you are asked to do so.
- Know the name, title, and the pronunciation of the interviewer's name.
- Do not sit down until the interviewer does.
- Do not talk too much about your personal life.
- Never bad-mouth your former employers.

BE PREPARED FOR COMMON INTERVIEW QUESTIONS

You can never be sure exactly what will happen at an interview, but you can be prepared for common interview questions. There are some interview questions that are illegal. Interviewers should not ask you about your age, gender, color, race, or religion. Employers should not ask whether you are married or pregnant, or question your health or disabilities.

Take time to think about your answers now. You might even write them down to clarify your thinking. The key to all interview questions is to be honest, and to be positive. Focus your answers on skills and abilities that apply to the job you are seeking. Practice answering the following questions with a friend:

- "Tell me about yourself."
- "Why do you want to work at this company?"
- "What did you like/dislike about your last job?"
- "What is your biggest accomplishment?"
- "What is your greatest strength?"
- "What is your greatest weakness?"
- "Do you prefer to work with others or on your own?"
- "What are your career goals?" or "Where do you see yourself in five years?"
- "Tell me about a time that you had a lot of work to do in a short time. How did you manage the situation?"
- "Have you ever had to work closely with a person you didn't get along with? How did you handle the situation?"

AFTER THE INTERVIEW

Be sure to thank the interviewer after the interview for his or her time and effort. Do not forget to follow up after the interview. Ask, "What is the next step?" If you are told to call in a few days, wait two or three days before calling back.

If the interview went well, the employer may call you to offer you the job. Find out the terms of the job offer, including job title and pay. Decide whether you want the job. If you decide not to accept the job, write a letter of rejection. Be courteous and thank the person for the opportunity and the offer. You may wish to give a brief general reason for not accepting the job. Leave the door open for possible employment in the future.

FOLLOW UP WITH A LETTER

Write a thank-you letter as soon as the interview is over. This shows your good manners, interest, and enthusiasm for the job. It also shows that you are organized. Make the letter neat and courteous. Thank the interviewer. Sell yourself again.

ACCEPTING A NEW JOB

If you decide to take the job, write a letter of acceptance. The letter should include some words of appreciation for the opportunity, written acceptance of the job offer, the terms of employment (salary, hours, benefits), and the starting date. Make sure the letter is neat and correct.

 STARTING A NEW JOB

Your first day of work will be busy. Determine what the dress code is and dress appropriately. Learn to do each task assigned properly. Ask for help when you need it. Learn the rules and regulations of the workplace.

You will do some paperwork on your first day. Bring your personal fact sheet with you. You will need to fill out some forms. Form W-4 tells your employer how much money to withhold for taxes. You may also need to fill out Form I-9. This shows that you are allowed to work in the United States. You will need your Social Security number and proof that you are allowed to work in the United States. You can bring your U.S. passport, your Certificate of Naturalization, or your Certificate of U.S. Citizenship. If you are not a permanent resident of the United States, bring your green card. If you are a resident of the United States, you will need to bring your work permit on your first day. If you are under the age of 16 in some states, you need a different kind of work permit.

You might be requested to take a drug test as a requirement for employment in some states. This could be for the safety of you and your coworkers, especially when working with machinery or other equipment.

IMPORTANT SKILLS AND QUALITIES

You will not work alone on a job. You will need to learn skills for getting along and being a team player. There are many good qualities necessary to get along in the workplace. They include being positive, showing sympathy, taking an interest in others, tolerating differences, laughing a little, and showing respect. Your employer may promote you or give you a raise if you show good employability skills. You must also communicate with your employer. For example, if you will be sick or late to work, you should call your employer as soon as possible.

There are several qualities necessary to be a good employee and get ahead in your job:

- be cooperative
- possess good character
- be responsible
- finish what you start

- have a strong work ethic
- work well without supervision
- work well with others
- possess initiative
- show enthusiasm for what you do
- be on time
- make the best of your time
- obey company laws and rules
- be honest
- be loyal
- exhibit good health habits

LEAVING A JOB

If you are considering leaving your job or are being laid off, you are facing one of the most difficult aspects in your career. The first step in resigning is to prepare a short resignation letter to offer your supervisor at the conclusion of the meeting you set up with him or her. Keep the letter short and to the point. Express your appreciation for the opportunity you had with the company. Do not try to list all that was wrong with the job.

You want to leave on good terms. Do not forget to ask for a reference. Do not talk about your employer or any of your coworkers. Do not talk negatively about your employer when you apply for a new job.

If you are being laid off or face downsizing, it can make you feel angry or depressed. Try to view it as a career-change opportunity. If possible, negotiate a good severance package. Find out about any benefits you may be entitled to. Perhaps the company will offer job-search services or consultation for finding new employment.

TAKE ACTION!

It is time for action. Remember the networking and contact lists you created when you searched for this job. Reach out for support from friends, family, and other acquaintances. Consider joining a job-search club. Assess your skills. Upgrade them if necessary. Examine your attitude and your vocational choices. Decide the direction you wish to take and move on!

Math Appendix

Number and Operations

▶ *Understand numbers, ways of representing numbers, relationships among numbers, and number systems*

Fraction, Decimal, and Percent

A percent is a ratio that compares a number to 100. To write a percent as a fraction, drop the percent sign, and use the number as the numerator in a fraction with a denominator of 100. Simplify, if possible. For example, $76\% = \frac{76}{100}$, or $\frac{19}{25}$. To write a fraction as a percent, convert it to an equivalent fraction with a denominator of 100. For example, $\frac{3}{4} = \frac{75}{100}$, or 75%. A fraction can be expressed as a percent by first converting the fraction to a decimal (divide the numerator by the denominator) and then converting the decimal to a percent by moving the decimal point two places to the right.

Comparing Numbers on a Number Line

In order to compare and understand the relationship between real numbers in various forms, it is helpful to use a number line. The zero point on a number line is called the origin; the points to the left of the origin are negative, and those to the right are positive. The number line below shows how numbers in fraction, decimal, percent, and integer form can be compared.

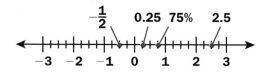

Percents Greater Than 100 and Less Than 1

Percents greater than 100% represent values greater than 1. For example, if the weight of an object is 250% of another, it is 2.5, or $2\frac{1}{2}$, times the weight.

Percents less than 1 represent values less than $\frac{1}{100}$. In other words, 0.1% is one tenth of one percent, which can also be represented in decimal form as 0.001, or in fraction form as $\frac{1}{1,000}$. Similarly, 0.01% is one hundredth of one percent or 0.0001 or $\frac{1}{10,000}$.

Ratio, Rate, and Proportion

A ratio is a comparison of two numbers using division. If a basketball player makes 8 out of 10 free throws, the ratio is written as 8 to 10, 8:10, or $\frac{8}{10}$. Ratios are usually written in simplest form. In simplest form, the ratio "8 out of 10" is 4 to 5, 4:5, or $\frac{4}{5}$. A rate is a ratio of two measurements having different kinds of units—cups per gallon, or miles per hour, for example. When a rate is simplified so that it has a denominator of 1, it is called a unit rate. An example of a unit rate is 9 miles per hour. A proportion is an equation stating that two ratios are equal. $\frac{3}{18} = \frac{13}{78}$ is an example of a proportion. The cross products of a proportion are also equal. $\frac{3}{18} = \frac{13}{78}$ and $3 \times 78 = 18 \times 13$.

Representing Large and Small Numbers

In order to represent large and small numbers, it is important to understand the number system. Our number system is based on 10, and the value of each place is 10 times the value of the place to its right.

The value of a digit is the product of a digit and its place value. For instance, in the number 6,400, the 6 has a value of six thousands and the 4 has a value of four hundreds. A place value chart can help you read numbers. In the chart, each group of three digits is called a period. Commas separate the periods: the ones period, the thousands period, the millions period, and so on. Values to the right of the ones period are decimals. By understanding place value you can write very large numbers like 5 billion and more, and very small numbers that are less than 1, like one-tenth.

Scientific Notation

When dealing with very large numbers like 1,500,000, or very small numbers like 0.000015, it is helpful to keep track of their value by writing the numbers in scientific notation. Powers of 10 with positive exponents are used with a decimal between 1 and 10 to express large numbers. The exponent represents the number of places the decimal point is moved to the right. So, 528,000 is written in scientific notation as 5.28×10^5. Powers of 10 with negative exponents are used with a decimal between 1 and 10 to express small numbers. The exponent represents the number of places the decimal point is moved to the left. The number 0.00047 is expressed as 4.7×10^{-4}.

Factor, Multiple, and Prime Factorization

Two or more numbers that are multiplied to form a product are called factors. Divisibility rules can be used to determine whether 2, 3, 4, 5, 6, 8, 9, or 10 are factors of a given number. Multiples are the products of a given number and various integers.

For example, 8 is a multiple of 4 because $4 \times 2 = 8$. A prime number is a whole number that has exactly two factors: 1 and itself. A composite number is a whole number that has more than two factors. Zero and 1 are neither prime nor composite. A composite number can be expressed as the product of its prime factors. The prime factorization of 40 is $2 \times 2 \times 2 \times 5$, or $2^3 \times 5$. The numbers 2 and 5 are prime numbers.

Integers

A negative number is a number less than zero. Negative numbers like –8, positive numbers like +6, and zero are members of the set of integers. Integers can be represented as points on a number line. A set of integers can be written {…, –3, –2, –1, 0, 1, 2, 3, …} where … means "continues indefinitely."

Real, Rational, and Irrational Numbers

The real number system is made up of the sets of rational and irrational numbers. Rational numbers are numbers that can be written in the form a/b where a and b are integers and $b \neq 0$. Examples are 0.45, $\frac{1}{2}$, and $\sqrt{36}$. Irrational numbers are non-repeating, non-terminating decimals. Examples are $\sqrt{71}$, π, and 0.020020002….

Complex and Imaginary Numbers

A complex number is a mathematical expression with a real number element and an imaginary number element. Imaginary numbers are multiples of i, the "imaginary" square root of –1. Complex numbers are represented by $a + bi$, where a and b are real numbers and i represents the imaginary element. When a quadratic equation does not

Math Appendix

have a real number solution, the solution can be represented by a complex number. Like real numbers, complex numbers can be added, subtracted, multiplied, and divided.

Vectors and Matrices

A matrix is a set of numbers or elements arranged in rows and columns to form a rectangle. The number of rows is represented by m and the number of columns is represented by n. To describe the number of rows and columns in a matrix, list the number of rows first using the format $m \times n$. Matrix A below is a 3×3 matrix because it has 3 rows and 3 columns. To name an element of a matrix, the letter i is used to denote the row and j is used to denote the column, and the element is labeled in the form $a_{i,j}$. In matrix A below, $a_{3,2}$ is 4.

$$\text{Matrix A} = \begin{pmatrix} 1 & 3 & 5 \\ 0 & 6 & 8 \\ 3 & 4 & 5 \end{pmatrix}$$

A vector is a matrix with only one column or row of elements. A transposed column vector, or a column vector turned on its side, is a row vector. In the example below, row vector b' is the transpose of column vector b.

$$b = \begin{pmatrix} 1 \\ 2 \\ 3 \\ 4 \end{pmatrix}$$

$$b' = \begin{pmatrix} 1 & 2 & 3 & 4 \end{pmatrix}$$

▶ Understand meanings of operations and how they relate to one another

Properties of Addition and Multiplication

Properties are statements that are true for any numbers. For example, $3 + 8$ is the same as $8 + 3$ because each expression equals 11. This illustrates the Commutative Property of Addition. Likewise, $3 \times 8 = 8 \times 3$ illustrates the Commutative Property of Multiplication.

When evaluating expressions, it is often helpful to group or associate the numbers. The Associative Property says that the way in which numbers are grouped when added or multiplied does not change the sum or product. The following properties are also true:

- **Additive Identity Property:** When 0 is added to any number, the sum is the number.

- **Multiplicative Identity Property:** When any number is multiplied by 1, the product is the number.

- **Multiplicative Property of Zero:** When any number is multiplied by 0, the product is 0.

Rational Numbers

A number that can be written as a fraction is called a rational number. Terminating and repeating decimals are rational numbers because both can be written as fractions.

Decimals that are neither terminating nor repeating are called irrational numbers because they cannot be written as fractions. Terminating decimals can be converted to fractions by placing the number (without the decimal point) in the numerator. Count the number of places to the right of the decimal point, and in the denominator, place a 1 followed by a number of zeros equal to the number of places that you counted. The fraction can then be reduced to its simplest form.

Writing a Fraction as a Decimal

Any fraction $\frac{a}{b}$, where $b \neq 0$, can be written as a decimal by dividing the numerator by the denominator. So, $\frac{a}{b} = a \div b$. If the division ends, or terminates, when the remainder is zero, the decimal is a terminating decimal. Not all fractions can be written as terminating decimals. Some have a repeating decimal. A bar indicates that the decimal repeats forever. For example, the fraction $\frac{4}{9}$ can be converted to a repeating decimal, $0.\overline{4}$

Adding and Subtracting Like Fractions

Fractions with the same denominator are called like fractions. To add like fractions, add the numerators and write the sum over the denominator. To add mixed numbers with like fractions, add the whole numbers and fractions separately, adding the numerators of the fractions, then simplifying if necessary. The rule for subtracting fractions with like denominators is similar to the rule

for adding. The numerators can be subtracted and the difference written over the denominator. Mixed numbers are written as improper fractions before subtracting. These same rules apply to adding or subtracting like algebraic fractions. An algebraic fraction is a fraction that contains one or more variables in the numerator or denominator.

Adding and Subtracting Unlike Fractions

Fractions with different denominators are called unlike fractions. The least common multiple of the denominators is used to rename the fractions with a common denominator. After a common denominator is found, the numerators can then be added or subtracted. To add mixed numbers with unlike fractions, rename the mixed numbers as improper fractions. Then find a common denominator, add the numerators, and simplify the answer.

Multiplying Rational Numbers

To multiply fractions, multiply the numerators and multiply the denominators. If the numerators and denominators have common factors, they can be simplified before multiplication. If the fractions have different signs, then the product will be negative. Mixed numbers can be multiplied in the same manner, after first renaming them as improper fractions. Algebraic fractions may be multiplied using the same method described above.

Math Appendix

Dividing Rational Numbers

To divide a number by a rational number (a fraction, for example), multiply the first number by the multiplicative inverse of the second. Two numbers whose product is 1 are called multiplicative inverses, or reciprocals. $\frac{7}{4} \times \frac{4}{7} = 1$. When dividing by a mixed number, first rename it as an improper fraction, and then multiply by its multiplicative inverse. This process of multiplying by a number's reciprocal can also be used when dividing algebraic fractions.

Adding Integers

To add integers with the same sign, add their absolute values. The sum takes the same sign as the addends. An addend is a number that is added to another number (the augend). The equation $-5 + (-2) = -7$ is an example of adding two integers with the same sign. To add integers with different signs, subtract their absolute values. The sum takes the same sign as the addend with the greater absolute value.

Subtracting Integers

The rules for adding integers are extended to the subtraction of integers. To subtract an integer, add its additive inverse. For example, to find the difference $2 - 5$, add the additive inverse of 5 to 2: $2 + (-5) = -3$. The rule for subtracting integers can be used to solve real-world problems and to evaluate algebraic expressions.

Additive Inverse Property

Two numbers with the same absolute value but different signs are called opposites. For example, -4 and 4 are opposites. An integer and its opposite are also called additive inverses. The Additive Inverse Property says that the sum of any number and its additive inverse is zero. The Commutative, Associative, and Identity Properties also apply to integers. These properties help when adding more than two integers.

Absolute Value

In mathematics, when two integers on a number line are on opposite sides of zero, and they are the same distance from zero, they have the same absolute value. The symbol for absolute value is two vertical bars on either side of the number. For example, $|-5| = 5$.

Multiplying Integers

Since multiplication is repeated addition, $3(-7)$ means that -7 is used as an addend 3 times. By the Commutative Property of Multiplication, $3(-7) = -7(3)$. The product of two integers with different signs is always negative. The product of two integers with the same sign is always positive.

Dividing Integers

The quotient of two integers can be found by dividing the numbers using their absolute values. The quotient of two integers with the same sign is positive, and the quotient of two integers with a different sign is negative. $-12 \div (-4) = 3$ and $12 \div (-4) = -3$. The division of integers is used in statistics to find the average, or mean, of a set of data. When finding the mean of a set of numbers, find the sum of the numbers, and then divide by the number in the set.

Adding and Multiplying Vectors and Matrices

In order to add two matrices together, they must have the same number of rows and columns. In matrix addition, the corresponding elements are added to each other. In other words $(a + b)_{ij} = a_{ij} + b_{ij}$. For example,

$$\begin{pmatrix} 1 & 2 \\ 2 & 1 \end{pmatrix} + \begin{pmatrix} 3 & 6 \\ 0 & 1 \end{pmatrix} = \begin{pmatrix} 1+3 & 2+6 \\ 2+0 & 1+1 \end{pmatrix} = \begin{pmatrix} 4 & 8 \\ 2 & 2 \end{pmatrix}$$

Matrix multiplication requires that the number of elements in each row in the first matrix is equal to the number of elements in each column in the second. The elements of the first row of the first matrix are multiplied by the corresponding elements of the first column of the second matrix and then added together to get the first element of the product matrix. To get the second element, the elements in the first row of the first matrix are multiplied by the corresponding elements in the second column of the second matrix then added, and so on, until every row of the first matrix is multiplied by every column of the second. See the example below.

$$\begin{pmatrix} 1 & 2 \\ 3 & 4 \end{pmatrix} \times \begin{pmatrix} 3 & 6 \\ 0 & 1 \end{pmatrix} = \begin{pmatrix} (1\times3)+(2\times0) & (1\times6)+(2\times1) \\ (3\times3)+(4\times0) & (3\times6)+(4\times1) \end{pmatrix} = \begin{pmatrix} 3 & 8 \\ 9 & 22 \end{pmatrix}$$

Vector addition and multiplication are performed in the same way, but there is only one column and one row.

Permutations and Combinations

Permutations and combinations are used to determine the number of possible outcomes in different situations. An arrangement, listing, or pattern in which order is important is called a permutation. The symbol P(6, 3) represents the number of permutations of 6 things taken 3 at a time. For P(6, 3), there are $6 \times 5 \times 4$ or 120 possible outcomes. An arrangement or listing where order is not important is called a combination. The symbol C(10, 5) represents the number of combinations of 10 things taken 5 at a time. For C(10, 5), there are $(10 \times 9 \times 8 \times 7 \times 6) \div (5 \times 4 \times 3 \times 2 \times 1)$ or 252 possible outcomes.

Powers and Exponents

An expression such as $3 \times 3 \times 3 \times 3$ can be written as a power. A power has two parts, a base and an exponent. $3 \times 3 \times 3 \times 3 = 3^4$. The base is the number that is multiplied (3). The exponent tells how many times the base is used as a factor (4 times). Numbers and variables can be written using exponents. For example, $8 \times 8 \times 8 \times m \times m \times m \times m \times m$ can be expressed $8^3 m^5$. Exponents also can be used with place value to express numbers in expanded form. Using this method, 1,462 can be written as $(1 \times 10^3) + (4 \times 10^2) + (6 \times 10^1) + (2 \times 10^0)$.

Squares and Square Roots

The square root of a number is one of two equal factors of a number. Every positive number has both a positive and a negative square root. For example, since $8 \times 8 = 64$, 8 is a square root of 64. Since $(-8) \times (-8) = 64$, −8 is also a square root of 64. The notation $\sqrt{\ }$ indicates the positive square root, $-\sqrt{\ }$ indicates the negative square root, and $\pm\sqrt{\ }$ indicates both square roots. For example, $\sqrt{81} = 9$, $-\sqrt{49} = -7$, and $\pm\sqrt{4} = \pm2$. The square root of a negative number is an imaginary number because any two factors of a negative number must have different signs, and are therefore not equivalent.

Math Appendix

Logarithm

A logarithm is the inverse of exponentiation. The logarithm of a number x in base b is equal to the number n. Therefore, $b^n = x$ and $\log_b x = n$. For example, $\log_4(64) = 3$ because $4^3 = 64$. The most commonly used bases for logarithms are 10, the common logarithm; 2, the binary logarithm; and the constant e, the natural logarithm (also called $ln(x)$ instead of $\log_e(x)$). Below is a list of some of the rules of logarithms that are important to understand if you are going to use them.

$$\log_b(xy) = \log_b(x) + \log_b(y)$$
$$\log_b(x/y) = \log_b(x) - \log_b(y)$$
$$\log_b(1/x) = -\log_b(x)$$
$$\log_b(x)y = y\log_b(x)$$

▶ Compute fluently and make reasonable estimates

Estimation by Rounding

When rounding numbers, look at the digit to the right of the place to which you are rounding. If the digit is 5 or greater, round up. If it is less than 5, round down. For example, to round 65,137 to the nearest hundred, look at the number in the tens place. Since 3 is less than 5, round down to 65,100. To round the same number to the nearest ten thousandth, look at the number in the thousandths place. Since it is 5, round up to 70,000.

Finding Equivalent Ratios

Equivalent ratios have the same meaning. Just like finding equivalent fractions, to find an equivalent ratio, multiply or divide both sides by the same number. For example, you can multiply 7 by both sides of the ratio 6:8 to get 42:56. Instead, you can also divide both sides of the same ratio by 2 to get 3:4. Find the simplest form of a ratio by dividing to find equivalent ratios until you can't go any further without going into decimals. So, 160:240 in simplest form is 2:3. To write a ratio in the form *1:n*, divide both sides by the left-hand number. In other words, to change 8:20 to *1:n*, divide both sides by 8 to get 1:2.5.

Front-End Estimation

Front-end estimation can be used to quickly estimate sums and differences before adding or subtracting. To use this technique, add or subtract just the digits of the two highest place values, and replace the other place values with zero. This will give you an estimation of the solution of a problem. For example, 93,471 − 22,825 can be changed to 93,000 − 22,000 or 71,000. This estimate can be compared to your final answer to judge its correctness.

Judging Reasonableness

When solving an equation, it is important to check your work by considering how reasonable your answer is. For example, consider the equation $9\frac{3}{4} \times 4\frac{1}{3}$. Since $9\frac{3}{4}$ is between 9 and 10 and $4\frac{1}{3}$ is between 4 and 5, only values that are between 9×4 or 36 and 10×5 or 50 will be reasonable. You can also use front-end estimation, or you can round and estimate a reasonable answer. In the equation 73×25, you can round and solve to estimate a reasonable answer to be near 70×30 or 2,100.

Algebra

▶ *Understand patterns, relations, and functions*

Relation

A relation is a generalization comparing sets of ordered pairs for an equation or inequality such as $x = y + 1$ or $x > y$. The first element in each pair, the x values, forms the domain. The second element in each pair, the y values, forms the range.

Function

A function is a special relation in which each member of the domain is paired with exactly one member in the range. Functions may be represented using ordered pairs, tables, or graphs. One way to determine whether a relation is a function is to use the vertical line test. Using an object to represent a vertical line, move the object from left to right across the graph. If, for each value of x in the domain, the object passes through no more than one point on the graph, then the graph represents a function.

Linear and Nonlinear Functions

Linear functions have graphs that are straight lines. These graphs represent constant rates of change. In other words, the slope between any two pairs of points on the graph is the same. Nonlinear functions do not have constant rates of change. The slope changes along these graphs. Therefore, the graphs of nonlinear functions are *not* straight lines. Graphs of curves represent nonlinear functions. The equation for a linear function can be written in the form $y = mx + b$, where m represents the constant rate of change, or the slope. Therefore, you can determine whether a function is linear by looking at the equation. For example, the equation $y = \frac{3}{x}$ is nonlinear because x is in the denominator and the equation cannot be written in the form $y = mx + b$. A nonlinear function does not increase or decrease at a constant rate. You can check this by using a table and finding the increase or decrease in y for each regular increase in x. For example, if for each increase in x by 2, y does not increase or decrease the same amount each time, the function is nonlinear.

Linear Equations in Two Variables

In a linear equation with two variables, such as $y = x - 3$, the variables appear in separate terms and neither variable contains an exponent other than 1. The graphs of all linear equations are straight lines. All points on a line are solutions of the equation that is graphed.

Quadratic and Cubic Functions

A quadratic function is a polynomial equation of the second degree, generally expressed as $ax^2 + bx + c = 0$, where a, b, and c are real numbers and a is not equal to zero. Similarly, a cubic function is a polynomial equation of the third degree, usually expressed as $ax^3 + bx^2 + cx + d = 0$. Quadratic functions can be graphed using an equation or a table of values. For example, to graph $y = 3x^2 + 1$, substitute the values −1, −0.5, 0, 0.5, and 1 for x to yield the point coordinates (−1, 4), (−0.5, 1.75), (0, 1), (0.5, 1.75), and (1, 4).

Math Appendix

Plot these points on a coordinate grid and connect the points in the form of a parabola. Cubic functions also can be graphed by making a table of values. The points of a cubic function from a curve. There is one point at which the curve changes from opening upward to opening downward, or vice versa, called the point of inflection.

Slope

Slope is the ratio of the rise, or vertical change, to the run, or horizontal change of a line: slope = rise/run. Slope (m) is the same for any two points on a straight line and can be found by using the coordinates of any two points on the line:

$$m = \frac{y_2 - y_1}{x_2 - x_1}, \text{ where } x_2 \neq x_1$$

Asymptotes

An asymptote is a straight line that a curve approaches but never actually meets or crosses. Theoretically, the asymptote meets the curve at infinity. For example, in the function $f(x) = \frac{1}{x}$, two asymptotes are being approached: the line $y = 0$ and $x = 0$. See the graph of the function below.

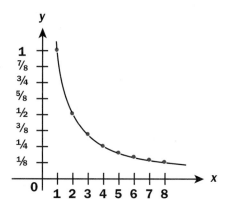

▶ Represent and analyze mathematical situations and structures using algebraic symbols

Variables and Expressions

Algebra is a language of symbols. A variable is a placeholder for a changing value. Any letter, such as x, can be used as a variable. Expressions such as $x + 2$ and $4x$ are algebraic expressions because they represent sums and/or products of variables and numbers. Usually, mathematicians avoid the use of i and e for variables because they have other mathematical meanings ($i = \sqrt{-1}$ and e is used with natural logarithms). To evaluate an algebraic expression, replace the variable or variables with known values, and then solve using order of operations. Translate verbal phrases into algebraic expressions by first defining a variable: Choose a variable and a quantity for the variable to represent. In this way, algebraic expressions can be used to represent real-world situations.

Constant and Coefficient

A constant is a fixed value unlike a variable, which can change. Constants are usually represented by numbers, but they can also be represented by symbols. For example, π is a symbolic representation of the value 3.1415…. A coefficient is a constant by which a variable or other object is multiplied. For example, in the expression $7x^2 + 5x + 9$, the coefficient of x^2 is 7 and the coefficient of x is 5. The number 9 is a constant and not a coefficient.

Monomial and Polynomial

A monomial is a number, a variable, or a product of numbers and/or variables such as 3×4. An algebraic expression that contains one or more monomials is called a polynomial. In a polynomial, there are no terms with variables in the denominator and no terms with variables under a radical sign. Polynomials can be classified by the number of terms contained in the expression. Therefore, a polynomial with two terms is called a binomial ($z^2 - 1$), and a polynomial with three terms is called a trinomial ($2y^3 + 4y^2 - y$). Polynomials also can be classified by their degrees. The degree of a monomial is the sum of the exponents of its variables. The degree of a nonzero constant such as 6 or 10 is 0. The constant 0 has no degree. For example, the monomial $4b^5c^2$ had a degree of 7. The degree of a polynomial is the same as that of the term with the greatest degree. For example, the polynomial $3x^4 - 2y^3 + 4y^2 - y$ has a degree of 4.

Equation

An equation is a mathematical sentence that states that two expressions are equal. The two expressions in an equation are always separated by an equal sign. When solving for a variable in an equation, you must perform the same operations on both sides of the equation in order for the mathematical sentence to remain true.

Solving Equations with Variables

To solve equations with variables on both sides, use the Addition or Subtraction Property of Equality to write an equivalent equation with the variables on the same side. For example, to solve $5x - 8 = 3x$, subtract $3x$ from each side to get $2x - 8 = 0$. Then add 8 to each side to get $2x = 8$. Finally, divide each side by 2 to find that $x = 4$.

Solving Equations with Grouping Symbols

Equations often contain grouping symbols such as parentheses or brackets. The first step in solving these equations is to use the Distributive Property to remove the grouping symbols. For example $5(x + 2) = 25$ can be changed to $5x + 10 = 25$, and then solved to find that $x = 3$.

Some equations have no solution. That is, there is no value of the variable that results in a true sentence. For such an equation, the solution set is called the null or empty set, and is represented by the symbol $\varnothing$ or {}. Other equations may have every number as the solution. An equation that is true for every value of the variable is called the identity.

Inequality

A mathematical sentence that contains the symbols < (less than), > (greater than), ≤ (less than or equal to), or ≥ (greater than or equal to) is called an inequality. For example, the statement that it is legal to drive 55 miles per hour or slower on a stretch of the highway can be shown by the sentence $s \le 55$. Inequalities with variables are called open sentences. When a variable is replaced with a number, the inequality may be true or false.

Solving Inequalities

Solving an inequality means finding values for the variable that make the inequality true. Just as with equations, when you add or subtract the same number from each side of an inequality, the inequality remains true. For example, if you add 5 to each side of the inequality $3x < 6$, the resulting inequality $3x + 5 < 11$ is also true. Adding or subtracting the same number from each side of an inequality does not affect the inequality sign. When multiplying or dividing each side of an inequality by the same positive number, the inequality remains true. In such cases, the inequality symbol does not change. When multiplying or dividing each side of an inequality by a negative number, the inequality symbol must be reversed. For example, when dividing each side of the inequality $-4x \geq -8$ by -2, the inequality sign must be changed to $\leq$ for the resulting inequality, $2x \leq 4$, to be true. Since the solutions to an inequality include all rational numbers satisfying it, inequalities have an infinite number of solutions.

Representing Inequalities on a Number Line
The solutions of inequalities can be graphed on a number line. For example, if the solution of an inequality is $x < 5$, start an arrow at 5 on the number line, and continue the arrow to the left to show all values less than 5 as the solution. Put an open circle at 5 to show that the point 5 is *not* included in the graph. Use a closed circle when graphing solutions that are greater than or equal to, or less than or equal to, a number.

Order of Operations
Solving a problem may involve using more than one operation. The answer can depend on the order in which you do the operations. To make sure that there is just one answer to a series of computations, mathematicians have agreed upon an order in which to do the operations. First simplify within the parentheses, often called graphing symbols, and then evaluate any exponents. Then multiply and divide from left to

right, and finally add and subtract from left to right.

Parametric Equations
Given an equation with more than one unknown, a statistician can draw conclusions about those unknown quantities through the use of parameters, independent variables that the statistician already knows something about. For example, you can find the velocity of an object if you make some assumptions about distance and time parameters.

Recursive Equations
In recursive equations, every value is determined by the previous value. You must first plug an initial value into the equation to get the first value, and then you can use the first value to determine the next one, and so on. For example, in order to determine what the population of pigeons will be in New York City in three years, you can use an equation with the birth, death, immigration, and emigration rates of the birds. Input the current population size into the equation to determine next year's population size, then repeat until you have calculated the value for which you are looking.

▶ Use mathematical models to represent and understand quantitative relationships

Solving Systems of Equations
Two or more equations together are called a system of equations. A system of equations can have one solution, no solution, or infinitely many solutions. One method for solving a system of equations is to graph the equations on the same coordinate plane. The coordinates of the point where the graphs

intersect is the solution. In other words, the solution of a system is the ordered pair that is a solution of all equations. A more accurate way to solve a system of two equations is by using a method called substitution. Write both equations in terms of y. Replace y in the first equation with the right side of the second equation. Check the solution by graphing. You can solve a system of three equations using matrix algebra.

Graphing Inequalities

To graph an inequality, first graph the related equation, which is the boundary. All points in the shaded region are solutions of the inequality. If an inequality contains the symbol $\leq$ or $\geq$, then use a solid line to indicate that the boundary is included in the graph. If an inequality contains the symbol $<$ or $>$, then use a dashed line to indicate that the boundary is not included in the graph.

▶ Analyze change in various contexts

Rate of Change

A change in one quantity with respect to another quantity is called the rate of change. Rates of change can be described using slope:

$$\text{slope} = \frac{\text{change in } y}{\text{change in } x}$$

You can find rates of change from an equation, a table, or a graph. A special type of linear equation that describes rate of change is called a direct variation. The graph of a direct variation always passes through the origin and represents a proportional situation. In the equation $y = kx$, k is called the constant of variation. It is the slope, or rate of change. As x increases in value, y increases or decreases at a constant rate k, or y varies directly with x. Another way to say this is that y is directly proportional to x. The direct variation $y = kx$ also can be written as $k = \frac{y}{x}$. In this form, you can see that the ratio of y to x is the same for any corresponding values of y and x.

Slope-Intercept Form

Equations written as $y = mx + b$, where m is the slope and b is the y-intercept, are linear equations in slope-intercept form. For example, the graph of $y = 5x - 6$ is a line that has a slope of 5 and crosses the y-axis at $(0, -6)$. Sometimes you must first write an equation in slope-intercept form before finding the slope and y-intercept. For example, the equation $2x + 3y = 15$ can be expressed in slope-intercept form by subtracting $2x$ from each side and then dividing by 3: $y = -\frac{2}{3}x + 5$, revealing a slope of $-\frac{2}{3}$ and a y-intercept of 5. You can use the slope-intercept form of an equation to graph a line easily. Graph the y-intercept and use the slope to find another point on the line, then connect the two points with a line.

Math Appendix

Geometry

▶ *Analyze characteristics and properties of two- and three-dimensional geometric shapes and develop mathematical arguments about geometric relationships*

Angles
Two rays that have the same endpoint form an angle. The common endpoint is called the vertex, and the two rays that make up the angle are called the sides of the angle. The most common unit of measure for angles is the degree. Protractors can be used to measure angles or to draw an angle of a given measure. Angles can be classified by their degree measure. Acute angles have measures less than 90° but greater than 0°. Obtuse angles have measures greater than 90° but less than 180°. Right angles have measures of 90°.

Triangles
A triangle is a figure formed by three line segments that intersect only at their endpoints. The sum of the measures of the angles of a triangle is 180°. Triangles can be classified by their angles. An acute triangle contains all acute angles. An obtuse triangle has one obtuse angle. A right triangle has one right angle. Triangles can also be classified by their sides. A scalene triangle has no congruent sides. An isosceles triangle has at least two congruent sides. In an equilateral triangle all sides are congruent.

Quadrilaterals
A quadrilateral is a closed figure with four sides and four vertices. The segments of a quadrilateral intersect only at their endpoints. Quadrilaterals can be separated into two triangles. Since the sum of the interior angles of all triangles totals 180°, the measures of the interior angles of a quadrilateral equal 360°. Quadrilaterals are classified according to their characteristics, and include trapezoids, parallelograms, rectangles, squares, and rhombuses.

Two-Dimensional Figures
A two-dimensional figure exists within a plane and has only the dimensions of length and width. Examples of two-dimensional figures include circles and polygons. Polygons are figures that have three or more angles, including triangles, quadrilaterals, pentagons, hexagons, and many more. The sum of the angles of any polygon totals at least 180° (triangle), and each additional side adds 180° to the measure of the first three angles. The sum of the angles of a quadrilateral, for example, is 360°. The sum of the angles of a pentagon is 540°.

Three-Dimensional Figures
A plane is a two-dimensional flat surface that extends in all directions. Intersecting planes can form the edges and vertices of three-dimensional figures or solids. A polyhedron is a solid with flat surfaces that are polygons.

Polyhedrons are composed of faces, edges, and vertices and are differentiated by their shape and by their number of bases. Skew lines are lines that lie in different planes. They are neither intersecting nor parallel.

Congruence

Figures that have the same size and shape are congruent. The parts of congruent triangles that match are called corresponding parts. Congruence statements are used to identify corresponding parts of congruent triangles. When writing a congruence statement, the letters must be written so that corresponding vertices appear in the same order. Corresponding parts can be used to find the measures of angles and sides in a figure that is congruent to a figure with known measures.

Similarity

If two figures have the same shape but not the same size they are called similar figures. For example, the triangles below are similar, so angles A, B, and C have the same measurements as angles D, E, and F, respectively. However, segments AB, BC, and CA do not have the same measurements as segments DE, EF, and FD , but the measures of the sides are proportional.

For example, $\dfrac{\overline{AB}}{\overline{DE}} = \dfrac{\overline{BC}}{\overline{EF}} = \dfrac{\overline{CA}}{\overline{FD}}$.

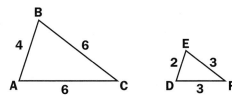

Solid figures are considered to be similar if they have the same shape and their corresponding linear measures are proportional. As with two-dimensional figures, they can be tested for similarity by comparing corresponding measures. If the compared ratios are proportional, then the figures are similar solids. Missing measures of similar solids can also be determined by using proportions.

The Pythagorean Theorem

The sides that are adjacent to a right angle are called legs. The side opposite the right angle is the hypotenuse.

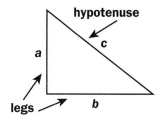

The Pythagorean Theorem describes the relationship between the lengths of the legs a and b and the hypotenuse c. It states that if a triangle is a right triangle, then the square of the length of the hypotenuse is equal to the sum of the squares of the lengths of the legs. In symbols, $c^2 = a^2 + b^2$.

Sine, Cosine, and Tangent Ratios

Trigonometry is the study of the properties of triangles. A trigonometric ratio is a ratio of the lengths of two sides of a right triangle. The most common trigonometric ratios are the sine, cosine, and tangent

Math Appendix

ratios. These ratios are abbreviated as *sin*, *cos*, and *tan*, respectively.

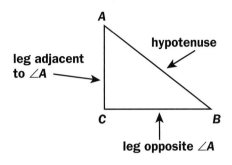

If ∠A is an acute angle of a right triangle, then

$$\sin \angle A = \frac{\text{measure of leg opposite } \angle A}{\text{measure of hypotenuse}},$$

$$\cos \angle A = \frac{\text{measure of leg adjacent to } \angle A}{\text{measure of hypotenuse}}, \text{ and}$$

$$\tan \angle A = \frac{\text{measure of leg opposite } \angle A}{\text{measure of leg adjacent to } \angle A}.$$

▶ Specify locations and describe spatial relationships using coordinate geometry and other representational systems

Polygons
A polygon is a simple, closed figure formed by three or more line segments. The line segments meet only at their endpoints. The points of intersection are called vertices, and the line segments are called sides. Polygons are classified by the number of sides they have. The diagonals of a polygon divide the polygon into triangles. The number of triangles formed is two less than the number of sides. To find the sum of the measures of the interior angles of any polygon, multiply the number of triangles within the polygon by 180. That is, if *n* equals the number of

sides, then (*n* – 2) 180 gives the sum of the measures of the polygon's interior angles.

Cartesian Coordinates
In the Cartesian coordinate system, the *y*-axis extends above and below the origin and the *x*-axis extends to the right and left of the origin, which is the point at which the *x*- and *y*-axes intersect. Numbers below and to the left of the origin are negative. A point graphed on the coordinate grid is said to have an *x*-coordinate and a *y*-coordinate. For example, the point (1,–2) has as its *x*-coordinate the number 1, and has as its *y*-coordinate the number –2. This point is graphed by locating the position on the grid that is 1 unit to the right of the origin and 2 units below the origin.

The *x*-axis and the *y*-axis separate the coordinate plane into four regions, called quadrants. The axes and points located on the axes themselves are not located in any of the quadrants. The quadrants are labeled I to IV, starting in the upper right and proceeding counterclockwise. In quadrant I, both coordinates are positive. In quadrant II, the *x*-coordinate is negative and the *y*-coordinate is positive. In quadrant III, both coordinates are negative. In quadrant IV, the *x*-coordinate is positive and the *y*-coordinate is negative. A coordinate graph can be used to show algebraic relationships among numbers.

▶ Apply transformations and use symmetry to analyze mathematical situations

Similar Triangles and Indirect Measurement
Triangles that have the same shape but not necessarily the same dimensions are called similar triangles. Similar triangles

have corresponding angles and corresponding sides. Arcs are used to show congruent angles. If two triangles are similar, then the corresponding angles have the same measure, and the corresponding sides are proportional. Therefore, to determine the measures of the sides of similar triangles when some measures are known, proportions can be used.

Transformations

A transformation is a movement of a geometric figure. There are several types of transformations. In a translation, also called a slide, a figure is slid from one position to another without turning it. Every point of the original figure is moved the same distance and in the same direction. In a reflection, also called a flip, a figure is flipped over a line to form a mirror image. Every point of the original figure has a corresponding point on the other side of the line of symmetry. In a rotation, also called a turn, a figure is turned around a fixed point. A figure can be rotated 0°–360° clockwise or counterclockwise. A dilation transforms each line to a parallel line whose length is a fixed multiple of the length of the original line to create a similar figure that will be either larger or smaller.

▶ *Use visualizations, spatial reasoning, and geometric modeling to solve problems*

Two-Dimensional Representations of Three-Dimensional Objects

Three-dimensional objects can be represented in a two-dimensional drawing in order to more easily determine properties such as surface area and volume. When you look at the triangular prism, you can see the orientation of its three dimensions, length, width, and height. Using the drawing and the formulas for surface area and volume, you can easily calculate these properties.

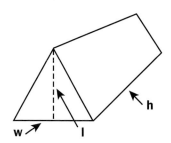

Another way to represent a three-dimensional object in a two-dimensional plane is by using a net, which is the unfolded representation. Imagine cutting the vertices of a box until it is flat then drawing an outline of it. That's a net. Most objects have more than one net, but any one can be measured to determine surface area. Below is a cube and one of its nets.

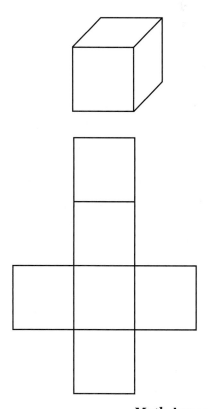

Math Appendix

Measurement

▶ *Understand measurable attributes of objects and the units, systems, and processes of measurement*

Customary System

The customary system is the system of weights and measures used in the United States. The main units of weight are ounces, pounds (1 equal to 16 ounces), and tons (1 equal to 2,000 pounds). Length is typically measured in inches, feet (1 equal to 12 inches), yards (1 equal to 3 feet), and miles (1 equal to 5,280 feet), while area is measured in square feet and acres (1 equal to 43,560 square feet). Liquid is measured in cups, pints (1 equal to 2 cups), quarts (1 equal to 2 pints), and gallons (1 equal to 4 quarts). Finally, temperature is measured in degrees Fahrenheit.

Metric System

The metric system is a decimal system of weights and measurements in which the prefixes of the words for the units of measure indicate the relationships between the different measurements. In this system, the main units of weight, or mass, are grams and kilograms. Length is measured in millimeters, centimeters, meters, and kilometers, and the units of area are square millimeters, centimeters, meters, and kilometers. Liquid is typically measured in milliliters and liters, while temperature is in degrees Celsius.

Selecting Units of Measure

When measuring something, it is important to select the appropriate type and size of unit. For example, in the United States it would be appropriate when describing someone's height to use feet and inches. These units of height or length are good to use because they are in the customary system, and they are of appropriate size. In the customary system, use inches, feet, and miles for lengths and perimeters; square inches, feet, and miles for area and surface area; and cups, pints, quarts, gallons or cubic inches and feet (and less commonly miles) for volume. In the metric system use millimeters, centimeters, meters, and kilometers for lengths and perimeters; square units millimeters, centimeters, meters, and kilometers for area and surface area; and milliliters and liters for volume. Finally, always use degrees to measure angles.

▶ *Apply appropriate techniques, tools, and formulas to determine measurements*

Precision and Significant Digits

The precision of measurement is the exactness to which a measurement is made. Precision depends on the smallest unit of measure being used, or the precision unit. One way to record a measure is to estimate to the nearest precision unit. A more precise method is to include all of the digits that are actually measured, plus one estimated digit. The digits recorded, called significant digits, indicate the precision of the measurement. There are special rules for determining significant digits. If a number contains a decimal point, the number of significant digits is found by counting from left to right, starting with the first nonzero digit.

If the number does not contain a decimal point, the number of significant digits is found by counting the digits from left to right, starting with the first digit and ending with the last nonzero digit.

Surface Area

The amount of material needed to cover the surface of a figure is called the surface area. It can be calculated by finding the area of each face and adding them together. To find the surface area of a rectangular prism, for example, the formula $S = 2lw + 2lh + 2wh$ applies. A cylinder, on the other hand, may be unrolled to reveal two circles and a rectangle. Its surface area can be determined by finding the area of the two circles, $2\pi r^2$, and adding it to the area of the rectangle, $2\pi rh$ (the length of the rectangle is the circumference of one of the circles), or $S = 2\pi r^2 + 2\pi rh$. The surface area of a pyramid is measured in a slightly different way because the sides of a pyramid are triangles that intersect at the vertex. These sides are called lateral faces and the height of each is called the slant height. The sum of their areas is the lateral area of a pyramid. The surface area of a square pyramid is the lateral area $\frac{1}{2}bh$ (area of a lateral face) times 4 (number of lateral faces), plus the area of the base. The surface area of a cone is the area of its circular base (πr^2) plus its lateral area (πrl, where l is the slant height).

Volume

Volume is the measure of space occupied by a solid region. To find the volume of a prism, the area of the base is multiplied by the measure of the height, $V = Bh$. A solid containing several prisms can be broken down into its component prisms. Then the volume of each component can be found and the volumes added. The volume of a cylinder can be determined by finding the area of its circular base, πr^2, and then multiplying by the height of the cylinder. A pyramid has one-third the volume of a prism with the same base and height. To find the volume of a pyramid, multiply the area of the base by the pyramid's height, and then divide by 3. Simply stated, the formula for the volume of a pyramid is $V = \frac{1}{3}bh$. A cone is a three-dimensional figure with one circular base and a curved surface connecting the base and the vertex. The volume of a cone is one-third the volume of a cylinder with the same base area and height. Like a pyramid, the formula for the volume of a cone is $V = \frac{1}{3}bh$. More specifically, the formula is $V = \frac{1}{3}\pi r^2 h$.

Upper and Lower Bounds

Upper and lower bounds have to do with the accuracy of a measurement. When a measurement is given, the degree of accuracy is also stated to tell you what the upper and lower bounds of the measurement are. The upper bound is the largest possible value that a measurement could have had before being rounded down, and the lower bound is the lowest possible value it could have had before being rounded up.

Math Appendix

Data Analysis and Probability

▶ *Formulate questions that can be addressed with data and collect, organize, and display relevant data to answer them*

Histograms

A histogram displays numerical data that have been organized into equal intervals using bars that have the same width and no space between them. While a histogram does not give exact data points, its shape shows the distribution of the data. Histograms also can be used to compare data.

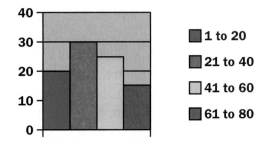

- ■ 1 to 20
- ■ 21 to 40
- □ 41 to 60
- ■ 61 to 80

Box-and-Whisker Plot

A box-and-whisker plot displays the measures of central tendency and variation. A box is drawn around the quartile values, and whiskers extend from each quartile to the extreme data points. To make a box plot for a set of data, draw a number line that covers the range of data. Find the median, the extremes, and the upper and lower quartiles. Mark these points on the number line with bullets, then draw a box and the whiskers. The length of a whisker or box shows whether the values of the data in that part are concentrated or spread out.

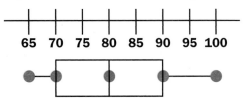

Scatter Plots

A scatter plot is a graph that shows the relationship between two sets of data. In a scatter plot, two sets of data are graphed as ordered pairs on a coordinate system. Two sets of data can have a positive correlation (as x increases, y increases), a negative correlation (as x increases, y decreases), or no correlation (no obvious pattern is shown). Scatter plots can be used to spot trends, draw conclusions, and make predictions about data.

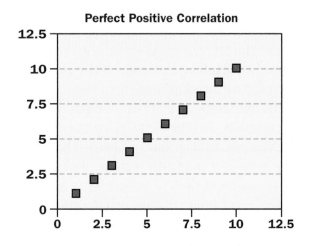

Perfect Positive Correlation

Randomization

The idea of randomization is a very important principle of statistics and the design of experiments. Data must be selected randomly to prevent bias from influencing the results. For example, you want to know the average income of people in your town but you can only use a sample of 100 individuals to make determinations about everyone. If you select 100 individuals who are all doctors, you will have a biased sample. However, if you chose a random sample of 100 people out of the phone book, you are much more likely to accurately represent average income in the town.

Statistics and Parameters

Statistics is a science that involves collecting, analyzing, and presenting data. The data can be collected in various ways—for example through a census or by making physical measurements. The data can then be analyzed by creating summary statistics, which have to do with the distribution of the data sample, including the mean, range, and standard error. They can also be illustrated in tables and graphs, like box-plots, scatter plots, and histograms. The presentation of the data typically involves describing the strength or validity of the data and what they show. For example, an analysis of ancestry of people in a city might tell you something about immigration patterns, unless the data set is very small or biased in some way, in which case it is not likely to be very accurate or useful.

Categorical and Measurement Data

When analyzing data, it is important to understand if the data is qualitative or quantitative. Categorical data is qualitative and measurement, or numerical, data is quantitative. Categorical data describes a quality of something and can be placed into different categories. For example, if you are analyzing the number of students in different grades in a school, each grade is a category. On the other hand, measurement data is continuous, like height, weight, or any other measurable variable. Measurement data can be converted into categorical data if you decide to group the data. Using height as an example, you can group the continuous data set into categories like under 5 feet, 5 feet to 5 feet 5 inches, over 5 feet five inches to 6 feet, and so on.

Univariate and Bivariate Data

In data analysis, a researcher can analyze one variable at a time or look at how multiple variables behave together. Univariate data involves only one variable, for example height in humans. You can measure the height in a population of people then plot the results in a histogram to look at how height is distributed in humans. To summarize univariate data, you can use statistics like the mean, mode, median, range, and standard deviation, which is a measure of variation. When looking at more than one variable at once, you use multivariate data. Bivariate data involves two variables. For example, you can look at height and age in humans together by gathering information on both variables from individuals in a population. You can then plot both variables in a scatter plot, look at how the variables behave in relation to each other, and create an equation that represents the relationship, also called a regression. These equations could help answer questions such as, for example, does height increase with age in humans?

▶ Select and use appropriate statistical methods to analyze data

Measures of Central Tendency

When you have a list of numerical data, it is often helpful to use one or more numbers to represent the whole set. These numbers are called measures of central tendency. Three measures of central tendency are mean, median, and mode. The mean is the sum of the data divided by the number of items in the data set. The median is the middle number of the ordered data (or the mean of the two middle numbers). The mode is the number or numbers that occur most often. These measures of central tendency allow data to be analyzed and better understood.

Measures of Spread

In statistics, measures of spread or variation are used to describe how data are distributed. The range of a set of data is the difference between the greatest and the least values of the data set. The quartiles are the values that divide the data into four equal parts. The median of data separates the set in half. Similarly, the median of the lower half of a set of data is the lower quartile. The median of the upper half of a set of data is the upper quartile. The interquartile range is the difference between the upper quartile and the lower quartile.

Line of Best Fit

When real-life data are collected, the points graphed usually do not form a straight line, but they may approximate a linear relationship. A line of best fit is a line that lies very close to most of the data points. It can be used to predict data. You also can use the equation of the best-fit line to make predictions.

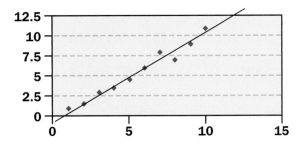

Stem and Leaf Plots

In a stem and leaf plot, numerical data are listed in ascending or descending order. The greatest place value of the data is used for the stems. The next greatest place value forms the leaves. For example, if the least number in a

set of data is 8 and the greatest number is 95, draw a vertical line and write the stems from 0 to 9 to the left of the line. Write the leaves from to the right of the line, with the corresponding stem. Next, rearrange the leaves so they are ordered from least to greatest. Then include a key or explanation, such as $1|3 = 13$. Notice that the stem-and-leaf plot below is like a histogram turned on its side.

```
0|8
1|3 6
2|5 6 9
3|0 2 7 8
4|0 1 4 7 9
5|1 4 5 8
6|1 3 7
7|5 8
8|2 6
9|5
```
Key: **1|3 = 13**

▶ Develop and evaluate inferences and predictions that are based on data

Sampling Distribution

The sampling distribution of a population is the distribution that would result if you could take an infinite number of samples from the population, average each, and then average the averages. The more normal the distribution of the population, that is, how closely the distribution follows a bell curve, the more likely the sampling distribution will also follow a normal distribution. Furthermore, the larger the sample, the more likely it will accurately represent the entire population. For instance, you are more likely to gain more representative results from a population of 1,000 with a sample of 100 than with a sample of 2.

Validity

In statistics, validity refers to acquiring results that accurately reflect that which is being measured. In other words, it is important when performing statistical analyses, to ensure that the data are valid in that the sample being analyzed represents the population to the best extent possible. Randomization of data and using appropriate sample sizes are two important aspects of making valid inferences about a population.

▶ Understand and apply basic concepts of probability

Complementary, Mutually Exclusive Events

To understand probability theory, it is important to know if two events are mutually exclusive, or complementary: the occurrence of one event automatically implies the non-occurrence of the other. That is, two complementary events cannot both occur. If you roll a pair of dice, the event of rolling 6 and rolling doubles have an outcome in common (3, 3), so they are not mutually exclusive. If you roll (3, 3), you also roll doubles. However, the events of rolling a 9 and rolling doubles are mutually exclusive because they have no outcomes in common. If you roll a 9, you will not also roll doubles.

Independent and Dependent Events

Determining the probability of a series of events requires that you know whether the events are independent or dependent. An independent event has no influence on the occurrence of subsequent events, whereas, a dependent event does influence subsequent events. The chances that a woman's first child will be a girl are $\frac{1}{2}$, and the chances that her second child will be a girl are also $\frac{1}{2}$ because the two events are independent of each other. However, if there are 7 red marbles in a bag of 15 marbles, the chances that the first marble you pick will be red are $\frac{7}{15}$ and if you indeed pick a red marble and remove it, you have reduced the chances of picking another red marble to $\frac{6}{14}$.

Sample Space

The sample space is the group of all possible outcomes for an event. For example, if you are tossing a single six-sided die, the sample space is {1, 2, 3, 4, 5, 6}. Similarly, you can determine the sample space for the possible outcomes of two events. If you are going to toss a coin twice, the sample space is {(heads, heads), (heads, tails), (tails, heads), (tails, tails)}.

Computing the Probability of a Compound Event

If two events are independent, the outcome of one event does not influence the outcome of the second. For example, if a bag contains 2 blue and 3 red marbles, then the probability of selecting a blue marble, replacing it, and then selecting a red marble is $P(A) \times P(B) = \frac{2}{5} \times \frac{3}{5}$ or $\frac{6}{25}$.

If two events are dependent, the outcome of one event affects the outcome of the second. For example, if a bag contains 2 blue and 3 red marbles, then the probability of selecting a blue and then a red marble without replacing the first marble is $P(A) \times P(B$ following $A) = \frac{2}{5} \times \frac{3}{4}$ or $\frac{3}{10}$. Two events that cannot happen at the same time are mutually exclusive. For example, when you roll two number cubes, you cannot roll a sum that is both 5 and even. So, $P(A$ or $B) = \frac{4}{36} + \frac{18}{36}$ or $\frac{11}{18}$.

Glossary

How to Use This Glossary

- Content vocabulary terms in this glossary are words that relate to this book's content. They are **highlighted yellow** in your text.

- Words in this glossary that have an asterisk (*) are academic vocabulary terms. They help you understand your school subjects and are used on tests. They are **boldfaced blue** in your text.

- Some of the vocabulary words in this book include pronunciation symbols to help you sound out the words. Use the pronunciation key to help you pronounce the words.

	Pronunciation Key	
a . . . . at	ô . . . . fork, all	ŋ . . . . sing
ā . . . . ape	œ . . . boeuf	th . . . thin
ä . . . . father	oo . . . wood, put	th . . . this
e . . . . end	ōō . . . fool	zh . . . treasure
ē . . . . me	oi . . . oil	ə . . . . ago, taken, pencil, lemon,
i . . . . it	ou . . . out	circus
ī . . . . ice	u . . . . up	' . . . . indicates primary stress
o . . . . hot	ū . . . . use	(symbol in front of and *above* letter)
ō . . . . hope	ü . . . . rule	ˌ . . . . indicates secondary stress
ȯ . . . . saw	u̅ . . . . pull	(symbol in front of and *below* letter)

A

à la carte (ˌä-lə-'kärt) menu A menu that offers each food and beverage item priced and served separately. (p. 310)

abrasion A scrape or minor cut. (p. 11)

* **abundant** Plentiful. (p. 406)

* **acceptable** Of good quality. (p. 572)

* **accessible** Available. (p. 663)

accident report log Shows the details of any accident that happens in a business. (p. 201)

accompaniment An item that comes with an entrée, such as a choice of potato, rice, or pasta and a choice of vegetable. (p. 312)

* **accompaniment** Something that goes well with another thing. (p. 416)

* **accurate** Correct and updated. (p. 78)

* **achieve** To do. (p. 619)

active listening The skill of paying attention and interacting with the speaker. (p. 85)

* **adapting** Positively changing. (p. 206)

additive Substance added to a food to improve it in some way. (p. 287)

* **adequate** Enough. (p. 190)

* **adhere** Follow. (p. 172)

advertising A paid form of promotion that persuades and informs the public about what a business has to offer. (p. 191)

* **affect** Act upon. (p. 38)

affirmative action Programs to locate, hire, train, and promote women and minorities. (p. 205)

aftertaste A secondary flavor that comes after the main flavor has subsided. (p. 742)

al dente "To the bite," meaning that the pasta is tender, but still firm. (p. 620)

albumin (al-'byü-mən) The clear white of an egg. (p. 433)

* **alter** To change. (p. 337)

* **alternative** Substitute. (p. 435); Option. (p. 771)

American-style ice cream Ice cream that has no eggs, is uncooked, and is made with milk, cream, sugar, and flavorings. (p. 771)

amino acid Small units that can be combined in certain ways to produce complete proteins. (p. 281)

* **analyze** Study all the components of. (p. 68)

angel food cake A type of foam cake that is made with egg whites, but not egg yolks. (p. 756)

* **anticipate** To predict. (p. 135)

antipasto (ˌan-tē-ˈpas-(ˌ)tō) Italian for before the meal. A typical antipasto tray includes cold meats, such as Genoa salami and various hams, assorted cheeses, olives, marinated vegetables, and sometimes fruits. (p. 481)

AP weight The weight of a product before trimming. (p. 351)

* **appeal** Attraction. (p. 314)

appetizer A small portion of hot or cold food meant to stimulate the appetite that is served as the first course of a meal. (p. 133)

apprentice One who works under the guidance of a skilled worker to learn a particular trade or art. (p. 65)

* **appropriate** Correct. (p. 461)

aroma Distinctive pleasing smell. (p. 410)

* **array** A wide selection. (p. 58)

* **artistic** creative. (p. 456)

* **aspect** Part of a problem or challenge. (p. 349)

aspic (ˈas-pik) A savory jelly made from meat or vegetable stock and gelatin. (p. 480)

as-purchased (AP) price The bulk price. (p. 349)

as-served (AS) portion The actual weight of the food product that is served to customers. (p. 350)

* **atmosphere** Overall mood. (p. 71)

au jus (ō-ˈzhü(s)) Accompanied by the juices obtained from roasting meat. (p. 499)

autocratic A management style in which information and policies move from the top down. (p. 172)

average check method Prices items near an average check that you would like each customer to spend. (p. 322)

avulsion (ˌə-ˈvəl-shən) An injury in which a portion of the skin is partially or completely torn off. (p. 11)

B

bacon Meat that comes from the side of a pig, and is cured and often smoked for flavor. (p. 432)

bacteria (bak-ˈtir-ē-ə) Tiny, single-celled microorganisms. (p. 14)

bag-in-the-box system A cardboard box with a bag of concentrated soda syrup inside. (p. 122)

bain marie (ˌban-mə-ˈrē) Water bath used to keep foods such as sauces and soups warm. (p. 242)

bake Cook with dry heat in a closed environment, usually an oven. No fat or liquid is used. (p. 382)

baker's percentage In a formula, includes the percentage of each ingredient in relation to the weight of flour in the final baked product. (p. 333)

baking blind To prepare pie shells in advance. (p. 767)

baking cup A paper liner that keeps muffins from sticking to the muffin pan. (p. 738)

baking powder A leavening agent made up of baking soda, an acid such as cream of tartar, and a moisture absorber such as cornstarch. (p. 694)

baking soda A chemical leavening agent that must be used with acid to give off CO_2 gas. (p. 694)

balance Dividing space to meet customer and preparation staff needs. (p. 182)

balance scale A scale with two platforms. One platform holds the item being weighed. The other platform holds weights. These weights are added or removed until the two platforms are balanced. (p. 335)

banquette (ban-ˈket) A type of seating arrangement in which customers are seated facing the server with their backs against the wall. (p. 146)

bar code A series of bars, spaces, and sometimes numbers that contain coded information and are designed to be scanned into a computer system. (p. 365)

barding Wrapping a lean meat with fat, such as bacon, before roasting. A few minutes before doneness, you remove the meat from the oven, unwrap the fat, put the meat back in the oven, and allow the surface of the meat to brown. (p. 588)

barley A hardy, adaptable grain that can grow in both warm and cold climates. (p. 626)

barnacle (ˈbär-ni-kəl) A crustacean that attaches itself to rocks, boats, or other sea life. (p. 552)

barquette (bär-ket) Dough formed into a small boat-shaped shell. (p. 502)

base A stock that is purchased in a powdered or concentrated form. (p. 510)

basic pie dough Sometimes called 3-2-1 dough. This ratio refers to the weight of three parts flour, two parts fat, and one part water. (p. 765)

baste A process in which fat drippings are spooned over a large bird every 15–20 minutes. (p. 577)

basting Moistening foods with melted fats, pan drippings, or another liquid during cooking. (p. 383)

batch cooking The process of preparing small amounts of food several times throughout a food-service period. (p. 300)

batonnet (ˈbä-tō-ˌnä) Matchstick-shaped cuts that are ¼-inch thick. (p. 259)

batter A semiliquid mixture that contains ingredients such as flour, milk, eggs, and seasonings. (p. 384)

Bavarian A dessert made of whipped cream, gelatin, and a flavored custard sauce. (p. 773)

beat Agitate ingredients vigorously to add air or develop gluten. (p. 699)

béchamel A basic French white sauce made with milk and a thickener. (p. 517)

bench box A covered container in which dough can be placed before shaping. (p. 718)

bench rest A time when rounded portions of dough are placed in bench boxes or left covered on the work bench. (p. 718)

* **beneficial** Helpful. (p. 472)

benefits Services or payments provided by an employer in addition to wages. (p. 110)

bid A price quote. (p. 359)

biscuit A small, round quick bread. (p. 445)

biscuit method Requires cutting or rubbing the fat into the dry ingredients. This is done until the fat and dry ingredients resemble cornmeal. Then, the liquid ingredients are added. (p. 731)

bisque ('bisk) Specialty soup that is usually made from shellfish and contain cream. (p. 531)

bivalve ('bī-,valv) A mollusk that has two shells that are hinged together. (p. 550)

blanching Using the boiling method to partially cook food. (p. 390)

blend A combination of herbs, spices, and seeds. (p. 404)

blending Mixing or folding two or more ingredients together until they are evenly combined. (p. 699)

blending method Combines the liquid, sugar, liquid fat, and eggs at the same time in baking. Then, the dry ingredients are added to the mixture. (p. 731)

blind taste test A food test in which food samples are not labeled so that the testers will not know which product they are tasting. (p. 424)

boiling A moist cooking technique in which you bring a liquid, such as water or stock, to the boiling point and keep it at that temperature while food cooks. (p. 389)

boiling point Temperature at which a liquid boils. (p. 389)

bolster Helps keep out food particles from between the tang and the handle on a knife. (p. 253)

boneless fish Fish that have cartilage instead of bones. Many boneless fish also have smooth skin instead of scales. (p. 542)

booth A type of seating arrangement in which the table rests against, or is attached to, a wall. (p. 145)

bouchée (bü-'shā) A shell made from puff pastry, used for appetizers or desserts. (p. 502)

bouquet garni (bü-'kā gär-'nē) A combination of fresh herbs and vegetables tied in a bundle with butcher's twine. The bundle is dropped into the stock pot and allowed to simmer. (p. 410)

bouquetière (,bü-kə-'tyēr) Bouquet of three or more vegetables. (p. 658)

braising A long, slow cooking process; meat is first seared and the pan deglazed before the moist cooking technique is used. (p. 392)

bread flour Flour that has a high gluten-forming protein content to allow bread to rise fully. (p. 688)

breading A coating made of eggs and crumbs. (p. 384)

break even When costs equal income. (p. 175)

breakfast meats Meats such as ham, bacon, Canadian bacon, sausage, hash, and steak. (p. 432)

brochette (brō-'shet) A combination of meat, poultry, fish, and vegetables served on a small skewer. (p. 502)

broiling To cook food directly under a primary heat source. (p. 387)

broth A liquid made from simmered meat and vegetables. (p. 527)

brown rice Rice with a tan color, a chewy texture, and a slightly nutty taste. (p. 625)

brown stock A stock that is made from either beef, veal, chicken, or game. It gets its color from roasting the ingredients without water, in a hot oven. (p. 511)

brunoise (brün-'wäz) $1/8$-inch thick cubes. (p. 259)

buffet A style of service in which all the food is attractively displayed on a table for the customers to see. (p. 148)

bulk Large quantities of a single food product. (p. 349)

business plan A document that describes a new business and a strategy to launch that business. (p. 76)

busser A foodservice worker who helps maintain an inviting table and keeps the service station stocked with supplies. (p. 118)

butler service The server carries the prepared food on a silver tray to standing or seated customers. Customers then serve themselves. (p. 148)

butterflied When a fish is dressed, then cut so the two sides lie open, yet are attached by skin. (p. 545)

bypassing When people or materials must walk or be moved past unrelated stations during foodservice. (p. 183)

by-products Usable leftover parts of food after prepreparation. (p. 351)

C

cafeteria A restaurant where customers serve themselves, or order at a counter. (p. 71)

cake flour Flour that is lower in protein than bread flour and pastry flour and produces a softer and more tender product than bread flour. (p. 688)

calamari The Italian name for squid. (p. 556)

calculate To work with numbers. (p. 84)

calibrate ('ka-lə-brāt) To adjust (as a thermometer) for accuracy. (p. 35)

California menu All three meals are available all day; some restaurants list them on the same menu. (p. 310)

Canadian bacon A breakfast meat from boneless pork loin. It is smoked and brined, with a thin layer of fat on its surface. (p. 432)

canapé ('ka-nə-ˌpā) An appetizer that is served on a small piece of bread or toast. (p. 456)

cancer The division and growth of cells that interferes with normal body functions. (p. 295)

caper A flower bud of a Mediterranean shrub, used for seasoning. (p. 563)

cappuccino (ˌka-pə-'chē-(ˌ)nō) A beverage made from espresso and steamed and foamed milk. (p. 123)

caramelization ('ker-ə-məl-ə-ˌzā-shən) The process of cooking sugar to high temperatures to create aroma and flavor. (p. 379)

carbohydrate The nutrient that is the body's main source of energy. (p. 280)

carcass What is left of the whole animal after it has been slaughtered. (p. 589)

cardiopulmonary resuscitation (ˌkär-dē-ō-'pùl-mə-ner-ē ri-ˌsə-sə-'tā-shən) Emergency care that is performed on people who are unresponsive. (p. 12)

cardiovascular (ˌkär-dē-ō-'vas-kyə-lər) Heart-related. (p. 282)

carryover cooking The cooking that takes place after you remove something from a heat source. (p. 382)

cashier The employee who correctly reads the amount of the bill, processes the payment, and makes change. (p. 118)

casserole A mixed food dish baked and served in a casserole dish. (p. 619)

casual-dining establishment Restaurant that features a relaxed environment and mid-range prices. (p. 142)

catering director Coordinates the food for each function. (p. 60)

cavity Hollow interior. (p. 582)

centerpiece A decorative object placed on tables to add beauty and interest. (p. 158)

cephalopod ('se-fə-lə-ˌpäd) A mollusk that has a thin internal shell. Cephalopods have tentacles, or false legs, attached to the head near the mouth. (p. 550)

certification Proof that you are an expert in a specific topic, such as culinary arts, baking, and pastry making. (p. 63)

chafing ('chā-fiŋ) dish A device that holds a large pan of food over a canned heat source. (p. 148)

chain restaurant A restaurant that has two or more locations that sell the same products and are operated by the same company. (p. 75)

chapatti (chə-pä-tē) An Indian whole-wheat flatbread. (p. 489)

* **characteristic** Feature. (p. 528)

charcuterie The name of a guild that prepared and sold cooked items made from pigs. (p. 458)

cheddaring A technique in which slabs of cheese are stacked and turned to squeeze out the whey; done for hard cheeses. (p. 471)

cheesecloth A loose-woven cotton cloth used in cheesemaking and cooking. (p. 518)

chef's coat A working coat that traditionally has two rows of buttons down the front, long sleeves, and turned-up cuffs. (p. 26)

chemical dough conditioners Substances that are added to hard lean doughs to strengthen the glutens that give hard lean dough products their dense structure. (p. 708)

chewy cookie A cookie with a high ratio of eggs, sugar, and liquid, but a low amount of fat. (p. 748)

chiffon (shi-'fän) cake A variation of a genoise cake made by using whipped egg whites to lighten the batter. (p. 756)

chiffonade (ˌshi-fə-'näd) To finely slice or shred leafy vegetables or herbs. (p. 255)

cholesterol (kə-'les-tə-ˌrōl) A fatlike substance that is found in all body cells and in all animal foods. (p. 282)

chowder A specialty soup made from fish, seafood, or vegetables. (p. 531)

chutney A condiment made of fruit, vinegar, sugar, and spices. (p. 642)

clarified butter Purified butterfat. This means that the butter is melted with the water and milk solids are removed. (p. 521)

clarify To remove particles as they float to the top of a liquid. (p. 528)

* **clarity ('kler-ə-tē)** How clear something is. (p. 518)

classical French service The most elegant and elaborate style of service; involves presenting or preparing some foods tableside. (p. 146)

* **classify** To sort. (p. 542)

cleaning Removing food and other soil from a surface. (p. 18)

clear soup Made from clear stock or broth. Clear soups are not thickened. (p. 527)

client base The customers who come regularly to a business. (p. 119)

clientele The people who will be a business's main customers. (p. 189)

clip-on A special list that is fastened directly to the menu. (p. 318)

club sandwich A triple-decker sandwich that features cold, sliced cooked turkey and ham, or bacon. (p. 499)

coagulate When proteins change from a liquid or semiliquid state to a drier, solid state. (p. 378)

cobbler A deep-dish fruit dessert. (p. 644)

colander A container with small holes in the bottom for rinsing and draining food. (p. 621)

cold soup A specialty soup that may be cooked or uncooked and then chilled. (p. 531)

cold-pack cheese Also known as club cheese; made from one or more varieties of cheese, finely ground and mixed until it is spreadable. (p. 474)

collagen Soft, white tissue that breaks down into gelatin and water during slow, moist cooking processes. (p. 588)

* **collapsing** Falling. (p. 756)

combination cooking Uses both moist and dry cooking techniques. (p. 376)

commercial operation An operation that earns more than enough to cover daily expenses. (p. 70)

commitment The dedication that you show to doing something. (p. 89)

* **compensate** Make up for the lack of something. (p. 92)

compensatory time Paid time off to reimburse workers for overtime. (p. 106)

competitor Business that offers similar products or services to the ones you offer. (p. 189)

competitors' pricing method Charges approximately what the competition charges for similar menu items. (p. 322)

* **complement** To go together well with another thing. (p. 416)

complete protein A protein source that provides all of the amino acids. (p. 281)

* **complex** Involved and possibly difficult. (p. 309)

* **composed** Made up of. (p. 588)

compote Fresh or dried fruits that have been cooked in a sugar syrup. (p. 642)

compotier (ˌkäm-pōt-tē-ˈyā) A deep, stemmed dish used to serve compotes, candies, and nuts. (p. 645)

compound butter Softened butter with seasonings added to it. (p. 521)

condiment Mustard, pickle relish, and ketchup, etc., traditionally served as an accompaniment to food. (p. 152); Something served as an accompaniment. (p. 416)

conduction Heats food by direct contact between a hot surface and the food. (p. 234)

* **confirm** To make sure. (p. 361)

connective tissue Tissue that holds muscle fiber together. (p. 571)

* **consistency** Texture. (p. 731)

* **consistent** Free from variations. (p. 330)

consommé (ˌkän(t)-sə-ˈmā) A concentrated, clear soup made from a rich broth. (p. 528)

contaminated Unfit to be eaten. (p. 14)

* **content** Amount. (p. 605)

continental menu A breakfast menu that provides mostly a selection of juices, beverages, and baked goods. (p. 311)

continuous breadmaking Also called commercial baking, mixing and kneading are done in a spiral mixer. (p. 715)

* **contrast** As a comparison. (p. 765)

* **contribution** Role. (p. 691)

contribution margin method A pricing method that uses a general contribution of customers to costs besides food for running a kitchen. You would add the average contribution margin per guest to the item's standard food cost. (p. 322)

convection A process in which the liquid closest to the bottom of the pan is heated and rises to the top. (p. 234, 389)

convection oven An oven that has a fan that circulates the oven's heated air. (p. 682)

conversion factor The number that comes from dividing the yield you want by the existing yield in a recipe. (p. 338)

convert To adjust ingredient quantities in a standardized recipe. (p. 335)

cooking line The arrangement of kitchen equipment. (p. 221)

cookware Pots, pans, and baking dishes. (p. 262)

corn A grain that can be eaten fresh or as a dried grain. (p. 627)

corporation A business formed when a state grants an individual or a group of people a charter with legal rights to form a business. (p. 77)

* **correspond** To compare closely to. (p. 714)

cost per portion The cost of a portion that you would serve to an individual customer. (p. 353)

cottage fries French fried potatoes that are cut into ½-inch thick circles, usually served during breakfast. (p. 443)

coulis (kü-ˈlē) A sauce made from a fruit or vegetable purée. (p. 518)

count The number of individual items used in a recipe. (p. 337)

counter scale A scale with a platform small enough to be placed on a counter. (p. 225)

counter service Customers sitting at a counter, rather than a booth, banquette, or table. (p. 143)

course A part of a meal that is served at one time. (p. 118)

couscous (ˈküs-ˌküs) A wheat product made from semolina that is milled from wheat. (p. 627)

cover An individual place setting that includes utensils, glasses, and dishes. (p. 127)

covers Individual meals served in a restaurant. (p. 322)

cream soup A velvety-smooth thick soup. It is made with cooked vegetables that are sometimes puréed. (p. 530)

creaming Vigorously combining softened fat and sugar to add air. (p. 699)

creaming method Sugar and pre-softened shortening are creamed together with a mixer on low speed until the mixture is light and fluffy. Eggs are then added one at a time. (p. 731)

crêpe (ˈkrāp) A small, thin pancake made with egg batter. (p. 489)

crisp cookie A cookie with very little moisture in the batter. It also has a high ratio of sugar. (p. 748)

* **critical** Necessary. (p. 714)

critical control point A step in the flow of food where contamination can be prevented or eliminated. (p. 32)

croissant A flaky, crescent-shaped roll. (p. 488)

cross-contamination The movement of harmful microorganisms from one place to another. (p. 14)

crosshatch Grill mark set at a 90-degree angle. (p. 579)

cross-train Giving employees work experience in many different tasks. (p. 59)

croutons (ˈkrü-tänz) Small pieces of bread that have been grilled, toasted, or fried and sometimes seasoned, used as a garnish for salads. (p. 463)

crudité (ˌkrü-di-ˈtā) Raw sliced vegetables served with dips. (p. 479)

crumb The internal texture of a baked product. (p. 688)

crust The outer surface of a bread or roll. (p. 708)

crustacean (ˌkrəs-ˈtā-shens) A shellfish with a hard outer shell and a jointed skeleton. (p. 553)

cuisine A style of cooking. (p. 69)

culinary scientist Sets new standards in food technology by creating new food products and cooking methods. (p. 60)

curdle (ˈkər-dəl) To separate, as in egg yolks and whites that have been cooked at too high of a temperature. (p. 437)

curing Preserving pork with salt, sugar, spices, flavoring, and nitrites. (p. 597)

custard Dessert made of eggs, milk or cream, flavorings, and sweeteners. (p. 771)

custard-style ice cream Ice cream made with cooked vanilla custard that consists of cream, milk, eggs, sugar, and flavorings. (p. 771)

cut in To mix solid fat with dry ingredients until lumps of the desired size remain. (p. 699)

cycle menu A menu that is used for a set period of time, such as a week, a month, or even longer. At the end of this time period, the menu repeats daily dishes in the same order. (p. 310)

D

Daily Production Report Shows how much food was used, sold, and left over each day. (p. 364)

daily value The amount of a nutrient that a person needs every day, based on a 2,000-calorie diet. (p. 290)

Danish pastry dough Dough that is sweeter and richer than croissant dough. (p. 711)

dark meat Parts of a bird that have more muscle and connective tissue. (p. 571)

* **deal** Amount. (p. 751)

debone To remove bones from meat, poultry, or fish. (p. 350)

deduction The money withheld from your gross pay for taxes, insurance, and other fees. (p. 109)

deep-frying To cook foods by completely submerging them in heated fat or oil. (p. 385)

deflate Cause dough to lose volume. (p. 734)

deglaze To use a small amount of liquid or fat to remove any leftover scraps of food from sautéing or searing from the pan. (p. 392)

dehydrated ((ˌ)dē-ˈhī-ˌdrāt-əd) Water has been removed. (p. 434)

dehydration (ˌdē-ˌhī-ˈdrā-shən) A serious fluid imbalance in the body. (p. 293)

delegate To give responsibility to another person. (p. 172)

* **delicate** Fragile. (p. 384)

demi-glace (ˈde-mē-ˌglas) A sauce that is half espagnole sauce and half brown stock that has been reduced by half. (p. 519)

demitasse (ˈde-mi-ˌtas) A half-size cup for espresso. (p. 124)

democratic A management style in which everyone is involved in the decision-making process. (p. 172)

design How the dining room, kitchen, and storage areas are laid out. (p. 182)

* **designate** To be a sign of. (p. 433)

* **desired** Wanted. (p. 739)

* **deteriorate** To go down in quality; to become worse in value. (p. 363, 740)

* **determine** To find out. (p. 207)

devein ((ˌ)dē-ˈvān) To remove a shrimp's intestinal tract, located along the back. (p. 553)

* **device** An item that serves a specific purpose. (p. 148)

diabetes An illness that affects the body's ability to convert blood sugar into energy. (p. 294)

diagonal A cut that results in an oval or elongated slice of a cylindrical fruit or vegetable. (p. 255)

* **dictate** To determine through necessity. (p. 309)

Dietary Guidelines for Americans Information on proper eating habits for healthy Americans ages two years and older. (p. 290)

digestible The nutrients, such as protein, are more accessible to the body. (p. 663)

* **diminish** To decrease. (p. 638)

dining room supervisor Coordinates and assigns duties to the hosts, servers, and bussers. (p. 60)

direct contamination Raw foods, or the plants or animals from which they come, are exposed to toxins. (p. 14)

direct labor cost Wages paid to employees. (p. 173)

direct marketing A form of advertising in which materials, such as letters and advertisements, are mailed directly to customers. (p. 192)

disability A physical or mental impairment that substantially limits one or more major life activities. (p. 206)

* **discard** To throw away. (p. 559)

discrimination Unfair treatment based on age, gender, race, ethnicity, religion, physical appearance, disability, or other factors. (p. 106)

disposable income Money that people have left over for extras after paying bills. (p. 321)

disposal point The point at which food remaining after being eaten is disposed of properly. (p. 44)

* **distinct** Separate. (p. 401)

distraction Something that turns your attention to something else. (p. 85)

docking Process of making small holes in the surface of an item before baking. (p. 722)

* **document** To write down the details of what happened. (p. 12)

dolly A small wheeled cart. (p. 225)

double pan A sheet pan placed inside a second pan of the same size. (p. 753)

double-entry bookkeeping Record-keeping in which transactions are recorded in at least two places so that records are balanced. (p. 173)

dough Combination of dry and liquid ingredients for a baked product; contains less liquid than a batter. (p. 698)

doughnut A sweetened, deep-fried pastry that often is ring-shaped. (p. 445)

drained weight The weight of a food product without the packing medium. (p. 652)

drawn Fish that have had their gills and entrails removed. (p. 544)

dredging Coating foods with flour; coating poultry parts with seasoned flour. (p. 384, 579)

dressed Drawn fish that have had their fins, scales, and sometimes their head removed. (p. 544)

dressing A sauce that is added to salads to give them flavor and to help hold the ingredients together. (p. 468)

dried milk solids Milk product used in baked goods. (p. 689)

drip loss The loss of moisture that occurs as a fish thaws. (p. 546)

drop batter Batter thick enough it needs to be dropped from a portion scoop. (p. 731)

drop cookie A cookie with soft batter or dough that uses the creaming process. (p. 751)

drupe A fruit that has soft flesh, thin skin, and one pit, or stone. (p. 638)

dry cooking technique Cooking technique that uses oil, fat, the radiation of hot air, or metal to transfer heat. (p. 376)

dry cure Food is coated in salt, sweeteners, and flavorings, and then wrapped in paper or cheesecloth. (p. 457)

du jour menu A menu that lists dishes that are available on a particular day. (p. 310)

* **duration** The amount of time something lasts. (p. 292)

dust To sprinkle very lightly with flour. (p. 766)

E

edible ('e-də-bəl) portion (EP) After preparation, the consumable food product that remains. (p. 350)

* **effect** Result. (p. 382)

* **efficient** Productive. (p. 222)

egg substitutes Substitutes for people with dietary concerns such as high cholesterol. (p. 434)

* **elaborate** Detailed. (p. 463)

elastic Stretchy and flexible. (p. 739)

elastin A hard, yellow tissue that does not break down during cooking. Also referred to as gristle. (p. 588)

electronic scale A scale that has a spring that is depressed when an item is placed on its platform. The weight is displayed on a digital readout. (p. 336)

* **elements** Parts. (p. 151)

emergency A potentially life-threatening situation that usually occurs suddenly and unexpectedly. (p. 9)

empathy The skill of thinking about what it would be like in another's place. (p. 107)

* **emphasize** Point out. (p. 502)

employee recruiter Helps businesses find the right employees. (p. 76)

employment agency A business that put employers in touch with potential employees. (p. 96)

emulsified shortening A type of fat that helps create a smooth consistency throughout the mixture. (p. 756)

emulsifier An additive, such as egg yolk, that allows unmixable liquids, such as oil and water, to combine uniformly. (p. 474)

en papillote (ən ˌpä-pē-ˈyō) A method of steaming that involves wrapping fish or shellfish in parchment paper with vegetables, herbs, and sauces or butters. (p. 559)

* **enforce** Carry out. (p. 198)

English muffin Made from bread dough that is cut into rounds and then toasted. (p. 446)

* **enhance** Increase the quality of. (p. 379)

enriched rice Rice that has a vitamin and mineral coating added to the grain. (p. 625)

* **entice** Attract. (p. 317)

entrée (ˈän-trā) Main dish. (p. 309)

entrepreneur (ˌänn-trə-p(r)ə-ˈn(y)ùr) A self-motivated person who creates and runs a business. (p. 74)

entry-level Jobs for which you do not need to have training or experience. (p. 64)

environmental impact statement Describes the impact of the proposed facility and any negative effects it might have on environment. (p. 200)

ergonomics (ˌər-gə-ˈnä-miks) The science of efficient and safe interaction between people and the things in their environment. (p. 207)

escargot (ˌes-kär-ˈgō) The French word for snails. (p. 557)

espresso (e-ˈspre-(ˌ)sō) A beverage made by forcing hot water and steam through finely ground, dark-roasted coffee beans. (p. 122)

ethics (ˈe-thiks) Your internal guidelines to distinguish right from wrong. (p. 108)

ethnic menu A menu that represents food choices from a speicific country. (p. 312)

ethylene (ˈe-thə-ˌlēn) gas An odorless, colorless gas that is emitted naturally as fruits ripen. (p. 639)

* **evaluate** Study. (p. 63)

evaluation A report of how well you perform your duties, and what you can do to improve. (p. 105)

evaporate To escape as vapor. (p. 376)

executive chef Manages all kitchen operations. (p. 60)

expense Money that goes out of a business. (p. 174)

extender An item made from leftover, low-cost ingredients. (p. 319)

extract A concentrated flavor such as lemon and vanilla. (p. 401)

* **extracted** Drawn out. (p. 392)

F

fabricated cut A smaller portion of meat taken from primal cuts. (p. 589)

* **factor** Issue. (p. 184)

factor method A common pricing method for restaurants with successful past performance records. You must first determine what the food cost percent should be. Then, take that food cost percent and divide it into 100%, which will give you your factor. Multiply the factor by the menu item cost. (p. 321)

family service Meal service in which food is delivered on a large platter or dish to an individual table and customers serve themselves. (p. 145)

fat Substance that regulates bodily functions and helps carry some vitamins through the system. (p. 282)

fat cap The fat that surrounds muscle tissue. (p. 588)

fatty fish Fish that have a relatively large amount of fat. (p. 542)

fermentation (ˌfər-mən-ˈtā-shən) A process in which yeast breaks down sugars into carbon dioxide gas and alcohol. (p. 694)

fermented ((ˌ)fər-ˈmen-ted) Chemically changed in brines or vinegars flavored and seasoned with dill, garlic, sugar, peppers, or salt. (p. 416)

fiber A unique form of a complex carbohydrate that does not provide energy. (p. 280)

* **field** Line of work. (p. 106)

fillets The sides of fish. (p. 544)

fine-dining restaurant A restaurant that provides an environment featuring excellent food, elegant decor, and superior service. (p. 71, 142)

finger food Hors d'oeuvres presented on platters from which each guest serves him- or herself. (p. 477)

first aid Assisting an injured person until professional medical help can be provided. (p. 9)

first in, first out An inventory system in which food products that are oldest are used first, so that all products are fresh when used. (p. 38)

fish stock A stock that is made by slowly cooking the bones of lean fish or shellfish. (p. 513)

fixed menu A menu that offers the same dishes every day for a long period of time. (p. 310)

flake Break away in small layers. (p. 559)

flaky dough A pie dough in which flour is not completely blended with the fat. (p. 766)

flambé (fläm-'bā) To cook a food tableside using flames as part of the preparation. (p. 147)

flammable Quick to burn. (p. 6)

flat A shallow box or container used to hold foods. (p. 349)

flat fish Fish that have a backbone running horizontally through the center of the fish. They swim horizontally and have both eyes on the top of their heads. (p. 542)

flatware Dining utensils, such as spoons, forks, and knives. (p. 155)

flavor enhancer Increases the way you perceive the food's flavor without changing the actual flavor. (p. 400)

flavored oil An oil that has been enhanced with ingredients such as herbs, spices, and garlic. (p. 416)

flavoring An ingredient that actually changes the natural flavor of the foods it is added to. (p. 400)

flexibility The ability to adapt willingly to changing circumstances. (p. 89)

floret A small flower that makes up the head of some plants. (p. 647)

flow of food The path food takes from when it is received by an establishment to when it is disposed of as waste. (p. 31)

fluting A manner of decorating crust by making uniform folds around the edge of the pie. (p. 767)

focaccia An Italian bread that is flavored with olive oil and herbs. (p. 489)

focal point A service point. (p. 145)

fold To use a rubber spatula to carefully mix the egg whites and batter to not lose volume. (p. 446); Gently adding light, airy ingredients such as eggs to heavier ingredients by using a smooth circular movement. (p. 699)

fondant A mixture of sugar, water, and flavorings that serves as a base for icings. (p. 762)

fondue Dipping foods into a central heated pot. (p. 645)

food allergy An allergic reaction triggered by the immune system in response to a particular food. (p. 294)

Food Code Guidelines for handling food safely. (p. 200)

food cost percentage The ratio of the cost of food served to the sales of food served. (p. 173)

food court A single area in malls or shopping centers with many quick-service restaurants. (p. 143)

food preparation Cooking and preparing foods to be eaten. (p. 42)

food thermometer A device used to check the temperatures of foods. (p. 34)

foodhandler A worker who is in direct contact with food. (p. 26)

foodservice consultant Offers advice and information to other foodservice business owners and managers. (p. 75)

foodservice director Manages the banquet operations of hotels, banquet facilities, hospitals, and universities. (p. 60)

forcemeat A mixture of ground, raw meat or seafood that is emulsified with fat. (p. 456)

forecasting Anticipating future trends. (p. 175)

formula A special type of recipe used in the bakeshop. (p. 331)

* **foundation** Starting point. (p. 488)

franchise A company that sells a business owner the right to use its name, logo, concept, and products. In return, the business owner agrees to run the business as outlined by the franchise company. (p. 75)

free enterprise A system in which businesses or individuals may buy, sell, and set prices with little government control. (p. 78)

free-form loaf Bread loaves that are shaped by hand, then baked, seam side down, on flat pans or directly on a hearth. (p. 718)

freezer burn Discoloration and dehydration caused by moisture loss as food freezes. (p. 546)

French toast Bread that has been dipped in a batter and then sautéed. (p. 448)

fresh cheese A soft cheese that is not ripened or aged after it is formed into a final shape. (p. 473)

frittata (frē-'tä-tə) A flat, open-face omelet. Eggs are beaten and mixed with the precooked filling ingredients, and then cooked over low heat without stirring. (p. 439)

frozen yogurt American ice cream with the addition of yogurt. (p. 771)

frying Cooking foods in hot fat or oil. (p. 384)

full-service restaurant A restaurant where servers take customer orders and then bring the food to the table. (p. 71)

fumet (fyü-'mā) A fish stock with lemon juice or other acids are added to the water; stronger flavor than fish stock. (p. 513)

* **function** An event. (p. 242); Purpose. (p. 445)

fungi ('fən-gī) Spore-producing organisms found in soil, plants, animals, water, and in the air. (p. 16)

G

garde manger (ˌgärd ˌmän-'zhā) The chef responsible for preparing cold food items. (p. 59)

garde manger brigade A team of chefs under the garde manger chef who handle cold food preparation. (p. 457)

garnish An edible food that is placed on or around food to add color or flavor. (p. 314)

* **gauge** Type and thickness of the material. (p. 262)

gelatinization (jə-ˌla-tə-nə-ˈzā-shən) The process of starch granules absorbing moisture when placed in a liquid. (p. 517)

general safety audit A review and inspection of all safety procedures and equipment. (p. 12)

genetically (jə-ˈne-ti-k(ə-)lē) engineered food Food that is made by recombining genes. (p. 199)

genoise (zhā-ˈnwäz) European sponge cake. (p. 756)

giblets The edible internal organs of a bird. (p. 571)

gipfels Tighter half circles made by Swiss and German bakers in croissant dough. (p. 710)

glassware Glasses used to hold beverages such as juice, water, iced tea. (p. 155)

glaze A stock that is reduced and concentrated. (p. 513)

glucose A usable energy source for your body. (p. 280)

gluten A firm, elastic substance that affects the texture of baked products. (p. 688)

glycogen (ˈglī-kə-jən) A storage form of glucose. (p. 293)

grading Applying specific quality standards to food products. (p. 198)

grain The direction of muscle fibers, or treads, in meat. (p. 607); A single, small, hard seed. (p. 624)

granola (grə-ˈnō-lə) A blend of grains, nuts, and dried fruits. (p. 444)

gravy A type of sauce made from meat or poultry juices; a liquid such as milk, cream, or broth; and a thickening agent such as a roux. (p. 521)

griddle A flat, solid plate of metal with a gas or electric heat source. (p. 386)

grilled sandwich A sandwich where the bread is browned on the outside on the griddle. (p. 496)

grilling A cooking method that places food on a heated grill. (p. 386)

gross pay The total amount of money you are paid for working. (p. 109)

* **guide** Something that provides information. (p. 321)

* **guidelines** Rules for doing things. (p. 75)

H

HACCP Hazard Analysis Critical Control Point; the system used to keep food safe from the kitchen to the table. (p. 31)

hair restraint Any barrier that holds back head or facial hair to keep it from contaminating food. (p. 26)

* **hallmark** Distinguishing feature. (p. 330)

hand sanitizer A special liquid that kills bacteria on your skin; it is often used without water. (p. 27)

hand service Bringing dishes to the table without using a tray. (p. 131)

hand tools Handheld items used to cook, serve, and prepare food. (p. 262)

hard lean dough A basic yeast dough often made solely from flour, water, salt, and yeast. (p. 708)

hard wheat flour Flour that comes from kernels that are firm, tough, and difficult to cut. (p. 688)

hash Chopped meat that is mixed with potatoes and onions, and then browned. (p. 432)

hash browns Potatoes that are shredded and may include onions and seasonings. (p. 443)

* **hasten** Speed up. (p. 647)

hazard A source of danger. (p. 14)

heat lamp A lamp that uses light in the infrared spectrum to keep food warm during holding. (p. 384)

heat transfer A measure of how efficiently heat passes from one object to another. (p. 262)

heat treated Glass that is heated and then cooled rapidly. (p. 155)

Heimlich maneuver A series of thrusts to the abdomen that can help dislodge something that is stuck in a person's airway. (p. 11)

herb A plant that grows in temperate climates; used as flavoring that adds color and aroma to foods. (p. 406)

high-fat cake A cake that generally uses baking powder as its leavening agent. (p. 755)

high-heat cooking Cooking methods such as broiling and grilling used for tender cuts of meat like tenderloins and strip steaks. (p. 605)

highlighting Emphasizing a particular menu item. (p. 128)

high-ratio layer cake A cake that contains a high ratio of both liquids and sugar, giving the cake a very moist and tender texture. (p. 758)

holding The process of keeping foods warm or cold before serving them. (p. 42)

hollandaise (ˌhä-lən-ˈdāz) A sauce made from lemon juice, butter, and eggs. (p. 517)

home fries French fries that are usually diced or sliced, served during breakfast. (p. 443)

hominy Corn product made by soaking dried corn in lye so that the kernels become swollen. (p. 627)

honesty When you are truthful and loyal in your words and actions. (p. 89)

hors d'oeuvre (ȯr-ˈdərv) A very small portion of food served before a meal. (p. 148)

hors d'oeuvre variés A combination of plated items with enough hors d'oeuvres for one person. (p. 477)

hospitality industry Provides food and lodging to customers. (p. 68)

host The employee who greets the customers by smiling warmly and welcoming them. (p. 116)

human resources Managing staff. (p. 172)

hummus ('hə-məs) A Middle Eastern dish made from mashed chickpeas, lemon juice, garlic, and tahini. (p. 478)

hydrogenation (hī-ˌdrä-jə-'nā-shən) A process in which hydrogen is added under pressure to polyunsaturated fats, such as soybean oil, and changes liquid oil into a solid fat. (p. 282)

hygiene Using good grooming habits to maintain health. (p. 26)

I

* **ideal** Perfect. (p. 38)

* **impact** To have a direct effect upon. (p. 293)

* **implement** To put into practice. (p. 350)

* **imprecise** Inexact. (p. 678)

* **improved** Made better. (p. 31)

in season During a fruit's or vegetable's main growing season. (p. 638)

income The money that comes into a business. (p. 174)

incomplete protein A protein source that does not provide all of the amino acids. (p. 281)

independent restaurant Has one or more owners and is not part of a national business. (p. 75)

* **indicate** To show. (p. 572)

* **indication** A sign. (p. 421)

indirect labor cost An operation's costs for employee health insurance, taxes, and vacations. (p. 173)

induction A heating source that uses electricity to heat cookware by magnetic energy generated by coils under the stovetop. (p. 234)

infuse To extract a substance's flavors by placing it in a hot liquid. (p. 124)

ingredient list In a recipe, includes all ingredients that will be used in the dish. (p. 333)

inhibitor (in-'hi-bə-tər) A substance that slows down the chemical breakdown of food. (p. 358)

initiative (i-ˌni-shə-tiv) The energy required to begin new tasks and see them through. (p. 105)

inspection A test of a business's practices against standards. (p. 198)

insurance A contract between a business and an insurance company. It provides financial protection against losses. (p. 78)

* **interact** To talk and work together. (p. 119)

internship A program in which an advanced student works at a business to get hands-on training. (p. 66)

interstate commerce Business that happens over two or more states. (p. 205)

* **invaluable** Very helpful. (p. 682)

inventory The amount of supplies a business has on hand. (p. 175)

invoice A bill from a supplier for providing goods or services. (p. 225)

IQF (individually quick frozen) Fish or shellfish that have been quickly frozen piece by piece. Because the freezing happens so fast, few ice crystals form. (p. 553)

irradiated (i-'rā-dē-ˌāt-ed) food Food that has been exposed to radiation to kill harmful bacteria. (p. 199)

island A kitchen counter or equipment arrangement that can be approached from all sides. (p. 221)

issuing The process of delivering foods from storage to the kitchen as needed for use. (p. 357)

Italian meringue (mə-'raŋ) Meringue that is made with a boiling sugar syrup instead of granular sugar. (p. 762)

J

job application A form that employers use to collect personal information and previous work experience from job applicants. (p. 96)

job description A list of specific duties and skills needed for a job. (p. 179)

job interview A formal meeting between you and your potential employer. (p. 97)

job lead Possible employment opportunity. (p. 96)

job portfolio A collection of papers and samples that can be given to a potential employer. (p. 96)

job rotation A system by which employees are rotated through a series of jobs, allowing them to learn a variety of skills. (p. 66)

julienne (jü-lē-'en) ⅛-inch thick matchstick-shaped cuts. (p. 259)

K

kaiser ('kī-zər) roll A round, crusty roll. (p. 489)

kale A cabbage with curly green or multicolored leaves. (p. 465)

* **keep** To stay fresh. (p. 547)

ketchup A tomato-based sauce used throughout the world as a flavoring. (p. 416)

keyword A word that makes it easier for employers to search for important information. (p. 98)

kind Species. (p. 570)

kitchen brigade A kitchen system where specific tasks are assigned to each member of the kitchen staff. (p. 59)

kitchen manager Orders ingredients and makes sure that they are prepared correctly. (p. 60)

kneading Working a dough by hand or in a bench mixer with a dough hook to develop gluten and evenly distribute ingredients. (p. 700)

L

* **labor** Hard work. (p. 619)

labor union An organization of workers in a similar field. (p. 106)

laceration (ˌla-sə-ˈrā-shən) A cut or tear in the skin that can be quite deep. (p. 11)

lacto-ovo-vegetarian (ˌve-jə-ˈter-ē-ən) Someone who eats both dairy products (lacto) and eggs (ovo). (p. 293)

lacto-vegetarian Someone who eats or drinks some dairy products, such as cheese and milk, but does not eat eggs. (p. 293)

lamb Meat that comes from sheep that are less than one year old. (p. 597)

* **lapse** Problem due to inattention. (p. 171)

larding Inserting long, thin strips of fat or vegetables into the center of lean meat. (p. 588)

latticework A grid pattern on a pie crust made with individual strips of crust. (p. 765)

law An established rule. (p. 205)

leach To dissolve. (p. 298)

leadership The ability to motivate others to cooperate in doing a common task. (p. 90)

lean fish Fish with little fat. (p. 542)

leavening agent A substance that causes a baked good to rise by introducing carbon dioxide (CO_2) or other gases into the mixture. (p. 694)

leavens (ˈle-vəns) Causes dough to rise. (p. 706)

legume (ˈle-ˌgyüm) The seeds and pods from certain plants. (p. 280); A plant that has double-seamed pods that contain a single row of seeds. (p. 660)

* **lend** To adapt. (p. 403)

* **lessen** To reduce. (p. 299)

* **lesser** Lower. (p. 638)

let down A condition in which the ingredients in a dough completely break down. (p. 715)

license A written permission to participate in a business activity. (p. 78)

light meat Lighter colored wing and breast meat found on birds that rarely fly. (p. 571)

line cooks/station cooks Cooks that work the food production line. (p. 59)

liner An ingredient that adds visual interest and texture in a canapé. (p. 477)

lipoprotein (ˌlī-pə-ˈprō-ˌtēn) A chemical package that circulates cholesterol through the bloodstream. (p. 282)

lockout/tagout OSHA procedure; all necessary switches on malfunctioning electrical equipment are tagged and locked from use. (p. 7)

log A written record of day-to-day activities and procedures. (p. 36)

loss prevention The steps a business takes to eliminate waste and theft. (p. 184)

lowboy A half-size refrigerator that fits under the counter in a work station. (p. 226)

low-fat cake A cake that is leavened from air that is whipped into the egg batter. (p. 755)

low-heat cooking The best method for preparing large cuts of meat, such as top round. (p. 605)

lug A box, crate, or basket in which produce is shipped to market. (p. 638)

* **luxury** Expensive and extravagant. (p. 549)

M

macrobiotics A diet that includes unprocessed foods and organically grown fruits and vegetables. (p. 293)

* **mainstay** Main part or support. (p. 443)

* **maintain** To keep. (p. 489)

make change To count back the correct amount of change to a customer from the money he or she has paid for a check. (p. 85)

* **mandatory** Required. (p. 549)

mandoline (ˌman-də-ˈlin) A hand-operated machine used for slicing vegetables and fruits. (p. 653)

manual dishwashing Washing dishes, glasses, cookware, and utensils by hand. (p. 45)

marbling Fat within the muscle tissue. (p. 588)

marinade (ˌmer-ə-ˈnād) An acidic sauce usually used to soak meat before it is cooked, to give the meat flavor and tenderness. (p. 410)

marinara sauce Made by adding olive oil and spices to a basic tomato sauce. (p. 520)

marinated vegetable A vegetable that has been soaked in a liquid, typically made of vinegar, oil, herbs, and spices. (p. 481)

* **mark** To show. (p. 651)

market form The form poultry is in when it is purchased. (p. 571)

market segment A particular type of clientele. (p. 189)

marketing plan A specific plan to market a business, including advertising, public relations, and promotions. (p. 191)

marketplace The location, people, and atmosphere of a particular geographic area. (p. 188)

markup-on-cost method A common menu pricing formula. To find the selling price, take the food cost of an item and divide it by the desired food cost percent. (p. 322)

masa harina (ˈmä-sə ä-ˈrē-nä) A finely ground hominy used in tortillas and breads. (p. 627)

mass marketing Marketing to all possible segments at once. (p. 189)

master work schedule A schedule which shows the work shifts of all employees of a business. (p. 181)

material safety data sheet Identifies any hazardous chemicals and their components. (p. 201)

maturity A bird's age. (p. 571)

mayonnaise A permanent suspension of egg yolks, oil, and vinegar or lemon juice. (p. 490)

meal-based menu A menu that shows dishes available for a single meal. (p. 310)

mealy dough A pie dough in which the fat is blended into the flour more completely than it is for flaky dough. (p. 766)

mealy potato A potato with thick skin and starchy flesh. (p. 650)

meat The muscle of animals, such as cattle and hogs. (p. 588)

* **mediocre** Average. (p. 517)

medium Meat that is browned on the surface with a thick outer layer of gray and a pink center. (p. 610)

medium rare Meat that is browned on the surface with a thicker outer layer of gray and a red to slightly pink center. (p. 610)

medium well Meat that is browned on the surface with a thick outer layer of gray and a center that is barely pink. (p. 610)

mentor An experienced employee who has a solid understanding of his or her job. (p. 180)

menu A listing of the food choices a restaurant offers for each meal. (p. 308)

menu board A handwritten or printed menu on a board on a wall or easel. (p. 318)

meringue (mə-'raŋ) Whipped egg whites. (p. 756)

mesclun ('mes-klən) A popular mix of baby leaves of lettuces and other more flavorful greens, such as arugula. (p. 466)

metric system A mathematical system that uses powers of 10 to measure things. (p. 335)

microwave An invisible wave of energy that causes water molecules to rub against each other and produce the heat that cooks food. (p. 234)

minerals An esssential part of your bones and teeth; regulates body processes. (p. 286)

minimum internal temperature The lowest temperature at which foods can be safely cooked. (p. 33)

minimum wage The lowest hourly amount a worker can earn. (p. 106)

mirepoix (mir-'pwä) A mix of coarsely chopped vegetables that is used in a stock to add flavor, nutrients, and color. (p. 510)

mise en place place (ˌmē-ˌzän-'pləs) Assembly of all the necessary ingredients, equipment, tools, and serving pieces to prepare food. (p. 222)

* **mode** Functioning arrangement. (p. 222)

modern American plated service Meal service in which the food is completely prepared, portioned, plated, and garnished in the kitchen. The servers carry the plated food from the kitchen and place the prepared dishes in front of the customer. (p. 144)

modified starch Also called waxy maize, a type of corn product used for fruit pies that will be frozen. (p. 767)

modified straight-dough method Method that breaks the straight-dough method into steps. (p. 713)

moist baking Adding vegetables and liquid to a large piece of fish or a whole fish. (p. 559)

moist cooking technique Uses liquid instead of oil to create the heat energy that is needed to cook the food. (p. 376)

mold A pan with a distinctive shape. (p. 686); A form of fungus. (p. 16)

mollusk ('mä-ləsks) A shellfish with no internal skeletal structure. Instead, it has a shell that covers its soft body. (p. 550)

monosodium glutamate A flavor enhancer. MSG comes from seaweed. It intensifies the natural flavor of most of the foods it is added to. (p. 403)

monounsaturated (ˌmä-nō-ˌən-'sa-chə-ˌrā-təd) fat A fat that is liquid at room temperature and does not raise cholesterol levels. (p. 283)

Monte Cristo A closed, shallow-fried or deep-fried sandwich. (p 497)

mother sauces The five basic sauces: béchamel, sauce espagnole, tomato, velouté, and hollandaise. (p. 519)

mousse ('müs) A light and airy dessert made with both meringue and whipped cream to enhance the lightness. (p. 774)

muffin A quick bread made with egg and baked in a cupcake mold. (p. 445)

muscle fibers Fiber in meat that determines the meat's texture and contribute to its flavor. (p. 588)

musculoskeletal (ˌməs-kyə-lō-'ske-lə-təl) disorder Workplace injury caused by repeated trauma to muscles or bones. (p. 207)

* **muted** Soft. (p. 480)

mutton Meat from sheep older than 1 year. (p. 597)

N

* **nature** Basic structure. (p. 100)

net pay The amount of money you actually receive after deductions. (p. 109)

net weight The weight of the contents of a can. (p. 652)

networking Making use of all of your personal connections to reach your career goals. (p. 94)

noncommercial operation An operation that works to pay for daily expenses. (p. 70)

nonedible A nonfood product. (p. 358)

nonperishable Items that will not spoil quickly when stored correctly. (p. 152)

* **notable** Well known. (p. 709)

* **note** To make a record of. (p. 225)

nourishing element Provides flavor, nutrients, and color to stocks; composed of fresh bones, meat trimmings, fish trimmings, or vegetable trimmings. (p. 510)

nut A hard-shelled dry fruit or seed. (p. 419)

nutrient A chemical compound that helps the body carry out its functions. (p. 280)

nutrient-dense food A food that is low in calories, but rich in nutrients. (p. 291)

nutrition label Information found on food giving serving size, calories, and nutrients. (p. 290)

O
---

oat berries Berries that do not have the outer layer removed, so they are a whole grain, with all the texture and nutrients found in other whole grains. Also called groats. (p. 627)

oats The berries of oat grass. (p. 627)

* **objective** Goal. (p. 127)

* **obtain** To get. (p. 499)

* **obvious** Easily spotted. (p. 179)

occupational back support A type of back brace with suspenders designed to support the lower back while lifting. (p. 4)

* **offset** To compensate for. (p. 116)

off-site catering A caterer prepares and delivers food from a central kitchen to different locations. (p. 71)

oil A fat that is extracted from plants such as soybeans, corn, peanuts, and cottonseed. (p. 690)

omelet ('äm-lət) An egg specialty dish made of beaten eggs that are cooked without stirring. Once the eggs are set, they are folded in half in the pan. (p. 437)

one-stage method A cookie mixing method in which all ingredients are mixed in a single stage. (p. 749)

on-site catering Food is prepared at a customer's location for special occasions. (p. 71)

* **opaque** Light-blocking. (p. 410)

open-ended question A question that requires more than a one- or two-word answer. (p. 179)

open-market buying Getting price quotes for identical items from several vendors. (p. 359)

open-spit roasting To roast food over an open fire. (p. 383)

operating cost Anything that is a cost of doing business. (p. 321)

* **option** Choice. (p. 625)

orientation A training session that is held for new employees to help them better understand the business. (p. 172)

* **outline** To describe in a basic way. (p. 105)

oven spring Final leavening effort, occurring before internal temperatures become hot enough to kill the yeast cells. (p. 722)

overhead cost Expenses other than food and wages. (p. 75)

overstaffing Scheduling too many people to work on a given shift. (p. 171)

ovo-vegetarian Someone who eats eggs in addition to foods from plant sources. (p. 293)

P
---

packing medium A liquid used in canned goods to protect the food product. (p. 652)

paella (pä-'ā-yə) A Spanish rice dish with meat or shellfish. (p. 414)

pan loaf Bread loaves that are rolled and placed, seam down, into prepared loaf pans. (p. 718)

pan-fry To cook by heating a moderate amount of fat in a pan before adding food. (p. 384)

pan Placing dough in the correct type of pan. (p. 718)

parasite ('pär-ə-sīt) An organism that must live in or on a host to survive. (p. 16)

parboiled rice Also called converted rice; rice that has been partially cooked with steam and then dried. (p. 625)

parboiling Foods are put into boiling water and partially cooked. The cooking time for parboiling foods is longer than for blanching. (p. 390)

pare To trim off. (p. 254)

parfait (pär-'fās) A frozen dessert flavored with heavy cream. (p. 774)

parstock The amount of stock that will cover a facility's needs from one delivery to the next. (p. 362)

partnership A legal association of two or more people who share the ownership of the business. (p. 77)

pasta A starchy food product that is made from grains. (p. 616)

pasteurize ('pas-chə-rīz) To heat a product at high enough temperatures to kill harmful bacteria. (p. 40)

pasteurized Food that is heated at very high temperatures for a short time to destroy bacteria. (p. 434)

pastrami (pə-ˈsträ-mē) A seasoned smoked meat. (p. 499)

pastries Also known as Danishes, made from yeasted, sweetened dough with butter. (p. 444)

pastry chef Responsible for making baked items, such as breads, desserts, and pastries. (p. 59)

pastry flour Flour that has a protein content between bread and cake flour. (p. 688)

pathogens Disease-causing microorganisms. (p. 14)

patronage (ˈpa-trə-nij) Spending money at a business. (p. 119)

peel A wooden board that a baker uses to slide breads onto the oven floor or hearth. (p. 706)

percentage A rate or proportion of 100. (p. 680)

* **perception** Awareness. (p. 422)

* **performance** The way a foodservice business operates. (p. 198)

periodic-ordering method A purchaser decides how much product will be used in a given time period. The purchaser then reviews the amount of product that is on hand, what will be needed, and how much parstock of the product is needed. (p. 363)

perishable (ˈper-i-shə-bəl) Products that can spoil quickly, especially if they are not stored properly. (p. 41)

* **perpendicular (ˌpər-pən-ˈdi-kyə-lər)** Standing at right angles. (p. 156)

perpetual inventory A continuously updated record of what a business has on hand for each item. (p. 362)

pesto (pes-(ˌ)tō) A sauce made with olive oil, pine nuts or walnuts, parmesan, and fresh basil, garlic, salt, and pepper. (p. 490)

phyllo (ˈfē-(ˌ)lō) A very thin, layered pastry dough. (p. 489)

physical inventory A list of everything that an operation has on hand at one time. (p. 362)

phytochemicals (ˌfī-tō-ˈke-mi-kəls) Natural chemicals such as those found in plants, fruits, vegetables, grains, and dry beans. (p. 295)

pigment The matter in cells and tissue that gives them their color. (p. 378)

pilaf method Sautéing a grain in oil or butter before adding liquid. (p. 630)

pilot light A continuously burning flame that lights the burner when you turn on the range. (p. 239)

pita (ˈpē-tə) A round-shaped bread cut open to form a pocket. (p. 489)

pith White membrane of a fruit. (p. 402)

plate composition The way in which foods are arranged on a plate. (p. 425)

platform scale A scale with a platform to hold large or heavy items to be weighed. (p. 225)

plating The arrangement of food items and garnishes on a plate. (p. 314)

poach To cook food in a flavorful liquid between 150°F (66°C) and 185°F (85°C). (p. 391)

point-of-sale system A system involving a computer that has either a number or a button code for each item on the menu that sends the order to the kitchen. (p. 130)

polenta (pō-ˈlenˈtə) Corn product made from cornmeal that is gradually sprinkled into simmering water or stock and cooked until it becomes a thick paste. (p. 627)

polyunsaturated (ˌpä-lē-ˌən-ˈsa-chə-ˌrā-təd) fat A fat that is liquid at room temperature. (p. 285)

pork The meat from hogs that are less than one year old. (p. 595)

porous (ˈpȯr-əs) For eggs, flavors and odors can be absorbed through the shell. (p. 433)

* **portion** Part. (p. 595)

portion scale A scale that weighs portions. (p. 225)

portion size The amount or size of an individual serving. (p. 331)

positioning The way a foodservice busines presents itself to the community. (p. 191)

positive reinforcement Praising an employee when a job or task is done correctly. (p. 180)

potency Strength. (p. 740)

poultry Birds that are raised for human consumption. (p. 570)

pound cake A cake that contains a pound each of butter, flour, sugar, and eggs. (p. 755)

pour batter Batter thin enough to be poured from the mixing bowl. (p. 731)

* **precise** Exact. (p. 335)

preferment The process of removing a portion of the dough. It is kept dormant for 8 to 24 hours and then added to the next day's bread products. (p. 713)

prep cook Prepares ingredients to be used on the food production line. (p. 59)

preparation procedure The steps you must take to prepare a dish. (p. 331)

prepared mustard Mustard that contains a combination of ingredients including ground white, black, and brown mustard seeds, vinegar, salt, and spices. (p. 416)

preprocessed legumes Legumes that have already been soaked. (p. 660)

preset To set items on the table before food is served. (p. 133)

preset menu A meal served to a group of customers who have decided in advance on the menu and the time of service. (p. 158)

pressure-frying Cooking foods more quickly and at lower temperatures. (p. 580)

primal cut Sometimes called wholesale cuts, large, primary pieces of meat separated from the animal. (p. 589)

* **principle** Rule. (p. 580)

printed menu Any form of printed menu list that is handed to customers as soon as they sit down. (p. 318)

prioritize Put things in order of importance. (p. 91)

prix fixe ('prē-'fēks) menu Offers a complete meal for a set price. With a prix fixe menu, the customer chooses one selection from each course offered. (p. 310)

probation (prō-'bā-shən) A short period of time when you first start work that gives your employer a chance to monitor your job performance closely. (p. 107)

* **process** Series of actions. (p. 298, 577)

processed cheese A combination of ripened and unripened cheese pasteurized with flavorings and emulsifiers and poured into molds. (p. 474)

processing Preparing and cleaning food so that it can be eaten (p. 40); the act of changing meat by artificial means. (p. 597)

produce Fresh fruits and vegetables. (p. 41)

product name A name given to a recipe. (p. 331)

product yield The amount of food product left after preparation. (p. 350)

profit The money a business makes after paying all of its expenses. (p. 70)

profit and loss statement A financial statement that shows exactly how money flows in a business. Also called an income statement. (p. 175)

* **promote** Advertise. (p. 142)

promotion A specific effort to market a particular item or special. (p. 191)

proofing Final fermentation stage that allows the leavening action of yeast to achieve its final strength before yeast cells are killed by hot oven temperatures. (p. 719)

proofing/holding cabinet Also called a proofer, a freestanding metal box on wheels that is temperature- and humidity-controlled. (p. 242)

proportion The ratio of one food to another and to the plate. (p. 315)

* **proportional** About the same size. (p. 502)

prosciutto (prō-'shü-(,)tō) Italian for ham; dry-cured, uncooked ham, usually served in thin slices. (p. 479)

protective clothing Clothing that is worn to help lower the chances of food contamination. (p. 26)

protein A nutrient that builds, maintains, and repairs body tissues. (p. 281)

* **provide** To make available. (p. 26)

psychological pricing method Menu pricing based on how a customer reacts to menu prices. (p. 323)

public relations Publicity and advertising that a foodservice operation uses to enhance its image. (p. 191)

publicity The free or low-cost efforts of a facility to improve its image. (p. 191)

pudding A dessert made from milk, sugar, eggs, flavorings, and cornstarch or cream for thickening. (p. 771)

PUFI mark Packed Under Federal Inspection; an inspection mark for fish and shellfish. (p. 549)

Pullman loaf A rectangular-shaped sandwich bread loaf with a flat top and an even texture. (p. 488)

pulse A seed of a legume that is dried. (p. 660)

punch The action of turning the sides of the dough into the middle and turning the dough over. (p. 716)

puncture wound An injury in which the skin is pierced with a pointed object, such as an ice pick, making a deep hole in the skin. (p. 11)

purchase order A document asking a supplier to ship supplies at a predetermined price. (p. 225)

purchaser Buys food and supplies according to his or her restaurant clients' current needs. (p. 61)

purée A food in which one or more of the ingredients have been ground in a food processor. (p. 300)

Q

Q factor Questionable ingredient factor; the cost of an ingredient that is difficult to measure. (p. 353)

* **qualities** Distinguishing characteristics. (p. 88)

quality control A system that ensures that everything will meet the foodservice establishment's standards. (p. 330)

* **quantity** Amount. (p. 225)

quantity The total amount a recipe makes. (p. 330)

quenelle (kə-nel) A purée of chopped food formed into shapes, used as a garnish. (p. 459)

quiche ('kēsh) A pie crust filled with a mixture of eggs, cream, cheese, and vegetables or meat. (p. 439)

quick breads A type of bread made from quick-acting leavening agents such as baking powder. (p. 445)

quick soak To soak beans by placing in a pot and covering with water. Bring the water to a boil for a few minutes, then turn off heat, cover, and let sit for one hour. (p. 663)

quick-service restaurant A restaurant that quickly provides a limited selection of food at low prices. (p. 70)

R

radiation Heats food by transmitting heat energy through air waves. (p. 234)

radicchio (ra-ˈdi-kē-ō) A cabbage-like plant with a slightly bitter, red leaf. (p. 466)

raft A floating mass that forms from the mixture of meat and eggs in a soup or consommé. The raft traps the impurities that rise to the top of the broth. (p. 528)

ramekin (ˈra-mi-kən) A small individual baking dish. (p. 440)

range of motion Using the fewest body movements without unnecessary stress or strain. (p. 223)

rare Meat that is browned on the surface, with a red center. (p. 610)

raw vegan (ˈvē-gən) Someone who eats only unprocessed vegan foods that have not been heated above 115°F (46°C). (p. 293)

ready-made bread Bread made in advance and delivered to restaurants. (p. 443)

ready-to-cook Food that has been prepared and packaged. (p. 571)

receiving Accepting deliveries of food and supplies. (p. 38)

receiving record A numbered record of everything received during a particular day. (p. 225)

receptors Cells that receive stimuli. (p. 421)

recipe An exact set of directions on how to use ingredients, equipment, and cooking techniques for a certain dish. (p. 330)

recipe conversion A change in a recipe to produce a new amount or yield. (p. 337)

Recommended Dietary Allowances The amount of each essential nutrient that will meet the nutritional needs of the majority of healthy Americans for a day. (p. 289)

recondition To coat a griddle or skillet in oil so that foods will not stick to it. (p. 239)

record-keeping system A system of flow charts, policy and procedure manuals, written descriptions, and food temperature readings taken at different times. (p. 35)

recovery time The time it takes for the fat or oil to return to the preset temperature after food has been submerged. (p. 386)

recycle To take a product at the end of its use and turn it into a raw material to make a different product. (p. 44)

reduce To decrease the volume of. (p. 391)

reduction The process of evaporating part of a stock's water through simmering or boiling. (p. 513)

reel oven An oven with shelves that move or rotate like a Ferris wheel to bake a quantity of similar items evenly. (p. 684)

* **refer** Reread briefly. (p. 231)

* **reflects** Shows. (p. 531)

* **regulate** Control. (p. 285)

regulation A rule by which government agencies enforce minimum standards of quality. (p. 198)

rehydrate ((ˌ)rē-ˈhī-ˌdrāt) To add water into. (p. 642)

reliable (ri-ˌlī-ə-ˈbəl) When other people can count on you to do what you say you will do. (p. 89)

relish tray An attractive arrangement of raw, blanched, or marinated vegetables. (p. 481)

relish Coarsely chopped or ground pickled items. (p. 416)

render To melt. (p. 577)

repetitive stress injury An injury that can happen to employees who must perform the same motions over and over. (p. 106)

* **replenish** Restock. (p. 242)

reputation The overall quality or character of a person or business. (p. 116)

requisition An internal invoice that allows management to track the physical movement of inventory through a business. (p. 363)

research chef Works closely with food scientists to produce new food products. (p. 60)

reservation An arrangement to have a table held for a customer at a specific time. (p. 116)

* **reserve** Keep. (p. 513)

* **resist** To avoid. (p. 597)

resource The raw material with which you do your work. (p. 91)

responsibility Your ability to be aware of what a particular situation demands of you. (p. 88)

rest To allow cooked meat to sit so that juices redistribute throughout the meat. (p. 607)

restaurant manager Oversees the operation of the entire restaurant. (p. 60)

* **result** Have an outcome. (p. 14)

résumé (ˈre-zə-ˌmā) A summary of your career objectives, work experience, job qualifications, education, and training. (p. 96)

* **reveal** To make known. (p. 591)

rice The starchy seeds of a cereal grass. (p. 624)

rind The outer surface of cheese. (p. 472)

ring A type of container that has no bottom. (p. 686)

ripe Fully grown and ready to eat. (p. 638)

ripening Process by which healthful bacteria and mold change the texture and flavor of cheese. (p. 471)

risk management Taking steps to prevent accidents from happening. (p. 185)

risotto A rice dish in which the grain has been sautéed in butter, and then simmered in a flavored cooking liquid, which has been added gradually to the rice until it has finished cooking. (p. 624)

risotto method A method in which the grain is sautéed, and then a small amount of hot liquid, often a soup stock, is added. The grain is stirred until most of the liquid is absorbed. This process of adding liquid and stirring the grain is continued until the grain is completely cooked. (p. 631)

risotto Milanese (ri-'so-(,)tō ,mi-lə-'nəz) An Italian dish that includes rice that is sautéed in butter before stock is added. (p. 414)

rivet A metal piece that fastens the tang to the knife handle. (p. 252)

roasting Cooking method that uses dry heat in a closed environment. Foods are placed on top of a rack that is inside a pan. This allows air to circulate all the way around the food. In general, roasting involves longer cooking times than baking. (p. 383)

* **role** Function performed. (p. 282)

roll cut Cutting a cylindrical fruit or vegetable as for a diagonal cut, rolling the fruit or vegetable by 180 degrees, and then doing another diagonal cut. (p. 255)

rolled-in fat yeast dough A dough made of many thin, alternating layers of fat and dough. (p. 709)

rondelle (rän-'del) A disk-shaped slice. (p. 255)

room service Having servers bring specially ordered meals to a customer's room. (p. 144)

rotate stock To place stored items in an orderly way so that older items are used first. (p. 363)

round fish Fish that have a backbone on the upper edge of their bodies. They have an eye on each side of their heads, and they swim vertically. (p. 542)

rounded Dough shaped into smooth balls. (p. 717)

* **routine** Regular set of actions. (p. 4)

roux (rü) A cooked mixture made from equal parts of fat and flour by weight used to thicken sauces. (p. 520)

rumaki (rə-'mä-kē) Appetizers that consist of blanched bacon wrapped around vegetables, seafood, chicken liver, meat, poultry, or fruits. (p. 503)

Russian/English service Each course is completely prepared, cooked, portioned, and garnished in the kitchen and then placed on a service plate or platters. Each customer is served a portion of the product from large platters. (p. 147)

S

sachet (sa-'shā) French for bag; used for herbs and spices. (p. 410)

salad A mixture of one or several ingredients with a dressing. (p. 463)

salad sandwich A sandwich that has a salad with a fatty dressing as the filling. (p. 499)

sales cycle The period between supply deliveries. (p. 358)

sales representative Helps chefs to select food and equipment that will best fit their needs and budgets. (p. 61)

salsa ('sol-sə) A fresh or cooked mixture of chiles, tomatoes, onions, and cilantro. (p. 416)

sanitary Clean. (p. 14)

sanitation Healthy or clean and whole. (p. 14)

sanitizing ('sa-nə-,tīz-iŋ) Reducing the number of microorganisms on the surface. (p. 18)

* **satisfy** To fill. (p. 605)

saturated ('sa-chə-,rāt-əd) fat A fat that tends to increase the amount of cholesterol in the blood and is solid at room temperature. (p. 283)

sauce A flavored, thickened liquid. It is usually formed by adding seasonings, flavorings, and a thickening agent to stock. (p. 517)

sauce espagnole (,es-pan-'yól) Made from brown stock and tomato product; one of the mother sauces. (p. 519)

sauerkraut ('saú(-ə)r-,kraút) Finely sliced cabbage that has been fermented in brine. (p. 491)

sausage A breakfast meat often made of ground pork that has been seasoned and stuffed into casings; also available as patties. (p. 432)

sautéing (so-'tā-iŋ) A quick, dry cooking technique that uses a small amount of fat or oil in a shallow pan. (p. 384)

savory ('sā-və-rē) Stimulating and full of flavor; sometimes included in the basic tastes. (p. 422)

scaling How bakers refer to weighing. (p. 679)

scone A type of quick bread similar to biscuits that is often cut into triangle shapes. (p. 445)

scoop Also called a disher, a tool to control portions during food preparation and serving. (p. 349)

scorch To burn with too intense of a heat. (p. 469)

score Make ridges in a diamond-shaped pattern with a fork. (p. 461)

seams The places where edges of the dough meet. (p. 718)

sear To quickly brown food at the start of the cooking process. (p. 383)

season Sealing the surface of a pan with a layer of baked-on oil to prevent sticking. (p. 438)

seasoning An ingredient that enhances food without changing the natural flavor. (p. 400)

section/station A group of tables that comprises a service staff member's responsibility. (p. 117)

seed A plant grain. (p. 419)

semi-à la carte menu A menu with the appetizers and desserts priced separately. (p. 310)

semiperishable Perishable items that contain an inhibitor. (p. 358)

semolina (,se-mə-'lē-nə) flour A hard-grain wheat flour that is high in the proteins that form gluten. (p. 616)

sensory evaluation The systematic tasting of food by consumers and foodservice professionals. (p. 424)

sensory perception How a person's eyes, nose, ears, mouth, and skin detect and evaluate the environment. (p. 421)

sensory properties Properties that affect how people perceive something. The sensory properties of food are color and appearance, flavor, and texture. (p. 421)

* **separation** Dividing. (p. 734)

serrated (sə-'rāt-ed) Toothed like a saw. (p. 254)

server The service staff member who has the most contact with the customers. (p. 117)

service station An area where supplies are kept for the service staff to reset tables between customers. (p. 118)

serviette A napkin-lined plate used to carry flatware. (p. 155)

sexual harrassment Unwelcome advances, requests for sexual favors, and other verbal or physical conduct of a sexual nature. (p. 206)

shape To form dough into the distinctive shapes associated with yeast products. (p. 718)

sheet pan A shallow, rectangular pan that comes in full, half, and quarter sizes. (p. 686)

sheeter A piece of equipment that rolls out large pieces of dough to a desired thickness. (p. 681)

shelf life The period of time a product can be stored and still be good to use. (p. 38)

sherbet Frozen dessert that combines fruit juices, sugar, water, and a small amount of cream or milk. (p. 771)

shirred ('shərd) Eggs covered with cream or milk and sometimes bread crumbs. Usually prepared in ramekins lined with a variety of ingredients. (p. 440)

shock A serious medical condition in which not enough oxygen reaches tissues. (p. 11)

shocking Plunging food into ice water after blanching. (p. 390)

shortening In baking, solid fats. (p. 689)

shrinkage The percentage of food lost during its storage and preparation. (p. 341)

shucked Removed from the shell. (p. 39)

side order An order of food in addition to what is served as the main dish. (p. 446)

side work Duties that service staff members have to perform before the dining room is open to customers. (p. 151)

sifting Passing dry ingredients through a wire mesh to remove lumps, blend, and add air. (p. 700)

simmering Food cooks slowly and steadily in a slightly cooler than boiling liquid. (p. 391)

simple syrup A syrup made of sugar dissolved into hot water. (p. 762)

single-food hors d'oeuvre An hors d'oeuvre that consists of one food item. (p. 477)

single-source buying Purchasing most products from a single vendor. (p. 359)

slash Making shallow cuts in the surface of an item just before baking. (p. 721)

sleeper A lobster in the process of dying. (p. 553)

* **slightly** A little bit. (p. 766)

smallwares Hand tools, pots, and pans used for cooking. (p. 262)

smoking A form of cooking using low heat, long cooking times, and wood smoke for flavor. (p. 382)

smoking point The temperature at which an oil will smoke in a pan. (p. 300, 580)

soft cookie A cookie that has low amounts of fat and sugar in the batter, and a high proportion of liquid, such as eggs. (p. 748)

soft medium dough A dough that produces items with a soft crumb and crust. (p. 709)

soft wheat flour Flour that comes from a soft wheat kernel. (p. 688)

solanine A toxic substance found in green potatoes that can upset your stomach and interfere with nerve transmission. (p. 650)

sole proprietorship A business that has only one owner. (p. 77)

solid waste Packaging material, containers, and recyclables. (p. 200)

sorbet (sȯr-'bā) The product left when the milk or cream is omitted from sherbet. (p. 771)

soufflé (sü-'flā) A puffed egg dish that is baked in the oven. (p. 434)

soup plate A shallow bowl-shaped plate. (p. 622)

sous ('sü) chef Supervises and sometime assists other chefs in the kitchen. (p. 59)

specialty soup A soup that highlights a specific region, or reflects, or shows, the use of special ingredients or techniques. (p. 531)

specification A written description of the products a foodservice operation needs to purchase. (p. 348)

spice A flavoring that blends with the natural flavor of foods. (p. 401)

spice rub A mixture of ground spices that is rubbed on raw food before it is cooked. (p. 607)

spinach Dark green, leafy vegetable that is full of calcium and adds color and flavor to salads. (p. 464)

spoken menu A server states what foods are available and the prices of each. (p. 318)

sponge cake Also called a foam cake, has an airy, light texture because of large amounts of air whipped into the eggs. (p. 756)

sponge method Dough preparation method that allows the yeast to develop separately before it is mixed with the other ingredients. (p. 713)

spread Expand. (p. 748)

springform pan A pan with a clamp used to release the pan's bottom from its wall. (p. 686)

* **stabilize** Support. (p. 755)

stack oven Also called a deck oven; a freestanding rectangular oven with a series of well-insulated compartments stacked on top of one another. (p. 682)

stainless steel A hard, durable metal made of chromium and carbon steel. (p. 252)

staling The process by which moisture is lost, causing a change in the texture and aroma of food. (p. 689)

standard An established model or example used to compare quality. (p. 198)

standardized accounting practices Reporting figures in a way that can be easily compared to the figures from other businesses. (p. 173)

standardized ('stan-dər-ˌdīzd) recipe A set of written instructions used to consistently prepare a known quantity and quality of food. (p. 330)

starter A mixture of flour, yeast, sugar, and a warm liquid that begins the leavening action. (p. 706)

steak sauce A tomato-based sauce that is tangier than ketchup. (p. 416)

steam table A food warmer; keeps prepared foods warm in serving lines. (p. 242)

steaming Cooking vegetables or other foods in a closed environment filled with steam. (p. 391)

stewing A combination cooking technique. Stewed foods are cut into small pieces, and completely covered with liquid during cooking. Cooking time for stewing is generally shorter than for braising. (p. 394)

stimuli Things that cause an activity or response. (p. 421)

stir-frying A dry cooking technique similar to sautéing done with a wok. (p. 384)

stirred custard A custard made on the range in a double boiler or saucepan. (p. 772)

stir Gently blending ingredients until they are combined. (p. 700)

stock The liquid that forms the foundation of sauces and soups. (p. 510)

storage Placing food in a location for later use. (p. 38)

straight-dough method Mixing all the ingredients together in a single step. (p. 713)

* **strategy** A plan of action. (p. 189)

streusel ('strü-səl) A sweet, crumbly topping made of flour, brown sugar, and granulated sugar. (p. 741)

stuffing Seasoned food mixture often made with bread. (p. 582)

* **subject** To expose to. (p. 378)

* **submerged** Covered in liquid. (p. 389)

* **substituted** Switched. (p. 774)

* **subtle** Understated; delicate. (p. 466)

* **sufficient** Enough. (p. 562)

* **suitable** Having the right qualifications. (p. 97)

sundae A dessert with one or more scoops of ice cream topped with garnishes, fruits, or syrups. (p. 774)

* **supplement** Addition. (p. 510)

surimi A combination of white fish and flavoring, minced and formed into shapes. (p. 557)

* **surround** Enclose. (p. 689)

sushi ('sü-shē) A Japanese dish of raw or cooked fresh fish or seafood wrapped in cooked and cooled rice. (p. 559)

sweating Cooking vegetables in fat over low heat in a process that allows them to release moisture. (p. 528)

Swedish meatball Made with ground beef or pork, onions, and served with a gravy. (p. 503)

sweet rich dough A soft, heavy dough that incorporates up to 25% of both fat and sugar. (p. 709)

Swiss meringue A meringue that is made by dissolving sugar and egg whites together over simmering water, and then beating them. (p. 762)

T

table d'hôte (ˌtä-bəl-'dōt) menu A menu that lists complete meals, from appetizers to desserts and sometimes beverages, for one set price. (p. 310)

table setting The specific arrangement of tableware, glassware, and flatware for a meal. (p. 156)

table tent Folded cards that stand on the table to list specials. (p. 318)

tableside At the table, in full view of the customer. (p. 146)

tableware Any kind of dish, from dinner plates to soup bowls to coffee cups. (p. 155)

tang The part of the blade that continues into the knife's handle. (p. 252)

tank system A system where two plastic lines are connected to each carbon dioxide tank in a soft drink machine. One leads to the CO_2 tank and allows it to pressurize the soda syrup. The other line permits the soda to pass to the dispensing gun. (p. 122)

target market The market segment you most want to attract. (p. 189)

tart pan A shallow pan that ranges in diameter from 4½ to 12½ inches. (p. 686)

tartar sauce A sauce made of mayonnaise and chopped pickles. (p. 563)

taste bud A specialized cell for tasting that is scattered over the surface of the tongue. (p. 422)

teamwork Learning to effectively communicate, resolve conflicts, and develop negotiation skills. (p. 89)

* **technique** Method. (p. 27)

* **tempted** Enticed. (p. 709)

theme restaurant A restaurant that tries to recreate another place or time. (p. 142)

thick soup A soup that is not clear or transparent. Thick soups include a thickening agent, such as roux; cream; or a vegetable purée. (p. 529)

thickening agent An ingredient, such as cornstarch, that adds body to a sauce. (p. 517)

tip A small bonus payment from a customer as a reward for excellent service. (p. 109)

tomato sauce Made by simmering a tomato product with flavorings, seasonings, and stock or another liquid; one of the mother sauces. (p. 519)

torpedo (tȯr-'pē-(ˌ)dō) roll A long, skinny sandwich roll. (p. 489)

tortilla (tȯr-'tē-yə) A flattened, round bread baked on a griddle or deep-fried. (p. 489)

total weight as served Multiply the number of portions by the portion weight when the food is served. (p. 352)

tournée (tōr-'nə) Turn vegetables using a tournée knife; creates a football shape. (p. 461)

toxin A harmful organism or substance. (p. 14)

trade publication A magazine or newsletter produced by and for members of the foodservice industry. (p. 95)

traffic path How people and materials move within a foodservice operation. (p. 183)

trans fatty acid An unsaturated fat that goes through the hydrogenation process. Also called trans fat. (p. 282)

* **transfer** To pass to food. (p. 252)

translucent Clear. (p. 422)

* **transmit** Spread. (p. 16)

tray service Bringing dishes to the table at the same time on a large tray. (p. 131)

tray stand A stand that has metal, wood, or plastic leg frames that will fold. Also called a tray jack. (p. 131)

trayline service Customers go through a food line and place items on their own trays. (p. 143)

trend A general preference or dislike for something within an industry. (p. 68)

trichinosis (ˌtri-kə-'nō-səs) An infestation by a parasite that can cause muscular pain, stomach upset, fever, weakness, and swelling. (p. 609)

trim To cut off excess fat or to cut food to a desired shape or size. (p. 350)

trim loss The weight of the waste material that was trimmed from the purchased product. (p. 351)

trueing Using a steel to keep a blade straight and to smooth out irregularities after sharpening. (p. 259)

trussing Tying up a bird's wings and legs against the body. (p. 575)

truth-in-menu guideline A guideline that ensures truthfulness in statements about nutrition, quantity, quality, grade, and freshness. (p. 315)

tuber The short, fleshy underground stems of plants. (p. 647)

tuile ('twēl) A Belgian molded cookie that comes out of the oven soft. (p. 751)

tunnels Large, irregular holes in bread. (p. 739)

* **turn** To become. (p. 748)

turnover rate The average number of times a seat will be occupied during a block of time. (p. 182)

U

underliner A dish placed under another dish to protect the table from spills. (p. 133)

uniform Clothing that is worn by a particular group to help identify workers. (p. 119)

* **uniform** Even in shape and size. (p. 255)

unit cost The cost of each individual item. (p. 349)

univalve ('yü-ni-ˌvalv) A mollusk that has a single shell. (p. 550)

* **upscale** For more affluent customers. (p. 322)

upselling Suggesting a larger size or better quality than the customer's original order. (p. 129)

V

vacuum packed Placed in air-tight containers from which the air has been removed to prevent the growth of bacteria. (p. 547)

* **variation** Change. (p. 496)

* **varied** Available in different kinds. (p. 471)

veal The meat from calves that are less than nine months old. (p. 599)

vegan ('vē-gən) Someone who does not eat any meat or animal products. (p. 293)

vegetable stock A stock made from vegetables, herbs, spices, and water. (p. 513)

vegetarian (ˌve-jə-'ter-ē-ən) A person who does not eat meat or other animal-based foods. (p. 293)

veined cheese A pungeant, semisoft cheese that has veins of mold running through it. (p. 472)

velouté (və-ˌlü-'tā) Also known as blond sauce, is made by thickening a light-colored stock with a light-colored roux; one of the mother sauces. (p. 520)

vendor A company that sells products to the food-service industry. (p. 61)

* **verify** To prove. (p. 36)

* **versatile** Adaptable. (p. 625)

vichyssoise (vi-shē-'swäz) A cold version of potato-leek soup. (p. 531)

vinaigrette (‚vi-ni-'gret) A salad dressing that has a ratio of three parts oil to one part vinegar. (p. 468)

vinegar A sour, acidic liquid used in cooking, marinades, and salad dressings. (p. 416)

violation Not following a rule. (p. 198)

viruses Simple organisms that are responsible for many food-related illnesses. (p. 16)

vitamin Substance that helps regulate many bodily functions. (p. 285)

* **volume** Amount. (p. 231)

volume The space occupied by a substance. (p. 262)

volume measurement A measurement that is expressed in cups, quarts, gallons, and fluid ounces. (p. 336)

W

walls The sides of a muffin. (p. 742)

warped Turned slightly from flat because of excessive heat and use. (p. 753)

washing Applying a thin glaze of liquid to dough's surface before baking. (p. 719)

waxy potato A potato with thin skin and less starch than mealy potatoes. (p. 650)

weight The heaviness of a substance. (p. 262)

well done Meat that is browned on the surface and gray on the inside. (p. 610)

wet cure A brine. Food is submerged in a mixture of sea salt, a sweetener, spices, and herbs that are dissolved in water. Then, the food is dried or cooked. (p. 457)

wheat A very versatile grain that is also milled into semolina and cracked wheat. (p. 627)

* **whet** To increase, as an appetite. (p. 477)

whetstone A sharpening stone made of either silicon carbide or stone. (p. 259)

whey The liquid portion of coagulated milk. (p. 471)

whip Vigorously beating ingredients to add air. (p. 700)

white rice Rice that has had the outer layers of the grain removed. (p. 625)

white stock A stock made from chicken, beef, veal, or fish bones simmered with vegetables. (p. 511)

* **withered** Shrunken and wrinkled. (p. 660)

* **withstand** To hold up to. (p. 262)

wok A large pan with sloping sides. (p. 384)

work ethic A personal commitment to doing your very best as part of the team. (p. 88)

work flow The orderly movement of food and staff through the kitchen. (p. 221)

work section Similar work stations that are grouped into larger work areas. (p. 220)

work simplification To perform a task in the most efficient way possible. (p. 222)

work station A work area that contains the necessary tools and equipment to prepare certain types of foods. (p. 220)

workers' compensation Insurance that pays for medical expenses and lost wages if you are injured on the job. (p. 106)

Y

yeast A living organism used as a leavener. (p. 694)

yield The amount of servings in a recipe. (p. 331)

yield grade Measures the amount of usable meat on beef and lamb. (p. 592)

yield percentage The ratio of the edible portion of food to the amount of food purchased. (p. 350)

yield test A process by which AP food is broken down into EP and waste. (p. 350)

yield weight AP weight minus trim loss. (p. 351)

Z

zest The rind of a fruit. (p. 402)

zoning A system that divides land into sections used for different purposes. (p. 78)

Index

A

À la carte menu, 310
Abrasion, 11
Accident report log, 201
Accompaniments, 312
    on menus, 319
    salads, 463
Active listening, 85
Activity level, nutritional needs and, 293
ADA (Americans with Disabilities Act), 206
Additives, 286, 287
    in baking, 697
    for desserts, 698
Advertising, 191–192
Affirmative action, 205
Age, nutritional needs and, 291
Age discrimination, 205, 206
Age Discrimination in Employment Act (1967), 206
Aging, of beef, 603
Air, as leavening agent, 694
Airline meals, 143
Al dente, 620
Albumin, 433
Alcohol service, 120
Alcohol use by employees, 181
Allspice, 411
Almonds, 417
American cuisine, seasonal, 68
American Culinary Federation, 65
American Grinders, 493
American omelets, 438
Americans with Disabilities Act (ADA), 206
American-style ice cream, 771
Amino acids, 281
Angel food cakes, 756, 760
Anise seeds, 411
Antipasto, 481
AP price. See As-purchased price
AP (as-purchased) weight, 353
Appearance, in plate composition, 425
Appetizer service, 133
Appetizers, 133, 318
    salads, 463
Apple corers, 263
Apple Wheat Germ Cake, 692
Apprentices, 65, 95
Aroma, 410
    cooking and, 379
    sensory perception of, 422–423
Arrowroot, for sauce thickening, 518
AS (as-served) portion, 352
Aspic, 480
As-purchased (AP) price, 351–352
As-purchased (AP) weight, 353
As-served (AS) portion, 352
Associate's degree programs, 63
Atmosphere, 191
Attitude, as service skill, 119
Au jus, 499
Audits, safety, 12

Autocratic leadership, 172
Average check method (menu pricing), 322
Avulsions, 11

B

Bachelor's degree programs, 64
Back braces, 4
Back injuries, preventing, 6
Bacon, 432, 435
Bacteria, 14–16
    battle against, 36
    glow test for, 39
    salmonella, 575
Bagels, 445
Bag-in-the-box system, 122
Bain marie, 242, 243
Baked custards, 772
Baked puddings, 773
Bakeries, careers in, 72
Baker's percentage, 333
Bakery ovens, 682, 684
Bakeshops
    formulas, 678–681
    ingredients, 688–697
    large equipment, 684
    measurements, 678–681
    mixing batters and doughs, 697–700
    smallwares, 684–686
Baking, 382
    biscuits, 733
    cakes, 759, 762
    cookies, 753
    fish and shellfish, 559, 560
    fruits, 644
    muffins, 741
    pasta, 619, 620
    pies, 769
    poultry, 577
    tools for, 685
    vegetables, 655
    yeast breads and rolls, 721–723
Baking blind, 767
Baking cup, 738
Baking powder, 694
Baking soda, 694
Balance
    in facility spaces, 182
    on menus, 314–315
Balance scales, 269, 336, 679, 680
Banquet facilities, careers in, 71–72
Banquette, 146
Banquette service, 146
Bar codes, 365
Bar cookies, 752, 753
Barding, 577, 588
Barley, 626–627
Barnacles, 552
Barquette, 502
Base, 510
Basic pie dough, 765, 768

Basil, 407
Basting, 383, 577
Batch cooking, 299–300
Batonnet, 259
Batters, 384
    drop, 731
    mixing, 697–700
    pour, 731
    scaling, 761
Bavarians, 773–774
Bay leaf, 407
Beating, 698
Béchamel Sauce, 517, 519, 522
Beef, 601–603
Beef Consommé, 533
Bench box, 718
Bench mixers, 232
Bench rest, 718
Bench scrapers, 267
Benefits, 110
Beverage service, 121–125
    alcohol, 120
    cold beverages, 127–128
    hot beverages, 128
    taking orders, 127
    water, 128
Beverages, on menus, 319
Bid, 361
Bins, for professional kitchens, 228, 229
Biological hazards, 14, 15
Biscuit method, 731
Biscuits, 445, 731–734
Bisques, 531
Bivalves, 550
Black pepper, 401
Blanching, 389–390, 655
Blenders, 233
Blending method, 698
    cakes, 758, 760
    muffins, 737
    quick breads, 731
Blends, flavoring, 404
Blind taste test, 424
Body language, 86, 121
Boiling, 389, 630
    pasta, 619, 620, 631
Boiling point, 389
Bolsters, 253
Boneless fish, 542
Boning knife, 254
Booth service, 145
Booths, 145
Bouchée, 502
Bouillon, 527
Bouquet garni, 400, 406, 510
Bouquetière, 657
Box graters, 266
Braising, 392–393
    grains, 631
    meats, 609
    poultry, 580, 581
    vegetables, 657
Brazils, 417

Bread crumbs, thickening sauces with, 518
Bread flour, 688–689
Bread service, 133
Breading, 384
Breads
    for breakfasts, 443–447
    quick breads, 730–742
    for sandwiches, 488–489
    yeast breads, 706–724
Break even, 175
Breakfast
    breads and cereals for, 443–450
    protein foods for, 432–441
    quick-service, 443
Breakfast menus, 311
Brochettes, 502
Broilers, 236, 239
Broiling, 386–387
    fish and shellfish, 560, 561
    fruits, 643
    meats, 607
    poultry, 579
    vegetables, 653, 655
Broth, 527
Brown rice, 625
Brown stock, 511, 513
Brown sugar, 691
Brunoise, 259
Buffet restaurants, 143
Buffet service, 149
Buffets, 149, 479–480
Bulk purchases, 351, 551
Burns
    first aid for, 10–11
    preventing, 5–6
    types of, 10
Bus stations, 152
Business ownership, types of, 77
Business plans, 76–77
Bussers, 118
Butcher knife, 254
Butchers, 589
Butler service, 148–149
Butter(s)
    for baking, 690
    compound, 520–521
    for sandwiches, 489
Butter cutters, 264, 460
Butterflied fish, 544
Bypassing, 183
By-products, 353

C
Cafeterias, 71
Cake flour, 689
Cakes, 755–763
    angel food, 756, 760
    baking, 759, 762
    chiffon, 757–758, 760
    cooling, 762
    foam, 756, 760

high-fat, 755
high-ratio layer cakes, 757–758
icing, 762–763
layer, 755
low-fat, 755
mixing methods, 759–760
pound, 755, 756
preparation methods, 760–762
sponge, 756, 760
storing, 762
Calamari, 556
Calculating numbers, 84
Calibrating thermometers, 35
California menu, 310
Can openers, 233
Canadian bacon, 432
Canapés, 456, 477–478
Cancer, 294–295
Canned foods
    fish, 547
    fruits, 639
    potatoes, 651
    storage of, 41
    vegetables, 651–652
Caper, 563
Cappuccino, 123
Caramelization, 379
Carbohydrates, 280
Carcasses, meat, 589, 590
Cardamom, 411
Cardiopulmonary resuscitation (CPR), 11
Cardiovascular disease, 282, 293, 294
Careers in foodservice, 58–72
    in bakeries and pastry shops, 72
    in banquet facilities, 71–72
    basic skills needed for, 84–88
    in catering, 72
    education for, 62–64
    employee responsibilities in, 104–105
    employer responsibilities in, 105–107
    for entrepreneurs, 74–78
    entry-level learning for, 64–66
    ethical behavior in, 107–108
    finding. See Job searches
    in hotels and resorts, 71
    leadership skills for, 90–92
    in management, 59–61
    in production, 38–39
    in restaurants, 70–71
    rewards and demands of, 61–62
    in service jobs, 58
    teamwork in, 107
    wages and benefits in, 108–110
    work ethic for, 88–90
Carry-out orders, 134
Carryover cooking, 382
Carving
    roasted meats, 607
    turkey, 578
Cashews, 417

Cashiers, 118–119
Casseroles, 619
Casual-dining establishments, 142
Catering, 72, 143
Catering directors, 60
Cavity, 582
Cayenne, 412
Ceilings, regulations for, 202
Celery seeds, 411
Centerpieces, 158
Cephalopods, 550
Cereals, 443–444, 448–450
Certification programs, 63
Certifications, 62, 63
Certified Professional Food Manager certification, 62
Chafing dishes, 149
Chain restaurants, 75
Channel knife, 460
Chapatti, 489
Charcuterie, 458
Checks, calculating and presenting, 134–136
Cheddaring, 471
Cheese slicers, 263
Cheese trays, 480
Cheesecloth, 518
Cheeses, 471–475
    cooking with, 473
    firm, 472
    hard, 471–472
    history of, 474
    on menus, 319
    for sandwiches, 491, 494
    sanitary handling of, 494
    semisoft, 472–473
    soft, 473–474
    specialty, 474–475
    types of, 471
Chefs
    history of, 63
    types of, 59, 60
Chef's coat, 26
Chef's fork, 265
Chef's knife, 253
Chemical dough conditioners, 708
Chemical hazards, 17–19
Chervil, 407
Chestnuts, 417
Chewy cookies, 748
Chez Panisse, 68
Chicken, 570, 577
Chiffon cakes, 758, 760
Chiffonade cuts, 255, 257
Chiffons, 774
Children, nutritional needs of, 292
Chiles, 412
Chili powder, 411
China cap, 266
Chinois, 266
Chives, 407
Chlorophyll, 379
Chocolate, 693, 696, 697

Index

Choking, first aid for, 11
Cholesterol, 282
Chowders, 531
Chutney, 642
Cilantro, 407
Cinnamon, 411
Civil Rights Act (1964), 206
Clams, 550-551
Clarified butter, 521
Clarify, 528
Classical French service, 146–147
Cleaning, 18
    equipment for, 239–240
    of kitchen equipment, 7
    of kitchens, 18–19
    safety of products, 18
Cleanliness, of foodhandlers, 26–29
Clear soups, 527–529
Clearing tables, 134
Client base, 119
Clientele, 189
Clip-on menus, 318
Closed sandwiches, 488
Closing restaurants, 183
Clothing
    for foodhandlers, 26
    for job interviews, 98
    protective, 4, 26
    for service staff, 119
Club sandwiches, 499
Coagulate, 378
Coarse sugar, 691
Cobblers, 644
Cocoa, 696, 697
Cocoa powder, 697
Coffee makers, 122–123, 125
Colanders, 266, 621
Cold beverage equipment, 122
Cold beverage service, 127–128
Cold cereals, 444, 449
Cold platters, 477–482
    hors d'oeuvres, 477–478
    preparation of, 479–482
Cold sandwiches, 499–500
Cold soups, 531
Cold-pack cheeses, 474–475
Collagen, 588
Color of foods
    cooking and, 378–379
    meats, 610
    in plate composition, 425
    sensory perception of, 421–422
Combination cooking, 376–377, 392–394
Combination steamer/oven, 237
Combination trays (cold), 481
Commercial dishwashers, 45–46
Commercial kitchens. *See* Professional kitchens
Commercial operation, 70
Commercial stock bases, 510
Commitment, as job skill, 90

Communication
    by foodservice managers, 171
    as service staff skill, 120, 121
Compensating, skills for, 92
Compensatory time, 106
Competition, analyzing, 189–190
Competitive buying, 361
Competitor, 189
Competitors' pricing method (menu pricing), 322
Complete protein, 281
Compote, 642
Compotier, 645
Compound butters, 520–521
Compressed yeast, 694
Computer skills, 92
Condiments, 152, 416
Conduct, standards of, 180–181
Conduction, 234
Confectioners' sugar, 691
Conflict resolution, 107
Connective tissue, 571, 588
Consommé, 528–529
Contamination, 14–17
Continental menu, 311
Continuous bread making, 715
Contract foodservice, 143
Contribution margin method (menu pricing), 322
Convection, 234, 389
Convection ovens, 238, 239, 682
Conversion factor, 337
Converted rice, 625
Converting recipes, 335, 337–342
Cooked salad dressings, 469
Cookies, 748–753
    baking, 753
    cooling, 753
    mixing methods, 749–750
    spread of, 748–749
    troubleshooting dough, 749
    types of, 748, 751–753
Cooking, 377–380
    combination, 376–377, 392–394
    dry, 376, 382–387
    general guidelines for, 43
    moist, 376, 389–392
    preventing nutrient loss during, 298–299
    techniques for, 376–377
    temperatures for, 341
    time required for, 339
Cooking equipment, 231, 234–239
Cooking line, 221–222
Cooking loss test, 353–354
Cookware, 262, 270–273
Cooling food, 17, 39
    biscuits, 734
    cakes, 762
    cookies, 753
    HACCP requirements for, 32–35
    legumes, 663–664
    safety guidelines for, 43–44

    stocks, 514–515
    yeast breads and rolls, 723
Corn, 627
Corn syrup, 691
Cornstarch, as thickening agent, 517
Corporate training programs, 65
Corporations, 77
Cost control, 350–357
    costing recipes, 354–357
    inventory control, 364–366
    portion control, 350–351
    and purchase of goods, 359–362
    and receiving goods, 362–364
    unit costs, 351–352
    yield percentages, 352–354
Cost per portion, 355
Costing recipes, 354–357
Cottage fries, 443
Coulis, 518
Count (recipes), 337
Counter scale, 225
Course service, 132–133
Courses (meal), 118
Couscous, 627
Cover letters, 98, 99
Covers (expected meals served), 322
Covers (place settings), 127
CPR (cardiopulmonary resuscitation), 11
Crab, 554–555
Crayfish, 555
Cream soups, 530, 689
Creaming method, 731
    cakes, 760
    cookies, 750
    muffins, 738
Credit card check payments, 136
Crème Anglaise, 773
Crêpes, 489
Crisp cookies, 748
Critical control points, 32–35
Croissants, 488, 710
Cross-contamination, 14, 592
Crosshatch, 579
Cross-training, 59
Croutons, 463
Crudités, 479
Cruise ship dining, 144
Crumb (of baked products), 688
Crumbing tables, 134
Crust (of breads), 708
Crustaceans, 553–555
Cryovaced, 642
Cuisine, 69
Culinary scientists, 60
Culture, menu items and, 309
Cumin, 412
Curdle, 437
Curing, 597
    beef, 603
    pork, 597
Custards, 771–773
Custard-style ice cream, 771

Customer base, 189
Customer preferences, 69
Customer satisfaction, assessing, 134
Customer service, 116–125, 127–136
    during and after the meal, 134
    beverage service, 121–125
    calculating and presenting checks,
      134–136
    for carry-out orders, 134
    opening service, 127–130
    serving the order, 131–134
    skills for, 119–121
    staff for, 116–119
Customers with special needs, 116
Cuts (injuries), 5
Cuts (of meat), 255–259
Cutting boards, 263
Cycle menus, 310

D

Daily values of nutrients, 290
Dairy products
    in baking, 689
    storage of, 40
Danish pastries, 444, 771
Danish pastry dough, 711
Dark meat, 571
Deaths, workplace, 207
Deboning, 352
Deck ovens, 238, 682
Decorating spatulas, 460
Deductions, paycheck, 109
Deep-fat fryers, 235
Deep-frying, 385–386
    fish and shellfish, 561
    fruits, 644
    poultry, 580
    vegetables, 655
Deflate, 733
Deglaze, 392
Dehydrated foods, 434, 651
Dehydration, 293
Delegation, 172
Delmonico's Restaurant, 142
Demi-glace, 519
Demitasse, 124
Democratic leadership, 172
Design of facilities, 182, 202–203
Dessert salads, 463
Dessert service, 133
Desserts
    additives for, 698
    Bavarians, 773–774
    cakes, 755–763
    chiffons, 774
    cookies, 748–753
    custards and puddings, 771–773
    frozen, 771
    on menus, 319
    mousses, 774
    pies, 765–769

salads, 463
    storing and serving, 774
Deveining, 553
Diabetes, 294
    and menu food choices, 316
    nutrition needs with, 294
Diagonal cuts, 255, 257
Dicing food, 255
Dietary Guidelines for Americans, 290
Dieting
    menu food choices for, 315–316
    nutritional needs during, 295
    soups for, 528
Digestible nutrients, 663
Digital scales, 336
Dill, 407
Dill seeds, 412
Diminished taste/freshness, 638
Dining environments, 142–149, 151–158
    dish, glass, and utensil choices,
      152, 155
    side work, 151–154
    table setting, 156–158
    types of meal service, 144–149
    types of restaurants, 142–144
Dining room supervisors, 60
Dinner menus, 312
Dips, 481
Direct contamination, 14
Direct labor costs, 173
Direct marketing, 192
Disability, 206
Discrimination, 106, 205, 206
Dish choices, 152, 155
Dishwashers, 239–240
Dishwashing, 45–46
Disposable income, 321
Disposal of food, 44–45
Disposal point, 44
Distractions, in listening, 85
Docking, 721
Dollies, 225
Double pan, 753
Double-entry bookkeeping, 173
Doughnuts, 445
Doughs, 697
    chemical dough conditioners, 708
    cookie, 749
    Danish pastry, 711
    fermentation of, 715, 716
    flaky, 766
    hard lean, 708
    mealy, 766
    mixing, 697–700
    modified straight dough method,
      713, 714
    pie, 765–768
    rolled-in fat, 709–711
    soft medium, 708–709
    straight dough method, 713
    sweet rich, 709
Drained weight, 652
Drawn fish, 544

Dredging, 384, 385, 579
Dressed fish, 544
Dressing, 468
Dried foods
    fruits, 642
    milk solids, 689
    pasta, 616, 619
    vegetables, 652
Drip loss, 546
Drop batter, 731
Drop cookies, 751
Drug use, 181
Drupes, 638
Dry active yeast, 694–695
Dry cooking, 376, 382–387
Dry cure, 457
Dry storage, 38, 41
Drying dishes, 46
Du jour menus, 310
Duck, 570, 577
Dusting, 767
Dutch-process cocoa powder, 697

E

Edible flowers, 466
Edible portion (EP), 352
Education, for foodservice careers,
    62–64
Eels, 557
Efficiency of kitchens, 223
Egg slicers, 264
Egg substitutes, 434
Eggs
    for baking, 693–694
    for breakfasts, 433–441
    composition of, 433
    cooking, 435–441
    forms of, 434
    grades quality of, 433
    internal cooking temperatures
      for, 34
    safety in preparing, 40
    storage of, 40
Eijkman, Christiaan, 293, 294
Elastic, 739
Elastin, 588
Elderly, nutritional needs of, 292
Electricity, for cooking, 234
Electronic ordering, 130
Electronic scales, 269, 336
Emergencies, 9
Emergency procedures, 9–12
Emergency reports and audits, 12
Empathy, 107
Employees
    evaluation of, 181–182
    managing, 179–182
    protection of, 182
    recruiting, 76
    responsibilities of, 104–105
    selection of, 179–180
    supervision of, 180–181

Index

temporary/part-time, 222
training of, 180
Employers, responsibilities of, 105–107
Employment agencies, 96
Employment laws, 205-205
for employee protection, 206–207
for equal opportunities, 205–206
responsibilities under, 207–208
Emulsified shortening, 756
Emulsifiers, 474
En papillote, 559
English muffins, 445
English service, 148
Enriched rice, 625
Entrée service, 133
Entrées, 309, 319
Entrepreneurial careers, 74–78
Entrepreneurs, 74
Entry-level learning, 64–66
Environmental impact statement, 200
Environmental Protection Agency
(EPA), 4, 200
EP (edible portion), 352
EPA. See Environmental Protection
Agency
Equal Employment Opportunities Act
(1972), 206
Equipment
cleaning and maintenance of, 226
cooking, 231, 234–239
for garde manger, 438–459
holding, 242–246
and menu items, 309
for portioning, 351
preparation, 231–240
regulations for, 202
selection of, 226
service, 246
specified in recipes, 339
storage, 227–228
Equipment handling, 185
Ergonomics, 207
Escargot, 556
Escoffier, Auguste, 63
Espresso, 122
Espresso machines, 123–125
Ethics, 107–108
Ethnic menus, 311, 312
Ethylene gas, 639
Evaluations, job, 105–107, 181–182
Evaporation, 376
Excellence, commitment to, 90
Executive chefs, 60
Expenses, 174
Extenders, 319
Extracts, 400

F

Fabricated cut, 589
Facilities management, 182–186
Facility maintenance, 202–203
Factor method (menu pricing), 321

Fair labor practices, 106
Falls, preventing, 4–5
Family, Career and Community
Leaders of America (FCCLA), 90
Family structure, trends in, 69
Family-style restaurants, 142
Family-style service, 146
Fat cap, 588
Fats
for baking, 689–691
in cooking meat, 608
as nutrient, 300
in poultry, 580
reducing, 300, 302
for roux, 521, 522
Fat-soluble vitamins, 284, 285
Fatty fish, 542
Fatty salad dressings, 468–469
FCCLA (Family, Career and Commu-
nity Leaders of America), 90
FDA regulations. See Food and Drug
Administration regulations
Federal Employment Compensation
Act (1993), 207
Fennel seeds, 412
Fermentation, 694
of vegetables, 416
of yeast doughs, 715, 716
Fiber, 280
FIFO (first in, first out), 38
Fillet knife, 254
Fillets, 544
Fillings
pie, 767, 769
sandwich, 484, 491
Fine-dining restaurants, 70, 71, 142
Finger food, 477
Finger sandwiches, 488
Fire extinguishers, 8
Fire safety, 7–9
emergency procedures, 9
fire protection equipment, 8–9
prevention of fires, 7–8
Firm cheeses, 472
First aid, 9–12
for burns, 10–11
for choking, 11
for wounds, 11
First in, first out (FIFO), 38
Fish, 542–547
canned, 547
cooking, 559–563
fresh, 544–546
frozen, 545–546
garnishing, 563–564
market forms of, 542–544
plating, 563
for sandwiches, 491
structure of, 542
Fish stock, 34, 513
Fixed menus, 310
Flakes, 559
Flaky dough, 766

Flambé, 147
Flammable materials, 6, 8
FlashBake ovens, 238
Flat fish, 351, 542
Flat-top ranges, 234, 235
Flatware, 152, 155
Flavor enhancers, 400, 425
Flavor of foods
cooking and, 379–380
in plate composition, 426
salad greens, 464, 465
sensory perception of, 422
Flavored oil, 416
Flavorings, 400, 403–404, 695–696.
(See also Seasonings and
flavorings)
Flexibility, as job skill, 89
Flexibility of menus, 316–317
Floors, regulations for, 202
Florets, 647
Flour
for baking, 688–689
for pastas, 616
for roux, 522
for sauce thickening, 517
Flow of food, 31, 38–45
cooling, 43–44
disposal, 44–45
in HACCP system, 31–32
holding, 42–43
preparation, 42–43
receiving, 38
reheating, 44
serving, 43
storage, 38–42
Flowers, edible, 466
Fluting, 767
Fluting knife, 460
FMPs (Foodservice Management Pro-
fessionals), 171
Foam cakes, 760
Focaccia, 489
Focal point (for booth service), 145
Fold, 446
Fondant, 763
Fondue, 644, 655
Food
contaminated, 14
flow of. See Flow of food
Food, Drug, and Cosmetic Act (1938),
199
Food additives. See Additives
Food allergies, 294, 316, 317
Food and Drug Administration (FDA)
regulations, 199–200
Food and Nutrition Board, National
Academy
of Sciences, 289
Food Code, 200
Food cost percentage, 173
Food courts, 143
Food handling inspections, 185
Food inspections, 176–177

Food mills, 266
Food molds, 267
Food orders
    carry-out, 134
    serving, 131–133
    taking, 129–131
Food preparation, 42
    avoiding contamination during, 42–43
    equipment for, 231–240
    tableside, 146, 147
    time required for, 339
Food processors, 231, 232
Food production businesses, 74
Food Safety and Inspection Service (FSIS),
    198–199
Food thermometers, 34–35
Foodborne illnesses, 14–17
    causes and symptoms of, 15
    outbreak response for, 17
Foodhandler, 26
Foodhandler cleanliness, 26–29
Food-handling hazards, in HACCP system, 32
Foodservice consultants, 75
Foodservice directors, 60
Foodservice industry, 58
    careers in. See Careers in food-service
    trend forecasts for, 69–70
    trends in, 68
Foodservice management, 75–76, 170–177
    effectiveness in, 170–172
    to maintain profitability, 173–177
    structures for, 170
Foodservice Management Professionals (FMPs), 171
Forcemeat, 456
Forecasting, 175
    in foodservice industry, 70
    for profitability, 175
Formulas (recipes), 331
Franchise restaurants, 75
Free enterprise, 78
Free-form loaves, 718
Freezer burn, 226
Freezers, 226, 228, 229
French omelets, 438
French toast, 446
Fresh foods
    cheese, 473
    fruits, 638–639
    pasta, 619
    potatoes, 651
    produce, 41
    vegetables, 647
Frittatas, 439
Frog legs, 556
Frozen foods
    desserts, 771
    fish, 545–546

fruits, 642
meats, 592–593
potatoes, 651
vegetables, 652
yogurt, 771
Frozen storage, 38, 41
Fruit corers, 263
Fruit trays, 480
Fruits, 638–645
    canned, 639
    cooking, 642–645
    dried, 642
    fresh, 638–639
    frozen, 642
    as garnishes, 459–461
    grading of, 638, 642
    on menus, 319
    purchasing, 638
    ripening, 638–639
Frying, 384
    eggs, 437, 438
    poultry, 579, 580
    sandwiches, 497
FSIS. See Food Safety and Inspection Service
Full-service restaurants, 70, 71
Fumet, 513
Fungi, 16
Funnels, 266

G
Game hens, roasting, 577
Garbage disposals, 239
Garde manger, 59, 456–461
    equipment for, 438–459
    garnish preparation, 459–461
    history of, 438
Garde manger brigade, 457
Garlic chives, 408
Garnishes, 314
    for fish and shellfish, 563–564
    fruits, 645
    in plate composition, 426
    preparation of, 459, 461
    for soups, 534–535
    tools for, 460
    vegetables, 657
Gas cooking, 234
Gelatinization, 517
General safety audit, 11
Genetically engineered food, 199
Genoise, 756
Giblets, 571, 574
Ginger, 413
Glassware choices, 152, 155
Glazes, 513–514
Glazing yeast breads and rolls, 723
Gloves, protective, 4, 595
Glucose, 280
Gluten, 688, 739
Glycogen, 293
Goose, 570, 577

Government nutrition guidelines, 289–291
Governmental regulations, 198–201
Grading, 198
    of eggs, 433
    of fruits, 638
    of meats, 591
    of poultry, 572–573
    of shellfish, 549
    of vegetables, 647
Grains, 607, 624–632
    cooking, 630–632
    rice, 624–626
Granola, 444
Granulated sugar, 691
Gravy, 520
Grease fires, extinguishing, 9
Green Beans in Garlic Sauce, 332
Green peppercorns, 401
Greeting customers, 127
Griddles, 235, 239, 386
Grill restaurants, 143
Grilling, 299, 386
    fish and shellfish, 560, 561
    fruits, 643
    meats, 607
    poultry, 579
    sandwiches, 496–498
    vegetables, 653, 655
Gross pay, 109
Guinea, 570

H
HACCP. See Hazard Analysis Critical Control Point
Hair, of food handlers, 26–27
Hair restraint, 26
Hallmarks, recipe, 330
Ham, 432, 434
Hand sanitizer, 27
Hand service, 131
Hand tools, 262–267
Hand-washing, 27–28
Hard cheeses, 471–472
Hard lean doughs, 708
Hard wheat flour, 688
Hard-cooked eggs, 437
Hash, 432, 435
Hash browns, 443
Hazard, 14
Hazard Analysis Critical Control Point (HACCP), 31–36
    critical control points in, 32–35
    flow of food in, 31–32
    food-handling hazards in, 32
    kitchen design in, 33
    structure of, 31
    system monitoring, 35–36
Hazelnuts, 417
Health
    of foodhandlers, 27
    and nutritional needs, 293–295
    for service staff, 120

Index

Heat lamp, 384
Heat sources, for cooking, 231, 234
Heat transfer, 262
Heat treated glass, 155
Heavy lifting, 6, 7
Height, in plate composition, 426
Heimlich maneuver, 11
Hepatitis A, 16
Herbs, 404, 406–410, 466
High-fat cakes, 755
High-heat cooking, 605
Highlighting (menu items), 128
High-ratio layer cake, 758
Holding equipment, 242–246
Holding food, 42–43, 299–300
Hollandaise sauce, 517, 520
Home fries, 443
Hominy, 627–628
Honesty, as job skill, 89
Honey, 693
Hood systems, 8–9
Hors d'oeuvre platters, 477–478,
    481–482
Hors d'oeuvre variés, 477
Hors d'oeuvres, 148
Hospitality industry, 68–72
    foodservice jobs in, 70–72
    trend forecasts for, 69–70
Hosts, 116–117
Hot beverage equipment, 122–125
Hot beverage service, 128
Hot cereals, 443–444, 448–449
Hot peppers, 402
Hot sandwiches, 496–400
Hotel pans, 242, 271
Hotel restaurants, 144
Hotels, careers in, 71
Human resources, 172
Hummus, 478
Hydrogenation, 282

I

Ice cream, 771
Ice makers, 122
Icebox cookies, 751
Illness
    foodborne, 14–17
    in foodhandlers, 29
Immigration and Nationality Act
    (INA), 207
Immigration laws, 207
Immigration Reform and Control Act
    (IRCA), 207
In season, 638
INA (Immigration and Nationality
    Act), 207
Income, 174
Incomplete protein, 282
Independent restaurants, 75
Indirect labor costs, 173
Individually quick frozen (IQF), 552
Infants, nutritional needs of, 292

Information, effective use of, 91
Infrared ovens, 238
Infuse, 124
Ingredient list, 331
Inhibitor, 360
Initiative, 105
Injuries, workplace, 207
Inspections, 198
    of food, 176, 177, 198–199
    of food handling, 185
    of meats, 591
    of poultry, 572–573
    of received goods, 363–364
    for safety, 184
    of shellfish, 549
Instant starches, thickening with, 518
Insurance, business, 78
Insurance, purpose and types of, 186
International soups, 531–532
Internet, as job resource, 96
Internships, 66
Interstate commerce, 205
Interviews. See Job interviews
Inventory, 175, 353
Inventory control, 175, 176, 364–366
Invoices, 225, 363
IQF (individually quick frozen), 552
IRCA (Immigration Reform and Con-
    trol Act), 207
Irradiation, 199, 597
    beef, 603
    pork, 597
Islands, kitchen, 221
Issuing (foods), 359, 365–366
Italian meringue, 763

J

Jewelry, removing, 26
Job applications, 96, 97
Job descriptions, 179
Job interviews, 97, 98, 100–101, 179–180
Job leads, 96
Job offers, responding to, 102
Job portfolios, 96
Job rotation, 66
Job searches, 94–102
    applying for jobs, 96–99
    interviews, 98, 100–101
    job offer responses, 102
    resources for, 94–96
Jobs. See Careers in foodservice
Journeymen, 95
Juicers, 233
Julienne, 259

K

Kaiser rolls, 489
Kale, 465
Ketchup, 416
Kettles, 237
Keywords, 98
Kind (poultry), 570

Kitchen brigade system, 58–59, 63
Kitchen equipment, safety with, 7
Kitchen managers, 60
Kitchen shears, 263
Kitchens
    cleanliness of, 18–19
    HACCP and design of, 33
    professional. See Professional
        kitchens
    sanitizers for, 44
Knives, 252–260, 460
    construction of, 252–253
    cuts with, 255–259
    gripping, 255
    sharpening and trueing, 259, 260
    skills in using, 254–259
    storing, 260
    types of, 253, 254

L

Labor costs, 173
Labor laws, 207
Labor unions, 106
Lacerations, 11
Lacto-ovo vegetarian, 293
Lacto-vegetarian, 293
Ladles, 269
Lamb, 597–599
Larding, 588
Latticework, 765
Laws, 205. (See also Employment laws)
Leach, 298
Leadership, 90
    by foodservice managers, 172
    skills for, 90–92
Leadership organizations, 90–91
Lean fish, 542
Leavening, 706
Leavening agents, 694
    for baking, 694–695
    for quick breads, 739–740
Legumes, 280, 660–664
    cooking, 663
    cooling, 663–664
    plating, 664
    purchasing and storing, 660
    storing, 664
    types of, 661–662
Lemon, 402
Lemongrass, 408
Lentil Stuffed Zucchini, 665
Lesser, 638
Let down (dough), 715
Letters of request, 98
Lettuces, 464
Licensing, 78
Lifestyle, nutritional needs and, 293
Light meat, 234, 571
Lighting, sensory perception of, 421
Lighting centerpieces, 158
Lind, James, 293, 294
Line cooks, 59

Linens, table, 158
Liners, for canapés, 477
Lipoproteins, 282
Liquid measures, 269
Liquids
    for baking, 689
    for sauces, 517
    for stocks, 510
Listening skills, 85
Loaf breads, 739–740
Loaf pans, 273
Lobsters, 553
Local regulations, 201
Location of business, 189
Lockout/tagout, 7
Log, 36
Loss prevention, 184
Lowboy, 226
Low-fat cakes, 755
Low-fat diets, menu food choices for, 315–316
Low-heat cooking, 605
Lug, 638
Lunch menus, 311–312

M

Macrobiotics, 293
Maillard reactions, 607
Main-course salads, 463
Maintenance
    in facilities management, 186
    of kitchen equipment, 7
Making change, 85
Management
    of employees, 179–182
    of facilities, 182–186
    foodservice, 170–177
Management careers, 59–61
Mandoline, 653
Manual dishwashing, 45
Maple syrup, 691
Marbling, 588
Margarine, for baking, 690–691
Marinades, 410
Marinara sauce, 520
Marinated vegetable, 481
Marjoram, 408
Market form, 571
Market segment, 189
Marketing, 77, 188–192
    advertising, 191–192
    analyzing marketplace, 188
    with atmosphere, 191
    direct, 192
    marketing plan, 191
    positioning, 190–191
    public relations, 191
    strategies for, 188–90
Marketing plan, 191
Marketplace, 188
Markup-on-cost method (menu pricing), 322

Masa harina, 627
Mass marketing, 189
Master recipes, 332
    American Grinders, 493
    Apple Wheat Germ Cake, 692
    Béchamel Sauce, 522
    Beef Consommé, 533
    Lentil Stuffed Zucchini, 665
    Monte Cristo Cheese
    Sandwiches, 498
    Omelet with Cheese, 436
    Pancakes with Maple Syrup, 447
    Polenta, 628
    Soft Rolls, 720
    Southern Vegetable Soup, 340
    Sweet and Spicy Broccoli, 656
    Vanilla Chiffon Genoise, 757
Master work schedule, 181
Material safety date sheet (MSDS), 201
Math skills, 84–85, 680–681
Maturity, 571
Mayonnaise, 489–490
McDonald's®, 65
Meal planning, 289–296
    government guidelines for, 289–291
    nutritional needs of specific
    groups, 291–296
Meal service, types of, 144–149
Meal-based menus, 310
Mealy dough, 766
Mealy potatoes, 650
Measuring and measurements, 84
    abbreviations used in, 336
    bakeshops, 678–681
    equipment for, 262, 268–269
    equivalents for, 337
    scaling, 714
Measuring spoons, 269
Meat tenderizer, 265
Meats, 588–593
    beef, 601–603
    for breakfasts, 432, 434–435
    cooking, 434–435, 605–610
    cross-contamination from, 592
    cuts of, 588–590, 595–603
    handling and storage of, 591–593
    inspection and grading of, 591
    internal cooking temperatures
    for, 34
    lamb, 597–599
    pork, 595–597
    purchasing, 590
    for sandwiches, 491
    storage of, 39–40, 599
    structure of, 588
    tenderizing, 589
    veal, 599–600
Melon ballers, 264, 460
Mentors, 180
Menu board, 318
Menus, 308–312
    categories of items on, 318–319
    design facilitating, 182

FDA regulation of, 199, 200
    importance of, 308
    influences on, 308–310
    planning principles for, 314–317
    pricing items on, 321–324
    selling, 128–129
    style and design of, 317–318
    types of, 310–312
Meringue, 758
Mesclun, 466
Metric system, 335
Microwave cooking, 234, 299
Microwave ovens, 236, 239
Military foodservice training pro-
    grams, 65
Milk, in baking, 689
Mincing food, 255, 259
Minerals, 284–286
Minimum internal temperature, 33
Minimum wage, 106, 207
Mint, 408
Mirepoix, 510
Mise en place, 222–223
Mixers, 231, 232, 681
Modern American plated service,
    144–145
Modified starch, 769
Modified straight dough method,
    713, 714
Moist baking, 559
Moist cooking, 376, 389–392
Molasses, 691
Molded cookies, 751
Molds (fungus), 16, 663
Molds (shapes), 683, 686
Mollusks, 550–553
Money, handling, 135–136
Monosodium glutamate (MSG),
    402–403
Monounsaturated fats, 283
Monte Cristo, 497, 498
Motel restaurants, 144
Mother sauces, 519–522
Mousses, 774
MSDS (material safety date sheet), 201
MSG. See Monosodium glutamate
Muffin pans, 273
Muffins, 445, 737–738, 741–742
Muscle fibers, 588
Musculoskeletal disorders, 207
Mussels, 551, 552
Mustard seeds, 413
Mustards, 416
Mutton, 597
MyPyramid, 290, 291

N

Napkins, folding, 152–154
National Environmental Policy Act
    (NEPA), 200
Neighborhood eating
    establishments, 143

Index

NEPA. *See* National Environmental Policy Act
Nerve endings, 423
Net pay, 109
Net weight, 652
Networking, 94–95
Noncommercial operation, 70
Nonedible items, 360
Nonperishable condiments, 152
Nonverbal communication, 121
Nourishing elements, 510
Nutmeg, 413
Nutrient-dense food, 291
Nutrients, 280–287
    carbohydrates, 280
    changed by cooking, 377
    cholesterol, 282, 283
    fats, 282–285
    fiber, 280, 281
    in fruits, 638
    in grains, 627
    in legumes, 660
    in meats, 588
    minerals, 284–286
    in nuts, 418
    in pasta, 616
    in poultry, 571
    preventing loss of, 298–302
    proteins, 281–282
    in quick breads, 741
    in salad greens, 464
    in sandwiches, 489
    and storage of foods, 365
    vitamins, 283–285
    water, 286
Nutrition
    meal planning, 289–296
    and menu food choices, 315
    preventing nutrient loss, 298–302
Nutrition Labeling and Education Act (1990), 199, 289, 290
Nutrition labels, 199, 200, 289–290
Nuts, 417–419, 697, 699

O

Oat berries, 627
Oats, 627
Oblique cuts, 255
Occupational back support, 4
Occupational Safety and Health Act, 182
Occupational Safety and Health Administration (OSHA), 4, 182, 201
Off-site catering, 72
Oils, 690
    for baking, 690
    commonly-used, 301
    flavored, 416
    as nutrient, 300
    and sensory perception of foods, 425
Omelet with Cheese, 436
Omelets, 436–440

One-stage method, 749
Onions, 402
On-site catering, 72
On-the-job training programs, 66, 95
Open-burner ranges, 234, 235, 239
Open-ended questions (job interviews), 179
Open-face sandwiches, 488, 497, 499
Opening restaurants, 183
Opening service, 127–130
Open-market buying, 361
Open-spit roasting, 383
Operating costs, 321
Oregano, 408
Orientation, employee, 172
OSHA. *See* Occupational Safety and Health Administration
Oven spring, 722
Ovens, 237–239, 682, 684
Overhead costs, 75
Overhead warmers, 243
Overstaffing, 171
Overtime pay, 108
Ovo-vegetarian, 293
Oysters, 550
Oysters Rockefeller, 561

P

Packaging, of yeast breads and rolls, 724
Packing medium, 652
Paella, 410
Pan loaves, 718
Pancakes, 445–447
Pancakes with Maple Syrup, 447
Pan-frying, 384
    fish and shellfish, 560–561
    meats, 608–609
    poultry, 580
Panning dough, 718
Pans, 272–273, 683, 684, 686
Pantry chefs, 59. (*See also* Garde manger)
Paprika, 413
Parasites, 16
Parboiling, 390
    rice, 625
    vegetables, 655
Parfaits, 774
Paring, 254
Paring knife, 254, 460
Parmentier, Antoine, 651
Parsley, 408
Parstock, 364
Partnerships, 74, 77
Pasta, 616–622
    cooking, 619–621, 631
    origin of, 619
    purchasing and storing, 616, 619
    quality characteristics of, 616
    serving, 622
    shapes of, 617–618

    stuffing, 621–622
    types of, 616
Pasteurization, 40, 434
Pastrami, 499
Pastries, 444
Pastry bags, 686
Pastry chefs, 59
Pastry flour, 689
Pastry shops, careers in, 72
Pastry tools, 267, 685
Pathogens, 14, 15
Patronage, 119
Pay, 108–110
Peanuts, 417
Pecans, 417
Peel (board), 706
Pepper, 401–402, 410, 413
Peppercorns, 413
Percentages, 680
    working with, 84–85, 323
    yield, 352–354
Performance evaluations, 106–107
Periodic-ordering method, 365
Perishable items, 41, 360
Perpetual inventory, 364
Personal health
    of foodhandlers, 27
    for service staff, 120
Personal hygiene, 17
    of foodhandlers, 26
    for service staff, 119–120
Personal injuries, 4–7
Personal protective clothing, 4
Pest management, 20
Pesticides, 19
Pesto, 490
pH scale, 38, 203
Phyllo, 489
Physical hazards, 20
Physical inventory, 364
Phytochemicals, 294–295
Pickled condiments, 416
Pie à la mode, 769
Pie dividers, 267
Pie dough, 765–768
Pies, 765–769
    baking, 769
    fillings for, 767, 769
    pie dough, 765–768
    storing and serving, 769
Pigeon, 570
Pigment, 378
Pilaf method, 631
Pilot light, 234
Pine nuts, 418
Pistachios, 418
Pita, 489
Pith, lemon, 402
Pizza cutters, 264
Plate composition, 425–426
Platform scale, 225
Plating, 314–315
    of breakfast meats, 435

of cold cereals, 449
of cold sandwiches, 499–500
of eggs, 441
of fish and shellfish, 563
of French toast, 446
of fruits, 645
of hot cereals, 448–449
of hot sandwiches, 497, 499
of legumes, 664
of pancakes and waffles, 446
of pasta, 622
of poultry dishes, 582
of vegetables, 657
Poaching foods, 299, 391
    eggs, 437
    fruits, 645
    poultry, 580
    vegetables, 657
Point-of-sale system, 130
Polenta, 627, 628
Polyunsaturated fats, 283, 285
Poppy seeds, 418
Pork, 595–597
Porous, 433
Portion control, 174, 350–351
Portion scales, 225, 269, 336
Portion size, 331
Portion size conversion, 338–339
Positioning, 190–191
Positive reinforcement, 180
Potatoes, 650–651
    for breakfasts, 445, 448
    green, 651
Potency, 740
Poultry, 570–575
    classifications of, 570
    cooking, 577, 579–582
    cutting up, 572–573
    evaluating, 571
    handling and storage of, 575
    inspection and grading of, 572–573
    maturity and tenderness of, 571
    plating, 582
    quality of, 572
    for sandwiches, 491
    storage of, 39–40
    stuffings for, 582
    thawing, 573
    trussing, 574
Pound cakes, 755
Pour batters, 731
Preferement, 713, 714
Pregnancy, nutritional needs during, 291
Prep cooks, 59
Preparation equipment, 231–233
Preparation procedure, 331. (See also
    Food preparation)
Prepared mustard, 416
Preprocessed legumes, 660
Preserved vegetables, 651
Preset menus, 158
Presetting food items, 133
Pressure steamers, 237

Pressure-frying, 580
Pricing, menu, 309, 321–324
Primal cut, 589
Printed menus, 318
Prioritizing, 91
Prix fixe menu, 310
Probation, 107
Processed cheese, 474
Processing, 40, 597
Produce, 41. (See also Fruits;
    Vegetables)
Product name, 331
Product yield, 352
Production careers, 38–39
Production schedule, 181
Production space, 183
Professional kitchens
    cooking equipment, 231, 234–239
    holding equipment, 242–246
    preparation equipment, 231–233
    receiving area, 225–229
    service equipment, 246
Professional organizations, 91, 95
Profit and loss statements, 175
Profitability, 173–177
Profits, 70, 74
Promotions, 191
Proofing cabinets, 682
Proofing dough, 719
Proofing/holding cabinets, 242, 243
Proportion, of plated foods, 315
Prosciutto, 479
Protective clothing, 26
    for foodhandlers, 26
    for safety, 4
    when working with meat, 595
Proteins, 281, 432–441
Psychological pricing method, 323
Public relations, 191
Publicity, 191
Puddings, 771–773
PUFI mark, 549
Pullman loaf, 488
Pulse, 660
Pumpkin seeds, 418
Punching dough, 716–717
Puncture wound, 11
Purchase orders, 225, 363
Purchase quantities, determining,
    360, 361
Purchasers, 61
Purchasing goods, 359–362
Purchasing procedures, 176
Purée soups, 529–530
Purées, 302

Q

Q factor, 355
Quality, commitment to, 90
Quality control, for standardized reci-
    pes, 330
Quantity, 330

Quenelle, 459
Quiches, 439
Quick breads, 445
    biscuit method for, 731–734
    loaf breads, 739–740
    methods for making, 730–731
    muffin method, 737–738, 741–742
    types of, 730
Quick soak, 663
Quick-rise dry yeast, 695
Quick-service breakfasts, 443
Quick-service restaurants, 70, 143

R

Radiation, 234
Radicchio, 466
Raft, 528
Ramekin, 439
Range of motion, 223
Ranges, 234, 235, 239
Rare, 610
Raw vegans, 293
Raw yield tests, 353
RDAs (Recommended Dietary Allow-
    ances), 289
Reading skills, 88
Ready-made breads, 443–445
Ready-to-cook poultry, 571
Receiving area, 225–229
Receiving goods, 38, 362–364
Receiving record, 225
Receptors, 421
Recipe conversion, 335, 337–342
Recipe costing form, 354–356
Recipes, 330. (See also Master recipes)
    costing, 354–357
    errors in, 342
    standardized, 330–333, 335–342,
    350–351
Recommended Dietary Allowances
    (RDAs), 289
Recondition, 239
Record keeping
    for HACCP, 35–36
    for profitability, 173
    for small businesses, 78
Recovery time, 386
Recycling, 44–45
Red pepper, 401
Reductions, 391, 513, 518
Reel ovens, 684
Refrigerated storage, 38, 41
Refrigerators, 226, 227, 229
Regulations, 198
    for facility maintenance, 202–203
    governmental, 198–201
Reheating food, 44
Rehydration, 642
Reliability, as job skill, 89
Relish trays, 481
Relishes, 416, 520
Render, 577

Index

Repairs, in facilities management, 186
Repetitive stress injury, 106
Reputation, 116
Requisition, 365
Research chefs, 60
Reservations, 116
Resorts, careers in, 71
Resources, 91
    effective use of, 91
    managing, 171–172
Responsibility, as job skill, 88
Restaurant managers, 60–61, 607
Restaurants
    careers in, 70–71
    entrepreneurial opportunities in, 75
    types of, 142–144
Résumés, 96–98
Rice, 624–626
    cooking, 630–632
    risotto, 631–632
Rind, cheese, 472
Rings, bakeshop, 686
Ripening, 638
    fruits, 638–639
    hard cheeses, 471–472
    soft cheeses, 473, 474
    vegetables, 647
Risk management, 185
Risotto, 624, 631–632
Risotto method, 631
Risotto Milanese, 410
Rivet, 252
Roasting, 383
    meats, 606
    open-spit, 383
    poultry, 577
Roasting pans, 271
Roll cut, 255
Rolled cookies, 751, 752
Rolled fancy sandwiches, 478
Rolled-in fat yeast dough, 709–710
Rolling pins, 267
Rolls
    for sandwiches, 489
    yeast rolls, 706–724
Rondelle cuts, 255, 257
Room service, 144
Rosemary, 409
Rotating stock, 365
Round fish, 542
Rounding dough, 717–718
Roux, 519, 521, 523–525
Rumaki, 503
Russian service, 148

S

Sachet, 406
Safety, 4–12, 256
    emergency procedures, 9–12
    facilities management for, 184–185
    fire safety, 7–9

and flow of food, 38–45
and foodhandler cleanliness, 26–29
HACCP system for, 31–36
with kitchen equipment, 7
with knives, 259–260
personal injuries, 4–7
personal protective clothing, 4
in professional kitchens, 229
training and certification for, 201
working conditions for, 106
Saffron, 412
Sage, 409
Salad dressings, 468–469
Salad sandwiches, 499
Salad service, 133
Salads, 463–468
    green, 464–468
    on menus, 318–319
    structure and arrangement of, 463
    types of, 463
Salamanders, 234, 238
Sales, profit vs., 176
Sales cycle, 360
Sales representatives, 61
Salmonella, 575
Salsas, 416, 520
Salt, 400–410, 695
Salt and pepper shakers, refilling, 151
Sandwiches, 488–494
American Grinders, 493
    breads for, 488–489
    cold, 499–500
    fillings for, 484, 491
    history of, 497
    as hors d'oeuvres, 478
    hot, 496–400
    on menus, 319
    preparing quantities of, 492
    spreads for, 488–490
    types of, 488
Sanitary, 14
Sanitation, 14–20
    with cheese handling, 494
    chemical hazards, 17–19
    and contamination, 14–17
    facilities management for, 185
    and flow of food, 38–45
    and foodhandler cleanliness, 26–29
    HACCP system for, 31–36
    of kitchens, 18–19
    of knives, 260
    of pastry bags, 686
    physical hazards, 20
    of preparation equipment, 231
    with raw fish/shellfish, 559
Sanitizers, kitchen, 44
Saturated fats, 283
Sauce espagnole, 519
Saucepans, 270
Saucepots, 270
Sauces, 416, 517–525
    ingredients for, 517–518
    for meats, 608

mother, 519–522
roux for, 521, 523–525
storage of, 519
thickening, 517–518
Sauerkraut, 491
Sausage, 432, 435
Sauté pans, 270
Sautéing, 383
    fish and shellfish, 560–561
    fruits, 644
    meats, 608–609
    poultry, 580, 581
    vegetables, 655
Savory, 409, 422
Scalds, preventing, 5–6
Scales, 225, 269, 336, 679, 680
Scaling, 679, 714, 761
Scallops, 552–553
Scones, 445
Scoops, 351
Scoring, 461
Scouring dishes, 45
Scrambled eggs, 437, 439
Scrubbing dishes, 45
Seafood, 556–557. (*See also* Fish;
    Shellfish)
    for sandwiches, 491
    storage of, 39
Seams (dough), 718
Searing, 383, 579
Season, 438
Seasonal cuisine, 68
Seasonings, defined, 400
Seasonings and flavorings, 400–404
    adding flavorings, 403–404
    condiments, 416
    herbs, 406–410
    lemon, 402
    for meats, 607–609
    monosodium glutamate, 402–403
    nuts and seeds, 417–419
    onion, 402
    pepper, 401–402
    salt, 400–410
    for sauces, 517
    sensory evaluation of, 424–426
    and sensory perception, 421–424
    spices, 410–414
    when to season, 403
Sections, service, 117–118
Seeds, 404, 411–413, 417–419
Self-service meals, 149
Semi-à la carte menu, 310
Semiperishable foods, 360
Semisoft cheeses, 472–473
Semolina flour, 616
Sensory evaluation of meals, 424–426
Sensory perception, 421–424, 480
Sensory properties, 421
Separate-course salads, 463
Serrated, 254
Servers, 117–118
Service careers, 58

Service equipment, 246
Service stations, 118
Serviettes, 155
Serving food, 43
    correct hand for, 145
    customer orders, 131–134
    guidelines for, 43
    types of meal service, 144–149
Sesame seeds, 418
Sexual harassment, 206
Shape, in plate composition, 426
Shaping dough, 718
Sharp tools, safety guidelines for, 5
Sheet pans, 686
Sheeters, 681–682
Shelf life, 38
Shellfish, 549–555
    cooking, 559–563
    crustaceans, 553–555
    garnishing, 563–564
    inspection and grading of, 549
    mollusks, 550–553
    plating, 563
    structure of, 549
Shelving units, 228, 229
Sherbet, 771
Shirred eggs, 439, 440
Shocking, 11, 390
Shoes, protective, 4
Shortening, 689
Shrimp, 553–554
Shrinkage, 341, 354
Shucked, 39
Side orders, 446
Side work, 151–154
Simmering, 390–391
    eggs, 440–441
    fruits, 645
    legumes, 663
    poultry, 580
    vegetables, 655
Single-food hors d'oeuvre, 477
Single-source buying, 361
Sinks, commercial, 239
Skillets, 271
Skills
    and available menu items, 309
    basic, 84–88
    for customer service, 119–121
    leadership, 90–92
    teamwork as, 89, 107
SkillsUSA, 90–91
Skimmers, 265
Slashing dough, 721
Sleeper, 553
Slicers (equipment), 231, 232
Slicers (knives), 234
Slicing, 255
Slips, preventing, 4–5
Small-business career opportunities, 74–78
Smallwares, 262–274
    for bakeshops, 684–686

cleaning and sanitation of, 274
cookware, 262, 270–273
hand tools, 262–267
measuring equipment, 268–269
Smoking foods, 382–383, 597
Smoking point, 300, 580
Soft cheeses, 473–474
Soft cookies, 748
Soft drink machines, 122
Soft drinks, carbonation in, 123
Soft medium dough, 708–709
Soft Rolls, 720
Soft wheat flour, 688
Solanine, 650, 651
Sole proprietorships, 77
Solid waste, 200
Sorbet, 771
Soufflé, 434, 438
Soufflé omelets, 438, 439
Soup plates, 622
Soup service, 133
Soups, 527–535
    clear, 527–529
    international, 531–532
    on menus, 318
    presentation of, 532, 534–535
    specialty, 531
    storage of, 535
    thick, 529–530
    vegetable, 529
Sous chefs, 59
Southern Vegetable Soup, 340
Spatulas, 265, 460
Speaking skills, 85–86
Specialty cheeses, 474–475
Specialty soups, 531
Specifications, 350, 360, 361
Spice rubs, 607
Spices, 401, 404, 410–414, 696
Spinach, 464
Spoken menu, 318
Sponge cakes, 756, 760
Sponge method, 713, 716
Spoons, 265
Spreads, 488–490, 748
Spring scales, 336
Springform pan, 686
Sprinkler systems, 8–9
Squab, roasting, 577
Squid, 556
Stack ovens, 682
Stainless steel, 252
Staling, 689, 723, 724
Standardized accounting practices, 173
Standardized recipes, 330–333
    converting, 337–342
    for cost control, 350–351
    measurements in, 335–337
    parts of, 331, 333
Standards, 198
    of conduct, 180–181
    for facility maintenance, 202–203
    industry, 198

Starches
    in pasta, 622
    for sauce thickening, 518
Starter, bread, 706
State regulations, 201
Station cooks, 59
Stations, service, 117–118
Steak (beef), 432, 435
Steak (fish), 544
Steak sauce, 416
Steam
    baking with, 722
    as leavening agent, 694
Steam tables, 242, 243
Steamers, 236–237
Steaming foods, 299, 391–392
    fish and shellfish, 560
    grains, 630–631
    vegetables, 655
Steam-jacketed kettles, 237
Stewing, 393, 394, 609
Stimuli, 421
Stir-frying, 299, 383–384
Stirred custard, 772
Stockpots, 270
Stocks, 510–515
    brown, 511, 513
    commercial bases, 510
    cooling and storing, 514–515
    elements of, 510
    fish, 513
    glazes, 513–514
    vegetable, 513
    white, 511, 512
Storage, 38–42
    of cakes, 762
    of cheese, 475
    of clean dishes, 46
    of condiments, 416
    of desserts, 774
    of fish, 545, 546
    of fruits, 638–639, 642
    of herbs, 409–410
    of knives, 260
    of legumes, 660, 664
    of meats, 591–593, 599
    of nuts and seeds, 418
    of pasta, 616, 619
    of pies, 769
    of poultry, 575
    preventing nutrient loss during, 299–300
    in professional kitchens, 225–229
    of received goods, 365
    of rice, 625
    of sauces, 519
    of shellfish, 550–555
    of soups, 535
    of stocks, 514–515
    of vegetables, 647, 650, 651
    of yeast breads and rolls, 724
Straight dough method, 713
Strainers, 266

Strains, preventing, 6
Streusel, 741
Stuffing pasta, 621–622
Stuffings, 582
Sugar bowls, refilling, 152
Sugars, for baking, 691
Sundae, 774
Sunflower seeds, 418
Superfine sugar, 691
Surimi, 556
Sushi, 559
Sweating, 528
Swedish meatballs, 503
Sweet and Spicy Broccoli, 656
Sweet rich doughs, 709
Sweeteners, for baking, 691, 693
Swiss meringue, 763

T

Table d'hôte menu, 310
Table setting, 156–158
Table tent menus, 318
Tablecloths, changing, 157
Tableside food preparation, 146, 147
Tableware choices, 152, 155
Tang, 252
Tank system (soft drinks), 122
Target customers, menu planning for, 308
Target market, 189
Tarragon, 409
Tart pans, 686
Tartar sauce, 563
Taste buds, 422
Tastes, sensory perception of, 422
Tea-making equipment, 124–125
Teamwork
    as job skill, 89, 107
    as service staff skill, 120
Technology, effective use of, 92
Teenagers, nutritional needs of, 292
Telephone calls, in job search, 96
Telephone skills, 86
Temperature
    cooking, for converted recipes, 341
    danger zone for holding foods, 33–34
    internal, 34
    in plate composition, 426
    sensory evaluation of, 424–425
    thermometers, 34–35
Texture
    cooking and, 377–378
    in plate composition, 426
    sensory evaluation of, 424–425
    sensory perception of, 423–424
Thawing foods
    fish, 546
    poultry, 573
Theme restaurants, 142
Thermometers, 225
Thick soups, 529–530

Thickening
    sauces, 517–518
    science of, 518
Thickening agent, 517
Thyme, 409
Tilting skillets, 236
Time management, 171, 223
Tips, 109, 135, 136
Toast, for breakfasts, 445
Tomato corers, 263
Tomato sauce, 519
Tomatoes, 515
Tongs, 265
Tools
    for baking and pastry, 685
    for garnishes, 460
    hand, 262–267
    for portioning, 351
Torpedo roll, 489
Tortillas, 489
Total weight as served, 354
Total yield recipe conversion method, 337–338
Tournée, 461
Tournée knife, 254, 460, 461
Toxin, 14
Trace minerals, 285
Trade publications, 95
Traffic paths, 183
Translucent, 422
Tray service, 131
Tray stands, 131–132
Trayline service, 143
Trends, 68
    in eating, menu items and, 309–310
    investigating, 190
Trichinosis, 609
Trim, 352
Trim loss, 353
Triple-decker sandwiches, 488
Trueing, 260
Trunnion kettles, 237
Trussing poultry, 574, 575
Truth-in-menu guideline, 315, 316
Tube pans, 273
Tubers, 647
Tuile, 751
Tunnels, 739
Turbinado sugar, 691
Turkey, 570
    carving, 578
    roasting, 577
Turnover rate, 182–183
240 Factor, 715

U

Underliner, 133
Uniforms, 119
Unit costs, 351–352
United States Department of Agriculture (USDA), 198–199, 290
Univalves, 550

Upselling, 129
USDA. *See* United States Department of Agriculture
Utensil choices, 152, 155

V

Vacuum packed, 546
Vanilla Chiffon Genoise, 757
Variety, on menus, 314
Veal, 599–600
Vegans, 293
Vegetable brushes, 267
Vegetable peelers, 263, 460
Vegetable purées, 490, 518
Vegetable soups, 529
Vegetable stock, 513
Vegetables, 647–657
    canned, 651–652
    classifications of, 647–649
    cooking, 652–653, 655, 657
    dried, 652
    fresh, 647
    frozen, 652
    frozen foods, 652
    as garnishes, 459–461
    garnishing, 657
    grading of, 647
    plating, 657
    preserved, 651
    purchasing and storing, 647, 650, 651
    ripening, 647
    salad greens, 464–468
Vegetarians, 293
Veined cheese, 472
Velouté, 519–520
Vending machines, 143
Vendors, 61, 362
Verbal communication, 120, 121
Verification (HACCP system), 36
Vichyssoise, 531
Vinaigrettes, 468
Vinegar, 416
Violations, 198
Viruses, 16
Vitamins, 285
    fat-soluble, 284
    water-soluble, 283, 284
Volume, 262
Volume measures, 269, 336

W

Waffle irons, 446
Waffles, 445–446
Wage laws, 207
Wages, 108–110
Walls, 202, 741
Walnuts, 418
Warped, 753
Washing dough, 719, 721, 723

Waste control, 174–175, 366
Waste disposal, 44–45
Water
    in baking, 689
    and sensory perception of foods,
        425
Water service, 128, 286
Waters, Alice, 68
Water-soluble vitamins, 283, 284
Waxy potato, 650
Weighing, 84
Weight, 262, 335, 336
Weight loss, nutritional needs
        during, 295
Wet cure, 457
Wheat, 627, 629–630
Wheat flour, 688–689
Whetstone, 259
Whey, 471
Whisks, 264
White pepper, 401
White rice, 625
White stock, 511, 512
Wiley, Harvey W., 200
Woks, 271, 383
Work, trends in, 69
Work areas, layout of, 183
Work ethic, 88–90
Work flow, 220–223
Work schedules, 181
Work sections, 220, 221
Work simplification, 222
Work stations, 220
Work tables, 233
Workers' compensation, 106, 207
Workplace injuries/deaths, 207
Wounds
    first aid for, 11
    of foodhandlers, 29
Wraps, 488
Writing skills, 87–88

Yeast, 694–695
Yeast breads and rolls, 706–724
    baking, 721–723
    cooling, 723
    dough preparation, 713–714
    glazing, 723
    hard lean doughs, 708
    origin of yeast doughs, 709
    packaging, 724
    rolled-in fat doughs, 709–711
    soft medium and rolls, 708–709
    stages of making dough,
        714–719, 721
    staling prevention, 723, 724
    storage, 724
    sweet rich doughs, 709
    troubleshooting, 724
    yeast dough ingredients, 706–707
Yield, 331, 352

Yield grade (meats), 591
Yield percentages, 352–354
Yield tests, 352, 361–362
Yield weight, 353
Yogurt, frozen, 771

Z

Zest, 402
Zesters, 264, 460
Zoning, 78

Photo Credits

Cover: Ed-Imaging; **1** Masterfile; **2-3** Stewart Cohen/Jupiter Images; **6** Getty Images; **7** McGraw-Hill Companies; **9** Renee Comet Photography, Inc./FoodStock; **10** Alamy; Alex Bartel/Photo Researchers, Inc.; Barry Slaven/The Medical File/Peter Arnold Inc.; Scott Camazine/Alamy; **11** Stockbyte/Alamy; **16** Jupiter Images; **18** Tony Freeman/PhotoEdit; **24-25** Ingram Publishing/SuperStock; **27** Jeff Greenberg/ PhotoEdit; **35** Roderick Chen/First Light/Getty Images; **42** Newhouse News Service/ Landov; **46** Jupiter Images; **56-57, 58, 61** Jupiter Images; **62** Corbis/Jupiter Images; **64** Tetra Images/ Jupiter Images; **65** Eric Futran/Jupiter Images; **68** Jupiter Images; **69** Rick Lew/Jupiter Images; **71** Knauer/Johnston/Jupiter Images; **82-83** Comstock Images/Jupiter Images; **86, 89** Getty Images; **94** Jim Sugar/CORBIS; **101** Edward Bock/CORBIS; **105** dbimages/Alamy; **107** Getty Images; **114-115** Getty Images; **117** Comstock/Jupiter Images; **118** Getty Images; **121** Stockfood; **122** CGM/ PhotoEdit; **124, 129, 130** Getty Images; **132** McGraw-Hill Companies; **140-141** CGM/PhotoEdit; **144** Jupiter Images; **147** Ben Fink/Jupiter Images; **148** McGraw-Hill Companies; **151** Jupiter Images; **157** McGraw-Hill Companies; **166-167** Westend61/Alamy;**168-169** Masterfile; **172** Jupiter Images/ BananaStock/Alamy; **174** ImageShop/Corbis; **175** Enigman/Alamy; **180** Nick White/Getty Images; **201** Michael Newman/PhotoEdit; **202** Realistic Reflections/Getty Images; **206** Stefano Scatà/Grand Tour/Corbis; **208** Jeff Greenberg/PhotoEdit; **216-217** Tina Hager/White, House/Handout/Reuters/Corbis; **218-219** Lew Robertson/Getty Images; **222** Corbis; **226** Lon C. Diehl/PhotoEdit; **233** The Edlund Co.; **235** Vulcan-Hart; **244** Cambro Manufacturing Company; **250-251** Owen Franken/Corbis; **280** Sam Stowell/Getty Images; **281** Cephas Picture Library/Alamy; **292** Todd Wright/Getty Images; **298** Masterfile; **306-307** James Carman/PhotoLibrary; **308** CGM/Photo Edit; **317** PhotoDisc; **321** CGM/Photo Edit; **328-329** Masterfile; **335** Michael Deuson/Jupiter Images; **336** Clive Streeter/ Getty Images; **337** Masterfile; **342** Luca Trovato/Getty Images; **348-349** McGraw-Hill Companies; **359** IPS Co., Ltd./Beateworks/Corbis; **374-375** Quentin Bacon/Getty Images; **376** Gentl and Hyers/ Jupiter Images; **382** Matt Armendariz/Jupiter Images; **389** McGraw-Hill Companies; **390** Studio Bonisolli-StockFood Munich/StockFood; **391** Sanderson, Dean-StockFood Munich/StockFood; **392** McGraw-Hill Companies; **398-399** Sophie Broadbridge/Getty Images; **400** Lew Robertson/Corbis; **402** Maximilian Stock–StockFood Munich/StockFood; **403** David Loftus–StockFood Munich/ StockFood; **407** Ted Mishima; **422** Food Image Source/O'Gara/Bissell/StockFood; **425** Thomas Barwick/Getty Images; **430-431** Sid Avery/StockFood; **432** Jupiter Images; **438** Kob–StockFood Munich/ StockFood; **439** McGraw-Hill Companies; **440** McGraw-Hill Companies; **444** Lannretonne–StockFood Munich/StockFood; **448** James & James Photography/Stockfood; **454-455** David Copeman/ Alamy; **457** Lehmann, Joerg (P)–StockFood Munich/StockFood; **458** Ann Garvin; Zabert–StockFood Munich/StockFood; **460** Freidr Dick Corporation; **464** Kate Everard Media; **468** McGraw-Hill Companies; **472-474** Kate Everard Media; **479** Joe Borrelli, Inc./StockFood; **481** John E. Kelly/Jupiter Images; **486-487** Gibson and Smith/Jupiter Images; **496** Jonelle Weaver/Jupiter Images; **499** David Fischer/Getty Images; **502** Roulier/Pardo/photocuisine/Corbis; **503** Envision/Corbis; **508-509** Eric Futran/StockFood; **513** Bon Appetit/Alamy; **519** Fleurent/photocuisine/Corbis; **525** Jupiter Images; **527** Plewinsky-StockFood Munich/StockFood; **530** Dorling Kindersley/Getty Images; **532** Masterfile; **540-541** Allison Dinner Photography/StockFood; **544** Larry Lilac/Alamy; **551** Koki Iino/Getty Images; **552** foodfolio/Alamy; **554** McGraw-Hill Companies; **555** Norbert Wu/Getty Images; Renee Comet Photography, Inc./StockFood; Studio K/Masterfile; **560** McGraw-Hill Companies; **561** CGM/PhotoEdit; **563** Brian Leatart/Jupiter Images; **586-587** Brian Leatart/StockFood; **606** McGraw-Hill Companies; **614-615** gulfimages/Getty Images; **624** Maximilian Stock–StockFood Munich/StockFood; **632** McGraw-Hill Companies; **636-637** Joe Pellegrini/Jupiter Images; **644** Comstock Images/Jupiter Images; **674-675** Bruno De Hogues/Getty Images; **682** Jim West/Alamy; **704-705** Fresh Food Images/PhotoLibrary; **707** Peter Rees–StockFood Munich/StockFood; **708** Foodcollection/Getty Images; **710** Food Image Source/Peter Hogg/StockFood; **721** Jupiter Images/Polka Dot/Alamy; **728-729** McGraw-Hill Companies; **730** PhotoBliss/Alamy; **734** Evan Sklar/Getty Images; **741** Ed Quinn/CORBIS; **746-747** Masterfile; **748** Envision/Corbis; **749** DK. Khattiya/Alamy; **755** Douglas Johns Studio Inc./StockFood; Element Photo/StockFood; **766** Acme Food Arts/Getty Images.